P9-CDM-887

The Labor Problems of American Society

THE LABOR PROBLEMS OF AMERICAN SOCIETY

by **Carroll R. Daugherty** · NORTHWESTERN UNIVERSITY

and **John B. Parrish** · UNIVERSITY OF ILLINOIS

HOUGHTON MIFFLIN COMPANY

The Riverside Press Cambridge

737

The Riverside Press
CAMBRIDGE, MASSACHUSETTS
PRINTED IN THE U.S.A.

TO

MARION ROBERTS DAUGHERTY

ANNE BULLOCK PARRISH

PREFACE

THIS INTRODUCTORY TEXTBOOK in labor problems, labor relations, and labor economics is a new book. It represents considerably more than a major revision of the senior author's *Labor Problems in American Industry*, which first appeared in 1933 and was revised a number of times, mainly in order to bring factual material up to date. The present volume is almost completely new writing rather than a patchwork of old and new materials.

It had to be new. The extraordinary developments in unionism and collective bargaining since 1933 have produced a tremendous shift in the balance of economic and political power among organized groups in the country and have raised problems of major dimensions for the entire society and its government. Government has undertaken vast legislative and administrative projects to cope with these problems and with other matters, such as social insurance, which appear to have lain beyond the competence of organized groups as well as of individual persons. And, mainly as a result of these trends, a wealth of new research material has become available from the scholars and agencies attracted to this dynamic controversial field.

All these developments have demanded re-analysis and re-appraisal for the new book. They have not only produced much new content in materials. They have also required a re-synthesis of the materials in an altered organizational form. In the earlier book, Part Two considered the problems of individual workers; and Part Three, in three sections, dealt respectively with unions', employers', and government's approaches to these problems. In the present volume, Part Two, in four sections, is concerned with the problems of private individuals and groups — individual workers, unions, employers, and union-employers jointly; and Part Three deals solely with the approach of government in handling these and its own problems and in achieving balance among the individuals and groups. The new organization is designed to reflect the necessity for the student to concentrate on the public interest and to respect the enhanced role of government in labor matters.

Yet the old and the new books have much in common. The order in which major topics are treated is substantially the same. The main concern of the authors is still the public welfare, although one's concept of what represents the common good may well change with changing circumstances. The first Part of each book contains material essential not only for the orientation of the student but also for analytical application by him to the materials presented subsequently. In both books the major organizational structure of a given chapter in a given Part or Section is repeated in successive similar chapters; this aims at making remembering easier. And in both books there is an effort to integrate the material in a given chapter with those in other chapters; this aims at facilitating understanding.

The authors decided to minimize the use of footnotes beyond that required for statistics, quotations, and the like. Teachers in the field will recognize that we have drawn widely from the work of the many specialists in the field. Students can be directed by their teachers to source materials. Our obligation to these specialists is heavy, and we take this occasion to pay tribute to them for their path-breaking work during the past decade and earlier.

Almost the entire manuscript was typed by the senior author's secretary, Mrs. Gretel Murphy. The authors wish to record their very special gratitude to her for her effective, untiring efforts. Miss Sue Eager and Mrs. Mildred Johnson are also to be thanked for important secretarial help.

C. R. D.
J. B. P.

CONTENTS

PART ONE

Background and Perspective

CHAPTER 1

The Nature of Labor Problems

A. WHAT, WHO, AND WHY

1. Introduction. This is a book introducing the student to an organized survey and analysis of labor problems in America. Therefore our first task is to learn what is meant by the term "labor problems"; who have or are seriously affected by labor problems; why the problems exist; and why people are concerned with the problems and their solutions.

Perhaps the student can be helped in part to his own answer to "what, who, and why" by a brief recital here of a recent labor event that was of high interest and importance to the whole country. On the afternoon of July 26, 1949, on the thirteenth floor of the federal courthouse in New York City, three men entered a richly furnished, oak-paneled courtroom filled with people, sat down in the judges' seats, called the meeting to order, and began listening to what the persons before them had to say. The men on the judicial bench were members of a so-called "fact-finding" board appointed by the President of the United States. Before them, on one side of the room, were representatives of a large, powerful labor organization, the United Steelworkers of America, C.I.O.; and on the other side of the room, representatives of the big corporations manufacturing the basic steel products used in the country. Up in the jury box, very appropriately, sat representatives of the nation's leading newspapers and wire services.

Why had the President asked the board to hold these hearings? Because the union had announced its intention to stop virtually all basic steel production by a strike. Such a stoppage, if sufficiently prolonged, would have resulted in a creeping economic paralysis for most of the nation. And why had the union threatened such drastic action? Superficially, because it had been unable to get the companies to yield to its demands for a wage-rate increase of 12.5 cents per hour and for medical and retirement benefits, or for some compromise thereof. But the real question is, Why had the union and the corporations failed to reach some sort of agreement on these issues?

If one is to come close to the right answers to this fundamental question, he must know a lot of things. He must be familiar with the "economics" of the industry, that is, with the conditions affecting the demand for and the supply of the industry's products and the labor helping to make the products. He must understand the technology or engineering processes of making the steel products. He must consider the relation of the steel industry and the steel union to the whole economy and to the whole labor movement. He must know something about "human nature"; that is, he must have grasped the fundamentals of human motivations, human behavior, and human relations, in both their individual and group manifestations. What do corporation executives and workers strive for as individuals? How do they act and interact among themselves and with each other? With this knowledge he can better understand certain basic "political" matters — not only Republican-Democratic party politics but also the political forces and rivalries that exist within a particular union, within the organized labor movement in general, within a particular corporation, and among the corporations as a group. These things must be understood in terms not only of a current labor-relations situation but also of historical background. No one could possibly grasp the full meaning of the steel labor hearings of 1949 without remembering, for example, that with the exception of a few industries like construction and coal mining, American unionism in general had, for a long time (until the middle of the "New Deal" period), been a barely tolerated minority movement; that unionism in the basic iron and steel industry had, after a period of strength during the 1880's and until 1937, been ruthlessly smashed and held at bay by the steel corporations; and that from 1937 to 1949 a pattern of more constructive and harmonious labor relations had begun to emerge. One would also have to know that the rapprochement of the forties had been hampered by a number of factors: the lack of delegation of adequate authority by top corporation management to their labor relations executives for the working out of harmonious relations with the union; the union's practice of setting a pattern on wage rates and other items for the whole industry through concluding an agreement first with some big, key company; the rivalries among top leaders within the labor movement; and the threat of left-wing unionism within the C.I.O., the federation to which the more conservative Steelworkers' union belonged.

It is not our purpose here to present information on the above-mentioned necessary items of information; that will come later. We wish now only to throw light on the nature of labor problems by stressing some of the knowledge that is essential to understanding — in this case, understanding of the steel situation in 1949.

With the exception of week-end recesses and one special recess of eight days, the fact-finding board held hearings continuously until the end of August on the three issues in dispute. During the proceedings there were at least two bitter verbal exchanges between the president of the union and certain top executives of the steel companies. Both sides used economists and lawyers to present evidence in support of their positions. The union stressed the companies' ability to meet its demands out of allegedly swollen profits. The companies attacked the union's estimates of their ability to pay. The union also emphatically asserted that the proposed wage-rate increase would be beneficial to the country as a whole, which had been experiencing a business recession since late in 1948; the union said that the increase would raise consumer "purchasing power" and bring back the economy from the brink of depression. The companies claimed that this represented fallacious economic reasoning.

On September 10 the board presented its findings of fact and its conclusions to the President, who approved them and asked the parties to resume negotiations on the basis of the board's recommendations. These included a suggestion that the union withdraw its demand for a wage-rate increase; a suggestion that the companies contribute 4 cents per hour per employee for medical benefits and 6 cents for pensions; and a suggestion that the issue of amounts of pension benefits in relation to contributions be re-negotiated after a joint study by companies and union.

This story did not at first have a happy ending. The government's objective of forestalling a strike was not achieved. In its renewed bargaining with the companies the union insisted that, in return for its relinquishment of its demand for a wage-rate increase, contributions to pension funds must be made solely by the companies. The companies agreed to make the 6-cent-per-hour contribution recommended by the board but insisted that the union members must also make some contribution. Each party brushed aside the board's recommendation for a joint study. Each side couched its arguments in stately and resounding language which honored "the humanitarian and democratic principles on which this country was founded." Perhaps these arguments were rationalizations of more fundamental things. Perhaps the union felt that it had to be intractable in order to maintain its prestige and its position of leadership within the family of unions that compose the labor movement, especially because of its announced intention to take the lead in purging the C.I.O. of communist-dominated unions. Perhaps some of the companies stood firm because they believed that the creation of the board involved the repayment of a political debt by the Democratic party, which the union had supported in the 1948 elections. Other companies may have wished to "teach the union a lesson."

In any case, there was agreement to settle the issue by economic force rather than peaceful compromise. An industry-wide strike was called by the union on October 1. By the end of that month the united front of the steel companies had been broken, and by the middle of November virtually all the companies had capitulated to the union on the pension issue, with the union agreeing (as it was willing to do before the strike) to no wage-rate increase and to joint union-company contributions for medical benefits. Labor peace came to the industry and continued through 1950 and 1951.

2. What are labor problems? This sketch of major labor events in basic steel for 1949 is not a unique one. The same sort of thing — open conflict between corporation management and workers' unions — has happened in other industries in other years. Even in an industry or company where a labor agreement has been negotiated without resort to pitched economic battle, there may be conflict over how the agreement is to be applied in the day-to-day relationships between management and union members. And even in plants where there is no formal unionization of the employees, one may find evidence of dissatisfaction and unrest in employer-worker relationships.

If we analyze these situations, we come to see something like this: Human beings have certain basic wants and needs. In America these human beings live and work together — that is, are organized — in a society that operates in accordance with the principles of economic and political democracy. Within the limits imposed by themselves or by other persons and groups or by government (because of the necessity of "getting things done" and because of the need for survival), they are free to make their own decisions. This freedom may bring the several individuals or groups into conflict. Thus, in the 1949 steel case the managers of the companies wished to keep unit labor costs and product prices at levels that would make profits high enough to allow for plant modernization and expansion, reserves against business depressions, dividends to stockholders, and bonuses for themselves. These desires ran counter to the wishes of the union and its members who were demanding higher and more secure wage incomes.

Many other examples of conflicting desires involving workingmen can be brought to mind. Within a given union one group of members may want the union leaders to make certain demands on employers and pursue certain tactics in order to achieve the demands; another group or clique may espouse other demands and methods. Or the wishes of the rank-and-file members may be at variance with those of the union leadership. Again, union officialdom can sometimes be a virtual bureaucracy more interested in keeping itself in office than in serving the membership. Similarly, there may be divisions within the ranks of management.

Even where there is no formal organization among workers (there is almost always *some* sort of organization among small groups, with commonly agreed-on informal rules of behavior enforced by group sanction or "natural" leaders), the wishes of the employees often run counter to those of supervisors and higher management on such matters as the level of wage rates, the length of work periods, the pace of work, the use of safety devices on machinery, the provision of rest rooms, and the granting of retirement benefits.

Let us see if we can devise a definition of "labor problem" from these examples. To begin with, it seems clear that, no matter whose point of view is being considered, a labor problem has to do, in one way or another, with those members of society whom we call "workers." Whether or not the interests and attitudes of stockholders, managers, unions, government, or the workers themselves occupy our attention, the focus is on the workers and not on the other groups.

This means that part of the task of defining labor problems is to define the term "worker." We may note first that certain groups do *not* come under the "worker" category. Persons who operate farms as owners or renters are not included in our definition; such persons, like those who own and operate other relatively small businesses (e.g., small trade and service establishments) are to be classified as *entrepreneurs.* The stockholders of corporations are excluded. So also are those engaged in managing the corporations, from the president down to the foremen who compose the lowest level of supervision. In short, neither the owners of small or large firms nor the higher-ranking employees of the larger firms are to be regarded as "workers," even though most of them do of course "work for a living."

We are left, then, with the great bulk of employees of firms — those below the rank of supervisor who are hired by firm-owners and managers to work for wages or salaries. In 1951 the total number of persons in the civilian "labor force" averaged about 65 million. Of these, about one-fourth, or more than 16 million persons, were in the *entrepreneur* and managerial groups. The remainder, almost 49 million, were those whom we have defined as "workers."

It will be seen, of course, that this definition is considerably narrower than the one used by the economist when he speaks of the factor of production, "labor." The economist includes all those who work for a living — the entire 1951 labor force of 65 million. And this is a proper inclusion, for the economist wishes to distinguish the human from the non-human agents of production. Our definition of "worker" is perhaps more social and political than economic; our purpose here is to distinguish that segment of the human productive factor which owns or "bosses" from the portion which does not.

The workers as defined are employed in a great variety of jobs or occupations. The federal census of occupations lists many hundreds of them. One major classification distinguishes between "white-collar" and "manual" jobs. Within each of these categories, the most numerous group of workers is found on "unskilled" jobs, e.g., errand boys in offices or common labor in steel mills; the second most numerous group is characterized as "semi-skilled"; and the least numerous group is composed of the "skilled" workers, e.g., secretaries in offices and tool-and-die makers in metal working.

Although the many jobs in which workers are employed differ widely, they have certain characteristics in common. In the first place, as we have noted, they rank below the position of supervisor. Further, the men and women who fill these jobs normally do not own the machines or tools or raw materials with which they work. They do not normally participate in the managerial function of directing the flow or process of work and of combining the "factors of production" to make products for sale. They usually have nothing to do with pricing and selling the products. And they have little control over when and where, in a given company, they are to work.

From this listing of these common traits, it should not be inferred that there is anything approaching a homogeneous "working class" in America. We have already said that the jobs of workers have many dissimilarities. Moreover, the workers themselves, as will be shown later in some detail, differ widely in individual make-up and attitude. For various reasons of heredity and environment such variety usually exists among groups of human beings. For example, workers in the white-collar occupations seem less amenable to unionization than manual workers; and manual workers in the South seem less so than manual workers in the North. In the United States, at least, there is sufficient opportunity and labor mobility to keep workers from feeling that they are sunk forever in the "working class." There is far from being an American "proletariat" in the Marxian sense; most American workers appear to accept the private enterprise ("capitalistic") system and do not look favorably on plans to overthrow it. Nevertheless, as recent studies have shown, many American workers have no hope of rising out of the group into which they were born. And many of them seem increasingly to be knit together by a vaguely felt awareness that they belong to the "bossed" rather than to the "bosses."

Granted, then, that labor problems are concerned mainly with "workers" as defined, we are left with the task of explaining what is meant by "problem." In the examples previously given, including the 1949 steel case, there was a lack of harmonious relationship and adjustment between or among individuals or groups; in greater or less degree, conflict existed because the individuals and groups had dissimilar, warring objectives and desires. This fact constituted the problem. The solution lay in reconciling the conflicting demands and in bringing the elements of the problem into more harmonious adjustment. To the extent that differences and grievances still existed after some adjustment had been made, the solution was only partial and the problem to some extent still remained.

As a matter of fact, in the field of human relations, of which labor relations are a part, the problems are usually so complicated and subtle that a complete solution is impossible. Most realistic students and participants are glad to settle for, say, 70 per cent of perfection. Furthermore, no solution, however close to perfection, can be expected to "stick" for long. In a dynamic world of continuous, often unexpected change, new problems or old problems in new forms are almost constantly arising.

"Labor problems" may then be defined as areas of maladjustment within or among the groups who are concerned with the conditions under which workers (as defined) live and are employed or seek employment. "Solutions" or "remedies" lie in correcting these maladjustments, partially or wholly.

The maladjustments in human relations in industry that we have termed "labor problems" may be viewed narrowly or broadly. In the narrow view, there are many separate problems on which one may concentrate. For example, one may speak of the problem of minimizing the exposure of workers to occupational diseases, or the problem of a plant manager in dealing with a bellicose local union representative, or the problem of top management in obtaining satisfactory acceptance and execution of its labor policies by foremen, or the problem of an individual union worker in getting adequate representation by an unfriendly or corrupt union official, or the problem of government in preventing inflation or mass unemployment. And so on, almost without end. There is virtue in this approach, for it permits the concentrated study needed for remedies. But there is also the danger of excessive compartmentalization, of failure to see the woods for the trees.

Students who take the broad view often speak of *the* labor problem; they mean that there is one basic maladjustment which underlies and lends unity to a study of all the specific problems. Cure this fundamental illness and all the particular symptoms will disappear, they say. This view also has merit. Why should the physician merely treat symptoms if he can eliminate the cause of the disease? The difficulty is, however, that the "symptoms" analogy is not very accurate. For example, it is possible to do something about "symptoms" like occupational diseases and union autocracy without finding and eliminating the causal elements common to both. Furthermore, it takes a great deal of time to locate the common trouble. There is at present no agreement on what it is or might be. The Marxists, of course, ascribe all our difficulties to the "capitalistic system"; their prescription is to replace this form of social organization by socialism and communism. Others believe that the solution will come from further intensive studies of human behavior and human relations. Still others would agree with the latter view in part, but would insist that there must be further significant studies in the fields of economics and government and that there must then be a grand synthesis of the findings in all the relevant fields.

Whether one takes the broad or narrow view, labor problems exist and people are trying to do something about them. It is the purpose of this book to analyze both the problems and the proposed solutions.

3. Whose labor problems? We have said that our study of labor problems will focus on the conditions under which workers live and are employed or seek employment. Does this mean that we shall consider only the workers' problems or all labor problems only from the workers' points of view? Emphatically not. As the preceding discussion must have made clear, there is much more to study than the workers' problems. Top management has very serious labor problems; so have the lower levels of management and supervision. Unions as organizational entities have pressing problems apart from those of their members as individuals. And society as a whole, especially through its organized agent the government, faces perhaps the most important labor problems of all.

The workers' problems include getting and holding a job in the face of possible unjust treatment by employers' supervisors or by union rules and officials and in the face of the various economic, technological, and other conditions that produce unemployment; obtaining an average income that is adequate in terms of reasonable goals of living and in terms of the incomes obtained by non-workers; and achieving protection against illness, accidents, and superannuation.

The problems of unions include obtaining, holding, and controlling members; and helping members (and officials) by dealing effectively with employers, other unions, and government. In short, a union strives for progress and security for the leaders, for the members, and for the union as an entity.

Employers (or management) also desire satisfaction for their drives. In their relations with individual employees, unions, and government they demand sufficient freedom and security to be able to expand their enterprises and to make adequate profits and incomes for themselves and for the owners of the firms (if the latter are persons distinct from the managers).

Finally, government's problems include such matters as protecting individual workers who, in relation to their employers or to the productive process, are too weak to help themselves; promoting harmonious and peaceful relations between employers and unions; enforcing the rights and duties of the various individuals and groups; and in general, trying to enlarge the amount of want-satisfaction experienced by the citizens under its jurisdiction.

No matter whose labor problems we shall be discussing, we shall not deal with them wholly or mainly from the workers' points of view. It may be that the troubles of workers are more serious than those of non-workers, and that workers' attitudes and beliefs merit particularly respectful attention because most workers have fewer and weaker resources and reserves than most non-workers. But the wants and needs of non-workers are no less important than those of workers. And the ideals of a society founded on democratic principles require that all individuals and groups be given "an even break." We shall therefore try fairly to present all points of view on any given issue.

It is the obligation of every student of labor problems to curb any biases or prejudices he may have acquired and to be objective in his investigations, analyses, and conclusions.

4. Why do labor problems exist? The answer to this question has already been hinted at in our discussion of the nature of these problems. The student will have a much fuller explanation after our sketch, in a later chapter, of some of the fundamentals of human behavior. It is enough to say here that the maladjustments we have called "labor problems" arise from the characteristics of human beings, especially as these are displayed in a world of scarcity. Given the fact of scarce economic and social resources in relation to the desires of men and given the nature of men as they now exist, there is bound to be conflict and competition among men for the use and fruits of the resources. The amount of satisfaction that men desire is virtually limitless relative to the amount that they are able to obtain from the scarce resources. Individuals and groups, including workers, are therefore bound to clash in their efforts to achieve larger shares of want-satisfaction.

5. Why are solutions to labor problems desirable? As we proceed with our studies, it will become clear that the various problems result in significant losses in physical output and in other aspects of want-satisfaction, both for most of the persons directly involved and for most of society as a whole. In other words, to whatever extent the problems can be resolved, most individuals and most of society will be better off. There will be a net increase in human well-being. This is the main reason for studying labor problems and for trying to do something about them.

B. THIS BOOK'S PLAN OF DISCUSSION

The point of view taken in this chapter has dictated the organization of this book. It may now be helpful for the student to get a bird's-eye view of the main features of the landscape.

The book has three main parts. Part One, composed of five chapters, is designed for orientation. It not only, as in this chapter, tries to explain the general characteristics of labor problems. It also attempts to provide perspective, background, and some conceptual and analytical tools or frames of reference. It is hoped that these chapters will importantly assist the student to achieve a fundamental understanding of the material presented in Parts Two and Three. Chapters 2 and 3 of Part One develop certain criteria and analytical concepts in respect to the goal of maximizing the satisfactions of the members of a society. Chapters 4 and 5 of Part One deal with the historical background of modern labor problems in terms of the growth and development of capital, technology and the managerial function, population, the labor force, unionism, employer organization, and the functions of government.

Part Two of the book considers the labor problems and points of view of the "private" participants in the production process. It is divided into four sections. Section A contains four chapters on the problems of workers as individuals — the problems mentioned above on page 10. In Section B there are seven chapters dealing with the problems of workers' unions as set forth on that same page. Section C has two chapters on the problems of employers. And the three chapters of Section D consider the problems of employers and unions and the issues between them in their joint dealings — the problems and issues of collective bargaining, in general and in particular industries and firms.

In Part Three the problems and points of view of society as a whole and of government are highlighted. This part is of paramount importance because the function of society, through government, is to treat the private participants evenhandedly and to try to assist in maximizing the well-being not of any particular group but of all individuals and groups as a whole. This idea may be taken as one of the central, unifying themes of the entire book.

CHAPTER 2

Psychological Aspects of Human Welfare

A. WHY STUDY HUMAN BEHAVIOR?

In this chapter and the next we shall introduce the student to certain concepts that we hope he will hold carefully in his mind, during subsequent studies of particular labor problems, in order better to understand the basic elements at work. The present chapter is devoted to a survey of certain significant elements that commonly characterize the behavior of the individuals and groups involved in labor problems.

Let us consider, at the outset, a few hypothetical examples that have their counterparts almost constantly, and much too widely, in the real world. Suppose that in a plant where there is no union, during a period when there is relatively full employment in the economy, the workers become dissatisfied with one or more terms of employment (such as wage rates, length of work periods, safeguards against accidents, the promotion system, or unfair arbitrary supervision), and the company's management is either unaware of the conditions which cause unrest or refuses to do anything about them. Here the workers do not come close to the fulfillment of their desires. So they react in a number of ways — lower the quantity and quality of their outputs, increase their rates of absenteeism, or quit outright. All these responses have the effect of increasing the company's production costs per unit of output and of decreasing the quality of the company's product. As a result of this situation, the workers are generally unhappier (and poorer if they are paid by the "piece" rather than by the hour); the company is poorer because of diminished profits; and the consuming public is worse off because of higher prices for the product or deterioration of quality, or both. These effects could have been avoided if the company had taken greater pains to "treat the workers like human beings" — if it had applied a little elementary psychology.

Or suppose that a union-recognizing company wishes to reduce its unit labor costs, increase its profits, and possibly lower its product-prices by introducing a wage-incentive system in place of its present time-rate plan. This company doesn't bother to consult the union officers or to educate its workers about the desirability of the new plan, but just suddenly, arbitrarily and unilaterally, puts it into effect one Monday morning. The workers are suspicious and refuse to cooperate. The union leaders are hostile and won't help. The new system falls far short of producing the economies that the engineers thought possible. It is a failure and ultimately is withdrawn. Why? Because here too the management forgot the human element.

Consider next the case of a union leadership that has negotiated a new labor agreement with the management of a firm, without consulting the rank-and-file membership of the local union about its terms. The negotiations took a lot of time and hard work. But it all went for nothing because the membership repudiated the agreement and further vented its dissatisfaction by indulging in a week-long "wildcat" strike. What was wrong in this picture?

It has almost become a rare week in which one cannot read in his newspaper about the successful completion of negotiations for new labor contracts — and also about the breakdown of other negotiations culminating in strikes. If one were to go behind the news and study each situation, the chances are that he would find a much better practice of human-relations principles in the successful negotiations than in the failures. Something in addition to favorable or unfavorable economic conditions probably brought about the happy and unhappy endings.

Suppose finally that, with the world at total peace, a full-blown economic cataclysm were to hit the United States and result in the long-term unemployment of, say, 15 million men. What is likely to happen to their attitudes toward economic and political democracy? Will they continue to cherish the private enterprise system and a freedom that to them has become little but the freedom to exist at near-starvation levels?

Such examples, on these as well as other aspects of human relations in industry, could be multiplied almost without end. The conclusion is this: It is easy to forget that production and other industrial activities are *human* activities, carried on by human beings for the satisfaction of human wants. Human beings are involved at every point, directly or indirectly. The use of machines and complicated systems of exchange does not obscure this fundamental fact. The welfare and happiness of human beings are, in the last analysis, the things that matter.

The labor problem is a human problem which exists because some individuals have failed to attain happiness and well-being out of their participation in economic enterprise. It arises from a lack of adjustment among the individuals or groups of individuals who are thrown together in the economic process, or from a lack of adjustment of the individual to the process itself. In order to study and understand the problem and in order to suggest and evaluate solutions, it is necessary to learn as much as possible about the nature and behavior of human beings. What are the forces that motivate human behavior? Under what conditions do men usually experience well-being? How satisfactorily does the industrial environment meet these conditions? Answers to these questions, even though incomplete and inconclusive, must precede a detailed survey of industrial relations. The student of labor problems must keep abreast of investigations and discoveries in the field of psychology; he is increasingly appreciative of the contributions made by industrial psychologists and psychiatrists.

The difficulty of understanding human nature should be squarely faced at the outset. There is no easy, precise, or definite answer to the "hows" and "whys" of human behavior. A chemist or physicist can rigidly control almost all of the factors entering into a given problem or experiment and can predict with relative certainty a given answer or result, but the psychologist, dealing with forces that frequently defy isolation and measurement, is rarely able to foretell human behavior with exactness or to account for it in simple terms. The wellsprings of thought and action lie deep beneath the surface.

The summary of psychological findings presented in this chapter attempts to set forth the material which is least controversial and which seems to be of greatest practical value in understanding human nature at work in economic affairs. It has been a notable advance for economists to turn to psychology and learn from it that man is not a purely rational creature of godlike intellect, an abstract being of simple and easily predictable behavior, as the classical economists of the eighteenth and early nineteenth centuries apparently believed. For them, economic self-interest was the dominating force in human behavior, and man was "the economic man," a person who was animated exclusively by the rational pursuit of economic gain and who always bought cheap and sold dear. His supposed preoccupation with base and materialistic ends, as the cardinal assumption of the older economics, brought undeserved stigma to the whole inquiry of political economy.

The concept of the economic man was an oversimplified abstraction. Private economic gain is not the exclusive factor governing individual conduct. People have been known to sacrifice personal economic advantages under the influence of patriotic ideals. Some employers, on behalf of class loyalties, have chosen to bankrupt their concerns in order to prosecute an anti-union campaign to the bitter end. Furthermore, students of social psychology increasingly have come to recognize that goals such as prestige with one's fellows and power over one's fellows are of enormous influence in shaping the conduct of human beings. Clearly, then, the older concept of economic man has become obsolete as a tool for understanding the behavior of human beings.

Nevertheless, the reaction against the concept of economic man must not be carried so far as to yield the opposite, erroneous conclusion that there are no economic influences upon human behavior at all. That would be like throwing out the baby with the bath. It is perfectly possible to reformulate the doctrine of the economic man to make it consistent with modern psychology. Or, to state the matter differently, it is possible to devise an explanation of human conduct that integrates all motives and influences, including the economic.

In the discussion which follows we shall deal with two main topics: first, the behavior of human beings as individuals; and second, human behavior in its group manifestations.

B. THE BEHAVIOR OF INDIVIDUALS

As in the illustrations of the preceding section, people fly certain recognizable storm signals when they are not experiencing the amount of well-being to which they believe themselves entitled. If one wishes to substitute satisfaction for dissatisfaction in the minds and actions of those (spouse, child, union leader, foreman, individual worker, vice-president, and so on) with whom one must live in any given situation, one comes to ask such questions as (1) What do they want? (2) How did they develop these wants? and (3) How do they try to obtain what they want? The discussion of this section is organized around these questions.

1. The objectives of individuals. When we talk here about what people want, we do not mean specific items, such as a book of "comics," or a fishing trip, or a seat at a concert by Horowitz. We do mean broad goals of living that in greater or less degree are held in common by virtually all human beings in our society. Among these goals, for our purposes, the following seem to be important: first, the desire for survival, in the sense of the will to live or continue in existence as a personality; second, the desire to experience sensory satisfaction from physical goods and services in accordance with the "standard of living" one admires and strives for; third, the desire for power or control over other men (especially men in our "class") and over non-human things (such as a bowling ball, a tenor saxophone, a horse, or a ladder); fourth, the desire for social recognition, i.e., the wish to be respected, loved, hated, feared, or envied, but in any case "noticed," in the roles we have chosen for ourselves; and finally, the desire for self-expression, which means that a man likes to "be himself," to feel that he is in some important degree master of his own fate, to have a congenial job that brings him "all out" but does not "lick" him.

These are the things that most men want. But underlying them seem to be three more generalized desires, each of which applies to the five items listed above. In the first place, it appears that men generally desire *freedom;* i.e., they wish to be free to adventure, to strive for survival, physical satisfaction, power, recognition, and self-expression. Second, they seem to want *security.* That is, they appear to like to have some sure base from which they can fare forth in quest of the five above-mentioned goals and to which they can return for shelter and comfort in case of temporary defeat or frustration. Moreover, they want to have assurance not only that any defeat is temporary but that they can have a modicum of achievement in their strivings. Third, freedom to try to achieve and a modicum of achievement are desirable; but they are not enough. In the United States, at least, men seem to set great store on *progress* toward their objectives. One hundred per cent achievement is not necessary so long as this year's accomplishments exceed last year's.

These, then, seem to be the goals which Americans strive for and which therefore motivate the things that they do from day to day. We may now ask, Where do these desires come from?

2. The sources of the objectives. The answer to this question is, in the first instance, this: Man's desires or goals are based on hereditary and environmental influences. But this answer, though correct, is too broad and general to tell us much. It is necessary to learn what "heredity" and "environment" mean.

a. Hereditary influences. By heredity is meant the sum of the traits with which a person is endowed at the moment of conception by the union of the germ cells of his father and mother. These traits at that time are of course potential rather than actually developed; they immediately become susceptible to environmental conditions, at first within the mother's body and later, after birth, outside in the "world." Through heredity each human organism is endowed with and predisposed toward (1) a certain sort of endocrine-gland system, the chemical secretions from which (known as "hormones") have important influences on the size and shape of the body and its parts and on an individual's temperament and personality; (2) a certain kind of nervous system, which acts as the agent for receiving stimuli from within and outside the organism and for setting in motion the organism's responses to the stimuli; and (3) certain kinds of systems of other organs (respiratory system, digestive system, circulatory system, and so forth), some of which, in the course of their functioning, set up strong internal tensions (such as hunger pangs) that drive the person to certain types of behavior in order to obtain relief or satisfaction.

Our interest in these three hereditary things lies in their influences on the behavior of the individuals involved in labor affairs. In the first place, although all human beings possess the same general kind of hereditary endowment, they differ widely among themselves in respect to the "quality" of their endowments. One person's glandular make-up is such that he is predisposed toward being pugnacious and aggressive; another individual is predisposed to be a Caspar Milquetoast; while still another is inclined to be phlegmatic and stolid. For example, the kind of "fighting" person who is effective in unionizing unorganized employees may not be fitted to do a good job as an administrative officer of an established union or as a persuasive negotiator in collective bargaining conferences with employers. This was a lesson learned by unionists after 1934. Again, some persons' organic systems are such that they are predisposed to be quick and dexterous; they make good typists and assemblers of small pieces. Others seem to have native aptitudes for being die-makers and machinists, while the "stupid but strong" seem fitted for little but heavy common labor. Another trait in which there are large individual differences is the ability to learn or be trained; some persons "catch on" quickly, while others are slow to learn. One of the human problems of industry is so to take account of individual differences that each person is slotted into a job for which he has an aptitude. "Square pegs in round holes" make for dissatisfaction and inefficiency.

Second, while there are wide differences in the ability to learn, every human being possesses it in some degree. This is an inherited characteristic, based on the nervous system, that man has in common with all the other forms of life. But man is far superior to other organisms in this trait. It should be clearly understood that only the *capacity* to learn is inherited. What is actually learned comes from a person's environment.

Third, man's inherited organic constitution gives him certain powerful *drives,* which must find adequate outlets. Frustration or repression of these drives usually leads to aggressive, neurotic, or other unhealthy and anti-social forms of behavior. Much of the unrest and conflict found in labor affairs today may properly be ascribed to the frustrations experienced by individual workers, union members, union officials, or managerial personnel. It is of course the environment that provides or withholds outlets for the drives; the environment can condition or train the drives into socially acceptable kinds of conduct, but it cannot repress them without damage to the individual and his society.

b. Environmental influences. The human goals or desires mentioned earlier in this chapter are *based* on the hereditary influences just discussed. But these desires as they are found in modern American society are much more than the product of heredity. They are also the result of environmental influences. By "environment" is meant the sum of external conditions that affect an individual from the moment of his conception. In general terms, man is not born human; *original* human nature (the inherited raw material) is not the same as human nature after a person has undergone socialization by his environment. We know this not only from deductive reasoning and from our own experiences as children and parents but also from authenticated reports of infants born of civilized parents and left by accident to grow up in isolated areas as true "wild men." With specific reference to the above-mentioned desires, it is clear that man learns from his environment the socially approved ways of satisfying them. Consider, for example, the desire for social recognition. We all want recognition. But the ways of obtaining it are learned from the cultural conditions of the society into which we are born and, more particularly, from the standards of the smaller group or groups to which we belong and by which we are controlled. Thus, in some societies or groups the way to "get ahead" is through military or athletic prowess; in others, distinction may be sought through religious work; and in still others, the accumulation of material wealth is highly regarded.

Two main sorts of environmental influences may be distinguished—the *physical* or natural, and the *social* or cultural. The former includes raw economic resources like coal, iron, and petroleum; climatic conditions such as temperature and rainfall; and topographical conditions (which of course also influence climate), such as the number and size and location of rivers, natural harbors, mountains, and so forth. These physical features affect man's attitudes and activities. For example, the mountaineer and the plainsman have different beliefs and ways of life in part because of their different natural environments. Labor problems and labor relations in Georgia may vary significantly from those in Massachusetts, Illinois, or Oregon; and here too, one of the reasons is the differences in climate, topography, and other natural conditions.

The social environment is all the environment other than the physical. It is man-made; it comes from the association of individuals in groups which range in size from the family to the national and even international community. It is composed not only of these *groups* themselves as *institutional entities* but also of the *cultural heritage* (informal, uncodified beliefs, attitudes, customs, and ideas; laws; and formalized knowledge in various fields, including technology or engineering know-how) which such groups have invented and developed from ancient times.

It would be hard to exaggerate the importance of these social influences on man's behavior. They begin their impact on him from the moment of his birth. So much that affects his conduct during maturity is learned in the early, formative, plastic years that the behavior is very deep-seated; it seems virtually unlearned or instinctive. It is from the social environment that the modern American obtains his beliefs and attitudes about "bosses," unions, economic and political systems, nationality groups, religious groups, the proper role of government, and many other things involved in or affecting labor problems. For example, one reason why unionization drives have been less successful in the South than in the North is because of the deep-rooted attitude of white Southern workers toward colored workers. Again, there is little chance for enduring harmonious labor relations to develop between a company whose president believes that all union leaders are corrupt power-seekers and a union official who thinks that all employers have horns and cloven feet.

3. The variability of human nature. If the social environment plays such an important part in molding human behavior and in making people "human" and if the same basic hereditary influences are the same in general for all men, it follows that in so far as this environment is significantly different in different areas or countries, human behavior and human nature varies there; and in so far as this environment changes over time, human behavior and human nature changes. As an example of spatial differences in environment, consider how difficult it is for Orientals and Occidentals to understand each other's behavior. As an example of the temporal differences, contrast the behavior of modern Americans with what we know of the nature and behavior of medieval Englishmen. It would appear that the statement, "You can't change human nature," has little validity.

4. Methods of attaining the objectives. How do individuals try to obtain satisfaction for their desires, as fashioned by the joint influence of heredity and environment? By a process of trial-and-error which has very much more of conscious, purposive direction than the almost wholly instinctive action of lower animals. Give a man a problem (i.e., something in his environment that keeps him from getting what he wants) and he will try to remember something in his own experience that will help him solve it; failing in that, he will try to profit from others' experiences as recorded in books or spoken by advisers; or failing there, he will try to puzzle the thing out himself. If his first effort is unsuccessful, he tries something else; and so on, until he has achieved a reasonably satisfactory adjustment — or until he acknowledges himself beaten and frustrated, whereupon he behaves aggressively or neurotically in ways that are directed not toward solving the problem but toward salving his wounded, thwarted ego.

But before admitting complete defeat in his attempts to achieve his objectives singlehandedly, man has one more device: He can band together with other men who have similar problems and are threatened with similar frustrations. He can organize, in the hope that he and his fellows, as a united group with pooled resources, will have the strength and cunning that each man lacked when acting alone. In doing this he has ample justification in human experience. Ever since man has been man, he has had "unions" of some sort — the clan, the tribe, the state, the church, the gild, and many others. And if one kind of organization was unsuccessful in solving the problems, it was scrapped and another was tried.

In modern times an individual usually belongs to more than one social group. Ordinarily this does not matter very much, for there is almost always one group that commands most of his interest and loyalty. Or the standards and requirements of the groups do not seriously conflict. Sometimes, however, there are two or more groups which are important to the individual and which impose conflicting obligations on him. Here his loyalties are divided; he is pulled apart, with resulting mental disorder.

Sooner or later, if he wishes to be an integrated person, he will have to withdraw from at least one of the groups. As illustrations of this sort of conflict, we may think of individual workers who are torn between loyalty to their firm and loyalty to their union; or foremen who are "in the middle" between an anti-labor top management and a local union with which they wish to have good relations.

C. THE BEHAVIOR OF GROUPS

Because the organization of groups is an important method whereby individuals try to satisfy their wants, we must now look at the way groups behave. The very fact that a group is composed of individual human beings means, of course, that the preceding discussion of individual behavior is applicable here. But an organization is more than the sum of its parts. The separate component cells are welded into something that becomes a distinct organism or entity in itself. A corporation or a labor union, for example, has an existence, a structure, and a number of functional aspects that are much more than those of any or all of the member units (stockholders or workers).

In our brief discussion here we shall consider two main aspects ot group conduct: (1) the goals and methods of the group in terms of its relationships with "outside" persons or with other groups; and (2) the internal relationships of the organization, i.e., the interactions among the group, its leaders, and its members.

1. "External" behavior. *a. General goals.* When we speak of the "goals" of organizations here, we refer to general goals rather than to the specific objectives of the groups. The latter of course vary among groups; one will be aiming at the prevention or cure of alcoholism, another at world federation among nations, still another at protecting wild life, and so on. Our concern is with the goals held more or less in common by all organizations. The more important ones may be listed as follows: (*a*) Normally, i.e., unless they wish to "go out of business" because of complete failure (or success), organizations wish *to survive.* As entities they wish to adapt their structure and functioning successfully to their environments or to control and change their environments enough to give their existing structure and functions survival value. (*b*) They wish *to have power vis-à-vis other groups.* (*c*) They wish *to be accepted* as a respected part of the community. As a rule any organization such as a corporation or a labor union wants "good public relations," wants to be thought "nice," wants not to be in the social or political doghouse, wants to be welcomed into the community of groups and be solicited for participation in community projects such as "chest" drives.

As with individuals, there are certain other urges that underlie those just listed. (*a*) Organizations want *security* in their relations with other groups. A labor union, for example, does not wish to spend most of its energies fighting for existence. It wants existence guaranteed; then it can concentrate on its specific objectives. (*b*) Groups demand *freedom* to pursue their goals. (*c*) They wish to experience *progress* toward the achievement of their specific goals. And in so doing, they try to help satisfy the needs of the membership (or at least the part of the membership that is considered important to the leadership).

It will be seen that these general goals are much like those of individual human beings. This is to be expected; a group is composed of human beings, and a group's aims necessarily reflect those of its leaders and members.

b. Methods of attaining objectives. Generally speaking, all the specific "external" policies and tactics adopted by organizations in order to achieve their general and specific goals within the society of all organizations may be subsumed under two main heads: (1) those directed at other groups with which the given organization has dealings; and (2) those directed at government — the organization that has supreme authority and control over all private groups.

(1) Methods in respect to other groups. The methods employed by an organization in respect to other private groups may in turn be classified as mainly *persuasive* and mainly *coercive.* There is of course no clear, sharp dividing line between these two sub-categories. Thus, one group may allow itself to be "persuaded" by another (e.g., a corporation by a union) because the former is fully aware of the latter's ability to exert effective coercion. In a society such as ours the power to coerce successfully is, in the last analysis, the most potent "persuader." By "coercion" is not meant chiefly the use of physical force (although farm groups, corporations, unions, and other organizations have been known to get rough at times), but the use of economic power to wring concessions from other groups. For example, even though a labor union may not resort to physical violence, it may bring an employer to his knees if it can deprive him or threaten to deprive him of customers (through a boycott) or workmen (through a strike) or substitute factors of production such as new, improved machinery (through resistance to technological change). Essentially, all these coercive strategies may be considered to involve *depriving the other organization of any course of action alternative to the one desired by the first.*

(2) Influencing government. An organization may turn to government for one or both of two reasons: to induce government to apply coercion or persuasion to one or more private groups that thus far have successfully resisted the organization's direct action; and to get government to help the organization achieve its objectives, even though the previous failure adequately to attain these goals has not been due to the direct resistance of other private groups. An example of the first is the federal National Labor Relations Act sponsored by labor unions in 1935 in order to force

employers to recognize unions. An illustration of the second is the legislation sponsored by farmers' organizations in order to raise the annual incomes of farmers.

Persuasion may be considered to be the chief method used to influence government. But in a democracy like the United States an organization may be able to induce its members to vote for or against the dominant political party if, as the government, the latter yields to or resists the organization's persuasion; this fact may be said to constitute an element of coercion.

There are thus two main methods of influencing government: first, trying on election days to elect or re-elect the organization's friends in the legislative and executive branches of government and to defeat the organization's enemies; and thereafter, no matter who has been elected, trying to obtain, by the process known as "lobbying," favorable decisions from the legislative and executive branches of government.

There is of course one other possible method of obtaining favors from government: If the organization is big and strong enough, it may form its own political party and attempt to get its candidates elected as the majority party and thus *be* the government. This method, although used extensively in Europe, has seldom been tried in America.

c. What happens if an organization fails. If a group is unable to achieve its general and specific goals by its chosen methods, it is frustrated, at least temporarily. Like any of the individuals of which it is composed, it then has the following main alternatives: (1) It may scale down its ambitions or goals. (2) It may change its policies and tactics. (3) It may alter its internal structure. Any of or all these moves may be called *adaptive behavior.* If they "work," the frustration disappears. If not, the frustration continues, and there will be further attempts at adaptation. If none of the successive changes is successful, there are other alternatives: (4) The organization may "commit suicide," i.e., disband. (5) It may adopt the special form of "adaptation" known as "aggressive behavior." For example, a union that is denied recognition by employers and by middle-class groups in general may become "violent," wrecking machinery, dynamiting employers' homes, slugging "scabs," staging sit-down strikes, and so forth. (6) It may adapt by turning "religious," going "underground," becoming a "movement." It was not by accident that union groups and their efforts to organize became known as the labor *movement.* Any "movement" (e.g., the prohibition movement and the woman's suffrage movement) is in behalf of some unpopular, minority-supported, underdog "cause." To the organization's members the goals are "noble" and inspire zealous pursuit. The movement almost always has its martyrs, saints, scriptures, and hymns.

2. Internal relationships. There is another very important aspect of "politics" with which organizations have to do — internal politics. Every organization has its internal political problems; this is inevitable because the group is composed of human beings and because, as our earlier discussion showed, individuals differ among themselves in personality, temperament, general intelligence, and aptitudes.

Within an organization there are a number of elements to be considered — the leaders who are appointed or elected (e.g., top management in a corporation and top officialdom in a labor union); the rank-and-file membership; and perhaps, especially if the organization is large, two or more sub-groups or factions.

Organizations today operate in a complex, interdependent world of rapid change. Each group must be able to adapt its policies and tactics quickly and effectively to such change. Furthermore, even if the changes were not rapid and drastic, many organizations are so large that the "legislation" passed by the membership or delegates at periodic conventions must be left for execution to the officers. Both of these factors have led to the *centralization of control* in the hands of the top leadership.

Bearing these things in mind, we may distinguish a number of possible internal situations: (*a*) An organization such as a union (and not infrequently a corporation) may be filled with rival, warring cliques and torn with dissension over proper specific goals and methods and over who is to lead the organization. The victorious faction may have difficulty in achieving the internal unity and cohesion necessary for success. (*b*) In many American organizations the rank and file, being concerned with their own private affairs, do not actively and continuously attend meetings or participate in other group matters. It requires a crisis to get them stirred up. This situation provides opportunities for active, militant minority factions to control the organization and to have their policies adopted. It also allows corrupt or self-serving leaders to pursue programs that may be inimical to the members' best interests. But if these interests are seriously jeopardized, it is usually true that no minority or leader can indefinitely stay in power. In the end he must "deliver the goods." (*c*) The leaders of the group may establish a veritable dictatorship in what is usually supposed to be a democratic organization. Dissension and even honest, mild discussion are often repressed. (*d*) Less commonly perhaps, an organization may operate like a true democracy, with active interest in group affairs, reasonable cohesiveness among the individuals and sub-groups, respect among them for honest differences of opinion on policies, acquiescence in majority rule, and reasonable respect for the rights of minorities. In truly democratic group operation, moreover, there is a nice balance between the wishes of the membership and those of the leadership; the leaders serve as a focus for the needs of the rank and file, and at the same time, possessing the qualities of real leadership, are able to get the members to accept policies that are deemed desirable from the leaders' superior vantage-points.

To function effectively a group must have not only a fair degree of unity, loyalty, and cooperation among its elements, but also an organizational structure suited to the functions it has to perform. One of the important reasons for labor's failure to unionize the large-scale manufacturing corporations before 1935 was the insistence by most of the top leadership that the workers in these plants be split up among a number of narrow craft or occupational unions instead of being united in single plant-wide organizations.

It was stated earlier in this chapter that one general goal of organizations is to help satisfy the needs of their members. Most groups are able to contribute in at least two ways to the greater want-satisfaction of many of their members. Not only do they aid members to attain specific individual objectives, such as higher incomes and better working conditions, and general goals like freedom, security, power, and social recognition in relation to the "outside" environment, but they also, within themselves, furnish outlets for members' desires. Thus, the members who participate in policy formation by attending meetings find avenues of self-expression not otherwise available. And election to even a minor office within the group helps satisfy the urge for power and for social recognition. On the other hand, of course, some members who are unable to influence policy or achieve office may be even more frustrated than they would be in the absence of organization.

For members, the most satisfying organizations are those within which the devices that Professor Bakke calls *bonds of organization*[1] have become well developed. For most leaders also, these "bonds" afford the most satisfaction and produce the most effective operation, partly because satisfied members, much better than dissatisfied or indifferent members, can be welded into a loyal, cohesive, actively cooperating unit. The bonds may be listed and explained, in paraphrase of Bakke, as follows: (*a*) The organization should have an *organizational charter*—a set of goals, methods, achievements, and traditions which give meaning to the group as a unit and enable members to say with pride in their hearts and voices, "I'm a G.M. man," or "I'm a Republican," or "I'm a United Mine Workers member." (*b*) Each member of the group should be given a satisfying *role* to perform and ample opportunity to fill it. Everyone should know what the content of this job is and how it is related to the roles or jobs of the other members. (*c*) Closely related to the matter of providing a role is the need for giving *status* to each member. Whereas "role" refers to productive work, "status" has to do with a member's rank within the organization. It is the "vertical hierarchy of authority and deference." (*d*) Exceedingly important is a properly fashioned and adequately functioning *system of communication*, from top leadership down to rank-and-file members, and from the members up to the leaders.

[1] See E. W. Bakke, in *Adaptive Human Behavior*, Yale University Labor and Management Center, New Haven, 1949, pp. 18 ff., and in *Bonds of Organization*, Harper and Brothers, New York, 1950.

From the top, orders or suggestions must be passed down promptly and clearly; from the bottom, reports and suggestions must be routed up with equal dispatch and effectiveness. Without adequate communications there can be no proper understanding of role and status, no proper sense of identity between leaders and members in the pursuit of common objectives — in short, no effective operation. (*e*) Finally, there should be a satisfying system of *rewards and punishments* — rewards that will provide true incentives for individual behavior consistent with the general and specific objectives of the group, and punishments that will discourage behavior inimical to group welfare. The rewards and punishments may be financial, such as bonuses paid to workers by corporations, and fines on union members for failure to attend meetings; or they may be non-financial, such as a plaque or banner for achievement and ostracism or suspension for failure.

In this chapter we have tried to learn in general terms what human beings want, individually and collectively; why they want what they do; and how they try to obtain what they want. In an economic and political democracy like the United States it is important for the student to know these things. Whether he is interested, as he should be, in enlarging want-satisfaction in the economy as a whole, or is concerned only with the welfare of particular individuals and groups, he needs some understanding of these psychological aspects of human welfare.

CHAPTER 3

Human Welfare in Terms of Available Resources

All the labor problems considered in this book have important human-relations or psychological facets. And all the solutions proposed or tried for these problems must be evaluated in human-relations terms. But all these problems also have broad, significant economic implications. And every suggested solution to a labor problem, whether proposed or used by a union, an employer, or government, must be appraised in economic as well as human terms. In other words, human welfare has economic as well as psychological aspects. That is why we present the very essential material in this chapter.

The student will find that we use the framework of analysis developed in this chapter throughout the book. It helps us, for example, to assess the social desirability of union security policies and union-employer pension plans, to appraise the social validity of a government minimum wage-rate law, and to make many other judgments from a rational vantage-point.

A. CHOICE AMONG ALTERNATIVE WANTS

1. The necessity for choice. We have seen that individual and group welfare depends on obtaining reasonable satisfaction for the fundamental human desires. It is not in the nature of things, however, for any person or organization to find complete fulfillment of all objectives. The reason for this conclusion is simple; but it is absolutely basic: For the satisfaction of wants, the means or resources — whether in respect to a single individual, a group, or the whole society — *are limited in relation to the number and intensity of the wants.*

a. What are the resources? In our meaning here, the resources for satisfying human desires include more than those commonly classified as "economic." To be sure, the latter are a most important part of a society's resources, for they embrace natural resources, man-made resources known as "capital" (machines, tools, raw materials, stocks of finished products, and so on), and human labor. But for our purposes here we include also other "social" resources: technological know-how; general social organization, e.g., democracy versus government dictatorship; specific social institutions, like corporations and unions, within the general social framework; customs, beliefs, laws, and so on; and the energies and skills, mental as well as physical, of the whole population (including housewives, children, and older non-working persons) rather than merely of those persons usually classified as being in the labor force. In short, we include all the people and their cultural heritage.

b. A given stock of fully employed resources. Real cost. The fact that human wants are limitless in relation to the resources available for satisfying them imposes, for the society as a whole and for any group therein, the necessity for human choice as to which wants and whose wants shall be satisfied, and to what degree they shall be satisfied. And, given the quantity and quality of his own resources, any one person must also decide which of his wants shall be satisfied, and to what degree. In other words, the fact of scarce resources means that the various specific and general goals of man "compete" among themselves for satisfaction. Man must therefore *economize* in the use of his resources. Given a fixed amount of fully utilized resources, any increase in the amount of satisfaction obtained for any particular want involves inevitably a loss in satisfaction for one or more other wants. To economists this fact is known as the principle of *real* or *opportunity cost.* (The word "opportunity" refers to *alternative* opportunities for using resources to produce want-satisfaction.) In the language of the man in the street, the principle means "you can't have your cake and eat it too." To illustrate: A consumer may want and buy a new automobile; but if he has only a fixed amount of money to spend on all goods, the acquisition of the car requires the giving-up of other wanted goods he might have bought with the money he spent on the automobile. Or, a society may want and obtain more medical and hospital services. But if the quantity and quality of the society's resources are fixed and fully utilized, the increased satisfaction for the desire for medical care is provided only at the expense of less satisfaction for other wants. Again, in broad terms, the more security a society wants and gets from its government, the less freedom there is for private individuals and groups. There is of course nothing "wrong" about enlarging the amount of satisfaction for any particular want; it is only necessary to understand that, given the fact of fixed and fully employed resources, a real cost is involved.

Given a fixed amount of fully employed resources, there is also, from the standpoint of society, real cost in the sense that whenever one individual or group succeeds in obtaining an increased share of want-satisfaction, some other individual or group gets less. In other words, the fact of scarcity of resources in relation to wants produces *competition* among individuals for the limited amount of want-satisfaction available from the resources. This competition intensifies the inclination of similarly situated individuals to organize. Within each group there is mainly *cooperation* toward common goals. Among organizations there is mainly competition. Both competition and cooperation exist, of course, within any given group and among different groups. Within a labor union, for example, the individual members cooperate to attain their common goals. But there is usually also competition among them in respect to what the goals and policies shall be and in respect to status and roles within the union. Again, nations in the modern world compete with each other for want-satisfaction, but they also cooperate at times in various "blocs." Within a given nation various private organizations like corporations and labor unions compete among themselves, but they also cooperate to aid the nation in its competition with other nations.

c. Choice under variable resources. The student will have noticed that several times in the foregoing discussion there was the proviso, "given a fixed amount of fully employed resources." This might suggest that if the quantity and quality of resources were not fixed or if a given amount of resources were not fully employed, the principle of opportunity cost would lose its validity. That is, if the quantity and quality of resources can be increased or if a fixed stock of resources, at first partially utilized, can be brought up to full employment, then it should be possible for a society, group, or person to obtain more of *all* goods (a "good" being defined as *anything* that satisfies a human want) and thereby more satisfaction for *all* wants. In other words, obtaining more satisfaction for any particular want by acquiring more of a particular good would not seem, in either of the two cases just mentioned, to require the sacrifice of satisfaction for other wants from other goods.

This conclusion would be erroneous. The principle of real cost is always operative. To be sure, it is possible to obtain more total want-satisfaction from a larger quantity of goods when the quantity and quality of resources are enlarged or when partially employed resources are given full utilization. But because the resources are still limited during these changes, there must be choice as to which resource items shall be increased and how much; hence there must still be choice as to which goods' outputs shall be raised and how much, and which wants' satisfaction shall be raised and how much. In other words, the resources available for making the increases are limited; and the more any one item is increased, the less any other one can be. Moreover, during the processes of enlarging the resources and attaining full utilization, there must be choice among alternative *methods* of achieving the results.

2. The need for and method of national choice. Granted that individuals and various organizations, including labor unions and government, must make choices among competing wants, the problem arises as to how these units can make their choices so as to get the most out of their limited available resources, i.e., so as to maximize or enlarge their want-satisfaction from the resources.

The problem of maximization makes it highly desirable that choices be *rational.* Irrational choices lessen the amount of want-satisfaction realized by the choosers.

a. Divisibility of alternatives. Let us see what "rational choice" means. There seem to be two main requirements of rationality in choosing. First, the alternative goods that satisfy competing wants should be what economists call *divisible.* They should not exist in big, indivisible "lumps" but should, if possible, be available in small units like phonograph records or lamb chops. If, in spending a given amount of income, a person is deciding between two divisible alternatives like apples and oranges, there is no "all or none" proposition. It is possible for him to obtain some of each good and thereby satisfy to some extent his desire for each. The problem of choice and maximization from his resource then resolves itself into discovering the optimum or best combination of quantities of the two goods; there will be one combination which gives greater utility from both goods than any other. But if the alternative goods are in large lumps (e.g., a house and an expensive automobile), the person of limited spending ability would find no combination of the two possible; the choice would lie, on the one hand, between all of the first and none of the second, or, on the other hand, between none of the first and all of the second. Here one of the wants must go unsatisfied, and the problem of maximization becomes very difficult. It is seriously to be doubted that the choice, when made, could be called rational.

b. The requirement of knowledge. The other requirement of rationality is *knowledge.* Two kinds of knowledge are needed. In the first place, the chooser should know whether the alternative goods are divisible or indivisible. But doesn't everyone know the size of the units in which such goods as apples, neckties, houses, automobiles, and yachts come? Perhaps. There are certain goods, however, such as freedom and security, about which many persons appear to have mistaken notions. Totalitarian governments, for example, seem to operate on the assumption that these two alternative goods are indivisible, that one must have all of the one and none of the other; and they typically choose security. The democracies, on the other hand, seem to believe that these goods are divisible; and they keep trying to discover the optimum combination.

The second kind of knowledge needed by a person or group for a rational choice among alternative goods is a knowledge of the utilities and costs (advantages and disadvantages) of the goods. And, to be accurate in economic parlance, he should know these data "at the margin"; that is, he should know the utility and the cost of each additional unit of each good as he acquires more units of the one good and gives up more units of the other good (or imagines himself so doing) in his effort to find the best combination of goods-quantities.

How common is this second sort of knowledge among the individuals and groups of the real world? It seems not to be very widespread; there is a great deal of ignorance. Knowledge, however, is a good which also has its costs as well as its utilities. Any cost detracts from total satisfaction. Perhaps many people decide that the costs of acquiring this kind of knowledge are not worth the benefits to be derived from it. If based on careful study, this conclusion can be said to be rational; if based on nothing but "laziness," it is irrational. Nevertheless, there appears to be a net loss in want-satisfaction because of lack of knowledge. If this were not so, there would be no point in trying to add to the sum of man's wisdom and understanding.

To hope for complete rationality in the making of choices would be useless. However, we may reasonably hope for more than now exists. As realists, we might well be satisfied with, say, 70 per cent of perfection.

3. Rational choice and maximization. If we assume that the requirements of divisibility and knowledge are met, then rational choice among competing alternatives is possible, even probable. And if the process of choosing is rational, then the maximization of want-satisfaction from a given scarce stock of resources follows.

How is a person or organization to know that any particular choice is rational and that maximization is thereby attained? The answer to this question is indeed hard to make in respect to any particular real-world situation. But the basic principles of maximization may be stated here in general terms: Consider a given resource — measurable in some unit such as dollars or labor-hours — which is to be allocated between two alternative goods, A and B. Then given the preferences between the goods of the person or group owning the resource, the optimum allocation of the resource, i.e., the best combination of quantity-of-A and quantity-of-B that can be bought with it, will occur when the net satisfaction obtained from good A (total gross satisfaction from A minus the resource-cost of achieving it) is the same as the net satisfaction from good B. At this point the shifting of one unit of the resource from A to B or B to A would result in a net loss in total net satisfaction. At this optimum point, if a unit of resource expenditure were shifted from A to B, there would be a gain in satisfaction from buying more of B and a loss from buying less of A. But the loss would be greater than the gain; there would be a *net* loss in the total net satisfaction obtained from both goods. The same thing would happen if the resource allocation were shifted by one unit from B to A.

The general principle of maximization explained above is applicable with greater or less precision to choices among the alternatives confronting all decision-making units, including households, firms, unions, and government. Households must allocate their hours of time between leisure and income, their income and past savings between present consumption and further saving, their labor-hours and savings among firms available for hiring them, and their spending among consumption goods — all in order to maximize satisfaction. Firms allocate their expenditures among the factors of production in order to maximize profits and other elements of satisfaction for that part of the ownership and management considered important by the firm's decision-makers. Unions must choose among alternative policies and tactics in order to maximize the satisfaction of that portion of the membership considered important by those who make the decisions. Government must decide how much of the total spending in the society shall be done by private units and how much by itself. It must also choose among alternative ways of obtaining funds (income tax, sales tax, and so on), and it must allocate these funds among various objects of expenditure (roads, education, defense, and so on) — all with a view to helping maximize the satisfaction of that portion of the citizenry which is deemed important by the government decision-makers.

In the following sections of this chapter we shall consider several aspects of maximizing and enlarging the total of want-satisfaction *in a whole society*, such as the United States. At various points in the discussion we shall have occasion to refer to the material presented in this section.

B. RESOURCE ALLOCATION IN THE ECONOMY AS A WHOLE

1. The allocation system. A democratic society like the United States is composed of many millions of households, millions of firms (including farmers), hundreds of labor unions, thousands of other private decision-making units. There are also thousands of local governments, some 50 state-territorial governments, and the federal government. Now, important and potent as the federal government is, it does not, during peacetime, control or direct in major fashion the choices made by the private units. There is, in fact, no top agency that performs this task, except in time of war. Consequently, there is no agency of human beings that arranges the allocation of the whole country's scarce resources among the many competing wants of all the individuals and organizations.

Yet the total resources of the society do get allocated. Let us initially consider how this is done, with government out of the picture. The allocation is accomplished by a sort of impersonal agency, a mechanism or institution known as the market-price system (or just the "price system"). It works like this: In the many market-places of the country, firms offer their various consumption products for sale to the households. In these markets the households express their preferences by voting their dollars for their favorites. Then the prices of the "elected" products tend to go up, thus tending to provide larger profits for the firms making and selling the products. And the prices of the less favored products tend to fall, thus tending to reduce the profits of the firms making such products. Then, seeking higher profits, the firms in the more profitable industries try to expand and the firms in the less profitable industries reduce their operations or try to enter the more profitable fields. This means increased demands and higher prices for resources (labor and capital) in the more profitable plants, with lowered demands and prices in the less profitable ones. Consequently, workers and the owners of capital have an incentive to move into the more profitable sectors.

Thus, if product prices and resource prices are able to rise and fall and if the households are willing to change the employments of the resources they own, the resources get allocated in the uses desired by the household as consumers, with the firms acting, in effect, as agents between the households as consumers and the households as resource-owners. This allocation takes place through the markets for consumption products and resources, with no dictation by any agency.

2. Conclusions on allocation. Without any further economic analysis or proof, we may state here certain very important generalizations in respect to the maximization of want-satisfaction in the economy as a whole from the standpoint of resource allocation. (We make certain arbitrary assumptions on other matters affecting maximization; thus, we take the distribution of income as given, we assume full utilization of resources, and we disregard economic progress.)

First, the general principle for the maximization of want-satisfaction by a single economic unit, as explained in Section A of this chapter, applies also to the whole society of millions of separate economic units when their choices are integrated by the market-price system: The economic and other resources of the society receive an optimum allocation — in other words, the society's well-being is maximized — at the point where the movement of resources to some other allocation, i.e., to the production of some other combination of goods, would result in a net loss in total satisfaction. If the allocation were altered from the optimum one in any direction, there would be a gain in satisfaction from the increased output of certain goods and there would be a loss in satisfaction from the diminished output of other goods. But the loss would exceed the gain, leaving a net loss to the society.

Second, the only kind of economy in which resources are certain to be given an optimum allocation, i.e., in which want-satisfaction is sure to be maximized from the standpoint of resource allocation, is one that has never existed and doubtless never could exist in the real world — the abstract, idealized economy in which there is pure and perfect competition on both the buying and selling sides of every product and resource market. This kind of market for any product or resource presupposes the following: (*a*) Each buyer and seller is an *atom*, i.e., is so small that he is powerless to influence the price of the product or resource, no matter how much he buys or sells. The prices are accepted as *given* by all buyers and sellers. (*b*) In any market each seller's product or resource is a *perfect substitute* for that of any other seller. (*c*) There is perfectly free *mobility* among all buyers and sellers. Each is able to move freely within any particular market and from one market to another.

Third, in modern real-world America the above-listed three market conditions exist only rarely if at all. The closest approach to those conditions may be found (*a*) in certain markets for staple agricultural products, where small-size farmer-sellers and small-size buyers act singly and without organization; and (*b*) on the buying side of markets for finished consumption products, where atomistic households act without organization. But in the sale of most products and in the buying of many, the units in the market are large enough to influence prices; that is, there exists some degree of monopoly (a situation in which there is only one seller) or monopsony (a situation in which there is only one buyer). And one firm's product or one household's resource is not a perfect substitute for those of other firms or households in the markets. Moreover, because of ignorance, laziness, or other reasons there is not full mobility within and among markets. Then in so far as these deterrents to and departures from perfect competition exist, there is almost certainly a failure to achieve optimum resource allocation and maximization of want-satisfaction in the economy as a whole. There may be tendencies toward "the best," but some misallocation almost surely takes place, with consequent net loss in satisfaction.

Fourth, if misallocation exists, the only agency big and strong enough to remove or reduce the degrees of monopoly and immobility that exist is the federal government (with assistance, perhaps, from state governments). The government might undertake through commissions to control or regulate monopolistic sellers and monopsonistic buyers so that the prices of products and resources in the various markets might approach more closely those that would prevail under perfect competition. Or the government might avoid direct control over prices and try to approach the perfectly competitive result by (*a*) breaking up labor unions and large, multi-plant corporations, thus restoring a degree of atomism in the markets; and (*b*) providing "free" information about prices and other market conditions (e.g., public employment offices for labor), thus increasing the mobility of buyers and sellers.

Fifth, whether or not the government attempts such methods to improve the allocation of resources is a matter which rests on the *political* decisions or choices of the country's voters. Not only are the adult members of American households free to cast dollar votes in the market polling places for economic goods (each adult possessing as many votes as he has dollars); they are also free to cast votes in the political polling places where each person, rich or poor, has only one vote on any set of offered alternatives (the alternatives usually being offered through the "platforms" of contending political parties and their candidates). In a democracy, if a majority of the voters were to tell their elected representatives to employ one or more methods, such as those listed above, to improve the allocation of resources, the government would presumably conform to this mandate. But here is the important point: The voters' majority decision to do or not to do this will have been a *rational* one only if they have come to be aware of the *costs* as well as the utilities of the kind of program they vote for. The chief utility of government controls over private resource allocation lies of course in the net gain in want-satisfaction that comes from the correction of misallocation. But there are also important costs that should be weighed by the voters: (*a*) Any thoroughgoing program of government control might well involve a very substantial reduction in the amount of democracy in the country, i.e., in the freedom to make one's own economic choices. Imagine how union members would feel if the government set limits on the wage rates or other terms of employment which they could demand, or compelled them to disband their unions; and similarly, how the owners and managers of enterprise would feel about governmental limits on the corporations' freedom to ask for certain product and resource prices and to combine or merge. (*b*) A significant portion of the country's resources (manpower and so on) would doubtless have to be shifted from the production of economic goods to the policing of governmental regulations. (*c*) The loss of freedom might be so large and so keenly felt that the owners and managers of enterprise might lack incentive to produce and to expand their operations. In other words, there might be a serious deterrent to economic progress in the economy.

All these costs mean losses in total want-satisfaction for the country's household members. Only if the voters, after careful weighing, were to decide that the utility — the gain in want-satisfaction resulting from the superior allocation of economic resources brought about by the government's program — was greater than the losses, would there be a rational choice among the alternatives.

But here again the alternatives might well be divisible; it might be possible to have *some* degree of government regulation and *some* considerable amount of economic freedom as well, rather than complete regulation versus complete freedom. Then the problem for the voters is to tell their government what they consider to be the optimum combination.

C. ECONOMIC PROGRESS AND WANT-SATISFACTION

1. The nature of progress. "Economic progress" is a term used to designate circumstances under which, in the economy as a whole, the amount of want-satisfaction experienced per person per period of time, such as a year, increases "secularly" over time. (Because actually it is impossible to gauge amounts of *want-satisfaction* from any or all goods, the usual measure of economic progress is *physical net output* of goods per person expressed over time in dollars of constant purchasing power.

"Net" output or income is value of gross physical output minus dollar amount of capital depreciation minus the total of excise or sales taxes plus total government subsidies.) For economic progress to exist, it is not enough for *total* want-satisfaction or net income to rise; there must be a *per-capita* increase if people in general are to be better off.

2. Causal elements. Economic progress can take place under either of two conditions: (*a*) when, relative to any increase in the satisfaction-experiencing population over time, there is an increase during that period in the *quantity* of the resources (capital and labor) which produce want-satisfaction; or (*b*) when, given any changes in population and quantity of resources, there is an increase in the *quality* of resources.

In respect to economic progress produced by a relative rise in quantity of resources, the most important resource-item is capital. That is, net capital accumulation is the chief way of raising the per-capita amount of satisfaction from the standpoint of quantity of resources. But even without net capital formation (or without a rise in the size of the labor force relative to population), economic progress would take place if the *quality* of existing amounts of capital and labor were improved. Improvement in quality takes place through *advances in technology*. Such advances occur because of inventions in the ways of embodying capital in tools and machines and because of inventions in the managerial methods of using labor with tools and machines. Better machines and managerial methods can be just as potent in producing economic progress as more machines and labor (relative to population). Usually, however, both forces work together during the same periods.

If economic progress depends in the first instance on relative changes in population and in quantity and quality of resources, the basic determinants lie in the conditions affecting (*a*) human decisions on size of family (birth rates), death rates, and migration into and out of the country (these are the main population factors); (*b*) human decisions on proportion of family that shall enter the labor market and on the allocation of time between leisure and income-getting (these decisions have to do with the size of the labor force); (*c*) human decisions, by firm-owners and managers (plus government officials to the extent that government engages in capital formation) on net investment in capital; and (*d*) human decisions on the development and use of technological improvements.

Most of the conditions affecting these decisions will be discussed at appropriate places in this book. The points to be emphasized here are two: First, all the decisions involve to some extent the theory of rational choice among divisible alternatives of known utilities and costs, as explained earlier in this chapter. Second, if an alternative that is good for society — in other words, that is conducive to economic progress — is to be chosen by a private decision-maker, he must be convinced of its utility *for him.* As a properly, humanly selfish entity in a democratic society, he cannot be expected to disregard his own interests for the good of society as a whole. The problem for society is to encourage private individuals to make choices that are not only directly good for them but also indirectly beneficial to the whole community. In short, economic progress is not likely to occur if the government of the society acts in such a way or allows private organizations in the society to act in such a way that there are serious general *losses* in the *incentives* for private capital formation and technological improvement.

It should be clear that an economy in which there are losses from the misallocation of resources can nevertheless experience economic progress. And, as suggested at the end of the preceding section, it is possible if not certain that too-stringent efforts by government to improve allocation might result in serious deterrents to progress.

Finally, government itself in a positive, direct sense may undertake major responsibility for economic progress by itself doing most or all of the net capital formation. This means government ownership and operation of most or all of the industries — in short, socialism. The society's voters, then, are faced with the alternatives of private enterprise and public enterprise. These alternatives, divisible in "theory," may well be largely indivisible in actuality. Can a nation exist for long "half slave and half free"? In any case, here again the voters cannot make a rational choice unless they know the costs as well as the utilities of each alternative.

D. INCOME DISTRIBUTION AND WANT–SATISFACTION

There is more to maximizing and enlarging the amount of want-satisfaction than obtaining the optimum allocation of resources and achieving economic progress. The degree of inequality with which the national income is distributed among the society's households is also an important factor. In order to concentrate on its influence let us continue to assume that resources are fully employed; and let us for the moment disregard the allocation of resources as well as any elements of economic progress.

1. What determines the distribution of income? The income of any household during a given period of time may be thought of as the number of dollar claims on goods providing want-satisfaction that it obtains during that period. This number of dollars depends mainly on two things: the *unit prices* paid to the household for the services of the productive resources that it owns and finds employment for in the markets; and the *quantity* of each resource that it owns and finds employment for.

A fairly detailed exposition of the conditions affecting the prices of labor resources is given in Chapters 6 and 8. It is enough to say here that, other conditions held constant, the scarcer the resource in the market, the higher the price it brings to its owner. A household offering skilled labor tends to obtain a higher prices for it in a given labor market area than a household offering unskilled labor, because unskilled labor is relatively plentiful.

Thus, one cause for inequality of incomes among households is inequality in the *quality* or grades of resources that they possess. But a much more important source of income inequality lies in the *quantity* of resources owned and employed. And most of the inequality in ownership is in the capital resource. As we shall learn, most of America's households possess no savings or capital, or at best very small amounts, whereas a small minority of households own the bulk of this resource.

Both factors together — unequal distribution of quality and quantity of resources — operate to make the distribution of income (before taxes) in the United States very unequal. The two factors usually go hand in hand; the scarcer, higher-priced resources are owned by the same families who own most of the resources.

2. The optimum distribution of income. In our consideration of income inequality here, we take no position in terms of social equity, morality, and so on. Our sole concern is with the maximization of want-satisfaction in the society as a whole as this is influenced by income distribution.

In order to understand what the optimum distribution of income or money claims is, we must first consider the distribution of something else — the capacity of the human beings in the various households to experience and enjoy want-satisfaction. A moment's thought suggests that, like any other human trait, this capacity is not equally shared; there are substantial individual differences, as in ability to play a musical instrument. Now, part of this inequality is the result of the individuals' differing heredities; some persons' glands tend to make them clods, while others' tend to produce extreme sensitivity and capacity to enjoy. But environmental influences are also extremely important. The opportunity to learn to enjoy comes from the environment, and here "rich men's sons" seem to have a distinct advantage. In other words, distribution of income can have a good deal to do with distribution of the capacity to enjoy. Nevertheless, modern mass-media advertising plus motion pictures and television would seem to provide a widespread opportunity for the acquisition of "tastes."

Let us start by treating the two distributions as given. It would appear that the distribution of the capacity to enjoy is in general much less unequally shared than are the money or income claims on want-satisfaction.

The principle of distributing income in optimal fashion may be stated as follows: The best income distribution — the one that maximizes the whole society's want-satisfaction — corresponds precisely with the enjoyment-capacity distribution. Therefore, if the former distribution is more unequal than the latter, the wealthier households should yield some of their incomes to the lower-income households. If this is done, society experiences a loss in want-satisfaction because of the losses to the rich; and society experiences a gain in satisfaction through the gains to the poor. But up to the point where redistribution of income becomes the same as distribution of the capacity to enjoy, the gain to the poor exceeds the loss to the rich, and there is a net gain to society as a whole. To make the income distribution *less* unequal than the other distribution would not do either, for here the loss to the rich would outweigh the gain to the poor. The optimum point is the one where the two distributions are identical. Here total satisfaction as a whole is maximized; here the marginal utility of an income-dollar becomes the same for every household.

3. Government action. This principle for achieving the optimum distribution of money claims on want-satisfaction is highly "theoretical." Although it is possible to measure the distribution of income among households before and after redistributing it, it is *not* possible to measure the distribution of the capacity to enjoy. Consequently, there must be reliance on some rough, "practical," rule-of-thumb method of redistributing income.

Clearly the only agency able to effect any thoroughgoing redistribution in the society as a whole is government. Certain organized groups like labor unions and farmers' associations may be in sufficiently favorable economic and political positions to raise members' incomes at the expense of non-members' incomes in certain sectors of the economy. But here, at least in the long run, it is always possible that the members' *real* incomes will not rise relatively, even though the prices of what the workers' and farmers' organizations sell (labor and farm products) do rise. This possibility exists because these prices are a part of the firms' production costs; and any increase in these costs may be reflected in higher prices for the products bought by workers and farmers. In other words, the efforts of these groups may not succeed because the price components of their incomes are set in resource markets and bargains that are in a production chain with the final-product markets. Any temporary success in the resource markets, where workers and farmers operate as organized sellers, may in the end be nullified in the product markets, where these individuals act mostly as unorganized buyers. Moreover, workers and farmers are not universally organized; and even if they were, their unions would not be equally strong in all sectors of the economy.

A progressive income tax system administered by government appears to be the most generally effective rule-of-thumb method of taking money claims away from the wealthier households. The tax funds may then be given to the lower-income households, either directly in cash, as in a family-allowance system, or indirectly, through government provision of "social services," such as free parks, libraries, roads, recreation, low-price housing, unemployment benefits, medical benefits, and pensions.

This system of redistributing income and of trying to reach the optimum distribution seems superior to the methods used by labor and farmer unions because it is universally applicable and because it falls on households *after* they have received their incomes, at the *end* and not in the *middle* of a chain of market transactions or bargains. In other words, the taxed households are not, in the narrow sense, able to shift their taxes to some other individuals or groups in other, subsequent market dealings.

In a broader sense however, there may be some significant "shifting" of the income tax to the society as a whole. And to whatever extent this happens, the imposition involves a social cost, a loss which, when one is trying to decide what the optimum distribution should be, must be added to the loss in consumer want-satisfaction experienced by the wealthier households when they are taxed. In other words, there are two losses which must be weighed against the gain in satisfaction experienced by the low-income households when they receive the "free" social services. This second possible cost or loss arises from the discriminatory nature of the tax. When income from high-grade labor is taxed, there is discrimination against work-for-income in favor of the good known as leisure. A tax on salary income constitutes a cut in salary and may thus, at the margin, lead the taxed person to decide to work less. If this happens, society suffers from a reduction in the amount of available managerial and highly skilled labor. When the income from the lending of savings (namely, interest income) is taxed, there is again discrimination, this time against saving and investing in favor of using income for consumption. This may cause the economy to suffer from a reduction in the amount of the capital resource available. In short, a progressive income tax system may involve a diminution of the incentives that, in a private enterprise democracy, seem to be necessary for a high rate of economic progress.

No one knows how steeply progressive an income tax system may be made before the possible losses from resource reduction become actual and significant. That there is such a point, however, can hardly be doubted. And to whatever extent such losses are brought about, there is a diminution in the rate of economic progress.

It is evident, then, that government action in the field of income distribution involves costs as well as utilities. As in the field of resource allocation, both costs and utilities must be carefully weighed by household voters if they are to make rational choices between the alternatives of government interference and no government interference. Here again, however, it is fortunate that the alternatives are not indivisible.

4. Relation to resource allocation. Finally, it should be clear that the distribution of income has a close relation to the allocation of resources within a society. For every different distribution of income there is a different optimum allocation of resources. This is because resource allocation is determined by the dollar votes of households as they express their preferences in the product markets. Under a markedly unequal distribution of income the richer households hold disproportionately high numbers of votes; resources are thus moved disproportionately into the production of the products they prefer. By the same token, any redistribution of income in favor of the low-income households gives the latter more claims over resources than before. Resources are moved to some extent away from the production of "luxury" goods and into the production of "necessity" goods. And if the optimum distribution of income were to be discovered, there would be an accompanying optimum allocation of resources for the society to aim at.

E. EXTENT OF RESOURCE UTILIZATION

The losses in total want-satisfaction to a society from misallocation of resources and markedly unequal distribution of income may well be serious. However, it is to be doubted — especially in view of the possible costs of government action to improve allocation and distribution — that these losses are nearly so large as the loss in satisfaction that occurs during a severe, prolonged depression, when a large percentage of the resources (both labor and capital) are unemployed. In other words, the most important necessity for a society seeking to make the level of satisfaction as high as possible is that there be full utilization of existing resources. It is therefore necessary for us to consider generally and briefly here (leaving details for later chapters) the causes of such underutilization and what government may do to eliminate them.

Obviously at this point we abandon our previous assumption that there is full employment of resources. We are now in the real world.

1. What causes low resource utilization? If "full employment" of resources is an essential element of maximizing satisfaction, we must first define the term. Does it actually imply 100 per cent utilization, or can we settle for some lower, more modest figure such as 95 or 97 per cent, which would mean about two or three million unemployed persons out of an American labor force of 65 million? The latter would seem to be much more realistic because, even when the level of business activity is very high, in a country of free labor markets there are always, on any one day, some workers who have left their previous jobs in search of better ones, and there are always some employers who are laying off workers because of reductions in demand for their products, increases in their production costs, technological innovations, and so on.

With this definition in mind, we may say that during any given period of time the level of employment or resource utilization depends in the first instance on the flow of total money spending in the society during that period. There is one particular level of spending that will provide full utilization, as defined.

Total spending is made up of government spending on goods and services (i.e., not including government disbursements that represent merely transfers of funds from one group, such as social security payments) plus two items of private spending: households' spending on consumption products and firms' spending on investment goods (durable plant and equipment, plus inventories of products and materials).

Let us assume for the moment that government spending is nonexistent; there are only the two items of private spending. Then we may note that when there is a decline in total spending, there will be a decline in employment, real or physical output, and money income; and these latter declines will be a multiple of the fall in spending. When, on the other hand, there is a rise in total spending, we must consider two situations — the one in which the economy is at a position of less than full employment when the increase in spending occurs; and the one in which there is already full utilization. In the first case, total employment, real output, and money income will rise by a multiple of the increase in total spending. In the second case, there can be no increase in employment and real output because we have assumed no economic progress and because there was full resource utilization to begin with. Here there will be only a (multiplier) rise in money income and an inflation of the price level.

What produces the decreases or increases in total spending? This question seeks the more basic causes of unemployment and of full employment without or with price inflation. In other words, what makes households spend less or more on consumption goods, and firms less or more on investment goods? The answers lie in the motivations and decisions of households and firm owners and managers (including bankers) as they try to adapt themselves to the conditions of a dynamic society in which change, often unexpected change, and uncertainty about the future are the rule. Both households and firms make plans into the future; they make present decisions about how much they will buy or sell now and at various possible dates in the future. These decisions are based in large part on the relationships that exist between the current prices of the products or resources bought and sold by households and firms and the prices expected to prevail in the future. Any change in the current and future price relationships will cause revisions in plans and thereby changes in the present amounts that households and firms have decided to buy or sell. Thus, if it is believed that future prices will rise relative to current prices, plans will be revised so that less will be sold now and more will be bought now; in other words, there will be a rise in current private spending. Or if future prices are expected to fall relative to current prices, purchases will be shifted to the future and sales to the present; there will be a fall in total current spending.

Uncertainty as to the accuracy of expectations about future prices is also important in affecting current spending. In general, the greater the degree of uncertainty, the shorter will be the lengths of the periods over which households and firms will venture to plan. They hesitate to make long-term commitments; they prefer to live "hand-to-mouth." The fewer the commitments into the future, the lower the amount of present spending in behalf of commitments.

In the dynamic economy a particularly important class of firms is the banks. This is because the banking system as a whole, within the limits of the ratio of reserves to loans set by government or the central bank (in America the Federal Reserve Board), is able to expand the quantity of money in the country by granting loans to other firms for investment spending. Conversely, the banking system is able to reduce the quantity of money by refusing to renew previous loans or grant new ones. These powers of the banking system thus affect directly the amount of investment spending and indirectly the amount of consumption spending.

Thus we see that the price expectations of households and of banking and non-banking firms, plus the factor of uncertainty, are very important determinants of the flow of spending during any period of time Great uncertainty, as long as it exists, makes for a low-level stagnation of spending, and thereby of income and employment. Expectations of relative falls in future prices lead to diminished present spending, income, and employment. Expectations of relative rises in future prices lead to increased current spending, income, and employment until the "full" point is reached, after which inflation develops.

What causes households and firms to have particular expectations or to be uncertain? The answers here lie deep within the wellsprings of human behavior. Experience with past circumstances similar to those of the present is significant. For example, households and firms who lived through the inflation of World War I could with certainty predict a similar rise in prices during and after World War II. Lack of experience, i.e., a strange new situation, often makes for uncertainty and timidity in planning into the future. Affecting all decisions is the fact that human beings, especially when ignorant or uncertain, are extremely suggestible to what others believe will happen. In other words, crowd behavior or "mob psychology" is common to human beings; they often stampede in one direction or another, i.e., are subject to mass moods of optimism or pessimism. Thus, during a period of prosperity we find businessmen almost unanimously "bullish," making generally future commitments in *waves* for investment in technologically improved machines and in inventories of products to be held for expected price increases. There is often much overreaching in such commitments; future demands for the inventories and for the machines' products have been overestimated by the firm-owners and by the bankers who lent the funds to finance the investment. Then comes reaction and pessimism as the country heads down into a depression.

2. Roles of government. We must now bring government into the discussion. Government policies can reinforce unfavorable trends in private spending, i.e., those making for unemployment or inflation; or they can be compensatory to private trends so as to offset the latter. Without going into detail here we may distinguish two main categories of government policy in this field: first, policies used by the central bank to encourage or discourage the making of loans by banks or other financial institutions to firms for investment spending and to households for consumption spending; and second, policies bearing on the amount of expenditure on goods and services by government itself, in relation to amount of tax revenue obtained from the private sector of the economy. The first kind of measure focuses on the control of private spending; the second emphasizes the government's own spending.

We shall reserve discussion of these measures until Chapter 22, where we deal with the government approach to unemployment. Our emphasis here is on the fact that certain costs as well as utilities are involved. And again the country's voters must weigh them in order to find the best rational combination of government action and no government action.

F. MAXIMIZING POLITICAL WANT–SATISFACTION

In Sections B through E of this chapter we have dealt with particular aspects of the principles of rational choice and of maximizing want-satisfaction in economic terms. In each case we have also shown what government's role might be, what the main utilities and costs of playing these roles might be, and what the voters would have to do to make rational choices about what the roles of government should be. It should have become apparent to the student, then, that the problem of choice and of maximizing and enlarging a whole society's want-satisfaction is political as well as economic. In this section we focus on these political matters in general terms.

Whenever, in the preceding sections, we have talked about the desirability of rational voters' choices among the divisible alternatives of government "interference" versus "no-interference," we might instead have spoken of a choice between *freedom* for private individuals and organizations to make their own decisions unaffected by government versus the *security* of having these decisions regulated or even made entirely by the sovereign over-all agency. In the political field, then, whatever the immediate, specific issue may be, the fundamental choice with long-run implications is between freedom and security.

It is important for the voters, when faced with a particular issue, to recognize that they are also choosing between these basic alternatives. In essence they are deciding what shall be the allocation of the country's total political resources. It is also important for the voters to know that these two goods are not indivisible — that the significant choice is not between all of one and none of the other. Rather, the problem is to obtain some of each in optimum combination. In order to do this the costs as well as the utilities of each must be known. Absolute freedom means anarchy. Absolute security is synonymous with death. But a reasonable base of security from which men can have freedom to venture, and to which they can return for solace from defeat or for rest from their labors, seems to promise the highest satisfaction in terms of what we have learned about the nature and behavior of human beings as individuals and in groups.

Even though a society might have attained maximum want-satisfaction from the standpoint of optimum resource allocation, optimum income distribution, full resource utilization, and economic progress, it could *not* be said to have maximized its over-all satisfaction from the *political* as well as economic sense unless the members of the society had had an opportunity to choose and had chosen rationally between freedom and security.

G. BASIC DETERMINANTS OF TOTAL WANT-SATISFACTION

As we know from Section A of this chapter, "maximization" refers to getting the most out of available economic and political resources. We know also that "resources" include economic resources, technology, and social organization. It follows from these definitions that, even though two nations had both maximized their respective satisfactions in the sense explained at the end of Section F, one of them would have a higher total and per-capita level of satisfaction if it possessed a superior quantity and quality of available resources. In other words, given the households' wants and preferences in any society, and apart from the problem of maximization, the level of satisfaction in that society is determined by the quantity of economic resources, the level of technology, and the structure of economic and political institutions, laws, customs, and ideas that is known as social organization.

CHAPTER 4

The Historical Background

In Chapter 1 we said that labor problems involved areas of maladjustment within or among the groups concerned with the conditions under which workers live and are employed or seek employment. Now, the conditions in the 1950's — economic, political, technological, and so on — under which workers live and are employed or seek employment did not just happen; they are the product of change and development over centuries. Similarly with the interested groups themselves — the owners and managers of industry, the consumers of industry's products, the workers, workers' unions, and government: Their very existence and the ways in which they are organized and function in order to achieve want-satisfaction cannot be fully understood without reference to the historical record.

The necessity for this review may also be considered in terms of the material and concepts presented in Chapters 2 and 3. Human beings have in common, although in varying degrees of intensity, certain general goals or desires. They also adopt certain specific goals in their efforts to attain the general goals. To achieve these general and specific objectives they try a number of strategies and tactics, including organization in groups and group tactics. The resources available for attaining group and individual goals (want-satisfaction) are limited. Therefore arise the problems of raising the quantity and quality of the resources and of making optimum allocation of existing resources among competing goals and groups. It is the history of efforts to solve these problems, with special reference to the ways in which workers have been involved, that we are undertaking to tell in this chapter and the next. What were the significant events and changes that left their mark on present-day economic resources, technology, and social organization?

A. THE "REVOLUTIONS" AND SUBSEQUENT CHANGES

Because the conditions affecting labor in modern American society have their origin in the society of Europe, and particularly of England, that emerged from the thousand-year medieval period, it is desirable for us to go back to the changes producing this emergence. Then we can consider the effects of these changes on the United States.

1. In Europe. During the Middle Ages society in Europe was relatively stable, static, and simple. Total and per-capita want-satisfaction was relatively low. The natural resources available for use (in the economic sense) were neither many nor ample; they consisted mainly of arable land, forests, a few minerals like coal and iron, and natural harbors and rivers. The stock of capital, the man-made resource, was relatively small. Technology was simple; its level was not much above that of ancient times. Security of existence and status was a more common, more highly regarded human goal than was individual freedom to raise one's level of existence and one's status. Much more attention was given to religious matters than in modern times; and in this field the authority of the Church was supreme. Society in general was organized under a system that smacked more of collectivism than of individual private enterprise. In the towns, productive activities were rigidly controlled by the gilds, which regulated prices, output, and sales. (The earlier merchant gilds were general in scope, whereas the later craft gilds were narrower organizations of master and journeymen producers of various products like cloth and apparel. But, aside from the very fact of organization, the gilds were not similar to modern labor unions, or forerunners of them. Nor were the gild members "workers," as that term was defined in Chapter 1.) In rural areas, the manorial system of social organization and common land utilization governed the social and economic activities of lords, freemen, and serfs, none of whom were "workers" in terms of our definition. The whole conglomerate of manors and towns, from the lowest-status serfs and apprentices to the highest-status lords and mayors, was linked to the king by the system of mutual rights and duties known as *vassalage.*

The urban and rural feudal systems were not absolutely static. There was some change, although it was gradual and slow. The tempo of the changes, however, became accelerated toward the end of the feudal period. Beginning about 1500 and continuing for three centuries or so thereafter, certain profound alterations took place in four fields — alterations that were so momentous as eventually to obliterate medieval society. Because of their far-reaching effects they have been called "revolutions" — the *commercial revolution,* the *agricultural revolution,* the *ideological revolution,* and the *industrial revolution.* None of these was a separate, compartmentalized movement. All overlapped and merged with each other over periods of time or at the same time; they were the joint products of the same underlying forces.

a. The commercial revolution. During the Middle Ages there was little trade. The manors were economically almost self-sufficient. There were a few traveling fairs, markets for the exchange of products, at favorably situated towns, and a small amount of sea-borne trade with other countries. But such obstacles as poor roads, feudal tolls, lack of a standard full-value currency, crude navigation techniques, and piracy prevented much commerce.

However, after the feudal system had become stabilized under strong national rulers, after wants had been stimulated by the contacts of Crusaders and sea adventurers with the products and ideas of the East, after new lands had been discovered in the West, and after the economic-political doctrine of *mercantilism* had arisen to furnish a justification for large increases in the export of staple domestic products, a number of significant developments took place. Trading companies, with special privileges and with the right to make and retain huge profits, far in excess of the medieval "just" amounts, in case of successful venturing, were chartered by the rulers (e.g., the East India Company, the Hudson's Bay Company, and the Hanseatic organizations). Many of these trading groups were joint-stock companies; that is, their capital was obtained from the savings of many rather than of one or a few persons. Here may be found a forerunner of the modern corporation. At the same time relatively stable, full-value national currencies came into being through royal edict or through the activities of money-changers and goldsmiths, who began to lend out money at interest, keeping as reserves against loans only a fraction of the currency entrusted to them by depositors for safekeeping. Thus, a banking system began to develop, and a spirit of commercial adventuring grew up among many people. Clearly, among these developments may be found some of the beginnings of the "capitalistic" or private enterprise system.

b. The agricultural revolution. This "revolution" refers to certain changes in land tenure and in farm technology which began in the sixteenth century and lasted through the eighteenth. It was particularly notable in England, where the changes were referred to as "enclosures." Under the manorial system most of the land was not enclosed or fenced. Small strips were worked in rotation for crops by the serfs, who paid the lord for the use of the land by giving him a portion of the output. Every third strip was allowed to lie fallow each year to renew its fertility. The lord kept some of his land for his own use; and he might add to his holdings by buying strips from the serfs, paying them cash therefor, or by taking over the land of serfs who had no sons.

When under the commercial revolution the demand for wool rose greatly, the lords were given an incentive to change from crop production to sheep grazing. With government approval and sanction they acquired land more rapidly and in larger amounts from the serfs and freeholders; they put it to pasture and fenced it in for sheep-raising. Then, because fewer men were needed for sheep-tending than for crop-growing, a large excess supply of labor developed in the rural areas. Here was a reservoir of labor for the factories that were soon to come.

c. The ideological revolution. We have already seen how important are the ideas and beliefs that men live by; they seem to need "spiritual" and intellectual support or rationalization for the policies and tactics they employ in trying to satisfy their wants. Such support was not lacking for the budding capitalists. Just as the medieval system of subordinating individual freedom and initiative to the collective quest for security was reinforced by the Church, whose authority held individual desires and actions subservient to its own, so the new system of private ownership of productive economic resources, private management of enterprise, and private appropriation of the profits of enterprise came to be buttressed by the Protestant movement, which emphasized individual "faith and works" as the "way to salvation." Clearly, if individual effort is good for the attainment of want-satisfaction in the hereafter, it is valid for achieving satisfaction in the here and now.

In the fields of political thought, economics, and philosophy there came also to be emphasis on the rights, duties, and welfare of the individual. This idea underlay the development of the *laissez-faire* or hands-off policy for government, of equalitarianism among human beings, and of emphasis on the "greatest good of the greatest number" in a society. In short, the "liberal philosophy" of the nineteenth century was based on the worth of the individual.

Of all the areas affected by the intellectual renaissance and the return to the ideas of early Greece and the East, perhaps the most important, in terms of ultimate influence, was science, pure and applied. Here was a field, long fallow, which was to bear fruit in the tremendous technological changes of centuries to come.

d. The industrial revolution. (1) Technological changes. The industrial revolution was essentially a technological one; but it was integrated with other developments, including those sketched above. Its end-products included the organization of production in factories, the consolidation of the private enterprise system, and the rise of a class of labor that worked for wages. The specific technological improvements (based, to be sure, on previous developments) were clustered in the eighteenth century and included Watt's steam engine plus five inventions in the field of textiles — two in weaving (Kay's flying shuttle and Cartwright's power loom) and three in spinning (Hargreaves' jenny, Arkwright's frame, and Crompton's "mule"). From textiles, technological inventions and innovations marched into mining, smelting, transportation, and many other areas. This march, of course, has never stopped; with occasional pauses for consolidation, it has gone on at an accelerated pace.

Technological innovation involves not only the use of improved tools and machines, but also betterments in methods of management, in ways of utilizing, combining, and controlling materials, tools, machines, and labor to produce goods or services. Accounting controls, such as double-entry bookkeeping and cost records, began to be developed in the century of the revolution. The "scientific management" of the early twentieth century and the production and personnel management of more recent decades were based on earlier efforts to improve the techniques of management. The division of product-making into specialized tasks — "division of labor" — was one of these. The "factory" itself, i.e., the enclosing of all the operations related to the production of one or more products under the roof of one building, was a managerial development directly related to the technological changes and to the availability of labor.

(2) The domestic and factory systems. We have already said that part of the necessary labor came from the farms after the enclosures had produced surpluses there. The other main source was an excess supply that resulted from the decline of the earlier "domestic" or "putting-out" system of producing woolen cloth. This system is of much interest for our review here, not only because its demise helped to man the factories but also because its existence provided another step in the growth of the private enterprise system. Briefly, the following elements were involved: The controls of the medieval gild system broke down under the earlier "revolutions" at a time when the growth of trade had greatly increased the demand for woolen cloth. An increasing number of persons began to spin yarn and weave cloth in their own homes with their own crude spinning devices and looms. They needed reliable sources of raw material (wool) and reliable markets in which to sell their products. This development gave certain merchant capitalists a chance to enlarge the scope of their operations. "Broggers" bought raw wool from the farms and sold it at a profit to other middlemen, who stored it and sold it as needed to the clothier-capitalists. The latter sold it to the domestic workers (the women and children usually specializing in spinning and the adult males in weaving), who after finishing the making of the cloth sold it back to the clothiers; these, in turn, sold the cloth to other merchants on the way to the final consumers. Then gradually came an increasing concentration of economic power in the hands of the clothiers. Instead of selling the wool to the domestic workers and buying back the cloth, they kept title to it and paid the workers in "wages" for the output. The clothiers solicited additional families into the making of wool cloth; and now the clothiers provided and kept ownership of the tools and machines. Next they decided to dye and finish the loom-cloth of various households at a central establishment. All these steps proved to be cost-reducing and profitable. Finally, after the invention of power machinery, it was a natural further cost-reducing step to enlarge these central finishing establishments and install the spinning and weaving operations there under the direct supervision of hired managers. Thus, by assuming the risks of loss involved in buying raw materials, manufacturing, and selling the products, the merchant capitalists were able to merge all the operations into unified, highly profitable ones. Private enterprise was vindicated in their eyes: Through the factory and wage systems they had devised, they

provided enlarged markets for farmers' wool, employment for the surplus labor from farms and towns, and increasing quantities of lower-priced cloth and garments to consumers.

What happened in woolens was repeated in shoes and other products. The industrial revolution was "rolling."

(3) *The condition of the working class.* The changes outlined above found their first and fullest expression in England; and England maintained its technological and "capitalistic" lead among all nations through the entire nineteenth century.

We have seen how private enterprise and the worker-wage system grew up. We must note that the changes in the three determinants of the level of total want-satisfaction — capital, technology, and social organization — greatly increased the per-capita output of most of the goods that provide satisfaction. There was, in other words, great economic progress by the middle of the nineteenth century, after the medieval period of relative stagnation.

But we must also note that these increases were very unevenly distributed among the members of the English society. The shift from the system of security to the system of freedom did not pay off evenly. For the owners and managers of the new enterprises there were enormous gains in virtually all the tangible and "psychic" elements that compose the total pattern of individual want-satisfaction. But for most of the members of the new working class it is to be doubted that there was much net benefit. For a while, there may even have been net losses in satisfaction. To come to these conclusions, one has only to read of the conditions under which people lived and worked. Not only men, but women and young children as well, were drawn to the factories for employment. Around the factory-clusters grew up cities in which the housing and other conditions were generally appalling. Filth and squalor characterized the greatly overcrowded streets, houses, and barracks where the workers lived. In the factories, wage rates and incomes were low, work periods were very long (twelve or more hours a day and seventy-two or more hours a week), and working conditions were both unsanitary and dangerous.

These conditions were a major reason for making workers, as sellers of labor, wish to form unions for self-protection, and as voters, wish to have government regulate and improve the conditions under which they lived and worked — all with a view to enlarging their share of the increases in satisfaction made possible by the industrial revolution. These were the two main alternatives of the British working class to remaining the way they were. Another possible alternative was migration to the New World.

2. In America. *a. The colonial period.* Of the four revolutions described above, the first three were under way during the colonization of America. The changes wrought by the commercial, agricultural, and ideological revolutions made many people available and willing to undertake the grand adventure. But, as might be expected under very different environmental conditions, the rise of industry in America came much later than in England. Before the war for independence the country was predominantly agricultural, with a little manufacturing of apparel and food products done in independent homes, and with the production of a few other goods (e.g., leather, shoes, and printing) performed on a small scale by artisans in the seaboard towns.

There was also a shortage of labor for hire. In those days, Americans possessed an alternative not available to stay-at-home Europeans — free land ready for clearing and farming; and many Americans took advantage of this opportunity to become economically independent, responsible for their own levels of want-satisfaction. (This condition of course persisted long after the colonial period had ended.) To relieve the resultant labor scarcity in the northern colonies an "indentured servant" system was devised, whereby free men in effect sold themselves into servitude for varying periods of time in return for ocean passage to the New World. In the South the system of Negro slavery or human capital was developed in order to provide labor for agriculture and handicraft industries.

Another important reason for the slow and late development of colonial manufacturing in factories was the economic-political philosophy and policy of mercantilism pursued by European rulers. They believed that the prosperity of the mother countries depended on obtaining raw materials from and selling finished manufactured products to the colonies at a profit. This meant, of course, that colonial manufacturing had to be prohibited, or at least taxed so heavily as to make it unprofitable. These restrictions were in fact a major cause of the American war for independence.

b. From 1790 to 1850. Independence having been won, the new nation did not experience an industrial revolution as rapidly as might have been expected. The government proposed to stimulate the growth of manufacturing with subsidies and tariff protection. But the development was gradual and slow, and it was not until about the middle of the nineteenth century that any significant shift away from the predominant agricultural economy became evident. One reason for this industrial lag was a continued shortage of labor (except in periods of business depression). Another was a relative lack of technological know-how. Still another was the lack of a large national domestic market for manufactured products.

But the period before 1850 was not static. There was an upward movement among the determinants of total and per-capita income and satisfaction. By 1810 there had been an accumulation of capital sufficient to permit the development of small "mill and furnace" establishments making lumber products, iron products, brick, and glass. Much as in England during an earlier period, merchant capitalists in cotton, wool, and shoes got together out of profits enough capital to transform the earlier American system of domestic and handicraft production into the beginnings of a factory system. As in England, their labor supply came from the home-workers and the artisans; here, too, these persons became increasingly members of a laboring class working under a wage system.

Technological improvements in transportation by water and by land gave more mobility to labor and capital and widened the market available for the products of any one producer. In other words, these changes broadened the area of competition among the owners of resources and the sellers of products who hired the resources. New manufacturing techniques were also invented, such as Whitney's gin for cleaning and straightening cotton fibers. In time, the English inventions in spinning and weaving came to be utilized. Accompanying the technological changes in both transportation and manufacturing was an increased amount of specialization. Firms in certain geographic areas like Pennsylvania concentrated on particular products like iron and steel. There was also more specialization in the jobs involved in making a given product. And because of this increased specialization, the parts of the economic mechanism became increasingly interdependent.

In 1837 the growing young nation experienced significantly for the first time one of the costs of the private enterprise system of economic organization — a serious financial and business depression of several years' duration. Tens of thousands of members of the new working class became unemployed, along with the tools and machines with which they worked, as total spending fell off sharply.

c. From 1850 to 1915. By the middle of the century the tempo of capital accumulation and technological change began to be accelerated, partly because of investment here by the private owners of capital in other countries. Much of America's rich virgin natural resources remained to be exploited and used for profit. Gold was discovered in the West. The formation of capital and the invention of new techniques in transportation and manufacturing were of course stimulated by the great scarcity of labor. Both of these changes were very important in the growth of the country, leading as they did to higher levels of income and to continuously widening markets for resources and products. But it is to be doubted that the rise of American industrialism would have been nearly so rapid and cumulative if there had not been at this time a very significant increase in the quantity of the scarcest resource, labor.

This "accumulation" of labor came mainly from without rather than from within the economy; that is, it came from immigration. Successive waves of European migrants beat upon America's shores, in search of economic opportunity or political and religious freedom. Some came of their own initiative; others, as a result of solicitation by representatives of manufacturing firms and steamship companies. From 1845 to 1915 the total number was in excess of 30 million. At first, most of them came from countries in the northern and western parts of Europe. But before the end of the century and until 1914, the immigration was predominantly from the southeastern areas of that continent.

Although a majority of the immigrants had been on farms in Europe, most of them (except the Germans and Scandinavians) took non-farm jobs, usually unskilled, in the East upon their arrival in the United States. They usually possessed neither the knowledge nor the financial resources to obtain farms or farm work here.

After the Civil War and before the first World War the capital resource grew more rapidly than ever. There were spurts of technological innovation in 1865–73, 1879–89, and 1898–1907. East-west and north-south, the country was spanned by a network of railroads. Markets became national in scope for most transportable products. By 1900, the economy of the United States had changed from a primarily agricultural to a predominantly manufacturing one, and important alterations in social organization were under way.

Among the most significant innovations was the corporate form of business enterprise, which was devised to provide indefinite life for a firm and to place under a single control, through the sale of stock to many savers, much larger aggregates of capital than would be available to most firm-owners as individuals or partners. An outstanding reason why large amounts of capital under a unified ownership were needed lay in the big, complicated, expensive machines that technological invention was making available for production. The corporations waxed rapidly in size and economic-political power.

Because of labor scarcity and the alternative of migration to the West, the wage rates and incomes of American workers seem in general not to have been so relatively low as those of English workers. The living and working conditions seem also to have been relatively better. Nevertheless their levels of want-satisfaction seem to have been sufficiently low to have caused them to try to form unions for self-help. Moreover, most workers seem to have felt they were losing their skills and occupational controls to the newly invented machines. The factory system, with its minute division of labor and its machine production, was making workers mere appendages to the machine. They had lost contact with the consumers of the products they were helping to make. They often found the work monotonous and stultifying. They had lost much of their control over when, how long, how hard, and where they were to work. All these things led many workers to turn to unionism. The earliest labor organizations came in the period between 1790 and 1850, discussed above; these were local in geographic scope and were short-lived for various reasons — the repressive attitudes of courts toward their activities, the ravages of the 1837 depression, unsuccessful tactics, or the opposition of employers. But the efforts to organize continued. There was experimentation with organizational structure and tactics. After such experimentation, extending from 1850 through the Civil War, enduring national labor organizations were formed among many of the skilled-worker groups. A federation of these was achieved in 1886, the American Federation of Labor.

Waves of labor violence in strikes and lockouts shook the country in the middle eighties and early nineties. The unions lost most of these contests, and many employers refused to deal with labor organizations. But by the middle nineties labor peace was restored. In that decade, for the first time in American history, labor-employer agreements reached by collective bargaining were reduced to writing and signed by both sides.

Because of the growing complexity and interdependence in the economic system and because of the increasing concentrations of economic and political power in the hands of certain corporations and labor unions (which tended to give them significant degrees of monopolistic control over small, unorganized buyers and sellers), there were two important developments in the field of government: first, an increasing centralization or concentration of governing power in the hands of the federal government; and second, a growing tendency to abandon *laissez faire* and regulate "big business" (e.g., through the Interstate Commerce Act of 1887 and the Sherman Anti-Trust Act of 1890) and to be concerned with relations between employers and unions (through both court decisions and statutes). These developments showed an increasing concern by government over the need for maximizing and enlarging want-satisfaction and for distributing satisfaction less unequally.

During this long period from 1850 to 1915 there were two severe business depressions (1873 and 1893), and at least two minor ones (1907 and 1914). Existing labor unions survived these economic storms. But their members, along with the members of other groups, suffered the usual diminutions in income and satisfaction.

d. After 1915. Because the student is undoubtedly somewhat familiar with the main events of the past three decades, they need only be mentioned here.

In the years during and immediately after both world wars the country learned the principles and practices necessary for an adequate control of resource allocation, income distribution, and inflation. After 1920, in the period as a whole, the *rate* of capital accumulation may have tapered off, but there were important spurts of net investment from 1923 to 1929 and after World War II. During these years of capital expansion there were important technological improvements — not only in tools and machinery but also in managerial techniques.

With the severe governmental restrictions put into effect after World War I, immigration ceased to be a major element in the growth of the American labor force. Most of the recruits came from the second generation of non-farm workers and from internal, domestic migration (i.e., the movement from farms to cities). During depressions like that of 1929–33, it is true, there were net movements from cities to farms, as unemployed workers migrated to rural areas in search of secure, independent subsistence. But over the longer period the net migration was farm-to-city, for there was an excess supply of labor on the farms. For one thing, the birth rate was much higher in rural areas than in the cities, because children were considered economic assets by farm households and liabilities by city households. For another, the increasing productivity of farm workers, due to the technological inventions, allowed a much smaller farm labor force to produce even more output than a larger force did previously.

Finally, a number of changes in social organization and ideas developed. Mobility between occupations and occupational groups tended to decline among workers. It became decreasingly possible for a worker to pass from one level of skill to another and, more important, from the worker class to the entrepreneur or "boss" class. During the twenties, moreover, the previously developing separation between the ownership and the managerial control of corporations became widespread. Managerial hierarchies became power-entities distinct from the (usually) large, unorganized groups of uninformed stockholders. At the same time, the corporate form of enterprise became overwhelmingly predominant in all the major fields of production except agriculture, construction, and professional service. And the large corporations became disproportionately powerful. In other words, the production of want-satisfaction products was increasingly concentrated in a few hands. In economic terms, this meant an increasing tendency toward monopoly in the sale of products and monopsony in buying labor — and thereby a rising tendency toward misallocation of resources. In social terms, these developments meant wider gulfs and diminished understanding between corporation management and consumers, on the one hand, and management and unorganized workers, on the other. These gulfs came not nearly so much from any consciously "evil" or anti-social attitudes of management as from ignorance, carelessness, and excessive concentration on management's immediate problems.

The prolonged and severe depression of 1929–33 shook many Americans' confidence in the judgment of American businessmen and in the ability of the private enterprise system to deliver sustained, high-level want-satisfaction in the absence of government intervention. A considerable change in the intellectual and emotional climate had occurred by 1932. A determination arose to enforce on management a degree of responsibility commensurate with its power. Whereas the resistance of large-scale manufacturing management to unionism during the twenties had seemed to have rather wide social approval and government sympathy (so that in general the strength of the movement waned somewhat during this decade), the mass unemployment of the next few years had changed the minds of numerous workers, legislators, and judges, and of not a few employers. Even before the Democratic Party's New Deal became a reality, Congress had passed legislation, e.g., the Norris-La-Guardia Act, favorable to the growth of unionism; and with the change in government came not only further legislation helpful to labor but also other controls over management in its other relations, e.g., with consumers, inventors, and competitive firms. Under these favorable conditions the economic and political strength of unionism increased very rapidly, so that by 1945 many of the employers who had been forced to deal with unions were asserting that now the employers were the underdogs and that therefore the unions needed some regulation by government. (Some such regulation was provided in 1947 by a Republican Congress in the Labor-Management Relations Act of that year.) A socially unfortunate aspect of the rise of big unionism was the split within the movement, between the A.F.L. and the C.I.O., which developed out of the inability or unwillingness of the older federation in 1934 and 1935 to attempt the unionization of the unorganized workers in mass-production industries like basic steel and automobiles. The split carried over into the fifties because of the struggle for power and the jealousies among the top leaders of the rival groups and because of the absence of any common external danger serious enough to demand the unity of amalgamation.

Another important development after World War I was the organization of farmers, whose power by 1951 had risen enormously. This was not so much the result of their forming cooperative marketing associations under government encouragement as of their political potency. Both political parties, and all candidates for office in areas where the farm votes were numerous, paid much attention to farmers' wants — so much so that during World War II and during the defense period beginning in 1951, when the wage rates of labor and the prices of non-farming firms' products were controlled, there were no adequate government limitations on the heights to which the prices of farm products might ascend.

From the above-mentioned changes in social organizations and ideas, two main conclusions may be drawn in respect to the role of government in the over-all social organization of households, firms, and their groups. First, the tendency, begun in the nineteenth century, of centralized government to regulate firms, organizations of firms, and unions so as to raise the total want-satisfaction and distribute it less unequally has continued at an increasing pace. Second, because the decisions of government have assumed such importance, organizations of farmers, of non-farm firms, and of labor have tried more and more urgently, in elections and through "lobbying," to influence these decisions in favor of increasing their respective shares of total satisfaction.

The second half of the twentieth century began, then, with a social organization in which big business, big unionism, and big farmerism faced each other in the economic and political arenas, with big government playing an increasingly important role trying to attain a measure of control over and balance among these organized groups — and with the unorganized individuals (e.g., professional persons and most other white-collar workers) more and more occupying positions of relative inferiority. This power pattern is in marked contrast to that existing before the "revolutions." During the Middle Ages it was the warrior-landowners, the gildsmen, and the churchmen who shared and struggled for economic and political ascendancy.

Finally, in the broadest sense the swing of the pendulum has brought men back from emphasizing freedom to stressing security. During the medieval period security had the major preference; in allocating political resources, men chose a much larger amount of security than of freedom. Then, with the revolutions, preferences shifted; the emphasis then was on freedom and adventure in all fields. But as the costs of unadulterated freedom became better understood by entrepreneurs and workers and their government, preferences once more swung toward security. In some authoritarian countries like Russia very little freedom has been chosen. In democratic countries like the United States and Great Britain there is an effort to have some of both; here, as previously stated, the problem is to find the optimum combination.

CHAPTER 5

The Historical Background (concluded)

B. POPULATION AND THE LABOR FORCE

At various places in the preceding chapter we have referred to certain conditions that produced changes in the American population (potential labor supply) and labor force (actual supply). In this chapter we shall focus on these matters. If we are to understand the problems in which American labor is involved, we must know more about the nature and growth of the group we have defined as workers.

1. Population trends. In any economy the size and composition of the population help to determine the size and composition of the labor resource. We shall consider here some of the major aspects of (*a*) the growth of total population and (*b*) the sex, racial, geographic, and age distribution of the population.

a. Total figures. (*1*) *Population.* Column 2 of Table 1 shows the population of the United States for the decennial census years, beginning with 1790. From the data in column 3 it will be observed that each decade registered an increase in absolute numbers; that the increase from 1860 to 1870, the Civil War decade, was very little more than the increase during the preceding decade; that the increase during the World War I decade was less than from 1900 to 1910; that the increase during the depressed 1930's was the smallest since the Civil War decade; but that the absolute increase during a third war decade (1940–50) was the largest ever experienced.

With the population base-number growing continuously, the percentage increases presented in column 4 are considerably more meaningful than the absolute ones in column 3. From column 4 we see that until the Civil War decade the percentage changes were uniformly very high — 33 per cent or more; that after that decade the rates of population increase fell, with especially sharp drops during the decade that included World War I and during the depression decade; and that the percentage rise during the 1940's, while less than during the 1920's or any other earlier decade, was twice as high as that during the 1930's. This sharp reversal confounded the estimators of future population. On the basis of the

TABLE 1 *Growth of Population in the United States*

Census Year	Total Population (in millions)	Increase over Preceding Census Year	
		Number (in millions)	Per Cent
1790	3.9	—	—
1800	5.3	1.4	36
1810	7.2	1.9	36
1820	9.6	2.4	33
1830	12.9	3.3	34
1840	17.1	4.2	33
1850	23.2	6.1	36
1860	31.4	8.2	35
1870	39.8	8.4	27
1880	50.2	10.4	26
1890	62.9	12.7	25
1900	76.0	13.1	21
1910	92.0	16.0	21
1920	105.7	13.7	15
1930	122.8	17.1	16
1940	131.7	8.9	7
1950	150.6	18.9	14

Source: For years 1790–1940, *Statistical Abstract of the United States, 1949*, p. 6; for 1950, U. S. Bureau of the Census, *Current Population Reports.*

decline during the thirties they had guessed that the 1950 figure would be substantially lower than it turned out to be; and they had been predicting that population in this country would stop rising by about 1980, with a peak figure of perhaps 165 million.

Whether the population rises, falls, or remains stable depends on the circumstances affecting birth rates and death rates and on the conditions influencing immigration into and emigration out of the country.

(2) *Birth rates and death rates.* By themselves, separately, birth rates and death rates and changes in each tell us little about population changes. It is the relationship between them that is important. When

TABLE 2 *Birth and Mortality Rates in the United States*

Period or Year	Number of Births per 1000 of Population	Number of Deaths per 1000 of Population
1915–1919, average	24.3	14.4
1920–1924, average	22.9	12.0
1925–1929, average	20.2	11.8
1930–1934, average	17.6	11.0
1935–1939, average	17.1	11.0
1940–1944, average	19.9	10.6
1945	19.6	10.6
1946	23.3	10.0
1947	25.8	10.1
1948	26.9	9.9
1949	24.0	9.7
1950	23.5	9.6

Source: Data 1915–47 from *Statistical Abstract of the United States*, various years; data 1948–50 from Federal Security Agency, Public Health Service, National Office of Vital Statistics, *Monthly Vital Statistics Bulletin*, various issues.

the number of births per 1000 persons in the population exceeds the number of deaths per 1000 persons, the population tends to grow; and vice versa. But the relationship between the percentage changes in each is also very important; it tells us whether the population is tending to grow at an increasing, decreasing, or stable rate. Thus, if the birth rate exceeds the death rate year by year but the rate of decline in the former is greater than that in the latter, the population tends to grow at a diminishing rate.

The data in Table 2 show that from 1915 (the first year for which the country had adequate vital statistics) through 1939 both the birth rate and the death rate were falling; but that the percentage declines in the birth rate exceeded those in the death rate. Therefore, unless the effect of these relationships were counteracted by net immigration, we could conclude that population was rising at a declining rate. But after 1939 the relationship changed. The death rate continued to drop somewhat, while the birth rate rose to unprecedented heights for the whole period. This fact is reflected in Table 1 in the population figures for 1950.

The conditions affecting birth rates are economic, technological, and social. Economic motives and advances in technology have had three main effects: First, higher incomes per family have been made possible, and their existence has stimulated parents to desire such incomes for themselves and for their children. Second, the industrialization and urbanization of the country resulting from technological change and capital accumulation have caused most parents to view large families as economic liabilities rather than assets; except on farms, the cost of having children is calculated to exceed their economic contributions. Third, given the *desire* to limit the size of families, technology has provided the *means* — in the form of contraceptive devices.

Other conditions affecting birth rates are the prevailing social and religious views on the propriety of using contraceptive methods and on the desirability of early marriage. Such views may have only informal sanctions or they may be backed by law, such as minimum statutory requirements for length of schooling. Moreover, governments concerned with military expansion often advocate large families in order to build large armies.

Advances in medical and industrial technology and in capital formation, in addition to the generally held humanitarian beliefs on the desirability of preserving individual lives, appear to have been mainly responsible for the continuing decline in the death rate. Improvements in production technology and the accumulation of capital have provided such higher national incomes that government has been able to make notable strides in public health work and education, at the same time that medical science has discovered new and better means of preventing and curing disease. As a result, the life expectancy of the population has risen sharply.

(3) *Net immigration.* By "net" immigration we mean the difference (positive or negative) between the number of immigrants arriving per period of time and the number of emigrants leaving during the period. In addition to the comments made in Chapter 4 on this subject, the data in Table 3 are presented here to show what an increasingly significant factor in population growth immigration was before World War I, and how much this factor declined in importance after the government decided, in 1921–24, to limit it very strictly by exclusion or by quotas.

b. Composition of the population. There is space here for no more than a summary of major facts about trends in the make-up of the population. At least a summary seems necessary, however, in order that we may better understand certain characteristics of the labor force.

Until 1950 the number of males has always been somewhat larger than the number of females. In 1820, for example, there were 103 males for every 100 females. This difference reached a peak in 1910, when the ratio was 106 to 100. By 1940, however, it had fallen to less than 101 to 100; and in 1950 the ratio was 98.1 to 100. This trend parallels the one in immigration, and it is doubtless true that the rise and fall in the importance of immigration has been mainly responsible for the abovementioned changes. Among the immigrants there was always a considerable preponderance of males. (It is true that there have always been about 106 male births to 100 female births; but the death rates among males have exceeded those among females for all age groups.)

In 1950 almost 90 per cent of the population was white, almost 10 per cent Negro, and a half of one per cent other races. The white race had been increasing and the Negro race declining in *relative* numbers for more than a century. The whites, of course, were not a homogeneous group, having come from many different European countries, as pre-

TABLE 3 *Immigration and Population Growth*

Decade	Number of Immigrants[1] (in millions)	Percentage of Population Increase Due to Immigration
1841–1850	1.7	27.9
1851–1860	2.6	31.3
1861–1870	2.3	27.4
1871–1880	2.8	27.2
1881–1890	5.2	40.6
1891–1900	3.7	28.5
1901–1910	8.8	55.0
1911–1920	3.7	27.0
1921–1930	3.2	18.7
1931–1940	−0.04	−0.4
1941–1950	0.9	4.5

Sources: For 1841–1940, J. F. Dewhurst and Associates, *America's Needs and Resources*, Twentieth Century Fund, New York, 1947, p. 32; for 1941–50, *Statistical Abstract of the United States, 1950*, and U. S. Department of Justice, Immigration and Naturalization Service, *Annual Report* (Fiscal Year Ending June 30, 1950), appendix, table 1, 2, and 13.

[1] Only figures for decades after 1910 show net immigration. For previous years, data are available only on immigration.

viously noted. With the severe curtailment in immigration, however, and with intermarriage among the various white sub-groups, the population was beginning to lose some of its heterogeneity. But the country was too large and geographically diverse for one justifiably to expect the sort of homogeneity found in certain European countries like Great Britain.

In 1790 almost 95 per cent of the population was rural (that is, living on farms or in communities with a population of less than 2500). The rural population outnumbered the urban until 1920, but the former's predominance after 1790 was a declining one. In 1950, 63.7 per cent lived in communities of 2500 or more inhabitants ("urban"), 20.6 per cent in smaller communities ("rural non-farm"), and 15.6 per cent on farms ("rural farm" population). Moreover, of the 96 million persons living in nine different sizes of urban communities in 1950, 30 per cent were located in cities of one million inhabitants or more; and this was by far the largest percentage class.

Most of the manufacturing establishments in the United States have always been located in the east-north states — roughly, those east of the Mississippi and north of the Potomac rivers. Here also, as would be expected, have lived about 60 per cent or more of the population. Most of the large cities are in this area.

Within the country as a whole there has been a considerable amount of migration. The east-to-west movement is of course classic and was the main one in the nineteenth and early twentieth centuries. But there have been other important internal migrations. Substantial numbers of Southern rural and urban Negroes have moved to the cities of the North and, to some extent recently, of the far West and Southwest. This trek was the combined result of diminishing opportunities for an agricultural livelihood in the South, the increase in job opportunities in the North and West, and the promise of greater political and economic freedom. The droughts in the Southwest during the middle thirties resulted in extensive migrations to California. Both these changes were part of the general farm-to-city migration previously mentioned. During World War II there were also important migrations to the industrial cities of the North and far West. Southern California has experienced the largest relative population growth among all areas in recent years.

The age composition of the American population has been undergoing striking alterations in recent decades. The conditions influencing the trends in birth rates, death rates, and immigration have led in general to the declining relative importance of the younger age groups and to the increasing importance of the older age groups. This development is expected to produce a corresponding change in the relative political and economic importance of the different age groups. For example, the recent pension drive by labor unions is not a mere happenstance; it is a reflection of these changes in the age composition of its members.

2. The American labor force. Population is the potential labor resource. Let us now consider the actual present-day labor force and the trends in its growth.

a. What is the labor force? How do we get from the potential to the actual force? There are two main considerations: *ability* to work, and *willingness* to work. Many individuals in the population are unable to work. Some are too young to fulfill work requirements. Others are too young, not for lack of physical or mental ability but because government or custom requires them to obtain a minimum of education. At the other end of the scale are the aged; either government or custom or physical and mental handicaps prevent them from entering the labor market. In between the too-young and the too-old are other more or less permanent unemployables — those who are also under enduring physical or mental or social disabilities.

Housewives are not counted as part of the labor force. This is not because they are unable or unwilling to work or because they do not in fact perform very important work. It is simply that they do not normally offer their services for hire in any labor market.

When the deductions from population are made for persons unable to work and for women occupied solely with the work of their own households, we are left with a balance of persons who could work if they wished. But even this group are not "the labor force" because they are free to choose between the alternatives of not-working and working-for-income, i.e., between the goods known as leisure and income. Many households can choose between having their children work and requiring them to obtain education beyond the minimum demanded by law. All households who are able to work can choose, within limits set by employers or government, how many hours they are willing to work per day, per week, or per longer period. And even when household members are working on jobs, they are often able, within limits determined by supervision or by the speed of the machines with which they work, to set the pace of their work so as to expand more or less energy per period. Absenteeism and tardiness are other ways in which workers, again weighing possible discipline by employers, vary the number of hours offered in the labor market.

Ideally, then, the labor force would be measured in terms of labor-hours of uniform quality. But to do this accurately in practice is statistically impossible. So those who count noses in census enumerations and those who make estimates for the years between censuses are compelled to measure the work force in terms of *persons.*

Whether hours or persons are used as the measure, we must note carefully that "the labor force" involves a considerably larger number of units than do "workers" as defined in Chapter 1. It includes "independent" professional persons, proprietors, and managerial persons in addition to the "workers" — in short, all those who offer their services in labor markets.

To use persons rather than hours greatly simplifies the problem of measuring the labor force. But let no one think that measurement thereby becomes simple. Let us look at some of the obstacles.

(1) The "gainful worker" concept, 1870–1930. Until very recently our knowledge of the American labor force was meager. Before 1940 we had to rely on the general population census taken every ten years. There were attempts in these decennial censuses to obtain information about workers and their jobs as early as 1820, but it was not until the ninth census in 1870 that a very serious effort was made to discover the total number of gainfully occupied persons. A "gainful worker" was defined as a person who "usually" worked at a given occupation from which he "earned money or its equivalent" or in which he "assisted in the production of marketable goods." Only workers who reported a "usual, gainful" occupation were counted as workers. This approach was followed with only slight change through 1930. It provided much valuable information about the occupational shifts taking place during a period of tremendous territorial and industrial expansion. But the "gainful worker" approach contained some very serious weaknesses and left wide gaps in our information.

First of all, a great many people were included as workers who should not have been included. Workers who were too old to work or who were permanently disabled reported themselves as having a "usual occupation" and were counted as workers. Actually they were not in the labor market, and most of them would never be again. Inmates of prisons had been asked by society not to work, but they too reported having "gainful occupations" and therefore were counted as workers. The same error applied to housewives who had worked at one time but had permanently withdrawn at the time the census was taken.

Second, other groups were *not* included in the census count who should have been. For example, new workers just out of school who had not yet obtained occupational experience could obviously not report a "gainful employment" when the census-taker called. They were classified as non-workers under the "gainful worker" concept. Actually they were in the labor market and very actively seeking jobs.

There were other serious technical deficiencies in the definitions used and numerous cases of underenumeration and overenumeration especially as regards "marginal" workers like housewives, children, and students. These persons often have a dual role, sometimes working and sometimes not working full or part time for pay. From the foregoing it is easy to understand why it was impossible from early census data to build up an accurate picture of the entire work force of the country.

In addition to the shortcomings noted above, one other proved serious. The time-consuming task of tabulating a census covering the entire population meant that the data were not available until two or three years after the enumeration. The census was already out of date for current usage when published. Ten-year intervals between censuses meant we had no knowledge of the year-to-year or month-to-month changes so essential to an up-to-date understanding of current problems.

(2) The crisis of the 1930's. Serious as these shortcomings were, they did not become critical until the 1930's. After the business cycle turned down in the fall of 1929, a series of supplemental questions were asked in the Fifteenth Decennial Census taken in April, 1930. These questions were designed to bring out more facts concerning the "current status" of workers. Census enumerators asked each person of working age if he was employed or unemployed. If unemployed how long had he been unemployed? Was he still looking for work? And so on. But because of the weakness in the "gainful worker" concept, a great many persons were excluded who should not have been, and others were included who obviously should have been left out. In some instances it was impossible to tell from the census returns what the status of the persons really was. For example, some persons were reported as "unemployed, having a job but on layoff without pay." If they were called back to work shortly after the enumerator visited the household, they clearly should be counted as employed. But if, as the business depression deepened, they were not called back, they most certainly should be classified as "unemployed." Once again the problem of the "new" worker plagued the statisticians. It became clear that, despite the extra effort in the 1930 census, probably a million persons had been classified as non-workers, not because they were not seeking work, but because under the "gainful worker" concept they could not report a "gainful occupation." Thus at the onset of a major depression we had very inadequate knowledge of our working population.

As the depression continued to worsen and unemployment rose into the millions, desperate efforts were made by business, labor, and government to estimate the total number of unemployed. All efforts used the same techniques. They consisted of (*a*) projecting an estimated labor force from the 1930 census "count" of total gainful workers; (*b*) estimating the number of employed workers (from non-census sources, which were themselves subject to an almost infinite variety of errors); and (*c*) obtaining "estimated" unemployment by subtracting (*b*) from (*a*). It is little wonder that the various "estimates" varied by as much as several million. In 1940 the "estimates" ranged from as low as 2 million to as high as 9 million. We can agree with Professor Douglas when he said in the late twenties that "the American statistics on unemployment are the worst of any industrial country in the world,"[1] and with Professor Hauser when he said, "we blundered through most of the critical decade of the thirties without ever knowing the actual magnitude of the mass unemployment with which we were confronted."[2]

[1] Paul H. Douglas, *Real Wages in the United States*, Houghton Mifflin Company, 1930, p. 12.

[2] Philip M. Hauser, "The Labor Force and Gainful Workers — Concept, Measurement, and Comparability," *American Journal of Sociology*, Vol. 54, No. 4, January 1949, p. 354.

(3) *Development of the "labor force" concept in the 1930's and thereafter.* As a result of this blundering, the efforts of statisticians and labor economists, both private and governmental, were focused after 1935 on the task of finding new techniques which would enable us to fill in the glaring gaps in our knowledge of the labor market. The objective was to find a way of obtaining information about workers which would (*a*) be current, i.e., available for use within a few weeks from the date of reference; (*b*) include non-workers as well as workers, since there is constant movement between these two groups; (*c*) include new and inexperienced workers as well as those with gainful work experience; and (*d*) provide not only an adequate classification of the entire work force but also an explanation of why workers found themselves in a particular "status." For example, if experienced workers were unemployed at the time of enumeration, was this unemployment voluntary (due to factors for which the worker assumed responsibility) or involuntary (due to factors for which society had to assume responsibility)?

Out of this period of study and experimentation, 1935–40, came two major advances. The first was the development of a sample census of the entire population which could be taken every month and the returns from which could be "blown up" to national proportions and published within a few weeks. The second was the development of the "labor force" concept, which, when applied on a monthly sample census basis, would yield the detailed information needed for an adequate understanding of the work force. The concept was first used in the Sixteenth Decennial Census of April, 1940. It has been used in a sample census every month since that time. The survey covers a rotating sample of 25,000 households in 60 representative counties. The enumeration takes place in the week containing the eighth day of each month. The results are published within three weeks by the U. S. Bureau of the Census in a release entitled the *Monthly Report on the Labor Force* (the *MRLF*). It can now be said that the United States has close to the best instead of the worst information on current employment and unemployment trends.

(4) *Understanding the current measurement of the labor force.* The best way to understand the new technique of measurement is to examine the *MRLF* for a given month. In Table 4 the basic information on population, labor force, employment, and unemployment is presented for September, 1951. Additional types of information are provided in each monthly issue of the *MRLF*, and special studies of particular problems are published from time to time.

The *MRLF* deals only with the adult segment of the population and excludes all those persons below 14 years of age who obviously have no work status. The adult population is divided into the non-labor force (housewives, students, and so on) and the labor force proper, with which we are primarily concerned. In peacetime, major interest centers in the

TABLE 4 *Population and Labor Force, United States, September, 1951*

Population — Total (all ages) [1]		154,853,000
Population — Civilian non-institutional (14 years of age and over)		108,956,000
Non-labor force		45,770,000
Keeping house	33,080,000	
In school	4,882,000	
Permanently unable to work	2,214,000	
Too old to work		
Retired	5,594,000	
"Other" [2]		
Labor force [3]		63,186,000
Employed		61,580,000
At work	58,476,000	
35 hours or more in week	34,928,000	
15–34 hours in week	21,506,000	
1–14 hours in week	2,042,000	
With job but not at work	3,104,000	
Temporary layoff	156,000	
New job or business	20,000	
Bad weather	144,000	
Industrial dispute	96,000	
Vacation	1,606,000	
Illness	622,000	
All other [4]	460,000	
Unemployed		1,606,000
Actively seeking work		n.a.
Temporarily not actively seeking work		n.a.
Illness	n.a.	
Indefinite layoff	n.a.	
No job available in regular line of work	n.a.	

n.a. — Not available

Source: U. S. Bureau of the Census, Population Reports, *Monthly Report on the Labor Force*, September, 1951, Release P–57, No. 111, October 5, 1951.

[1] Provisional estimate.

[2] Includes "seasonal workers for whom the survey week fell in an 'off' season," voluntarily idle, and persons doing incidental unpaid family work of less than 15 hours in census week.

[3] Excludes armed services force for which data not published after beginning of hostilities in Korea. Unofficial estimates place armed forces at between 3.0 and 3.5 millions in September, 1951, making nation's total labor force at least 66 million.

[4] Includes "personal" reasons such as illness of other members of family, personal business, etc.

civilian labor force and the extent to which its members are employed or unemployed.

It is the measurement of the "employed" and "unemployed" that requires considerable study for a proper understanding. The *MRLF* divides the employed into those "at work," a category which is self-explanatory, and those "with a job but not at work." This latter group is divided into some seven types (see Table 4). The workers who are classified in this group are persons who were away from their jobs when the census was taken but who cannot be considered jobless because their jobs are being held for them. Their absence is *temporary*. It is due to illness, weather, vacations, or similar factors. Before the *MRLF* was devised, this group was often misclassified or not counted at all.

The unemployed are also divided into two groups — those "actively seeking work," which is self-explanatory, and those "temporarily not actively seeking work." The latter are workers who are without jobs but who for special reasons (see Table 4) are not actively seeking work for the time being. A worker who is seriously ill is out of work but obviously not in the labor market in the same sense as an unemployed worker who is knocking on the employer's door every day asking for a job.

The new monthly measurement of the labor force represents a very great advance in understanding our economy. It provides a barometer for the condition of business in general. It provides a current yardstick for measuring the extent to which we are utilizing our labor resources. From 1941–45 it proved useful in gauging our success in mobilizing secondary labor reserves for wartime purposes. It provides the current data necessary in carrying out the full employment policy in the Employment Act of 1946. Finally, it provides a vast amount of data which students of labor may utilize in analyzing the complex functions of our labor market.

b. Trends in the labor force as a whole and as a percentage of population. The figures in Table 5 are roughly suggestive of the growth of the American labor force and of the relationship of the force to total population, even though, as explained in the preceding section and in the footnote to the table, the data are not wholly comparable. In 80 years the size of the force rose more than fivefold. And over this long period there was a noteworthy increase in the proportion of the total population offering to work for income.

The second of these two conclusions may be expressed in another way. Statistics on trends in the size of population and labor force show that in 1890 there were 182 persons not in the labor force for every 100 persons in the labor force, whereas fifty years later the ratio had dropped to 147:100.[3]

This increase in willingness to sell labor services in the market meant that the economy's labor resource in 1950 was much larger than it would have been if the inclinations of 1870 or 1880 had held. If only 33 per cent of the population had entered the labor market in 1950, the labor force would have numbered only about 50 million, or 15 million less than it actually did. This would undoubtedly have meant a substantial reduction in the national output of goods and services.

There were conflicting influences at work on the nation's inclination and ability to labor for hire. Fewer young people were able to work because of the rise of the compulsory-school-attendance age. But this inability was somewhat offset by the declining relative numerical importance of this age group in the whole population. The rise of the old-age group in relative importance, together with the increased financial provision for their

[3] See J. D. Durand, *The Labor Force in the United States*, Social Science Research Council, New York, 1948, p. 43.

TABLE 5 *Growth in American Labor Force, 1870–1950*

Year	Number (in millions)	Percentage of Total Population
1870	12.9	32.5
1880	17.4	34.7
1890	23.3	37.2
1900	29.1	38.3
1910	37.4	40.6
1920	42.4	40.1
1930	47.6	38.8
1940	53.3	40.5
1950	64.6	43.0

Sources: For 1870–1940, Dewhurst and Associates, *op. cit.*, p. 542; for 1950, U. S. Bureau of the Census (preliminary estimate; includes armed forces). The data for 1870–1920 are not closely comparable with those for 1930–1950, the earlier figures being somewhat higher than they would have been if the methods of later years had been used. The 1930 figure has been adjusted to comparability with that for 1940 and 1950.

retirement, was also a factor operating against any increase in the percentage of labor force to population. But the industrialization and urbanization of the economy freed women from non-labor-market housework and led many of them to enter gainful employment. As the data in columns 5 and 7 of Table 6 suggest (see page 71), it was this condition that outweighed all the unfavorable factors and produced the rise shown in the last column of Table 5.

In recent years approximately 1.8 million young men and women change annually from economic dependency to maturity and enter the labor force for the first time. During each year about 1.0 million persons *leave* the labor market as a result of injury, retirement, or death. In other words, recently there has been a net addition to the labor force of about 0.8 million job-seekers per year.

It should be noted that we have thus far been considering long-term or *secular* changes in the labor force. Over shorter periods of time, such as the years of prosperity and depression in a peacetime *business cycle*, it is to be doubted that there are any significant changes in the proportion of the population that is able and willing to work. During a bad depression there might well be an increase in physical and mental disability because of human deterioration among the long-term unemployed persons. But this tendency toward a reduction in the size of the available labor force might be offset by an increased willingness to work on the part of persons not normally in the labor market, such as housewives, who now seek employment because of lowered household income. During the prosperity phase of the cycle, there might be increased ability to work, offset by lessened willingness.

There are definite *seasonal* fluctuations in the size of the labor force and in the proportion of labor force to total population. The low point during any year comes in January, after the Christmas-month splurge in employment; and the high point comes in July, when the labor force becomes swollen with temporary workers (mainly students and housewives) who take employment in canneries, on construction jobs, at vacation resorts, and so forth. The difference between the low-month and high-month labor forces has recently been from 4 to 5 million. Thus, any annual figure for the labor force is either an average for all twelve months or a figure for some "medium" month like April.

c. Composition of the labor force. The foregoing discussion has already suggested that some of the reasons for the change in the percentage of total work force to total population lay in changes in the labor-force participation of young people, old people, and women. For this reason, and because of the inherent interest and value of the data, we review here various aspects of labor-force makeup, past and present.

(1) Males and females in the labor force. The figures in Table 6 establish that, while the total numbers of both males and females rose markedly from 1870 to 1950, the rate of increase for females was significantly higher. In 1950 the males in the work force outnumbered the females by about 2.5 to one, but this numerical superiority was much smaller than in previous decades because the percentage of all labor-force females to total female population more than doubled during the 80-year period, whereas after 1870 the percentage of labor-force males to total male population rose only a few percentage points.

(2) Age groups. The declining relative numerical importance of the low- and high-age groups and the rising relative numerical importance of the "middle"-age classes, discussed above, is shown by the figures presented in Table 7.

(3) Racial groups. Available data on the racial composition of the labor force indicate that the number of white persons in the force has always far exceeded that of non-white groups; that the relative numerical importance of the whites has gradually been increasing at the expense of

TABLE 6 *Sex Composition of American Labor Force, 1870–1950*

Year	Number (in millions)		Percentage of Force		Percentage of Population Ten Years Old and Over	
	Male	Female	Male	Female	Male	Female
1	2	3	4	5	6	7
1870	11.0	1.9	85.2	14.8	74.9	13.3
1880	14.7	2.6	84.8	15.2	78.7	14.7
1890	19.3	4.0	82.8	17.2	79.3	17.4
1900	23.8	5.3	81.7	18.3	80.0	18.8
1910	29.9	7.4	80.1	19.9	80.8	21.5
1920	33.8	8.6	79.6	20.4	79.9	21.4
1930	37.0	10.4	78.1	21.9	82.1	23.6
1940	40.3	13.0	75.6	24.4	79.7	25.7
1950	45.9	18.7	71.0	29.0	84.4	33.0

Sources: For the years 1870–1940, Dewhurst and Associates, *op. cit.*, p. 543; for 1950, U. S. Bureau of the Census. Data for 1930–50 in columns 6 and 7 are for population 14 years of age and over. Data for 1950 cover non-institutional population.

TABLE 7 *Per Cent Distribution of the Labor Force by Age Groups for the United States: 1890, 1940, 1944, and 1950*

Age	1950	1944	1940	1890
14 years and over	100.0	100.0	100.0	100.0[1]
14 to 19 years	7.5	11.8	7.8	15.1[2]
20 to 24 years	12.2	14.2	14.4	16.8
24 to 44 years	45.6	43.2	46.6	43.6
45 to 64 years	29.9	26.6	27.1	20.1
65 years and over	4.8	4.2	4.1	4.5

Source: Henry S. Shryock, Jr., "The Changing Age Profile of the Population," in *The Aged and Society*, symposium, Industrial Relations Research Association, 1950, p. 22.

[1] 10 years and over.

[2] 10 to 19 years.

Negroes and Asians; but that the percentages of the non-white populations still in the non-white labor force are larger than the percentage of the white population in the white labor force; and that with the restrictions on immigration the sub-group differences within the white American labor forces have been becoming smaller and less important.

(4) Occupational groups. Let us turn now to the different kinds of work performed in or offered to different industries by the members of the labor force. For this purpose the two kinds of classification discussed below are meaningful.

(a) Major industries. Since, as already explained, the aims and methods for enumerating labor-force members were considerably changed in 1940, it is very difficult to harmonize accurately the census results for 1940

TABLE 8 *Distribution of Employed Labor Force by Major Occupational-Industrial Groups, 1950*

Line	Occupational-Industrial Group	Number	Per Cent of Total
1	Total	59,269,838	100.0
2	Primary Industries	8,543,838	14.4
3	Agriculture	8,317,000	14.0
4	Forestry and Fishing	226,838	0.4
5	Secondary Industries	18,106,000	30.6
6	Mining	904,000	1.6
7	Construction (contract)	2,318,000	3.9
8	Manufacturing	14,884,000	25.1
9	Tertiary Industries	32,620,000	55.0
10	Transportation and Communication (excluding postal service and garages)	4,010,000	6.8
11	Trade (including garages and repair services)	9,524,000	16.0
12	Finance, Insurance, Real Estate	1,812,000	3.1
13	Domestic Service	1,805,000	3.0
14	Professional and Related Services	4,798,000	8.1
15	Hotels, Laundries, Motion Pictures	4,761,000	8.0
16	Government Service	5,910,000	10.0

Source: Data lines 6–8, 10–12, 15–16 from *Monthly Labor Review*, Vol. 73, No. 4, October, 1951, pp. 485–488; data lines 3, 13, 14 from U. S. Bureau of Census, *Annual Report on the Labor Force, 1950*, p. 26; data line 4 from *Statistical Abstract of the United States, 1950.*

and 1950 with those of 1870–1930 when occupational groupings in major industries are considered. Accordingly, we present here only the classification for 1950 (see Table 8). It will be observed that less than one-sixth of the labor force was in the primary or basic industries, less than one-third in the secondary (mainly manufacturing) industries, and more than one-half in the tertiary (mainly service) industries. This distribution means that in 1950 the United States was a mature, industrialized nation, wealthy in terms of per-capita incomes. All countries having a high concentration of the work force in the tertiary occupations are relatively well off.[4]

The United States was not always in this position. The occupational data for the census years before 1940 are sufficiently comparable with those for 1940–50 to establish that as late as 1870 more than half the work force was in the primary industries; and that by 1910 these industries had been outstripped by both the secondary and tertiary groups, the latter taking first rank in that year.

(b) Social-economic groups. Another, equally significant occupational classification of the labor force may be made in terms of the social-economic status of the labor-force members. Whatever the industry to which they are attached, what kind of work do they perform? Are they "independent," more or less "their own bosses," employed in professional and managerial positions? Or are they "dependent" and "bossed"? This is the sort of classification that brings us close to our previously stated definition of "worker," for the "workers" are in the lower-level, dependent groups of the labor force.

The data in Table 9 present some answers to these questions for 1950. It will be seen that about one-fourth of the persons constituting the labor force were in the upper-level categories. Roughly three-fourths were "workers," as we have defined that term. Among these, about 25 per cent were in white-collar occupations and about 75 per cent in manual jobs. Of the manual workers the most numerous were the unskilled.

The statistics for census years before 1940 are not accurately comparable with those for recent years. Nevertheless, certain trends are unmistakable. The "independent" classes have declined somewhat in relative numerical importance, though not in functional importance. By the same token, the proportion of the "worker" groups to the total number of persons in the labor force has risen. Within the "independent" classification, however, the relative numerical importance of professionals and managers has increased, whereas that of the farm group has declined. Within the "dependent" or worker classification the relative numerical position of the white-collar groups has been raised considerably at the expense of the manual groups, which show a small decline. Within the manual class, the relative numerical importance of the skilled workers

[4] See Colin Clark, *The Conditions of Economic Progress,* The Macmillan Company, New York, 1942, pp. 176 ff.

TABLE 9 *Social-Economic Composition of American Labor Force, 1950*

(Thousands of persons, 14 years of age and over)

Class of Person	Number	Per Cent of Total
Total Number	61,764	100.0
"Independent" classes	15,174	24.6
Professional and semi-professional	4,798	7.8
Farmers and farm managers	4,150	6.7
Urban proprietors, managers, and officials	6,226	10.1
"Dependent" classes	46,590	75.4
White-collar workers	11,476	18.6
Salespersons	3,925	6.4
Clerical and kindred workers	7,551	12.2
Manual workers	35,114	56.8
Skilled workers	8,086	13.0
Semi-skilled workers	12,540	20.3
Unskilled workers	14,488	23.5
Domestic and other service	6,416	10.4
Farm laborers	4,167	6.7
Other laborers	3,905	6.4

Source: U. S. Bureau of the Census, Current Population Reports, *Annual Report on the Labor Force, 1950*, Series P–50, No. 31, March 9, 1951, p. 26.

has declined slightly and that of the unskilled considerably, with a significant rise for those workers classified as semi-skilled.

All these changes are to be attributed to the technological, economic, political, and social developments outlined in Chapter 4 or earlier in this chapter.

(5) Geographic distribution of the labor force. The location of the members of the work force may be considered from two standpoints: first, the numbers living in the various states or regions, and second, the kind of industry in which they are employed. From the first standpoint, the geographic distribution of the labor force closely approximates that of the population itself. The second point of view has more significance; here we consider the distribution of labor in terms of the location of particular industries. Thus, in agriculture, cotton labor is found in the Southeast and the Southwest, staple-food-crop labor mainly in the Midwest, beetfield workers in Michigan and Colorado, and so on. Lumbermen are concentrated chiefly in Maine, the Southeastern States, and the far West; coal miners, in the southern and northern Appalachian mountain areas; metal miners, in the mountain states of the West. Most manufacturing, and hence most manufacturing labor, is in the North and East. Construction is a local industry. Workers in the rail transport, truck transport, and communications industries, when not actually engaged in moving things or people, are concentrated largely in the population centers. Water transportation labor is found on the East, West, and Gulf coasts; "service" labor, chiefly in the population centers; and so on.

(6) Mobility within the labor force. We saw in Chapter 3 that mobility of resources (including labor) is necessary for proper resource allocation. The ability to move "horizontally" from one job to another or

"vertically" from lower-skilled to higher-skilled jobs is also necessary for the full realization of economic and political democracy. The question thus arises, How much mobility is there within the labor force as a whole?

There are perhaps three main aspects of labor mobility. One is *geographic.* Here the material presented above on the internal migration of population is wholly relevant and need not be repeated. A second aspect of labor mobility is *occupational-industrial,* i.e., the movement from one job to another at about the same level of skill and socio-economic status. This sort of mobility is "horizontal." It may be within a given plant, between or among plants in the same industry and labor market area, or between or among plants in different industries of the area. A third kind of mobility is the "vertical," "up-the-ladder" movement *from one level of skill and status to another.*

Clearly, mobility is a matter of concern to the individual worker, to his union, to employers, and to society as a whole. We shall deal with this topic in more detail in later chapters where the problems of these groups are discussed.

(7) Some other aspects of the labor force. (a) Variations in number of hours offered for work by individual workers. Some members of the labor force offer their services for full-time jobs, i.e., for the full daily and weekly numbers of hours prevailing in the market. Others are able or willing (or both) to work only part-time, i.e., for fewer daily and weekly hours than those prevailing. Still others work in excess of the normal full-time numbers of hours scheduled for their particular jobs; they do this by working overtime on their regular jobs or by taking part-time jobs in addition to their regular ones. All workers at various times — whether on full-time, part-time, or more than full-time jobs — become unable or unwilling to work the full numbers of hours made available to them by employers; they regulate their hours through tardiness and through absenteeism (staying away from work because of temporary physical disability, dissatisfaction with work conditions, and various personal or family necessities).

The percentage of the labor force that works part-time is always changing. A special study made by the federal Census Bureau in August, 1949, showed that about 8.3 million persons — roughly 15 per cent of the entire labor force — were on part-time jobs. Of these, about 48 per cent were *voluntarily* working part-time; that is, for their own personal reasons they were unable or unwilling to work full-time. This group of about 4 million is of chief interest to us here, because we are now emphasizing the *supply* of labor rather than the demand for it. The remaining 52 per cent were involuntarily part-timers; they were able and willing to work full-time if the employers' *demand* for labor had made it possible. Of these 4.3 million persons, three-fourths usually worked full-time but were temporarily on part-time because of such conditions as shortages of raw materials and repairs to machinery in their plants. The other one-fourth said that they usually worked part-time because they could not obtain full-time jobs anywhere.

The multiple job holders are usually a considerably smaller percentage of the labor force than the voluntary part-timers. A special Census Bureau study for July, 1946, found about 1.3 million persons holding more than one job — a little more than two per cent of the labor force as a whole. Most of these "multiples" were in the agricultural and self-employed segments of the labor force.

(b) Variations in number of workers per household. If we consider membership in the labor force from the standpoint of the household rather than of the individual worker, the households who hold such membership may be classified on the basis of number of individuals offered for employment. Some households decide to offer only one person in the labor market, usually the father. Others offer the mother too. Still others send also one or more children of working age into the market. A special Census Bureau study for March, 1950, found that, among the approximately 40 million households in the United States, over 8 million (more than one-fifth) had both husband and wife working. About 2 million additional families had one or more children in the labor force. Obviously, if other conditions are equal, the wage incomes of multiple-earner households exceed those of single-earner ones.

In Part One we have defined our subject and tasks, and we have provided certain conceptual and informational tools that we believe the student should possess in order better to understand the labor problems and "solutions" that are discussed in the remainder of the book. We pass next to a consideration of the labor problems of individual workers.

PART TWO

The Labor Problems of Private Groups

SECTION A

Labor Problems of Individual Workers

CHAPTER 6

Getting and Holding a Job

A. INTRODUCTION

We have stated that one of the basic human desires or objectives is security; that security is attained at the cost of some degree of economic and political freedom; that security and freedom are not, however, indivisible alternatives but goods which may be combined; and that the main problem for any individual or group is to work out the best possible combination of the two. We have also suggested that there have been long-term fluctuations in the strength of the urge for security. It was very strong during the medieval period; it was relatively weak during the "revolutionary" period of rampant individualism; and in recent decades, for many persons in many countries, it has again become very potent.

In Chapters 6–9 we shall consider the labor problems of individual workers — and we shall find that these problems are based in significant part on the security needs of individual workers. First of all, we shall consider the problem of job security — the getting and holding of a job which, to the worker, is his source of income and hence his means of livelihood.

Now if a person feels insecure about something, he is afraid he will lose it if he has it, or he is afraid he won't be able to get it if he doesn't have it. In other words, job insecurity for an individual worker means that he is afraid he will lose his existing job or will not be able to obtain a job if he hasn't one. The question thus arises, What or who makes him afraid? What or who threatens to take his source of work-income away from him or to prevent his getting a job?

There seem to be two main sources of the fear of losing one's job. One source may be characterized as "personal," the other as "impersonal." By "personal" we mean that certain human beings with whom workers have to deal — e.g., management officials like foremen or union officials like business agents or shop stewards — have the power to deprive workers of jobs. The problem here is one of human relations. And this is true no matter what the impersonal conditions may be. By "impersonal" we mean the factors that are not directly involved in any human relationships the workers may have: the economic, technological, governmental, and other conditions, over which no employer or union has much control, which may operate to deprive workers of jobs. The personal elements (such as a foreman's likes, prejudices, and grudges) are usually highly selective in respect to individual workers. Ordinarily they do not cause all or a significant number of the workers in a particular plant to lose their jobs in any given period. On the other hand, the impersonal conditions, such as a sharp decline in the demand for a firm's products, are much less selective. They often threaten all workers or groups of workers, usually without singling out particular individuals.

In the real world — for example, when layoffs out of a firm are required by a fall in the demand for its products — the personal and impersonal elements may often act together or be intermingled in respect to particular workers. The impersonal conditions result in the layoffs, but the personal relationships between managerial employees and the workers may well determine which workers are to go. Nevertheless, for analytical purposes we shall find it useful to distinguish between the two kinds of circumstances — particularly in our discussion of the *causes* of and *remedies* for unemployment. Actually, whether a worker loses his job or is unable to get one for personal or impersonal reasons or both, he is unemployed. And for the duration of this involuntary idleness the effects on him and his family are the same.

Our treatment of each of the problems of individual workers will follow a common schematic plan. We shall consider first the *nature and extent* of the problem; second, its *effects* on workers as individuals; third, its causes; and fourth, in later chapters, the efforts to "solve" the problem, i.e., the *remedies.*

B. NATURE AND EXTENT OF UNEMPLOYMENT

Whenever a society's resources (including the labor resource) are not fully utilized, there is a loss in physical output and want-satisfaction for the society as a whole. It is this fact, as well as the harmful effects experienced by unemployed workers as individuals (these are of course part of society's losses), which moves us first to consider in fairly precise terms just what unemployment is. If unemployment is to be prevented, i.e., if the problem is to be solved, its causes must be known. And the very first requirement for any agency interested in learning the causes and solving the problem is to know exactly what the problem is.

1. The definition of unemployment. In Chapter 5 we said the labor force is composed of those who are *able* and *willing* to work. By "ability" to work we did *not* mean ability to *find* jobs; finding jobs depends mainly on employers' *demands* for labor. We were concerned with conditions affecting the *supply* of labor. To be employable, persons must not be so physically or mentally handicapped that they are unable to enter the labor market. By "willingness" to work we meant that, given the ability, persons must wish to retain or obtain some sort of gainful employment.

Broadly speaking, then, we may say that unemployment exists within the labor force when part of the labor force is involuntarily idle. Some persons who are able and willing to work cannot find jobs. But when anyone involved in making a census of unemployed persons tries to use this general definition, he is very apt to run into difficulties, for there are almost always a number of borderline or marginal cases whose status is not clear under the terms of the definition.

Let us consider some of these borderline cases. First, look at those who we have said are "unable" to work. Sometimes such persons are called *unemployable.* It is easy to see that many bedridden persons, e.g., complete paralytics, cannot be enumerated as part of the labor force. They are totally disabled. But what about those who, for example, are paralyzed only from the waist down? Such persons are able, if they like, to do what is known as "homework." They might do embroidery or finish garments or make artificial flowers or Christmas cards or wrap small products like powder puffs in cellophane for employers producing such goods. Are they members of the labor force? And what about certain persons who (from the demand side) are superannuated? They have been compelled, under the rules of their employers, to retire at the age of 65; but, still judging themselves able to work, they take odd jobs of various sorts. Are they in the labor force? Again, there are persons who have some mental disability. Is a "moron" who is capable of doing simple repetitive operations on a machine a member of the labor force?

Second, let us regard the matter of "willingness." How shall we classify the hobo who sometimes takes casual or temporary jobs when "scrounging" fails to pay off? What about workers on strike or those "locked out" by their employers in labor disputes? What about those who would be in the labor force if they were not in prison? How do we classify workers who have been laid off because of a drop in the demand for their firms' products or because of technological improvements, and who have resorted to government "relief" jobs or apple-selling or door-to-door canvassing? In view of their willingness to do such work in order to have some income, are they employed or unemployed?

To most of these questions on the so-called "marginal" persons there are no completely satisfying answers. Frequently the decisions must be arbitrary. In general the United States Bureau of the Census and other agencies include in the labor force most of the groups mentioned above except seasonal workers "out of season" and persons who are substantially disabled for physical, mental, or moral reasons. The test used for the "substantially disabled" group is whether firms are willing to hire them. Clearly, since this is a labor-demand test rather than a labor-supply test, it is inadequate. From the experience of World War II, when there was a great scarcity of labor because of the needs of the armed forces and because of the increased demands for products, we know that many persons (numbered in millions) from this hard core of "unemployables" can do acceptable work and hence become a part of the employed labor force. Nevertheless, because there seems to be no adequate way of separating by enumeration the truly from the partially unemployable, the Census definition may be accepted.

It is important to remember that our definition of unemployment includes not only those "able and willing" persons who have lost their jobs and are looking for other acceptable ones but also those who are looking for jobs for the first time (e.g., young people just out of school). In other words, the army of the unemployed contains both veterans of and recruits to the labor force.

2. Extent of unemployment past and present. *a. Total amounts.* Given the definition of unemployment and the Census Bureau's decisions on applying it, what information do we possess about the amount of unemployment at various times in the United States and about the percentages which these amounts have been of the total labor force?

In Chapter 5 (refer to pages 65–69) we discussed the old and the new methods of measuring the size and make-up of the labor force. Here we also had something to say about measuring and estimating the amount of unemployment. And we presented Table 4 showing the composition of

TABLE 10 *Labor Force, Employment, Unemployment, 1940–1950*

(Numbers are in thousands of persons 14 years of age and over)

Years	Total Labor Force Including Armed Forces	Armed Forces	Total Civilian Labor Force	Total Employment	Unemployment	Per Cent Labor Force Unemployed	Excess of Actual Over "Normal" Labor Force[1]	
							Number	Per Cent Excess
1940	56,030	390	55,640	47,520	8,120	14.5		
1941	57,380	1,470	55,910	50,350	5,560	9.7	390	0.7
1942	60,230	3,820	56,410	53,750	2,660	4.4	2,400	4.0
1943	64,410	8,870	55,540	54,470	1,090	1.7	5,720	8.9
1944	65,890	11,260	54,630	53,960	670	1.0	6,650	10.1
1945	65,140	11,280	53,860	52,820	1,040	1.6	7,200	11.1
1946	60,820	3,300	57,250	55,250	2,270	3.7	2,320	3.8
1947	61,608	1,440	60,168	58,027	2,142	3.5	2,598	4.2
1948	62,748	1,307	61,442	59,378	2,064	3.3	3,238	5.2
1949	63,571	1,406	62,105	58,710	3,395	5.3	4,877	8.4
1950	64,599	1,500	63,099	59,957	3,142	4.8	5,434	9.2

Source: Data in first five columns from *The Economic Report of the President*, January 6, 1950, p. 157, based on estimates of the U. S. Bureau of the Census and the U. S. Bureau of Labor Statistics. Data in last two columns from U. S. Bureau of the Census, Population Reports, *Normal Growth of the Labor Force in the United States: 1940 to 1950*, Special Reports, Series P–44, No. 12, June 12, 1944; *Labor Force Trends in the United States*, Series P–45, No. 11, December 21, 1945, and *Annual Report on the Labor Force*, Series P–50, for the years 1945–50.

[1] Based on 1920–1940 trend.

Details will not necessarily add to totals because of rounding.

the employed and unemployed segments of the work force for April, 1951, in terms of the labor-force members' relationship to jobs. The details of that table illustrated the Census Bureau's application of the unemployment definition.

The Bureau began to use its definition in 1940. Table 10 presents data

TABLE 11 *Total Labor Force, Employed, Unemployed, "Extras" in Labor Force, 1900–1939*

Number of Workers (in thousands of persons 14 years of age and over)

Year	Total Labor Force	Employed	Unemployed	Extras in Labor Force	Per Cent Labor Force Unemployed	Per Cent Extras in Labor Force
1900	29,025	27,378	1,647		6	
1901	29,959	28,238	1,721		6	
1902	30,905	30,405	500		2	
1903	31,842	30,319	1,523		5	
1904	32,605	31,175	1,430		4	
1905	33,653	33,032	621		2	
1906	34,647	34,790	n.a.	143	n.a.	0.4
1907	35,631	34,875	756		2	
1908	36,580	34,284	2,296		6	
1909	37,454	36,735	719		2	
1910	38,133	37,580	553		1	
1911	38,668	37,097	1,571		4	
1912	39,089	38,169	920		2	
1913	39,500	38,482	1,018		3	
1914	39,789	37,575	2,214		6	
1915	40,083	37,728	2,355		6	
1916	40,314	40,127	187		1	
1917	40,752	42,685	n.a.	1,933	n.a.	4.7
1918	41,088	44,187	n.a.	3,099	n.a.	7.5
1919	41,159	42,029	n.a.	870	n.a	2.1
1920	41,897	41,339	558		1	
1921	42,445	37,691	4,754		11	
1922	42,966	40,049	2,917		7	
1923	43,760	43,011	749		2	
1924	44,549	42,515	2,034		5	
1925	45,009	44,192	817		2	
1926	45,962	45,498	464		1	
1927	46,939	45,319	1,620		4	
1928	47,914	46,057	1,857		4	
1929	49,440	47,630	1,550		3	
1930	50,080	45,480	4,340		9	
1931	50,680	42,400	8,020		16	
1932	51,250	38,940	12,060		24	
1933	51,840	38,760	12,830		25	
1934	52,490	40,890	11,340		22	
1935	53,140	42,260	10,610		20	
1936	53,740	44,410	9,030		17	
1937	54,320	46,300	7,700		14	
1938	54,950	44,220	10,390		19	
1939	55,600	45,750	9,480		19	

n.a.—Not available.

Source: Data for 1900–1938 are those of National Industrial Conference Board as quoted in *Historical Statistics of the United States, 1789–1945*, U. S. Department of Commerce, Washington, D. C., 1949, Series D 62–76, p. 65. Workers cited in table as "extras in labor force" are referred to by the N.I.C.B. in the classification as "negative unemployment." Data 1929–39 are those of U. S. Departments of Labor and of Commerce quoted in *The Economic Report of the President*, January 6, 1950, Washington, D. C., 1950 (81st Congress, 2d Session, House Document 388), Appendix Table C–9, p. 157.

on total labor force and on total unemployment for 1940 through 1950. It will be seen that whereas in 1940, when war-preparation efforts had barely gotten under way, more than 8 million persons (almost 15 per cent of the labor force) were involuntarily idle, the number of unemployed had dropped to 0.7 million (one per cent of the force) by 1944. There were increases at the end of and after the war, but in general the high level of employment was maintained until the recession of 1949. Even then there was much less unemployment than just before the war. And there was a business recovery in 1950.

It is unfortunate that we do not have data of adequate accuracy for the pre-1940 years. But the figures for these years have enough validity to permit comparisons with the high-employment forties. Table 11 presents data for 1900–39. Before 1930 the only year of serious mass idleness was during the relatively short-lived depression of 1921, when an average of 11 per cent of the labor force is estimated to have been unemployed. But the record for the thirties is a gloomy one. It is estimated conservatively that in no year was average unemployment less than 14 per cent of the work force. From 1932 through 1935 the percentage of idleness was 20 or more, 1932 and 1933 having been especially bad years. (In March, 1933, at least 30 per cent were idle.)

From both tables it will be noted that there were years (almost all of them war or immediate postwar years) when there was "excess employment" or "negative unemployment." That is, the size of the labor force became inflated by the entrance of persons who would normally not have entered the labor market. This influx compensated in large part for the losses of the civilian labor force to the armed forces. In 1945, for example, these persons numbered 7.2 million. A special study by the federal Census Bureau found that about half of them entered the labor force as the result of an accelerated movement from schools and colleges. Another 40 per cent were housewives (mostly without children), including the wives of members of the armed services. The remainder were marginal workers, previously retired or partially handicapped.

b. Composition of the unemployed group. The data on total unemployment are very important in helping to give us a picture of the extent to which the labor resource has been utilized and the national output maximized. But it possesses the defects of all totals and averages: it fails to throw any light on the incidence of idleness among particular groups within the labor force. Unemployment, like any social disease, does not mow down its victims evenly. Some get very "sick"; others are affected very little.

A number of private and government studies have been made which throw light on the composition of the afflicted part of the nation's work force. First, the *duration* of unemployment is different for different groups of workers at any given time. This is particularly true during depression years. There is a relatively small nucleus of unemployed workers who have been idle for a year or more, a somewhat larger group (including the first) that has been unemployed for nine months or more, a still larger group for six months or more, and so on, with the great bulk of the workers idle for only a few weeks or more. In other words, during any one year the army of the unemployed has a core of long-service veterans to which new recruits are constantly being added and from which there are continued desertions. And on any one day the jobless army is very much smaller than the total number who have been unemployed during the whole year. The figures in Tables 10 and 11 are averages for the year; they do not represent the total number of different persons who became idle during any one year.

Second, there are *occupational, industrial, size-of-firm, and geographic differences* in the incidence of unemployment. Other factors equal (such as sex, age, and race), the unskilled workers have less job security than the skilled. Unemployment during depression happens more frequently and lasts longer for workers attached to industries making durable goods than for those in industries making non-durable goods. Among the durable-goods industries the incidence of unemployment is higher for capital-goods plants (e.g., those making machine tools or locomotives) than for consumption-goods firms (e.g., those manufacturing automobiles or breakfast cereals). Joblessness during depressions is less bad among consumption-goods companies making "necessity" goods like food and shoes than among those making "luxury" goods like automobiles. It appears also that the reduction of employment during such years is in general greater among large plants than among medium-size and small plants. And because all the different kinds of firms mentioned above vary in location, there are geographic differences in the incidence of unemployment. Thus, the workers of Pittsburgh, a center of the steel and other capital-goods industries, and of Detroit, the heart of the automobile industry, experience heavier unemployment than those of Philadelphia and Boston, where production is more diversified, more given over to the output of consumption and non-durable goods.

Third, the *sex, age, and race* of workers also make for differences in the extent and duration of unemployment during depressions. In respect to sex, it seems necessary to distinguish between women who are regularly a part of the labor force and those whom the depression (through unemployment of the male earners in families) drives into the labor market temporarily. If we consider only the first class of women, we find more unemployment among male workers than among females. This is probably due to the fact that most women are regularly employed by companies (such as retail stores) that experience less reduction in product demand than do the firms that employ mainly men. However, if we group both classes of women together, we appear to find more unemployment among females; at least, as depression continues, unemployment among them tends to rise more rapidly than among males.

Among the age groups of the work force, the members of the very young and of the older groups tend to lose their jobs first and stay jobless longer during a depression than do the middle groups. The percentage of unemployment among the young becomes particularly high because the new accretions to the work force from schools and colleges find it most difficult to find jobs.

Finally, the research done on these matters establishes that the incidence of unemployment is higher and its duration longer for colored and foreign-born workers than for the native whites.

c. Part-time employment during depressions. When it becomes evident that the country is truly in the grip of a considerable business depression, as in 1921 and 1931, a great many firms, either on their own initiative or under government or union pressure, adopt the policy of "spreading work." That is, instead of laying off much larger numbers of workers and working the remaining ones full-time, they retain substantial percentages of their forces by dividing the available work among them. Most workers then work only part-time. Thus, in March, 1932, it was found that, among some 6500 firms employing almost 3.5 million workers in 1929, only 27 per cent of these workers had been laid off. The remaining 73 per cent (about 2.5 million) were still working. Of these, 56 per cent were on part-time, and their weekly hours averaged about 60 per cent of full-time.

These facts suggest that during depression years the statistics on amount and percentage of unemployment greatly understate the extent to which the available labor force is under-utilized. Thus, in March, 1933, when almost one-third of the work force was wholly without jobs, i.e., when almost one-third of the force was wholly unemployed in terms of the number of *persons* offering their services at existing wage rates, it may well have been that more than half of the labor resource was idle in terms of the number of *labor-hours* that the labor force was ready to supply at prevailing wage rates.

C. EFFECTS OF UNEMPLOYMENT

Unemployment, particularly the prolonged kind that so many workers experience during a business depression, has very serious effects not only on the workers themselves but also on their unions, on employers, and on the society as a whole. Since we are dealing in this section of the book with the problems of individual workers, however, our discussion is confined to what idleness does to them.

1. Effects of depression unemployment. Unemployment places heavy economic, physical, mental, and moral burdens on workers. Their financial reserves, if any, are soon exhausted and their levels of living greatly lowered, so that they are brought to such straits as getting deeply into debt, accepting the meanest kinds of jobs, appealing to charity, taking in lodgers, or sending wives and children out for work of any description. This last step, of course, means adding to the already overcrowded labor market, with the result that wages and hours may be further lowered and sweatshop or homework conditions encouraged. Continued idleness leads to loss of job skill. Reduction in the status of living means physical deterioration for whole families affected by unemployment. Lowered vitality increases susceptibility to disease, especially for women and children. Added to this are the mental agonies of continual worry and discouragement, which often lead to shiftless and drifting habits, moral breakdown, and loss of self-respect, ambition, will-power, and sense of responsibility. Insanity, desertion, and suicide are all too frequently the end-products of prolonged joblessness.

To support the belief that as human beings the wage-earners lose much more from unemployment than any other group, there is a great deal of evidence, ranging from detailed case studies of individual unemployed persons to statistical summaries of pertinent data. Typical information was provided by two volumes published in 1931,[1] both using case material made available through the Committee on Unemployment of the National Federation of Social Settlements. They exploded the notion then current among certain people that a majority of the unemployed during that depression were a shiftless lot, with no real desire to find work. These studies also established the existence of unfavorable economic, physical, and mental effects. The economic effects included using up savings; going into debt for food and shelter; moving to cheaper quarters; borrowing money from friends, relatives, and neighbors; borrowing money on possessions from loan agencies; pawning jewelry; selling furniture; allowing insurance to lapse; allowing installment purchases and house payments to lapse; wife and children trying to find work; taking in boarders or lodgers; "doubling up," or sharing living quarters with relatives or other families; taking casual jobs; giving up relaxation and amusement activities; removing children from school; sending children to relatives or institutions; appealing at last to charity.

There were also harmful physical and mental effects. The amount and quality of food was "trimmed," including milk and green vegetables. Evidences of malnutrition were common and clothing often inadequate. Homes were poorly heated and barely furnished. Respiratory diseases such as pneumonia and tuberculosis were sometimes discovered. In four of the families studied, deaths were traceable to unemployment hardships. The mental effects of continued joblessness were plainly discernible. Almost all the families were discouraged and worried about the future. Some were humiliated at having to accept charitable aid.

[1] C. Calkins, *Some Folks Won't Work*, Harcourt, Brace and Co., New York; and M. Elderton, *Case Studies of Unemployment*, University of Pennsylvania Press, Philadelphia.

Others had lost morale and self-respect. In some homes cooperation had been heightened by the emergency, but in most there was an atmosphere of unhappiness and irritation. There were a good many cases of juvenile delinquency. Among the adults were found such anti-social behaviors as temporary desertion, cruelty toward wife and children, excessive drinking, crime (such as stealing, forgery, and drug peddling), and suicide.

Not the least of the mental effects of prolonged unemployment on individual workers is a growing bitterness toward the established social order. Workers begin to question the validity of an economic and political system that has failed to provide them with the means of adequate living. They tend to become susceptible to the promises and blandishments of demagogues who arise to preach the gospel of revolution. They come to believe that security is all-important compared to an economic and political freedom that has become meaningless. What does it matter to them if security is attained through a political dictatorship?

No one can comprehend just what unemployment means to the average wage-earner unless he has been in the army of the jobless himself or has had first-hand contact with actual cases. A few afternoons at a welfare agency or on the back streets of an industrial city during a depression will be decidedly more convincing to the student than any discussion within the walls of a classroom or the covers of a textbook.

By 1952 it had been more than a decade since there was an "army" of the unemployed. The younger workers of that year had never experienced depression unemployment. But the older ones had. And in the United States, as in other democracies, their memories were long. If one may judge by their voting in elections, they appeared to be determined that there should not be a repetition of the economic conditions of the 1930's. They seemed to favor some sort of government action, short of authoritarianism, to maintain high employment.

2. Effects of non-depression unemployment. As the statistics presented earlier in this chapter show, some unemployment exists during even the most prosperous years. Some workers voluntarily quit their existing jobs in order to find other work. Moreover, there are non-cyclical fluctuations in *firms' demands* for labor. For example, production in some firms, such as those that pack or can fresh fruits and vegetables, is highly seasonal, and employees are laid off at the end of the work season. Other industries, such as metal mining in certain areas and the industries related to "horse and buggy" transportation, may decline or die out, often leaving "ghost" communities from which the unemployed workers have fled. Or technological improvements in production methods may displace particular kinds of workmen. Finally even in the absence of the above-mentioned conditions certain individual workers may lose or be unable to obtain jobs because of discriminatory treatment by employers or unions or both.

Unemployment resulting from any of these conditions does not have to be nearly so prolonged as that existing in a big depression. In so far as it is not, the harmful effects on particular workers are less severe. But in many cases there are very considerable stresses created by necessary readjustments. In a time of high general employment a worker who has been displaced by a new machine or discharged by an unfriendly foreman or prevented from getting or holding a job in the plant of his choice by a "union shop" agreement between management and union can obtain some kind of job somewhere else without too much trouble. He can, that is, *if* he is willing to bear the costs. And these costs may be high. A technologically displaced skilled worker may find that the investment he made in acquiring his skill has been lost; he may have to take an unskilled job at a much lower rate of pay. A discharged worker may have to bear the expense of moving into another labor market; he may be "blacklisted" in the market where he used to work. The highly individualistic worker who wants no part of unionism may have to swallow his pride and join one if he wishes to keep his existing job or get another one. In all such cases the monetary and psychological losses for particular workers may be heavy.

D. CAUSES OF UNEMPLOYMENT

We have learned enough about the nature, extent, and effects of unemployment among American workers to be convinced that it can be a very serious problem for them, individually and collectively. Having this conviction, we are forced logically to either or both of two conclusions: the effects must somehow be *alleviated*; the effects must somehow be *prevented.*

If most of us were given our choice between the alleviation and the prevention of any disease, our preferences would lean heavily toward prevention. The two goods are divisible; that is, it is possible to have some of each. But the optimum combination for most people would be a great deal of prevention and no more alleviation than that necessary to take care of those workers for whom our preventive measures had proved unsuccessful. An ounce of prevention is worth a ton of alleviation.

How do you achieve prevention? Obviously you must first discover the causes. Then you prescribe remedies that aim to remove or neutralize the causes.

In the discussion that follows we separate the conditions causing involuntary idleness among individual workers into the two categories suggested at the beginning of the chapter: (1) the conditions that are mainly impersonal; and (2) the conditions that are personal, involving human relations.

1. Impersonal causes of unemployment. From our use of the descriptive term "impersonal," it should not be inferred that the causal elements to be discussed here arise from some mysterious source external to and uncontrollable by the human beings involved. The choices and decisions of human beings, as individuals or in groups, are most important at every step. To be sure, in some cases (such as a major crop failure) unemployment may appear to have been created by "acts of God." But ultimately it is the human, subjective decisions in response to the objective conditions that produce the unemployment. It is conceivable, indeed, that under certain circumstances an objective event like a crop failure would lead to human decisions making for more employment rather than more unemployment.

If human decisions are always involved, why use the term "impersonal"? Because, as explained at the beginning of the chapter, it is a way of distinguishing the *human-relations* from the *non-human-relations* causes of job loss. The "impersonal" conditions are not in the main concerned with the behavioral interactions of individual workers and management or union officials.

Let us now get a bird's-eye view of the territory we propose to survey. Wherever unemployment of workers exists — in respect to a particular firm, area, or industry, or in respect to the whole society — there is in the economic sense an *excess* supply of labor at the wage rate (and other terms of employment) prevailing in the markets for labor. That is, at the prevailing wage rates (and other terms of employment) the quantity of labor demanded by one or more firms is smaller than the quantity supplied. Our purpose is to consider the reasons for possible excess supplies.

In the real world most of the group unemployment that merits serious attention is that produced by the conditions which cause reductions in the *demand* for labor relative to more or less given labor supplies. Sometimes increases in labor supply relative to more or less given labor demands have produced the excess supplies we have defined as unemployment; examples are immigration during certain years before World War I and the annual graduation of young people from schools and colleges. But in the main we may think of unemployment as caused chiefly by decreases in labor demand — in particular firms, industries, and areas, and in the economy as a whole.

a. Unemployment from particular firms. Textbooks on labor problems often discuss in general terms such topics as cyclical unemployment, frictional unemployment, technological unemployment, seasonal unemployment, and casual unemployment. Each of these "types" of unemployment can be fitted into an analytical framework for an individual firm.

(1) Analytical frame of reference. If labor unemployment represents an excess of labor supply over labor demand, we must know a few simple things about the conditions determining the supply of labor avail-

able to a particular firm and about the conditions affecting a firm's demand for labor.

(*a*) *Labor-supply conditions for the firm.* The number of labor hours which a worker is willing to offer to a firm at any given wage rate depends on two main sets of preferences in the worker's mind: (*i*) his preferences between enjoying the good known as leisure and all other goods, which are purchasable with the money he can earn by working; and (*ii*) his preferences between the job conditions offered by a given firm and those offered by other firms. In balancing these preferences the worker tries to obtain the same satisfaction (at the margin) from one good as from the other. As a result, there are certain numbers of hours he is willing to offer to any firm at the various wage rates which might be offered by the firm.

While there seems to be no precise relationship between the amount of the wage rate offered by a firm and the number of hours offered by the worker, it appears that the wage rate is the most important condition influencing workers' preferences among different firms. In general, the higher the wage rate offered by a firm, the more labor-hours a worker will supply to it.

However, there are at least seven other conditions influencing a worker's inter-firm preferences: (*i*) the physical working conditions, such as amount of exertion required, degree of cleanliness, heat, wetness, noise, and so on; (*ii*) the social prestige of the job and firm; (*iii*) the degree of independence and freedom from close supervision on the job; (*iv*) the security which the job affords in terms of steady work and protection from the arbitrary actions of supervisors; (*v*) the opportunities for advancement and the fairness with which workers are treated in respect to promotion; (*vi*) relations with fellow workers — kinds of people in the same shop and degree of cooperation among them; and (*vii*) the degree of interest and challenge to capacities which the job possesses.

It should not be thought that the typical worker shops around actively and with determination in order to compare various firms' jobs on the basis of the above-mentioned characteristics. His preferences are based on a limited amount of investigation and hearsay from friends and relatives. Actually, the only way a worker can learn about a job is to try it out for a while. His selection of a job and a firm is often most haphazard. Furthermore, once on a job, he is usually disinclined to move because of ignorance of alternative opportunities; attachment to his present job and place of residence by social ties and sheer habit; the bother of moving and other elements of inertia; and the fear of using up financial resources before another job can be found.

Nevertheless, except in times of mass unemployment some workers do move; there is a fair amount of labor turnover in any one plant. This is enough to establish a sort of positive or direct relation between a firm's wage rate and the worker's supply of labor-hours.

The total labor supply to a firm is the aggregate of the quantities of labor-hours offered at various wage rates by all the individual workers in the labor market. Obviously, if a minimum wage rate is set by law or by unemployment compensation or by formal or informal organization among the workers, no labor-hours will be offered at wage rates below the minimum.

(b) Labor-demand conditions for the firm. The number of labor-hours that a firm is able and willing to hire at any given wage rate depends on three things: (*i*) the technological conditions of producing the firm's product; (*ii*) the supply conditions affecting other factors of production, such as machines and raw materials; and (*iii*) the conditions affecting the demand for the firm's product.

i. Technological influences. By technology we mean the methods of producing goods. It includes types of machines and productive processes, plus managerial know-how. A technological improvement is an invention which raises the amount of output per hour which a worker can produce. At any given level of technology there is a fact of supreme importance: After a certain point has been reached, the more labor-hours an employer hires in conjunction with a given input of fixed plant and equipment, the lower the output per labor-hour. This represents the operation of the principle of diminishing returns or productivity. And it follows from this principle that, with no improvement in technology, the larger the number of labor-hours a firm hires in conjunction with given plant and equipment, the lower the wage rate he is able to pay.

A technological improvement, i.e., a rise in the level of a firm's production techniques, usually has one of two effects on the firm's demand for labor. Let us say the improvement is a new and better machine. If the machine is a *substitute* for labor, the firm's demand for labor *in the first instance* tends to be reduced. But if labor must be used with the new machine, i.e., if the machine is a *complement* to rather than a substitute for labor, then the firm's demand for labor may stay the same or be increased.

Technology determines another important matter: the percentage which labor cost is of total production cost at any given level of output. In general, the higher the proportion of labor cost to total cost, the more sensitive the firm is to imposed changes in the wage rate, i.e., the more elastic is its demand for labor-hours; and vice versa. It is easy to see why this is so. Suppose that, as in coal mining, labor cost is 60 per cent of the total cost of production. Then a 20 per cent rise in wage rates means in the first instance a 12 per cent increase in total cost (60 per cent of 20 per cent). But if, as in petroleum refining, labor cost is only 6 per cent of total cost, then a 20 per cent rise in wage rates means only a 1.2 per cent boost in total cost. Clearly a coal-mining firm's demand for labor-hours is much more sensitive or elastic than a petroleum refinery's.

ii. Supplies of other factors. Raw materials are complements to labor;

machines may be complements or substitutes. In any case, the nature of the supplies of these non-labor factors affects the demand for labor. If complementary raw materials and machines are easy and cheap to buy, the firm's demand for labor is higher than otherwise. If substitute machines are easy and cheap to get, the demand tends to be lower.

iii. Product-demand conditions. It is easy to see that the nature of the demand for a firm's product affects the firm's demand for labor, for the latter is *derived* from the former. An increase in the demand for the firm's product is almost always reflected in a rise in the firm's demand for the labor that helps make the product; and vice versa.

The *price elasticity* of the demand for the product is often as important as the amount of demand. (By "price elasticity" of product demand we mean the responsiveness of consumers to changes in the price of the product. If consumers are very responsive to price increases or decreases, i.e., if the quantity of the firm's product which they buy falls or rises more than proportionately to the percentage change in price, we say the demand is elastic; if less than proportionately, inelastic.) In general, if product demand is elastic or inelastic, the firm's demand for the labor which goes into the product tends to be elastic or inelastic. Thus, if the firm raises its product price in the face of an inelastic product demand, the quantity of labor-hours hired by the firm will tend to be reduced much less than if the product demand were elastic.

(2) *Cyclical unemployment and the firm.* "Cyclical" unemployment refers to the mass unemployment generated during business depressions. We shall consider this matter from the standpoint of the economy as a whole later on in the chapter. Our interest here is in how any single firm is affected during the downswing of a typical American peacetime business cycle.

We know from Chapter 3 and from the foregoing discussion that one of the determinants of the demand for a firm's product is the amount of income available among households for spending on all products; that when this spending rises or falls, this demand tends to increase or decrease; that the demand for a firm's product is one of the determinants of the firm's demand for labor; and that during a business downswing total spending per period of time declines continuously. It follows, then, that at such times a firm's demand for labor (and for all other productive factors) keeps declining. The firm thus is in virtually continuous disequilibrium; there is a continuous, increasing excess supply of labor — unless the labor supply decreases commensurately, which is highly unlikely during a period of general unemployment. The increase in unemployment for the firm (whether in the form of layoffs of workers or of providing only part-time work) will not stop until there is an end to the decrease in total spending which caused the demand for the firm's product to drop. And the excess supply of labor will not be removed until total (real) spending has returned to the full-employment level.

(3) *Seasonal unemployment.* (*a*) *Nature and causes.* Employment in a given firm is said to be "seasonal" when it fluctuates rather regularly from certain "high" months within the period of a year. Seasonal unemployment exists, then, when workers are laid off or given part-time work during the months of low employment. (The increase in unemployment, however, is usually not so large as the decrease in employment, because many workers leave the labor market entirely at the end of their "seasons.")

Virtually all the major fields of production (agriculture, mining, construction, manufacturing, transportation, trade, and so on) experience seasonality in some degree. So also do almost all the subdivisions in these fields, e.g., wheat production, coal mining, house building, steel, automobiles, commercial canning, clothing, railroading, retail trade, and so on. But the degree of seasonality is much higher in some industries than in others. In retail trade, for example, during a given year employment in the low month may be only from 10 to 15 per cent below that for the peak month. Similarly moderate fluctuations may occur in railroad transportation, public utilities, and the manufacture of certain necessity staples like soap and processed foods. On the other hand, in particular localities or areas production in some other fields like construction, farm products, and the packing and canning of fresh fruits and vegetables often may range from zero during one or more months to the peaks of employment.

Sometimes there are also variations in degree of seasonality among firms in the same industry and area. Certain firms may be better able than others to plan their operations so as to avoid extreme seasonal fluctuations in employment. They may also introduce other products whose seasonal peaks and troughs come at other times during the year.

In most seasonal industries, such as clothing, skilled construction work, and coal mining, most of the workers consider themselves "attached" to the industry. That is, they do not leave the industry at the end of "the season." Either they remain idle during the slack months, depending on their previous earnings to tide them over until their firms recall them; or they take such temporary odd jobs as they can find. In a few industries, such as farm products, packing and canning (at least in some areas), and Christmas retail selling, the work force personnel may be largely different from season to season. In any case it is important to remember that the seasonal spurts in the demand for labor are not filled mainly by pirating labor from non-seasonal firms. The seasonal labor demand is met for the most part by seasonal increases in the labor supply.

The basic causes of seasonality in labor demand may be listed as follows. First comes weather, or climatic changes. The succession of the seasons conditions the growing and ripening of agricultural products. Crops must be harvested and picked when ripe; and the more perishable the product, the more feverish is the climax of productive activity, with complete shutdown later on. Sometimes, as in outdoor construction, the weather affects the actual production processes. In the northern part of the country the amount of building that can be done during the coldest months tends to be extremely limited. The climatic seasons also influence the consumption of certain products and thereby also tend to seasonalize the production of these products. Domestic fuel and overcoats are used mostly in the winter; garden tools, fishing tackle, bathing togs, and many other products in the spring and summer.

A second cause of seasonality is to be found in certain social conditions. "Style" or "fashion" is one of these. Changes in the weather do lead consumers to want certain kinds of apparel at particular times during the year. But the fickleness and unpredictability of public taste in response to style and model changes cause all firms but the leaders to hold up production until the last possible moment; then, sensing which styles are "catching on," they plunge into hectic activity. Custom decrees, moreover, that certain products shall be used at certain regular times during the year: new bonnets for Easter, greeting cards for Christmas, firecrackers for the Fourth of July in the North and for Christmas week in the South.

(*b*) *Relation to supply-demand analysis.* Now let us try to fit the facts of seasonality into the analytical framework developed above. Suppose that certain workers, such as the wives and daughters of farmers and coal miners, offer to work for a certain firm, such as a nearby food-processing plant, only during a month or so each year in response to the firm's solicitation when perishable fruits or vegetables are being canned. Then we find a considerable increase of the firm's labor supply as the new workers add their labor-hour offerings to those of the firm's core of stable, year-round workers. On the other hand, when the special canning season is over and the seasonal workers retire to their homes, the supply decreases again.

But most of the employment disequilibrium created by seasonality is reflected by what happens to the demand for labor. When the season begins, this demand rises a great deal. In fact, if the cannery or other establishment has been shut down during the off-season, the demand "appears from nowhere." When the season ends, the demand for labor disappears completely.

Which determinants of labor demand change to produce these shifts? Style and custom and weather changes which affect the timing of consumption operate through changes in the product-demand determinant. The climatic seasonality that governs the growing and ripening of agricultural products also operates through the supply curves of productive factors that are complementary with labor. Thus, when tomatoes ripen, their supply rises very substantially; and labor, being complementary to this raw material in the canning process, must be hired in increased numbers. After the season the supply of tomatoes vanishes; and so does the demand for the labor needed to help can the tomatoes. Again, weather affecting the production process as such operates through the technological determinant. Thus, when zero weather stops construction work, technology wipes out the demand for the time being, and all the labor on such a job is in excess supply.

Finally, it should be noted that seasonal unemployment becomes a much more important problem during the periods when cyclical unemployment is severe. We have seen that normally many seasonal workers do not wish to work throughout the year. During depressions, however, when one or more other members of their households may have lost their jobs, they may change their minds and desire steady work. But the chances are against finding it at such times. Moreover, there are some seasonal workers who even in prosperous periods turn to other work for support in the "off" season. These workers may also be balked during depressions.

(4) *Casual unemployment.* In a few industries there is another kind of irregular employment within the period of a year or less. This sort of irregularity differs from that found in the industries we have called seasonal because it lacks the rhythm or periodicity of seasonal employment. The best example is to be found in the loading and unloading of ships by longshoremen. The arrival and departure of ships from the docks is sporadic, but the workers hold themselves ready for calls to go to work. We can thus consider their labor supply as fixed, while the shippers' labor demand appears and disappears intermittently because the complementary productive factors appear and disappear intermittently. During the disappearance periods, of course, the dockworkers are unemployed.

(5) *Frictional unemployment.* By "frictional" unemployment we mean the excess supplies of labor that are temporarily created by or in particular firms in particular localities when they go out of business because of financial insolvency, migrate to other localities, merge with other firms, or substitute capital for labor in their productive processes. When any of these things happen to or in a firm, time is required for the displaced employees to find other jobs. There are barriers to the easy, immediate movement of these workers to new places of employment. No central authority exists to transfer them swiftly to job vacancies in other firms. They must spend days, even weeks and months, in looking for new work. Sometimes they must move to other localities, or be re-trained for other jobs. These things constitute the frictions in the labor market.

Frictional unemployment may also be considered to include an important item on the labor supply side: the new workers who have just finished school and are seriously entering the labor market for the first time. Being untrained and inexperienced for the most part, these persons often have more difficulty getting properly placed than do displaced experienced workers.

Entirely apart from casual and seasonal unemployment, some amount of frictional unemployment exists during even the most prosperous years of a business cycle. In a dynamic society of continuous change there is always a sizable group of workers who are unemployed at any one time for one or another of the five reasons mentioned in the preceding paragraphs. This group of workers experiences additions and subtractions each day as new layoffs are made by certain firms and as other firms fill job vacancies.

As suggested by the data in Tables 10 and 11 (pages 82 and 83), the amount of normal or frictional unemployment that exists even during years of high employment ranges from one to five per cent of the total number of persons in the labor force (as defined).

(*a*) *Insolvency among firms.* A firm becomes insolvent when its sales revenues are too small to permit it to cover its costs over a period of time long enough to convince the firm's owners or creditors that the loss situation cannot be rectified. When a firm is threatened with insolvency, it can go out of business, migrate to some other location where it hopes to become profitable, or merge with some other firm. The threat of insolvency may arise from conditions affecting the firm's costs or from product-demand conditions or from both. In terms of our analytical framework, the supply of labor and other productive factors may have diminished so much as to raise the wage rate too high; or labor demand may have decreased too much because of an inadequacy or a large decrease in product demand, or because of insufficient knowledge or inefficient use of available techniques of production. If the interaction of labor supply and demand provides a wage rate which is higher than the firm's estimated worth of the quantity of labor employed at that wage rate — and if this situation persists in spite of efforts to improve it, the firm, if economically rational, will go out of business, at least under its present ownership and in its present location. Then the firm's demand for labor disappears, and the firm's workers lose their jobs and are compelled to seek employment with other firms in the same community or elsewhere.

Available statistics indicate that the average annual number of failures among firms since 1900 has been well over 15,000. The percentage of insolvencies to total numbers of firms has averaged about one per cent over the same period. Both the numbers and the percentages have been much higher in depression than in prosperous years. The industries, such as apparel, in which most of the firms are small and in which competition is severe have much higher mortality rates than the industries, such as steel, in which the firms are large and competition is less keen.

(*b*) *Migration and mergers among firms.* As already suggested, sometimes a firm that has consistently been losing money has one or more alternatives to being declared bankrupt. It may be able to move to some other location, or it may sell out to or combine with one or more other firms, with changed ownership and management. In either case it hopes that its move will provide profits because of lower wage rates, interest rates, raw material costs, taxes, and other costs, or because of higher product demand or improved managerial efficiency. For example, a firm in a highly unionized metropolitan community may believe that it can lower its labor and other costs by "running away" to some much smaller city in a rural, non-union area. The small community may even solicit such moves by providing free plant sites and tax exemptions.

The level of employment in a given community is affected not only by the migration of firms threatened by insolvency, but also by the removal of profitable firms that believe they will make even higher profits in some other locality. Moreover, the owners of newly projected firms may decide to establish their plant in some other locality. Over time and on a large scale, these separate decisions of individual firms set the industrial-migration pattern for the whole country — a pattern to which we shall refer under "secular trends" in our later discussion of employment in the economy as a whole.

When firms merge, unemployment may be created, depending on the nature of the merger. There may be little or no disturbance of existing personnel, as when small independent stores or bakeries are bought up by a chain organization. On the other hand, there may be considerable labor displacement in the interests of greater efficiency, as when two or more banks in the same small locality are consolidated into one operation.

(c) Technological displacement of labor. As in the cases of industrial migration and cyclical fluctuations, we shall consider the over-all aspects and effects of technological change in our discussion of unemployment in the economy as a whole. Our concern with the matter here is confined to what happens to the employment equilibrium of an individual firm when a technological innovation occurs in that firm or some other firm.

Let us consider the content of technology a little more fully than we did above. Technology includes the nature and kinds of the goods or products themselves. It embraces also the methods of developing and utilizing power and energy sources, from animal power on through direct water power, steam, electricity, and atomic energy. It covers the development and improvement of raw materials such as new farm products, synthetic fibers, plastics, and metal alloys. It includes all non-mechanical and mechanical production *processes.* It has to do also with machines of all sorts. And it covers all kinds of managerial techniques for organizing the human and non-human productive factors into an effective producing unit.

The "level" of technology means "the state of the industrial arts" or techniques — the degree of "advancedness" in production methods. The level in modern America is doubtless higher than in any other national economy; and in all modern industrialized economies it is very far above that existing, for example, among savage tribes in mid-Africa today.

Technological "change" means, usually, an improvement or raising of the level of technology. As previously noted, the level of technology did not rise much during the Middle Ages. But the "industrial revolution" marked a great advance, the end of which is not foreseen, especially with the unlocking of the atom's energy.

We have seen that, depending on the technological conditions, the various kinds of labor and other productive factors may be mainly substitutes for or complements to each other. Or they may be more or less neutral in these matters. Whether or not a given technological improvement in the first instance displaces labor in a particular firm depends in part, as we said earlier, on whether the capital with which the new technique is involved is a substitute for or a complement to labor. If the relationship is one of substitution, the labor input of the firm will at first be reduced. If the relationship is a complementary one, there will be an initial tendency to increase the firm's employment of labor. But if the relationship is one of neutrality, there may be no initial tendency in either direction. For example, the introduction by building contractors of metal sashes in place of wooden ones for windows and doors tended to replace carpenters with sheet-metal workers. But no matter which group of workers did the work, there was no *net* tendency to raise or lower the labor input on a given construction job. Again, some new techniques may not tend to replace any kind of labor with another kind or to replace labor with capital. Thus, the introduction of automatic firing devices on steam locomotives displaced no firemen in the first instance.

Note that we use the terms "tend," "tendency," and "in the first instance" in speaking of the effect of a technological improvement on labor input in a given firm. This is because, after the first impact, the net employment effect of a given new technique is often very hard to discover. A complicated chain of reactions is usually set up.

Let us consider this matter a little more fully, first in respect to a firm which introduces a technological change, and second in respect to other firms. When a firm makes such an innovation, it expects its unit production costs to be lower and its profits higher. Now, if unit production costs are lower, the firm may lower the price of its product. Whether or not it does so depends on the degree of competition with other firms in the product market. Thus, under oligopoly, where sellers wish to avoid price wars, the firm is not likely to lower prices. Here, given the demand for all the firms' products, there is likely to be no change in the quantity of product sold by the firm and therefore no change in labor input *from this source.* All that happens is a rise in the firm's profits and a free rein to the *technological* tendency to reduce or increase or leave unchanged the input of labor.

Where some degree of price competition prevails, the firm is likely to be led to reduce its product price. Then the quantity of the product sold will rise unless product demand is zero-elastic. And the more elastic the demand for the product is, the more will the quantity sold increase in relation to the price decrease. Thus here, even if a given technological improvement tends to *displace* labor, there will be some offset to this tendency unless product demand is zero-elastic. And with considerable elasticity of demand, the offset may well be so large that there is a net *rise* in the number of labor-hours employed by the firm after the effects of the new production technique have worked themselves out.

A technological improvement of a firm's *product* will cause an increase in the demand for the firm's product, if the improved product "catches on" with consumers. Then the demand for labor increases, and labor input is raised. This kind of technological change is always directly beneficial to the employment of labor in the firm making the innovation.

Now let us turn to a consideration of the effects of a technological improvement on labor employment in firms other than the one making the innovation. It is this study that shows us how complex the reverberations of a given change are. Consider first the case mentioned just above. Employment was increased in the firm that improved its product. But if we assume no rise in total spending in the economy as a whole, then employment must have decreased in one or more other firms. For when households' preferences turned toward the improved product of the first firm, their preferences must have turned to some extent against the products of other firms. That is, when the product demand of firm A inceased, thus raising its labor input, the product demand of one or more other firms must have been reduced. And these shifts must have decreased the latter firms' labor demand, thus reducing labor employment in these firms. Are the workers who are laid off by the other firms suffering from "technological unemployment"?

The same effect on other firms' employment is found (under our assumption of no change in economy-wide spending) in another case above — the one in which firm A introduces a labor-saving improvement in its production methods, followed by a decrease in product price under conditions of elastic demand. When demand is elastic, a price reduction results in an increase in total expenditure on the product because the quantity bought rises more than proportionately to the price decrease. If spending on product A rises, then the expenditures on other firms' products must fall. In other words, their product demands fall, and so do their demands for labor. Labor inputs in these firms are reduced. Are the laid-off workers here also technologically idle?

If the demand for firm A's product is unit-elastic when the price is reduced (i.e., if the quantity bought rises just proportionately to the reduction in price), there is no change in the expenditures for its products or for the products of other firms. Here employment in all firms is unchanged from the standpoint of product demand. If the demand is inelastic, there will be a drop in spending for firm A's product and a net drop in its employment; and there will be rises in expenditures for other firms' products and *increases* in their employment.

Suppose the firm making the technological innovation is an oliogopolist and does not change the price of its product. It is content with the higher profits made possible by the lower unit costs at the present product price. If we assume that these additional profits are not hoarded by the firm's owners, then other firms may find their labor inputs enlarged. For the added profits will be spent either on consumption products or on investment products (new plant and equipment); in either case, other firms' product demands and labor demands rise.

It must also be remembered that many if not most technological innovations involve the introduction of new, improved tools and machines. Since both labor and capital must be employed to make these new items of capital equipment, the firms specializing in their production have increases in their product and labor demands. Employment is increased in these plants at least temporarily, even though it may fall in the plant making the technological innovation.

Firms may be especially stimulated to introduce labor-saving devices by some condition that makes labor expensive, i.e., by some circumstance that in effect reduces labor supply, such as the raising of wage rates by a union or the introduction or amendment of a minimum wage law. Such conditions may make profitable certain labor-saving technological improvements that were previously deemed too expensive. The firm wishes to raise the average worth of its labor-hours in order to bear the increased average outlays. Here the question always arises, Are the workers displaced in such a situation technologically unemployed? Which event caused them to be made idle — the wage-rate increase or the new machines?

The manifold, reverberating effects of a particular innovation may be illustrated by what happened to labor employment in various firms after 1925, when steel plants began to introduce the new automatic, continuous mills for rolling steel sheets and "strips." Before this improvement these products were made by workers who, aided only by hand tongs, passed the heavy hot steel plates, with great exertion and skill, back and forth between revolving rolls mounted in small, individual stands or frames until the sheets were of the specified gauge or thinness. In the new, continuous mill there is a series of rolls and tables in tandem (stretching out for a quarter of a mile or more) which are controlled by one or two highly skilled and responsible workers in a little "house" above the rolls. Through these the steel plates start and run very swiftly and automatically like a ribbon until, at the end of the run, they are coiled up on huge spools. The capacity of such a production unit per period of time is many, many times greater than that of any one of the old hand mills. Yet considerably fewer workers (even including the skilled maintenance men and the unskilled clean-up men) are needed than before for the rolling of a given tonnage of sheets.

Here, then, was high direct net displacement of labor. The innovation was *labor-saving*. It was also *labor-changing*: different kinds of labor were needed after the change. Furthermore, it was *labor-serving*: it made the labor of the new worker much lighter and cooler than before. Finally, in an indirect way the improvement was *labor-creating*: it provided jobs for many workers in the firms of other industries.

Let us look at these effects a little more closely. The direct displacement of the old hand rollers in the plant in which the new mill was installed is easy to see. But a big steel corporation usually has many plants, and employees in some of these may also be displaced by a big innovation in the first plant. Thus, when the United States Steel Corporation introduced automatic mills in the Pittsburgh district during the thirties, there was direct labor-saving in that locality. But many miles away were other U.S. Steel sheet mills that became obsolete, in small communities like Farrell, Pennsylvania. These towns almost became "ghosts." The sheet mills had been the main industry, and almost all the other firms — stores, banks, and so on — had depended on them. The continuous mills in the Pittsburgh district displaced most of the workers in these other localities.

On the other hand, the introduction of the automatic sheet-rolling mills *created* many man-hours of employment. This happened, first, when the new mills were built and installed, and second, when the price of steel sheets was reduced, because of lowered unit production costs, and when therefore the quantity produced and sold was increased. In the first case, the firms building the mills had higher employment. In turn there was increased output and employment for the firms supplying materials to the mill-building firms — all the way back to the ore, coal, and limestone mines and the railroads transporting these materials. The earnings of employees in these firms, moreover, provided employment for firms in many different industries. In the second case, the increased sales of steel sheets not only made more jobs for salesmen and white-collar record keepers in the steel plants but also created more work in all the supply industries.

b. Unemployment in the economy as a whole. Now let us consider employment and unemployment among *all* firms, i.e., in the economy as a whole. In order to do this it will be necessary for the student to go back to pages 35–37 and 41–44 of Chapter 3 and pages 59–63 of Chapter 5 for a thorough review of the nature and causes of economic progress, population changes, and cyclical fluctuations in economic activity.

(1) Economic progress and labor supply and demand. First we shall go beyond the confines of any particular business cycle; we shall look at the long-term changes in employment. In doing this it will be convenient to take first an "external" or over-all view of the economy, and then an "internal" view.

(*a*) *The over-all view.* In Chapter 3 we said that, given the households' wants and preferences among various goods (including leisure), the level of output and want-satisfaction available to the households was determined and limited by the quantity of resources, the state of technology, and the nature of the organization for production. This means that, given full employment of available resources, output and satisfaction can be increased if the quantity of resources is enlarged, if technology is improved, or if the efficiency of the social organization is raised. As previously stated, these are the roads to economic-political progress.

When we speak of increasing output and satisfaction, we mean total output and satisfaction in relation to size of population. We mean an increase in per-capita satisfaction. One cannot say that an economy has progressed if total satisfaction has risen merely in pace with the increase in population. Economic progress occurs only when total satisfaction increases *faster* than total population. Only then is more of everything available for everybody.

Over long periods of time — without regard to cyclical fluctuations — there are secular trends in the supply of labor and in labor demand. All the conditions affecting population growth, as shown in Chapter 5, influence labor supply. In addition there are changes in households' preferences between not-working (leisure, schooling, and so on) and the goods purchasable with money income. All these bear on the size of the labor force and the number of hours per day, week, and year that the force is willing to work. For the United States we found a steadily increasing labor force, one that rose more than proportionately to the growth in population. But because of the notable decline in the length of the work-week, the labor supply *in terms of labor-hours* did not keep pace with population growth. In other words, while the population rose at a diminishing rate, the rate of growth of the man-hour labor supply diminished even more.

On the side of secular demand for labor, the two main components of economic progress — net capital formation and technological improvements — greatly increased the ability of all firms to hire labor. If we look at the whole economy as a unit, there can be no question that capital (machines and materials) and labor are complements rather than substitutes. Then we must conclude that every increase in the quantity and every technological improvement in the quality of capital raised the demand not only for capital but also for its helpmate, labor. In the long run there can be and was no such thing as over-all technological unemployment. Technological progress not only produced more and better products, but also more and better ways of enjoying leisure, and more and better jobs. Whatever short-run hardships were entailed in particular cases, capital accumulation and technological improvements were of vast benefit to the population as a whole. They did not make for permanent unemployment disequilibria; they did not prevent post-depression business recoveries to levels of full employment. On the contrary, they created more jobs than they destroyed. And everyone, on the average became better off.

Statistics on real per-capita income establish beyond doubt that there was economic progress as defined above. From 1800 to 1919 output per person more than trebled. From 1919 to 1950 it doubled.

The main reasons for this sixfold increase since the early days of the nation are, first, the increase in labor supply mentioned above; second, an accumulation of capital at a rate much greater than the rate of population growth or the rate of labor-force increase (there are no accurate long-run statistics on the capital item); and third, a number of spurts in technological improvement, such as those in the years 1866–73, 1879–89, 1898–1907, 1923–28, and 1946–49. Of these three factors, the latter two were outstanding.

Additional evidence of the effects of the changes in these two determinants may be found in the data on output per labor-hour collected and compiled by government agencies like the Bureau of Labor Statistics. These statistics show the average physical-product output for the number of labor-hours employed during various years; that is, they show average labor productivity, being obtained by dividing total hours worked into total physical output. If such figures are available for successive years and if the data for a given year are selected as base figures, series of index numbers can be worked out, showing the trends in productivity. See Table 12.

The increase in per-capita satisfaction undoubtedly was considerably greater than the sixfold rise in per-capita output. The latter figures make no allowance for the gains in leisure. During the century and a half

TABLE 12 *Average Labor Productivity, Selected Industries and Years*

(Index Numbers: 1930 = 100)

Year	Physical Output per Labor-Hour in						Output per Worker in	
	Manufacturing	Bituminous Coal Mining	Anthracite Coal Mining	Petroleum Refining	Steam Railroads	Mechanical Trades[1]	White-Collar Trades[1]	Agriculture
1	2	3	4	5	6	7	8	9
1909	48.8	62.1	87.2	65.9	—	—	—	73.9
1914	56.2	69.0	92.3	59.1	66.3	—	—	88.4
1919	56.2	76.1	102.8	54.5	75.0	—	—	90.4
1925	83.3	89.5	100.9	97.7	91.9	85.5	100.1	98.7
1930	100.0	100.0	100.0	100.0	100.0	100.0	100.0	100.0
1935	116.7	102.3	129.0	154.5	115.1	116.1	103.3	97.4
1940	135.5	126.2	—	—	138.2	134.7	107.6	115.1

Source: J. F. Dewhurst and Associates, *America's Needs and Resources*, pp. 552–553.

[1] Data on mechanical trades come from mining, manufacturing, railway transportation, electric power and gas utilities, and construction. Data on "white-collar" trades come from wholesale and retail trade, communication, finance, personal and professional services, and miscellaneous occupations.

under consideration here the average length of the work-week declined by about 50 per cent — from about 80 to 40 hours per week.

(*b*) *Internal disruptions.* As some of our previous statements (as well as the figures in Table 12) have suggested, the rate of economic change for a whole society is an average. Within the economy the different industries and geographic areas experience varying rates of change. Some are growing much more rapidly than the national average, others more slowly. Some, indeed, are declining. This unevenness within the economy makes for long-term changes and dislocations in employment.

On this point much of the discussion, in Chapters 4 and 5, of trends in the composition of the labor force is relevant. We saw there that technological developments in products and production processes in various fields (including transportation) led to the rise of manufacturing, the relative decline of agriculture, and, finally, the growth of the service industries. Each of these broad developments over time meant declining employment opportunities in some fields and greatly expanding opportunities in others. The automobile affords an outstanding example of a technological innovation in the field of *products* followed by great innovations in the *processes of production* — the mass production of standardized parts assembled into a finished product on moving lines. Numerous other industries rose or expanded enormously in the work of automobile manufacture — petroleum production and refining, rubber tires, glass, sheet steel, miscellaneous parts, road construction, garages and filling stations, taxicab, bus, and truck transportation, and so on. At the same time that employment was rising tremendously in these fields, it declined notably in the industries connected with horse-and-buggy transportation. Wagon and carriage workers, harness makers, livery stable workers, and others lost their jobs.

Technological progress also invaded many particular occupations. As shown in Chapter 5, it lowered the importance of both skilled and unskilled workers in many industries and raised the importance of semiskilled machine tenders.

In part, the technologically induced growth of new industries and the decline of old ones involved a rise of employment in new geographic areas and the creation of unemployment in established industrial areas. The development of Detroit and other localities is a case in point. But there are other reasons for industrial migration, such as the discovery of new natural resources, the availability of labor, the development of new kinds of energy and power, and special governmental inducements such as low taxes or free sites. Among the best-known examples of employment-unemployment resulting from industrial migration are the rise of the South and the decline of New England in cotton textiles (in 1900 three-fourths of the textile workers were in New England, whereas by 1940 three-fourths were in the South); the movement of the lumber industry from Maine to Michigan and Wisconsin, then to the South and the Pacific Northwest; the migration of the shoe industry from New England to the Middle West; the development of cotton growing in Texas, Arkansas, and Oklahoma; the growth of manufacturing in Southern California; the decline of employment opportunities on farms and the rise of big-city manufacturing; and some later tendency to decentralize, i.e., move from large cities to smaller communities.

All these changes involved internal disruptions of employment equilibria. Such dislocations will continue to occur. Over time the adjustments are usually made successfully. But individual workers who lose their jobs during the process experience considerable hardship.

(2) *Cyclical unemployment in the whole economy.* When the changes in total spending mentioned on pages 41–44 occur, there are cyclical oscillations around the secular trend discussed above. Decreases in the consumption spending of households and in the investment spending of firms, caused by the unfavorable price expectations of these economic units and by reductions in the quantity of bank-created money, result in mass unemployment unless the reduction in private spending is compensated for by increased deficit spending by government.

(*a*) *American examples of cyclical unemployment.* Let us now briefly consider a few illustrations of cyclical employment disequilibrium created under these real-world conditions in the United States. A real-world business cycle is "typical" only in that it is composed of a downswing, an upswing, and a "bottom" and "top." In severity and duration each cycle is unique. Moreover, some cycles are mainly "financial"; they affect mainly the security and money markets, and have relatively little influence on real output and employment.

Among the approximately twenty dips below the level of reasonably full employment since the Civil War, the depressions of 1873–78, 1893–95, 1920–22, and 1930–39 are probably best remembered. Of these, the first three appear, in perspective, to have been relatively unimportant, temporary breathing spaces in the country's almost headlong development of its rich natural resources. Before 1930 there was little uncertainty about the essential validity of American economic and political institutions. But the depression that began with the stock market crash of 1929 was another matter. By March, 1933, the productive mechanism of the country had almost broken down. Households' confidence in the solvency of banks had been severely shaken; there had been many "runs" on banks; many banks had failed, and the government was forced to close the others. A third of the labor force had become wholly unemployed, and at least another third was working much less than full-time. According to Dr. Kuznets, of the National Bureau of Economic Research, a conservative estimate of the amount of output lost from 1930 through 1938 because of resource unemployment would come to about $135 billion (output being valued at 1929 prices). It had become popular also to question the "rightness" and social desirability of the other economic and political institutions that people had hitherto accepted with little question. The American businessman had fallen from the pedestal which he had attained in the golden twenties.

It may be helpful to consider what occurred between October, 1929, and March, 1933, and thereafter, in the technical terms that we have used to describe what happens during busines cycles. Shortly after the stock market panic President Hoover called business leaders to Washington and asked them to agree not to reduce wage rates. (The President was an adherent of the "consumer purchasing power theory" of business cycles: He doubted the efficacy of wage-rate cutting as a cost-reducing stimulus to business spending. Rather, he emphasized that a general wage-rate decrease would reduce wage income, and by thus reducing consumption spending would worsen the recession that had begun.) The business leaders agreed. In the first half of 1930 there were, in fact, more wage-rate rises than decreases; and it was not until October, 1931, that there was any general round of sizable wage-rate cuts.

The maintenance of wage rates did not prevent the recession from deepening into a significant downswing and depression. But neither did the round of 15 per cent wage-rate decreases in October, 1931, or the second round of 10 per cent decreases a year or so later. Households and firms had very unfavorable price expectations, and they were increasingly uncertain about the future. The wage-rate decreases doubtless led to expectations of further cuts and hence to greater uncertainty. As voters in the 1932 elections, households turned out the Republicans in favor of the Democrats, just as primitive peoples throw out impotent medicine men. But the change in administration could not come until March, 1933, and by that time many people had begun to wonder if there was any "bottom" short of total collapse.

There was. The new man in the White House inspired confidence. The new Congress rushed through various pieces of "recovery" legislation. Confidence was fortified. Price expectations turned favorable. Business and employment began to improve.

The most important piece of legislation in 1933 was the National Industrial Recovery Act. While providing for wage-rate increases, the Act as administered also encouraged government-fostered cartel-like arrangements among the firms in each industry. Firms liked this, for higher product prices were permitted and encouraged.

But the new government desired reform as well as business recovery. It believed that certain business practices had led to the economic cataclysm, and it wished to prohibit such practices so that there would be no recurrence. Accordingly, a number of other statutes were passed during 1934 and 1935, in rapid succession, to protect the consumer, the household lender, and the worker from "exploitation" by business.

The country got indigestion from this surfeit of reform legislation. There can be little doubt that it was needed. But, perhaps because another election was scheduled for 1936, it came too fast. The man who saved the country in 1933 became unpopular in business circles. Business recovery became impeded. Investment spending by firms was inhibited because of their lack of confidence, their uncertainty about the future. In spite of a minor boom in 1936–37, the country failed to reach reasonably full employment. It "stagnated." The continued unemployment of from eight to ten million workers led Professor Hansen of Harvard to announce that economic maturity had been reached with the passing of the geographic frontiers, and that henceforth senility would set in unless the government made up the deficit in private business investment.

The events just before and after America's participation in World War II proved the incorrectness of this hypothesis. After 1939, when the war started in Europe, price expectations in America turned upward and favorable. Certainty began to replace uncertainty — business confidence began to be restored. Households and firms remembered what wars do to prices, business activity, and profits. Even before government spending reached high levels, total spending rose toward the full employment level. From 1942 to 1945, after the United States had entered the war, tremendous amounts of government spending were of course added to the increases in private spending, so that price and wage-rate controls were needed to avoid a tremendous price inflation. But when, following the end of the war, government spending was greatly reduced, there was no significant business recession. Private expectations remained favorable and certain. Private consumption and investment spending held at very high levels. And with price and wage-rate controls removed, we had inflation. There was no hint of stagnation from 1946 to 1951.

(b) Relation of technological progress to cyclical fluctuations. Earlier we discussed technological change in respect to the secular trend of employment. Now, as the last topic in our analysis of the causes of unemployment in the economy as a whole, we must determine whether technological change is a factor in cyclical oscillations of employment.

To do this we have first to note whether such fluctuations affect the timing of the technological improvements made by firms. Then we have to learn whether the timing of these improvements in turn influences the cyclical fluctuations.

In attacking the first point we must remember to distinguish between the two kinds of technological innovations — new, improved machines and new managerial methods. And we must also distinguish the desire to make these two kinds of changes from the ability to do so.

Then we may observe the following: During business downswings the desire of firms to make both kinds of innovations rises because there is an increased need to reduce unit production costs. However, there is also an increased need to guard financial reserves. Therefore, we find managerial improvements being introduced at an accelerated pace; but the introduction of new machines is held up until better times.

On the other hand, during business upswings the situation is reversed. The desire to make cost-reducing innovations of either kind is probably less keen. But the ability to do so is much greater. Therefore, we find firms making new-machine improvements in great waves. A very large rise in firms' investment spending occurs about the middle of the upswing.

Now let us consider whether these effects of cyclical fluctuations in turn influence the fluctuations. During the downswing the introduction of cost-reducing managerial improvements probably tends to lessen the length and severity of the depression. It helps firms to be ready for a business upturn and tends to change their expectations from loss to profits. But once business recovery is under way and the wave of concentrated investment spending on improved machines takes place, we have the basis for a boom that takes the economy to a great inflationary height from which the plunge into depression can be long and devastating. During the boom the machine-producing firms and industries are fully employed. But once the new machines are produced and installed, the demand for machines is saturated; they are durable and do not need the quick replacement that many consumption goods do. Then employment and wage income and spending decline in the machine-making firms at the same time that increased quantities of consumption goods from the new machines reach the market. Firms find that their expectations were too rosy. The new machines are not so profitable as was anticipated because total spending is not so high as was expected. Things would not be so bad if the workers previously employed in making the machines now moved into the firms making consumption products. But this does not happen sufficiently to compensate for the drop in employment and wage income in the machine-making industries. So firms' expectations in general turn unfavorable and a business downswing gets under way.

2. Personal and human-relations causes of unemployment. We now turn to a brief consideration of the unemployment among individual workers caused by "personal conditions," as that term was defined at the beginning of this chapter. Involuntary idleness produced by one of these conditions may be just as grim for a particular worker as that resulting from the installation of a labor-saving machine or the migration or insolvency of a firm. Any discussion of the problem of "getting and holding a job" would be incomplete without mention of these circumstances.

It is convenient to classify these personal conditions (which prevent individual workers from getting jobs or cause them to lose jobs) under three main heads: (*a*) inherent characteristics of the workers themselves; (*b*) managerial policies; and (*c*) the policies of labor unions.

a. The workers' own characteristics. It would be unfair to say that all workers who are fired, laid off, or unable to obtain jobs find themselves in such circumstances because of the attitudes and policies of their bosses or of union officials. The workers themselves, within the total situations of intra-plant and extra-plant living, are also often to blame. For reasons of heredity or environment or both, many workers are not well adjusted or successful in their jobs; they are "square pegs in round holes." Or as jobless persons seeking work, they are seen to be poor prospects by firms having vacancies. They have a hard time getting placed in all but the tightest labor markets. In a free society such persons are to be pitied and should be helped in one way or another to become suitably adjusted in industrial employment. But no one can reasonably be expected to experience a feeling of rankling injustice over their difficulties in so far as these are the result of their own deficiencies rather than of the hostile, anti-social acts of other persons. The most that can properly be looked for in an economic and political democracy is equality of opportunity and treatment. Every man and woman should be given a fair chance to develop his natural endowments and train his inborn aptitudes. Every person is justified in asking that the same rules and tests for successful performance be applied without favor or prejudice to him and all others. Beyond that, he is on his own in respect to getting and holding a job.

b. Managerial policies. Unfortunately we have evidence that the ideal of equality of opportunity and treatment is not always honored in the hiring and layoff policies of firms. Frequently there is discrimination against one or more kinds of workers. Sometimes these policies may be rather well founded on experience; a firm's management has to develop an effective production organization, and some classes of workers have been found, after fair trial, not to fit. More often, however, there is no rational basis for discrimination; it is the result of irrational bias and prejudice.

There appear to be four main kinds of discrimination that have existed for some time in greater or less degree: (1) against workers for joining or being active in a labor union; (2) against certain age groups; (3) against certain race groups; and (4) against women workers. Let us consider each of these briefly.

(1) Anti-union discrimination. Before unionism became widespread, powerful, and safeguarded by law, a great many employers — except in a few well-unionized industries such as construction and train operation — actively discriminated against union members and leaders. The "yellow-dog" contract of employment was frequently used and had legal protection. Here a job applicant promised in writing, as a condition of getting and retaining work in a plant, not to join or assist in forming a union. Failure to keep this promise meant, on discovery, discharge. Not only that: Anti-union employers in a given market area circulated blacklists among themselves. If a union "trouble maker" showed up as an ap-

plicant at the employment office of some other of these employers, he was refused a job. And even if the yellow dog and the blacklist were not used, workers were usually discharged at the first sign of union organizing or other union activity.

During the thirties these and many other anti-union practices were made illegal, and today there is relatively little anti-union discrimination except in certain isolated areas, mainly in the South.

(2) Age hiring limits. Some firms are reluctant to hire young, inexperienced workers except in times of labor scarcity. But the chief kind of discrimination based on workers' ages is found at the other end of the scale. It is not so much that firms are inclined to lay off disproportionate numbers of older workers; men above fifty or sixty have little difficulty retaining their jobs if they do not quit their firms. But if for any non-age reason they are separated from their previous employment, they often have trouble in finding new jobs.

It appears that almost half of the firms employing more than 500 persons have formal or informal policies to give hiring preference to younger workers when the conditions of the labor market permit. There is definite aversion to hiring unskilled or semi-skilled workers over 40 or 45 years of age and skilled workers over 45 or 50 years old. Thus, so far as hiring is concerned, a worker tends to become "old" or superannuated when he reaches forty.

This sort of discrimination is a particularly significant problem because it has come into existence at a time when, as was shown in Chapter 5, the proportions of persons above age 40, 50, and 60 in the population and the labor force have been increasing. It means that in years of other than full employment the percentages of unemployment tend to be considerably higher and the periods of unemployment to last longer among the older groups of workers.

Why do so many firms have maximum-age hiring limits? They seem to feel that modern production is a high-speed operation, sometimes dangerous, requiring fast, dexterous reactions; and that younger workers possess the necessary traits more than older men. In other words, the older workers are said to be more prone to injury and more susceptible to disease; to have lost some of their skill; to be harder to train in work and morale; and, in general, to be less productive and more expensive to employ. Those who oppose such discrimination insist that available data do not support these beliefs. They cite Bureau of Labor Statistics and other data showing that absenteeism from illness and other causes is somewhat lower for workers over 40; accident frequency rates are generally lower; accident severity rates but little higher; and productivity very little lower. And they maintain that the older workers more than make up for any possible inferiority on these counts by their superior loyalty, reliability, and general stability.

One reason for age limits in hiring has attained special importance in recent years. The widespread adoption of company pension plans under union pressure has worked against the hiring of older workers in two ways. In the first place, most of the plans provide for retirement benefits of a certain amount to be paid to workers of 25 or more years of service with the company when they reach a given age, say 65 (or 68). Retirement is compulsory at such age. Workers having only from 10 (or 15) to 25 years of service receive proportionately smaller pensions. These provisions mean that the young worker who starts working for a company at the age of, say, 25 years will have a much larger contribution (including compound interest) built up for him by the time he reaches retirement age than the worker who is, say, 40 or 45 years old when he is hired. That is, for a young worker the company contributions plus interest are much lower in relation to the size of pension than for an older worker. Because of the pension plan it is much cheaper for the company to employ younger men.

Pension plans operate in another way, also, against the employment of older workers. Under the plans, workers of only 10 (or 15) years' service get no pensions at all. Many of these workers therefore wish to work beyond the age of 65 (or 68). If the firm permits them to do so, it may be accused of discriminating against the men eligible for pensions, who must be retired at the given age. On the other hand, if it doesn't permit non-pensioners to work after they are 65 (or 68), it may be accused of being unfair to *them.* In other words, the company gets into trouble on either count. So it decides to avoid trouble by not hiring men in their fifties, who will be ineligible for company pensions.

(3) Racial discrimination. Many firms are located in cities such as New York, Chicago, Pittsburgh, Cleveland, and Detroit, where the labor forces contain diverse racial elements. There are whites who in the first or second generation have come from various foreign countries; and there are Negroes. Under these circumstances the managements of a good many firms come, rightly or wrongly, to look on the members of certain racial groups as trouble-makers; they tend to limit these groups to certain small percentages of their work forces. The members of other groups are considered good and desirable workers; they are preferred job applicants. Again, the members of one group are believed to be antagonistic to those of another; they must not be allowed to work in the same department.

Of all the racial groups, Negroes appear to be most subject to discrimination in hiring, promotions, and layoffs. During periods of substantial general unemployment, higher percentages of colored workers become and stay idle than of any other class of workers. With little foundation or justification in fact, the notion becomes prevalent that they are inefficient workers or that they are fitted only for certain kinds of work, usually unskilled and menial. This seems to be particularly true in the South. Even these traditional types of work — e.g., barbering, elevator operation, and waiting on table — become invaded by white workers during times of depression.

(4) Discrimination against women. Some employers — a declining number in recent decades — also believe that women make inferior, more expensive workers. Because absenteeism is usually higher among women than among men, because a number of women work briefly for "pin money" and hence are only transient members of the labor force, and because firms must often provide special facilities (such as work-seating and rest rooms) for them, it may well be that the employment of women does entail additional expense. But most women do not work for pin money; they are permanent members of the labor force. And the evidence weighs heavily in favor of the conclusion that, on jobs to which their capacities are suited, they are at least as productive as men. An increasing number of firms have abandoned any discrimination based on sex. (One reason, of course, has been that employers are often able to discriminate against women in the matter of wage rates. For jobs capable of being filled by either men or women, firms can often hire women at lower rates. See Chapter 7.)

c. Union policies. Firms are not the only agencies that discriminate against certain classes of workers. Labor organizations also have been in a position to restrict employment opportunities.

In our chapters on unionism we shall find that unions are very active in protecting the job security of their members against possible discrimination by employers. Because many of the unions are relatively young and have only recently won recognition from formerly anti-union firms, the unions are also zealous in providing for the security of the union as an organizational entity. Seniority or length of service as a basis for promotion, layoff, and rehiring, plus anti-discrimination and "union shop" provisions in union contracts (Chapter 14), are the chief ways used to provide security for members. Moreover, some form of "union shop," whereby the employer agrees to give preference to union members in hiring or to keep only union members in his employ, is the chief measure of security for the union as an entity.

Now, so long as any member of the managerial hierarchy of a firm is likely to discriminate against union members in the matters of hiring and job tenure and promotion, these union policies are fine for the members and for the union. (Of course, if all management is thoroughly sold on unionism and operates with fairness and wisdom on job tenure, the policies are superfluous except as a safeguard against managerial backsliding.) But in fairness to *all* free Americans who wish to work and to attain security, progress, and justice, in respect to the goals mentioned in Chapter 2, two further questions must be raised: (1) Are all workers in the occupation or plant or industry eligible for membership in the union which controls employment destinies and provides employment benefits for its members? That is, does the union purposefully exclude from membership any workers who would willingly join in order to participate in the security which the union is able to provide? (2) Do unions, through their security measures, prevent workers who do not wish to join the unions from getting and holding jobs?

We shall study union policies in Chapters 10–16. From the material there, more detailed answers to these questions will be available. But certain summary statements can be made here.

Most unions actively solicit members and welcome all who wish to join. A sizable minority, however, by one device or another exclude various kinds of workers. For example, the high initiation fees and dues and the apprenticeship regulations of the building trades unions tend to restrict membership. Furthermore, these and other unions may have certain provisions in their constitutions or in their initiation rituals that exclude women, Negroes, or others from membership. Sometimes it is only the unwritten law of common consent which effects the exclusion.

If these means of exclusion are combined with arrangements whereby employers dealing with these unions agree to keep only union members in their employ, the job opportunities of the non-unionists are severely limited. They may well wish to belong to the union but be unable to do so. Clearly they must turn to some other industry where the union will accept them. It is difficult to find any social justification for such union practices.

But what about the highly individualistic, strong-minded workers who are able but unwilling to join unions and thereby are also excluded from many job opportunities? Most union men say such workers deserve no pity. They make a free choice to stay out of the union. Why, unionists argue, should this kind of non-unionist get a free pass on the union gravy train? That is, why should a man obtain all the benefits of a union contract (higher wage rates and many other improved terms of employment) without subjecting himself to union discipline, rules, dues, and so on? Is it fair for the non-unionist to reap where he has not sown?

It is not hard to understand this point of view. On the other hand, neither are the opposing arguments to be dismissed lightly. Why, it is said, should a man be coerced into doing something he prefers not to do? Is it anti-social to exercise one's American freedom to try to better one's self by one's own efforts? By what logic can the penalty of unemployment be justified for a person who practices the principles on which this country was founded?

Obviously there is here a conflict of rights and freedoms — the right of free men to associate or band together for common betterment versus the right of free men to achieve progress and security by individual effort. The student will have to decide for himself how the conflict should be resolved. Government is the agency which settles such differences. We shall discuss the policy of government on this issue in a later chapter.

This concludes our discussion of the nature, extent, effects, and causes of unemployment among workers. We have seen that there are many economic and non-economic conditions that influence workers' willingness and ability to get and hold jobs. One of these conditions is the level of wage rates and wage income. The level of wage rates affects employers' willingness to hire labor. Wage rates and wage income affect workers' willingness to supply labor. It is necessary, therefore, for us to focus our attention on the level and structure of American wage rates and income.

CHAPTER 7

Obtaining Adequate Income

A. INTRODUCTION

1. Relation of income problem to employment problem. For the ordinary worker the problem of getting and holding a job is inseparable from and virtually identical with the problem of obtaining an adequate, secure income. Usually he wants a job not for the joy of working but for the wage income that permits him to buy goods that will satisfy his wants. In short, the obtaining of adequate income is the main problem of the worker.

Most workers own no resource or productive factor other than their own labor. That is, they rely largely on wage income; they own few or no savings from which interest income is received. A number of statistical studies attest to this fact.[1] In 1929, a prosperous year, it was estimated that 84 per cent of total family savings out of income in the United States were made by the 8 per cent of households that had received $5000 or more of income during that year. There was very little saving done by the 60 per cent of the families that had less than $2000 of income; and most of the workers were in this income class. In 1935–36, moderately depressed years when the average annual wage was less than $1000, there were no savings made in the income classes below $1250. In 1949, a relatively prosperous year, 29 per cent of the households had no savings or liquid assets, and another 28 per cent had less than $500.

When we talked about getting and holding a job in Chapter 6, we meant a full-time job. It will be recalled that in most of the discussions we dealt with labor-hours of employment rather than with men or workers. In our usage, unemployment exists not only when a worker has no job at all, but also, to some extent, when a worker is employed only part-time on his job. In other words, given the wage rate and other terms of employment, a worker allocates his time between leisure and real income;

[1] See, for example, M. Leven, H. G. Moulton, and C. Warburton, *America's Capacity to Consume,* the Brookings Institution, Washington, 1934, pp. 93, 126; National Resources Committee, *Consumer Expenditures in the United States, 1935–1936,* Washington, 1938; and *Economic Report of the President,* various semi-annual issues, Appendix B, Washington.

he decides thereby how many hours he wishes to work for income. And to the extent that the number of hours he decides to offer is not matched by the number of hours firms are willing to employ him, he is unemployed. He is not obtaining the amount of wage income he wishes.

Some households are composed of single, unmarried persons. Other households include two or more persons but have only one worker. Still other households are not only composed of two or more persons but also have two or more wage-earners. In any case, we are concerned here more with household or family income than with individual-worker income. This is because the household is usually the unit that decides how much labor to offer and how much to spend and to save.

As stated in Chapter 3, the amount of money income received by a household per period of time depends in the first instance on (*a*) the number of units of each kind of resource (each kind of labor and capital) owned or controlled by the household and hired by firms; and (*b*) the unit price of each such resource. Price times quantity sold equals money income from each resource whose services are hired. And the sum of the incomes from all the resources hired equals the household's money income for the given period.

2. The plan of discussion. Because we are interested here in workers' problems and because most workers own and sell the services of little more than some kind of labor resource, our discussion will focus mainly on wage income. A household's wage income per period of time, such as a week or year, is the product of the wage rate times the number of hours worked during the period, i.e., times the amount of employment the household gets.

In the pages that follow, we shall deal first with the *nature and extent* of the wage-income problem. Here our main concern is with appraising the adequacy of workers' incomes. Second, we shall consider briefly some *effects* of inadequate incomes. And third, we shall try to analyze the "causes" of the income problem. That is, we shall study the economic and human-relations conditions that influence the wage-rate component of wage income; and we shall relate these conditions to those affecting the employment component of wage income — hours of work.

B. NATURE AND EXTENT OF THE PROBLEM

1. Income standards. What number of workers' households have adequate incomes? What percentage of all workers' households is this number? What percentage is it of all households, including non-workers'?

Anyone trying to answer these questions must obviously first define "adequate." This is a very difficult task. Whose standards shall prevail in fashioning the definition? Those of government officials? Social workers? Reformers and do-gooders? Employers? The wage-earners themsel-

a. General considerations. (1) Determinants of income standards. No matter who undertakes the task, a major requirement is that the definition be attuned to the realities of the world in which the workers live and labor. There is no sense in letting one's ideals or fancies run away with him. "If wishes were horses, beggars would ride" is a picturesque way of saying that what man *wants* to have must be curbed by what he is *able* to have. We must thus begin with the hard economic fact that the average or per-capita income in any economy depends on its organization for production and on the quantity of resources and the level of technology. An "adequate" income must always be related to and based upon these fundamental economic determinants.

If one society possesses quantities and qualities of resources and a social organization superior to those of some other economy, the former will tend to have a higher per-capita *plane* of living or income than the latter. And its *standard* or *goal* of adequate living for all households should also be higher.

But is this last statement supportable? Granted that the average household in a "backward" country has a lower realized income than the average household in an "advanced" country, doesn't each household need the same quotas of calories, vitamins, minerals, and other requirements of health and satisfaction? Isn't there some absolute minimum standard applicable to both? Not necessarily or probably. For one thing, the household in the "poor" country might not know about the things considered desirable by the rich-country household. For another, it might not want these things if it did know about them. It might belong to a religious or ascetic society which considered such gadgets wicked or silly. And suppose it did wish for as well as know about the things included in the rich country's minimum standard of living: Failing to obtain them, the household in the poor country would probably not be nearly so badly off, mentally or physically, as a household in the wealthy country which was unable to reach the standard. The former would see very few other households in its land living up to the rich country's standard; there would be very little to covet and feel frustrated about. And presumably this household would, like its neighbors, be properly adjusted for physical survival in the poor country. We learned in Korea how much less the Chinese soldier needed than the American for survival.

We conclude that not only the actual plane or level of living but also the standard or goal of adequate living and income must be related not only to the beliefs, customs, and wants of the households in an economy but also to the quantity and quality of resources and social organization. This being so, it follows that as wants change and as resources and organization improve over time, the standard of income-adequacy is very likely to rise.

We see also that, whatever the level of income chosen as adequate, it is a household's *relative* position in the society that is of prime importance. No household is likely to be seriously upset or resentful over failure to meet a given standard if it believes it has been given a fair chance to attain the standard, and if other households have also failed. It may well be that the resources and technology of an economy are such as to permit the achievement of a certain *minimum* per-capita income; and failure to reach this minimum may be considered reprehensible for any person or for the society. But beyond this amount, it is one's relative income position that matters.

The setting of income standards by any person or group, then, involves two things: the determination of a minimum amount of income below which no household or person should fall; and the determination of how any "surplus" income in the economy should be distributed. Anyone who tries to set up a minimum standard must, as already shown, consider how much the economy's resources and technology can afford. He must set different minima for different sizes of households. Obviously a single worker living alone needs less than a man and wife and four or five dependent children. Furthermore, the minimum income is actually a minimum amount of *real* rather than money income; it is concerned with the products and services that can be bought with money income. This fact means two things. First, the minimum amount of money income representing the real goods must be changed up or down when the prices of the goods rise or fall. (This change is of course independent of any change in the real standard made possible by an increase in the quantity and quality of resources.) Second, for any given size of family at any given time the money income necessary to support the goods-standard will vary as the cost of living varies among localities. Thus, the cost of the goods that compose the standard may be lower in a small town than in a large city.

Still another matter that must be considered in determining a minimum standard for a given size of family in an economy is that the real goods themselves may vary in amount among various communities. For example, a family in a small town lives a different kind of life from one in a big city; the items on the two budgets could not reasonably be expected to be identical. Similarly, a deep-South family needs fewer clothes and less fuel than a far-North one.

Now suppose we multiply the minimum for a given size of family by the number of families of that size shown by a census to exist in the economy. We obtain a total minimum amount of income for that class of household. If this is done for each size of family and if all the totals are then summed, we have a minimum total income for all households. This total, if realistically determined, should be substantially less than the full-employment total income for the economy. Thus, the next question is how the difference or "surplus" should be distributed among the households. The answer to this question would determine a household's relative income position, which we have said is of major importance.

(2) Principles of income distribution. The question of income standards virtually boils down to the principle of income distribution that is generally accepted in a given economy. There are two main possible bases for distributing a society's total income among its households: (*a*) productivity, and (*b*) need.

(a) The principle of productivity. The principle of productivity is the one that largely prevails in a democratic, private enterprise society. In the popular conception, it means that a worker's income is determined by his "contribution" to the economy's output; the bigger or more significant his contribution, the larger his income. Actually, it means that a man's income varies directly with his "market advantage." That is, a person's income depends on the quantity of resources or productive factors he manages to acquire, and on the unit prices of these resources as determined by the various conditions affecting market supply and demand. High market advantage exists when a person inherits or obtains by his own efforts a large portion of resources whose prices are high because their total market supplies are limited. Low market advantage exists when a person owns a small quantity of resources whose prices are low because their total market supplies are relatively plentiful. Thus, a household having two tool-and-die makers tends to have a high wage income compared to a household having only one common laborer, both because the first household owns more labor resources and because the total market supply of skilled workers like tool-and-die makers is much smaller than that of unskilled workers like common laborers — the hourly wage rate of a tool maker is much higher than that of a common laborer. But this does not mean that the skilled workers necessarily work any harder or more industriously than the unskilled. "Productivity" or "contribution" is not necessarily in direct relation to effort. No teacher, for example, is required to give a student a grade of A merely for effort. The rarer, highly skilled student, who may or may not be lazy, is the one who gets the A's.

Market advantage is based on a variety of hereditary and environmental conditions. Some workers are born with the mental and physical traits necessary for performing highly skilled work. Others are not. Among those adequately endowed by heredity, some get the opportunity to develop or train their native aptitudes; others do not. Thus, both heredity and environment operate to determine which households possess the high- and the low-priced resources.

Through laws governing the inheritance of the non-labor resource, capital, the environment also influences the *quantity* of resources owned. In most private enterprise economies a household or person may acquire a large quantity of this productive factor from his parents rather than through his own efforts.

High prices for some resources may be "artificially" induced. That is, an "artificial" scarcity may be created if one or more owners of a resource manage to control and limit the market supply, i.e., manage to become monopolistic sellers. Thus, the exclusive owner of a patented machine is in a position to restrict its supply and raise its price above the level that would exist if there were a number of competitive sellers of the machine. And some labor unions, through artificially restricting their memberships by a variety of devices and through requiring firms to hire only union members, are able to raise their wage rates beyond the "natural" competitive level.

The main virtues of the "productivity" principle of income distribution are said to be that it is in accord with "human nature," is regarded as fair, is therefore calculated to call forth a person's best efforts, and hence is beneficial to the whole society. There may be a flaw or two in this chain of reasoning. For one thing, it assumes human nature to be such that each household wishes to work only in behalf of its own want-satisfaction. This may or may not be true, depending on what the prevailing social code is. If every child were taught that the way to "get ahead" is to help other people or to serve the state, he might try to be as productive as possible without much thought about his own satisfaction. Second, even though the maximization of one's own satisfaction appears to be a main objective of human behavior in a private enterprise society, it does not follow that the pursuit of this goal will make everyone work harder and more skillfully. As we have just seen, a person's income in such a society may be made larger when he restricts rather than increases his output. To whatever extent this happens, society is poorer rather than richer.

(b) The principle of need. The so-called "productivity" principle, which turns out to be one of market advantage, may not have all the virtues that are sometimes ascribed to it, nor have them in as great degree. But is there any other principle of income distribution that is more just, or that could be viewed as more just by the individual, more satisfying to his basic desires, and more beneficial to society as a whole? This significant question leads us directly to consider the only alternative principle of distribution — that of *need.*

The classical communists of pre-Soviet days held that output-production and income-distribution in the ideal society would be organized in accordance with the formula, "From each according to his ability, to each according to his need." That is, they envisaged an economy in which human nature would be such that everyone would work as hard and skillfully as possible for the common good, without regard for payment proportionate to effort and ability. Every household would share in the society's total output on the basis of relative need or capacity to experience want-satisfaction. Here the households that were larger or had more ailing, dependent members would be given the larger incomes no matter what quantity or quality of resources they possessed.

In time it came to be recognized that it might be very hard to calculate or measure each household's relative need or enjoyment-capacity. So the modern advocates of this principle have said that the simplest way of giving effect to it would be to distribute income equally among all households. There might well be cases of individual hardship if this were done — as well as cases where households got too much. Capacity to enjoy satisfaction would not be closely related to size of income in these cases. But in a society of millions of families the hardship and the bonanza cases would tend to cancel each other out. And a net gain in total satisfaction would result from taking away from the rich and giving to the poor.

Because this principle has never been put into effect on a sufficiently large scale for a sufficiently long period of time, there is no inductive or historical evidence on its relative merits. One is reduced to theorizing. Those who espouse the need principle assert the following: Since one man thinks he is as good as another, the principle would seem fairer than the one which makes for income inequality. Human nature can be changed, and people can be taught to be productive regardless of amount of personal income. The greater a household's need, the harder it will work. Society will suffer no loss in total physical output and will experience a gain in total well-being, which depends in part on non-physical things.

Those who oppose the need idea make these points: This principle, especially if expressed through income equality, will not impress most people as fair. On the contrary, there will be resentment that income is not allowed to vary in accordance with ability and achievement. Human nature cannot be changed except under an ironclad dictatorship, and such a system is repugnant to most households. If a household knows that its income will be the same as every other's, why should it put forth its best efforts? What incentive is there to hard and skillful work if one is not to starve or to suffer relatively? Any attempt to slice up the output pie equally will therefore result in a significant reduction in the size of the pie. Society, and each household along with it, will end up much poorer than before.

(c) Can the principles be combined? These, then, are the two main alternative principles of income distribution. If our discussion at the beginning of Chapter 3 has taken root, the student will ask at once, Are these alternatives divisible or indivisible? Must one be chosen to the exclusion of the other, or can some of both be had?

It would seem that they are divisible. Most modern societies, whether democratic or authoritarian, have tried to combine them. The principle of need is observed through statutory provisions for minimum incomes (through minimum-wage-rate laws, unemployment compensation and relief, and so on). The productivity principle is given force through permitting income differentials to exist above the minima.

(3) Who selects income standards and principles? Anyone who concerns himself with minimum income standards and with the sharing of

the total output which an economy's resources and technology affords is in reality trying to answer the broad question, Among all the households of the society, whose wants and desires shall be satisfied how much? We come back, then, to the matter of who should give a definitive answer to this question.

Any individual student or layman can and often does try his hand at an answer. But the significant and definitive determination of income standards must of necessity come from organized private groups or from the supreme, sovereign organization, government. The two main private groups having views on the problems are associations of households in labor unions and associations of firms. Usually the views of these organizations are expressed through their policies on only one of the components of wage income, namely wage *rates*. But labor unions, especially in Great Britain and to some extent in America, have come in recent years to ask for guaranteed annual wage incomes — which means that they are concerned with not only the wage rate but also the hours-worked component of wage income.

No labor union or federation of unions and no association of employers has yet been in a position to speak for all households — worker and nonworker alike. The only agency able to do this has been the national government of a country. Government can approach the problem of income standards in two ways. First, it can adopt standards which it believes are good and proper for the households under its jurisdiction, without regard to the households' own wishes and preferences. Such an approach is much less likely in a democracy than in an authoritarian state. Consider, for example, how difficult it was in 1951 for the United States government to get workers and farmers to agree to income sacrifices in behalf of the defense program. Compare this situation with the relative ease with which the Soviet government had for decades forced or propagandized its households to accept low incomes for the sake of industrialization and defense. The second way in which government may approach the problem of income standards is to conform its standards to what it believes are those of its households. Although this may be done under a despotic government, it is much more likely in a democracy.

How does a democratic government learn about households' views on income standards and distribution? Through their votes on issues presented by rival candidates, through their communications to elected representatives, through editorial opinions expressed in the newspapers and magazines published by organized groups, through private polls of public opinion, and through studies made by particular government agencies like the federal Bureau of Labor Statistics.

But no matter what agency — private or governmental — defines income standards, the prime requisites for definition are knowledge and realism.

b. Some American income standards. With all these things in mind, let us now consider some attempts to determine adequate standards of living and standards of income distribution for American households.

(1) Minimum standards of income. Since the beginning of the twentieth century, private economists, sociologists, research groups, and government agencies have at different times published their estimates of what constitute minimum adequate amounts of annual income for one or more sizes of American households living in various parts of the country in communities of various sizes. These estimates have differed in many ways. Some, like those of the Heller Committee for skilled workers' families of five members in San Francisco, were confined to a single locality and class of household. Others, like those of the federal Bureau of Labor Statistics for wage-earners in 34 large cities, were much more comprehensive in geographic, size-of-family, and degree-of-skill coverage. Some, like those of the federal Works Progress Administration in 1935, were based on the notions of the estimators about the nature, quantities, and qualities of the products the households were supposed to be able to buy. Others, like the post-World War II studies of the B.L.S., reflected much more the ideas, habits, and standards of the households themselves. Some, like those of the Technocrats in the early thirties, were exceedingly rough, unrealistic, and idealistic estimates. Others, like those of the B.L.S., were relatively very careful and painstaking and represented much more conservative thinking. Some, like those of the W.P.A., allowed little more than subsistence living. Others, like those of the Heller Committee, were designed for living planes of modest "comfort."

Any person or agency that attempts to make a serious, objective estimate of a minimum adequate standard of living goes through two main steps: (*a*) Budgets are devised for one or more sizes of household. The principal budget items include food of various sorts; items of apparel; housing, utilities, and household equipment; transportation; medical and dental care; recreation; education; miscellaneous items; and perhaps savings. For each item in each budget category, quantity and quality are specified. (*b*) The budget items are priced in the stores of one or more localities to which the standard will apply.

Clearly, as households' consumption patterns change, the content of the budgets must be revised. For example, a place must be found for spinach and for television sets as these products become popular. Such revision recognizes the influence of technological progress. Furthermore, the budgets must be re-priced from time to time, especially during periods of significant general price changes. If neither kind of revision is made, the income standard based on the original budget loses its current validity and becomes only of historical interest.

There is space in this book for only the most recent efforts to define minimum adequate income standards by the agency — the B.L.S. — that has had most and broadest experience in the field and is best fitted to do the job. Yet even the published studies of the B.L.S., as it would freely concede, fail to give comprehensive coverage. Data for all sizes of households are not given. Households are not classified by number of workers. And families in rural areas and smaller cities and towns are usually not surveyed.

In an effort to arrive at a minimum standard of income adequacy that would be commonly accepted, the Congress asked the U.S. Bureau of Labor Statistics in 1946 to develop and price a minimum budget for urban families. This budget was published in 1947 as the City Worker's Family Budget and represents the nearest approach yet made to a scientific yardstick for measuring adequacy under contemporary conditions. The budget has been described as representing not a "mere existence level nor a luxury level" but a "modest but adequate standard of living." It attempts to set a minimum amount required by families at that vague but nevertheless real point in the income scale where "the struggle for more and more gives way to the desire for better and better quality." That is to say, below this budget level, families are struggling to get enough to attain a "physically adequate existence," while above it they have enough income to think about improving the quality of living.

In arriving at the appropriate quantity and quality of goods required by such a budget, the Bureau's technicians based their estimates not on an "ideal" living standard or on what technicians might think families ought to have, but rather on the actual purchasing habits of working-class people. The City Worker's Family Budget thus reflected community judgment as to what goods and services were necessary. If these goods were not obtained, the households experienced a feeling of serious depreciation. Once the quantity and quality of goods required by such a budget were determined, the items were priced in 34 major cities of the country.

By the end of 1951 the B.L.S. had priced the budget three times — in June, 1947; October, 1949; and October, 1950. In the last-named month the total annual cost of goods and services ranged from about $3180 in New Orleans to about $3580 in Washington, D.C., for a typical wage-earner's household of four members — man, wife, and boy and girl aged, respectively, 13 and 8 years. The national average was roughly $3400. If personal taxes and insurance are included, the range was from $3450 in New Orleans to $3930 in Milwaukee, with a national average of roughly $3700.

(2) Standards of income distribution. Bearing in mind what we have previously said about the nature and importance of relative size of income among an economy's households, we find that no persons or agencies, private or governmental, have made objective studies of what the distribution of income ought to be. On the other hand, almost everyone has felt himself free at one time or another to express himself qualitatively about what the prevailing principle of distribution should be.

These facts should surprise no one. The very nature of the problem precludes scientific inductive study and leaves the field wide open for the expression of subjective value judgments. As previously stated, it is impossible to measure different persons' needs or capacities to enjoy satisfaction and then to determine the distribution of these needs or capacities among the nation's households in order to compare this distribution with the distribution of money incomes (which can be objectively determined). Furthermore, even if the distribution of enjoyment-capacity could be discovered, it would be impossible to state with assurance that money income should be shared by an identical distribution. For, as pointed out in Chapter 3, if the two distributions are to be made identical, the government must redistribute income by some system of taxation and benefits; and the process might well seriously diminish the incentives to produce.

Let no one conclude, however, that these difficulties have deterred households or government from adopting and acting on certain standards of income distribution. In America a large majority of the people have always adhered to the view that, in peacetime at least, the nation's output should be distributed on the basis of the principle of productivity, whether or not they have realized that in practice this principle really means market advantage. And very probably they would not have changed their minds if they had understood that productivity means market advantage; most people recognize, honor, and try to practice market advantage virtually every day of their lives.

But this is not the whole story. A majority of the household members who belong to labor unions and a majority of those who vote have not been satisfied to let alone the results of adopting the market-advantage principle. That is, they have not thought well of the very unequal distribution of income resulting from the operation of this principle. The labor unions have continually tried, by demanding wage-rate increases and other benefits from employers, to divert to the lower-income households a larger share of the national income. A majority of the voters have supported the efforts of government to establish equality of opportunity to secure larger individual incomes — through such measures as free public schools and universities. The voters also have approved government efforts to redistribute income through progressive income taxation and free services. In fact, they felt so strongly about the desirability of redistribution that they went to the great trouble of amending the national constitution in 1916 to permit such taxation. Furthermore, during the thirties they approved laws giving more power to labor unions, providing for large-scale, government-organized unemployment compensation and relief, and establishing state and federal minimum wage rates for most unskilled jobs.

In short, a majority of American households may be said to have groped their way toward finding the optimum combination of the two income-distribution principles: market advantage and need or capacity to enjoy.

Now if we were to try to interpret these actions of the voters, we might say that their bare minimum standards on relative incomes have been as follows: First, no household shall receive less than a certain minimum income, much less starve. Second, the distribution of incomes and want-satisfaction shall be considerably less unequal after than before taxes. Third, over time, the minimum income must rise; and the distribution of income before taxes must at least not become more unequal than in previous comparable years.

2. American incomes in the light of the standards. Having considered the nature and methods of determining adequate income standards, we may now attempt to answer the questions posed at the beginning of this chapter-section (page 117). First of all, what numbers and percentages of American workers have achieved the American income standards?

a. Minimum adequate amounts of annual income. At the outset we must admit that, good as American statistics are compared to those of most other countries, we just do not have enough information to give accurate, comprehensive answers to the questions in which we are interested here. As already stated, the Bureau of Labor Statistics or other agencies have not published income *standards* for various sizes of workers' families in various kinds of localities. Similarly, there are no published data showing the incomes actually earned by households of various sizes and various numbers of workers in different localities. Much of the available income data is also for families as such; that is, we are not told how many of a given group of low-income households are workers' families and how many are farm families or widows or retired couples who are subsisting on small incomes from property or pensions.

In the absence of complete information one is reduced to making rough estimates. We shall first present some tentative conclusions about the historical trend and the current situation for all households in the country as a whole. Then we shall consider the income problems of particular groups such as women and Negroes.

(1) All households' incomes. In making our historical sketch we shall make the assumption (undoubtedly unrealistic) that the income standards for the various years — 1929, 1932, 1935–36, and 1950 — are based on budgets which are reasonably comparable and which differ mainly because of changes in consumption patterns and because of higher standards of consumption, both due to improvments in resources and technology. Where this assumption is known to be false, we may try to make an allowance in our estimate. For example, the budget for 1935–36 was the "maintenance" budget of the federal Works Progress Administration, as priced by the B.L.S. There is no question that this budget represented a considerably lower standard for a family of four persons than did the City Worker's Family Budget of 1950 developed and priced by the B.L.S. Not only did the intervening years bring improvements in the country's re-

sources, technology, and level of employment, but the 1935–36 budget represented little more than minimum "subsistence," whereas the 1950 budget stood for minimum "adequacy."

The data in Table 13 give the authors' best guesses on the percentages of all four-person households (worker and non-worker) whose incomes could be called reasonably adequate in terms of America's capacity to produce with the resources, technology, and social organization prevailing in the given years. In respect to other sizes of families, a sample study for 1935–36 by the Social Security Board suggests that larger percentages of households with three or fewer members meet their income standards than the percentages shown in Table 13; and by the same token, smaller percentages of families of five or more members attain theirs. Because the average household is roughly four, however, the Table 13 data may well represent the over-all situation for all urban households. The conditions under which small-city and rural families work and live are so different and the published data are so inadequate that it is not possible to say with assurance just what differences the inclusion of these households would make in the figures in Table 13. However, the sample survey of consumer finances sponsored in 1950 by the Board of Governors of the Federal Reserve Board, conducted by the University of Michigan's Survey Research Center, and reported in part in the January, 1951, *President's Economic Report*, revealed that 51 per cent of all the surveyed households receiving less than $1000 income in 1949 lived in rural areas, while only 23 per cent of the households receiving $3000 or more in that year were rural. It may well be that the costs of adequate budgets for households living in such localities are considerably lower than those for big-city families (there are no definitive data on this matter). Nevertheless, the findings just mentioned, plus other scattered data, suggest that, if a table for *all* households were prepared, the percentages of adequate-income households shown in Table 13 would be considerably lower for all the years, especially those before 1950.

TABLE 13 *Estimated Percentages of All Four-Person Urban Families Whose Annual Incomes Met Standard of Adequacy, Selected Years*

Year	Percentage
1929	55
1932	25
1935–36	40
1950	65

Sources: For 1950, Bureau of Labor Statistics and Bureau of the Census studies of family income, budgets, and expenditures for urban workers. For 1935–36, National Resources Committee, *Consumer Expenditures in the United States,* plus related studies of B.L.S. and Social Security Board. For 1932, Department of Commerce data from study of urban housing. For 1929, a budget or income-standard figure was estimated from later budget studies by allowing for changes in cost of living and labor productivity; income distribution data from Leven, Moulton, and Warburton, *op. cit.*

In any case, in respect to the households included in Table 13, the figures seem sufficiently trustworthy to justify at least two conclusions. First, it is evident that in prosperous years like 1929 and 1950 smaller percentages of such American households are beyond the pale of adequate incomes than in bad depression years like 1932 and semi-depression years like 1935–36. Second, there appears to be a movement toward a greater degree of income adequacy, inasmuch as the percentage for prosperous 1950 is substantially higher than that for prosperous 1929. Whether this 18-year development will persist long enough to become a secular trend remains to be seen.

(2) Incomes of particular groups of households. Now let us go behind the general figures and consider the income problems and status of certain groups that appear to be located disproportionately in the low- or inadequate-income class. As in our discussion of all households, we shall at this point look only at the groups' income conditions, reserving for later discussion (Chapter 8) the reasons for these conditions. As a basis for our review we have the 1948–49 analysis of low-income classes made by the Joint (Senate-House) Committee on the (President's) Economic Report.

(*a*) *Women workers.* In the latter years of the forties, only about 25 per cent of the urban households headed by white males were found to be substandard — that is, to have inadequate annual incomes. But 55 per cent of the urban households headed by white females had substandard incomes. The difference between colored male and female workers' earnings as urban family heads was smaller but still considerable: About 45 per cent of the male Negro family heads had inadequate incomes, compared to 75 per cent for the female Negro family heads.

The import of these data is substantiated by numerous publications of the Women's Bureau of the United States Department of Labor, as well as by various other private and governmental reports. The figures in Table 14 show that the median annual income of all women workers in

TABLE 14 *Annual Earnings of Women and Men, All Workers and Full-Time Workers, 1946*

Earnings	Men		Women	
	All Workers	Full-time Workers	All Workers	Full-time Workers
Median	$2,134	$2,588	$1,045	$1,661
Per cent Earning:				
All Amounts	100	100	100	100
Under $1,000	19	4	48	15
$1,000, under $1,500	12	8	19	25
$1,500, under $2,000	14	14	17	30
$2,000, under $2,500	17	21	9	18
$2,500, under $3,000	12	17	4	7
$3,000 and over	26	36	3	5

Source: U. S. Women's Bureau, *Handbook of Facts on Women Workers*, Bulletin No. 225, 1948, p. 19. All civilian workers aged 14 and over in urban and rural non-farm areas are included.

manufacturing industries for 1946 was not quite half that of all male workers, although the median earnings of *full-time* female workers in that year were about 65 per cent of the males'; moreover, the percentages of the female workers (either full-time or all workers) in the low-income brackets were very much higher than the percentages for male workers.

There are no adequate data on annual earnings to tell us whether the relative income position of women workers has improved since the turn of the century. However, as will be shown later on, there has been a significant decrease in the differential between the job rates and hourly earnings of male workers and those of female workers; and this fact suggests that there has been a somewhat comparable improvement in the relative annual incomes of women workers.

(*b*) *Negro and Mexican workers.* The data reviewed above in comparing white female with white male workers and colored female with colored male workers also establish the existence of Negro-white income differentials. There have been a good many other studies in support of the conclusion that the percentages of Negro households receiving inadequate or substandard annual incomes are much higher than those for white families. Thus, the survey of consumer finances previously mentioned revealed that Negro households were a disproportionately large percentage of those receiving less than $1000 income in 1949, and at the same time they were a disproportionately small percentage of families receiving more than $3000. As with the male-female comparison, there is no direct evidence that the relative income position of colored workers has improved since 1900. But the fact that discrimination against Negroes in respect to kinds of jobs, job rates, and hourly earnings appears to have been declining somewhat suggests that their annual earnings have risen relative to those of white workers.

Unfavorable as the relative income position of Negro households has been and is, it is highly unlikely that their incomes are, on the average, as far substandard today as those of Mexican workers, particularly the "wetbacks" (wet from swimming the border rivers) who have recently entered the United States illegally — about one million a year — and who work almost entirely in the Southwestern states (and to some extent in California) under conditions of virtual servitude or peonage, including very low wage rates.

(*c*) *Young and old workers.* Another factor affecting income inadequacy is the age of the workers who head or support households. The data in Table 15 establish the rise and decline of income as we pass from the very young to the higher age groups. Other studies (including the survey of consumer finances for 1949) support this conclusion and show in addition some variations by sex and occupation. Thus, women workers' earnings reach a peak when the women are about 30 years old, male manual workers' when they are about 40, clerical workers' when they are about 45.

TABLE 15 *Median Income of Various Age Groups' Spending Units, 1948*

Age of Head of Spending Unit	Median 1948 Income
18 to 24	$2,020
25 to 34	3,090
35 to 44	3,430
45 to 54	3,130
55 to 64	2,560
65 and over	1,100

Source: 1949 Survey of Consumer Finances conducted for the Board of Governors of the Federal Reserve System by the Survey Research Center, University of Michigan. Quoted in *Low Income Families and Economic Stability,* Joint Committee on the Economic Report, 81st Congress, 1st Session, 1949, p. 88.

(*d*) *Migratory workers.* Among all the groups and classes of wage-earners in this country, perhaps none is so interesting as the heterogeneous army which is included under the heading of "migratory workers." Up and down the coasts and from the Gulf to the Great Lakes are hundreds of thousands of workers who have no steady, regular occupation or job, who shift from city to city or farm to farm or from farm to city and back again to meet a highly seasonal, fluctuating demand for their services.

It is important to remember that the term *migratory* workers does not refer to all wage-earners employed in seasonal industries, but only to those who are not considered "attached" to an industry. Employees in the clothing industries, for example, are laid off for two seasonally slack periods every year, yet they are practically sure of their jobs again when the industry renews operations — they are almost permanently "attached" to their work. Not so with the migratory worker, who is likely to be a homeless, shiftless vagrant — here today, gone tomorrow; a lumberjack one season, a wheatfield worker the next, a construction "stiff" after that, and perhaps a longshoreman next year. These "floating" workers most certainly are more hobo-like than the "attached" workers.

The nature of migratory work makes very difficult the collection of accurate and complete information regarding the number and condition of the laborers. It is probable, on the basis of recent material reported by government agencies (including the President's Commission on Migratory Labor of 1950), that in prosperous years there are about 1.5 million migratory workers in the country, most of whom help pick and harvest the various agricultural products. Wheat is the chief employer, and the western half of the United States the main field. Beginning in northern Texas in early summer, hands are recruited from Southern lumber camps, cotton and oil fields to harvest the great staple crop. By the time the Kansas wheat is ready, over a quarter of a million men are in the fields, drawn from many neighboring sections. Northward the course of wheat empire takes its way, on up into Canada, where lumber workers and metal miners join the ranks. After the harvest is over, the workers disperse into various other regions and get other jobs if and when they feel like it. There is still corn to be brought in, as well as fruits, sugar beets, and hops in most of the states from Michigan to California. In the Southwest, Mexicans are extensively used in casual agricultural labor. In the eastern part of the United States there are fewer such jobs, yet in the aggregate the fruit and truck farms from Florida to Maine use many thousands of workers — Maryland, New Jersey, and New York being the chief fields. Again, the lumber camps in Maine, the Great Lakes region, the Gulf section, and the Northwest use a casual labor force of over 100,000 men in the season.

The only manufacturing industry that could really be called casual is canning. Although not all plants are highly seasonal, a great many operate for only a comparatively short period at a time. Other industries that attract large proportions of floaters are metal mining, construction, railway maintenance of way, ship loading and unloading, and sheep shearing.

The President's Commission found that the average number of days worked by migratory workers in 1949 was about 100. From this average employment the average wage income for that year was $550. This income included "perquisites" or non-cash items such as room and board provided by employers.

(*e*) *Other groups.* The Joint Committee on the Economic Report found particularly low incomes among certain other classes of workers. (These of course overlap to a significant extent with the groups already discussed.) Obviously, level of income and degree of training and education are directly related; there is much more income inadequacy among the poorly trained workers' households, who have had no more than grade-school education, than among the skilled. Another group of households whose annual earnings are at least temporarily substandard is composed of families whose earners have been disabled by sickness or accident or whose earners have deserted, died, or left the household for other reasons.

(*f*) *Summary.* In reviewing these classes of workers and factors in income inadequacy, one sees that some of the groups are only temporarily in a substandard position (e.g., many young workers and those suffering temporary physical disability), some are experiencing gradual improvement (e.g., women workers), and some are in a static or worsening position (e.g., aged workers and Mexicans). Looking at income substandardness as a whole, then, we find that, just as with the army of the unemployed during a prolonged depression, there is a hard core of more or less permanent low-income households; and, for the rest, the low-income army discharges many families and obtains new recruits every year. In other words, in any given year many households are only temporarily in the substandard income class, while others are permanently there.

b. Other approaches to income distribution. Our discussion of income adequacy in terms of a reasonable budget of goods and services involved a consideration of income distribution. But it was income distribution in terms of a single break-point — how many households were getting less and how many more than a single minimum-adequate amount of annual income. We have now to look at the sharing of the economy's total income from two other points of view: (1) the distribution of the economy's income among all households, grouped in income classes from low to high; and (2) the distribution of income among households classified roughly on the basis of the nature of the chief resource or productive factor owned — labor, capital, and so on.

(1) Distribution by size-of-income class. Suppose, for any given year, we had a list of all the households in the country (almost 45 million in 1951) with the total money income received by each during that year. We would also, by summation of these household incomes, have the total money income of all households for that year. Suppose, next, that we arranged this list by amount of each household's annual income from lowest to highest and divided the total number of households in this ranking into equal fifths or quintiles. Suppose further that we summed the incomes of all the households in each quintile. Division of each quintile total by the national total money income would give us the percentage of the latter received by the households in each quintile. If we did this for a number of different years, we might be able to discern a trend in the distribution of the national income among the five income groups. That trend would be helpful in telling us whether one of the voters' relative-income standards — the one which says that over time the distribution of income should at least not become more unequal — had been realized.

Of course, we should have no direct or precise information on the economic well-being of workers compared with that of non-worker groups. This is because, as previously asserted, there are many non-worker families (farmers, small capital-owners, and small businesses) that are in the low-income groups. Nevertheless, a distribution like the one mentioned above does throw some light on the relative position of workers because the percentages of workers' families in the lower quintiles are very high — much higher than in the top fifth of the income-receivers. The figures in Table 16 show for three different years the results of efforts by government statisticians to estimate income distribution, by the method described above, from family-income data collected by the Bureau of Labor Statistics and other agencies. It will be observed from columns 2–4 that, in so far as the data for these years can be said to portray a trend, the minimum relative-income standard of American voters has been achieved for the lowest quintile of income-receivers and has been surpassed for the second, third, and fourth classes.

The decline in the relative importance of the top fifth substantiates this conclusion. Nevertheless, the high-income 20 per cent of all households still obtained more than 45 per cent of the total national income.

TABLE 16 *Distribution of Incomes Among Families and Single Persons in United States, by Quintiles, Selected Years*

Quintile	Percentage of Total Civilian Money Income			Average Income in Each Quintile (dollars of 1948 purchasing power [2])			Per Cent Increase in Purchasing Power	
	1935–36	1941	1948 [1]	1935–36	1941	1948	1935–36 to 1948	1941–48
1	2	3	4	5	6	7	8	9
All groups	100.0	100.0	100.0	2,664	3,396	4,235	59	25
Lowest fifth	4.0	3.5	4.0	534	592	848	59	43
Second fifth	8.7	9.1	11.0	1,159	1,546	2,326	101	50
Third fifth	13.6	15.3	16.0	1,810	2,597	3,380	87	31
Fourth fifth	20.5	22.5	22.0	2,734	3,816	4,663	70	22
Top fifth	53.2	49.6	47.0	7,083	8,418	9,946	41	18

Source: Prepared by the staff of the Joint Committee on the Economic Report from data provided by the Council of Economic Advisers. Quoted in *Low-Income Families and Economic Stability*, Joint Committee on the Economic Report, 81st Congress, 1st Session, 1949, p. 138.

[1] Estimated on the basis of figures given in 1949 Survey of Consumer Finances, Board of Governors, Federal Reserve System, part III.

[2] Deflated by consumers' price index adjusted for understatement of price increases during price-control period. (See table D–5, footnote 3, Midyear Economic Report of the President, July, 1949.)

The data in columns 5–7 show the average annual *real* incomes of the households in each quintile, and the figures in columns 8 and 9 show percentage changes therein. It is significant that there were sizable increases for all income classes from 1935–36 to 1941 and 1948. In other words, the typical families in all five groups got richer. Part of this increment was due to the fact that unemployment of resources was much lower in 1941 than in 1935–36, and in 1948 it was lower still. But another reason for increased income among all groups was the improvement in the quantity and quality of resources.

Two other matters are also worth noting: First, although adequately comparable data are not available for years before 1935, the information that does exist (e.g., for 1910 and 1929) suggests that the trend noted above has been going on for a considerable length of time. Second, the 1935–48 figures in Table 16 probably understate the shift to less unequal income distribution. The years 1935–36 were semi-depressed ones. The year 1948 was relatively very prosperous. Available data such as those in Table 17 establish that labor income is always a larger share of total income in depressed than in prosperous years. This suggests that if 1935–36 had been as prosperous as 1948, there would doubtless have been an even greater decrease in income inequality over the 13-year period.

(2) Distribution by class of chief resource owned. When we come to consider income distribution in terms of the shares of total net output going to households classified on the basis of the main economic resource they own, we can approach the matter in two ways: (*a*) We can turn to the national income data compiled by the federal Department of Com-

merce. This information enables us to compare, for any relatively recent year and over a period of years, the total *annual* income of worker households with that of various classes of non-worker families. Or (*b*) we can look at the product-price and wage-rate statistics compiled by the B.L.S. and other government agencies. This information enables us to compare, from one period to another, changes in the price of labor with changes in the prices received by the owners of other resources. Clearly this comparison, as a basis for measuring relative changes in the annual incomes of worker and non-worker groups, has validity only for different periods in all of which there has been reasonably full employment. This is because price is only one component of income, the other being quantity sold. Suppose we were to try to compare average annual farmer income with average annual worker income between a boom year and a depression year. We know that, especially under unionism, wage rates are relatively rigid — that is, they do not fall very much during a depression. But the quantity of labor-hours hired falls a great deal. On the other hand, farm product prices may fall considerably, with only a moderate fall in quantity sold. In both cases annual incomes would fall. But if we were to use only the prices as indicators of income changes, we would reach the wholly erroneous conclusion that farmers' incomes fell substantially while workers' did not. However, if we compare farm *prices* with labor *prices* in two different years of *high* employment, we may say with considerable justification that we have a pretty fair comparison of farmers' average annual *income* with workers' average annual *income.* There will have been no change in either income component — price or quantity — for either farmers or workers because of depression. Then if, from one period to the next, either group's price has risen or fallen more than the other's, the chances are that its annual average income will have risen or fallen relatively.

(*a*) *Annual total worker versus total non-worker income.* Data on this kind of income distribution are presented in Table 17. A number of interesting points stand out. With respect to total labor income (which unfortunately includes the salaries of corporation heads as well as the wages of common labor, and covers not only unionized manual workers but also non-union white-collar employees), we see that household income from the sale of labor services has increased in relative importance over a half-century, having been generally less than 60 per cent of all income before the thirties and well above that percentage thereafter. This fact reflects a number of conditions. For one thing, as the table shows, labor income always rises in relative importance during years of business depression (because profits almost disappear but wage income is still received in spite of the unemployment); and almost all of the thirties were depression years. But in the secular or long-run sense, the marginal and average productivity of labor has risen as greater quantities of capital have been accumulated and have been embodied in technologically su-

TABLE 17 *Income Distribution Among Resource-Owning Classes, Selected Years*

Year	Total National Income (in billions of current dollars)	Percentage of Total National Income Received By						
		Household Sellers of All Grades of Labor[1]	Household Lenders of Capital[2]	Household Equity-Owners of Firms[3]				
				Total, All Firms	Unincorporated Firms			Corporations
					Total	Business and Professional	Farms	
1	2	3	4	5	6	7	8	9
1909	28.7	57.2	13.2	29.6	21.9	11.8	10.1	7.7
1914	33.9	59.6	13.9	26.5	20.9	12.6	8.3	5.6
1919	68.1	56.3	10.4	33.3	24.9	13.8	11.1	8.4
1921	51.9	69.9	13.7	16.4	16.4	10.2	6.2	.0
1929	87.4	58.1	14.1	27.8	16.0	9.5	6.5	11.8
1932	41.7	74.1	18.9	7.0	11.8	7.7	4.1	−4.8
1937	73.6	64.8	10.2	25.0	16.6	9.0	7.6	8.4
1940	81.3	63.7	9.5	26.8	15.5	9.5	6.0	11.3
1946	179.6	65.3	5.1	29.6	19.5	11.6	7.9	10.1
1950	239.0	64.2	5.6	30.3	15.1	9.3	5.8	15.2

Source: For years before 1929, Department of Commerce and National Bureau of Economic Research; for 1929 and later years, Department of Commerce.

[1] Includes wages, salaries, and supplements.

[2] Includes net interest and "rental" income to individuals.

[3] Figures for firms (as for other classes) are before taxes.

perior forms. And the rise of unionism, as well as government minimum-wage and social security legislation, has probably helped labor get more of its marginal product. If previous cyclical fluctuations in labor's share of the national income had been repeated since 1940, one would expect lower percentages than the ones shown for 1946 and 1950. But unionism and government seem to have been important factors in keeping these percentages well above 60 per cent.

It should be noted that the larger labor share does not by itself necessarily mean that the average household-seller of labor is better off in relation to households selling the services of contract or equity savings. If the number of labor-selling households had increased as fast as or faster than the increase in the labor share of total income, such households would, on the average, be relatively no better off, or would be worse off. Available data indicate, however, that in spite of the trend from "independent" small business and farming to "dependent" labor-selling, the percentage increase in labor-selling households has been less than the percentage increase in labor's share of income.

With respect to interest income on contract (loaned) savings, this share has declined over the half-century. Here again we would need to know the trend in number of lending households before we could conclude that, on the average, their position has worsened. The relative fixity in dollar amounts of this kind of income is seen from Table 17 when we compare the depression years, 1914, 1921, and 1932, with the other years; cyclically, interest-income is a larger share of total income in depression years, a smaller share in boom years, especially if the latter are badly inflationary.

The residual income-receivers — the owners of firms and the holders of equity savings — have an opposite cyclical experience: Their shares tend to rise in boom years and slump badly in "bust" years. There seems to be no pronounced secular trend, however, in this ownership share, at least as a whole. However, it does appear that the shares of farm-owners as a class have tended to decline somewhat. It took the devastation of the European continent during World War II to rescue the American farmers from their worsening position. (It should be remembered, however, that the lot of the *individual* farmer improved because the number of farmers decreased significantly.) Small non-farm business also may be said to have gradually lost ground as a class.

(*b*) *Relative price changes.* Let us now consider the relative movements of the prices affecting the income positions of workers, farmers, and capital owners from the prosperous twenties to the prosperous years after World War II. The data in Table 18 indicate that workers in manufacturing fared best during this period and farmers next best, with households owning mainly the capital resource (house space, equity capital) generally standing third. By 1948 the hourly earnings of factory workers (an item which is indicative of the price of labor in manufacturing) rose one and a half times, almost 150 per cent, while the prices of the products bought by such workers increased less than 35 per cent. In other words, the "real" price position of factory workers improved a great deal; the price of this labor rose more than four times as high as its cost of living, providing a "real" increase of 85 per cent.

It must not be thought that workers as a whole fared as well as those in manufacturing. Those in labor unions in the fields of mining, construction, and transportation may well have done so. But there are large numbers of unorganized agricultural and domestic workers, as well as white-collar workers, who, according to available data, failed to some extent to

TABLE 18 *Relative Price Changes, Selected Goods, 1924–1951*

ITEM	Percentage Change from 1924–27 to	
	February, 1948	February, 1951
Manufacturing labor, average hourly earnings	+148	+201
Consumption goods used by workers, prices	+ 34	+ 47
Farm products, prices received by farmers	+ 90	+115
Products bought by farmers, prices paid	+ 48	+ 67
House space, rents	− 23	− 11
Equity capital, prices of industrial stocks	+ 40	+124

Source: For 1924–27 and 1948, F. C. Mills, *The Structure of Post-War Prices*, Occasional Paper No. 27, National Bureau of Economic Research, 1948, pp. 6, 30. Data for 1951 supplied by Professor Mills.

keep up with the parade. Farmers became better off after the twenties. By 1948 the prices of what they sold increased 90 per cent while the prices of what they bought went up only a little more than half that much; their real-price position was bettered by 28 per cent. Nevertheless, they were far outstripped by factory labor. The same conclusion holds for 1951.

Up to 1948 both groups fared much better than the owners of capital. Landlords' rents declined by almost 25 per cent. Stock prices experienced an average rise of 40 per cent, the increase reflecting a rise in the money earnings of industrial corporations. Apparently the average stockholder was not very much better off in 1948 than he had been 20 years earlier. By 1951, however, after Korea, the prices of stocks rose a great deal. Nevertheless rents still lagged.

3. Conclusions on income adequacy and distribution. On the basis of the foregoing discussion we may state the following conclusions about the income position of American workers.

From the standpoint of secular trend, everyone's standards of income adequacy have risen as the economy's resources have improved in quantity and quality. Even in the light of higher standards every household has, on the average, become richer (has obtained higher real income and want-satisfaction) for the same fundamental reason; and part of the gain has been taken in more leisure, i.e., shorter work periods. Because of organization and government policies of protection, the workers as a class — and on the average as individuals — have in recent decades obtained larger shares of the national income; in other words, their relative income positions before taxes have improved at the expense of other groups, mainly the capital-owning households. Because of the government's structure of progressive income taxes, whereby in effect income is taken from the high-income households and distributed to the low-income ones, labor's relative real income position has improved considerably more than the before-taxes statistics indicate. Finally, the percentage of households (worker and non-worker) that receive substandard incomes before taxes is still too high for anyone to feel complacent over the achievements of the economy in respect to economic progress and income distribution.

From the standpoint of cyclical fluctuations in economic activity, it appears that the percentage of households receiving adequate incomes is much lower during depressions than during prosperous periods. Labor's relative income position tends to improve during depressions and to grow worse during booms, although in recent years the worsening during booms has been much reduced, mainly because of widespread unionism. But the improvement during depression is only *relative*: although non-workers' incomes (such as dividends) decline more than wage incomes, workers' actual incomes do decline seriously, and the workers have much slimmer reserves to fall back on.

C. EFFECTS OF INADEQUATE INCOMES

One of the main reasons why there should be no complacency about the economy's over-all economic progress or about the improvement in the workers' relative economic positions is to be found in the effects of income inadequacy on the sizable fraction of households (both workers' and non-workers') that have failed to obtain the minimum income considered necessary for well-being.

Some of the effects of low annual incomes were discussed in Chapter 6, in relation to the effects of unemployment on workers. (The student should review pages 86–89 at this point.) Obviously, most of the harmful results of unemployment make themselves felt through curtailment of income. It is possible, nevertheless, for steadily and fully employed workers to receive substandard incomes and suffer thereby. Our interest here is in the effects of such incomes on workers, regardless of why the incomes are low.

A number of detailed studies [2] made by sociologists and economists substantiate what is evident to even the casual observer: that underpaid laborers and their families are under average in physical well-being. To begin with, members of wage-earners' families have a shorter average life expectancy and are more likely to die than persons in wealthy homes. The death rate of the lower class of workers is over three times that among the well-to-do. The death rate from specific diseases, such as tuberculosis, Bright's disease, scarlet fever, pneumonia, and influenza, is decidedly higher in the poverty-ridden slum districts than in the better residential areas. Mortality among mothers at childbirth, as well as the incidence of non-fatal disabilities accompanying child-bearing, is more common among the poorer classes because they are unable to pay for competent pre-natal, natal, and post-natal care. There is also a cause-and-effect relation between the amount of the fathers' earnings and the ability of live-born babies to survive. Thus, the United States Children's Bureau found, from an investigation that covered more than 21,500 live births in seven different cities, that the lower the fathers' earnings were, the higher was the death rate per 1000 live-born infants; the range was, progressively, from 166.9 deaths per thousand when the fathers' annual incomes averaged less than $450, to 59.1 deaths per thousand when the fathers were earning $1250 and more per year.

Nor are the members of workers' families at a physical disadvantage only during the birth period. There is a great likelihood that the babies who do survive will not get enough food or the right kinds of food to permit proper physical development during childhood. A number of researches have established the fact that there is a relationship, sometimes indirect, between economic status and the weight and height of chil-

[2] For a good summary, see H. G. S. Bossard, *Social Change and Social Problems*, Harper and Brothers, New York, 1934, chapter VIII.

dren. The adults may also suffer from malnutrition; this lowers their vitality and resistance and makes them easier prey to sickness and disease, while lack of medical care decreases the probability of recovery, as already noted. Inadequate housing and clothing also play their parts in producing physical weakness. The United States Public Health Service has shown that the number of cases of disabling sickness per thousand individuals and the amount of working time lost thereby was decidedly greater among the low-income groups than among the better paid.

Wage-earners also suffer mentally because of economic insufficiency. Any sharp distinction between "mind" and "body" is of course artificial because the human organism is a unit made up of interdependent parts, each affecting the others in greater or less degree. Nevertheless, that part which may be termed the "conscious self" is specifically and directly affected by economic well-being, or the lack of it. Malnutrition may retard the development of intellectual powers in a physical way, and inadequate income all too often prevents children from obtaining ordinary training and education. Poverty may be a blessing to the exceptional individual and spur him on to unusual achievement, but its effect on the average person is stultifying and repressive and often leads to behavior which is individually and socially unwholesome. Feelings of inferiority, a tendency to blame others for one's shortcomings and failures, and continual bitterness against society are frequently found among people in the lower income groups. Worry over inability to provide the necessities of life helps rob them of bodily and mental health. It would be wrong to conclude that all unskilled employees are continually torn with anxiety and are never happy, but it is impossible to disregard the fact that they have to face contingencies rarely known by those with higher incomes. There can be no doubt that the chances for adequate satisfaction of basic desires are much less among members of low-income families than among members of the higher income groups.

CHAPTER 8

Obtaining Adequate Income (concluded)

D. CAUSAL FACTORS IN WAGE INCOME

1. Introduction. In the previous chapter we learned about the sizes of workers' annual wage incomes and we compared these incomes with those of non-workers. Our task now is to find out something about the conditions that influence the absolute and relative sizes of workers' wage incomes.

We know that there are two components of a person's annual wage income: the price he receives for his labor per unit of time such as an hour — the hourly wage rate; and the number of work-hours he sells to firms per year. In Chapter 6 we learned something about the conditions that influence the size of the second component, employment. Therefore our discussion in this chapter focuses on the conditions affecting the first component, the wage rate.

Actually most of our discussion here will deal with job rates rather than wage rates. In this book we define the job rate more narrowly than the wage rate. The latter is taken to be the same as gross average hourly earnings; it includes not only the job rate but also the average hourly amount of such additional compensation as overtime pay, vacation pay, and so on.

Our plan of discussion is to deal first with an individual firm or plant, second with a locality, and then with the economy as a whole. It is necessary also for us to distinguish wage (or job) rate *structure* from wage (or job) rate *level.* The former means the hierarchy of rates that exists within a given firm (or plant), locality, or society for all the different jobs within the unit. The general level of rates means the weighted average of all the different rates in the unit's structure.

2. The American wage rate structure. *a. An individual firm.* In dealing with an individual firm we shall be thinking mainly of a typical manufacturing establishment. However, the things we shall learn apply rather generally to non-manufacturing firms also.

(1) Kinds of jobs and job rates. (a) Unskilled. The labor force of the individual firm may be conveniently divided into three levels of skill.

At the lowest level are the unskilled jobs. In these occupations workers are usually paid on a time basis, that is, so much per hour. Such wage payments are known as *hourly rates*. The tools used by unskilled workers are few and simple. The work requires little or no training. In the case of unskilled workers doing very heavy work, slightly higher rates may be paid since the work may be unpleasant or involve some danger Ordinarily, unskilled labor does not lead directly to higher-pay jobs.

(b) Semi-skilled. The second level of jobs includes the semi-skilled tasks. They involve principally (1) the operation of machines producing parts or materials; or (2) the assembly of parts. The work is usually light and repetitive and calls for dexterity and a sense of timing. The cycle of work is usually short, ranging from a few seconds to a few hours. Such jobs require some training, ranging from a few days for the simplest tasks to a week or more for the more complex operations. The worker must learn to operate his equipment efficiently and to judge whether his work meets minimum standards laid down by management.

The emphasis in semi-skilled jobs is on output. Some workers are paid on a time basis, but many are paid on an incentive basis; that is, they are paid for each article produced rather than for the amount of time expended. Still others may be paid on the basis of time and output combined.

The variety of incentive methods of wage payments is so great that we can do no more than mention the subject here. Some incentive systems are based on *straight piece work*. A worker may receive so many cents per acceptable unit turned out, and his entire earnings during the week will depend on production. A common variation is a guaranteed *minimum plus a bonus*. The worker is thus assured of a minimum payment per hour plus a bonus for each unit turned out above a given standard. Some bonus systems are "ascending," in that the bonus rises with output above standard. Other bonus rates taper downward, and still others share all output above a standard norm equally between the worker and management. In cases where a particular sequence of operations is performed by several workers in a team, the bonus may be in terms of the group rather than the individual.

The role of the semi-skilled workers in industry has risen in importance with the expansion of the mass-production system of making standardized articles, so characteristic of consumer-goods industries. The spread of hourly earnings for the semi-skilled is very wide, frequently ranging from only 5 or 10 per cent above unskilled work to a level which may equal or even surpass the earnings of skilled workers. It has been estimated that the average semi-skilled worker earns about 30 to 35 per cent more than the unskilled. Within the semi-skilled group the incentive workers earn about 20 to 25 per cent more on the average than the hourly rated workers. This latter differential is based on the assumption that workers paid on the basis of output will produce that much more per hour than workers paid by the hour. This assumption, of course, makes sense. If a worker on straight piece rates working at top speed could earn only 5 per cent more than a worker paid by the hour working at a more leisurely pace, there would obviously be no adequate incentive for piece-rate workers to expend the additional effort. They would rightfully complain of inequitable earnings. On the other hand, if the amount paid per piece was so generous as to permit a piece-rate worker to earn 100 per cent more at a rather leisurely pace than an hourly rated worker could earn, then no one would want to work on hourly rated jobs. Further, management would consider an incentive system pointless if most of the gains of greater output were absorbed by the worker.

The semi-skilled workers attach considerable importance to remaining with the same employer. The unskilled worker has little or no skill to lose in transferring from one employer to another. The skilled worker can take his skill with him. But the semi-skilled worker who has advanced to a highly specialized single-purpose task, on which he has learned numerous short cuts which enable him to obtain high hourly earnings, may not find a similar job if he is forced to change employment. His earnings may well drop precipitously. For this reason, job security is highly important to him. Labor turnover is lowest in this group.

(c) Skilled jobs and rates. The third and highest class of jobs is composed of the skilled occupations. In most manufacturing firms the skilled workers are of three main types. First, there are the maintenance craftsmen: both those who maintain, repair, or remodel portions of the plant and its structures — e.g., carpenters, bricklayers, painters, and other construction workers; and those who adjust, repair, or rebuild the machines in the production line — e.g., machinists. Maintenance workers are sometimes paid the prevailing community job rates for the same kind of skill. However, because their jobs may be steadier and more secure, they may be paid lower job rates than in some other industries, such as construction. Both kinds of maintenance workers are usually paid hourly job rates. A second group of skilled workers are the tool-and-die makers who translate engineers' drawings into dies and tools which are used in forming, forging, stamping, or cutting metal parts. Such work requires considerable knowledge of practical mathematics, familiarity with metals and tools, and ability to work to very close tolerances. These highly skilled workers are usually at the top of the manual occupational hierarchy. Their hourly earnings, usually based on hourly job rates, normally average 50 per cent more than those of the unskilled workers — and often run over 100 per cent more. A third class of highly skilled workers are those who participate directly in the line-production process. They are represented by such crafts as the cutters in the clothing industry, the tiremakers in the rubber industry, the electrotypers in the printing industry, and the heaters and rollers in the basic steel industry. These workers are commonly paid under some kind of incentive wage system.

(2) Wage-rate inequities. (a) Personal rates versus job rates. Within these broad classes of skill are a large number of related occupations which go to make up the occupational structure of the firm. If the rates paid by the firm to its workers are based on management's judgment of each worker's ability, loyalty, and so on, with little regard to his job as such, we say that the wage structure is on an *individual* or personal basis. If the rates paid are based on the kind of job performed regardless of the particular individual on the job, we say the wage structure is based on a *schedule or plan of job rates.* A few decades ago, it was common for the foreman to determine what each individual worker should get. The personal judgments of various foremen naturally differed. As might be expected, this process resulted in haphazard and irrational wage structures with some workers doing comparable work getting different rates of pay and others doing different types of work getting the same rates of pay. Inequities were numerous. A huge turnover of workers was a common result of dissatisfaction over such inequities. Today the more progressive firms have some form of job-rate plan or schedule which attempts to base wage payments on objective rather than subjective standards, to relate wage payment to job content, and to rank each job in relation to all other jobs on the basis of content. One of the most useful tools in determining equitable rate differentials between and among jobs is the technique of job evaluation. It is not possible here to consider this subject in detail except to note that it is designed to provide for the proper study and description of jobs; the systematic classification and ranking of jobs in order of their relative degrees of skill and other requirements; and the assignment of job rates based on relative job worth (see Chapter 15).

(b) Rate ranges versus single rates. Some firms prefer a single rate for each job in the plant and others use a rate range, from minimum to maximum, for many jobs. The rate-range system permits workers to be advanced within a given range on the basis of merit or length of service.

(c) Removal of inequities. In recent years great strides have been made by American management, unilaterally or in conjunction with trade unions, in developing more equitable and rational job-rate structures. This is not to say, of course, that inequitable job rates no longer exist within particular firms. They do — even among those who have tried to rationalize their structures. Among these inequitable wage differentials two types deserve special mention. One is the lower rates often paid to Negro workers in contrast to the rates paid to white workers on comparable jobs, and the other is the discriminatory job rates paid to women workers.

The differentials based on color center largely in the South. They have been narrowing somewhat in recent years and may well in time disappear. Rate differentials for the same jobs based on color have not been common among Northern firms. It should be pointed out, however, that it is possible to discriminate against minority workers by assigning them only or mainly to the lower classified jobs as well as by paying them lower wages on the same jobs. Discrimination in work assignments still seems to persist in firms in all parts of the country.

Women workers have often been paid at rates 10 to 25 per cent lower than those given men on the *same kinds of jobs.* Such differentials are still widespread among firms, but there is considerable evidence that the practice is declining. Both the existence of differentials and the evidence of their decline were established by data presented in 1945 before the United States Senate Committee on Education and Labor, which was holding hearings on a "bill providing equal pay for equal work for women."

(3) Trends in firms' wage-rate structures. The developments in particular firms' job-rate and hourly-earnings structures that have occurred during the past fifty years may be summarily stated here. There has been an increase in the number and percentage of jobs and workers covered by incentive systems of wage payment; in 1951 roughly one-third of all manufacturing workers were so paid. There has been a growing tendency among the larger firms at least, to reduce intra-firm job-rate inequities through job evaluation and rationalization of the internal job-rate structure. Specific race and sex job-rate and hourly-earnings inequities and differentials have also tended to be diminished in amount and frequency. The job-rate and earnings spread between unskilled and skilled jobs has narrowed considerably because of technological improvements that have diluted the content of many skilled jobs and raised many unskilled jobs to the semi-skilled level. With the increase in the relative importance of semi-skilled production-line jobs, the unskilled-skilled hourly-earnings differential has narrowed, according to the Bureau of Labor Statistics, from about 100 per cent in 1900 to about 55 per cent in 1950. In other words, the average hourly earnings or wage rates for skilled jobs now average less than 60 per cent above those for unskilled jobs.

b. The job- and wage-rate structure of a locality. Firm and industry differentials. Under theoretical economic analysis for a purely competitive labor market, the job rate and the wage rate for a given grade of labor are respectively equalized when a given labor market is in equilibrium. In most theory there is a *tendency* toward such uniformity even when the market is imperfectly competitive. The question now to be raised is, Do we find any such uniformity or tendency thereto in a real-world labor market?

The answer is no, with few exceptions. A number of investigations, mainly by the Bureau of Labor Statistics, have revealed a great variety of job rates and hourly earnings for similar jobs in different firms in the same local area. Skilled and semi-skilled job rates and earnings (wage rates) often vary from 25 to 50 per cent, unskilled jobs sometimes 100 per cent. During World War II, for example, when under the wage stabilization program the National War Labor Board was given the task of determin-

TABLE 19 *Distribution of 85 Industrial Plants in Cleveland by Hiring (Job) Rates for Common Labor, February, 1947*

Wage Class	Number of Plants
50–69 cents an hour	4
70–74 " " "	2
75–79 " " "	1
80–84 " " "	12
85–89 " " "	13
90–94 " " "	22
95–99 " " "	17
$1.00–1.04 " "	6
1.05–1.09 " "	8

Source: Sumner H. Slichter, "Notes on the Structure of Wages," *The Review of Economics and Statistics,* Vol. 32, No. 1, February, 1950, p. 80.

ing whether hundreds of thousands of applications for job-rate increases should be granted, the applications, as well as independent studies made for the Board by the B.L.S., turned up very few cases of local job-rate uniformity. Sometimes powerful unions had effected job-rate standardization for a given city, e.g., the building trades unions in Chicago. Yet even in such cases the wage rates (as we have defined them) were likely to differ somewhat.

An example of local job-rate spread is given in Table 19, which shows a distribution of 85 Cleveland plants in terms of the hiring rates existing in 1947 for unskilled, common labor. This is a fairly typical distribution for such jobs. A few firms pay very low rates, a few very high; and most of the firms are clustered within a much narrower range of rates.

The data in Table 20 also show the wage-rate differences that can exist in a local labor market for semi-skilled and skilled jobs.

c. The national job- and wage-rate structure. Now let us look at the economy as a whole. Here we find staggeringly large job-rate and hourly-earnings differentials. They are of three main sorts: (1) differences among industries; (2) differences among communities of similar size

TABLE 20 *Average Hourly-Earnings Differences in Philadelphia Machine Tool Plants, Selected Occupations, 1927*

Occupation	Average Hourly Earnings in Lowest Paying Plant	Average Hourly Earnings in Highest Paying Plant	Per Cent Low Is of High
Drill press operator	$0.348	$0.868	40
Milling machine operator	0.408	0.925	44
Engine lathe operator	0.488	0.986	50
Screw machine operator	0.498	0.966	52
Turret lathe operator	0.513	0.909	56
Boring mill operator	0.613	0.995	62
Planer operator	0.600	0.791	76

Source: H. L. Frain, *Earnings in Certain Standard Machine Tool Occupations in Philadelphia,* University of Pennsylvania Press, 1929, p. 14.

located in different geographic areas; and (3) differences among different sizes of community in the same section of the country.

(1) Inter-industry differentials. As we shall learn later on, one of the conditions responsible for rate and earnings differentials for similar, comparable jobs in the same locality is that many different industries are represented in the locality. (We define "industry" loosely here to mean a group of firms in one or more localities making the same general kind of product, such as aspirin, razor blades, fine cotton textiles, rubber tires, or automobiles.) Each industry has its own special situation in respect to product-market competition within the industry and with other industries. There are other inter-industry differences, such as the nature and level of technology — a factor which influences an industry's ability to pay high wage rates and determines the proportions of skilled to semi-skilled and unskilled jobs. These differences help make for local wage-rate variations. (However, it must not be thought that the rate for a given job would necessarily be uniform among, say, ten firms in the *same* industry in a given large locality. As we shall see, there are a number of other

TABLE 21 *Distribution of 132 Manufacturing Industries and Their Employment, by Average Hourly-Earnings Classes, October, 1948*

Average Hourly Earnings, October, 1948 (Dollars)	Industries		Percentage Distribution of Employment [1]
	Number	Per Cent	
Total	134	100.0	100.0
.75– .79	2	1.5	0.4
.80– .84	0	0.0	0.0
.85– .89	1	0.8	0.4
.90– .94	3	2.2	1.0
.95– .99	3	2.2	0.5
1.00–1.04	6	4.5	1.5
1.05–1.09	5	3.7	1.6
1.10–1.14	8	6.0	13.4
1.15–1.19	10	7.5	10.9
1.20–1.24	10	7.5	6.4
1.25–1.29	9	6.7	3.9
1.30–1.34	7	5.2	7.2
1.35–1.39	9	6.7	4.1
1.40–1.44	12	9.0	7.5
1.45–1.49	17	12.7	12.5
1.50–1.54	13	9.7	6.1
1.55–1.59	4	3.0	2.9
1.60–1.64	8	6.0	4.7
1.65–1.69	3	2.2	11.6
1.70–1.74	2	1.5	1.1
1.85–1.89	1	.7	1.0
1.90–1.94	1	.7	1.3

Source: U. S. Bureau of Labor Statistics, *Wage Movements; Changes in 1948*, War and Postwar Trends, Series 3, No. 1 (undated), p. 15.

[1] Refers to *production* worker employment in industries having the specified average hourly earning

reasons for local wage-rate variation.) As a matter of fact, a large community is in some ways the best place to study inter-industry wage-rate differences, for the effects of regional and size-of-city differentials are thereby ruled out.

In Table 21 we present for the country as a whole the number and percentage of 134 manufacturing industries (together with the percent-

TABLE 22 *Average Hourly Earnings, Selected Industries, October, 1950*

Industry	Average Hourly Earnings	Per Cent of Average for All Manufacturing
All manufacturing	$1.501	100
All durable goods	1.577	105
All non-durable goods	1.405	94
Selected durable-goods industries		
Agricultural machinery	1.645	110
Aircraft engines and parts	1.750	117
Aluminum, rolling and drawing	1.574	105
Automobiles	1.830	122
Basic steel	1.686	112
Bricks and hollow tile	1.316	88
Foundries, gray iron	1.586	106
Furniture, household	1.280	85
Glass	1.584	106
Locomotives and parts	1.824	121
Lumbering (saw mills and planing mills)	1.402	94
Machine tools	1.678	112
Radios, phonographs, television sets	1.373	92
Shipbuilding	1.664	111
Selected non-durable goods		
Canning and preserving	1.210	80
Clothing (men's and boys' suits and coats)	1.366	91
Clothing (women's suits, coats, skirts)	1.971	131
Cotton, silk, synthetic fiber	1.269	85
Dairy products	1.287	86
Fertilizers	1.138	76
Hosiery, seamless	1.011	67
Leather	1.472	98
Paper and pulp	1.518	101
Petroleum refining	1.967	131
Printing, books	1.639	109
Printing, newspaper	2.207	147
Rubber tires and tubes	1.837	122
Shoes	1.166	78
Slaughtering and meatpacking	1.529	102
Tobacco products	1.077	72
Woolen goods	1.439	96
Construction, contract	2.025	135
Coal, bituminous	2.022	135
Farm workers	.55	37
Laundries	.874	58
Metal mining		
Railroad, Class I	1.544	103
Trade, retail (general merchandise)	.984	66
Utilities, gas and electric	1.626	108

Source: U. S. Bureau of Labor Statistics, *Monthly Labor Review*, February, 1951, pp. 225–240.

age of total employment in these industries) whose average hourly earnings for all occupations in October, 1948, fell within the earnings classes listed in column 1. It will be observed that the average earnings ranged from $0.75 to almost $2.00 per hour, with most of the workers concentrated between $1.10 and $1.70. If all the workers had been employed full-time, their wage incomes would have shown comparable differences.

A number of studies establish the fact that average rates for similar particular jobs like common labor also vary a great deal among different industries in the country as a whole.

It may be of interest to observe the average actual wage rates (gross average hourly earnings) paid by various industries on a country-wide basis during a particular month. Such data are given in Table 22. It will be seen that the range between the very low industries (e.g., laundries) and the very high (e.g., newspaper printing) is very wide — much more than 100 per cent.

Table 23 presents the second, more meaningful kind of data on industry variations in wage rates — those for a particular locality, with regional and size-of-city factors out of the picture. It will be observed that in the large, diversified Chicago labor market in 1945 the inter-industry differentials in average hourly earnings for production work forces were very large, in spite of the elimination of the above-mentioned factors.

TABLE 23 *Average Hourly Earnings of Production Workers, Selected Industries, Chicago Labor Market, 1945* [1]

Industry	Average Hourly Earnings	Per Cent of Earnings for Upholstered Wood Furniture
Aircraft engines, parts	$1.16	116
Bread and bakery products	0.85	85
Corrugated, fiber boxes	0.82	82
Dresses, women's and misses'	1.16	116
Iron and steel forgings	1.29	129
Iron and steel foundry products	1.06	106
Jewelry		
Costume	.90	90
Non-costume	1.41	141
Machinery, miscellaneous	1.03	103
Machine tools	.96	96
Motor vehicles, bodies	1.15	115
Power laundries	.67	67
Radios, radio equipment	.86	86
Retail stores		
Men's and women's clothing	.89	89
Department stores	.76	76
Shoes	.91	91
Structural clay products	1.06	106
Tool and die jobbing shops	1.24	124
Wood furniture		
Upholstered	1.00	100
Not upholstered	.89	89

Source: Occupational wage-rate studies, Chicago Regional Office, U. S. Bureau of Labor Statistics.
[1] Differentials are only approximate because surveys were made at various periods within 1945.

TABLE 24 *Regional Differences in Median Job Rates, Manufacturing Industries, 1945–1946*

Region	Median Relation in Per Cent with Northeast = 100
Fat West	115
Middle West	101
Northeast	100
South	85

Source: U. S. Bureau of Labor Statistics, *Trends in Wage Differentials, 1907–1947,* Serial No. R. 1932 (undated), p. 5.

(2) Regional wage-rate differentials. As already stated, one reason why wage rates differ among industries on the national level is that they vary so greatly among regions. A B.L.S. study of job-rate differences among manufacturing workers by region for 1945–46 revealed the variations shown in Table 24. The Far West was found to pay rates averaging about 15 per cent above those in the Northeastern and Midwestern states and about 35 per cent above those in the South. It was found that these wide regional differences have persisted without much narrowing since 1900. Not only is there a remarkable persistence over time, but there appears to be a high consistency within each region. That is, if a region pays relatively high rates in a few industries, it is likely to do so in most others. Thus, most industries in the Far West pay relatively high job rates, and most industries in the South pay relatively low rates.

A more detailed regional breakdown of job rates and wage rates provides the following ranking, from high to low: the Pacific states (particularly in Seattle and San Francisco), the Middle Atlantic states, the states in the Great Lakes region, New England, the Middle West (except the Great Lakes area), the Southwest, and the Southeast.

Although virtually all industries exhibit these regional job-rate and earnings differences, some industries do so much more than others. Thus, the North-South differential is relatively small in cement, glass, leather, and paper and pulp; and it is relatively large in ceramics, chemicals, and lumber. Particular Southern firms, in fact, may pay the same or higher rates than some Northern ones.

There are also differences in the *trend* of regional differences. In some industries, such as construction and furniture, the North-South differentials have widened since 1900, while in others, such as chemicals, cotton textiles, hosiery, and paper and pulp, there has been a significant reduction.

(3) Size-of-city differentials. In order to detect the influence of size of city on wage rates we need data for single industries in the same geographic region, located in different sizes of communities. That is, if we are to isolate the effects of city-size, we must not allow inter-industry and inter-regional wage-rate differentials in the picture.

The data on job rates and average hourly earnings published in various bulletins of the Bureau of Labor Statistics enable us to make such proper comparisons. Thus, workers in such industries as retail trade, shoes, meat packing, metal trades, bakeries, and printing within a given region have been found in general to have the highest average hourly earnings in large metropolitan communities of a million or more population and the lowest in small towns of five thousand or less. The latter may be as much as 35 per cent below the large-city averages. As a rule (to which there are of course exceptions), earnings in communities of intermediate size lie between the two extremes just mentioned.

Table 25 presents hourly earnings data for a few selected representative occupations and industries in large and small communities within the Great Lakes region. It will be seen that in all but the last three occupations and industries the hourly earnings were higher in the larger communities. But the differences varied a great deal.

It will also be noted that in the last three industries the higher rates were to be found in the smaller cities. Does this fact rob our previous generalization of its validity? Only in part. The higher small-city rates for these three industries may have been due to the fact that some large companies with a high wage rate policy had located large plants in small communities but continued to pay high rates. Moreover, if metropolitan communities of, say, 750,000 or more had been compared with small communities of less than 10,000, the differences would have been larger and

TABLE 25 *Average Straight-Time Hourly Earnings, Selected Manufacturing Industries (Representative Occupations) and Years, by Size of Community in Great Lakes Region* [1]

Industry, Occupation, and Year	Size of Community[2]		Per Cent Which Earnings in Small Cities Were of Earnings in Large Cities
	Large	Small	
Shoes (male cutters, vamp and whole machine, 1944)	$1.27	$0.95	75
Grain milling (male flour packers, 1948)	1.22	0.94	77
Cotton garments (1949)			
Men (machine cutters)	1.47	1.21	82
Women (sewing machine operators)	0.98	0.79	81
Metal working (clerk typists, 1945)	0.69	0.58	84
Machinery (production machinists, 1948)	1.24	1.07	86
Canning (all plant workers, Indiana, 1948)	0.80	0.71	89
Shoes (female fancy stitchers, 1945)	0.81	0.72	89
Petroleum refining (cracking stillmen, 1948)	2.23	2.06	92
Wood furniture (female cover sewers, 1949)	0.82	0.76	93
Radios (Class C female assemblers, 1947)	0.92	0.89	97
Industrial chemicals (Class A operators, 1946)	1.25	1.26	101
Wood furniture (male upholsterers, 1945)	1.13	1.20	106
Structural clay products (hand molders, 1945)	0.90	0.99	110

Source: U. S. Bureau of Labor Statistics, *Wage Structure* studies, Series 2, Nos. 1, 13, 16, 19, 23, 25, 30, 65, 71, 72, 75.

[1] This area includes Illinois, Indiana, Michigan, Minnesota, Ohio, and Wisconsin.

[2] "Large" cities are defined as those with populations of over 100,000, except for cotton garments and canning (over 25,000). "Small" cities are defined as those with populations below 25,000, except for petroleum refining, wood furniture, and radios (under 100,000) and canning (under 2,500).

more striking. Nevertheless, the large-small city pattern of wage-rate differentials is not universal. And it may well be that some other pattern is a more valid and appropriate one. A few examples lead one to suspect the existence of a sort of "concentric" geographic rate structure, in which the concentrated, major portion of the industry is the high rate center, while the successively more distant communities pay lower rates. This condition doubtless exists in the rubber tire industry, where Akron, not a very large city, is the high rate center. Another example is the tool and die industry, which centers in high rate Detroit; here outlying cities pay lower rates — even a city like Chicago, which is much bigger than Detroit.

It should also be noted that for some time size-of-city wage-rate differentials have been narrowing in most industries.

3. Trends in the general level of American wage rates. Having studied in summary fashion the main characteristics of the American wage-rate structure, let us next consider the general level of wage rates in the country — the thing, we said, that must be distinguished from internal wage-rate structure.

To consider the general level of wage rates as of any one date is virtually meaningless. It is the trend in the level that interests students. And the trend in the money level is much less significant than the trend in the real level. In other words, our main concern here is with the changes in the level of money wage rates (gross money average hourly earnings) corrected by the changes in the cost of the goods labor buys that occurred at the same time.

TABLE 26 *Indexes of Money and Real Average Hourly Earnings and Cost of Living, 1820–1946*

(1914 = 100)

Year	Money Average Hourly Earnings	Cost of Living	Real Average Hourly Earnings
1820	35	86	41
1830	36	71	51
1840	40	78	51
1850	42	72	59
1860	46	80	57
1870	82	117	71
1880	65	84	77
1890	73	75	96
1900	76	75	101
1910	92	92	100
1920	242	200	128
1925	245	175	140
1930	248	166	149
1935	247	137	181
1940	296	140	212
1946	486	194	251

Source: Compilation of J. T. Dunlop presented in G. F. Bloom and H. R. Northrup, *Economics of Labor and Industrial Relations,* The Blakiston Company, Philadelphia, 1950, p. 67.

Statistics on the trend for most of the economy's industries are presented in Table 26 for the years 1820 to 1946. The statistics for the years before World War I are based on information that is substantially less complete and accurate than for the later years. Nevertheless, they are sufficiently reliable to establish the trend. From the data in Table 26 we see that during the century and a quarter after 1820 the level of money wage rates rose almost fourteenfold, after the beginning of World War I almost fivefold, and after 1920 about twofold; that because the cost of living was rising also, the increases in real earnings were a good deal less than in money earnings — a little more than sixfold from 1820 to 1946, about 2.5 times from 1914 to 1946, and about twofold from 1920 to 1946; and that from 1820 to 1946 the *average annual percentage* (not compounded) rise in real earnings was about 4.4 per cent, from 1914 to 1946 about 4.6 per cent, and from 1920 to 1946 about 3.6 per cent.

Indexes of changes in money and real average hourly earnings for three major industries from 1914 to 1946 are presented in Table 27. The main conclusions from these data are that in each of the industries real hourly earnings more than doubled during the 33 years; that from 1914 to 1946 the largest increase occurred in manufacturing, the smallest in mining; and that from 1930 to 1946 the increases were by about the same percentages in manufacturing and mining, with railroads falling behind.

TABLE 27 *Indexes of Money and Real Average Hourly Earnings, Three Major Industries, 1914–1946*

(1914 = 100)

Year	Money Average Hourly Earnings			Real Average Hourly Earnings		
	Manufacturing	Mining [1]	Railroads [2]	Manufacturing	Mining [1]	Railroads [2]
1914	100	100	100	100	100	100
1919	218	209	216	114	110	114
1925	250	224	240	143	127	137
1930	250	206	256	150	124	154
1935	250	218	256	182	159	187
1940	300	250	284	214	178	203
1946	491	406	444	253	209	229

Source: Based on compilations of J. T. Dunlop presented in Bloom and Northrup, *op. cit.*, pp. 67, 68.
[1] Includes anthracite and bituminous coal and metal mining.
[2] Class I railroads, which include 98 per cent of total railroad mileage.

As stated previously, American workers have experienced greater benefits over time than those involved merely in the rise in real wage rates. For there has also been a decrease in the lengths of work periods. This fact is brought out for manufacturing workers by the data in column 4 of Table 28, which establish a decline of almost 20 per cent in the average number of hours worked per week. As a result, from 1914 to 1950 real weekly earnings have risen by a smaller percentage (about 125 per cent) than real hourly wage rates (175 per cent).

Although the trend in weekly hours has been definitely downward, the influence of cyclical and war conditions is to be seen from the figures in the table. During the depressed thirties, weekly hours went abnormally low, and during the war years they came back to the level of the twenties. But during the prosperous postwar years the downward trend became evident.

TABLE 28 *Money and Real Earnings and Hours of Work in Manufacturing, 1914–1950*

Year	Average Hourly Earnings	Average Weekly Earnings	Average Weekly Hours	Indexes (1939 = 100)				
				Actual Hourly Earnings	Actual Weekly Earnings	Consumers' Prices	Real Hourly Earnings [1]	Real Weekly Earnings [1]
1	2	3	4	5	6	7	8	9
1914	$0.223	$11.01	49.4	35.2	46.1	72.2	48.8	63.9
1919	.477	22.08	46.3	75.4	92.5	124.5	60.6	74.3
1923	.522	23.82	45.6	82.5	99.8	122.6	67.3	81.4
1924	.547	23.93	43.7	86.4	100.3	122.9	70.3	81.6
1925	.547	24.37	44.5	86.4	102.1	126.2	68.5	80.9
1926	.548	24.65	45.0	86.6	103.3	127.2	68.1	81.2
1927	.550	24.74	45.0	86.9	103.7	124.7	69.7	83.2
1928	.562	24.97	44.4	88.8	104.7	123.3	72.0	84.9
1929	.566	25.03	44.2	89.4	104.9	123.2	72.6	85.1
1930	.552	23.25	42.1	87.2	97.4	120.1	72.6	81.1
1931	.515	20.87	40.5	81.4	87.5	109.4	74.4	80.0
1932	.446	17.05	38.3	70.5	71.5	98.2	71.8	72.8
1933	.442	16.73	38.1	69.8	70.1	93.0	75.1	75.4
1934	.532	18.40	34.6	84.0	77.1	96.3	87.2	80.1
1935	.550	20.13	36.6	86.9	84.4	98.7	88.0	85.5
1936	.556	21.78	39.2	87.8	91.3	99.7	88.1	91.6
1937	.624	24.05	38.6	98.6	100.8	103.3	95.5	97.6
1938	.627	22.30	35.6	99.1	93.5	101.4	97.7	92.2
1939	.633	23.86	37.7	100.0	100.0	100.0	100.0	100.0
1940	.661	25.20	38.1	104.4	105.6	100.8	103.6	104.8
1941	.729	29.58	40.6	115.2	124.0	105.8	108.9	117.2
1942	.853	36.65	42.9	134.8	153.6	117.2	115.0	131.1
1943	.961	43.14	44.9	151.8	180.8	124.3	122.1	145.5
1944	1.019	46.08	45.2	161.0	193.1	126.3	127.5	152.9
1945	1.023	44.41	43.4	161.6	186.1	129.3	125.1	144.0
1946	1.084	43.74	40.4	171.2	183.3	140.1	122.2	130.8
1947	1.221	49.25	40.3	192.9	206.4	160.2	120.4	128.8
1948	1.327	53.13	40.0	209.6	222.7	172.2	121.7	129.3
1949	1.401	54.92	39.2	221.0	230.1	170.1	129.9	135.2
1950	1.465	59.33	40.5	232.2	248.6	172.9	134.2	143.7

Source: U. S. Bureau of Labor Statistics. Data are based on revision and extension of data in "Wages, Hour, and Productivity of Industrial Labor, 1909–39," *Monthly Labor Review*, September, 1940. The earnings shown are "gross"; they include such items as premium pay for overtime and late-shift work. Changes among firms, industries, and areas and changes in the distribution of employment also affect the general level of earnings.

[1] Money earnings adjusted by Consumers' Price Index of B.L.S.

4. Some reasons for the wage-rate structure and level. We have seen that the American job-rate and wage-rate structures are very complex and have been subject to certain changes over a long period of time. Within a given plant there are many occupational and personal wage-rate differentials. Among the plants in a given locality, comparable common jobs are often paid at different rates, even among firms in the same industry. In the country as a whole, there are industry, regional, and size-of-city differentials in job rates and average hourly earnings (wage rates). And there have been changes in all these things.

We have also noted the upward trend in hourly earnings, the downward trend in length of work periods, and the upward trend in real weekly and annual wage income.

We now come to our chief task — an explanation of *why* these wage-rate and income factors are what we have found them to be. Because, as previously stated, the conditions affecting wage-rate structures and levels are to a large extent the same as those influencing the amount of employment and unemployment, the nature and shape of our analysis will have to be somewhat similar to that used in Chapter 6. That is, we must consider the conditions affecting the supply of and the demand for labor-hours in the firm, locality, industry, and entire economy.

a. The job and wage-rate structure. (1) The rate for any particular job. Our task will be simplified if we begin by surveying the conditions that affect the determination of a rate for any single job in any firm in any industry, locality, or region.

In Chapter 6 (pages 91–92) we reviewed the general conditions affecting the preferences of workers between leisure and income and among various firms' jobs, all of which operate to determine the quantity of labor-hours that the workers in the market are willing to offer to this or that firm at various possible wage rates. These are the general labor supply conditions. We also found that there are special conditions for particular groups of workers, such as women and Negroes.

It should also be noted that we may define "leisure" broadly enough to include workers' refusal to work (i.e., workers' willingness to go on strike) if the wage rate offered for a given job in a given firm is lower than the rate that workers believe necessary for decent living. This socially influenced rate tends to be the minimum that the firm has to pay.

In Chapter 6 we learned also that the quantities of labor-hours a firm is able to buy at various wage rates depend in general on the nature and level of technology in the firm; the supplies of complementary and substitute productive factors, such as raw materials and machines; and the amount and elasticity of the demand for the firm's product. These are the general labor demand conditions. They influence an employer's estimate of how much the average worth of any given input of labor-hours is to him. Thus they affect his guess as to how high a wage rate he is *able* to pay for quantity of labor-hours to be hired. He figures that he certainly can't pay a higher wage rate for a given labor input than the amount of the estimated average dollar worth of this input. He hopes, of course, that he can get the labor for less.

What do we mean by the "estimated average dollar worth of a given labor input"? We mean that the number of labor-hours (the input of labor) hired by a firm helps to produce a certain estimated amount of physical output which can be sold in the product market at a certain estimated price, thus producing a certain estimated amount of dollar revenue. If from this gross revenue the costs of other productive factors are subtracted, a net figure remains attributable to labor. Divide this estimated net dollar amount by the number of labor-hours in the labor input, and we have the estimated average revenue or worth of the labor per hour.

It is the conjunction and interaction of these general and special labor supply and demand conditions which determine the wage rate paid for any particular job anywhere. If workers were as knowing and as mobile as they are supposed to be under perfectly competitive economic theory, and if employers were as completely wrapped up in maximizing profits as that theory assumes, then the workers would shop around for jobs very thoroughly (under full-employment conditions in the whole economy) and offer their hours only to the highest bidders; and the wage rates the firms *had* to pay to get the hours would just equal what they were *able* to pay, namely the estimated average worth of the input. For any job each firm would just break even on its input of labor. The rate would be set, in the end, at just what the firm is *able* to pay.

Actually, however, workers do not shop around very much to learn about alternative employment opportunities. Individually they are not very well able to play one employer off against another. In other words, unless the workers are well organized in a union, most employers are in much the stronger economic position. In relation to the workers, the employers are usually to some extent in a position of monopoly (more accurately, monopsony) in buying labor services. This means that in the absence of unions most employers do not *have* to pay as high a wage rate as they are *able* to pay. *There is often a sizable margin between the two.*

Now if a margin exists between the wage rate that a firm has to pay for a given job and what it is able to pay, the firm has considerable latitude or discretion in choosing the rate it actually does pay. Thus, there is a substantial difference between the workings of an imagined perfectly competitive labor market and a real-world one. For real-world analysis we must consider what a firm is *willing* to pay as well as what it *has* to pay and is *able* to pay. Estimated ability sets an upper limit, "must-ness" a lower limit. Willingness determines where, between these limits, the rate will actually be.

It must also be noted that in the real world many employers are unable to learn enough about the nature of the demands for their products to be able to estimate accurately the average worth of the labor input hired for a particular job. They may have accurate engineering and cost data on physical outputs yet be unable to predict how much of the output they can sell at what price. In other words, they have only hazy ideas what wage rate they are able to pay for any given employment of labor-hours.

But a wage rate does get determined for the job. One firm is willing to pay as high a rate as it thinks it is able to. It may be moved to do so by its desire for social esteem and good public relations; this motive may be mainly non-economic. Or it may have one or more economic motives. First, it may believe that it can obtain especially good workers if it adopts this policy and other firms do not. If it does attract the better, more efficient workers, its unit labor costs may well be low even at high job rates. Second, the firm may be a public utility or government contractor. Then it has a cost-plus deal; it can pass on higher labor costs to the customers with little or no loss in sales. Third, the firm may conclude that it might be better to pay out a large part of its revenues in the form of higher wages than to pay it to government in the form of higher taxes. The firm is no worse off in the former case.

(2) The structure of rates within a given plant or firm. What is true of the rate set for any single job is true of the rates paid for all the different jobs in a firm's plant. In so far as the supply conditions or the demand conditions reviewed above — or the relationships between the two — are different for the various jobs, we may expect the wage rates to differ. Each job or each group of similar jobs in the plant usually bears a different rate.

(a) Differences in labor supplies. i. General reasons. On the supply side, the total number of hours offered to a given firm usually varies from job to job because of different ratings that workers give the jobs and differences in workers' abilities to perform (or to be trained to perform) the jobs. Workers have subjective ratings of jobs, often based on objective experience with them. Some jobs rank high in prestige and desirability, others low. But many workers, for reasons of heredity or environment, are unable to perform the more desirable jobs. Garbage collecting, for example, may not rate very high; but some workers may be able to do little else. Managing a firm may be considered one of the most desirable jobs; but few workers have the native or acquired capacity to be managers. Workers are in fact often separated into what economists sometimes call "non-competing groups" because of these differences in ability.

ii. Special groups of workers. In Chapter 7 we reviewed the relative inadequacy of annual income for certain special groups of workers — women, Negroes and Mexicans, young and old workers, and migratory farm workers. One of the reasons for these relatively low wage incomes is the relatively low level of the wage-rate components of the incomes. And some of the reasons for the relatively low wage rates received by these classes of employees are to be found in the conditions affecting their labor supplies.

Consider, first, women workers. Most female employees lack occupational skill. They are concentrated in the unskilled, or at best semi-skilled, "light" machine-tending and assembling operations, where wage rates are relatively low. They are also concentrated in industries, e.g., dresses and shoes, in which the average wage rate is usually low. Moreover, in some firms there is a wage-rate discrimination against women, even for jobs on which they are as productive as men; that is, they are paid lower rates than male workers for the same jobs and outputs.

Why is the percentage of women workers who lack skill and industrial versatility larger than that of male workers? Partly because of lack of opportunity for training, partly because of biological differences, and partly because of lack of desire for training. Law, custom, and social attitudes have often designated certain occupations as "men's work," others as "women's work." Some jobs, indeed, seem too heavy or hazardous for females. But others seem especially suited to their dexterity and other traits. In any case, many women have "gone along" with prevailing attitudes; they seem to have no special urge to break down irrational occupational barriers. Some (a distinct small minority) are in the "pin-money" class, working to avoid boredom and not needing income to support themselves or dependents. Others, "hunting a man" and looking on marriage and home-making as their main, ultimate objective, consider themselves only temporarily in the labor market; why, then, invest in training and apprenticeship? Most women workers, however, need income and are permanent members of the labor force. But they are usually deprived of much mobility because of being attached to the maintenance of a home along with their occupation. They are unable or unwilling to move about much in search of better-paying jobs. For all these reasons also, women as individuals are weak in economic and political bargaining power. And many have been only lukewarm about organization to remedy their bargaining deficiencies. (Many unions, as we shall see, have also been less than ardent about trying to organize women workers.)

Some of the reasons for the relatively low level of women workers' wage rates also explain why non-white workers' wage rates are lower than those of white workers. Here too there has been a concentration in the lower-wage unskilled and semi-skilled occupations which may be explained in large part by lack of opportunity for training in skilled work. But, at least so far as male non-whites are concerned, there may have been less acquiescence in occupational barriers and a greater desire for and native ability to perform skilled work than among women workers as a whole. There is also greater mobility, i.e., willingness to move toward the better-paying jobs.

The young workers in industry are exceptionally mobile. But because they lack training and experience, their wage rates are relatively low. Old workers are in an opposite situation. They have lost most of their mobility but have considerable occupational experience. But this experience, without mobility and the bargaining power that comes from having alternative employment opportunities, is of little avail in maintaining their wage rates.

From the standpoint of labor supply, the wage rates of migratory farm workers are low because, for the most part, they are unskilled and unorganized. In other words, as individuals they are in a very weak bargaining position in both the economic and the political sense.

(*b*) *Differences in labor demands. i. General reasons.* Within a given firm the management's estimate of product demand influences its demand for all the different grades of labor equally. That is, when the firm tries to estimate the average worth of the labor needed for each different job, the same product demand applies to each. This of course is because all the different kinds of labor in the productive process contribute to making the same product and product revenue. Therefore no differences in the firm's demands for the different grades of labor can arise from this source.

But with respect to the other two main determinants of labor demand — technological conditions and the supplies of complementary and substitute productive factors — the situation is different. The techniques of producing the product are such that the firm rates some jobs as being more important than others; that is, it estimates the average worth of the labor inputs on some jobs at higher figures than the estimates of average worth for other jobs. Thus, in a metal-working plant one key job is tool-and-die making. The firm considers a tool-and-die maker much more valuable than a common laborer. Similarly, weavers and loom fixers in a textile mill are rated much more valuable than sweepers and janitors.

In the same way, operations on which it is easy to substitute machinery for labor tend to be rated lower than those for which substitute productive factors are not available or are hard to get.

These differences influence the rates a firm thinks it is *able* to pay for the various jobs. The previously mentioned conditions affecting a firm's *willingness* to pay what it is able to may also bear with varying weight on different jobs. Thus, in a foundry it may not matter much to an employer what he pays for common floor labor; but he may be moved by the desire for prestige or other non-economic reasons to pay skilled workers very close to what he thinks he can afford.

ii. Special groups of workers. In respect to *women workers*, it should be noted that the technological developments leading to the mechanization of production processes have made many more jobs available to women's work capacities. In the wage rates for a particular job, however, a firm may pay less to women than to men. For one thing, the firm's bargaining power is greater vis-à-vis women than men. Moreover, the firm's management may share the social prejudice that considers women workers less productive than men; or perhaps the firm actually has facts to show that it costs more to employ women (because of greater absenteeism and because of the necessity of providing special facilities, such as work-seating and rest rooms) and therefore to support its contention that the equal-pay-for-equal-work principle should not apply here.

Willingness to hire *non-white workers* is based on a mixture of economic, technological, political, and social conditions. As previously noted, most of the discrimination against these workers is in the kind of jobs for which they are hired rather than in the wage rates for particular jobs. However, some wage discrimination does exist, particularly in the South. It is based mainly on the largely unsupported social belief that such workers are less productive than whites. That is, the non-whites are thought to provide fewer standard labor-hours per capita than the whites, so that a firm's estimate of the average worth of such labor is lower than for white labor. Also, like all substandard wage-rate groups, these workers when unorganized, are in a very inferior bargaining position with relation to the employer.

The reasons for the inferior wage-rate circumstances of the other special groups — the very young and old and the migratory workers — are much the same as those for women and non-white labor.

(c) Interaction of supply and demand. i. General considerations. If we consider the different supplies of labor-hours offered by workers for different jobs in relation to the differing worth of these jobs as estimated by the firm, we can understand the chief reasons for the variety of job rates within a single plant, ranging from low to high. In general, the larger the supply of hours for a given job, the lower the rate paid. Not many workers possess the native aptitudes or the training needed to perform skilled jobs. Their supplies are limited relative to those available for unskilled and semi-skilled jobs. Firms are therefore compelled to rank skilled jobs higher than other jobs, to estimate the worth of skilled jobs as higher than the worth of the other occupations. And sometimes non-economic circumstances make it likely that they will be more willing to pay the full amounts of their worth-estimate for skilled jobs than for others.

For reasons of habit, custom, and their higher living standards, the minimum rate which skilled workers are willing to accept is higher than that which the less skilled believe is necessary. Technologically, moreover, the skilled workers are usually in strategic, bottleneck positions in a plant. Their bargaining power in relation to the employer greatly exceeds that of the less skilled. They are often in a position to compel the employer to pay close to what he believes their work is worth.

ii. Reasons for trends in intra-firm wage-rate differentials. Earlier in this chapter we stated that during the past half-century there has been a definite trend toward a narrowing of the wage-rate differentials between unskilled and skilled jobs and between the rates paid to special groups of workers, e.g., women, and those paid to white male workers. How are these trends to be explained?

The explanation lies, of course, in changes in the supply and demand conditions discussed above. On the supply side, there has been an improvement in the extent and quality of training available to the low-wage-rate groups. With the spread of effective unionism into the mass-production industries and the consequent organization of the unskilled workers, the improvement in the bargaining position of these workers in relation to firms has been greater than that of the skilled workers. Union leadership has been attentive to the wishes of the unskilled in these industries because these workers have so many votes. The positions of the low-rate groups were also bolstered by the setting of minimum wage rates by various government agencies in peacetime, and by the decisions of the National War Labor Board during World War II, which granted much higher percentage increases in wage rates to the unskilled than to the skilled.

On the demand side, the mechanization of industry seems to have raised the productivity of the low-paying jobs more than that of the high-rated jobs. In other words, the increase in labor demand due to technological improvements had been greater for the low-rate jobs than for the high-rate jobs. A half-century ago workers on common labor jobs were not very productive. Digging ditches or stacking goods by hand was slow, inefficient work. Today the simplest tasks of loading, sorting, stacking, digging, and so on are performed with the aid of machinery. Second, social attitudes, manifested directly or through government regulation, have changed in respect to both the desirability of employing women and non-whites on better-paying jobs and the undesirability of discriminating against these groups in the wage rates paid for particular jobs.

(3) The structure of rates within a given city. We saw in Table 23 that the average hourly earnings of workers in the Chicago labor market varied a good deal in different industries. One reason for this variation undoubtedly lay in the varying compositions of the job structures among the industries. In the plants of one industry paying high average earnings the proportion of workers on skilled, high-rate jobs was doubtless much greater than in the plants of some other industry paying low earnings. A difference in techniques of production is the responsible condition here; technology determines the proportions in which the inputs of the various productive factors are hired. It is an important factor, for example, in explaining some of the differences in Table 23. The earnings in non-costume jewelry and in tool-and-die shops are much higher than in costume jewelry and department stores, partly because the latter industries use so much higher percentages of unskilled and semi-skilled workers.

Our concern at this point, however, is not directly with the reasons for inter-industry wage-rate differences as such. We wish to know now why different plants in the *same* industry and city can and do pay different rates for the *same-named job.*

(a) Supply conditions. Again we must analyze such variations in terms of labor supply and demand. On the supply side we need merely note again the inter-firm preferences of workers, plus the habits, attachments

(inertia), ignorance, and other conditions which keep them from moving freely from firm to firm in search of the best opportunity. All these operate to provide different labor supplies to different firms for a given job.

The unionization of workers and the unions' rules and policies may make important differences in the nature and amounts of labor supply for various jobs. As we shall see, union seniority rules tend to reduce labor mobility. Workers tend to stay put so as not to lose the advantages of accumulated service. The rules of some unions restrict output, hours, and availability of workers. In short, they restrict labor supply. Unions raise the minimum rates that workers are willing to accept without striking. Unions press for uniformity of wage rates for similar jobs in a given market. They do this to protect the union as an entity and to provide "equal pay for equal work" to members. Unions greatly increase members' bargaining strength and skill relative to those of employers.

(b) Demand conditions. On the demand side we must again distinguish ability from willingness to pay. From the standpoint of *ability,* we may note, first, that different firms in the same industry and locality may employ different *techniques of production.* Thus, although jobs may have the same name, they may differ substantially in content among firms. One firm may have its workers concentrate solely on operating a given machine, such as a loom, while another may have such workers performing a number of auxiliary tasks. Other things being equal, the latter firm may well rate its job at a higher average worth. Again, the wage or job rate per unit of labor *input* is not the same as unit labor cost per unit of *output.* One firm may be very efficient in utilizing and managing its labor, materials, and machines; another may be inefficient. In the former, labor cost per unit of output will be much lower than in the latter. Therefore, the former is *able* to pay a much higher wage rate. In the second place, from the standpoint of ability one firm may be in a better position than another in respect to the *supplies of complementary and substitute productive factors.* If so, it probably can afford higher wage rates. However, inter-firm differences are probably not great here. Third, in a world of product differentiation in the minds of customers, one firm's *product demand* may be greater, more stable or secure, and less elastic than another's. The former firm tends to be able to pay the higher wage rate. On the matter of product demand we may note again that firms selling products to government or private customers on a cost-plus basis are able to pay higher rates than those operating in a highly competitive private market.

In respect to firms' *willingness* to pay what they are able, a number of other points must be noted, all of which make for inter-firm wage rate differences in the same industry and community. First, the firms may have an anti-pirating, oligopsonistic labor market arrangement. This means that they agree not only to avoid proselyting workers away from each other but also to change wage rates for similar jobs in concert rather than singly and competitively. They may all pay different rates for the same job. But they *change* their rates up or down only in unison. Second, as previously noted, a few firms prefer to pay high rates because they believe they can obtain more efficient workers, while a few other firms are content to pay low rates as an offset to inefficiency among their poorer-grade workers. In between are the bulk of the firms in the market; these pay middle-range rates. If the calculations of the firms are correct, their labor costs per unit of output are probably much closer to uniformity than their wage cost per unit of labor input. Third, some firms tend to fill most of their higher job vacancies by promotion from the labor forces already within their own plants. This reduces their "open-market" demands for labor and, given a certain degree of ignorance and inertia on the part of the workers, tends to relieve the firms of the necessity of biddings up wage rates. Fourth, as previously noted, the willingness of some firms to pay is increased by heavy taxes on profits. Fifth, wage- and job-rate differentials among firms tend over time to become habitual. Both firms and workers come to look on any one firm's relative wage-rate position as normal and customary. This fact tends in normal times to institutionalize each firm's willingness to pay a given rate for a given job. It usually takes decreased ability to pay a rate or to obtain workers (during business downswings or upswings or during a time of marked "abnormal" increase in product or labor market competition) to jolt a firm out of its customary willingness to pay.

(c) Supply and demand interaction. Under non-union conditions of labor supply, there are ample real-world labor supply and demand differences to explain variations in the wage rates paid for a particular job by firms in the same industry and locality. Under unionization there is a tendency not only for the whole range to move upward, because union pressure and economic coercion raises firms' "willingness" to pay higher rates, but also for the range to narrow considerably, because of the union policy of wage-rate uniformity for similar jobs.

(4) Inter-industry differentials. Actually the wage-rate differences for a good many similar jobs that exist in a given locality (for example, the spread of rates for common labor shown in Table 21 for Cleveland) are the result not only of the circumstances just reviewed but also of the different conditions that exist among the firms in *different* industries. Let us consider these inter-industry wage-rate variations, focusing on a single locality in order to rule out any effects of inter-regional and size-of-city differences in labor supply and demand conditions.

In respect to supply, there is only one thing to add to the points already made: If different industries are considered, there are more firms among which workers may choose if they wish. And there are greater differences among the employment policies of the firms. Therefore, there may well be larger variations in inter-firm labor supply.

The demand conditions are the important ones in any explanation of local inter-industry wage differences. The techniques of production are very different in various industries. An iron and steel plant, for example, has a much higher capital input per worker than a clothing shop. In general, the higher the capital input in relation to normal labor inputs, the higher the physical output and the value of output per worker — and therefore the higher the wage rate the firm is *able* to pay. Among industries, moreover, there may be significant differences in the availability of complementary and substitute productive factors. But this item is likely to be a minor one in explaining wage-rate differentials.

A major condition affecting relative ability to pay lies in the differences in firms' product demands. When we consider product demand differences, we must include the whole market for an industry's product, which may be national rather than local. Here the degree of competition in each industry's product market is of prime importance. In general, the more competitive the product market of an industry, the lower the wage rate which any firm-member of the industry is able to pay. One reason why wage rates are higher in steel and automobiles than in work clothing and cotton textiles is, as we have said, the higher capital investment per worker in the former. But another reason is that automobile and steel firms sell in oligopolistic product markets, whereas the clothing and cotton textile markets are relatively very competitive.

Under union conditions covering all industries with equal strength, inter-industry wage-rate differentials seem to be little affected. This is because different unions are in power in different industries; there is not the same need for equalizing wage rates if wage-rate differences do not jeopardize union security. The only uniformity is in wage-rate *changes;* here unions tend to keep pace with each other, industry by industry. Yet even here there may be differences because industries vary in ability to pay.

In respect to *willingness* to pay, there is little to add to the points made above. With different industries in the locality, there is undoubtedly a wider variation in willingness. But the same factors as those previously mentioned are at work.

When one or more industries are unionized but others are not, the organization of the latter at a later date may well tend to result in some narrowing of the former wage-rate spread. But once this happens, the new spread tends to persist because of the basic technological and product market differences.

(5) Inter-regional and size-of-city differences. Our labor supply and demand analysis can also be used to explain area differences in wage rates. We shall confine ourselves here to the North-South spread. When we consider labor supply conditions in relation to labor demand conditions for the South compared with the North and for small compared with large communities, we come closer to an understanding of the reasons for the wage-rate differentials. Fundamentally, in Northern large

cities labor is scarcer in relation to the demand for it than in the South generally or in small communities generally. This basic fact may be stated in two ways: (*a*) The degree of industrialization is greater in Northern large cities. (*b*) In the South, or in small communities, firms are much closer to actual or potential labor surpluses, because they are closer to agriculture; but in these areas there are not yet enough firms to wipe out the surpluses and make severe the competition for labor.

Earlier in the chapter we saw that these differentials have been narrowing for some time — a development that is to be expected, if competitive theory has any real-world validity at all. Thus, in spite of the labor immobilities which stand as an obstacle to the perfect working-out of the theory, the higher wage rates in the North and in large cities have *helped* to attract labor from the South and from small cities. Labor supply has been increased in the former and reduced in the latter. At the same time, the lower rates in the South and in small cities have been *one* of several factors inducing Northern big-city firms to move to the low-rate areas or open branches there. Thus, labor demand may well have risen more in the South and in the small communities than in the other localities. Both these movements have doubtless tended to narrow the previous differentials.

b. The national wage-rate level. Now let us turn from a consideration of the conditions responsible for the wage-rate differentials that make up the national wage-rate structure. Let us try to learn the reasons for the changes in the *general level* of wage rates portrayed in Tables 26 to 28 (pages 152–154). In addition to showing a downward trend in the length of work periods (i.e., an increase in the amount of leisure), these tables established, first, a long-term increase in the level of real wage rates, and second, cyclical variations in the levels of money and real wage rates.

In order to explain these movements we must refer back to the discussion of Chapter 6 on employment and unemployment in the economy as a whole. There we sketched the conditions affecting the over-all supply of labor and the conditions determining the over-all demand for labor under secular and cyclical circumstances.

(1) The secular trend. As pointed out in Chapter 6, the meaningful approach to the general level of wage rates is in terms of "real" rates, i.e., the money price of labor in relation to the money prices of other goods. This approach is the only significant one when the trend in the wage-rate level is being considered.

(a) The economy's ability to pay higher real wage rates. Over the past century the level of real rates has risen because the over-all supply of labor (as determined by individual households' decisions on births and retirement and on the allocation of time between leisure and income, union policies on lengths of work periods, advances in medical science, and government policies on the lengths of work periods and in the field

of public health) has increased much less rapidly than the total real demand for labor (as determined by the quantity of capital, the level of technology, and the nature of the general social organization for production). That is to say, capital has been accumulated and the techniques of production have been improved faster than the population and the labor force have increased. As a result, physical output per worker has risen: The economy has been able to afford higher real wage rates.

Evidence of the economy's increasing ability to pay is presented in the average labor productivity data of Table 12 (page 104). The increases during the 30-year period 1909–40 were striking in all fields except those in which white-collar workers were employed.

Comparable data for 1950 are not yet available. Before World War II, over a long period of time, the average annual rise in labor-hour productivity in the economy as a whole was about 2.5 per cent. This increase may or may not have continued through 1945. In any case it undoubtedly was resumed after 1945 because of the wave of investment spending by firms on new, technologically superior capital equipment during the postwar years.

(b) The economy's willingness to pay higher real wage rates. Continuing to look at the economy as a whole, we must next ask whether, in view of the way in which the productive activity of the economy was organized (i.e., through the private enterprise system), the economy was *willing* to pay what the data in Table 12 suggest it was *able* to pay. This question has to do with the *distribution* of the productivity gains resulting from capital accumulation and technological progress.

There are three main channels for such distribution — labor, consumers, and firm-owners. That is, the over-all increases in productivity may go to labor-owners in the form of money wage rates which rise faster than non-labor prices; or to consumers, in the form of lower product prices and improved product quality; or to firm-owners, in the form of increased dividends or higher values of stock equities. Actually all three groups share in the gains. Labor-selling households and firm-owners as a whole are double beneficiaries because they are also consumers.

The data in Tables 26–28, in conjunction with those in Table 12, suggest that the average yearly rise in average real wage rates just about kept pace with the average yearly increase in physical productivity per labor-hour. Thus, according to the figures in the last column of Table 26, the average (compounded) annual increase in real wage rates from 1910 to 1940 for most industries was about 3.0 per cent; and, if we can assume that, in respect to Table 12, the 1910 composite index number for "mechanical trades" in 1910 would be about 65, the average annual productivity increase for this 31-year period would be about the same as the rise in real wage rates. In other words, there seems to have been sufficient competition among firms and sufficient bargaining strength among workers to produce a significant rise in real hourly earnings. Given the ability to pay, the economy's firms, operating within the private enterprise form of social organization, were willing to pay.

This fact of course does not mean that owners of the firms and consumers as a group failed to obtain a share of the benefits from increased productivity.

(2) Cyclical fluctuations. As we learned in Chapters 3 and 6, a fall in the total flow of spending (households' consumption spending, or firms' investment spending, or both) per period of time below the level required for full employment results in a decline in total output, employment, and money income, as well as a fall in the general level of all prices. This is the sort of thing that happens during a business downswing.

We also learned that there are certain institutional resistances to falling prices. Some firms, as oligopolists or monopolists, may be in a position to avoid reductions in their product prices; other, more competitive firms may be unable to do so. The question then arises, Do money wage rates fall more or less than or the same as product prices? In other words, during a business downswing do real wage rates fall, rise, or stay the same?

A similar question arises in respect to a business upswing, when an increase in total spending leads to a rise in the general level of all prices: As product prices go up, do money wage rates rise at the same rate or more or less? In other words, do real wage rates stay the same or rise or fall?

To answer these questions, we must distinguish union from non-union conditions. In the absence of unionism, most firms are in a position to choose the amount and the timing of wage-rate reductions during a business downswing. Studies of what happened to money wage rates during the 1930–32 and 1937–38 periods suggest the following conclusions: Wage-rate reductions are not made *en masse* or simultaneously by all firms. Some firms take the lead and cut rates early in the downswing. Others hold off for considerable periods. Small firms and unprofitable firms (the members of these two groups are not necessarily identical) usually make the first and largest wage-rate cuts. For public relations or other non-economic reasons the large firms are disinclined to rush into such action unless their financial position is weak. Financial pressure to reduce rates (i.e., unprofitability) is greatest among firms whose product prices are forced down by competitive market conditions, and among firms with production techniques in which labor cost is a high percentage of total cost. Under competitive theory, the industries having the most unemployment should make the first and largest wage-rate reductions. But this is just the opposite of what actually happened. By the end of the downswing, however, almost all firms in all industries will have reduced their money wage rates. It appears (see, for example, column 8 of Table 28) that the fall in money wage rates is smaller and slower than the decline in product prices until late in the downswing. In the end, however, the former tends to catch up with or exceed the latter. In other words, real wage rates rise at first, then fall.

Much the same conclusions emerge from a study of changes in money wage rates during a business upswing. Again the various firms and industries do not keep step. The more profitable and the more public-relations-minded firms raise their rates first and farther. Usually the more profitable firms are those who sell their products in markets permitting price increases. Firms in which labor cost is a small percentage of total cost can clearly afford wage-rate increases better than those in which the opposite situation exists. During the first part of the upswing the rise in money wage rates tends to lag behind the rise in product prices; real wage rates tend to fall. In the end, however, money rates may more than catch up; real rates will then have risen.

What effects does widespread, powerful unionism have on the two patterns just described? In respect to a business downswing, there is as yet no conclusive evidence; we have had no important downswing since World War II, from which organized labor emerged so powerful. It is true that in the 1930–32 period the industries in which unions were strong experienced as many and as large wage-rate decreases as the non-union industries, in spite of the avowed union intention to accept "no reductions." But it is to be doubted that one is justified in concluding from this experience that a powerful, united labor movement would be unable to resist wage-rate cuts in some future depression. It would at least seem reasonable to believe that this sort of unionism could compel a significant lag in reductions.

In respect to business upswings, the experience of the country with five successive "rounds" of wage-rate increases from 1945–46 to 1950–51, during which real wage rates rose, suggests that widespread powerful unionism is able to reduce greatly the previously noted tendency of money rates to lag behind product prices in rate of increase.

CHAPTER 9

Maintaining Physical and Mental Well-Being

A. INTRODUCTION

Our study of unemployment and incomes established a reciprocal relationship among these two aspects of workers' well-being. We saw that unemployment, which reduces the size of the hours-worked component, leads to low incomes. We also found that low incomes, whether caused by a low level of the wage-rate component or by a low level of the employment component, have physical and mental effects on workers and economic effects on society which often lead to more unemployment (including part-time employment) and lowered productivity. On the other hand, high employment tends to create high incomes, which in turn tend to make for more employment. In short, the reciprocal relationship between employment and income can involve cumulative effects; there can be a vicious or a beneficent circle.

Unemployment was defined as involuntary idleness among workers who are able and willing to work. The use of the word "able" means that absence from work because of injury or sickness or superannuation is not counted as unemployment. This distinction is wholly proper, for the absence from work called "unemployment" is caused by conditions essentially different from those producing the other kinds of work absence. Yet the latter are very important because the end product — reduction of income — is the same as from unemployment, as defined.

We see, then, that there is a third significant aspect of workers' welfare, one that is closely and reciprocally related to the employment and income aspects. Physical disability and superannuation are part of the vicious-circle relationship between unemployment and low income. Physical well-being before voluntary retirement is part of the beneficent circle of full employment and high income.

To emphasize the income and economic effects of physical disability and superannuation is not to minimize such other effects as pure physical suffering and mental anguish. Obviously, everything possible should be done to eliminate or alleviate these aspects of disability, even if all workers were guaranteed high incomes when hurt or ill or aged. Moreover, individual workers can be free of injury or disease or be earning high incomes and still be mentally upset if they feel themselves subject to repression by the attitudes and policies of employer or union. All-round well-being involves more than steady, high-income employment and physical health; there must also be adequate opportunities for self-expression.

In the discussion which follows, we shall consider the nature, extent, effects, and causes of, first, the problem of accidents on and off the job; second, the problem of occupational and non-occupational illness; third, the problem of caring for aged workers; and fourth, the problem of industrial autocracy.

B. ACCIDENTS TO WORKERS

1. Occupational injuries. *a. Nature and extent. (1) Definition of injury.* To begin with, it is essential to formulate a definition of the term *industrial accident,* a definition that is accurate and has general acceptance. This is not so easily done as one might suppose. For example, what exactly is meant by the statement that there are almost 2 million accidents in industry each year? Does this figure include minor scratches and abrasions, which require only a few minutes' treatment at the plant dispensary, as well as industrial fatalities? Just when is a man "statistically" injured? Strictly speaking, an industrial accident seems to be any sudden happening which robs a worker in the plant of his physical well-being and results in death or in disability for any length of time. The most widely accepted definition, however, says that an accident is "an injury which results in the loss of time beyond the day or shift in which it occurs." This means that the unexpected happening is not a statistical accident if the worker's injury permits him to resume work the next day or shift. Such a conception undoubtedly fails to include a large number of injuries. But it may be agreed that for practical purposes an arbitrary line must be drawn somewhere and that the definition just quoted is as good as any which could be devised. As in the case of unemployment, the important point is that everyone should accept and use the same definition. This desideratum, unfortunately, has not been realized. Accident statistics are supplied partly through the various state workmen's compensation agencies, and many of these report only compensable accidents for covered employees. As to what a "compensable injury" is, each state is a law unto itself: in some there are waiting periods up to ten days before an employee is entitled to compensation. The laws also vary in coverage, with agricultural and domestic workers the most usual large exclusions. Finally, it has become a fairly common practice for plants which are participating in accident-prevention drives or contests to give injured workers medical treatment and keep them in the plant on full wages rather than besmirch their "no-accident" records by reporting them to the state as lost-time accidents.

(2) *Meaning of frequency and severity rates.* There is thus ample room for improvement in the reporting of accidents. But a good deal of progress has already been made. For example, it was soon realized that merely to give the absolute number of accidents was not enough. It would be much more significant to compare the number of accidents with the opportunities for getting hurt. That is to say, there should be relative figures which would take into account the number of employees in each plant and the hours worked — in short, the "exposure" to possible accidents. Thus, if a large plant and a small plant each had the same absolute number of accidents, the small plant would show a poorer record because the number of its employees and their total hours would be less than that of the large plant. This ratio between number of accidents and man-hours of exposure, usually expressed as so many injuries per 1,000,000 man-hours, is known as the *accident frequency rate.* It is very useful in comparing the accident records of different plants, industries, and localities. Yet it falls short in one respect: it fails to give statistical recognition to the fact that accidents are not alike but vary greatly in seriousness of effect on the worker. In other words, they differ in severity, ranging all the way from minor injuries, which result in the loss of only one or two working days, to those which cause permanent disability or death. On this account the better agencies always demand that reporting firms show whether accidents are fatal or non-fatal, and if non-fatal, the duration of lost time after the shift in which the accident occurred. From these data accident *severity rates* can be calculated; here the numerator is the total number of days lost, the denominator is again the man-hours of exposure, and the quotient is multiplied by 1000. An arbitrary number of lost days is applied to fatalities and permanent disabilities. Severity rates, then, tell the number of days lost (rather than number of accidents) per given periods of exposure.

(3) *Classification of injuries by type and cause.* It was also found desirable to know the number and the frequency and severity of occupational injuries by type and by cause of injury. Industrial accidents are classified in four main categories as to severity and duration: fatalities, permanent total disability, permanent partial disability, and temporary total disability. The meaning of each should be rather obvious. "Permanent total disability" designates accidents that completely incapacitate workers for the remainders of their lives. A "permanent partial disability" is an injury involving the loss or impairment of one or more members or portions or functions of a worker's body (e.g., eye, hand, leg) for the rest of his life; but the disability is not such as to prevent his employment at some kind of work once the wound has healed and the immediate total disability has passed. All other injuries (as defined) involve total absence from work for only a temporary period of more than a day, followed by complete recovery and re-employment.

Other advances in the statistical handling of accidents have been the requirements that firms report accidents as to cause and by major departments and occupations. Detailed data of this nature furnish a much more definite basis for accident-prevention work, which of course is the chief reason for the collection of all facts about injuries. Thus, the New York (State) Department of Labor has classified the causes of accidents under nine main heads: handling objects, falls, machinery, vehicles, hand tools, falling objects, explosions, heat, and hoisting apparatus. There are appropriate subheads under each.

(4) *Number, frequency, and severity of various kinds of occupational injuries.* For a good many years data on industrial accidents have been collected by several government agencies and have been published mainly by the federal Bureau of Labor Statistics. Private agencies, particularly the National Safety Council, also collect and publish statistics on occupational and non-occupational injuries.

Our sole concern here with accident statistics is in respect to the welfare of the group whose problems we have been discussing in this section of the book — individual workers. This means that the data on number, frequency, and severity of various kinds of industrial accidents for any given year have significance for us only in so far as they can be related to an appraisal of workers' well-being.

Two kinds of perspective are important: First, what has been the trend in number, frequency, and severity of occupational injuries? Are workers better off now than previously? Second, how do these injuries stand in relation to other killers and maimers, such as war, and to other causes of occupational idleness, such as unemployment, strikes, non-occupational idleness, and occupational and non-occupational sickness?

TABLE 29 *Estimated Number of Disabling Occupational Injuries, 1936–1949*

Year	Total Number of Injuries	Fatalities [1]	Permanent Total Disabilities	Permanent Partial Disabilities	Temporary Total Disabilities
1936	1,407,200	16,000	—	66,200	1,325,000
1937	1,837,300	19,600	—	126,000	1,691,700
1938	1,375,600	16,400	—	98,900	1,260,300
1939	1,573,500	16,400	—	109,400	1,447,700
1940	1,889,700	18,100	—	89,600	1,782,000
1941	2,180,200	19,200	—	100,600	2,060,400
1942	2,267,700	18,100	1,800	100,800	2,147,000
1943	2,414,000	18,400	1,700	108,000	2,285,900
1944	2,230,400	15,900	1,700	94,400	2,118,400
1945	2,020,300	16,500	1,800	88,100	1,913,900
1946	2,056,000	16,500	1,800	92,400	1,945,300
1947	2,060,800	17,000	1,800	91,800	1,950,200
1948	2,019,900	16,000	1,800	86,700	1,915,400
1949 [2]	1,870,000	15,000	1,600	79,400	1,774,000

Source: U. S. Bureau of Labor Statistics, as reported for 1936–47 in D. Gagliardo, *American Social Insurance*, Harper and Brothers, New York, 1949, p. 345, and for 1948–49 in *Monthly Labor Reviews*.

[1] Includes permanent total disabilities through 1941.

[2] Data for 1949 not strictly comparable with those for earlier years, because of inclusion of improved data for agriculture and construction in the latter year. Data for 1950 not yet available.

(*a*) *The trend. i. Statistics on industrial accidents.* The data in Table 29 suggest the following conclusions. Temporary total disabilities are by far the most numerous type of accident, permanent total disabilities by far the least numerous. There are cyclical fluctuations in the annual numbers of all kinds of occupational injuries. This is to be expected, because exposure is much greater in prosperous years than in time of depression. Moreover, when unemployed workers resume their jobs after long layoffs, they have lost much of their skill in protecting themselves; their proneness to injuries has risen considerably. During World War II there was an upward bulge, partly because of the greatly accelerated recruitment of green workers. From the unrefined statistics on *numbers* of accidents it is impossible to establish any trend except in the case of fatalities, which showed a significant downward movement in spite of the greatly increased exposure after 1940.

In order to obtain a clear idea about the trend in occupational injuries, then, we must relate their numbers to the amount of exposure. That is, we must look at the data on frequency and severity of industrial accidents over a period of years. This sort of information is presented in Table 30. It will be seen that during the past quarter of a century there has been, for all kinds of occupational accidents, a notable decline in both frequency and severity, with no great cyclical deviations from the trend; and that the greatest gain in workers' safety came in the most serious kinds of injury — death and permanent total disability. The year 1949 was a record year in all respects.

Other accident facts involving details too numerous for presentation here but of interest for our purpose may be briefly summarized.

First, what industries have the best and the worst accident records? On the average, among the broad industry groups, transportation, construction, and mining have the highest frequency and severity rates, communications the lowest. Some industry groups, such as manufacturing and trade have rather high frequency rates and low severity rates. Within the broad industry groups, notably "safe" industries are as follows: in respect to frequency, aircraft manufacture, electrical equipment, steel, and rubber; in respect to severity, printing, tobacco, trade and service. The worst maimers and killers are, in respect to frequency, lumbering, coal mining, metal mining, railroading, marine transportation, and wood products; in respect to severity, coal mining, lumbering, railroading, metal mining, and quarrying.

Second, the larger plants and firms appear in general to achieve lower accident frequency and severity rates than the smaller ones.

Third, in any given plant or industry the frequency of industrial injuries seems to be higher among the younger workers than among the older. On the other hand, accident severity is higher among the older workers.

ii. Reasons for the statistical trends and differences. We have seen

TABLE 30 *Injury-Frequency and Severity Rates, Manufacturing,*[1] *and Indexes of Injury-Frequency Rates by Extent of Disability, 1926–1949*

Year	Injury-Frequency Rates	Injury-Severity Rates	Indexes of Injury-Frequency Rates by Extent of Disability (1926 = 100)			
			All Injuries	Death and Permanent Total	Permanent Partial	Temporary Total
1926	24.2	2.6	100.0	100.0	100.0	100.0
1927	22.6	2.6	93.6	107.1	96.3	93.3
1928	22.5	2.6	93.2	107.1	104.6	92.5
1929	24.0	2.4	99.2	92.9	109.2	98.7
1930	23.1	2.8	95.5	107.1	111.0	94.6
1931	18.9	2.6	78.0	92.9	102.8	76.5
1932	19.6	2.9	80.9	107.1	113.8	78.9
1933	19.3	2.2	91.8	85.7	110.1	90.8
1934	20.2	2.7	93.6	107.1	128.4	91.6
1935	17.9	2.3	88.1	92.9	121.1	86.2
1936	16.6	2.1	85.7	85.7	114.7	84.1
1937	17.8	2.3	85.8	85.7	122.0	83.7
1938	15.1	1.6	71.7	71.4	78.9	68.1
1939	14.9	1.4	73.4	71.4	80.7	73.9
1940	15.3	1.6	75.3	71.4	84.8	75.6
1941	18.1	1.7	85.8	80.3	93.7	86.2
1942	19.9	1.5	93.5	70.7	83.4	94.1
1943	20.0	1.4	94.4	70.7	83.4	95.0
1944	18.4	1.4	88.3	62.8	75.4	89.7
1945	18.6	1.6	81.9	62.8	72.3	83.0
1946	19.9	1.6	84.3	60.1	77.9	85.3
1947	18.8	1.4	78.4	51.7	70.1	79.3
1948	17.2	1.5	69.8	51.7	67.3	70.6
1949	15.0	1.4	61.2	44.3	61.9	61.6

Source: Data in first two columns from files, U. S. Bureau of Labor Statistics; in last four columns from *Work Injuries in the United States During 1949*, U. S. Bureau of Labor Statistics, Bulletin No. 1025, August, 1951, p. 23.

[1] Rates for years 1926 to 1935 are unweighted averages of reports received for 30 leading manufacturing industries, and refer to wage-earners only. Data for 1936 and subsequent years are based on a considerably expanded sample and include representation of all important manufacturing industries. Administrative, office, and all other employees are included in the scope of the coverage. The rates of individual industries were weighted by the estimated total employment to obtain the average for all manufacturing. Prior to 1939 injury information was obtained from Workmen's Compensation records of various states; beginning in 1939 data on both hours of exposure and number of injuries were obtained through voluntary reports from employers.

that the industrial accident record of the United States has improved substantially over the years; that the record is, however, still pretty bad; and that the problem is concentrated in certain kinds of plants, industries, and workers. Why are these things true?

To answer this question fully, we have to know the causes of industrial accidents. This topic is discussed below. But certain observations may be made here. Some industries, such as construction, railroading, steel, and explosives are *potentially* much more hazardous than others, such as trade and service. Yet some of the potentially dangerous industries, like steel and explosives, are actually much safer than others of considerably lower hazard-potential. This can only mean that steel, explosives, and similar industries have made special and successful efforts to cope with the known causes of occupational injuries. Various safety devices have been used to protect workers from dangerous equipment. Workers have been educated to be careful. Accident-prone workers have been removed from points of hazard. And a spirit of competition among firms and groups of workers has helped spark the drive for improved safety records.

(*b*) *Industrial accidents compared to other causes of lost time.* Now let us look at occupational injuries from our other point of perspective. What is their relative importance as a cause of lost work time and lost income among workers?

The figures in Table 31 represent the results of an effort to compare the number of work-days lost through industrial accidents with the number lost through five other causes. These data must be used with care and with knowledge of their meanings (see table footnote). Thus, the data in line 7 show the estimated number of man-days lost by the workers directly involved in the years in which the accidents actually occurred. This is a minimum figure. Clearly, if an accident is very serious (e.g., a fatality or a permanent total disability), the number of work-days lost extends beyond the year in which the accident occurred. (This would be true

TABLE 31 *Approximate Average Annual Number of Man-Days Lost in Industry from Selected Causes, 1947–1950* [1]

	Average Annual Number of Man-Days (in thousands)	Per Cent Distribution
All Factors	1,559,952	100.0
Unemployment	695,422	44.6
Sickness	406,550	26.1
Vacation	263,835	16.9
Strikes	46,370	3.0
Bad weather	43,485	2.8
Work injuries	41,175	2.6
Temporary layoff	35,165	2.2
New job or business	27,950	1.8

[1] Except for unemployment and work injuries, estimates must be considered as crude because of the inadequacies of the data for this purpose. Work injury data are from the U. S. Bureau of Labor Statistics. All other data are from the U. S. Bureau of Census, *Annual Report on the Labor Force* for the years 1947–50. The weekly averages obtained from the labor force sample census were multiplied by 52 to obtain annual man-weeks and the product multiplied by 5 to obtain total man-days. In the case of sickness and strikes the resultant estimates were doubled to allow for under-representation. It should be noted that the estimate of man-days lost from strikes is somewhat above that of the U. S. Bureau of Labor Statistics using different collection procedures. The Bureau's data show the average annual man-days lost from strikes 1947–50 to be 39.5 million. For a discussion of the technical differences in the procedures of the two agencies, see Thomas K. Hitch, "Meaning and Measurement of 'Full' or 'Maximum' Employment," *The Review of Economics and Statistics,* Vol. 33, No. 1, February, 1950, footnote 3, table 1, p. 4. Work injury data minimize man-days lost from this cause relative to other causes, since annual losses from death or permanent physical impairment extend on into future years. Estimated average annual total man-days lost from this cause, including future effects, for this same period is estimated at 217,175,000 man-days. The man-days lost in terms of equivalent full-time employment is estimated at 137,250 workers annually. (See *Monthly Labor Review,* 1947–50, various issues.)

also of serious non-occupational accidents, occupational sicknesses, and non-occupational sicknesses.) Experts in the field of industrial accidents estimate that the time lost in post-accident years is roughly five times the number of work-days lost in the year of the injuries. Furthermore, when workers who are hurt or ill lose time, other workers' time is affected. The accident itself often results in damaged equipment; until it is repaired, there is a production bottleneck, and other workers lose time and sometimes earnings. Even if no equipment is damaged, the injured workers' associates take time off to assist him or to recover from shaken nerves and morale. All this slows down production and output. The National Safety Council estimates that industrial accidents result in approximately five times as many days lost by other workers as by the injured ones in the year of the accidents.

Unemployment that is severe enough to rob workers of skill and morale also tends to lessen work time and income during years subsequent to the one in which the idleness occurred. On the other hand, most strikes do not last long enough to have this effect in significant degree.

With these things in mind, we see that Table 31 shows industrial accidents to be neither the least nor the most important cause of lost time among workers. They cause much less lost time than sickness and unemployment. In the years considered by the table, strikes caused considerably more direct lost time than work injuries. But 1947–50 was an inflationary period of abnormal strike activity.

(*c*) *Summary and conclusions.* From both points of view — the trend and the relative position of industrial accidents as a cause of lost time — the statistical record justifies some pointing with pride. The accomplishments and progress of particular industries like basic steel and explosives in accident prevention during recent years is especially a reason for satisfaction. Yet the fact that in 1949 there were still about 15,000 work fatalities and almost 2 million work injuries of all kinds is a warning against complacency. There is still much to be done. If we assume an average work year of 250 days, the 45 million man-days lost in 1947, for example, can be translated into a loss of about 180,000 man-years of employment. In the absence of industrial accidents (a Utopian ideal, of course), there would have been the equivalent of that much more employment and output.

b. Effects and costs of industrial accidents. Early in this chapter we emphasized the relation of disabling occupational injuries to workers' incomes. And in Chapter 7 we pointed out the various harmful effects of low incomes on individual workers. There is no need to repeat these discussions here. In respect to industrial accidents, we may merely say now that to these effects must be added the physical suffering and the mental pain of the workers involved in the accidents.

However, it may be of interest to try to arrive at some estimate of the income losses suffered by workers as a group from industrial injuries.

There are two main kinds of loss: (1) the direct wage-income loss; and (2) the indirect loss resulting from the higher product prices charged by firms because of the costs of accidents to the firms.

We may arrive at a figure approximating the first loss by multiplying an estimated average daily wage payment by the estimated number of days lost from industrial accidents during a given year. Available wage-rate data such as those presented in Chapter 8 suggest that $1.25 per hour, or ten dollars per eight-hour day, would be a conservative average amount. Then the direct wage-income loss for 1947 (with no allowance for wage loss in subsequent years from serious injuries occurring in 1947) would have been about $450,000,000 (45 million man-days time $10 per day). If it is true that the wage loss in later years resulting from industrial injuries in a particular year is about five times the direct, immediate loss, the total wage-income loss ultimately caused by 1947's injuries would be at least $2.7 billion (450 million plus $2250 million), again on the conservative assumption that ten dollars represents the average daily wage throughout the period.

These figures can be accepted only if we make the rather doubtful assumption that the days lost through injuries would actually have been spent at work instead of at the ball park or beach or sick in bed at home. Just how much our estimates should be reduced because of these possibilities cannot be guessed. Perhaps we have already made sufficient allowance by using a low average daily wage in making the estimates.

Any figure representing the indirect loss falling on workers from higher product prices is less reliable than the "direct" figures just given, not because the indirect costs to employers cannot be estimated satisfactorily but because it is impossible to say just what percentage of these costs is passed on to consumers in the form of higher prices. However, we can be fairly certain that in a prosperous year of high total product demand — like 1950 — virtually all increased costs are shifted to consumers.

One of the first thoroughgoing attempts to estimate employers' total accident costs was made in 1931 by H. W. Heinrich of the Travelers' Insurance Company.[1] He divided the employer's accident burden into direct and indirect costs. The direct costs for employers as a group were made up of compensation paid to workmen under the state laws, payments to hospital and doctors for medical treatment, administrative costs of state boards or private funds, and legal expenses where court action was undertaken, as in states that had no compensation laws. Four times as important as these direct expenses were the indirect costs, which were composed of the following items: the cost, to the employer, of the worker's lost time after the accident; the cost of the time lost by other employees who stop work out of curiosity and sympathy or to be of assis-

[1] See *Proceedings of the Seventeenth Annual Meeting of the International Association Industrial Accident Boards and Commissions*, U.S. Bureau of Labor Statistics, Bulletin No. 536, pp. 171–179.

tance; the cost of the time lost by foremen or other executives on account of assisting the injured workers, investigating the cause of the accident, selecting, training, or breaking in a replacement for the vacated job, and preparing accident reports or attending hearings; the cost of time spent on the case by first-aid attendants and hospital staff, unless compensated for by insurance; the cost due to injury to materials, machines, tools, or other property; the cost due to interference with flow of production; the cost under the employee benefit or welfare system; the cost of paying full wages to the injured employee after his return even though his productive efficiency is temporarily impaired; the cost resulting from lowered efficiency and shaken morale; the overhead costs that continue while the injured employee is a non-producer.

The total of direct costs in Heinrich's estimate amounted to $912 million. The indirect or hidden costs were estimated at $4098 million, making a grand total of $5 billion. It should be noted that this estimate included the costs of minor and no-injury (as defined) accidents, as well as those for which compensation was paid under the law. The direct and indirect costs of the compensable accidents were said to be $3.7 billion out of the grand total of $5.0 billion.

More recently the National Safety Council estimated the employers' direct and indirect costs for lost-time occupational injuries at $2.4 billion for 1946, a year in which prices were roughly 50 per cent higher than in the year involved in Heinrich's estimate. But no estimate was given for minor and no-injury accidents. However, if we assume that in 1946 the latter were about the same proportion of a grand total as they were in 1931, we may guess that the aggregate cost to the employer may have been about $3.2 billion for 1946. But with the value of the 1946 dollar only two-thirds that of the 1931 dollar, we must reduce this figure to about $2.2 billion in order to compare it with the Heinrich estimate. This is still a staggering amount. But if the two figures are comparable, it represents real progress.

According to the data in Table 29, there were 186,000 fewer lost-time injuries in 1949 than in 1946, and all kinds of injuries seem to have been reduced in about the same proportion (roughly 10 per cent). But prices were about 20 per cent higher in 1949. Then we may estimate the employer cost of all industrial injuries at about $3.5 billion in 1949 dollars ($3.2 billion, minus 10 per cent, plus 20 per cent). Adding this figure to the $0.5 billion direct wage-income loss, we have about $4.0 billion as the total financial loss to American workers from occupational accidents during that year.

c. Causes of industrial accidents. Who or what are to be blamed for industrial accidents and the losses just cited? The word "blame" should be used only in the sense that, in order to get action calculated to prevent or minimize the frequency and severity of accidents, the responsibility for accidents must be assessed to the proper causes and to the persons able to remove the causes.

Thus, one person might be inclined to say: It is the profits system, the private enterprise organization of production that is to blame. Employers in frantic quest of maximum profits are too stingy, greedy, or careless to introduce expensive programs of accident prevention. Introduce socialism, make the government the sole employer, and you will see a tremendous lowering of accident frequency and severity rates.

But another person might well answer: It is not the profits system that is chiefly at fault. Granted that a few firms, mostly the smaller ones, are as you have described them, and granted that severe competition in some product markets make certain other employers unable, even if willing, to spend the necessary sums on accident prevention; still it would be silly to do away with the whole private enterprise system just because of a few erring or impotent members. You'd be throwing out the baby with the bath. Look at Russia. It is a socialist state, and yet it has millions of industrial accidents every year. No, the fault seems to lie in the technological developments that have produced mechanized production processes — high-speed, complicated, dangerous machines ready to maim and kill.

Still another person might argue: There are elements of truth in what each of you has said. The accident *potential* of modern mechanized industry is certainly much higher than that of the handicraft methods of production used before the technological revolution. The destructive power of a modern steel plant is certainly much greater than that of ten thousand blacksmith shops. A buzz saw in a power mill can do much more damage than a hundred hand saws. Much factory work is noisy, high-speed, nerve-fraying, and fatiguing. Other factory work is very monotonous. Under these conditions it is easy for workers to lose the alertness necessary for the avoidance of accidents. But note that some of the most potentially dangerous industries have been made by conscious human effort into actually the safest to work in. And consider that more than a third of all accidents (industrial and non-industrial) occur in the home, which is hardly a place filled with big, high-speed, frightening, fatiguing machinery. A bathtub is much more dangerous than an automatic loom. It seems to me that, all things considered, it is human beings who must bear the blame, whatever the environment. A careful person never breaks his leg or head getting into a bathtub. A careful worker never falls into a ladle of molten steel or gets his arm caught in the gears of a power machine. A careful employer guards the dangerous parts of his equipment, rock-dusts and prevents gas accumulation in his coal mine, and educates his workmen to be always on guard against carelessness and horseplay. Manufacturers of machines can insure against their breakdown by careful production, inspection, and instruction for use.

This third point of view seems to be the reasonable, correct one. In the final analysis, human failures somewhere along the line cause almost all industrial accidents. If the behavior of human beings were one hundred per cent perfect from beginning to end, there would be only a handful of injuries. But human beings are obviously far from perfect. The most one can hope for is improvement. One should never hesitate to settle for 75 or 80 per cent of perfection.

If we look only at the *immediate* causes of occupational injuries — that is, if we disregard, for example, the fact that an accident like a broken flywheel resulted from the carelessness of someone in the foundry that made the casting — we may classify these causes as "mechanical" and "human." The mechanical causes are those involving imperfections in machines, tools, and other equipment, as well as the dangers inherent in certain kinds of equipment and production processes. The human causes reside in both management and workers.

On the management side, there is often failure to provide proper light, heat, humidity, and ventilation; failure to guard dangerous machines and processes and in general provide good plant housekeeping; failure to alleviate the dangerous effects of fatigue by rest periods and shorter work periods; failure to select non-accident-prone workers for employment on hazardous jobs; failure to educate all employees, accident-prone or not, in safety-conscious methods of work and behavior; and failure to enforce approved safety codes and rules by appropriate disciplinary measure.

On the workers' side, we frequently find carelessness and disobedience in respect to known safety rules. But, as an increasing number of studies has shown, there is an important minority of workers who, although not truly or willfully ignorant, careless, callous, or disobedient, are scantily equipped to labor safely in inherently or potentially dangerous workplaces. Their reaction times are slow; they are unable to concentrate for more than very short periods; they have poor nerve-muscle coordination; or they have one or more physical defects such as poor vision or hearing. These are the so-called *accident-prone* workers (of any age group) whose employment on potentially hazardous jobs is almost a guarantee that accidents will happen.

If these are the causes of work accidents, whose is the major responsibility for eliminating or minimizing them? The responsibility of the workers, particularly if they are organized in a union, is not to be understated. Without their cooperation a plant safety program is doomed. But because the firm owns the machines, equipment, and processes and because the workers who labor thereon are subject to management's direction and control (in short, because management *is* management), the main responsibility would appear to rest on its shoulders.

Because the human causes of industrial accidents are so overwhelmingly important, management's accident-prevention problem is essentially one of human relations. The first step is of course to safeguard dangerous machines and processes, to provide good working conditions generally, and to limit the length of work-stretches to the capacities of workers. Before the work-week of five eight-hour days or less became the rule and before rest periods during the work-day were introduced, work periods were so long and continuous that fatigue set in and wore down the workers' resistance to accidents and disease. (Fatigue is defined as *cumulative* physical and nervous exhaustion — wear and tear not required because of insufficient rest and relaxation.) Workers came to lose the mental alertness and physical well-being needed to avoid injury in the presence of danger. But because of shorter work-stretches fatigue is much less common than previously. Nevertheless careless and indifferent workers who are ignorant of safe behavior get hurt in the absence of fatigue. It appears that the major problem today is to get the workers to cooperate in the use of safety devices and in generally careful behavior.

That management can successfully shoulder its responsibility for safety is not to be doubted. Evidence for this conclusion lies in the downward trend in accident frequency and severity, and particularly in the records of potentially very dangerous industries like coal mining and basic steel. In 1949 one of the most highly mechanized and hazardous industries — explosives — was the safest to work in, from the standpoint of the accidents that actually occurred.

Not all firms' managements have felt able or willing on their own initiative to undertake accident prevention work on an adequate scale. It then becomes the duty of government or labor unions to impose responsibility on the firms. These matters will be considered in later chapters. We may say here, however, that, where collective bargaining relations exist between managements and unions, the latter perforce must share with management the responsibility for plant safety.

2. Non-industrial accidents. Our handling of this topic will be very brief, since non-occupational accidents usually do not arise out of the employment relationship, at least not directly. It is true that if fatigue (as defined) exists among employees because of long work periods or other wearing work conditions, they may become more prone to injury away from their plants; here the plant employment relationship indirectly affects what happens elsewhere. It is true also that some employers, particularly those in isolated communities in the Southern and Mountain states, own the houses in which their employees live, own the stores in which the workers buy goods, and in fact control almost every aspect of the workers' lives. Under such circumstances, non-industrial accidents may be said to arise out of the employment relationship. Here an employer may be said to have a large measure of responsibility for the safety of his employees away from the plant. For example, his houses should be safely constructed and maintained. But where working conditions and work periods are satisfactory and where the relations between management and men are confined to the plant, non-occupational accidents are not, in any meaningful way, the responsibility of the employer.

In any case, all such injuries *affect* the employment relationship. They cause absence from work, which raises firms' costs and lowers workers' incomes. In fact the losses to workers (who are the focus of our present concern) are much higher than those from plant accidents. In 1949, when there were 15,000 industrial fatalities and a total of 1.9 million lost-time injuries (Table 29), there were 31,000 home accidents resulting in death, and a total of 4.7 million other home injuries causing loss of potential work time; and there were 45,000 accidental fatalities in public places (streets, highways, and so forth, including 30,000 deaths in which that great instrument of destruction, the automobile, was involved), and a total of 3.0 million non-fatal injuries in such places.

C. SICKNESS AMONG WORKERS

1. Occupational sickness. *a. Nature, extent, effects.* The spectacular manner in which industrial accidents usually happen and the suddenness with which sound workers are killed or crippled serve to impress the general public, as well as immediate observers, with the serious nature of the accident hazard as a menace to physical well-being. But there are other equally serious industrial hazards which threaten to kill and maim. They work more subtly, however. Although their total effects are in the end quite comparable to those of accidents, they operate unnoticed for months and perhaps years and almost never gain front-page attention from the newspapers. But wage-earners realize that among the chief enemies of their health are the conditions under which they have to labor.

Illnesses which are definitely the result of exposure to noxious working conditions over a period of time are known as *occupational diseases.* This definition is rather narrow; it includes only those trades which "definitely" give rise to diseases that are peculiarly industrial. It does not embrace occupations which produce no specific disease, but which may so weaken the employee that he falls an easy prey to other ordinary diseases like influenza. In actual practice, however, it is often very difficult to make distinctions. For example, a disease like tuberculosis may be found both within and without industry, but if it occurs persistently among a large proportion of the workers in an occupation, such as typesetting, there is reason in such cases for calling it a specific occupational disease.

The number of disease-breeding occupations is very large. Various students have attempted to classify them under main heads, but there is no general agreement. Some have used, as a basis for classification, the nature of the industrial process which produces the disease; others have used the nature of the disease as found among the workers. However, in practice most writers combine these two bases, as we do below. There seem to be nine major job groups in which one or more diseases are definite hazards.

1. *The dusty trades.* Here minute particles of matter are thrown into the air and inhaled by employees. There are two main kinds of dusty occupations

— those involving inorganic materials and those producing organic dust. The inorganic dusts are either metallic (such as those given off in foundry work, grinding and machine tool work, metal polishing, file cutting, iron and steel plants, and jewelry work) or mineral (such as those found in coal mines, glass plants, stone quarries, and rock drilling). The organic dusts are either vegetable fiber (such as those common to cotton, tobacco, flax, paper, and flour mills) or animal (such as those in woolen, fur, felt hat, and carpet factories). The action of dusts is either mechanically irritative or chemically poisonous. Irritation leads to obstruction of the air passages or fibrosis of the lungs and respiratory tract, which in turn results in tuberculosis, pneumonia, or other less serious respiratory diseases. The dusts which are chemically absorbed, such as mercury, lead, and tobacco, produce various deadly types of poisoning. Germs may also be inhaled with dust.

2. *The poisonous trades, other than dusty.* This group includes a great number of occupations in the metal, printing, and chemical industries, where substances like lead, brass, mercury, arsenic, formaldehyde, naphtha, and benzol are taken into the system by ingestion through the alimentary tract, inhalation of fumes, and possible absorption through the skin. Lead poisoning or plumbism is the chief killer and ruins the health and lives of workers wherever lead is used; its ravages are widespread in the printing trades, in the manufacturing and use of paints, in the pottery and enameling industries, and in lead smelting. The "hatters' shakes" is an expression long used to describe the palsy and ague which follow exposure to mercury in the process of making felt hats. The "brass chills" are the common result of inhaling zinc fumes in brass foundries. "Phossy jaw" signifies the necrosis or eating away of the bones which often happens to workers in plants using phosphorus. Carbon monoxide inhaled through the lungs and aniline absorbed through the skin poison the blood and sooner or later kill their victims. And so on. The list of diseases caused by the absorption of poisons could be extended almost indefinitely.

3. *Occupations producing germ diseases.* Infection by bacteria is likely in all work. Reference here, however, is to such cases as the infection of wage-earners in tanneries — and other plants or trades using animal products — by the anthrax germ through a break in the skin; and the infection of coal miners by the hook-worm parasite.

4. *Occupations producing skin infections.* Constant contact with irritating acids or other substances like powders and oils produce annoying, although seldom fatal, dermititis or eczema. Employees who work with radioactive substances, as do the painters of luminous watch dials, are very likely to die from damage to the skin and other body parts.

5. *Occupations involving extremes in temperature.* Work in factories where lacquering and japanning is done and in iron and steel plants and glass factories often requires sudden changes from great heat to cold, and vice versa. This leads to respiratory diseases and, because great quantities of water are drunk, to digestive disturbances.

6. *Occupations involving work in compressed or rarefied atmospheres.* Divers and subway or tunnel workers are often afflicted with "the bends" or caisson disease, which results from too sudden change from high to low pressures; it is characterized by the formation of air bubbles in the blood and may produce deafness, paralysis, convulsions, and death.

7. *Improper lighting.* This, if bad enough and prolonged sufficiently, may produce spasmodic eye movements such as miners' nystagmus.

8. *Occupations requiring constant use of certain parts of the body.* Continual use of a member of the body frequently produces neuritis (even in orchestra conductors) or cramp (as with telegraphers, stone cutters, and drillers who use pneumatic tools).

9. *Processes requiring artificial humidity.* The spinning and weaving of cotton, wool, flax, and silk necessitate a very damp air which is usually provided by artificial means. Together with a high temperature, this condition often leads to tuberculosis.

The extent, costs, and relative importance of occupational illness are indicated by the data presented in column 4 of Table 31 above. If we multiply the man-days-lost figure for a given year by an average daily wage, a total direct wage loss may be estimated. As with industrial accidents, to this estimate should be added the loss from higher product prices due to the costs of occupational diseases to employers. Unfortunately, there have been no authoritative efforts to obtain a figure such as the one developed by Heinrich for accidents. But there can be doubt about the deadliness of the occupational-disease hazard to workers' real incomes and general well-being.

b. Causal conditions. As in the case of non-occupational sickness, some workers are much more susceptible to occupational diseases than other workers; this difference may be based on inborn traits or environmental circumstances or both. As in the case of industrial accidents, some workers are careful to avoid contamination and to obey management's rules about using precautionary devices, such as nose masks and ventilators when working in dusty places. Other workers are careless, disobedient, or ignorant of what to do. In short, there are "human" causes of occupational disease; and among these, some are attributable to workers and subject to their assumption of responsibility and control.

Given the "mechanical" causes of such diseases, i.e., given the existence of production techniques and processes which expose workers to occupational sickness, employers — or employers and unions jointly — must assume the main responsibility for prevention or minimization. The argument here is the same as that outlined in our discussion of the causes of industrial accidents. Management is the chief agency in a position to control the installation of safety devices, the selection of employees less prone to contract the diseases, the education of employees to the use of safety devices, and the accumulation of fatigue from long work periods.

2. Non-occupational sickness and disability. *a. Nature, extent, effects.* By "non-occupational sickness" we mean, of course, illness that is not the specific result of a particular occupational hazard. We mean illness from diseases such as typhoid fever, pneumonia, and cancer, which are of general incidence among non-workers and workers alike.

As non-industrial accidents are to industrial ones, so non-occupational sickness is to occupational sickness. Non-occupational illness may or may not, directly, arise out of the employment relationship between firms and workers. But it certainly does affect this relationship.

Our interest here centers in several main questions: What are the latest figures on the incidence of non-industrial sickness? What has been the trend in the nation's health? Is the frequency and severity of non-occupational disease greater among those whom we have called "workers" than among non-workers? What are the costs of this kind of sickness? What is the ability of workers to bear these costs?

(1) Sickness disability in the population as a whole. There have been no comprehensive health surveys since World War II to give us a current view of sickness disability among American households. The thirties were the decade during which such studies were made, e.g., by the President's Committee on Medical Care and by the United States Public Health Service in its National Health Survey.

On the basis of these studies, however, we may make the following observations. On any given day, depending on the season of the year, between three and four per cent of the population are incapacitated by non-industrial sickness of varied duration. In any given year, close to half the population are free from disabling illness, about one-third are ill once, and the remaining fifth are ill two or more times. The frequency rate of sickness lasting more than six days is more than 160 cases per 1000 persons of all ages. If shorter-period illnesses were included, the rate would of course be much higher. The duration (severity) of illnesses lasting more than six days is about ten days per person in the population. But the number of days lost per sick person averages more than fifty, including those acutely ill for relatively short periods plus those chronically ill for long periods.

The experience of the armed forces with selective service registrants during World War II is also suggestive of the poor physical condition of a large segment of the population. Out of 16 million persons examined, half were found unfit for service. It is of course true that military standards of fitness for fighting are considerably higher than private industry's for employment.

(2) The trend. There are no time series of data on sickness frequency and severity. Therefore we are unable to note the trend in these items directly, as we did with industrial accidents. We are compelled to fall back on our knowledge of what has been happening to death rates from various causes. We know that the death rate has declined continuously for a number of decades (Table 2, page 60). This has been mainly the result of our successful efforts to control the diseases attacking young people, e.g., diphtheria and typhoid fever. If we had been equally successful in balking the attacks of the degenerative diseases that attack older persons (e.g., cancer and heart ailments), the decline in the death rate

would have been much greater. The net fall in the death rate has of course meant a considerable increase in the life expectancies of infants — for white infants, from about 50 years in 1900 to about 65 years in 1950. For older persons (above 60) there has been little change in the number of years they may expect to live.

Available information thus establishes a decline in *mortality* from disease. As to *morbidity,* i.e., non-fatal sickness, there are no conclusive data to make us sure that the nation's health has been improving.

(3) Workers versus non-workers. The mortality statistics of the Metropolitan Life Insurance Company for its male policy-holders show that the death rates of workers from illness are significantly above those of *all* its male policy-holders (including workers), especially in the age groups between 25 and 54, where the workers' rates are 50 per cent higher. If the data for the insured persons were broken down into those for male workers and non-workers, the differences would of course be even more marked.

This evidence is buttressed by other statistics which establish that the frequency and severity of non-fatal sickness is considerably greater among low-income households than among middle- and high-income families. Proportionately more worker than non-worker households are in the low-income group.

Among women, however, the severity of illness is greater among housewives than among the gainfully employed women. In general, the severity among females is higher than among males.

(4) Costs of illness. As in the cases of occupational injuries and illnesses, workers who become sick from non-occupational causes stand to lose work-time and income. And there is also always physical and mental discomfort and hardship. But, as we shall learn later in more detail, a considerable amount of medical care and compensation for loss of income is provided by government or employers for most workers seriously stricken by industrial accidents and disease. This is not nearly so true for workers suffering from non-industrial sickness.

As shown in Table 31, the estimated number of man-days lost from this source in 1947–50 was about 407 million — a much larger figure than those estimated for occupational injuries and illnesses. At an average daily wage of ten dollars, the direct wage loss comes to $4 billion. To this figure again would have to be added a very substantial sum reflecting the higher product prices resulting from costs borne initially by employers. These outlays include not only any contributions made by employers to private medical-care plans, plus any taxes paid for medical services provided by government, but also the costs of hiring and training workers needed to take the place of those who quit their jobs or are absent because of sickness, plus the losses involved in delays on the production line, additional record-keeping, and so on. No authoritative estimate of these costs has been made.

(5) Cost and distribution of medical care. In 1948, according to figures on income and expenditure published by the federal Department of Commerce, the people of the United States spent directly on medical care 3.7 per cent of their disposable private money incomes totaling more than $200 billion. The average per-capita cost of medical care was thus about fifty dollars ($7.5 billion divided by 150 million).

For purposes of perspective we may note also that considerably more was spent on alcoholic beverages (about 6 per cent) and on recreation (also about 6 per cent). Whether these expenditures bore one way or the other on the amount of illness, it is impossible to say.

In any case the distribution of the $7.5 billion spent for medical services was very unequal. A number of studies show that the *amount* spent per household rises sharply with size of income. Yet the percentage of income devoted to medical care falls substantially as income rises.

Of the total personal expenditure of $7.5 billion on medical care, it is impossible to say how much was spent by those we have designated as workers. Workers are three-fourths of the labor force; but since they reside mainly in the lower-income classes, their medical spending would not be in proportion to their numerical importance. Perhaps $2.5 billion would be a fair estimate of their expenditure on medical service. This figure added to the $4.0 billion wage loss gives a total cost of $6.5 billion — still without the addition of the unknown amount involved in employers' costs and reflected in higher product prices.

About one-third of the population is covered by some sort of hospitalization insurance, and a much smaller fraction has some kind of insurance protection against a part of the cost of physicians' services. In addition, a not insignificant amount of free medical care is provided in clinics to low-income patients. Yet it seems to be agreed that the supply of doctors, dentists, nurses, hospital services, and other medical facilities is far from adequate to meet over-all needs. And this is especially true for the low-income households, among whom we have said the frequency and severity of illness are highest.

b. Causes of non-industrial sickness. Why do people become ill? Who or what is to blame for sickness and for the inadequate amount of medical service? Here again we may conclude that the primary responsibilities are those of the workers themselves, of employers, and of the community (government). Some persons are *inherently* susceptible, some *inherently* resistant to disease. All are susceptible or resistant in part because of the unfavorable or favorable environmental conditions under which they work and live, and in part because of the neglect or the care they exhibit in following the rules of good health.

In so far as workers easily fall prey to disease for hereditary reasons, there is little that can be done. But the protection of such workers is important, and this fact emphasizes the necessity for maintaining favorable working and living conditions.

A favorable environment is little less important for workers who are constitutionally stronger. As already emphasized, persons subject to fatigue, strain, tension, and wet, noisy, hot, cold, dangerous, and otherwise unpleasant working conditions become prone to illness, no matter how inherently strong they may be. Long, unbroken work periods and low wage incomes are part of the circle of cause-effect relationships. Employers have the responsibility for making their working conditions as good as possible.

Poor housing, unsanitary living conditions, lack of attention to other aspects of public health, and ignorance of rules of health are equally important causes of high sickness frequency and severity. The responsibility for these things must rest mainly on the community's government — although where employers provide housing and other items of community living, they too must assume responsibility. A great deal can be done and has been done to raise the general level of community health by a thoroughgoing public-health program.

D. SUPERANNUATION AMONG WORKERS

1. Nature and extent of the problem. *a. Who are the "old" persons?* A superannuated person may be defined as one who because of his age is unable or unwilling to work, i.e., a person who for any reason related to his age is forced against his will to retire from participation in the labor force or does so voluntarily.

In this definition several points stand out. Lack of employment or participation in the labor force for this group is related to the age element. *Age* disability is the crux of the matter, not disability directly resulting from industrial or non-industrial accidents or from occupational or non-occupational sickness. True, injuries or illness may help to age a person prematurely. But persons who have never been injured or ill nevertheless reach a point where they are unable or unwilling to continue working. Some superannuated persons would like to be employed but cannot work because of some age factor. Others retire from work for reasons of age because they wish to retire, even though they might be able to work.

Our definition thus covers older workers under company pension plans or company rules who, although physically and mentally fit, are compelled to retire in order to obtain their pensions or to make way for younger workers; workers who have worn out physically or mentally and admit themselves to be unfit for further gainful employment; and workers who, although fit for further employment, wish to concentrate on the enjoyment of leisure for the rest of their lives. The definition does not include those aged 40 or more who, having lost their jobs for any reason, are willing and physically able to work but are unable to find jobs because of the age hiring limits of certain employers. This is to be thought of as a special problem of unemployment.

b. Why is superannuation a problem? We are concerned with superannuation among individual workers because of the income question. We may recognize the human problems that come from aging as such. But our main interest here must lie in the answer to the following questions: Are the persons whom we have called superannuated financially able to care for themselves when their wage incomes cease? How many such persons are there, and what is the extent of economic dependency among them?

(1) Extent of superannuation among workers. We are forced to say at once that there are no data telling us precisely how many superannuated persons there are (as we have defined that term) or what percentage of the total population and of their own age group they comprise. The best we can do is to obtain some hints from the statistics on age groups in the population and the labor force.

(a) Increased numerical importance of aged persons. The problem of superannuation and old-age dependency has *potentially* become one of greatly increased significance during the past half century because of the large increase in the numbers and population-proportions of persons aged 45 to 64 and persons aged 65 or more. Census data indicate that in 1900 there were 10.4 million in the 45–64 years group and 3.1 million in the 65-and-over group; these were, respectively, 13.7 per cent and 4.1 per cent of the total population of that year. In 1950, persons from 45 to 64 years old numbered 31.0 million, or 20.5 per cent of the population; and those 65 or over numbered 11.5 million, or 7.6 per cent of total population.

The reasons for this development include the decline in the birth rate, which tended to reduce the percentages of children in the population; the decline in the death rate from diseases attacking the younger persons, which has increased their life expectancies and allowed much larger percentages of them to reach maturity and old age; and the great reduction in the numbers of immigrants, who had been primarily below 45 years old.

(b) Increased economic opportunity? Whether, in the light of the changes just noted, the potentially greater problem has become an *actually* greater one depends on whether economic opportunity and income for the older workers has advanced in proportion to their numerical importance. Have the opportunities for being self-supporting increased as rapidly as the need? The remainder of our discussion is pointed toward answering this question.

i. Older workers in the labor force. We saw above that, in respect to population from 1900 to 1950, the percentage of persons aged 45 to 64 rose from 13.7 to 20.5 per cent, an increase of about 50 per cent in relative importance. At the same time the percentage of those 65 and over went up from 4.1 to 7.6 per cent, a rise of about 85 per cent. Let us assume for the moment that all these people in 1950 wished to obtain work.

Then the participation of these two age groups in the labor force should have risen by the same percentages (50 and 85 per cent).

Is this what actually happened? It almost did for the 45–64 group. In 1900 these persons comprised 20.4 per cent of those gainfully occupied, while in 1950 this group was about 29.9 per cent of the labor force, a rise of 46 per cent in relative numerical importance. But the 65-and-over group did not come close to matching its increase of 85 per cent in population percentage. In 1900 it was 4.0 per cent of the gainfully occupied, and in 1950 it was 4.8 per cent, a rise of only 20 per cent in relative numerical importance.

ii. Significance of the figures. We see, then, that *if* the groups of older workers were physically able to work and wished to work, the opportunities for doing so decreased from 1900 to 1950 for those 65 years and over. But we cannot be sure that nearly all of them did wish to work or were able to do so.

In the first place, the health of the members of this age group appears no worse than it used to be. Many more persons die of the old-age diseases (heart trouble, cancer, and so on) than formerly. But there are many more old persons, and the frequency and severity rates of these ailments seem not to have risen. True, the life expectancy of persons 65 years old (about 12 years) has not risen significantly; but neither has it fallen. We conclude that the physical ability of these persons to work has not been impaired.

In the second place, there may well have been a significant reduction in the desire of the over-64 group to continue working. It might be expected that, as a part of the general shift in preferences toward leisure a large percentage of these older workers might wish, if possible, to retire and "enjoy life." If this were true and if economic security were available to permit retirement, we would be no more justified in bemoaning the failure of this group's labor-force participation to keep pace with its population participation than we would in mourning the reduction of the length of the work-week from 72 to 40 hours.

Data supporting the notion that an increased proportion of older workers are willing to retire are those showing the percentages of the persons in each population age group which are in the labor force. Refer to Table 7, page 72. Here we see that the workers from 45 to 64 were in appreciably smaller percentage of all persons in their age group in 1950 than in 1920. For those aged 65 or more, the decline was even more marked.

What has been happening, then, for workers aged 20, 30, or 40 years is this: Their life expectancies have been rising at the same time that their work-life expectancies have increased scarcely at all. In other words, their retirement expectancies (the number of years of life remaining after retirement) have been increasing considerably.

Retirement at 65 has come to be considered the normal thing in

America. (Both governmental and union-company plans have settled on this age.) But this does not mean that many men (and women) over this age are not in the labor force. In 1950 2.9 million persons 65 years or over (25 per cent of the 11.5 million in this age group of the population) had jobs of some sort, according to estimates made by the Federal Security Agency on the basis of Census and other data.

iii. Estimate of superannuation. We may now approach a numerical estimate of superannuation for persons 65 and over in 1950. Let us assume that the 2.9 million just mentioned *wished* to continue working and, of course, were able. (This assumption may be valid in view of the income alternatives provided by government and private pension plans.) To this number add 0.9 million wives of these workers; our total is 3.8 million who were *not* superannuated in that year. The remainder of 7.7 million persons (67 per cent of those over 65)—beneficiaries of government or private pension programs or of their own savings or of assistance from relatives—may be considered members of the superannuated class. Of these, a little more than half were women; how many of these had been workers before reaching 65 cannot be ascertained.

The figure of 7.7 million does not include superannuated persons below 65 years of age. There are no data on these. In any case, we have a total figure which is more than 5 per cent of the whole population.

(2) Extent of economic dependency. By "economic dependency" we mean the condition under which superannuated persons are not self-supporting financially. The dependent aged have incomes and resources so low that they must be supported in whole or in part by relatives, friends, private institutions, or government. Under this definition we exclude those aged persons whose own savings are sufficient for their needs or who have economically sufficient incomes from pensions to which they are entitled by legal right under company, union, or government plans; the pensions are built up by their own and others' savings. We include as dependent those who are the objects of "charity" from their own relatives, friends, private or public "homes," or government.

Among the 7.7 million superannuated persons in 1950, 3.0 million were receiving private or public pensions as a matter of legal right, and 2.7 million were receiving benefit payments under the federal-state program of "old-age assistance," under which need or dependency must be proved before payments can be received. The figure of 2.7 million (35 per cent of the 7.7 million superannuated persons) undoubtedly represents economic dependency, as we have defined this term. But does the figure of 3.0 million represent economic independence? And does the remainder of 2.0 million (7.7 million minus 3.0 million minus 2.7 million) also represent independence? The answer to both questions is "no." Among the 3.0 million must have been many whose pensions were inadequate for maintenance; additional support from some source must have been received. And many of those not receiving benefit payments of any sort (legal or charitable) may nevertheless not have been self-supporting; many may have been living with grown children or other relatives or staying in "old people's homes."

We conclude that the 2.7 million recipients of federal-state old-age assistance represent the bare minimum of old-age dependency in 1950. But it is impossible to say how many more aged persons among the remaining 5.0 million superannuated ones were dependent in that prosperous year. As a matter of fact, some of the 3.8 million aged 65 or over whose incomes came from employment and whom we have excluded from our definition of "superannuated" may have come under our definition of "dependency"; their incomes may have been too low for full self-support. Evidence to this effect comes from Census data, which show that almost one-fourth of those employed at 65 or over are part-time rather than full-time workers.

We learned in Chapter 6 that unemployment is more frequent and severe among older workers than among those below 45 (except for the very young workers); and that the proportion of low-income households is considerably higher among the workers over 64. Both these facts point to old-age dependency.

More detailed income data are available than those mentioned in Chapter 6. The Bureau of Labor Statistics priced a modest but adequate budget for elderly couples living in large cities. In 1949 this budget averaged about $1700. Let us reduce this to, say, $1500 in order to allow for lower living costs in smaller communities. Then we find that, according to Census Bureau data on annual incomes, more than 80 per cent of all those aged 65 and over had incomes below $1500.

The percentages given above must not be considered to represent the extent of dependency, for we have not defined this term to mean any aged household receiving less than a stipulated amount of annual income. Such a definition might be proper. But living standards or goals are flexible things, and many an elderly couple prefer to maintain independence and self-respect by getting along at a level below $1500. In any case, the data do establish the likelihood of a high proportion of dependency among the aged.

Another bit of evidence is to be found in the data (pages 116–117) showing that the overwhelming bulk of savings is done and most of the liquid assets are held by the upper-income households. Most workers, being in the lower-income groups, do not have savings nearly high enough to care for their retirements in the absence of contributions regularly made to some pension plan from an early age. At an interest rate of 4 per cent, an annual retirement income of $1000 would require a saved fund of $25,000.

For more than thirty years various organizations and students of the problem have made estimates of the extent of old-age dependency (as we have defined the term) from time to time. These estimates, inconclusive for the 1950's (the latest one was for 1943) have ranged from 45 to 65 per cent of all persons aged 65 and over, or roughly 65 to 90 per cent of those we have called superannuated.

What has been the trend in extent of old-age dependency? The studies just mentioned probably lack comparability; it would be difficult to establish a trend from them. But we may reason as follows: When the country was mainly agricultural, old-age dependency was probably much less prevalent than during the first decades after it became mainly industrial and urban. This occupational and geographical change produced a notable increase in pace of work and a notable decline in opportunities for self-employment and in family care for aged members. During the later period (1900 to 1930) the extent of old-age dependency must have risen a great deal. As a result, there was a movement for private and government pension plans. This in turn, once the programs got under way, would serve to reduce the extent of dependency. But the plans had not really become widespread or showed their full effects by 1950; this must wait until perhaps 1970 or 1980. Consequently, it may well be that in 1950 at least 60 per cent of the superannuated and 40 per cent of all those over age 64 were dependent.

2. Effects of superannuation and dependency. Growing old is a sad business. The fact that aging and care for the aging have been perennial problems during all of man's history is small comfort to those who are reaching the end of their relatively healthy and productive lives. Most bitter of all is the knowledge or fear that retirement, instead of bringing recreation and happiness, will mean misery, unhappiness, and dependency on others, who are made unhappy too.

There is no need to dilate here upon the physical and mental suffering of aged dependents and paupers. As we have seen, all the problems of individual workers discussed in this section of the book bear down with special weight on the older workers and ex-workers. The dreariness and deadliness of life in most charitable institutions is well-known. Life with children or relatives or friends leaves little independence or happiness for either the old or the young. No self-respecting person of any age likes to be a burden on anyone else. Charity under any circumstances carries an unwanted stigma.

The problem of dealing with inevitable superannuation is thus to make it at least tolerable for those who experience it. This means that the health and happiness of persons 60 or 65 and over must be a matter of particular concern to those who are younger. Ways must be and are being found to make life after 60 healthy, self-respecting, and contented.

3. Causes of old-age dependency. Who or what are responsible for the existence of the problem? Thus far in man's history there has been no avoiding the matter of aging; everyone has to wear out and die. But why do so many have to die financially dependent?

Some people may believe that the workers themselves are to blame. The argument runs thus: Except for those who have had the hard luck to be permanently disabled by accident or disease, aren't most workers too stupid or lazy to give thought to saving for their retirement periods? This is a free country — every man for himself. Why, then, don't workers assume the responsibility that goes with freedom and provide for their own old age? If old-age dependency is so abhorrent when it comes, why don't workers strive mightily to avoid it by saving out of their work incomes when they are young?

This is a serious question, not lightly to be dismissed. In a society like ours, who *does* have the responsibility for building up a fund adequate to take care of the depreciation in the human machine? If the workers were slaves, one might reasonably expect employers to bear the full burden. But workers are not slaves. They are free to try to better their income positions. Why shouldn't they bear the full responsibility of caring for themselves?

Anyone trying objectively to answer this question must grant a certain amount of improvidence among many workers. He must also recognize that it is difficult for the average young worker to visualize and anticipate his needs and feelings many years hence. Again, he must admit that a large number of workers have incomes high enough to permit sizable savings if the workers were sufficiently impressed with the need for saving. But there are other facts that must be faced also. One is that all the sales managers in the country, through all the potent advertising media and with the application of all the best psychological principles appropriate to seduction, are constantly doing their best to get workers *not* to save. Competition in the ownership of various gadgets has become a social fetish. Another fact is that many workers' incomes are too low to permit adequate savings without serious inroads on the consumption spending necessary for minimum health and maintenance. Again, the accumulation of savings does not guarantee old-age independence. Many workers able to save seem to have concluded that the future utility of an anticipated competence after retirement is too uncertain to be worth the sacrifice in current consumption. They have experienced or heard about depressions and other economic misfortunes which wipe out the savings of many a household. Or they have seen how inflation can halve the current value of hard-won past savings. In view of all these circumstances one cannot judge workers too harshly for failing to provide for an independent old age.

If workers are not to carry the whole responsibility for the problem of old-age dependency, who may be asked to bear the rest of it? Employers are one group, at least in the first instance. They cannot fairly be saddled with the whole problem, for, as already stated, we live in a free society and workers are not slaves. But workers do depreciate under employers' managerial direction. Workers' alternatives are not so various and attractive that they can refuse to work under conditions contributing to superannuation. These conditions are subject to employers' control, and employers may fairly be asked to assume some of the burden of building up depreciation funds for workers' retirements.

In the long run, however, employers contribute only in the first instance. Their contributions are part of their costs and as such tend to be part of the prices paid by everyone (including workers) for products. In other words, the financial payments of employers tend to come not out of their profits but out of the income of the whole economy.

This brings us to the broader, social aspects of causal conditions. As already suggested in our discussion of trends in old-age dependency, the fundamental reason lies in the failure of economic opportunity and care for the aged to change commensurately with the shift in the age composition of the population and the work force. When the economy was mainly agricultural, self-employment on farms and small non-farm enterprises at a self-appointed speed of work was a major way of earning a living. Economic independence and self-reliance were much more prevalent than now. Caring for superannuated persons was much more commonly a matter of family responsibility. The industrialization and urbanization of the country changed most of this. Workers became dependent on employers. Employers' machines dictated the pace of work; the workers had to adjust themselves to the machine rather than vice versa. Families became smaller; young people left home; there was no one left to care for the aging patriarchs and their spouses.

The changes wrought by the technological and related revolutions in production were social changes, not brought on merely by the decisions and actions of any one individual or group, such as employers. Society has benefited tremendously from these changes, but they have also raised many serious problems, including that of old-age dependency, in respect to which there was a lag in social adjustment and solution. The main responsibility is that of society, through government. And, as will be shown in later chapters, society is now determined to acknowledge its responsibility and solve the problems.

E. REPRESSION AND AUTOCRACY

1. Nature, extent, effects. Any treatment of the labor problems of individual workers is incomplete that fails to deal with the loss in well-being caused by autocratic policies of employers and unions. Workers who have never been injured or sick and who have adequate, secure incomes are nevertheless not whole men if their basic needs for self-expression and social recognition are not met in the plant within which they work or in the union to which they belong.

As we saw in Chapter 2, nothing is truer than the proverb that man does not live by bread alone. The desire for self-expression and the urge for social approbation are major, fundamental parts of the over-all pattern of human needs. And the physical and social environments must provide outlets for all basic urges before all-round well-being can be experienced. Unfavorable environmental circumstances mean repression or inadequate expression for men's desires; and the result is dissatisfaction, unrest, and usually overt anti-social action of varying frequency and severity.

We do not mean to suggest that physical well-being and high, stable incomes do not contribute significantly to workers' self-respect and social esteem. They do. We are merely saying that they are not the whole story. There must be something more — the feeling that one is being treated as a man of importance rather than as a machine in the plant and as a co-equal rather than as a menial in the union. American workers are taught from early childhood to believe in the principles and practices of political democracy: self-determination, majority rule, respect for the rights of minorities, free elections, free speech, free assembly, and so on. But the practice of political democracy is ordinarily not a close, day-to-day experience for most workers. The kind of democracy that has most meaning to them is that provided where they work and where the union meets and operates. If they are prevented from practicing democracy there, they suffer repression and autocracy; there is a significant loss in total welfare.

In the last part of Chapter 6 we dealt with the effects of industrial autocracy on workers' employment opportunities and tenure. Here we are concerned with something else that is just as important: the lack of mental well-being that workers may experience while holding a job. Suppose that a given worker is male, white, and under forty years of age. He is able to get a well-paid job suited to his capacities — in spite of any possible discriminatory hiring practices by his firm against women, Negroes, and older workers. Yet he may be badly adjusted to his work. He and his fellows may restrict output and give other evidences of indifference toward their jobs and distrust of and resentment toward the management. What he needs, as a number of studies [2] have shown, is an assurance that his superiors recognize his worth and take an interest in his personal problems, a voice in determining the conditions under which he works, a knowledge of how his job fits into the whole productive process, a feeling that his job is important to management and fellow workmen, a feeling of teamwork — in short, a feeling that his role is important and his status respected. These studies have also shown that, when management tries sincerely to provide these things, workers' cooperation, as shown by higher output and regular attendance, has increased greatly.

Workers often feel that a union is the best or only way to achieve self-

[2] For a popular summary and selected bibliography of these studies, see Stuart Chase, *Roads to Agreement,* Harper and Brothers, New York, 1951.

determination and prestige. Employers who try on their own initiative to help the workers achieve these ends frequently find that their best and most sincere efforts are not enough, especially in large plants where top management is several levels above the workers and too distant from them, or in firms where the workers suspect that management is motivated by a desire to fend off unionism. The experience of the Harwood Manufacturing Corporation in Marion, Virginia, is a case in point. After a well-developed management-initiated program which elicited much greater output and cooperation, the workers nevertheless voted to be represented by the Ladies' Garment Workers' Union.

But suppose that an employer is aggressively anti-union. He is benevolent toward his workers as individuals, willing to give them a measure of self-expression and recognition as individuals. However, he wants no part of unions. Under these conditions the employee may be able to hold his job as long as he refrains from "talking union" or joining one and as long as he takes in silence many acts by his supervisors that he privately considers arbitrary and unjust. He is a "good boy"; and while he remains one, his employer may well do numerous things for him such as distributing Christmas baskets and providing group life insurance, sickness benefits, pensions, and so on. But behind this benevolent paternalism there is always the mute threat of what will happen if he stops being a good boy. In short, this worker has a job but he "burns up inside." And given the opportunity, by law or secret organization, he and many of his fellows will in time give overt, often violent expression to their pent-up feelings against their employer. This sort of thing has happened again and again in American labor history.

Suppose next that, in spite the employer's opposition to unionism, an organization among some of the men gets started, either spontaneously or through the efforts of an outside union organizer. American labor history is also replete with employers' hardboiled efforts to smash such organizations. In the old days, not only were known union members fired, but union organizers were beaten up and thrown out of town by company police or by the police of friendly local governments. Spies were planted within the union to learn about plans and to influence policies. Strikes were provoked, picket lines broken by police and armed guards, and strikers replaced by strikebreakers. It was this sort of opposition that made unionism a "movement."

Now suppose that a firm has none of these repressive characteristics. For many years it has permitted freedom of expression to its workers. They are organized in a union with which the employer has had friendly, cooperative relations. Collective bargaining agreements have been negotiated and adhered to in good faith. Workers' grievances under the labor agreement have been handled fairly and expeditiously by union and management representatives. And then there is a change in union officialdom. A power-seeking clique sweeps into leadership and ruthlessly quells any opposition to its policies. Gone is free expression of opposing opinions on controversial issues within union meetings. Dissenters are shouted down or thrown out by the clique's strong-arm henchmen. Under such circumstances the practice of democracy becomes a mockery. Here too is autocracy, this time imposed by labor.

Consider further the case of the worker who, while desiring freedom of expression and fair treatment from his employer, is so much an individualist that he dislikes power concentrations wherever he finds them; and to him this means wishing to stay out of the union. Suppose that the union and the firm have no agreement whereby the firm promises to hire and retain only union workmen. In other words, this worker is not forced to lose his job because of the union. But by staying out of the union, he is unable to get his grievances "processed." He is left without an adequate vehicle of expression. Is he too a victim of industrial autocracy? Many would say he is. Many others would deny this, or would agree at least that the loss in self-expression suffered by him is the result of a decision that he himself was free to make.

What are the criteria by which one can judge whether labor autocracy or labor democracy exists for individual workers within a given firm or union? From what has already been said, it is clear that a firm is operating democratically if its workers are given a meaningful voice in the determinations of the conditions under which they work — wage rates, length of work periods, physical working conditions, job tenure, handling of grievances, and so on. "Meaningful voice" refers, of course, to the workers' freedom to organize unions if they wish. Experience has demonstrated that, except in small plants, almost the only way in which workers can be significantly and respectedly vocal about their desires is through self-organization.

It is clear also that a union's affairs are being conducted democratically if all the principles of political democracy mentioned earlier in this section are being conscientiously practiced by both leaders and ordinary members.

How much autocracy and repression, whether practiced by management or by union, exist in industry in the United States today? To this question there can be no statistical answers like those we gave in respect to accidents and illness. But of the trend there can be little doubt. On the employers' side, there is a very great deal less than there used to be. All but the subtlest forms of employer opposition to unionism have been outlawed by statute for many years (since 1935). Under government protection and encouragement (a tremendous shift from the former attitude and policies) unionism has reached unprecedented heights of numerical and financial strength and economic and political power.

On the side of organized labor, the rise of big unionism has of course increased the possibility of intra-union autocracy. But it is to be doubted that there has been anything like a proportionate actual rise in this form of repression. The public spotlight has been focused on union affairs as never before. And government itself has provided some statutory protections for individual union members.

2. *Causal factors.* Why does autocracy exist in the field of labor? Why does it exist or why has it existed in some firms and unions and not in others? Why have there been changes from autocracy to democracy in many firms and in some unions?

Complete and precise answers to these questions are not possible. We do not know enough about human individual and group behavior and its variants to draw up a thoroughgoing scheme of causation. We shall therefore have to content ourselves with some suggestions.

Some persons would maintain that the system of private enterprise, profits, and "capitalism" is to blame. If this system is the culprit, how do we account for the fact that under it some firms and unions have practiced labor democracy while others have not? How do we account for the trends toward democracy noted above? And how are we to explain the autocracy in socialist, non-capitalistic Russia and its satellite countries, where free labor unions are not even permitted to exist? To say that labor democracy is practiced in the political field in those countries is no answer; for there is no political democracy either.

Does the responsibility lie with the technological revolution, which made possible unprecedented gratification for men's desire to achieve power through large-scale monopolistic organization of production? We may say at once that technological progress, by requiring huge amounts of capital for the purchase of big, complicated machinery, was a major factor in the development of the corporation. It has had a great deal to do with the trend toward the *centralization* of power in government as well as in business and unions. In a complex, interdependent world of large organizations someone must have the authority to make decisions quickly. Town-meeting democracy is too slow and cumbersome; responsible representative democracy is the best that can be hoped for. Thus, we may say that technology made modern industrial autocracy possible or *more likely.* From the great height at the top of a corporate or union empire it is easy to forget that responsibility must go with power. It is easy to be ignorant or indifferent about the problems, needs, and rights of groups one does not often see or hear from — much easier than in a small firm, where the owner has close, daily contacts with his workmen. But big business does not *have* to be autocratic in its relations with workers, consumers, and stockholders. Many big corporations are operated with due regard for the rights of these other groups. The same holds for big unionism.

Granted that technological advance made autocracy more likely, what made it an actuality in many firms and in some unions? Autocracy certainly did not arrive with the revolution in technology. It is about as old as man himself. The technological revolution was barely getting under way in England when the political revolution in France deposed some of the outstanding autocrats of the time. Moreover, Russia had Genghis Khan, Ivan the Dread, and other despots long before technology was raised beyond the primitive agricultural level in that country. These facts suggests that the answer to our question lies primarily in the conditions affecting human behavior and human relations.

In broad outline we may say that, given the hereditary basis of man's behavior, his relations with other human beings depend largely on prevailing social attitudes and beliefs. In the nineteenth century, after the technological revolution had gotten under way and after the political and religious revolutions had established economic, political, and religious democracy as the accepted way of life, free rein was given to the individual pursuit of economic gain, "salvation," and other personal goals. It was doubtless believed that organizations would be so small, and relationships among human beings so close and personal, that responsibility commensurate with power would be enforced through face-to-face contacts. But technological progress intervened to make organizations large. Close relationships disappeared in many sectors of society. Opportunities for autocratic relations multiplied. A tremendous lag developed in social beliefs. And it was not really until the bitter experiences of the Great Depression in this country (1930–32) that the gap between social thinking and the realities of economic-political life began to be closed. The change in society's beliefs and policies was effectuated by government. Government, expressing the will of a large majority of the voters, decided to enforce the responsibility for labor democracy on those firms which it felt had avoided such responsibility. The change was tremendous. Unionism grew apace, favored also by prosperous economic conditions and a high demand for labor. A decade later a majority of the voters asked government to impose a higher degree of responsibility on big unionism.

This discussion brings us to the end of Section A in Part Two, which has focused on the major problems of individual workers. As already suggested, for many decades workers have tried to do something about their problems, partly by organizing in unions and dealing with employers and government through unions, and partly by dealing directly with government as voters. In Section B of Part Two, to which we now pass, we shall consider American unionism — not only in relation to the problems of the individual workers who belong to the unions but also, perhaps mainly, in respect to the problems of the unions as organizational entities.

PART TWO

The Labor Problems of Private Groups

SECTION B

The Problems of Labor Unions

CHAPTER 10

The Development and Present Status of American Unionism

A. THE NATURE OF UNIONISM

1. Unionism as collective action. In Part One of this book and in Section A of Part Two we have given detailed consideration to the questions of what individual workers want and the extent to which these wants have been and are being satisfied. In Chapter 2 we learned that men desire freedom, security, and progress in attaining such things as physical survival, material comforts, power over other men and over things, social recognition, and self-expression (a voice in determining the conditions affecting the degree to which their other goals are achieved). In Chapters 6–9 we studied the extent to which all these objectives have been realized by individual workers. We looked at their circumstances in respect to job security and tenure, wage income, and physical and mental well-being. We noted real progress toward the attainment of their goals.

One of the reasons for this progress — only *one* of the reasons but an important one — has undoubtedly been the rise of unionism to a position of power and eminence. Most students appear to believe that workers have gone farther through collective action than they would have as individuals. They have achieved higher levels of all-round want-satisfaction through the strength developed by organization than they would have if they had remained individually weak in the face of powerful employers. For, as the employing units expanded in size and in economic and political potency, individual workers' freedom of choice or decision and range of alternatives became increasingly restricted. They came to have little voice in or control over any of the terms of employment under which they worked. This would not have happened in the idealized perfectly competitive economy where employers as well as workers are visualized as atoms. But it did happen in the real world where, as the level of technology rose, significant elements of monopoly and monopsony developed among employers as individual units and in formal or informal associations. As a result, workers in many fields long ago yielded to the universal human urge for *organization* to attain their goals. Frustrated in greater or less degree in their individual efforts, they decided to form unions.

However, whether or not these unions have brought workers closer to the attainment of their objectives is not really our main interest at this point in our discussion. Our chief concern here is that many workers must have *believed* that unions *would* mean a net gain in welfare. True, union members must bend their necks to the collective will; and for many, this loss of freedom to make certain decisions of their own must involve considerable disutility. But usually the members can participate democratically in the collective decision-making; this involves utility for them. And the strength of the group enables them to obtain many concessions otherwise unattainable or only partially attainable. To most workers, then, the utilities outweigh the disutilities. They believe in or envision a net gain in satisfaction.

Unionism thus means essentially that workers undertake group or collective decision-making and action at the same time that employer's alternatives and freedoms in decision-making are restricted. In other words, when collective dealings are substituted for individual-worker dealings with employing units, the workers expect substantial improvement in their relative bargaining positions. And thereby they expect to achieve greater net total want-satisfaction.

The collective action of unions may not be and usually is not confined to bargaining with the firms employing union members. It is also brought to bear on various agencies of government whenever government action on one or more matters is deemed necessary. In other words, the political aims and methods of unionism may be just as important as those that are more directly economic.

2. The complexity of unionism. American unionism today is "big business." There are more than 200 unions of national scope, tens of thousands of local units, and many federations among these local and national units. Some fifteen million workers belong to them, and many big, basic industries are almost completely unionized. The economic and political potency of the labor movement is tremendous, rivaling if not exceeding that of employers.

All these organizational units of labor have certain important characteristics in common. Yet, for reasons to be developed in more detail later on, there are also significant differences among them. There is no such thing, really, as a typical union or a typical kind of unionism. There are almost as many types as there are unions.

The specific reasons for differences among unions will be considered toward the end of the next chapter. In general, the reasons lie in differing environmental circumstances among trades and industries, and in differing kinds of human reactions, among union members and union leaders, to the industrial and political environment. For in the broadest sense unionism as a whole, and the ways in which particular unions are organized and the things that various unions do, are social group responses to environmental conditions. Just as an individual biological organism develops a certain structure and a certain pattern of functional reactions to its environment, so a social organism like a labor union works out by trial-and-error experimentation what seem to it the most effective form of organization (structure) and the most effective policies and tactics (functions).

Unlike subhuman organisms, human beings and their organizations are able to exert significant *control* over their environments. That is, the structures and functions of human associations are not directed merely toward adaptation to environmental conditions. They also are pointed in part toward changing these conditions for their own purposes. Consider, for example, the great change in the industrial environment brought about by the National Labor Relations Act, which was sponsored by unions and which compelled employers to discard many of their anti-union weapons.

The structural and functional differences among unions will become apparent in our brief survey of union history below. We may note here, however, a few important ones. Structurally, a labor organization in a given plant may be composed only of skilled workers having a given homogeneous occupational background and training; or it may include all the workers in the plant, unskilled as well as skilled; or a labor organization may include the workers in many plants without regard to occupational, plant, or company distinctions. The first kind of union is known as a *craft* union, the second as an *industrial* or *plant-wide* union, and the third as a *labor* union. As already suggested, there may also be loose *federations* of autonomous unions. Another structural difference lies in geographic or area coverage: A *local* union (craft or industrial) is made up of members from one or more plants in the same locality. A *district* union is composed of local unions in a given economic or political region. A *national* union embraces all the locals of the craft or industry in the whole country. Federations of unions may also be local, state-wide, or national.

Functional differences of policy and tactics to be watched for in our survey of the history of the American labor movement are these: Is the union strictly a business one, i.e., does it concentrate almost wholly on an economic program, or does it go in mainly or importantly for political action? Economic- or political-minded or both, does a union accept the existing private enterprise organization of society, or does it wish to alter the social order? If the latter, does it want to have violent revolution now or soon, or is it willing to work for the change, e.g., democratic socialism, peacefully and gradually? Whether conservative or radical, is a union militant, aggressive, and warlike in its immediate relations with employers, or is it friendly and cooperative? Whether militant or cooperative, is it honest and straightforward in its dealings, or are the militancy and cooperation cloaks for double-dealing, extortion, and the like? A given union may have been all these things from time to time during its history, depending on the nature of environmental conditions and the nature of leaders and members.

3. Unions as organizational entities. In Chapter 2, we said that a social organization, like a biological organism, is composed of various cells or parts; yet the whole is much more than the mere sum of its parts. So with a labor union; it is much more, structurally and functionally, than the sum of its members. It is a configuration of membership and leadership organization — a pattern in which the members, committees, officers, and so on are arranged in certain relationships with each other. This means that a union, while it could not exist apart from and without its membership, has a life of its own as a total entity. And this life is apart from the separate lives of the members who compose the union. Sometimes the union will do certain things that are directed toward assuring the survival or the progress of the union as such, entirely apart from the immediate interests of the individual members.

From the internal point of view, a labor union is inevitably a *political* organization. (The term "political" here has nothing to do with the term as used above, when we mentioned unions' relations with and attitudes toward civil government.) This is because it is composed of human beings who react to each other in various ways and who must elect officers, committees, and so on, if the business of the organization is to be carried on. (Let the student review the latter part of Chapter 2 on this point.) Within a union as a political entity there may be opportunities for individual workers to practice democratic principles in ways and in frequency that would not otherwise be available. Workers thus may find much satisfaction within the organization as such. It represents a charter of freedom for them.

4. Unionism as a movement. In Chapter 2 we noted that, when certain groups try to organize and other groups resist such organization, the drives of the former tend to become "movements." Unionism fits this characterization perfectly. From the beginning, the labor movement exhibited all the traits mentioned on page 23.

5. Definition of union. From all the above, a labor organization or union may be defined as a free, voluntary association of workers organized for the common purpose of attaining the workers' and the union's objectives through collective bargaining with appropriate employers and through collective dealings with government.

6. This chapter's plan of discussion. In the sections which follow in this chapter and the next, we shall consider, first, the statistical evidence of organized labor's growth and present position; and second, the actual history of its development in terms of environmental conditions and changes, and of structural and functional manifestations and changes. The final section will be the most important one: It will summarize the "lessons" from union history in terms of the environmental determinants and the structural and functional responses and policies that have brought unionism to its present eminence.

B. STATISTICS OF UNION GROWTH AND STRENGTH

1. Introduction. The strength and influence of any organization or movement cannot be measured merely in numbers. Nevertheless, a study of statistics on union membership over a period of years does give some indication of present and past importance and of rising or falling strength.

Figures on union membership should not be accepted blindly; they doubtless fall short of being completely accurate and reliable. The published reports of particular unions in any given year may be "padded" or may understate actual membership. For example, a union might wish to conceal from outsiders statistical evidence of losses it had suffered during the year; it might well overstate its membership. On the other hand, a union might wish to conceal evidence of growth or strength; here understatement would be in order. National unions belonging to the American Federation of Labor or the Congress of Industrial Organizations pay per-capita taxes or assessments to these federations. The larger the membership is, the higher the total payment must be to the federation. A union can save money by understating its numerical strength. Again, if a union reports only dues-paying members, the membership figure will fail to include members temporarily relieved of dues payment because of unemployment or work stoppages.

Nevertheless, the statistical story of union membership can be accepted without too much reservation. When the membership figures of all unions are added together, many of the discrepancies cancel out. Certainly long-run changes in total union membership are discernible.

What do we wish to know about union membership? First, what trend is shown in the total membership over a period of years? Second, and much more significant, what percentage has *actual* membership been of *potential* membership? Third, in what union groups has the membership been concentrated? Fourth, in what major industrial fields and specific industries?

2. Total actual and potential union membership. *a. Changes in actual membership.* Study the data in Table 32. The figures in column 3 tell us certain definite things about trends in union membership. During the half century from 1897 to 1947 the numerical strength of American unions rose by about 3400 per cent. There have also been cyclical fluctuations in

TABLE 32 *Total Labor Force (1900–1950), Union Membership (1897–1950), and Percentage of Union Membership to Total Labor Force*

Year	Total Labor Force (in thousands)	Union Membership (in thousands)	Per Cent (3) is of (2)
1	2	3	4
1897	[1]	440	[1]
1898	[1]	467	[1]
1899	[1]	550	[1]
1900	29,025	791	2.7
1901	29,959	1,058	3.5
1902	30,905	1,335	4.3
1903	31,842	1,824	5.7
1904	32,605	2,067	6.3
1905	33,653	1,918	5.7
1906	34,647	1,892	5.5
1907	35,631	2,077	5.8
1908	36,580	2,092	5.7
1909	37,454	1,965	5.2
1910	38,133	2,116	5.5
1911	38,668	2,318	6.0
1912	39,089	2,405	6.2
1913	39,500	2,661	6.7
1914	39,789	2,647	6.7
1915	40,083	2,560	6.4
1916	40,314	2,722	6.8
1917	40,752	2,976	7.3
1918	41,088	3,368	8.2
1919	41,159	4,046	9.8
1920	41,897	5,034	12.0
1921	42,445	4,722	11.1
1922	42,966	3,950	9.2
1923	43,760	3,629	8.3
1924	44,549	3,549	8.0
1925	45,009	3,566	7.9
1926	45,962	3,592	7.8
1927	46,939	3,600	7.7
1928	47,914	3,567	7.4
1929	48,354	3,625	7.5
1930	49,006	3,632	7.4
1931	49,597	3,526	7.1
1932	50,132	3,226	6.4
1933	50,691	2,857	5.6
1934	51,267	3,249	6.3
1935	51,769	3,728	7.2
1936	52,237	4,164	8.0
1937	52,692	7,218	13.7
1938	53,229	8,265	15.5
1939	53,811	8,980	16.7
1940	53,466	8,944	16,7
1941	54,156	10,489	19.4
1942	54,859	10,762	19.6
1943	55,564	13,642	24.6
1944	56,184	14,261	26.0
1945	56,769	14,796	26.1
1946	57,520	14,974	26.0
1947	60,168	15,414	25.6
1948	62,748	15,500 [2]	24.7
1949	63,571	15,500 [2]	24.4
1950	64,599	15,500 [2]	24.0

Source: Column 2 — *Historical Statistics of the United States*, U. S. Bureau of Census, Table Series D 62–76, p. 65, for the years 1900–1947; subsequent years from *Annual Reports on the Labor Force*,

total membership. During prosperous and inflationary periods membership tends to rise, as during World Wars I and II. During business downswings and depressions membership tends to fall, as in 1921 and 1931–33.

But, as we shall see later, membership is affected by many conditions other than those producing business cycles. By and large, the years from 1895 to 1900 were subnormal in business activity. Yet unionism grew rapidly in those years, as indeed it continued to do in the prosperous years from 1900 to 1904. On the other hand, business continued prosperous until the close of 1907, whereas union membership stopped growing in 1904. Again, after the drop in membership during the 1921–22 depression, there was no recovery to match the business prosperity of 1923–29. But after 1933, during the depressed thirties, union membership trebled by 1939. In short, there have been spurts of growth followed by leveling-off plateaus, unrelated in any direct way to business fluctuations. It is entirely possible that unionism entered another plateau period about 1947.

b. Actual versus potential membership. (*1*) *The statistics of Table 32.* Columns 2 to 4 of Table 32 show the relationship of total union membership to the total number of persons in the labor force since 1897. It should be clearly understood that the labor force data in column 2 do not represent total potential union membership, for, as explained in Chapter 5, they include *all* who work for a living and receive money compensation for their efforts. That is, these figures include self-employed persons (farmers and professional persons) and managerial employees as well as those we have called "workers." Nevertheless, to relate union membership to the labor force as a whole is not without significance. If the percentage of the labor force belonging to unions has risen substantially during the past half-century, we are justified in concluding that the power of unionism has risen at a similar pace.

This indeed is the conclusion to which Table 32 leads us. Since the middle of World War II, organized labor has had about 25 per cent of the nation's labor force on its rolls. The percentage began a notable increase in 1937, when the C.I.O.'s organizing efforts started to bear fruit. Before 1937 the proportion had never been as high as 10 per cent except during the years immediately after World War I. The percentages dur-

---

Bureau of Census. The data for 1940 and subsequent years are not strictly comparable with the figures for the years prior to 1940. The data for 1940 forward are based on the labor force concept adopted in 1940. The data for prior years are based on the gainful worker concept. The 1940 figure, using the gainful worker concept, would have been 54,308,000. For a discussion of the differences in the application of the two concepts, see *Historical Statistics of the United States*, pp. 55–56.

Column 3 — U. S. Bureau of Labor Statistics, *Handbook of Labor Statistics*, 1947, p. 130, and subsequent releases of the Bureau.

Column 4 — computed.

[1] Not available.

[2] For the years 1948–50 the U. S. Bureau of Labor Statistics estimated total union membership at from 14,000,000 to 16,000,000. Data are not available for a more definite estimate. A rounded figure close to the 1947 one has been arbitrarily chosen here.

ing the first decade of the century averaged little more than 5 per cent, and they were not much higher from 1925 to 1935.

(2) *Other data.* Since the data in Table 32 do not purport to compare actual with potential union membership, we must turn to figures that do. That is, we must reduce the labor force figures for recent years in Table 32 to those representing organizable *workers* eligible for union membership and sought after by unions. Table 9 (page 74) provides a clue. By excluding professional, proprietary, and managerial persons (including farmers and farm managers) we obtain a figure of 46.6 million wage and salary workers. Union membership is 33 per cent of these workers, a much higher proportion than the 25 per cent mentioned above.

But perhaps even this higher percentage unfairly understates the numerical potency of organized labor. For a number of reasons (including lack of interest, anti-union attitudes, scattered location, and the migratory nature of the workers) white-collar workers, farm laborers, and domestic servants have been found hard to unionize and hard to hold as union members, once organized. They are not regarded as good union material and thus far have not been sought after with anything like the organizing resources and energies employed in transportation, manufacturing, mining, and other fields. If these poor prospects are excluded, our potential membership figure is reduced to 24.5 million. Actual membership in the "eligible" fields is about 14.0 million, or 57 per cent of the potential.

3. Workers affected by union agreements and union sentiment. The influence of American unionism is wider than that suggested by the percentage mentioned above. First, in trades, in plants, or firms where the terms of employment are determined by collective bargaining between management and labor and where union membership is not a condition of getting or holding a job (i.e., where some form of the union shop does not prevail), there are often sizable fractions of the work force who do not belong to the unions involved. Yet their wage rates and other employment conditions are set by the union-employer agreements. Surely such workers are very much within the power orbit of unionism. On this point consider the specific industries listed in Table 33 for the year 1946. In many manufacturing and non-manufacturing industries and occupations very large percentages of the workers, non-union as well as union, had their terms of employment set by union action and agreement.

Second, so great is the effect of key labor contracts negotiated by major unions that the union terms of employment significantly affect those of workers in wholly non-union plants. The threat of unionization has always had important influences on the wage-rate and other decisions of non-union employers. By providing employment terms as good as or better than those obtained or promised by outside unions, employers tried to forestall the organization of their workers by such unions. The example of unionism is more potent today than ever before.

TABLE 33 *Proportion of Wage-Earners under Union Agreements in 1946*

MANUFACTURING INDUSTRIES				
80–100 per cent	60–79 per cent	40–59 per cent	20–39 per cent	1–19 per cent
Agricultural equipment Aircraft and parts Aluminum Automobiles and parts Breweries Carpets and rugs, wool Cement Clocks and watches Clothing, men's Clothing, women's Electrical machinery Furs and garments Glass and glassware Leather tanning Meat Packing Newspaper printing and publishing Nonferrous metals and products, except those listed Rayon yarn Rubber Shipbuilding Steel, basic Sugar	Book and job printing and publishing Coal products Canning and preserving foods Dyeing and finishing textiles Gloves, leather Machinery, except agricultural equipment and electrical machinery Millinery and hats Paper and pulp Petroleum refining Railroad equipment Steel products Tobacco Woolen and worsted textiles	Baking Chemicals, excluding rayon yarn Flour and other grain products Furniture Hosiery Jewelry and silverware Knit goods Leather, luggage, handbags, novelties Lumber Paper products Pottery, including chinaware Shoes, cut stock and findings Stone and clay products, except pottery	Beverages, nonalcoholic Confectionary products Cotton textiles Dairy products Silk and rayon textiles	None
NON-MANUFACTURING				
80–100 per cent	60–79 per cent	40–59 per cent	20–39 per cent	1–19 per cent
Actors and musicians Airline pilots and mechanics Bus and streetcar, local Coal mining Construction Longshoring Maritime Metal mining Motion-picture production Railroads Telegraph Trucking, local and intercity	Radio technicians Theater-stage hands, motion-picture operators	Bus lines, intercity Light and power Newspaper offices Telephone	Barber shops Building servicing and maintenance Cleaning and dyeing Crude petroleum and natural gas Fishing Hotels and restaurants Laundries Non-metallic mining and quarrying Taxicabs	Agriculture [1] Beauty Shops Clerical and professional, excluding transportation, communication, theaters and newspapers Retail and wholesale trade

Source: *Monthly Labor Review,* Vol. 64, No. 5, May, 1947, p. 766.
[1] Less than 1 per cent.

Third, in recent years unionism has entered more American households than ever before. It is in the air. Except in the three low-organization fields mentioned previously, and in certain areas (mainly in the South) that have remained largely non-union, there are relatively few worker-households who do not contain a union member or who do not know intimately some other union household. In polling a sample of all sorts of households in all walks of life on the question, "Are you, or is anybody in your family, a member of a labor union?" one study [1] found that almost a third of the households had husband, wife, or other family member in a union. But the percentage would have been much higher if the study had been limited to workers' families.

4. Extent of interest in unions by members. We may grant, then, that the army of American unionists is large, influential, and formidable. Before looking further into its composition, however, we must ask an important question: What percentage of this army is made up of members who are actively interested in union affairs — interested enough to run for union offices, attend meetings regularly, vote and debate on policy questions, perform union functions, and otherwise exert themselves in behalf of the labor movement?

This is an important question. It is applicable to any organization of human beings — church, fraternity, lodge, political party, and so on. To say that most members are actively interested in an organization is to suggest that the organization is filling a vital need in their lives and fully commands their loyalty, cooperation, and respect. On the other hand, to say that most members are passive participants in an organization's affairs may mean a number of different things. It could mean that the organization is weak and unable to win a fight for victory or survival. But such a conclusion does not necessarily follow. In a fight the interest of passive members might be quickly and easily activated. It all depends on how closely the members identify their own interests with those of the organization as an entity. When the going is easy and routine, many Americans are inclined to busy themselves with personal affairs and leave the operation of their organization in the hands of those who, for one reason or another, like to be active participants. But when the life or progress of the group is threatened, most members usually rally to its support.

In any case, to leave the organization in the hands of a minority during "normal" times is to avoid the assumption of democratic responsibilities and the practice of democratic principles. It is also to invite the possibility of usurpation of power by minority factions or use of the organization for personal aggrandizement by self-seeking officers.

[1] See C. W. Mills and T. E. Anderson, "People in the Unions," in G. B. S. Hardman and M. F. Neufeld, eds., *The House of Labor*, Prentice-Hall, New York, 1951, pp. 48–49.

No definitive study has been made to answer the question posed above. However, some persons close to the labor movement have estimated[2] that out of 15.5 union members only a little more than two million are active. If correct, this estimate states that only about 15 per cent (one member out of seven) exhibit a direct and active concern in union operations.

5. Membership in main union groupings. Organized labor in the United States has never been monolithic or united in objectives and policies. It has always been split into two or more main groups of national unions on various grounds. It is split today.

In 1950 there were about 210 national unions ("international" if local units existed in Canada or other neighboring countries). There were some 70,000 local unions, the vast majority of which belonged to the national unions. The national union is the organizational unit of overwhelming importance in the labor movement. Although it and its local units may belong to one or more federations, it retains its autonomy or sovereignty; it is essentially free to make its own decisions in pursuit of its own objectives.

a. The A.F.L., C.I.O., and other groups. Among the national unions there was great variety in affiliation with one another and in size, age, structural make-up, and functional manifestations. The largest group of national unions (107) belonged to the American Federation of Labor. The Federation's total membership was about 7.1 million, which included not only the combined numerical strength of the 107 national unions but also that of some 1700 local unions which, not belonging to any national organization, were directly affiliated with the A.F.L. The second largest group of national unions (30) were affiliates of the Congress of Industrial Organizations, whose total membership in 1950 was about 5.5 million.

The remaining 70 or so national unions are known usually as "independent"; that is, they do not belong to either of the two great federations, A.F.L. and C.I.O. Their membership in 1950 totaled about 2.9 million, or almost 20 per cent of the country's unionists. As might be expected, the differences among these independents were wide.

Among the unaffiliated unions were six railroad unions, led by the "big four" train-operating brotherhoods — the Locomotive Engineers, the Firemen, the Conductors, and Trainmen. These unions were "conservative" or "right wing" in policies. For common action on problems arising in the railroad industry, the chief executive officers of the Brotherhoods were organized in the Railway Labor Executives' Association with the leaders of fifteen A.F.L. unions and one C.I.O. union whose memberships were also wholly or partly in that industry.

A second group of unaffiliated unions might be called the "non-railroad

[2] See J. B. S. Hardman, "State of the Movement," in Hardman and Neufeld, *op. cit.*, p. 62.

TABLE 34

Labor Union Membership: 1897 to 1950

Year	All Unions Total Membership	American Federation of Labor			Congress of Industrial Organizations			Independent or Unaffiliated Unions	
		Number of Affiliated National Unions	Total Membership		Number of Affiliated National Unions	Total Membership		Total Membership	
			In Thousands	Per Cent of All-Union Total		In Thousands	Per Cent of All-Union Total	In Thousands	Per Cent of All-Union Total
1	2	3	4	5	6	7	8	9	10
1897	440	58	265	60				175	40
1898	467	67	278	60				189	40
1899	550	73	349	63				201	37
1900	791	82	548	69				243	31
1901	1,058	87	788	75				270	25
1902	1,335	97	1,024	77				311	23
1903	1,824	113	1,466	80				358	20
1904	2,067	120	1,676	81				391	19
1905	1,918	118	1,494	78				424	22
1906	1,892	119	1,454	77				438	23
1907	2,077	117	1,539	74				538	26
1908	2,092	116	1,587	76				505	24
1909	1,965	119	1,483	76				482	24
1910	2,116	120	1,562	74				554	26
1911	2,318	115	1,762	76				556	24
1912	2,405	112	1,770	74				635	26
1913	2,661	111	1,996	75				665	25
1914	2,647	110	2,021	76				626	24
1915	2,560	110	1,946	76				614	24
1916	2,722	111	2,073	76				649	24

TABLE 34 (continued)

1917	2,976	111	2,371	80				605	20
1918	3,368	111	2,726	81				642	19
1919	4,046	111	3,260	81				786	19
1920	5,034	110	4,079	81				955	19
1921	4,722	110	3,907	83				815	17
1922	3,950	112	3,196	81				754	19
1923	3,629	108	2,926	81				703	19
1924	3,549	107	2,866	81				683	19
1925	3,566	107	2,877	81				689	19
1926	3,592	107	2,804	78				788	22
1927	3,600	106	2,813	78				787	22
1928	3,567	107	2,896	81				671	19
1929	3,625	105	2,934	81				691	19
1930	3,632	104	2,961	82				671	18
1931	3,526	105	2,890	82				636	18
1932	3,226	106	2,532	78				694	22
1933	2,857	108	2,127	75				730	25
1934	3,249	109	2,608	80				641	20
1935	3,728	109	3,045	82				683	18
1936	4,164	111	3,422	82				742	18
1937	7,218	100	2,861	40	32	3,718	51	639	9
1938	8,265	102	3,623	44	42	4,038	49	604	7
1939	8,980	104	4,006	45	45	4,000	44	974	11
1940	8,944	105	4,247	48	42	3,625	40	1,072	12
1941	10,489	106	4,569	44	41	5,000	47	920	9
1942	10,762	102	5,483	51	39	4,195	39	1,084	10
1943	13,642	99	6,564	48	40	5,285	39	1,793	13
1944	14,621	100	6,807	47	41	5,935	40	1,879	13
1945	14,796	102	6,931	47	40	6,000	40	1,865	13
1946	14,974	102	7,152	48	40	6,000	40	1,822	12
1947	15,414	105	7,578	49	41	6,000	39	1,836	12
1948	15,500	105	7,200	46	40	6,000	39	2,300	15
1949	15,500	107	7,200	46	39	6,000	39	2,300	15
1950	15,500	107	7,100	46	30	5,500	35	2,900	19

Source: Data 1897–1945 from U. S. Department of Commerce, *Historical Statistics of the United States*, 1789–1945, p. 72; data 1946–50 from U. S. Bureau of Labor Statistics. See footnote 2 of Table 32.

right-wing independents." These unions were not associated in any way; they had in common only the traits designated in the characterization given above. But they embraced most of the workers in the postal and other government service. And they included one of the largest and most powerful unions in the country — John L. Lewis' United Mine Workers, with 600,000 members in coal mining and various other industries.

The third group of unaffiliates might be labeled the "non-railroad left-wing independents." These unions were the eleven former C.I.O. national organizations (now reduced to eight through mergers) which were expelled from the C.I.O. in 1949 and 1950 for refusing to follow majority policies against communist influence and alliances.

The figures in Table 34 show the trend in the membership of the A.F.L., C.I.O., and independent unions over a period of years. It will be seen that after 1900 and up to 1937, the year when the C.I.O. became a separate force in the labor movement, the A.F.L. included from three-fourths to four-fifths of the country's union members. Since 1937 the Federation has averaged less than (but close to) one-half. The C.I.O.'s share has averaged about 40 per cent, although voluntary defections (such as those of the Mine Workers and the Ladies' Garment Workers before 1945) and forced expulsions (such as those of the left-wing unions in 1949 and 1950) have caused a gradual reduction of relative numerical importance to the 35 per cent of 1950. The relative strength of independent unions has undergone substantial fluctuations.

b. Major centers of organization. As previously suggested, American unionism is concentrated in certain occupations, industries, and areas. And thereby, certain unions are much bigger and more powerful than others. In 1950 more than 70 per cent of all union members were employed in mining, construction, transportation and public utilities, and three groups of manufacturing industries: metal products (including basic steel and automobiles); textiles, apparel, and leather; and lumber and its products.

Statistics from various sources suggest other kinds of concentrations and differences in union membership. Thus, the numbers and especially the percentages of unionization in 1950 were much higher in the Northeast, Midwest, and West (an average of about 32 per cent of non-agricultural workers) than in the South (about 12 per cent); in the large cities — those of more than 50,000 inhabitants (about 31 per cent) — than in the small (about 10 per cent); among manual workers (about 34 per cent) than among white-collar employees (about 13 per cent); among male workers (about 33 per cent) than among female workers (about 22 per cent); and among white workers (about 32 per cent) than among Negro workers (about 18 per cent).

The variation in size among the more than 200 national unions was tremendous. The range was between Siderographers (a printing trades union), which had 60 members in three locals, and the Teamsters (drivers of automotive vehicles) and Warehousemen, which had 1.1 million mem-

TABLE 35 *Number of National Unions, by Size of Membership and by Affiliation, December, 1949* [1]

Number of Members	Affiliated with A.F.L.	Affiliated with C.I.O.[2]	Inde-pendent	Total	
				Number	Per Cent
Under 1,000	10	1	11	22	10.6
1,000 and under 5,000	12	1	18	31	15.0
5,000 and under 10,000	7	4	11	22	10.6
10,000 and under 25,000	17	4	5	26	12.6
25,000 and under 50,000	18	9	8	35	17.0
50,000 and under 100,000	21	12	3	36	17.4
100,000 and under 200,000	13	2	1	16	7.7
200,000 and under 300,000	3	2	2	7	3.4
300,000 and under 400,000	1	2		3	1.4
400,000 and under 500,000	3			3	1.4
500,000 and over	2	2	2	6	2.9
Total	107	39	61	207	100.0

Source: U. S. Department of Labor, Bureau of Labor Statistics, *Directory of Labor Unions in the United States,* 1950, p. 3.

[1] Although exact membership data are not available for all unions listed in this directory, sufficient information is available to place all but two independent unions within the groups in this table.

[2] Includes seven unions expelled in 1950 by the C.I.O. executive board.

bers in 896 locals. Table 35 presents a 1949 grouping of A.F.L., C.I.O., and unaffiliated unions in eleven size classes. For unions as a whole, only 17 per cent had more than 100,000 members. The A.F.L. and the C.I.O. each had about 20 per cent of its unions above this number; the independents, 8 per cent. Yet the twelve largest unions of the country had almost half of the total union membership.

The six largest unions, having memberships of over 500,000, were the Teamsters (A.F.L., 1,103,000 members); the Steelworkers (C.I.O., 961,000 members); the Automobile, Aircraft, and Agricultural Implement Workers (C.I.O., 948,000 members); the Carpenters (A.F.L., 735,000 members); the Mine Workers (independent, 600,000 members); and the Machinists (A.F.L., 582,000 members).

c. Age and structure. About 35 per cent of the 200-odd unions existing at the end of 1950 had been established before 1900. Only one of the C.I.O. unions was pre-1900 in date of birth, the great majority of the remainder having been formed after 1930; but about 60 per cent of the A.F.L. organizations were more than fifty years old. About half of the independents were formed before 1900.

Most of the A.F.L. and the independent unions were craft in structure, whereas almost all the C.I.O. unions were industrial. Yet some of the A.F.L. unions, such as the Carpenters and Electricians and the Machinists, had large industrial branches. Looking at the labor movement as a whole, we find that almost two-thirds of the 1950 membership was in some kind of industrial union.

C. HIGHLIGHTS OF UNION HISTORY [3]

We have said that American unionism today is big and powerful. We have obtained some idea of its numerical strength and have learned that its potency is concentrated in the strategic sectors of the economy—mining, construction, basic manufactures, and transportation and communication. Now let us briefly sketch the story of its rise to position and power.

If unionism may properly be regarded as a social group effort by workers to adapt themselves to environmental conditions and to control or change these conditions, it is desirable to note, for the different periods in American history, first the environmental circumstances and then the structural and functional responses of unionism. Three kinds of environmental conditions are important for us: the level of technology in transportation, manufacturing, and other fields of production; the economic nature of the markets for products and productive factors; and the prevailing political and social conditions, including mainly the attitudes of employers and government toward unionism.

The first true labor organization in America was born almost with the republic, at the end of the eighteenth century. Not until early in the twentieth century, however, after more than a hundred years of rapid technological, economic, and political change and flux, did the country approach maturity. The same is true of unionism. We shall find that there was much that is familiar and "modern" in the structural and functional manifestations of unionism during its formative years. We shall also find much that seems strange and bizarre from our present perspective. There had to be a great deal of experimentation, almost blind trial-and-error groping, before the best and most appropriate policies and organizational devices could be discovered.

With the approach to maturity there could be a crystallization of structure and function. Yet society is dynamic, and the environment keeps changing. Therefore unionism, and every other institution, must continue to adapt itself if it is to achieve survival and progress.

Our historical sketch will consider four main periods: (1) the formative years, roughly from 1790 to 1850; (2) the beginnings of national unionism and federation, 1850 to 1890; (3) the predominance of the American Federation of Labor, 1890 to 1935; and (4) the rise of the rival Congress of Industrial Organizations, 1935 to 1952. The student will find it helpful to review at this point our survey of the country's economic and political history in Chapter 4.

[3] Large portions of this section in this and the next chapter are taken from Chapters 30 and 44, by C. R. Daugherty, in H. F. Williamson, editor, *The Growth of the American Economy*, Prentice-Hall, Inc., New York, 1951. Reproduced by permission of the editor and publisher.

1. The formative years, to 1850. *a. Local craft unions and economic functions.* American labor organizations, as we now think of them, can trace their origins back to the unionism which appeared at the end of the eighteenth century. They were and are the product of conditions brought about by the technological revolution. They are not the descendants of the English gilds which flourished during the fourteenth and fifteenth centuries, nor of the "companies of mechanics" which were formed in America during the eighteenth century. These were combinations which included masters and merchants with journeymen for the purpose of regulating quality, quantity, and price of product. There was no division into opposing employers and employee groups. During the so-called colonial period, manufacturing was either domestic or handicraft — not factory-housed. The workingmen's associations that did come into existence during the first half of the eighteenth century were benefit societies with purely welfare functions; their purposes were to supply financial help to needy members and to facilitate social activities. Little or no attention was devoted to the improvement of job conditions.

The technological and economic environment began to change soon after the Revolutionary War and the formation of the new nation. A powerful movement was launched, with the government's full support, for the development of manufacturing industries which should supply at home those products formerly imported from England. The factory system and the use of power-driven machinery thus began to appear. The individual establishments were as yet only small, and the markets for products, though broadening, were still mainly local. But a new factor appeared which was of great significance to the craftsmen. The technology of transportation improved sufficiently to permit some movement of workers and products among major cities. The increased mobility of workers threatened the labor standards of a given locality. The mobility of products widened the area of competition also. The marketing function came to be the specialized province of merchant-middlemen capitalists, who wholesaled the products of manufacturers from different seaboard cities and who gradually were able to exert great pressure on the manufacturers in the matter of price. This in turn led the latter to seek wage reductions. Thus the outside competition precluded the possibility of workmen and manufacturers agreeing, as in former times, to hold product prices and wage rates at certain levels. The common point of view was being lost; no longer did both parties see eye to eye. Many employers tried to meet this competition and this pressure from the merchants by using unskilled men on machines wherever possible or substituting "green" hands for journeymen. The old apprenticeship rules and requirements came to be ignored or diluted. Wages were frequently reduced and hours lengthened.

What functional and structural responses did wage-earners make to the new situation? As the need for mutual aid became increasingly plain, they formed the first true labor organizations in this country. In Philadelphia the carpenters organized during 1791 and the cordwainers (shoemakers) during 1794. In New York during the latter year also appeared the Typographical Society, while in 1795 there was formed the Baltimore Tailors' Association. The first years of the new century saw the birth of other unions in other cities, such as the printers and tailors in Boston and New Orleans. All these were local craft organizations.

Functionally, interest in these first years was centered chiefly in "business" policies and methods, although, as in previous decades, welfare activities played an important part. (The chief uplift work consisted of mutual benefit plans to provide sickness and death assistance for unfortunate members.)

The local unions sought for agreements with their masters; they presented unilateral demands for shorter hours and higher wages and for the enforcement of apprenticeship regulations which limited the amount of work to be done by such "inferior" workmen. Other objectives were a shop closed to workers who refused to join the union; that is, the unions wished employers not to hire non-union workmen. Failure to secure these demands was often followed by strikes, sometimes partly successful. There was no give-and-take negotiation and bargaining (as we now know these things) over the terms of employment.

During these years employers fought back, not only through the courts but also by forming local associations for combatting strikes and blacklisting (refusing to hire) union members. Even when employers agreed to union demands, they did not give the unions the security of written contracts, such as are common today.

The nature of these early but familiar and "modern" economic demands of the unions, of the strikes called to enforce them, and of employers' reactions brings us to the third set of early environmental conditions, the political. Union journeymen soon discovered that government, especially the judicial branch, was a potent ally of their employers. At first, as in the Philadelphia Cordwainers' case of 1806, the mere combination of workers in unions for the purpose of bettering their terms of employment was condemned by the courts as constituting conspiracy, punishable by fine or imprisonment in a criminal action or actionable by an aggrieved party (employer or non-union workman) in a civil suit for money damages. Later on, as in the case of *Commonwealth (of Massachusetts) v. Hunt* in 1842, the doctrine of conspiracy was softened to cover only the unlawful objectives of unions or the unlawful methods employed to achieve the objectives; unionism in itself was not held to be a conspiracy. But as to what constituted lawful and unlawful objectives and lawful and unlawful methods, the decision was up to the judge or judges handling any particular case. And the judiciary, with a few noteworthy exceptions, looked with disfavor on most union activities that directly or indirectly harmed employers or non-unionists.

Here was an obstacle that barred the path toward improvement for almost all unionists everywhere. Another environmental condition of major general concern was the business depression of 1817–21 that followed the end of the Napoleonic wars. This downswing wiped out most of the local unions previously formed; their financial resources were too slender to withstand the loss in membership and dues payments and the deterioration of labor standards that resulted from unemployment among union workmen. Then, when business became prosperous again, from 1822 to 1837 (there was a recession during 1829–32), more local craft unions than ever came into existence. By 1836 there were several hundred in the Eastern cities, with a combined membership of about 300,000. But an inflation in bank credit produced a serious inflation in the cost of living. Here too was a problem affecting all workers. There were also other difficulties, such as very long work periods, lack of educational opportunity, lack of universal manhood suffrage, imprisonment for unpaid debts, inequitable taxation, and injustices in the availability of western lands for settlement.

b. Federation and political action. These country-wide environmental conditions brought forth a new structural response: the formation of loose city and regional federations of the local unions for mutual aid and pooling of resources. There was also a new functional reaction: political activity. Not only did these federations work directly to elect friendly legislators and executives so as to obtain governmental redress of the common grievances; they also helped to establish political parties in various states for the same purposes. The first city federation of labor — the Mechanics' Union of Trade Associations — was formed in Philadelphia during 1827, following an unsuccessful strike by the trades for a ten-hour day. A year later in the same city came the organization of the first known labor party in the country — the Working Men's Party, which spread into Ohio, New York, and New England and was influential for several years. The political program included a universal ten-hour day, universal manhood suffrage, free schools, free public lands, control of banks, equal taxation, abolition of debtor imprisonment, and regulation of the labor of women and children.

One reason why union membership melted away during depressions and why, after prosperity returned and unionism revived, the unions turned to a political program of broad reform was the lack of belief among workers that they were permanently stuck, without alternatives, in a separate hard-and-fast working class. Most workers seem to have been perfectly aware of the development and existence of a separate employee class and of an employer-worker relationship that was very different from the old master-journeyman relationship. But most of them certainly did not resign themselves to indefinite membership in the worker class. Free land in the West and the possibility of saving enough out of wage income to become a "small business man" afforded real alternatives for many.

c. Return to separate craft unionism and economic action. Political activity failed to produce noteworthy immediate results, although many of labor's proposals came in time to be enacted into law. So in 1833, the structural and functional policies veered back to emphasis on separate craft unionism and direct economic action vis-à-vis particular employers. Technological developments in manufacturing were beginning to dilute the skills of craftsmen, but the incidence of this development was uneven, demanding specific, separate action by the unions involved. Business was prosperous from 1833 to 1836.

During this four-year period more improvements in the technology of transportation caused a further widening of product and labor markets. The increase in competition caused the locals in five different crafts (carpenters, comb makers, handloom weavers, printers, and shoemakers) to attempt a new structural device — the formation of national unions in their respective trades. The purpose of this move was to resist the competitive pressure on wage rates and other terms of employment. Henceforth, each local of a given craft was to insist on the same terms as every other local in the craft; the terms of employment were to be made uniform in all cities.

The year 1836 was especially noteworthy because, in terms of *percentage* of all workers, the 300,000 union members previously noted represent the high-water mark of unionism during the nineteenth century. As a matter of fact, on this relative basis the numerical strength of American unionism did not become so great again until after 1935.

d. Humanitarianism and utopianism. This prosperity and labor strength did not last long. The financial panic of 1837 ushered in a business depression that lasted with little exception until 1850. Down once more crashed the house of labor. Almost none of the unions survived. Thereupon the country began to be caught up in the backwash of the revolutionary movements that had begun to surge in Europe. The 1840's were the decade of the American humanitarian movements. Thoughts about day-to-day, bread-and-butter unionism yielded to political allegiance to bizarre reforms and utopias offered by intellectuals and do-gooders who had never been a part of the labor movement. Cooperative societies were formed in the fields of production and consumption; working-class congresses were once more organized for political action on land reform and other unfulfilled dreams; and a few collectivist (truly communist) communities were formed (as at New Harmony, Indiana, and Brook Farm, Massachusetts).

2. The beginnings of national unionism; attempts at federation, 1850 to 1890. Almost all these efforts fell short of their objectives. Without the substance of achievement, the workers' basic needs were not fulfilled, and the cycle of utopianism ended in the failure and dissolution of the organizations. A number of events conspired to swing most American workmen back to more practical and conservative unionism during the fifties. The discovery and use of California's gold helped to establish an industrial revival. With further improvement in transportation, including the railroads, the commodity and labor markets and the area of competition widened considerably. Technological developments in manufacturing began increasingly to displace labor and change the skills and abilities needed by workmen in particular occupations. And the first of the great waves of immigration began to beat upon the nation's shores.

a. Unionism before the Knights of Labor. During this decade (1850) the first national craft union of permanence was formed. It was created by the printers — the union long known as the I.T.U., the International Typographical Union of North America. By 1857 five others — the Stonecutters, Hat Finishers, Molders, Machinists, and Blacksmiths — had organized nationally. Each of these craft unions tried not only to control its members as they moved from market to market but also to achieve the general union objective of uniform conditions of employment in all labor markets, that is, to take wage rates out of employers' competition in the various product markets.

Another depression began in 1857. Only the I.T.U. and the Molders survived it. But recovery from the depression came as the country was plunged into civil conflict. And, as in all wars, labor became scarce in relation to the greatly increased demand for it. Men were needed for the armies. Some workers took advantage of the Homestead Act of 1862 and moved west. Once more, unions were formed, and some twenty were national in scope. Of these, the Cigar Makers, the Bricklayers, the Plasterers, the Locomotive Engineers, and the Railway Conductors survive to this day.

During the war and postwar periods these national unions for the most part adopted narrowly selfish "business" or conservative policies and tactics that were influenced by the further development of transportation and the broadening of markets. But there were also common problems for these unions, for the large group of workers still in local unions, and for the mass of the unorganized. These problems included a severe inflation of the price level before 1873, competition from immigrants who had been brought over during the war, and a serious depression beginning in 1873. Consequently, in this period — in the land of hope and free ideas and of freedom to keep hope alive by trying out the ideas — we still find some flirtation with "panaceas" and with broad organizational forms. Small business, farmers, and other non-union workers were usually invited to join. The objectives were, first, legislative enactments providing universally for a reduction in daily hours from ten or eleven to eight (this was the pet hobby of Ira Steward, a famous member of the Machinists); and second, a cheap money policy (easily obtainable loans at low interest rates) by the federal government so that workers could freely establish producer and consumer cooperatives or could set up in business for themselves. It is noteworthy that for the most part, these aims, while visionary from the standpoint of workability, were not radical in the sense that they betokened a desire to do away with the private enterprise system. Rather were they an expression of the desire to give reality to the American dream of an equal chance for all common men to acquire economic independence and security. Cooperatives also had an especially practical appeal to local union members who had lost strikes and had later been unable to obtain work because of employers' blacklists against them.

The objectives met no permanent acceptance or realization. A few states passed eight-hour laws, but they lacked enforcement teeth and were not effective. The federal Congress stopped issuing "greenback" money; there was to be no cheap currency of this sort. And the cooperative movement exhibited no signs of durable strength.

Three organizations of this period (the post-Civil War years up to about 1880) may be singled out for brief mention: (1) The National Labor Union was a conglomerate national association that convened for the first time in Baltimore in 1866 and met annually thereafter until 1872. The delegates at these conventions represented a variety of constituent organizations — city assemblies (loose local federations of local craft unions), national craft unions, farmers' organizations, women's rights groups, and various other "reform" associations. Peak membership amounted to about half a million. (2) The Knights of St. Crispin was a national craft union of shoemakers that began in 1867 as a response to the threat of labor-saving machinery and the competition of "green hands." The word "Knights" is suggestive of the idealism of the times. The union experienced a phenomenal growth, claiming the allegiance of some 50,000 by 1870. Miscalculations in political maneuvering and untrustworthy leadership led to just as rapid a decline, and the organization went under in the 1873 depression. (3) Just before the depression began and soon after the decline of the National Labor Union, the national craft unions, which numbered about thirty by this time and which had never been much of a factor in the N.L.U., organized a loose federation called the Industrial Brotherhood. As might be expected, the more skilled workmen of these unions took a more hard-headed view of attainable objectives. They decided to abandon political activity and to confine themselves to the more immediate issues, such as exclusion of immigrants and regulation of apprenticeships.

This organization and all but eight of its constituent national craft unions collapsed during the long, severe depression beginning in 1873. Once more a serious business recession took a heavy toll in the labor movement. During the five years of low-level employment, financial resources of unions were sapped, and the membership of the organizations that managed to survive dwindled greatly. There were successive rounds of wage-rate reductions against which workers protested with numerous bitter strikes. Two of these are noteworthy: the bloody strike of 1874–75 in anthracite coal, where a secret organization of miners, the Molly Maguires, terrorized whole communities; and the equally violent railroad strikes of 1877, which involved widespread rioting, bloodshed, and destruction of property. Most of the conflicts were lost, for the employers consistently had the greater staying power (sometimes with the aid of government, as when federal troops were used to break the railroad strikes). And when the unions lost their strikes, they usually lost "recognition" from the employers. Blacklisting of active unionists was a common practice.

b. Knights of Labor. These conditions, combined with a further invasion of skills by technological progress in manufacturing and a further widening of markets through technological advances in transportation and settlement of lands to the west, doubtless made American workmen feel as never before the need for strong unionism. But not until the end of the depression in 1879 were most of them able to find fulfillment of the need. When the demand for labor had picked up sufficiently, they found an organization ready and anxious to receive them — a curious association, unique in American labor annals. Begun in 1869 by a Philadelphia garment cutter named Uriah Stevens, it had managed, by dint of great secrecy (including the use of ritual, signs, passwords, and "grips"), to survive on a small scale throughout the rigors of the depression. This organization was the Noble Order of the Knights of Labor.

Before reviewing the organizational make-up and the aims and tactics of the Knights, let us pause to consider the beliefs of American workmen about 1880. The country was still young; there were still frontiers to be settled, rich new resources to be exploited, new claims to be staked. Workmen were still far from being unanimous in feeling that they were rooted in the worker class with no chance of escape. All that many asked was a fair chance to become self-employed, to go into business for themselves. Those who entertained little hope of rising out of the wage-earning class were not of one mind about how to improve their positions. And the workers in the East might well have views different from those held by workers who lived farther west.

There were, in fact, at this time, as there had been in previous decades, a number of alternative, competing notions about how labor organizations should be organized and about what they should do. Most of the skilled craftsmen believed that they were in sufficiently strategic market positions to be able to help themselves, provided that the courts and other government agencies did not raise serious obstacles to organization and provided that the government would pass laws restricting the competition of hard-to-organize workers, such as immigrants, women, and children. These skilled craftsmen for the most part wished to be organized in national craft unions and wished these unions to be bound together in a federation for the purpose of influencing government on their common problems. A second group of workers — the less skilled and the less strategically situated of the skilled group — were susceptible to the broad, sometimes visionary measures advocated by various non-labor, middle-class reform groups — measures that, as we have seen, included monetary and banking legislation, anti-trust proposals (for the combination or trust movement had already begun among firms), producers' cooperatives, and free-land laws. These workers believed mainly in an all-inclusive form of organization. A third group, relatively small and composed chiefly of recent immigrants in the East, had socialistic aims (labor-government ownership of basic productive facilities) and leaned also to the broadly inclusive organizational type. In addition, there was a small number of anarchists, who believed in no government at all, complete freedom of worker enterprise, and violent dispossession of employers; and a little later there was to develop an organization favoring syndicalism (operation of industries by workers' corporations, with government non-existent or negligible).

During the remainder of the nineteenth century the first two of these groups were by far the largest and most important. But the other three made up somewhat for their lack of numerical, economic, and political weight by a disproportionate amount of noise, agitation, and sometimes violence. It should also be noted that many of the individual members were not irrevocably committed to their group's structural and functional ideals for the labor movement. They changed their minds and passed from group to group, particularly between the first two groups mentioned. Such shifts often depended on which phase of the business cycle the workers were living in; the broader reform goals frequently became more popular during periods of severe business deflation (or inflation), whereas high-level, stable economic activity often evoked the conservative, business type of unionism. Nevertheless, during the formative periods under consideration here, with social and economic conditions still very much in flux, there was by no means a precise and exclusive coordination between business-cycle phases and the structural and functional manifestations of the American labor movement. This last statement is borne out by the period when the Knights of Labor was the country's outstanding labor organization. Most of the years of its ascendancy (1879–90) were prosperous ones. Yet, as we shall see, this union was far from typifying the strictly "business" sort of function.

The Knights began to move after 1881, when, under a new leader ("grand master workman" T. V. Powderly), they abandoned their rituals and other elements of secrecy. The year of peak membership was 1886, when they numbered about 700,000. By 1890, the organization had dwindled to about 100,000. Its popularity in 1886 may be ascribed mainly to two circumstances: (1) The public got a highly exaggerated idea of the Knights' strength from the press, especially after their success during 1885 in conducting strikes against the railroads controlled by the powerful Jay Gould, who was temporarily in a weak financial and competitive position. (2) The rapidly growing and spreading sentiment among workers for a universal eight-hour day reached a climax in 1886. Although the Knights' leadership had given no official support to this drive and was in fact cool to it, because of the union's financial flabbiness and organizational looseness, the mass of workers rallied to the Knights' local units as the only groups that could lead them to victory. In May of that year more than 300,000 workers were out on strike for the eight-hour day. Most of these conflicts were lost. And when the official attitude became known, many workers angrily withdrew their membership and support. (But, as will be shown, there were more basic reasons for the subsequent demise of the union.)

The Knights were in part blamed by the general public for another happening of early May, 1886 — the Haymarket affair. Centering in Haymarket Square in Chicago, this was a violent two-day outbreak, involving severe rioting, bombing, and gunfire between mobs and the police. More than two hundred on both sides were killed or wounded.

As already indicated, the organizational make-up of the Knights was loose and conglomerate. As a whole, they were "one big union," including almost any person who wished to join, regardless of craft, degree of skill, creed, sex, or color. Even "fair" employers were allowed to join; one of the Knights' cardinal principles was the brotherhood of man, and they did not hold that being an employer automatically put a person beyond the pale of polite labor society. Many people in the professions were also admitted. In fact the only exclusions were those whom the Knights thought of as "social parasites" — stockbrokers, bankers, lawyers, gamblers, and those producing or selling intoxicants. The local units of the national organizations were called *local assemblies.* These were of two kinds — *mixed* and *trade.* The former were heterogeneous in membership, admitting anyone except those in the excluded groups. The trade assemblies were composed of members from only a single craft. (Occasionally even a national craft union was consulted as a local assembly.) Five or more locals made up a *district assembly.* The latter were then united in the General Assembly, the supreme law-making body of the Knights' organization. This Assembly and its officers exercised, at least in theory, a complete and centralized control over the district and local assemblies. It had final jurisdiction on the granting and revocation of charters, the calling and termination of strikes, and other matters.

The general objective of the Knights was not to replace the private enterprise system with socialism. Rather did they aim to replace the wage and banking systems with a society of cooperatives. Their methods for the most part involved political action and education instead of collective bargaining and strike action against employers.

After the great upheaval of 1886 the popularity of the Knights began to decline swiftly. In 1886, many of the skilled craft unions of the country, dissatisfied with the broad reform goals, the ineffective tactics, and the confused structure of the Knights, banded together in a new association, the American Federation of Labor, which was committed to the observance of craft-union autonomy and exclusive jurisdiction and to the immediate objective of improving workers' conditions of employment through the tactics of business unionism. After a bitter struggle with the Knights over membership, centering mainly in the New York cigar-making industry, the Knights were thoroughly beaten and proceeded to disintegrate. By 1900, to all intents and purposes they were no more. After almost a century of alternate swings between craft-conscious business unionism, on the one hand, and the more inclusive forms of organization and political utopianism, on the other, the former structural and functional measures began to assume an ascendancy that was to last almost fifty years.

The reasons for the demise of this unique organization are of large importance to the student of the American labor movement. First, the Knights' membership was too polyglot and its organizational structure too mixed for the welding of a cohesive, smooth-functioning machine. The Knights' leaders wrongly believed that the interests of all classes and groups of workmen were harmonious under the American conditions of those years. Second, the local and district assemblies and the member craft unions became rebellious because they were not given enough freedom of action; there was too great a concentration of authority in the General Assembly and its officers, at a time when a good deal of autonomy was needed. Third, the aims and methods of the Knights were ill suited to the day-to-day needs of the membership. The reform goals were too broad and idealistic. The program of political action was ill-conceived and ill-executed. The cooperative ventures were mismanaged, and they failed.

CHAPTER 11

The Development and Present Status of American Unionism (concluded)

C. HIGHLIGHTS OF UNION HISTORY (concluded)

3. The Predominance of the American Federation of Labor, 1890 to 1935. The A.F.L. was to demonstrate that its organizational structure and its tactics (briefly mentioned above and explained at greater length below) had much greater survival value; that is, they were a much better adaptation to environment than those of the Knights. Before considering the manner of the Federation's survival and reviewing its rise to predominance, we must look at the environment itself.

a. To the end of World War I. By the middle 1880's the pace of the technological revolution had been stepped up. Most workers became acutely aware of the machine's threat to their particular jobs and to their physical welfare. New materials and products were being developed, the former blurring the lines of demarcation among particular crafts (the use of steel instead of wood in building, for example), and the latter causing shifts in employment from declining to expanding industries. The country had been spanned east-west and north-south with a network of railway lines. The markets of many products for a rapidly expanding population (this expansion coming partly from an accelerated immigration) had now become truly national. Large, powerful, integrated corporations and combinations of corporations (trusts) were being formed — in petroleum, steel, and railroading, for example — whose monopolistic and discriminatory practices were to lead Congress to pass the Sherman (Anti-Trust) Act of 1890. Employers in some localities and industries were beginning to organize associations for the purpose of presenting a united front in dealing with organized labor or of preventing the unionization of their employees.

All these problems were common to almost all wage-earners. This was one reason for the temporary success of the Knights. But they affected the various industries and crafts in different degrees and in different ways. Moreover, the effects on the skilled workmen were different from those on the unskilled.

In the decades after the Civil War an increasing number of national craft unions were formed in response to the above-mentioned conditions. Railway train operation was becoming highly organized. So were the building trades and the printing industry. In the metal industries the Blacksmiths, the Boilermakers, and the Iron, Steel, and Tin Workers were added to the Molders. There was substantial organization also in glass, pottery, and miscellaneous manufactures.

These craft unionists, almost without exception, had never been more than lukewarm toward the Knights of Labor. The Knights' leaders issued charters to assemblies rather indiscriminately, and the jurisdictions or coverages in the charters were seldom clearly defined; there was much overlapping. This was exceedingly irksome to skilled workmen who had invested considerable time, energy, and money in learning their trades. Many of the craftsmen thought of themselves in a sense as small businessmen. They had not a little contempt for the masses of unskilled laborers so eagerly sheltering under the wings of the parent body. And, as small businessmen, the craftsmen wished to deal in a business way with the employer-buyers of their labor, rather than go off on wild-goose chases after utopian reforms. True, many of the skilled workmen — like Gompers and Strasser of the Cigar Makers, who were to become leaders in founding and promoting the growth of the A.F.L. — inherited from European backgrounds a belief in socialism. But they were not believers in revolutionary violence; they wished to work with the private enterprise system while it existed (and in time they worked themselves out of their original beliefs). Furthermore, each national craft union wished to run its own internal affairs and to develop its own tactics for dealing with employers, free of interference or dictation from a central union authority. It wished, in other words, to enjoy what is known as autonomy, and it desired to federate with other, similar unions only on common problems (such as legal restrictions on union activities) that were broader than those involved in bargaining with employers or employers' associations.

An abortive attempt to organize a federation composed of national and local craft unionists holding the views outlined above was made in 1881 by the Federation of Organized Trades and Labor Unions. For various reasons that need not concern us here, this move failed. But five years later Samuel Gompers and Adolph Strasser launched a successful revolt against the Knights and took the lead in establishing the American Federation of Labor. Gompers was elected first president by his fellow craft unionists; until his death in 1924, he held this office every year except during 1894–95.

The path of the new federation was thorny at first. Not all the leaders of member unions wanted war with the Knights; some wanted unity. Gompers' view prevailed, however. Then came the fight; and for a while it was bitter. But the A.F.L. emerged victorious. There was another split on policy within the Federation; the socialists were strong at first and demanded a political program that included government ownership and operation of the means of production. In 1896 many of the A.F.L.'s members were attracted by the Bryan free-silver-coinage campaign and wished to hitch the organization to the Democratic bandwagon. It was not until after 1896 that the business, non-political unionists prevailed. The organization of the two great political parties (Republican and Democratic) had crystallized two decades earlier, and Gompers recognized that it would be unwise for labor to attach itself to either party or form its own party. Rather, he believed, labor should try to elect friendly legislators and executives from each party. Still another obstacle was the severe depression in business activity that began in 1893. But more than ever before, the trade union movement gave evidence of its staying power; it successfully weathered the economic storm. The opposition of powerful corporations such as the Carnegie Steel Company and the Pullman Company also confronted some of the constituent unions. Carnegie beat the Iron, Steel, and Tin Workers badly in 1892, and the strike of 1894 against the Pullman Company was also lost.

The latter defeat is especially noteworthy because it involved a new form of assistance to employers by government — the court-in-equity injunction restraining unions from exerting economic pressure through strikes or through boycotts. The injunctive weapon came to be utilized with increasing frequency and effectiveness by employers in later decades. Its effectiveness lay in the ease and promptness with which it could be obtained from friendly judges and in the severe penalties attached to disobedience of the court orders. Failure to obey an injunction meant "contempt of court"; that is, union violators (such as Eugene Debs, a leader in the strike of 1894) could be sentenced to fine or imprisonment or both by the judge who issued the injunction, thus depriving the union of its leadership and breaking up the collective action. It is clear that the injunction, although based on an application of essentially the same common law principles (the conspiracy doctrine) as those governing ordinary criminal and civil suits, was calculated to give much swifter and fuller relief to anti-union employers than would criminal and civil suits.

Not all the events of the Federation's first fifteen years were unfavorable. By 1900 an increasing number of employers and employers' groups had begun to deal with the constituent unions and sign collective bargaining agreements. The first agreement of real substance was concluded in 1891 between the Molders and the firms in the stove foundry industry. This was truly a business deal of far-reaching significance. During the period of the agreement, whether during prosperous or depressed years, it gave unprecedented security to the union in respect to all the conditions of employment covered by the agreement. Here, then, were tangible benefits that solidified the resolve of craft unionists to avoid chasing the rainbows of broad, vague reform. They could now concentrate on tactics for improving the conditions of employment (wage rates, hours, and so forth) for organizing the non-union plants in their crafts and industries, and for making these terms of employment uniform among all plants in order to minimize inter-worker and inter-firm competition. These immediate business things become the chief goals of the A.F.L. unions.

Until about 1904 the Federation's success was, on the whole, notable. By that year the membership of its constituent unions totaled about 1.6 million, whereas fifteen years earlier it had numbered less than a quarter of a million. But it was not until 1915 that the 2.0 million point was attained. In other words, the rate of growth after 1904 dropped off sharply. This retardation was in part due to the business recession of 1907. But the fundamental cause lay in other conditions. The member unions seem pretty much to have reached the end of the list of employers willing to deal with them. The violent, prolonged strike of 1902 by the Mine Workers in the anthracite coal mines, which required the intervention of President Roosevelt and his "big stick," served to alienate unionism from the esteem of a large portion of the middle-class public. Many employers became fearful of the strength of the labor movement. Besides, they wished to be free of union restrictions in order to play freely with the newly discovered technological toy known as scientific management, which promised large reductions in production costs and much higher profits. So a variety of union-resisting measures, such as vigilante groups, citizens' committees, and strikebreaking organizations, were used with considerable success. And, as was usual in those days, most federal and state courts interpreted the common and statutory law to the disadvantage of the unions. Great was the alarm of the A.F.L. when in 1908 the United States Supreme Court, in the Danbury Hatters case (*Loewe v. Lawlor*), judged the Hatters' union to be liable under the provisions of the Sherman Act to triple damages of almost $300,000 for conducting an effective secondary boycott in some twenty states against the hats produced by the Loewe company. Consternation mounted when in 1911 the Court approved an injunction against the A.F.L. for helping the Molders to prosecute an effective secondary boycott against the Buck Stove and Range Company of St. Louis. Samuel Gompers was sentenced to jail for contempt of court when he disregarded the injunction.

The A.F.L. decided to marshal its non-partisan political program against such court actions. By 1914 it thought it had achieved success when the Congress included, in the Clayton Act amendments to the Sherman Act, provisions legalizing peaceably conducted strikes and secondary boycotts. Gompers hailed the Clayton Act as organized labor's Magna Charta. But, as we shall see in a later chapter, the courts interpreted these provisions in such a way that labor was no better off than before.

In 1914 World War I began in the midst of a business slump in America. But as various commodities became scarce under war conditions, business revived. When the United States entered the conflict in 1917, business boomed. The labor market became "tight," partly because of the increase in the demand for labor and partly because of the cessation of immigration. These circumstances are always favorable to union organizing activity, and the A.F.L. unions rose to the opportunity. Further, most employers abandoned their anti-union tactics during the war, and union leaders became members of councils advising the government on the prosecution of the home-front war. By the end of the war and the subsequent inflation they were above the four-million mark.

We may summarize this period of union history as follows: (1) In spite of growing opposition by employers and courts, the strength and influence of the American labor movement, as typified by the A.F.L., rose considerably during the period from 1886 to 1918. The A.F.L.'s structural and functional features for that period appear to have represented the most appropriate response thus far discovered to the changing American environment. (2) Structurally, the Federation was composed mainly of national craft unions, organized on the principles of exclusive jurisdiction and union autonomy. The big craft unions were (and are) the predominant influence within the Federation. (3) Functionally, during this period the A.F.L. developed its program of opportunistic business unionism. It concentrated on the control of job opportunities and uniform terms of employment through trade agreements and economic pressures; it avoided reliance on government except for removal of court restrictions and removal of competition from groups hard to organize, such as women, children, and immigrants. And it avoided alliance with any political party as such.

Our story of unionism during this period would not approach completeness without mention of certain non-A.F.L. groups. From 1886 to 1918, an average of about 25 per cent of the total union numerical strength was in non-affiliated national and local unions. Most of this strength was concentrated in nationals like those in railroad train operation — e.g., the "big four" Brotherhoods — and in government service. One union — a "labor" or all-inclusive union called the Industrial Workers of the World (the I.W.W. or "Wobblies") — was of unique interest in the history of American labor. It was formed in 1905 from such various dissident, left-wing elements as the Western Federation of Miners, the Socialist Trade and Labor Alliance, and other "splinters" dissatisfied with A.F.L. craft exclusiveness and conservatism and sharing a hatred of the private enterprise system. With its program of sabotage and general or sympathetic strikes, this loose organization was the cause of much turmoil in the mining communities of the West and the textile centers of the East. It persisted through World War I but finally yielded to the "anti-red" campaigns of 1918–20.

b. From 1918 to 1935. After the armistice there were almost two years of severe price inflation. Unions held and increased their wartime gains and total membership rose to above five million in 1920. But in that period of labor unrest caused by the rapidly rising cost of living, there were ominous forebodings of what was to happen to the labor movement in the "natural" environment of the next decade or so. First, there were two great labor conflicts in 1919 — the steel strike and the coal strike. Since the Homestead strike, the basic steel industry had been regarded as a citadel in the defense of the country's big manufacturing industries against unionization and against collective bargaining between unions and employers. The steel companies were foremost among the proponents of the so-called "open shop" (a term that, although ostensibly used to designate a condition under which union members and non-unionists worked harmoniously and democratically together for a benevolent employer, actually cloaked a situation in which an anti-union employer was free to weed unionists out of his plant and operate without collective bargaining). Some fifteen unions of the A.F.L. banded together to unionize the racially conglomerate work force of the steel industry, concentrating mainly on the United States Steel Corporation. Apart from vigorous efforts of the steel companies and local government agencies to break the strike, and apart from the problem of communicating with and uniting these immigrant groups of varying languages and backgrounds, the conditions were propitious. The demand for steel labor was high and there were significant issues for arousing the workers, such as the exhausting twelve-hour day and the poor working and living conditions. But the A.F.L. unions were not up to the task. The drive fell apart from lack of unity among the participants, lack of financial resources, and lack of imagination and energy.

In the same year the coal strike, conducted by durable, experienced, united leaders and members of the United Mine Workers, was also lost. This time the cause was the government. Under the still-existing war powers, Federal Judge Anderson issued a memorable injunction forbidding most of the activities (even to the payment of strike dues) that are necessary to success in striking.

These two big labor upheavals raised public apprehension over the matter of unionism. The public had recently also been disturbed by the strikes and unrest caused by the I.W.W. during the war. Added to these causes of anxiety was the postwar spread of "radicalism" in Europe, centering mainly, of course, in the new Bolshevik state, the Soviet Union. A "red scare" developed in the United States, with witch-hunting on a considerable scale led by Attorney General Palmer.

This scare, together with the steel and coal victories, fortified most of the employers in manufacturing and metal mining in their resolve to resist unionism. There was further fortification from government. Kansas passed a compulsory arbitration law for public-interest industries in 1920. In 1917 the United States Supreme Court, in a case arising long before the war in the non-union West Virginia coal fields, had declared it unlawful for union organizers to try to get non-union workers to break their so-called "yellow-dog" contracts with employers. (These contracts required that, as a condition of obtaining and retaining employment, a worker sign an agreement not to join or help organize a union.) This decision strengthened one of the principal anti-union weapons. Then, in the midst of the 1921 depression, came two other Supreme Court decisions that left unionists in no doubt as to whose ally this branch of government was. So far as organized labor was concerned, Sections 6 and 20 of the Clayton Act (which presumably legalized peaceably conducted strikes and secondary boycotts in labor disputes broadly defined) were wholly nullified in the *American Steel Foundries* case (where mass picketing in furtherance of a strike had occurred) and in the *Duplex Printing Company* case (where a boycott of printing presses had been made effective in New York City by a machinists' union that had struck the manufacturer in Michigan).

Perhaps nowhere was the adamant anti-union attitude of most employers more pointedly revealed than at the national labor-management conferences called by President Wilson in 1919 and 1920 for the purpose of developing constructive principles and procedures of sound, harmonious labor relations for the postwar years. The employer and union delegates to these conferences split wide apart over the issue of union recognition and collective bargaining versus the open shop.

Of all the early postwar events unfavorable to unionism, the rather severe (if relatively brief) depression of 1921 possibly did the movement the most immediate injury. In this period of unemployment and reduced worker incomes, union membership fell off sharply, mainly among the recently organized unskilled laborers. Many additional employers declared for the open shop. Thus was the usual story of unions during depressions in part retold.

Ordinarily, in previous decades, business recovery had brought union recovery. It was not so this time. When economic activity became high-level again in 1923, total union membership was about 3.6 million. By 1929, after seven fat business years, the total was about 0.2 million less. Existing union strength was concentrated in certain industries — such as railroad train operation, water transportation, street railways, construction, coal mining, and, within the manufacturing group, clothing and printing. But most of metal mining and almost the entire field of large-scale mass-production manufacturing — steel, automobiles, rubber, petroleum refining, chemicals, metal fabricating, lumber, and textiles, for example — were non-union.

The main reason for this "stagnation" of the labor movement has already been suggested — employer opposition, with considerable assistance to employers from government. This continued throughout the decade. Employers' positions were strengthened by a greatly accelerated rate of invention and technological change; improvements in production methods further diluted or altered skills, making it easier for employers to dismiss union members and hire non-unionists. Part of the technological development came in the field of human relations. The techniques of so-called "personnel management" and industrial psychology, which had received much stimulus in the selection and training of soldiers during the war, came to have important peacetime uses. The smarter firms adapted them to industrial uses for the purpose of making more careful selection of employees and for maintaining them in contentment on their jobs. These techniques could be used effectively and subtly against unionism in two ways: (1) to keep unionists out as employees, and (2) through various "welfare" measures (such as employee representation plans or "company unions," bowling leagues, soft-ball teams, pensions, group insurance, and housing) to make existing employees so well satisfied that they would not care to join unions. Wage-rate increases were also sometimes part of the drive to take workers' minds off unionism.

In addition to using all these "soft" welfare measures, employers reverted to the hard-boiled anti-union tactics developed during the century's first decade. Blacklisting of union members, espionage, strikebreaking, vigilance committees, and other tactics were employed by numerous firms, individually and in local and national associations.

As already suggested, the structural and functional responses of unionism to this environment were inadequate for progress and barely enough for survival or maintenance of the status quo in the industries where craftsmen were still in a strategic position. There were a few unions, such as the Amalgamated Clothing Workers in men's clothing and the Ladies' Garment Workers in women's clothing, that developed new policies and techniques for winning and holding new members and for gaining and retaining recognition from employers. These unions duplicated and even improved on employers' "welfare" programs; that is, by means of such measures as workers' education, housing, banks, recreation centers, medical and dental service, and summer camps these unions tied their members loyally to them by filling almost every corner of their lives and providing outlets for almost all the basic human drives. As the Amalgamated Clothing Workers demonstrated in their unionization of the nonunion Philadelphia market, these unions had learned smart new tactics for limiting employers' alternatives, while broadening their own alternatives and developing a favorable attitude on the part of the public. But such things were exceptional. That the organizational and functional devices of craft unionism were obsolescent in respect to the task of organizing the big manufacturing and metal-mining industries cannot be doubted. Moreover, the attitude of the public as a whole remained in general hostile to unionism, being fed from material supplied by both pro- and anti-labor critics of the union movement. It was a rare month when some story of labor extortion or racketeering, lack of democracy within unions, or jurisdictional bickering and strikes between craft unions was not told to the public. Much too often these stories appear to have been true.

One matter that received favorable publicity and attention was union-management cooperation. This term referred to joint programs worked out by local unions and their employers for the purpose of improving production methods and efficiency, thereby lowering costs, improving the employers' competitive positions in the produce markets, and increasing the employment opportunities and security of the union members. This was undoubtedly a constructive, socially beneficial development — a far cry from other unions' policies of output-restriction and of opposition to technological advancement. Unfortunately, it was practiced by only a very small minority of local units of national unions. There were some notable examples, as in the shops of the Baltimore and Ohio Railroad and in a number of textile and hosiery mills; but actual application of the principles of union-management cooperation was confined almost entirely to partially unionized, rather competitive industries in which the job security of union members depended importantly on the ability of union-recognizing employers to develop some offset to the competitive advantage enjoyed by non-union employers, who of course had much greater freedom to reduce wage rates.

Another constructive functional feature of unionism in the twenties was the A.F.L.'s enunciation of a "social wage policy." This policy emphasized labor's wish to raise the incomes of union members in proportion to the increases in the national income occasioned by productivity-raising technological improvements. The A.F.L. did not care who was responsible for the technological and output gains; it wanted the members of its constituent unions to share in them. But no noteworthy practical techniques beyond wage-rate increases were developed for measuring and sharing these gains.

The political program of organized labor remained, in general, about the same. True, just after the war, when the government had virtually taken over the railroads, the Railway Brotherhoods came out for permanent government ownership and operation of the lines. The Mine Workers similarly wanted nationalization of the mines, and the A.F.L. talked about nationalizing all public utilities. But these proposals met with only hostility from the rest of the nation and came in time to be dropped by labor itself. With respect to political parties, the A.F.L. maintained its traditional policy of not tying itself to any one group, choosing, rather, to elect friends and purge enemies from all parties. With respect to the legislation to be sought from friendly legislators, the program was also, with one exception, the traditional one — pass laws to curb the courts and pass laws to curb the wage competition of the hard-to-organize. In short, give us no help except that which we need in order to be able to help ourselves. The exception was in the field of old-age security; by 1927 the A.F.L. was forced to admit that the old-age benefits systems of its unions were entirely inadequate to cope with the income problems of superannuated union members.

It was during the 1920's that international communism made its appearance in the American labor movement. This was the form and direction of labor radicalism that in the next decades was to supplant all other kinds of revolutionary unionism in America. During most of the twenties the official "line" was to bore from within the existing conservative unions in an effort to elect communist party members or sympathizers to important policy positions within these unions, to make the unions adopt more progressive and militant policies, and to instill class-consciousness among the rank and file. There were fair-sized communist minorities in some of the unions — in clothing, textiles, and lumber, for example — and these were given organization direction through the Trade Union Educational League. These minorities became sufficiently vocal and annoying to lead the conservative majorities to conduct purges in 1926 and 1927. As a result of the expulsions, the communist leaders were compelled in 1928 to form a separate, rival federation of labor. But, in this form, communist unionism turned out to be ineffective.

To sum up the position of organized labor in the twenties, it may be said that, while the country as a whole was completing its transition from the horse-and-buggy era to the automobile age, the labor movement as a whole — though generally handicapped by employer opposition and government unfriendliness — remained in the horse-and-buggy stage.

Then came the great depression. The events of this period of economic cataclysm may well have done more than the happenings of any other time to change the face of American unionism and to make it what it is today — a big, powerful economic-political force. One of the most important things that had happened by the end of 1932, when unemployment had reached the staggering total of 15 million or about 30 per cent of the national labor force, was a loss of faith in the godlike infallibility of the big business man, a questioning of the rightness of his attitudes and decisions on many matters, including those on labor unions. All groups, including most of the business community itself and most members of the political party in power, participated in this questioning. There is some indication also that important parts of the organized labor movement were asking why they should not be free to organize unions among the masses of unorganized workers.

Perhaps the chief piece of evidence on the changing attitude of the public toward unionism during these last months of the pre-New Deal period was the enactment in 1932 of the Norris-La Guardia Act by the still-Republican government. There had been a forerunner to this event in 1926 and 1930. In 1926 the Congress passed the Watson-Parker Act, dealing with labor relations on interstate railroads, where unionization had been almost complete in train operation but very spotty among maintenance, repair, clerical, and other non-operating workers. One significant provision was aimed at banning the employers' anti-union activities, such as the previously legalized and protected yellow-dog contract. Railroad companies were forbidden to discriminate, in hiring or firing, against employees who joined or organized unions for the purpose of collective bargaining. There had been a similar provision in the Erdman Act of 1898 for railroads. The Supreme Court had invalidated it, however, in the case of *Adair v. U.S.* But in 1930 the court reversed itself; in the *Texas and New Orleans Railroad* case it upheld the protective clauses of the Watson-Parker Act.

This decision was encouraging to those who favored the enactment of the Norris-La Guardia Act. It showed that even that ultimate legislator, the United States Supreme Court, was being affected by the change in men's thinking. The Act stated it to be public policy that workers should be free to unionize. It forbade federal courts to issue injunctions protecting employers' use of yellow-dog contracts. By various substantive and procedural provisions, it sought to undo most of the previous nullification by courts of the labor provisions of the Clayton Act, which had legalized peaceably conducted strikes and boycotts in labor disputes broadly defined. The Norris-LaGuardia Act further sought to remedy a number of other abuses into which the use of the labor injunction had fallen, such as "blanket" provisions, acceptance of *ex parte* evidence, and too easy issuance.

This Act was not enough to assuage the distaste of the voters for the political party under which economic catastrophe had befallen the country. In November, 1932, the Republicans were voted out of office. The New Deal was about to take over.

4. The rise of the C.I.O.; the split within unionism, 1935 to 1952. *a. Before World War II.* The trend that had begun in the last days of the Republicans was greatly accelerated under the Democrats. The first half of the thirties clearly marks a momentous shift in the attitude of government toward unionism. A century and a half before, government's attitude had been one of suppression. During the previous century the attitude may be said to have been one of toleration. But now it was to be one of encouragement. Whereas the hearts of government officials had previously bled for employers, now for many years they were for the most part to bleed for labor. All branches of government exhibited this new point of view, but the change seems to have been most marked in the administrative branch.

In the early days of the New Deal there was no noteworthy alteration in employers' attitudes toward unionism. Here and there came a defection from the ranks of the anti-union group, but it took about five years for most of them to be convinced that the tide had turned for an indefinite period and that consequently they had better learn to live with their labor partners.

Early in 1933 the National Industrial Recovery Act was passed to help bring the country back from the state of economic-financial collapse into which it had fallen at the time President Roosevelt was inaugurated. One of its sections (7a) was a forerunner of what was to come. Section 7a repeated in essence the policy previously enunciated for railway workers in the Watson-Parker Act of 1926 and in the public-policy statement of the Norris-La Guardia Act of 1932. Under its stimulus a number of unions launched vigorous and successful organizing movements. Conspicuous among these was the drive of John L. Lewis, president of the United Mine Workers, whose membership — as a result of the competitive pressure of non-union operators during the twenties, the competition of other sources of energy, and the later depression conditions — had fallen to an unprecedented low of less than 100,000. By 1934 virtually all the mines had been re-won to unionism and the membership was close to 500,000.

Many other unions, however, did not do so well, partly because of their own ineptitude or lack of interest, partly because of continued employer opposition, and partly because the N.I.R.A. provided no adequate means for enforcing the policies stated in Section 7a. In 1935 two new events of great moment for organized labor took place. In that year, after the Supreme Court junked the N.I.R.A. (for reasons not directly connected with labor matters), the Congress passed the National Labor Relations Act; and when it became clear that the A.F.L. majority did not intend to try seriously to unionize the big non-union manufacturing and metal-mining industries, John L. Lewis of the Miners and seven other union presidents formed within the A.F.L. a Committee for Industrial Organization to undertake the task.

The National Labor Relations Act of 1935, as it was conceived by its sponsors and as it was administered by labor's friends on the National Labor Relations Board, was one statute that truly deserved to be called the Magna Charta of organized labor. It contained two main sets of provisions. (1) Upon complaint by unions and after hearings by the Board, the Board was authorized to issue cease-and-desist orders to employers found guilty of the unfair labor practices of interfering with the freedom of workers to form unions; discriminating against union members in hiring, firing, or tenure; fostering or dominating labor organizations (this was the anti-company union clause); or refusing to bargain collectively with a bona fide, duly certified labor organization. In cases of non-compliance with its orders, the N.L.R.B. was empowered to obtain enforcement from an appropriate federal Circuit Court of Appeals; here were "teeth" at last. (2) On its own motion or upon request by a union, the N.L.R.B. was authorized to hold a secret, free election among an employer's workers to determine or "certify" which union, if any, was the proper representative of the workers for collective dealing with the employer.

The C.I.O. was formed because the A.F.L. majority (composed of craft unionists) refused to take advantage of the organizing opportunities afforded by the successive favorable statutes culminating in the N.L.R.A. The craft unionists refused to surrender their jurisdictional rights in the highly mechanized mass-production industries, while the progressives headed by Lewis argued that the inclusive *industrial* form of union organization was much more appropriate than a conglomeration of loosely federated crafts. After a bitter fight at the 1935 A.F.L. convention, the Lewis group was outvoted. Thereupon it decided to go ahead without official sanction and established the Committee mentioned above, still holding affiliation to the Federation. Calling upon the combined financial and human resources of its eight member unions, the C.I.O. set up a number of organizing committees for these industries, concentrating first on basic steel. New organizing methods were employed with marked success. In 1936 the A.F.L. suspended most of the C.I.O. unions, the suspension taking effect at the local and state levels as well as at the national. But the C.I.O. members were undeterred from their task.

The year 1937, the least unfavorable in a decade of economic depression and stagnation, was another notable one in American labor history. There were at least four major events. First, the National Labor Relations Act was declared constitutional by the Supreme Court in the *Jones and Laughlin* case. Many anti-union employers, on advice of counsel, had been disregarding the Act's provisions in the belief that it would be held invalid. Now the supreme authority on such matters had spoken. Second, a month earlier the United States Steel Corporation, the very core of the country's previous anti-unionism, agreed, without one shot being fired, to bargain collectively with the steel union. The psychological impact of this about-face was shattering. The same year witnessed the capitulation of another major industry, automobiles. Third, there were many union-employer contests in which shots *were* fired. The Steelworkers' union fought a very difficult and unsuccessful battle with the big "independent" steel companies during a series of bitter strikes in the summer. This also was the year in which the new techniques of slow-downs and sit-down strikes were most widely practiced. In the end, in spite of court disapproval of the sit-downs and in spite of other temporary reversals, the unions were victorious. Fourth, the A.F.L. and the suspended C.I.O. unions were unable to work out arrangements whereby the labor movement might be united on mutually accepted principles of structure and function. In self-defense the A.F.L. was compelled to try to organize the mass-production industries itself. Willy-nilly it usually had to accept the industrial form of unionism. The Committee for Industrial Organization, on the other hand, was forced to organize its members into a rival federation of labor, known now as the Congress of Industrial Organizations. As a result, the National Labor Relations Board, the employers, and the general public got caught between the rival claims and drives of the two federations. The provisions of the N.L.R.A. came to be used as much for settling disputes between the A.F.L. and the C.I.O. as for handling issues between organized labor in general and employers.

The Congress of Industrial Organizations developed internal organizational and governmental forms not very different from those of the A.F.L. The C.I.O. is a federation mainly of industrial unions. Legislative work is accomplished at the annual convention. Administrative and judicial functions are performed by an executive board. There are state and local councils that deal at these levels with the problems common to the C.I.O. local units in the respective areas.

It was in its functional aspects (objectives and tactics) that the C.I.O. came to differ most markedly from the A.F.L. Like the latter federation, it accepted the private enterprise system and tried to practice the precepts of business unionism within it. But in general the C.I.O. appeared somewhat more militant, had a much larger communist-led element, and depended much more on government. With its main strength in the mass-production industries, where the unskilled and semi-skilled workers outnumbered the more strategically placed skilled craftsmen, it was unable or unwilling to utilize the restrictive (and occasionally racketeering) practices that characterized some of the A.F.L. organizations. During its first five years most of the C.I.O.'s energies were devoted to organization drives, in which it not only showed uncommon imagination and vigor but also an unusual ability to use effectively for its purposes the administration of such statutes as the N.L.R.A., the Fair Labor Standards (Wage and Hour) Act, and the Walsh-Healey (government contracts) Act. The C.I.O. followed the A.F.L. in its relation to political parties; that is, it too adopted the non-partisan principle and tried to elect labor's friends and defeat its enemies. But it spent much more effort on building effective organizations (political action committees) to get out and influence the vote than did the A.F.L. at this time. And in general it was much more of an ally of the Democratic Party than was the rival federation.

By 1940 there were about 9 million members in the ranks of American unions. Almost half of these were in A.F.L. affiliates, about 40 per cent in C.I.O. unions, and a little more than 10 per cent in non-affiliated organizations. Thus, under the encouraging conditions of the New Deal, union membership almost trebled from 1932 to 1940, and most of the manual workers in the country's major industries were becoming organized.

b. The World War II period and its aftermath. Great as were the numerical gains of organized labor by the end of the thirties, and much as it grew in economic and political strength, there was one environmental condition lacking in those days, a condition that prevented even more sweeping conquests. This was a "tight" labor market, a condition of full employment. In 1940 there were still about 8 million unemployed — almost 15 per cent of the total labor force. In earlier years, except during the 1936–37 upswing, the percentage of unemployed had been even higher.

It is a commonplace that workers are more likely to organize when labor is relatively scarce, and this was the kind of labor market that largely existed throughout the 1940's. First came the defense program, with government beginning to supplement total private spending with large expenditures for war materials. By 1941, unemployment amounted to only about 5.5 million. Then came the war, with government spending on a staggering, unprecedentedly large scale. By 1944, with the greatly increased demand for goods and with about 12 million men withdrawn from the labor supply for service in the armed forces (and with these men not wholly replaced by the entrance of women into the labor market or by increases in labor productivity), unemployment had fallen to less than a million.

This sort of labor market continued to prevail through 1950. There was a short period of temporary increase in unemployment in the early part of 1946, when many firms paused in their operations to convert from war to peacetime productive equipment and products. There was also a temporary business recession during the first half of 1949, with a rise in unemployment. But in general the postwar years were high-employment ones; for the most part, the total demand for products kept pace with the "natural" increase in the country's labor force.

Under these circumstances — and with no significant diminution in government encouragement of unionism — the A.F.L., the C.I.O., and the unaffiliated unions prospered. As shown in Table 34, total union membership by 1950 was about 15.5 million, with roughly 45 per cent in the A.F.L. affiliates, 35 per cent in the C.I.O. unions, and 20 per cent in the unaffiliated organizations.

The economic and political potency of organized labor rose with the increase in numerical strength. The ordinary middle-class citizen seemed to become aware for the first time of the existence and potency of big unionism and of the problems raised by its growth. Each of the twelve largest unions had more than 350,000 members. Three had about a million or more. Their treasuries bulged with dollars counted in the millions. Seventy per cent and more of the employees in mining, manufacturing, construction, and transportation (plus public utilities) were working under collective bargaining agreements. (As usual, the percentage of unionization in agriculture and in the white-collar fields of trade, finance, and public and private service were low — 20 per cent or less.) Labor leaders were making pronouncements on various economic and political issues in the domestic and international areas. Non-partisan political action was undertaken on an unprecedented scale, particularly by the C.I.O. and usually in behalf of Democratic candidates and proposals.

But the thing that seemed most to draw the attention of the man in the street to the new position of unionism was the ability of the big unions to shut down all or major portions of the country's basic industries. This economic power was first manifested in 1946, when there were more strikes, more strikers, and more man-days lost from strikes than in any other year of our history (including 1919, also a postwar year, which had previously led in these respects). The years 1947–49 were also marked by uncommon labor conflict. The indirect effects, on employment and business, of stoppages in industries like coal and steel were also evident, if hard to measure. As a result, there was much questioning about how to make collective bargaining work in a manner that would eliminate such stoppages, and how to direct the power of unionism into channels that would be constructive in terms of the common welfare.

Broadly conceived, the problem of obtaining successful collective bargaining is the problem of developing successful, harmonious human relations between managerial personnel, who wish to be secure and free to organize the non-human and human factors of production, and union officials (from the shop representatives or stewards or business agents up to the top leadership) who wish to advance the economic interests of the membership, to keep themselves securely in power, and to obtain respected social status. These interests, sometimes identical and often conflicting, must be composed without substantial impairment of communication between management and the rank and file of employees and between union leaders and the rank and file of union members. Thus conceived, the problem of socially desirable collective bargaining involves much more than the successful negotiation, every year or two, of new labor contracts; it involves also living harmoniously together during the life of the contract.

The general problem can be better understood if two environmental conditions — one during the war and the other during the first few postwar years — are considered. Both had considerable influence on the course of collective bargaining during the forties.

Unionism had just come to many of the big, basic industries before the defense effort started. There had been very little opportunity to develop procedures, techniques, and attitudes for successful and harmonious living together. Such things take time; and just when such things might have gotten under way, the war began. The country, desiring speedy total victory, could not afford to risk strikes in basic industries; the home front had to be stable, all out for continuous high production to support and supply the armed forces. The government recognized the inevitability of inflationary pressures and knew that price inflation would bring labor unrest and low, interrupted production, resulting from high labor turnover (as workers shopped around for higher-paying jobs) and from strikes (as workers quit collectively to enforce demands for higher pay). It instituted price control through the Office of Price Administration and wage-rate control through the National War Labor Board. Recognizing also that product-price wage-rate stabilization would not itself be a complete guarantee against work stoppages, the President got management and unions voluntarily to agree to give up the strike and lockout and other major forms of economic coercion in return for representation on the War Labor Board, which, if government mediation failed, was in effect to act as an agency of compulsory arbitration for unsettled labor disputes.

Now this no-strike, no-lockout agreement and the creation of the N.W.L.B. meant in essence that, in the national interest, much of the collective bargaining that normally would have been successfully conducted day by day between the parties themselves would be carried on in Washington or in regional offices by the tripartite Board or its subsidiary regional counterparts. There would be some bargaining at the "bench level," of course, and there would be bargaining in Board offices by management and labor representatives on the Board, with the public members casting the deciding votes when necessary. But by and large there would not be the free, peacetime sort of relationship. In short, during the war many disputes came to the Board that ordinarily would have been settled at "home," peacefully or by economic force; and many times one side or the other came to the Board, believing that it could get a better "break" there than at home. Such practices meant the atrophying of the practices of two-party bargaining. In the newly organized industries, real collective bargaining had very little chance to develop normally.

Then came the second — the postwar — circumstance referred to above. There was a severe price inflation, and all the labor unrest and strife that had been controlled during the war broke out in a wave of strikes. After V–J day, in the fall of 1945, the War Labor Board — with the agreement, even urging, of most of its members — was abolished. In effect the wage-rate controls were largely removed (in spite of their nominal continuance under a Wage Stabilization Board), and the collective bargaining game was given "back to the boys" in the hope that they would restore their collective bargaining muscles and develop harmonious relations. But, with the removal of the product-price controls a year later and the resulting rise in living costs, there was much less restoration and development than had been anticipated.

There were other postwar obstacles to the growth of stable, equable labor relations. Most of these remained after the price inflation ended (at least temporarily) in 1949. And most of them were evident at the National Labor-Management Conference called by the President in November, 1945. The employer representatives at this conference showed an attitude toward unions that was in marked contrast to the attitude of employer representatives at the Wilson conferences of 1919 and 1920. They indicated an acceptance of unionism and collective bargaining that had been almost wholly absent 25 years before. But they did have some grievances against unions, and they wanted the union representatives to agree to redress the grievances, voluntarily or through legislation amending the National Labor Relations Act. First, the employers wished labor to agree to remedy abuses — such as strikes against the results of elections conducted by the National Labor Relations Board to determine the proper collective bargaining agency — which arose out of the A.F.L.–C.I.O. conflict or out of jurisdictional disputes among A.F.L. unions. Employers were tired of being innocently caught in the middle of rival union disputes. Second, they wished labor to limit its demands to items that would not further "infringe on the prerogatives of management," and they asked in general that unions be reasonable in the nature and number of their demands. Third, employers wished labor to cease its drive for industry-wide or multiple-employer bargaining; the employers wanted the bargaining area no broader than the individual company. Fourth, employers asked unions to agree to curb certain "unfair practices," such as the coercion of non-unionists into membership, the use of secondary boycotts, and bad-faith bargaining. Fifth, there was the question of what the proper role of government should be in respect to the handling of unsettled labor disputes in basic industries. Some employers wanted the government to have the power to settle such disputes.

The union representatives refused to give ground on these matters. Like the conferences of 1919 and 1920, the conclave of 1945 broke up without agreement on major issues. It will be seen, however, that, whereas 25 years earlier the basic employer-union issue was the desirability of unionism and collective bargaining, the fundamental cleavage of 1945 came on the nature and permissible scope of collective bargaining and union activities. There had been a notable change in the attitude of employers since 1919. Unionism had won an unprecedented degree of acceptance. But the possibility remained that failure to reassure and give security to employers on the matters troubling them might in the end lead them to revert to some form of anti-unionism.

Upon the break-up of the conference, each side had the alternatives of trying to develop the kind of relations it desired through peaceful collective bargaining, or trying to get what it wanted through economic and political pressure. As is usual in American democracy, each side tried some of each. The employers drew first blood in the political field. In the 1946 elections the Republicans wrested control of the Congress from the Democrats, and by 1947 there was on the statute books a National Labor Relations Act that had been significantly amended by the Labor-Management Relations (Taft-Hartley) Act.

Organized labor (A.F.L., C.I.O., and unaffiliated unions) was and continued to be united in bitter opposition to the amendments, which, employers claimed, would merely restore a measure of balance between management and organized labor. Employers argued that under government encouragement the pendulum had swung too far in favor of unions; the employers were now the underdog. Government must be neutral and evenhanded in union-employer relations. The power of each side must be kept in balance. This, they said, would truly be in the public interest.

The original Act of 1935 had three main sets of provisions: (1) those empowering the N.L.R.B. to proscribe unfair labor practices of employers, (2) those empowering the Board to hold elections and certify the collective bargaining agency in a bargaining unit or area determined by the Board, and (3) those enabling the Board to obtain enforcement of its orders and decisions in the Federal Circuit Courts of Appeals. The Act of 1947 substantially retained these provisions.

The amendments of 1947 that are important here may be grouped under five heads: (1) limitations on what unions can do exert pressure on employers, (2) limitations on what unions and employers can agree on, (3) limitations on unions' relations with individual workers, that is, with non-unionists and union members, (4) limitations on unions' exercise of political pressure, that is, on unions' influence on government, and (5) procedures for bringing the power of the federal government to bear on unsettled labor disputes affecting national safety and welfare.

These, then, were the chief amendments aimed at redressing the balance of labor-relations power. That in the remaining years of the forties organized labor suffered a loss of strength because of these changes would be difficult to discover or prove. But labor did not cease to work for their elimination. By the end of 1951, however, the Congress had altered the Act only to the extent of dropping the requirement that a "union shop" could be agreed on by a union and an employer only if a majority of the employees in the bargaining unit voted in favor of such an arrangement.

The amended N.L.R.A. attempted to handle unsettled "national-emergency" labor disputes by resort to delay or "cooling off," temporary federal injunctions against work stoppages, and compulsory investigation of the dispute by *ad hoc* fact-finding boards, which were to have no power to make recommendations in respect to settlement. This measure was invoked by the President a number of times from 1947 to 1951, with fair success.

With or without the amended N.L.R.A., no one could say by 1951 that labor relations had reached a stage of reasonable stability and maturity. The issues that split the President's Conference of 1945 remained unresolved in the minds of management and unions. Unions were still afraid that employers had not been converted to the gospel of the labor movement. Unionism had come a very long way, indeed, from its humble beginnings. But there was still the feeling of insecurity, the lack of full social acceptance, the fear that employers (during the next depression or Republican administration) would backslide into union-smashing. On their side, employers also felt insecure. Unions were beginning to ask for things far beyond their demands during the horse-and-buggy days. Guaranteed annual wages, pensions, medical benefits, and a host of restrictions on freedom to manage — plus the C.I.O.'s outspoken desire to guide government policies on such matters as income taxation, control of the business cycle, and corporation price policies — all these were among the things that made management wary and fearful.

In short, by the end of the forties the development of harmonious relations and mutual good faith and confidence between employers and unions remained one of the major domestic problems of the country. An equally important, related problem was this: Given harmonious relations between employers and organized labor, how could the consciousness of social responsibility be developed among both groups so that their joint decisions would not be incompatible with the criteria of over-all social welfare discussed in Chapter 3?

Recent status of A.F.L.–C.I.O. rivalry. Personal animosities, jealousies, and struggles for power; the craft versus industrial unionism conflict; and the need for unionizing unorganized workers were potent factors responsible for the A.F.L.–C.I.O. split. But the chief reason for the schism appeared to be the dissatisfaction of the progressive, aggressive C.I.O. leaders with the attitudes and policies of the A.F.L. leaders (who happened to be craft unionists).

Whether the labor movement has suffered because of the split cannot be stated; the competition between rival unions may have been beneficial. But that employers and the public have often been hurt by the conflict can hardly be doubted.

What are the prospects for a resolution of this dual unionism? This is a perennial question. Several times negotiating committees from the two federations have met to find an answer. The first was in 1937 at the invitation of the C.I.O. after the October conventions of the rival federations, as a result of pressure from the rank and file and, unofficially, from the government. It was abandoned because the parties were unable to agree on methods of getting the C.I.O. affiliates back into the A.F.L. without loss of "face" by either side. The A.F.L. conceded the C.I.O. request that the executive council's power to suspend be curbed. It proposed that the original C.I.O. unions be taken back into the Federation, all rights intact, and that the status of the other C.I.O. unions — some twenty organizations, most of them set up after the suspension of the original C.I.O. unions — then be decided by further negotiation among the dual groups. The C.I.O. negotiators feared that once again inside the A.F.L. the outnumbered original unions would be unable to secure prompt or "just" action for their dual unions because of the die-hard attitude of certain A.F.L. leaders; so they demanded that the entire C.I.O. membership be received into the A.F.L. at once and that the dualism settlements be negotiated immediately thereafter. Inasmuch as this proposal would undoubtedly have given the industrial unionists more votes and power within the Federation than the craft unionists had, the A.F.L. declined it, and the conference ended, each side trying to convince the public that the other's unreasonable demands had caused the breakdown.

Other, later efforts to heal the breach also ended ingloriously. Perhaps the country was fated to continue indefinitely to have two great rival labor federations. After 1947 employers became less concerned about the split, since the Taft-Hartley amendments made it an unfair practice (punishable through damage suit by employer or by cease-desist order of the National Labor Relations Board or restrainable through court injunction obtained by the Board) for a union to make effective a raid on another union's membership by calling a strike. Another circumstance, from the union point of view, was the fact that a consolidation of the two federations would have reduced the bureaucracies of both in size and would have lowered the relative prestige of many of the leaders in each. Thus, there could be only one president of a united federation, and there would be fewer lesser dignitaries.

One hope — a rather important one — remains. This is the need for unity on the national and international political front. As previously noted, the A.F.L. has tended to be more conservative and more inclined to rely on its own efforts and less on government than the C.I.O. This and other circumstances have often caused splits in the political arena. Sometimes the two federations have supported rival candidates for election to legislative, executive, and judicial posts in government. They have also sometimes opposed each other in lobbying on particular legislative or administrative proposals. With government action on domestic and foreign affairs looming more important every year, the need for a united front on such matters became imperative after the beginning of the Korean episode. Organized labor could not afford to neutralize its power by a canceling-out process between the federations. Thus, in December, 1950, a United Labor Policy Committee was created, composed of the presidents of the A.F.L. and C.I.O., the president of the (then) independent Machinists, the head of the Railway Labor Executives Association and ten other leading union officials (but not John L. Lewis of the Miners).

During the first year of its existence this Committee was effective in obtaining government revisions of policy and administration in respect to wage-rate stabilization and manpower controls under the country's defense program. It was hoped that the high degree of inter-union unity obtained in this major political area during a period of national emergency would in time be translated into a unity of organic structure and other functions. But in August, 1951, a majority of the A.F.L. executive council, perhaps believing that the C.I.O.'s influence in governmental circles was much more than proportionate to its relative size, withdrew from the U.L.P.C. and, at least temporarily, dashed any hopes for organic unity.

D. CONCLUSIONS FROM UNION STATISTICS AND HISTORY

What conclusions may be drawn from our analysis of statistics on unionism and from our recital of the main features of its development?

1. General considerations. *a. Unionism as a response to environment.* Our studies must have established the validity of a basic statement made at the beginning of this chapter: Unionism is a social group response to technological, economic, political, and social stimuli. The environment raises certain problems, certain obstacles to the workers' achievement of want-satisfaction. Workers organize in order to cope with the problems and obstacles. The structure of their organizations and the way they function (their objectives, strategy, and tactics) are not only adaptations to the environmental conditions but also efforts to control and change them. Workers join and stay in unions because, given the environment, they believe their basic desires are better met with unions than without them.

b. Pragmatic nature of American unionism. Second, the structural and functional manifestations of unionism are not usually the result of long-range preconceived plans developed in the minds of idealistic, theorizing, "intellectual" friends of the labor movement, but are hard-headed, pragmatic measures developed by home-grown leaders and rank-and-file members to meet immediate situations. The leadership of Sam Gompers in the A.F.L. shows how a theoretical or ideological approach gets modified in the light of immediate environmental circumstances; American conditions led him to slough off his socialistic concepts and to develop a hard-headed, conservative business unionism.

c. Experimentation with structural and functional responses. Third, the best and most successful forms of organization and kinds of policies evolve through a process of experimentation, of trial and error. Unsuccessful measures, without merit in terms of survival and growth, are discarded. Successful ones are retained and improved.

This experimentation with structural and functional devices has characterized the labor movement during the entire century and a half of its existence; and will continue to do so, because society is always dynamic and changing. But there was more experimentation during the earlier decades than during the later ones. This is to be expected. For one thing, the rate of change in environmental conditions was more rapid while the country was being settled than after it had attained a degree of maturity. For another, it takes time for any organism to discover the most effective measures of adaptation to and control of its environment.

Nevertheless, because the environment never stops changing, adaptation thereto and experimentation with new responses cannot cease without endangering the ability of the organism to survive and make progress. Any pronounced lag in adaptation involves this risk. The structural and functional ineptitudes of most of the A.F.L. unions from 1920 to 1935 is the best recent example of this point. The C.I.O.'s leaders showed that new structural forms and new organizing methods could produce successful adaptation, and could, moreover, control the new environment to a large degree.

It is true that the environment had become much more favorable to unionism beginning in 1932. But even so, the A.F.L. seemed relatively helpless to take advantage of it before the C.I.O. demonstrated what could be done. On the other hand, it is interesting, if useless, to speculate whether the C.I.O.'s program would have been effective when government sided mainly with employers, as during the twenties. Certainly the C.I.O. would have had an enormously more difficult time of it.

The split between the A.F.L. and the C.I.O. has had a number of unfortunate effects — excessive demands, organizational strikes, and so forth — on the employers, workers, and other citizens who have been caught willy-nilly in the middle of it. It is unfortunate that there had to be a split in order that the labor movement could move ahead. Yet the competition between the federations has had the effect of leading most unions to the appropriate forms of adaptive behavior. The structural and functional differences between the two groups were much less in 1951 than in 1937. And apart from personal rivalries and antagonisms between the leaders in the two camps, it became increasingly clear that there were no really good reasons why they should not amalgamate. Perhaps, however, unity in the labor movement would have to await the advent and compulsion of a hostile environment.

d. The growth processes of unionism. (1) Willingness to organize. Fourth, like any other organism, unionism first took root and grew most flourishingly where the environmental conditions were the most propitious. Then, once having established itself, it spread to less favoring areas. Thus, our historical review establishes that unionism began among the skilled manual workers in the large Northern cities and spread not only to unskilled and semi-skilled manual workers and, to some extent, to white-collar workers in those cities, but also to many workers in smaller communities in all parts of the country. Why did it happen this way? In order to answer this very important question we must distinguish *willingness and desire* to organize from *ability* to do so. We have already noted that the *desire* for unionism sprang from certain technological, economic, political, and social conditions in the environment.

(a) Technological conditions. The technological improvement of transportation widened both the labor and product markets, i.e., broadened the area of competition among workers. Labor mobility increased when more workers could travel more easily and quickly from place to place. The labor standards of any one community were jeopardized when itinerants moved in to compete with resident workmen. The enlargement of the product market also made competitors of the workers in many cities; thus, if shoes made in Boston could compete in New York with those made in Philadelphia, the shoe workers in Boston were competing with those in Philadelphia.

The technological improvements in manufacturing processes diluted and modified the skills of craftsmen, robbing them of some of their strategic bargaining power and making them wish to protect themselves by unionization.

Advances in technology meant huge machines, assembly lines, and so on. Firms had to be large because of the large investment in fixed capital that was required. The larger the firms became, the more impersonal were the relations between management and workers and the greater the need for protection against arbitrary, unilateral managerial decisions affecting workers' welfare. In small firms workers ordinarily feel much less keenly the urge to organize, because they have almost daily personal contacts with top management. Here management tends to be more solicitous about the well-being of workers it knows well, and it knows most of them well. Most large plants are in large cities. Here, then, on the "willingness" side is a reason for the start of unionism in the big communities.

(*b*) *Economic conditions.* There seem to have been two sets of economic conditions affecting workers' desire to organize during the history of unionism: those existing throughout the economy, and those existing in particular industries and firms.

i. The economy as a whole. The widening of product and labor markets was an economic matter based on the technological developments in transportation mentioned above. The reaction of workers to these technological-economic changes was an economic one. In any one city they wished to organize in order to protect themselves against the increased competitive pressure that, operating through the "merchant capitalists," tended to lower their wage rates and other conditions of employment. These conditions bore most heavily on the skilled workers of large cities.

The cyclical nature of economic activity also increased the intensity of workers' desire to form unions, especially in large communities where farming was not a practical alternative or supplement to other work. During boom periods the cost of living rose, cutting workers' real earnings and leading to demands for higher wage rates. These demands could not usually be made effective without organization. During business downswings, the rising tide of unemployment and the cutting of wage rates by firms trying to reduce costs also enhanced the urge if not the ability to form unions.

Until the country had extended itself to the limits of its geographical frontiers, all workers, particularly those of large cities, wished to broaden the range of their economic alternatives. They wished to be able to leave the worker class by becoming businessmen — either as farmers through the settlement of free western lands, or as manufacturers or merchants through the obtaining of easy credit. This desire could be made effective only through unions acting as political agitators.

ii. Particular industries. For technological reasons the firms in some industries (like apparel) require only small capital investment in order to get into production; and labor cost is a high percentage of the total cost. Such firms are small, and there are a great many of them. Competition is therefore keen, and the pressure on wage rates is tremendous. In such industries, as our review has shown, the *need* for unionism has been great. In any one firm the workers have desired to improve their conditions. But this has been impossible so long as the workers of competing firms remained unorganized. Job tenure, wage rates, and other terms of employment in unionized plants have always been threatened so long as non-union firms, who were able to exercise unilateral control over *their* terms of employment, competed with the unionized firms in the product market. Thus, the security and very survival of a union in a competitive industry have depended on unionizing the entire industry and establishing uniform terms of employment therein.

In other industries (such as steel and automobiles) where for technological reasons the capital investment per firm is necessarily high, there are relatively few firms. Oligopoly replaces severe competition in the product market. The pressure on wage rates is light; and because of the relatively large capital investment per worker the level of wage rates is relatively high. Here, apart from the important matter of impersonal labor-management relations mentioned above, our historical review suggests that the *desire* for unionism has tended to be less keen.

(c) Political and social conditions. We have found that internal union politics, the attitude and activities of government, and general social beliefs are important conditions influencing both the desire and ability of workers to form unions. On the side of desire for unionism the following points may be noted.

A clique in power within a union or a federation of unions may block the desire of others to unionize other plants or industries if the ruling group is satisfied with its own position and is willing to let well enough alone or if it fears that the inclusion of more members or unions would jeopardize its power and position.

On the other hand, in the absence of such circumstances the desires for security and progress in the attainment of power and social recognition are important drives toward the expansion of unionism. Most unions, as well as both federations, have large staffs of paid full-time organizers whose success is measured by and whose promotion within the labor movement depends on their ability to keep bringing in sheaves of new unionists. Within the movement and in our society as a whole the power and prestige of a union's top leadership have come to be determined in large part by the size of the union's membership and treasury. Lesser officers and the rank-and-file members also get a significant portion of their psychological "kicks" out of the importance of the labor organization to which they belong.

If employers and government try to stifle workers' urges toward organization, a natural reaction is to increase the intensity of the desire to form unions. Freedom to practice democratic principles daily in the work place is apt to seem more precious to those to whom it is denied.

Finally, the prevailing social attitudes of workers as a whole and of particular groups are very important. In general, the fewer the alternatives open to individuals for making a living outside the worker class, the more they feel they must seek want-satisfaction within that class and the more likely they are to organize. One of the reasons why workers turned periodically to the pursuit of broad social and humanitarian reforms during the nineteenth century was their desire to become self-employed as farmers or small businessmen. The ultimate ascendancy of pure business unionism came when most workers had resigned themselves to more or less permanent membership in the working class. Such workers make good unionists; the others do not.

Additional support for this conclusion may be found among particular groups of workers. Many women look on industrial employment as a temporary stop on the road to marriage and home-making; women are usually hard to organize. Many white-collar workers cherish the hope of rising into the ranks of management; and unionization among them is still spotty. Unionization has also lagged among the workers of small communities. Such workers are usually much closer to the agricultural way of living and thinking and have more opportunity than big-city workers to turn to farming in lieu of industrial employment. They are therefore more individualistic — less ready to surrender their freedom of decision and action to the collective will of a union. In any group of workers — whatever their occupation, age, sex, location — there are those who share this individualistic point of view.

Many workers, perhaps most, have appeared to be rather indifferent about unionism. In part this attitude is to be explained by the fact that their unions have obtained satisfactory conditions for them; in the absence of specific important grievances, they seem to be passive. Yet they are willing to join and stay in unions, because they want to go with the crowd, avoid social ostracism, and hold the union as insurance against future trouble.

The over-all social attitude toward unionism is of prime importance. To this day, many persons think that unions are not quite "nice." This attitude is of course much less prevalent now than it used to be. But whenever and wherever it has existed, this view may have deterred some workers from joining unions. Other workers, on the contrary, have undoubtedly been fired with crusading zeal because of it. In any case, we saw that the events of the Great Depression made an enormous difference in many persons' attitudes about the desirability of unionism as an institution and about the necessity for letting workers be free to join them.

(2) Ability to organize. Let us look now at the conditions paving the way for or operating as obstacles to the unionization of workers. Given the various conditions affecting the willingness or desire to form unions, what factors tend to facilitate or block organization?

(a) Technological and economic conditions. First let us go back to one of our original questions: Why did organization begin with the skilled manual workers? Why were these workers so long the backbone of the labor movement? Why even recently have they been so important in the plant-wide unions of the mass-production manufacturing industries?

i. Strategic position. There are a number of answers, some to be mentioned below as "sociological." But a factor of major importance may be designated as *strategic position.* This term has an economic meaning and a technological foundation. Economically, a group of workers may be said to occupy a superior strategic position when their bargaining strength vis-à-vis their employer or in the economy is high. And their bargaining strength is great when their alternative courses of action are superior to those of other groups. They have more "other places to go" than their employers or other workers. They can get along better without their employers than the latter can without them. In short, they have their employers over an economic barrel.

It is primarily technology which gives certain skilled groups their economic advantage. We may consider technological influences both from the standpoint of a particular firm and from the whole economy's standpoint. Within a firm, certain skilled workers are of critical importance in the process of production. More than any others, they are essential and decisive. If they strike, the whole productive operation comes to a halt. Examples are locomotive engineers in railroading, loom-fixers in textile weaving, cutters in clothing plants, heaters and rollers in the basic steel industry, and molders in foundries.

Likewise, in the economy as a whole certain firms and therefore their employees (particularly the skilled ones) are strategically placed at the very heartbeat of productive activity from raw materials on. The interdependence of almost all economic units in the economic system under modern technology is well known. Shut down the crucial plants or industries and the whole productive mechanism is in danger of grinding to a stop. Firms in this position are often able to exert monopolistic power; and their workers and unions are in a position to appropriate much of this "gravy" (economic rent). Examples are the Teamsters in the trucking industry, the train-operating unions in the railroad industry, the Miners in the bituminous coal industry, and the Steelworkers in basic steel.

ii. Competitive situation of firms. In our historical review the economic nature of the market in which a firm sells its product was found to be important in another respect. Not only did the desire for unions tend to be greater among workers in competitive than in oligopolistic industries; employers' desire for such unions (i.e., workers' ability to get them) in competitive industries like clothing tended to be greater also. This was because the employers felt that they would profit if a union organized all the competitors and put a uniform "floor" under wage rates. The union was believed to be a stabilizing agency for the industry. On the other hand, oligopolists could stabilize their industries unaided. Unions were not needed for this purpose; by most such firms they were believed to be nothing but nuisances.

In general, the advances in technology which helped lead to the development of the corporate form of business organization and of firms of great size diminished the workers' ability to organize. Larger firms had larger resources for resisting unionization unless they were unprofitable. Low-cost, profitable firms could provide wage rates and employment terms superior to those demanded by unions. High-cost firms were much less able to resist unionism. Many unions began organizing industries by attacking first the financially weaker firms.

iii. The business cycle. In the economy as a whole, we saw above, the existence of cyclical fluctuations in business activity increased the desire of workers for unionism, during both upswings and downswings. From the standpoint of *ability* to organize, however, only the upswings were propitious. Under the rising unemployment of downswings, jobs got much scarcer and wage incomes smaller. Workers' alternatives seriously deteriorated. They became afraid to join unions and unable to support the financial obligations involved in membership, no matter how much they may have wished to. In our review we learned how union strength has invariably declined a great deal during depressions.

(b) Political and social conditions. i. Composition of work force. We learned above that the *desire* for unionism varied among different groups of workers — women, white-collar workers, ex-farm boys, skilled manual workers, and so on — depending on their beliefs and their possession of alternatives to industrial employment. By the same token, from the standpoint of a union, these workers varied in organizability, i.e., ability to be proselyted to unionism. Not the least of the reasons why unionism started among skilled manual workers in separate local craft units was the *homogeneity* of such employees in training, experience, skill, social status, economic alternatives, financial resources, race, sex, and general cultural outlook and interests and beliefs. It appears that only after stable, continuing unionism had become established among these workers did the time become ripe for expanding the same kind of organization to other groups. Even when unionism reached the mass-production manufacturing plants, it was usually the skilled workers who took the lead and gave stability to the drives for unionization. In general, as was learned in the great steel strike of 1919, the more heterogeneous a work force is, the harder it is to organize into a stable union.

A high labor turnover makes a given plant easier to organize, for here unionists have relatively little difficulty in obtaining jobs. But by the same token, the maintenance of a stable union is harder under these conditions. When the membership of a work force is continually in flux, the organizational work tends to be never-ending.

ii. Attitudes and actions of employers. We found that for more than a century most employers were averse to unionism. They disliked the unions' restrictions on their freedom to manage their enterprises as they saw fit. Unless, as in the competitive industries, they believed unions could help them profit-wise, they tried to operate non-union shops. The anti-union warfare measures used in the 1920's were about the same as those employed in the 1820's. In more recent decades, however, we found positive welfare measures being used against unions, in addition to the repressive warfare ones. The employer who welcomed unionism and sought to develop a pattern of constructive, harmonious human relations in his plant through dealing with a union was exceptional in most industries.

Given the role of government in labor relations, the attitudes and actions of big business were a major obstacle to widespread unionism so long as employers were legally free to fight organization with every available weapon.

iii. Attitudes and actions of government. One of the most striking things about the development of modern big unionism in the United States is the important relationship of the role of government to workers' ability to organize and *stay* organized. Our historical review enables us to distinguish perhaps five phases in this relationship. (*a*) At the very beginning the courts tended to deny the right to organize as such. (*b*) Soon, however, the courts permitted unionism to exist as such, but for the most part rather severely circumscribed their self-help activities vis-à-vis employers, non-unionists, and employers' customers. This may be (and has been by several writers) characterized as an attitude of *grudging tolerance.* It lasted for about a century, roughly from 1830 to 1930. (*c*) In 1932, in the Norris-La Guardia Act the Congress (and a number of states) by statute told the federal (and state) courts to cease being allies of employers. It deprived employer-employee anti-union (yellow-dog) contracts, when broken under union-organizing drives, of court protection. And it greatly restricted the issuance of anti-union injunctions in labor disputes by courts at the behest of employers. The main purpose of this legislation was not to forbid employers to use various measures for fighting unions but to make government more impartial in its relationship to employers and unions — and thus *to help unions help themselves* in their organizing efforts and in their relations with employers. This phase, which strictly speaking lasted only a few years, may be characterized as one of *relative government impartiality.* (*d*) The reaction from the horrors of the Great Depression seems to have been too severe to permit a continuance of this attitude. The way in which the federal courts interpreted the Norris-La Guardia Act and other federal statutes pertaining to labor (e.g., the Sherman Act) after 1935, and the passage of the National Labor Relations Act in that year and its subsequent administration and interpretation, show that all branches of government had decided not only to help unions help themselves, but also, by curbing unfair labor practices, to prevent employers from helping themselves. This attitude placed government on the side of unionism; and this phase, which lasted until 1947, may be called one of *union encouragement.* (*e*) In 1947, the postwar political reaction that put a Republican Congress into power led to the Taft-Hartley amendments to the N.L.R.A. These amendments were intended to curb certain alleged excesses of unions and of union organizational efforts. This phase, which continued through 1951, was considered by some students an attempt to swing the pendulum back to middle-of-the-road government impartially. Others averred that, come the first real depression, the Taft-Hartley amendments would be utilized by employers to renew their efforts to smash unions. Time alone can tell which view is correct.

In any case it is clear that the attitude of government has been and will always be of paramount importance to unionism's survival, security, and progress. Of all the environmental conditions it is perhaps the most crucial.

iv. Quality of union leadership. The caliber of union leaders and organizers was shown to be a very weighty factor in the spread of unionism. Perhaps without the change in governmental attitudes the C.I.O.'s leaders and salesmen of unionism would not have been successful. The point is, however, that they knew an environmental change when they saw one, and they were quick to take advantage of it when the A.F.L. leaders were not. They adapted their sales promotion methods to the needs and techniques of the times. Furthermore, the organizing success of such leaders as Hillman of the Amalgamated Clothing Workers and Dubinsky of the Ladies' Garment Workers, in the face of the employer-governmental anti-unionism of the twenties, shows what can be done in competitive industries even when many unfavorable environmental conditions exist.

e. The ultimate destiny of American unionism. Our survey shows that, even though unionism has seemed from time to time to reach plateaus of membership and strength, during which recent gains are being consolidated, it has ultimately moved into hitherto unorganized occupational and geographic areas. Unions have acted like other organizations of human beings; as entities they have desired security, freedom, and progress in striving for survival, power, and social recognition.

This means that the basic problems of unionism are to hold existing members and win new members through appropriate internal operations and through successful dealings with employers and government. And it suggests that the past trend will continue in spite of possible short-run fluctuations. In due course most of the presently unorganized workers (white-collar, domestic, agricultural, and small-town) will probably be enrolled under the banner of unionism. In other words, the big unionism of 1952 is likely to become the even bigger unionism of 1962 or 1972.

The question then must arise, Where is this unionism going to take the country? That is, will America become a "laboristic" state, with or without the retention of real democracy? Or is the ultimate goal socialism? Or will continued big unionism provoke a fascist reaction by non-labor groups?

Opinions on these points must necessarily be conjectural. The student should not attempt to make even tentative answers until he has read and thought about the material in the rest of this book.

2. Specific developments in union structure. Our study of union history revealed the emergence of at least five organizational and governmental characteristics that had survival value.

a. The formation of national unions. First, as the area of competition widened to national scope in the product and labor markets because of the technological improvements in transportation and communication, the various separate local unions in a given craft became faced with the problem of obtaining uniform terms of employment among all the competing firms employing men working in the craft. As we have seen, this led to the establishment of national craft unions. These national organizations exhibited much greater cohesion and staying power during depressions and other hard times than did the other organizational form tried during the early days — local federation.

b. The centralization of authority in national unions. Second, as industries expanded and new firms entered them, as the necessity for uniform employment terms increased, and as the need developed for quick, forthright action on various problems during inter-convention periods, power came to be increasingly centralized in the national unions, and especially in the hands of the nationals' officers. It was the national office of a union which had to assume the task of organizing locals in new plants so as to prevent non-union competition. Naturally, such locals owed their existence and gave their loyalty to the national union. Moreover, the existing as well as the new locals had to be supervised in their relations with employers if uniform terms of employment were to be maintained. National officers came more and more to participate in local collective bargaining with employers. They also found it necessary to control the locals' calling of strikes; too many strikes would soon deplete the national "war chest" for paying strike benefits to workers and for making other strike disbursements. Not only did strike funds become "nationalized"; so too did other monies such as those for unemployment and old-age benefits. The financial tie and control was a very powerful one. Another important control that developed was the right of the national officers or convention to suspend or expel locals, thus depriving the latter of the moral and financial support of the labor movement. Still another control was the building of political machines in the locals; the national officers could usually count on the loyalty and assistance of the members of these machines. All these developments greatly strengthened the locals' loyalty to and dependence on their respective national unions.

There were no such potent economic and financial ties to other locals of other crafts in the same city. Until the last two decades or so, local federations were formed mainly for political action on common local problems. And after the demise of the Knights of Labor political action became a minor part of the program of unionism. The dominance of the national union was to be expected when the emphasis shifted to and stayed on economic or "business" dealings with employers.

In general, the centralization of union power in the hands of national unions and their officers has been part of the move toward the concentration of power nationally in the governments of all organizations, private and public. This trend has followed inevitably from the technological and economic changes that have made nations, separately and collectively, one interdependent world.

c. The sovereignty of national unions. Third, the autonomy and independence of the national unions came, with the rise of the A.F.L., to be accepted as a cardinal principle of union organization. (It is sometimes known as *voluntarism.*) Within the labor movement sovereignty came to reside mainly in the national union. No matter how many alliances and affiliations a given national might make in order better to solve problems common to it and other nationals, the national retained its freedom of action. These alliances were expedient to the solution of the national's *own* problems. In the last analysis, so long as business unionism remained the dominant function, the national union was the only organization able to exercise any real controls over and apply any real sanctions to any other labor unit. The two great federations, A.F.L. and C.I.O., important as they were and are, had no such controls or sanctions, fundamentally. When a national expels a local, the latter is likely to die, like a foot amputated from a body. When a federation expels a national or a national disaffiliates itself from a federation, no such dire effect is probable. For example, during the last two decades the Miners have been in and out of the A.F.L. and the C.I.O. like Groucho Marx in and out of Mrs. Quackenbush's bedroom in *A Night at the Opera.* But the Miners have kept rolling along in very good condition. Neither have the Carpenters or the Machinists experienced rough going when out of the A.F.L.

d. The importance of federations. Fourth, dominant and sovereign though the national unions became, the great majority did feel the need for federation, at three levels — national, state, and local. There *were* problems common to all — such as the competition of immigrant and women workers and the attitude of courts — which could not be solved by direct economic action and bargaining with employers but demanded united effort on the political front. On such problems the federations proved to be effective.

The question may properly be asked, If centralization of power has been a universal trend of the times, why hasn't it been manifested in the labor federations? Isn't this an example of cultural lag, i.e., failure adequately to adjust to the environment? The answer seems to be, There has been some small tendency toward greater influence by the federations. The C.I.O. especially — because it is a central organization itself and has organized many of its affiliated unions by direction from headquarters — appears to exercise considerable control over member-union policies. To many persons outside the labor movement, moreover, it is the federations that have the prestige and speak for organized labor. But until economic action and collective bargaining with employers yield in importance to political action (and perhaps the formation of a separate labor party) as a major function, the national union will continue to be the dominant structural form. This, furthermore, is not aptly to be designated as an example of cultural lag. But if action by the federal government continues to increase in importance on the problems of unemployment and on changes in the level of wage rates, the need for trying to influence or control government will become more pressing. It may well be that in time labor will have to present a much more closely knit, united front on such matters. Then, unless the federations merge and exert more control over the national unions, cultural lag may well be said to exist.

e. The rise of industrial unionism. Finally, the history of unionism and the organizing successes of the C.I.O. have established the propriety of the plant-wide or industrial form of union for workers in the large-scale manufacturing and similar industries, where the great majority of employees are semi-skilled and unskilled and where the skilled workers are found only in maintenance or repair occupations (such as machinists and bricklayers) and in a few top-level groups (such as rollers in steel mills and cutters in clothing shops). The pro's and con's of industrial unionism will be outlined in a later chapter.

3. Specific developments in union functions. We have said that the problems of unions as entities may be summarized as the getting and holding of members through appropriate structural forms of organization and government and through appropriate policies of dealing with existing members, potential members, employers, and government. Our study of union history should have thrown considerable light on what policies, i.e., functional responses, have been appropriate in the changing American environment.

Structure and function are interdependent. Each helps to determine the other. How anything operates (functions), whether an automobile engine, a human body, or a labor union, helps to determine how it is built from part to whole (structure); and vice versa. The ascendancy of the national unions, within the loose bonds of the A.F.L., over all other kinds of labor organization represented not only the superiority of their organizational forms but also of the policies they stood for and carried out.

The cardinal functional principle of the A.F.L. unions was conservative business unionism. They emphasized action on the immediate economic front. Away with utopianism, intellectualism, and political action for socialism or other broad, long-range social reforms! We want more bread and butter now!

How do we get it? By organizing the unorganized in our crafts. By holding our memberships together (not only by what we get for them from employers but also by having them contribute to benefit funds in which they have a stake). By controlling the supplies of employers' workers (closed shop). By enlarging our economic alternatives while limiting those of employers. By bargaining with employers for higher, uniform wage rates, shorter work periods, and more security of job tenure (seniority rules and so on), while holding the threat of economic reprisal (strikes, boycotts) conspicuously in the background. By using political pressure for government action only in cases where we are not able to help ourselves (laws regulating competition of women, children, and immigrants, and laws preventing courts from siding with employers).

With this approach the A.F.L. vanquished its rival, the Knights, and achieved a considerable measure of recognition and success. But the business policies were not applied with much imagination. The successes were mainly in the crafts and industries where the unions' strategic positions (technological and economic) were naturally very strong (construction, transportation, coal mining). The policies, as applied, were not adequate for the organization of large anti-union manufacturing firms assisted by government.

It remained for the clothing unions to show how the basic business methods could be streamlined and embellished for successful organizational work among employees and successful conquest of employers in highly competitive industries (see Chapters 15 and 16). It remained further for the C.I.O. leadership to show how the program of business unionism could be adapted to organizing oligopolists, and how the A.F.L.'s traditional methods of using pressure in the political field could be developed into influencing a government whose operational interest in unionism and other labor matters had increased enormously.

The main cleavage between the C.I.O. and the A.F.L. today lies not in the structural question of craft versus industrial unionism but in the functional problem of whether the labor movement should depend on government. The older federation still holds pretty much to its traditional self-help principle. The C.I.O., born and nurtured in the favorable climate of the New Deal, seems not at all frightened by the A.F.L.'s specter of ultimate government control over and possible suppression of unionism.

Will organized labor's enlarged concern with government be pushed so far as the organization of a separate labor political party? This is a question on functional development whose answer depends mainly on the same conditions that will determine the answer to the structural question previously asked, Will all unions in time unite in a single federation of large control over its national affiliates?

Having reviewed the statistical and historical evidence of organized labor's rise to power in the United States, we may now turn to a more detailed consideration of the structural and functional characteristics of modern American unionism.

CHAPTER 12

Union Structure and Government

A. INTRODUCTION

1. Union problems in relation to structure and government. As noted in Chapter 2, a social institution like a union desires to be free and secure and to experience progress in the pursuit of survival, power, and social recognition. Let us see what these rather abstract notions mean specifically in respect to unions.

A union wishes to be free to try to organize non-union workers, to exert economic pressure on employers in order to help individual members attain their own basic objectives, and to exert political pressure on government for the same purpose. Success in these endeavors means progress. And if the gains are held, the union has security. As a result, the union not only survives; it achieves power in the society, and it gets the social respect that power commands.

a. Nature of structure and government within a union. If a union is to be successful in performing its functions (i.e., in attaining its objectives by the use of selected policies, strategems, and tactics), it must have a structure and a system of government that are suited to the functions — just as any animal, such as a muskellunge, or any machine, such as a pile-driver, must be built appropriately for the job it has to do in the environment in which it exists.

By union structure we mean the way it is organized or built up from the smallest unit, the members, on up through the shop or department committees or stewards for local unions, to the largest — which of course is the whole organism. The structure of an animal begins with the smallest units of matter (electrons, protons, and so on), on up through atoms, molecules, and cells; the cells are grouped in organs and parts of the body; and the whole system of organs and parts is tied together in a certain pattern of relations. So, in general, with a union: The members are organized in various units for the performance of particular functions. Each member and each organizational unit has a certain status in the next larger unit and a certain role to perform. And all the members and units are arranged together in a certain complex of relationships and interdependence.

Now let us consider what is meant by union government. Within a given union structure there are different levels of status. And there are increasingly important roles to be played by the union members and the organizational units occupying the successively higher levels. Those playing their roles to the satisfaction of persons in the same level and in lower and higher levels are usually rewarded by promotion to higher status. Those failing to obtain approbation are usually punished by demotion to lower levels or "to the ranks." They may even be fined, suspended, or expelled. The most important roles are those performed by the persons occupying the highest status. Those persons, the top leaders and officials, are the "bosses" of the union organization. They give the orders to those occupying lower statuses and playing inferior roles. Yet they are elected by and ultimately responsible to the latter. If the members and officials are to work together effectively, an adequate two-way system of communications must exist in the hierarchy. The leadership must issue, and clearly explain the nature and reasons for, instructions to those in all lower levels. In reverse, there must be open channels whereby the rank-and-file members and lower union officers can quickly and effectively make their views and needs known to the top officialdom. Among the actions taken by the elected leaders, some will be legislative in nature; some administrative (carrying out the laws); and some will be judicial, in the sense of deciding disputes among those in the lower status levels. All these things are involved in what we call union structure and government, just as in any organization of human beings. Without them a union fails to perform its functions successfully.

b. The problems of rank-and-file union members. In any union the great majority of the members of course occupy the lowest or "rank-and-file" status. As individuals they have the same desires and to a large extent the same problems when they are union members as they would have without a union. That is, as individual union members they still wish to have freedom, security, and progress in achieving physical survival, physical comforts, individual power, individual recognition from society, and individual self-expression. They wish to improve their physical well-being by getting higher wage rates, shorter work-periods, better physical working conditions, vacations, medical benefits plans, and so on. Through these and other things (including satisfactory grievance settlement by the employer, protection from arbitrary treatment by the employer, and recognition of seniority) they hope to gain power, improve their general social position, and find outlets for the urge for self-expression.

But as union members, individual workers see these problems through a different focus. Although their basic desires are the same and they want the same specific things from their employers and the community, their problems now include getting their union to help them obtain these things. They wish to influence union policies and activities so as better to achieve their own goals. They wish to be effective within the union.

For many workers this means attending union meetings, making speeches at the meetings, working on committees, running for office, and so on. In respect to a union's internal structure and government, then, the chief problem of such individual workers is to obtain equitable treatment and fair hearings within the organization from those in superior positions. As pointed out at the end of Chapter 9, the opportunity for self-expression within a union through the frequent practice of democracy is great. But satisfaction for this basic need is not obtained in an autocratically led organization.

As already suggested, many workers, probably a majority, normally take no active interest in union affairs. They rarely attend union meetings or participate in the voting. Some, indeed, may have been coerced by various kinds of pressure into joining. For all such workers, the problem of finding power, recognition, and self-expression within the union does not include being rewarded for interest and activity. But it very definitely does include being treated fairly in the handling of grievances and other matters of personal welfare; obtaining their "dues' worth" of satisfaction in the form of higher wage rates and the other specific gains mentioned above; and obtaining as many and as frequent improvements as the members of other unions.

c. The problems of union leaders. In many situations the officials of a union *are* the union. This applies not only to the top leaders but also to minor committeemen and officers at various levels in the hierarchy. Wherever and whenever these men serve as the focus for the needs and desires of that part of the membership subject to their authority and represent these membership units in dealings with management and the "outside world," they are the union, to all intents and purposes. As such, their problems are the problems of the union as an entity.

Yet all these leaders operate in particular situations and thus have intra-union problems peculiar to these circumstances. For one thing, they have their constituents to satisfy. Contented constituents mean votes for re-election; officials like the power and prestige that go with their jobs, and they wish to be re-elected. This is not to be regarded cynically. On the contrary, it is a good thing — part of democracy. It would also be a mistake to believe that nothing but this self-serving motive underlies leaders' efforts to please members. There is also undoubtedly a lot of pure altruism involved, just as when employers do things for workers.

The problem of satisfying constituents and keeping ahead of rival cliques and candidates is in part the problem of making successful bargains with employers. No union officer can remain in power indefinitely unless he delivers the gains desired by the membership. These gains are regarded mainly in relative terms. The members wish their wage-rate progress, for example, to keep pace with employers' advances in profits and with the increases obtained by other unions.

Sometimes the economic conditions affecting a firm or industry are so unfavorable that it is impossible, at least in the present, for a union leader or bargaining committee to obtain what the members want. Then the leadership has the difficult problem of "sitting on the lid." Somehow the membership must be mollified with a satisfactory explanation of why the anticipated gains were not forthcoming.

d. Who is the union? The meaning of this question may be made clearer if we ask a similar one about a more familiar, smaller social unit, the family. Who is the family? The head of the family (usually the father), the mother, children, or all of them together? The answer depends on one's point of view or focus. To an outsider the family is ordinarily the person with whom he has direct, immediate contacts. The other persons in the household are seen rather dimly in the background. They exist and are real, but the outsider judges the family by the representative with whom he deals.

To most outsiders it is usually this way with a union. To a foreman the union is mainly the members in his shop or the union steward or both. To the top management of a plant the union is mainly the top local leaders and the national representatives with whom it must deal. In such cases the other, dimly apprehended parts of the union stand in the background most of the time. But occasionally, as during an industry-wide strike, the focus broadens to include the whole of the organization.

We as students must constantly keep the wide focus. To us the union is a complex or pattern of organizational relationships among all the members, including the hierarchy of officials. When we concentrate on the particular problems of individual rank-and-file members, we must not lose sight of the problems of the leaders; and vice versa. Nor must we forget that, since both together comprise the union as an entity, the members and the leaders have many if not most of their problems in common.

2. The plan of discussion. In the three main sections that follow in this chapter and the next, we shall consider, first, unions' policies on obtaining members. Here we are concerned with membership inclusions and exclusions of various kinds. Second, we shall survey the ways in which existing union members are organized and governed within the unions. Third, we shall try to appraise the adequacy of union structure and government.

In dealing with all these topics we must bear in mind that the various unions differ among themselves in many ways, depending on the nature of the environmental conditions and on the responses of union officials and members.

B. THE INCLUSION AND EXCLUSION OF JOBS AND PROSPECTIVE MEMBERS

When any group of persons forms an organization, such as a college fraternity or a labor union, it has to decide whom to include and whom to exclude. When the group makes this decision, it consciously or unconsciously adopts certain standards or criteria for inclusion and exclusion. An "exclusive" organization is one confined to only those few, relatively rare persons who can meet the high and varied requirements for membership. An inclusive organization is one having few and easily met standards.

All labor organizations have some standards for including and excluding members. Some unions are inclusive, some exclusive. Our interest here is in the nature and effect of these standards.

1. Union jurisdiction. The main standard used by a given union to decide whether it wants a given person as a member is this: Is the person employed, or is he trying to obtain employment, on a *job* and in a *locality* over which the union claims control? (When we speak of a union claiming "control" over jobs, we mean that the union wishes to be the sole agency for bargaining with firms having such jobs over the terms of employment — wage rates and so on — applicable to the jobs.) Thus, when the Philadelphia cordwainers organized late in the eighteenth century, they decided they wanted control over all shoe-making jobs in that locality. Therefore they wished to enroll as members all the cordwainers in Philadelphia. Again, the United Steelworkers of America in 1952 wished to control all the production jobs in basic steel and steel fabricating plants in the country. Accordingly, all the production workers in such plants were eligible for membership. The occupational and geographic areas over which a union claims control and in which it therefore seeks to enroll members comprise the union's claimed *jurisdiction.*

As previously noted, every unit of union organization — local or national — that is not subject to and controlled by some larger organizational entity is sovereign and independent. The chief sovereigns are the separate national unions. Just as sovereign nations in the realm of international politics and diplomacy claim exclusive control over the areas of their announced respective jurisdictions, so each national union claims *exclusive* control over the jobs or groups of jobs within the boundaries of its announced jurisdiction.

To claim jurisdiction is not necessarily to have it universally recognized. Some other sovereign union may dispute a given union's claims in whole or in part, just as one sovereign state may object to the boundaries claimed by some other state. The nature, effects, and causes of rival union jurisdictional claims will be considered later on in this section.

Suppose that no other union quarrels with the claimed jurisdiction of a given union. Then the latter has two more main tasks: getting the firms who have the claimed jobs to recognize the union's claims, and getting the firms to agree that only members of the union shall be employed on these jobs. Only when all three of these objectives have been achieved does the union feel secure.

Suppose now that the union has obtained this threefold security. Then there is a further decision to be made: Shall the union welcome into membership all the workers who are eligible in terms of the union's job jurisdiction, regardless of sex, race and color, age, and so on; or shall the union restrict its membership in one or more ways? If a policy of restriction is to be followed, then standards for inclusion other than job-area jurisdiction are adopted. Later on in this section we shall look at this matter also.

a. Ranges of job or occupational jurisdiction. (1) Structural types among American unions. (a) Classification. i. Single unions. In our survey of union history we noted two general types of occupational coverage — craft unions and industrial or plant-wide unions. For our purpose at the time, this classification was sufficient. But now that we are focusing in some detail on union structure, we must be more precise. Actually there are more structural forms than these two main ones.

First is the *craft union*, narrowly defined. (Our previous, broader definition emphasized the skilled, relatively narrow character of craft unionism, but neglected to distinguish the varieties of the general type.) A true craft union is composed of workers performing only one skilled operation in a given process of production. Examples are the Sheep Shearers (A.F.L.), the Window Glass Cutters' League (A.F.L.), and the Pattern Makers' League, (A.F.L.).

Second, the *amalgamated craft union* is also composed only of skilled workers and thus is very much like the pure craft union. But it is broader. Its members do not perform just one skilled operation, but a number of different (but nevertheless closely related) kinds of skilled work. As the term itself suggests, some of these unions were formed by mergers of pure craft types. Examples of this kind of union are the Plumbers and Steamfitters (A.F.L.), the Upholsterers, Carpet, and Linoleum Mechanics (A.F.L.), and the Railroad Trainmen (independent).

Third, some craft unions, such as the Printing Pressmen and Assistants' Union (A.F.L.), accept as members all semi-skilled and unskilled workers and helpers if these perform operations closely connected with the work of the skilled craftsmen. Yet such a union is far from being an all-inclusive industrial union; for, as in the printing and publishing industry (where at least four other separate craft unions exist in the production end), there are many skilled and unskilled workers in other unions in a given plant. We may call such a union a *modified craft union.*

Fourth, a closer step toward complete industrial unionism is to be found in what may be termed *semi-industrial unions.* Here all the skilled craftsmen plus the semi-skilled and unskilled workers in the production line are included in the membership. But maintenance mechanics, packers, shippers, and other workers of an auxiliary nature off the direct line of production are excluded. Examples are found chiefly in the apparel industries, e.g., the Amalgamated Clothing Workers (C.I.O.) and the United Hatters, Cap, and Millinery Workers (A.F.L.).

A fifth structural type is the true *industrial union,* which includes all the workers of every kind (except usually the office and clerical employees) in a given plant or firm. Examples are the United Mine Workers (independent) in bituminous coal mining and the United Steelworkers (C.I.O.) in basic steel plants.

The exigencies of organizing non-unionists and the conditions in particular plants and industries often produce special variants from the pure industrial form. Some unions, like the United Brewery, Flour, Cereal, and Soft Drink Workers (C.I.O.) and the United Automobile, Aircraft, and Agricultural Equipment Workers (C.I.O.), are *multiple industrial unions.* (A particularly intriguing multiple-industrial example is to be found in District 50 of the United Mine Workers. This organizational group is not made up of coal miners at all but is a sprawling, catch-all division composed of units of chemical workers, unskilled railroad workers, dairy farmers, and portions of the personnel in several other industries.) Yet in some of the plants under their jurisdictions some of the workers, such as truckdrivers and technical workers, are members of other unions. Again, some of the A.F.L. amalgamated or modified craft unions, such as the Carpenters and the Electricians and the Machinists, have formed semi-industrial or industrial union divisions for mass-production operations (in lumbering and woodworking, electrical equipment, and metal-working plants, respectively) in order to meet the organizational challenges of the C.I.O.

Sixth and last comes the *labor union.* Under this form, all workers of all degrees of skill and in all industries are accepted as members. Examples are the mixed assemblies of the Knights of Labor during the 1880's, the One Big Union of Canada, and the so-called federal labor unions directly affiliated with the A.F.L. (see below).

A few American unions, such as the Hod Carriers, Building and Common Laborers (A.F.L.) in the construction industry and the Brotherhood of Foundry Employees in the foundry industry, are not classifiable in any of the above-mentioned types. The memberships of these unions are confined to unskilled workers in their industries.

ii. Federations of unions. As already shown in our story of the development of American unionism, local federations of separate, autonomous unions came into being at an early date in the nineteenth century. And as unions grew into national size, national federations were attempted. Of those formed during that century, one — the American Federation of Labor — has survived.

Two kinds of federations may be distinguished: the *general* federation, and the *industrial* federation. The first embraces all the unions affiliated to a parent body like the A.F.L. The second is confined to the unions in a particular industry, e.g., construction.

At the national level there were in 1952 two leading general federations, the A.F.L. and C.I.O. The structure and government of each will be explained in some detail in the next chapter. In addition, a third federation, more loosely set up than the other two, was reported to have been formed in 1949 as the Confederated Unions of America; it claimed the affiliation of 70 non-A.F.L.-C.I.O. unions, with over 100,000 members. In Chapter 10 we also noted the existence of the Railway Labor Executives Association.

Within both the C.I.O. and the A.F.L. there are state and local general federations whose nature will be explained later. Just as the national federations were established by member national unions for joint action on national problems that were common to all and were too big for successful action by any one union, so the lower-level federations, composed of local units of the national unions, were created for joint action on common state and local problems.

The industrial type of federation is found within the A.F.L. at the local and national levels. (Because the C.I.O. is almost entirely composed of industrial unions, such federations would be largely unnecessary and superfluous for it.) In a manner to be described later on, the craft unions in a few industries, such as local printing and publishing and national railways, combine for over-all treatment of common problems.

Whatever the industrial and geographical scope of a federation of unions in America, two outstanding structural principles prevail: first, the autonomy or freedom of action of each member union (the principle of voluntarism); and second, exclusive jurisdiction for each union over one or more occupations and areas. Under the first principle, the parent federation exercises no more control over the organization, government, and policies of any affiliated union than it is able to exert through moral suasion and the force of its own prestige. Each union is free to follow or to disregard the policies mutually agreed on by the federation's members. Its loyalty and compliance are purely voluntary.

Under the principle of exclusive jurisdiction, each member union is supposed to rule as sole sovereign over a given, recognized occupational and geographical territory. Within a given territory all the workers are subject, as actual or potential members, to only one union. No union is to be permitted to transgress any other union's borders.

(*b*) *Relation of structural types to environmental conditions and to functions.* We have repeatedly stressed that unionism, structurally as well as functionally, is a response to environmental conditions and changes therein. If unions are to survive and grow, their structural form and occupational coverage must be adequate. The amalgamation of separate related skilled crafts and the rise of industrial unionism came about as the result of technological and economic developments which diluted or changed the nature of required skills and which led to large-scale business enterprise. Under modern conditions many skills and aptitudes have become peculiar to just one industry or even one plant. These skills cannot easily be transferred, as they could previously, from industry to industry or plant to plant. Most vacancies occurring on such jobs within plants are filled by upgrading and promotion from within rather than by hiring workers from the outside who had learned the same jobs in other plants. Exceptions are of course the maintenance jobs using carpenters, electricians, machinists, and so on. Here craft or amalgamated craft unions may still be an appropriate structural form. But for the other jobs in most industries, industrial unions appear to afford a more adequate structural adaptation.

We have also emphasized that union structure is related to and depends on union function; and vice versa. Thus, it is no accident that the unions composed of skilled craftsmen have usually been more conservative, inclined more to economic action and self-help, and less to political action, than the industrial and labor unions of broad membership, mostly semi-skilled and unskilled. In situations where even conservative craft unionists have believed political pressure desirable, they have banded together in federation form rather than organize industrial unions to carry out this function.

(2) The relative merits of craft and industrial forms for union survival and growth. All of this raises the question of which main structural type — craft or industrial — has the greater survival value. We may answer at once that each type has survival value under the technological and economic conditions appropriate to it. Looking at the matter objectively, it is impossible to say that *on general principle* one form is superior to the other.

During the twenties and early thirties many persons who were anxious to see the citadels of anti-unionism in the big mass-production industries breached, and who had witnessed the past failures and existing unwillingness of craft unions to breach them, opposed the craft structure on principle and advanced a number of arguments against it. They cited the economic and social losses of jurisdictional disputes among craft unions (see below); the "scabbing" of one craft against another, as when the Firemen ran locomotives for the railroads during a strike by the Engineers; and the ability of an employer dealing with several crafts to play one off against another by having their agreements expire at different times, so that concerted action is impossible and one craft, often the weakest, sets the pattern of new employment conditions for the others. The opponents of craft unionism also pointed to the ability of one craft in a "bottleneck" position to shut down a whole plant for its own selfish reasons, while none of the other crafts has any quarrel with the management; and conversely to the ability of an employer dealing with several crafts to defeat any one of them (unless it is in a strategic bottleneck position) in a strike by hiring strikebreakers or by having the craft's portion of the production operation performed by an outside firm, so that in either case the plant keeps going — something that would be impossible if all the workers were in a single industrial union and struck together. Another argument was the waste in officers' salaries and other administrative expenses that could be avoided by consolidating the crafts in a given industry into one industrial union. Finally, the industrial unionists asserted that a small craft union or a combination of such skilled unions was helpless in the face of large employers.

Those who espoused craft unionism on principle argued that there was no evidence that there would be fewer or less wasteful jurisdictional disputes among industrial unions than among craft unions (experience since 1937 has lent considerable support to this point); and no evidence, either, in terms of actual experience, that the other arguments of the industrial unionists would stand up. Because the members of most craft unions are employed in a number of different industries, they asserted, there is much less likelihood that a single strike would involve all the members. Therefore the loss of any one strike would be much less likely to inflict serious damage on the organization in finances, membership, and other elements of strength. Moreover, if a united front to a large employer or industry were necessary, it could be obtained by federation among the crafts involved. (Experience has not provided much support for this argument, at least in large-scale manufacturing.) Unity and harmony, said the craft unionists, are much more likely among the members of a craft union than within an industrial union. The reason is that the former are a much more homogeneous group, bound together by common skill, social status, experience, customs, and outlook. The members of an industrial union, on the other hand, are heterogeneous in race, skill, background, and interests; close-knit unity is not to be expected among them.

There are certain elements of truth in most of the points made by each side. Yet, as previously stated, the main test of the validity of either structural type lies in its appropriateness to the economic and technological conditions which it faces. In applying this test we must distinguish two kinds of craft unions: first, those whose claimed members are confined almost entirely to a single industry, as the printing and publishing craft unions are; and second, those whose claimed members work in a number of different industries, as, for example, the craft Electricians and Machinists and the Bricklayers and Painters do. The former kind of craft union has virtually no quarrel with industrial unionism; the latter does have a quarrel. It should cause no astonishment that the Printers (the International Typographical Union) were among the eight original member unions of the A.F.L. which formed the Committee for Industrial Organization in 1935. Even though this union had long before agreed with its fellow craft unions to break up the former semi-industrial union in its industry into the constituent crafts (thus showing no approval of the principle of industrial unionism for printing and publishing), it felt no threat from any of the unions the C.I.O. proposed to form. It had no members in steel, automobiles, and so on. On the other hand, the Electricians, Machinists, and other similar craft unions did have claimed members in these mass-production industries; accordingly, they opposed the C.I.O.'s industrial unionism.

Thus we see that if the labor market over which a given craft union claims jurisdiction includes several industries and if this union's members do in fact move from one of these industries to another, there is a solid economic-technological reason for the existence and survival of such a union in its craft form. And there is a solid economic reason for its opposition to the industrial form. Given this mobility, craft unionism best protects the labor standards of workers having particular skills; it is better able than industrial unionism to make the terms of employment uniform from industry to industry.

But the members of the printing and publishing industry's craft unions do not move from industry to industry. When they do leave one shop, they move only to another one in the same industry. Why, then, are the compositors (typesetters), pressmen, photoengravers, stereotypers and electrotypers, and others in separate craft unions? There was and is an important economic reason. The non-typesetting craftsmen felt that in the former semi-industrial union they were in danger of being dominated by the most powerful group, the compositors. They believed that their own special economic interests could best be protected by separate craft unions. These interests were mainly the control of the supply of craftsmen — the limitation of their numbers so as to raise the price of their services. Each group of craftsmen would be in a more strategic economic-technological position vis-à-vis their employers if they acted separately.

Now, unless jobs are skilled ones requiring considerable periods of apprenticeship or training, the workers holding such jobs are not in a strategic position and their supply cannot be limited or controlled. But supply and membership can be controlled by skilled craftsmen. Therefore, the printing trades unions had ample economic justification for their decision to operate in the craft form.

This factor is applicable also to the kind of craft union whose members move from industry to industry. In short, this kind of union has two significant economic reasons for holding to the craft form: first, the protection of uniform labor standards for inter-industry craftsmen; and second, the limitation and control of membership. The intra-industry craft union has only the second of these reasons; but this single factor is enough to justify the craft form.

Consider now the technological and economic conditions prevailing in most large-scale mass-production plants. As previously noted, most of the jobs here are specialized; the skills are not transferable to jobs in other industries and plants. Therefore the first reason mentioned above for craft unionism — the protection of inter-industry labor standards — does not exist. What about the second reason — limitation and control of the supply of labor? In the mass-production plants, the great bulk of the jobs are semi-skilled and unskilled. They can be learned in a few days or weeks.

Consequently most of the workers on such jobs are not in a strategic position and their supply cannot be effectively controlled. Here the industrial type of union is the more appropriate structural response.

b. Conflicts among unions' jurisdictional claims; rival unionism. (1) Nature. During part of our discussion above we stressed the principle of exclusive occupational and geographical jurisdiction for each autonomous, sovereign union. All American unions in all federative organizations adhere religiously to this principle. But it would be wrong to think that every union carefully respects the jurisdictional claims of every other union. Just as it used to be and sometimes still is with sovereign nations, there have been and are disputes about the precise territorial borders of various unions' jurisdictions. Technological and economic developments may destroy or change certain occupations; the work over which a given union claims jurisdiction may be wiped out or so altered that another union can claim it. (This is what happened when metal windows and doors and frames were developed and replaced wooden ones to some extent. Previously the Carpenters had had exclusive possession of the installation of the wooden ones, but now the Sheet Metal Workers claimed the metal ones.) Or new industrial lands may be "discovered" which were never previously claimed by any union. Then there is a mad scramble for "settlement," just as when the New World was opened to the nations of Europe by the discoveries of explorers. (This is illustrated by the events of the thirties which made possible the unionization of hitherto non-union industries.) Or, in the absence of any special technological, economic, or governmental change, a given union may decide to raid and conquer the jurisdictional territory of some other union. (This sort of thing has happened repeatedly during the struggle between the A.F.L. and the C.I.O. unions and, more recently in some industries, during the struggle between certain C.I.O. unions, like the International Union of Electrical, Radio, and Machine Workers, and certain of the expelled left-wing unions, such as the United Electrical, Radio, and Machine Workers.)

Rival unionism is a good term to indicate all sorts of inter-union disputes over jurisdiction. The term "jurisdictional disputes" historically connotes "border" conflicts among A.F.L. craft unions and therefore seems too narrow to cover A.F.L.–C.I.O. and similar disputes. We may formally define rival unionism as conflict between two or more unions over the right to control certain kinds of work or workers.

The disputes between or among rival unions may be classified in two main ways. The first and more meaningful basis is the *source* of the conflict. Here there are two kinds — job disputes and membership disputes. The second classification is based on the *nature of the disputants.* Here there are three kinds of disputes: those between craft unions, those between a craft union and an industrial union, and those between industrial unions.

The *job* kind of dispute is, as was suggested above, the classic jurisdictional conflict between two A.F.L. craft unions over which shall control a particular kind of work, i.e., over whose members shall perform a particular job. Labor history abounds with examples: Shall carpenters or sheet metal workers hang metal doors and windows and lay the related metal frames? Shall carpenters or plasterers nail up plaster board? Shall carpenters or plumbers bore the holes in floors and walls through which water and steam pipes pass? Shall carpenters or roofers or asbestos workers put asbestos shingles on a house? Who shall install metal lath—carpenters, sheet metal workers, or lathers? Which union shall install and dismantle machinery—the Carpenters, who claim jurisdiction over millwrights, or the Machinists? Shall the Stonecutters or the Granite Cutters control the work on artificial stone? Shall the Railway Clerks or the Teamsters control the driving of Railway Express trucks? Which union shall install telephone conduits in buildings—the Electrical Workers or the Telephone Workers? Who shall unload trucks at warehouses—the truck drivers or the warehousemen? And so on.

In the *membership* kind of dispute the question is not which kind of craftsmen shall perform a particular kind of work but which union shall have as members the workers who, all agree, are rightfully on the jobs. For example, no one argues that skilled cooks should not prepare the meals on board an ocean liner, but there has been much strife over the question of whether they should belong to the Seamen's union or to the Hotel and Restaurant Employees. The Seamen have also run afoul of the Marine Engineers in the same way. At one time there was a grave dispute between the United Mine Workers and the Carpenters, not over the question of whether carpenters should do the woodwork around and in mines, but whether these carpenters should belong to the U.M.W. or the Carpenters' union. Much hostility has developed between the Brewery Workers and the Teamsters over a similar question: to which of these unions should the drivers of the brewers' trucks owe allegiance? Again, which industrial union should have the textile workers who make tire cords in a plant owned by a rubber tire firm—the Textile Workers or the Rubber Workers?

Membership disputes may occur between unions in different fields or industries whose claims of membership overlap only at one or a very few points, examples of which have been cited in the preceding paragraph. On the other hand, they may occur between unions in the same field whose jurisdictional claims completely overlap. This "dual unionism" that exists when two or more unions contend for the entire body of workers in the craft or industry is illustrated by the above-mentioned strife between certain A.F.L. unions (such as the Brotherhood of Electrical Workers) and certain C.I.O. unions (such as the Electrical, Radio, and Machine Workers), and between certain C.I.O. unions and the left-wing unions expelled in 1949–50. Occasionally such disputes have existed between unions which belong to neither federation, as in the case of the two Railroad Yardmasters' organizations.

(2) Extent and effects. The data on the extent and costs of all this internecine labor conflict are not very satisfactory. Nevertheless, we have enough facts to permit us to obtain perspective and to get some idea of a trend. From the strike statistics collected by the federal Bureau of Labor Statistics from 1927 to date, it appears that, out of all the man-days lost from all sorts of strikes or work stoppages since the earlier year, the job kind of inter-union dispute averaged only about one per cent and the membership kind a little less than three per cent. It also appears that the frequency and severity of both kinds of conflict have diminished significantly in recent years. In short, rival unionism has never been a major cause of strikes and loss therefrom, and its relative importance has been declining.

But the record is still not one for complacency. The effects of this sort of industrial strife are always wholly bad, except possibly for the union whose selfish ends are gained in winning the dispute. Even so, the victory is not unmixed or complete. The basis for future conflict may be laid, and the union's tactics may lead to a loss of prestige and respect among other unions, employers, and the public. The last two groups are the ones who suffer most. They are caught in the middle. Employers may benefit sometimes, as when a docile, conservative union wins over a militant or left-wing union. But usually they must stand helplessly by while the feuding unions fight it out, to the detriment of output, costs, and profits. Sometimes labor groups try to enforce their jurisdictional claims by attempting to get employers, under threat of calling strikes, to bring pressure on their rivals. Such methods also work hardship and injustice on employers, and, in the event of strikes, lead to great economic loss for them and the public. Sometimes, of course, employers try to take advantage of conflicting claims by getting one union, whose wage rates are lower, to "scab" on its adversary.

The whole labor movement is partly discredited by jurisdictional disputes. Many liberal-minded people who would be inclined to sympathize with the aims and principles of unionism have been alienated by this continual, socially fruitless dissension.

(3) Causes of disputes. The losses occasioned by this inter-union warfare are so serious that one is impelled to search for causes and, if possible, to find means for eliminating them. There are two kinds of causes: those based in the nature of human beings and of human organizations; and those residing in the nature of modern industry. In respect to the first kind, we find the desires of unions and their leaders and members for security and power. Winning a jurisdictional conflict with another union means more employment and earnings for a given union's members. It also means more members, power, and prestige for the union and its leaders. In respect to the second kind of causes, we find the extremely

complex nature of modern industry, the continually changing processes of modern industry, and the existence of unions in narrow craft forms. The extreme specialization and subdivision of tasks, the increasing use of machinery and labor-saving devices, the discovery of new designs, processes, and methods of work, and the substitution of new or different materials (such as artificial stone and plaster or metal trim) — all these give rise to new problems of craft authority. As soon as one is settled, others tend to keep coming up. Before the Industrial Revolution there were clear-cut demarcations among the crafts, but twentieth-century conditions have so blurred them that they are often hardly recognizable.

In the face of these conditions, each union whose skill has not been largely impaired by modern conditions still clings to its narrow and exclusive form of organization. Each new encroachment of machinery and scientific management whittles away some operation that used to belong only to it; now the operation can be done either by an unskilled workman or with equal validity by a worker in another craft. Therefore, in order to save itself further narrowing, each craft fiercely maintains a claim over the new material or process. If all the workers in the industry were in one union, however, instead of (say) ten, one of the gravest sources for friction would be removed.

But it would be a mistake to believe that jurisdictional disputes would disappear if all unions were industrial rather than craft in form. As shown above, such disputes can and do exist in significant numbers within the C.I.O. and between the C.I.O. unions and their industrial rivals.

(4) Remedial measures. Thus far in our discussion of union jurisdiction we have noted, among various things, that given certain technological and economic conditions, the craft form of unionism appears to be a valid structural adaptation; that jurisdictional conflicts among unions would not disappear even if there were only industrial unions; and that the causes of these disputes lie deep in the nature of the technological-economic environment and in the nature of human beings and unions.

It follows, then, that jurisdictional conflict as such cannot be eliminated. The best that can be hoped for is to get the disputes settled in an orderly and harmonious way before they get to the stage of strikes and other kinds of serious social loss.

As in disputes between unions and employers, the best program of settlement is one that is worked out and operated voluntarily by the parties themselves, without outside compulsion from or participation by government. Such efforts have not been lacking.

(a) Within the A.F.L. From the time of its formation, one of the functions of the A.F.L. was considered to be the airing of grievances and the settlement of all sorts of disputes among its affiliated unions. The specific agencies involved in the performance of this function from time to time were the Executive Board, the various Departments, the annual convention, and local federations. (These A.F.L. organizational units are dis-

cussed later on in the chapter.) Special committees were also sometimes appointed to investigate particular jurisdictional problems. And for the construction industry at least three plans for the arbitration of unsettled jurisdictional job disputes at the national level have been tried over the years.

The most recent arbitration program for this industry may be briefly noted here. Spurred by certain sections in the Taft-Hartley amendments to the (federal) National Labor Relations Act passed in 1947, the A.F.L. national building trades unions joined with the Association of General Contractors to establish in 1948 a National Joint Board for the Settlement of Jurisdictional Disputes in the construction industry. (The relevant sections in the amended N.L.R.A. directed the National Labor Relations Board to decide within ten days which among the disputing unions in a given case should perform the disputed work; and made a union guilty of unfair labor practices, liable to damage suits by injured parties, and subject to court injunctions by the N.L.R.B., if the union engaged in a strike or boycott to force an employer to assign work to it rather than some other group of workers.) Under the new plan, if a given jurisdictional dispute of the job type, arising almost always on a particular construction project between or among locals of the national construction unions, cannot be settled by the locals involved, it goes to a board of trustees, made up of four employer and four union representatives. This board decides whether the dispute is like one previously settled by some earlier arbitration decision or inter-union agreement. If it is, the previous ruling or agreement ordinarily is applied to the new case. If settlement of the dispute on the basis of precedent appears to be impossible, the case goes to the National Joint Board, which is composed of a neutral chairman and two union and two employer representatives chosen by the chairman from a panel of twelve unionists and twelve employers. The union and employer board members must not be connected with the dispute. The decision of this board is supposed to be final and binding, and at no time may the disputants engage in a strike or other coercive activity.

Thus far (1952) this plan has operated successfully in a number of cases. Whether it continues to do so depends on the will and good faith of the member unions, the skill and consistency of the arbitrators, and the continuance of the governmental threat in the background. The sovereignty principle of national unionism plus a lack of consistency in decisions and a yielding to expediency operated to destroy somewhat similar programs in the past. Once a given powerful union had decided to rebel against an unfavorable decision, it was free to withdraw from the Federation and, thereby, from participation in the dispute-settlement scheme. For example, under the National Board for Jurisdictional Awards, established in 1919, the metal window, door, and trim controversy was decided in favor of the Sheet Metal Workers and against the Carpenters in 1924. Thereupon the latter union took its toys home and refused to play; it seceded from the Building Trades Department and threatened to leave the A.F.L. entirely. Its size and prestige were so great, however, that the A.F.L. yielded; and the Awards board was quietly buried as the Carpenters came back. Again, under a later program of settlement (before 1948) the Machinists seceded from the Federation and became independent when decisions went against them and in favor of the Carpenters. And the Brewery Workers transferred to the C.I.O. when worsted by the Teamsters within the A.F.L. on the classic dispute (of the partial-overlap membership type) over which union should have the brewery truck drivers. Perhaps the 1948 plan described above for the job kind of dispute in the construction industry will have a better fate if government continues to stand ready to prevent jurisdictional strikes, which are the time-honored weapon used to win these disputes.

In addition to the above-mentioned methods of trying to secure peace in this field, one other measure has been used successfully and quite frequently within the Federation — the amalgamation or merger of the disputing unions. Many of the names of present-day unions give evidence of the earlier amalgamation of competing, overlapping, similar unions whose jurisdictional boundaries became increasingly blurred by technological changes. An example is the United Hatters, Cap and Millinery Workers' Union which was created by merging the United Hatters with the Cloth Hat, Cap and Millinery Workers.

(b) Within the C.I.O. As already noted, certain unions affiliated with the C.I.O. have also had jurisdictional conflicts. For example, the Auto Workers tried to move into plants which the Farm Equipment Workers claimed were wholly within the latter's jurisdiction. However, until 1950 these conflicts appear not to have been serious enough or numerous enough to justify the establishment of settlement machinery as elaborate as that used by the A.F.L. From time to time the C.I.O. executive board and a three-member standing jurisdictional committee had worked on inter-union disputes. But in 1951 the need for more formal and effective measures became apparent. At the C.I.O. convention of that year a contract, enforceable in the courts, was signed by the affiliated national unions, whereby they agreed to try to settle their jurisdictional differences, first, by direct bargaining between top officials of the unions involved; second, through mediation by the executive vice-president of the C.I.O.; and third, through arbitration by an impartial outsider, who renders final, binding decisions.

(c) A.F.L. versus C.I.O. and independents. Most of the jurisdictional conflict among unions belonging to different federations or to no federation has been of the complete-overlap membership kind. Instances of voluntary efforts to settle such disputes have been rare. During the latter part of the war the Auto Workers of the C.I.O. and the Machinists (first in and then out of the A.F.L.) operated under a truce whereby they

agreed not to raid each other's organizational possessions. But most unions strained every sinew to increase their strengths by organizing non-union plants or proselyting previously unionized ones. And in so far as they were not members of the same federation, there was no agency for settling such disputes except the (federal) National Labor Relations Board. As will be explained in Part Three of this book, the National Labor Relations Act authorizes the Board to hold elections among the workers of plants where rival unions are pressing organizational claims. The union winning such an election is certified by the Board as the exclusive bargaining agency for the workers.

2. Eligibility standards for union membership. *a. Establishing recognition and jurisdiction.* It is clear that if a given union wishes to secure its jurisdictional claims, so that no other union disputes the occupations and the geographical area which the union wishes to control, the union must actually win and hold control of this jurisdictional territory. This usually means, first, getting the workers in these occupations and this area to join the union; and second, getting the firms employing these workers to recognize or deal with the union as the sole representative of the workers.

The enrollment of the workers gives the union economic and political power in relation to the firms and in relation to rival unions. The union gets this power when it, rather than any other union, controls the supply of the labor which the firms must have in order to produce. As a rule, an employer will not recognize a union as the representative of its workers for bargaining over the terms of employment unless it is convinced that the union has organized the workers and commands their loyalty.

(1) Obtaining recognition from employers. How is an employer convinced? If he is friendly rather than hostile to the idea of dealing with a union, the union may obtain recognition by showing him its membership cards or other evidence of employee support. A few employers have even been known to make "sweetheart" agreements with national union officials whereby the employers helped the union to organize their workers. But if an employer is hostile, the union would not even show him membership cards, for fear of possible reprisal against those who had signed up; and this or other, similar evidence would not be effective in any event. In such cases an organizational strike is often required. If the strike is won by the union, the firm capitulates; it now has excellent evidence that the union commands the support of its workers. Another convincer much used since 1935 is the winning of a Labor Board election by the union.

Whatever the methods used by a union to obtain recognition from an employer, it is rarely necessary for the union to enroll all the workers in its claimed jurisdiction within the firm. Many a union has won exclusive bargaining rights through strike or election with an initial enlistment of substantially less than half of the eligible employees. A strike can be won through effective picketing by the union minority. And after the firm has yielded recognition, most of the remaining workers can be induced or required to join the union. Similarly, a majority for the union can often be obtained in an election through effective campaigning by the original unionized minority of the workers. Most non-unionists are usually so indifferent that they either stay away from the polls or go along with the aggressive union crowd. (Under the Labor Relations Act an election is won if a majority of the actual voters rather than of all eligible voters casts ballots for the union.)

Employers' ability to fight the unionization of their workers has been severely restricted under the federal and state labor statues. See Chapter 25 in Part Three.

(2) Enrolling union members. How does a union organize non-unionists who work on jobs and in an area subject to the union's jurisdictional claims? As already noted, in a few cases friendly employers have handed over their workers more or less "on a platter." In a few other instances the workers in certain plants have spontaneously flamed into some sort of organization all by themselves and have solicited assistance from and membership in some appropriate national union or federation. In most situations, however, new members for existing locals and new locals for existing national unions or federations are added to the ranks of organized labor by the hard, persistent, effective organizing tactics of the paid, professional organizers hired by local unions, national unions, or the federations.

Industries and areas that are wholly or mainly non-union have often been attacked through organizing "drives." Here the campaigns are carefully planned and adequately financed; and a whole "host" of organizers invades the area, usually picking on one or more key objectives (such as financially or competitively weak companies) rather than attacking along the whole front simultaneously. Examples are the successful work of the Steelworkers' Organizing Committee, set up by the Committee for Industrial Organization, from 1936 to 1938; and "Operation Dixie," the partially successful effort of the C.I.O. to organize Southern workers after World War II.

Seldom does an industry or area capitulate *en masse.* There are usually non-union salients and resistance points that remain to be reduced. New firms arise, too, which must be organized. Seldom can a union sit back and view its work not only as good but completed, its jurisdictional claims wholly fulfilled.

Whether the work of organization is by wholesale drive or in piecemeal bits, experimentation has developed certain methods that have proved effective. There is of course no single pattern of devices. Each campaign must be suited to the special conditions confronting the organizers. In the old hard days, before employers were stripped of most of their offensive and defensive weapons, many a union organizer was forced to sneak into town, staying in some contact worker's home or in an unobtrusive hotel and meeting secretly at night behind barred doors and shaded windows with those bold souls who braved the employers' ability to spy and to work retribution. Employees were gradually signed up; but not until a substantial fraction of them had joined was the cloak of secrecy and conspiracy thrown off.

Since 1937 in most places the work of organizing has become much easier. Communication between organizers and workers is open, loud, and long. The radio, newspapers, leaflets, sound trucks, mass meetings, parades, and all the other devices for whipping up mass enthusiasm are freely employed. The support or neutrality of teachers, clergymen, the public press, civic organizations, and others capable of influencing public opinion is assiduously cultivated. Merchants are visited and told how much better off they will be when the purchasing power of the workers is increased through higher wage rates.

Whatever the particular organizing tactics are, the campaign is made to hinge on two main elements: first, the enlistment of key, local, popular workers at a very early date; and second, the selection of one or more labor issues of paramount importance to the workers who are being solicited. Except in large metropolitan areas it will not do for the anti-unionists to be able to pin the label of "foreign" on the campaign. No community or group likes to be told what is good or bad for it by "outsiders." "Damyankees" are not very effective in unionizing the Deep South. Similarly with the issues: The non-union workers can't be expected to get excited over some imported ready-made grievance or issue. The campaign must be fought out over things that are bothering the local employees. As a rule these are not hard to find; once found, they can be blown up to suitable proportions. Furthermore, these issues have had their counterparts in other places organized by the union; and the union has no difficulty in proving to the workers, through copies of union contracts and other documents, how it was able to obtain substantial redress of these grievances, wage or otherwise. The need for unity and for standing together is stressed.

b. Maintaining control of the labor supply. (1) Job control. Suppose now that a union has organized a sufficient fraction of the workers in a given firm to obtain, by persuasion or strike or election, recognition as the exclusive representative and bargaining agent for all the workers. Its problem now becomes one of *holding* its newly gained power. In the long run this problem involves getting and doing enough for the local members to increase or retain their loyalty. The sales talk need not stop; but there must also be a delivery of goods. This takes time. The delivery cannot all be made in the first contract negotiated with the management. (Naturally this first contract is very important. It must be made to look like a great victory. But in most cases the substantial gains for the membership come only after the new members have developed into a united, solid group and after good relations have grown up with the firm's management.) So in the short run it is highly desirable for the union to insure its survival and security by inducing the firm to hire — or hire and retain in its employ — only union members. In other words, the union finds it very advantageous to obtain some form of union-favoring shop (see Chapter 15 for explanation of types).

(2) Membership control. Let us suppose that the union is able to do this. Then it controls all the jobs in the firm subject to its claimed jurisdiction. From the *job* standpoint, its economic bargaining strength is complete and its security and survival assured. But even if the firm agrees that at any one time there will be only union members working on its jobs, the union might still decide that it could improve its security and economic power. It might make this improvement by doing two related things: by refusing membership to certain groups of persons, such as women and Negroes, whom it might believe to be lacking in union loyalty and stamina; and by limiting the size of the membership by other devices, thus restricting the labor supply available to the firm and tending to raise the wage rate. Let us consider each of these devices.

(a) Union membership policies on certain categories of workers. There are three main classes of workers to be considered here: women, Negroes, and left-wingers (communists or their sympathizers). Merely to name these groups is to understand that the possible exclusion or special treatment of them by unions has more than the economic basis emphasized just above. Social, political, and ideological attitudes are also very important.

i. Women workers. Women are not newcomers to industry, nor is unionism new among female wage-earners. Nevertheless, just as women have become a really important segment of the labor force only in recent decades, so their importance to and in unions has in general been pretty much confined to the past half-century. The American Federation of Labor, composed mostly of skilled craftsmen in autonomous unions, was for a long time something less than ardent in its efforts to carry out its policy, enunciated from the first, of organizing women employees. The growing mechanization of industrial processes and the accompanying increases in the competitive employment of women, however, led to the use of paid organizers at different times for the purpose of forming women's locals or bringing them into existing unions of male wage-earners. But the most important impetus toward the unionization of women workers before World War II came from the C.I.O., whose unions practiced as well as preached the principle of including these employees. The success of the C.I.O. unions in their competition with A.F.L. unions also led many of the latter to relax their formal or informal exclusions of women workers and to become less cool toward organizing them.

Why was unionism so long in taking hold among women workers? The reasons are to be sought, first, in the attitude of male unionists and the policies of their unions toward female employees; and second, in the attitude of women workers themselves. The skilled craftsmen for the most part took the view that women, by the fact of their sex, were out of place in industry and, by the fact of their lack of skill, were beyond the pale of craft unionism. Even when technological developments diluted men's skills and made possible the employment of women in certain trades, the men's unions only grudgingly admitted the fact of women's competition and the need for unionizing them.

The attitude of male unionists was partly based, with some justification, on the attitude of women workers themselves. Experience has shown that one of the toughest of all the organizational problems of unions is to *keep* workers organized; and of all workers hard to organize and keep organized, women seemed to be the most difficult. The reason for many women's lackadaisical attitude toward unionism lay in their feeling of impermanence and instability in the status of worker. The conditions determining this attitude were outlined in Chapter 8.

The withdrawal of large numbers of men from the labor force for service with the armed forces during World War II greatly stimulated the employment and the unionization of women. By 1950 only about eight unions had formal provisions in their constitutions barring women as members. Perhaps an additional twelve or so acted informally to exclude women. Virtually all these unions still practicing restrictions were skilled craft ones. About half of them were in the railroad industry, covering occupations where women are thinly employed, if at all. Almost all the non-railroad restrictive unions also had jurisdiction over occupations in which few women were employed.

Another piece of evidence on the increasing importance of women in unions was the abandonment by many organizations of the practice of keeping the female members in separate locals. By 1950, in plants employing both women and men, mixed locals were almost universal, whereas twenty years earlier sex separation had been rather common.

The effect of all the conditions leading to the increased unionization of women may be seen statistically. In 1910 there were only 75,000 female unionists — only about 3.5 per cent of all union members. In 1940 there were about 800,000 women unionists, or 9 per cent of total membership. And by 1950 they numbered about 3 million, or roughly about 19 per cent of the total.

It is rather unlikely that a woman will ever be chosen as president of a big national union. But in the lower reaches of the leadership hierarchy the contrast with prewar days is nonetheless rather striking. In at least fifteen national unions one or more women are on the executive board. Many women hold such national-union posts as vice-president, secretary-treasurer, committee chairman, and director of education or of research or of organization. And in the district or local units of unions having substantial female memberships the number of women having positions of leadership is considerable. The rising trend of women's importance within the labor movement bids fair to continue.

ii. Negro workers. Another group or level of workers whose union membership has in the past been very inconsiderable is made up of the Negroes. As in the case of women workers, the number of Negroes in American unions before 1935 was very far from being proportionate to their numerical importance in the labor force. (In 1929 only about 2 per cent of all unionists were Negroes.) At the end of 1950 the disproportion still held, but to a considerably smaller extent. Negroes in unions at that time numbered about 1.1 million, or about 7 per cent of total union membership; but Negro workers were about 12 per cent of all workers. Stated differently, about 32 per cent of white non-agricultural workers were in unions, while only 18 per cent of Negro non-agricultural were organized. Three unions — the Automobile Workers (C.I.O.), the Steelworkers (C.I.O.), and the Mine Workers (independent) — had at least 100,000 Negro members each.

What were the causes for the inferior position of these workers in the earlier years? One reason was their concentration in non-union, hard-to-organize occupations — unskilled and semi-skilled work in the mass-production industries, in agriculture, and in domestic and other service. But, as in the case of women workers, the main causes were to be found in the attitudes of white craft unionists and in the attitudes of the Negroes themselves. Racial prejudices are by no means confined to the South, although they may be made effective somewhat differently there. Part of the craft-union exclusiveness was anti-Negro as well as anti-woman. And why should the Negro workers be much interested in white men's unions when Jim Crow policies were the rule; why shouldn't they, as they frequently did, act as strikebreakers for employers?

The improvement in the position of Negroes in the labor movement since 1935 has been the combined result of several conditions. For one thing, the C.I.O. unions have preached and required the practice of anti-exclusion policies for their locals rather rigorously. The C.I.O. unions' policies were based in part on a real desire to eliminate race prejudice and in part on the necessity for enrolling all elements in the work forces subject to their jurisdiction.

During World War II, moreover, the manpower shortages demanded the employment of Negroes as well as of women. A federal Fair Employment Practices Committee (F.E.P.C.) was established by the President to get employers voluntarily to abandon any discriminatory hiring and promotion policies based on racial or other grounds. New York and New Jersey in 1945 (and a few other states since then, as well as a number of cities) passed legislation prohibiting such discrimination. All this helped to increase the employment of Negroes in previously closed occupations and lent considerable support to the policies of those unions concerned with abolishing discrimination. Such a union's ability to help member and non-member Negroes is limited in part by the ability of Negroes to get jobs. Moreover, during and after the war there were a number of United States Supreme Court decisions upholding the removal of discrimination against Negro workers, students, travelers, and others. And Negro athletes like Jackie Robinson began to break into previously all-white athletic events and leagues. The aggregate anti-discrimination impact of all these factors was substantial.

Once a gain of this sort has been made, there is seldom a retreat. Unions interested in helping Negro workers have been able to get many employers to eliminate discrimination in wage rates, hiring, layoff, and promotion. These achievements give Negroes reasons for wanting to join such unions. The Taft-Hartley amendments to the National Labor Relations Act, as will be explained in Part Three, banned the closed shop and thus in effect prevent unions from making employers refuse to hire Negro workers if the employers wish to. Northern corporations opening branches in the South usually extend their employment practices to the new plants; many such firms have non-discrimination policies. Finally, the continued drive for more thorough organization and union power inevitably enhances the need for including colored workers.

The record of Negro members' participation in "white-union" affairs, once membership has been obtained, is probably not so good as that of women, but it is improving. A few Negroes have achieved vice-presidencies in national "white" unions, and a number have attained lesser offices in nationals or locals. To wipe out discrimination against Negro workers is indeed a long-range objective. But gradual progress is to be noted.

iii. Communists and other revolutionaries. A 1946 study [1] found some 30 national unions, in this case many of the large ones, constitutionally denying membership to persons holding beliefs that would involve overthrowing by revolutionary force the American system of government and production. Today the number of such unions is doubtless larger because of the rising conflict between Communist Russia and the United States. And there can be no question that, in view of this development, the exclusive provisions are aimed chiefly at American communists.

Both communism and fascism, once they have taken over the government of a nation and established totalitarianism, abolish the free union movement as it has been and is known in private enterprise democracies. There are no free labor unions in Soviet Russia or fascist Spain, and there were none in Nazi Germany or fascist Italy. But in democratic countries communism has always seemed the greater menace to free unionism. It professes extreme devotion to the working-class proletariat and identifies the interests of the workers with those of communism (in fact, communism is supposed to be established through the dictatorship of the prole-

[1] See C. W. Sommers, "Admission Policies of Labor Unions," *Quarterly Journal of Economics,* November, 1946, pp. 66–107.

tariat), whereas fascism involves the violent reaction of the employing and middle class against the power acquisitions and aspirations of the revolutionary working class. In short, communism has seemed much more able than fascism to attract and seduce workers and union members.

It is greatly to be doubted that a majority of the members of any national union or important local unit in America have ever been real died-in-the-wool communists or even "fellow travelers." But from time to time a number of national and local unions have been communist controlled and oriented. How is such a thing possible? Because those who are really communists have been very well schooled in the tactics of taking over and controlling any kind of organization. They know all the parliamentary tricks. They know how to split and fragmentize the opposition while maintaining the strictest unity and discipline within their own cliques. They know how a small, well-planted, and well-trained minority can control union meetings when the opposition is disorganized, dispirited, or absent playing soft-ball. They understand that to most Americans union meetings are a bore; there is little interest in union affairs so long as the union leaders — whether good, honest Americans, racketeers, or communists — obtain improvements in the terms of employment and handle individual members' shop grievances satisfactorily. In short, *any* man or group of men can usually control and run a union for their own selfish purposes so long as they are devoted to their purposes and can deliver a minimum amount of satisfaction to the members. Eternal vigilance by the members is the price of maintaining democracy in any organization. If most members are not willing to practice democracy within their unions, the will of a minority can prevail. The communists are well aware of all this.

The favorite communist tactic has been to "bore from within" the unions that compose the labor movement. That is, rather than try to organize workers into separate, or "dual," avowedly communist unions, the labor arm of the communist movement much prefers to get its members into the regular unions and then, by using the above-mentioned tactics, influence these unions' policies or take over and control the unions.

In America the "boring" began in 1921, with the creation of the Trade Union Educational League by the Communist Party. A good deal of success attended these efforts, particularly in the clothing and textile industries. By 1926, however, the non-communists were frightened into counter-action and the communists were purged out of most unions. Thereupon the "party line" was shifted. Separate communist unions were organized in a Trade Union Unity League in 1928. These unions were not very successful and seem never to have mustered as many as 100,000 members. One reason was most workers' lack of interest in the communist program. Another was the excessive "splintering" of doctrine among rival communist cliques. In 1934, with the revival of unionism under the New Deal, the communist policy changed back to boring; the

T.U.U.L. was dissolved, and the members and leaders of the affiliated left-wing unions were directed to work within the non-communist organizations. When the C.I.O. was formed, its leaders accepted the support of known communists on the theory that they were good organizers, that every possible resource and assistance should be used to break the strongholds of anti-unionism, and that the communists could be controlled.

The communists and fellow travelers do appear to have been helpful in organizing non-union workers. But, as usual, they also became obnoxious to the non-communist leaders. By the end of World War II they had worked themselves into positions of top leadership and control in at least a dozen C.I.O. national unions. One or two A.F.L. national unions and a number of locals were also affected.

As a consequence of this state of affairs, together with the growing antipathy toward the theory and practices of international communism, another purge seemed to be due. In 1946 the election of Walter Reuther as president of the United Automobile Workers (C.I.O.) settled the communist issue in favor of anti-communism and in time brought internal peace to this most faction-ridden of all unions. In 1947 and 1948 the top leadership of two other C.I.O. unions — the National Maritime Union and the Transport Workers' Union — turned its back on communism. Meanwhile, the C.I.O. as a federation began to lay plans for the ousting of left-wing unions. As early as 1946 the convention voted that it would not tolerate interference in C.I.O. affairs by the Communist Party. In 1948 the leftists were warned by President Murray that, unless their policies were drastically altered, appropriate measures would be taken against them at the next convention. No such changes were made, so the 1949 convention, after stormy sessions, adopted constitutional amendments declaring ineligible for any C.I.O. office any person who was a member of an anti-democratic organization; giving the C.I.O. Executive Board power to remove any officer of a C.I.O. union who was such a member; and authorizing the Executive Board to revoke the charter of (expel) any union guilty of following left-wing policies.

Immediate action followed. On November 4, 1949, the United Electrical, Radio, and Machine Workers (the "U.E.") and the Farm Equipment and Metal Workers were expelled from the C.I.O. Hearings were held by the Executive Board on ten other affiliates, with ex-communists providing most of the damaging evidence. By late August, 1950, nine more unions had been ousted: the (Metal) Mine, Mill, and Smelter Workers; the Food, Tobacco, and Agricultural Workers; the United Public Workers; the Office and Professional Workers; the American Communications Association; the Fur and Leather Workers; the (West Coast) Longshoremen's and Warehousemen's Union; the Marine Cooks and Stewards; and the Fishermen and Allied Workers. A twelfth union, the Furniture Workers, avoided excommunication by electing an anti-communist slate of officers in 1950.

These expulsions made a sizable hole in C.I.O. strength, the eleven unions having perhaps a total of 900,000 members. Consequently the C.I.O. took steps to wean the rank and file away from the left-wing leaders. In a few instances rival unions — such as the "I.U.E.," the International Union of Electrical, Radio, and Machine Workers — were set up for this purpose, while in other industries existing unions like the Automobile Workers conducted raiding operations. By the end of 1951 the C.I.O. had made very substantial inroads, but the battle remained to be decided.

(*b*) *Closing the union in order to restrict labor supply. i. Determinants and objectives of inclusion and exclusion.* A given union's attitude and policy toward including or excluding one or more of all the categories of workers discussed in the preceding pages is determined by the technological and economic conditions peculiar to the occupation or industry over which it claims jurisdiction, and by the prevailing social attitudes toward such workers. Further, inclusion or exclusion has certain economic, political, and social objectives.

Clearly the economic objective of including all sorts of workers is to control and limit (i.e., reduce) the labor supply in the occupation or industry and remove atomistic competition from among the workers as individuals. If the job or jobs require relatively little training (as in much of large-scale manufacturing) and if employers are free to hire nonunionist as well as unionists, the union will wish to enroll all workers regardless of sex, race, age, and so on. The union may also wish to do so on the basis of social principle. But if successful work on the job requires a considerable apprenticeship-training period and if employers can be forced to hire only union men, the economic basis for organizing all sorts of workers largely vanishes. The union can do better for its members and leaders from the economic standpoint if it restricts its membership, i.e., if it operates what is known as a partially or wholly "closed" union.

There may also be political and social reasons for such a policy. From the internal political standpoint the union may be a more compact, united organization if diverse racial and other elements are excluded. The leadership may have less trouble with factionalism, may have less indifference to cope with. Or the existing members and leaders may just have irrational but deep-seated prejudices against certain kinds of workers.

It should also be noted that within a given national union the actual exclusion or inclusion of members is done by the local units. From locality to locality the conditions mentioned above may differ sufficiently to foster different policies. Some locals may wish to include, others to exclude, certain classes of workers from membership. The national union, expressing the views of its top officers or the majority views of delegates to the national convention, then has the task of obtaining acquiescence to national policy among all locals. In general, the national unions are considerably less inclined than their locals toward a policy of exclusion. The locals are more likely to take a short-sighted view. The national officers are more likely to realize that too much exclusion may not only turn public opinion against the union but also result in the growth of a potentially dangerous body of non-union workers. On the whole, most national unions have been rather ineffective if not half-hearted in their efforts to achieve uniform inclusion policies among their locals in cases where exclusion is possible and profitable. The printing and construction nationals have the settled policy of allowing their locals a great deal of latitude in respect to including or excluding workers.

ii. Methods of exclusion for economic reasons. By what methods, other than the formal and informal practices already discussed (constitutional provisions, rituals, tacit agreement, etc.), do unions restrict membership or entry to the jobs they control and thus make themselves "closed" for economic purposes? There are five principal measures: age requirements; apprenticeship requirements; high initiation fees and dues; simple refusal to take in new members; and the permit system.

Age requirements. Many of the restrictive unions have a minimum age requirement such as 16 or 18. Some have maximum age limits, such as 50 or 55, for new members. And some require that existing members leave the union when they reach, say, 55 or 60. The upper age limits for new members are found mostly among the organizations that have old-age benefit or retirement plans for members. Obviously a union cannot afford to pay such benefits to persons entering the organization only a few years before retirement; there is insufficient time to build up reserves for such persons. (Some unions having benefit plans have no maximum age limit but do not permit older entrants to participate in the plans.) It appears that employers are not the only ones to prescribe age limitations on workers.

Apprenticeship. An apprentice is a person who is learning the operations of a skilled trade over a period of several years. Suppose that employers dealing with a union having jurisdiction over a particular skilled occupation have agreed to hire only skilled union men. Then if the union can control the training of all persons aspiring to learn the skill, it can control the number of entrants to the occupation, and thereby the number of unionists available to the employers. On the other hand, if employers can hire non-unionists as well as union men and can train their own apprentices or obtain those trained in government schools, the union's control over the supply of skilled workers is broken.

Apprenticeship systems of some sort are almost as old as history. There were strict regulations among the medieval craft guilds. And they have persisted to this day in occupations, such as printing and construction, whose skills have not been destroyed or significantly eroded by technological change. The number of such occupations, however, has steadily diminished; and so has the number of unions requiring formal apprenticeship training for admission to membership. Perhaps thirty do so today.

This trend of course does not mean that the adequate all-around training of a sufficient number of young workers in the remaining skilled occupations — tool-and-die making, skilled machine trades, construction work, printing and publishing, and others — is not now of paramount importance. On the contrary, an adequate supply of such workers is a requisite for continued economic progress. For example, before and during World War II not enough young men learned bricklaying and other skilled construction occupations. Consequently there were not enough bricklayers and other skilled craftsmen to meet the demand for new housing after the war. Too few houses were built. And those built were over-expensive because the craftsmen were paid bonus wage rates above the official union scale, in addition to time-and-a-half for many hours of overtime work. This was good for the unionists whose numbers had been limited, but it was not good for the more numerous group of citizens who wanted new housing.

The unions control the training of apprentices by limiting their numbers; prescribing the length of the training periods; and prescribing the content of the training. Most skilled craft unions achieve a numerical restriction on apprentices by setting a ratio of number of apprentices to number of journeymen. One to five is the most usual, although one to ten is frequent also. (Some unions also specify that only the sons and nephews of journeymen can be admitted to apprenticeship.) The prescribed length of training period varies from two to six years among the different crafts. As to content of training, unions usually insist on all-round initiation instead of the specialized, partial training preferred by many employers.

Most unions interested in apprenticeship have given up insisting that the training be supplied wholly by union journeymen. They do not object to training by employers' agents or under government-sponsored plans and schools so long as the content is adequate for the unions' purposes.

Initiation fees and dues. When a worker joins a union, he must usually pay a sum of money known as an *initiation fee.* After he is in, he must make regular, periodic payments known as *dues.* He may also be subject to occasional *special assessments* for particular purposes.

Obviously, high fees and dues act as deterrents to prospective members. The great majority of unions charge initiation fees of from \$2 to \$5. Those of most C.I.O. unions are within this modest range. But some of the A.F.L. skilled craft unions go considerably higher, the common range being \$25 to \$50. Particular locals at times have gone up to \$300, \$500, and \$1000.

Membership dues range usually from \$2 to \$3 per month for A.F.L. unions, \$1.00 to \$1.50 for C.I.O. organizations.

The amended National Labor Relations Act of 1947 tends to limit the amounts of fees and dues properly chargeable by American unions (see Chapter 24).

Other restrictions. Sometimes local craft unions simply refuse to receive any more members for a period of time, no matter how many competent applicants may be clamoring for admission. Often this measure is adopted because of substantial unemployment among existing members. At other times it is used to secure the control of the local. If employers complain at not being able to obtain needed workers, the union may issue temporary work-permit cards to outsiders capable of performing the jobs.

As we come to the end of this discussion of exclusiveness among American labor unions, it is important to note that only a minority of the unions (as in construction and printing) are in a position to employ restrictive measures successfully; and the trend has been toward a reduction in their use. In other words, the practice of closing unions for economic reasons (in order to restrict the labor supply) is declining in much the same way as the practice of shutting out special categories of workers, such as Negroes and women.

CHAPTER 13

Union Structure and Government (concluded)

C. THE ORGANIZATION AND GOVERNMENT OF EXISTING MEMBERS

We shall now look at the internal arrangements of unions and federations of unions. Our focus shifts from job-worker jurisdiction and control to the ways in which the existing members are organized in various units, the members and the organizational units are related and controlled, and the business of the unions and federations gets transacted. We shall review first the general structure of the labor movement. Then we shall consider in succession the organization and government of local unions, national unions, and federations of unions.

1. General structure of the labor movement. In our discussion of union history in Chapters 10 and 11 and in our treatment of membership inclusions and exclusions in Chapter 12, the general structural make-up of American unionism should have emerged rather clearly. Nevertheless it is desirable now to concentrate on the matter of structure in order to remove any possible misunderstanding.

First, as a unionist an individual worker is a member of a local union. The individual worker is the smallest particle in the organizational pyramid of unionism. The local union to which he belongs may or may not be a unit of a national (or "international") union. There are three possibilities in respect to a local union's affiliations with labor organizations of national scope: (*a*) It may be a unit of a national union. This is the most usual condition. Here the individual worker is a member of the national union by virtue of being a member of the local unit of the national. (*b*) The local union may not be a part of a national union, but it may be directly affiliated with a national federation, such as the A.F.L. or the C.I.O. At any one time there are many such locals. But for any one of them such affiliation is usually temporary; in the end, it is usually taken into some existing national or combined with other, similar locals into a new national. Whether the direct affiliation with the national federation is temporary or indefinite, the individual worker belonging to such a local is never a member of the national federation; he belongs only to the local. (*c*) The local union may be neither a unit of a sovereign national union nor affiliated with a national federation of such sovereigns. This situation is not a usual one but occasionally exists in firms where the workers want only an unconnected plant union.

Second, local unions in the first two categories given above almost always have connections in addition to those just mentioned. At the local level in a big city they may belong to company-wide or city-wide grouping of locals belonging to the same national union. Here the individual worker is not a member of the group of locals. A given local may also be part of one or the other or both of the two kinds of local federations mentioned early in Chapter 12 — the all-inclusive federation (the city central of the A.F.L. or the local industrial union council of the C.I.O.), or the industrial federation, such as the local printing trades councils or the local building trades councils of the A.F.L. Most local unions belong only to the all-inclusive kind of local federation. Here too the individual member of a local is not a member of the local federation as such.

At the district (regional) or state level a given local union, if part of a national union, usually has two or more connections: It may be part of a district, regional, or state grouping of locals in the same national union. And it may be part of an A.F.L. state federation of labor or a C.I.O. state industrial union council. If the local is not part of a national union but is affiliated directly with a national federation, it belongs to an appropriate state federation or council. In all these cases the individual member of the local does not belong to the group as such.

At the national level a local union that is part of a national union may also be a member of an industrial subdivision of the national federation to which the national union is affiliated. These industrial subdivisions are called "departments." Examples are the Metal Trades Department and the Building Trades Department of the A.F.L. Again the individual union worker does not belong to the department.

2. Organization and government of the local union. Just as in the United States there are three levels of governmental jurisdiction — the local, state, and national; so in most national unions there are at least three levels — the local unions, the intermediate organizations (district, regional, or state), and the national. The local unions thus form the basic foundation of the national's structure.

The local union is overwhelmingly the unit whereby the individual member has his relations with his national union and with the labor movement in general. It is here that he has his say, if any, in the determination of policies affecting his welfare and satisfaction. In considering the internal make-up of local unions we shall deal with their size and scope; their relation to the national union; the nature, duties, and powers of local union officers; and local union finances.

a. Size and scope. How large a given local is and how many plants or firms it covers depends on historical, technological, and economic conditions plus the nature of the membership and administrative expediency and convenience for the union officers. If in a given locality the firms or plants in which a given national union is recognized are small, a local unit of the national may well cover a number of plants or firms. This situation is rather usual for most craft unions, such as the Bricklayers and Plasterers. But it may also exist, as in the apparel industries and in the tool-and-die shops subject to the jurisdiction of the United Automobile Workers, for some industrial or semi-industrial union locals. On the other hand, in the large-scale mass-production industries, where individual plants are large, a local is ordinarily confined to one plant; and a multiplant firm will be dealing with a number of different locals. This situation is common for most industrial unions.

There are many exceptions to the above rules. The locals of some unions are city-wide even though the employing plants or firms are large. Thus, all the members of the Hosiery Workers living in Philadelphia, a major center of the industry, are in one local, which is so large that it comprises one-fourth of the national union's total membership. Or in a given large city, as with the Automobile Workers and the United Electrical, Radio, and Machine Workers, the locals may be company-wide, even though the company has several large plants in the area. Again, an industrial union like the Amalgamated Clothing Workers may set up separate locals for particular craftsmen like the cutters. The Flint Glass Workers and the Bookbinders have separate locals for unskilled members and the Automobile Workers for plant white-collar workers. The Teamsters have separate locals for different branches of trucking, such as milk-wagon drivers, laundry drivers, and taxicab drivers. Moreover, as noted in Chapter 12, separate locals have been established by some unions for women, Negroes, and special nationality-language groups like the Italians.

In all these cases the size and coverage of the local has been the result of the size of the plant or firm, the composition of the membership, or the administrative or political convenience of the union leadership. The last-named factor is sometimes of major importance. Thus, large locals combining the union memberships of several plants are usually easier to control by top leadership than a number of separate, small ones. They also make it easier for a smart minority faction to seize power in the union. Suppose that a minority clique wishes to obtain control over a big local in a given large city. To do this it must control the executive council which governs the local and which is composed of one representative from each plant covered by the local. If the clique concentrates on winning the votes of the members in the small plants, it may well obtain a majority on the council and thus get into power over the members of all the plants.

As a result of the operation of all these factors there is a tremendous range in size among the more than 70,000 locals in the country. The national Association of Letter Carriers has a few locals of only two members. At the other extreme we find Local 600 of the Automobile Workers composed of some 60,000 members working at the River Rouge plant of the Ford Motor Company near Detroit; Lodge 72 of the Boilermakers with over 60,000 members (during the war); and Local 89 of the Ladies' Garment Workers with more than 35,000 members. In general, the average size of the C.I.O. unions' locals is considerably larger than that of the A.F.L. unions' locals.

b. Degree of control by national unions. In our discussion of union history we noted the trend toward and the conditions making for the centralization of power in the hands of national unions' conventions and officers. Centralization has existed in almost all national unions, but it has been much more pronounced in some than in others. In general, power in the C.I.O. unions is more concentrated than in the A.F.L. unions. The conditions affecting this matter include the age and size of the local, the nature of the national leadership, and the scope of the market for the industry's product. The older and bigger a local union is, the less likely is it to submit with docility to national control. Some locals antedate the creation of the national and feel relatively independent and superior. Clearly also, national leaders with strong personalities and power drives are more likely to bend locals to their wills than weak leaders. Again, the markets for many products are national; but in some fields, such as construction, newspaper publishing, building service (elevator operation, cleaning, etc.), and barbering, the markets are local. In national-market industries each national union feels keenly the need for making all its locals follow the same policies in dealing with firms. In the local-market industries this need is weak; consequently, national control is usually much weaker in these industries.

c. Local union meetings, officers, and committees. The great variety in the size and scope of local unions makes it difficult to generalize about the ways in which the business of these units is conducted. However, some common characteristics may be noted.

(1) Meetings. Usually the interested members of local unions assemble once a month for a regular meeting. Special sessions are sometimes called to discuss and vote on special matters, such as the ratification of a new collective bargaining agreement.

The meeting-places vary a great deal in appearance, size, and attractiveness. A small, run-down local will hold its sessions in a small, poorly furnished, dimly lighted second-floor room over a bar or a poolroom. A big, prosperous local will meet in a "Labor Temple" whose appointments are at least as luxurious as those provided by most corporations for stockholders' meetings.

Many, perhaps most, local union sessions come as close as anything we have left in America to practicing the town-meeting sort of democracy.

They are often dull and routine, but they can be exciting; much depends on the kind of leadership, the character of the membership, and the vitality of the issues being discussed. The interested student should avail himself of opportunities to visit local meetings and learn how matters of local and national import are treated; here he may learn much about the advantages and faults of democracy.

As previously noted, attendance at routine local meetings is usually poor. It takes some big problem or crisis like a new contract with employers or a crucial challenge to the leadership by an aroused opposing faction to bring out the vote. In other words, union members are just like other Americans in other organizations. When do most citizens, most stockholders, or most church members bother to go to the polls or to business meetings?

To point out these parallels is not of course to condone indifference on the part of the rank and file. Absenteeism at union meetings, as in other organizations, is an open invitation to control by minority cliques, racketeers, or others who would pervert the uses of democracy to their own ends.

A good many unions have tried to reduce such absenteeism — either negatively by the levying of fines for non-attendance or positively by providing refreshments, special talks, entertainment, lottery prizes, and so forth.

(2) Officers and committees. (a) Regular officers. Local union meetings are presided over and inter-meeting local union affairs are handled by the usual kinds of officers and committees, supplemented by some that are peculiar to unions. There is a local president, a vice-president or two, a secretary and a treasurer (or a secretary-treasurer), perhaps an executive board composed of three officials, and the usual committees for routine and special assignments. The larger the local, the larger and more complicated is its official set-up.

The above-mentioned officers are elected, at a local union meeting or (in the case of very large locals) by referendum or mail vote, for a period of one or two years. The committeemen may be elected but are usually appointed by the president; in the first case, they owe their jobs to the electorate, in the second to the president, thus providing him with some "patronage."

The turnover in local union office is usually rather high (tenure averaging two to four years), but not necessarily because the membership is regularly dissatisfied with the existing officers. Turnover also occurs partly because there are contests for the honor and prestige of officialdom (with campaigning inexpensive); partly because, once elected, the officers find the burden of work to be great in comparison with the pecuniary and realized non-pecuniary compensation; and partly because local union officers are often promoted up into the national official family or are seduced by management into foremanships or superintendencies.

In most of the smaller local unions the officers work at their own plant jobs along with the rank-and-file members who elected them. They perform their union duties on their own spare time, mostly at night. The special compensation for their union work is usually small and informal, sometimes a few hundred dollars voted by the membership and paid like a bonus at the end of the term of office. In these circumstances, the officers are likely to be close to and share the views of the rank and file; they are subject to the same environmental conditions. This benefit, however, is likely to be offset by a lack of objectivity and perspective in dealings with management.

The larger locals usually require full-time service from some of their officers. And, being large, these locals have treasuries big enough to pay for full-time work. Here the advantages and disadvantages are reversed: There is a gain in objectivity in dealing with management, but there is a loss in understanding the workers' problems.

The salaries paid to full-time local officers are rather modest in all but the exceptionally large locals. Many unions pay their officers the highest regular wage rate received by local members working in the trade, although a few raise this rate by some amount, say a dollar per hour, or pay foremen's compensation. Other locals pay stipulated annual amounts rather than follow the rate paid to foremen or fellow union members; these amounts probably do not today average very much above $4000 per year.

(b) The shop steward. In addition to the above-mentioned customary group of officers and committees, there are special union functionaries. In many unions one of these is the *shop steward* or *committeeman.* Although sometimes appointed by the local's officers, the steward is usually elected by a given local's members in the shop, department, or plant in which the members are employed. In a large plant with large departments there is usually one steward to each department. If the departments are small, one steward may serve several of them.

A shop steward's duties are numerous and varied. He is the local's initial and immediate contact with the rank and file. He is often a collector of dues; an enforcer and applier of union rules and policies in respect to management and union members; an organizer of non-unionists in his department; a general "talk-union" man; and sometimes an employment-agent go-between (a job-getter and job-filler) for unionists and management. In short, he represents the local union to the workers of his department. But his main function almost always is to represent his constituents and bring their grievances to the attention of the foreman of his department. That is, in the first instance he represents the union to management. He is thus very much a key man in the day-to-day labor relations of the plant. Along with the foreman he can make or break the union-management relationship. For no matter how great the good will and no matter how proper the policies in the relationship between top management and top union officialdom, the quality of the plant relationship depends on the lowest level of practitioners on both sides. And the plant relationship in the last analysis is the crucial one.

The shop steward is supposed to spend most of his time working on a regular job in the department which he represents. As a worker he is of course paid by the management. Clearly, however, if he is to perform all the functions listed above, he must frequently be absent from his workplace. At such times he is compensated at a rate equivalent to his average hourly earnings either by the union or by management or by these two jointly.

(c) The business agent. In certain industries (such as small metal working, clothing, and construction) the plants are so small or so impermanent that the shop steward system is not appropriate. Here we find the *business agent* (or "walking delegate") as a very important local union official. He is as old as unionism; as may be understood from the statement above on the kinds of industries in which he is found, he certainly antedates the shop steward because the plants in most industries were small and impermanent in the early days. In the early days there were additional reasons for establishing this union job. The business agent possessed knowledge and bargaining skill not found in ordinary members. Being paid by the union, he could take a strong stand against employers without jeopardizing his job tenure. Being a full-time agent, he could devote all his energies to union affairs.

The business agent may not have been — though he usually has been — a worker in the craft or industry. As in the case of a labor lawyer who takes the job, he may even not be — but he usually is — a member of the union he represents. He is sometimes appointed by the local union officers; perhaps more commonly he is elected by the membership.

In any case, the business agent's functions are very much like those enumerated above for the shop steward. But, unlike the latter, he is a full-time union officer paid wholly by the union. And he has one other function which is not regularly part of a shop steward's job, namely, playing an important role in the negotiation of new contracts with employers.

Most business agents have undoubtedly been found, by the unionists and employers with whom they deal, to be honest and reasonable as well as effective. However, in a few industries, particularly construction, a business agent has exceptional opportunity for being crooked and domineering if he is so inclined. Investigations by various government agencies after World War I and in 1930–31 and 1935–37 have disclosed the following: In construction a business agent can exercise control over contractors because, although the latter cannot affect the agent's job tenure, he is empowered to call strikes at a moment's notice. The contractor has posted a bond or forfeit to complete the building within a stated period of time. A strike causes lost time and makes the contractor lose his forfeit. Each craft usually works on the building for only a short period; but its presence is absolutely essential for this period. The collective bargaining contract between the contractor and the union contains a great many rules and regulations governing the conditions of work. It is not hard to find the contractor violating some minor rule. An honest, reasonable business agent winks at such violations. But a domineering, dishonest one uses them as a club over the contractor's head and threatens to call the men out on strike — unless of course the contractor is willing to make a nice little "insurance" payment to the agent for refraining from calling the stoppage. If the contractor balks at such extortion, he may be "persuaded" not only by the strike but sometimes also by a bomb at his home, a fire at his new building, or a slugging by the business agent's strong-arm squad. For a while, in some big cities like New York and Chicago, contractors regularly added ten per cent or so as strike insurance to their costs in bids on construction work.

With their "take" on these projects, some business agents in construction have also set themselves up in business as suppliers of building materials or machinery. Contractors have then been "persuaded" to confine their purchases to these sources. Naturally the prices were exorbitant.

Of course, many contractors are not too much upset by all these practices. Their operations are pretty much cost-plus; they can pass the increased costs on to the buyers of office buildings and dwellings. They figure that the demand for construction is income-elastic but not price-elastic. That is, so long as the economy's resources are fully employed and national income is high, they feel they have little to worry about from rising construction costs and prices.

A business agent's power is not confined to employers. If he wishes to exercise it, he has a great hold on union members also, particularly in construction. In this industry he is usually not responsible to national-union officers but only to his own constituents. These he controls in part because of his job-getting function; they are dependent on him for the number, frequency, and nature of the jobs they get during the year. The agent can build up a political machine of loyal henchmen and supporters by giving them the best jobs. Those who object to his activities find themselves without jobs or with the poorer ones. Other controls sometimes found include the power to give or withhold union benefit payments for sickness, unemployment, and retirement; the power to let a worker temporarily off payment of dues; the power to press or withhold action on workers' grievances; and the accumulated experience of the business agent, which makes him valuable and hard to replace.

It is not unusual to find a business agent in the thick of local government politics. As a labor boss it is easy for him to become a political boss, for he controls or influences a great many local-union votes. As a political boss he is able to obtain political preferment for his supporters. And he can influence zoning and other ordinances affecting the quantity and location of new construction, thus giving him an additional hold over contractors.

Some of the more notorious names in the history of this rather nasty business have been Skinny Malden in Chicago (1905), Bob Brindell (1920) and Pat Comerford (1931) in New York, and Czar Brandle in northern New Jersey (1935). It is indeed to the credit of the unions in the construction and other industries that the list of such men has been relatively short.

(d) Important local committees. In most local unions there are three especially important committees: the negotiating committee, the grievance committee, and the trial or judicial committee or board. The names of these groups denote their functions. The negotiating committee is the one which bargains with one or more employers over the terms of new contracts. Its composition varies among different locals. In some, all the main local officers are automatically on this committee, and one or more additional persons may be elected by the membership or appointed by the president. In other cases, no officers or only one or two need be on the committee, the members again being elected or appointed. The "international" representative of the national union often participates in the negotiations in order to see that the terms of the contract accord with national policy as well as to assist the committee in reaching an agreement. Usually any agreement that is negotiated by this committee must be submitted to the rank and file for approval.

During the life of an existing contract grievances of workers over managerial actions and disputes over the interpretation and application of the contract arise. As a first step the shop stewards or business agent try to settle such matters with the foreman involved. If these efforts fail, the next step often brings in the local union grievance committee and a higher level of management. This committee is usually composed of all the shop stewards or of an elected or appointed fraction of their number. Occasionally the elected or appointed committee members are non-stewards.

The trial committee of a local union handles cases involving charges against union members which, if judged proven, result in some form of disciplinary action (fine, suspension, and so forth) against the guilty person or persons. This committee holds hearings on the charges. It may be composed of the elected officers, or it may be a standing or temporary elected group of non-officers. This committee's findings and recommendations must usually be submitted to the local membership for ratification or rejection. (See later sections in this chapter for further discussion of union disciplinary procedure.)

d. Local union finances. We have said several times that much of American unionism is big business. This means that a large union's annual income and expenditures run into six or seven digits. Most unions have a broad range of functions, and they have to spend a great deal of money to perform these functions adequately. Therefore their expenditures are high, and their incomes must be high.

(1) Income. Most of the income obtained by a national union originates in and funnels through the local units. Money in the local treasury comes from four main sources — initiation fees, regular dues, special assessments, and occasional fines on members for breaking union rules. Part of the money thus collected is used for local purposes, part may be given to a district or state division of the national union, and part is sent in to the various funds administered by the national union. A local may also raise money for special purposes by such devices as dances, picnics, tag days, raffles, and so forth. The funds are usually cared for by a treasurer or financial secretary (often bonded). Sometimes there is a standing auditing committee which periodically scrutinizes receipts and expenditures. Usually a representative of the national office also audits each local's books once a year.

(2) Expenditures. The portions of local gross income paid to its district and national union are of course "expenditures" for a given local. From one-third to two-thirds may go out in this fashion for various items, such as the death benefit fund, strike fund, and so on.

Of the local's net income — the money left after payments to higher union levels — there are substantial out-payments on administrative salaries and materials, organizational work, donations to various labor and liberal causes, perhaps strikes, and so on.

4. Organization and government of national unions. To most people "the union" means the national organization. This is natural because of the previously mentioned gradual concentration of power in its hands. Except in the cases pointed out earlier, it is usually the national body which determines most of the important policies and dominates almost every phase of the union's legitimate activities. Its governmental functions, like those of any other group, may be considered under three heads — legislative, executive, and judicial. These powers, like those of the United States government, are set forth and defined in a written constitution and set of bylaws.

a. The legislative function. For unions the legislative function includes making amendments to the constitution, passing rules on a great variety of subjects (such as organization drives, apprenticeship rules, union label, and demands to be made on employers), levying taxes (such as special assessments), appropriating funds for various expenditures, voting on strikes or boycotts, and electing officers. The legislative function may be carried on by a national convention or by direct referendum vote of all the members, or by both.

(1) The convention. In almost every union the convention is officially the most important body. It is supposed to be the supreme law-making group, having the final word on all questions of general significance.

(a) Frequency of meeting. The great majority of national constitutions provide for periodic conventions. A small minority, however, make no

official requirement for a convention. In the latter unions the referendum is usually used for legislative work; and if a convention is proposed by leaders or members, the referendum is employed to obtain membership approval. A few unions have gone for very long periods (such as 30 to 40 years) without holding a convention.

Among the unions whose constitutions require periodic conventions, the biennial gathering appears to be the most common, with the annual meeting a close second. However, conventions every three, four, or five years are found among a good many national unions. The trend has been away from annual meetings. One reason is the high cost of conventions. Whether the national bears the entire financial burden (as is often the case) or makes the locals do so (as is rarely the case) or splits the expense with the locals (as sometimes happens), a large union spends a great deal of money on these affairs. A quarter of a million dollars or more is not uncommon.

(b) Basis of membership representation. The convention is a delegate body composed of representatives elected by the various locals of the parent union. Only locals in good standing, i.e., those who are paid up in all their financial obligations to the national and have honored all the rules and regulations of the national authorities, can expect to have their delegates seated. The large national unions may have from 1500 to almost 3000 delegates at their conventions.

How many delegates does each local elect and send? The simplest basis of representation is the proportional one — one delegate for, say, every 200 or 300 members or major fraction thereof. Many unions use this plan, which clearly may permit a few large locals to dominate the convention. The small locals of some unions, however, like the small states in this country, have feared domination by large locals; preferring an equal number of delegates regardless of size, or a progressive plan of some sort, these locals have opposed the proportional plan with such vigor that they have succeeded in securing at least a compromise which gives the bigger locals proportionately less voting strength. This result is produced by setting a limit to the total number of representatives allowed from any local or by broadening the representation base (e.g., one delegate for the first 100 members, a second delegate for the next 200 members, a third for the next 500 members, and so on) or by both.

(c) Procedure and work. At the convention the procedure or order of business is generally similar to that of any other national conference such as a fraternity convention or a church conference. The delegates' credentials are first scrutinized by a special committee, and if two or more factions are fighting for control of the organization, there is plenty of opportunity at this point for the display of rancor or dirty politics. The next main feature is the reading of the reports of the national officers. Then the various subjects for action (embracing all or most of the topics mentioned at the beginning of this section on "legislation"), which ordi-

narily include proposals and petitions made by various locals as well as those introduced by the national officers, are referred for discussion and report to a great number of committees. These committees may urge favorable consideration or modify the proposal or pigeonhole it. The main work of the convention consists of debating the proposals reported back to it. Those which are approved acquire the force of law for the union until the next meeting. In this way the convention may become the wellspring of most of the shifts in the policies and tactics by which unionism is known. Toward the end of the session officers are elected and installed for the next period.

The convention often also takes unto itself certain executive and judicial functions. Local unions, officers, and committees may submit grievances and disputes to it for decision. Often locals' disciplinary actions in respect to individual members (mentioned above) come before the convention on appeal. So also may the inter-convention decisions of the national officers. The convention may have the authority in many cases to fine, suspend, or expel local unions and individuals. Frequently its committees do administrative and executive work.

(2) The referendum. Some unions (almost half of the larger ones), desiring to make their governments more subject to democratic control by the rank and file, have used the referendum a great deal as a legislative medium for certain important matters. Often the initiation of measures directly by locals is also provided for. The nomination and election of officers, amendments to the constitution, calling of strikes, and ratification of important policies initiated by locals or endorsed by conventions are the things most commonly referred to popular vote. For certain proposals, such as constitutional amendments and changes in dues, a two-thirds majority of a minimum vote is required. There is no union which uses the referendum exclusively instead of the convention. In almost all the chief labor groups there is a combination of the two. But in most, the convention is the more important; the referendum is reserved for matters of special moment, and the trend has been somewhat away from its use.

(3) Relative value of convention and referendum. The advantages claimed for the referendum are as follows: it is superior in recording the wishes of the rank and file; it reduces the chances for autocratic domination by cliques or officers; it allays suspicion of such domination; it is educational and promotes more interest in union affairs; and it gives minorities greater opportunity to become articulate. Many students feel that these theoretical merits have not been realized. Super-democratic control in all kinds of government leaves something to be desired. The referendum has often proved cumbersome and wasteful of time, energy, and money. A great many members are not interested enough to vote, except perhaps on a momentous question such as a general strike. Minorities often seem indifferent to this chance for expression of opinion. The

ordinary union man may not be well enough informed to vote intelligently.

The convention, on the other hand, probably brings together the cream of the union crop, men whose intelligence is above the average and who are better equipped to decide important issues. The convention's forum provides a much greater opportunity for open and free exchange of ideas than the referendum. It is distinctly stimulating to meet under such conditions, and most delegates come home with a broadened outlook and new enthusiasm. Union solidarity is promoted when delegates from one section rub elbows with those from other places. The delegates' contact with leaders and officers is often invigorating for both.

The experiences of the great majority of unions seem to bear out these theoretical advantages of the convention. Nevertheless, the fact that the referendum has been retained would indicate that a judicious combination of the two best fulfills the legislative function.

b. The executive function. Wide as is the scope of the convention's work, there are certain administrative and executive functions which it cannot fulfill. During the periods between conventions many weighty problems arise which demand immediate solution and require prompt decision. Therefore it is highly necessary that a compact group of able men be selected to guide the course of the national organization by giving to its affairs their complete attention throughout the year. The most important of their numerous duties include (1) the enforcement and interpretation of all rules passed by the convention or already listed in the constitution; (2) the negotiation of agreements with employers or officers of employers' associations, subject sometimes to later ratification by referendum; (3) the calling of strikes when the time is ripe and the rescinding of strike orders when conditions are unfavorable (it is true that the calling and calling off of strikes are subject to referendum vote in some unions, but because delay gives employers more chance to use countertactics and industrial conditions may change and rob the strike of its effectiveness, it has seemed better to allow a large measure of discretion to the national officers); (4) the organization of new locals and the granting of new charters; (5) the temporary suspension and even expulsion of refractory locals; (6) the removal of local officers; (7) the deciding of appeals and grievances from subordinate units in the union; (8) the appointing of convention and inter-convention committees; (9) the collection of revenue and the levying of special assessments in times of need; and (10) the coordination and unification of the locals' activities and interest through international representatives, intermediate units, correspondence, and publication of a weekly or monthly journal.

(1) The elected national executive officers. (a) Who they are and what they do. In most national unions these functions are performed by a group of full-time officers and by an executive board. The chief executive is usually the president, and the second most important official is ordi-

narily the secretary-treasurer. The president's job includes presiding at conventions and general supervision of most of the administrative work of the union. When the executive board, mentioned below, is not in session, the president performs most of the functions listed above. The secretary-treasurer performs or supervises most of the clerical and correspondence work, sometimes (except in large unions) edits the union periodical, and usually is in charge of union finances.

In the larger unions there are also one or more vice-presidents. Sometimes these are the heads of the intermediate units discussed above. Usually the union's constitution allocates the vice-presidencies on the basis of geographic location or of industrial or craft division within the union. Occasionally some of the vice-presidents are required to be actual workers.

In the larger unions there are also one or more vice-presidents. Sometralization of power over subordinate units in the national union meant growing authority for the national president. To avoid despotism by this official, executive boards or councils were created by the conventions of many unions. A number of the president's functions (such as the granting of charters to new locals, the suspension of existing locals, and the levying of special assessments) were transferred to these boards. Frequently the boards were authorized to serve as courts of appeal from the president's decisions.

In some unions the executive board is merely the whole group of executive officers (president and so on) mentioned above. In a few other unions the personnel of the board is entirely different from that of the other officers. Commonly, however, there is some overlap: The board includes some of the officers, plus others whose only official duty is to sit on the board.

Frequently the official subordination of the national union president to the executive board has failed to curb the power of the president. For one thing, the president is usually on the job all the time, whereas the board assembles only occasionally, sometimes only at the call of the president. More important, the president is usually in a position to control or influence the board members. He is usually the head of a political machine, built up by his power to grant various favors, appoint friendly national organizers and representatives, supervise local and intermediate activities, and present his own actions in a favorable light to the membership through the union press. The members of the executive board ordinarily find it desirable to follow his wishes, for the maintenance of their own positions often depends on his good will.

In general, it appears that the concentration of power is greater among some of the A.F.L. unions than among most C.I.O. unions. But there are notable exceptions to this generalization, and centralization has been growing among the C.I.O. unions.

(b) Characteristics of top union officials. The great majority of leaders

of national unions have come up from the ranks of ordinary workers and union members. Their fathers and relatives have usually been members of the working class. They have "arrived" by dint of hard work and long hours of devotion to the cause of organized labor and to the methods of winning political preferment and membership allegiance. Only a minority have had an education above the high-school level. Thus far, there has been little evidence of any shift from the traditional antipathy of American unionists toward outside, "intellectual" leadership.

After winning his way to a top position and holding it for some time, a union leader has developed to a fine point the art of dealing successfully with people, both within and outside his own organization. He tends to look and act like a combination of businessman and politician. He has a comfortable salary from a job with prestige, and he wants to keep it. He is much farther from direct contact with the rank and file of local union members than are local union officers. This means that he may get out of touch with their needs and sentiments. By the same token, he is less susceptible to short-sighted, impatient, emotional approaches to workers' problems. Through bargaining with management he has accumulated much insight and experience in business and managerial difficulties and is much more apt than a local leader to understand and sympathize with management's point of view. Not that he is likely to sell his membership down the river or forget all about the ideals of the labor movement he has helped to build; he gets much satisfaction from the victories he wins for his followers. But he is usually content to take the longer view and work for the longer pull.

(c) Manner of election and tenure of office. In most unions top union officials are elected by vote of the delegates to the union convention. In a minority of unions the rank and file vote directly through referenda.

Officially, the tenure of national office is not long. That is, under most union constitutions the term of office is one or two years. Some unions allow three or four, a few five years. But the actual tenure of most top leaders is much longer. They tend to be re-elected time after time. This is in striking contrast with the rapid, frequent turnover among most local union officers.

Very often an existing union president is unopposed in seeking re-election. This is especially true among the older A.F.L. unions, but has been much less the case among the new C.I.O. organizations. The International Typographical Union has a unique two-party system; the Progressives and the Independents each support a full slate of candidates and have relatively equal access to the membership (through the union periodical and otherwise) in presenting their programs. Here the elections are hotly contested, and the degree of interest and participation by the high-grade membership is large. In most A.F.L. unions, however, and to an increasing extent in the older C.I.O. unions there is usually little organized opposition to existing incumbents, and the members are more or less indifferent (save where the communist issue is important). In one A.F.L. union, the Longshoremen, President Ryan has been elected for life!

Tenures of 30 to 50 years as union president have not been uncommon in American labor history. The average among the older unions is about 20 years. Thus, Dan Tobin of the Teamsters came into power in 1907; Bill Hutcheson of the Carpenters was first elected in 1916, yielding the office to his son in 1951; and John L. Lewis became president of the Miners in 1920. There have been a good many others in their tenure class.

A variety of conditions make such long terms of office possible. (*i*) The membership may recognize the worth of the leader's experience in running the union and in dealing with employers and government. Such experience is not easily or quickly acquired by new incumbents. (*ii*) The membership may be apathetic toward the desirability of removing existing leaders. Why should they bother about despotism or even dishonesty at the top so long as the leaders keep pace within the union and win from firms and government concessions that improve members' day-to-day living in plant and home? (*iii*) The control of the union periodical and the political machine that the union president develops through his power to appoint his supporters to positions of preferment in various spots throughout the union (these supporters in turn being able to create adherents by passing out petty favors among the members) give the president and his associates a tremendous advantage over less well-known and well-situated opponents. Almost every organizer, every international representative, and every subordinate official is inclined to talk about the "boss" as a "great guy." Unless there is an organized opposition party, as in the Typographical Union and in the American political system, the members have little chance to learn about rival candidates. (*iv*) Some union leaders have brooked no opposition, using ruthless, often extra-constitutional methods (expulsion, demotion, and so on) to remove rivals from the field. If members are indifferent, appeals from such actions are likely to be ineffective.

The disadvantages of long office tenures are fairly obvious. (*i*) Some long-term leaders tend to lose their "zing" and aggressiveness. Their patience with employers' points of view may degenerate into sell-outs. (*ii*) They may get too far out of touch with members' needs. They may come to think too much about their own job tenures, i.e., believe that the welfare of the union and their own well-being are identical. (*iii*) They may lose the knack of adaptation to changing conditions, the ability to make proper decisions promptly. In short, long-time labor leaders sometimes seem to be afflicted with all the ills commonly associated with aging. (*iv*) Young, promising unionists may be discouraged or thwarted from seeking office and making contributions to the welfare of members and union. (*v*) The process of maintaining one's self in power may involve a denial of democratic rights and privileges to the membership.

The advantages of having one set of officers in power for a long time may be less obvious to those concerned with democracy within unions. But there *are* utilities. (*i*) The union and its members have a big asset in the experience and reputation of the top leadership. The president's ability and prestige may win concessions from business and government that a younger, greener leader could not obtain. (*ii*) Top corporation officials usually have long tenures. There seems to be no particular reason why union leaders should be in office less long. (*iii*) Long tenure can mean continuity of policy and the ability to make and carry out long-range plans. (*iv*) Most important, the development of successful, harmonious, stable, long-term relations between a union and the employers with which it deals depends in part on the continuity and security of the leaders on both sides. When the personnel of the bargainers on each side is frequently changed, there is rarely an opportunity for the necessary personal knowledge of and adjustment between the parties. If a union negotiator is constantly worrying about re-election and membership reactions, he is in a poor position to take a long view, to make necessary concessions, to deal frankly, and to build up confidence in his ability and integrity.

(d) Salaries. National union presidents, as would be expected, are considerably better paid than are local union officers. Yet even the largest, most financially strong nationals pay their presidents much less than most corporations give their top executives. Apparently power and prestige, plus the sense of accomplishment in their devotion to the welfare of the common worker, are important items in the over-all compensation of union officials.

From available, somewhat limited data it appears that the average annual salary of union presidents is less than $9000 (plus an expense account of varying dimensions). Most receive less than $7000. But the average is pulled up by a few relatively high salaries, such as the $30,000 received by Tobin of the Teamsters (A.F.L.); the $25,000 paid to Lewis of the Miners (independent), Hutcheson of the Carpenters (A.F.L.), and Harrison of the Railway Clerks (A.F.L.); and the $20,000 paid to Murray of the Steelworkers (C.I.O.), Ryan of the Longshoremen (A.F.L.), and Petrillo of the Musicians (A.F.L.), who also receives $25,000 from his local in Chicago. In general, the salaries of officers in A.F.L. unions are higher than those of C.I.O. union leaders. Although the rule is far from invariable, it does appear that the smaller unions tend to pay the lower salaries.

(2) Subordinate appointed officials and staff. Most national unions have, in addition to the elected top officials, sizable staffs of employees who are appointed by the officers to perform specific work. These staff employees may be divided into two main classes: first, the international organizers and all-round administrative-bargaining representatives, who commonly are members of the union and have risen to some prominence

out of the rank and file; and second, the professional group of specialists — attorneys, economists, statisticians, research workers, educational director and staff, public relations men, editors, and so forth — whose advice and assistance have been found essential to the success of the many different activities conducted by the complex union enterprise.

The members of the first group spearhead organizing drives and assist locals in all sorts of local activities, the most important of which is bargaining with employers over grievances and new contracts. Through these men the national office tries to obtain uniform application of all union policies affecting the internal and external relationships of the local and intermediate units. It is also partly through these representatives that the national office builds its machine of political patronage and consolidates its political controls. Obviously these persons owe their jobs to the national officers. If the latter are defeated in an election, the representatives are swept out also. Hence it is to their interest to sell the top leadership to the lower units and members and to insure loyalty by distributing petty patronage themselves.

The technical and office staff workers need not have been union members. Their job is to give advice when asked for it and to perform the specific tasks assigned by the union policy-makers. The attorneys tell the leadership which tactics are legal, which illegal. Economists and statisticians are asked to justify demands for wage-rate increases or to forecast business conditions or to perform other jobs related to the economic aspects of union activities. Editors and public relations men run the union's newspaper or periodical and publicity campaigns. The educational director and his staff perform the training work noted in Chapter 16. In short, this sort of staff work is very much like that found in a corporation, trade association, or government agency. And the professional staff is allowed no more freedom in the union than in these other organizations. Theirs not to reason independently, but to rationalize the decisions of the top policy-makers.

c. The judicial function. The judicial function is not clearly differentiated in labor organizations; that is, there is no separate tribunal entrusted with the sole task of weighing and deciding intra-union disputes. It has already been mentioned that the convention votes on numerous questions of a judicial nature. The president also settles many such problems during the convention interim. Perhaps the chief judicial agency at the present time is the executive board. If it does not at once decide all the matters that come up, it frequently is the court of last resort, hearing appeals from decisions on union rules and on cases arising between local members, between a local member and his local, between different locals, between a local and its district body, or between a local and the national.

One of the most important classes of cases on which national judicial action is taken are appeals of individual members from disciplinary action (fine, suspension, expulsion, and so on) by their local unions. Most national unions provide for two or three successive appeal steps, for example to the national president, then to the executive board, and finally to the convention. The time within which appeals must be filed is often limited, 30 days being the most common. In at least half the unions the local's penalty on the member is not suspended during the appeal procedure.

Sometimes a local's disciplinary decision is reversed on appeal, but more often it is not. One reason is the lack of detailed, specific, effective provisions in union constitutions governing the procedural and other requirements essential to fair trials. Another reason is the disinclination of unionists to give accused members the benefit of doubt about their guilt. Unions, being in conflict a great deal of the time with employers and other unions, are forced to require strict discipline and conformity among members, much like an army. Emotions usually run high when someone has seemed to commit a traitorous act. Perhaps the main obstacle to a completely judicial approach to appeals and verdicts, however, lies in the political nature of the union. National presidents and boards ordinarily dislike to reverse a local verdict because of the likelihood of antagonizing officers and members whose political support is needed. Furthermore, the action of the accused member may be interpreted as a challenge to the political control and prestige of the top leadership. Even if the convention is the final agency of appeal, a fair trial is not easy to get, for the case is usually given, in the first instance, to a committee on appeals, whose members are appointed by and are adherents of the president or board. Such a committee is not likely to recommend to the convention a verdict not wanted by its superiors. Appeals decisions in unions often illustrate the necessity for an independent judiciary in any kind of democratic government.

d. The finances of national unions. Reference has already been made to the significance of national finances as a centralizing force. Because of the need for flexibility in times of emergency, the funds in the treasury of the national union are not always kept rigidly separated for different uses, but most organizations try to keep adequate reserves for the various major items of expenditures. There are the usual administrative, operating, and overhead expenses, including officers' salaries, correspondence, publication of the official organ, organizers' expenses, rent, expenses for travel, research, legal work, education, publicity, and so on. Part of the revenue may be kept in a special strike or defense fund for the support of locals. Some of the most important funds are those devoted to the payment of sickness, death, disability, and unemployment benefits.

The chief source of national monies is a specified share of the dues collected by the local unions; this share is usually taken in the form of a per-capita tax of, say, forty cents per member per month, or one-half or two-thirds of the dues paid by each member. The national union also takes about half of the money raised locally through initiation fees. Other sources of income include charter fees to new locals (say $25); special assessments on the entire membership (a very important source of rapid increase in resources for special purposes, such as organizing campaigns); subscriptions to and advertising in the union paper; and returns on investments, if any.

As previously stated, American unionism is big business. It is not nearly as big as the aggregate of private business enterprise itself; nor, in fact, is it as big in terms of financial assets and net worth as any single one of the very large corporations. But it is large all the same. The annual gross income of all unions must be close to a billion dollars and their net worth close to a half billion.

Whenever unions become strong, anti-unionists propagandize about the looseness of union finances and records, with the implication that most union officers misuse and misappropriate the union funds. The fact is that in the existing economic system union officers are about the same as other businessmen. There is probably no more embezzlement of union funds than of other business funds. And union accounts today are probably as good or as bad as those of most other businesses. Corporation executives often publish misleading or meaningless statements concerning their financial conditions, in order that stockholders, competitors, customers, and employees shall be unable to discover their actual affairs. Union officers often do the same thing so that union members, employers, and "competitors" cannot learn the truth about their financial conditions. Certified public accountants are given, proportionately, as much work by unions as by other business organizations.

The point is made, of course, that the handling of funds and accounts by both unions and other businesses could be greatly improved. Two wrongs of omission or of commission in such matters do not make a right. And unions themselves usually do not object to publicity for their accounts once employer opposition to unionism has disappeared.

In recent years there has been substantial improvement in union accounting and in the clarity and completeness of union financial statements. (An outstanding example is to be found in the statements released by the Ladies' Garment Workers.) This development has in part been a voluntary one and has in part resulted from the provision in the amended National Labor Relations Act which requires that unions, before they can become beneficiaries of the Act, must file annually full financial statements with the federal Secretary of Labor. Not all unions, however, comply with this requirement. A few, such as the Hod Carriers and the Operating Engineers, are so firmly established that they do not need to take advantage of the Act; and they prefer to continue keeping their members in the dark about what happens to their dues and other payments.

5. The structure and government of the two big national federations of

unions. In Chapter 12 we described in general terms what federations of unions are like. Now let us consider in some detail the actual organization and government of the country's two leading union groups, the A.F.L. and the C.I.O.

a. The American Federation of Labor. (1) Structure. The Federation's structure is somewhat complicated. There are six kinds of organizations which are directly affiliated, namely, national unions, federal labor locals, federal trade locals, city central bodies, the departments, and the state federations of labor. As previously emphasized, most important of these, from every standpoint of membership, power, and finances, is the *national* or *international union.* Each national body controls all the local units on this continent in its own craft or industry; the whole union acts as a unit in matters of general import. In August, 1950, 107 national unions belonged to the Federation, with a total reported membership of almost 7 million.

The *federal labor locals* are mixed organizations made up of workers in many different trades and industries in a given community and having no affiliations with national bodies. They are usually found only in small localities where there are not enough employees in each craft to form separate craft locals. As soon as the workers in the different trades increase in number, the Federation requires organization on a craft basis. Federal labor locals are directly represented in the A.F.L.

The *federal trade locals* are thus a step farther on than the labor locals. The trade locals are craft organizations in a given community which are directly affiliated with the Federation because no national unions exist in their areas or trades. The A.F.L. always requires locals to connect themselves with national bodies, however, whenever convenient or possible. Frequently the Federation has organized a number of locals in the same trade in different cities over a period of years and then, issuing a new charter, has asked them to combine into a national association. In August, 1950, there were 1204 federal trade and labor locals directly connected with the A.F.L. and having a combined reported membership of about 188,000.

It was soon learned that many local problems, such as the formation of a strong employers' association or the existence of grave jurisdictional disputes, were common menaces to the welfare of all local unions. These bodies, whether federal trade locals or the local units of different nationals, therefore federate themselves together for united local action and mutual protection. They represent the interests of organized labor in every community and concern themselves with such matters as vocational training and workers' education, recreation campaigns, local legislation, and various economic problems. The local federations are called *city centrals,* or *central trades and labor councils,* or *central labor unions.* In August, 1950, there were almost 900 of them in existence, each directly represented in the A.F.L.

In large cities there are other local federations besides the all-inclusive city centrals. These are the *industrial* or *local departmental councils* which are composed of all craft locals interested in a particular local industry, such as the building trades' council and the printing trades' council. They have been established to care for jurisdictional troubles and other problems peculiar to the industry. They are not directly affiliated with the Federation in their local form but find representation through their national *departments*, which were established by the Federation, after about 20 years of experience with jurisdictional troubles among the national unions in different industries, to serve as clearing houses for their common difficulties. There were five in existence from 1907 to 1923: the building trades, railway employees, metal trades, union label, and mining. After the coal miners and metal miners had resolved their difficulties, the last-named department was dissolved in 1923, leaving only four, which have continued to function. A new department, for the maritime trades, was created in 1946, making a total of five once more. The union-label department is made up of some sixty national unions which use labels, buttons, or cards on their products to promote the sale thereof. Membership in the departments is frequently overlapping; for example, the national Machinists belong to both the railway and the metal trades groups.

There are fifty *state federations of labor* belonging to the national Federation. All the locals, councils, and city centrals in each state elect delegates to an annual convention where full-time officers are chosen to carry out measures for the benefit of organized labor throughout the state. These organizations deal mainly with labor legislation and educational proposals, although some economic functions are also performed, such as the promotion of the purchase of union-label goods and the furtherance of boycotts.

In spite of its apparently very loose and awkward organizational structure, the A.F.L. has become a powerful and often dominating factor in the unions and councils of which it is composed. The means whereby the Federation officers have achieved a measure of centralized power are outlined below.

(2) Government. The government of the American Federation of Labor is no less important than its organization. The different member bodies elect delegates to its annual convention, where are decided, after the reports of different committees, various questions of national policy and action. Technically the decisions thus worked out have only the force of recommendations; they are the majority's suggestions, which the affiliated national organizations may or may not follow, according to their own lights. Actually, the convention's resolutions and the Executive Council's decisions have a good deal of influence on most national unions. The state federations usually follow the parent body closely, while the federal trade and labor locals must obey or face suspension and expulsion directly by

the A.F.L. officers. Suspension and expulsion of national unions can be accomplished only by a two-thirds roll-call vote at a convention. The "moral power" and the prestige of the Federation tend to keep them in line.

Representation of national unions at conventions is based on paid-up membership. Each such union is entitled to one delegate for fewer than 4000 members; two delegates for 4000–7999 members; three delegates for 8000–15,999 members; four delegates for 16,000–31,999 members; and so on, proportionally. At the convention each delegate of a national union is permitted to cast one vote for each one hundred members, or major fraction thereof, whom he represents. The voting ascendancy of the large national organizations is purposely kept paramount by the provision of only one delegate and one vote for each of the other affiliated groups, such as state federations, city centrals, and labor locals. The system also makes for conservatism — that is, for keeping the "in's" in — because, in effect, no radical or opposition movement within a national union can secure a vote at the convention unless it has managed to attain a majority control of the member union itself.

The convention does the legislative work of the Federation. The system and procedures are about the same as those described above for a national union. The executive and most of the judicial functions are performed by the Executive Council, a group of fifteen men elected annually by the convention and composed of the Federation president and secretary-treasurer (full-time officials) and thirteen vice-presidents (heads of national unions, who meet with the other two officers at least four times a year for the determination of policies and the execution of convention decisions). These men are usually of higher than average caliber and have risen from the labor ranks. Through utterances on the platform and radio and in the press they acquaint the general public with the Federation's goals and policies. Other important duties include the direction of organizing activities in non-union sections, the granting of new charters and the suspension of old ones, the guidance of lobbying for favorable labor legislation, and the planning of measures calculated to cope with all the major problems of the day. Each year the Council must prepare a detailed report of its activities and a full list of recommendations for the convention to consider.

The various activities of the Federation are financed mainly by the collection of per-capita dues of three cents per month per member from national unions and thirty-seven cents per month per member from federal labor and trade locals. Prompt payment is usually assured by the constitutional provisions that if a union's dues are in arrears, its delegates shall not be seated at the A.F.L. convention; and three months' arrears mean automatic suspension from the Federation. About one-third of the total collections are kept for the support of member bodies in times of strikes; the other two-thirds carry the various current expenses.

In practice the Executive Council is the most powerful agency in the A.F.L., and the main force on the Council has been the majority bloc of powerful craft-union leaders. These leaders, controlling the delegates from their own unions to the A.F.L. conventions, have often been able to dominate the convention by political machine methods, securing the election of a Federation president to suit their tastes and deciding which resolutions should or should not pass. Between conventions they have been able to control the direction taken by the labor movement through their control of Federation funds and expenditures (for organizing and other assistance); their direct control of federal locals; their indirect control of city centrals, state federations, and departments through control of delegates from their own unions; and their power to ostracize unions from the fellowship and moral support of their branch of the labor movement.

b. The Congress of Industrial Organizations. (1) Structure. In the rush of organizing during its formative years, the C.I.O. was not able to proceed by careful blueprint plans of structure. The main objective was to grasp time by the forelock and get the unorganized workers into some sort of affiliated union. It was largely a question of which existing union was available with its organizers to do a given job. Thus, the Mine, Mill, and Smelter Workers took over the task of unionizing tunnel workers, and the Mine Workers tried to organize chemical workers. As a consequence, there were by 1940 certain anomalies of structure that promised later jurisdictional difficulties if the unions doing the original organizing were to acquire a vested interest in such members. Even if careful pre-planning had been possible, however, there would have been many knotty problems. Should the new industrial unions be organized according to the financial structure of companies and industries or according to products? For example, should the workers in General Motors' electrical products plants go into the Auto Workers or into the Electrical Workers?

By the end of 1940, the structure of the C.I.O. was not dissimilar to that of the A.F.L., and this was true also in 1950. The backbone of the organization, as with the A.F.L., was made up of the federated national unions. There were also some four hundred directly affiliated local unions of industrial form. As noted above, there were also state and local industrial councils or federations roughly comparable to the similar A.F.L. groups. As yet no national "departments" had been established, but there was the possibility that a few divisions representing the major industrial fields might in time be set up.

(2) Government. At the 1938 convention the C.I.O. adopted a definite form of government. By 1950 the national officers, each a member of some affiliated union and elected by majority vote of the convention, were a president, nine vice-presidents, and a secretary-treasurer. These eleven men *ex-officio*, together with representatives of the national unions and organizing committees (one representative is given to each affiliate after

nominations by the affiliate and election by the convention), constitute the Executive Board, which performs executive and judicial functions. Clearly this group is much larger than the A.F.L. Executive Council.

The legislative work of the C.I.O. is done by the annual convention. Delegates thereto are apportioned among the member bodies as follows: to local industrial unions and to councils, one delegate each; to national unions, according to membership. Thus unions having 5000 or fewer members get 2 delegates; from 5000 to 10,000 members, 3 delegates; from 10,000 to 25,000, 4 delegates; from 25,000 to 50,000, 5 delegates; from 50,000 to 75,000, 6 delegates; from 75,000 to 100,000, 7 delegates; and over 100,000, 8 delegates, with one additional delegate for each additional 50,000 members or major fraction thereof. The delegates have one vote per member represented, except that each *council* delegate has only one vote. Thus, as with the A.F.L., the power of the Congress is wielded by the national unions.

C.I.O. funds are raised by a per-capita tax of five cents per member per month (established for the national unions) and fifty cents per member per month for directly affiliated locals. The institution of this tax, decided on by the affiliated unions in March, 1937, followed closely the institution of dues collection among members of newly organized unions, such as the one in steel.

Among the many problems of organization and government which arose during the C.I.O.'s first years, the most important appeared to be, first, the development and maintenance of democratic procedure among the unions in the C.I.O. as a whole and within the several new unions; second, the parallel development and maintenance of discipline (self-discipline) among members; third, the development of strong leadership in the new unions; and fourth, the smoothing-out of factionalism within the affiliated unions. There was the danger that the top C.I.O. officials might fall into the habit, begun naturally enough when the new unions were raw and inexperienced, of "suggesting" policies and procedure for these unions. By the end of 1937 there were already expressions of dissatisfaction among some of the new unionists over the direction of their affairs by "outsiders." The second and third problems were closely related to the first: the experienced C.I.O. leaders and organizers hesitated to relinquish control and to leave the inexperienced new unionists to their own devices. A series of unauthorized or "wildcat" strikes, mainly among unionists in the automobile industry, had given employers opportunity to propagandize the public with regard to union irresponsibility, and thus, because of the need for disproving such charges, there developed, at a time when the experienced leaders' attentions were greatly occupied with organizing the unorganized and dealing with the A.F.L. situation, a pressing need for education in elementary parliamentary procedure and in other discipline-producing measures.

The problem of factionalism within the C.I.O., although not essentially different in nature from similar problems within any large organization of human beings, was especially grave because it often involved communism; because of the lack of seasoned discipline among the new members; and because of the need for united fronts in all the unions whose battles for recognition had not been completely won.

D. ADEQUACY OF UNION STRUCTURE AND GOVERNMENT

Having completed our description and analysis of union structure and government, we must try to appraise these things in terms of the degree of satisfaction which they afford to prospective members and to existing union members, including both the rank and file and the family of officials; and in terms of the contribution they make to the realization of American democratic ideals.

1. Prospective members. One of the principles of democracy that has probably been honored more in the United States than elsewhere is equality of opportunity among individuals to obtain want-satisfaction. A main way of obtaining want-satisfaction is of course to have a job which provides the money income necessary for purchasing want-satisfying goods. We saw in Chapter 12 that most unions seek security as organizations by trying to control jobs, i.e., by trying to get employers to hire or retain only union men. If only union members can hold jobs, it clearly is necessary for workers to join unions in order to obtain job incomes that will enable them to buy the things they want.

a. The case in which workers do not wish to join unions. There may be some workers who for various reasons wish not to belong to labor organizations. So the questions arise, Aren't the unions that pursue this policy refusing to honor the democratic principle of equality of opportunity? Is such a policy socially justifiable?

On the first question the answer is fairly clear: To prevent non-union workers from laboring on the jobs of their choice — jobs which would otherwise be available to them — *is* a denial of equal opportunity. If union organization were universal and if this union-security program were in universal effect, such persons could not work at all except perhaps at some kind of self-employment. But the second question is much harder to answer. In general we may say that this union policy is socially justifiable only if the social loss experienced through the denial of equal opportunity to non-unionists is canceled out by some social gain experienced by other persons, such as union members and employers.

It is not possible to measure this social loss felt by non-unionists or other individuals or by society as a whole, nor is it possible to calculate the social benefit accruing to various groups and to society as a whole. All we can do is to point out the chief arguments made against and in behalf of exclusive job control by unions (union security) and then let the student make his own rough qualitative judgment as to whether the gain equals or exceeds the loss, i.e., whether there is a net gain or loss.

(1) Arguments against union-security shops. The arguments against union security or job-control measures include the following. (*a*) As just stated, these measures are antithetical to the democratic principle of equal opportunity. (*b*) Employees forced by economic or political circumstances to join unions make poor union members. They are not likely to be loyal, cooperative, and disciplined. Rather do they tend to be indifferent, rebellious, and susceptible to factionalism. It is much better for unions to try to sell themselves to workers in such a way that the latter wish to belong voluntarily. (*c*) Under the tighter form of "union shop," workers who do join the union are subsequently at the mercy of a one-party political system within the union. They must vote with the machine or run the risk of expulsion on various charges, thereby losing their union-controlled jobs. (See Chapter 24 for information on how the amended National Labor Relations Act tries to prevent this sort of thing.) In short, unions or union leaders are endowed by union-security arrangements with the power to discharge workers for certain reasons. (*d*) Because of this power the public through government is forced to become concerned with the ways in which unions' internal affairs are conducted. (*e*) Employers operating under a closed union shop are severely restricted in building up competent work forces. Union membership is not the main criterion of worker efficiency.

(2) Favoring arguments. Unionists, union sympathizers, and some employers have points that must be given a respectful hearing. (*a*) First is the "free rider" argument. Why should non-unionists, who make no kind of contribution to the organization, be allowed to work in a shop in which the terms of employment have been improved through the sacrifices of loyal, dues-paying unionists? Why should anyone be permitted to reap where he has not sowed? (*b*) Until employers have convinced unions that management would not try to destroy unions if it could, unions must demand the security of job control. To permit an employer to hire and retain non-unionists is to invite the undermining of union strength in his plant. With normal labor turnover he could keep hiring non-unionists until they outnumbered the unionists. In the end the union would disintegrate. No shop can long continue half union and half non-union unless the employer is sympathetic with unionism. (*c*) A good many employers find that a union shop is conducive to responsible unionism and improves labor relations in general. They hold that a strong, secure union is easier to live with than one tormented with anxiety over its survival. A plant whose work force contains a sizable fraction of non-unionists is often strife-torn and low in morale. A union cannot maintain effective discipline and devote itself to constructive labor relations unless it controls all the workers. (*d*) It may well be true that it is better for a union to be composed wholly of voluntarily loyal members than partially of those who

join under the compulsion of a union shop. As a practical matter, however, voluntary loyalty is not always inculcated by such constructive measures as low-cost medical and dental service in a union health service. Some unions attempt to generate loyalty by first deliberately stirring up grievances and then pressuring management to settle them in favor of the union members. In such cases, the employers suffer along with the union for the latter's feeling of insecurity. (*e*) Some form of union shop not only insures a union's survival against possible employer antagonism, but also tends to prevent successful raiding by a rival union. And this is usually beneficial to the employer also. The latter's operations may be severely impeded or interrupted by the deterioration in workers' morale and efficiency which often results from competing organizational drives.

b. The case in which workers wish to join unions but cannot. Next we must consider, in respect to prospective union members, the social consequences of the exclusion policies of some unions. Here we have the situation in which non-unionists would join a union if they could, but are prevented from doing so by the union's restrictions. And if the union has thorough job control, the outsiders are thus prevented from obtaining work in the craft or industry.

Such policies cannot be defended on any rational grounds from the standpoint of a society dedicated to the practice of democracy. The closed union in conjunction with the closed shop is the ultimate in denial of equality of opportunity in the labor field. It also represents the ultimate degree of labor-market monopoly that a union can achieve. It restricts the alternatives of non-members much more than any other union policy. In the case previously considered, a non-unionist is barred from the job only if he chooses to stay out of the union. Here there is no question of choice; the non-member is simply barred from the job.

Exclusionary policies are of course good for the union that is strategically enough placed to be able to practice them. They enable the union to restrict the supply of labor available to employers and thus tend to raise the wage rate and improve the other terms of employment. Any monopolistic seller of a product or productive factor achieves this sort of result. But society does not benefit; on the contrary, it is worse off because of such union practices.

2. Existing members. Now let us look at the workers who are in the unions. How effective in getting union business done is the kind of organization and government that has been developed? How democratic are the union's operations? How satisfying to members' desires?

There are of course no precise objective and quantitative measures for providing definite answers to these questions. Of necessity any appraisal must be mainly subjective. Nevertheless, from the attitudes and behavior of union members and leaders and the behavior of unions as entities, it is not impossible to make some reasonable judgments.

a. Organizational effectiveness. (1) Need for efficiency. In so far as unionism is still a "movement" because it must still struggle to achieve the full measure of security, prestige, and social recognition that it desires, it must be an effective fighting force. In all effective fighting forces the leaders must have some degree of military authority, and the rank and file must be subject to some degree of military discipline. Decisions cannot wait for the operations of democratic procedures. Leaders must be free to change tactics at a moment's notice. Then if progress toward security and recognition is the criterion of efficient organization and government, we must conclude that the kinds developed by American unions have been successful, for in organizable industries most of these unions have won unprecedented, almost complete recognition from (if not acceptance by) employers, and in government their views are given careful attention. It is also not too much to say that, among American unions in general, the ones with well-oiled, somewhat autocratic political machines have done rather better than the others.

We cannot be sure that some other kinds of structure and government would not have been even more effective than the ones which actually developed. But the fact that the existing kinds are a product of evolution and have survived, while other forms were discarded as ineffective, bends one to the view that the existing union structure and government are reasonably adequate.

(2) Standards of effectiveness. But to say that union government and structure have been reasonably adequate is not to suggest that they are perfect. Far from it. Let us consider how they might be improved. At the end of Chapter 2 we listed five "bonds of organization" that may be used to appraise the effectiveness of an organization and to judge the satisfactions which it provides for leaders and for rank-and-file members. Any organization, we said, should have a "charter" (prestige value for members); give a satisfying role to each member; confer an appropriate status on each member; possess an adequate two-way system of communication; and develop a proper system of rewards for good performance of roles and penalties for poor performances.

It should be noted that these criteria are applicable to autocratic as well as democratic organizations. All these "bonds" may be fully and effectively developed in an organization, and yet the group may not function as a democracy at all. Thus, the fact that communications must operate from bottom to top as well as from top to bottom does not imply that the organization must be democratic. All that is necessary is that there be an adequate channel open from the lower levels for making reports on how orders have been carried out and for making suggestions on how the organization can function more efficiently. Our focus at this point is on the effectiveness of the union organization rather than on democracy.

To what extent do unions seem to have worked out these "bonds"?

First, it appears that for the most part they have been organizations of which their members are proud. They undoubtedly have helped their members stand erect in American society. They have helped significantly to satisfy the desire of their members for social recognition and esteem.

Second and third, there seems to be little doubt that the various roles or union jobs have been rather well defined, from bottom to top, and that each member's status within the organization is accurately related not only to his role but also to the statuses of other members.

It is in respect to the fourth and fifth criteria that the organization and government of a good many unions seem to have lacked a certain amount of effectiveness. There is of course a communications system. As we saw, delegates to union conventions help make policy and inform their constituents on changes in policy. The trouble is that in some unions conventions are not held very often. We also learned that the top leaders use the union paper or magazine to inform members of problems and policies. The difficulty here, however, is that the information is often not complete or accurate. Too often this channel is used to further the political fortunes of those who control the union. International representatives also transmit orders and policy directives to locals and members. And here again, the information is often colored by political considerations.

In view of these things it appears justifiable to conclude, in respect to top-to-bottom communications, that the channels are open and (except where conventions are infrequent) are rather extensively used; the channels are effectively used for the transmittal of orders and policies approved by the leadership; but they are often not well used for the purpose of disseminating full knowledge among the rank and file. In short, this sort of communication contributes to the efficiency of the organization and to the tenure of top officials if not to the practice of democracy.

How about bottom-to-top communications? How well is the leadership informed about the problems and views of the rank and file and the lower officers? We have noted that local unions send instructed delegates, petitions, and resolutions to the convention; that some unions have made considerable use of the referendum although in general it is less used than formerly; and that international representatives continually keep their ears to the ground and transmit local sentiment to top leadership. It is to the interest of every labor leader, autocratic or democratic, to be well informed about what is being said and done at the lower levels. We conclude that this channel of communication is open and effectively used. It is beside the present point that it, like the other channel, is often employed for efficiency and for political purposes rather than for giving full effect to the wishes of the rank and file or of minorities within the union.

Being a social organization, a union has a formal and informal system of rewards and punishments for the kinds of performances given by the members in their several roles and statuses. Every member is supposed to perform his role in accordance with the rules and regulations laid down in the union's constitution and bylaws and with all other written or informal directives provided by membership or leadership. Successful performance is often rewarded by appointive or elective advancement to higher union jobs. Unsuccessful performance and failure to abide by or operate in conformity with the rules and directives may be punished by appointive or elective demotion or by fine, barring from union meetings, suspension, or expulsion — not to mention such informal expressions of disapproval as ostracism and physical beatings.

Disloyalty to the union is one of the gravest offenses of which a member can be guilty. Such disloyalty may consist of "slandering" or otherwise "abusing" union policies to outsiders or to other unionists. In practice it may also consist of talking against or otherwise opposing the union leadership. As previously pointed out, the officers' power to mete out punishment or recommend it to a controlled membership often makes it possible to trample the rights of minorities and silence all opposition. This power is abetted by the absence of independent tribunals and the lack of adequate provisions, in most unions' constitutions, spelling out in detail the precise procedural steps to be followed in trials of accused members and appeals from lower-level decisions. But again, one's concern over this failure to observe democratic principles should not blind one to the fact that the existing system may add to the union's effectiveness.

b. Intra-union democracy. (1) Relation to efficiency. Now let us focus on intra-union democracy. It is often stated (and in fact may be said to have been implied in our discussion above) that organizational efficiency and intra-organizational democracy are antithetical. People who say this have in mind such situations as the following: A general cannot take the risk or the time to let the privates vote in town meetings if he wishes to win a battle or a war. A corporation chairman cannot afford to assemble all the stockholders and let them vote on policy. A mayor of a large city cannot function if he has to submit questions to a mass meeting of the citizens. To permit democratic freedom of discussion and voting in any of these situations would mean a great waste of time and energy and tremendous inefficiency. There would in fact be something close to anarchy.

But this is not the point. No one expects the town-meeting kind of democracy to prevail among large organizations; representative democracy is the most that can be expected. Policy is made and executed by freely elected representatives.

But isn't even representative democracy in conflict with organizational efficiency? Probably it is in the short run and for the duration of emergencies. In the long run, however, the matter is not so clear. If the organization's members are interested rather than wholly apathetic about the welfare of the organization and of themselves, it may well be that democracy and efficiency are not incompatible. So one might conclude from the experience of the two-party Typographical Union. No organization can be effective for long if the rank and file are chafing over autocratic restraints. The cooperation of all or most members seems to be essential for long-run efficiency.

This appears to be the crux of the matter. Unless the members are completely indifferent, they must be sufficiently satisfied with their roles and statuses, with communications, and with rewards and punishments, to cooperate with and be loyal to the leadership. But it does not appear that this cooperative attitude must necessarily rest on a democratic base. An autocracy might well be able to keep itself in power indefinitely and operate the organization with efficiency if it were sufficiently benevolent and responsive to the basic desires of the members, if it were able to provide satisfaction for most of these desires, and if it were able to prevent rivals from having access to the members.

For many years there have been successful autocratic, one-party labor organizations, such as the Mine Workers and the Carpenters, as well as some successful democratic ones like the two-party Typographical Union. We have noted the long tenure of the autocratic leaders who have ruled by political machine methods, sometimes without holding conventions or elections for years. But it would be a mistake to think that the presidents of these unions would not be overwhelmingly re-elected by the members if free elections were held tomorrow. In spite of their ruthless quelling of opposition, these leaders have delivered satisfaction to most of their memberships.

We conclude, then, that intra-union democracy is not incompatible with efficiency of operation except under special emergency circumstances; and that intra-union autocracy is also probably compatible with effective operation if the autocrats are benevolent and responsive as well as strong and capable.

(2) Criteria of intra-union democracy. To admit the success of any kind of autocracy is not to condone or espouse it. In a country that gives more than lip service to the practice of democracy, most organizations should also practice it. Otherwise the general belief in the value of democracy is sapped and dies. For the organizations within the over-all society are the ones in which the ordinary citizen can practice democracy most frequently.

All this is especially true of unions, which developed in part because of the denial of the democratic freedoms to workers by employers. It would be more than ironic if after this denial workers found another within their own organizations.

Freedom of choice among alternative candidates and their policies at frequent elections is of course an important criterion of democracy. Measured by it, unions do not fare too well. We have seen that in too many unions there is only one set of candidates, at least for national office. Opposition, where it exists, is not often strong or vocal.

A second tenet of democracy is majority rule. Unions often honor this principle more in the breach than in the observance. For one thing, majority rule implies at least two sets of alternative candidates and policies. Frequently these do not exist. For another, the apathy of members and political maneuverings have often permitted minority groups, ideological or racketeering, to control union policies and activities.

But there is much more to democracy than free voting for representatives and the rule of the majority. Other standards include freedom of speech, equality of opportunity within the organization, safeguards for the rights of minorities, and fair trials (due process of law) by an independent judiciary for those accused of anti-organization acts. Here again we have found that unions often fail to measure up. There is no need to repeat or summarize the evidence presented in earlier pages.

Are unions worse "sinners" than other social organizations in America? Undoubtedly not. They are composed of human beings all of whom are conditioned by the same general environment. Indifference to the practice of democracy, lack of moral fiber, corruption, autocracy, and other antisocial characteristics exist in all sorts of associations. So do the socially desirable traits. But because of what unions stand for basically and because of the origins of the labor movement, perhaps one is justified in expecting a little more from them than from many other groups.

CHAPTER 14

Union Policies and Activities

A. UNION POLICY–MAKING AND POLICIES

1. What is union policy-making? By union policies we mean the decision on or choice of a certain plan of action or program of activities from among a number of alternative plans or programs. Policy-making involves a choice of objectives and a selection of measures or tactics intended to achieve the objectives. To illustrate, let us consider a union's relation to government. A union (or a federation of unions) has first to decide whether it wishes to try to obtain favors from government, i.e., to rely on government. If it decides affirmatively, it faces a further choice between forming a separate labor political party or working with existing parties. If the non-partisan approach is adopted, then various measures for influencing the existing parties must be selected. All these decisions constitute an example of making union policy.

2. Who makes union policy? In Chapters 12 and 13 we studied union structure (how a union is built up from a large number of small units at the bottom to a small group at the top) and we studied union government (the hierarchy of relationships among the units from top to bottom). We did this in order to further our understanding of just what a union is and what its problems are. Among the details that we reviewed, we were particularly interested in, first, the union's relation to non-member workers; and second, the relationships between the union's leaders and its other members, with a view to discovering the locus of control in union government and policy-making — just who "runs" the union and decides what it is going to do.

This second point becomes especially important to us as we discuss, in this chapter and the next two, what the unions actually have done and are doing. It serves to emphasize again that the structural aspects of unionism are very closely related to the functional aspects.

We must now note another important influence on union policy — one not previously emphasized — namely, inter-union relationships. A given union is related policy-wise to other unions in two ways: first, as an ally within a formal industrial or inclusive federation or in an informal combination; and second, as a rival. In respect to the first, some of the policies of a particular union may be unique because they are related to unique conditions in the trade or industry over which the union claims jurisdiction. But, even though a given national union is a sovereign organization, many of its policies will be similar to those of other unions in the federation to which it belongs. One reason why the federation exists is because of the need for a united front on common problems. In respect to the second point of relationship, some unions — almost always the large, powerful ones having imaginative, dynamic leaders — take the lead in formulating demands and other policies. For example, Petrillo of the Musicians and Lewis of the Miners led off in 1944–45 in demanding employer contributions to pension and welfare funds for their members. If the new policies are a success, other unions' members hear about it and want the same things. Inevitably the leaders of other unions must adopt the same policies and make the same demands, as Murray of the Steelworkers did in 1948–49. This fact explains in part the prevalence of "pattern" bargaining after World War II, when unionism had become widespread and strong.

There is another kind of rivalry that influences a union's policies — that involved in dual unionism or conflicting jurisdictional claims over the workers of a given plant or craft. The competition and conflict between certain A.F.L. and C.I.O. unions led in many cases to the adoption of extravagant and unrealistic policies and demands in order to win or proselyte the workers from adherence to rival unions.

3. General nature of the policies. Summary preview. Before launching into a detailed account and analysis of present-day union policies and activities, let us try to obtain a broad view of the ground we propose to cover. Let us consider union objectives and methods in summary form.

a. Long-run policies of American unions. It is logically difficult to distinguish consistently between aims and methods. For example, the strike is clearly a method for winning one or more union demands, such as a wage-rate increase, or for bolstering union morale or for getting revenge on an employer or for attaining other objectives. The strike is scarcely ever to be thought of as an objective in itself. But if a wage-rate increase is an objective in the first instance, it is also a means or method for attaining some less immediate goal, such as a less unequal distribution of income, or more union power, or greater physical welfare for union members. In short, we should bear in mind, in our summary of ultimate and immediate objectives below, that the latter are really measures for achieving the former.

However, the distinction has its uses. We shall start here with broad, ultimate union goals and work down to more immediate ones. As in the case of any individual or group faced with the problem of allocating limited resources among competing, alternative uses, the general goal in a union is to get the most out of union resources. That is, there is an effort to maximize something. But what does "the most" refer to? What is to be maximized? In the broadest sense, there is an attempt to maximize the satisfaction of that portion of the members whose wants are deemed important by the policy-making group of the union. The portion of the members may be all of them (including the leaders), or a clique or faction which is in power, or merely the top officials.

Whenever maximization is being considered as the goal of a person or an organization, the time factor enters. To what period of time is the maximization objective applicable? Is immediate satisfaction demanded? Or are the goals moderately long-range, or truly long-range? Success in attaining an immediate goal might spell defeat in the long run; and vice versa. In general, where the membership is the policy-maker, as in some local unions on policy matters delegated to this level, the maximization objective is usually a very short-run one; on national union policies, where the top national leader is securely in power, the time period tends to lengthen considerably; but even national union policies are seldom very long-range in character.

The fact that most union policies are short-run in nature causes many observers to criticize unions and their leaders for lack of "statesmanship." Undoubtedly this criticism has some validity, although the relatively recent rise of unionism to national power will inevitably compel the top leaders to take a broader view and show more interest in long-range considerations. Are there any rational explanations for the short-run approach that prevails among most unions? Apparently there are.

First, the nature of a modern, dynamic, private enterprise economy favors short-run policies. Change is continually taking place, and the changes are often unexpected and unpredictable. No one can be certain what the effect of a given policy will be; its expected long-run influences are often obscured and obliterated by unforeseen intervening events. Why not take what can be had now, without regard to consequences that are so uncertain? In the 1946–48 period, for example, many an economist told the unions publicly that demands for wage-rate increases, if successful, would only add fuel to the inflationary fires, and would so raise the cost of living that the unions would achieve no real gains. This was doubtless true. But no one could assure the unions that without wage-rate increases there would be no inflation of living costs. There might well have been such an inflation because of the rising demand for investment goods by firms. In this case, the unionists would have suffered *losses* in real income.

A second explanation for the prevalence of short-run policies lies in the fact that each sovereign national union, to the extent that it determines its own policies, operates in disregard of what other unions do. Each one feels, with considerable justification (except in respect to the big unions who set the "pattern" of policy), that it is too small a segment of the economy to influence the conditions that determine the level of income and employment in the economy as a whole. Only when the conditions governing income and employment in a particular craft or industry are of dominant importance (as when the craft or industry is split into union and non-union parts and the union might price its employers out of the market), does a union seriously consider the income and employment effects of its own policies. Here it can be relatively certain that, if it aims too high, its own survival and power will suffer.

Although it is true that the maximization of some group's satisfaction is the main general goal of a union, "satisfaction" is too broad and abstract a term to have much meaning. More specifically, the policy-makers desire freedom, security, and progress in establishing the survival of the union as an entity and in attaining power and social recognition for the union. They desire, further, to find satisfaction for the wants of the members (or part of them) as individuals, in so far as this individual satisfaction does not conflict with the survival, power, and prestige goals of the organization.

Wishing to move down still farther from the rarefied air of abstraction, we ask next, How do the policy-makers try to achieve these three union goals? Do they plan ultimately to do away with the economic and political system of private enterprise, or do they accept it and try to achieve maximization within it? In recent years this has been a question of great concern to many employers and other "outsiders" whose power and control have seemed to be threatened by the tremendous growth of unionism and by the ever-widening range of demands made by unions in their dealings with firms and government. What do unions want and where will they stop? The answer is that the great majority of union policy-makers are "conservative"; they are not communists, socialists, fascists, or devotees of any other anti-capitalistic "ism." Not only are they not unsympathetic with employers' problems; they have also shown little real desire to usurp management's functions on a broad scale. Union leaders are pragmatists and opportunists, focusing on what they hope will be the best short-run solutions to immediate problems. Continuous, relatively small advances instead of huge spectacular gains is the usual program.

But won't the continuous small advances in the end bring unions to the point where there is no more to be gotten out of the economy as now organized? It may take longer to move to this point, but won't it finally be reached? Isn't the internal political make-up of unionism such that the leaders, in order to stay in favor with the members, must continually make new demands which in time will very seriously encroach on management's ability to operate in a free society? No one, of course, can answer with complete assurance. But this line of questioning implies a static society rather than a dynamic, progressive one in which new developments are almost constantly creating new particular problems for unions and in which there is always the general problem of maintaining one's relative position. It also implies that the spectacle of what happened to unions in totalitarian states (such as Germany and Russia, where free unions were destroyed) has made no impression on American unionists.

b. Shorter-run policies. Given the general lack of a negative attitude toward the private enterprise system, what immediate aims have union policy-makers developed for insuring the union's survival and for achieving power and prestige? We may divide the immediate aims into three groups: those to be achieved mainly through dealings with employers; those to be granted chiefly by government; and those to be attained by working directly with union members.

In dealing with employers, the policy-makers try first to obtain what has come to be known as "union security" from employers. That is, they shoot first for "recognition" of the union as the exclusive bargaining representative of a firm's workers; and then, as noted in Chapter 12, they try to get the employer to agree to employ only union members on the jobs included under the union's jurisdiction. These security aims are the main ones which concentrate directly on the welfare of the union as an organizational entity. The other employer-oriented aims have to do chiefly with the welfare of individual members; but these of course also contribute to the survival, power, and prestige of the union as such. Among them are security for members through restrictions on employers' freedom to promote, demote, transfer, lay off, discipline, and discharge workers; security for members through restrictions on employers' freedom to introduce new machines and methods of work; improved economic position of members through all the direct and "fringe" wage-rate policies of unions that focus on employers; leisure and security of members through all the hours-of-work demands made of employers; and physical welfare of members through demands pertaining to working conditions.

In respect to union policies that focus on government, we may again distinguish those which bear chiefly on the union as an entity and those which have chiefly to do with individual members. In the first group are efforts to obtain governmental statutory assurance that the courts and other government agencies will not operate as allies of anti-union employers and that government agencies will prevent employers from using union-smashing tactics. In the group of objectives related to government aid for individual members we find minimum wage laws, hours laws, and various kinds of social security laws (on accidents, sickness, disability, and superannuation).

The third main aim — the one to be attained by dealing directly with workers through measures summarized in a later chapter — has two facets. The members must be tied to the union in such a way that they will be loyal and retain membership in the union no matter how adverse the circumstances; this insures the survival of the union and enhances its power and prestige. And the members are glad to be loyal because there is also altruism in these measures; the workers' own welfare is increased thereby.

4. The distribution of benefits from union policies. We said above that the main general objective of a union is to maximize the satisfaction of that portion of the membership whose wants are considered important by the policy-makers. The decision on whose wants are to be satisfied how much signifies a choice among alternative patterns of *distributing* the benefits derived from successful policy-making.

Most of the decision on distribution is made when the policies themselves are formulated. It is not a question of devising any old set of policies and later doling out the benefits. True, this is done to some extent by union officials or by membership vote when the system of rewards (promotions, and so on) and punishments (fines, suspensions, and so on) is applied to particular individuals. But for the membership as a whole, the policies themselves predetermine the distribution.

A union, like any social group, is composed of diverse elements often having opposing desires. In an industrial union there are different skilled crafts as well as masses of unskilled and semi-skilled member-workers. In any union — industrial or craft, there are usually different age groups, geographic sectors, and racial-language elements. There may also be a substantial out-of-work segment versus the employed group, hourly-rate workers versus incentive-rate workers, and ideological or religious cliques, and so on. The policies selected by majority vote or by top-official judgment help determine how each group fares. For example, the Automobile Workers' drive for a company-supported pension plan in the Ford Motor Company was held up until 1949 because the large proportion of younger workers in the Ford Department of the union preferred present wage-rate increases to far-off pensions. Again, members of locals in big-city high-wage-rate areas try to keep the union from settling for lower wage rates to be paid to the members of locals in smaller communities. This has happened in the clothing and printing unions.

Whatever the sources of conflicting intra-union interests, union policy-makers face the problem of (*a*) minimizing the conflicts by adopting at least one policy that will satisfy each interest-group and (*b*) adopting policies favoring the group (or groups) that are most important for the survival and progress of the union or union leadership.

5. The plan of discussion. In this chapter and the next we shall follow much the same order of topics developed in our summary above. That is, we shall consider union policies and tactics first in dealing with employers, second in relation to government, and third in relation to the members. We may also note that the discussion deals only with *union policies* on the topics covered. It does not deal also with the policies of employers or government, or with the extent to which the unions have succeeded in obtaining employer and government acceptance of their policies. These other matters will be handled in the chapters on collective bargaining and on government policy.

B. DEALING WITH EMPLOYERS

1. Union security policies. From recognition to closed shop. In order to give rational continuity and perspective to our discussion of membership inclusion and exclusion in Chapter 12, we were compelled to make some mention of union job control and security policies. For the same reason, in our appraisal of unionism as a democratic institution at the end of Chapter 13 we presented the arguments for and against these policies. These points need not be repeated here; the student is referred to them to refresh his memory.

Our present discussion, then, is confined to the equally important matters of the nature of the various kinds of union security arrangements; the prevalence of the policies among American unions; and the economic significance of the policies. Again we emphasize that the main objective of these policies is the survival and increased power of the union as an entity. Success in the policies usually, of course, contributes to the survival and power of the union's officials. Individual members tend also to profit, because a strong union can better protect their job tenure and other interests. Nevertheless, the paramount consideration is the welfare of the union itself.

a. Kinds of union security policies. There are two main policies aimed at preserving the position of a union in a given plant: (1) some sort of "shop" in which the hiring of union members rather than non-unionists is emphasized; and (2) some sort of arrangement, called the *check-off*, whereby the employer deducts union dues from the pay of union members and transmits them to the union.

(1) Kinds of shops. (a) The open shop. If we consider a given plant in which a given union has been able to organize some of the workers subject to its claimed jurisdiction, we find that the situation providing the least security for the union as an organizational entity is the so-called "open" shop. Here, in classroom theory at least, non-union men work along with union members. Any existing worker is free to join or not to join the union. And the employer is free to hire either unionists or non-unionists as he pleases. But — and here is probably the crux of the matter — in almost all versions of the open shop the employer does not recognize the union as the collective bargaining agent for even its own members. Determination of the conditions of employment remains unilateral, wholly in the firm's hands.

At first glance this sort of shop looks like a very democratic place to work in. It seems to give full freedom of choice to both workers and employer, while preserving the freedom of the union to organize the non-unionists if it can. (This is why during the first two decades of this century many employers and their associations, such as the National Association of Manufacturers, had a good deal of success in propagandizing the uninformed public that all then-known forms of union security were undemocratic and that the open shop epitomized "the American way.") The trouble is that it assumes too much good will in human behavior and too much of a static condition in the plant's personnel; and it disregards a major reason for the existence of unionism. Every plant experiences some labor turnover; job vacancies occur almost every day and must be filled. In an open shop, of course, the management fills them. To assume that the employer has enough good will or even indifference toward the union (with its rules that restrict his absolute freedom to run his plant as he pleases) to distribute the vacancies about evenly between union members and non-members is to be (in most cases) utterly unrealistic. And to assume that there will be no friction or rivalry between the two groups of employees is equally unrealistic. In the great majority of cases the open shop develops into a passively non-union or actively anti-union one.

The open-shop theory fails, finally, to recognize that the main reason for the existence of a union is the collective wish of its members to substitute collective bargaining and joint, employer-union determination of the terms of employment for so-called individual bargaining between worker and employer, which in practice means unilateral control by the employer. To expect a union to put up with a situation in which it has members but no power to bargain for them is of course to make a most unrealistic interpretation of what a union is for. In short, the open shop provides no real union security at all.

(b) Bargaining for members only. The first step in obtaining real union security, then, is to get "recognized" by the employer. The most limited kind of recognition — such as that granted by the United States Steel Corporation to the C.I.O.'s Steelworkers' Organizing Committee in 1937, the first year of its relations with organized labor — is an agreement to bargain with the union over the terms of employment for the union's members only. Such arrangements may exist where, in the absence of any rival union or of employer antagonism, the union now counts only a minority of employees as members, or where, even if it has enrolled most of the workers, it is not in a position to take advantage of state or federal laws, such as the National Labor Relations Act, which provide for elections to determine an exclusive bargaining representative.

Clearly there is not very much security here, and the situation is an unstable one. Why then does a union agree to it? Because it represents a "foot in the door," an entering wedge whereby, given sufficient good will in the employer, the union can enroll more employees and work from minority weakness to majority strength.

(c) Exclusive bargaining shop. Suppose that the union has now achieved

majority support. Suppose further that the employer, either voluntarily or under the compulsion of statute, recognizes the union as exclusive bargaining agent for all the plant's workers. This is the next higher level in union security. In the union's contract with the employer there is still no provision that non-union workers have to join the union; they can still work alongside union members without jeopardizing their own job tenure. The firm can also still hire non-unionists for job vacancies. But during the term of the agreement the firm may not deal with any rival union nor, on the general terms of employment, with any non-union worker as an individual. The employer and the union — and no other organization or individual — jointly bargain the conditions under which *all* employees work.

This sort of shop clearly represents an advance for the union. It is likely to increase the degree of its majority support if it bargains and operates wisely and smartly. For non-union as well as union workers may well come to look upon the union as the source of satisfaction for their desires.

Nevertheless, there is still danger for the union here. The employer is not prevented from hiring only non-unionists for job vacancies if he wishes to. He can still gradually undermine the union. On balance, however, the union achieves a fair degree of security under exclusive bargaining.

(d) Closed shop, union shop, preferential shop, and maintenance of membership. As suggested in Chapter 12, for fullest security the union would like the employer to agree that every worker presently employed on a job under the union's jurisdiction in the plant must belong to the union *and* that the employer will fill job vacancies only with applicants who already belong to the union. Such a situation is known as the *closed shop.* Here the union's control of job opportunities and plant workers is complete. Not only is the union exclusive bargaining agent, but the employer cannot undermine the union by hiring or retaining non-union men. In effect the union operates as an employment agency, not only for its own members but also for the employer.

Suppose the employer is strong enough to refuse this degree of union security. Or suppose, as is actually the case, that this kind of shop is in effect prohibited by federal statute (the amended National Labor Relations Act) or by state law. Then the union tries for the next best — the so-called *union shop.* Here all workers must have joined the union within a certain period after the date of hiring (thirty days was the minimum allowed by the N.L.R.A. before 1952 if most workers had voted for the union shop). Under this kind of shop at any one time all but a sprinkling of newly hired workers are union men. But for job vacancies the employer is allowed to introduce workers without regard to their relationship with the union. Here the union's control is less complete; however, there is little real opportunity for the employer to undermine the union.

Now suppose that the union-employer relationship or the attitude of government is such that not even the union shop can be obtained. Then some kind of compromise on union security may be worked out. There are two of these to be noted: the *preferential shop;* and *maintenance of membership.* Under the former, as we shall see, the compromise favors the union a good deal. Here the employer usually agrees to give preference to union members in hiring, promotion, transfer, layoff, and re-employment after layoff. As to hiring, the firm promises to fill job vacancies with union members if the union, as a sort of employment agency, is able to supply workers of requisite ability and experience within an agreed-on period of time. If the union cannot provide such men, the firm is free to hire non-unionists. And, once hired, these workers are not compelled to join the union; they can work on their jobs for indefinite periods as non-unionists. But the other preferential arrangements might make them wish to join the union eventually: Non-unionists are supposed to be the last to be considered for promotions and desirable transfers. They are also to be laid off first when the firm's employment decreases, and re-employed last when business picks up again.

Preferential shops often operate through the medium of a "hiring hall," which is usually under the control of the union, although it may nominally be administered and controlled jointly by employers and unions. It is especially favored by unions in industries characterized by small firms, much seasonality of operation, and work forces that sometimes include large percentages of casuals or "floaters."

A high degree of union security is provided by this kind of shop. Some concessions are made to the employer's desire to be free to manage his work force as he pleases; and it might appear that he would be able to undermine the union by hiring non-unionists after successfully insisting that the workers referred to him by union are incompetent. But in practice it has not worked out in this fashion. Actually employers have usually become dependent on the union as an employment agency. This has been the experience in most industries where preferential hiring is widely used, notably clothing and maritime shipping. Thus the preferential shop turns out not to be very much of a compromise between the closed shop and employer freedom; as a rule, the union gets much more than the employer.

Because many preferential shops actually resemble closed shops (which were outlawed in 1947 by the amendments to the National Labor Relations Act), there has been a good deal of doubt about their legality.

Maintenance of (union) membership is a union-security compromise given prominence during World War II by the efforts of the public members of the National War Labor Board. The employer members of this tripartite agency stood firm in upholding the wish of most employers to operate untrammeled by the restrictions of the closed or the union shop. Although they did not insist on the open shop, as they had 20 or 25 years earlier, they objected to any extension of union security brought on by the tight labor-market conditions, which greatly increased unions' bargaining strength. The employers' minimum demand was maintenance of the pre-war status quo. On the other hand, the union representatives on the board wished unions to be free to obtain the closed or union shop if they could. The compromise was designed to protect unions against the chance of loss in membership and security and at the same time protect employers against restrictions to which they would not have agreed in peacetime. Under maintenance of membership the employer does not have to hire only union men for job vacancies, nor do those of his existing workers who are non-unionists have to join the union. But during the life of the agreement between the employer and the union, the workers who are union members must remain so or lose their jobs. Freedom of choice (between membership and non-membership) for all workers is preserved by the so-called "escape" period (usually fifteen days) which is provided at the beginning of each new or renewed collective bargaining contract. During this period all the workers (both non-union and union) under the union's job jurisdiction in the plant are free to decide whether they wish to join, get out of, or stay in the union. Those who tell the union and the employer by the end of the escape period that they wish to be in the union must maintain their membership until the expiration of the contract. (However, there is usually no maintenance of non-membership during the life of the contract. Like workers newly hired after the escape period, existing non-union workers may join the union any time they change their minds.)

Before the change in late 1951, the amended National Labor Relations Act of 1947 probably put the maintenance-of-membership shop into the same class with the union shop. That is, to be legal it had to be approved, in a secret-ballot election conducted by the National Labor Relations Board, by a majority of the recognized bargaining agency's members eligible to vote in the bargaining unit.

(2) The check-off. A union that has a check-off agreement with an employer has persuaded him to act as a sort of tax collection agency. He deducts (checks off) regular dues, initiation fees, fines, and special assessments from the earnings of the union members in his plant and turns the money over to the union's treasurer.

It is plain that this is a security measure which differs from the "shop" kind discussed above. It is aimed at insuring the union's income and financial solvency rather than at job control. Nevertheless, most unions look on it as a necessary or desirable measure for achieving survival and power. In most American organizations, union or otherwise, most members are not zealously interested in organizational affairs — at least not so zealously as to be regular, reliable dues-payers. Hence it is safer for unions to make collections automatic via the employers. It is also cheaper, and it saves the time and energy of union officers for other matters.

A minority view among unionists on the check-off is that in the long run it is better for the union if it collects its own dues. If the union is its own collection agency, it must keep on its toes to continue selling unionism to its members. Shop stewards and other local officers are kept in closer touch with the members and are more responsive to them.

There are two kinds of check-off: the compulsory or automatic, and the voluntary. The former is the more attractive to unions because it provides the greater security; every union member is willy-nilly subject to it. However, if an employer is strong enough to resist the compulsory variety or if (as in the amended National Labor Relations Act) a statute forbids its use, the union is willing to settle for the voluntary kind. Here a union member must individually authorize the employer in writing to make the check-off; otherwise the union itself must collect the dues, fees, fines, and assessments. Voluntary check-offs are, in turn, of two kinds: irrevocable and revocable. Under the former, the voluntary authorization by a union employee must endure throughout the life of the collective bargaining agreement. A voluntary revocable check-off arrangement, however, permits a unionist to withdraw at any time his authorization for payroll deductions. (Under the N.L.R.A. irrevocable check-offs are permitted, but only for the period of a year or until the expiration of the contract, whichever is shorter.)

b. Prevalence of security policies among American unions. Among the labor movements of various industrialized countries, the American one appears to be unique in its emphasis on the security measures discussed above. Why is this? The arguments (some of them rationalizations) for union security were presented at the end of Chapter 13. We are interested here in underlying causes. Undoubtedly the main reason has been the long-enduring opposition of most American employers to unionism. Since 1935, when government definitely turned from being chiefly an ally of employers, a good deal of this anti-unionism has been disappearing. But in most industries unions are by no means convinced that, given such circumstances as a bad depression or a Republican government, many employers would not revert to union-smashing.

There is no such fear of employer antagonism in countries like Great Britain, France, and Sweden. There the unions seem to be convinced that they have been fully accepted by the employers and that the latter have sufficient good will not to attempt any sort of union-breaking.

A second reason, which has in part offset any effect of the softening in employers' attitudes, has been the rivalry among A.F.L., C.I.O., and independent unions since 1935. Union security agreements help to repel raids by competing unions. Here again the American situation is not paralleled by anything similar in most other countries.

Third, we must note again the apathy of many union members toward their unions. Throughout the history of the American labor movement a major problem of the unions has been to *keep* workers organized once they have joined. Real unionization of workers has usually been a harder task than organization. It would indeed be a mistake to believe that most American workers eligible for membership in unions do not want to belong to them and are coerced into membership by union strong-arm methods or by union security agreements with employers. From July, 1947, through June, 1950, the National Labor Relations Board conducted roughly 46,000 elections on the union shop issue under the requirements of the Taft-Hartley amendments to the National Labor Relations Act. In these tests about 85 per cent of the workers eligible to vote actually participated. And of these voters about 92 per cent cast ballots for the union shop. But the typical American worker is not very class-conscious and is anything but fanatical in loyalty to his union. This is in marked contrast to most unionized workers in other countries. Consequently, American union leaders feel a good deal safer under the protection against defection which is afforded by strong union-security arrangements.

Not all American unions have followed the general pattern. A notable exception was the railroad industry before 1951. In the train-operating branch the Big Four Brotherhoods (Locomotive Engineers, Firemen, Conductors, and Trainmen) found the conventional union-security policies, such as the union shop and the check-off, needless, because of the security provided by their strategic position, and impractical, because their members' employment often fluctuated back and forth between two crafts.

The trend among American unions is still for security. Almost all of them appear to want the maximum allowed by law. Some are so strong that they actually do not need a union shop. Nevertheless they demand it. At the other end of the scale, a few unions are so weak that they need security badly. They too demand it. Almost all unions are still afraid that the favorable conditions since 1935 may not last. Until they are convinced that employers will not try to break them, until most eligible workers are really unionized, and until rival unionism has largely disappeared with a united labor movement, little abatement in this policy may be expected.

c. Economic meaning of union-security measures. Now let us think of the union-security measures in terms of the analytical concepts developed in Chapter 8. We pointed out there that an employer's ability to hire labor depended on technological conditions, the conditions affecting the supply of substitute factors of production, and the conditions affecting the demand for the employer's product. Which one of these sets of conditions is influenced by the closed shop or other forms of union security?

Security measures clearly aim in part at depriving the employer of access to non-union labor. So far as union labor is concerned, non-unionists constitute a substitute factor of production. So long as non-union workers are freely available to the employer (that is, so long as the supply of non-unionists to the employer is elastic), his demand for union workers tends to be decidedly elastic. This is economically bad for the union and its members. For example, a union-inspired wage-rate increase may tend to reduce the employment of union men considerably. It is much better for the union if the firm's demand for its members' labor-hours is inelastic. One way of achieving this desirable result is to make the supply of non-union labor inelastic. In fact, it is best of all if this supply can be entirely wiped out by getting the employer to agree *never* to hire non-unionists.

2. Job security for members. As we have said before, the survival and power of the union and its leaders depend in large degree on how well the desires of the individual members are satisfied. We saw in Chapter 2 that one of the most urgent of individual human desires is for personal security. We learned in Chapters 6 and 7 that the important sources of insecurity — the conditions that threaten the workers' investments in their jobs and skills and earning capacities — are the arbitrary unilateral decisions that foremen and other levels of management often make in respect to the job tenure of individual workers; the slackening of the demand for the products made by the firms employing the workers; and the introduction of technological improvements (in machines and managerial methods) in particular plants and occupations. Let us see what policies and practices unions have developed to handle these problems.

a. Protection against unjust disciplinary acts by management. Under the common or court law and in the absence of statutory modification thereof, an employer's right to discipline employees for infractions of plant rules was virtually absolute. He could demote, suspend, discharge, or otherwise punish a worker for any reason that seemed appropriate to him. Top management usually delegated discipline to its foremen, who often made decisions that seemed arbitrary, unfair, and discriminatory to the workers.

It was not that most workers objected to management's disciplinary rights on principle. In the abstract, the need for a company system of rewards and punishments was usually conceded. But the fact of its frequent use to weed out or otherwise discriminate against union workers, plus its unilateral nature, bred resentment.

Workers inevitably come to feel they have some rights in their jobs after working in a plant for some time. Whether these are called "property" rights does not matter. The important fact is their belief that they have made some sort of investment in their training and work and that this investment must be protected.

It is not surprising, therefore, that unions have always sought to provide such protection. They worked for the passage of the National Labor Relations Act, which prohibits the discriminatory discipline of workers for union activity. They have appealed almost innumerable times to the N.L.R.B. for protection against such discrimination. On cases not related to union activity as such, they fight directly with management to protect members against unreasonable decisions. They concede the necessity for managerial discipline. They admit the firm's right to make discharges, disciplinary layoffs, and demotions for "cause," and are ordinarily willing to specify that drunkenness in the plant, proved incompetency, dishonesty, and disobedience to posted shop rules constitute "cause." But to insure against unfair applications they usually demand that warning notices be issued to workers whom management contemplates disciplining; that the grievance procedure, including arbitration (see Chapter 20 for discussion of grievance steps), be applied in contested discipline cases; and that back pay for lost earnings be provided by the company in cases of unjustifiable discipline.

b. Union seniority rules. Demotions and layoffs may have to be made for reasons other than discipline. If the demand for the firm's product falls off from seasonal, cyclical, or other causes, the firm may wish to reduce the size of its work force. In order to retain skilled, loyal, and efficient workers, management may temporarily demote them to lower-paying jobs. Then they "bump" the existing incumbents, and in the end there are layoffs among the lower grades of workers.

At other times, in the normal course of business, the work of particular departments may expand or contract. The transfer of workers into or out of the departments may solve personnel problems in such cases. Normally also, job vacancies occur in plants because of labor turnover (quits, discharges, and so on).

In all such cases the question of the individual worker's equity in his own or some job in the plant arises. Workers usually do not wish to grant management the right of unilateral decision on who is to be laid off, demoted, promoted, or transferred. Here too they fear abuse of this function. They have seen or heard about workers slipping money to foremen or doing other favors in order to win promotions. They know about cases in which long-service employees have been laid off while company "pets" were retained. So the members of many unions insist on length of service as the sole or major criterion for all these changes in jobs. The length-of-service principle goes by the name of *seniority.*

(1) Application of seniority. Length of service seems like a simple, easy rule to apply: Let the workers of longest service be the last to be laid off, the first to be re-hired, and the first to be promoted or transferred to more desirable jobs. Actually the application of seniority rules involves a host of difficult, complicated problems.

(a) Straight and modified seniority. First, shall seniority be the sole, unqualified criterion? If it is, we have what is commonly known as *straight seniority.* If it is to be used only in conjunction with other standards, such as skill or ability to perform the given job or jobs, we have what may be called *modified seniority.* Here the union recognizes management's desire to obtain efficient operations by rewarding superior performance with promotions or with tenure during layoffs. Unions may say, "Given equal seniority, management may promote or lay off on the basis of

ability." Or "Seniority shall control unless employees are not competent to perform the work." These modifications favor the union. If the union is weaker or stresses seniority less urgently, it may agree to this qualification: "Ability and efficiency being equal among workers, seniority shall govern layoffs, promotions, and so on." Depending on the looseness of the modification and the relative strengths of the parties, management may use seniority chiefly or rather infrequently as the criterion. But almost always the unions strive for a tight application of the principle.

(b) Scope of employment conditions covered. Second, shall the length-of-service rule apply only to layoffs, or shall it also cover demotions, promotions, transfers, and other items? All unions stressing seniority focus on layoffs and re-employment because these items are the most vital elements in worker security. They are more likely to demand straight seniority here than for promotions. But no union that desires seniority for layoffs professes disinterest in the principle for promotions. In trying to gain acceptance of seniority some unions go a good deal beyond the items mentioned previously. Thus, if a plant has rate ranges rather than single rates for its jobs, these unions demand that progression from the minimum to the maximum rate of the range be based on length of service rather than "merit" or ability. Other demanded applications include length of paid vacations, amounts of sick leave, selection of the more desirable shifts to work on, and amount of overtime work.

(c) The unit of application. Third, what is the unit within which the seniority principle is to apply? Shall it be company-wide (if the firm has more than one plant), plant-wide, department-wide, occupation-wide, or some combination of these? In general, save under special circumstances, unions demand broad units for applying seniority, usually broader units than employers do. This is because the longer-service employees are given a wider area within which their vested job rights must be observed. Suppose that seniority is valid only within separate departments. Then with a transfer or promotion into a given department a worker must begin to accumulate seniority all over again. And in the case of necessary layoffs, if one department were hit harder than another or if the average length of service were much greater in one department than another, workers of, say, twenty years' seniority might lose their jobs in the first unit while two-year men might be kept on in the other.

However, plant-wide seniority has at least one important general disadvantage for union members. Although it extends greater security to the older workers, it often adds to the insecurity and uncertainty of the younger ones. By the time the older union members have been transferred around a large plant to different departments, a great many workers will have been "bumped" off their jobs, each bumpee in turn bumping some younger-service worker, with the very short-service ones finally shoved into the street. Under departmental seniority the younger workers know better where they stand and are less likely to receive bumps.

Because each kind of unit has disadvantages as well as benefits, many unions have adopted the policy of asking for some combination of plant and departmental seniority. Thus, for layoffs plant-wide seniority may be demanded, with department-wide service determining promotions. Or seniority may be allowed to *accumulate* plant-wide but be *applied* only within a worker's existing department.

(d) When and for whom seniority begins and ends. Most unions demand that the accumulation of seniority for any worker should begin as of the date when his employment with the firm begins. However, a good many unions have acquiesced in the establishment of a probationary period for new employees, during which they are tried out and during which they have no seniority privileges. This period ranges from thirty days to six months in various plants. If an employee successfully passes his trial period, he either begins accumulating seniority the first day thereafter, or he may be allowed seniority retroactively back to the day he was employed, i.e., from the start of the probationary period.

Under what circumstances are unions willing to agree that a worker loses his seniority in a given plant or department? They do not argue against the principle that his seniority ends or is lost when he quits or is fired from his job. But what about less final kinds of job-leaving? As a rule unions do not insist that seniority be preserved for workers laid off more than a year, sometimes six months. They often agree also that seniority is lost if a worker fails to report back for work within a week after notification of the end of his layoff or after he has been granted a leave of absence. Excessive unexplained absence is also usually accepted as justification for loss of seniority. But unions generally insist that leaves of absence for such reasons as union activity, sickness, death in family, or service in the armed forces shall not deprive a worker of his accumulated seniority.

Shall seniority continue to accumulate during layoffs and leaves of absence; or shall such periods not be counted, i.e., shall they be treated as hiatuses in the accrual of seniority? Most unions have argued for continued accumulation, but many have accepted the other point of view.

In addition to the probationary employees mentioned above, certain other classes of workers are often accepted by unions as having a special relationship to the seniority system. Temporary and seasonal employees are commonly excluded. Local union officials such as shop stewards, and sometimes armed-forces veterans, are often placed in a "superseniority" bracket. This means that they are privileged to "bump" other employees regardless of length of service. Unions in some industries, notably automobiles, also agree to exempting from the operation of seniority a small, select group of key skilled workers chosen by management as being essential to the working of the plant.

(2) Prevalence of and conditions determining seniority policies. Not all unions stress the seniority principle. Its prominence today dates mainly

from the organization of the mass-production manufacturing industries since 1935. Before then its application was found mainly in the railroad industry, which still furnishes the outstanding example of straight seniority for layoffs and promotions, and in some of the printing crafts.

If unions vary in their attitudes and policies on seniority, then there must be — in addition to the previously mentioned general wish to curb unilateral action on layoffs, promotions, and so on by management — certain circumstances that importantly influence these attitudes and policies.

As we shall see below, one way of protecting union members from the insecurity and uncertainty that occurs when a plant begins laying off men for any reason is to ask the employer to divide the available work among existing workers. Here there is a reduction in the length of the work-week rather than in the size of the work force. Some unions prefer this measure to layoffs on the basis of seniority.

Why have some unions stressed seniority and others work-sharing? In the first place, the application of seniority may tend to establish a political cleavage within the union. The younger, shorter-service members may be at odds with the older members who receive preferred treatment under seniority. Unions in which this is an important matter may wish to avoid too much emphasis on length of service when a firm's operations are curtailed and total work-hours must be reduced. Second, in highly seasonal industries such as clothing, shoes, construction, and coal mining there are large, regular, short-term reductions in demand once or twice a year which affect almost the whole work force at one time rather than particular crafts or departments at different times. Here general equal division of work is preferred to discriminatory layoffs based on seniority — at least down to the point where work-sharing means poverty-sharing. Some of the unions in these industries demand equal division of work down to a certain point, such as 30 hours of work per week for each employee, with layoffs to be made on the basis of seniority if the firm's operations must be further curtailed. Third, in industries where the average length of service is low (e.g., some industries employing mainly women, many of whom look on marriage as their main goal), unions see little point in stressing seniority. Fourth, in small-sized firms unions are less concerned with the kind of protection provided by seniority. Not only are arbitrary, unjust decisions on layoffs less likely in such plants, but the techniques of production are likely to be such that inter-job movements of workers are not feasible. In the large-scale mass-production plants, on the other hand, most jobs are semi-skilled or unskilled; here technology is such that senior workers can easily transfer and bump junior workers. Fifth, where layoffs are often long or permanent, there is apt to be considerable emphasis on seniority. Long layoffs occur in the durable capital and consumption goods industries (e.g., steel and automobiles) during business depressions. Permanent layoffs are found where technological change is rapid and sweeping.

(3) Possible effects of seniority. Favoring arguments. Unions and their friends advance a number of reasons why seniority is a desirable policy. The student will have to evaluate these arguments for himself in terms of what seems good for the union, the employer, and society. (Employers' arguments against seniority will be reviewed in Chapter 18.)

It is argued that: (*a*) Seniority provides security for individual workers against possible arbitrary, unreasonable decisions by management. (*b*) Seniority contributes significantly also to the security of the union as such. It helps keep loyal to the union the less efficient, less aggressive, less successful workers who otherwise would be left behind in a non-union world of competition among individual workers. It also helps keep the older, more stable workers tied to the union. (*c*) Seniority does not really hurt employers. Employers may object to the principle because they believe, emotionally rather than objectively, that it interferes with the building up of an efficient work force. But most employers have no certain objective standards for measuring the relative worths and efficiencies of individual workers. Their layoffs and promotions are based mainly on guesses and favoritism. Seniority provides an accurate, easy basis for layoff and promotion. By and large, the longer a worker serves a firm, the more efficient and valuable he becomes. (*d*) Seniority confers other positive benefits on employers. It improves workers' morale because it makes them feel more secure; and this makes them more efficient workers. Furthermore, because seniority makes it much harder for an employer to "divorce" an employee, it makes the former much more careful in his choice of a "mate"; that is, it leads the employer to do a better job of selecting and training new workers. This gives him more efficient workers and helps reduce labor turnover and its costs. Labor turnover is also reduced because the seniority system makes workers loath to lose their job rights by quitting the plant. Remember, further, that most unions are willing to use modified rather than straight seniority. This allows employers to exercise considerable discretion and judgment in the interests of efficiency. (*e*) For the sake of argument, assume that seniority does cause an employer to retain less efficient workmen. Against this assumed loss to him must be set certain gains to society. Seniority is a way of distributing among employers the less capable workers of long service rather than having them cast as a burden on society in times of general unemployment. Such unemployment is a social misfortune, and no one class of workers (or employers) is responsible for it. It should therefore be shared by all workers and should not fall mainly on the older, less efficient ones. If such workers were let go at such times, they would have great difficulty in finding other jobs. Seniority permits them to work until retirement time, and society gets the benefit of their contributions to total output. But even if this were not true, even if there were a net loss rather than gain in total physical output because of their employment, this loss would be outweighed by the psychological and morale gains.

(4) Economic analysis of seniority. Is it possible to fit union seniority policies into the framework of economic analysis developed in Chapter 8 for the determination of employment and wage rates in a firm? What, if anything, do these policies do to labor supply or to the firm's ability to hire?

A firm's ability to hire labor-hours at any given wage rate depends, we said, on the nature and level of technology, the nature of the supplies of other productive factors, and the nature of the demand for the firm's product. Do seniority policies affect any of these three categories of determinants? The demand for the firm's product could be affected if workers were made to feel more secure under seniority, so that they were less uncertain about the desirability of buying products in the present. In such an event, the current product demand might become more stable and increase somewhat. This conclusion of course is purely speculative; there is no evidence on the matter. In any case the effect would be small — very much smaller than the effects of other conditions influencing product demand.

It is also difficult to see how seniority rules would have any effect on the elasticities and amounts of the supplies of substitute or complementary productive factors — loan funds, machinery, raw materials, and so on. If the application of seniority made workers less efficient, i.e., more costly to hire (there is no objective evidence on this matter), employers might be stimulated to use substitute labor-saving factors. But this does not mean that the supplies of these factors to employers are changed.

How about the nature and level of technology? Only if employers believed, rightly or wrongly, that seniority made workers less efficient might they search for labor-saving improvements. In this case, at least in the short run, the firm's demand for labor would tend to decrease.

What about the effect of seniority rules on the *supply* of labor-hours? If the firm believes that its workers are less efficient under seniority than formerly, this belief means that to the firm the wage cost or rate per labor-hour has gone up. And this means that the supply of labor-hours has been reduced. The firm has to pay a higher rate for the same number of such hours; or, to state the same thing differently, the firm gets fewer such hours for the same wage rate.

It is this change which might inspire an employer to look for labor-saving improvements. But, as we have said, there is no real evidence that seniority rules actually do shift labor supply in the way just mentioned. Certainly seniority may alter the *composition* of the work force in terms of *men.* Employers are restricted in their freedom to promote the men considered most efficient and to lay off, in times of reduced product demand, the workers considered least efficient. But it must be remembered that under most plans efficiency is considered jointly with seniority in making promotions and layoffs; straight seniority is not common except in a very few industries like railroads. And the union argument that the greater the length of service, the higher the efficiency of workers, cannot be dismissed as having no substance whatever. Therefore, in terms of labor-hours rather than in terms of work-force composition, one may seriously doubt that the application of seniority rules makes much difference.

c. Work-sharing. We have seen that the seniority principle is applied by unions to many items, the most important of which in terms of worker security is layoff occasioned by a reduction in the demand for a firm's product or by a labor-saving technological improvement. In the course of our discussion, we have also learned that the conditions in some industries and unions are such that, in respect to layoffs threatened by reduction in product demand, the unions' attitude toward seniority is rather negative. Unions prefer to forestall the layoffs by asking the firm to divide the available work equally among the existing regular union work force.

There are two principal ways in which the equal work-sharing policy is effectuated by the unions which espouse it. Which of the two measures is used depends on the nature of the industry's operations, that is, on whether the industry shuts down entirely one or more times during the year or merely curtails its operations to a low point without complete cessation. Thus construction in the northern part of the country ceases almost entirely during the coldest months. And maritime shipping and ship loading and unloading are intermittent. When a ship reaches port, the seamen are off and the longshoremen on; when it leaves port, the employment situation of the two groups is reversed. Each group is finished and paid off at the end of its stint. The Seamen and the Longshoremen have used the union hiring hall not only as a way of insuring that only union men shall be employed but also as a way of sharing available work. This aim is accomplished by application of the principle of "first off, first on." That is, the seamen who have been longest on shore get the first call when a ship is ready for a new crew. And the gang of longshoremen who have unloaded the latest ship to reach port go to the bottom of the hiring hall's job list and will not be called for work again until all the gangs ahead of them on the list have successively had ships to work on. Similarly, some of the construction unions have tried to see that the men laid off first when the cold weather sets in get the first jobs in the spring.

In coal mining and some of the apparel industries there are one or two seasonal peaks and lulls in production. But usually production does not stop entirely. Here we find the second kind of work-division — a reduction in the length of the work-week so that none but probationary workers need to be dismissed.

In considering this second measure we must carefully note that the reduction in the length of the work-week is quite a different matter from the reduction in the lengths of the work-day and work-week which unions have demanded from time to time during the past century in order to obtain more leisure without reduction in take-home pay. In the present case the unions are on the defensive economically. Their objective here is to spread evenly the effects of unemployment, chief of which is loss of wage income; there is no talk of raising the hourly wage rate in order to maintain earnings and thus compensate for the shortening of the work period. In the other case (see below, Chapter 15) the unions are on the economic offensive during a prosperity era; and they do ask that a wage-rate increase accompany the hours reduction.

As previously mentioned, work-sharing is not pursued to the bitter end. That is, if the demand for a firm's product falls off to such an extent that an equal division of the total available labor-hours would reduce the per-capita average below 30 per week, the union agrees to some layoffs. And these are to be made on the basis of seniority.

d. Make-work rules. Featherbedding and restriction of output. One of the most serious charges against unions is that, through various devices, they approve or demand restriction of output by members, require the use of unneeded men, and insist on the performance of unneeded work. Sympathy for union objectives is often alienated among many persons by the notion that all unions in these ways obstruct economic and social progress. It is therefore desirable for us to inquire into the nature, prevalence, and rationale of these policies that have come to be blanketed in the popular mind under the general term, "featherbedding."

(1) Nature of make-work policies. Without at present considering how widespread these union rules or policies are, we may classify them as follows: (*a*) direct limits on daily or weekly output; (*b*) measures that restrict output indirectly; (*c*) requirements that workers be employed who are not needed for the performance of the job; and (*d*) requirements that unnecessary work be done.

(*a*) *Direct restrictions on output.* Among the unions restricting output, almost none insist that a maximum amount for any job shall be set forth explicitly in the collective bargaining agreement with a given employer. Sometimes, however, a union (e.g., the Molders, Stonecutters, Lathers, and Printers) demands that a worker, to become a member and work at the trade, must be able to turn out a certain number of product-units per period of time, such as an hour or a day. In practice this minimum standard of output tends to become the maximum. As a matter of fact, virtually all direct output limitation is informal and tacit. It is simply agreed among the members of a given local union that they will not turn out more than what seems to be, among them mutually, a reasonable amount of work. Members who "rush," "push," or speed up so as to produce more are subject to the informal punishments of ostracism or physical roughing-up. Occasionally they may be penalized more formally, e.g., by a fine.

(*b*) *Indirect restrictions.* Much more than direct restrictions, indirect limitations on output may be achieved by formal as well as informal rules.

In either case a great variety of practices exists. In the construction trades, members are forbidden to act as or receive extra pay for being pace-setters. Bricklayers' locals have been known to forbid the laying of bricks with both hands. The Plumbers and Steamfitters used to prohibit vehicular transportation of members betwen shops and jobs. Apprentices or helpers are often not allowed to use a journeyman's tools at the same time as he does on a job. The Painters have limited the width of brushes to be used. The Carpenters have often prohibited the use of small, portable, electrically driven tools. The longshoring unions on the East and West Coasts have limited the size of the sling loads in working on ships' cargoes. Many unions, notably those in construction and transportation, are able to hold down output by undue emphasis on safety; safety measures are of course desirable within reasonable limits. The building unions also achieve some restriction by excessive emphasis on quality; here again a laudable objective (avoidance of slipshod work on a very expensive product) is turned into a make-work device.

Another indirect method of limiting output is to demand a reduction in the length of the standard work-day and work-week. We shall consider the "hours" problem in some detail later on, as a separate topic, because it is related to wage-rate matters and also to questions of leisure, health, and safety. But work-period reduction is another example of a measure that is in part laudable and desirable and in part a device for making work.

Still another union policy (also discussed more fully below) is not all "black" or all "white": the objections to the "speed-up" and the "stretch-out." In union parlance the speed-up means a too-fast speed of operations on tools or machines that are not mainly automatic but require almost constant attention and manual work by employees. It is quite possible that management, in its concern over cost reduction, would wish the operations to be performed at a pace which over a period of time would undermine the health and safety of the workers. Unions usually object to increases in operational speed on such grounds. This would seem to be a main reason why the Automobile Workers have insisted on joint union-employer determination of the speed of automotive assembly lines. But an element often strongly present is the members' fear that they will work themselves out of jobs.

The stretch-out is a related union term, originating and still mainly used in the textile industries, which signifies that management has unduly increased the number of operations a worker has to perform or the number of machines (e.g., spinning frames or looms) a worker has to tend. Here too there is not only a concern about physical well-being but also a fear that the work will not last.

(*c*) *Employment of unneeded workers.* Sometimes unions demand that a minimum or extra crew of workers be employed for the performance of a particular operation. Here the make-work policy stands naked and unashamed; there is no dilution of the motive to create jobs for members.

The now classic example is to be found in the demand of Caesar Petrillo's Musicians' union: Radio-broadcasting stations sending out recorded music or transmitting "live" musical programs originating in other cities must hire an orchestra to "stand by" and "fill in" in the event that something goes wrong in the broadcast. Because such an emergency has almost never been known to occur, the stand-by musicians are for all practical purposes paid the full union wage scale for doing nothing.

Other examples of this kind of policy are the demand of the Locomotive Engineers and of the Firemen for an extra man on the new, more powerful Diesel locomotives used by the railroads; the full-crew laws for railroads passed by many states for "safety" reasons as a result of the lobby organized by the railway operating unions; the demand of the Motion Picture Operators for two operators for each projector; the Theatrical Stage Employees' requirement of minimum-size crews for each performance, whether needed or not; the Pressmen's demand for minimum-size crews on the large web presses; and many unions' demands that employers and foremen shall not work at the trade.

(*d*) *Performance of unnecessary work.* Additional jobs for members may also be obtained by unions if employers can be induced or coerced into providing certain kinds of work. When a technological change in products or production methods occurs, the demarcation lines between craft jurisdictions are often blurred. Two or more craft unions may claim control over the work. Then we have the job kind of jurisdictional dispute discussed in Chapter 12.

But this is not a good example of "made" work. True, each competing union tries to compel the employer to give the work to its own members. But the job is there to be done. What we are interested in here is a union's effort to obtain employment for some of its members through a demand that certain wholly or partly unnecessary operations be performed.

The classic example in this field is the policy of certain unions in the printing industry on the setting of "bogus." It has long been customary for newspapers and periodicals to circulate the durable matrices for advertising and certain other printed matter among themselves; these plates can be used again and again. But the unions demand that one or more men in each newspaper or periodical printshop be used to set up and make a duplicate matrix for each such circulated one. After this is done, the bogus duplicates are destroyed; there is no need for them.

There are a good many other examples, such as the demand of certain building unions that work must be done at the site of the job even though it has already been or could be done more easily and cheaply elsewhere, e.g., in a manufacturing plant. Thus, the Plasterers have demanded that all the larger casts (for use on ornamental work for walls, fireplaces, ceilings, and so on) be made on the job and have often had the molds broken up after a single use. The Painters have required members to work over with dry brushes seats, cabinets, and other articles already finished at the factory. The Electrical Workers have often refused to install switchboards or other complicated pieces of electrical equipment in buildings unless the factory wiring was torn out and the whole job re-done by union members. The Plumbers have frequently declined to install factory-assembled fixtures and factory-cut and threaded pipe; here they tear down and re-assemble the fixtures and cut and re-thread the pipe. It is easy to imagine how all the construction unions feel about pre-fabricated houses.

(2) Prevalence of these policies. The determining conditions. How common are union make-work policies? What conditions tend to favor or prevent their practice?

(a) General analysis. Let us begin to answer the first question by looking at output restriction broadly. The practical experience of persons in industry and the observations of special, objective investigators establish that some degree of restriction is practiced almost universally by workers, *whether they are union members or not.* Socially sanctioned norms of production seem to exist among the workers in all shops. Speeders and pushers and pace-setters are generally despised.

Why is this? There may be many reasons. One is an almost instinctive desire to avoid the harmful physical and nervous effects that result from the strain and tension of concentrated, fast, driving, prolonged work. All of us try to work only at a normal pace. We may not mind occasional spurts of effort, but we dislike having to keep it up.

But "normal" pace for some is too slow or too fast for others. Why this social pressure for a commonly adhered-to speed of work? First, there is the economic and social cleavage between ownership and management, on the one hand, and workers, on the other. A self-employed person sets his pace chiefly on the basis of his own physical and mental needs. He has no one to quarrel with over the division of his firm's revenue. He has an incentive to work hard if he feels like it. But in modern industry, not only do workers usually object on principle to taking orders from others on speed of labor; they have no guarantee that they rather than the owners and managers will benefit from faster work. There is little incentive. Second, workers' experience with various kinds of unemployment and its effects have indelibly stamped on their minds the impression that jobs are scarce. With scanty financial resources to fall back on, they have an all-pervading sense of insecurity about getting and holding jobs. If they have a job, they wish to make it last. Consciously or unconsciously, they adhere to what has sometimes been called the "lump of labor" theory: There is just so much work to be done. Why should a few men working fast get what a lot of men going slow can do? Spread it around; don't work yourself out of a job. Third, most workers, union or non-union, feel intuitively the need for a united front on this matter. A speed artist who hopes to be president of the company by the age of fifty or a worker with no such ambitions but with a normal pace that is substantially beyond that of the average in the group breaks the solidarity of the group and must be curbed in the interests of the majority.

A union is the only agency whereby a truly united front can be achieved and whereby group rules can be enforced by appropriate sanctions. A union can protect its members from employers' insistence on speed-up. And it can punish workers who violate the code governing pace of work.

(*b*) *Particular unions.* But some unions can do much more than others. This brings us to the second main part of our analysis. The student will have noticed that almost all our examples of make-work policies came from among the A.F.L. or independent skilled craft unions and almost none from the C.I.O. industrial unions in the mass-production industries. Why is this so? Are the C.I.O. unions more socially "virtuous" than the others?

The fact that some unions practice featherbedding more than others is chiefly attributable to differences in the technological and economic conditions affecting the product and labor markets in the various industries in which the unions operate. These conditions affect both the *desire* or need and the *ability* to practice make-work; and we must distinguish between desire and ability in our analysis. As to the former, all unions — C.I.O., A.F.L., and independent — object to speed-ups and stretch-outs and wish to control them. In large-scale manufacturing the problem of the C.I.O. unions on these matters is undoubtedly more acute than in the industries and occupations where the A.F.L. craft unions hold sway. But even in manufacturing one must distinguish situations where the machines are automatic and need only casual attention from their worker-tenders (e.g., an Owens automatic bottle-making machine) from those in which the machines require constant worker collaboration and operation (e.g., a punch-press machine or a paper box stapler). It is usually only the latter which present a serious speed-up problem.

On the other hand, apart from controlling the speed of operators, the C.I.O. and other industrial unions in the mass-production industries have less need for make-work policies than the skilled craft unions. Technological change is much less likely to undermine a union's position if it includes semi-skilled and unskilled workers as well as skilled. A major labor-saving invention, however, could rob craftsmen of their skill and almost break the union.

Another condition, affecting craft and industrial unions equally so far as desire to make work goes, is the seasonality of the industry, as in construction and the theater. Still another is the fact of secularly declining employment, as on the railroads and in live music.

As to ability to make work, it is mainly the craft unions in certain industries like construction, newspaper publishing, music and theatrical entertainment, and local trucking that successfully demand the performance of unnecessary work and the employment of unnecessary workers. One economic trait of these industries is that the markets for their products are local; there is little or no competition from other localities to undermine the monopolistic status of the unions here. Moreover, these organizations operate to an unusual degree under the technological and economic circumstances mentioned in Chapter 11 (pages 254–56) which make for "strategic position." They can "get away" with make-work policies much better than most industrial unions.

In most unions the policy of output restriction is promulgated and made effective by the local unions. It may and does vary from locality to locality. However, the leadership of the national union, having more perspective and a longer-range view, sometimes tries vigorously to alter the nature of the control devices and diminish their severity.

Many of the make-work rules are obsolete today in terms of the needs of the union members or of the industry in which they work. That is, when originally introduced many years ago, they served at least a moderately useful purpose, whereas today they are pure make-work. For example, the Printers' "bogus" device goes back into the nineteenth century when compositors were on piece work and the circulation of the advertising matrices among newspapers cut heavily into their earnings. Again, the system of paying operating employees on the railroads — whereby a day's work is defined as eight hours or a run of 100 or 150 miles — was fair to both unionists and management when it was devised decades ago. It tended to protect unionists from the harmful effects of over-long work periods and at the same time helped management achieve safety and efficiency. But the different technological improvements on the railroads (such as double tracking and much more powerful locomotives) today make it possible to cover 100 or 150 miles in much less than eight hours. In most cases the rule is now nothing but a make-work device.

(3) Economic analysis of make-work policies. Finally, let us see if we can fit union output-restriction policies and make-work rules into our scheme for employment and wage-rate analysis developed in earlier chapters. It is not hard to see where the practices outlined in our sections on direct and indirect output controls belong. When, for example, bricklayers limit the number of bricks to be laid per hour and painters limit the width of their brushes, they are in effect limiting the supply of labor available to an employer. That is, they are reducing the number of labor-hours that he can buy at any wage rate. Or, to put the matter differently, such rules tend to raise the wage rate and wage cost of the employer for any given number of labor-hours.

The answer is not so clear in respect to the rules requiring employers to pay for unneeded work or men. But it appears that these practices have the same effect as those mentioned above: They make for higher labor cost (wage rate) per labor-hour; for any given number of such hours the firm must pay a higher rate. Here too, then, the supply of labor-hours is reduced.

e. Union policies on technological improvements. As in our chapters on unemployment, we define technological improvements to embrace not only the introduction of new machines, equipment, and tools but also the use of new management methods. The latter include incentive wage-rate systems and job evaluation plans, which, because they bear mainly on wage rates and earnings, will be discussed in the union-wage-policy section of the next chapter. However, motion and time study and the improvement and standardization of work methods and output, which often precede and accompany the introduction of wage-rate incentive programs, will be dealt with here.

(1) Policies on introduction of improved machines. We may distinguish three kinds of union attitudes and policies on new machines: obstruction, competition, and adaptation. All three have often existed and now do exist simultaneously. But in terms of the date when the attitude took hold among unions, the listing just given may also be taken as roughly suggesting the historical development.

Before going into details we may note a few useful guiding generalizations. First, craft unionists are much more likely to suffer serious losses in earnings, security, and prestige from technological change than are most industrial union members. New machines and managerial methods whittle away at the skills acquired through an investment of years of training and experience. Craft unions are composed of skilled workers. On the other hand, the skilled members of an industrial union are in the minority. Second, in no field is the conflict that sometimes exists between the immediate interests of the rank and file and the survival and progress of the union as an entity more striking. National union leadership, interested in the union as a whole, has repeatedly taken a longer view on how to deal with new machines and methods than has the membership. Severe internal conflicts have often developed. Third, whatever the policy adopted, the unions that were most successful were those whose strategic position continued to be strong in spite of the inroads of technological change. If the innovations in machinery or management methods are so sweeping that employers can dispense with the skill of the unionists and can operate with semi-skilled or non-skilled non-union workers, the union loses its strength and position unless it can organize the new workers also. A union can continue strong only if it controls all the jobs in all the plants making the product.

(a) Obstruction. This term signifies active opposition and resistance to the introduction of new mechanical devices. In the early days of the technological revolution the opposition was often very direct and violent, as when the hand spinners and weavers in England smashed the new frames and looms that threatened to dilute their skills. But this kind of action ran so counter to prevailing social and legal standards that it has long since been abandoned. Opposition came to take the form of strikes or threats of strikes and rules forbidding members to work with the new machines or their products. Thus, in 1870 the Knights of St. Crispin refused to work in the same shop with the new shoe-making machines or with the "green hands" brought in to operate the machines. This union

died. So, some forty years later, did another union in another industry, which adopted the same policy: the National Window Glass Workers' Union. The Cigarmakers almost suffered the same fate for the same reasons, until the obstructionist policy was changed.

It would be wrong to conclude from the above that all unions adopting an obstructionist policy have been doomed to extinction or near-extinction. As already stated, a great deal depends on the strategic position of the union, i.e., on how well it controls the supply of labor that can be used on the new machines and on how much its obstruction weakens its employers in the competition of the product market. If the union can prevent the employer from using unskilled non-union labor on the new devices, the union may lose strength but not mortally so. If it can see to it that other firms in the same or other industries do not undermine the sales of its own employers, its bargaining position remains pretty much intact. Thus, when the Street and Electric Railway Employees (A.F.L.) resisted the change-over to one-man operation of streetcars, it encouraged the development of bus transportation. But it was able to organize the bus drivers also (yielding to one-man operation in the end, however). Other illustrations are the unnecessary-work policies of the construction unions previously mentioned. These unions are so entrenched that they can get away with obstructionist tactics.

(*b*) *Competition.* By this policy we mean that the union tries to make it worth while to the employer not to introduce the machine. The most common competitive measure is to accept a sizable wage-rate reduction, thus making the machine's savings smaller. Outstanding among the unions trying this measure was the Glass Bottle Blowers. This union also gave up its summer shutdown (a previously effective way of protecting members from the furnace heat and of restricting production so as to keep product prices high), and it agreed to permit three-shift operation.

Occasionally a union has set up in business for itself in order to compete with machine plants. The Window Glass Workers tried this (unsuccessfully) before giving up the ghost. In essence, this method involves wage-rate reductions also; they are necessary in order to keep product price competitive.

(*c*) *Adaptation.* This kind of policy may be thought of as an effort to insure union survival and growth in the face of technological change. By policies of adaptation we mean measures which, while permitting employers to use the inventions, attempt to prevent any sudden and devastating effect on members or union and to preserve the integrity and power of the union as an entity. For example, unions have attempted to limit the pace at which the new machines are introduced, so that the displacement of union members is spread over a considerable period of time; and to insure that only union members will be trained and used for the new machine jobs (as was done by the Typographical Union for hand printers when the linotype machine came in at the turn of the century, and as was tried by the Glass Bottle Blowers when the automatic bottle-making machines were introduced in 1907). Employers have also been required to retrain displaced unionists and transfer them to other jobs. Again, the unions have tried to obtain a share of the machine-produced savings by insisting on much higher wage rates for members employed on the new machines — a measure which also serves to act as a brake on the rate of introducing the equipment. They have sought to shorten work periods in order to cushion and spread the effect of technological unemployment. Finally, unions have attempted to get the employer to pay "dismissal compensation" (usually a lump sum of from $100 to $500) to displaced workers for whom there are no other jobs in the shop. The Amalgamated Clothing Workers have been uncommonly successful with this last policy.

In respect to the attitude and policies of adaptation, two main generalizations may be stressed. First, most unions are willing to go along with management on new machinery only if management agrees with and tries to implement the principle of sharing the benefits of the new machines with the union members. Such sharing in practice means paying higher wage rates to unionists who work on the machines, giving dismissal wages to displaced union workers, and in general taking joint action on all the problems that are involved. Second, some unions are forced to adopt a cooperative policy willy-nilly, for they have inadequate control over all the jobs in the industry. That is, if some of the firms in the industry recognize the union and others do not, the union is often compelled to cooperate with the organized firms in order that the latter may be able to compete with the non-union firms in the product market. The non-union firms are free to introduce new machines and methods whenever they wish. They can also lower or raise wage rates without interference by the union. In short, their unit costs of producing the product are much more flexible than those of the unionized firm. And they may therefore be able to undersell the latter in the product market. Unless the union helps its firms reduce costs in a cooperative way, the firms' sales may fall and union members lose their jobs.

(2) Policies on introduction of new management methods. (a) Nature of these changes. The installation of new machines is ordinarily to be thought of as producing a more or less sudden, striking change of considerable magnitude in a firm's production processes; but such changes are relatively infrequent. A change in management methods, on the other hand, is usually to be thought of as being of much smaller magnitude; but such changes happen much more often — virtually every day. Over substantial periods of time the total effects of new machines and of new methods may be about the same.

These day-to-day changes in management methods include rearranging machines; introducing minor labor-saving tools; running machines faster; removing unskilled operations from skilled men's work, giving such operations to low-paid workers, and requiring the skilled workers to do more skilled work; studying the operations and content of various jobs so as to eliminate waste effort and improve efficiency; and setting time-output standards for workers on various jobs.

These last two items are generally known as "motion and time study." Plant engineers or outside consulting engineers come into a department of the plant and analyze the work of men on different jobs. All the motions on a given job are studied with a view to discovering the best way of performing the job. After wasteful and unnecessary motions have been eliminated, the sequence of the remaining, best motions is broken down into elements, which are then timed by numerous stop-watch observations. Obviously, in the quest for the "one best way" to do a job, much depends on the ability of the worker and on the degree of cooperation in his attitude. In respect to timing the job elements, also, a fast, cooperative worker will provide a much shorter total time for all the elements needed for producing an output-unit than either a naturally slow man or a worker who deliberately goes slow because he suspects that the change will injure his status and lower his earnings. The motion-time-study engineers insist that they are usually successful in choosing only normal-pace workers and in obtaining their cooperation. They also make certain allowances for workers' personal needs and for other contingencies. The total adjusted time for completing the sequence of motions to produce a unit of output is said to represent a reasonable time-output standard for any average worker.

Motion-time-study determination is usually associated with incentive wage-rate systems. But this relationship is not a necessary one. Some incentive wage-rate systems are not based on job study. And motion-time study may be used for "measured day work" or some other system of hourly-rate pay rather than incentive rates.

(*b*) *Unions' attitudes and policies.* Because these changes in management methods happen so frequently and their aggregate effect is so great, they usually make workers feel almost as insecure as the big, new-machine changes, particularly if they are introduced unilaterally by management. It is to be expected that union workers would ask their leaders to provide some protection against this sort of insecurity.

Unions' efforts in this direction have varied about as much as their policies in respect to new machines. Some unions are obstructive, some reluctantly tolerant, and some adaptive, even positively cooperative. All unions (as well as much of modern management itself) agree in challenging early-day management's well-worn argument that the engineers' approach is "scientific" — and therefore not subject to debate or questioning. They may grant that it is less unscientific to set time-output standards on the basis of job analysis and motion-time study than by rule-of-thumb or guess. But they assert that there is still a wide area for error in human, subjective judgment. The selection of the workers to be studied, the choice of job elements and "best motions," the discarding of abnormally high and low times for the elements or motions, and the allowances given for workers' personal needs, fatigue, and delays — all these leave ample room for mistakes and prejudice. Workers will not cooperate, when studied, unless they feel sure they will not be hurt by the results. Experienced workers often know better ways of improving job motions than the engineers can dream of; but workers will not reveal them if they are afraid. In many cases the output standards cannot be attained day after day because of management's own failure to maintain a steady flow of materials to the workers' machines and to provide sufficient maintenance to keep the equipment from breaking down. And workers' experiences with incentive wage-rate systems based on motion-time study (see the next chapter) has conditioned them to believe that employers use such study to exploit rather than help workers.

Proceeding from this general common attitude have come the three specific kinds of policies previously mentioned. Some of the strategically placed unions, notably the skilled crafts in the construction industry, such as the Bricklayers, have refused to allow job study, asserting with some justification that each job is different and the necessary requisite of standardized conditions impossible to attain. Other unions tolerate job study. They allow management to do motion-time study and install time-output standards unilaterally in the first instance; but they reserve the right to challenge all such standards under the grievance procedure. Still other unions have adopted a much more positive approach. They have their own engineering departments. They stand ready to study and improve job methods jointly with or separately from management's engineers, but in any case insist that time-output standards be subject to joint determination and agreement. As evidence of their good faith in cooperating with employers to reduce costs (and thereby keep jobs for members), they cite cases in which they have proffered the services of their engineers to money-losing companies and, the offer being accepted, have transformed these firms into efficient, profitable operations.

(3) *Economic analysis of policies on technological change.* Union policies on both kinds of technological change — machine and managerial — can be fitted into the analytical concepts developed in Chapter 8. The level and nature of the technological conditions in a given plant are determinants of the firm's ability to hire labor-hours. We have already made an analysis in these terms of the effects of technological change on the employment of labor under various conditions; the student should review pages 98–106 at this point. Now, the members of a union perforce take a short-run and particularistic view of the effects of a given change which threatens their job security. They are not impressed with the notion that in the long run more workers than ever may be employed after the initial displacement of their own labor by the new machine or method. All they are concerned with is the fact that the innovation is robbing them now of all or part of their life's investment in skill and experience. They

are not inclined to cooperate with management on the change unless management or their leaders can convince them that they would be even worse off in the absence of the innovation or that resistance to it is futile. So, given the variety of conditions mentioned earlier — strategic position of the union, control of leadership over local membership, and so on — we have the different union policies just discussed.

The out-and-out obstructionist policies, if successful (as among some of the building craftsmen), cut off the employer from the supply of a rival, substitute factor of production. This tactic has two effects on the demand for labor. In the first place, it tends to make that demand much less elastic than it would be in the absence of the restrictions. This means, for example, that a successful demand for a wage-rate increase will have a less unfavorable effect on employment than if the firm, after the rate increase, could resort to new machines or improved managerial methods as a substitute productive factor. In the second place, a successful policy of obstruction means that the demand for this particular grade of labor is prevented from being reduced at *any* wage rate. This means an absence of even temporary technological employment.

The adaptive but not positively cooperative union policies constitute a sort of delaying, rear-guard action. From the economic standpoint, such policies as dismissal compensation for displaced unionists and the insistence on much higher wage rates for members retained to operate the new machines tend to make the innovation more expensive and less attractive to the employer. Consequently, for the grade of labor that is threatened by the invention, the demand at any wage rate is less reduced and is less elastic than if the firm had complete freedom of action.

The fully cooperative policy, which is not often adopted when a union is in real control of an industry, subordinates short-run, particularistic considerations to broader, longer-range ones. Unions in industries that are partly non-union reason that any reduction in labor-demand caused by technological improvements is much less harmful than the reduction that would occur if the union firms' product-demand was seriously cut because of successful competition by the non-union firms. In fact, the unions hope that the reduction for technological reasons will be more than offset by an increase that would occur if the union firms, helped by the cost-reducing innovations, win the product-market struggle with the non-union firms.

Even if a union is in full control of an industry, so that the product-market competition of non-union firms is not a problem, there are often high-cost firms that are having difficulties competing with other unionized firms in the product market. The union, wishing to keep its members employed in such firms, may cooperate with them if they move to increase efficiency. Or the union may even take the initiative in such cost-reduction measures. In either case the economic analysis is the same as that given in the preceding paragraph.

f. Union policies on physical working conditions. The final item of union policy to be considered in this chapter is that bearing on physical working conditions within the plants and shops where members are employed. Workers usually object to spending 40 hours or more per week in workplaces that are dirty, noisy, wet, very hot, or dangerous. They frequently ask their unions to do something to improve these conditions.

How do unions operate to obtain such improvements? In respect to the other elements of members' security and well-being for which we have reviewed union policies, we found that some of the policies (e.g., seniority) were initiated and enforced from the national-union level and some (e.g., make-work rules) at the local level. Some, such as most make-work rules, were effectuated merely by local union rules governing the behavior of members; and others, such as seniority, were made effective in collective agreements negotiated with employers. The working-conditions policies are given force mostly by a third method: the use of the grievance procedure. That is, the improvement of working conditions is clearly not to be achieved through rules governing members' activities, outputs, and so on. Nor can it usually be handled in contract negotiation because the variety of these conditions is too great to permit their handling by general principles. Therefore each improvement must be sought through the day-by-day contacts of union shop stewards and grievance committees with appropriate management officials. (A notable exception to this generalization exists in railroading, where collective bargaining agreements contain a great many pages on a large variety of "rules" and working conditions.)

CHAPTER 15

Union Policies and Activities (continued)

B. DEALING WITH EMPLOYERS (continued)

3. Union wage policies. *a. General nature.* In the last analysis the strategy and tactics that labor organizations adopt in respect to wage rates and wage income form the keystone of their policies. More than any other policy or group of related policies, a union's wage objectives and methods represent its best thinking and efforts toward achieving survival, power, and social status for the union as such and toward satisfying the needs of the members as individuals. Successful wage policy helps provide security and status as well as physical well-being for individual workers, and satisfied members help insure union survival and expansion. Successful wage policy adds to a union's prestige and power; it helps beat off attacks by rival unions, serves as a weapon for the invasion of rival unions' jurisdictional territory, and commands respect from employers and the community at large.

In our survey here we shall consider, first, the "political" determinants of the wage policies adopted by a given union. Then we shall deal with various aspects of wage policy affecting the individual firm, an industry of firms, and the economy as a whole.

b. The internal politics of union wage policy. It will be remembered that in introducing our discussion of union functions, at the beginning of Chapter 14, we gave attention to the question, Who makes union policy? To no aspect of the whole of union policy is our discussion there more relevant than to union wage practices. It is especially true of wage policy that a union's internal political situation and its relationships with various other unions and with various employers are of great importance.

c. External factors. (1) Relations with other unions. The current or recent wage demands and successes of other unions have a great deal to do with the wage policies adopted at a particular time by a given union. If other unions have obtained a general wage-rate increase of, say, 15 cents an hour, the leadership of the union can ill afford to accept less. Its prestige with its own membership, with other unions, employers, and the public, would be seriously undermined. This is especially true if the other unions are close, direct rivals in jurisdiction.

But wage policy may be an offensive as well as defensive weapon. An aggressive union may try to raid its rivals by promising their memberships higher wage benefits than their present leaders can get or have obtained for them.

Within the labor movement as a whole a few unions and their top officials take the lead in formulating wage policies. At one time or another in the last decade or so the Mine Workers, the Musicians, the Amalgamated Clothing Workers, the Steelworkers, and the Ladies' Garment Workers have initiated one or more wage demands or practices that have been followed by numerous other unions. In these organizations the top leadership had been relatively secure and free from internal political pressures. This has meant greater ability to take a broad, long-range view of wage policy.

(2) *Relations with employers.* Another important influence on the wage policies of a union is its relationships with the employer in its industry. Here we must distinguish between a wholly and a partially unionized industry. Suppose the union is recognized by only a fraction, say half, of the firms in the industry. Then the union's ability to obtain wage benefits is often seriously limited if the product market is competitive, as it is in cotton textiles, hosiery, and cotton garments. Thus, unless the Textile Workers are fairly sure that the non-union firms in the South will not cut prices and wage rates, so as to endanger the competitive position of the union firms (and thereby jeopardize the employment security of the union members) in the North and South, it will have to be modest unless it believes that the non-union mills will come close to matching the wage benefits desired by the union. And this matching is unlikely unless business is prosperous and full employment exists or unless the union has launched a drive to organize the non-union plants. During depression conditions a union in such an industry may have to adopt that most repugnant of wage policies, a wage-rate reduction, in order to preserve its membership and strength. This is what the Hosiery Workers did in the early thirties, when the non-union firms, having the ability to reduce wage rates and other costs without resistance by a union, almost bankrupted the union mills by lowering product prices.

Suppose now that a union has been recognized by all the firms in its industry. So far as product-market competition is concerned, all that the leadership has to worry about is the rivalry of firms in other industries. Sometimes this is not unimportant. The Mine Workers cannot disregard what will happen to the sales of bituminous coal if because of wage-rate increases the coal operators raise the price of their product so high as greatly to encourage consumers to substitute petroleum and gas. This shift would not matter so much to the union if the workers in these other industries also belonged to the Mine Workers. But they don't; they are in other unions. Similarly, the railway unions cannot be wholly unmindful of the competition between the railroads and motor and air transport.

By and large, however, the unions that are recognized by all the firms in their own industries are not seriously restricted as to wage demands by product-market competition.

In such situations, so far as relations with employers are concerned, the problem presented by wage policy formulation is to make demands for wage benefits (or resist employers' demands for the reduction of wage benefits) which will not seriously impair any firm's ability to pay them. This means that wage increases (or opposition to decreases) must not be so large as to (1) make firms wish to run away from the industry center and cause them to re-open as non-union plants in some small-town area; or (2) endanger the solvency of any firm recognizing the union, whether or not the firm contemplates migration. In other words, for the sake of the union's security, as well as the security of the members, union policy-makers cannot avoid being concerned with the possible employment effects of various alternative wage demands.

In recent years some students of unions' operations have asserted that there is little or no evidence to support the conclusion that unions are concerned with the employment effects of wage policies. This may well be true in the sense that the policy-makers make no effort to estimate a firm's or an industry's formal or exact demand curve for labor hours. It is also doubtless true that union leaders and negotiators listen with considerable skepticism to employers' claims about being unable to bear the financial burden of wage-rate increases. They have seen too often the refutation of such claims by events subsequent to the winning of the increases. That is, in a great many cases in which firms have declared that the granting of wage benefits would cause them to go out of business, the unions have discovered, after extracting the wage concessions from the firms, either that the employers were not talking in good faith or that later on something (such as improvement of market conditions or of managerial efficiency) happened to better the firm's financial position. Too many cries of "Wolf!" do tend to make one callous about the possibility of real danger. Frequent success in getting away with possibly extravagant wage demands tend to make unionists indifferent to possible unfavorable long-run effects that may well never be realized.

But all this need not justify the belief that union wage-policy-makers are not at all concerned with the employment effects of the policies. Such concern is visible enough in the case of the partially non-union industry. It is also evident when the country is heading toward or has fallen into a business depression. Under the latter circumstances unions are not only definitely restrained in their wage demands but are usually confined to fighting delaying actions in the matter of wage-rate reductions. The belief is apparent also in the demands of some unions in 1944–45 for guaranteed annual wages. Fearing a postwar depression, these unions (notably the Steelworkers) wished to bargain not only for wage rates but also for a minimum annual amount of employment.

These facts make one wonder if the proponents of the unions-don't-care belief are not basing it mainly on the experience of the inflationary years, 1942–48, when, because of the tremendous increases in product demand, large wage benefits could be and were granted by employers without substantial inroads on profits and employment potential. If these conditions can be called normal, then the belief has considerable validity. But is anyone yet prepared to assert that inflationary full employment will persist indefinitely in this country?

c. Wage policy in respect to the individual firm. Now let us begin considering the content of union wage policy. We shall deal initially with the individual firm, first in respect to its method of wage payment, second in respect to its wage-rate *structure*, and then in respect to its wage-rate *level*. Then we shall look at union wage policy as it bears on the economy as a whole.

(1) Wage-rate systems. It will be recalled from our discussions in Chapter 8 that there are two main systems of paying workers for their efforts: by unit of time, such as the hour; and by amount of output. Under the hourly-rate systems, we learned, there may be a chaotic group of personal rates, or there may be an orderly system of single rates or rate ranges; there is a variety of incentive rate systems, also. We shall deal here separately with union policies on hourly-rate systems and on incentive-rate systems.

(a) Union hourly-rate policy. The standard rate. What are union policies on the hourly-rate systems? In general, the unions favor single rates rather than rate ranges. And they abhor what we have described as "chaotic" wage-rate structures. This is because a single rate prevents firms from discriminating among workers in ways inimical to the security of the union and of the workers. It is part of a fundamental principle of union wage policy, namely *the standard rate*. Most unions wish an employer to pay one rate to all the qualified employees — no matter what their sex, nationality, or age group — who are working on a given job. Sometimes this principle is also termed "equal pay for equal work." It helps to build the united front or solidarity so necessary for successful collective bargaining. When union members receive differential rates, the possibility exists that individual bargaining will replace collective bargaining to some extent. The solid, united front of the union would tend to be cracked if individual workers could bargain with management about their positions within a rate range or about their personal rates in a chaotic structure. The union might then feel it necessary to bargain with the employer on all the individual rates. But this would not only be time-consuming and bothersome; it would also tend to stir up rivalry and trouble among the members. In any case, the survival of the union would be endangered.

Unions often assert that the standard rate is only a minimum rate and that they do not object if the employer chooses to pay more than the maximum to exceptionally fast or able workers. They say that if an employer does so, the responsibility for discriminatory rates is on him; the union members getting only the standard rate will blame the employer rather than the union. Actually the standard rate in most cases tends to be the maximum as well as the minimum because of the previously mentioned informal union rules against speeding up.

The standard single-wage-rate policy has often been attacked as stifling incentives to increased productivity and as reducing all workers to the dead level of mediocrity. Those who defend it argue that it really encourages increased productivity because it promotes the security of both the union and the union members and it raises the workers' morale. Workers' morale and productivity are said to be low in plants where wage-rate discrimination and inequities exist. In addition, high worker morale in itself, i.e., without regard to productivity, is said to be socially desirable.

Some unions — mostly affiliates of the C.I.O. — do not object to rate ranges for various jobs. This might seem like an abandonment of the principle of the standard rate and the united front. But it is not. The principle finds application even among these organizations. Even though at any one time the unions allow the workers on a given job to receive different rates, they almost always insist that progression from the minimum to the maximum rate be automatic on the basis of job seniority. They frown on the system whereby the employer unilaterally determines which workers merit intra-range advancement.

A few local unions have accepted the merit principle of progression when they have believed that its operations are sufficiently safeguarded. That is, they have gone along with pure merit if the firm agreed to joint union-management judgment of merit. Other unions have yielded no further than to agree that merit shall govern progression from the midpoint to the maximum of the rate range, with individual increases from the minimum to the midpoint based on length of service. A few unions have agreed to unilateral managerial judgment of merit in cases where the union was weak or management was fully trusted.

(b) Union policy on incentive wage-rate systems. When an employer introduces an incentive wage-rate system, he in effect says to his workers, "I wish to increase output and lower unit costs in order to improve my competitive position and make more profits. You wish to take home more pay every week. I have a system here that will make it possible for both these objectives to be attained. If you work harder and produce more, I will pay you more. At the same time you will help me reduce unit costs and increase my profits. Let's work together."

i. The pre-scientific-management period. When non-union workers first heard words like these, soon after factory manufacturing began in America, most of them thought the idea sounded pretty good. Like almost all workers, they had not outdone themselves laboring for their employers' advantage under hourly rates of pay. Informal but effective social pressure had enforced a very moderate pace of work. But a plan that offered more pay for more work seemed to give workers an opportunity to share in the profits resulting from harder, faster work.

At first, as a rule, the system operated as predicted. In some plants, of course, the workers never cooperated. This was because their employers introduced the system arbitrarily and autocratically, with no explanations of what it was supposed to do and with no pleas for cooperation. Here the workers were suspicious and resentful from the start. In some plants, also, many workers feared to cooperate because they carried in their heads the perennial lump-of-labor notion that there is only so much work to be done and jobs are always scarce. Why work harder and speed yourself out of a job? But in many plants the inaugurations of the incentive system seemed auspicious. The workers really "put out," and they were usually rewarded with much higher weekly earnings. But in many cases a period of disillusionment followed. Most workers, whether non-union or union, came to have bitter resentment against "piece work."

How did this happen? For one thing, the workers often found there was no very direct relation between their own pace and amount of effort, on the one hand, and their output and earnings, on the other. If their machines broke down, there were often long delays in getting them repaired. And there was no pay, for they had no output. Or the flow of materials to their workplaces stopped or was retarded by the failure of fellow workers or managerial work schedulers and routers to keep the stream moving. Again no output and no pay. For another thing, many workers pushed themselves too hard at first. The lure of higher wage income led them to work-paces that could not be maintained. Their health suffered from fatigue and nervous strain. They had to go more slowly. But they had tasted much higher earnings, and they resented not being able to continue getting them.

But the main source of resentment was the cutting of the incentive rates of pay. In many cases the harder-working employees began to earn as much as 50 or 100 per cent more than they had under hourly rates. To some employers this seemed "unnatural" if not "immoral"; workers just didn't earn that much. Most employers, however, decided they had set the rates too loosely. And they probably had; the workers were earning much more, but the firms' unit costs were not being reduced as anticipated. The employers therefore chose to reduce the rates. The workers became bitter after the rate cut, for they had now to work much harder if they were to take home as much pay as in the first weeks under the plan.

Most of the earlier plans had the virtue of being simple; the workers did not find them hard to understand. They were what is known as *straight piece work*, with each unit of output paid for at a certain rate. This system is still widely used today. There are three variants. First, as output increases, the rate per piece decreases and moderately. So long as the rates do not fall so rapidly as to eliminate all incentive to the workers, this plan is beneficial to the employer, for there is a reduced unit wage cost as well as a reduced unit overhead cost as output rises. It is not liked by workers. Second, as output increases, the piece rate rises. This plan favors the workers. It may confer no benefits on management if the rates rise rapidly enough. The reduction in unit overhead cost resulting from spreading fixed costs over higher outputs is offset by the rise in unit wage cost. The firm's total unit cost may thus be held constant or even rise. Here the incentive for management to cooperate is gone. In the third version, the piece rate remains constant for all outputs. This compromise plan seems fairest to all concerned — provided that the piece rate is not unjustifiably cut later on — because it tends to split the gains between workers and management.

ii. Scientific management. Most employers could understand why workers so violently resented the cutting of piece rates. They could also see that resentful workers would not produce much, but they felt that they had to cut their original rates if any cost reduction was to be achieved. In short, they were in a dilemma. Then a few shrewd managers and engineers began to see the conditions that had caused the trouble. They came to understand that education and explanation should have preceded the introduction of the plans; that a minimum hourly rate equal at least to the pre-incentive rate should have been guaranteed for all "down" time caused by machine breakdown, lack of materials, or other causes; and that management should have assumed full responsibility for preventing or quickly repairing machine breakdowns and for insuring a steady, adequate flow of materials to each worker. Most important of all, they learned that there should have been an analysis of each job before incentive rates were set. No effort had been made to discover how many pieces an average worker could produce per unit of time when stimulated by the lure of higher earnings to abandon his former habits of output restriction and when trained to perform the job in accordance with the methods and motions discovered by job study. Foremen had simply made a guess based on past output records and work methods and the piece rates had then been set so as to provide daily or weekly earnings moderately higher than the old wages under hourly rates. Very few managers were prepared for the flood of output turned out by "hot" workers.

Motion and time study, as described in Chapter 14, were developed to remedy this defect. Improved techniques for avoiding the other defects were also worked out. And new kinds of incentive systems were devised. Although many variants came into existence, the feature common to most of these later plans was the setting of a standard "task" (amount of output) per period of time — so many pieces per hour or per day, or so many minutes or hours per piece (unit of output). If the time-output standard or a high percentage thereof (e.g., 80 per cent) was not achieved, the worker received only his "base" hourly rate. This amount was guaranteed. If the standard or high percentage thereof was attained, he received his base rate plus the incentive bonus.

What about the crucial problem of rate-cutting under the newer approach? Management promised not to reduce the incentive rates so long as there was no substantial change in the job. Obviously, if a new machine or tool or flow of materials made the job really a different one, management would have to re-study and re-time it. Otherwise the worker would get all the benefit from a management-initiated technological improvement. But small, minor changes would not be used as an excuse to cut the rate unless a number of successive small changes added up to a substantial or major one.

Although the newer approach was introduced and maintained successfully in a great many firms, in many other plants it met resistance and sometimes failed totally. There were a number of reasons for this failure. Workers were suspicious of "scientific," "inhuman" men like management engineers — especially since there was some evidence that their methods were not so scientific as they purported to be (recall our discussion of motion and time study in Chapter 14). Management too often failed to enlist the workers' understanding and cooperation by proper human-relations measures, and hence to allay the workers' general mistrust of any change which may threaten their established habits of work and their investments in skill. In addition, the workers disliked the complicated methods of calculating earnings under the new incentive systems, and often found them almost impossible to understand. The incentive systems also fell into disrepute through being applied to operations in which the unit of output is too large (e.g., a Diesel engine) or too non-standard (e.g., a construction electrician's work) to be amenable to time-output measurement. And they were seriously discredited through the tendency of some firms to introduce fake improvements on jobs in order to cut rates that they found to be too high. Of course, as the workers formed low opinions of the incentive systems, those systems had less chance to succeed.

iii. Union policies. Our discussion above should have made it clear that, where workers' resistance to incentive wage-rate systems exists, it is not confined to unionists. But union workers have a much better chance to be articulate and to implement their attitudes. They can communicate their feelings to their employers through their representatives. And what the union representatives or leaders say carries a good deal of weight. Employers usually cannot afford to ignore it.

But not all union members and unions are opposed to incentive plans. Many individual union workers like the higher earnings that go with such plans. Furthermore, in a sense the worker becomes his own boss; since his earnings depend on his own effort, he can be left free from constant supervision and nagging by his foreman. Again, he can benefit considerably from the increased earnings that accrue when either he or management makes improvements on his job, provided that management deems those improvements too small to justify cutting the incentive rate. All these things tend to make incentive work attractive to many unionists. Nevertheless, they also desire security. They don't want to be pushed around arbitrarily by management, have their rates cut and their skills diluted, or be compelled to work too fast. Faced with these costs as well as the utilities of incentive work, then, many union workers try to strike a balance by saying, We are willing to accept wage-rate incentive systems if we are protected against abuses by management.

What about the union as an entity? Don't these plans threaten union survival because they foster differences in effort and earnings among members? Doesn't an incentive system tend to break the united front and to some extent substitute individual for collective bargaining? Doesn't it tend to create dissension among members and tear the union apart when some members fare better than others? In short, isn't such a system the antithesis of the standard rate principle?

At first thought it might appear that the answer to these questions must be an unqualified "yes." But further consideration suggests some necessary qualifications. First, in a few unions, such as the Amalgamated Clothing Workers and the Ladies' Garment Workers, the more capable workers are a large proportion of those working on certain jobs. They actually wish to be distinguished from the less effective employees by differentials in earnings. They believe that an incentive system is the best way of making rewards proportionate to capabilities and effort. There would be much more dissension within the union if there were no incentive system.

Second, the things that work against or contribute to the survival of a union as an entity are many and various. From the internal political standpoint, the wishes of the membership on incentive plans cannot be disregarded by the leadership. If the members are dead set against incentives for any reason, the officers have a very hard task of education ahead of them if they believe incentives are desirable. On the other hand, if the members desire such plans, after balancing the costs and utilities, the leaders may have to bow to this view even if they believe the plans unwise. Again, in an industry only partially unionized, incentive systems may be a way of contributing to union survival because they help reduce unit costs and keep union firms competitive with non-union firms in the product market. This was a main reason why the unions in textiles, hosiery, men's clothing, and coal mining began to espouse piece work. These unions had to risk some degree of threat to survival from possible internal dissension over the administration of the plans, because the non-union hazard to survival was much more important.

Third, why was the standard wage-rate principle adopted by a union in the first place? To protect individual members and help insure union survival. But there are other ways to achieve these objectives. And if the other measures are effective, then the standard rate principle need not be adhered to with absolute rigidity. Under an incentive system this principle is abandoned to the extent that certain differences in output and take-home pay are permitted among individual union members working on the same job. But the principle is retained in two ways: Each member working on a given job must be paid at the same incentive rate. And formal rules or informal pressures can be (and are) exerted against any overly ambitious or individualistic member who might work so hard as to invite management to find an excuse for cutting the rate.

What protective measures can be adopted to replace the standard wage-rate principle in so far as the latter is not rigidly adhered to under an incentive plan? In the first place, the unions themselves may take over the setting of time-output standards and the determination of appropriate incentive rates. This of course is the ultimate in protecting the individual member and insuring union survival. And in the industries where it is done (men's and women's clothing, and to some extent hosiery and textiles), it is not considered an intolerable infringement on managerial prerogatives. The firms in which union engineers do the whole job are usually too small and financially weak to be able to pay for motion-time-study men or a rate-setting staff of their own. The desirability of incentive rates being mutually agreed on, these firms are glad to accept the help of the unions. In the second place, both union and management may have rate-setting engineers who study jobs and determine incentives jointly. Here also there is protection for the union and its members. A variant of this approach is found where management is allowed to set the time-output standards unilaterally (with the determination subject to review under the grievance procedure) but the incentive rates themselves are jointly negotiated by union and management. A third security measure common among unions that favor or tolerate incentive plans is not to have union engineers study jobs and set rates unilaterally or jointly but to permit management both to make the studies and to set the rates. The rates are called "temporary." But they become "permanent" after a stated period of time, such as four weeks, unless challenged within this period through the regular grievance procedure. In general, the minimum security requirement in respect to any aspect of the operation of an incentive system is an appeal from managerial decisions via the grievance routine.

Among the unions actively in favor of incentive plans, special note should be taken of the Amalgamated Clothing Workers, whom we have previously cited. To most unions the standard rate means not only wage-rate uniformity for all the workers on a given job within a given plant but also, as we shall see, some approach to inter-plant wage-rate uniformity. The latter aims at achieving union survival and power by "taking the competition out of wages." That is, it aims to prevent the pressure originating in firms' competition in the product market from pushing down wage rates in the labor market. The theory is that if all the firms in the industry have to pay the same wage rates, their labor costs per unit of output will be the same; and no firm will be able to obtain a competitive advantage by reducing wage rates. Now union leaders know full well that uniform wage rates among firms are not the same as uniform unit labor costs; managerial efficiencies and other conditions vary a good deal so that one plant's labor costs per unit of output may be much higher or lower than another's. But in the nature of things the great majority of unions can exert little or no control toward obtaining uniform labor costs beyond that afforded by uniform wage rates. The Amalgamated is one of the few exceptions. In 1939, in the men's suits and coats branch of the industry, it introduced a Stabilization Program intended to achieve uniform labor costs for each of six grades of garments. The fundamentals of this plan were two: standard operations (uniform time-output standards) for each kind of clothing in all plants; and uniform incentive rates in all plants for each kind of clothing. The success of this program in a highly competitive, seasonal industry indicates how a "smart" union can utilize an incentive system to its own marked advantage.

Some unions are adamant and long-standing in their complete opposition to incentive systems. In most plants where they are recognized, the Machinists and the Automobile Workers are good examples. The former's attitude is based mainly on the bitter experience of its members with such plans and on the fear that job study will make further serious inroads on their skills. The Automobile Workers' position is founded mainly on this thesis: The speed of operation on many machines, including assembly lines, is paced by the machine rather than by the worker. The worker has to adjust himself to the machine rather than vice versa. It is really not to the benefit of management itself to use incentive rates for such jobs because the worker cannot increase output by laboring harder; he merely has to keep up with the machine. (If he can't, presumably he deserves discharge or transfer, unless the machine is being operated at an unreasonable speed.) However, suppose that incentive rates are introduced on such operations. It is management's responsibility to see that the machine does not break down. But if a breakdown does occur, the worker suffers much more than management. The worker gets only his guaranteed base rate pay for "down" time; this may be 20 per cent or more below average hourly incentive earnings. Thus, in such operations management is said to shift to the worker the losses from its own failures.

Other noteworthy unions resolutely opposed to incentive rates are those in printing and construction. A few of the latter feel so strongly that they, like the Machinists, have included a formal prohibitory paragraph in their constitutions.

Evidently, then, national union policy on this method of wage payment is decidedly non-uniform. Moreover, the various locals within a given national union often differ among themselves on incentive systems. Some of them may refuse to go along with official national policy. This has been true even of the Machinists and Automobile Workers. Again, both the United Steelworkers and the United Electrical, Radio, and Machine Workers approve incentive plans, but each of these national unions has certain locals that decline to follow the top policy.

(2) Wage-rate structure within a plant. So much for the method of remuneration. Now, for the sake of simplicity, let us assume that all the jobs in a given one-plant firm are paid on the hourly, single-rate system. Do unions have any policies on what the relationships should be among the rates paid for the different jobs within the plant? If so, what are the policies?

(a) General political considerations. Unions do have policies on the internal wage structure of a plant. But it must be clear that we are concerned here mainly with the attitudes and policies of industrial unions, for they are the ones which have jurisdiction over all the jobs in a plant, from the least skilled to the most skilled. We may dismiss the craft unions with the statement that in any plant in a given industry, such as printing or construction, each tries at least to maintain its relative wage-rate position. This means, first, that relative position is usually maintainable only at the times when *changes* in wage rates are being considered; and second, that relative position is to be held by keeping a *percentage* rather than a *cents-per-hour* differential between or among the respective crafts' rates of pay.

In respect to industrial unions, let us start again with individual workers. As union members with votes they often strongly affect local and top policy. We saw in Chapter 7 that *relative* wage-rate and wage-income position is a very important determinant of social status. That is, workers dislike being subject to what came to be known, under the National War Labor Board's administration of wage-rate stabilization, as "intra-plant inequities." They believe that workers doing similar work should get about the same rates of pay. And they have rather definite ideas about how much "better" or "poorer" the workers on other jobs are and how much higher or lower their rates should be. These ideas, of course, are based to a large extent on what the workers have become accustomed to.

When one or more union members in a plant have wage-rate grievances of this sort, they can have them attended to by a shop steward through the grievance procedure, if the problem is to give the worker the proper rate among a number of existing job rates. Or, if the problem involves changing the job rate itself, the grievances may be resolved through the negotiation of a new agreement or contract. Our interest here is mainly in the alignment of *job* rates as such rather than in the "slotting" of workers into existing job rates.

Clearly the handling of job-rate inequities for various groups of workers is one of the ways in which local and national officers can serve these workers and command their political support. A general, across-the-board wage-rate increase for all the workers in a plant does not make much distinction among the different occupations. (It is true, of course, that a general rise given in cents favors the lower-paid jobs somewhat; and a percentage increase may be said to favor the workers on the higher-skill jobs.) But if rates are negotiated job by job rather than in terms of a general change, it is possible to favor certain jobs and workers one year and other jobs and workers the next year, and so on. In this way, over time, union officers can hold the loyalties of most of their constituents.

Such political wage-rate negotiation also has much the same net economic effect as an across-the-board change. When a sizable increase is obtained for one job or group of jobs, the union negotiators do not willingly agree to a rate reduction for other jobs. Over time, consequently, the whole schedule of job rates is effectively whipsawed upward.

(b) Job evaluation. Nature and administration. There is a relatively rational (as opposed to political) way of correcting intra-plant job-rate inequities. It goes by the name of *job evaluation.* Although not a new technique, its recent growth in favor among employers has been the result of the government's wage stabilization program during World War II and of the growth of unionism. Employers seized on it, with the frequent approval of unions, as a back-door way of obtaining wage-rate increases during the wage control period. (The use of job evaluation for this purpose need not concern us here.) Employers continue to like it now, not only because of its value in improving worker morale but also because it helps to balk the political, whipsawing wage-rate demands of unions.

Without going into technicalities we may explain job evaluation as follows: There are two main phases — rating all the jobs in the plant in ascending order of importance, from low to high; and applying to the various jobs wage rates which reflect these rankings. The first phase is the evaluation proper. To begin with, a group of rating criteria or elements must be chosen. These include such items as education, experience, physical effort, mental effort, judgment, initiative, responsibility for safety of workers or consumers, responsibility for equipment and materials, responsibility for work of others, and working conditions. Then a maximum number of points is assigned to each rating element. The relative numbers of maximum points given to the various elements show their relative weights or importance in the minds of the evaluators. Usually many more points are given by employers to education and experience and initiative, which make for skill, than to effort and working conditions. The next step is to study and describe each job in the plant in terms of these rating criteria. Then, in respect to each criterion a number of points is assigned to each job. The points for all the criteria are then summed for each job; in other words, a total point score is obtained for each job. After this is accomplished, the jobs can be ranked from bottom to top. If there are a great many different jobs and the point differences among many of them are small, the jobs may be slotted into a much smaller number of "labor grades," say twelve, fifteen, or twenty. For example, if the sum of the maximum numbers of points assigned to the criteria is 600, then all the jobs whose total score is from, say, 530 to 600 may be put into Labor Grade One, all those scoring from 450 to 530 in Labor Grade Two, and so on.

The second phase — applying dollar wage rates or rate ranges to the evaluated jobs or labor grades — involves, first, the determination of proper rates for two or more key or "anchor" jobs. In the absence of a union, management usually does this by obtaining information on what rates are being paid for such jobs by other plants in the area or industry. (Here we see how influential the economic conditions of the labor market and the product market are.) Management then decides whether to remunerate the key jobs at, above, or below the prevailing rates. After the key-job rates have been set, the rates for the intermediate jobs are determined by their point relationships to the key ones.

Clearly, when a job evaluation plan is put into effect, it is jobs rather than workers that have been rated. In normal times — that is, in the absence of inflationary pressures in a tight labor market or in the absence of various union demands — it is possible to draw the "evaluation line" from lowest to highest rated jobs in such a way that there is no net increase or decrease in the average of job rates. This means that, in terms of the wage rates assigned to the jobs after evaluation, some pre-evaluation job wage rates are higher and have to be reduced, and some are lower and have to be raised; and the amount by which the higher rates are brought down is about equal to the amount by which the lower ones are brought up. But for reasons of morale and equity, although the workers on the jobs with rates that have to be raised are given the new, higher rates, the workers on the jobs whose rates are lowered are kept at their previous rates. In other words, upon the inauguration of the plan some workers are given increases but no workers are given decreases. Thus, although there may be no net change in job rates as such, there usually is a considerable net increase in the rates of the workers as persons.

This fact does not defeat the purpose of the evaluation. In time, labor turnover will remove from their jobs the workers whose personal rates stayed above the newly evaluated job rates. And the new workers hired to replace them will be paid at the proper job rates. But all the workers who were on a job of this sort when the plan was initiated do not leave the job at one time. They drift away gradually, so that at any one time there are some old and some new workers on the jobs. Then the latter, who are receiving the actual job rate, may feel unfairly treated because the pre-evaluation workers are still paid at their higher personal rates.

Once a job evaluation system has been in effect for some time, two other major problems arise in its administration. First, market conditions may change so that labor for one or more jobs becomes hard to get and hold. Shall the "engineered," evaluated wage rate yield to a more "economic" one? If so, and if this happens often enough, what becomes of the evaluation system? A second problem arises out of the fact that the content of many of the jobs, because of technological improvements or for other reasons, may change over time. Usually such changes are in the direction of greater simplicity and fewer skill requirements. This means that most such jobs are given lower ratings and are assigned lower wage rates. A morale problem is created if the workers assigned to such a job came from the previous, higher-pay job and are now paid at the lower rates. This can be avoided by doing what was done when the whole system first went into effect: Pay such workers their former rates until they leave the job.

(c) Union policies. National union attitudes toward the job evaluation method of removing intra-plant wage-rate inequities are not uniform. And again there are local union deviations from a given national policy. However, it may be said in general that most local and national union officers would not grieve too much over the loss of opportunity to whipsaw the job-rate structure upward for economic and political purposes. There is still plenty of scope for serving constituents by arguing with management over the workers' personal wage-rate inequities under a job evaluation plan; arguing about the job-rate problems (mentioned above) that arise over time under the administration of a plan; and arguing about job and personal rates at the time when the plan is being set up.

As with incentive systems of wage payment, industrial unions do not seriously oppose the introduction of job evaluation plans if they are given a voice in both the construction and the administration of the plans. This is the crucial point — avoidance of unilateral judgment and action by the employer in order to protect the survival of the union and the security of members. The steel, electrical products, pulp and paper, and other industries have shown what constructive union-management cooperation can achieve in the systematic reduction of intra-plant inequities.

(3) The plant's level of all wage rates. We have seen that a union can effect a rise in the general *level* of a firm's job wage rates by any of three methods: first, a whipsawing process whereby, under the guise of redressing inequities in the internal job-rate structure, first one set of jobs and then another (and back again to the first) are given higher rates, so that in the end the whole level is boosted; second, a job evaluation system under which the key job rates are set so high (and the evaluation or rating line is therefore so high) that many more job rates are raised than are lowered; and third, an across-the-board increase for all job rates and workers, under which everyone obtains the same amount of raise, either cents-wise or percentage-wise.

(a) Conditions influencing policy. Our interest now is not in *how* a

union changes a plant's wage-rate level, but *why* and *under what conditions and rationalizations.* These matters are of special moment because most union bargains with employers are still plant- or firm-wide rather than industry-wide. All the discussion, early in this chapter, of the politics of union wage policy-making is relevant here. In addition, our discussion of union wage policy in respect to the economy as a whole is very important also; such policy is given effect in large part through dealing with individual firms. To summarize, a given union's wage demands on a given firm depend on such conditions as the following: (*i*) the relationship between union leadership and the membership, in terms of presence or absence of factions, weakness or strength of national political machines, and so on; (*ii*) what other unions have obtained in other crafts or industries or areas; (*iii*) what other employers (non-union as well as union), have granted in the same industry or in other industries and areas; (*iv*) the degree of unionization in the industry; (*v*) the degree of competition in the industry's product market. Another important factor is (*vi*) the nature of the markets in which the firm buys complementary productive factors like raw materials and substitute factors like labor-saving machinery (thus, if the firm buys materials as a monopsonist, it has some extra "gravy" that the union may be able to extract; and if inexpensive labor-saving machines are readily available to the firm, the union's wage-rate demands tend to be temperate, for too high a wage-rate increase may well cause the firm to make extensive substitution, thus causing unemployment and dissatisfaction among the members). Still other conditions influencing union policy are (*vii*) the phase of the business cycle in which the union is operating (Is the cost of living rising or falling and are business profits large and growing or small and declining?); and (*viii*) the union's attitude on obtaining an adequate share of the increased income made possible by general technological progress and capital accumulation.

In brief, a union asks a firm for a level of wage rates that the union believes will contribute to the survival, prestige, and power of the union as such and will add to members' satisfactions (rather than diminish them by harming the firm that employs them). This level is sought over time by demanding changes of one sort or another in the existing structure and level of the firm's rates.

(b) Rationalization of demands. Whatever the *real* reasons for and the actual conditions affecting a union's demand for a wage-rate-level change, the demand must be rationalized, explained, and argued for in a way intended to impress the public, hearten the membership, and put the employer at a psychological and public relations disadvantage. A union's rationalizing arguments in behalf of its position include one or more of the following.

First, the cost of living has risen. Therefore hourly wage rates must rise by at least the same percentage. Otherwise workers' real incomes and satisfactions fall in an economy in which the long-term trend has always involved a rise in per-capita real income. (If the rise in the hourly earnings of the firm's workers has outpaced the rise in the cost of living, so that the workers' real incomes have been increasing, the union may claim that the cost-of-living index does not adequately reflect the actual changes in the prices and qualities of products bought by workers. This argument was made by C.I.O. and A.F.L. unions during the wage-rate-control period of World War II.)

Second, the firm is able to pay higher wage rates. This ability-to-pay argument takes one or the other or both of two forms. (*a*) The firm's financial and income statements show amounts and rates of profits that are more than necessary for the maintenance and expansion of its plant and equipment and for the payment of a fair rate of dividends to stockholders. The excess should go to labor. (*b*) The average man-hour productivity of the firm's (or the industry's) labor has risen by a larger percentage than has the increase in its workers' real wage rates. The workers have not been receiving their fair share of this gain. The larger gain in productivity establishes the firm's ability to pay higher money wage rates.

Third, government (or private) agencies have made studies and concluded that an annual income of, say, $3500 is necessary for the attainment of a modest standard of living for an average worker's family. The average annual income of this firm's workers last year was, say, $300 less than this minimum amount. Their wage rates should be raised enough to permit them to reach this standard.

Sometimes additional arguments are advanced in particular cases where they seem applicable. One of these is the maintenance of take-home pay discussed later on under union policy on length of work periods. When unions ask for reductions in the length of work periods, they often demand simultaneous proportionate increases in wage rates so that weekly earnings will not be diminished. Another argument sometimes heard, particularly in big pattern-setting single-firm cases, is that workers' "purchasing power" must be raised so that business depressions can be avoided or minimized.

It is not our purpose here to make a critical analysis and appraisal of these rationalizing arguments. That will come later on in the book (Part Three, Chapter 23, where we deal with public welfare and with government policy on wage matters. We must note here, however, that unions often employ these arguments with admitted and open inconsistency. The cost-of-living principle cuts both ways; it can also be used to justify a decrease in wage rates when the level of consumption-product prices is falling. But unions usually turn their backs on the argument when the cost of living is declining. Similarly, unions eye coldly the ability-to-pay rationalization, when advanced by an employer who claims he is losing money. The fact is that unions use these arguments only when union purpose is served thereby. Their main objective is the one consistent element in the whole business: more, always more. They believe this is a truly American objective, shared with them by employers and virtually all other individuals and groups. And, like these others, they will use, inconsistently if necessary, whatever argument comes to hand.

(4) Special wage policies. Under this heading we note three main kinds of comparatively recent union policies affecting wage rates or wage income: (*a*) "fringe" or supplementary wage items; (*b*) the demand for guaranteed annual wage income; and (*c*) policies affecting wages indirectly.

(a) Fringe items. The "fringe" or supplementary wage items are those involving money payments to workers from sources other than the direct hourly or incentive wage rate. They include the following categories: (*i*) Payments for time not worked, such as vacations with pay (e.g., one week for one year's service and two weeks for five years' service), paid holidays (usually six per year), pay for certain periods of sickness, paid lunch periods, paid rest periods, paid time for travel (such as travel to and from a non-plant job or from plant "portal" to workplace at the beginning of the workday and from workplace to plant "portal" at the end of the workday), paid clean-up time, paid call-in time (payment for a minimum number of hours, such as four, when a worker is called back to his job after having left the plant for the day), paid call time (payment for a minimum number of hours when an employee reports for work at his regular time and is sent home for lack of work to be done), and payments to unionists for time spent in handling grievances or other negotiations with the management; (*ii*) special premium payments for special hours worked, such as time-and-a-half for hours over eight per day and/or forty per week, double time for work on Saturdays, Sundays, and holidays, and premiums (so much per hour) for working second or third shifts or for working on particularly unpleasant or hazardous jobs; and (*iii*) "welfare" plans financed partly or wholly by employers and providing payments for permanent layoff, sickness, injury, retirement, or death.

Many of these items are not new in American industry. Some of them were in fact inaugurated by numerous employers before their workers became unionized, partly in order to forestall such organization. But these fringe provisions are today much more usual and varied than they used to be. Unions turned to them during the wage control period of World War II as a way of getting additional wage-rate increases after they had used up their allowances under other aspects of the War Labor Board's stabilization policies. Fringes are a fertile area for union activity, since to help the union as well as its members, a union is always searching for new ways of protecting members against possible abuses from employers and against the general hazards of employment.

There is space here only for special attention to unions' demands for employer-financed welfare plans. These are to be distinguished from the benefit plans (discussed in the next chapter) which are purely union affairs — financed out of members' dues payments and providing payments against unemployment, sickness, disability, superannuation, and death. Among the major unions the Amalgamated Clothing Workers and the Ladies' Garment Workers were the first to ask their employers to contribute to a joint fund to protect members against one or more of the above-mentioned hazards. (Dismissal wages or severance pay for workers laid off permanently because of technological improvements or for other reasons was a part of these arrangements.) In 1944 the War Labor Board approved a plan whereby unemployed members of the Musicians' Union were to be supported out of a fund accumulated from "royalties" on phonograph records paid by the record-making companies. In 1946 the Mine Workers obtained from the government (who at that time under war powers was operating the bituminous coal mines because the private operators refused to grant the union's demands) a welfare plan covering sickness and pension benefits and financed by "royalties" on tons of mined coal. This program remained as a condition for the return of the mines to the private owners. Spurred on by these achievements and by the failure of Congress, after the postwar inflation, to raise the benefits payable under the federal Social Security Act, the two chief C.I.O. unions, the Steelworkers and the Automobile Workers, began asking for employer-financed company medical and hospital benefits and pensions. The companies refused; but in the latter part of 1949 the unions' efforts met success, after favorable recommendation by a fact-finding board appointed by the President to settle the dispute in the steel industry, and after a subsequent industry-wide steel strike.

Since these 1949 events, a difference in policy has become evident between most of the C.I.O. unions and most of the A.F.L. and old-line independent unions. The two latter groups are in general older, and many of these unions still operate their own long-standing benefit plans. After years of opposition they also had changed their minds about government social insurance; they had come to believe that government plans are the most comprehensive and inexpensive. For example, the railroad independents have been covered by their own government pension program since 1937. Many A.F.L. and independent unions have therefore been lukewarm about company pension systems. Most of the C.I.O. unions, on the other hand, have espoused them vigorously.

Among the A.F.L., independent, and C.I.O. unions asking for company plans, another policy cleavage has become visible. The A.F.L. and independent unions appear mainly to ask for "contributory" systems, under which the workers as well as the firms make payments to the pension and medical funds. Most of the C.I.O. unions, on the other hand, have adhered to the non-contributory principle of obtaining payments solely from the companies.

To date most unions have not taken a strong stand on dismissal wages. The policy is a good deal more prevalent now than it was before World War II, but it is still far down on the list of union "musts."

Employers' views and questions of public policy (including an economic analysis) on welfare and pension plans will be presented in Chapters 18 and 23.

(b) Guaranteed annual wages. There has also been a policy difference between A.F.L. and C.I.O. unions in respect to guaranteed annual wage income. The former are lukewarm; the latter are strong advocates.

By a wage guarantee is meant that an employer agrees not only to pay a certain schedule of wage rates but also to pay these rates to a certain percentage of his workers (usually those having a stated length of service, such as two or five years) for a certain number of work-hours per year. The guarantee thus actually relates to a minimum amount of annual employment. Guarantee that, and you guarantee a certain amount of annual income.

Like welfare plans, wage-income guarantees are not new; and where they were adopted or still exist, the majority were initiated by management. (However, if unions now exist in plants having such plans, the guarantees are usually subject to collective bargaining.)

The C.I.O. move for secure wage income began in 1944, when the Steelworkers asked the steel companies to agree to them. The companies declined, whereupon the issue went to the War Labor Board. The Board refused to order the firms to adopt such plans but recommended that the President appoint a committee to study the problem.

The demand for the guarantee in steel and other industries, such as automobiles and meat packing, appears to have been variously motivated. One reason lay in the desire to provide security against unemployment for members; another in the desire to contribute to union survival and power, for unemployed members are usually not very good unionists. In 1944 the memory of the unemployment of the thirties was still very vivid. There was also a widely held belief that there would be a severe postwar depression. The actual full-employment prosperity of 1946 to 1951, however, did much to alleviate such fears. Consequently, the demand has not been pressed hard until recently. Another reason for the 1944 policy may have been to use the demand as a means of forcing government to adopt alternative approaches to unemployment: raise the level of unemployment compensation payments, and use fiscal and monetary measures to achieve indefinite full employment.

Chapter 23 contains a critical analysis of this union demand from the standpoint of public policy.

(c) Indirect wage policies. By "indirect" we mean union policies that have the intended effect of raising wage rates, even though such policies do not focus on demands for wage-rate changes. In terms of our analysis of labor supply and demand presented in Chapters 6 and 8 and used from time to time above, many of the non-wage policies that we have been discussing tend to have a wage-rate effect. The membership-limitation and output-restriction policies and the opposition to incentive

wage systems tend to reduce labor supply and thereby, given the labor demand conditions, to raise wage rates. On the labor demand side, we have noted that the measures pointed toward the control of substitute factors of production (e.g., the closed and union shops against non-union labor, and union restrictions on the use of labor-saving machines and management methods) tend to make labor demand less elastic or prevent it from being reduced (or both), thus tending to raise wage rates or prevent them from falling. It is also to be noted that union-management cooperation policies in the field of production tend, in the longer run, to increase the demand for labor in a particular plant or industry.

This economic analysis need not blind us to the fact that all these measures also have "political" purposes — to increase the job security of union members and to facilitate the survival and increase the power of unions as entities.

We come now to a new set of union policies whose political purpose is also to increase members' job security and achieve union survival and power and whose economic purpose is to make the firm's or industry's demand for labor less elastic and higher. These policies concentrate on the demand for the industry's or the firm's product, this condition being a major determinant of the demand for labor.

First may be noted the *union label campaigns* conducted by the unions belonging to the A.F.L.'s Union Label Department and by a few unions belonging to the C.I.O., such as the Amalgamated Clothing Workers. The objective of these unions is to "educate" union members and the general public into buying only dresses, suits, cigarettes, printing, and other products that bear the standard label of the union whose members help make the products. As with all advertising, the effect of successful efforts of this sort is that the demand for these products (and thereby the demand for the union workers) becomes less elastic and larger.

Second, with or without union labels, a good many unions, on their own motion or in cooperation with one or more employers, have paid wholly or partly for advertising campaigns to promote sales of the firms' products. Thus, the unionists employed by the Atlantic Coast Line railroad engaged in such promotion when their jobs were jeopardized by the threatened insolvency of the road. Similarly, the Ladies' Garment Workers' Union has spent large sums to establish New York as the style center for dresses; the Hatters, Cap, and Millinery Workers sponsored a movement to get young bareheads to wear hats; and the Painters have helped contractors try to persuade houseowners to repaint more frequently.

Third, a number of unions whose firms have been subject to competition from abroad have tried to de-elasticize and increase their firms' product demands by helping to lobby for tariffs against the foreign substitute products.

Fourth, a union may help its firm in bargaining a lower price from sellers of raw materials (thus tending to raise the demand for labor) or a higher price from buyers of the firm's product (the same effect).

Fifth, unions may compel their employers or get them to agree to shut down their operations, so as to reduce output supply and raise product price. Thus, the Glass Blowers' early-day program for a summer shutdown was motivated not only by the union's desire to protect the health of its members during the hot months but also by its wish to have the employers obtain higher product prices so as to be able to pay higher wage rates. The latter motive was also a main one in the decision of the Mine Workers to work only three days a week for several months in the fall of 1949.

Sixth, a few unions, chiefly in construction, have promoted collusive arrangements among employers so as to keep competing firms and products out of the area and raise local product prices. Thus, the Electrical Workers of Local No. 3 in New York refused to work on "imported" electrical products. Construction unions have frequently used their political influence upon city councils to obtain ordinances making it hard for new contractors to enter the locality.

Seventh, a few unions try to get government to legislate for their industries in such a way that competition is "stabilized" and higher product prices and wage rates are possible. Thus, in 1935 the Mine Workers obtained a federal law establishing a National Bituminous Coal Commission for such objectives. And the Barbers have sometimes obtained state laws governing sanitation and other matters, which have the effect of raising the price of haircuts and barbers' wages.

d. Wage policy in respect to an industry. As already indicated, the wage-rate level (and even structure) demanded of a particular firm by a given union is influenced by what the wage-rate level is or is expected to be in other firms in the industry or area or both. Our interest now is in the attitudes and policies which unions adopt toward the whole group of firms in a given industry with which they have or would like to have bargaining relations. These policies focus on two questions: (1) Shall all the firms in the industry be required to pay the same rates for similar jobs, regardless of the region or size of city in which they are located? (2) Shall this matter of inter-firm wage-rate differentials (as well as the related question of whether *changes* in the *general levels* of the various firms' wage rates shall be in uniform amounts or percentages) be handled by dealing separately with the individual firms or plants in the industry or by dealing with all the firms together through what has come to be known, rather imprecisely, as "industry-wide bargaining"?

Answers to both questions clearly involve policy-making at the national rather than the local level.

(1) Regional and size-of-city differentials among firms. Union policies vary a good deal on this problem. As might be expected from our previous statements that the locals are allowed wide latitude because the product markets are local, the construction and printing craft unions permit regional and size-of-city differentials in wage rates to persist. (But

within a given locality all firms are asked to pay the same rates.) Given a good deal of immobility in such labor so far as inter-city migration is concerned, it is not necessary to have uniform rates throughout the country.

At the other end of the scale, at least two major unions — the United Automobile Workers and the United Mine Workers — have succeeded in eliminating regional differentials. The U.A.W. has been aided in this policy by the favorable attitudes of the three major oligopolists with which it deals (separately) — General Motors, Ford, and Chrysler. The U.M.W., however, operates in a highly competitive industry (bituminous coal) which had been accustomed to all sorts of wage differences. Its no-wage-differential policy was part of a general program for stabilizing (curbing wage competition in) the industry.

Between these extremes stand the other unions, of whom we may say this: They are moving gradually in the direction of wage-rate uniformity in all sections of the country, but they agree to differentials without too much of a fight where they believe special circumstances exist. Thus, the Steelworkers have wiped out differences among almost all Northern plants but have only narrowed the North-South differential because of the higher costs which the Southern firms must incur to reach the major, Northern markets for steel products. The policies of the unions in textiles and rubber are other illustrations.

In general, although nation-wide inter-firm uniformity of wage rates for similar jobs is a logical ultimate extension of the principle of the standard rate, most unions have not pressed very hard for it unless impelled to do so by special conditions such as severe competion. Within a given area or region, however, uniformity is demanded. And in time an extension of the principle to the whole country is to be expected.

(2) Multi-employer bargaining. When a union demands changes in the level of a firm's wage rates or the removal or narrowing of differentials between a firm's job rates and those of other firms, it has several alternatives in respect to the area of bargaining to be selected for the accomplishment of these objectives. Within its industry it may bargain separately with each firm. In fact, if some of the firms have more than one plant, the union may choose to deal separately with each plant. Another possibility is bargaining with all the employers in a city or associated area. Still wider in area would be a region, such as New England or the West Coast or the Southeast. Widest of all would be the entire industry — bargaining that is national in scope if the industry is.

From a union's point of view each alternative has costs as well as utilities. A major determinant of these is again the degree of competition in the product market. Severe competition among the industry's firms makes a broad area of bargaining desirable. Unions want wage-rate uniformity in highly competitive industries, particularly if labor cost is a high fraction of total production cost. It is costly and expensive to try to attain this goal plant by plant or firm by firm, and the outcome is more doubtful. But a keenly competitive industry has a great many firms. Industry- or region-wide bargaining may be hard to get. It requires the organization of an effective association among the firms. However, the firms may be eager to form such an association because the union is so much stronger than any one of them.

In an oligopolistic industry like steel or automobiles, a broad bargaining area is much easier to obtain if the firms do not object on principle to such an area, as they often do, because *they* do not need it (see Chapter 17). But the need of unions for a broad scope is also less urgent here. The firms are accustomed to "cooperate" in the product market—and often in the labor market. There is not much pressure on wage rates.

The area of the product market is important also. There is little or no inter-market competition in retail trade, in the hotel and restaurant industry, in newspaper publishing, and in construction. Therefore there is no need for nation-wide bargaining. But within each separate market the competition may be keen enough to lead the unions to demand city-wide bargaining.

To summarize, the main economic impetus toward industry-wide bargaining on a national scale is severe competition among many firms in a national product market. The main technological factor is the high importance of labor costs. Multi-employer bargaining greatly facilitates the union's effort to stabilize and control wage competition in the industry. Thus, we find it in several branches of the clothing and hosiery industries and in anthracite and bituminous coal. But the union must be recognized in a major portion of an industry before such stabilization-bargaining can be effective. Hence it is not as yet found in some competitive industries like cotton textiles.

In industries in which product-market competition is not so severe, unions may or may not favor multi-employer bargaining. The trend is definitely toward broadening the scope, but union attitudes are not now uniform. This is in part because they evaluate differently the other costs and utilities of the various areas of bargaining. Some unions have favored individual firm or plant bargaining because a single firm in their industries is usually much weaker than the union. The other firms in the industry continue to operate if the union calls a strike against one firm. While the latter is idle, the others "steal" its customers, many of whom may never come back after the strike is over. If there are not too many firms in the industry, then, the union can obtain more from each and, in the end, from the whole industry by picking off the firms one at a time, starting usually with the weakest. By the time they come to the stronger firms a "pattern" has been established.

The other non-economic conditions found on the side of multi-employer bargaining are as follows: (*a*) Dealing with a group of employers is easier and much less time-consuming and expensive than making many separate bargains with individual firms. A union can concentrate its best research men and negotiators on the master bargaining area. (*b*) Multi-employer bargaining tends to enhance the prestige of the national officers and to increase the degree of their control over the union's affairs and policies. (*c*) It also is said to lessen the chances of dissension or rivalry among locals of the union. This is because more inter-local uniformity in wage-rate conditions and changes may be obtained in an over-all bargain. (*d*) Multi-employer bargaining is almost a necessity in industries — such as the maritime industry (both sailors and longshoremen), certain branches of the clothing industry, and the building trades — where many or most of the workers shift from employer to employer in the course of one or more years. Here uniform wage rates are a "must" and are much more likely to be obtained by group-employer bargaining. (*e*) If employers are organized in an association, they can be induced — indeed, they are often eager — to apply various pressures against any firm that refuses to abide by the terms of the master agreement. In other words, a union is likely to have less contract violation in multi-employer bargaining. (*f*) A large bargaining area helps repel raids by a rival union. Usually the rival cannot raid more than one or a few plants at a time. The way in which rival union claims are settled is by an election held by the National (or a state) Labor Relations Board. If the bargaining unit includes numerous plants and firms and has been in existence for some time, the Board will tend to select the whole multi-employer area as the election unit. This means that the rival union must obtain a majority of the voters in all the plants as a whole — a difficult feat.

Sometimes, as in the basic steel industry, a union can achieve what amounts to industry-wide bargaining by concentrating on the negotiation of an agreement with a leading firm, like the United States Steel Corporation, and then taking the new contract around to the relatively small number of other firms, demanding that they sign up.

Employers' views on multi-employer bargaining are presented in Chapter 17.

e. Union wage policy and the whole economy. American unionism has not obtained sufficient general social acceptance or unity to have reached the point where one over-all federation of labor bargains with a similar federation of employers or with government about the broad outlines of a national wage policy. This does not mean that the leaders of some unions and union federations have not considered wage policy in broad national terms. It does mean that, so far as relations with employers are concerned, such broad policies can only be effectuated by key, pattern-setting collective bargains made by big, powerful unions with big corporations in major industries like steel or automobiles or with big industries like railroads. So far as relations with government are concerned, the existing labor federations are in a position to exercise considerable influence on certain matters affecting wages, such as minimum wage-rate laws and unemployment compensation.

Whatever the kind of relationship (with employers or government), union wage policies having to do with the economy as a whole are made with an awareness of the implications of secular economic progress and of cyclical fluctuations in economic activity. Our discussion below will be subsumed mainly under these two headings. We should note also that in these broad fields the leading unions and the federations have come to lean heavily, much more than in almost any other field of union policy-making, on the advice of hired or friendly intellectuals — in this case, economists.

(1) Participation in the fruits of economic progress. As we stated in Chapter 3, economic progress is revealed by long-term rises in "real" per-capita national income and is caused by capital accumulation and technological advance. For more than twenty-five years (beginning with the A.F.L. convention of 1925) American organized labor has had what used to be called a "social" wage policy. It has insisted that workers must have a "fair" share of secularly rising real national income; and it has held that this objective is attained only when workers' real wage rates (money wage rates corrected for changes in living costs) rise at least proportionately with rises in real output per labor-hour.

(2) Cyclical wage policy. Unions wish the real wage rates of their members to rise secularly, i.e., over longish periods of time; but this must happen in a cyclical setting. In the absence of unions in most of the economy, this is what *did* occur over past decades. In any one business cycle, during the prosperity phase, money wage rates usually tended to lag behind increases in the cost of living until the end of the upswing. In other words, real wage rates tended to fall during most of a boom period. But after the downswing had started, money wage rates held for a while. And as the depression deepened, with its deflation of living costs, money wage rates tended to fall less rapidly. That is, real wage rates tended to rise. Considering the cycle as a whole, the loss in real rates during most of the boom was more than compensated for by the gain during the downswing; there was a net gain over the whole cycle. In particular industries, of course, the pattern was far from uniform; but in the economy as a whole the secular rise in real rates appears to have taken the cyclical path just described.

Now when unionism becomes widespread, its cyclical policies on wage rates tend in general to do two things: to reinforce the downswing movement, and to reverse the upswing. During an upswing such as the one that occurred after World War II, unions are quick to ask for the re-opening of wage-rate agreements with employers. They wish their members' money wage rates to at least keep pace with rises in living costs. They may even ask for formalization of the keep-pace policy in an automatic escalator clause, whereunder the workers' money rates are raised periodically (every three or four months) in proportion to increases in the consumers' price index of the federal Bureau of Labor Statistics. The Automobile Workers did this in 1948, and many other unions have since followed their example. Thus, through frequent contract re-openings and formal cost-of-living escalator arrangements, unions have successfully tried to maintain or raise real wage rates during upswings.

These escalator arrangements are supposed to cut both ways; money wage rates are supposed to be reduced automatically when the price index falls during business downswings. For a short while unions may hold to such an arrangement. But in time they chafe at it a great deal. They are in general opposed to reductions in *money* wage rates and do not willingly accept them unless compelled to do so by the product-market competition of non-union plants or by other forces which tend significantly to reduce the product prices of their employers.

There are a number of reasons for this policy of resistance. For one thing, unions are always struggling to raise money wage rates, and the struggles are hard. They hate to see years of effort go for naught, necessitating their starting all over again when the upswing begins. In the second place, the basic money wage rate is, to a union and its members, the major measure of achievement. More than anything else, the level of this rate shows how successful the union has been. Depression-time concessions are more readily made in other elements of the bargains with firms. A third reason why unions oppose reductions in money wage rates is their uncertainty about future economic movements. They prefer to take a chance on an improvement in business. They can never be sure, either, that yielding to a demand for a wage cut will not encourage firms to expect and ask for further cuts. Finally, most unions believe that a wage-rate reduction, if general enough, will reduce "purchasing power" and thereby lower the demand curve for labor in a firm or industry.

Let us consider this purchasing-power tenet a little more fully. For decades it has been a cardinal union argument for opposing general wage-rate reductions and for demanding wage-rate increases. So far as its use by unions is concerned, it was given its most sophisticated presentation in 1949 by the Steelworkers in their case before the President's fact-finding board. Their chain of reasoning, based on an unsophisticated reading of the late Lord Keynes' theory of employment, ran something like this: Wage income is the main component of total spending in the economy as a whole. Reduce wage income and you decrease total spending. This brings on a depression or worsens an existing one. Raise wage income and you increase total spending. This prevents a depression from developing or brings the economy out of an existing one. When wage *rates* are cut, wage *income* is reduced. When wage rates are raised, wage income goes up. Therefore economy-wide wage-rate increases are desirable at all times.

The student may wish now to analyze the correctness of this argument in terms of the concepts and thought-tools developed in Chapter 3. Our own analysis appears in the discussion of public policy on wage rates, Chapter 23.

(3) Wage-rate and income floors. Finally we must note union policy on government establishment of minimum wage rates and of unemployment benefits.

(a) Minimum wage rates. Before the advent of the C.I.O. the traditional attitude of most A.F.L. unions was that government should not interfere in the determination of wage rates — except in respect to workers, such as women, who were hard to organize. In other words, these unions believed strongly in self-help rather than government help. They never spearheaded movements for general state or federal minimum wage-rate laws. They feared that if workers got benefits from government, they would have less reason for joining or retaining membership in unions.

The C.I.O. unions did not share this fear. They believed that a general minimum wage-rate statute like the federal Fair Labor Standards Act ("Wage and Hour Law") not only was desirable because it placed a floor under wage-rate reductions during business downswings but also could be useful in promoting unionization. Thus, C.I.O. organizers would go to the workers in outlying non-union shops in the cotton textile, seamless hosiery, work clothing, and other low-wage industries and say: "A federal law has been passed at our insistence to see that your bosses don't pay you starvation wages. We want to have you get the protection intended by this statute. But you can be sure your employer will evade the law if you don't have a union to make him obey it. Unorganized, you will be afraid to complain about him to the Wage and Hour Division of the Labor Department, which the Congress set up to help you get the benefits of the law. Join our union. Your boss can't hurt us. And we'll make sure he pays you what the law says you should get."

The Walsh-Healey Act is another federal statute that C.I.O. unions have used to advance unionism as well as help individual workers. This law requires an administrator to set minimum rates for jobs in plants producing products for the government. The basis for determining such rates is the "prevailing" wage rates for similar jobs in the "locality." As with the F.L.S.A., the unions not only appear at hearings which are held before the administrator to determine on how high the rates should be; they also use the Act as an organizing device in the way explained above. Thus, during their organizational drive in the late thirties the Steelworkers were able to get the Act used to eliminate wage-rate differentials among Northern steel mills.

Many of the A.F.L. unions have to some extent abandoned their negative attitudes toward government action on minimum wage rates and have emulated the C.I.O. The unions in the construction industry make excellent use of a federal statute called the Davis-Bacon Act, which authorizes the Secretary of Labor to set minimum rates on government construction jobs on the basis of the rates prevailing in the locality for private jobs. The Secretary has the power to define "locality" as well as "prevailing." In many cases the construction unions have been able to obtain a very broad definition of locality and a high definition of prevailing, so that the wage rates on the government projects have been higher than those on private jobs in the immediate area. Thereupon the unions have required the private contractors to raise their rates to the government levels — an example of whipsawing at its best.

(b) Unemployment compensation. We have learned that unemployed unionists are not very good unionists. Knowing this full well from past experience, unions have lobbied vigorously for adequate levels of state unemployment compensation, including increases to make up for rises in living costs.

The traditional union attitude, as typified by official A.F.L. policy before 1932, was against government action in this field. The basic reasons were the same as those stated above for the policy on government minimum wage rates. It was believed that each union should have its own system of unemployment or out-of-work benefits; the union fund was to be built up out of a portion of each member's dues, and benefits to unemployed members were to be disbursed by the nationals or its locals. This would help to hold members' loyalties during depressions.

Many unions had such plans. But no one foresaw a depression like that of 1930–32. The union funds were not large enough to pay benefits to such large percentages of members for such long periods of time. It seemed undesirable to raise the contributions of employed members enough to keep the funds solvent. There was nothing to do but abandon the negative policy toward a government system. So, beginning in 1932, the A.F.L. lobbied for a statute like the one which was passed by the Congress in 1935 (see Chapter 22).

A union rationalization of its changed policy was the maintenance of "purchasing power" during business downswings.

4. Union hours policies. We have frequently stressed the relationship between wage rates and the lengths of work periods. They are the two components of wage income. We shall find that unions are far from being unaware of this fact.

In Chapter 14 we had something to say about the hours policies of the unions in respect to spreading work — or spreading unemployment, to state the same thing differently. This temporary equal-sharing of available work-hours during periods of slack business activity is not the sort of thing in which we are interested here. Our focus now is on hours policy during times of full employment — or perhaps more accurately, on hours policy in the secular rather than the cyclical sense.

a. Historical sketch. (1) Trend in lengths of work periods. Earlier in this book attention has been called several times to two outstanding developments during the past century and a half: first, a notable rise in the real wage rates and weekly and annual earnings of workers and in real annual income per person in the population; and second, a notable increase in the availability and use of leisure.

The latter increase means, obversely, that the lengths of the work-day and the work-week have decreased a great deal. For some decades after the United States won its independence work periods in the towns and cities were pretty much patterned after those in agriculture — sunup to sundown. Work-days from 12 to 16 hours long, and 72- to 96-hour weeks were usual. Today the peacetime rule is 40 weekly hours in five days of eight hours each. Even industries or firms whose work-weeks exceed this standard rarely go beyond 48 hours. And for almost twenty-five years there has been serious talk among unions of moving on to a 30-hour week of five days.

(2) Reasons for the trend. (a) Changed attitude toward leisure. In the early days of the country the saying, "An idle mind is the devil's workshop," characterized the social attitude toward leisure versus work. Idleness was sinful to most people in a predominantly agricultural economy. They doubtless *wished* (at least secretly) for more leisure. But with the scarcity of capital and with the relatively primitive nature of the tools and machines, making a living was difficult; people had to "scratch" hard and long. They could not *afford* much leisure.

But gradually the religious and economic buttresses of this belief about leisure were weathered away. It may not have been too unhealthful to work a 72- or 96-hour week out in the open fields of farms. But long periods of work in crowded, unsanitary factories and mines, poorly lighted, ill-heated, and badly ventilated, were another matter. Religious and social leaders came to see that, although too large and sudden a dose of unaccustomed leisure might be "sinful," there was also the devil to pay for the broken health of the men, women, and children who labored in many of the non-agricultural pursuits. A humanitarian base was thus laid for the "shorter hours" movement.

(b) Basic economic justification. On the economic side, the country gradually came to be able to afford more leisure as well as wish for it. Capital accumulation and technological improvement made it possible successively to reduce the lengths of work periods. As we know, the benefits of economic progress may be enjoyed in two forms: higher per-capita real or physical output and higher per-capita leisure. We have seen that, allowing for spurts and "rest periods" during our history, average labor-hour productivity has risen by from two to three per cent per year because of the above-mentioned increases in the quantity and quality of capital; and per-capita real income has grown several fold. But the latter increase would undoubtedly have been larger if the population had not wished to have more leisure — both for its own sake and in order to have more time to enjoy all the shiny new gadgets that came tumbling off the new production lines. There can be little question that if firm-owners in, say, 1925 had worked the new machines and their labor forces as many hours as their grandfathers had theirs, total and per-capita output would have been considerably higher.

(c) Union pressure. Someone has to spearhead a movement that is gradually acquiring social approval and economic justification. There seem to have been three main spearheads in the order of importance named, but very much overlapping in point of time: organized labor, government, and progressive employers.

If we turn our minds back to our recital of union history in Chapters 10 and 11, we will recall how often the shortening of work-hours was mentioned as a major union objective. Already in the 1820's unionists in the Eastern seaboard cities had begun driving on the economic and political fronts for the ten-hour day. Before the Civil War many skilled craftsmen, especially those in the building trades, had obtained it by economic action. These craftsmen also secured the eight-hour day in the 1890's. However, in the public's mind it was first the National Labor Union (soon after the Civil War) and later, especially, the Knights of Labor in the 1880's who typified and dramatized, with strikes and flamboyant parades, labor's efforts to win the eight-hour day. These efforts failed. Except for the above-mentioned strategically situated craftsmen, the ten-hour day remained standard, e.g., in manufacturing, until the 1920's.

Two events in the decade of World War I made the public conscious again of labor's drive for shorter hours. In 1916 the railway train-operating Brotherhoods, by threatening a nation-wide strike, got the Congress to pass the Adamson Act, which established the basic eight-hour day for their members. Three years later came the spectacular strike by a group of A.F.L. unions against the basic steel companies. Here a major issue was the abolition of the twelve-hour day and the seven-day week. Although the strike was lost, public opinion had become sufficiently aroused to make the companies in 1923 reverse their position that the eight-hour day and six-day week were "impracticable" for steel plants.

Soon after World War I the construction unions obtained the 40-hour week. By 1929 the great majority of unionists were working on this schedule. But after the depression was well under way, there were demands for the 35- or 30-hour week. In a few industries in relatively recent years (e.g., ladies' garments and coal mining) the unions have obtained a 35-hour week.

During World War II, manpower shortages led unions temporarily to agree to work-weeks longer than 40 hours, with time-and-a-half wage rates for the hours above forty. With the end of the war employers returned to the 40-hour week. Under the full-employment conditions of the postwar years few unions renewed their drive for weekly hours below that figure. But if a business downswing were to get under way and endure, there would undoubtedly be such a renewal.

Up until the New Deal period, unions controlled only a small minority of organizable workers in the economy as a whole. It is also true that the *percentage reduction* in weekly hours from 1890 to 1925 was as high for non-union as for union firms.[1] But these facts should not lead one to conclude that unions were not a very important factor in the reduction of the length of work periods. In the first place, in each of those years the *actual hours schedules* were considerably shorter among non-union firms. The percentage reductions may have been the same, but the union firms started from a lower hours base and maintained this differential over the years.

Second, the unions were strong and strategically placed in certain industries like construction, railroad train operation, printing, and coal mining. Their hours achievements in those industries served notice on non-union industries or industries with weak unions as to what might be expected if the firms in those other industries did not emulate the achievements. As with wage rates, "welfare" measures, and other conditions of employment, so with hours before the New Deal: One effective way of avoiding unionization was to keep up with or ahead of the union parade.

Third, unorganized workers seem to be particularly weak, i.e., have poor alternatives, in dealing with their employers on hours. There are inter-firm and inter-industry differentials in wage rates; and non-unionists have a variety of alternative employment opportunities if, under full employment, they choose to exercise them when dissatisfied with the wage rate paid by their existing employers. But in respect to length of work periods there is much more uniformity among firms, at least in a given industry and area. Suppose that most workers' preferences are to work 40 rather than 60 hours per week. Suppose also that the firms are all operating six 10-hour days. How are workers, in the absence of a union, to make their preferences effective? By laying off two days every week? They would be fired, one at a time, for absenteeism of this amount. Without a union or union influence their labor supply could not be reduced to reflect their true preferences so long as the employers maintained an unbroken front.

(d) Government leadership and legislation. State and federal governments (particularly the federal government) have aided the more-leisure movement substantially. As employers of labor, they have taken the lead and served as hours models for private employers. Thus, in 1840, the 10-hour day was established in government navy yards. All federal employees have had the eight-hour day since before World War I. As protectors of citizens employed in private industry, the federal and state governments have passed laws limiting the work hours of special groups, such as women workers and children, and of workers in general. Particularly noteworthy were two pieces of legislation: the National Industrial Recovery Act of 1933–35, which established the basic 40-hour (sometimes 36-hour) week in its "codes of fair competition"; and its successor in the matter of

[1] See P. H. Douglas, *Real Wages in the United States,* Houghton Mifflin Company, Boston, 1930, pp. 112–115.

hours, the Fair Labor Standards Act of 1938, which penalized a work-week of more than 40 hours with a premium pay rate of time-and-a-half, thus exerting indirect pressure on employers not to exceed the standard.

(e) Progressive employers. As already suggested at the end of our discussion above of union influence on work periods, given full employment and a united front among employers, the determination of actual lengths of work-days and work-weeks appears to be considerably less subject to competitive supply and demand conditions operating in the product and labor markets than are wage rates and total hours worked. The total number of hours employed by a given firm at any given wage rate are clearly affected by labor supply, technology, supplies of substitute and complementary productive factors, and product demand. But the distribution of the employed hours among people and work periods seems to provide wide latitude of decision to employers, with little direct influence by the determinants of labor supply and demand.

One reason for the relative lack of competition among firms in respect to length of work periods has been their uncertainty about the effects of reductions on unit costs of production. As we shall see later, in times of full employment workers are usually not willing to accept a decrease in weekly earnings when weekly hours are reduced. They wish to maintain weekly income at its former level, which of course means an increase in the hourly wage rate. Now, as we shall find in Chapter 23, where we make an economic analysis of this problem in terms of public policy, this means an increase in unit cost unless there is a compensating increase in worker effort and efficiency or unless there is a compensating decrease in machine or overhead costs. The conditions, short-run and long-run, affecting these two possible compensators are many and various, and it is almost impossible to predict what will actually occur.

However, there have not been unbroken fronts among all employers at all times and under all conditions. Some have been willing to risk an increase in costs following an hours reduction. We label such employers, always very much in the minority, "progressive" here — not because they have been especially humanitarian but because they have had the will and the ability to take the lead, often in the absence of any serious threat of unionism. The will came in part from an appreciation of possible favorable long-run results. The ability came in many cases because the firm had a secure, partially monopolistic position in selling its product or in buying its raw materials.

When a firm like this takes the lead in reducing daily and weekly hours, its motives may be much like those of a firm which deliberately undertakes to pay higher wage rates than other firms in the market. The firm that pays higher rates does so in the hope of attracting the best workers; i.e., it tries to obtain labor-hours of above-standard efficiency. If it succeeds, as it often does, the firm's unit wage *costs* may be as low as or lower than those of firms paying lower wage *rates.* The same thing may be true of the firm that pioneers in hours reduction: When it shortens work periods and at the same time raises wage rates so as to maintain weekly earnings, it may attract such superior workers that its wage-cost position is not only not worsened but bettered. In addition, the efficiency of the existing workers may be increased because of lessened fatigue and generally better mental and physical health. Still another advantage to such a pioneer is an improvement in its general "public relations." The firm may also wish other firms to follow its lead. It may be making a product whose consumption would rise if most workers were given shorter work periods by their employers.

Considerations such as these undoubtedly weighed heavily in the minds of such hours-reduction pioneers as Henry Ford, when he introduced the five-day, 40-hour week in 1927.

b. Union policies and their motivations. The foregoing historical sketch was presented in order to provide perspective for an understanding of union hours policies and their influences on the trend in lengths of work periods. These policies may be summarized as follows: (1) Shorten daily and weekly work periods and maintain weekly earnings by a compensatory rise in wage rates. Unions have never forgotten the jingle attributed to the eight-hour-day zealot, Ira Stewart, head of the Machinists and organizer of the Grand Eight-Hour League of Massachusetts in 1866 — "Whether you work by the piece or the day, decreasing the hours increases the pay." (2) Achieve the reductions either by an outright prohibition on hours beyond the agreed-on maxima or by penalizing employers with premium pay rates for hours worked in excess of the standards. Most unions have adopted the latter method. It allows some flexibility to firms who have emergency or special production problems. And it permits some union members to work excessive hours if they prefer the higher earnings to the forgone leisure. A few unions, like the Ladies' Garment Workers, enforce the maximum rather rigidly and allow no overtime.

What are the reasons for the hours-reduction policy? Apart from the desire to "share the work" during depressions, one of the objectives of the shorter hours policy has undoubtedly been to protect the health of union members. But this aim would seem to become progressively less important as successive hours reductions are achieved. Granted that the speed of work tends to rise as work periods are shortened, there can be little doubt that worker fatigue is less today than it was a half century ago.

Another objective is to provide increased leisure and the opportunity to enjoy what goes with it. This goal would seem also to become weaker as successive shortenings are gained.

The main aim appears now, as it probably was throughout the past century, to be an economic one. Given the pervasive attitude among workers that jobs are always scarce and that there is only a certain lump of labor to be done, unions try to limit the amount of work done by each member so that the lump can be shared by more men. Like some unions' output-restriction policies, their hours measures have the effect of reducing the supply of labor to a firm or industry.

c. Unions' rationalization of hours policy. These real reasons, particularly the last one, are not always made explicit when unions present demands to employers or try to enlist public support for their policies. The health argument, of course, is usually used and made available for public inspection. Often the argument for leisure is, too. But the economic basis for hours reduction is usually concealed behind a "front" of other arguments, which are in themselves valid in greater or less degree.

When unions use the leisure argument to buttress their proposals, they usually stress the benefits to employers and to the nation more than the welfare of union members. They say that workers will have more time and at least as much money to consume the products of industry. In other words, they bring out the "purchasing power" argument. They also argue that shorter work periods give workers more time to learn how to be good citizens and to practice what they have learned. Many will read more and take adult education courses. The general level of learning will be raised.

Nor is the health argument confined to what is good for the workers. Unions assert that healthier workers will confer economic benefits on employers and on the nation. When they are less fatigued and more refreshed, they are more efficient in output (both as to quantity and quality), less prone to accidents, and less likely to be absent or tardy because of illness or fatigue. The unions cite studies by private and government research agencies showing that a five-day, 40-hour week is the optimum work schedule. Although they ordinarily do not say so explicitly, they imply that any tendency toward unit-cost increases from the compensatory rises in wage rates will be entirely offset by these gains in worker efficiency. That is, they imply that when hours are reduced from, say, 54 or 48 per week to 40, output per worker per day or week will be as high as before. But they fail to make clear how, if this is true, the union can expect to divide the lump of labor among more workers than before.

CHAPTER 16

Union Policies and Activities (concluded)

B. DEALING WITH EMPLOYERS (concluded)

5. Policies and tactics of coercion. *a. General nature.* In Chapters 14 and 15 we dealt with union policies from the standpoint of the things that unions try to obtain from employers in order to achieve union survival, power, and prestige and in order to help members satisfy their individual desires. In this chapter we consider the various methods and tactics that unions may employ to reach their goals — collective bargaining, strikes, boycotts, picketing, and racketeering.

Bear in mind that union policies in respect to government and to their own members, discussed in Sections C and D of this chapter, are also measures for attaining these union objectives in so far as they affect union relationships with employers. Our reason for dealing with government and union members separately is that these union measures impinge on and cover much more than relations with employers.

All these methods and tactics involve in greater or less degree the use of coercion against employers. "Coercion" is a word which, narrowly or popularly defined, may have somewhat ugly connotations. But we use it broadly here to mean the bringing of pressure to bear upon employers. Pressure may be exerted in many ways. If, in trying to get someone else to do you a favor, you speak to him in the softest, gentlest, most disarming manner, you are nonetheless exerting pressure. When you do what someone else wants in order to get him to do what you want, you are applying pressure to him. In short, coercion is not confined to physical violence or financial ruin or social ostracism or penal statutes or to threats thereof. It is part and parcel of day-to-day human relations within and among all social institutions. That is why we include peaceful collective bargaining as well as extortion and violence in our list of union coercive weapons.

Our interest here is in the nature of these weapons, not in their legality. Some of them have full social approval and are not in any way prohibited by society's agent, government. Others are downright illegal. But these matters are reserved for Chapter 24 in Part Three.

b. Collective bargaining. In Chapters 19–21 we shall deal with the procedures, content, achievements, and failures of collective bargaining between unions and employers. Our concern now is with its use by unions to get what they want.

Let us assume that, with due regard for all relevant political conditions within the organization, a set of demands embodying union security, member security, wage rates, hours, and other items has been formulated for presentation to an employer. These demands reflect in varying degree what the different members think they want and what the leaders believe is necessary for the welfare of the union as an entity and of themselves as its officers who wish to remain in power. The demands are a resultant (as they say in physics) of all the pushes and pulls within the union.

The serving of the demands on the employer is the first step in the negotiation of a new contract. It may be the first contract; the union may have been recognized only a short time ago. In any case this step makes it entirely clear that collective coercion or pressure has been substituted for the situation in which non-union workers' welfare is determined pretty much unilaterally by an employer who can say "take it or leave it" to them. This substitution is fundamental in collective bargaining.

The employer cannot say "take it or leave it" to the union now unless the latter is woefully weak. This must mean that through organization the workers have greatly widened the range of their alternatives. Usually the union cannot say "take it or leave it" to the employer either. But the workers' bargaining position — which may always be considered in terms of their alternatives versus the employer's — has vastly improved.

By alternatives in bargaining we mean of course, What can I do to you and where else can I go if you don't do what I want you to? This question is of great importance to the union as it looks at the employer, and vice versa. It applies to each party. It is vital in what is sometimes known as "the power struggle" between labor and management.

The time for serving demands on the employer is important. From the union's standpoint it should be a time when its alternatives are at or close to a maximum and the employer's are poor. If the time is set by the automatic expiration of a previous agreement and if this is not the best time in the above terms for exerting maximum coercion, the union may sometimes be able to drag out the negotiation period (by asking for recesses on various pretexts, talking interminably, and so forth) until a more auspicious moment has arrived.

When are the union's alternatives good? When its war chest or strike-benefit fund is full. When the membership is interested, loyal, and united. When the weather is not too cold and striking members who are not on duty on the picket line won't have to be in their wives' way at home but can go fishing or hunting. When other firms in the industry have already made "liberal" settlements with the union. When brother unions can be counted on to donate heavily to the war chest if need be. When part-time temporary jobs are available for members in a full-employment market. When the public is on the union's side in the controversy. And so on.

When are the employer's alternatives poor for him but good for the union? When the union's measures for denying him access to substitute productive factors (such as non-union labor and machinery) are effective. When the employer is heavily indebted and his loans are coming due. When he is to be financially penalized if he doesn't deliver a big order in accordance with his contract with the customer. When his surplus and reserves are depleted. In short, when he stands to lose a good deal of money if he doesn't agree with the union.

It is part of the union's job, through spies, gossip, well-placed friends, or otherwise, to discover how weak or strong the employer is and when he is weakest or least strong. It is also part of its job to conceal, if possible, any weaknesses it may have and to give the employer the impression that it is stronger than it really is, i.e., to make him think its alternatives are better than they really are (this latter tactic is of course known as "bluffing").

Suppose now that the union and the employer begin negotiating about the union's demands. All the above-mentioned things are in the minds of its negotiators. So are the settlements made this year by rival unions in the same or other industries. The "psychology" of the membership is particularly important if this is the first contract to be negotiated. The union organizers will have raised high hopes among the recruits with promises of how much the union would get for them. The union negotiators can ill afford a poor settlement at this juncture. Yet if they force a strike by holding out for extreme demands, can they depend on the new members' endurance and loyalty? Similarly, if previous contracts have been negotiated, the union's internal political condition is important. A strong vocal minority faction can make considerable trouble, perhaps can even defeat the incumbent officers for re-election if the new settlement is not a good one.

All these considerations virtually resolve into the principles of choosing among different courses of action, as explained in Chapter 3. Suppose the union negotiators have a fairly good idea of what is the best agreement they can extract from the employer short of a strike. This settlement involves certain utilities and certain costs, i.e., certain advantages and disadvantages, which must be estimated. Not to agree — in other words, to strike — also has certain utilities and costs. The negotiators must, however roughly, judge which course of action — agreement or strike — promises the higher net amount of utility over cost, and act accordingly.

What we have said about striking applies in some degree to the other main union weapons of economic warfare, the boycott and various kinds of picketing.

We come to see, then, that the union's weapons of economic warfare and coercion are an integral part of collective bargaining. Because their use is costly and involves the risk of serious loss to the union as well as the employer, the possibility of their employment exerts pressure on both sides to come to an agreement. Let us find out something about these measures.

c. The strike. (1) Nature and classification. A strike is a collective stoppage of work by a combination of wage-earners who, although temporarily suspending shop activity in order to win a particular labor controversy, attempt to keep their places as employees.

Strikes may be classified in various ways. On the basis of *scope,* a strike may be purely local and confined to the workers of one plant, or one trade within a plant, or it may involve all the workers in a given trade or industry throughout the plants of a certain section or of the whole country; or it might possibly include the workers in all trades and industries in a given section or the whole country. Strikes are thus by trade or by industry or "general"; and local, sectional, or national. Different combinations are possible, the broadest being a national general strike and the narrowest a local trade dispute.

Strikes may be initiated to win further concessions on wages, hours, and working conditions from employers, in which case they are sometimes called "positive" or "attack" strikes. They are known as "negative" or "defense" strikes when used to maintain existing employment terms and to resist employers' demands to lower them. Whether a given strike is an attack or a defense depends largely on whether the original demands came from workers or the employer. In practice — as where, under a system of union collective bargaining, demands have been presented by both sides almost simultaneously — it is often impossible to classify a strike as "attack" or "defense."

There are also *outlaw* or *wildcat* or *unauthorized strikes, sympathetic strikes,* and *jurisdictional strikes.* The outlaw (or wildcat or unauthorized) strike is one called by a local union in disobedience to orders from national headquarters. The sympathetic strike is one carried on by a group of workers who have no particular dispute with their own employer, but who wish to help another group on strike in some other plant, shop, or trade. The jurisdictional strike is a stoppage called to enforce a union's jurisdictional claims in the kind of rival-union conflict designated as "job dispute" in our discussion in Chapter 12. Here the employer, e.g., a contractor in the construction industry, usually has given a certain kind of work to another union, and the other claimant strikes to reverse his decision.

During the period of organized labor's struggle for status and power — and even today, if to a lesser extent — perhaps the most meaningful classification of strikes was one based on whether or not the struck employer had bargaining relations with the striking union. Thus, a *bargaining* strike (either attack or defense) is one called to enforce union demands on a firm or industry with which the union has already had collective dealings, while an *organizational* strike is called to force an employer to recognize and bargain with the union for the first time.

(2) Purpose and methods. The purpose of a strike is to keep the employer off the labor market; that is, the workers try to control the supply of labor and withhold it from the employer so that he shall be unable to continue production and profit-making. By striking, workers try to demonstrate how strong they are as bargainers in the labor market.

The orthodox method of striking is for the workers to leave their jobs in a body and stay outside the employer's plant or place of business. Picket lines made up of small or large numbers of workers (the latter is known as "mass picketing") are established at plant entrances to try to keep all existing or potential workers off the employer's labor market (i.e., strong efforts are made to prevent individual selling of labor). In 1935–37, however, the *sit-down* or *stay-in* strike came into wide use for a while. Here the workers (sometimes only a relatively small number), instead of leaving the plant, simply stop their machines and refuse to work, staying inside the employer's place of business. Strictly defined, a sit-down strike lasts more than a day or a shift. If the in-plant stoppage lasts for a shorter period, it is known as a *quickie*. Another type of "inside job" is the *slowdown*. Here there is no actual cessation of work. The workers merely decrease the pace of their operations considerably.

Nowhere is skillful strategy more necessary than in the calling and prosecution of strikes. There are three main factors involved throughout: economic strategy, warfare tactics, and social control. A great many economic factors must be considered, such as the phase of the business cycle, the nature of the industry and its sources of raw materials, the seasonality or regularity of the employer's business, its competitive situation with relation to other firms (union and non-union), the nature of the employer's market, the marketing system of the company, the employer's bank connections and the terms of his indebtedness to them, possible sources of strikebreakers, the condition of the union's strike reserves and the probability of support from other unions, and the possible support that the employer will obtain from other employers. In the pioneering days it was often sufficient for the union to pick what seemed to be an opportune moment, call the strike, and then concentrate attention on keeping strikebreakers away from the employer while supporting the strikers. Under present conditions such tactics, when used alone, are crude and rarely successful. Modern strike strategy demands that the union study the total situation of the employer's economic, political, and social connections and competently manipulate all the various related factors. During the prosperity phase of the business cycle, for example, employers are more likely to yield than during depression years. Similarly with seasonal operations; when the clothing unions strike, for example, they almost always choose the beginning of the semi-annual periods of brisk activity in late winter and summer. Furthermore, by investigating a company's markets, sources of raw materials, and bank arrangements, a union may be able to strike a short time before an employer's orders, notes, and bills must be met. These customers and creditors may fear that he will not be able to meet his obligations, and the union, if able to convince them that it is a constructive force in the industry, may succeed in getting them to exert pressure on the employer to end the conflict and accede to the union's demands.

The necessity for meeting the employer in all fields demands the exercise of methods of social control with regard to government agencies, the public, and the workers, union and non-union. The favor, or at least the neutrality, of politicians and government officials who might otherwise help the employer with men and munitions is usually cultivated. Labor boards which have been set up to curb employers' repressive anti-union tactics are often appealed to. A favorable public attitude must be built up. Thus, the union may let it be known that a strike will be called in a certain community. The public in the city must be influenced into believing that the union's demands are just. Officers of the organization may get themselves invited to speak by liberal civic bodies, so that the community will learn that they are not ignoramuses or radicals and that they espouse an "American" cause. Challenges to debates may be issued. Liberal newspaper support may be won, and an advertising campaign may be carried on, not in terms of violent denunciation but rather in phrases of "sweet reasonableness."

In short, no stone is left unturned in building up to the initiation of the strike. The workers themselves must not be neglected. Their grievances must be played up and a genuine fighting mood established. Every effort must be made to instill a compelling spirit of "do or die," an enthusiasm which may reach a pitch of almost religious fervor. Non-unionists are appealed to on various grounds such as individual gain, manhood, and class solidarity or group welfare. Their wives, children, or relatives may be importuned, sometimes threatened. Occasionally non-unionists are slugged and their homes bombed. Most unions, however, admonish their adherents not to use threats or violence, lest public opinion turn against the union.

Then, when the union believes the resistant employer to be pressed financially and most anxious to secure and finish orders, when the competitive season is at its peak, the men are called out and the test of strength begins in earnest. Union vigilance must be redoubled on every front. The strikers' morale must be maintained by providing food and shelter from relief funds and by furnishing emotional and spiritual food as well. Ladies' auxiliaries are organized; soup kitchens and tent shelters may be provided. "Conflict moods" must be kept alive, alternating with opportunities for recreation and relaxation. "Flying squadrons" of picked, loyal workers may speed in automobiles from plant to plant or from gate to gate in order to bolster any wavering line. Loudspeaker equipment on sound trucks is often used as part of such tactics. Sanitation and songs, food and fanfare — all must be provided.

Favorable public opinion must also be held in line. Radio broadcasts and press releases are often used for this purpose. Instead of attempting to coerce the public, every effort is made to discredit the employer and to identify the strikers' interests with those of the community. In order not to alienate sympathy, the union forbids its pickets to use violence against strikebreakers or employer's guards. If it finds that the employer is resorting to shady practices, such as bribing policemen to make unwarranted arrests among pickets or hiring thugs to set off dynamite and stir up riots which are then blamed on the strikers, it may feel compelled to counter with under-cover tactics of its own. It may, for example, set up secretly a bogus employment agency to furnish the employer with "scabs" who, once within the plant, manage to spoil work and so hold up production that the firm's orders are canceled by irate buyers and customers. It may outbid the employer for the support of the police. If the police make arrests, the union may try to get so many pickets taken that the jails are soon filled to overflowing and the police chiefs are forced to discontinue such tactics. Or lawyers may be hired and bonding companies retained so as to secure quick release of prisoners, especially the strike leaders. Money and political connections may play a big part in the campaign. By roundabout means all sorts of economic and political pressures may be brought to bear on the management so that in the end it may come to believe that it costs less to yield the union its demands than to keep up the fight. But a union can expect such a successful outcome only if it has taken the pains to plan everything in advance, only if it has built up reserves and staying power.

d. The boycott. (1) Nature and kinds. Another weapon of economic warfare used by unions to coerce employers is the *boycott*. Whereas the strike is employed to deprive the employer of access to a substitute factor of production (non-union workers or traitorous unionists) in the labor market, the boycott is used to bar the employer from his product market. We may accordingly define this measure as an organized refusal to buy or to let other persons buy the employer's product.

Two main kinds of boycotts must be noted. The distinction is based on who refuses to buy the firm's product and on whether the product is a consumption good or a factor of production. If the product is a consumption good bought by wholesalers or retailers in behalf of households, and if one or more of these three groups refuse or are persuaded to refuse to purchase the product, we have a *consumer* boycott. If the firm's product is used as a factor of production (raw material or machine) by one or more other firms and if the union employees of these other firms refuse to work with this product or coerce their employers or other firms not to buy it, we have a *factor* boycott.

In respect to the *scope* of either kind of boycott, there are two types: the *primary* boycott and the *secondary* boycott. A primary consumer boycott is one in which only the workers (and their family members) of the union directly in dispute with the employer refuse to patronize him. A secondary consumer boycott is one in which the disputant union brings pressure on wholesalers or retailers or other consumers not to purchase the disputed firm's product. A primary factor boycott is one in which the disputant union workers simply refuse to work on the disputed firm's materials or machines when these are purchased or intended to be purchased by the firm for which they work. A secondary factor boycott exists when the union strikes against or otherwise coerces union firms in order to make them refuse to buy the disputed firm's product.

In practice the distinction between primary and secondary *factor* boycotts is a hazy one. Actually almost all factor boycotts are secondary in nature because some element of coercion against the purchasing employer almost always exists, even if no word is spoken to him by the unionists. Strikes and boycotts may be and often are used together by a union. Thus, in the famous *Danbury Hatters* case (see Chapter 24) the members of a Hatters' local in Danbury, Connecticut, struck against the Loewe Company there; and in order to improve their chance of winning the dispute, they instituted a secondary consumer boycott involving wholesalers, retailers, and other households in twenty states. In the equally famous *Duplex Printing Company* case (Chapter 24) a Machinists' local in Michigan struck against the company there (which manufactured printing presses) and at the same time, with the help of other unions' members, "persuaded" the newspaper and job-printing companies in New York City (the major center of printing in the country) to stop buying Duplex presses. And in the *Bedford Cut Stone Company* case (same chapter) union members of the Stonecutters' union employed in helping to construct stone buildings in various cities walked off their jobs because the contractors had bought stone quarried and dressed at the Bedford Company's non-union plant in Indiana.

(2) Methods of conducting boycotts. The last two examples just cited above are suggestive of the ways in which a union can conduct factor boycotts. In addition, picketing and other devices may be used to coerce the purchasing firms into doing what the union wishes.

In respect to consumer boycotts a number of methods are employed. Dealers are visited or circularized and, after being told about the dispute, are asked not to sell the employer's products. Dealers' establishments may also be picketed by workers who, by word of mouth or by banners, handbills, and placards, try to influence the patronage of consumers. Labor organizations often print lists of employers who are "unfair" to unions and ask members and others not to buy their products. Sometimes unions use the opposite procedure and circulate lists of "fair" employers who should be patronized. A method similar to the fair list is the union label which union-recognizing employers are asked or permitted to put on their products; consumers are then asked to give preference to union-label goods. It will be seen that the fair-list and union-label methods produce a sort of negative or indirect boycott.

e. Picketing. Picketing or patrolling is one of the methods used by unionists to win a strike or further a boycott. When picketing is employed in a strike, it attempts to prevent "blacklegs" or "scabs" from entering the plant and taking the jobs vacated by the strikers. When part of boycotting activities, it tries to persuade wholesale or retail merchants and individual consumers not to purchase the firm's products. Basically it is a means of social control, made up of a wide variety of devices ranging from sensible, peaceable reasoning to physical violence, and including the circulation of handbills, the displaying of banners and placards, the making of veiled threats, the ostracism of strikebreakers, jeering, slugging, and stone-throwing. Picketing may be carried on by relatively small picked groups of loyal unionists or by large numbers of unionists (in which case there is *mass picketing*).

Stranger picketing is a device that was rather widely used from 1935 to 1947. It is the picketing of a plant by workers who are not employees of the firm with whom the union is having a dispute. Usually, however, the "strangers" are members of the same union from other plants in the same area. Such picketing is used where the union is weak in the struck plant; the employer and non-unionists find it harder to retaliate against strangers.

f. Violence. Because the courts have almost always outlawed violence, intimidation, and fraud in connection with picketing, union leaders as a rule have tried to impress their men with the necessity for abstaining from acts of such nature. At least so one may judge from their public utterances. But in the heat of labor conflict passions run so high and emotions are so easily aroused that it is an exceedingly difficult matter to confine picketers to peaceful persuasion. When one man sees another running off with the job and wages he considers rightfully his own, or when he sees customers indifferent to the "cause" patronizing the enemy as before, he often fails to heed sober council, especially when the struggle is reaching a critical stage and has lasted long enough to draw nerves taut. Union men have contended that in the old days the employers' use of detectives and police guards, such as the coal and iron constabulary in Pennsylvania, was an open invitation to violence. They have claimed that private detectives and gunmen, in order to hold their jobs, often committed outrages which they caused to be blamed on innocent unionists. If in addition the strike was big enough to attract irresponsible hoodlums, camp-followers, and radicals, the odds were all in favor of incidents which brought discredit on the bona-fide strikers.

A good deal of support for the above-mentioned union contention is to be found in the notable peacefulness with which most of the many big strikes from 1946 to 1951 were conducted. There was little violence because employers were not trying to break the unions. The industry-wide steel strike in 1949 was one of the most peaceful in any industry at any time. This was in marked contrast to the steel strikes of 1919 and 1892.

g. Racketeering. A few of the "businessmen" who have headed local unions in certain industries have given evidence of complete mastery over the seamier, more sordid tactics that have developed in America. They have grafted in the best manner of petty politicians; they have extorted sums of money from employers and union members; and they have sometimes used outside or professional gangsters to carry on these activities. All these anti-social, dishonest practices may be grouped under the head of union racketeering, a term which may be defined as the private enrichment, by various coercive and corrupt tactics, of union officials at the expense of workers, employers, and the public.

Not nearly all union officials and union locals are racketeering, or ever have been. Neither are certain unions always or continually racketeering. It takes an unusual combination of circumstances to produce this functional type. The racketeering unions are generally conservative business unions that have temporarily "gone wrong." Because of the lawless and secret nature of their activities it is difficult to determine how many there are or have been. Whenever their operations are brought to light, wide publicity is given them because they are "news." Certain writers with a flair for the sensational play them up in special feature articles which it is almost useless to challenge, inasmuch as there are very few accurate data on the subject and no one knows just how widespread the use of racketeering tactics is. Occasionally, after some particularly flagrant happening, an aroused populace will demand an investigation, such as those of the early years after World War I (e.g., the Lockwood Commission in New York and the Dailey Commission in Chicago) and the 1935–37 period (e.g., the Dewey investigations in New York). The subsequent disclosures usually lead unthinking persons to believe that all unions wear garments similar to those displayed at the public washing. But it seems safe to say that most union leaders are law-abiding and honest.

(1) Graft. The present discussion is interested in the corrupt minority. Among the grafting practices that certain local union officials have been found to carry on are the padding of expense accounts to amounts many times their official salaries; the outright embezzlement of union funds; the selling of supplies or real estate to employers or to their unions at exorbitant prices (sometimes the officials set themselves up in some business for the express purpose of making such sales); and the taking of bribes from employers ("selling out" the union) for "sitting on the lid" and holding the rank and file from strikes or other employer-disturbing activities.

(2) Extortion. Union grafting is petty compared to certain extortion practices. These are the real racketeering. Extortion is likely to exist

when an unscrupulous union leader attains a great deal of power through exercising the prerogatives of his office. Local business agents in the building trades seem to be stronger than any other officers, and it is probably mostly in this industry that racketeering unionism has existed, at least before World War II. The factors responsible for the power of business agents over union members and employers have already been described (Chapter 13).

(3) Labor gangsterism. Although conditions in the building trades are peculiarly propitious, other industries have also suffered from hold-up tactics. The 1930–31 and 1935–37 investigations on racketeering in New York discovered extortion in the clothing industry, motion-picture projection, laundries, food distribution, restaurant operation, ship-loading, and other trades. The fact that it was revealed during legal action against gangster rackets is significant. During the inter-war period (even before the end of the prohibition era) the wide and varied repertoire of illegal activities carried on by gang czars such as Al Capone and Bugs Moran also included union domination. An unscrupulous business agent might hire gangsters to coerce an employer on a particular job or to frighten off a rival union official or a contestant for his union office. Having found it profitable once, the racketeers might then force the union to use them regularly and pay them the usual monthly "protection." Once having tasted "blood," the mobsters often "muscled in" on other unions, unasked and unwanted. Thus, the union became subject to the underworld and a tool for all manner of crooked dealings. Local politics were also frequently involved, for business agents controlled labor votes which were utilized by gang leaders in courting the favor of the higher-ups.

Sometimes, as in the New York restaurant industry, outside gangsters organized "fake" unions among the workers (i.e., they coerced workers into joining an association where none existed before and collected dues from these workers) at the same time that they organized the employers in "associations" and collected dues from them; thus, money was extorted from both sides.

How much of the above-mentioned grafting, extortion, and labor gangsterism exists today is impossible to say. Undoubtedly there is some, though probably less than before World War II. But until some "Kefauver Committee" makes a thorough study, no one can be sure.

C. DEALING WITH GOVERNMENT

1. The main policy questions. Unions may wish to obtain help from government (federal, state, or local, depending on the circumstances) in order to deal more effectively with employers. They may try to obtain statutes or court decisions curbing the competition of non-union workers, such as women and immigrants; restraining employers from using certain coercive tactics against unions; and favoring the use of their own coercive tactics.

There are other reasons why unions may wish to get assistance from government — reasons not directly related to union-management dealings. Some problems, such as the mass unemployment of depressions, are too big to be handled by means of negotiations with any one firm or industry of firms. The unions may believe that direct action by the federal government is the only way in which these major problems can be solved. Furthermore, during the past century more and more problems of this sort have arisen, and more and more authority has been taken by government to handle them. This is part of the world-wide trend toward the centralization of power in the hands of national governments as a result of the increasing complexity of economic and political life that has come with modern technological developments.

In respect to relations with government, the first fundamental policy issue facing unions is this: Shall organized labor attempt to gain its ends chiefly through the state or shall it continue to rely mainly upon direct economic action and pressure on employers? If through the state, shall labor devote a large portion of its energies to the formation and support of its own independent political party or shall it remain non-partisan and continue its traditional policy of working through the two chief existing parties? The answers are not easy, and the issues are still not definitively resolved. It is doubtful, moreover, that they will be settled for a good many years to come.

a. Union attitudes toward government help. Regarding the general matter of legislation or action through the government, there is a lack of unanimity which springs from the fundamental differences in policy among the chief kinds of unionism. The very conservative, strictly business unions (mainly certain A.F.L. unions) are still rather inclined to dislike any form of state paternalism. They oppose any laws which might hinder their freedom to organize and strike (e.g., arbitration laws) and they view with distaste legislation which tries to give to workers benefits that could be obtained by direct bargaining with employers (e.g., minimum wage laws for men). They favor only two chief kinds of governmental interference — regulations for weak, relatively unorganizable workers, such as children and immigrants, whose competition menaces union standards; and legislation which restricts the power of courts to block union activities. Unions with the broader outlook (chiefly, the C.I.O. organizations), however, are much less opposed to government action, so long as it is favorable and non-restrictive. They apparently attach little weight to the view that what the state gives it can also take away, with compound interest. The socialists and communists of course believe in ultimate complete governmental control over industrial organization through the employees.

The attitude of any labor group with regard to state interference must necessarily be determined in the light of peculiarly American circumstances. Experience in other countries is of little value. There are a number of factors arising out of the governmental system of the United States which make it an extremely difficult and uncertain matter for unions to secure adequate and uniform labor legislation. The strictly business attitude is partly based on previous unhappy experience with it. These obstacles are apart from the political situation, which will be discussed later.

In the first place, there are forty-nine governmental systems in this huge land. Instead of being able to concentrate upon one central legislative group, as English workers can do, American labor is confronted with the disheartening task of overcoming opposition on a great many fronts. It has had to nibble away on one or two at a time, with varying success, so that one of the great weaknesses of labor legislation in the United States has been its lack of uniformity. Thus, employers in states with severe statutes may be at a competitive disadvantage with those in states having little or no regulation. Another obstacle is the form of government which divides the law-making power among two legislative houses and a chief executive with veto privileges. Such a system is well designed to preserve the existing order of things but is highly discouraging to any group working for progressive legislation or reforms. Many a bill has passed one house only to be scotched by the other, and even if it secures the approval of both groups, a veto may await it. If the executive approves the law, there is then the problem of judicial interpretation, a third difficulty which arises out of the fact that the federal and state constitutions are rigid written instruments which often preserve in a state of embalmment the old *laissez-faire* philosophy of individualism; under the system of checks and balances, the judges of the higher courts are empowered to remove any labor law which they believe in conflict therewith. (Because of changes in the composition and attitudes of the judiciary, however, this problem is much less important now than it used to be.) In the fourth place, moreover, even if such laws are declared constitutional, the standards which they set up may be lower than those already obtained by unionists and may be considered as maxima by employers instead of minima. In other words, unions are always pressing forward for higher standards, whereas most kinds of legislation set up stationary standards beyond which employers usually claim they are not compelled to go and which can be improved only by successful union efforts to fight through another law. In the fifth place, a law on the statute books is something entirely different from a law actually in effective operation. Adequate administration, an absolute essential in labor legislation, has sometimes been so lacking that the law has for the most part failed in its purpose and remained an example of wasted work. Finally, unions have learned that employers are often as powerful an opposition in the legislative field as in the industrial. Their lobbying has frequently blocked labor's attempts to win statutory relief.

Nevertheless, in spite of these obstacles and deterrents, a majority of unionists have turned more and more to government for help since the first New Deal years. The reasons for this shift in attitude were the decreasing effectiveness of purely economic or business unionism during the 1920's in the face of employer opposition; the increasingly unfavorable attitudes of certain government agencies to unionism during that decade; the inability of purely business unionism to meet the problems of depression; and opportunities presented by the union-favoring attitudes of government agencies under the New Deal. In other words, most unionists — recognizing their inability to cope with anti-union employers on equal terms on the economic field, aware of their inability to protect their members against the vicissitudes of depression, and discovering what a great difference a favorable government made in their fortunes — came to regard government as an agency which could turn the tide in their favor.

b. The question of non-partisan political action versus a separate political party. Once unions have decided to utilize government, the problem of getting labor measures successfully through the law-making bodies inevitably brings up the question of independent political action. Organized labor must choose between practicing the non-partisan measures outlined below and developing a political party of its own to a point where it can elect enough representatives to pass the legislation it wants. Conservative unionists are traditionally opposed to the formation of a separate party, being wedded to a policy of non-partisanship with regard to the two old political groups and professing to support either Republican or Democratic candidates, depending on which ones have the better labor records and make the more favorable pledges. Most progressives, socialists, and communists believe that in the long run such a policy is inadequate and insist that lasting gains for labor as a whole can be effected only through the agency of an independent, inclusive labor party.

The conservative attitude is not hard to understand. It is pragmatic and firmly founded on the lessons of union history in this country. Independent political action has failed in the United States, say the A.F.L. and the C.I.O. in elaborating their official policies, for reasons bound up in our economic and political systems; there is no cause for believing that these forces are ceasing to operate, no justification for thinking that a separate labor party today would be any more effective and successful than those tried in other decades.

A number of difficulties are frequently emphasized. In the first place the two-party system is traditional in this country, and third parties have always begun at a psychological disadvantage and ended in failure. Both the big political organizations, having been well established before anything resembling class feeling developed, can appeal for the support of working people, whereas in European countries each of the many parties usually represents a definite class or economic segment of the population.

A second reason is to be found in the loyalty of worker-voters to these old parties. Political affiliations, like religious beliefs, are a most potent part of the folkways and *mores* absorbed by individuals at an early age. They produce such a powerful emotional response that, unless something unusual happens, such as low wheat prices in the case of farmers or wage decreases in the case of the Brotherhoods after World War I, it is very hard to pull a worker away from his habitual political groove for any length of time. Many a union meeting has been disrupted by fights between Democratic and Republican members who fell out over some question of party politics. Workers, of course, have other interests besides their jobs; like other human beings, they belong to numerous other social groups. It has become a by-word that union leaders cannot guarantee to "deliver the labor vote."

In the third place, astute action by politicians has often beaten the new party line before it has been fairly launched. They may bid for labor support by including temporarily in their platforms the very planks on which the independent movement was started. They may also try to stir up factional strife in the new party or seduce its active workers by promises of greater and more immediate political rewards and preferment which only the most disinterested and unselfish can resist.

A fourth problem arises from the difficulty of building up and financing the intricate organization or "machine" which seems to be so necessary for political success in modern times.

Another factor which works against cohesive action in a new party is the heterogeneous, mixed nature of the working population. In other nations there are not usually so many diverse elements. It is also pointed out that a labor party in England has succeeded because the wage-earners are more than 50 per cent organized, whereas a smaller fraction belongs to unions in this country. Furthermore, it is said that employees in a relatively new country are more individualistic and tend to rely on economic rather than political action. This argument might seem to be refuted by the existence of a strong labor party in Australia, but the homogeneity of the population and the fact that, as in England, unions are almost completely recognized help to account for the situation there.

Still another factor that results in keeping workers within the old parties in the United States is the "primary" system of nominating candidates. In England, where nominations are largely made in caucus among the party leaders, it is almost imperative for labor to have its own party in order to get its candidates on the ballot. But in this country the primary enables workers to express their preferences directly without forming a separate party. Union leaders have also realized that a political party is something bigger than a labor group. That is to say, they have seen that organized labor at present desires only a few specific favors from the government, and that once these are granted, it will wish to carry on only economic activities. But to continue in existence a political party must create and press new issues. Therefore it would have to seek all betterment through governmental legislation and in the end would probably be forced, as in England, to advocate socialism and state control of industry.

Finally, the union conservatives rely mainly on the actual experiences of labor and other groups with independent politics in the United States. They do not forget that the Knights of Labor and many of its predecessors fell apart largely because of internal political dissension, and they wish to avoid chancing any such result. They also remember vividly that the path of politics in this country is strewn with the wrecks of ambitious third-party movements.

All these factors have influenced the A.F.L. and C.I.O. and most of the independent unions to continue their adherence to Samuel Gompers' doctrine of non-partisanship. Party politics are taboo. Although political matters do receive full discussion, the endorsement of any party as a party or the formation of a separate labor party are topics studiously avoided. Two well-known slogans express the official attitude — "Elect labor's friends and defeat labor's enemies," and "We are partisan to a principle and not to any party." In other words, the conservative unions, instead of endorsing parties, support candidates who favor labor's aims.

2. The non-partisan policy in action. *a. Methods of operation.* What are the strategy and tactics now employed by these unions to secure the laws they want? There are of course two chief stages: first, the development of a legislative program; second, efforts to get the program written into law. The latter consist of trying to elect legislators who will favor the program, and maintaining lobbies to influence the lawmakers while in session.

The program of laws which labor organizations wish to have placed on the statute books of the various states or national government is worked out in the councils of high officers and in union conventions. The national unions and the federations generally occupy themselves with federal legislation, while state laws are proposed during the annual conference of locals, city centrals, and local councils in the A.F.L. state federations of labor and the C.I.O. state industrial councils. Care is usually taken to select a propitious time of meeting, such as a week near the opening of legislative sessions or before elections, when legislators or candidates have attentive ears close to the ground. At the conventions, laws are proposed by the officers or local unions, referred to appropriate committees and, if favorably reported, passed or rejected by vote of the delegates. A complete program is thus finally created.

The real obstacles arise when the unions try to secure the passage of the proposed laws. In trying to elect the more friendly of the candidates already put up by the standard parties, there are two main methods employed to learn the attitude of the nominees. First, a complete record of the vote of every senator, congressman, and assemblyman on labor questions is kept in a card index by the legislative committees of the national and state federations. Before elections union members are asked to support those candidates who have proved themselves favorable to labor legislation and to work against all those who have been antagonistic. If both aspirants have been unfriendly or if either is a new man or if both have equally satisfactory records, the second method becomes important. Union legislative committees almost always approach each candidate with labor's platform and ask him to endorse it or to state his position on it. The one who makes the more suitable pledges is likely to receive labor's backing. Sometimes a nominee will accede to the unions' demands because he believes that they hold a balance of voting power. Another will turn a deaf ear because he believes from past experience that labor leaders have seldom been able to "deliver" the labor vote.

Getting out the vote is the next step. For this purpose committees are set up in most of the locals. House-to-house visiting among most voters is carried on. Non-workers and non-union workers in the lower-income classes are talked to, as well as unionists. Unions have come to realize that the success of their legislative programs rests in part on their ability to enlist the support of white-collar and farm groups.

The making of campaign pledges is notoriously one of those political gestures which may mean almost nothing. For this reason there remains the important task of securing the post-election redemption of pre-election promises from successful candidates. This involves, of course, the maintenance of lobbying committees whose duty it is to keep a close watch over any legislation in Congress and in the several state legislatures which affects labor. The union legislative program is brought to the attention of the lawmakers, while all bills which might injure the cause or hamper the activities of organized labor are strongly opposed. Labor lobbyists must therefore get their proposals introduced by friendly legislators, interview many others, present briefs to and attend hearings before appropriate committees, carry on publicity campaigns to influence public opinion, and have letters and telegrams sent to legislators from the voters at home. All these responsibilities demand the exercise of great watchfulness, care, tact, and perseverance. At present each state federation of labor keeps a committee active while the legislature is in session in its state. Federal legislation is given attention by the national legislative committees of the A.F.L. and C.I.O. and by a group of lobbyists from the various national unions, including the railway Brotherhoods.

Lobbying is not confined to legislation. Once a law is passed it needs administration friendly to labor. Therefore labor committees appear at administrative hearings and visit government officials.

It is manifestly impossible to make an exact appraisal of the success of organized labor's legislative tactics. There are too many other unmeasurable and subtle factors entering into the determination of legislators' votes. Further, one or more other, non-labor organizations may have been working for a certain law. Even with these qualifications in mind, however, one seems justified in concluding that union efforts have exerted powerful influence and borne much fruit.

b. Union political organizations. As organized labor grew stronger under the New Deal, the unions (mainly C.I.O.) that looked with favor on the policy of getting help from government began to consider how they might organize effectively for non-partisan political action. In 1936 they formed Labor's Non-Partisan League, which helped to mobilize the labor vote for President Roosevelt's re-election in that year and for the election of various other friendly candidates for national, state, and local office. In those days there was also the so-called American Labor Party in New York, which helped the progressive Republican, La Guardia, defeat Tammany Hall in the mayoralty contest. Individual unions also contributed substantial sums to the political party campaign managers of various candidates. When such contributions were prohibited under the Smith-Connally Act of 1943, the C.I.O. created a successor to the above-mentioned League — the Political Action Committee — which was to receive direct contributions from the unions and operate through local, district, and state labor organizations to get out the member and non-member vote and disseminate pre-election propaganda. The A.F.L. set up a similar organization in 1947, Labor's League for Political Education. In that year, however, an amendment to the National Labor Relations Act prohibited expenditures by unions as such for any political purpose, thus forbidding the contributions of unions as entities even to their own political arms, such as the P.A.C. It then appeared that, unless this provision were to be repealed (which has not happened), the money to support political action would have to come from union members as individuals.

The A.F.L. has a National Legislative Committee and the C.I.O. a Legislative Department whose duty it is to examine and analyze all bills introduced in the Congress and in state legislatures and to advise the federations as to policy thereon.

3. What do unions want from government? We have already answered this question in terms of broad categories of objectives — at the beginning of this section. In general, labor wishes government to do things that will help union members and unions to achieve their goals. This means inevitably that unions press for measures favoring the common man.

Unions interpret this general objective broadly. Top union officials, union lobbyists, and union publications take political positions on a great variety of subjects. One week the A.F.L. makes a pronouncement on what it believes should be the government's foreign policy for combatting communism. The next week the C.I.O. will say what it thinks about the Congress' failure to implement President Truman's Point Four program on the development of backward areas in the world. And the A.F.L. will have had something to offer on the subject of aid to Spain. The C.I.O., considerably more than the A.F.L., is interested in averting depressions through government fiscal and monetary action and in curbing inflation through price controls. But whatever the matter being considered by government, the unions of both federations try to make certain that there shall be equity for labor when there is either sacrifice or the fruits of progress to be shared.

D. DEALING WITH MEMBERS

1. General nature of policies. In this section we are interested in what has sometimes been termed *welfare unionism.* A union's welfare policies are pointed mainly toward its members and confer direct benefits on them as well as important indirect benefits on the union as an entity. In Chapter 13 we dealt also with union policies having to do with members. Our focus there was on the governing and controlling of members and on the extent to which they are given a voice in the determination of policy. Here we concentrate on the things a union does for its members from within the organization, without regard to the forms and procedures of union government.

In trying to understand the nature of our present topic we should also distinguish it from employer- and government-oriented union policies. Clearly, unions aim to help and provide benefits for their members when they bargain with employers and pressure government. But in respect to the welfare policies we are about to discuss, the relationship is almost wholly confined to a direct one between the unions and their members.

The welfare programs of labor groups may be much like those operated by many employers in their industrial establishments. The chief labor relations function of employers is of course a business one, but many of the personal activities in any important plant are welfare in nature. This is so even though it be recognized that there may be a business motive underlying a company's entire welfare program. So with unions; what is true of *welfare capitalism,* in this respect, is true of *welfare unionism.* A business motive may well be the main one behind such union uplift measures as unemployment benefits or old-age pensions. These things assist the union member, but they also further union survival and power and help it realize its business aims. Nevertheless, it is legitimate to distinguish between unions' welfare and business activites. Business unionism is preoccupied with the various factors of immediate and direct job control. The relation of the welfare function to the daily job is roundabout; its direct concern is the physical and mental health of union members and its measures are not merely economic.

In actual existence all conservative unions — that is, those which accept the present economic system and confine their efforts to improving it and remedying abuses in it — combine both business and welfare functions. There is not necessarily any conflict between these functions; in fact, the most successful unions, like the Amalgamated Clothing Workers, seem to be those which have developed both together into an integrated force that fills almost every part of the members' lives. According to this idea, a union will mean much to a man and will claim his devotion and loyalty in proportion to the success with which it satisfies the many different needs of his existence as a human being. And claiming all members' loyalties and attracting new members with its welfare program, a union is able much better to achieve a complete collective selling of labor and a good control of employment terms, which are the main goals of business unionism.

The welfare measures which are briefly reviewed here are: union benefit and relief plans; union health work; union recreational work; union housing; union counseling work; and workers' education. In their efforts to attain both their business and humanitarian goals, labor organizations have initiated and operated a variety of benefit or relief plans. Realizing that the average worker as an individual fails through financial incapacity or ignorance to provide for himself and his family against the risks of modern economic society, almost all labor organizations have made efforts to relieve their members by providing special homes or making money payments upon loss of jobs or earning power due to accident, sickness, old age, death, or unemployment. Further recognizing the value of prevention instead of relief, several unions have actively interested themselves in health campaigns, the provision of inexpensive medical advice and service, the sponsoring of recreational programs, and the establishment of inexpensive and adequate housing facilities. And, aware of members' need for knowledge of political, economic, and union affairs, in order that union power may be increased and intra-union democracy and self-discipline developed, a number of unions have gone into educational activities on a considerable scale.

2. Union benefits. For many years a good many unions (mostly the older A.F.L., C.I.O., and independent unions) have provided some sort of financial relief for members or members' families when the members died or became sick, disabled by accident, superannuated, or unemployed. (As we saw in our survey of union history, some of these organizations, such as the Big Four Brotherhoods, were originally created as much for the purpose of providing certain low-cost benefits as for bargaining with employers.) This relief has taken one or both of two forms: money payments and institutional care.

Regular dues, special or separate dues, and special assessments were the sources of income for the different benefit funds. The administration of national benefit funds was sometimes in the hands of secretaries, treasurers, or secretary-treasurers and sometimes under the control of an executive council. Local benefits were cared for by similar officers or the business agent; many nationals, however, required uniform dues, disbursements, and accounting among all locals. The passing of members from city to city made standardization necessary in this respect as well as in job conditions.

For participation in these benefits there were of course almost always certain conditions which had to be observed. Most unions required a membership period of one year, while in some the disbursements increased with length of affiliation. All claimants had to be members in good standing with paid-up dues and assessments, except in cases where continued lack of work necessitated the temporary suspension of this requirement. Eligibility requirements for disability benefits were especially strict. The Bridge, Structural and Ornamental Iron Workers provided, for example, that such relief should go only to members who had been in good standing for fifteen consecutive years, whose helplessness had not been brought on by their own "improper conduct," and who were unable to work or find any other source of support. The railway Brotherhoods also barred injuries caused by the use of intoxicants or by participation in "unlawful acts."

Death benefits are paid almost always in a lump sum to the member's survivor. They are not large, on the average; the main objective is to defray the expense of a modest but decent burial. The range is from about $50 to $1500, the average about $200. This is the most important benefit paid by unions. In 1949, out of 108 A.F.L. unions and the four independent railway Brotherhoods, approximately 68 unions provided this sort of relief. In some cases the total payments were very small, in others substantial. Out of a total amount of $43 million disbursed for all kinds of benefits except those labeled "miscellaneous," almost $19 million were for death. None of these figures include information for any C.I.O. union or for the Mine Workers and the Machinists.

Sickness benefits range up to $15 per week over periods varying from 8 to 16 weeks. Total payments by 21 A.F.L. unions and one railway Brotherhood amounted to about $7.3 million in 1949. Permanent disability payments were made by 15 A.F.L. unions and two Brotherhoods in 1949. The total benefits amounted to $1.4 billion. Most of the few unions providing this kind of relief made lump-sum rather than periodic payments.

Old-age compensation was second in importance to death benefits, both in respect to number of unions (23 A.F.L. unions) and amount disbursed (almost $15 billion). Three unions — the Carpenters, the Electrical Workers, and the Typographical Union — accounted for almost 80 per cent of this total.

Unemployment or out-of-work payments were the smallest item in the group of five items, amounting to only $0.8 million in 1949. This was in part due to the fact that unemployment was not high in that year. Mainly, however, it was because most unions had given up such payments following the disastrous experience of 1930–32.

A few unions — notably the Carpenters, the Typographical Union, the

Printing Pressmen, and the railway Brotherhoods — provided institutional care for financially and physically disabled members of long and good standing. The buildings, grounds, and services of these "homes" were in general extensive and of good quality.

Many adverse criticisms have been directed at the handling of union benefit funds, not nearly so much at the possibilities for dishonesty among officials as at the loose accounting. Strike benefit moneys were often not kept separate from the "friendly" benefit funds and no attempt was made (nor was it usually possible) to put the systems on a sound actuarial basis. Realizing this and admitting also the frequent inadequacy of the benefits as to amount and duration, a number of unions, including the Conductors, Engineers, Firemen, Trainmen, Leather Workers, and Machinists, added regular life insurance to their national programs or, like the Boilermakers, Cigarmakers, and Sleeping Car Conductors, adopted such insurance to the exclusion of all other benefits, leaving the older forms of relief optional with the locals. Most of this insurance was group rather than individual. A few unions took their insurance from some "old-line" commercial company, but most carried it through one or the other of two general union insurance companies, the Union Co-operative Life Insurance Company, established by the Electrical Workers, or the Union Labor Life Insurance Company, sponsored by the A.F.L. Some of the unions required all fit members to take out or participate in the insurance. Some of the plans covered death, accident, and sickness, while others were limited to life insurance.

3. Health work outside the shop. All union efforts to safeguard members' health have a certain welfare basis, but those which focus on shop conditions of work are mainly business because they are an important aspect of the struggle for standard conditions and job control. Measures for improving the physical status of members outside the shop, however, possess a large welfare as well as business aspect. They include specific medical service of various sorts to the members, educational work along health or medical lines, and the encouragement of sports and outdoor recreational activities by the locals. One of the most notable examples of a varied medical service is to be found in New York City where in 1919 the nine locals of the International Ladies' Garment Workers' Union, with a membership of about 45,000, cooperated to establish and operate a Union Health Center. A building was purchased wherein were installed complete medical and dental facilities under the direction of a number of full-time graduate physicians and dentists. Members of all the New York labor organizations came to be permitted to make use of the services, which were provided at unusually low costs and included health information, examinations (including X-ray work and all sorts of clinical observation), and treatment (including prescription-filling at the drugstore).

Locals of the Amalgamated Clothing Workers in Cincinnati and Chicago have also organized for health work, emphasizing the preventive aspects through examinations and educational measures. The Locomotive Engineers have for a number of years tried to reduce the death rate among members by asking them to use the union's inexpensive health service. A number of unions, such as the Flint-Glass Workers, the Photo-Engravers, and the Stonecutters, conduct a health or medical department in their official magazines or publish occasional special feature articles on the subject. In general, however, there is much less preventive health work and medical aid among unions than might be expected. It would seem much more desirable and probably not more expensive to promote such activities than to pay benefits for preventable sickness, disability, and death. The measures most widely used — perhaps because bound up with diversion, relaxation, and social contacts — are sports and outdoor recreation.

4. Recreational activities. Sports and games, both indoor and outdoor, are strong influences in the building of union morale and solidarity. They are mentally stimulating and provide normal outlets for many of the workers' deeper needs. For this reason progressive union leaders have always fostered intra-labor recreation as a powerful socializing force, both in arousing the interest of non-union workers and in keeping a union group intact. Outdoor games also promote vitality and disease-resisting qualities; the printing unions, for example, have long sought to interest their members in the formation of baseball, basketball, and golf teams as protection against the occupational hazards of tuberculosis and lead poisoning. Although recreation may be a national policy, it is of course carried on and supported mainly by locals. Among indoor social events, dances, smokers, card parties, and dinners are reported in greatest number, with occasional musical concerts and amateur theatrical entertainment. In large cities locals of the same or different unions have joined in the building and maintenance of "labor temples" or buildings where clubrooms, classrooms, lounges, reading rooms, card rooms, billiard rooms, bowling alleys, assembly halls and stages, motion pictures, radios, kitchens and dining rooms, and other social features are provided. Many headquarters buildings of national and local unions are also well equipped for recreation.

Outdoor recreation during both summer and winter months at special camps is sponsored by the locals of a number of unions. Outstanding for many years (since 1918) has been Unity House, located in the Pocono mountains of Pennsylvania and owned and operated by the I.L.G.W.U. (Ladies' Garment Workers). The property, which serves the members of this and other unions, includes a lake and all the facilities for boating and swimming; an amphitheater for drama and music; facilities for golf, tennis, and riding; and numerous other attractions.

5. Union housing and other consumers' services. At various times since

1920 certain local and national unions have established enterprises to provide their members with consumers' goods and services at low cost. In this field particularly, there is little difference from true consumer cooperation, except that the control is vested in the union as a union and the benefits are usually limited to union members instead of being open to all workers. The most notable achievements have been in supplying *housing facilities.* A number of labor groups in several states have at various times organized home-loan companies to assist members in building and owning their own dwellings. Two unions have undertaken the actual construction of homes or apartments. In New York City the Amalgamated Clothing Workers have built large apartment houses, financed chiefly through their own bank, and sold or rented the apartments to members or other workers. Tenants buy ice, milk, coal, electricity, and food on a cooperative basis. The success of this venture has led to plans for similar projects in other locations. In Philadelphia the Hosiery Workers have also sponsored a notable cooperative apartment development.

A few other unions, blessed with more space to work in, have preferred to sponsor the building of houses rather than apartments. Thus, the South Bend, Indiana, local of the United Automobile Workers started a cooperative project in 1946 involving the construction of some 600 six-room brick houses. And about the same time a Virginia local of the Textile Workers' Union began a 150-house development.

6. Union counseling and social work. Union members are of course like other human beings in that they are often beset with various personality or behavior difficulties, family problems, work frustrations, and so on. Many have no idea of where to go for legal or psychiatric advice, and most cannot afford such professional service. Beginning mainly with World War II, a number of unions, both C.I.O. and A.F.L., set up counseling services for their members in large cities like Detroit and Brooklyn. The benefits to both members and unions were so plainly to be seen that since the war such services have expanded a great deal.

The counseling work of unions has largely taken two forms. First, the members of a few unions, like the seamen who belong to the National Maritime Union (C.I.O.), are in such special circumstances, e.g., not really a part of any one community for long, that the union employs its own professional social workers, legal advisers, and so forth to advise and serve these members in the chief cities where they live or visit. Second, more usually, however, the counseling is sponsored by a C.I.O. local industrial council or an A.F.L. city central rather than by the locals of a single national union; and except for minor problems of the members, the counseling is used to direct the needy members to appropriate professional social work agencies. The C.I.O. and A.F.L. have more than 5000 counselors each in close to 100 industrial communities. The counselors are given training courses before they begin work.

If union members are to be served by community chests and other voluntary social agencies, it is to the interest of the union councils that these agencies be adequately financed, staffed, and managed. Therefore we find the unions asking for and in most cases receiving representation on the citizens' committees that handle community fund drives and advise the social agencies.

These developments have not only helped individual union members a great deal; they have also been excellent "public relations" for the labor movement and have added significantly to its prestige and acceptance in the local communities.

7. Unions' educational work. *a. Nature and causation.* The term "workers' education" has historically been used to designate the efforts of labor organizations (or of any other groups and individuals definitely interested in the labor movement) to instruct workers in certain fields of knowledge, familiarize them with the basic aims of organized labor, and teach them the tactics necessary to attain those aims. It is almost entirely apart from specific job training or even apprenticeship. In many cases the field is as wide as or wider than that of so-called "adult education." The approach and emphasis, however, are usually different; that is, the material and subject matter, instead of being handled mainly to train students for citizenship or business and professional activities or the enjoyment of leisure or the attainment of culture, is interpreted in the light of the labor movement, its past and future. Usually it is not primarily learning for the sake of learning or for the sake of any other goal but the welfare of the workers themselves and the organizations and movement of which they are a part.

In the United States the organized effort toward workers' education is relatively recent, having had its beginning in the first decade of the present century and its most notable development since World War I. The first century of the labor movement was a period of struggle for existence and of experimentation with structure and function. Almost every energy was focused on the fight for recognition and the immediate betterment of employment conditions. Only after these things were at least partially won and stability was achieved, was organized labor free and able to afford the "luxury" of an educational program.

During the upsurge of unionism in the past fifteen years the need for such education became urgent. Millions of workers new to the labor movement needed general training in the nature of unionism and in parliamentarism. Thousands of local leaders had to be developed.

b. Aims, curricula, and agencies. The aims of education for wage-earners cannot be stated in simple, unequivocal terms. Like the aims of any other controversial movement, the terms in which they are formulated depend on the nature and attitude of the person who is stating them. The goals of workers' education as conceived by any given person reflect his views on the objectives of the labor movement in general, for the teaching of wage-earners is a means to a larger end and not an end in itself. The conservative unionist looks upon it as a method for training workers in the economics of the existing order and the particular problems of business unionism. The welfare unionist regards it as a means of giving workers a chance to live a richer, fuller life by learning some of the things they may have missed in their previous schooling — an opportunity to become acquainted with broadening, cultural knowledge in the fields of the arts and the natural and social sciences. This view is, of course, practically identical with the aims of so-called "adult education." All views agree that honest and able labor leaders can best be developed through an educational program.

There is great variety in the field of workers' education. In respect to content, we must distinguish lectures and courses given to the general membership from the more intensified training given to young local officers or to those of potential leadership timber. In a few unions, such as the Ladies' Garment Workers, the locals offer to the rank and file many different "cultural" as well as utilitarian courses; the members can study anything from music, literature, and painting to job evaluation and motion-time study. Usually, however, courses for the membership are confined to union matters such as the history of the labor movement, the economics of wages and hours, labor law and legislation, union administration, collective bargaining procedures, and parliamentary law. The leadership-training courses require much more participation by students and are more intensively geared to the things a leader will have to do and the problems he will face in operating a local union and in dealing with management. In addition to the regular union courses given to members and officer-candidates, there are also occasional special institutes on particular topics or groups of topics, such as "labor in the defense program."

In respect to control over and sponsorship of workers' education, we must distinguish unions from outside agencies. There seems to be a tendency in recent years for unions to take over more of the control and direction. And the national unions and federations appear to be increasingly occupied with directing the educational activities carried on at the local level.

The extent of educational work by unions is not so great as one might expect. In 1950 only 48 national unions (less than one-fourth of the total number) had education departments. Of these, 21 were affiliated with the A.F.L., 14 with the C.I.O., and 13 were unaffiliated. However, most of the large organizations were in this group. The A.F.L. has a Workers' Education Bureau which serves the A.F.L. national unions, state federations, city centrals, and local unions interested in workers' education. The Bureau, in existence for 27 years but formally made part of the Federation only in 1950, furnishes a variety of information to these units, publishes a monthly news letter, and helps organize special institutes throughout the country. The C.I.O.'s Department of Research and Education performs similar functions.

Among the outside agencies concerned with workers' education, but not part of the labor movement as such, are the American Labor Education Service, which arranges institutes and conferences, publishes various information, holds an annual meeting for training teachers in workers' education, studies new teaching techniques (films, radio, and so forth), and conducts an annual summer school for office workers; two residence schools, the Highlander Folk School in Tennessee and the Hudson Shore Labor School in upstate New York; and a number of universities (including Harvard, Cornell, and Wisconsin), which give courses for union leaders and members during their regular sessions or in extension work or in special summer sessions and institutes.

E. DEALING WITH THE PUBLIC

No matter how big, powerful, and strategically situated a given union may be, it cannot afford to take the public-be-damned attitude expressed by a few business leaders in the late nineteenth century. A friendly or at least tolerant public is needed whether the union is at peace or at war with the employers in its craft or industry. Otherwise the survival, power, and prestige of the union are in jeopardy.

Unions have probably always recognized the truth of this. But when most of them were struggling to achieve recognition in the face of employer opposition and government unfriendliness, they perhaps concluded either that the union was too weak financially to afford "good public relations" or that any expenditure of energy and resources on this sort of thing would be wasted.

The leaders of a few unions, notably those in the clothing industries, took a different view. They believed and demonstrated that the public could be successfully wooed while the union was fighting for status and could be held after the union had achieved recognition. Perhaps no union has matched the success of the Ladies' Garment Workers in winning public esteem. Its open and detailed financial statements have been mentioned in a previous chapter. From 1937 to 1940 it staged a musical revue, *Pins and Needles,* which was cast, written, and played on the professional stage by some of its talented members and which won universal acclaim from critics and public. In general, this union has succeeded by these and other means in convincing the public that the union's leaders and members are "good guys" and "nice people" and that the organization is genuinely interested in the welfare of the nation and of the communities in which it operates.

There are five chief media for presenting labor's story to the public: the labor press, the commercial press, pamphlets, lectures or addresses, and radio broadcasting. Others are used occasionally, such as books, the commercial magazines, movies, and the drama. The labor press includes 250 monthly magazines and 650 weekly or bi-weekly papers, which are published and sent mainly to members by almost all the large national unions, as well as by certain city central bodies. They are financed through block subscriptions or by portions of local dues. Dailies have not been successful for any length of time.

Before 1935 the appeal of the labor press was chiefly to union members, and the editors' duties were centered on the problem of making the journals a constructive, vital force in their lives. Too often the editors regarded the publications as an unimportant, routine job; many were union secretaries weighed down with a host of other responsibilities. Today the consensus is that editors should be practically full-time and should abandon the use of much syndicated labor news along with the too prevalent shears-and-paste-pot methods. It is estimated that union periodicals now reach more than 20 million readers, including many non-unionist. Many carry items of general interest as well as union news.

In recent years organized labor has not been slow to seize opportunities for free advertising in the daily commercial press. It has not failed to take a few leaves out of the books of high-pressure publicity agents and "public relations" departments of big corporations who get their clients' activities into print because, although those activities are often but thinly disguised propaganda, they have real news value. Many labor happenings are also "news" to the general public. In addition, the big unions emulate the big corporations in paying for full-page advertisements during strikes or debates on vital national issues. Both the A.F.L. and the C.I.O. have their own press services.

Direct contact with the public has also been achieved through pamphlets or booklets, through addresses, and, especially in recent years under the C.I.O., through radio. In the field of radio broadcasting, certain labor groups have made promising starts. Two of them operate their own AM stations, Chicago labor "going on the air" as WCFL and the Debs Memorial Radio Fund broadcasting from New York City as WEVD. Labor also operates five FM stations: three by the Ladies' Garment Workers in New York, Chattanooga, and Los Angeles; and two by the Auto Workers, in Detroit and Cleveland.

We have reached the end of our discussion and analysis of American unionism. We have learned something about how labor is organized and how it operates to help satisfy the needs of members and to achieve the survival, power, and prestige of unions as entities.

We shall not try to make an appraisal of unionism at this point. Before we do that, it is desirable to consider employers' attitudes and activities and to study union-employer relations. Then we can appraise both unions and employers and their relations from the standpoint of social welfare, which is the authors' point of view in this book.

PART TWO

The Labor Problems of Private Groups

SECTION C

The Labor Problems of Employers

CHAPTER 17

The Structure and Labor Policies of American Management

A. INTRODUCTION

Thus far in this book we have dealt with the labor problems — and with the attitudes and policy decisions related thereto — of two economic-political units: individual workers (and their households), and workers' unions. Now we turn to consider a third unit and its labor problems, the unit we have been variously labeling as "employer," "firm," "company," "business enterprise," and "management."

1. What is an employer? "Firm" is a term well adapted for use in discussing the relatively impersonal economic decisions of a business enterprise. But "employer" sounds like more than a legal and economic person. It has a "human" connotation; and most of the time we used this term rather than "firm" during our discussion of workers' and unions' problems.

"Management" also has a human connotation. It is perhaps the best term of all because it suggests a fact of large moment: In enterprises in which labor problems are of critical importance — namely the larger enterprises — the employer is much more than a single person. As pointed out in Chapter 1, an employer is a whole group or hierarchy of individuals, from top policy makers down through various levels of managers to the lowest plane of supervision.

It is commonplace but largely true that in small firms the labor problems of the human-relations sort (i.e., problems arising because of the interactions of employers and individual workers as people and not because of impersonal economic conditions, such as severe competition in the product market or a cyclical decline in total spending) are usually of decidedly lesser magnitude than they are in large enterprises. A plant having only a few employees, say less than fifty, is ordinarily owned by a single person. As in small retail establishments, the owner may work along with his workers. His output may be just like theirs. At the least, as both owner and manager, he sees all of them almost every day and tends to be in direct, friendly contact with them. He does all the hiring, promoting, and firing of workers. Their grievances and problems are a matter of personal observation and concern for him. He tends to be keenly aware of the fact that his own business welfare depends in large part on his workers' well-being. And the workers, being able to see rather directly how prosperous or dull business is, are usually impressed by the fact that their welfare depends in large part on their employer's.

But, as we saw in Chapter 4, the human-relations problems of owners, managers, and workers in large firms having many hundreds or thousands of workers are another matter. Almost all such firms are corporations, owned by stockholders who almost never see the workers in the plant or at their homes and who hire professional managers to operate the enterprise. The top managers themselves seldom are in direct contact with the workers, and vice versa. In comparison with the small shop, there may be ignorance, lack of understanding, and even suspicion, contempt, or hatred on both sides because of the wide gulf in status and background and because of failure to meet as human beings having common problems.

Our interest in this section of the book, then, is almost wholly in the labor problems of corporate employers. But are there enough of these to justify such discrimination? There certainly are. In 1950 there were some 11 million firms in the United States. Of these, about 60 per cent were individually owned farms and perhaps 25 per cent were individually owned or partnership-owned retail trade shops, service establishments, and construction firms. Perhaps half of the remaining 15 per cent were corporations, mainly in mining, manufacturing, transportation, communications, public utilities, and finance. Their number was thus relatively small. But these corporations produced at least 60 per cent of total private business income and employed almost that percentage of the workers found in private establishments. If we exclude agriculture from our consideration, the relative importance of corporations becomes even greater. Thus, in manufacturing more than 90 per cent of the workers had corporate employers during 1950.

For any branch of industry the corporate employer is typically a large one. This follows from the fact that the technology of producing the product requires an amount of capital investment which is usually beyond the means of one person to supply; that is, the pooled savings of many owners or stockholders are required. More than half of manufacturing workers in 1950 were in plants having more than 500 workers. If certain industries, such as lumber and its products and the cheaper kinds of clothing (in which the typical establishment is relatively small) are excluded, the percentage of workers in plants of more than 500 employees rises considerably.

2. The locus of corporation control. Who rules these large corporate firms? Whose attitudes and beliefs are important? Who determines the policies which govern the corporation's operations, including those affecting labor? We shall deal in some detail with the internal structure and government of a corporation in the next section. Our concern here is with the further identification of "employer."

Theoretically, the owners of a corporation — the stockholders — determine its policies by democratically voting for and electing representatives to its main governing body, the board of directors. True, some amount of democracy may be lost by application of the rule of one vote per share of stock rather than one vote per stock-owner; under this rule those owning the larger blocks of stock cast more votes than the smaller holders. But in most large corporations the holdings are rather widely diffused; few owners possess more than one per cent of the total number of shares.

Nevertheless the typical stockholder has little to say about "his" corporation's policies. One reason is that he usually doesn't care to inform himself on policies or bother himself with them so long as he continues to receive his dividend checks. Ignorance and inertia are present here, just as with workers in respect to alternative job opportunities. Another reason is that, given knowledge and desire, the typical stockholder has no effective way of making his views count with his representatives on the board of directors. Communications to them and appearances before them at the annual meeting of stockholders can be safely disregarded by the directors. As a result, about the most a discontented shareholder can do is to sell his stock.

The most important reason for stockholders' impotence, however, is the conjunction of the diffusion of holdings with several other conditions. First, top management — usually the president of the corporation and his chief vice-presidents — is usually the only group that knows much about the operations of the business. Therefore, although not absolutely essential, it is usually desirable that these officers be treated as more than mere hirelings of the directors. It is desirable to induce them to buy sizable blocks (but still less than one per cent) of the corporation's stock on especially favorable terms in order to increase their interest in the success of the enterprise. And it is desirable to get them elected to the board, rather than have them merely report to it, so that they can have a hand in the determination of the policies that they must administer. Second, once the professional managers are on the board, they are often in a position to dominate it or significantly to influence its decisions. Here again their much greater familiarity with the problems and operations are a major factor. Third, where the rank and file of stockholders are consulted by referendum on policy matters, the managerial group is in a good position to obtain votes in accordance with its wishes; this is done by making suggestions or recommendations to the uninformed owners. Fourth, when new directors are to be elected, top management again is usually able to obtain the men it wants through its control of the proxy voting arrangements.

What it all comes down to, then, for the typical large corporation is this: As pointed out in Chapter 4, the control of corporate decision-making rests in the hands of top management and is largely exercised independently of ownership. That is, ownership has come to be divorced from control.

Thus the locus of corporation control is in top management. And, as we shall see, within the structure and government of the corporation as such there are no democratic checks and balances on the exercise of this control. This government is essentially an authoritarian one. The only checks are those which top management may impose on itself, in accordance with its own traditions, principles, and beliefs; or those which may be imposed by the necessity for obtaining the cooperation of the governed.

This condition may well be regarded as similar to that existing in local or national labor organizations that are subject to the dictatorial control of labor bosses. But it also may be considered to stand in significant contrast to local, state, and national government and to the government of other unions in which considerable degrees of democracy prevail, and in which, therefore, control and authority flow up to the top from the rank and file of the governed rather than vice versa.

If corporation control resides in top management, it follows that when in this section we talk about the labor problems of employers, we shall usually be dealing with the problems of these decision-makers.

3. The general problems of management. Like a labor union, church, or fraternity, a corporate (and non-corporate) firm is a social organization, as we defined that term in Chapter 2. Its specific goals and methods — and the things that measure the success of the methods in achieving the objectives — will be discussed later on. In general terms, we may say here that the problems of the corporation as a social entity are to have freedom, security, and progress in attaining survival, power, and social recognition. In so far as top management identifies itself with the corporation which it controls, i.e., in so far as it considers its own objectives to be identical with those of the firm as an entity (and it usually does), the above-mentioned general goals are also those sought by the managers. Furthermore, as in a union, in so far as management has come to recognize (and in general it has) that the good will and cooperation of those with whom it deals — e.g., customers, suppliers, stock-owners, and the workers it governs wholly or partly — are necessary to the success of the enterprise as an entity, it aims to contribute to the welfare and satisfaction of the members of these groups as individuals, particularly the workers.

More specifically, in the field of labor, management may be said to have the following problems: first, enlisting the cooperation and loyalty of all employees so that they work as a team to help attain the objectives of the enterprise; second, resisting encroachments from any source on the freedom to make managerial decisions and exercise the controls calculated to achieve the enterprise's objectives.

4. Plan of discussion. The general outline for dealing with the labor problems of management will be much the same as the one we used for unions. Our first main topic will be the structure and government of the corporate form of enterprise. Here we shall consider the "managerial hierarchy" and its relations with the rank and file of employees; and we shall have a look at managerial politics. Here we shall also consider the structural aspects of "federations" or associations of firms banded together for united action on common labor problems. The second main topic will be the labor functions of management. Here we discuss attitudes and specific objectives; and we deal with the specific measures adopted to reach the objectives. In this part of our study we shall have to distinguish between measures oriented toward individual workers and those directed toward workers' unions. Here again we shall deal with employers' associations, this time from the standpoint of how they operate.

B. STRUCTURE AND GOVERNMENT

When we discussed union structure and government, we did not explicitly distinguish "formal" from "informal" organization. But this distinction was certainly implicit in what we said. The formal organization was the "paper" or "chart" picture that we drew verbally in respect to (*a*) the way a typical national union is built up from members through local and district units to the national office; and (*b*) the governmental relationships that, according to the union constitution and bylaws, are supposed to exist between the people who have specified statuses and roles in the respective levels of the structure. The informal organization had to do with internal union politics. It was the way the people in the various roles and statuses actually behaved as human beings in the relationships formally assigned to them or informally developed by them. In this connection we talked about such things as the political machines of labor bosses and the degrees of democracy within various unions.

The same distinction is valid now for our discussion of the hierarchy of relationships that comprise what we have called "management." Let us see if we can make the distinction improve our understanding of a firm's objectives and measures in dealing with labor.

1. The formal organization. *a. Structure.* The formal organization of a business enterprise is a tool for accomplishing the enterprise's aims, such as the profitable manufacture of one or more products and the attainment of corporate power, survival, and prestige. It is top management's task to devise the kind of organization that is best calculated to fulfill these aims.

Let us concentrate on a manufacturing firm. What we say about it will apply also to other kinds of enterprises. In economic terms, the profitable production of a product requires a combining of the factors of production (raw materials, machines, and various grades of labor) in least-cost proportions. In engineering terms, the manufacture of the product requires that men, materials, and machines be present in the right amounts at the right times. In human-relations terms, management's job is to direct and coordinate the activities of all employees, from bottom to top, in such a way that full effort and cooperation will be forthcoming.

This human-relations task requires the determination of what roles must be performed by various persons. Roles must be based on the determination of necessary jobs and job specifications. There must be clear definitions of authority and responsibility; this is a prime requisite of good management. The jobs and roles must then be ranked or graded in respect to relative importance. These ratings confer intra-firm and community status on the persons who perform the roles.

A formal organization is a bureaucracy composed of all the jobs or roles in relation to each other, from those of rank-and-file workers up to those of top management. The "bottom" jobs of similar nature or related to a common specific function are grouped in shops. To coordinate these jobs and obtain cooperation among those who perform these job-roles, the lowest managerial job of foreman or supervisor is created. Next, similar or related shops are grouped in departments under department heads; then similar or related departments are grouped into divisions under division superintendents; and the divisions are placed under a plant manager, who "reports to" the vice-president in charge of production. He in turn reports to the highest role-filler, the president of the firm.

This or some similar arrangement of job-role layers or segments is known as "the line." It is the organization directly involved in manufacturing the firm's product or products. "Line" refers to the direct channels of communication through which policies and orders originating at the top are transmitted for execution to the bottom and through which reports on the success or failure of execution pass from bottom to top.

In addition to the job-roles and employee-statuses of the line, there is another class of job-roles and statuses in our typical firm's organization. These mainly comprise what is known as "the staff." Staff departments are groups of jobs related to the performance of a particular function, such as engineering, accounting, sales, finance, and personnel and public relations. Each of these departments is headed by a chief, sometimes known as a "director," sometimes labeled a "vice-president." With each such department there is again a hierarchy of various job-roles and employee-statuses.

Of all the staff departments in a firm, the ones that are most important in our study are those embracing personnel recruitment; other personnel work in respect to individual workers; relations with one or more unions, if these exist; wage rate and salary engineering and administration; and health and safety work. Sometimes all these functions affecting workers are combined in a single department, with different functional subdivisions, all under a director or a vice-president. (It is symptomatic of how much more important personnel work and labor and human relations have come to be regarded by top management that in the last two decades an increasing number of companies have elevated their chief labor executives to vice-presidencies. Before 1930 such officerships were very rare for labor men.) In other cases the functions may be separated in different departments. Thus, wage rate and salary administration may be in one organizational unit, with time-output standards determined by time-study men in the engineering department. Safety work may also be under engineering. The recruitment and selection of employees may be in a separate employment office. Other personnel functions may be in a personnel department, and union-management relations in a labor relations unit.

b. Government. The direct line is an authoritarian or quasi-military kind of government. Orders and authority move in only one direction — down the two-way communications line from the president (general) through successive levels of administration and supervision to the ordinary workers (privates). What moves back up the communications channel is not orders or directives but responsibility: suggestions and reports on compliance, on objectives won or lost, or missions completed or unfinished. Orders and reports are normally communicated in written form.

In the line the top executive cannot possibly oversee and give orders on every aspect or detail of the work that must be done in all job-roles for the attainment of the firm's objectives. He is supposed to develop broad policies in general terms and then, by order to the next in line, to *delegate* his authority and responsibility for the execution of the policies. Vice-presidents in turn make similar delegations. And so on down. They are supposed to be experts in delegating such matters (natural laziness helps a great deal); they must "keep their desks clear" for policy decisions, check-ups on subordinates' performance, and decisions on unexpected, emergency matters.

From this it follows that the extent of authority, responsibility, and discretion in decision-making diminishes continuously through successively lower levels of management. True, the lowest levels of supervision (foremen) have some discretion in executing orders from department heads. They plan shop work; they place and discipline workers; and they deal with workers' representatives in the first step of the grievance procedure. But except through suggestions they have little or nothing to say on major policies.

The top staff officers, while supreme in their own bailiwicks, almost never have any direct control over officers or workers in the line so far as the main business of the line is concerned. Consider, for example, the personnel department. The personnel director and his employees may deal directly with the workers on matters only indirectly related to production, such as housing, recreation, safety, and the pension system. But in respect to hiring, firing, discipline, promotions, and other matters having a direct bearing on line production, they exercise only an advisory or service function. That is, they are limited in this field to developing and trying to "sell" labor policies; and if adopted, such policies are supposed to be executed only by line executives.

There is a system of rewards and punishments governing both line and staff. On the basis of personal observation and of reports received, the corporation generals and subordinates are supposed to reward successful missions, task-fulfillments, and noteworthy efforts with appropriate promotions to higher ranks or with appropriate medals, awards, and so on. Those who fail to carry out orders with sufficient effort or success are supposed to be punished with lack of promotion or with demotion, dismissal, or other formal discipline.

2. Informal structure and government. *Obstacles to successful operation.* Let us assume that the formal organizational structure and governmental system for a given corporation is as good a blueprint as could be devised for achieving the firm's objectives. Then the success of top management is in large part measured by how closely it can get actual performance to conform to the blueprint. Being successful here means getting human beings to cooperate so that each does well what the chart says he is supposed to do. More and more during recent decades top executives have come to recognize that good management means good human relations from top to bottom in the organization.

As in any organization of human beings, the employees of a firm have their own individual desires for freedom, security, and progress in attaining survival, personal integrity, physical comfort, self-expression, power, and social esteem. The firm as an entity has its own goals, as previously stated, most of which can be explained or rationalized in terms of the personal desires of the top executives. The problem, as in a union, is to strike a balance between and effect a synthesis or integration of these various desires, many of which may be in more or less direct conflict. Thus, top management may realize that its objectives and those of the firm-entity can in the long run be only very imperfectly realized unless it makes a serious effort really to satisfy the desires of the workers and of lower management. In similar vein, the workers and foremen may be brought to understand that in the end their welfare is bound up closely with that of the firm and its higher management.

But, one may ask, suppose the workers belong to a union; isn't the union then competing with management for the loyalty and cooperation of the workers? Suppose the union is effective; it knows its business in respect to developing loyalty. If management competes with equal sincerity and effectiveness for the workers' loyalty, won't there be split personalities or mental conflicts within the workers, with resulting loss in morale and efficiency? Wouldn't it be better to leave the field to the union and take what's left from the workers?

On answers to these questions there is no unanimity of opinion among management or others. One "smart" view, however, is this: Both top management and top union officialdom can obtain the workers' loyalties without tearing the workers apart, provided that there is real, effective cooperation between management and union at the upper level, with effective communication from top to bottom and back in both organizations and effective communication between management and union at all important levels of contact.

a. Choked communication channels; distortions in orders and reports. Communications are of supreme importance if the informal or actual human organization is to measure up to that presupposed in the formal design. Orders must be transmitted with undiluted clarity and vigor through various managerial levels down to all the workers if top decisions are to be executed as intended. Reports must come back up from the bottom giving the whole truth about progress in executing the orders and about problems that have arisen therewith. Otherwise policies are at best made only partially effective; and top management fails to learn what actually goes on below.

(1) Failures within management. Some of the failure to achieve adequate communication must be laid at the door of the high executives themselves. Orders may not be clear to begin with. Proper explanation of the reasons for the orders may be lacking. The line is not so authoritarian that top management can reasonably expect blind obedience to unexplained orders.

This failure is most striking in respect to foremen's execution of labor relations policies. The success of these policies is particularly dependent on the full understanding and cooperation of foremen. To most workers in a given shop the foreman is the company. They see or hear no other managerial representative or executive. The way he interprets and carries out his orders on labor matters makes or breaks the policies, no matter how much good will and good intent exists at the top. Therefore intelligent management has been careful to have intensive foreman-training classes conducted in order to explain the reasons for the firm's orders.

But top management is not the only group responsible for poor communication. Sometimes orders from the front office must necessarily be given only in general terms. It is left to successive levels of management to provide needed interpretation in terms of the details with which only these executives are familiar. Here there is serious danger of misinterpretation and ambiguity, willful or unintentional. The farther down the line a policy order goes, the greater is the need for specificity and clarity.

Reports from foremen to the top may also be distorted, with essential matters filtered out at successive stages. No subordinate, from foreman up, wants to look bad to his superior. Promotions are usually hard to win. What could be more natural than to cover up failures and stress achievements when one writes a report to the boss on executing orders. Problems that should receive immediate attention higher up may be played down or omitted in the report. Or suppose that some honest lower executive, or one with a guilty conscience, tells all in a report to his superior — a report that is ultimately destined to reach the latter's own boss. This superior may believe that he will be held responsible for the shortcomings of his subordinate, so he may screen out much of the unfavorable information to save his own neck.

All distortions and blockages in managerial communication seriously affect also the equitable administration of the system of rewards and penalties. Failure to understand and hence execute ambiguous, garbled orders may unfairly result in demotion or dismissal. Promotions may unjustly go to those who most ably display their achievements and hide their failings.

(2) Failures in communication from workers to management. Another communication difficulty is often to be found in the inability of management to learn about its workers' problems. Suppose that management does realize the necessity for satisfying workers' desires in order that its own objectives may be realized. To know that workers want security, self-expression, physical comfort, social esteem, and so on is not enough. One must discover the *specific content* of these general desires. What specific things do the workers want which will give them esteem, security, and so forth? Too often management is prone to think that this content is the same for workers as for management. This is usually a fatal mistake. It may lead management to initiate policies which it considers good for the workers yet which may produce derision or resentment rather than cooperation. But suppose management is aware that workers want different specific things from those desired by management. Then equally fatal is a management's belief that it knows what the workers want anyway. In the absence of some open, frank way for workers to communicate with top management it is rarely possible for management to get a complete, accurate impression. As we shall see, a union with a well-operated union-management grievance procedure can be superior to most other systems of bottom-to-top communication.

It is clearly part of management's responsibility to keep free and open the channels of communication in both directions.

b. Cliques, cleavages, and inter-personal rivalries. When we studied the internal structure and government of unions, we found that, as political organizations, they are often split into factions or cliques on one or more bases, including level of skill, language, nationality, cultural background, age, sex, religion, geographic location, inter-personal rivalries of leaders, and so on. The same thing happens within the managerial hierarchy in a large corporation. An aggressive division head may develop a clique by distributing petty favors to "loyal" subordinates and by making social contacts with weaker peers. An equally pushing rival at the same level may operate similarly. Then the two vie with each other in currying favor with top management. Staff departments may feud with line divisions, one plant manager with another, and so on. There are as many bases for competition and rivalry within a large firm as in a large union.

All these cleavages and rivalries add to the likelihood of poor communication and inequitably administered rewards and punishments. It takes an able, vigorous administrator to minimize such centrifugal forces and establish harmony and cooperation. We do not mean to imply that all competition and rivalry among same-level executives is hurtful to the firm. On the contrary, it may stimulate more effective operation all around. But carried to the personal extremes sometimes found, it can lead to very unequal enforcement of labor and other policies among different departments and plants. Workers learn about these things. Their morale is unfavorably affected and those in some divisions claim inequitable treatment.

3. Associations of firms. Just as unions are a natural response of workers to common problems, so organizations of employers are a natural response to common problems that seem too big to be handled successfully by any one firm in a given industry or locality. *Employers' associations* is the name usually applied to such organizations.

An employers' association may be formed to handle certain labor policies collectively in the absence of unions. But, as we shall see in the historical review presented in Chapter 18, the great majority in the past as well as present have come into existence either to fight or to deal collectively with labor organizations. As we saw in Chapter 10, one of the first local unions to be formed in this country (in 1794) was the Philadelphia Cordwainers. Only four years later the master shoemakers organized to break up this union. Since that time a great many employers' associations have been formed. Several hundred exist today.

a. Structural types. Our discussion at this point is confined to certain structural aspects of these organizations. From this standpoint the associations may be classified on the basis of geographical and industrial scope. They may be local, such as the building contractors' organizations in the various large cities; district, such as certain coal operators' groups; state, such as the Pennsylvania Manufacturers' Association; or national, such as the National Founders' Association or the National Association of Manufacturers. As regards the industrial coverage; some organizations are confined entirely to employers in a given industry, such as the National Metal Trades Association or the American Newspaper Publishers' Association; others include employers from many different lines of manufacturing — for example, the San Francisco Employers' Council, the Illinois Manufacturers' Association, and the National Association of Manufacturers.

It is plain that these different employers' groups are in some ways the counterparts of the various employees' organizations. A degree of parallelism might be expected wherever areas of negotiation and conflicts of interest between the two groups arise, depending always on the nature of the industry. Thus, a local industrial council among unions in the printing industry or the building trades is often met by a local group of newspaper publishers or building contractors; or a city central union may be paralleled by a city organization of all local employers. The district organization of coal operators is coextensive with the coal miners' district union, and the state employers' association is roughly comparable to the state federation of labor. Nationally, the employers' groups in different industries correspond to the national unions, at least to those of the industrial type, while the inclusive employers' associations in a way resemble the general federation of labor. The student must, of course, guard against the error of believing that this structural parallelism is always exact or neat or pre-planned. Employers' associations have been, like unions, largely the product of a trial-and-error evolution, and there are many differences among these complex economic groups.

b. Organization and government. Here also a number of similarities may be found between employers' associations and labor organizations. This is to be expected since both groups are facing the same problems, although from different sides. Where the industry is mainly local, as in building construction, employers are organized in local groups. Where the industry is nationally competitive there will be a national employers' organization to meet a nationally centralized union.

The national employers' association, like the national union, is divided into district and local groups because of the necessity for united dealing with purely regional problems. Each of these has its own elected officers who transact district or local business. The government of the national group is usually the most important because the same economic and financial forces which led to the centralization of power in the hands of national union officers have been responsible for a similar situation in employers' associations. Financial reserves are accumulated by means of initiation fees, annual dues, and special assessments. Sometimes these are flat sums, the same for all; sometimes they are proportional to the amount of payroll or volume of business. Discipline is maintained among members by the posting of bonds or by the loss of accrued rights in the reserve fund. Membership is theoretically open to any employer in a given industry or to those who employ workmen in given trades, provided they believe in and act in accordance with the principles of the organization. Actually many groups limit their memberships to employers who manage to be free of recurring labor disputes.

The legislative phase of association government is usually carried on in an annual convention composed of all the members or of elected delegates, depending on the size of the organization. In large associations the referendum is occasionally employed. The executive duties fall to the elected chief officers and especially to a salaried official known as the commissioner or executive secretary, who, like the union business agent, spends his full time in investigating labor troubles, dealing with unions, and in general protecting the interests of his group. Decisions of a judicial nature are commonly made by the national governing council or board.

C. MANAGEMENT'S GENERAL LABOR ATTITUDES AND POLICIES

Now let us turn to consider the attitudes and beliefs that dominate management's thinking and the general labor policies that flow from these attitudes and beliefs. In doing this we shall distinguish policies bearing on individual workers from those having to do with labor unions.

1. Managerial objectives and attitudes. *a. For the enterprise.* What are the goals of top management? We have already answered this question in broad social terms; we said above that it was management's job to see that the enterprise as an entity survives and waxes in power and prestige. But what content do these very general objectives have? We must answer this question before we can consider particular aims in respect to labor.

The economist assumes that management's sole goal is the maximization of profits, the difference between total sales revenue and total production and sales costs. There is nothing wrong with this assumption; it must be made if one is to focus his thinking on the economic aspects of a firm's operations. The economist merely says this: *If* a firm's management knows the demand curve for its product and the supply curves for its productive factors and *if* it is solely interested in maximizing its profits, it will produce an output at which marginal cost is just equal to marginal sales revenue and at which the marginal outlay on each productive factor is just equal to the factor's marginal revenue product. This is a valid statement if the "ifs" are valid assumptions. But are they valid? Are they in accord with reality? Some economists become so enamored of their abstract economic models that they neglect to revise their conclusions in terms of real-world conditions. They overlook the fact that it is very difficult for firms in a dynamic world to know much about future product demand and factor supplies; that in practice it would be hard in any case to compute marginal amounts; and that the firms therefore resort to certain other accounting methods of determining their profits or losses and their financial positions. Economists also often forget that all decision-making units are likely to have more than a simple, direct economic objective; there are others equally weighty.

It will not do to reject the economic or profits motive. We must simply get in the right perspective. To survive, a firm must stay solvent; it cannot lose money indefinitely, and it would much rather make a lot of money than a little. Management is much concerned with increasing or at least maintaining its sales volume or market position. It is also much interested in reducing costs or at least in maintaining its existing level of efficiency. The balance sheet and the income statement serve as guides for many decisions. Top management's own standing and prestige depend in large measure on keeping the enterprise well out of the red. At every level of management below the top, a man's achievement is in large part measured by his ability to keep his costs down to or preferably below the amount set in the firm's budget plan.

Nevertheless, revenue increase, cost reduction, and profits are far from the whole story. To say that profits are important is not to agree that a firm tries to *maximize* them at any one time or even, as might be more likely, over a rather long period of time such as a whole business cycle. Top management may well be — the evidence suggests that it is — content to earn a "fair," stable return. Why? In the first place, management is sometimes lethargic about cost reduction. Management is popularly supposed to be frantically and continuously searching for ways to reduce costs. But there are numerous examples of managements that more or less rest on their oars until impelled by some objective circumstance (such as severe price competition in the product market or a successful strike by a union or a business downswing) to seek greater efficiency. It often takes a threat to a firm's survival to jolt its management out of the rut of "letting well enough alone." Then it starts taking mental exercise to eliminate wasteful fat. Clearly the management of a firm in a highly competitive industry must be ever watchful. As pointed out in Chapter 15, union leaders have often heard the cry of "Wolf"; management has often said with real sincerity that to grant a wage-rate increase would ruin the firm. But once the increase has been granted, management has usually found ways of reducing costs and maintaining profits unimpaired.

Another condition that works against maximization of profits is management's fear of encroachments from the outside — by unions or by government. Very high profits might lead a union to ask for a very large wage-rate increase. If granted, this might raise costs a great deal. And the company would probably be stuck with this situation thereafter, for unions vigorously resist firms' demands for wage-rate reductions when business gets bad. Thus, after World War II the demand for such products as steel, automobiles, and gasoline was very high. But the firms in these industries did not raise their product prices nearly so high as the traffic could have borne. One reason may well have been the fear that very high profits would have caused unions to ask for very large increases; or government to make an investigation of possible monopolistic practices; or the companies to lose public esteem.

If profits are only one objective of a firm, what are some others? Good public relations, i.e., prestige, is looked on as very important. Particularly after the loss of face suffered during and because of the Great Depression, big business has come to be very concerned with being well thought of. Much of the advertising in periodicals, radio, and television is calculated to create a favorable attitude in the public mind as well as to sell products.

It will not do to be too cynical about public relations campaigns. It is undoubtedly true that many top executives have sincerely come to regard themselves as public servants occupying positions of trust and having large responsibilities to society. A sort of code of business ethics, governing relations with stockholders, customers, suppliers, creditors, and labor, has begun to take hold.

Prestige to firms also involves their being regarded as leaders in the public mind and in the minds of other firms' managers. Leadership means being in the vanguard in improving the quality of existing products, introducing new products, new kinds of advertising, new labor relations methods, new management measures and production methods, and many other things.

Prestige and leadership mean, too, that a firm likes to have a reasonable share of the total sales volume in its industry. At worst it feels it must retain its present market position. Preferably it would like to improve its position. Such an objective may well lessen profits; costs may be increased more than revenues.

These things being true, firms seek "adequate" rather than maximum profits. Adequacy is defined mainly in terms of the firm's being able to build up liquid reserves sufficient to (1) finance ordinary needed technological and other improvements and capital expansion; and (2) meet any conceivable financial emergency.

Finally, in trying to attain these objectives of adequate profits and prestige, management wishes to be *free*. That is, in making decisions in any field it desires to be impeded and restricted by no forces or controls save those which its own conscience and beliefs impose. It doesn't want any union representative or government official to come around and tell it what it may or may not do. It wishes to run its enterprise solely according to its own lights, whether or not these are strictly in accord with what outsiders would agree are the highest ethical and moral principles and ideals. At worst, such freedom would tend to make a corporation president a ruthless tyrant. At best he would tend to be a very just, benevolent emperor.

b. For top management. Top executives, as human beings, have the usual individual human desires noted in Chapter 2, conditioned of course by the environment in which, as quasi-professional persons, they grew up and now live. They believe profoundly in private enterprise and in freedom of decision-making. They are not unaware of their positions as leaders, innovators, organizers, trustees, and builders. They and their colleagues from other neighboring enterprises tend to lunch together, live in the same suburbs or city apartment houses, and have fairly frequent social contacts at their homes or clubs. Naturally they come to think and act in much the same pattern.

In most cases the objectives of these men are identical with those of their enterprises as entities. This of course is because the chief executives identify their own welfare with that of their firms. They are in fact the firms. Yet occasionally it is possible to see a rift between the interests of a chief executive and those of his firm as an entity. This is the sort of thing that happens when boards of directors vote themselves huge bonuses at the expense not only of stockholders but of the financial soundness of the firm, or when corporation presidents with phobias on labor unions decide to fight them to the bitter end. For example, during the late thirties Tom Girdler, head of the Republic Steel Corporation, was finally sued by some of his stockholders for his bitter, intractable, expensive opposition to the Steelworkers. He and his subordinates also caused a noteworthy loss in the firm's prestige, for they were responsible for the "Memorial Day massacre" of unresisting unionists by gunfire during a strike at South Chicago in 1937.

Management is management wherever the organizational and coordinational functions must be performed, no matter what the size of the firm. But the kind of management we have been talking about in this chapter exists in the relatively large firms in which labor relations and labor problems are most important. In such firms top management, being mainly free of control by stockholders, is relatively secure politically. It has a pretty sure base from which it can fare forth to perform its functions of leadership and innovation. It is also economically secure because the markets in which large firms sell their products are not severely competitive.

c. Objectives in respect to labor. The discussions above of the objectives and attitudes of business management in respect to the enterprise as a whole should help us understand management's aims and beliefs in respect to labor matters. In general, we see that, if maximization of profits is not the be-all and end-all of managerial living, there is financial leeway for most firms to experiment with various measures in dealing with labor. It may well be true that many measures are expected to pay for themselves in time. But it is also likely that most of them would have been introduced in any case, as part of a program for improving the firm's prestige and position of leadership.

(1) Determinants. (a) Economic and technological. In this connection

we must stress again the influence of product market conditions on management's labor attitudes and aims. In an oligopolistic product market, where competition is restricted and a firm's position is relatively secure from price wars and the entry of new firms, there is much more leeway for experimentation in labor policies than in severely competitive markets which make for financial insecurity. Thus, a union might be opposed as an obstructing, interfering force by the management of a firm in the first kind of industry; the management might believe that a union could make no contribution toward the attainment of the firm's main objectives. But in the second kind of industry a union might be welcomed by most firms as a stabilizing force, one that made a considerable contribution to the security of each firm.

Another economic determinant of the labor attitudes and aims of management in a firm is how susceptible the industry is to cyclical fluctuations. Both a firm in the machine tool industry and a firm making a staple product like bread or soap might have the objective of providing secure, year-round jobs for their workers. But the first firm would be very much less likely than the second firm to introduce a guaranteed annual wage and employment plan, because the first is virtually always shut down during bad depression years while the second has a relatively very stable demand for its product.

The same sort of contrast is found between a firm in an expanding industry, i.e., one for whose product demand is rising secularly over time, and a firm in a contracting one. Profits are relatively high and almost automatic in the first, low (if any) and uncertain in the second. Obviously the firm in the expanding industry can raise wage rates and introduce various other labor measures much more easily than the firm in the contracting industry.

A fourth determinant lies in the nature of the production technology under which a firm operates. Here a main condition is the proportions in which the inputs of the productive factors must be used. In some operations, e.g., coal mining, the labor input is normally large in relation to capital input. In others, e.g., petroleum refining, it is relatively small. Then, given the prices of both classes of factors, the proportion of labor cost to total cost is high for a firm in the first kind of industry, low for a firm in the second. And the introduction of new labor measures in the first tends to be much more expensive and thus must actually be much more carefully weighed in the first than in the second.

We must also note that improvements in a firm's level of technology tend to reduce the relative importance of labor costs and thereby to increase management's willingness to employ various labor measures.

(b) Non-economic. A number of other conditions, mainly "political" or "human" rather than economic, help to determine the attitude of a firm's management on various labor measures. The size of the firm has a political as well as economic connotation. The economic contrast between

large and small firms was given above. From the political standpoint, management is relatively very close to ownership in the small firm; owner and manager in fact are often the same person. In the large enterprise, as we have seen, there is a very significant separation which frees management to experiment with various labor measures.

At the same time, the larger the plant, the greater the *need* for various personnel methods and practices. We have already commented several times on the increasing impersonalization of relations between management and workers as plant size grows. The top executive, when reminded of this tendency, used to say, "Any employee can see me any time. My door is always open." Today he has come to realize how silly that statement was. For one thing, employees do not relish the idea of "barging in" on a stranger like the big boss. For another, the invitation is bad management: It asks a worker to go over the heads of all intervening supervisors and executives, thus disrupting the prescribed organizational flow of authority and responsibility. Third, if all the workers actually took the boss at his word, he would have no time for his proper duties. Nor, to a lesser extent, would they for theirs.

Unionism or the threat of unionization can affect managerial attitudes and aims in various ways. A management that wishes to avoid organization may be stimulated by the threat of unionism to introduce measures that it otherwise might not, in order to divert its workers from any intention to join a union. A firm newly unionized may choose one of two main courses: It may enlarge and intensify its efforts in behalf of individual workers, trying hard to compete with the union for their loyalties. Or it may abandon some or most of its pre-union program and concentrate on dealing bilaterally with the union.

Government's attitude and activities (the attitudes and decisions of legislators, administrators, and judges) are also important. We shall see in later chapters how much management's attitudes towards unions and other labor matters were affected by various pieces of labor legislation and court decisions.

(2) Management's objectives in respect to individual workers. (a) Basic attitudes and objectives. Given the above-mentioned general and specific objectives and attitudes of management for the firm as a whole, its basic belief in respect to the work force of the firm can be represented as something like this: The firm needs workers to man its jobs and contribute to the attainment of the firm's objectives. The workers need the jobs in order to reach their own objectives. By working hard and loyally the workers can at once serve their own ends and those of the firm. Therefore the interests of management and of workers are very much bound up together if not identical. No real divergence between these interests need exist.

From this attitude or belief comes management's basic labor objective — to convince workers that management's belief is valid. If workers can be led to believe that management is working for them and that they must therefore work for management, their attitude will be one of active loyalty and their aim will be active cooperation. They will be well-functioning parts of the whole organizational team, and there will be glory and gain for every member of the team as it drives steadily toward the goal.

Any of us who have been interested in the success of an athletic team, for example, must necessarily be sympathetic to this basic attitude and objective of management. We know that the survival and the progress of the group toward its goals is greatly jeopardized if the players, managers, and coaches lack interest or cooperate half-heartedly. We have seen potential championship football and baseball teams fade "in the stretch" because of factionalism among the members or half-hearted playing. We know, too, some teams fail because one or more members are in on a "fix" with a gambler. Like any other organization, a ball team cannot realize its potentialities if some of its members are loyal to some objective foreign to the welfare of the group as a whole. On the other hand, we often also see ordinary teams play inspired ball and win unexpected victories because of the unusual degree of mutual loyalty and cooperation among players, managers, and coaches.

Now, as already indicated, there is a greater likelihood that a good team can be developed, without extra-special effort on the part of the coach or manager, if the number of players is small. In respect to business, in the absence of special attention and effort by the boss a small firm is more likely than a large one to have a work force which is cooperative and recognizes mutual interests. But as business expands into the large corporate form, top management "naturally" loses personal contact with and direct interest in the workers and their welfare. It is not that the high executives hate or despise or don't care about their workers. They just don't know them or know about them; and what one doesn't know doesn't concern him. So, with no one caring directly or specially about their welfare, the workers tend to lose interest in the welfare of the firm and of top management. A player who is continually ignored by the coach isn't likely to be on fire to cooperate when he gets into the game. Therefore, in a big company extra-special measures are required for enlisting the workers' cooperation and loyalty. They have to be convinced that top management is sincerely concerned with their welfare.

Executives were a long time coming to realize this. They were too busy, too wrapped up in trying to satisfy their own desires to give much thought to what is now by way of becoming a managerial commonplace in the most enlightened firms: In any organization you can't in the end obtain high satisfaction for your own desires if you don't give the other members of the outfit a chance to obtain high satisfaction for theirs. That is, you can't expect others to help you solve *your* problems if you don't convince them you are interested in helping them solve *theirs*.

(b) Evolution of progressive managerial thinking. Let us note a few main historical steps in the working-out of this managerial Golden Rule. The first noteworthy development came in the form of piece-rate wage systems during the nineteenth century. Managers figured that their own objective of cost reduction could be achieved at the same time that the workers' goal of higher earnings and more steaks was attained. The deficiencies of these early plans have already been noted (on pages 364–67 of Chapter 15). The student should review them now. It is enough to say here that in most firms both management and workers were sorely disappointed with the results; and the fault lay mostly with management because of its disregard of workers' feelings in introducing and operating the systems.

The next step was the "scientific management" movement headed by the zealous Frederick W. Taylor at the close of the century. Taylor introduced job analysis and motion and time study as a basis for setting incentive wage rates for various jobs (see pages 355–56). His methods and those of his disciples represented a distinct improvement over the previous haphazard guesswork used to determine output standards for piece rates or bonus plans. His methods could have been notably beneficial to both workers and management. But here again there was much disregard of the "human element." Workers were treated too impersonally, almost like machines. And, by and large, they refused to team up with management.

The years during and just after World War I saw the next major development — *personnel management,* or *labor management.* There appear to have been four main reasons for this innovation in dealing with workers. First was a realization of the shortcomings of scientific management. Before the war the managements of the more progressive firms had begun to understand some of the reasons why scientific management had failed to realize its potentialities. They saw that time-study and production engineers had been prone to think of workers as mere appendages of machines rather than the most important parts of the various job units. Second, during the war there was a very tight labor market; workers were hard to get and hold. As a result, management felt impelled to search for ways to reduce the extent and costs of labor turnover and to create loyalty among workers. Third, a few industrial psychologists and personnel experts were employed during the war by the government to devise and supervise methods for selecting and training millions of civilians as soldiers. Private management observed and admired the work of these men and decided that such specialists could help industry select, train, and maintain efficient, cooperative work forces in peacetime. Fourth, the Bolshevik revolution in Russia and the postwar wave of strikes in this country by unions that had gained much strength during and just after the war made management fear the growth of radical unionism. Management believed that expert personnel methods could contribute much toward weeding out undesirable workers and toward making the desirable workers so contented that they would not wish to join unions.

Concomitant with the rise of personnel management, and perhaps to be considered a part of it, was a fourth development which may broadly be termed *welfare work.* Top management of large enterprises believed that such things as group insurance, pension plans, housing, and recreation programs would help satisfy workers' desires and win their loyalty and cooperation.

These later changes represented a notable advance in managerial thinking. Management was beginning to understand the importance and significance of good human relations. In a number of firms, where all the levels of management, including foremen, were successfully trained and imbued with this belief, and where there was close and effective coordination between the line and the personnel staff people and therefore adequate fulfillment of the planned program, workers in general seemed to respond rather well. But in many other firms — even in some where adequate foreman training and line-staff cooperation existed — the expected favorable response from workers failed to materialize.

Why was this? Evidently something essential was lacking. The necessary labor relations ingredient that was missing was management's failure to discern one very important basic desire of most workers: self-expression or self-determination. Most people seem in time to become resentful or, at best, unappreciative of things that are done *for* them by others. Furthermore, they tend not to relish what is done for them if they suspect the motives of those who profess to be interested in their well-being. In terms of employers' personnel and welfare programs, this desire for self-expression meant that the workers would have liked to have a voice in the administration of many of the programs affecting them. And many of them sensed or were convinced that a main reason for the introduction of the personnel and welfare measures was management's desire to avoid dealing with an important agency for worker self-expression — namely, labor unions.

The managements of some companies were not unaware of their workers' need for self-determination. So they organized what *they* called "employee representation plans" and what outside unionists called "company unions." Some of these were formed at about the time when the companies' personnel and welfare programs got under way. Others were set up in 1933 or soon after, when it became clear that the New Deal administration intended to put the weight of government on the side of helping workers to achieve self-determination in outside unions. A few of the employee representation plans appear to have been operated in such a way that the workers felt they were being effective in helping decide certain matters affecting their own welfare. In other words, these few plans seem to have achieved a measure of success. But most of the plans seemed not to satisfy the workers. On the various items discussed by the employee committees under these programs, the workers' representatives gave advice and suggestions and were for the most part attentively listened to by management. But the power of unilateral decision remained in management's hands. Most workers understood this. And unless they had decided to throw their lot in on the side of management, hoping for promotion to foremanships and higher executive positions, their cooperation with management was limited.

(3) Attitudes and objectives in respect to unions. (a) The basic problem. Our sketch of the development of progressive management's Golden Rule has brought us squarely up to the question of the attitudes of all management on unionism.

It appears to be a fact that workers, as human beings, possess a strong desire for a voice in the making of decisions on the terms of employment. It also seems to be true that most workers believe labor organizations — independent of and uncontrolled by management — are the best agency for obtaining and making effective this desire for self-determination. Then if top management is sincere in believing that the interests of management and workers are generally identical and that workers' cooperation and team spirit are essential to the full success of the enterprise, does it not follow that management must welcome unionism with open arms if its Golden Rule is really to be practiced?

Let us see: The management of any given firm is wrapped up in the success of that firm. Normally the desires of the managers as human beings are satisfied when the firm achieves the objectives they have set for it. To managers, then, society is virtually compartmentalized. There are many firms competing for the favors of customers and of suppliers of productive factors. The fact that different firms' managements often cooperate with each other on economic and political fronts and that as persons the top managers of different firms have social contacts with each other does not obscure the fact of this vertical division and competition. If its own firm does not achieve managerial objectives and hold its own in the product market and elsewhere, the management has failed, and its inter-firm cooperation and inter-personal social contacts are gone. Hence management's Golden Rule in respect to workers is confined to its own employees. It needs *their* cooperation, not that of any other firm's workers. It may be perfectly willing for its own workers to have an independent union. But for them to belong to a union which claims the loyalty not only of the firm's own workers but also of many other firms' employees in the same industry may be another matter.

To a union and its leaders society is for the most part horizontally stratified. The aims of management and the firm are only to a limited extent those of the workers and their union. Management cannot be interested in the workers' well-being to the exclusion of its own well-being (and that of the firm). On the contrary, it must place the latter first. To the union, this means that conflict between the two is bound to arise.

For union workers to have a voice in decisions on the terms of employment means inevitably, in the union mind, a basic horizontal "competition" between the managerial class and the working class over the division of the firm's revenues, and a certain amount of antagonism between the bosses and the bossed over how much bossing is proper. Further, unionists say that an organization of workers confined to one firm has little economic strength. Its resources must of necessity be much smaller than those of a union embracing many firms. When a local of a national union strikes or threatens to strike against its firm, it knows it has the resources of the whole union plus the moral support of other locals (in fact of the whole labor movement) at its command. The firm's management knows it too. In short, real self-determination can exist only when the workers belong to a strong national organization.

So we must ask ourselves whether the management view is compatible with the union view. Can progressive management's Golden Rule be extended to cover the development of amicable relations in a given firm with an outside union when in essence the union seems to compete strongly with management by asking the latter's employees to be loyal to the union (including the union's members in all the other firms the union covers) rather than to the management?

There can be no categorical answer to this question. It all depends on the circumstances. By "circumstances" we mean mainly the economic position of the firm and the political and human nature of the union and its leaders. There have been notable examples of carrying the Rule to its logical conclusion in spite of the divergence of views just mentioned. Given economic necessity or economic ability and given sufficient will and good faith on management's side, a successful marriage can be developed, with a reconciliation of the divergent approaches, if there is also sufficient will and good faith on the part of the union.

What does management think? There are as yet wide differences among the beliefs of various executives. The determinants of these varying attitudes are the same as those outlined above in our discussion of management's general labor objectives (pages 440–42); we need not repeat them here, but we must use them. We shall consider first management's attitudes toward unionism in general and second its position on three main controversial matters — union responsibility, management prerogatives, and industry-wide collective bargaining.

(b) Kinds of attitudes toward unionism. As previously noted, one determinant of what management does in respect to labor is what government says it must do. It is the law of the land that if a majority of a firm's workers voting in an election held by the National Labor Relations Board decide they want to be represented by a given outside union, the firm's management must recognize and bargain collectively with this union.

Under this law unionism has made the strides previously noted, and the great majority of corporations have for some years been dealing with one or more labor organizations. But this does not mean that all managements have accepted the principle and fact of unionism in their hearts and minds. Today there are still in truth two main attitudes toward it, which we may label "positive" and "negative." Without regard now to government compulsion, these attitudes are determined in part by the economic and in part by the non-economic conditions previously discussed.

i. The negative attitude; its varieties. Disregarding the economic determinants, let us consider the socially conditioned negative attitude toward unions. There have been three main varieties in practice, which will be noted below. But common to all of them is the belief that unionism represents a fundamental challenge to management's freedom to attain its objectives. Executives holding this belief feel that it is impossible to reconcile the previously discussed divergent approaches of management and unionism on social organization and functioning.

One other point should be noted. Unionists look on themselves, at least in their rationalizing, more idealistic moments, as champions of practical democracy, supporters of the underdog classes, and crusaders for social equity and progress. Managements having a negative attitude believe, just as strongly and sincerely, that unionism is a deterrent to social and economic progress. They cite unions' restrictive policies and their infringements on managerial freedom to make unilateral decisions as cases in point. They see unionism in the same light as government control; both, they say, stifle managerial initiative and seriously dampen the incentive to make innovations and be productive. As a result of union policies, they believe, there is a definite lowering of the rate at which per-capita national income increases.

The three specific expressions which come out of the general negative attitude may be called *warfare, competition*, and *containment*. As we shall see, they are not mutually exclusive; at least two may be found in the same management at the same time. The first involves the use of a number of measures that will be reviewed in the next chapter, all calculated to smash or wipe out the union to whatever extent it has been organized in the firm. Physical force and other weapons of warfare, including assistance from the police and judicial arms of local or state government are used. This kind of policy is relatively rare today because of the changed attitude of government and the much greater strength of unionism. It is confined now mainly to small, outlying communities, perhaps mostly in the South.

By *competition* we mean that management's previously mentioned personnel and welfare measures in respect to individual workers can be and have been used to fend off unionization or to weaken a union already organized. Unlike most of the warfare program this policy is perfectly legal and is still used by a goodly number of managements, including many who recognize and bargain with unions. Before the New Deal it was often used along with the warfare program. More accurately, it was the first line of defense, with the rough methods held in reserve — a velvet glove enclosing a mailed fist. Essentially the competitive policy involves various subtle ways in which management tells its union-member employees, "Anything the union can do I can do better, when it comes to satsfying your needs. You can have a union if you want it, of course. But frankly, I don't see what it gets you." This is a direct competition for the employers' loyalty.

Containment means holding off the unpleasant union object at arm's length and regarding it coldly. Management's every action vis-à-vis the union is punctiliously correct in point of law. But there is no warmth in the relationship. The union is tolerated because the government says it must be. But management is still tough. It will not give an inch beyond what is dictated by legal necessity and the union's strength. This icy attitude toward the union may of course be combined with a warm attitude toward many individual workers as the management competes with the union for the workers' affections.

The negative attitudes of competition and containment are still probably in the ascendancy if the economy as a whole is considered. Possibly a majority of managements would revert to non-unionism if they were able to. But an increasing number of top executives have given up any hope that the hands of the clock will be turned back; they think big unionism is here to stay. And the negative approach is losing some of its dominance as younger, more liberal men succeed to the positions of managerial responsibility vacated by the elderly gentlemen of the old school.

ii. The positive attitude. Although doubtless still somewhat in the minority, the ranks of top executives who take a positive approach to union-management relations are getting new recruits every year. In essence the thinking of such an executive may be summarized thus:

"I have my own objectives and problems. I wish the firm I manage not only to survive but also to grow in strength and community stature. I get my own kicks out of achieving these goals and solving the problems that come up. I can't make the grade without the full-hearted cooperation of lower management and workers. Getting this cooperation is one of my very biggest problems. Now maybe I can get this union to help me. The officers have the confidence and loyalty of my workers; and if I can get the confidence and respect of these union leaders, they can help me get the confidence and cooperation of the workers. Then I'm in. But I know I haven't a chance to win union leaders or men unless I can convince them they have *my* respect and confidence and unless I can show them by actions as well as words that I'm sympathetically aware of *their* objectives and problems and willing to help them. They want assurance of survival and growth in power and prestige, too. Okay, I'll give it to them. I'll stop competing with them. No more going to the workers over the leaders' heads with unilateral actions and utterances. If I think it would be a good idea for my company to give the workers a group life insurance plan or a new housing development or anything else, I won't announce these things unilaterally and try to make the union officers look foolish. I'll call them in and tell them what I'm willing to do and then suggest that they 'demand' these things of me in the next negotiations, so that they can get most of the credit from the workers for these improvements. The same way with union security measures; if the union asks me for them I'll grant them in negotiations after a few arguments. And another thing: I've come around finally to see that a union outfit is somewhat different from a business organization. We have politics in our management; but union politics is not quite the same. None of the people below me in management votes me into or out of my office; I tell *them,* they don't tell me. But these union fellows can get voted out if I don't let them look good. So I have to understand that some of the things they demand and some of the ways they talk and act are the result of the union political set-up. I can't expect them to behave in just the same way as the salesmen of my suppliers or the purchasing agents of my customers. Now, I believe that if I operate like this, I'll win the cooperation I need. I'll communicate with my employees through their union representatives as well as through my foremen. And they'll communicate with me through both channels, too. This will be a lot better than my old system of communication, under which I was misinformed half the time or didn't know what was really going on. The cooperation I need will have to come through the union, not over its head or any other way. Looks as if this is the only way I can win."

This is progressive management's Golden Rule carried to its logical conclusion. It works. It is working increasingly in the United States today.

It would be wrong for anyone to get the impression that such an attitude is all sweetness and light or that management has to give away everything, including its shirt, in order to get anything back, including its shirt. The executive whose thinking was paraphrased above would be the first to say that this is not so. He could not gain the respect of the union if he never took strong positions and opposed certain union demands in good faith. He can even be unyielding on particular points so long as he convinces the union that in general he accepts it wholeheartedly, wishes to help preserve its strength and help solve its problems, and is willing to compromise on most disputed issues.

This positive attitude can take two expressions, which may also be successive stages. The first may be called *acceptance and accommodation,* the second *union-management cooperation.* The first is everything implied in the discussion above. Management negotiates agreements in good faith, gives up obdurate devotion to principles as such, abandons legalistic interpretations of the clauses of the agreement, tries to help to get workers' grievances settled expeditiously and fairly through the union-management grievance procedure, and uses the union for communication to the workers on many other matters, such as safety programs, incentive wage systems, and job evaluation plans. The whole attitude is one of cooperation.

Why, then, distinguish another aspect of the positive approach by calling it "union-management cooperation" when the one just noted involves cooperation too? Because the term "union-management cooperation" has a special, historical meaning in labor relations. It includes not only the "acceptance" attitude but also the relationship under which the *union* adopts a distinctly positive attitude on one of *management's* main problems, the economic welfare of the firm. In return for management's commitment to protect the security of the union and its members from technological and other threats, the union agrees to help management discover technological improvements and other methods of reducing unit costs and of increasing product demand.

(c) Union responsibility. Now let us consider management's attitudes on the three matters previously announced — union responsibility, union encroachment on managerial prerogatives, and unions' demand for multi-employer bargaining.

When we talk about "union responsibility," we mean the extent to which unions are willing to adhere to their written or oral commitments with management. The ethical precepts which guide top management include rigid adherence to contracts with suppliers of productive factors and with customers who buy the firm's products. And if for any reasons this precept is disregarded, the injured party can normally obtain redress ("damages" or an order requiring performance) in an appropriate court. It is not difficult to understand why managers, as businessmen, expect to adhere to their commitments with unions just as they keep their promises to the suppliers of non-human productive factors, such as raw materials; and why they expect unions, like the suppliers of other productive factors, to adhere to their commitments with firms. It is also not hard to be sympathetic with management when it expresses outrage over wildcat strikes; requests for contract re-openings at times not provided for in the existing contracts; requests for bargaining on issues excluded by previous commitments; and other apparent breaches of promise.

Top executives unanimously agree that union responsibility is desirable. They believe that unionists, from officers to rank and file, should be scrupulous in adhering to the letter and spirit of collective bargaining agreements. They also believe that union leaders and members should be sober and statesmanlike in formulating their demands in the collective bargaining and political fields. They say, in general, that union responsibility must be proportionate to union power and influence.

But there is no unanimity on how union responsibility can best be obtained. Some executives believe in damage suits or other primitive action in order to make the unions rigidly accountable. At one time it was difficult to sue unions and collect damages from them because they were held by the courts to be voluntary, non-profit associations which could not be reached as entities but only through the various individual members. Because legal action against members was expensive, time-consuming, and financially unproductive, many firms demanded compulsory incorporation of unions so that they could be sued as entities. More recently this demand has subsided because both court decisions and statutes have held unions liable as entities.

Another approach, taken mostly by managements having the negative attitude toward unions, has been to take disciplinary action, including discharge, against union members who violate union contracts.

Other executives, having a more positive view of unionism, might agree to disciplinary actions in cases of clear-cut infraction of contract. But they look coldly on damage suits, believing that the desired cooperation of workers and union cannot be fostered by hostile acts and that good labor relations cannot flourish in the legalistic atmosphere of courtrooms. They would say that a man who wants to live amicably with his wife cannot hope to do so by suing her when she commits a disagreeable act or violates some part of the marital code. It is much better, they say, to look for the cause of the act and try to remedy it. In labor relations the cause may lie in the perversity of one or more union people. But it may also lie in the behavior of some uninstructed foreman or in the unresolved insecurity of the firm's workers. It takes time to make a responsible, harmonious marriage, and it takes at least as much time to develop harmonious, cooperative, responsible labor relations. Train your foremen and use every other means to convince the union of your good will and responsibility; then you will get theirs. New union officers will often be elected. These will be of the negotiating type, rather than the aggressive fellows who made good organizers when the union was fighting for recognition.

(d) Preservation of management's prerogatives. It is a cardinal principle of good organization in any field of human association that, when you give anybody a certain amount of responsibility in his group, you must give him enough authority and freedom of decision-making to permit him to fulfill his trust. Responsibility without authority can in the end mean only frustration and futility for the person and failure for the organization.

This principle stands in the forefront of executives' minds when they are confronted by successive union demands which seem to limit their freedom and discretion to make the decisions they have traditionally deemed necessary for the fulfillment of their responsibilities to their enterprises. An executive may say something like this:

"My job is to keep this business going and profitable and well regarded. I can't do this job unless I can operate without hindrance an effective system of rewards and penalties which will stimulate efficiency and loyalty and deter inefficiency and lack of cooperation. How can I live with a union that tries to tell me whom I can hire and whom I can promote, lay off, and discipline? All this union shop and seniority stuff and this joint review of discipline ties my hands in developing an efficient, loyal work force. And they keep trying to undermine me more and more every year. Often they want to look at my books when I say I can't afford to raise wages. Then, too, I hear top union men like Murray of the Steelworkers and Reuther of the Auto Workers say they want sometime to have management and labor form industry councils or some such thing. They say that then management and labor would jointly determine price policies, output and employment policies, new investment, rate of technological change, plant location, and other matters, as well as the usual matters — wage rates, hours, and so on. This is really something. Looks like syndicalism or the corporate state in Mussolini's Italy. This is taking away or dividing up my *job,* not just removing part of the *authority* I had to carry out my sole responsibility. I guess they won't stop till they've taken everything away from us."

This point of view, undoubtedly held by many if not most top managements, is understandable. It underlies much of the general negative attitude toward unionism. A positive minority view of rising importance, however, runs something like this:

"You've made two main points: Under the first you say you have the whole responsibility for running the show and the union takes away some of the authority you need to meet the responsibility. Under the second you say the union wants to share your main responsibility as well as your authority. Let's look at the first point. An executive's job today is just as you have stated it. He does have that responsibility. And we agree that, human behavior being what it is sometimes, there must be some adequate system of rewards and penalties, which cannot safely be abandoned. But there are various ways of obtaining and exercising the authority necessary for the fulfillment of responsibility. Maybe a legalistic adherence to a stiff rewards-and-punishments system is the best way. Maybe not. One way is to temper justice with mercy. That is, one way of meeting responsibility is to deal with the union in such a way that many more rewards than penalties will be meted out. If most workers labor harder and are more cooperative because you have made them and their union more secure, a union shop and a seniority system may well have made your job easier and more successfully performed than your previous unilateral system of rewards and penalties. Furthermore joint union-management review of disciplinary penalties need not hamstring management's ability or freedom to make such decisions in the first instance. Management can go ahead and take immediate action on any such matter so long as the union has a chance to obtain a review of alleged unfair treatment under the grievance procedure.

"Now let's look at the second point. When a union asks me for a wage increase and I oppose it by saying I can't afford it, and then the union wants me to prove my claimed inability by showing them my accounts, I don't like it much. But unless I've really won their respect and their belief in my honesty, I can't expect them not to doubt my claim. I can't blame them for wanting factual evidence. In any case, I don't think their request to see the books means they want to usurp any of my responsibility. But on this other matter — this industry council stuff — there does seem to be an intent to split up top management's responsibility as well as authority. I can understand where the idea came from; it seems to be based on private enterprise's inability to provide full employment from 1929 to 1940. But if the labor boys are serious in this proposal, I am against it. The stockholders hire me, not Murray, to run the business. If the business does poorly, the stockholders suffer and I get the blame, not the labor leaders. Of course, they and the workers suffer too when business is bad. That is why the best way to keep the labor boys from getting serious on this deal is to keep the country's resources fully employed. There must be some way to do this without setting up these councils."

(e) Multi-employer collective bargaining. Finally, another issue that divides management (as well as a majority of managements, on the one hand, from most unions, on the other) is what has come to be known as "industry-wide bargaining." This is perhaps better termed "multi-employer bargaining" because, whereas there are relatively few collective bargaining systems that really cover an entire industry in the country-wide sense, there are a good many systems covering all or most of an industry's employers in a given locality or region.

On this issue the economic-technological determinants are just as important as the non-economic and ideological ones. If there are many firms in an industry and they sell their products in highly competitive markets (e.g., most of the men's and women's clothing industries, cotton textiles, hosiery, pottery, and bituminous coal), the firms' managements tend to favor uniform labor agreements for all firms because wage-rate cutting is prohibited, labor costs tend to be more uniform, and therefore product-price competition tends to be less severe. This advantage is particularly important if the technology of production is such that labor cost is a high percentage of total production cost.

On the other hand, if there is only a relatively small number of large firms in an industry (as in automobiles and steel) so that the product market is oligopolistic rather than severely competitive, there is little downward pressure on product price and wage rates, even though labor cost may be a high proportion of total cost. The managements of such firms are not whipped by economic necessity into welcoming a master labor agreement covering all firms. Here ideological and other reasons may have much greater sway.

Most managements of such firms vigorously oppose multi-employer bargaining; they believe that union-management relations are primarily a matter of dealings between the firm and its own organized workers. On labor relations in general, some of these managements have what has been called in these pages the "positive" outlook of accepting and trying to cooperate with unions. Basic to all their arguments and rationalizations on this matter is their belief in the previously mentioned vertical organization of society. They simply do not see why they should have to be concerned with the labor problems of other firms or other firms' workers.

The few executives of oligopolistic firms who do not oppose multi-employer bargaining operate on the basis of another fundamental belief. In essence it is like the positive attitudes expressed above on managerial prerogatives and union responsibility. It holds that the security of the union workers in any one firm depends in part on their feeling of solidarity with the members of the same union who work for other firms; that this security is usually heightened by union-management dealings on a multi-firm front; and that any one of the firms will benefit from this greater worker security — it will obtain more effort and loyalty from its workers.

Apart from the basic belief noted above, the arguments (some of them rationalizations) used by those who oppose multi-firm bargaining may be listed as follows: (1) Under this sort of relationship the union is stronger than the firms. It is united as rival firms cannot be. The latter's defense is no stronger than that of the weakest firm in the market. The union thus exercises monopolistic power and has the power to shut down the whole industry, which is disastrous to all concerned, including the public especially if the industry is a basic one like bituminous coal or steel. (2) The union tries to impose uniform employment conditions on all the firms. This is inequitable because each firm is faced with special conditions and problems. It also tends to stifle competition among firms. (3) The uniform conditions sought by the union are those already in effect or possible of being put into effect in the most favorably situated firm in the industry. Such conditions would be very burdensome for most of the other firms. (4) Under these circumstances the union limits the entry of new firms in existing and especially *new* areas. Wage rates and other conditions of employment are raised so high that promoters are unwilling to venture and take the risk of not living through the usual initial period of inefficient, high-cost operations. (5) There is another danger to competition: collusive agreements between managements and the union, as in the construction industry, which raise labor costs and product prices unduly high to the consumer. (6) For each company industry-wide negotiations take more time and are much more cumbersome than if the union bargained with each separately. From each firm there must be several management as well as union representatives. Bargaining can degenerate into a town meeting. The union doubtless saves time and trouble but not the firms. (7) Similar job titles among firms do not necessarily mean similar job contents. By applying uniform wage rates to jobs of the same name but different contents, the union can create many wage-rate inequities within any one firm. (8) Some companies, as in tires and automobiles, make a great variety of products, i.e., are members of several industries, and must deal with several national unions. Industry-wide bargaining would greatly increase their difficulties in obtaining balance among the labor agreements covering their different operations.

Now let us look at some of the arguments and rationalizations (in addition to the matters already mentioned) advanced by managements who do not oppose multi-firm bargaining: (1) Such bargaining enables both management and union representatives to take a broader, more statesmanlike view of the problems of the whole industry, as well as those of the individual firms. (2) By and large there will be fewer strikes in the industry. Most of the time the industry conference will produce agreement. Then all the firms are at peace during the next term. Under individual-firm bargaining one or more companies are likely to have strikes each year. (3) The bargaining power of small firms and the opportunity of their getting a fair hearing is increased when they are members of a solid industry front. (4) In fact, the bargaining power of all firms is enhanced. The union is prevented from "whipsawing," i.e., from picking off one firm at a time, starting with the weakest and extracting concessions from it which it then applies to other companies. (5) Multi-firm bargaining is almost a necessity in local industries where workers typically (as in longshoring, construction, and clothing) are employed by different firms from month to month or year to year. Unions rightly claim that such workers need the protection of uniform terms of employment. (6) Rival unionism, which is a great bother to firms, can be more easily avoided if the bargaining unit is a multi-employer one (recall pages 383–84 of Chapter 15). (7) Under individual-firm bargaining a firm struck by the union may lose customers permanently to the firms that continue to operate. This cannot happen in an industry-wide strike. (8) Bargaining may be more cumbersome but certainly less onerous or time-consuming for any one firm under multi-employerism. The whole industry's staff of superior experts can take over the burden of research and preparation that each firm would otherwise have to do for itself. (9) Whipsawing by the union in the *interpretation* of the agreement can also be avoided. Standard, uniform rulings can be obtained and applied to each firm's operations.

CHAPTER 18

The Structure and Labor Policies of American Management (concluded)

D. SPECIFIC POLICIES AND TACTICS

In this chapter we shall consider in summary fashion the methods used by firms, as individual entities and as groups organized sometimes in employers' associations, to deal with individual employees and with unions in order to achieve the objectives and make effective the attitudes discussed in the previous chapters.

1. Individual firms. Our treatment of the specific labor policies of individual firms will at first assume that there is no union in the picture; here management will be considered to be dealing with its employees as individuals. Then we shall assume that there is a union; here we shall discuss management's policies and tactics in dealing with the union and with the union's members.

a. Relations with workers as individuals. In this discussion our material can be subsumed under four heads: (1) telling employees what the management wants and expects of its employees; (2) finding out what the employees want and expect of management; (3) implementing what management expects of workers; and (4) paying attention to the wants of employees. The first two are mainly matters of communication. The third has mainly to do with management's system of rewards and penalties. And the fourth bears on other managerial techniques for enlisting employee cooperation and loyalty.

(1) Communication from top management to employees. Orders from a firm's top management on production matters are transmitted through successive levels to the shop foremen, each of whom has the responsibility of making work assignments and directing the flow of work for the employees under his supervision. The foreman may also be used to inform workers of numerous other matters not directly related to production. But in a company with well-developed personnel functions there is top-to-bottom communication through a number of other channels. When a

worker is hired, he is given an *employee handbook* which explains a great many things about the company's labor policies, including the method of wage payment; the time and place of wage payment; the various benefit and "welfare" plans and activities, such as group insurance, retirement program, housing, and recreation; the shop rules; and the penalties (discharge, disciplinary layoff, and so on) for violation of shop rules. These things are part of an employee's *indoctrination* and are usually also explained orally (because most employees are unlikely to read the handbook on their own) by some supervisor or trainer.

After workers have been hired, other channels of communication can be used. These include company newspapers or magazines, bulletin boards, in-plant public-address (loud-speaker) systems, letters from top management, and talks at shop or department meetings.

Rumor by the grapevine is usually distorted and unsettling. It is much better for management to be open and frank. Sharing information on the plant's orders and prospects, higher personnel changes, contemplated technological changes, and various existing and new policies is one way of raising employee morale and cooperation.

(2) Employee-to-management communication. How does top management learn what workers want and expect of management? Some managements have been known to employ undercover agents, i.e., spies, and stool pigeons; these men work as employees and make oral or written reports to appropriate high executives. Although sometimes this technique may be used with good intentions, it is not highly regarded. The spies are likely to try to "make work" for themselves by presenting exaggerated or false reports. And if the ordinary workers learn about the existence of these special employees, the former are likely to become bitterly resentful at the management.

Foremen are of course a source of information about what workers are thinking. So are other management representatives (such as time-study engineers) who are sometimes in contact with the workers. Some firms use oral opinion surveys, written questionnaires, and interviews by personnel men with workers, especially those who are quitting their jobs. Still another source is an employee suggestion system under which the workers are invited to make and are usually rewarded for suggestions for the improvement of their job processes and conditions. Helpful also are follow-up interviews with newly hired employees after they have been on their jobs a few weeks. Probably the best source of unbiased information is the counseling service introduced by a number of firms, whereby workers with special family or work problems are given advice and guidance by expert psychologists, social workers, and vocational guidance men.

(3) The system of rewards and penalties. In general, management wishes to develop and hold a loyal, efficient work force. One way of doing this is to give rewards and mete out penalties. Rewards, such as promo-

tions and in-grade wage-rate increases, go to those who are regular in attendance, obey plant rules, have the best production records in terms of quantity and quality, and have the best safety records. Disciplinary measures, such as demotion, temporary layoff, lack of promotion, or discharge, are applied to those who disobey plant rules, are frequently absent or tardy, get hurt often, or are inefficient in production.

A number of personnel functions are built around such a system. We shall briefly discuss here *(a)* labor turnover, absenteeism, and accident studies; *(b)* job analysis; *(c)* recruitment, selection, and placement work; *(d)* employee training; and *(e)* employee rating for reward or penalty.

(a) Studies of reasons for leaving jobs. Workers may quit or be laid off or discharged from their jobs. This is known as *labor turnover.* Work-force turnover is usually calculated as the percentage which the separations are of the total work force per period of time such as a year.

A certain amount of turnover is desirable. Inefficient, unruly, disloyal employees can be weeded out and replaced with better workers. But turnover above this amount is undesirable and expensive. The cost of losing good workers and of finding, training, and indoctrinating replacements may average as high as $500 per man per year. It takes time and money to develop new workers to the point where they are efficient, loyal, not wasteful, and not accident-prone.

Unduly high labor turnover in normal times is a symptom that something is wrong in management's handling of its employees. Before management can take remedial steps, the personnel department must learn where the trouble spots are. This means making studies to discover turnover rates for different departments and shops, age groups, sexes, nationalities, and reasons for quits and discharges.

Absenteeism and tardiness must also be studied; statistics must be obtained in the same breakdowns as those mentioned just above for turnover. Obviously the flow of production is retarded when workers are late or abandon their jobs for one or more days. Investigations of the causes not only will help reveal deficiencies in managerial labor policy but also will help to determine which workers should be rewarded, which punished.

(b) Job analysis. Before management can properly judge a worker's performance so as to reward or penalize him, it must know exactly what the job requires. This knowledge is obtained by studying the content of the various jobs and then writing a list of job specifications in terms of the kinds of workers needed to perform the jobs successfully.

Job analysis is broader than the motion and time study mentioned in Chapter 15, though often including it. Job analysis involves getting the following information: data concerning the technical nature of the operation, which includes a description of the process in terms of materials, tools, machinery, other equipment, motions, and time-output standards (the latter facts are usually obtained from cooperating production engineers); data on the environmental conditions of the job (such as its hazards) and their effects on the employees' physical and mental nature; all facts regarding hours and rates of pay, possible deductions and fines, etc.; the chances for promotion and the methods of measuring success; the necessary qualifications of the worker, including native and acquired skills, physical and mental capacities; and facts showing the relation of the job to other jobs in the factory and to the whole process of production.

The importance of job analysis cannot be overemphasized, for its uses are many. No selection and placement man can hire new employees intelligently without knowing the nature of the jobs and the kinds of workers needed on them. No instructor can teach green men how to operate their tools and machines without being entirely familiar with all the processes. Job analysis, moreover, often leads to the discovery of better methods of work and more equitable time standards and wage rates. In addition, it may forcibly bring unsafe or unhealthful working conditions to the attention of those who will take steps for improving them. Finally, it helps serve as a basis for the rating of employees.

(c) Recruiting and selecting new employees. It is not fair to discipline or penalize employees for lack of success on their jobs if the workers' capacities are not suited to the requirements of the jobs. No management wants square pegs in round holes. Therefore, when the firm has job vacancies that are not to be filled by promotion from the ranks of the workers now on lower-rated jobs in the plant or by the transfer of existing employees from other jobs, it is very important that new employees having the right qualities be recruited.

i. Recruitment. The first problem is to get job applicants into the offices of the employment branch of the personnel department. The phase of the business cycle has a lot to do with the ease or difficulty of this task. Thus, the tight labor market of a boom period makes labor scarce; during depressions, of course, applicants at the gate are plentiful. A most usual source for a non-union firm is suggestions from existing employees, who are asked to tell their friends about the vacancies. Management likes this source, for existing workers are prone to recommend new men who will be more congenial, cooperative, and easy to break in than strangers. Foremen are also considered a desirable source for applicants; they have a large number of contacts among workers and are likely to recommend only those with whom they believe they can get along. Public schools are sometimes approached and prevailed upon to send their graduates. State public employment offices are often used; but some managements do not like to rely on this source very much because the employment office does more preliminary weeding out than most managements like, and the workers registered at such an office are often of lower average quality than the community work force (potential applicants) as a whole. Newspaper advertising is also used, mostly in a tight labor market. It should be noted also that most managements formally or informally agree not to "pirate" or proselyte workers from each other, thus removing a large element of competition on the buying side of the labor market.

ii. Selection and placement. In the old days the foreman did all the hiring and training of employees for his shop. Later, when most personnel functions were put into a separate department, specialized employment officers took over this work. This move took away from the foreman some of the authority he felt he needed in order to fulfill his responsibility for getting work out of his men. Most managements have therefore restored at least part of this authority by the following arrangement. The employment office does a preliminary weeding out, in ways noted below, and sends several men, if possible, to the foreman, who picks the one he thinks most desirable.

The selection process invariably includes one or more interviews with each applicant. These are used to judge personality and behavior traits; it is important to learn whether a candidate will be able to work cooperatively with the foreman and the existing workers. For the same purpose, references from former employers are also used to some extent. If the specifications for the vacant jobs show that special aptitudes or capacities to learn the jobs are needed, certain standard tests may be given to the applicants. Where past experience, i.e., already acquired capacity to do jobs, is demanded, special performance tests on the jobs are often given.

(d) Training and indoctrination. If the newly selected workers are to fill jobs unique to the firm, or if they do not already possess job experience, they must be trained for successful performance. And all new employees, experienced or not, must be "broken in" to shop rules, plant practices, and general labor policies.

Here we shall consider only job training, for indoctrination has been previously discussed in connection with management-worker communication. If the jobs are highly skilled and if trained applicants are not available, management is likely to have or to install some sort of apprenticeship training system, covering one or more years, or cooperate with and help finance some group-employer or city-employer system of apprenticeship. However, if the jobs can be learned in a few days or weeks, a less elaborate plan of instruction is used.

Two main kinds of such job training may be distinguished. "On the job" instruction may be given directly in the shop, at the machine or with the tools with which the neophyte will be expected to work. The training may be supplied by fellow workmen or by the foreman or by both. However, this method delays production because the fellow employees or the foreman have to give up their own duties temporarily in order to conduct the training. Therefore some managements in large plants employ special trainers who devote all their time to such work. These persons are supposed to be fully informed on the job specifications and on how to do the job. In addition, they are supposed to be expert in the techniques of imparting knowledge.

The second kind of job instruction is done by these special teachers "off the floor," in special quarters, sometimes known as "vestibule schools." Some kinds of work, e.g., being a telephone operator, demand this sort of training. Other kinds do not, but it is used because of its greater speed and effectiveness. Obviously this system can also be used for training transferred or promoted employees on their new jobs.

In some large plants, where a certain amount of absenteeism and a number of temporary job vacancies exist each day, there may be a special group of workers trained to do many different jobs. These "floaters," sometimes called the "service squad," are prepared to fill in on almost any kind of vacancy. They are also a source for filling minor executive positions.

(e) Rating the success of employees. Applying rewards and penalties. Let us suppose that over a period of time the selection and training system has been successful in fitting round pegs into round holes, i.e., in obtaining workers whose qualifications meet the specifications of the respective jobs. There is still no guarantee, management recognizes, that workers will actually work efficiently and be loyal and cooperative. In the day-to-day life of any shop there are too many variables (family discord and unforeseen personality clashes, to mention only two) affecting human behavior for anyone to be able to predict how any given employee will perform or get along with fellow workers. Therefore, management feels the need for further labor relations activities — methods of rewarding "good" employees and punishing "bad" ones, and measures aimed at obtaining cooperation and teamwork.

In respect to the system of rewards and penalties, three questions arise: Who shall apply and enforce the rewards and penalties? On what bases shall rewards and penalties be distributed? What shall the rewards and penalties be?

i. Who executes rewards and penalties? This question is not easy to answer. The foreman is responsible for discipline in his shop and for efficient operation. As previously stated, a cardinal principle of good organization is that authority must be commensurate with responsibility. Therefore, a good case can be made for giving the foreman the power to reward and to punish.

But unless the foreman has been thoroughly trained and well-grounded in how to exercise this power properly and evenhandedly, or unless he is "just naturally" adept in such matters, serious abuses may arise. The record is packed with cases of arbitrary, unjust penalties and of gross favoritism in the distribution of rewards.

One method of handling such possibilities and yet not depriving the foreman of authority is to permit him to initiate action, such as discharge or promotion, but make it subject to the review of a line superior in conjunction with a labor relations staff man. Another is to have a committee, including the foreman, decide the appropriate reward or penalty in the first instance and then have the foreman execute the decision. Still another, which may or may not be used in conjunction with the second method, is to have some sort of grievance-settlement procedure whereunder aggrieved employees may appeal from the decision to higher levels of management. This method, of course, normally works best where there is a union.

ii. The bases for reward and penalty. In any case, progressive managements usually insist that whoever has the power to reward or punish (foreman or committee or higher executive) shall try to be as objective as possible in rating the worth of employees. Some measures of relative success are objective: The figures on quantity and quality of production, frequency and severity of accidents, and regularity of attendance speak for themselves. But there are other traits of a personal nature that must also be considered, such as general cooperativeness, initiative, imagination, and judgment. There are very few adequate objective measures of such traits. In the absence of objectivity, the problem is to squeeze as much subjectivity as possible out of the ratings made by foremen and others. For this purpose various employee rating systems have been devised. In a typical one, a number of personal traits are listed. Five degrees or grades, from low to high, in which the trait may be possessed are explained in words. The rater is asked to check which one of the five most nearly describes the behavior of the ratee. On each trait the ratee is given a point score which represents the rater's judgment. The points may then simply be added together to get the ratee's total score. Or, if some traits are regarded as more important than others on the particular job, they may be given special weights. Here the end-product is a weighted total point score.

Employees may be rated periodically, say every three months. The objective and subjective data together then form the basis for decisions on which workers should receive rewards, which penalties, and which neither.

In the absence of unions, almost all managements would prefer to grant rewards or administer penalties on the basis of "merit," as shown by workers' records and ratings, rather than on the basis of seniority (length of service) or any other criterion. In some firms one noteworthy exception to this principle may be found in the matter of temporary layoffs. (Layoffs for economic reasons of course can scarcely be counted as a disciplinary action.) Here length of service may be an important factor. Need, as shown by size of the workers' families, may be another.

iii. What shall be the rewards and penalties? Most of the rewards and penalties used by management are well known. Promotion to a better paying, more highly regarded job is a standard reward. However, transfer to a job having the same wage rate but more prestige or more agreeable working conditions and more congenial fellow workers may be considered a reward.

Firms whose jobs have rate ranges rather than single rates may confer intra-range rewards on certain workers without moving the workers from their existing jobs. This is done by giving "merit" wage-rate increases of five or ten cents per hour within the range for successful performance.

Still another kind of reward, not found so commonly, is the giving of special banners, scrolls, plaques, or some such thing to meritorious employees. Where used, this non-pecuniary kind of reward is usually applied to groups of employees rather than to individuals.

Piece-rate and incentive-wage-rate systems may be regarded as providing automatic pecuniary rewards for superior performance.

In addition to these methods of showing managerial approval, there are of course a host of less formal ways in which discrimination may be exercised in the distribution of rewards. Foremen can be adept in giving their favorites all sorts of "breaks" such as better washroom facilities and lockers, better machines and tools, days off, and so on. Because such rewards usually stir up strife and discontent rather than cooperation, they are not considered a desirable part of good labor relations.

The customary *penalties* against workers include temporary disciplinary layoffs or suspensions; discharge; demotion; and transfer to a less highly regarded job. In addition there are many other less formal means of intimating to workers that they are in disfavor, such as the withholding of usual benefits and perquisites (e.g., free medical treatment by the company doctor or free car-parking space); the withholding of possible or anticipated rewards, such as a year-end bonus or a promotion or a chance to learn a better-paying job; especially close supervision by the foreman; disregard of suggestions; and lack of attention to grievances. Not many of these less formal ways of expressing managerial displeasure are well thought of in terms of good labor relations.

(4) Enlisting cooperation by helping satisfy workers' desires. There is some overlap between this topic and the previous one dealing with the system of rewards and penalties. Obviously rewards help to satisfy the wants of the workers who receive them. But perhaps most of the workers do not receive them. To be effective, a rewards system must usually be selective or discriminatory. This point marks the distinction between the main substance of our present topic and that of the previous one. The measures about to be discussed apply to all employees; that is, they are not primarily selective.

We may divide these measures into two main classes: pecuniary and non-pecuniary. In the first group we consider employers' wage policies (in the absence of unions); employment regularization; dismissal compensation; profit-sharing plans; employee stock ownership; and various "benefit" plans, including pensions. In the second group are health and safety work and various welfare and service activities, such as the provision of recreational facilities. It may be considered that all measures related to satisfying employees' desires are used in order to help management satisfy its own desires and achieve its own goals.

(a) Wage policies. Company wage policies in the absence of unions may be considered under four main heads: method of wage-rate payment, internal wage-rate structure, general level of wage rates, and guaranteed annual wages.

i. Method of wage rate payment. In other connections we have discussed the *nature* of various systems of paying wages by the hour and by amount of output and the *nature* of job evaluation plans for developing an equitable intra-plant structure of occupational wage rates (Chapter 15). Consequently our discussion here may be restricted largely to certain problems arising in the *administration* of these plans.

In respect to hourly wage-rate systems, some managements prefer single rates to rate ranges because the former are much simpler to administer. Other managements prefer rate ranges because they provide additional ways of rewarding efficiency and punishing inefficiency. In respect to piece-rate or incentive-wage-rate systems, most managements will not introduce them, or, having introduced them, will abandon them if one or more of the following conditions exist: (*a*) The unit of output is not homogeneous; that is, successive units vary in size, shape, and other characteristics. Thus, a firm making castings of various sizes and qualities to order would find it difficult to "pay by the piece." (*b*) The unit of output, such as a house or a locomotive, is too large. (*c*) The amount of output on a job is not closely related to the amount of effort expended by the workers. This is the case where the speed of the machine rather than of the worker determines the pace of the job. It also occurs on assembly line operations where one man's output depends on another's. However, in this case a group incentive system, which puts a premium on teamwork, may be effective. (*d*) The materials being worked on are very valuable, e.g., in watch-making. A worker who concentrates on quantity of output and therefore tends to work at rather high speed is often likely to waste and spoil materials. Then management's gain from increased output may be more than offset by the loss in materials. (*e*) The product is changed or varied frequently. In this case two unfavorable results are likely. First, there is too much "down time" for the worker; for such time he is paid only his base rate, which is usually considerably lower than his average hourly incentive earnings, and he resents this. Second, the "run" on any one product is too short to let the worker get warmed up and reach normal earnings. He resents this, too. (*f*) The technology of production on the operation is in such a state of flux that considerable improvement in work methods may occur rather frequently. In such cases output rises substantially. And unless management were to cut the incentive each time this happens, the worker's earnings would rise tremendously. But rate-cutting angers workers. Hence it is usually best to pay hourly rates in such cases until the work methods have become stabilized. (*g*) Workers are sometimes intractably opposed to incentive systems, for historical reasons or other causes beyond management's control. If management's best and most sincere efforts are unavailing in breaking down this attitude, an hourly rate system is the only rational solution.

Let us suppose that the job and product conditions and the attitudes of workers are such as to give an incentive system the chance of success. Then progressive management interested in obtaining workers' cooperation has found it desirable to take full account of most of the workers' objections to such a system (Chapter 15). Thus, management consults the workers in setting time-output standards; agrees not to cut rates except for substantial improvements in job methods; tries to make the system simple and easy to understand; and takes the necessary steps to insure a steady flow of materials and to guard against machine breakdown.

ii. Job evaluation plans. The firm's internal wage-rate structure. Job evaluation engineering (Chapter 15) may be applied to either an hourly (single or rate range) system of wage rates or to the respective base rates in an incentive system. In any case, certain problems of administration arise which make it difficult to hold the cooperation of the employees. These difficulties have caused a number of firms to abandon their plans after several years of experience. However, the number of new plans recently introduced has been larger; the trend is still upward.

What have the problems been and how have they been handled? As in the case of incentive-wage-rate systems, workers are likely to resent a mechanistic or engineering approach to making a wage-rate structure equitable. Management has found it desirable to give weight to the human relations aspects by consulting the employees on the number and nature of the human traits to be considered in relation to the various jobs and on the weights to be given to the traits. If workers' cooperation is judged to be important, as it must be, such consultation is essential.

In any case, the job wage rates based on the point weightings or evaluations of the respective jobs must not be permitted to get very far out of line from the respective market evaluations of the jobs. Fortunately, three conditions make it possible to keep the two kinds of evaluations pretty much in line if workers' wishes are consulted and if the "religious" attitude of the job evaluation engineers is not allowed to hold sway. For one thing, some (often many) of the jobs are unique to the particular firm. Market wage rates, as usually conceived, do not exist for such jobs. Second, even when the jobs are common to many firms in the labor market, there is no uniform market rate for a given job but rather, as we have seen, a fairly wide band of rates. This fact allows leeway to a given firm's rate-setter. Third, workers resent inter-plant as well as intra-plant wage-rate inequities. Their own evaluations of a firm's jobs are therefore not going to be far out of line with the market evaluations or ratings.

After an evaluated job-rate structure has been put into effect, technological changes occur frequently in respect to the contents of many of the jobs and the methods used on them. Most of these managerial improvements seem to be in the direction of job simplification; that is, the worker qualities needed for successful performance become less high than before. This makes it possible for management to put jobs of this sort into lower labor grades paying lower wage rates. But the workers on such jobs resent this action. Thus the question arises, Should such devaluation be done? Wouldn't it be better to be satisfied with the output increases which technological changes permit? Managements that stress the necessity for obtaining workers' cooperation are inclined to avoid devaluation unless the change in job content is really substantial.

Whether or not a formal job evaluation plan is in effect, the internal job-wage structure of a firm is seen to be the resultant of the interplay of human relations and economic conditions. Workers' loyalty and cooperation are necessary for the achievement of management's objectives. Therefore they must be convinced that the relationships among the various job rates are equitable. As we say in Chapter 8, the labor supply and demand conditions for any given job are such in the real world that, in the absence of a union, there is likely to be a considerable difference between the rate that management feels it *is able* to pay and the rate that out of economic necessity it *has* to pay. This difference provides a margin wherein its willingness to pay can be operative. And management's willingness is inevitably affected by its desire to obtain employee cooperation. If such a margin exists for all jobs, there is leeway for the redress of intra-plant inequities, i.e., for the development of an equitable internal wage-rate structure.

iii. The general level of a firm's wage rates. Let us consider now managerial policy in respect to the general level of wage rates to be paid by the firm. Mostly this policy can have meaning only in terms of the relationship between a given firm's level of rates and the levels of other firms in the same locality or in the same industry.

This relationship may be viewed as of any one moment or in terms of general wage-rate changes over a period of time. In either case we must again recognize that for all the jobs in the firm together, as well as for any single job, there is usually leeway for an "administered" or "managed" wage-rate policy. In a given firm, management's *willingness* to pay usually has plenty of elbow room to operate between what it conceives it *has* to pay and what it believes it is *able* to pay. The analysis of Chapter 8 is again relevant here.

A few points may be added or re-emphasized here. In the chapters just mentioned we noted that there are significant differences in the wage rates that different firms have to pay, are able to pay, and are willing to pay. The conditions making for these three sets of differences are such that the general wage-rate levels of firms vary a good deal within a given locality or industry. Some firms are or can be high rate ones, others low, most others medium. We found also that, once a firm has taken a certain rank in the band of rate levels in a given locality or industry, custom and social acquiescence tend to keep it there unless something big or serious happens to change its ability to pay or unless its top management makes an about-face in respect to its willingness to maintain its former position. Management's usual desire to preserve its customary wage-level ranking explains in part the "pattern" or more or less uniform changes from time to time in all firms' wage-rate levels in a locality or industry. Alterations in rankings do occur sometimes. But the general adherence to previous positions is notable.

All the managerial objectives discussed in Chapter 17, such as fair profits, company expansion, adequate financial reserves, social prestige and leadership, and employee cooperation, affect managerial policy on what its relative wage-rate position should be.

The managements of firms that are in industries containing large companies and having products clearly defined and differentiated from those of other industries — e.g., automobile assembly, airplane assembly, rubber tires, basic steel, glass, and railroads — usually guide their wage-rate policies more by what the other firms in their industries do than by wage-rate patterns in the locality. Smaller firms in less well-defined industries are more likely to be guided by locality relationships.

A good many companies have plants in different localities. The managements of some of these companies set the wage-rate levels of their plants in accordance with the patterns existing in the communities where the plants are respectively located. The managements of other such companies have adopted the policy of, first, keeping in line with the community in which their main operations are located; and second, paying the same rates in all other plants as in the main one, regardless of what rates are paid by other firms in the other localities. One reason for this company-wide uniformity is that it facilitates the inter-plant transfer of employees. Another is that it is of help in maintaining the same job evaluation program in each plant.

How does the management of any one firm learn what wage rates are being paid by other firms? It asks. Wage-rate data are not considered top secret. Most firms are not afraid to divulge such information to competitors. Frequently the data are collected and disseminated by industry trade associations, local chambers of commerce, or local employers' associations.

iv. Managerial policy on guaranteed annual wages. Managements seriously interested in enlisting employee cooperation might be expected to be anxious to introduce programs of guaranteeing a certain amount of employment (and thereby wage income) every year for their workers. A guaranteed annual wage would mean a great deal to the employees in terms of security.

But most managements are against such a policy, mainly because of the dynamic economic conditions under which their firms operate. They feel there are limits to what their firms can do in trying to satisfy their employees' needs. To guarantee employment and annual wage income to a substantial fraction of the work force means changing a large variable cost (labor) into a fixed one. Only firms whose product demands and sales revenue are relatively stable from year to year over the period of a business cycle can anticipate always being able to cover such a fixed cost in addition to the usual overhead items. In times of depression, the product demands and revenues of all firms except those making staple necessity goods like soap and food are so greatly reduced that very large fixed costs could not be met.

In 1946 there were only about 200 firms guaranteeing some percentage of full-time annual wage income (such as 40 or 48 weeks of work) to some fraction of their total work forces (such as those having two, three, or five years of service with their firms). Substantial restrictions on amount of guarantee and on eligibility for participation made many such plans operate like a roundabout, complicated seniority plan of layoffs. All these programs covered only about 60,000 workers and were found mainly in small companies producing or selling staple consumption products. Among the larger companies the best-known plans were those of the Procter and Gamble Company, the Nunn-Bush Shoe Company, and George A. Hormel and Company (meat packing).

(b) Stabilization of employment. Related conceptually to annual wage guarantees are plans for employment stabilization or regularization. Obviously, if a firm manages to hold employment at a high, stable level, the annual wage incomes of its workers are also maintained at such a level, and are in a sense guaranteed without the formality of an actual promise.

Employment regularization methods apply to two main kinds of business fluctuation — seasonal and cyclical. The measures may be classified as having to do mainly with three managerial functions: sales, production, and personnel or labor. In practice, of course, the three must be coordinated.

Sales measures try to stabilize product demand. They include the following: (*i*) market research into possible outlets and sales volumes for products; (*ii*) trying to forecast the level of general business activity; (*iii*) development of new uses for existing products; (*iv*) development of new products whose seasonal demands are the opposite of those for existing products; (*v*) redoubling advertising and sales promotion work when depressions threaten; (*vi*) giving customers special discounts during dull seasons; (*vii*) raising the commission rates of salesmen during such seasons; (*viii*) bringing out new models or styles of products, such as automobiles, during slack seasons; (*ix*) changing the product-distribution system, as when Procter and Gamble began to sell soap products directly to retailers rather than to jobbers, so as to eliminate spasmodic bursts of demand based on speculative buying; (*x*) standardization of products and elimination of styles or varieties subject to unexpected vagaries in consumer demand; and (*xi*) adoption of conservative expansion programs during booms.

Production measures include (*i*) manufacture of style products for stock or inventory during slack periods; (*ii*) careful purchase of adequate stocks of raw materials so as to avoid hold-ups in production; (*iii*) careful scheduling and budgeting of production for the same purpose; and (*iv*) scheduling of plant repair and expansion for slack periods.

Along with the above sales and production policies certain personnel measures have been successfully used, such as (*i*) equal division of available work among employees by reduction of the scheduled work-week; (*ii*) training of workers to do more than one job; and (*iii*) transferring such workers from slack to busy departments.

For any one firm such measures may be very effective in regularizing employment during seasonal fluctuations and, if the firm produces staple necessity products, in minimizing tendencies toward cyclical declines in employment. What would happen if *all* firms' managements were to use such measures is another matter.

(c) Dismissal compensation. Dismissal compensation, or severance pay, has been adopted by a few managements as a way of alleviating the hardships borne by workers permanently laid off due to technological improvements (labor-saving machines or methods), product abandonment, mergers of firms, migration, or other causes. Under the usual plan each such worker is given, at separation time, a lump sum of money, e.g., $500 to $1000, in order that he may be sustained during his search for and training in another job. Sometimes the amount of such compensation varies directly with an employee's length of service and previous rate of pay.

The managements using this measure justify it in terms of the larger amount of cooperation obtained from employees having this additional buttress against job insecurity. They admit that it adds to the cost of making certain improvements but believe that the additional cost is made up by greater loyalty and efficiency among employees.

(d) Plant credit unions; savings and loan plans. Because of lack of opportunity or inclination, many workers fail to develop habits of systematic saving for the emergencies of life. Hard times find them at the mercy of various consumers' loan companies, which charge high or exorbitant rates of interest. Labor organizations and independent credit unions have been the wage-earners' own independent agencies for overcoming this difficulty, and for a number of years certain employers have also initiated and fostered plans for the pooling of loanable savings.

Company savings plans may be classified as to what is done with the savings and as to how they are administered. Regarding the first basis of classification, there are four chief methods: Some firms deposit the workers' savings in outside banking institutions, which pay the market rate of interest thereon. Others, in order to secure a higher, more attractive rate of return, help to invest the funds in securities in accordance with the investment-trust idea; the 1929–33 depression, of course, showed the danger of such a plan. A third way has been to lend the pooled savings in small amounts to employees who need temporary tiding-over and can establish worthiness according to the usual credit union standards; after 1935, under favoring federal and state legislation, credit unions experienced a tremendous growth and by 1937 were the chief savings and loan plan in industry. Still another plan uses savings in the building-and-loan manner to encourage home-building among the workers. All of these except the second seem to be desirable and safe methods of investment. The loan plans, of course, are doubly serviceable and worth while.

As regards administration, the savings associations or clubs may be operated solely by the employer through a personnel subordinate, or entirely by representatives of the workers, with advice from the management, or by a joint committee representing both the employer and the employees.

(e) Mutual benefit associations. Group life and health insurance. Although state workmen's compensation laws provide for certain payments to employees for accidents, death, and (sometimes) illness brought on by employment in industry, no compensation is given for any of these misfortunes if occasioned by circumstances not related to industrial work. For this purpose many employers, even in the absence of unions and their pressure, have aided in the formation of mutual benefit associations among their workers in order to make possible the diffusion of risk and the support of those afflicted beyond their ordinary financial means.

Numerous studies made by both public and private agencies have brought to light some interesting facts. The administration of the mutual aid plans, like that of the thrift organizations, may be in the hands of the employer, the employees, or both, usually the last. The funds are accumulated from members' weekly or monthly contributions, usually deducted from pay, which average about fifty cents per month, from initiation fees in about half the companies, and from special assessments in times of deficit. In about half the cases employers add to the reserves in a number of ways: they may contribute monthly amounts equal to those of the employees, pay a lump sum each year, bear the costs of administration, or merely agree to make up any deficit.

Although membership in most plans is still voluntary, there has been a trend toward compulsory membership. Certain requirements are common, such as the passing of a physical examination (often waived when required for employment in the company), a minimum period of employment ranging from one week to six months, and an age less than the maximum of 50 or 55 years.

The provisions regarding the payment of benefits vary widely. The standard, old-fashioned kind of mutual benefit association does not provide medical care directly but confines itself to paying money benefits. For sickness and accidents there is a waiting period of from three to seven days in order to prevent malingering. Payments may last for periods ranging from 13 to 52 weeks. The weekly amounts are not large, averaging about twelve dollars. Death or funeral benefits are, of course, paid in a lump sum, ordinarily about $200 or $300.

Mutual aid societies are entirely plant affairs; they have existed for a long time (since before 1890) to provide a measure of protection against some of the physical risks of industry. Group life insurance was a newer development. Begun in 1911, it brought outside insurance companies into the industrial welfare picture. Since then a greatly increasing number of managements have used it to provide for their employees and improve their loyalty. Such insurance may be contributory or non-contributory; that is to say, the employees may join with the employer in paying the premiums or the employer may bear the whole cost. The amount of group life insurance per employee is about $1500 to $2000, which, although seemingly small, is much greater than the average policy which workers have been able to take out through their own efforts. The cost of ordinary coverage, resulting from the large overhead expenses of writing ordinary policies, is beyond the means of the common wage-earner; not so with the small contributions required under the group plan.

During the past decade, partly because of union pressure but also partly because of management's recognition of the general increase in the demand for low-cost, easily available medical and dental care, there has been a notable increase in the number of company plans providing such care, entirely apart from weekly cash benefit payments for disability. These plans may operate under regular insurance companies or be tied in with other voluntary health insurance organizations, such as Blue Cross and Blue Shield. A variety of hospital, medical, and dental services and benefits may be provided. Frequently the coverage is extended to employees' family members. Membership in the plan may be voluntary or compulsory. Contributions may come from the firm only, or from employees only, or from both.

(f) Industrial pensions. Industrial pensions are periodic money payments made by a company to its superannuated workers. Up until 1936, when the old-age benefits section of the federal Social Security Act began to be administered, there was a growing interest and a substantial expansion in company pension plans. In 1935 there were about 750 such programs. Because the Congress refused to exempt employees under such plans from contributions to the federal fund, however, there were for a while only a few new pension systems adopted after 1935 and a fair number of existing plans were stopped or changed. However, during World War II firms began to turn to pension plans again because the government's wage stabilization program restricted the allowable amounts of rate increases that could be given employees. Another stimulus came

after the war, when the Congress failed until 1950 to raise old-age benefits in the face of large increases in the cost of living.

We shall not consider collectively bargained union-employer plans here (for those, see Chapter 20). Industrial pension plans may be classified in a number of ways. In the first place, it is well to distinguish between informal and formal plans. *Informal* plans are found mainly among small companies. They are almost no plans at all; that is, there are no rules, restrictions, or set amounts. Each superannuated employee is dealt with according to the merits of his own case and pensions awarded on the basis of his own peculiar needs. Large companies have *formal* pension systems. These are characterized by generally rigid rules regarding age of retirement, length of service, withdrawal of employee, amount of pension, administration, and other matters.

Formal plans may themselves be classified mainly as *contributory* and *non-contributory.* The first term designates plans which are supported by the employees jointly with the employer. The second refers to pensions paid solely out of the company's funds. Pension plans may further be classified as *contractual, non-contractual,* and *limited contractual* as regards the right or ability of the company to abandon or change the system. Although, as is the case when a firm buys retirement annuities for its workers from an insurance company, there are a few plans under which employers guarantee to maintain the provisions and employees have legal holds on their pensions, there is probably no truly contractual system which legally binds the firm to continue the arrangement indefinitely. Most of the contributory plans are limited contractual, for employees have a legal right to their contributions, although not always with interest. Sometimes the employer also binds himself to continue paying pensions once granted. Most of the non-contributory systems are non-contractual; the employer reserves the right to modify or give up the plan at his discretion.

A number of provisions common to most systems are worth noting. Some are compulsory, and in some the participation of employees is optional. Eligibility may be confined to employees below the rank of foreman. Two invariable requirements for receiving pensions are a specified length of service, ranging from ten to thirty-five years, and a retirement age such as 65. However, in case of permanent total disability the age requirement may be waived and the pension paid to employees with good service records. If a worker leaves his job because of strikes or voluntary quitting, he loses his pension standing but gets a refund of his own contributions, if any. Short-time layoffs and leaves of absence usually do not constitute breaks in service. The amount of monthly pension is sometimes figured as a percentage (e.g., 1 or 2.5 per cent) of the average monthly wages for the whole period or the last five or ten years, multiplied by the number of years of service. Minimum and maximum amounts are usually stipulated. In a few cases the pension is extended to widows after the husbands have died. Administration is usually in the hands of a special pension board, which often includes the personnel manager and sometimes representatives of the employees.

The failure of company pension plans to provide real protection against old-age insecurity was one of the main reasons for the enactment of the federal old-age security provisions. Many company plans were actuarially unsound; reserves were insufficient to take care of accrued liabilities. And there were too few of them; only a small fraction of all American workers were covered; and those who were under the plans could not, for the most part, count with certainty on their pensions.

Most of the previously existing company plans have been amended to take account of the increase in living costs that occurred after 1940. Most of the old and new plans provide higher benefits than those stipulated in the amended federal Social Security Act. But they also provide that the company is to pay only the difference between the company pension and the amount of the federal benefit.

(g) Profit-sharing. Company welfare programs have included two other plans for improving the economic status of employees — profit-sharing and employee stock-ownership. These measures are similar to pensions, group insurance, and benefit and thrift plans in that their use by employers is motivated by the same aims, namely, the reduction of labor turnover and a measure of protection to employees against the risks of industry. But profit-sharing and stock-ownership, it should also be noted, are basically different from the other measures in that they try to attain these aims by giving the workers a more direct share in the success of the company. Profit-sharing thus gives the employees a part of the net income resulting from prosperous operation, while stock-ownership, in addition to doing this, also provides some degree of control over the profit-getting operations themselves. It will therefore be seen — and this cannot be too strongly emphasized — that both plans go farther than the others because they try to substitute an identity or at least community of interest in place of the old conflict of interests between employer and employees. That is to say, whereas there was an antagonism between the employer with his desire for profits and the worker with his desire for higher wages, there is now to be a joint, more harmonious striving after the same goal, namely, the employer's profits, because the worker is to share in them. Finally, the other plans as a whole make money payments only when certain contingencies (such as accident, sickness, death, or old age) arise, whereas under profit-sharing and stock-ownership the cash supplements to the workers' wages are periodic and more immediate.

Profit-sharing may be defined as a system whereby, according to an arrangement voluntarily made by the management, a number of employees in a business enterprise receive in addition to their regular wages a definite, previously determined part of the net income. This statement should make it clear that what each man gets depends, not directly on output (as it does in the case of incentive wages), nor on time put in (as in day wages), nor on contributions to a fund, but on the success of the management in making profits out of the business conditions which it must face. Profit-sharing should also be distinguished from three other matters — from the Christmas-gift bonus; from product-sharing, which involves a split-up of the actual output, as in agriculture and fishing; and from the sliding-scale system of wages, employed mostly in England, under which wages go up or down according to fluctuations in the selling price of the company's product. In this last case workers indirectly share profits and losses, but only do by agreement what actually happens to almost all other wage-earners during the alternations of prosperity and depression.

Firms which decide to introduce profit-sharing must make decisions on three main points: the basis on which profits are to be divided, the form in which payments are to be made, and the requirements which must be met by employees in order to participate. As regards the first item, it is of course provided that the partition shall come out of *net* income; that is, the usual fixed and overhead costs, such as bond charges and depreciation, are deducted along with variable costs. Some plans first pay dividends to stockholders (the investors of capital) at a fixed rate, such as 7 per cent, before sharing profits with employees (the investors of labor). Others make no such deduction. Whichever method is followed, the real problem is how to split the net income or what is left of it. Some companies give the worker group as a whole a fixed annual percentage, ranging from 5 to 50 per cent of net earnings. Others divide the profits according to certain ratios, the most common being the total annual amount of wages to the total amount of stock outstanding.

Then there still remains the question of dividing the workers' total share among the individual employees. The usual method is to make payments proportional to annual wages, although some firms provide for equal amounts to all. Still another way is to give each workman a certain percentage of his yearly earnings without specific regard for any ratio of distribution between company and working force.

The second main question — as to the form of payments — has been decided by various plants in three principal ways. The most common is the cash payment at the end of the fiscal year or at stated shorter intervals. Another is the deferred-payment plan, in which each employee's share is placed by the management in a savings fund or superannuation account bearing from 3 to 6 per cent interest. A third plan is to give the men company stock instead of money or an account. This is, of course, not the same as the employee stock-ownership which is based on savings out of wages, discussed in the next section.

The third main point that profit-sharing companies must decide is the requirements for participation. Some plans are limited to major and minor executives and have been very successful because such men are directly responsible for production and sales. Other systems are confined to the skilled and stable part of the working force. There are always length-of-service requirements, varying from a few weeks to a number of years. Some plans exclude workers below a given age or those making more than a certain salary or wage. Many bar employees who are guilty of wasteful work, irregular attendance, or unsatisfactory conduct, such as disobedience or striking.

As a part of labor management, profit-sharing has had a longer history than almost any other financial incentive or welfare measure. At one time, in Europe as well as in America, it was hailed as the great solution to labor-relations problems, and even after it failed to exhibit panacea or cure-all properties, it was adopted by a good many companies as a desirable welfare measure. Its failure to realize the high hopes of its sponsors may be attributed to arbitrary introduction by management; paternalism and lack of democracy in operation; failure of workers to relate infrequent profit-sharings with daily efficiency on their jobs; and ill will engendered among workers when management failed to make expected profits or when "drone" workers received as large shares as efficient workers. The experience of almost a century has shown that profit-sharing works well only in small companies and among supervisory-executive employees.

(h) Employee stock-ownership. Because of the failures of profit-sharing, many employers turned to another method, which they believed would give workers a more direct interest in the prosperity and success of the firm — namely, the acquisition of stock by employees. Employee stock-ownership is similar to profit-sharing in certain ways, but differs widely in other respects. Sometimes the two exist in the same plan, as in the cases where the deferred-profit shares are held for employees in the form of company stock. But ordinarily stock-ownership exists independently of profit-sharing and operates differently. Profit-sharing makes payments without requiring any money investment on the part of the worker, whereas under stock-ownership each participating employee does invest some savings and identifies himself to that extent with the fortunes of his company. He is thus a risk-bearer in a new sense and takes the chance of sharing losses the same as gains. Theoretically he also shares in the management of the firm to the amount of his holdings, and in rare cases, where the aggregate employee investment is a large percentage of the total company stock, becomes an actual as well as potential partner in the business.

The various plans show differences in a number of their specific provisions. Employees may come into possession of stock through the company in one or more of four main ways. The most common is cash or installment purchase entirely out of their own savings or wages. The company sells them stock at market price, at par value, at book value, or at a price somewhat below the market value. This plan is contributory from the management's standpoint if the stock has to be bought on the market and is then sold to employees at a lower price. A second way is for the company to make joint-purchase payments with the employees. To match or assist the workers' installment is, of course, to make the plan definitely contributory. In the third place, deserving employees may receive gifts of stock as reward for long and useful service. The fourth way in which workers may acquire company stock is to receive it as their share in a profit-division plan.

How successful have these stock-purchase programs been and how important are they in modern industrial relations? The answer appears to be much the same as it was for profit-sharing: Management's high hopes were dashed and employee stock-ownership is now a rather minor part of industrial relations programs. During the roseate, golden, New-Era years of the twenties, many people believed that employee stock-purchase plans would result in the democratization of industry and in the abolition of the class struggle. Every worker was to become a capitalist. But although in some large corporations very substantial proportions of all the employees were stock-owners, the proportions of total stock which they held were very small and insignificant, and the unskilled workers participated very little. Employees who did own stock were unable or unwilling to take much interest in voting their stock ("sharing in management"). In industry as a whole both the number of employee stockholders and the total amount of their stock were relatively very small. And the depression administered the *coup de grâce*: Stock prices fell abysmally below levels at which employees had bought, and dividend payments were suspended by most companies. This cataclysm showed workers that they had violated a basic investment principle: They had put all their eggs in one basket. Rightly or wrongly, many workers blamed their employers, and any good will that might have been built up under the arrangement was largely dissipated.

(i) Accident prevention and treatment. Now let us turn to look briefly at the measures which we said, so far as the workers are concerned, are mainly non-pecuniary. First come the safety programs of progressive managements. Recognizing that industrial ill-health and accidents result from both mechanical and human defects — that is, from poor conditions of work and the shortcomings of the workers — the more forward-looking managements have attacked the problem of safety at these sources. The hazards to which employees are exposed, of course, vary with the nature of the industry, and the program adopted by any plant depends in addition a great deal upon its size and resources, but almost no firm has failed to undertake some measures to reduce the toll of accidents and disease. The personnel work of large corporations includes many health and safety activities, directed toward improving the working environment, remedying the workers' faults, and taking care of sickness and accident cases which happen chiefly because of the temporary failure of the preventive programs.

Improving the working environment. The better firms usually go farther in improving conditions of work than the minimum standards laid down in most state laws. Machinery, tools, belting, gears, floors, elevators, and other equipment are safeguarded and made as foolproof as possible. Efforts are made not to subject employees to unhealthful and disagreeable processes any more than is necessary. On the basis of research much attention is given to proper lighting, heating, ventilation, and seating. Plant sanitation and housecleaning are part of the drive against possible spread of communicable diseases. Washing and bathing facilities and rest rooms are often provided for the employees.

Dealing with the human factors. The health and safety movement was not many years old before it was driven home to employers with increasing emphasis that attacking industrial disease and accidents from the mechanical side of working conditions, while very desirable and helpful, was not enough to stem by itself the rising tide of casualties. The best safeguards were never entirely foolproof, and firms came to see that a major part of the work would have to be concentrated on the human side — on making the workers less "foolish," or, in other words, on correcting their physiological and psychological deficiencies. Consequently, plans of attack have been developed and plant organizations built up to deal with these phases of the situation. In the course of time a number of important features have been found effective. Doctors, nurses, and dentists are employed to examine applicants and older workers in order to weed out those with physical defects and contagious infections or to cure them by proper treatment. It is possible, of course, as certain companies have found, to use employees having certain physical or mental defects without danger to others or loss in production. But it is now widely recognized that certain kinds of persons are much more *accident-prone* than others; and the policy is either not to hire them at all or to place them only on "safe" jobs."

Fatigue studies have also been made and rest periods instituted and refreshments provided during the day where the work is monotonous and tiring, with resulting increases in output, reduction of labor turnover, and decreases in accidents. Periodic transfers often effect the same end.

Equally important is the work of educating employees in the prevention of accidents and disease. Ignorant, careless, reckless, disobedient, depressed, and preoccupied workers are responsible for accidents just as much as are the physically unsuited. For this reason every effort is made to overcome these psychological obstacles. Publicity is directed at the employees in a never-ending stream by means of bulletin-board advertising, the plant paper, motion pictures, and safety rallies or conferences. Every worker is taught what the hazards are and how to avoid them. Investigation of home and family circumstances often reveals poor sanitation and diet on the physical side or mental conflicts which tend to depress the worker, all of which is reflected in disease and accidents and can frequently be remedied by tactful action. A great deal depends on organization. In large plants there is a safety engineer who sets up safety committees among foremen and among the workers in each shop and stimulates practical accident-prevention discussion. First aid is taught and competition spurred among departments in the matter of no-accident records. Employees are encouraged to make suggestions for improved safety devices.

The treatment of infection and accident cases. Imperfect human beings have never been, and probably never will be, able to prevent all accidents or disease. The medical division is therefore needed for more than the examination and prophylactic work. Many plants have emergency stations for first aid and some have elaborately equipped hospitals and dispensaries for every sort of surgical and medical work, from the treatment of minor abrasions in order to prevent infection to the use of X-ray machines and basal metabolism tests.

Exchange of information. In addition to these individual plant measures, many firms have acted collectively to prevent accidents by fostering certain organizations, such as the National Safety Council, the Safety Code Committee of the American Engineering Council, and the Personnel Research Federation, which act as clearing houses for all sorts of safety and accident information and attempt to promote the best safe practices. The members of the National Safety Council, for example, report accident statistics to the Council and receive regular bulletins giving the trend for the whole country and stressing the need for more zealous accident-prevention work.

(j) Welfare and service activities. Progressive managements were not slow to discern the fundamental psychological truth that their employees' lives and interests are not confined solely to the factory and the jobs. Labor service means much more than providing fair wages, proper hours, and safe working conditions. It involves consideration of the worker's "total situation" — that is, all the aspects of his being which have significant effect on his attitude and efficiency. It includes stimulating undivided loyalty by filling almost every phase of his life. Thus, management often feels it necessary to concern itself with such matters as what its workers do with their leisure time, what they eat, what kind of homes they live in, what they do with their savings, and even occasionally how happy their family life is.

Personnel activities concerned with these things are usually known as *welfare work.* In its broadest sense welfare work may be defined as "all those services which any employer may render to his work people over and above the payment of wages." This would include, however, some of the measures already discussed under other phases of personnel management. It seems better to limit the term to the items noted above, inasmuch as their relation to job efficiency is more indirect.

Be that as it may, it is in carrying on these "service" activities and dealing with every aspect of the human factor that the employer lays himself open to the charge of paternalism. From his standpoint "proper regard for the well-being of the workers" means, in addition to the things discussed in the preceding chapter, furnishing such items as recreation facilities (including sports fields, bowling alleys, softball teams, libraries, gymnasiums, and indoor clubhouses and game rooms), lunchrooms, restrooms, housing, stores, and plans for economic betterment (including thrift associations, mutual benefit associations, group life insurance, pensions, unemployment benefits, profit-sharing, and stock-ownership). A few employers may be motivated chiefly by altruism, humanitarianism, and a belief in fulfilling their social responsibilities, but the dominant drive in most cases is the belief that "it pays" in dollars and cents. The workers themselves seem to sense this, and that is one reason why they have often received employer welfare work with something less than enthusiasm.

Many employers are aware of the danger of playing the benevolent autocrat, and realize that welfare work, if used at all, must be handled very tactfully, lest the opposition of employees be aroused to such a point that all the benefits are lost. It has been generally discovered that the best way to avoid this pitfall is to put the installation and execution of the different service measures as much as possible into the hands of the workers themselves, and to limit the management's participation to subtle suggestion and indirect supervision. Thus conceived and carried out, welfare work may attain its ends and become really a part of the joint relations program.

Furthermore, it is doubtless true that some measures like recreation, housing, and bathing facilities in the plant are really necessary from the nature of the community, such as isolated mining camps and textile-mills villages, or the kind of industry, such as iron and steel. Employees may come to accept and even expect such things.

b. Policies in respect to unions. Our next concern is with managerial policies having to do with outside unions. We noted in Chapter 17 that there were three negative attitudes (warfare, competition, and containment) and two positive attitudes (acceptance and cooperation) among firms in respect to unionism. Our purpose here is to note the specific measures that flow from these attitudes.

(1) Warfare measures. Warfare strategy and tactics are or have been used by firms' managements under two main conditions: (*a*) in order to resist unionization; and (*b*) in order to win a strike called by or forced on a union with which management has already been dealing. Warfare under the latter circumstances, of course, is not necessarily based on a negative attitude toward unionism; sometimes managements who accept and cooperate with unions get into temporary positions out of which strikes may develop.

(a) Resisting unions' organizing efforts. The warfare measures used under these circumstances are today chiefly of historical importance; that

is, the "rough" tactics of management are found nowadays only in isolated areas. This is partly because of the changed attitude of most segments of government since 1933, as expressed in union-encouraging statutes and court decisions; and partly because of the tremendous organizing headway made by unions under government encouragement since that date. But the historical record, outlined in Chapters 10 and 11, is of great importance. The student should know it in order to have the perspective necessary for understanding current labor relations problems.

The union-smashing tactics may be classified under two heads: cold-war measures, and open-warfare tactics.

i. Cold-war measures. One long-employed measure used to avoid unionization was the *anti-union ("yellow-dog") contract,* under which, as a condition of getting and holding jobs in a given firm, all existing and newly hired employees agreed in writing not to join unions or help union-organizing efforts. All individual workers understood that if they violated these contracts, they would face immediate discharge. Their economic and political weakness vis-à-vis most firms made them sign the contracts.

Another weapon of long standing was discrimination of various kinds against union members who were seeking jobs or who inadvertently had been hired by management. Known unionists were refused jobs, the technique here being the circulation of written or word-of-mouth blacklists by and among the employers in a given locality or industry. Although in some states this tactic became illegal long before the New Deal, it persisted because in practice its use was difficult to detect.

Discrimination among various nationalities in hiring was also used to prevent any one group, such as the militant Irish, from becoming too strong in the plant. "Divide and rule" was the principle applied here.

In firms not using anti-union contracts, unionists sometimes got employed in spite of the discriminatory hiring policy. Then various other kinds of discrimination were possible and were frequently used to discourage unionization. These ranged from outright discharge upon discovery of membership to various more subtle measures. Non-union men were given the promotions, the better jobs and working conditions, and the better treatment in respect to the different welfare measures. When lay-offs had to be made for any reason (e.g., reduction in product demand or technological improvements of the labor-saving sort), the key union men were the first to "get the axe."

Often, when union organizers moved into a small or medium-sized community to start a full-scale drive for members, the company police or the town or county officers (who were usually connected politically with the firm's management) would break up these efforts with physical violence. Sometimes, of course, social ostracism and other non-violent tactics, such as refusal to permit union meetings in any public indoor or outdoor place were sufficient to convince the organizers that their cause was hopeless. More often, however, more severe coercion was needed. The organizers would sometimes be thrown into jail on the pretext of violating some ordinance; then they would be released on promise to get out of town. On other occasions the action was even more direct: Organizers were simply beaten up and dragged to the city limits. Union offices were broken into and smashed up. And other acts of violence and intimidation were committed.

Espionage was also a usual anti-union weapon. Managements fighting unionism hired their own spies from among former city detectives or F.B.I. agents or employed professional "private eyes" from Burns, Pinkerton, or other detective agencies. These men were paid for "inside" or "outside" work. That is, they worked inside the plant like ordinary employees, spreading anti-union propaganda and reporting to management any "agitation" they might have heard. Or they joined the union and worked themselves up into local officerships, where they were in a position to bribe other officers, sow dissension, learn union secrets and plans, and report to management thereon. Because the spies' work and pay depended on the existence of a union threat, many of them saw to it that this threat should not disappear too quickly. That is, they often made work for themselves by reporting fictitious occurrences to keep management worried and desirous of continuing the espionage service.

ii. Open-warfare tactics. All the above-described tactics were "cold-war" measures. That is, with the exception of espionage (which obviously continued during the "hot" war of a strike), they were used to break up unionization activities before any union capable of calling a strike could be formed. Let us see now what weapons were used by anti-union managements in situations where the "cold" measures had failed to prevent the organization of an unrecognized union.

As we saw earlier, as soon as a union feels it has sufficient numerical strength and membership morale, it asks for recognition from the firm's management. In the old days an anti-union management would almost always refuse. Then it had to decide whether to take the offensive or wait for the union to do so. At first, firms would often use the *lockout.* That is, they would shut down the plant in order to coerce the union members, with their slender financial resources, into abandoning their union. If the union made a fight of it, as it almost always did, then management used most of the weapons described below in respect to a strike initiated by the union. But management came to find a bit of social or public stigma involved in starting open warfare by locking out its employees. So it decided it would be better to provoke the union into beginning the overt conflict.

Once the "hot" war had been declared, management had quite an array of weapons. As we know, the union uses pickets to bar the employer from access to the labor market; the union tries to keep management from hiring "scabs" and thereby tries to keep the plant shut down. It may also conduct a secondary boycott in order to bar the firm from the product market; this also helps keep the plant shut down. So management's problems were the reverse of the union's — to keep the plant operating and, if necessary, to defeat the boycott. This meant breaking the union's picket lines; breaking the strikers' morale; hiring non-unionists or getting loyal workers back to their jobs, protecting them and the plant from possible violence; influencing public opinion; obtaining government help for these purposes, if necessary; and obtaining government action against a boycott if one existed.

A number of specific measures were used to achieve these objectives. Before the strike the plant might be fortified with small arms and ammunition, tear gas guns and bombs, floodlights and searchlights, barbed wire (sometimes with arrangements for charging it with electricity), live steam pipes with vents, and cots and supplies for strikebreakers. Sometimes management engineered a strike vote before the strike and then claimed (rightly or falsely) that only a minority of employees supported the union and wanted a stoppage. After the beginning of the strike, professional strikebreakers were often hired from one of several companies specializing in such work, for the purpose of breaking up union picket lines, protecting plant property from possible union violence, and protecting loyal workers who might wish to return to their jobs at a propitious moment. Management would then attempt to hasten the propitious moment by organizing citizens' vigilante groups committees, propagandizing among those (such as retailers) who were unfavorably affected by the strike or who were ideologically opposed to unionism, getting help from local or state police, publicizing the results of the strike vote, and otherwise making the unionists appear to be a minority group of radical agitators. A back-to-work movement would be organized among loyal workers and lukewarm unionists whose morale had been weakened by the development of public sentiment against the strike. Finally a date would be set for the final action — the forcible breaking of the picket lines and the re-opening of the plant.

Before and during the early New Deal period of union activity a number of strikes and unions were smashed very effectively by measures like the above. But no strikebreaking accomplishment excited so much admiration among anti-union employers or served so well as a model for later efforts (e.g., the breaking of the "Little Steel" strike in 1937) as that of James H. Rand, Jr., president of Remington Rand, Inc., who in 1936, through use of what came to be known (after publicity to all members by the National Association of Manufacturers) as the "Mohawk Valley Formula," beat the unions in six of his plants, where strikes had been called because of his refusal to deal in good faith with the unionists. The Formula included all the measures mentioned above.

In addition to using the law-enforcement arm of government to help break strikes, employers often turned to the courts, as we saw in Chapters 10 and 11. Damage suits were sometimes used; but, as we shall learn in

Chapter 24, the much preferred legal weapon was the labor injunction. By getting judges to issue blanket prohibitions of all acts and on all persons connected with the direct or indirect conduct of strikes, a great many stoppages were beaten, for refusal to obey such court orders was punishable, by fine or imprisonment, as contempt of court.

(b) Strikes caused by failure of collective bargaining. Sometimes strikes occur even though management and the union have been dealing collectively with each other for years. If the employer's attitude toward the union is basically negative, he might use the strike as a pretext for breaking the union by methods such as those described above. And before the New Deal this did sometimes happen. But nowadays the attitude of government and the strength of the union are such in most situations that management is unable to break the union. Then, as during the steel strike of 1949, there is nothing to be done but sweat it out and take the loss. The union now has a relatively easy time; its pickets are unmolested, and many of the members go fishing or hunting or do odd jobs around the house. But the resources of the union and its members are far from unlimited. In the end economic necessity causes a re-opening of collective bargaining sessions and brings about an agreement (if government mediators have not already effected such a denouement).

(2) Competition with the union. Management may compete with a union for its employees' loyalty with all or most of the personnel measures described earlier in this chapter. Such competition may have begun long before actual recognition of and bargaining with the union. And it may continue for a good while thereafter.

Specifically, the competition may take the following forms. Where a union is still not recognized, management may make bigger and more frequent wage-rate increases than are given in union plants. The welfare and service measures, both pecuniary and non-pecuniary, may be used to focus employee interest and loyalty on the company. There may be subtle discrimination against ardent unionists in favor of "company" workers in the administration of the system of rewards and punishments (promotions, layoffs, settlement of grievances, and so on). Such discrimination today must be truly subtle; otherwise the union, if one already exists in the plant, will cite the company to a government labor relations board for unfair labor practices. Management may use the top-to-bottom communication system (company magazine, bulletin board, speeches, and so forth) to convince employees how deeply management is concerned for their welfare. Unionism may be deprecated, within the limits of the law, as stifling workers' freedom and initiative. If a union is already recognized, management refuses for the most part to use it as an avenue of communication and a means of doing things for the employees. It often decides on and announces directly and unilaterally, over the union's head, certain benefits like group insurance (as did General Motors in 1948).

In most cases such competition has not been successful. A few companies, such as the American Rolling Mill Company and the National Steel Corporation, have been notably successful in avoiding unionization from the outside in some of their plants. But most firms have not managed to do so.

Once an outside union is recognized, it is usually able to eliminate a good deal of the competition. For one thing, management is at a great disadvantage in trying to make its employees believe that management, which after all appears to have some objectives antithetical to those of the workers, is more interested in their well-being than their own organization. The union, for example, can press for settlement of grievances in such a way as to make it appear that management is opposed to justice for the workers. It can also devise and operate a welfare or benefits program at least as good as management's. Or, as with the union pension drive in recent years, it can compel management to alter and liberalize the company welfare program; and the union gets the credit for such improvements. In the second place, the union is usually able to force drastic change in management's system of rewards and penalties. Seniority is made to be a major if not the sole basis for promotions and other elements in the system. Here too, credit goes to the union for the greater security which this alteration gives most workers.

(3) Containment or passive resistance. (a) General approach. This managerial attitude begets not only measures for competing with the union but also, mainly, tactics for resisting the union's encroachment on management's prerogatives or freedom of decision-making. In the negotiation of new agreements management's representatives are doggedly tough in opposing union demands. Its own counter-demands are in the direction of greater managerial freedom and are designed to put the union definitely on the defensive. Thus, management tries to strengthen and enlarge the section found in most agreements which guarantees certain managerial prerogatives. Not only does it insist on the usual freedoms to enforce discipline and make various disciplinary moves (subject of course to workers' protest under the grievance procedure); plan, direct, and control products, materials, and plant operations; assign workers to such jobs as it sees fit; and determine shop and safety rules and regulations. Management also aggressively opposes such forms of union security as the union shop and the closed shop. Maintenance of membership represents the most it is willing to settle for. It will not yield on the seniority principle further than to agree that, among workers of *equal* ability, length of service shall be decisive for promotions, layoffs, and so on. It resolutely insists on managerial freedom unilaterally to make technological changes, to set time-output standards for new jobs and incentive wage rates based thereon, and to evaluate the worth of new jobs in terms of the plant's whole internal wage-rate structure. In these matters the most that management is willing to concede is that objections of workers in respect to its decisions may be handled under the grievance procedure.

Any suggestion that these production and wage items be jointly determined in the first instance is received with shock and horror; to do this would be to yield much too far on the question of prerogatives.

If they are in an economic position to do so, managements of this sort are in the forefront of the ranks of those who oppose multi-employer bargaining. We have reviewed their arguments and rationalizations in Chapter 17.

So much for the negotiation of new agreements. In interpreting existing agreements and living with the union thereunder, managements having the resistant attitude tend to be excessively legalistic and adherent to principle. That is, they guide their own day-to-day decisions in accord with the letter rather than with the spirit of the agreement. They are scrupulously religious about contract observance and expect the union to be the same. When they think they are right, they fight grievances toughly and grimly through all the steps, including arbitration by a third party, if necessary.

(b) Management's arguments against union security. In Chapters 13 and 14 (pages 319–20, 332–39) we reviewed the unions' case for some kind of union security. What does resistant management have to say against this union demand? (*i*) It is often not good for the union. In the first place, to compel workers to join against their own judgment and will is to court dissension and indifference within the union. It is much better for the union to do a positive selling job and win workers into membership by constructive achievements in their behalf. In effect, union security makes the employer the recruiting agent for union membership. A union made strong by its own selling efforts really does not need a union or closed shop. In the second place, the job and worker control that the union and closed shops give unions will in the end compel the government to interfere in the affairs of these organizations. As labor monopolies, unions will have to be regulated in respect to wage-rate and other policies. As determiners of job opportunities (because non-unionists are not allowed to work), the internal procedures and practices of unions in respect to dues, members' rights, expulsion, general dictatorship by officers, and so on will have to be controlled by government. (*ii*) If management is to be compelled to follow a hands-off policy in respect to whether its employees should join a union, so also should the union. Let the individual worker be free to decide for himself, without compulsion from any source. (*iii*) Union security arrangements substitute union discrimination in employment for employer discrimination. They make union membership the condition necessary for holding a job. This is unfair to workers who prefer not to belong to unions. (*iv*) As already stated, union security gives the union monopoly power. If business monopoly is socially undesirable, so also is union monopoly. (*v*) No firm can build up an efficient, loyal, disciplined work force if its choice in hiring and holding workers is restricted to union members. Society suffers from

higher costs and prices. (*vi*) The closed shop is especially iniquitous. It hampers both management's freedom of employee selection and workers' freedom of choice, and it encourages internal union autocracy considerably more than the union shop.

(*c*) *Managerial arguments against seniority.* What arguments do we find resistant management making against seniority measures designed to make individual union members (and of course thereby the union itself) more secure? Most such managers are able to accept "modified" seniority, for it enables them to reward superior efficiency rather effectively (but see below). They do not like "straight" seniority, however. (*i*) They say it may hurt the union itself. Dissension may arise between the younger and the older members, because the latter are favored. (*ii*) Seniority is said to make for an inefficient work force and hinder economic progress. The incentive for superior individual performance is removed. Management is unable to do a good job of weeding out inefficient workers. There is no positive correlation between length of service and efficiency. (*iii*) As to fairness, seniority is just as discriminatory as promotion and layoff based on merit. It merely substitutes one kind of discrimination for another. Seniority exploits the better employees to the advantage of the union and the less efficient employees. (*iv*) Modified seniority is not too bad, but it has one effect which weighs rather heavily against it: Its application breeds a disproportionately high number of grievances.

(*4*) *Acceptance and cooperation.* (*a*) *General approach.* The general nature of these positive kinds of management attitude was also analyzed in the preceding chapter. There is a will to agree and a degree of good faith and good will toward the union that is almost wholly missing in the negative attitudes. Underlying any specific measures is a willingness on the part of management to use the union as a major up-and-down channel of communication with the workers and to avoid most of what could be unilateral decision on matters affecting employees. In other words, an accepting and cooperating management is committed to consultation and even joint action with the union at all appropriate levels on matters directly (and sometimes indirectly) affecting the workers. Such managements have drawn no hard and fast line beyond which they will not yield on managerial prerogatives. They doubt that the union wishes to bother with sales, finance, the procurement of materials, and other management matters that impinge on the workers only very indirectly. They believe that management and unions can get mired down in a morass of semantic difficulties if they worry about, argue about, and try carefully to define managerial prerogatives.

(*b*) *Managerial arguments for union security.* A number of managements — almost all of them in the positive-attitude class — favor giving unions some form of security. The general position is simply a further expression of the managerial Golden Rule: Management wants survival, expansion, prestige. So does the union as an entity. Give the union with sincerity what it wants, and it will respond by giving management what it basically wants. From this general attitude come several specific arguments, based mainly on actual experience: (*i*) Union security reduces inter-union competition and thereby tends to spare management from being caught in the middle between rival union organizing drives. (*ii*) Union responsibility tends to vary directly with the degree of union security. If the union gets a union shop, its suspicion of managerial hostility is substantially reduced. It is then much more willing to discipline unruly members, eliminate phony grievances, and abide by its contractual obligations. (*iii*) A secure union is less likely to try to restrict managerial freedoms than an insecure one. The union agreements not having union security clauses contain considerably more other security provisions for employees (such as restrictions on management's right to discharge and lay off workers) than those containing such clauses. (*iv*) When union leaders and members are secure, they spend much less time worrying about and fighting against managerial discrimination. They can then work constructively with management to help solve *its* problems. (*v*) All these things mean a more stable, efficient, loyal work force.

(*c*) *Managerial arguments for seniority.* Here too there is a field of application for management's Golden Rule: Help the union and its members on their security problem, and they will help management on its problems. This means that managements having a positive theory of labor relations go along pretty much with the third and fourth union assertions presented in Chapter 14, page 344.

(*d*) *Union-management cooperation.* To what specific measures does management commit itself in engaging in the special form of union acceptance known technically as union-management cooperation (recall pages 450–51)? The joint-consultation approach is used here to cover the introduction of technological improvements, work-output standards, and wage rates. In return for the unionists' promise not only not to oppose management's cost-reducing improvements but also to try constructively to think some up themselves, management agrees, first, to introduce the improvements so as not to displace workers permanently; and second, to reward workers for their suggestions and cooperation by sharing with them the gains of increased productivity and cost reduction through higher wage rates. Management tries to fulfill its side of the bargain by transferring displaced employees to other jobs; undergoing the expense of retraining them when necessary; dividing work equally when necessary; paying wage rates as high as possible after allowance for normal profits and plant expansion; and paying dismissal wages to workers unavoidably displaced. In short, this is the deal: Management gets help from the union on its problems of profits, financial security, and social prestige; and in return it is willing to help the union on its problems of survival and prestige and to help the workers on their problems of getting higher incomes and more secure employment.

2. Employers' associations and their labor policies. The labor policies of employers' associations reflect of course the attitudes of the firms who belong to them. The associations were formed to give greater effect to the attitudes of the individual members. So we distinguish here also the negative and positive approaches to unionism.

a. Reasons for existence. We can understand this distinction better if we consider first in more detail why firms have organized employers' associations. The development of unions in membership, financial reserves, and bargaining skill enabled them to challenge in many industries the absolute power of the individual employer. In fact, at times the single employer came to find himself distinctly at a disadvantage in the rising struggle for control. As a rule he was no match for the union officer in bargaining on labor matters, and he was frequently worsted in the pitched battle of strike or lockout. Faced with increasing demands for concessions which he could not yield if he was to adhere to the belief in his traditional "right" to run his business without interference, he and his fellows responded to the changed conditions by forming associations through which they hoped at least to equal the strength of unions and to block further restraints on their profit-seeking activities.

True, in many associations a firm loses much of its freedom to make decisions on its own labor policies. But this loss appears smaller than the loss that would occur if the firm were on its own, at the mercy of the union.

In its larger aspects the development of employers' associations represents an interesting and important step in the struggle for industrial control in modern society. It is one of the answers of the "haves" to the "have nots," the response of a group in power to a group challenging that power.

b. Functional classification. We have already seen that, structurally, employers' associations may be (1) local, state-wide or regional, or national, and (2) confined to a single industry or industry group, or cover many industries. Our concern here is with what the associations do.

Historically, there have been two main classes of associations in respect to function: (1) the "belligerent," union-hating and -smashing kinds; and (2) the "negotiatory" or union-recognizing and -bargaining kind. The belligerent associations used to build up war chests from members' contributions in order to help any member who was having union difficulties fight and break the union. All the warfare tactics of anti-union employers mentioned above were employed. The association furnished funds, non-union workers, professional strikebreakers, spies, propaganda, and political influence. Fellow members were often asked to fill the orders and supply the customers of a struck member.

The negotiatory or conciliatory kind of association has two main variants: those who confine themselves to negotiating — or helping members negotiate — new agreements with unions; and those who both negotiate agreements *and* administer them for members.

All the technological-economic and other conditions which we said, in Chapter 17, determine individual employers' attitudes are determinants of associations' attitudes and policies toward unions. The newspaper publishers were conciliatory because their highly skilled unionized employees could prevent the appearance of the newspapers which must come out every day. The time element in building construction, plus the skill demanded of workers, explains why most contractors in the large cities were negotiatory. In job printing and in clothing manufacture some employers' groups felt compelled to deal with unions in order to avail themselves of the selling worth of the union label and the stabilizing effect of union wage-rate uniformity. Where competition among employers is severe, as in the bituminous-coal, clothing, building, and stove industries, the larger employers tended to combine in asking the union to help, by strikes and organizing activities, to drive out non-union competitors.

Since the late thirties there have been several noteworthy developments. First, under government encouragement of unionism, with the growth of powerful unions, and with the increase in the union drive for multi-employer bargaining, a number of new associations have been formed. Some of these are industry-wide, some locality-wide. Second, virtually all associations today are negotiatory in the sense that they deal with or help members deal with the unions rather than try to break them. But there is still a basic functional cleavage among them; some are negative, believing in competition and containment, while others accept unions more willingly. It is probable that the associations having the negative approach substantially outnumber those with the positive attitude. Third, some rather important firms have declined to join associations to which they are eligible. They prefer to conclude their own individual agreements with their unions, either on special terms or following the pattern set first by the respective associations. They would rather take their chances alone with the union than be compelled to follow the rules and policies of associations whose officers and members they may distrust or dislike. Majority decision is felt to impose too onerous a burden, especially if a firm knows that this majority can cause the firm to have a work stoppage at a time when the firm believes it could obtain a peaceful settlement with the union. Fourth, following a few earlier examples, a number of associations have become *administrative* as well as negotiatory. That is, not only does the association's negotiating committee work out and sign with the union (or unions) agreements that are binding on all the members. It also settles grievances and interpretive disputes arising under and during the life of the master agreement; these settlements are also binding on all members. This development indeed restricts the freedom of individual managements. But it prevents a still greater restriction, one which would be imposed by the union if individual-firm grievance settlement were permitted: The union would be likely to obtain a very favorable settlement from the weakest firm and then whipsaw this settlement into effect in all the others. The San Francisco Employers' Council is probably the outstanding example of an association combining the negotiation and administration of labor contracts.

PART TWO

The Labor Problems of Private Groups

SECTION D

Union-Employer Relations

CHAPTER 19

Collective Bargaining, Theory and Practice

A. THE NATURE AND EXTENT OF COLLECTIVE BARGAINING

In Section A of Part Two we discussed the basic needs and desires of workers as individuals, in terms of the specific problems they meet in trying to get and hold jobs. In Section B we dealt with unions as agencies for helping individual workers solve their problems. We saw that unions as entities have their own problems and that in order to solve them the unions have adopted certain organizational and governmental forms and certain policies in dealing with members, employers, and government. In Section C, we learned about management's problems in respect to employees and their unions, and we considered the organizational devices and the various attitudes and policies adopted for meeting these problems. The purpose of this concluding section of Part Two is to try to bring the problems of all three units and the policies of unions and management together into one structure of interaction and interrelationship.

1. Basic meaning of collective bargaining. From those earlier discussions we can see now that, broadly speaking, we have a sort of two-pronged vertical structure based on the workers. That is, at the bottom are the workers; and rising above them vertically we may visualize a House of Organized Labor and a House of Organized Management. The House of Labor is ruled by top officials elected by the workers as union members. The House of Management is ruled by top officials not elected by the workers but appointed by the officials themselves or by representatives of the stockholders. Thus, in theory, top union officialdom is responsible to the workers, but top management is not. However, in practice the relationship of the rulers in each House to the "subjects" is not too different. Top management knows that the workers are not slaves, particularly when organized in a union. Therefore, to achieve its own goals top management must in some significant degree be responsive to the workers and their desires. And union leaders, as we saw, manage to organize things so that they need not be too sensitive and responsive to the workers. The officers must of course "deliver"; but they lead and direct and are not usually driven by the members.

Within each House there is the need for the leaders to develop a hierarchy of roles and statuses, an adequate system of two-way communication, and an acceptable arrangement of rewards and penalties.

Now the fact that both Houses rest on the same foundation, the workers, creates difficulties and problems for each — and for the workers also. Each House (and its top officials) needs the loyalty of the workers if it is to prosper; hence there may be competition and conflict rather than cooperation and good will between the Houses. The workers conceivably could be torn apart mentally by the opposing pulls; but most of them avoid this unhappy result by giving the union most of their affection. This resolution of the dualism is not unnatural, for after all the union is the workers' own organization.

The fact that in the last analysis the union is the workers' own organization offers a solution of the possible conflict between the House of Management and the House of Labor. Management and the union may be able to adjust or accommodate themselves to each other in such a way that management directs the workers partly through and with the help of the union, while the union helps its member-workers and achieves its own goals as an entity because it is accepted as a limited partner.

In the broadest sense, *collective bargaining* is a term which may be used to describe this fundamental process of adjustment and accommodation between management and organized labor. Thus conceived, it embraces all the relationships between the two Houses within the area which both have agreed covers their direct, face-to-face dealings. It includes not only the periodic negotiation of new labor agreements or contracts but also all the day-by-day relationships between the parties to the agreement as they live under it, interpret it, and enforce it on themselves and on each other. In short, it covers the whole range of institutional, organized, direct relationships between the parties.

The phrase "collective bargaining" is supposed to have been used first near the close of the nineteenth century by Sidney and Beatrice Webb, noted analysts and chroniclers of the British labor movement. To them, it appears, the term had a narrower meaning than the one we have just formulated. The words meant pretty much what they said: "Bargaining" meant "trading," "haggling," or "negotiating" over the terms of employment. "Collective" was opposed to "individual." Presumably management is in any case a representative of collectively organized stockholders. (An employers' association is simply more "collective" on management's side.) But there can be no collective dealing or bargaining over the conditions of employment unless a firm's workers are organized in a union. Otherwise there is said to be only "individual bargaining." (Actually, except in the case of very scarce skilled workmen, there is no individual *bargaining* when employees are unorganized. When management sets the terms of employment unilaterally, a take-it-or-leave-it ultimatum is in effect handed to the workers. And they usually take it.)

a. Collective bargaining as joint determination of terms of employment. Since the Webbs' time, experience in their country, as well as in other democracies, including our own, has made it clear not only that a union is more than a cooperative marketing association organized by workers for the sale at higher prices of their labor services, but also that collective bargaining is more than a way of negotiating a contract covering the terms of such a sale. True, a union is in a sense such an association; and collective bargaining is in a sense a way of settling on a labor contract. (Under modern court and statutory law a breach of the terms of a labor contract by either party is actionable in a civil suit for damages.) But both are more. And there are important differences from other marketing associations and other contracts.

When a labor agreement is worked out between a firm and a union, the firm does not usually promise to buy a given quantity of labor-hours nor does the union guarantee to supply any given quantity. Furthermore, although in a sense the union acts as a sales agent for its members, the labor agreement binds any one member only if he and the firm agree (make an individual contract) that he shall work in the firm's plant. The worker is legally free to work for some other firm. The agreement does set the minimum terms of employment, and no unionist can work at the particular firm for less nor can the firm hire for less. But it is clear that the labor agreement is not like a contract for the sale of some non-human commodity.

b. Collective bargaining as a system of government. If it is granted that collective bargaining between a management and a union includes the negotiation of a contract which sets the terms of employment for the workers employed by the firm, yet is more than merely such a contract, in what terms shall the entire relationship be described and analyzed? Some authorities look on the relationship in governmental terms. They look on the relationship as a sharing of sovereignty, which involves application of the democratic principle of compromise. They see the labor agreement as a "constitution" which establishes and limits the authority and responsibility of each party, creates governing bodies (such as labor-management grievance committees), and provides for the interpretation and enforcement of such laws (e.g., shop rules) as the parties may mutually agree on. The governing bodies' decisions set up a cumulating body of labor law (industrial jurisprudence). This is a legislative function if the grievance committees' decisions supplement or add to the rules in the constitution. A judicial function is involved if these committees' decisions do nothing but interpret the provisions of the constitution or contract. Judicial interpretation also results from the decisions of neutral umpires or arbitrators on unsettled grievances if the constitution provides for such persons. The executive function is given to management, which has the right to initiate action on such matters as time-output standards and new incentive rates. But the right is limited by the labor agreement's constitutional system of checks and balances. The union has a veto right on many matters affecting the workers. That is, under the labor constitution's system of joint sovereignty, management's executive authority is subject to the legislative and judicial work of the joint grievance committees and the judicial decisions of neutral arbitrators if such exist.

c. Collective bargaining as a method of management. Another way of looking on the collective bargaining relationship is in terms of running a business, i.e., in terms of how the managerial function is exercised. When management recognizes a union, it knows that it is going to have to perform many of its managerial functions in respect to its workers through the union and jointly with the union. Collective bargaining may therefore be viewed as a method of labor management, a way of making managerial decisions on labor matters. Top labor policies are jointly decided during the periodic negotiations of the labor agreement. They are embodied in the agreement. But most agreements cannot possibly cover every little specific aspect of the day-to-day conduct of labor affairs in the plant. Like top unilateral managerial policies, labor agreements must be in rather general terms, leaving specific application, interpretation, and compliance in the hands either of those working at the lower levels, namely foremen and union stewards, or of those persons settling grievances at higher levels, such as arbitrators. This point of view helps one to understand how important the *spirit* of the relationship is and how much everything in the relationship depends on the attitudes and actions of lower-level personnel in day-to-day contracts.

d. Collective bargaining as a political struggle for power. Still another way of looking at collective bargaining is "political" (as distinguished from governmental). Organized management and organized labor are viewed as being involved in a struggle for power. But the validity of this view depends on how "power" and "struggle" are defined. In this and preceding chapters we have learned enough to know that the union-management relationship involves much more than the question of which House is to be the "boss" in the operations of a firm. This element is indeed present to some extent in respect to certain matters (like the disciplining of workers), especially if management's attitude toward the union is negative and defensive. But such a narrow definition of power cannot cover everything that happens in a truly cooperative relationship, where both parties think and act positively and constructively. Here power has to be defined broadly. It must mean more than an aggressive, conniving, ruthless drive for control. It covers all methods for achieving group objectives. Thus, if management's main goals are survival, prestige, and growth for its enterprise, it may well believe that the workers' cooperation is essential. Then if management's main labor goal is to enlist the cooperation of its employees, and if management believes that the best way of attaining this goal is to work through and with the union to help satisfy the workers' own needs, we may say broadly that management is striving for power. Similarly, if a union's objectives are satisfaction of wants for its members and survival, prestige, and growth for itself as an entity, and if the union believes that the best way of achieving these aims is to deal cooperatively with a positive-minded management, we may also say broadly that the union is striving for power. But each side may be "struggling" for power *with* rather than *against* the other.

e. Summary. Each of these points of view can contribute something to our understanding of what collective bargaining is and what it involves. It does involve the negotiation of a contract embracing the terms under which workers' labor services are bought and sold. It is a system of industrial democracy and government which goes far beyond such negotiations. It is a method of managing labor. And it does involve a struggle for power in which the parties struggle *against* each other in so far as their interests and objectives are divergent, and in which they struggle or work *with* each other in so far as their interests and objectives are the same. Let us always remember, however, that "collective bargaining" refers to the institutional organization of the whole range of direct relationships between management and union within the bargaining area or unit.

2. Human relations aspects of collective bargaining. *a. Principles of organization.* We have repeatedly emphasized that the effectiveness of any organization can be measured by the success with which (*a*) the roles and statuses of the individuals and sub-groups within the organization have been clearly defined and arranged in a hierarchy of authorities and commensurate responsibilities; (*b*) there is an open channel of communication from top to bottom whereby orders, suggestions, and information can be transmitted without distortion and without bypassing anyone (going over anybody's head) to successively lower levels of roles and statuses; (*c*) there is an equally open and no-bypass channel of upward communication for the transmittal of undistorted reports, suggestions, and information; and (*d*) there is a well-defined, acceptable system of rewards for good role performances and punishments for poor ones.

These standards apply to the management of a non-union firm and to the operation of a union separately. And when a firm has recognized a union, they also apply to the joint organization of management plus union, as well as (still) to the separate management and union organizations. On management's side, relations with the union will very probably be bad if, for example, top management bypasses and neglects middle management in dealing with foremen; or if top management fails to train middle management and foremen in the proper attitudes and techniques of handling labor matters; or if top management fails to encourage and heed suggestions from lower management; or if responsibility is delegated without sufficient authority; or if top management fails to administer rewards and penalties fairly for superior and inferior performance in applying such training in day-to-day labor relations. To give just one example, failure to instill foremen with the right attitude toward relations with unions or to train them in how to deal with union members and shop stewards is a frequent cause of wildcat strikes or production slowdowns.

On the union side, relations with management will probably be poor if the top officials fail to consult with the rank and file or to consider their expressed wishes, or permit the members to pressure top management directly (as in a mass demonstration before the front office), or fail to train shop stewards in proper attitudes and techniques, or neglect to inform the members of the progress of negotiations or the reasons for the settlement. To give one example, top union officers might settle with top management in an agreement wholly unacceptable (or "unsold") to the membership. The members might then openly revolt and refuse to live under the agreement or might indulge in undercover sabotage of the agreement.

As already stated, the same principles apply to the joint organization of management and union for the performance of their joint functions. The collective bargaining agreement and system of jurisprudence must clearly define the roles and statuses of workers, foremen, shop stewards, middle management, union grievance committee, top levels on each side, and arbitrators (if any) in respect to grievance settlement and other relationships. At each level, authority and responsibility must be clear and commensurate. The success of contract negotiations, as well as of grievance settlement, is often imperiled by an inadequate delegation of authority to the participants. Frequently both sets of negotiators are willing and able to reach a settlement but find it jeopardized by the necessity for referring the proposals back to respective higher authorities, who, being absent, have missed the attitudes and interactions leading to the proposed agreement. On the union side there is some reason for the necessity of referral: The union is supposed to be a democratic institution, and it may be proper to submit the tentative settlement to the members, even though they may reject it. But on the side of management it is hard to find rational justification for referral of the settlement by management negotiators to top management. Management, as previously noted, is essentially authoritarian in government and operation.

Not only must there be adequate two-way *vertical* communication within the House of Management and the House of Labor separately. There must also be proper two-way *horizontal* communication between the two Houses at all levels above the worker foundation. Foremen and shop stewards must have ready access to each other in the settlement of grievances. So must middle management and the union grievance committee. And so must top management and top unionists.

But what about a joint system of rewards and penalties; is such a thing possible or desirable? It is possible, of course. Management might sue the union for damages if the latter failed to perform its agreed-on role, e.g., broke a provision of the contract. Or management might cook up some excuse for firing a shop steward if he seemed to exceed his contract-designated authority. Or, on the union side, a shop steward might "discipline" a foreman for lack of cooperation or for favoritism by drowning him in a flood of spurious grievances. Or top union officials might tell the boys to go on a slowdown or a quickie strike to let top management know how dissatisfied the union was with management's performance. But all these unilateral actions are undesirable in terms of good labor relations. They make for antagonism and bitterness, for bad morale and inefficiency, for lack of cooperation. Co-partners or sovereigns should not try to discipline each other. Such efforts mean war. Peace is desirable. And peace can be achieved only if each side disciplines itself and jointly agrees on the discipline of poorly performing agents. Self-imposed discipline is the best kind in all relationships.

b. Attitudes. This brings us to the second element of human relations to be stressed here: the attitudes of the participants at all levels on both sides. As we saw in Sections B and C, the attitudes of each party dominate its own policies, tactics, and actions. We found a variety of union and management attitudes — and therefore a variety of policies and actions. We must now note here, in addition, that there is a pattern of interaction: Each side's attitudes and actions are importantly influenced by those of the other. Like begets like. It takes a real saint on either side to preserve unswervingly an attitude and policy of cooperation when the words and deeds of the other side are unpleasant and antagonistic. But if either party says, in effect, to the other, "I see what your problems are; let me see if I can help you solve them," and then acts in accordance with these sentiments, it is likely in the end to hear the same words back and get a reciprocal amount of helpful action.

This is one of the best results of a successful plan of what is known technically as union-management cooperation. The plan itself, i.e., the successful partnership, is a joint product beyond the reach of either side alone. Then, especially if it has received favorable publicity and social acclaim, each party is very proud of the program, gets a "kick" out of it, and is anxious to preserve it.

3. Essential economics of collective bargaining. *a. Economic versus human aspects.* As we said before, there is a mutuality of interests and objectives between management and labor. But this mutuality may not be complete; there may be a sizable area within which their interests are or appear to be in conflict. Thus, both parties wish the enterprise to remain solvent (survive) and to expand. But there may well be a difference of opinion about how low a level of wage rates is necessary for the attainment of this joint objective. Then "bargaining" must take place. And within the limits imposed by the law and by their own human attitudes toward their relationship, each side attempts to impose its will on — i.e., coerce — the other.

"Impose" and "coerce" are rather rough words. They imply the use of economic force, the threat of strike, and so on. But this does not rob of significance the things we have been saying about mutual good will and cooperation. Human nature being what it is, a little coercion is good for the soul. That is, each side respects the other in part because it is able to exercise coercion. And really good relations come to exist when each side, recognizing the power of the other to use force, refrains from doing so. Good relations between management and a union do not often exist when one side is much stronger than the other.

We are saying, then, as we did early in Chapter 14, that the ability to apply economic pressure is an integral part of collective bargaining. It helps resolve the issues in dispute. A strike is costly and burdensome to both sides. Normally, rather than undergo these costs, both parties are willing to effect a compromise.

b. A range for bargaining. To simplify our discussion of the basic economics of collective bargaining, suppose that the only issue in dispute is the union's demand for, say, a fifteen-cent wage-rate increase throughout the plant. Let us go back to our discussion of wage-rate determination in Chapter 8. There we distinguished three items — what an employer thinks he *has* to pay, what he thinks he is *able* to pay, and what he decides he is *willing* to pay. Let us further simplify by imagining that the firm hires only one grade of labor for one kind of job; that is, the wage rate for this grade of labor will be taken to represent the average or level of wage rates for all the various labor grades and jobs actually existing in the plant. Then in terms of a non-union firm, the wage rate the employer thinks he has to pay is governed mainly by his estimate of the conditions of labor supply facing his firm: How high a wage rate must I pay to get the quantity of labor-hours I must hire to produce the amount of output I expect to sell? Next, the wage rate the employer thinks he is able to pay is governed by his estimate of the average market worth of an hour of the labor input he expects to hire. This estimate is in turn based on three factors: (1) the employer's guess about the price he can get for the output of the product he expects to produce; (2) the employer's estimate of the average physical output of an hour of the expected labor-hours (input) to be hired, as determined by the production technique used in the plant; and (3) the prices of the productive factors that are complements to and substitutes for labor (e.g., raw materials and certain labor-saving machines). Given the preferences of consumers among various products, the estimated price of the product depends in large part on the degree of competition among firms selling the same or similar products. Clearly, as explained in Chapter 8, the lower the proportion of labor cost to total cost, the higher the wage rate the firm feels able to pay. When labor cost is a low percentage of total cost, there is a high capital investment per worker, and labor's average output and worth are high. And the prices of the other productive (non-human) factors depend on the degree of competition among the firms making these factors in relation to the degree of competition among the firms (including our firm) buying them.

In a non-union labor market the wage rate that the employer thinks he has to pay is usually lower than the rate he judges he is able to pay. In other words, there is a margin within which the employer may exercise discretion. This is where willingness comes in. The rate he is willing to pay, in the absence of a union, depends mainly on such non-economic things as his desire for social approbation.

When a union enters the picture, it has this margin between "must" and "able" to work on. It tries to get the wage rate raised up as high as possible toward the "able" level. (And its estimate of what the firm is able to pay may well be higher than the employer's own.) From the employer's standpoint, the union may affect all three of the items — what the employer has to pay, is able to pay, and is willing to pay. The union certainly changes the first; it raises the minimum rate below which the workers prefer not to work for the firm at all. If the union is a cooperative one, it may also increase the employer's ability to pay. It can do this if the members work harder, i.e., are more efficient, make good suggestions for technological improvements, or help with sales promotion and advertising. On the other hand a restrictive, non-cooperative union is likely to enforce rules which reduce the firm's ability to pay. Finally, as we shall see, the union is likely to raise the wage rate which management is willing to pay. The union's coercive power makes it costly for management not to yield to the union's demand.

The range between the minimum rate that the union will accept without striking and the maximum rate that the employer estimates he is able to pay (or decides he is willing to pay) normally affords leeway for collective bargaining between the parties. The union's minimum rate is determined by a number of conditions (both economic and non-economic), such as the members' notion of the rate necessary to produce an annual wage income which will provide the plane of living considered minimal; or the officers' notion of the minimum rate necessary to keep them in power; or the rate won by some other union's leaders. The employer's maximum rate may actually be his estimate of what he is able to pay. But lack of willingness based on one or more non-economic conditions, such as a dislike of unionism, may reduce the employer's maximum below the ability level. Such conditions, in other words, might cause him to prefer a work stoppage rather than pay as much as he thought he could afford.

c. The determination of the bargained rate. Let us suppose that, prior to the negotiation of the wage rate, a range does exist between the minimum the workers would accept if they were unorganized and the maximum rate the employer estimates and firmly believes he is able to pay. This range sets the limits within which a wage rate may be negotiated. Suppose the minimum is $1.20 per hour and the maximum is $1.60.

(1) Indeterminacy of precise result. But within these extreme limits, where will the rate actually be set? We do not know. The precise point is what we call *indeterminate.* It is indeterminate because some of the conditions affecting the result cannot be precisely measured.

In order to understand why this is so, as well as to understand how the rate does get set, let us follow through the main features of the negotiations or bargaining. The bargaining starts when one of the parties, usually the union, presents a "demand" to the other. The union will almost always ask for a wage rate higher than it really expects to get; in this case, let us assume that $1.70 is the rate demanded. The union expects to have to retreat, during the process of bargaining, from this "asking price" to some lower figure. Similarly the management in its "counter-demand" stipulates a rate considerably lower than the one it expects eventually to have to pay, let us say $1.10.

Here again we have a range. Which of the two ranges — the one between the workers' true minimum and the firm's true maximum, as previously described, or the one between the the two asking prices, as stated just above — is the range of indeterminacy? It seems better to consider the first range as representing the actual limits within which the rate will be negotiated. For they define the extreme limits of the union's willingness to accept and the firm's willingness to pay.

We are thus back once more to the question of *willingness.* During the negotiations the firm's problem is to induce the union to reduce the rate it is willing to take; and the union's problem is to get the firm to raise the rate it is willing to pay as high as possible toward the absolute top it thinks it is able to pay.

Two sets of conditions govern how successful each party is. We may label one the elements of bargaining *strength* or *position* and the other the elements of bargaining *skill.* The former conditions are in existence before the negotiations begin, although these conditions may of course change during the course of the bargaining. The elements of bargaining skill are employed during the bargaining.

(2) Bargaining strength. What are the elements of bargaining strength on each side? What conditions determine the parties' *relative* bargaining positions? Fundamentally, it is a matter of the number and importance of the employer's *alternatives* in relation to the number and importance of the union's. The employer's alternatives to yielding to the union include forcing the union into a strike; getting strikebreakers or nonunionists to man the jobs; getting government help in case of a strike; obtaining financial help in time of strike; getting other firms to fill his orders if there is a strike; enlisting public opinion against the union's demands; replacing labor that has become more expensive with machines that have become relatively less expensive (in case there is no strike);

leaving the locality for some lower wage, non-union area; and selling his present business and investing in a new one. The union's alternatives to yielding to the employer include enlisting public opinion in favor of its demands; going out on strike; obtaining financial help for members during the strike; obtaining jobs in other firms for members; and obtaining government support during the strike.

In building up to the negotiations, and perhaps during them, each side strives not only to improve its own bargaining position but also to worsen the other's. That is, it tries to increase the number and importance of its own alternatives while limiting those of its opponent. Thus, the union may present its demands at a time when its spies tell it the employer is in financial trouble with its bankers. It is prepared to throw picket lines around the plant in case of strike so as to bar the employer from getting non-union substitute labor. It may be ready to conduct a secondary boycott against the firm in the product market. It may try to obtain assurances that local or state police will not help the firm break the strike. And so on. The employer prepares appropriate counter-measures to bolster its relative position.

Some unions are in exceptionally strategic bargaining positions because of economic and technological conditions. The jobs their members fill are highly skilled and require long training. This makes it hard for the employer to get substitute non-union labor and, sometimes, substitute machines. Their jobs may be technologically in bottleneck positions; if the members strike, the whole plant must shut down. The industry they work in may also be a bottleneck one, like transportation. Thus, we find truck drivers, railroad train operating employees, building construction workers, coal miners and certain other skilled craftsmen with relatively high bargaining strength. On the other hand, the unions dealing with big corporations employing relatively unskilled men tend to have relatively low bargaining power.

(3) Bargaining skill. Given the relative bargaining strengths of the management and the union, the negotiations begin. Here is where relative bargaining skills become important too. The elements of bargaining skill stand first among the items that cannot be measured and that therefore make it impossible to know just what the negotiated wage rate, if any, will be. By bargaining skill we mean ability to endure the physical and nervous strains resulting from numerous long bargaining sessions on hotly disputed issues; finesse in discovering the bargaining strength (alternatives) of the other side, by use of spies, published information, or clever verbal sparring during the bargaining session; ability to hide one's own weaknesses from the other side; and ability to "bluff," i.e., to make the other side believe one's own alternatives are better than they really are.

(4) Settlement or work stoppage? As the negotiations proceed, the influences of both bargaining strength and bargaining skill are in operation. If the union's bargaining strength is superior to that of the employer, or if

its negotiators are better at wheedling, cajoling, bridling, yelling, pounding the table, and other tactics, they may be able to push the wage rate up close to what the employer thinks is the most he can afford to pay. That is, the union may drive his "willingness" rate up near his "ability" rate. And vice versa; the management may be able to beat the union down.

During the whole process each party is engaged in weighing as closely as possible the costs versus the utilities of each one of its alternatives. As the negotiations proceed, each side's estimates of those costs and utilities (disadvantages and advantages) may change, depending on its bargaining skill. The essential economic principles involved in the weighing of costs and utilities are those explained in Chapter 3, where we discussed the theory of choice. The main alternatives of the employer are accepting the union's best (to him) offer versus undergoing a work stoppage. He must estimate the advantages and disadvantages of acceptance and compare them with the advantages and disadvantages of a strike. If the net gain (utility minus cost) from the former is larger than from the latter, the employer will lean toward acceptance. If not, he will tend to reject the union's offer. The employer who has a relatively inelastic product demand in a monopolistic market, a low ratio of labor cost to total cost, and costly, inelastic supplies of substitute productive factors will tend to rate acceptance higher than an employer operating under opposite conditions.

Similarly, the union's main alternatives are accepting the employer's best (to it) offer versus calling a strike. The union, too, will be inclined to choose whichever course offers the greater net advantage.

In the great majority of collective dealings between firms and unions, there is a range which permits a rate to be negotiated. In almost all cases also, the negotiators will work out a compromise settlement which roughly reflects their relative bargaining strengths and skills.

Settlements in the real world are facilitated by the fact that there is usually not just a single wage rate to be negotiated, but instead several wage issues as well as a number of non-wage issues. When the wage rates for many jobs are debated, the employer can yield on one job rate in return for a concession by the union on another job rate. (This would not be true, of course, if only a general, across-the-board change in the wage rate were up for discussion.) Similarly, the employer can trade a concession on wage rates obtained from the union for some managerial concession on a non-wage issue, such as the union shop or seniority.

Sometimes, of course, there is no range within which a compromise can be negotiated. There are two sets of circumstances in which this can happen. Under the first, the very lowest rate that the union members can be persuaded to accept is higher than the employer's highest estimate of his ability to pay. This sort of situation might exist during a business depression, when the demand for the firm's product had fallen a great deal.

Or it might happen in "normal" times if the market in which the firm sold its product were severely competitive and product price were thereby driven down.

The second set of circumstances involves a clash of "willingness" rather than "abilities." So far as ability is concerned, a range exists. But the lowest rate the union negotiators are willing to accept is higher than the highest rate the management is willing to pay. Here the human and political factors loom large. The union leaders may be inhibited from making concessions because of the threat to their internal leadership raised by a strong minority faction which might use a poor settlement to turn the rank and file away from the existing leadership at the next election or even sooner, e.g., when the settlement is referred to the members for a vote of approval or disapproval. Or the union officers may believe they will lose face in the labor movement as a whole if they settle for anything less than what other leaders of rival unions have won.

On the firm's side, the management may also be stopped by non-economic circumstances from making economically rational concessions. It may hate unionism and think it can break the union by forcing a strike; here, too, the estimated utility of a strike stands high in relation to its estimated cost. Or it may think that concessions will cause it to lose face in polite managerial society. Or it may underestimate the strength and staying power of the union.

4. Determinants of collective bargaining relationships. From all that we have said thus far about the human-political and the economic-technological aspects of collective bargaining (as we have defined this term), we can proceed to a summary statement of the main conditions that determine the kind of collective relationship one finds in a given firm or industry.

Clearly the attitude and acts of government agencies are of prime importance, as we saw in Chapters 10 and 11 and will see even more fully in Chapter 24. The willingness of legislatures, executive and administrative agencies, and courts to help one side or the other (or both, as in mediation and fact-finding) limits or expands, as the case may be, the alternatives of the parties.

Given the attitude of government, we note next the attitudes of the parties themselves. Their attitudes influence the objectives they have set for themselves, their feelings toward each other, and their feelings about the kind of relationship they ought to have. Favorable attitudes alone cannot make a good relationship. But unfavorable attitudes can break one. This is just as true on the union's side as on management's. A union officialdom that is unbendingly aggressive or ideologically militant or crookedly racketeering can ruin any structure of cooperative relationship that friendly management might wish to create.

The "politics" or power structure and the organizational relationships within the House of Labor and the House of Management separately are significant determinants of the collective bargaining relationship, as we have just seen. The locus of authority and responsibility on either side, the nature of the communications system, and the nature of the rewards-penalties system can also make or break the relationship.

Equally important is the inter-group, union-management structure of organizational and power relationships. Here too the nature and adequacy of definitions of joint responsibility and authority, of intercommunication, and of self-discipline are of first-rate significance.

Economic and technological conditions combine to produce two kinds of situation. They may make for circumstances in which unionism is hard to bear for any one firm in an industry but is often ardently desired by the industry's employers as a group. Or they may produce situations in which unionism is relatively easy to tolerate in a single firm or in the entire industry. Here the human-political conditions, such as attitudes of management, are especially important; they may lead to a positive acceptance of unionism or to a negative policy of resistance. It is no accident that to date most of the examples of union-management cooperation have been found in firms who were at a competitive disadvantage in their product markets and whose production technologies were such that labor cost was a high percentage of total cost (i.e., capital investment per worker was low). If part of such an industry, such as hosiery, textiles, or work clothing, is non-union, the necessity for union-management cooperation is especially great. But such a relationship is not abandoned if all the firms become unionized. All of them hail the union as a stabilizing agency for "taking the competition out of wages" and making inter-firm labor cost differences much smaller. They do not quibble much about union encroachment on managerial prerogatives when a union like the Amalgamated Clothing Workers takes joint managerial responsibility to achieve such stabilization.

On the other hand, managements of firms operating in oligopolistic or monopolistic product markets and having production techniques which make for high capital investment per worker (relatively low percentages of labor cost to total cost) are under no particular economic or technological compulsion to accept unionism — unless some union is in a strategic bottleneck position (such as the Printers or the Stagehands or the Locomotive Engineers) or unless there is some special feature about the product, such as the high "perishability" of daily theatrical performances. (Theatrical producers and newspaper owners, believing that "the show must go on" or "the paper must come out," are very vulnerable to the demands of strategically placed unions and are inclined to have good relations with them.) In the absence of such special circumstances, firms selling their products under conditions of oligopoly or monopoly and buying labor that is mostly semi-skilled under conditions of oligopsony or monopsony, are in a position to take unionism or leave it. Such firms do not need unions in order to prosper. Therefore, much depends on the social conditioning and attitudes of their managers. Government may force them to take unionism; but their attitudes and policies toward it may still be negative.

5. Kinds of collective bargaining relationships. Our summary outline above and our previous fuller discussions of the determinants of collective bargaining give us a frame of reference or set of conceptual tools that can be used for studying and understanding the kinds of collective bargaining relationships that exist in various plants, companies, and industries. In so far as information exists, we shall try to use these tools in Chapter 21, where we tell the story of union-management relations in three specific situations.

At this point we may briefly describe several kinds of relationships that have developed in this country.[1] This classification brings together certain management types with certain union types. First we may note the relationship of *containment-aggression.* Here the union is the "aggressor." It is on the offensive to enlarge the scope of its control. It appears to demand successive "encroachments on managerial prerogatives." And management vigorously tries to resist these demands, to contain the union within what management believes are the proper, traditional bounds of union activity. Relations here are polite but not cordial. There is likely to be an excessively legalistic insistence on strict adherence to the letter of the agreement. But the spirit of mutual good will and friendly cooperation is conspicuously absent. This sort of relationship is to be found mostly among the large oligopolistic firms mentioned above, who are relatively new to union dealings and reluctant to enter into the collective relationship, though compelled by government and union pressure to do so. The relationships between the United Automobile Workers and the large automobile manufacturing corporations during the 1940's afford as good an example as any.

Second, we may note that certain of the collective bargaining newcomers among unions and corporations have managed to get beyond the relationship described above. They have accepted each other, have a healthy respect for each other, and have begun to try to live together amicably. An underlying spirit of cooperation, of trying to help solve each other's problems, is developing. The union is losing its fear that management would smash it if given a chance. Management is forgetting to be worried by the bogey that the union is trying to usurp its functions. This development represents a distinct shift away from aggression and resistance. We may call it *mutual accommodation.* A good example is to be found in the large companies in the glass industry, non-union before 1934.

[1] For a similar but more detailed classification of bargaining types, see B. M. Selekman, S. K. Selekman, and S. H. Fuller, *Problems in Labor Relations,* McGraw-Hill Book Co., Inc., New York, 1950, pp. 5–9.

Third, from this position the relationship may move into what we have been calling "technical" *union-management cooperation.* Anyone who is interested in the development of good labor relations but who is realistic should be willing to settle for mutual accommodation in the country as a whole. But union-management cooperation is even better, and there are enough examples of it to let one entertain the hope that it may be extended (without developing into the industrial syndicalism feared by some students). The danger of collusion is present, it is true. But such a development is by no means certain. And a watchful government could control it under the anti-trust laws.

We shall not repeat the details of union-management cooperation here. But we may note that economic necessity has been a powerful stimulus and that the collective bargaining relationship has usually been one of long standing. The best examples are to be found in highly competitive industries like clothing, where for decades the unions have been a constructive force.

A fourth kind of relationship may be called *power bargaining.* (Here "power" is more narrowly defined than earlier in the chapter.) It is perhaps best illustrated by the dealings of long standing between the coal companies' associations and the United Mine Workers and by those between the railroads and the train-operating Brotherhoods. "Power" bargaining stands midway between containment-aggression and mutual accommodation. The parties have come to accept each other and the relationship; there is nothing else to do. But the spirit of true cooperation seems to be lacking. Each side tries to extract from the other the last ounce of concession that economic-technological conditions and its strategic position permit.

If power bargaining is product-market-wide, i.e., if the union deals with an association of all the firms selling products in the market, and if these firms operate as a group monopoly in their product market, then power bargaining may also develop into or be part of *union-management collusion.* Here the interests of the consuming public are very likely to suffer. The demand for the firms' product is relatively inelastic. In this case, yielding to the union's demands may not be too expensive. Management knows that increased labor costs can be passed on to the consumers in the form of higher product prices without much loss (if any) in sales volume and profits. In return for concessions the union helps the employers restrict entry into the industry; the union makes it hard for new firms to get into the business. There is thus a double-barreled monopoly leveled at consumers. Such a relationship is said to have existed between the unions and the contractors in the construction industry of large cities.

It is much to be doubted that any actual real-life collective bargaining relationship in this country is a pure representative of any of the five types described above. A given relationship may have elements of two or more of the types. And it may change over time. Nevertheless, at any one time collective bargaining between a given union and a given company or industry is closer to any one of these types than to any other.

Our treatment of the nature of collective bargaining must not be permitted to close without heavy emphasis on this fact: In a country as large as this — with such diverse economic-technological and human-political conditions among firms, industries, and areas — each collective bargaining situation is in some respects unique. There are similarities. But there are also wide differences. Viewed as a whole, collective bargaining is a very complex, internally diverse institution.

6. Development and extent of collective bargaining. Workers form unions to deal collectively with their employers. From this one might suppose that collective bargaining in the United States is as old as the first local union, which, as noted in Chapter 10, was organized before 1800. One might also conclude that the history of unionism is in part a history of collective bargaining. But a moment's thought would lead one to doubt the validity of these conclusions. In terms of our definition, a *prime prerequisite* of collective bargaining is the *recognition of unions* by employers.

Now if employers refused to recognize the early unions there could have been no collective bargaining. The unions would have failed to gain their objectives. Furthermore, our definition means that there must be actual bargaining or negotiations over matters of concern to unions and employers. But if either party tried to impose its will unilaterally, without negotiation, then there was no true collective bargaining.

A study of the history of labor relations and unionism establishes the correctness of these last conclusions. Before the Civil War, when local or regional unions of shoemakers, carpenters, and printers were formed, employers usually organized to defeat them; recognition as we know it today was usually refused. But in the minority of cases where the unions were tolerated, there was still no bargaining: The unions presented their wage scale and other demands to the employers unilaterally; the employers had to take it or leave it. When a union demanded a wage rate of, say, 15 cents per hour, it meant just that figure; the 15 cents was not an asking price. There was thus no room for negotiation.

It was not until the 1860's that certain unions became convinced that this tactic was no way to win employers and influence the public. No one in a democracy likes to be the object of unilateral decree. So here and there, when the smart labor leaders presented demands to employers, they let it be known indirectly and subtly that these *were* asking prices subject to "talking it over." And wherever and whenever employers agreed to negotiate, there was true collective bargaining.

The really epoch-making event in the history of union-management bargaining came in 1891, when after some thirty years of intermittent conflict between the Molders and the firms in the stove foundry industry a national agreement was negotiated by the union and the employers' association and was reduced to writing. By the end of the century this example was followed in printing, construction, and coal mining.

Since 1900 the history of collective bargaining *has* been pretty much the story of the rise and fall and rise again of unionism and union strength. Once the pattern of recognition and negotiation (of grievances as well as contracts) had been set as the heart of collective bargaining, the latter waned and waxed with unionism. Therefore we need not repeat the recital of Chapters 10 and 11 here. We need merely remember the tremendous increase in collective bargaining and labor agreements since 1933; recall the data of Table 33 (page 211), which show the percentages of workers covered by such agreements in the various manufacturing industries; and note that the total number of agreements in 1951 has been variously estimated to be from 60,000 to 100,000.

B. THE SCOPE OF COLLECTIVE BARGAINING

By "scope" we mean what is covered in the relations between unions and employers. We shall accordingly deal here with two main topics: (1) the area of collective bargaining, and (2) the contents of the agreements arrived at through collective bargaining. The first has to do with the scope or coverage of the bargaining unit. Is it confined to a single craft, or does it embrace all the production workers? Is it confined to a single department or a single plant of a single company, or does it cover many plants of many companies? The second topic has to do with the subject matter or topics over which the union and the management in a given unit bargain — wage rates, work periods, and so on.

1. The area of the bargaining unit. By bargaining unit we mean the group of workers represented by negotiators at a collective bargaining conference with one or more employers and covered by the agreement worked out at such conference. Our interest here is in (*a*) the kinds of bargaining-unit areas; (*b*) the variety and range of areas existing in the United States today; and (*c*) the conditions that determine the area in any given situation.

a. Kinds of areas. There are two kinds of areas that one must bear in mind when he considers the scope of bargaining units. One has to do with the jurisdiction of the union and stems mainly from the wishes of the organized workers themselves. The other has to do with the size and scope of the business organization (or organizations) covered in the collective bargaining conference.

(1) Union jurisdictional area. As we know from our study of union structural types, union jurisdictions range from the narrow craft type to the all-inclusive industrial union. In any given firm a variety of bargaining units is possible. Consider a manufacturing company. The

broadest kind of bargaining unit would be one including all the firm's employees — not only the workers on the production line but also the maintenance crafts (painters, electricians, machinists, and so on), the "auxiliary" workers (truck drivers, power-plant employees, cafeteria workers, and so on), and the white-collar, office employees. But many firms deal with narrower units. Each maintenance craft and each group of auxiliary workers might have a separate bargaining unit if that is what the workers have voted for. The production-line employees and the office workers also might well be (and usually are, if the latter are unionized at all) in separate units.

All these things are true also of other kinds of enterprises, such as department stores, public utilities, railroads, and construction.

(2) Business organization area. The range in the size of the bargaining unit from the standpoint of the employer's organizational set-up is from a single shop in a single department of a single plant in a single firm to all the firms in a given product market (industry) in the country or all the firms in a given local labor market. Consider a company making steel forgings. It has, say, twenty plants. In each plant is a maintenance department. In each maintenance department is a tool-and-die shop; there the highly skilled workers make and repair the dies used in the forging machines. Now if these tool-and-die makers are organized in a separate union and bargain separately, plant by plant, with the respective plant managers, we have about as narrow and small a bargaining unit as can be found.

The next largest bargaining unit in this company would be a departmental one. For example, all the workers in the maintenance department of a given plant might be organized for bargaining purposes in a single group rather than in separate crafts.

Next suppose that in each of the twenty plants there is an all-inclusive industrial union. But each local plant union bargains separately with the management. This is the next largest bargaining unit. Then suppose that the same national union has an industrial local in each of the plants and that the firm agrees to bargain collectively with representatives of all the locals. This gives us the next largest area, which may be called a multi-plant, single-firm unit (or multi-plant, company-wide unit).

Beyond the confines of a single company we get into a number of situations. Here we have what is known as multi-employer bargaining. It is convenient to distinguish multi-employer bargaining based on product-market relations among the employers from that based on labor-market relations. In respect to the product market, employers may combine locally, regionally, or nationally to deal with a given union or group of unions. How wide the area is depends on the area of product-market competition. Thus, in the construction industry the product cannot normally be transported from one community to another; competition among contractors is local. Therefore, the contractors' association is local, the unions have a lot of local autonomy, and bargaining is on a local basis. Similarly with local trucking. On the other hand, as in the pottery industry, competition in the product market is nation-wide; and multi-employer bargaining with the Potters' union is on that basis.

In respect to local labor market conditions, multi-employer bargaining units often (but by no means always) transcend industrial lines of demarcation. The local employers' association in a large city usually includes firms or plants in many different industries. And sometimes these associations, as in San Francisco, bargain formally with various unions in behalf of the employer members recognizing the unions.

We see, then, that if we bring union jurisdiction together with employer organization an almost infinite variety of bargaining units is possible. And in point of fact an almost infinite variety exists in the country today.

In this connection we may also note that further variety obtains because of what may be termed "combination" bargaining arrangements. If there is multi-plant bargaining in a single large corporation, the large unit may negotiate only a master or general agreement, leaving subsidiary agreements to be negotiated locally in each plant on the details of labor relations and conditions peculiar to each plant. Similarly an employers' association in a given industry may work out a master agreement with one or more unions covering all the main, general labor matters of common concern. But special matters peculiar to each may be negotiated regionally or locally.

b. Bargaining arrangements in the United States since World War II. In Chapters 15 and 17 we reviewed the attitudes and arguments of unions and employers on the question of the proper scope of the bargaining unit, with special attention to the problem of multi-employer bargaining. Our concern here is with the kinds of bargaining units that have actually been worked out by agreement of unions and employers.

(1) The situation in 1950. As of 1950 we may distinguish the following bargaining-unit areas, all from the standpoint of employer organization: single plant, single-employer multi-plant, national multi-employer, regional multi-employer, and local multi-employer. The most significant measure of the importance of each of these units is relative number of workers covered. Data collected by the U. S. Bureau of Labor Statistics for 1950 provide the basis for the following tabulation:

Per cent of workers in		
Single-employer bargaining units, total	67	
Single plant		28
Multi-plant		39
Multi-employer units, total	33	
National		4
Regional		6
Local		23

It will be seen, then, that multi-employer bargaining covered one-third of the employees working under union agreements. Two-thirds were in single-company units. Of the former, the majority (70 per cent of 33 per cent) were in local multi-employer units. Only 6 per cent of the grand total (19 per cent of 33 per cent) were in multi-employer regional units, and only 4 per cent (11 per cent of 33 per cent) were under nation-wide multi-employer bargaining.

Of the employees working under single-employer bargaining units, 28 per cent of the grand total (42 per cent of 67 per cent) were in single-plant units and 39 per cent (58 per cent of 67 per cent) were in multi-plant units. Thus, multi-plant single-employer bargaining was the most important kind of all, in terms of percentage of workers covered.

There were marked geographical differences in the prevalence of multi-employer bargaining. In New England and the South fewer than 10 per cent of the bargaining units were of this sort. (The percentages of workers covered were probably even lower, but geographical data on this item are not available.) But on the Pacific Coast almost half (48 per cent) and in the Mountain states more than a fifth (22 per cent) of the bargaining units were multi-employer. It is also noteworthy that in at least seven western communities (Denver, Los Angeles, Phoenix, Reno, Sacramento, San Francisco, and Tacoma) the multi-employer bargaining embraced more than one industry; it was multi-industry.

There were also noteworthy differences between A.F.L. unions and C.I.O. unions. Multi-employer bargaining units were much more prevalent among the former; almost a third of the A.F.L. units were of this sort, compared to only 7 per cent for the C.I.O. Data on percentages of workers covered in the various kinds of bargaining units are not available for distinguishing A.F.L. from C.I.O. unions. However, the known C.I.O. strength in large-scale manufacturing and the known scope of the agreements made by its chief unions (such as the Steelworkers and the Automobile Workers) justify the conclusion that most of its membership works under single-employer multi-plant agreements. Similarly, there is reason for believing that most of the A.F.L. members are in single-employer single-plant bargaining units, with multi-employer units a close second, and multi-plant single-employer units a poor third.

It should be understood that all the above data are based on a *sample* of union-employer agreements rather than on all the 60,000–100,000 agreements believed to exist in the country. Whether the sample is truly representative of the much larger total is hard to say. It may well be that the data given above understate the relative importance of the single-plant single-employer kind of bargaining unit.

Table 36 presents 1950 figures by industries on three areas of bargaining units, from a sample of labor agreements studied by the Bureau of Labor Statistics. Employment data were available for more than two-thirds of the agreements. It will be seen that, in terms of workers covered, single-

TABLE 36 *Distribution of Agreements and Workers Covered, by Type of Bargaining Unit, 1950*

Industry	Agreements: Number	Agreements: Unit of Bargaining — Per Cent of Total: Single Plant	Multi-Plant	Multi-Employer	Number of Agreements with Employment Data Available	Workers Covered: Number	Workers Covered: Unit of Bargaining — Per Cent of Total: Single Plant	Multi-Plant	Multi-Employer
All industries: Total	3,376	68	12	20	2,460	4,408,000	28	39	33
Manufacturing: Total	2,454	81	8	11	1,888	3,031,400	36	44	20
Machinery (except electrical)	227	95	3	2	199	197,000	91	7	2
Fabricated metal products	272	92	4	4	174	134,000	68	21	11
Petroleum and coal products	53	92	6	2	42	42,000	73	27	—
Professional, scientific, and controlling instruments	31	90	7	3	27	23,100	88	11	1
Chemicals and allied products	157	89	8	3	110	92,400	60	34	6
Leather and leather goods	134	89	2	9	119	77,300	48	4	48
Paper and allied products	107	86	9	5	83	88,600	39	31	30
Rubber products	42	86	14	—	27	123,000	18	82	—
Transportation equipment	103	85	14	1	74	667,000	25	75	—
Textile mill products	196	84	11	5	181	227,000	50	29	21
Electrical machinery	90	82	15	3	78	214,000	41	26	33
Primary metal industries	195	80	13	7	142	453,700	18	73	9
Furniture; finished wood products	66	80	3	17	51	26,900	79	6	15
Stone, clay, and glass products	185	79	13	8	156	104,000	35	37	28
Lumber and timber basic products	71	78	7	15	62	40,500	36	6	58
Food and kindred products	225	65	11	24	154	163,000	39	43	18
Tobacco	23	65	26	9	19	32,700	23	58	19
Printing and publishing	107	51	3	46	58	27,000	35	2	63
Apparel and other finished textile mill products	105	36	11	53	76	272,000	3	5	92
Miscellaneous manufacturing [1]	65	77	5	18	56	26,200	73	8	19
Non-manufacturing: Total	922	37	21	42	572	1,376,600	9	29	62
Mining, crude petroleum and natural gas production	66	66	23	11	45	489,000	2	1	97
Transportation	212	50	14	36	125	194,000	31	7	62
Wholesale and retail trade	215	37	8	55	118	92,600	17	10	73
Services [2]	189	30	8	62	103	124,000	4	3	93
Utilities: Electric and gas	132	27	68	5	117	151,000	12	78	10
Communications	33	12	85	3	27	278,000	7	89	4
Miscellaneous nonmanufacturing [3]	75	21	—	79	37	48,000	4	—	96

Source: U. S. Bureau of Labor Statistics, *Monthly Labor Review*, Vol. 71, No. 6, December, 1950, p. 697.

[1] Includes jewelry and silverware, buttons, musical instruments, toys, athletic goods, ordnance, and ammunition.

[2] Includes financial, insurance, and other business services, personal services, hotels and restaurants, automobile repair shops, amusement and recreation establishments, and medical and other health services.

[3] Includes construction, farming, fishing, educational institutions, non-profit membership organizations, and governmental establishments.

plant single-employer bargaining predominated in eleven industries or industry groups; multi-plant single-employer bargaining in eight (rubber, transportation equipment, steel and other basic metals, glass and clay products, food, tobacco, utilities, and communications); and multi-employer in eight (lumber, printing and publishing, apparel, coal and other mining, transportation of various kinds, trade services, and miscellaneous non-manufacturing).

(2) The trend. Even during the comparatively short period from 1946 to 1950 there is evidence of an extension of the trend toward larger (particularly multi-employer) bargaining units. Data collected by the Bureau of Labor Statistics in 1946 show that only 27 per cent of the workers covered by union-employer agreements in that year were in multi-employer units. By 1950, as shown above, this percentage had risen to 33 per cent.

c. Determinants of bargaining-unit areas. We have noted a tremendous variety in bargaining-unit areas and a trend toward multi-employer ones. What are the conditions responsible for the variety and for the trend?

Let us first assume that government has no influence on these things. Then the scope of the bargaining unit, like other issues, is a matter for collective bargaining between and joint agreement by unions and employers. In previous chapters we have noted union attitudes and policies on this issue; and we have also noted those of employers. Earlier in this chapter we also reviewed the economic-technological and the human-political determinants of collective bargaining relationships in general. Our task here, then, is to bring these previous discussions together and highlight the particularly relevant points.

(1) Conditions making for multi-unit bargaining. It is desirable to distinguish two multi-unit bargaining situations: (*a*) where a union bargains with a single employer for most or all of his plants; and (*b*) where one or more unions deal with a number of employers.

(a) Single-employer multi-plant bargaining. A union and a multi-plant employer sometimes agree to negotiate at least a master agreement for all the plants operated by the employer because, in the first place, it is more convenient to do it that way. Both save time and money thereby. The best brains and top abilities on each side can be conserved and brought to focus on their respective problems in a broader perspective. Special local conditions can be handled in subsidiary local-plant agreements. If there were plant-by-plant bargaining, the main features of the agreement negotiated at the first plant would probably be incorporated in the other local agreements anyway. A further convenience arises if an arbitration arrangement for contract interpretation and last-step grievance settlement is desired by both parties; here it is much better to have the arbitrator set up and paid for under a master agreement. Finally, both employer and union are aware that there is likely to be less trouble from a rival union under a multi-plant agreement: The rival union would have to crack most

or all of the plants before it could convince the company that it merited consideration.

A second main reason for desiring a multi-plant unit stems from the desire of each side to increase its relative bargaining power. The employer often feels he can increase his bargaining strength and skill by agreeing to one over-all negotiation. Frequently under plant-by-plant dealings the national union will not permit its locals to deviate from the nationally decided demands. In effect, then, these demands are unilateral. And the employer is unable to win compromises or concessions on a local basis, as he might if he were negotiating a master agreement with the national officers themselves. Most unions do not object to the possibility of an improvement in the company's relative bargaining position if they can effect the above-mentioned savings; as a matter of fact, because of these savings the union actually does not lose much in bargaining position. Furthermore, one of the problems a union always faces in plant-by-plant dealings with a multi-unit company is to get to the fountainhead of managerial decision-making; bargaining with local plant managers is often frustrating because they lack ultimate authority to make concessions.

Third, we must note again the influences of economic conditions and of internal union politics. The union covers more than one company. One of its principles is inter-plant and inter-firm wage-rate uniformity for similar jobs. The political or human-relations reason for this is that uniformity appeals to the union members' notions of social equity. The economic reasons in respect to a single multi-plant company are two: first, to prevent competition among workers; and second, to facilitate the attainment of *inter-firm* wage-rate uniformity.

On the employer's side there may well be no objection to inter-plant wage-rate uniformity, unless the plants are located in widely separated communities having distinctly different wage-rate and other standards. A good many large firms with plants scattered all over the country paid uniform wage rates even before the advent of unions in these localities.

(b) Multi-employer bargaining. So far as convenience is concerned, most of the conditions listed above in respect to multi-plant bargaining have been operative also to promote the growth of multi-employer bargaining. The need and desire of small employers to raise their relative bargaining strengths and skills is considerably more of a factor here than in the multi-plant situation. As shown earlier, these employers, faced by strong national unions, have banded together for mutual assistance and protection, just like workers in their organizations. Again we find no objection from the unions.

Most important of all, however, is severe competition in the product market under technological conditions (low capital investment per worker) which make labor cost a high percentage of total cost. Under these conditions it is most difficult for the union to protect its members from wage-rate degradation unless it can deal with the employers as a group and obtain enforceable wage-rate uniformity. At the same time the employers in such industries welcome the union as a stabilizing agent able to mitigate the severity of competition in both product and labor markets.

Even in industries where oligopoly rather than keen competition prevails in the product market the small firms may wish to have industry-wide bargaining. In such industries there is often "pattern" bargaining; the union negotiates an agreement with a leading firm and then demands almost unilaterally that all other firms sign similar ones. This is a sort of left-handed industry-wide bargaining arrangement. Here the small firms may believe that they would have better representation and receive fuller consideration of their special problems if they were part of an industrial negotiating group facing the union at one time.

(2) Conditions working against multi-unit bargaining. But in such industries the big employers, as noted in Chapter 17, are unlikely to feel any economic compulsion toward a multi-employer bargaining unit. These are the firms that now for the most part oppose such relationships with the union. This attitude is not likely to change unless the greater convenience of group relations becomes more appealing or unless the union becomes so strong as to be able to dominate any one company and whipsaw greater concessions than could be obtained from united employers.

One obstacle to multi-employer bargaining in such industries is the difficulty of obtaining a united front. The smaller firms may feel it better to follow the pattern set by the big fellows than to be outvoted and ignored by these large companies in an employers' association. The large firms often wish to retain the prestige that goes with being a pattern-maker. The organizational problems are often imposing. As suggested by the defection of the Bethlehem Steel Company from the ranks of the basic steel industry during the strike called by the United Steelworkers in the fall of 1949, some industries would need almost a czar to achieve employer solidarity.

Two other obstacles in any industry, oligopolistic or competitive, are wide geographical dispersion of firms and plants and inter-firm differences in product-mix. The first not only makes it difficult to obtain cooperation and solidarity among firms because of differences in environmentally determined attitudes and policies (e.g., Northern versus Southern); it also may work against the development of anything but the most general kind of master agreement because of wide inter-regional differences in the supply and demand conditions operating the labor market (again the North and South afford a good example in many industries). The second obstacle — differences in the relative importances of the products made by firms in the same general industry — also tends to inhibit a united front in the same two ways. The markets for some of the products may be less competitive and more prosperous than those for the other products. Then the firms concentrating on the first kind of product may be more able and willing to pay a given level of wage rates asked by the union than the firms having an opposite sort of product-mix. This is what happened before the war in the West Coast pulp and paper industry. The pulp mills were much better off financially than the paper mills, and the regional multi-firm bargaining system broke down temporarily because only the companies concentrating on pulp felt that they could afford to meet the union's demands.

(3) *The attitude of government.* Now let us bring government into the picture. We must note at once that no government agency has anything direct to say about the area of the bargaining unit in cases where employers have been recognizing a given union for some time but fail to agree with the union on a change in the scope of the bargaining units. This issue is normally decided solely by collective bargaining. But, as we shall learn in Chapter 25, in two other kinds of cases the National Labor Relations Board is empowered under the National Labor Relations Act to decide how broad or how narrow the bargaining unit shall be. Suppose, first, that a given union, hitherto unrecognized by one or more employers in a given area or industry, has made progress in organizing the plants of the employer (or employers), asks for recognition, is refused, and then petitions the Board for an election to determine whether the employees of the firm (or firms) wish to be represented by the union. Before running the election the Board holds hearings on several matters, including the nature and size of the unit in which the votes shall be counted to learn whether a majority of the voting workers want the union. By its decision on this point the Board determines the size of the unit to be used for future collective bargaining in case the union wins. The same sort of thing happens in the second kind of case, namely, when rival unions dispute over the right to recognition and collective bargaining with the employer.

CHAPTER 20

Collective Bargaining, Theory and Practice (concluded)

B. THE SCOPE OF COLLECTIVE BARGAINING (concluded)

2. The content of agreements. We turn now to a brief consideration of the second main topic under our heading of the "scope" of collective bargaining. What subjects do we find included in the agreements negotiated by employers and unions? How much and what sort of items are covered under each topic? We learned in Section B what the unions want for themselves as entities and for the members as individuals. And in Section C we found out what management wants. What has collective bargaining between the two produced?

a. Classifying the content of agreements. There appear to be three main ways of arranging the topics covered in union-employer agreements. One is simply to list them pretty much as found in typical contracts. Most of them begin with some sort of preamble which names the parties, sets forth one or more "whereas-es," and says "now therefore the parties agree as follows." Then usually comes an article or section on union recognition, in which the company agrees to deal with the union as the exclusive agent for its members or for all employees in the bargaining unit as therein defined. Next come sections on management's rights, the union's rights, and promises that there shall be no strike or lockout during the life of the agreement. Frequently the next section deals with methods and procedures for the administration and interpretation of the contract and for the settlement of grievances arising under it. Then come major sections on wage rates and other items of compensation, on hours of work, and on working conditions and rules. There is also a lengthy statement of principles and procedures governing individual-employee job tenure. Other sections may deal with special matters peculiar to the plant, firm, or industry. At the end is usually a relatively short section setting forth the duration of the agreement and the provisions governing its re-opening, continuance, or termination.

The other two ways of arranging the topics of labor agreements are more meaningful because they subsume the above-mentioned subjects under significant main headings. Thus, a second method of classification divides the contract provisions into those having to do mainly with employees' wage rates and incomes and those concerned mainly with human relations between management and union, and management and employees. A third way of classifying topics in the contract is based on the group which derives chief benefit from a given section in the agreement — management, the union as an entity, or individual union members. Thus, the section on managerial prerogatives clearly is of chief value to the firm's management; the section on union security is mainly for the union as an entity; and such sections as those on wage rates, seniority, and grievance settlement may be considered to focus mostly on the welfare of individual union employees. All provisions of course affect all three groups to some extent.

Realizing full well that there is almost infinite variety among union-management contract provisions, let us briefly consider certain important provisions that are common to most of them. We shall deal first with wage and income matters, second with hours of work, third with union security provisions, fourth with worker security provisions, fifth with management security, and finally with grievance settlement.

b. Wage-rate and income provisions. As shown in previous chapters, unions and managements have certain policies on what the general job-rate level of the plant or firm or industry (depending on the scope of the bargaining unit) should be; on what the relationships should be among the rates for the different jobs or grades of jobs; on methods of wage-rate payment; on various supplementary or "fringe" wage items; and on guaranteed annual wage income. These are the wage matters that are bargained about. And, naturally, most of them are covered in union-management agreements.

(1) Systems of wage-rate payment. In industries where some kind of piece or incentive wage-rate system is feasible (see Chapter 18) probably about 30 per cent of unionized workers are paid on this basis. In other words, the unions under whose jurisdiction these workers come have agreed with management that, under appropriate safeguards, this system is acceptable. Among the major industries so covered are most of metal and coal mining, about 35 per cent of manufacturing, railroad train operation (in part), retail and wholesale selling (in part). The remainder of the workers are on time rates. Construction is an industry in which time rates are universal.

Among the agreements in which piece or incentive rates are approved, three main kinds of provisions are found. First, as in coal or glass, the actual schedule of rates is bargained out at the negotiations and is set forth in the agreement — either in the body thereof or in an appendix. Second, as in shoes and clothing, a procedure for joint union-management determination of the rates is spelled out in the contract, but the actual rates are usually not mentioned, being left for separate later determination. Third, as in steel, again the rates are usually not given as such; the rates in existence during the negotiation are presumed to continue in effect. But changes in such rates are left in the first instance to managerial discretion. That is, management is permitted to alter existing rates unilaterally, subject to later review or protest by the union under the grievance system.

Most union workers who are under time-rate systems are on single rates rather than rate ranges. Where the latter exist, progression from the minimum to the maximum of the range is about evenly divided between the merit basis and the automatic length-of-service basis. However, where agreements provide for merit progression, only a small minority leave it solely to managerial discretion. The others either permit managerial initiative, with review through the grievance procedure, or provide for joint union-management determination of the employees who are to receive merit increases. Still other agreements establish a combination of merit and automatic progression, such as automatic to the midpoint of the range and merit progression thereafter.

(2) The general level of wage rates. Of all the wage items in the agreement (and probably of all the items as a whole) the general level of rates for all the jobs is usually the most important single matter to be negotiated. We have previously seen that over a period of several years it is possible to whipsaw the general level upward by raising first the rates for one or more grades of jobs and later raising the rates for other grades. We have also seen that a job evaluation plan can be used to accomplish the same result. But usually the general level is changed by an across-the-board increase or decrease which is the same for all the job rates.

Across-the-board changes may take one of two forms: Each job rate may be changed by the same number of cents per hour; or each may be changed by the same percentage. Under the former method the *cents* differentials among the various job rates are preserved. Under the second, the *percentage* differentials among the job rates are maintained. In different words, a general wage-rate increase in cents per hour narrows the percentage differentials between the rates for skilled jobs and those for less skilled jobs, thus worsening the relative position of the skilled workers. On the other hand, a general rise of a given percentage (say 15 per cent) preserves the relative positions of all workers while widening the cents differentials among their job rates.

Before World War II most wage-rate changes, up or down, were in percentage terms. During the war, however, under the War Labor Board's wage stabilization program the relatively modest general increases that were allowed were granted in terms of cents per hour. During the postwar inflationary years until 1950 most general increases continued to be agreed on in the cents form. However, the skilled union members began to protest against this system, and in that year and thereafter many unions negotiated increases either in straight percentage terms or in cents terms with special, additional raises for the skilled groups.

In 1950, in a sample of 2754 agreements studied by the Bureau of Labor Statistics,[1] 55 per cent (1517 contracts), covering almost two-thirds of the workers under the agreements, provided for a re-opening of the agreements during their life for negotiation of new general wage-rate levels or for automatic changes therein (see below).

(a) Pattern increases. Two main conditions — the widespread growth of unionism after 1935 and the rapid rises in the cost of living after government price and wage-rate controls were removed in 1945–46 — were responsible for a series or number of "rounds" of wage-rate increases after World War II. A large, powerful union (such as the Mine Workers or the Steelworkers or the Automobile Workers) would negotiate, with or without a strike and government intervention, a general wage-rate increase with a basic or important industry or key corporation therein. This agreement then became the "pattern" for a whole "round" of similar increases negotiated with other firms and industries. To be sure, certain firms or certain industries might deviate from the pattern to some extent, depending on special circumstances such as a fall in money demand for the particular product or products of the firm or industry. But the existence of a pattern during each of five or six rounds by 1952 was plainly to be seen.

Whether this sort of thing would continue under generally stable but non-inflationary economic conditions is a hard question to answer. Then differences in the wage-paying abilities of different firms and industries might well begin to reassert their influences and cause wage-rate changes of varying amounts to be negotiated by different unions. On the other hand the human or political consideration of maintaining equities among various groups of workers through fairly uniform changes in rates might take precedence over economic considerations.

To whatever extent key bargains on wage rates do continue to develop into patterns, there will be, as there has been since 1945, a centralization of the real collective bargaining function on the wage-rate item in the hands of the top leaders of the big unions. Several interesting consequences flow out of this leadership. For one thing, on the union side it tends to reduce rank-and-file participation and control in the formulation of demands and in the negotiation and approval of agreements. For another, it tends to increase the rivalry among and the prestige drives of the top officials of the big unions. Third, it tends to reduce the area of compromise and the practice of collective bargaining among firms dealing with lesser unions. Real bargaining and compromise in these cases tend to be found mainly in respect to matters other than wage rates and incomes. (But bargaining on these other matters may also be significantly affected by what happens in the big key negotiations.) Fourth, it exerts some pressure toward the formation of multi-employer bargaining units;

[1] *Labor-Management Contract Provisions,* 1949–50, Bulletin 1022, Washington, 1951, pp. 28–29.

even big firms may be moved to band together in order to meet the big industry-wide union on more favorable terms.

Most important of all, however, the key bargains tend to decide what the national policy on wage rates shall be. This is a development of tremendous import. When the Steelworkers and the basic steel corporations appeared before the Presidential board mentioned early in Chapter 1 and argued the merits of their unsettled dispute over the union's demand for a general wage-rate increase of 12½ cents per hour, a major portion of their arguments dealt with the alleged effects that this increase would have on *the economy as a whole.* And the board, as a temporary agency of government, knew that its recommendations, if accepted by the parties, would very probably set the pattern on the disputed issues for that year (1949) and possibly for years to come. In short, if the parties had themselves negotiated a settlement without recourse to government, they would have established a national 1949 policy on wage rates (and industrial pensions and health plans); and, failing to agree bilaterally, they came in time to accept the recommendations of a government agency which perforce had to determine a national policy for that year.

Thus, key bargains which set a pattern of settlement for lesser firms, industries, and unions place an enormous responsibility on those who negotiate the key agreements. Inevitably these men must take an economy-wide perspective. And inevitably certain basic questions arise, such as, Can collective bargaining successfully stand the strain imposed by these circumstances? Will the end product be bargaining on fundamental issues between representatives of a master association of employers and representatives of a united federation of labor? Can government stand by for long without taking a hand in such bargaining in order to protect the public interest? In short, into what kind of political economy will pattern bargaining in time lead us if it continues, as it may well do?

(b) "Escalator" wage-rate increases. In Chapter 15 we saw that one of the arguments used by unions to justify or rationalize demands for wage-rate increases during times of price inflation is the increase in the cost of living. The least that unions are willing to accept during such periods is *maintenance of real wage rates.* They argue as follows: Although an increase in wage rates made on this basis may lead to further price inflation or cost-of-living increases (thus causing further wage-rate increases and still more price inflation, on and on), considerations of social equity require that workers be allowed to preserve their living planes and relative income positions.

In 1948 one of the largest and most successful of all American corporations — General Motors — decided to agree with this union argument and to embody in a two-year contract with the Automobile Workers the principle which it expresses. In 1950 the new, epoch-making five-year agreement between the parties reaffirmed the principle and its operation. Henceforth, in general terms, the union members' wage rates were to be raised (or lowered) across the board in accordance with increases (or decreases) in the cost of living. In specific terms, wage rates were to be adjusted every three months on the following basis: a change of one cent for every change of 1.14 *points* in the Bureau of Labor Statistics Consumers' Price Index. The ratio of 1:1.14 was based on the relationship between the Index on April 15, 1948, to the average hourly earnings of G.M. workers in May of that year. The Index in April stood at 169.3 and the average rate stood at $1.485 in May, 1948. Then 169.3 points divided by 148.5 cents equals 1.14 points for each cent. Suppose that thereafter the cost of living had risen by 10 per cent; that is, the Index had gone up by 16.93 points. Dividing 16.93 points by 1.14 points gives 14.85 cents, the amount by which wage rates would then have gone up under the agreement. This increase, which is obviously 10 per cent of the previous average hourly wage rate, keeps the workers, on the average, abreast of the rise in the cost of living.

Since 1948, but particularly since the 1950 agreement, many other firms and unions have emulated the G.M.-U.A.W. example. In other words, these key bargains led to a "pattern." Some of the other contracts took over the G.M. ratio between the Index-change and wage-rate-change. Others adopted the simpler formula of a one-cent wage-rate increase for each one-point rise in the Index, thus raising wage rates by a higher percentage than the rise in the C.P.I. Others more properly worked out their own ratio based on the relation between their own average hourly earnings and the number of Index points as of their own base date.

By no means all union-management agreements contained escalator clauses. As a matter of fact, according to the B.L.S. survey cited above (page 522), only 4 per cent of the 1517 agreements permitting changes in the wage-rate level during the life of the contract provided for automatic escalator increases. The others merely established the right of union or management to re-open the wage-rate-level provisions during the life of the contract. But the firms having escalation were large ones: Of all the workers covered by the 1517 agreements permitting interim changes, 45 per cent were subject to automatic or escalator wage-rate advances. And by 1952 the number of workers under such clauses must have risen a great deal. Thus, by May, 1951, about one million railroad unionists had been brought under an escalation contract signed by 15 unions with the railroads.

(c) "Improvement factor" wage-rate increases. The agreements of 1948 and 1950 between G.M. and the U.A.W. contained one other notable path-breaking provision on wage-rate increases which also appeared by 1952 to be setting something of a pattern. This provision again meant giving concrete expression to a principle of wage-rate determination argued by unions and many employers alike for several decades. The principle can be stated in two ways, both amounting to the same thing: (*i*) Wage rates (actually *real* wage rates) should be based on ability to

pay. (*ii*) Workers should obtain a proper share of the higher per-capita real income made possible by economic progress (net capital formation and technological advance). In other words, not only should workers' real wage rates be *maintained* by increasing money rates in pace with rises in living costs; real wage rates should also be raised in pace with increases in average man-hour productivity.

Specifically, the 1948 G.M. contract provided for an annual automatic raise of three cents per hour as an "improvement factor"—i.e., in recognition of the improvement in output per labor-hour due to the two main elements of economic progress. The 1950 agreement raised this annual increase to four cents.

Where did the three and four cents come from? Why were these particular amounts chosen rather than others? They represent roughly 2 to 2½ per cent of the average hourly earnings of G.M. workers. And the 2 to 2½ per cent is a fairly conservative estimate of the average annual increase in national man-hour productivity over a period of several decades. In other words, these per cents represent the estimated increase in the ability of *the economy as a whole* to pay higher real wage rates.

Note that last sentence carefully. The 2 to 2½ per cent does not indicate G.M.'s increased man-hour productivity or ability to pay higher real wage rates every year. It applies to the average of the whole economy of millions of firms and scores of industries.

But why shouldn't the General Motors agreement have focused on G.M.'s ability to pay rather than on the whole economy's? The chain of reasoning is as follows: Productivity gains (increased ability to provide higher returns) may be distributed in a number of ways. (*i*) Workers may be given an increase in money wage rates which is higher than the increase (if any) in the cost of living. (*ii*) Consumers (who of course include workers) may benefit in the form of lower product prices (decreased cost of living), with no change in money rates of income; improved quality of products (better products at the same prices); or both. (*iii*) The owners of firms may benefit through higher rates of profit on their capital investments. Now suppose that G.M. is an especially profitable firm, which it is. If wage-rate increases for G.M. workers were geared solely to increases in G.M.'s productivity and profitability, which are higher than the national average, G.M.'s customers and stockholders would receive substantially smaller shares thereof. Consumers would have less incentive to buy General Motors automobiles. Stockholders would have less incentive to maintain and increase their investment in the corporation. Management would have less incentive to make further increases in G.M.'s productivity and profitability. G.M.'s workers in the end, as a group, might be worse off because of a decrease in the company's ability to pay higher wage rates and provide high employment.

According to the United States Bureau of Labor Statistics, in 1951 more than 1,000,000 unionists were covered by collective bargaining agreements which included wage-rate increases based on an annual improvement or productivity factor.

(3) Intra-plant wage-rate relationships. So much for bargained changes in a plant's or firm's or industry's general level of wage rates. What do we find in union-management contracts about the relationships among the rates attached to the different jobs or grades of jobs within a given plant?

Whether the plant pays rates on a time or incentive basis, many agreements set forth the various rates in the body of the agreement or in an attached appendix. How are these worked out, apart from any across-the-board change in all the rates? There are three main negotiation approaches: Only a few rates may be dealt with when the contract is worked out, the other relationships remaining as under the previous agreement. Or all the rates may be established during the negotiations. Or, because in most cases the latter procedure is a very time-consuming one, the agreement may simply set forth general principles to govern the later determination of the various job rates. In this instance — for example, in the application of a job-evaluation system — the agreement either states that the rates shall be jointly determined by a union-management committee, or gives management the right to initiate the rates and relationships unilaterally, with any union objections to be handled under the grievance procedure.

(4) Supplementary or "fringe" compensation items. A considerable number of bargained labor contract provisions deal with other wage-rate and income matters. We have space for only a brief summary here.

(a) Premium rates of pay for overtime. The oldest "fringe" item, dating far back into the nineteenth century, concerns penalty rates for working employees longer than the standard, agreed-on number of hours per day or per week or than the standard, agreed-on weekly work-days. Today almost all labor agreements provide for daily overtime premiums; at least three-fourths provide for weekly overtime premiums; almost half penalize Saturday work with a premium pay rate; about two-thirds penalize Sunday work; and in cases where the technological nature of the production process (as in basic steel) makes Saturday or Sunday work unavoidable, there are similar premium penalties against a firm's using men on the sixth or seventh day of a work-week of consecutive days.

The usual agreed-on premium rates are time-and-half for hours worked in excess of eight per day, hours worked above forty per week, Saturday work as such, and sixth-day work in a work-week; and double time for Sunday work as such and seventh-day work in a work-week.

The computation of the "regular" rate of pay on the basis of which the premiums are paid is extremely complicated, whether workers are on time or incentive rates. It might seem that the regular rate is merely the agreed-on hourly rate in the case of time workers or the average hourly earnings (total earnings divided by total hours worked per day or week) in the case of incentive workers. But, as we shall see, union workers are often paid for time not worked. Shall this pay and these hours be included in the computation? They are also granted sick leave and other time off without pay. Shall these hours be counted in dividing earnings by hours? Union agreements often have many paragraphs covering such matters in detail.

One other kind of provision should be noted. Suppose an agreement states that premium rates shall be paid daily for hours over eight and for weekly hours above forty. Suppose then that an employee works ten hours on Monday and eight hours the other four days, making forty-two for the week. Is he entitled to overtime on two hours twice? Or suppose he works ten hours on Monday, twelve hours on Tuesday, eight on Wednesday and Thursday, and six on Friday. On a daily basis he has six hours of overtime, on a weekly basis four. Does he get premium pay for ten hours, six, or four? Most agreements try to avoid the "pyramiding" of overtime. In the first case the worker would receive premium for only two hours, not four. In the second case, the usual provision would give him either the daily *or* the weekly overtime, whichever is greater, but not both. In other words, he would be credited with six overtime hours.

(b) Vacations and holidays with pay. During the past decade vacations and holidays with pay have become standard in the great majority of union-management contracts. In 1949 the above-cited study of the B.L.S. found that 93 per cent of the agreements in the sample analyzed provided for paid vacations and 73 per cent stipulated paid holidays. This development was greatly stimulated during World War II, when such "fringe" items were a way (approved by the War Labor Board) of extracting as much as possible out of the wage stabilization program.

The usual vacation plan varies the length of the paid vacation with the unionist's length of service. Typically, one week of vacation is given to workers having one year of service and two weeks to those with five years' service. Some plans are even more liberal, providing three or four weeks to employees of ten, fifteen, or twenty years' service. The trend is toward increasing vacation time and reducing length-of-service requirements.

The amount of pay received per week by a given worker during his vacation period is ordinarily calculated by multiplying his average straight-time hourly earnings for the preceding two or three months by the standard number of hours in the work-week or by the average number of hours worked by him per week during the previous two or three months. Sometimes a minimum and maximum number of weekly hours is stipulated.

Sixty per cent of the agreements studied by the B.L.S. provided six national holidays with pay. The range was from one holiday to ten. The pay on each holiday is for the standard number of daily hours multiplied by the worker's existing standard hourly rate or average straight-time hourly earnings. Most agreements also provide that, if for any reason, e.g., an emergency, the firm requires a worker to be on duty during these holidays, he shall be paid at double (sometimes triple) his regular wage rate.

(c) Special wage-rate differentials. Agreements often have a variety of clauses providing special wage rates for special groups of workers. The most common of these is the *shift differential,* which also received great stimulus during the war. Some industries, like basic steel and petroleum refining, operate continuously — twenty-four hours a day and seven days a week — because of technological conditions. Here each worker labors a forty-hour week. But he may be on the day shift one week, the early night shift the next week, and the "graveyard" shift the third week. (He also may rotate his days of the week during the process; i.e., each worker may get some Saturday and Sunday work in his work-week of forty hours from time to time.) In prosperous times other industries, like cotton textiles, may put on an extra shift or two at night. Whatever the industry, night work is not considered desirable by most employees. They demand extra pay for undergoing the inconvenience. And most employers have agreed to pay premium wage rates for the late shifts. These premiums vary mainly from three to six cents per hour for the second shift and from five to twelve cents for the third. Four-eight and five-ten are the most usual.

Firms and unions sometimes agree on special rates for particularly dangerous or unpleasant work. Most contracts specify no wage-rate discrimination based on race or sex; however, the union sometimes agrees that, if a female employee on a given job is not able to produce according to standard, a special rate may be negotiated for her. Unions also often agree that substandard rates may be paid to learners and to handicapped, temporary, or part-time workers.

(d) Payments for time not worked other than vacations and holidays. By this we mean not only the kind of thing typified by the Musicians' successful demand for stand-by crews in radio broadcasting stations (Chapter 14) but also such items as those mentioned on pages 377–78. In respect to *call-back pay,* the guaranteed-pay range in union-management agreements for workers recalled for work after their regular shifts is from two to six or eight hours, with four hours of pay the most common. For *call-in pay* the range is similar; and again four hours is the most usual. In addition to this sort of provision, many contracts provide for paid wash-up or clean-up time, tool-care time, paid lunch periods, paid rest periods, paid grievance-settlement time, and paid down time (minimum pay for the time during which a worker's machine is "down" — i.e., not operating — for any reason). In a few industries, notably coal mining, metal mining (mainly copper), and logging, employers have also agreed to pay employees for time spent in traveling from the entrance of the

plant to the place of work. Travel or portal-to-portal pay would undoubtedly be much more prevalent today if the Congress in 1947 had not passed the Portal-to-Portal Act relieving employers of the statutory obligation to include travel time in their computation of hours worked for the purpose of determining whether premium overtime payments should be made under the requirements of the federal Fair Labor Standards Act.

(e) Dismissal or severance compensation. Severance pay, long demanded by numerous unions, has thus far not become a common provision in American labor agreements. In the previously cited 1949 study of the Bureau of Labor Statistics, only about eight per cent of the 2100 agreements in the sample were found to have formal provisions guaranteeing minimum amounts of pay for workers permanently laid off through no fault of their own (e.g., by labor-saving machinery). However, this percentage was twice as high as that found in a similar B.L.S. study five years earlier. Most of the agreements were in the rubber, printing, railroad, and communications industries. Almost all the agreements specified lump-sum payments, and most of them varied the amounts of the payments in accordance with employees' previous lengths of service.

(f) Negotiated welfare and pension plans. In the field of supplementary compensation no recent development in collective bargaining has been of greater significance than the successful postwar demands of unions for employers' contributions to private funds out of which pensions and medical benefits are paid under stipulated conditions to employees of the companies.

i. Development of the movement. We have noted previously that a good many unions had their own old-age benefit plans for several decades, a few also providing medical benefits; that a number of the larger corporations installed pension and group insurance plans during the twenties; and that the inadequacy of benefits and the insufficiency of coverage under both these kinds of plans led in the thirties to a successful movement for government action in the pension field and an unsuccessful demand for government action in the health field.

During the 1940's several circumstances combined to produce the union drive for employer-financed company pension and medical or "welfare" plans. Fundamental, of course, was the desire of individual union members, particularly the older ones, for financial security after retirement, usually at the age of 65. Another factor was the rivalry among the leaders of the big national unions for the prestige of obtaining the most for their own memberships. In 1944 James Petrillo, head of the Musicians' union, obtained War Labor Board approval of his proposal that a "welfare" fund, mainly for unemployed musicians, be built up by a "royalty" on each phonograph record sold by the record-producing companies. In 1946 John L. Lewis of the Mine Workers obtained from the federal government, which had temporarily taken over the coal mines to keep them operating during the union's dispute with the private owners, an agreement to develop a "welfare" fund for the payment of pensions and medical benefits from a royalty on each ton of coal mined. Naturally most other outstanding labor leaders were moved to emulate these successes.

Two other wartime conditions played an important part in the development of welfare and pension plans. For one thing, the direct wage-rate controls exercised by the War Labor Board during the war led to union pressure for "fringe" benefits of various kinds as a way of obtaining increased compensation for members beyond the amounts permissible in the form of wage-rate increases. Pensions and medical benefits were among these fringe items. Employers themselves, with or without unions, were for the most part not loath to introduce such plans, for they needed to hold existing workers and attract new ones in a very tight labor market; and at that time they did not greatly mind incurring increased labor costs because the government's excess profits tax took away all net revenue (gross revenue minus total costs) above a certain percentage anyway; and in any case, many firms had cost-plus contracts for producing war goods for the government. The second wartime factor that encouraged negotiated welfare and pension plans was price inflation. There was some price inflation during the war and a great deal in the postwar years, when the controls were removed. The increases in the cost of living made the benefit payments under the federal government's Old-Age and Survivors' Insurance plan inadequate. Yet even by 1949 the Congress had failed to amend the Social Security Act so as to increase these benefits.

Still another circumstance aiding the unions' private pension drive was the series of decisions of the National Labor Relations Board from 1947 to 1949 (upheld in the courts) that pensions and welfare payments are a part of "wages" under the National Labor Relations Act and as such are properly the subject of collective bargaining. That is, if unions include these items in their demands, employers are obligated to bargain about them. Most of the labor organizations spearheading the movement for company pension and welfare plans were either independent, such as the Mine Workers, or affiliated with the C.I.O., such as the Automobile Workers and the Steelworkers, rather than with the A.F.L. The success of the Steelworkers in obtaining from the fact-finding board mentioned early in Chapter 1 a recommendation that the steel corporations negotiate such plans with the union was the final factor leading to their widespread adoption in a number of industries.

A statistical story of the growth of private pension plans is presented in Table 37. The two great spurts in the number of plans will be observed in the 1945 and 1950 figures of column 2. Whereas before World War II the great majority of the workers covered by such programs were in companies that had installed the plans unilaterally, by 1950 about 60 per cent of the workers under private pensions (columns 3–5) were in companies that had either bargained the plans with unions initially or had modified their own pre-union plans as a result of bargaining with the union.

TABLE 37 *Approximate Number of Private Industrial Pension Plans and Number of Workers Covered in the United States, 1900–1950*

Year	Number of Private Plans	Number of Workers Covered by Private Industrial Plans			Number of Workers Receiving Monthly Benefits from Employer
		Total	Collectively Bargained	Employer Controlled	
1900	12				
1910	60				
1920	270	3,000,000			
1930	420	3,500,000			140,000
1932	430	4,000,000			
1935	750				
1937		3,000,000			175,000
1945	6,860		500,000		
1946		3,700,000			
1948			1,650,000		
1949	9,000	7,500,000			300,000
1950	14,000	8,500,000	5,123,000	3,377,000	

Sources: M. W. Latimer, *Industrial Pension Systems in the United States and Canada*, Industrial Relations Counselors Inc., New York, 1933; Social Security Board, *Social Security in America*, p. 172; Federal Reserve Bank of Chicago, *Business Conditions*, September, 1950, p. 5; Marjorie Shearon, "Economic Status of the Aged," *Social Security Bulletin*, March and August, 1938, as adapted by Domenico Gagliardo, *American Social Insurance*, 1949, p. 45; Robert M. Ball, "Pension Plans Under Collective Bargaining: An Evaluation of Their Social Utility," *Proceedings*, Industrial Relations Research Association, December 29–30, 1950, p. 127; Sumner H. Slichter, "The Pressing Problem of Old Age Security," *New York Times*, October 16, 1949; Actuary, Social Security Administration, Federal Security Agency; U. S. Bureau of Labor Statistics, Release of December 29, 1950; U. S. Bureau of Internal Revenue, Release of August 31, 1946.

Data not available for spaces in lines and columns left blank.

Of the 5.1 million workers covered by collectively bargained private pension systems in 1950, about 55 per cent were in C.I.O. unions, about 25 per cent in A.F.L. unions, and about 20 per cent in unaffiliated unions. The railway organizations have been covered by a special government retirement-benefit program since 1937 (see Chapter 23).

The same general trend exists for medical benefit plans. Although the majority of workers covered by such plans are under non-bargained programs, the percentage of employees under bargained plans has been rising. More than 7 million workers were under bargained plans in 1950. Of these, about 50 per cent were in C.I.O. unions, 30 per cent in A.F.L. unions, and 20 per cent in unaffiliated unions. Most of the workers covered by bargained private pension and welfare (medical benefit) plans in 1950 were found in manufacturing. Second in importance came transportation (excluding railroads), communication, and public utilities. Third in coverage was mining (coal and metal) and quarrying. Among the manufacturing industries the metal products group (basic steel, automobiles, machinery, and so on) stood out, followed by textiles, apparel, and leather products. The percentages of workers covered were highest in metal products, mining, transportation and communication, paper and allied products, petroleum products, chemicals, and rubber.

ii. Main characteristics. What were the main features of the bargained pension and medical benefit plans? As to *the source of payments into the funds*, about 75 per cent of the workers covered did not contribute to their retirement benefits. That is, in terms of workers covered, the great majority of the pension plans were non-contributory or solely employer-financed. For C.I.O. and unaffiliated unions the percentages were about 80 per cent, for A.F.L. unions about 60 per cent. On the other hand, more of the bargained medical benefit plans involved contributions from the workers. Only about 55 per cent of the workers covered were under non-contributory plans.

In respect to *the nature of the benefits provided*, the main characteristic of the private bargained pension plans is a monthly payment of $100 or $125 for employees eligible for the benefit at the retirement age, usually 65, and for permanently disabled employees. These benefits are "gross" ones; that is, the fund actually pays out to a retired employee each month only the difference between $100 or $125 and whatever amount the employee receives under the federal government's old-age insurance program. The chief eligibility requirement is a specified length of service, which varies in the different plans from 15 to 35 years. The bargained health plans and funds provide a number of benefits which, in order of importance (as determined by relative numbers of workers covered), include life insurance, hospitalization, surgical or medical care or both, cash payments for loss of work time resulting from temporary sickness and non-plant accidents, and cash benefits for accidental death or dismemberment.

As to *operation of the plans and funds,* unions have demanded joint union-company administration, and most have succeeded in obtaining it.

A critical analysis of the adequacy of these pension and welfare plans is made in Chapter 23.

(5) Guaranteed annual wages. The nature of guaranteed annual wage plans and of unions' policies thereon has been discussed in an earlier chapter (Chapter 15). Our interest here is solely in the extent to which such plans have been bargained out between unions and companies. The answer is that, although there may be some such development in the future (as there appears to have been in Great Britain since World War II), unions have thus far had very little success with this demand in the United States. They had in fact not pressed it during the full-employment years of 1946–50. However, it was included by the Steelworkers as one of their 1951 demands (possibly a "blue-sky" one). In 1951 only about 50,000 workers, mostly in small firms, were covered by union agreements which contained guarantees of employment for the longer-service portions of the work forces.

c. Hours of work. As noted many times previously, hours of work are very closely related to rates of pay and wage income. This accounts for our having already discussed under wage rates many of the items (such as vacations and holiday pay, premium overtime, and payments for time not worked) that could appropriately be dealt with here when we focus on union contract provisions dealing with work-hours. Because we have already considered these special hours matters above, we shall stress here only the following points: (1) The great bulk of union-management agreements provide for a standard work-week of five days of eight hours each. A few unions, such as the Mine Workers and the Ladies' Garment Workers, have succeeded in obtaining a work-week of fewer than forty hours, such as thirty-five. (2) In respect to periods of slack output, most unions have succeeded in getting employers to agree on equal work-sharing among employees, down to the point where the average per worker is thirty or thirty-two per week. Sometimes the employer manages to bargain a provision that a certain percentage of the work force (such as 10 per cent) can be laid off before the work-sharing principle is put into effect.

d. Union security agreements. What kinds of "shops" have unions been able to obtain from employers? What is the status of the check-off in current labor contracts?

(1) Kind of shop. For the country as a whole over a period of almost ten years the relative importance of the various kinds of union security arrangements demanded and obtained by American unions through collective bargaining may be seen from the percentage figures given in Table 38. In spite of the outlawing of the closed shop as such by the Taft-Hartley amendments to the National Labor Relations Act, the trend has been unmistakably toward a higher degree of security for the unions as entities. From 1942 to 1950, the second weakest form of security — that is, exclusive bargaining agency for all employees in the bargaining unit, whether or not they are union members — dropped from 40 per cent to 29 per cent, in terms of percentage of agreements studied by the Bureau of Labor Statistics. (In terms of workers covered, in 1950 there

TABLE 38 *Union Security Provisions in Union Contracts, Percentage Distribution of Agreements, Selected Years, 1942–1950*

All Types	Percentage Distribution			
	1942	1944	1946	1949–50
	100.0	100.0	100.0	100.0
Closed Shop	45.0	28.0	33.0	[3]
Union Shop		18.0	17.0	50.0
Membership Maintenance	[1]	27.0	25.0	21.0
Sole Bargaining	40.0[2]	27.0[2]	25.0[2]	29.0

Source: U. S. Bureau of Labor Statistics. Data for 1941–46 from *Monthly Labor Review*, May, 1947, p. 767; data for 1949–50 from *Monthly Labor Review*, August, 1950, p. 224.

[1] Not available.

[2] Includes agreements with security contracts that may be classified as providing for preferential hiring (not estimated separately 1949–50). For the years 1941–46 this type constituted between 2 and 5 per cent of all agreements.

[3] Closed shop invalidated by the Taft-Hartley Act of 1947.

were 36 per cent under sole-bargaining contracts, 24 per cent under maintenance of membership, and 40 per cent in union shops.) At the same time the relative importance of another weak form of security (maintenance of membership) also declined, while that of the union shop rose.

This conclusion is buttressed by the fact that, as previously noted, under the Taft-Hartley amendments, which require government-supervised elections among the workers in order to establish a union shop, more than 90 per cent of the voters in about 46,000 elections expressed a preference for this form of security.

Behind the over-all figures were some interesting differences in 1949–50. Among 20 industry groups in manufacturing the relative importance of the union shop ranged from 10 per cent of all the agreements in the petroleum and coal products industries to 88 per cent in apparel and finished textile products, 75 per cent in printing and publishing, 72 per cent in paper and allied products, and 71 per cent in food and kindred products. In four other manufacturing industry groups more than half the agreements provided for the union shop.

Among the agreements studied by the B.L.S. for eight non-manufacturing industry groups, the 1949–50 range for the union shop was from 12 per cent in communications to 19 per cent in hotels and restaurants.

Of the union shop agreements a little less than 10 per cent were found to require that workers must be members of the union before they are hired, whereas more than 90 per cent required union membership only within specified periods after hiring.

There were also differences among the A.F.L., C.I.O., and unaffiliated unions in 1949–50. The A.F.L. contracts contained by far the largest percentage of union shop provisions (67 per cent); whereas among both the C.I.O. and the unaffiliated unions' agreements, only 35 per cent established this kind of union security.

Noteworthy variations also existed among geographic areas in 1949–50. In the three Pacific Coast states, 71 per cent of the agreements studied provided for this sort of shop. Almost 60 per cent of the contracts in the New England and Middle Atlantic states also contained such provisions. On the other hand, relatively few of the employers in the Southeast and Southwest had granted the union shop (13 per cent in the West South Central states, 22 per cent in the South Atlantic states, and 31 per cent in the East South Central states).

In leaving this topic we should bear in mind that apparently there is wide disregard of the Taft-Hartley union security provisions and prohibitions in certain industries and areas. That is, union shops are agreed on tacitly by some employers and unions without regard to the elections required by the Act. There also appear to be numerous "bootleg" closed shops, in spite of the Act's prohibition of this strongest form of union security. In short, the over-all degree of union security is doubtless higher than that revealed by the figures of Table 38.

(2) The check-off. Among the 2159 agreements studied in 1949 by the B.L.S., about 65 per cent provided for some kind of check-off. Only 40 per cent of the A.F.L. contracts had this form of union security, but 90 per cent of the C.I.O. and 65 per cent of the unaffiliated contracts included it.

Among the 20 manufacturing industry groups the lowest percentage of agreements containing check-off provisions was in printing and publishing (19 per cent), the highest in textile mill products (95 per cent). Tobacco and rubber also stood above 90 per cent; and in all, 19 of the 20 groups had a check-off provision in more than half of their contracts. In non-manufacturing the range was from 30 per cent in transportation to 90 per cent in mining, crude petroleum, and natural gas production.

The relative importance of the various geographical regions in respect to the check-off in 1949–50 was very different from that which we said existed in respect to the union shop. Thus, it has long been a practice in Southern states to deduct from workers' weekly gross pay various amounts for rent in company-owned houses, food bought in company stores, and other items. It is therefore not unnatural for union-recognizing Southern employers to agree to deduct their workers' union dues while at the same time they fight bitterly to preserve both their own right to hire non-unionists and the right of non-union workers to stay out of the union. Over 75 per cent of the Southern union agreements provided for the check-off. On the other hand, in that year the Pacific Coast employers, who were so liberal in respect to the union shop, were rather stony about the check-off: Only a third of the contracts in that area provided for it.

Looking at those agreements which do contain check-off provisions, we find that about half allowed only the deduction of dues; 27 per cent allowed the check-off of dues and initiation fees; and 23 per cent, of dues, initiation fees, and assessments.

e. Seniority rules for the security of individual workers. As we learned in our discussion of union policies on seniority, the subject is a very complicated one and has almost innumerable facets and ramifications. We must now note also that there is great variety in the agreements which unions and employers have negotiated on the subject. It is therefore very difficult to summarize them in the way we have summarized provisions for union security.

We shall accordingly content ourselves with the following brief observations: (1) The overwhelming majority of labor agreements contain some provision on seniority. (2) Strict or straight seniority prevails in a few industries like railroads and printing. But in most industries modified seniority prevails, and the trend has been in that direction. (3) In respect to the scope of application for the seniority principle, the most common field is layoffs and rehiring. Second and a close third are promotions and transfers. Only a small minority of agreements apply seniority to such matters as selection of time for vacation, selection of shifts, and opportunity to work overtime. But the trend is toward broader scope of application. (4) In respect to the worker unit within which seniority applies, the most common is the entire plant, with the department not far behind. Combinations of the two for particular applications are gaining in prevalence. (5) The most usual methods of calculating the amount of seniority for particular employees is from the time and day of hiring.

f. Provisions on management security and prerogatives. We have already discussed the attitudes and policies of unions and employers on the question of management's rights and prerogatives. At this point we are not concerned with the basic elements of this issue, although we shall return to them later on in the chapter. Our interest here is in what has thus far been agreed on and written in contracts by labor and management.

In virtually all agreements there is a section or article that declares "management's right to manage" in general terms and names a noninclusive list of functions and rights, such as the discharge of employees for cause and the planning, direction, and control of plant operations, which, the union agrees, are the province of management. Where the exercise of these rights and functions in particular cases directly affects the workers, as with discharge for cause, the agreements may provide, in the same or other sections, for appeal from managerial decisions by the union through the grievance procedure.

g. Provisions for the settlement of grievances. In labor relations parlance, a worker has a "grievance" against management when, for whatever reason, he is dissatisfied in his relationships with the conditions (people, such as his foreman; or things, such as his physical working conditions or his wage rate) over which management exercises control. If management wishes the worker to be loyal, cooperative, and efficient, it must obviously concern itself with banishing or lessening his dissatisfaction, preferably by attacking the cause.

Similarly the union may have a grievance or complaint against the company's management over the way the latter is interpreting some clause in the contract. The union may believe that its own survival or progress as an entity is threatened by management's application of, say, the union shop section. And management, on its side, may also experience dissatisfaction with the behavior of the union during the life of the agreement. In both such cases there is again a need for peaceful resolution of the difficulties.

It is clear, then, that it is to the interest of both managements and unions to specify in their contracts a more or less formal way of taking care of one another's grievances during the terms of the contracts without resort to economic coercion, such as wildcat strikes or slowdowns or punitive discharge.

"Grievance procedure" is the term usually applied to contract provisions of this sort. Virtually all labor agreements spell out in some detail a series of three, four, or more steps to be followed in the processing of a grievance from any source. The grievance procedure is of supreme importance in building up harmonious day-to-day relations and in serving as a channel of communication between management and workers and between management and union.

So significant is the grievance procedure that we shall give it fuller consideration in the section that follows.

C. COLLECTIVE BARGAINING PROCEDURES AND PRACTICES

As explained in Chapter 19, collective bargaining covers the whole range of continuing relationships between a union and its members, on the one hand, and the management of a firm, on the other. It thus includes not only the very important matter of contract negotiation but also the administration, application, and interpretation of the contract in day-to-day problems. Accordingly, in this section we shall deal with (1) the ways in which labor contracts are negotiated and (2) the ways in which the contracts are given force during their terms.

1. Negotiation procedures and practices. In Chapter 19 we considered the determinants of the bargaining relationship in any given union-management situation. We also dealt with the occupational and geographical scope of the bargaining unit. Because these determinants vary so much from situation to situation and because there is so much variety in the size and composition of the bargaining unit, there is also much variety in bargaining procedures and practices. For this reason, as well as because of space limitations, we shall confine ourselves here to a summary of the features that are common to most bargaining relationships. Our topics will be (*a*) the make-up of the negotiating parties; (*b*) their preparation for the negotiations; (*c*) pre-negotiation procedures; (*d*) negotiation procedures; and (*e*) the final agreement.

a. The negotiators. For simplicity, let us assume that the bargaining unit is a local unit of a national industrial union dealing with a manufacturing corporation having a single large plant. This is perhaps the most usual situation. Then the negotiations are between a single union and the corporation's management, and the agreement covers all the non-office employees of the corporation.

(1) For the union. Let us also assume that the corporation is important in its industry. A contract negotiated by it might well set a pattern for competitors to follow. Then we may be sure that the national union will be keenly and directly interested in the outcome of the negotiations. The president of the national or some other important person out of the national office — perhaps some "international representative" — will participate in the bargaining on the union's side. Usually he will not serve as the head of the union's bargaining committee. But he will be available

for advice to the committee, will try to steer a nice course between the interest of the national and that of the local, and will enter into the bargaining discussions at any critical point where he believes his experience and skill can be helpful and definitive.

The local's negotiating committee is usually composed of from five to ten local leaders. Too many members tend to spoil the broth and make the proceedings cumbersome and chaotic. Too few members usually means a failure to tap the local's resources fully. A bargaining group needs various kinds of personalities — the aggressive fighter for hard punching; the soft-spoken, pleasant person who can mollify ruffled feelings; the dogged, tough-minded man who can stay with the opposing party through long, wearying sessions; the quick-witted one with a flair for figures and reasoning, who can pick flaws in the opposing presentation; and so on. Too few members also often means that all the main departments of the plant are not directly represented. This is bad from the standpoint of obtaining the whole membership's acceptance of the new agreement.

The union committee may be appointed by the local officers or elected by the local's membership. It usually includes the chief officers, such as the president and secretary-treasurer, plus representatives from major plant departments. The latter may or may not be shop stewards. The local's business agent, if there is one, is commonly included.

(2) For management. On the employer's side, the bargaining committee will be headed either by the chief labor relations executive (a staff officer) or by a major line official, such as the vice-president in charge of production. The former usually knows more about bargaining, labor conditions in the plant, and labor relations in general. But the line man has to "live with" the new agreement; the success of his operational efforts depends in large degree on the kind of provisions it contains. In any case he is usually included on the company's bargaining committee.

As with the union, the other committee members for management typically include representatives (superintendents) from the several major operating departments. The superintendents' knowledge of conditions in their own bailiwicks is obviously important during the course of the debate over the parties' demands.

Management often includes legal counsel in its bargaining group, as a rule more frequently than does the union. There may be some advantages to this for both sides. A lawyer may know better the statutory and legal limits within which the agreement must be consummated. He may be able to produce a clearer, less ambiguous written document expressing the substance of the agreements resulting from the negotiations. He may be a more effective debater than his colleagues. But there are usually also serious liabilities in his presence on a bargaining committee. He ordinarily has a good deal less knowledge of plant conditions than the union and management men. He often is inclined to be excessively argumentative and legalistic rather than conciliatory in debate. And frequently his legalistic slant tends to cause him to overload the new written agreement with "lawyer language" which foremen and union members find hard to understand and interpret. Because of these disadvantages he is often used, if at all, only as an adviser, silent unless and until called upon.

b. The parties' separate preparations for the negotiations. As previously noted, most collective bargaining agreements run for definite terms, such as one or two years. Many provide for re-opening, after due notice, one or more subjects (at least wage rates in years of price inflation) during the life of the contract. If the agreement cannot be re-opened during its term, under the law and, even more important, under good collective bargaining practice, due notice (such as thirty days before the agreement runs out) must be given by either side if it wishes to change the terms of the contract.

When either side gives the other party notice of its wish to alter the agreement, it often (but not always) accompanies or soon follows up the notice with a statement of its demands or desired changes and a proposal as to the date and time (sometimes also place) of the first bargaining conference. Then, after an exchange of communications and an agreement on time and place of meeting, each side engages in feverish preparation for the bargaining sessions.

At this point we are concerned with the separate preparations of each group. The joint preparations that sometimes occur are considered below.

As a matter of fact, if the union and the management are alert and foresighted (and they usually are), they will have begun their preparations some time before the serving of notice and demands. Some demands, as we have seen, stem mainly from what other unions or other locals of the same union or other managements have asked for or succeeded in obtaining in key bargains. Inter-union or inter-local or inter-company rivalry sees to that. But some unions or locals or companies *set* the pattern (make the key demands and bargains). And in any case there are almost always some conditions peculiar to each bargaining situation. How are the key demands and the proposals dealing with these special conditions worked out?

In the first place, in a case such as the one we have assumed, both parties have been living with the existing agreement for almost one or two or more years. The local union will have duly noted the points at which the most numerous and the most serious grievances have arisen under the contract as it has been administered day by day. These grievances afford the basis for one or more demands for modifying the contract or for inserting new provisions. Management will also have studied workers' grievances and of course in addition will have analyzed its own and its foremen's reactions to the operation of the existing agreement. Second, each side will have been studying economic conditions in the whole economy, in the particular industry of which the corporation is a part, and in respect to the corporation itself. They will have their own research staffs or specially hired economic consultants collect information on recent general economic trends, on the state of the industry, and on the corporation's profits, and other matters affecting ability to bear higher labor costs. In directing such studies each side will be thinking not only of rationalizing its own demands but also of opposing the other party's proposals. The ability to anticipate and prepare for the other side's demands is an important element of bargaining effectiveness.

As noted in an earlier chapter, there has been a growing tendency for national unions to exert control over their locals' contracts with employers. This is especially true of key bargains. Some nationals, in the first instance, seek suggestions and advice on demands from the locals. These may be transmitted to the national office directly or via international representatives; or the suggestions may take the form of resolutions offered to the national convention. In other unions the main demands are worked out by the top leaders and are then submitted for criticism and suggestions to the locals, directly, or through representatives on a large "policy" committee.

c. Joint preparations; pre-negotiation procedures. In some cases, each side's demands are not finally formulated in advance of any joint meeting between the parties. But usually they are, sometimes (in big cases) with considerable public fanfare.

The practice of issuing public statements about one's own and the other party's demands cannot in most cases be regarded as desirable from the standpoint of sound, harmonious union-management relationships. It tends to try the case before the public at a time when the public is not well enough informed to make a reasonable judgment on the merits of the opposing contentions. It tends to foster the making of extreme demands at a time when restrained, moderate, face-to-face dealings away from the public spotlight are necessary. Each side tends to go out on a limb — and later finds itself unable to get off without losing face with the public. In short, the practice almost always makes for conflict and works against restraint, compromise, and cooperation, which are necessities for successful negotiations.

Whether or not there is publicity about the proposals, the making of extreme demands or the setting of unrealistically high "asking prices" for tactical bargaining advantage is not conducive to harmonious relationships. On the union side, at least, the membership learns about the demands. The leaders may know very well that the extreme demands are unrealistic and cannot possibly be won; but the members, being much less well informed, may come to believe that the corporation can agree to the proposals if it only will. Here again the leaders are risking their jobs as well as their "faces" if they make the necessary compromises. It is much better to formulate less unreasonable demands.

A rather common union practice before the beginning of negotiations is to take a strike vote among its members and announce the results. Usually the vote, at least if publicized, is overwhelmingly in favor of striking unless the union's demands are met. The union's purpose here, of course, is to show doubting management that the membership is solidly behind the union negotiators; the union believes that its bargaining power is thereby enhanced. But management already knows that one of the union's alternatives is to strike. And from the standpoint of good relations there seems to be little that is desirable in publicly brandishing and pointing such a weapon at management.

To avoid such excesses, in recent years the pre-negotiation conference has been developed, though as yet it is not very widely used. Here the parties meet and informally explore one another's viewpoints. There is an airing of problems which each side can be asked to help solve. The posing of each party's problems and the request for help from the other side creates an atmosphere for the formal presentation of demands that is very different from the usual climate at the bargaining table. Almost inevitably a constructive, restrained approach develops. Furthermore, in such a conference there can be informal agreement on the facts needed to help solve the various problems. Frequently the parties can agree on the joint collection of necessary data, such as statistics on absenteeism and on the wage rates paid for similar jobs by other firms in the locality and industry. It is much better to have joint collection of basic information — and hence agreement on it — than to find each party coming into the formal negotiations with its own assortment of hand-picked, slanted data.

At the pre-bargaining conference the parties can also determine the place and hours of meeting and agree on the general procedures to be followed during the negotiations proper.

d. Procedures during negotiation conferences. We may conveniently discuss this topic under three headings: (1) the organization of the conference; (2) the order of business; and (3) techniques for reaching agreement.

(1) Organization. By organization we mean the arrangements that the parties make for facilitating the business of the meetings. Obviously, conference organization covers the provision of a properly large and comfortable suite of rooms (preferably in neutral territory, e.g., in a hotel, rather than on company property) — a main conference room adequately equipped with large and small tables and chairs, adjoining smaller rooms for caucuses and subcommittee meetings, rest rooms, and so on. But it also includes decisions on whether there shall be a chairman for the meetings; a leading, authoritative spokesman for each side; a parliamentary, formal mode of discussion, or the free give-and-take of informal discussion; a recording secretary to take minutes on main points in the discussion, or a full verbatim transcript of everything said, or no record at all; and similar matters.

In respect to these last items one may say, first, that it is usually not necessary to have a conference chairman if the negotiating committee on each side is small and if relations between the parties have been reasonably amicable and of fairly long duration. Larger negotiating groups, however, have found chairmen helpful. A common practice is to have a management man preside one day, a union man the next, and so on. A chairman's responsibility is to "recognize" speakers; maintain some sort of order during the meetings; and, if possible, minimize the introduction of antagonistic and irrelevant statements. It is hard, of course, for a partisan person to become as neutral as a chairman should be. Nevertheless a good many of the larger conferences have found such an arrangement helpful. A few have introduced a third party for chairman, either a man who has already participated in grievance settlements for the parties or a conciliator from a state or federal agency.

It is generally agreed that it is desirable for each side to have a leader, even though all members of each committee participate in the bargaining. Some such centralization of authority and responsibility facilitates final agreement. On the desirability of formal parliamentary discussion and of formal records of the discussions there is no unanimity of opinion. Formality of any important sort may stultify free and open discussion and promote suspicion and distrust, even though it may contribute to speeding the order of business.

(2) The order of business. Sometimes the union's demands and the employer's counter-proposals have been made known before the first bargaining session. In other cases the first meeting is the time when they are exchanged. The union may present a complete draft of the new contract it desires; so also may the management. Or there may simply be an exchange of requested changes in the existing contract. In any case, if the exchange takes place at the first session each party is likely to ask for time to study the other's proposals. The first session then is actually likely to be little more than a pre-bargaining conference, at which procedures and other matters are worked out. At such a meeting, however, each side may make an "opening statement," trying to explain and justify its proposals more or less formally in fairly general terms. Even if there has been a previous exchange of demands and a true pre-bargaining conference, the bargaining may well begin with such beginning statements.

Once the preliminaries have been taken care of, the real bargaining begins. Here three related procedural matters are of considerable importance. First, shall the parties meet head on at once in respect to the tough, really controversial issues, or shall they first take up the easy demands on which they are already not far apart, or shall the latter be sandwiched here and there among the controversial items? There is something to be said for trying to get the hard items settled while the negotiators are still fresh rather than frazzled. On the other hand, if disagreement on the disputed matters is serious, the conference may make very little progress and may be overcome by a feeling of hopelessness. It may, then, be better to dispose of the non-controversial issues first, so as to establish the mood and habit of compromise and agreement. Alternating the discussion of hard and easy issues also helps to foster a spirit of agreement and a sense of progress.

Second, shall there be a fixed agenda or order of topic-discussion, to be rigidly adhered to, or shall there be complete flexibility? Experience seems to dictate the latter. Suppose the parties do begin with a tough issue and find themselves hopelessly deadlocked at the outset. There is no reason for them to conclude that all negotiations should be broken off and a strike called and endured. They can "pass" the moot point for the time being and move on to something else, coming back to it later under possibly more hopeful circumstances. Flexibility during negotiations would appear to be of paramount importance.

Third, as agreement is reached in discussion on a given issue, should it be initialed and thought of as finally and completely settled; or should the parties merely agree "tentatively," subject to what happens to the other issues? In other words, should they take a piecemeal or a "basket" approach to the various items? There is something to be said for the first alternative. Not only does it get settled issues completely out of the way; it also tends to get each side to consider each issue strictly on its own merits. But there are important disadvantages. An employer usually prefers to learn what the whole contract "package" is going to cost him before he agrees finally to any one item. The union negotiators also may well wish to see the whole agreement that they will have to sell to the membership, before agreeing conclusively on any particular issue. Moreover, the other alternative largely precludes either side's trading off one demand in return for obtaining concessions on another. This trading is a frequent occurrence during the course of many negotiations. In many bargaining conferences a compromise arrangement is effected: The issues are divided into pecuniary and non-pecuniary items. The latter are handled and finally agreed to on an individual basis, while the pecuniary issues are looked at whole, i.e., as a "package" or in a "basket."

(3) Some techniques for reaching agreement. The student will note that we are here considering methods for winning mutually agreeable compromises, not methods whereby either side can get its own way, at least directly.

There is of course no standard book of rules that are invariably successful as applied to all kinds of bargaining situations. Nevertheless, managerial and labor negotiators who have approached their conferences in good faith, with the intent to write an acceptable contract if possible, have learned that certain things are usually helpful toward that end and certain other measures are deterrents. These may be briefly listed as follows: (*a*) The negotiators should not try their case before the public. One of the surest ways to antagonize is to issue exaggerated statements to the press over the head of the other side. (*b*) Arguments should be factual and impersonal rather than emotional and personal. Attacks on the good faith, integrity and beliefs of persons on the opposite committee are anything but conducive to good relationships and agreement. (*c*) Debate over principles as such should be avoided. Sticking to facts and particulars is the much easier path to compromise. (*d*) Falsification, exaggeration, and various sharp practices and tricks almost always not only boomerang on those indulging in them but also serve to block agreement. (*e*) Patience in listening respectfully to the arguments of the other party pays off in terms of obtaining a fair hearing for one's own contentions and of reaching a workable compromise. (*f*) Short recesses during bargaining sessions are desirable, especially at times when tension has been accumulating. (*g*) Sometimes subcommittees can profitably be appointed to explore avenues for settlement, to consider complicated factual material, and to report thereon. (*h*) On both sides the negotiators should have broad grants of authority to make conclusive commitments or agreements and to bind their principals. Almost nothing is more stultifying to bargaining than the knowledge or fear that the person with whom you are dealing has to go out and telephone his superiors for approval or instructions every time you get close to agreement. On management's side, adequate authority can be obtained by the appointment of a high-rank officer (e.g., production vice-president) as the head of the committee. On the union's side, it is true that in most cases any agreement is subject to ratification by majority vote of the membership. This may well be a desirable thing from the standpoint of preserving intra-union democracy and avoiding opportunistic sell-outs by the union leadership. It would appear to be especially desirable in unions where the top leadership is able, by political machine methods, to prevent the membership from using the usual democratic method of registering discontent with executive achievement, namely, refusing to re-elect the officials. But in such unions the machine would also be almost certain to obtain ratification of the agreement. In the more democratic unions ratification might not be necessary because the rank and file would be able to vote out the leaders if the agreements they negotiated were not acceptable. It seems that full delegation of authority to union negotiators could be made by the members without impairing democratic processes, provided free and frequent elections of officials were held and provided the leaders took the pains to educate the members in the economic and political realities which the leaders must face in negotiating with management.

e. The final agreement. Let us suppose that, as happens in the overwhelming majority of cases, the parties in one way or another finally reach a meeting of minds on all the clauses of the new agreement. There remains the work of finding language properly to express the mutual intent of the parties on each point. In other words, the contract has to be written in final form.

This is no mean task. To perform it or to assist in performing it lawyers are sometimes called in. In any case, the final draft should be as simply worded as possible and should be carefully scrutinized by everyone on both sides; and there should be verbal agreement among the negotiators on the meaning and intent of each paragraph. At the end of the negotiations everyone is worn out and is anxious to get back to his regular job. The temptation is great to rush away without undergoing this last effort to make sure that everybody understands what the new contract says. But both sides should remember that here is the legislation under which they must get along for the next year or more. It is well worth the extra time and effort to make sure they agree on its specific purposes and meanings.

2. Administration of the contract. Grievance settlement procedures. *a. General considerations.* We come now to procedural aspects of the relationships of the parties as they live together day by day under the new contract. As in the case of legislation in any other field, the really important matters are those that occur during the administration of the statute. A statute is nothing until it is administered.

Every statute contains provisions dealing with the principles, procedures, and agencies under which it is to be administered. Union-management agreements are no exception. But no statute can spell out all the details. Much must be left to the discretion of the administration.

Some labor agreements, e.g., those in the railroad industry, are very long and cover scores of pages. Almost everything that arose as an issue between management and the union during the preceding year seems to get itself included in the new contract. Even so, the agreement cannot possibly cover every eventuality. New problems will arise in the coming year. Perhaps they can be solved by application of some clause of the new contract. If not, they must be settled, at least tentatively, before the next agreement is negotiated.

There are two senses in which administration of labor agreements may be considered. First, it is possible to say that the administration of the contract rests primarily or in the first instance on management as it engages in the operation of its plant. Here the union is viewed as checking up on management and making its position known through the grievance procedure or through special conferences with an appropriate managerial group. Second, in the broader sense one may look at contract administration as being a joint union-management matter. This approach rightly emphasizes that, in the last analysis, no matter who takes the initiative on any given matter, the union and the employer are jointly responsible for the successful operation of the agreement.

b. Introduction and explanation of the new contract. Whichever view is taken, it is certain that the new agreement will be more successfully administered if each side takes the pains to explain its provisions in simple language to all those who must live under it. In civil life ignorance of the law is no excuse for disobeying it or avoiding penalties thereunder. In union-management relations the same principle applies; and there is the additional very real possibility that ignorance will worsen relations or prove a barrier to the improvement or continuance of mutual understanding.

Recognizing these things, progressive employers take pains to explain the new contract to the lower levels of management, particularly the foremen who must operate under it day by day. Frequently a manual is prepared not only to clarify the several clauses in simple language but also to show their application to hypothetical cases. Similarly, progressive unions prepare simple written expositions for shop stewards and members. These explanations are not merely distributed for possible reading at some vague future date. They are read and discussed at special meetings — management with its foremen, the union with its stewards and then with the whole membership. In some cases, where union-management relations are good enough to make it profitable, joint meetings may be held.

c. The settlement of disagreements during the life of the contract. (1) Need for settlement. We have said that it is important for the negotiators to agree on the meaning of the new contract's clauses before they go home. (Some of the provisions are not new, of course; and their interpretation has been built up by a great many previous negotiations, agreements, and arbitrators' decisions.) If an agreement on meaning is reached, and if foremen and stewards have been adequately educated in the agreed-on interpretations, the chances are good for harmonious living under the contract. But human beings are fallible; because of ignorance or emotional conflicts there are almost bound to be some failures at all levels, but particularly at the worker-steward and foremen levels, to agree on the meaning of certain provisions and on how they should be applied to particular situations. Moreover, as already indicated, the new contract can never foresee all possible exigencies; during the term of the contract some cases will almost certainly arise which demand prompt solution but which are not governed by express provisions.

The grievance procedure and the special conference between union leaders and appropriate levels of management are the two methods of settling differences between the parties on these matters during the life of the contract. When the contract is being negotiated, the threat and possibility of strike or lockout or other form of economic warfare exists in all cases but those few in which management and union (as in the local transportation industry and the printing and publishing industry in many cities) have previously agreed to submit their unsettled disputes to an impartial arbitrator. But when the new contract is agreed on, a usual paragraph provides that during the life of the contract neither side will resort to economic warfare to win its point in a dispute over the interpretation or application of the terms or over any other matter that requires solution. Labor peace is supposed to be guaranteed for both parties during this period. And grievance procedures plus special conferences are the safety devices that are supposed to relieve the parties of any necessity for using strikes or other such weapons. Both sides bind themselves to exert pressure only through these "lawful" measures.

(2) Grievance procedures. (a) General nature. As previously shown, grievance procedures are formalized in a section of the contract. The details of the procedures may vary a good deal from firm to firm and from union to union. But typically they provide for the settlement of disputes through a series of successively higher union-management "steps," the last step for unsettled issues (in more than four-fifths of the contracts) being final decision by an impartial arbitrator. In the smaller plants there may be only three steps, in the large ones four or five.

The first and lowest step involves, for management, the foreman. On the union side under the amended National Labor Relations Act an individual employee has the right to present his own grievance to the foreman (or to higher management) and settle it with them. But the union's steward or committeeman has the right to be present at all stages; and the settlement must not be contrary to the provisions of the contract. The reasons for this compromise arrangement must be clear: Management likes to deal directly with aggrieved workers; it almost always wishes to preserve as many direct contacts with employees as possible, and sometimes it is eager to show them that a union is not needed for the equitable settlement of grievances. Non-union workers, if they exist in the plant, also prefer to avoid dependence on the union. On the other hand, the union wishes to make non-unionists feel dependent on the union (in the absence of the law, unions have sometimes refused to handle or to let management settle grievances of non-union workers) as well as to let union members know they are getting their money's worth. And certainly the union cannot permit management to settle with non-unionists on terms better than those given to unionists; to allow such a thing would be to flout the principle of solidarity or no-discrimination and to undermine union security and strength.

If an individual worker wishes the union to handle his grievance, the grievance terms of the contract apply. In some cases the worker himself first approaches the foreman, without the active participation of the shop steward, who, however, will previously have assisted the worker in formulating his grievance. The shop steward may or may not be present; usually he is. In other cases the shop steward alone deals with the foreman. In still others there is a joint presentation by the steward and the grievant.

If settlement comes in any of these first-step arrangements, the issue is considered to be finally determined. If not, it goes to the next higher step "on appeal." It is in the number of "next steps" that contracts differ. In small plants there may be only one more before outside arbitrators are called in. Here the local union president or the business agent or a union committee meets with the plant manager or the firm's president. In large plants or firms, the second step may involve, for management, a middle-level line executive, such as a superintendent, or the labor relations (staff) department; and for the union, the chief steward (or chairman of the plant grievance committee of five to ten members) or the business agent.

The third step may involve the local plant's top management official and the plant's union grievance committee or the local union president. An international representative of the parent union may also assist.

If the firm has only the one large plant, the fourth step on unsettled cases would then be outside arbitration. But if the firm is a multi-plant one, the fourth step may involve the corporation's top management and some high official of the national union, such as a regional president or even the national president. Then outside arbitration would be a fifth step.

The final step of arbitration means that in almost all cases a third person decides all issues that have not been resolved by use of the preceding steps. The smaller companies and unions usually have too few unsettled grievances to justify the employment of a full-time "umpire" or "impartial chairman." In such cases *ad hoc* or temporary arbitrators are chosen — by mutual agreement or, in case of failure to agree, by having him appointed by some outside agency such as the American Arbitration Association, the federal or state mediation and conciliation service, or the state department of labor. Sometimes, however, as in the clothing industries, a number of firms dealing with a single union may combine to hire a full-time arbitrator, jointly paid by management and union. A number of corporations (e.g., General Motors and United States Steel) and their unions are big enough to provide employment for full-time umpires.

This kind of voluntary arbitration is a necessary terminal point to the whole grievance procedure. It gets the unsettled grievances and problems decided during the life of the contract. It thus helps insure labor peace during this term. True, each side may lose its case in any given dispute, and it may feel deeply about the principle involved. But there is a net gain for all; the gains outweigh the losses. The arbitrator doesn't like to lose his well-paid job. He tends to be pretty even-handed; over a period of time one side will be likely to win about as many cases as the other. Furthermore, an arbitrator tends to get one or the other or both sides "off the hook" in particular cases. He gets paid not only for hearing cases, making awards, and writing opinions but also for taking the blame on decisions averse to the immediate interests of lower management or of union members. This is especially important for the union leaders in their political situations. Because their offices are elective, the leaders often feel they have to press grievances which they actually believe unjustified. They can make a great show of militance in behalf of their constituents, hoping that the arbitrator will decide against them — or at least not caring how the decision goes. In any case, their faces are saved.

(b) Special problems. A first requirement of any grievance procedure is that it handle grievances promptly and expeditiously. Nowhere is delay more stultifying and aggravating to one or both parties than in labor relations. This fact has led to limiting the number of steps in the procedure, especially in large corporations (for instance, only four steps are provided in the G.M.–U.A.W. contract). It has also resulted in setting deadlines or time limits for the consideration of grievances at each step in the procedure. Such time limits help to prevent stalling by either side and to avoid large accumulations of unsettled grievances. One or two days are usual limits for the first and second steps. For the higher steps a time limit of a week or so may be set; or there may be a provision requiring unsettled cases to be handled at weekly or bi-weekly meetings. Failure to meet the deadlines automatically moves the case up to the next step. Sometimes time limits also apply to arbitrators' hearings and decisions. In a few instances an over-all time limit is provided.

Another important aspect of avoiding delay and waste is to get the great majority of complaints settled at the first step, without having appeals to the higher levels. This can be accomplished if the relationship between the union and the management is such that they try to remove the sources of grievances rather than just win cases; if the foremen and the shop stewards are given adequate delegations of authority to make settlements; and if foremen and stewards are relieved of their jobs if, after training, they refuse to cooperate with each other.

Still another aspect of avoiding delay is to make each side's representatives almost continuously available to his constituents and to the other side's representatives. Several specific contract provisions are frequently designed to assist on this point. Although a few unions prefer to pay their own stewards in order to relieve them of any dependence on the employer, most contracts provide that management shall compensate workers' representatives (at their average hourly earnings) for time spent on grievances during plant work hours. Many contracts establish the number of shop stewards in terms of a ratio with the number of workers in the plant or department — one steward for a given number of employees, say one to 100. Some contracts provide for one or more deputies for each steward. These substitute for him when he is out sick or on leave of absence. Stewards are often given super-seniority in order to prevent their being laid off during periods of work-force reduction.

At what stage should a grievance be reduced to writing? The usual requirement is that any grievance not settled at the lowest level must be put in writing. In many cases, however, written grievances are required from the beginning. The belief is that, although some hardship may be involved for those not adept at written expression, the requirement tends to reduce the number of phony grievances because men must usually think before they write and may find it hard to justify formally a position that they might be casual about in conversation. It also tends to help both union and management representatives understand and settle the case, and to help both sides study the nature and causes of grievances.

Some contracts, or the actual practices thereunder, limit the scope of the grievance procedure. It seems clear that, given the statute governing the relations of management with the union and its members, there should be no limit on who can bring up what matters when. That is, although obviously it would almost always invite chaos to re-hash the issues that were settled by negotiation for a given period of time when the new contract was signed, there is no good reason for refusing to permit an airing of grievances on matters not covered by the contract as well as on matters involving an interpretation and application of the contract. It is essential to a harmonious relationship that either party should be free to bring up both kinds of problems at any time. Otherwise, things are unsettled and unrest accumulates in certain areas. Yet we find that in some cases the grievance procedure is used almost exclusively by the union; management makes little use of this channel of communication. And we also find management refusing to listen to any complaints that cannot be grounded on some clause of the contract. Clearly this is a legalistic rather than a human approach to labor relations. The problem is to discover labor problems and their causes and then solve them through joint action. The only rational way to limit the number of grievances would seem to be to search for and remove their sources.

Arbitration, the final step in grievance settlement, may well present a special case. It may be desirable to exclude from such appeal all matters not involving an interpretation or application of the contract's provisions, i.e., grievances on matters unrelated to or unforeseen by the contract (which are best settled by direct negotiations between the parties) and grievances on matters reserved by the contract to management, such as the setting of output standards and wage rates under incentive plans or the control of production processes and methods. (We may also note here that arbitrators in grievance cases are not permitted to alter the provisions of the contract.)

We have already mentioned in other connections that both sides should have a diagnostic rather than a legalistic approach to grievance settlement. Let us focus on and emphasize this point here. If management thinks mainly of standing firm on the rights guaranteed to it by the contract or tries to win as many cases as possible in order to make the union look bad to the workers, the union will almost always respond in kind. It will press hard on every grievance — petty or big, imaginary or real. It has the ability to make every foreman's life a misery and to bedevil every higher manager by stirring up and bringing in floods of all sorts of complaints. Similarly, if the union, on its own initiative, does things in order to win the loyalty of the workers and impress management with its power, it can expect to meet a fighting, uncooperative management. Both parties end by being utterly unhappy; and under the law there is very little prospect of getting a divorce. It is therefore just good sense and good policy for each side to exercise restraint at all levels, to respect the authority of the other's representatives, and to consider the other's grievances as problems that must be sympathetically heard and cooperatively investigated and settled. Grievances should be regarded as symptoms of things that may be wrong in the day-to-day conduct of the union-management relationship. The basic problem is to discover and remove the causes.

In many cases management (sometimes acting jointly with the union) studies the grievances of the past six months or year, classifying them, in the steps at which they were settled, under various headings — by department, type, cause, time consumed, contract clause involved, and so forth. Such an analysis can be very helpful in discovering trouble spots and applying remedies. It also gives a clear review picture of the body of interpretative law that is being built up to govern the parties' relations.

What penalties, if any, should be meted out to either side or its representatives for failure to keep its contractual promise to use the grievance procedure rather than economic force during the life of the contract? The Taft-Hartley amendments to the National Labor Relations Act authorize management to sue for damages in federal courts if the union members engage in wildcat strikes or otherwise breach their contracts. As a result, some unions have refused to renew their contractual no-strike pledges. But not many companies have chosen to sue in any case. Such action is hardly conducive to harmonious relations. A positive approach is usually much better. To assert this is not, of course, to say that all penalties are useless and should be abandoned. But to sue a whole local union is to attack it as an entity and threaten its prestige and security. It is one thing to penalize and antagonize the whole group and quite another to punish the particular persons who are responsible for the violation. Numerous contracts provide that management may discharge such proven ringleaders and discipline others who have participated in the breach of contract. In some cases the union itself fines or otherwise penalizes its guilty members. Management also often discharges or disciplines foremen who may have been partly responsible for the unionists' actions.

D. APPRAISING THE SUCCESS OF COLLECTIVE BARGAINING

Suppose that you were asked to study the collective bargaining experience of a union and management in a given plant or firm or industry, with a view to discovering the conditions there that had made for a good, socially desirable relationship or for the reverse. How would you know whether the relationship had been good or bad? And as a working hypothesis, what conditions do you think you might list tentatively as tending to make the relationship good or bad?

1. Standards of appraisal. *a. The strike record.* As a start, let us briefly consider a few criteria for appraising the kind of relationship that exists in a particular collective bargaining situation. One that comes to mind immediately is the frequency and severity of strikes. This is a standard that does not involve too many difficulties of measurement. Suppose that you are studying two plants of the same size with virtually identical economic-technological conditions in the same industry. Statistics over a period of years on the number of strikes, the number of workers involved, the number of man-hours lost, extent of violence, and other relevant items are readily available; and the strike record of plant B is much worse than that of plant A. Does this fact point unequivocably to the conclusion that union-management relations in A have been much better than in B?

Not necessarily. An absence of strikes in plant A might mean a good, strong, constructive relationship. We may go so far as to say that there would be a strong presumption in this direction. But it might also mean that, given no difference in the strengths of the two plants' managements, the union in plant A was much weaker than the one in plant B. Again, it might be a reflection of much more favorable economic conditions in plant A.

In general, we may say that the absence of overt conflict such as that involved in strikes is suggestive but not conclusive evidence of a good relationship. As a matter of fact, a strike occasionally improves rather than embitters subsequent relations; for it forcefully reminds the parties how expensive is failure to practice compromise and cooperation.

b. The record on grievances and arbitrations. Another measure of how well a union and an employer have been getting along with each other is the frequency and severity of grievances, including appeals to neutral arbitration. Here again, high rates give a presumption of an unsatisfactory relationship; and vice versa. But here too we must be cautious in our interpretations and conclusions. High rates might point to a contract that is poorly written and hard to understand. Or they might represent excessive zeal on both sides. Low rates might have resulted from sluggish stewards or an over-docile labor force. A great many possible causal conditions must be scrutinized in any analysis of the grievance record.

c. Production records. The trends in quantity and quality of production must also be scrutinized. So must records of absenteeism, tardiness, accidents, and so on. Favorable developments in these areas may well betoken a high degree of union-management cooperation. But again, not necessarily. For example, a weak union in conjunction with a tough, efficiency-minded, innovating management might result in noteworthy improvements in all these respects.

d. Attitudes and sentiments. Given the economic and technological framework within which the parties deal with each other, the attitudes and sentiments of the union leaders and the union rank and file and the persons in the various levels of management are of paramount importance.

Changes in attitudes and sentiments are particularly significant. How can these be discovered? No one has yet succeeded in developing a wholly trustworthy attitude-detector. But by means of well-planned interviews with those who have participated in union-management dealings and by careful study of the written records of negotiations between the parties on new contracts and on contract administration (including grievance settlement), experienced researchers are able to obtain rather objective information on the human-political conditions affecting the relationship. From such information it is possible to conclude which of the kinds of relationships explained in Chapter 19 existed at any one time, as well as what changes have occurred and why.

2. Summary of conditions favoring good relationships. At various points in many of the preceding chapters we have had occasion to discuss the factors that make for success in union-management relations. Let us list them in summary fashion here: favorable economic circumstances for the firm or industry; not too rapid a rate of technological change; explicit, concrete expression of willingness by each side to respect the other's desire to survive and progress; consequent avoidance of a legalistic, win-at-all-costs attitude and adoption of an attitude of mutual consideration and helpfulness in problem-solving; keeping unduly aggressive personalities out of negotiations; avoidance of going over the other party's head to its constituents or to the public; avoidance of unilateral actions by both sides; avoidance of arguments over principles and adherence to the factual, problem-solving approach; full, free, two-way vertical communication within the union and within management; adequate horizontal communication between union and management at all levels; education of foremen by management and of rank and file, stewards, and local officers by the union in necessary attitudes and procedures; clearly delineated and respected roles and statuses for all participants in the relationship; and adequate system of rewards for successful performances within and between the two organizations.

At this stage of our knowledge of factors affecting human relations, there is of course no sure prescription for curing all labor-relations ills and for maintaining continuous labor-relations health. The number of variables is bewilderingly large, and conditions change almost from day to day. The conditions listed above provide no guarantee of stable, harmonious union-management relations, but they are helpful.

3. The basic problem of collective bargaining. Now, as we leave this general discussion of collective bargaining and begin to study real-world examples of it, as well as prepare to consider, in Part Three, what public policy on collective bargaining should be, let us broaden our perspective and consider the fundamental problem involved in union-management relations for the country as a whole. Big business and big unionism are not the whole of American society. There are the farmers, organized and unorganized; there is much small business; there are many self-employed people, including professional people, and many unorganized employees. But big business and big unionism certainly cover very large and important sectors of the economy. And their ability to achieve an over-all stable, balanced, harmonious relationship is surely of vast import to all citizens. It is not too much to say that the maintenance of economic and political democracy as we have known it depends in large part on the success with which this sort of relationship is worked out.

Prediction Number One. There are many who see unionism as a challenge to management's power; big business and big unionism are conceived to be engaged, essentially, in a struggle for power and control over the nation's resources. And these observers appear to believe that the struggle can end only with the complete ascendancy of one group and the utter defeat and death of the other. In other words, the ultimate resolution of the conflict is said to involve the creation of fascist capitalism or of revolutionary socialism through the organization and use of political power. In either case, it is asserted, economic and political democracy of the traditional sort — including free, private enterprise and free unionism — will disappear. To bolster their case, these observers cite what happened in Italy, Germany, Spain, Russia, and elsewhere.

Prediction Number Two. Other students agree that there is such a struggle and that it will in time be transferred from the economic to the political arena. But they deny that the end product need be or will be a dictatorship of the right or of the left and a destruction of democracy, at least in the political field. They foresee a peaceful evolution to a "welfare" democracy of the sort found in Britain and other English-speaking countries.

Prediction Number Three. A few others believe that in the end we shall have an American form of syndicalism. That is, they predict that big unionism will succeed in making successive encroachments on managerial prerogatives and will come in time to participate as true partners in the making of decisions on all business matters, including price and sales policies, procurement of machines and raw materials, and capital investment of all sorts. Under these conditions all unorganized persons are seen as being reduced to passive economic subservience, and government is visualized as playing a minor economic and political role. The important decisions will be made by the pattern-setting top labor leaders and corporation executives. In support of this view they cite the increasing pace of recent encroachments, the postwar requests of the U.A.W.'s Mr. Reuther for joint union-management determination of price and investment policies, and the developments in Sweden.

Is any one of these forecasts correct and inevitable? Let us examine some of their assumptions. Persons holding the first view summarized above appear to believe that among the leaders in both camps the basic drives and desires — for survival, power, and prestige — are so strong that neither side can compromise. Once labor gets rolling, it acquires an unstoppable momentum. Its leaders couldn't halt its onward movement even if they were so inclined. But their own drives will not incline them to make the attempt. Labor will always be asking for more, always seeking new encroachments. Management is inclined at first to yield, on matters directly affecting the workers. But when unions keep asking for more and more, they reach at last a point where they demand participation in managerial decisions that affect workers only indirectly. Some managements, sensing the trend, will vigorously resist further penetration. And after a few more lines of defense have been yielded, most managments will unite with all their resources to protect their "inherent" rights. Their own drives for survival, power, and prestige are such as to make them do so. On this assumption, the survival of both sides and a sharing of power and prestige are impossible because the drives of both sides are such as to make compromise impossible.

Thus we see that the first view is based essentially on a particular assumption about human motivation and behavior. So are the other two views. But both of the latter seem to assume that there is enough flexibility in human nature to permit a large measure of political and economic democracy. Neither side has to go "whole hog" in either arena. Political and economic power can be shared, and both sides can be permitted to survive without serious suppression of anyone's basic human drives.

Which assumption about human nature is correct? Much depends on whose human nature we are talking about. We saw in Chapter 2 that the nature and potency of human desires are conditioned by both hereditary and environmental conditions. The same person in considerably different environments might well exhibit different "human natures" or behaviors. And in the same environment different behavior patterns are found among different persons. One would not expect most Englishmen to go to the same political extremes that certain Germans and Russians have. But some Englishmen have tried to lead authoritarian movements; and many Germans and Russians have loathed and fought against their dictatorships. So we come to see that the future of labor-management relations depends a great deal on the kinds of leaders that unions and management have, and on what the leaders and those whom they lead have been taught to believe in. And on the above grounds we may conclude that the rise of the labor movement does not necessarily presage any particular form of social organization.

Let us carry our discussion a bit farther. Consider first the unions and their members. We have seen that the prestige and power of union leaders depend on the survival, power, and prestige of their unions as entities. We have also seen that the survival, power, and prestige of the unions depend in significant degree on their utility to satisfy the desires of most of their rank-and-file members for prestige, physical well-being, self-expression, security, and other things; members seek higher, more secure incomes, self-realization, and other satisfactions through their unions. Does the effort to satisfy all these desires mean that ultimately union leaders will guide their members into demands to control the whole of industry through government or to participate equally in all managerial decisions at the top level? Some unions, in the preambles to their constitutions, have language suggesting that the ultimate goal is worker ownership of the means of production. Do the leaders and members really mean it?

Now let us consider management. We have seen that the prestige and power of executives depend on the survival, prestige, and power of the entities known as firms which they manage. Many of these executives have come to look on themselves as "trustees." That is, they tend to think of themselves as a group which, having received in effect a grant of power from society, has the responsibility of safeguarding the interests not only of the owners of industry who theoretically employ them but also of their employees and the public in general. They also often tend to believe that they are peculiarly fitted to insure the survival and expansion of their firms and to fulfill the above-mentioned responsibilities. Then along come the unions with a demand that management shall share some of these functions and responsibilities. Do management's beliefs and desires mean that it must fight unionism and ultimately wipe it out? Or can management be induced to share some of its decision-making authority; and if so, how much?

By and large, there is little evidence that organized labor as a whole really wishes, on any theoretical or ideological basis, to share in top-management decisions or to usurp the managerial role *in toto.* It would appear that unions will continue their traditional pragmatic, opportunistic, trial-and-error approach to their immediate problems as they arise. But this is not a proper answer to the questions raised above. The real issue is, Will union's efforts to solve their day-to-day problems in a practical way lead them ultimately and inevitably to demand a half share in top control or to seek full top control for themselves? There is of course no certain answer to this basic question. But a few observations may be relevant.

It may be significant that union leaders always refuse to commit themselves on the issue of managerial prerogatives. That is, they refuse to say to management, "Here is a line beyond which we promise we will not move in asking for joint determination of decisions affecting our members." This refusal was perhaps the main reason why in 1945, soon after the war's end, the Labor-Management Conference called by President Truman broke up without agreement on the main issues of collective bargaining. A similar conference had been called in 1919 by President Wilson. That one broke up in disagreement over whether outside unions should be recognized as the proper agencies for dealings by management with employees. At that time most employers refused to recognize outside unions; they wanted the "open" shop or, at most, company unions. Twenty-five years later this issue was virtually non-existent. Unions, with governmental assistance, had gained a great deal of ground, and apparently employers were reconciled to dealing with them. There had been a notable change, then, in management's attitude. The fundamental issue in 1945 was not the acceptance of unionism as a principle but the proper scope of collective bargaining after union recognition. But failure to settle the 1945 issue to the satisfaction of both sides might in the end cause the 1919 issue to be revived; management's attitude might revert to what it had been after World War I.

For some time the unions in the severely competitive clothing industries have shared in a considerable number of top managerial decisions. In fact, in some areas the unions may almost be thought of as doing more managing than management. If those on management's side in these industries are very much upset over this development, they have not been vocal about their feelings. The main point about the union's sharing of decision-making in the apparel industries is this: It resulted from the efforts of unions and managements alike to help themselves by helping one another to solve their common problems in a practical way. It was not brought about by adherence to any particular theory or ideology. Thus, the members and leaders of the Amalgamated Clothing Workers wished, among many things, to have job security, higher incomes, and union survival and progress. The clothing firm executives wanted stability and security also. The Amalgamated's stabilization program was the pragmatic, mutually satisfactory answer to all these problems and desires.

Most managements in the less competitive (and generally bigger, more important) industries would be horrified to be asked seriously to yield similar ground. This is in part because there is much less mutuality of problems here. It is one thing for an enlightened management to believe that on matters directly affecting its workers it is best to use the union as a way of managing, i.e., to share decision-making with the union. Here the problems of management and of the union have much in common; both entities can advance their respective interests by trying together to satisfy the employee-members' basic desires. And management is often prepared to grant that the union may know more than management does (or at least as much) about these desires and how to satisfy them. In other words, the union can make a real contribution to good management in the field of employee relations. But it is quite another thing for management in the big industries to let the unions help decide such matters as price and investment policy. True, such decisions do affect the workers' welfare, if only indirectly. The union may well feel concern over them. But if management allows the union to share in such decisions, it is in effect admitting that the union knows as much about this kind of managing as management itself does. Very few managements would be willing to concede such a point. They would say, "If a union man knows enough to help make such decisions, we ought to take him over on management's side. Under any form of social organization — socialist, fascist, or private enterprise — the job of managing has to be done. The question is, by whom? Under our present system management makes top policy decisions that affect almost everyone — not only employees but also customers, suppliers of raw materials, and government. If the union view were carried to its logical conclusion, the top management of a given corporation ought to include representatives of *all* these groups. Then where would we be? No, managing has to be performed by a separate group. This group, in making its decisions, should properly consider the wishes of all the other groups and be their trustee. But to include these others in management itself would be to invite deadlock and chaos. Someone in the end must be the boss in decision-making and in trying to reconcile conflicting interests."

Union leaders might reply: "Management's logic fails to meet the test of practicality. In our world, customers and suppliers and others affected by managerial decisions have more and better alternatives, are in a much more secure position, and have higher incomes than our members. In other words, managerial decisions affect us much more directly and seriously than the members of any other group. Our people have to *live* with management. The others don't. Therefore, much more than any other group, labor is justified in asking to participate in managerial decision-making."

Let us suppose, for the sake of argument, that union leaders have agreed to draw a line beyond which they would not go in respect to managerial prerogatives. On the untouchable side of the line would be decisions on price and sales policy, procurement, investment, and similar matters. Let us suppose also that the union leaders have come to feel secure about the survival of their organizations; management by its acts as well as words has convinced them that it accepts unions completely and will never try to break them. In short, the survival and progress of both parties appear to have been assured.

There is at least one serpent in this Eden of good will. It is the inability of the private enterprise system by itself to guarantee and maintain full employment of resources. Every union member wants badly the chance for stable, continuous employment. His memory of experiences during previous depressions is vivid and bitter. Union leaders can not afford to disregard this desire. Suppose now that the economy falls into another bad business slump. Then the union leaders are going to feel they must do something about it.

What are their alternatives? One is to break their promise not to encroach further on managerial decision-making. Maybe some economist whom they like and who likes labor has convinced them that the main cause of depressions is price rigidity; everything would be all right if the big corporations would lower their product prices the way it happens in agriculture. Then much more of everything would be bought and many more workers would have to be hired. If the union leaders hold strongly to this belief, what else can they do (in view of their responsibilities to their members and to themselves) but ask management to let them help decide price policy? Then management "burns"; and both sides are out of Eden. One original sin may well lead to another. But in the end the unions may win joint control. Then we shall have a form of syndicalism, as prediction number three (page 554) is realized.

The other main alternative is to work through government. Maybe the economist who holds the confidence of the labor leaders is one who believes that the government budget can be manipulated so as to cure and prevent depressions. Then the leaders have two sub-alternatives: They can form a political party and try to become the government so as to have direct control over the budget. Or they can operate as they do now, trying to elect legislators favorable to the idea and lobbying for statutory enactment and administrative application of the idea. If they choose the first sub-alternative, either prediction number one or number two (page 554 above) may be fulfilled. But if they decide on the second sub-alternative, then none of the three predictions need come to pass. Government may remain relatively neutral, management may retain its major prerogatives, and economic and political democracy may be preserved.

For, as pointed out in Chapter 3, once economic knowledge has replaced ignorance in men's minds, there seems to be no valid, serious objection to giving governmental budget control a thorough, fair trial. It operates only at the top level and does not interfere below with anyone's freedom to make his own private economic and political decisions. In short, this approach appears to merit experimentation because it promises to provide, in the socially least expensive way, for the avoidance of unemployment and the maintenance of liberty.

This approach would also seem to hold promise as a solution to the fundamental problem of collective bargaining. Under such a program there would be little social justification for unions to try to usurp or share the making of top managerial decisions. And it is hard to believe that without important social justification union leaders would try very hard to move in that direction. In fact, one can imagine without too much difficulty that smart union leaders would try to enlist management's support in trying to get the budget-control program adopted by relatively neutral government. It is also fairly easy to imagine that smart management would go along if aware of the basic alternatives.

We have just finished discussing the possible future of collective bargaining. How far into the future the various possibilities extend, no one can tell. It might not be very far if international peace were suddenly to break out and a big depression were thereafter to blanket the land. However, such peace seems unlikely so long as the communists continue their efforts to proselyte mankind.

CHAPTER 21

Some Collective Bargaining Experiences

In Chapters 10–16 and 17–20 we explained the technological-economic and the behavioral conditions which determine the attitudes and policies of unions and of employers, and which influence the relations between unions and employers. With these things in mind, let us consider how unions and managements have lived together in three collective bargaining situations – bituminous coal, automobiles, and a particular plant of the Inland Steel Company.

In each of these situations we shall deal first with the economic-technological and human relations conditions, and second with the collective bargaining experiences of the parties in the light of these conditions.

A. THE BITUMINOUS COAL INDUSTRY

1. The setting for relations. The bituminous coal industry is a fruitful area for study. Coal appeared on the commercial market as early as 1745, and the growth of the industry paralleled the transformation of the United States from a predominantly agricultural nation to an industrialized urban nation. Unionism in the bituminous coal industry has existed for over 100 years. In the beginning, it was insignificant and helpless in the face of competitive economic forces. Today it is nation-wide and powerful. Today the decisions at the bargaining table of this industry immediately affect the economic welfare of the country.

a. Economic conditions. (1) In the product market. Labor-management relations in the coal industry have been continuously affected by the peculiarities of coal production and distribution. Therefore it is desirable to consider the nature and effects of some basic characteristics of the product market.

(a) Economics of coal marketing. The demand for coal is relatively concentrated, whereas the supply is relatively dispersed. The demand for coal is derived from its use as a source of energy, heat, and chemical derivatives. The great users of coal are manufacturing, utilities, and railroads; these together in 1949 consumed about 80 per cent of the total

coal output. The remainder is purchased largely by householders. Hence demand is concentrated in the great centers of population and industry. In contrast, coal reserves are abundant and widely distributed. So is production. Coal is mined commercially in 28 states. These fall logically into three major coal regions. The Appalachian Field (Pennsylvania, West Virginia, Ohio, Maryland, Virginia, eastern Kentucky, Tennessee, and Alabama) is the largest, producing about 75 per cent of the nation's output. The Central Field (including Illinois, Indiana, and western Kentucky) produces about 15 per cent; and the Western Field, which includes all mines west of the Mississippi, produces about 10 per cent of the total. Some coal moves only a few miles to market; other coal moves 500 miles or more. The struggle *between areas* to capture major markets and overcome differences in transportation cost, quality of coal, accessibility, and so forth has made for severe competition.

Labor cost is a high proportion of total cost at the mine. Labor constitutes between 60 and 65 per cent of this cost. Hence competition between producers *within* the same region places great pressure on wages, since wage costs are the key to success or failure in capturing a market, other costs being equal.

Transportation cost is a high proportion of the total cost to the consumer. The cost of transporting coal to market will run from 20 to 50 per cent of the delivered price. Thus coal may cost $5 a ton at the mine and $10 delivered at the market. This is significant for several reasons. In order to permit outlying regions to compete in a given market, the railroads have granted lower rates *per ton-mile* for long hauls than for short hauls. This has intensified competition. Because the total freight revenue from coal is very high, individual railroads have encouraged the opening up of new areas in order to benefit from the revenues. Freight rates, however, are inflexible. Since they are a high proportion of the price and cannot be easily lowered, competitive pressures are shifted back to the mines and particularly to wage costs. It obviously takes a considerable cut in wage costs to bring about a major reduction in delivered prices.

The cost of coal is a small part of total costs to industrial users. A manufacturer using coal for fuel will find that a reduction of, say, 20 per cent in coal prices will not affect his total manufacturing costs as much as one or two per cent. As a result, demand tends to be relatively inelastic to the point where a user may substitute a competing fuel. The cost of coal may be reduced drastically at the mine without stimulating short-run demand very much. A single coal producer may gain something for himself by sharp price and wage reductions, but his gain will in the short run be at the expense of other coal producers.

The number of producing units in this industry is very large, and most of the units are small. In 1950, there were about 9000 mines of commercial size in the 28 principal coal states operated by about 5000 companies. No single firm accounted for as much as 5 per cent of total output and only about 10 companies produced as much as one per cent each.[1] This extreme decentralization exists despite the fact that for many decades there has been a trend toward concentration. In 1905, the larger mines producing 200,000 tons or more annually accounted for 40 per cent of the total; in 1948, they accounted for 65 per cent.[2] The multiplicity of ownership compounds the competitive factors in the industry.

The capital required to exploit coal resources is small, but once invested is highly immobile. Especially in the past, before mining became highly mechanized, it was easy for a few individuals to pool their resources, lease coal land, and start mining. But once a mine is opened, capital cannot be retrieved except over a long period through depreciation and depletion allowances. Mines cannot be closed except at very great expense and very great risk. Areaways must be kept ventilated to avoid the accumulation of gases, pumped to avoid destruction by water, timbered to prevent collapse of ceilings. "Maintenance of idle property may be more costly than operation at a loss."[3] Under such conditions, expansion may take place very quickly, but contraction takes place very slowly. Marginal producers stay in the industry even when forced to sell below cost in the hope of recovering at least some of their capital. Further, contraction is prolonged by the fact that, while one group of owners may go bankrupt, other purchasers may secure the coal property at great discount and continue producing coal with lower capital charges.

As a result of all these factors, the ordinary function of price is greatly modified in the product market of this industry. The function of price is the balancing of supply and demand. When demand for coal suddenly moves up rapidly, production does respond readily. Old mines work longer hours and add to their labor force. New mines are opened. But when demand falls, production may continue as before or decline slowly for the reasons cited above. Prices become unprofitable over considerable periods as operators produce at a loss and frantically try to lower costs. Both management and labor suffer from the short-run demoralization during such periods of "cutthroat" competition typical of this industry. One must keep in mind these hard economic facts of life in the product market of the coal industry, in order to appreciate the attitudes of both management and labor toward their respective problems.

(b) Operation of supply and demand. i. The era of expansion, 1850–1923. Following the Civil War and accompanying the development of heavy industry in this country, the coal industry entered a period of brilliant expansion. From an output of only 10 million tons in 1860 the industry expanded so rapidly that by 1900 output was 260 million tons a

[1] Bituminous Coal Institute, *1950 Bituminous Coal Annual,* p. 8.

[2] *Ibid.,* p. 55.

[3] Temporary National Economic Committee, *Competition and Monopoly in American Industry,* Monograph No. 21, 1941, p. 25.

year and the United States had passed Great Britain as the foremost world producer. The rate of expansion slowed down somewhat after 1900 but was still rapid until World War I. There were many reasons why the outlook was favorable. Not only was population growing, but the per-capita consumption of coal had risen steadily despite occasional periods of overproduction. World War I brought even greater demand. Private enterprise responded quickly. In 1923, some 9331 mines produced the unprecedented output of 564 million tons.[4] Profits from 1918–23 were extraordinary.

ii. Contraction and adjustments, 1923–50. After 1923 the outlook for coal demand clouded and then darkened. The industry suddenly found itself with chronic over-capacity, falling prices, ruinous competition, severe wage-cutting, and strikes. Two main forces were at work. First, temporary stimulants to demand disappeared. Much of the demand from 1918–23, which brought so many new mines into production, was war-born and non-continuing, leaving many operators with no logical markets.

Second, "normal" peacetime demand leveled off and then declined. Per-capita consumption no longer increased. Instead it declined. At least two factors explained this sudden change within a single decade, both of them originating from the cumulative impact of technology. For one, a large portion of the rising demand for energy in the United States came to be met by competitive fuels. In some cases outright displacement took place; railroads, for example, replaced coal-fired locomotives with oil-burning Diesels. In the early 1920's bituminous coal provided about 70 per cent of the nation's fuel and power. By 1950 this share had declined to 45 per cent as coal gave way to oil and natural gas. Another important factor was the increased efficiency in the utilization of coal. In 1920 utility power plants required 3.2 pounds of coal per kilowatt hour of electricity produced. In 1948 they burned only 1.3 pounds. In 1920 iron and steel mills required about 3000 pounds of coking coal per ton of pig iron. In 1948 they burned a little less than 2800 pounds.[5] The collapse of temporary stimulants and the expansion of competing fuels brought chronic over-capacity in the 1920's and 1930's, estimated at from 25 to 30 per cent even in the best years. To add to the industry's woes came continued expansion of coal capacity in the South Appalachian region which was able to undersell most of the older Northern properties. This tended to concentrate the over-capacity in the older Northern coal areas and hence to intensify the struggle for markets there.

Amidst unrestrained and desperate competition brought on by over-capacity, prices declined steadily from $2.68 at the mine in 1923 to $1.31 in 1932. Yet liquidation of mine capacity was slow and was concentrated in the smaller mines. Despite a rising cycle of business and despite gov-

[4] Bituminous Coal Institute, *1950 Bituminous Coal Annual,* pp. 12–13.
[5] U. S. Department of Interior, *Minerals Yearbook,* 1948, p. 280.

ernment stabilization efforts after 1932, the industry continued with excess capacity and severe internal and external competition until relieved by the unusual demands of World War II. By 1950 the pressures of external competition were again being felt.

(2) The labor market. We now turn to a consideration of those who constitute the labor force of this industry. How do miners live? What are their needs? How have their jobs affected their attitudes towards their union, toward coal management, toward the community at large?

(a) Size and occupational composition of coal's labor resources. There are today about 375,000 workers who normally make their living from coal, with perhaps another 25,000 who work part-time in the mines.[6] These figures reflect the sharp decline from the peak employment of 700,000 reached in the year 1923. During the era of expansion to World War I, the labor force was largely recruited from abroad, the skilled English and Welsh miners coming over during the early days, followed by the Irish and then by a wide variety of immigrants from eastern and southeastern Europe. The influx of such a mixed group was a major deterrent to collective action. Underground mining tasks fall into two broad classes. The "tonnage" workers dig out the coal at the working face of the mine. They are usually paid on an incentive basis of so much per ton. The "day" men are the service workers who carry out the auxiliary tasks of haulage, timbering, ventilation, power supply, and maintenance. They are usually paid by the day. "Tonnage" workers made up nearly two-thirds of the work force during the early days of hand mining. Mechanization has reversed the ratio. In the process many miners found their skills no longer needed.

(b) The "physical and cultural isolation of miners." Mining communities must be built where coal resources lie, whether that be "a narrow valley between big hills, as in West Virginia, Utah, or eastern Kentucky, or under prairie lands as in Illinois, Indiana, Ohio . . ."[7] Before the coming of modern highways the isolation of these communities was almost complete. It is important even today. Miners feel they are on their own, set apart from the rest of society. Coal is usually the only source of employment outside of marginal agriculture. This gives the miner a precarious economic basis that makes for a feeling of insecurity. It has been estimated that over 40 per cent of all the nation's coal workers live in 36 widely scattered "single industry" counties.[8] Miners thus live under extreme dependence. When the mine whistle fails to blow, the entire community is without means of support. The typical coal-mining town has been dirty, smoky, and dusty, with substandard housing and inadequate community facilities. The town usually had to be built by the company.

[6] Bituminous Coal Institute, *1950 Bituminous Coal Annual,* p. 143.

[7] *Ibid.,* p. 136.

[8] W. C. Trapnell and Ralph Ilesley, *The Bituminous Coal Industry with a Survey of Competing Fuels,* Federal Emergency Relief Administration, 1935, pp. 6–8.

Since the coal resources in a particular locality would last only so long, the company reasoned, why build adequate housing? It is beyond our scope to recount here the story of the "company town" of the past, but the student would do well to review its history.[9] The deprivation of civil liberties as well as the exaction of economic servitude in return for employment is one of the sordid chapters in American industrial development.

(c) Dangers of mining. Mining is the most dangerous of major occupations. This fact plays an important role in the attitude of the miner toward himself and his community. When John L. Lewis cries out that "coal is already saturated with the blood of too many widows and orphans," he voices the deep and abiding sense of risk involved in making a living from coal. The average injury severity rate for all U. S. industries is 1.02. For coal it is 6.84.[10]

From 1900 to 1930, nearly 2000 miners were killed every year. In recent years the industry has made considerable progress in reducing hazards, but nearly 1000 are still being killed every year, and 50,000 injured.[11] The odds are very great against a coal miner's working throughout his life without a serious injury. As one writer recently put it,

> Statistically, he can work only about seven years without being overtaken by violent death or injury. He has only about a 10 to 1 chance to survive thirty years of working in the coal mines, and little better than a 4 to 1 chance of escaping being totally or partially disabled for life.[12]

This adds up to 55,000 miners killed in accidents from 1920 to 1950. In addition, nearly 125,000 were crippled, and injuries totaled 2,000,000.

(d) Chronic under-employment since World War I. Mining is normally subject to seasonal variations which reduce man-days per year to 260 at best. Mine breakdowns and accidents further reduce working time. Since World War I the secular dislocation of the industry resulted in spreading out the work; in the 1920's average work-days per year were only about 200. The vulnerability of coal to the major cyclical decline of the early 1930's reduced annual man-days to around 175. Not until after 1940 did the average rise above 200. These statistics emphasize the importance to the miner of his hourly or incentive wage rate. It must be high to compensate for irregularity of employment.

(e) Relative immobility of the coal labor force. An experienced miner has a specialized skill. It is not easily transferred to other types of work. The community in which he works is usually one with a single industry

[9] See, for example, Lois MacDonald, *Labor Problems and the American Scene,* Chap. 5, "Company Towns: Coal Camps," pp. 77–91; and L. Gilfillan, *I Went to Pit College,* Blue Ribbon Books, Inc., 1934.

[10] National Safety Council, *Accident Facts,* 1950, p. 26.

[11] U. S. Bureau of Mines, Release of June 22, 1948.

[12] David G. Wittels, "The Bloody Price of Coal," *Saturday Evening Post,* February 12, 1949, p. 16.

— coal. Alternative employments are not available. Leaving the community means an uprooting of such magnitude that few miners past 30 years of age will undertake it except under extraordinary economic pressure. Contraction of coal demand has not been followed by a proportionate contraction in the labor force in short-run periods. "Pulling in" workers to expand output has been fairly easy. "Pushing them out" has been slow.

(f) Implications in terms of human relations. The miner's way of living has made him extremely conscious of his need for security. Sensitive to outside criticism, he is quick to defend what he believes will protect him and his family from want. His memories of the past, of life in company coal towns, of the death of his co-workers, his experience with months of unemployment, his feeling of being in a world apart — all these add up to an attitude of aggressiveness in getting more from the economic system than he has obtained in the past.

b. Technological conditions. In the last four decades the bituminous coal industry has undergone a technological revolution. Prior to the 1890's mining was a handicraft industry. The first step in mechanization began with the undercutting of coal seams about 1890. Today nearly 90 per cent of coal is cut mechanically. Electrical power replaced animal power in haulage after 1910. Mechanical loading began in the early 1920's. Today nearly 70 per cent of the coal is so loaded. Productivity per man-hour is nearly three times greater in strip mining than in underground. Strip mining expanded rapidly after 1920. Over-all production per man-hour has risen from about .40 tons in 1914 to .85 tons in 1949. Since 1935, output per man-day has risen from 4.5 to 6.4 tons. The latter is more than twice the output per man-day of any other country.[13]

The force behind this revolution has been twofold. In the era of expansion, the principal goal of individual producers was to increase output and capture a larger share of the market. In the period of contraction the objective was to keep unit costs down in order to offset the rising pressure on wage costs by unionism and the pressure from competitive fuels. Had the industry not mechanized, the contraction in consumption would have been markedly greater.

The achievements in mechanization have brought both gains and losses to coal miners. Coal mining is easier and safer than ever before. Greater productivity has made possible advancing wage rates. At the same time it has reduced the size of labor force required and has thus added to the employment problem of miners who remain in mining. This may be readily seen from the fact that in 1947, the peak year of output in coal's history, the industry produced 631 million tons, or 62 million tons *more* than in 1920, but with 220,000 *fewer* miners.[14]

c. Relation to government. Government has for many decades closely

[13] Bituminous Coal Institute, *1950 Bituminous Coal Annual,* pp. 14 and 150.
[14] *Loc. cit.*

observed or intervened in the production and marketing of coal. As early as the 1890's both state and federal governments undertook social and economic investigations of the coal industry. These early studies were not intended to serve as the basis for changing the competitive nature of the industry but rather to focus public attention on the causes of conflict between labor and management and the low living standards of the mining population. A second phase of government relations came when government intervened in behalf of the public. In order to assure adequate wartime coal supplies, the government fixed coal prices high enough during World War I to keep marginal mines in profitable operation and to encourage the opening of new mines. The success of this policy is seen in the fact that between 1916 and 1919 the number of mines increased about 50 per cent. Government policy was thus a major factor in the over-expansion at that time. In return for participation in the World War I "Washington Agreement," labor was given a wage-rate increase and the right to maintain unions without interference from employers. Again in World War II the federal government fixed both prices and wage rates under wartime stabilization policy in the public interest. A third type of intervention has been in behalf of and at the request of the union and the industry. Coal prices and wage rates fell steadily from 1923 to 1933 until checked by government price and wage-rate-fixing programs desired by labor and by a large segment of management. These programs began with the N.I.R.A. in 1933 (declared unconstitutional in 1935) and were carried on through the thirties by the Bituminous Coal Conservation Act of 1935 and its successor, the Bituminous Coal Act of 1937. This peacetime price "stabilization" program was shelved during World War II and not revived through 1951. It should be understood that in its quest for higher wage rates the United Mine Workers tried to do with the aid of government what the Amalgamated Clothing Workers tried to do (with success) on its own motion, namely, stabilize a highly competitive industry. The miners' union, with the support of most of the industry, got the government for a while to provide for higher coal prices so that higher wage rates could be afforded.

In the area of labor-management relations, government has intervened *in behalf of labor* since 1933. Beginning with the N.I.R.A. (Section 7a) and continuing later with the National Labor Relations Act of 1935, government guaranteed workers the right to select representatives of their own choosing without interference from employers (see below).

The history of government intervention to avert or end strikes and lockouts *in behalf of the public* is too long to be adequately reviewed here. The legislative branch of the federal government has not only laid down national labor policy for all industries, but on occasion has passed legislation clearly designed for special application to the coal industry (e.g., the Smith-Connally Act of 1943). The judiciary through court injunction has frequently issued restraining orders on labor or management or both. The executive branch has intervened through the services of the government's mediation and conciliation service, the President's seizure of the mines under wartime emergency authority, and the appointment of fact-finding boards under the amended National Labor Relations (Taft-Hartley) Act of 1947.

The significance of government intervention in coal is twofold. First, the community has been *willing* to intervene for the purpose of assisting one or the other of the parties in the industry. Both parties on occasion have *requested* the assistance of the community. It follows that the community has believed it *desirable* to render assistance to promote the welfare of labor or management. Second, the community on other occasions has found it *necessary* to intervene to protect not the parties, but the community itself. The national economy cannot stand a prolonged work stoppage without impairment to the health, welfare, and safety of the community.

d. The parties to bargaining. (1) General nature of employers. Employers in the coal industry have had several prominent characteristics. First, *competitive interests have not been similar.* As we have already pointed out, coal operators in various areas have wanted to be free to operate individually in the market, that is, to adjust their costs and their output so as to achieve the greatest competitive advantage. In the absence of unionism they have desired flexibility in wage rates, the big cost item. If unionized wage uniformity had been established by 1910, many Southern mines would never have been opened. Second, *ownership interests have not been the same.* About 85 per cent of coal is mined by independent concerns. About 15 per cent is produced by "captive" mines owned by steel companies, utilities, and railroads. Thus, the marketing interests of the owners have often been dissimilar. Third, *the number of employers has been extremely large* and their location scattered. As previously stated, the number of management units has been upwards of 5000, located in 28 states from Alabama to the state of Washington. Agreement on policy among so many firms is extremely difficult. Fourth, *there was no need for industry-wide unity until after 1933 because until then there was no industry-wide union.* Even today, despite the fact that members of the United Mine Workers produce 90 per cent of the nation's coal, there is no single employers' association. The two largest organizations, however, the Northern and the Southern Appalachian operators, with their numerous sub-associations, account for probably 70 per cent of total coal output and set the pattern for the rest of the industry.

(2) General nature of the union. (a) Role of unionism in the mining community. The union plays a more important role in the life of the average mine worker than it does in the life of many other types of wage-earners. It has of course been an economic agency for betterment, as in other industries. As such, unionism is synonymous with the notable

progress in raising the miner's living standard. But it is much more. Among miners living in "physical and cultural isolation" it is a social institution, a focal point for social gatherings, discussions, and community celebrations. It provides an outlet for miners' interests. It serves as *personal compensation* for the deficiencies in their lives, such as the lack of adequate education. And it serves as *group compensation* for the limited variety of community facilities in single-industry counties.

(b) History of unionism. i. The struggle for permanent unionism, 1850–90. The first local unions appeared about 1850. They were weak and shortlived. In 1870 the first regional union successfully negotiated a contract with an employers' association. But it lasted only a few years. Unionism consumed its energies in trying to survive. The obstacles were formidable and included the difficulties of organizing workers speaking a variety of languages, the unrelenting opposition of employers, the recurring price wars which threatened the solvency of the operators, the lack of experience of miners in negotiating contracts, the great dispersal of the industry, and the struggles between rival union organizations. At no time did union membership rise above 20 per cent of eligible workers.

ii. Permanent unionism: The United Mine Workers of America, 1890 to date. As a result of disastrous local strikes in 1889 the two largest regional federations, the National Federation of Miners and the Knights of Labor, formed the United Mine Workers of America in 1890. No sooner had the union been formed than the acute depression of 1892–96 demoralized labor; membership dropped to an estimated 4000 members or around five per cent of the nation's miners. Yet despite its admitted weakness, the U.M.W. called a strike in 1897 as a result of the miners' desperate plight following persistent price and wage cuttings. To the amazement of the industry, 150,000 miners walked out of the pits.[15] With the signing of a regional contract with employers, membership jumped spectacularly to 115,000 by 1900 and to 247,000 by 1903. Labor market stringency during and just after World War I enabled the U.M.W. to claim 440,000 members by 1920, or almost three-fourths of all coal miners. But the economic difficulties of the industry during the twenties, together with the U.M.W.'s inability to organize the mines of West Virginia, Kentucky, and Alabama (because of hard-boiled employer opposition, court injunctions, and unfriendly police), almost led to the union's undoing.

The New Deal and the business recovery that began in 1933 brought another swift change in the fortunes of the U.M.W. Under the protection of the N.I.R.A. and the National Labor Relations Act, the union's vigorous organizing drives brought the great majority of miners back into the fold and enabled its president, John L. Lewis, to claim by 1940 that almost 90 per cent of the industry had been unionized, including most of the

15 Waldo E. Fisher, in *How Collective Bargaining Works, Twentieth Century Fund*, 1942, p. 236.

South. In 1951 the U.M.W. had a membership of 600,000 and included more than 90 per cent of the nation's bituminous coal miners.[16]

Several aspects of this growth should be noted. The development of unionism in coal, while steadily upward over the long run, was accompanied by numerous setbacks, and in 1932 by an almost complete collapse after eighty years of effort. As shown by the willingness of unorganized miners to follow the U.M.W. out of the mines, the importance of coal unionism has always been much greater than indicated by mere membership figures. The desire to organize has been deeply rooted and persistent in the minds of coal miners since the beginning of the industry, as also shown by their readiness to join the U.M.W. when they could do so without fear of loss of employment. The successful unionization of the entire industry is a very recent accomplishment. It has depended heavily on government interference in the affairs of the industry and on the economic well-being of the industry. The union has never been able to withstand for long the forces accompanying serious cyclical or secular decline.

iii. Internal union characteristics. It is not our purpose here to deal at length with the internal administration of the U.M.W. Two points, however, should be noted. First, the administration of the union has always been highly centralized — a circumstance that may have been made necessary by the decentralized nature of mining, but one that has also led to ruthless and autocratic control over union affairs. Second, internal friction over policy matters has persisted over long periods, as some local groups have resisted top leadership decisions. The only successful open revolt occurred in 1932 when some rebellious Illinois locals, with a membership of around 15,000, seceded and formed the Progressive Mine Workers of America. The P.M.W. has generally followed the patterns established by the U.M.W.

iv. The U.M.W.'s leadership and relations with other unions. The Mine Workers' leadership has always been vigorous. Since the rise of John L. Lewis, the union has been in the center of the American labor movement. In 1935–38, Lewis and the miners took the leadership in forming the C.I.O. and in organizing the steel industry. At that time the miners left the A.F.L. A short time thereafter they left the C.I.O. (1942) and in due course rejoined the A.F.L. (1946). But this affiliation again became distasteful to the individualistic leader of the miners, and the U.M.W. soon withdrew to become an "independent" in 1947.

Since the end of World War II the miners have been in the forefront of labor's fight for higher wage rates and "fringe" benefits, notably pension and welfare funds. They have served as a bellwether for other unions and have often set the pattern for successive "rounds" of achievements. The intense rivalry between the leadership of the U.M.W. and that of

[16] U. S. Bureau of Labor Statistics, *Directory of Labor Unions in the United States*, 1950, p. 35. The figure 600,000 includes the anthracite miners and the non-miners of District 50.

other unions has been a major obstacle to the emergence of a unified national labor movement.

2. The collective bargaining experience. *a. History and development.* The history of collective bargaining in coal may be thought of as passing through two stages. From 1898 to 1927 the U.M.W. and the operators in the Central Competitive Field had a collective pact which at times covered over half of the nation's coal output. The collapse of this pact in 1927 saw the deterioration of bargaining, until by 1932 unionized output was less than 20 per cent of the total. The second phase from 1933 to the present has witnessed the achievement of industry-wide unionization by the U.M.W.; but the union-management relationship is still on a multi-employer-association basis. Throughout the entire period bargaining has been difficult. "Honeymoon" discussions between the parties have been followed by pitched battles in the coal towns. From 1900 to 1950, strikes preceded the signing of contracts in over half the peacetime years. What has been the cause of this chronic breakdown in industrial relations? We shall try to seek the answer in terms of key factors which run continuously through the whole bargaining history.

(1) Basic issues between the parties, 1898–1929. (a) Union recognition and security. Contrary to widespread opinion, the employers in coal have not been uniformly opposed to granting the U.M.W. recognition and giving it security. A substantial segment has always been willing to recognize the union if the rest of the industry did likewise. But some operators have always opposed recognition and in recent years have accepted unionism only under great pressure.

Why does such a hard core of adamant anti-unionism exist? Some operators have objected to the inflexibility which comes from a union contract. Others have personally disliked the leadership of the U.M.W. and the way Lewis "throws his weight around." But the underlying factor has been disagreement over union wage policy and its competitive implications.

(b) The area of bargaining. Many coal operators have disagreed both with the union and with other employers over the area of bargaining. The union has constantly tried to extend the area of bargaining to cover the entire industry. Some Northern operators, in favorable competitive positions, have agreed with this policy. Others, however, have opposed it. Under the Central Competitive pact in the years 1898–1927, Ohio and Pennsylvania operators refused to admit the higher paying Western operators to conference discussions, fearing that these might join with the union to peg wages to Western rates. These same Ohio and Pennsylvania operators, however, urged the union to organize the lower-wage Southern mines so that Southern operators would be forced into the conference. Many small mine owners wanted the area of bargaining to be kept small lest they be swallowed by the policies of the big operators. Management

units have frequently changed positions with altered market conditions.

(c) The fundamental issue of wage-rate policy. It is abundantly clear that the success or failure of the parties to bargain in coal has rested primarily on the competitive conditions of the market. And the key issue here is labor cost, which in turn rests on wage-rate policy.

What has been the union's wage-rate policy? It first took form under the Central Competitive pact of 1898–1927. The parties had to decide three fundamental questions. The first was how to set *wage-rate differentials* between and within competing coal areas. The operators wanted tonnage workers to be paid equal tonnage rates, which would make for uniformity of unit labor costs and hence for competitive equality. This would result in unequal earnings by the miners because the thickness of the coal seams and other conditions differed widely among the areas. The miners wanted equal earnings for equal effort. This seemed fair and equitable, but would require unequal tonnage rates — higher in the poor mines, lower in the good ones. The result would be unequal labor costs per ton to the operators. In general, the needs of employers for "competitive equality" were accepted in principle, with due regard wherever possible for the desires of the miners. The goal was agreed to be "uniform costs in fields with common markets," in order to keep operator's "selling prices up to reasonable rates.[17] The union early recognized that price and product market conditions were prerequisite to stability. The second question that the parties had to decide under the Central Competitive pact was one of *wage-rate level.* In actual practice wage-rate levels were related to the higher Western rates rather than to the lower Southern rates. The third question concerned the manner of *negotiating and administering wages* for many specific occupations and hundreds of separate mine properties. This was solved by using several districts within the Central Competitive Field as "basing points for fixing rates for key occupations. Detailed rates for most occupations were left to district and sub-district negotiations.[18]

By means of bargaining the union hoped to raise the living standards of union members, to extend union standards to the rest of the industry, and reduce strife in the coal fields. How well did the union (and the operators) succeed?

From 1898 to 1923 the union was able to secure "substantial wage increases for its members" and to maintain "rates of pay well above those prevailing in non-union mines." Union members not only got higher hourly and annual earnings but worked shorter hours. In its drive to organize the entire industry the union made considerable progress, increasing the percentage of coal mined under union contract from about 20

[17] Waldo E. Fisher, "Bituminous Coal," Chapter 5 in *How Collective Bargaining Works,* p. 238.

[18] Carrie Glasser, "Union Wage Policy in Bituminous Coal," *Industrial and Labor Relations Review,* Vol. I, No. 4, July, 1948, p. 611.

per cent in 1898 to nearly 75 per cent in 1919. Bargaining did not reduce industrial strife. The percentage of man-days lost through strikes in Illinois, Indiana, and Ohio between 1898 and 1927 was nearly three times as great as in the rest of the industry.[19]

One reason for the union's success during 1898–1923 in making economic gains and extending unionism was the fact that this was a period of expanding demand for coal. Internal competition was kept moderate by rising demand. At times very high prices could be charged by individual operators because demand was so high. During World War I, output was limited by labor supply, not by ability to compete in the product market. Employers relented their opposition to unionism. For another thing, external competition from competing fuels had not yet become a major concern. Finally, a friendly government during the war years strengthened the union's hand.

From 1923 to 1933 the story was entirely different. The industry was confronted with falling demand, cutthroat price competition, the growing output of non-union Southern mines (which had begun to cut wage rates), chronic over-capacity, and constant strife in the union fields. The U.M.W. and its leader, John L. Lewis, had to make a hard decision. Should the union continue to hold union wage rates firm? The favoring arguments were impressive. Miners had not fought to build a union just to let union leadership accept wage-rate cuts. They might as well have gone non-union. Over-capacity could never be liquidated unless the marginal mines went out of business, yet drastic wage-rate reductions would keep them in. Acceptance of wage-rate decreases in the union fields would only result in disproportionate cuts in the non-union fields. Union miners argued that "we'd just be racing non-union wages down the hill." The argument against holding union wage rates up was simple but formidable. If the union fields didn't meet the competition of non-union fields, the latter would capture the market. Despite a deteriorating market, the U.M.W. decided to hold wage rates in the North and to try to unionize the South. Lewis said there would be "no backward step."

The union's policy did not succeed. From the non-union mines came such severe, low-cost competition for Northern union mines that a number of small mine operators there repudiated the high-wage Jacksonville agreement of 1924 and operated non-union before 1927, when the agreement expired. The large Northern operators were forced to ask for wage reductions at the Miami union-operator conference of 1927. When the union refused to grant them, the conference broke up without agreement, and most of the Northern mines, defeating the union in a bitter strike, began to operate non-union. By 1932, only a part of the Illinois bituminous field and the entire anthracite field remained in the union fold, and the dues-paying membership had declined to about 100,000.

[19] Waldo E. Fisher, "Bituminous Coal," Chapter 5 in *How Collective Bargaining Works*, p. 250.

Why did bargaining almost cease to function after making such progress up to 1923? We have already touched on some of the answers. First, the union and union operators were helpless to do anything about the chronic over-capacity on the supply side and the declining demand on the market side. Second, the shrinking over-all demand brought ruinous price and wage-rate competition, which forced employers to either break with the union or go out of business. They chose the former. Third, the non-union Southern fields operated under complete freedom to adjust wage rates and prices to market conditions. From 1923–33 they steadily widened differentials in their favor, which enabled them to acquire an increasing share of the market and concentrate the over-capacity in the Northern unionized mines. That is, capacity in the South increased as Northern mines were forced to shut down. The percentage of total coal produced in the non-union states of West Virginia and Kentucky jumped from 22 per cent for 1916–20 to 36.1 per cent for 1931–35.[20] In the face of economic disintegration, the U.M.W. not only failed to organize the rest of the industry; it could not hold what it had won. Ironically, in its efforts to hold what it had gained, the U.M.W. engaged in such continuous strife with the operators that the interruption of production in the Northern fields added to the ability of the non-union South to take over markets. By 1933, collective bargaining was almost ended after three decades of effort.

(d) Some non-wage aspects. Failure in bargaining was not complete, however. Bargaining on certain non-wage issues had made real progress and was quickly resumed when the economic climate improved. One issue was the development of grievance machinery which began with the worker and his foreman or pit boss and continued up through successive levels of union-management discussion to arbitration.

(2) Basic issues between the parties, 1933–51. (a) Union recognition and security. So desperate was the plight of workers and management alike in 1933 that the economic and industrial relations program of the Roosevelt administration was quickly accepted in the industry. Management got price-fixing. Labor got the right to organize without employer interference. Hundreds of U.M.W. organizers and volunteers moved into the coal fields. Within twelve months, the union had organized 90 per cent of the miners including a large proportion of the former non-union coal workers of the South. Through government protection the union achieved in one year recognition that it had not been able to obtain in the previous forty years. By 1939 the union felt strong enough to demand the union shop. Within a few years, through strike pressures and government assistance, the U.M.W. secured the union shop from both Northern and Southern operators and a modified union shop from the most bitter hold-outs of Harlan County, Kentucky. In ten years the union

[20] Carrie Glasser, *op. cit.*, p. 612.

had secured industry-wide security, something it had failed to attain in the previous fifty years.

(b) The area of bargaining. The principal bargaining conference established under the N.R.A. in 1933 produced what was known as the "Appalachian Agreement." It included the states of Pennsylvania, Michigan, Ohio, Maryland, Virginia, West Virginia, eastern Kentucky, and Tennessee. This region produces over 70 per cent of the nation's coal, and agreement therein sets the pattern for the industry. The conference avoided the basic weakness of the old Central Competitive pact of not including the important, growing mines of the Southern field. The conference lasted until 1939, when the Southern associations chose to walk out as they had in previous decades. But this time the threat to stability was short-lived. Now that the union was industry-wide it gained the upper hand by playing one regional association off against another. In 1943 the union succeeded in getting essentially the same contract with all associations through negotiations extending over a year. In 1945 all associations, including the captive mine operators, were invited to a revived Appalachian Conference. All employer associations signed, thus establishing the first truly national wage conference in coal. The union had achieved in about twelve years what it had failed to do in the previous forty. The area of bargaining was now industry-wide, although bargaining on the employer side was still multi-associational. There have been occasional dissensions within management's ranks since 1945, but these have not been disruptive. All units of management signed a "pre-stabilization" contract on January 18, 1951, to expire on March 31, 1952. In effect, a powerful nation-wide union had forced the operators to merge in order to raise their bargaining power to the level of the union's. This is a relatively recent turn of events in the coal industry.

(c) The issue of wage-rate policy. After 1933 the U.M.W. made it clear that it would not repeat the mistakes of the 1920's. From the very first it sought and obtained higher wage-rate increases for Southern mines than for Northern. In so doing the union had the encouragement and actual bargaining assistance of Northern management. The Southern mines could no longer hold out as in the past. The union could and did make compacts with Northern operators, while keeping Southern mines closed down with consequent loss of markets. For all practical purposes the North-South differential was eliminated in the contract of 1941. Industry-wide uniformity had been achieved in eight years and another threat to internal stability eliminated.

(d) Some non-wage issues. Other achievements of unionism were noteworthy during this period. The union miner achieved protection on the job through contractual rights covering hiring, transfer, promotion, discharge, elaborate machinery for handling of grievances, protection against short weighing, and numerous other aspects of day-to-day operations.

Of special significance was the development of protection for the miner who was unable to work because of injury or superannuation. In 1946 the union demanded a fund to provide this protection. It proposed a royalty tax on each ton of coal. In a sense, this would be an industry excise tax to be passed on to the consumer. Management argued that wage-rate increases could be offset by mechanization but a royalty tax could not. Marginal mines might have to absorb it out of profits. This would reduce ability to finance capital improvements. The union argued that marginal mines should not remain in the industry. To many, the union proposal appeared at the time as just another of the measures used by Lewis to demonstrate that he could obtain more for his members than other, less aggressive union leaders. This was a superficial view. The fund was desired to meet two basic needs of the men who work in coal. First, it was designed to relieve the miners' overwhelming concern with security in an industry characterized by erratic employment and daily hazard. Second, it was designed to give the miners a feeling of social prestige and status. It would provide compensation for some of the disadvantages of coal mining. The welfare fund issue stalemated negotiations in 1946. The government seized the mines, and in the Krug-Lewis Agreement of May 29, 1946, the government granted the union demand. The royalty payment was begun at 5 cents a ton and raised subsequently to 30 cents. The welfare fund provides for a retirement pension over and above federal pension payments; death benefits for survivors of men killed in mine accidents; disability benefits for injured miners; rehabilitation assistance; hospitalization (and medical care when connected with hospitalization) for miners and members of their families.[21]

(3) The changing status of miners, 1933–50. The coal miners have made some remarkable gains since 1933 in terms of higher wage rates, shorter hours, and welfare benefits. In 1932, the average miner received about $6 a day for 8 hours of actual work. He traveled within the mine on his own time, which amounted to 45 minutes or more. By 1950, this same miner was getting nearly $19 a day for working only 6¾ hours "at the face"; his travel time from portal to portal and a half-hour lunch period were paid for by the operators. He was among the highest paid workers in the nation. In terms of annual earnings he had moved from well below average in the depression to well above average. In 1932, annual earnings per full-time employee in the United States were $1136; for the average full-time bituminous coal miner they were $748. In 1947, the peak postwar year of coal output, the annual average for all full-time employees was $2598, and for the coal miner $3212.[22]

b. Crucial present human-relations matters: achievements and prob-

[21] For details of the health and welfare fund, see *Monthly Labor Review,* December, 1950, p. 707.

[22] Data from U.S. Department of Commerce, National Income Studies, quoted by Bituminous Coal Institute, *1950 Bituminous Coal Annual,* p. 139.

TABLE 39

Work Stoppages Arising from Labor Management Disputes: All Industries and Bituminous Coal Industry, 1944–1950

Year	Number of Work Stoppages			Number of Workers Involved[1]			Number of Man-Days Idle			Non-Agricultural Labor Force in U. S.		
	All Industries	Bituminous Coal	Per Cent Coal of Total	All Industries	Bituminous Coal	Per Cent Coal of Total	All Industries	Bituminous Coal	Per Cent Coal of Total	Total	Bituminous Coal	Per Cent Coal of Total
1944	4,956	792	16.0	2,115,637	229,907	10.9	8,721,079	1,056,341	12.1	(In thousands)		
1945	4,750	598	12.6	3,467,000	581,500	16.8	38,025,000	5,007,000	13.2			
1946	4,985	485	9.7	4,600,000	834,000	18.1	116,000,000	19,500,000	16.8			
1947	3,693	415	11.2	2,170,000	490,000	22.6	34,600,000	2,190,000	6.3	44,371	431.8	
1948	3,419	561	16.4	1,960,000	582,000	29.7	34,100,000	9,560,000	28.0	44,201	438.2	1.0
1949	3,606	421	11.7	3,030,000	1,130,000	37.3	50,500,000	16,700,000	33.1	43,006	399.0	1.0
1950	4,843	430[2]	9.8	2,410,000	165,000[2]	6.8	38,800,000	9,320,000[2]	24.0	44,124	375.6	.9

Source: U.S. Bureau of Labor Statistics.

[1] Proprietors, self-employed, domestic servants, personnel of armed forces excluded.

[2] General coal stoppage, January–March, 1950, included in 1949 data since stoppage began in June, 1949.

lems. We have observed that many of the basic conditions that destroyed bargaining before 1933 have since been resolved. Offhand, it would appear that the relations between the parties should have improved steadily. A glance at Table 39, however, quickly dispels this notion. No record in industrial relations has been more turbulent in the last fifteen years than coal. Only a few contracts have been negotiated without work stoppages, some of them lasting off and on for nearly a year.

As shown in Table 39, bituminous coal miners constitute only about one per cent of the nation's non-agricultural labor force. Yet since 1945 the miners have constituted as high as 37 per cent of all workers involved in work stoppages. They have accounted for as high as one-third of the total annual number of man-days lost in this country through stoppages. The most that can be said is that the 1951 agreement was achieved with more harmony than any other recent one; but in this case the parties were trying to beat the time table of government wage and price stabilization orders. Government intervention in the affairs of the industry has been almost continuous.

How do we explain the fact that, although many issues have been resolved, human relations apparently have not improved? First, it may be noted that the process of resolving the issues was a basic cause for turmoil and hard feeling. The union has done the gaining and management has made the concessions. Settlement in the union's favor doesn't guarantee future peace; but at least the issues of union recognition and security, areas of bargaining, and wage uniformity are not likely to cause strife in the future unless management tries to return to earlier conditions.

Second, the U.M.W. has followed an aggressive policy designed to get more for the miner than is obtained by other workers. This has been a "restoration" policy based on the assumption that the coal miners fell behind in the depression years. Naturally management has resisted. Can we assume that the miner has now been restored to his "proper place in industry"?

A third factor has been the leadership on both sides. On labor's side, John L. Lewis has been bold and unpredictable in his use of strategy. His policies have brought both successes and failures, but more of the former. He has without doubt antagonized both management and government with uncompromising demands and ruthless exercise of ability to gain them. On management's side, leadership in the 1930's was tough and adamant. Concessions were made slowly and grudgingly. Many Southern operators were particuarly bitter and antagonistic. But by 1950, there were abundant signs that management leadership was changing in the direction of more moderation and greater unity among employers.

Fourth has been the factor of timing. The union believed that high product demand during the war and in the early postwar years was temporary, would be followed by a serious decline. Therefore, it was desirable to get all that was possible in a hurry. Lewis and the miners often led the parade of postwar "rounds" of wages after 1945 and initiated the union drive for private pension plans. In general, it can be said that the internal forces which wrecked bargaining before 1933 have been successfully met through bargaining.

Bargaining progress in coal since 1933 has been made in a generally improving economic climate. But what if the demand for coal in the 1950's declines substantially, bringing competitive pressure on marginal mines and outlying regions? The fact remains that the parties have done little to improve the competitive position of coal in relation to other fields. External competition looms as a threat to coal's internal stability. Management has frequently stated its belief that the union's wage-rate *level* policy has "priced coal out of some markets." If this should prove correct, then internal progress has been obtained at the cost of external weakness. Gains in daily wages may have been obtained at the cost of future employment. Should widespread under-employment return, the union may well face again the problem of internal dissension and management may face the secession of former non-union fields from the national bargaining table.

3. Appraisal. *a. Lessons from the past.* Our review of collective bargaining in bituminous coal suggests a number of conclusions. First, in an industry in which there are many producers under severe competitive pressure and in which labor cost is a high proportion of total cost, labor is particularly vulnerable to competitive wage cutting unless there is industry-wide unionization. Until the industry was unionized, stability and good relations between the parties were well-nigh impossible.

Second, although it took labor nearly a hundred years to unionize the coal industry, the persistence of this effort indicates the fundamental need for unionism in meeting the human problems of the coal communities. The bitterness attending this effort, moreover, has contributed to current difficulties between the parties. It is likely to carry over into the future for a considerable time.

Third, the study of coal reveals the limitations of collective bargaining as a means of increasing workers' living standards and security. A strong union can obtain advances for its members in an expanding industry. To protect its members against economic and technological conditions which lessen the demand for the product is much more difficult. In an environment of declining demand, a union by holding wage levels too high, may actually increase the insecurity of many of its members.

Fourth, a large part of the gains of coal miners in terms of economic advancement and political and social freedom has been due to governmental assistance. This has taken the form of various kinds of protection against mining hazards, guarantees of workers' rights to organize without employer interference, wage and price fixing programs, conciliation, and favorable government labor contracts under mine seizure. The community has a vested interest in this industry.

Fifth, the student of collective bargaining must keep in mind the very great change in the balance of power which has taken place in the coal industry. Until the late 1930's the balance of power usually swung heavily in management's favor. Today this is no longer true. The U.M.W. is stronger than any individual mine operator or any regional association of operators. It has demonstrated its ability to more than hold its own even against a united front of management. Moreover, the union has often been able to break this front when to do so worked to the union's advantage.

Sixth, even if we grant that "taking wages out of competition" through industry-wide unionization is a desirable social goal, it is not without social cost. Since the elimination of the wage-rate differentials which favored Southern operators, no further significant shifts in production to that region have occurred. Therefore, we may conclude that union policy, assisted by Northern operators, has been influencing the allocation of one of the nation's great resources. Whether this is in the interest of a long-run national economic welfare is an open question.

b. Important questions for the future. One very important question for the future is the nature of public policy when bargaining between the parties breaks down and a coal strike or lockout imperils the health and safety of the community. In some industries a work stoppage is important to the parties but of little consequence to the nation's economic welfare. Not so in coal. A coal shortage can speedily bring the wheels of industry to a halt and create widespread unemployment and distress. When this question was raised with Mr. Lewis during his testimony before a Congressional committee in 1947, he was reported as saying, "Let the parties fight it out." He went on to say that you can't compel a worker to sell his labor if he doesn't want to, nor can you compel a buyer to buy if he doesn't want to. But fighting it out may take months. And meanwhile the public suffers. (See Chapter 25 for an analysis of the various alternatives in terms of government policy.)

A second and closely related question concerns the concentrated power of an industry-wide union in a basic industry. This may be illustrated by events in 1949 and 1950. The contract between the U.M.W. and the operators expired on June 30, 1949. Coal stocks in May were at a postwar high of 75,000,000 tons. The union announced that it would undertake to reduce these stocks in order to protect prices and wages. In July and August the miners east of the Mississippi were ordered on a three-day work-week. In September and October they went on a "no-day work-week." Meanwhile, negotiations dragged. In November, Lewis ordered three weeks of full output and then a return in December to a three-day week. Coal stocks had declined and were declining rapidly. January and

February, 1950, saw a return of the "no-day work-week." In February, coal stocks fell to a new postwar low of 25,000,000 tons. On March 5 a new contract was signed.

Several aspects of this union action are significant. First, it is inconceivable that similar action by coal operators could have occurred without public prosecution under anti-trust laws. Yet, the U.M.W. insisted that the miners stayed out of the mines individually, and under our Constitution no worker may be forced to work against his will. Further, trade unions, as organizations, are exempt from the anti-trust laws for all practical purposes, as noted elsewhere in this book. The question is, Did the union go beyond its proper sphere in withholding labor to the point where in effect it regulated output and hence determined the price of a basic commodity? So recently in our industrial history have unions had the power to take such sweeping action that public policy in 1950 was not formulated to the point where it could deal with this problem in the coal industry.

There are some big economic as well as political issues posed. Union-enforced industry-wide restrictions of production in times of sagging demand will keep marginal mines in business and keep marginal workers in coal's labor force. May this not result in a mal-distribution of national resources and a lower level of real income?

A third major question is directly related to the first two we have raised. If both labor and managemnt are highly organized, might the two parties cease opposing each other and engage in collusion at the expense of the public? In the coal industry the pressures of competing fuels may prevent this, but it is a possibility that cannot be overlooked.

Our fourth question for the future stems from all of the foregoing discussion. It concerns the distribution of the gains from economic progress. In the past, with labor weak and management units competing against each other, perhaps most of the profits in the bituminous coal industry went to the consumer. For example, from 1923 to 1932 the average hourly earnings of coal miners dropped from 85 cents to 52 cents. Coal operators reported deficits every year. The average value of coal at the mine declined from $4.02 per ton in 1922 to $1.31 in 1932 (around $7.00 retail).[23] The consumer was the principal gainer through lower coal prices. Since 1933 this situation has been reversed. Miners have made large economic gains, as previously shown. Management has reported increasingly profitable operations. But the retail price of coal has risen steadily from around $7.65 per ton in 1933 to around $16 in 1950. Labor appears to have been able to obtain a large part of these increases in higher wages, shorter hours, and welfare benefits. Coal wholesalers and retailers have benefited, though perhaps less than the miners. But in these later years

[23] Waldo E. Fisher, *Collective Bargaining in the Bituminous Coal Industry: An Appraisal,* Labor Relations Council, Wharton School of Finance and Commerce, University of Pennsylvania, 1948, p. 39.

the consumer has lagged as a participant in the industry's gains. How is the consumer, particularly the fixed-income consumer, to be protected? Will the government in the future find it necessary to shift its protective policy from labor or management to the consumer?

B. THE AUTOMOBILE INDUSTRY

1 The setting for relations. The automobile industry has typified the growth of mass-production techniques in America. Collective bargaining in automobiles has a short history, beginning not long before World War II. Yet so large is the industry and its union that today the bargaining decisions of the parties often set the pattern for a large segment of the manufacturing economy.

a. Economic conditions. (1) In the product market. Production in autos is highly concentrated.[24] The "Big Three" (General Motors, Ford, and Chrysler), with which we shall be primarily concerned, account for 80 per cent of the total car output. Price competition is very limited. Competition takes place in terms of quality, style, economy, and service facilities rather than prices. In short, the industry affords a good example of what economists call "oligopoly." This has not always been true, however. During the years from 1900 to 1915, when automobile manufacturing was transformed from handicraft to mass-production techniques and the product brought down from the luxury class to the average consumer's level, price competition, led by Ford, was extremely keen. It has been estimated that out of the 2000 models which several hundred competitors at one time or another placed on the market, only about 50 survive today.[25]

The industry has been very profitable for the survivors. Whenever a company has obtained widespread consumer acceptance, profits have been high. Even in the depression years 1927–37, General Motors averaged a 36 per cent net return on invested capital, and Chrysler 29 per cent. In fact, during this period General Motors "made more money than any other manufacturing corporation in the United States." [26] Profits were reduced to a modest 10 per cent during World War II, but have since risen sharply.[27] The big automobile companies are among the financial giants of American industry, with large reserves and vast resources for obtaining additional capital. The net worth of General Motors is esti-

[24] This the result chiefly of "economies of large scale operation and consumer preference for makes having far-flung dealer service stations." See W. H. McPherson, "Automobiles," Chapter 11 in *How Collective Bargaining Works,* The Twentieth Century Fund, 1942, p. 574.

[25] U.S. Congress, 80th, 2d Session, *Corporate Profits,* Hearings before the Joint Committee on the Economic Report, December 6–21, 1948, Washington, D.C., 1949, p. 512.

[26] Clair Wilcox, *Competition and Monopoly in American Industry,* Monograph No. 21, Temporary National Economic Committee, 76th Congress, 3d Session, Washington, D.C., 1940, p. 197.

[27] U.S. Congress, 80th, 2d Session, *op. cit.,* p. 538.

mated at one and a half billion dollars.[28] That of Ford and of Chrysler is listed in the neighborhood of one-half billion dollars each. Some of the eight "small" firms have net worths of around fifty million dollars each. The economic power of such enterprises in both product and labor markets is obvious.

(2) The market for productive factors. (a) Labor. The area of Detroit and lower Michigan early became the center for the automobile industry. Expansion was almost continuous from 1900 to 1929. Labor was chronically short and had to be pulled in from other areas, especially Kentucky and Tennessee in the 1920's. The industry has paid relatively high wage rates. It was *willing* to pay high in the early days of the industry in order to get enough labor. Then and since, it has been *able* to do so because labor cost on assembly is a small proportion of total cost (only around 10 to 20 per cent) and because automobile production is highly profitable for successful producers whenever demand is adequate.

The labor force of the industry, including the auto body and parts plants, was around 850,000 in 1950. Contrary to popular opinion only about 20 per cent of the labor force is used directly on the assembly lines. The majority of workers are used in the production or assembly of parts and in stocking, servicing, or maintenance. The technical achievements of management have been so great that "skill has been built into the machines and processes" with the result that the average worker's skill requirement is low. "Over a fourth of the occupations in the industry require no experience, while less than a tenth need more than a year of training." [29] Thus, except for this upper tenth (e.g. tool-and-die makers) the automobile labor force is semi-skilled. Producers can easily meet most of their labor supply needs in the general labor market. The weak bargaining power of any one person or small group in this semi-skilled force is obvious. The ability of the industry to "machine out" specific jobs further lowers the bargaining power of individuals or small groups.

(b) Non-labor factors. The big auto firms require a tremendous stream of raw materials, parts, sub-assemblies, accessories, and equipment from thousands of suppliers.[30] So great is their buying and bargaining power that they are able to induce high competition between these suppliers. The materials purchased make up nearly 70 per cent of the value of the finished automobile. Competition in the over-all automotive industry is

[28] The gross revenues of General Motors in 1942 were about twice as great as the gross revenues of the states of New York, Illinois, and Ohio combined. See U.S. Congress, 80th, 2d Session, *op. cit.*, p. 479 and 667.

[29] W. H. McPherson, "Automobiles," Chapter 11, in *How Collective Bargaining Works*, p. 576.

[30] Mr. Edsel Ford said in 1940 that his company, which produces more of its own parts than the other two major producers, had between 5000 and 6000 suppliers. There were about 16,000 parts in the 1940 Ford. Source: U.S. Congress, 76th, 3d Session, *Investigation of Concentration of Economic Power*, Hearings before the Temporary National Economic Committee, Part 20, April 10, 1940, Washington, D.C., 1940, p. 16323.

thus felt most severely in this supplier product market. It is here that an automobile assembly company will be made or broken, profit-wise. The pressures are pushed out of Detroit to the surrounding supply area. This situation is in sharp contrast to the coal industry, in which 60 or more per cent of mine cost per ton is labor cost, a fact which pulls the competitive pressures to labor.

b. Technological conditions. The technological achievements of the automobile industry are so well known as to make a detailed analysis unnecessary here. The development of the motor vehicle industry is almost synonymous with the growth of mass-production methods. In no other segment of the economy have rationalization, specialization, integration, and general mechanization of the productive processes been more highly developed. These technical developments have included such improvements as standardization of parts, simplification of tasks, creation of specialized and multiple-purpose tools, automatization of processes, synchronization of parts conveyors, and the perfection of final assembly techniques. As a result, the industry has had a remarkable record for improving quality, raising labor productivity, raising wage rates, and reducing prices. Henry Ford reduced the price of his car from around $5000 in the early years of output to $400 in the early 1920's. The industry as a whole reduced labor requirements 60 per cent and prices 40 per cent between 1919 and 1936.[31] A government investigation into the extent of competition in automobiles concluded that consumer benefits "have probably been more substantial than in any other large industry." [32] Since 1935 the industry has tended to translate technical advances into higher wages and improved quality rather than lower prices.[33]

It is important here to note that because of the low ratio of labor cost to total cost, because of the relatively low overhead costs, and because of the other economic-technological conditions making for oligopoly and oligopsony, competition of the kind experienced in coal has not occurred and the big automobile makers have not had an incentive to cut wage rates. During the early growth of the industry from 1900 to the mid-1920's, the loss of individual jobs through rapid technological displacement was more than offset by the growth of employment resulting from expanding sales. Net total employment expanded almost every year. This

[31] H. Dewey Anderson, et al., *Technology in Our Economy,* Monograph No. 22, Temporary National Economic Committee, 76th Congress, 3d Session, Washington, D.C., 1941, p. 259; based on Works Progress Administration, National Research Project, *Production, Employment, and Productivity in 59 Manufacturing Industries, 1919–36,* Part II, 1939.

[32] Clair Wilcox, *op. cit.,* p. 196, quoting the Federal Trade Commission.

[33] See W. H. McPherson, in *How Collective Bargaining Works,* p. 578. M. E. Coyle, executive vice-president of General Motors in testimony before a Congressional committee, December 20, 1948, pointed out that the $1300 Chevrolet of 1948 greatly excelled the company's $1300 Buick of 1929 in horsepower, maximum speed, fuel economy, interior room, etc. Source: U.S. Congress, 80th, 2d Session, *op. cit.,* p. 517.

meant industry-wide though not job security. The depression beginning in 1929 brought contracting sales; and until recovery came in the late 1930's, net job displacement took place on a considerable scale. Since the end of World War II over-all employment has grown to new high levels. The postwar trend in productivity per worker has sometimes been the subject of disagreement between labor and management. The evidence is rather inconclusive.

c. Relation to government. Except in wartime the government has not interfered with the production or marketing policies of this industry. It has occasionally investigated the extent of monopoly practices; but the industry has generally been given a clean bill of health. In the field of industrial relations, however, government investigation has been extensive and important. The revelations of the LaFollette (Senate) Committee, 1937–39, that the industry had resorted to the anti-union (and sometimes brutal) use of company police, labor espionage, blacklisting, and other forms of discrimination when workers tried to organize, darkened the social prestige of the big companies and undoubtedly operated to modify the nature of their labor policies. As sellers to the great mass of consumers, the firms in this industry have become sensitive to public approval or disapproval.

d. The parties to bargaining. (1) General nature of employers. The big automobile employers have never been organized as a group for the purpose of dealing with labor. They have preferred independence and have been financially powerful enough to be independent.[34] Although in pre-union days some companies did combine in a number of anti-union organizations, most of them (excepting Ford in particular) have belonged only to a *trade* association, the Automobile Manufacturers' Association. This organization has limited itself principally to non-labor issues.

The very corporate size of the "Big Three" has created enormous problems of internal management. With hundreds of plants, thousands of minor supervisors, and great variability in working conditions, it has been a difficult administrative task for top management in each concern to keep informed of day-to-day developments at the lower levels and to make major policy decisions and communicate these to the lower levels through a technically competent but complex hierarchy of officials.

(2) General nature of unionism. Unionism in the automobile industry was practically non-existent in 1933, although a few earlier attempts had been made to organize the industry. But in that year, encouraged by a liberal federal administration, the intense interest of the workers, and expanding unionism in other industries, about 100 spontaneous "grass roots" locals sprang up with a membership of around 60,000. By the spring of 1934 these had received affiliation with the A.F.L. as federal locals.

As a result of inexperience, ineffective aid from the A.F.L., and the de-

[34] For example, General Motors absorbed a loss of $1,000,000 a day during the 113-day strike, November 23, 1945, to March 13, 1946.

sire of the latter to organize the industry along craft rather than industrial lines, union membership declined to a mere 30,000 members by 1936. The A.F.L. reluctantly granted a degree of autonomy to the locals, which then combined into the United Automobile Workers of America. Internal dissatisfaction, however, was great. The new union split into two separate unions, U.A.W.–A.F.L. and a second, larger U.A.W., which affiliated with the nascent C.I.O. Vigorous organizing brought U.A.W.–C.I.O. membership to 370,000 by July, 1937, and to around 750,000 by 1940. During World War II the U.A.W.–C.I.O. reached a peak of 1,242,659 members, including workers in the greatly expanded aircraft industry. During the early postwar reconversion, membership declined to around 550,000 but recovered to a new peacetime high of 950,000 in 1950. In 1941 U.A.W.–C.I.O. changed its name to the United Automobile, Aircraft, and Agricultural Implements Workers of America but retained its old initials. Meanwhile the U.A.W. branch that had remained with the A.F.L. stayed small and unimportant in the industry; it had only 54,000 members in 1950.

The U.A.W.–C.I.O., to which we shall confine our discussion, is the third largest union in the nation. It has about 1000 locals ranging in size from a few hundred members to the "world's largest local," Ford Local 600, at River Rouge, Michigan, with 60,000 members. Contract negotiation is by "departments," which tend to be company-wide in automobile assembly and to be product- or area-wide in other sections of the far-flung metal working and electrical products industries which supply the big producers with parts. Day-to-day relations with automotive management are handled for the union by shop committees and stewards. In complexity the union organization here rivals the hierarchy of management.

2. The collective bargaining experience. *a. History and development. (1) The struggle over recognition of unionism, 1933–41.* Although concerted effort to unionize the automotive industry may be said to have begun in 1933, it should be noted that sporadic local efforts to organize occurred as early as 1913.[35] They were met by uncompromising management opposition, which persisted until 1937.

What were the sources of management's opposition? For one thing, auto management prided itself on technical competence; it wanted no interference in the interdependent operations of mass-production techniques. Management feared efficiency would be impaired by unionism. It believed that the majority of workers were satisfied without unions — and this was perhaps true until 1929. Moreover, there were psychological barriers to the recognition of unions. Top management in automobiles, best exemplified by Henry Ford, Sr., had built the industry. It was anathema to Ford even to think of turning over any fraction of deci-

[35] For a description of these early struggles, see *Ammunition,* U.A.W.–C.I.O., Vol. 9, No. 4, April, 1951, pp. 6–7.

sion-making to men on the assembly line who had been given employment and high wage rates by the skill and energy of industrialists like himself. The left-wing philosophy of some early union advocates also helped to throw a political block between management and labor. The traditional American guarantee of private property rights included the right to use that property without interference from those who voluntarily offered their labor for employment by the property owners. Finally, the financial strength of the automobile makers made the feeble efforts of early unionists look like David stalking Goliath. Why should management take seriously something it didn't want and didn't have to accept?

As already noted, labor's desire for unionization in this industry was weak before 1930. Why did the automobile workers' attitude change so fundamentally after 1930? We can only summarize briefly here. To begin with, the Great Depression brought the first prolonged industry-wide fear of unemployment. In turn, this overwhelming fear created for the first time a feeling of solidarity among workers in various levels of skills and in different companies and localities. Second, the scarcity of employment brought a fear of arbitrary and discriminatory supervision involving discharge, transfer, and so on. Third, it brought fear of excessive "speed-up" in operations. Although the factual evidence on "speed-up" is not conclusive, workers testified that "fighting the line," i.e., the rate of speed of operation on assembly lines, became an obsession with the auto workers. Fourth, there developed a fear of age discrimination. As recovery set in after 1933, the automobile companies tended to hire new and inexperienced young workers for assembly jobs, leaving the older experienced men on continued layoff. Fifth, regardless of their level of employment, the workers had a growing sense of personal insecurity and helplessness in dealing with the giant, impersonal automobile corporations. Sixth, the protection offered to labor by a friendly government under which unionism made great strides in other industries encouraged the automobile workers after 1933. And finally, the tactics of management itself helped to create the very pro-union sentiment they were intended to dispel. These tactics included the use of company police and spy systems, arbitrary discharge for union activity, anti-union campaigns in the newspapers, adamant refusal to meet with workers' committees, and so forth. It is a long and rather unpleasant story that cannot be reviewed here.

Two incidents will serve to illustrate how management's anti-union efforts alienated those who otherwise might have been greatly interested in unionism. In May, 1937, a little-known union official, Walter Reuther (now U.A.W.'s president), attempted to distribute leaflets on a street overpass to automobile workers as they changed shiftts. He and another official soon found themselves surrounded by a crowd of 150 men. He testified later at a National Labor Relation's Board hearing:

> . . . They picked me up and threw me bodily on the concrete floor of the

> platform. Then they kicked me again and again. They tried to tear my legs apart. Seven times they raised me off the concrete and threw me down on it. They pinned my arms and shot . . . jabs to my face. I was dragged to the stairway. I grabbed the railing and they wrenched me loose. I was thrown down the first flight of iron steps. Then they kicked me down the other two flights.[36]

Although the company claimed the crowd was composed of "loyal workers," the evidence supported the account quoted above and indicated that the crowd was made up of members of the company's private police or "service" department.

The second illustration is taken from events during a prolonged strike for recognition. Thousands of workers were without income. Many were on relief. An automobile manufacturer thought to discourage the continuance of the strike. He had a large display sign erected. As workers drove or walked along a cold and dreary winter street, they read, "I can eat for the next twelve months, can you?" The workers were not discouraged. They were alienated and incensed. The drive for unionism became more than an economic issue; it became an emotional crusade.

Not only did union membership rise rapidly after 1936; it threatened to get out of hand before union officials could properly organize their campaigns. Events moved fast. In January, 1937, sit-down strikes broke out so rapidly that by the end of the month 140,000 workers were out in Detroit, and General Motors was shut down. After weeks of exhausting negotiation, General Motors recognized the U.A.W. on February 11, 1937. Chrysler followed suit on April 6, after a prolonged strike. Ford did not sign until June 20, 1941, after an N.L.R.B. election indicated that an overwhelming majority of Ford workers wanted the union.

It is important to note that, except during the depression years, harsh economic pressures have not been the primary problem of workers in automobiles as they have been in the coal industry. Rather, the source of unionism has been the human problem of adjustment to living in large, impersonal industrial centers and performing semi-skilled, highly repetitive tasks in a vast occupational structure under a far-removed and complex managerial hierarchy.

(2) Bargaining experience of the parties after union recognition. (a) The strategy of bargaining. In general, management in the industry has attempted to contain the union, that is, to fight a defensive battle in the hope of preventing too much interference with managerial decisions and in the hope of maintaining the loyalty of workers to the company rather than to the union. In turn, the union has struggled to secure the loyalty of the workers and to expand its power and authority in the industry both to improve its bargaining position and to assure its own security as an entity. Only in recent years — e.g., in the 1948 and 1950 contracts of General Motors with the U.A.W.–C.I.O. — do we sense the beginning of a positive, constructive relationship.

[36] Herbert Harris, *American Labor*, Yale University Press, 1938, p. 275.

On the union side, policy is formed from two directions. The top echelon of union officials usually determines the over-all wage demands in terms of national trends. Union demands concerning specific job or working conditions come up from the bottom. Before a new contract is to be negotiated with such multi-plant firms as General Motors, the union holds a national conference with delegates from all the corporation's locals. "The individual demands from each local are organized into general demands to cover similar situations all through the corporation."[37] Meanwhile the union's research department attempts to support with statistical or other evidence the final demands to be presented by the union's top level bargaining committee.

Somewhat similar activities go on in management. The practice in one of the big companies will serve as illustration.[38] Its director of industrial relations has said that preparation for bargaining "goes on the year around." Final policy is formulated by a top level committee of twenty executives representing such areas of the company as "finance, legal, economic, analysis, sales, public relations, engineering, manufacturing, etc."[39] In support of this committee is a planning and analysis department, within the division of industrial relations, which coordinates the activities of eight specialized departments. The planning department analysts try to anticipate union demands, review prevailing practices in industry, calculate the cost of various possible union demands, summarize and document the company's dissatisfaction with the existing contract, determine what the workers are currently thinking in order to evaluate union demands, and compile evidence in support of management's demands on the union. Both sides are well armed when discussion begins. The negotiators on both sides represent the work and judgments of hundreds of individuals. Behind the management's proposals is the right to refuse to sign a new contract. Behind the union's demand is the threat to strike. Between the parties lies the use of bargaining skill, of stalling tactics, of resort to public opinion through publicity channels, and of vague contract phraseology which "gives room to move around in." Both sides are constantly concerned with the long-range implications of current bargaining. The 113-day General Motors strike (December, 1945–March, 1946) is illustrative. Outsiders saw only the economic losses to the parties in this worst postwar conflict. Actually there was much more than a struggle over wage rates. There was a struggle to determine the balance of power in bargaining as much for the future as for the present. Each side demonstrated its ability and willingness to hold out.

It is significant that there has been no repetition of this encounter between G.M. and U.A.W. Both sides learned how costly a strike like that one can be. It is a salutary experience that perhaps every bargaining duo

[37] *Ammunition,* U.A.W.–C.I.O., Vol. 8, No. 4, April, 1950, p. 15.

[38] Ford Motor Company, as described by the Director of Industrial Relations and reported in *Ammunition,* Vol. 8, No. 4, pp. 14–16.

[39] *Ibid.,* p. 14.

should have, at least once, so that they can be impressed thereafter with the desirability of amicable relations and give-and-take.

(b) Basic issues in bargaining. In recent years the most significant aspect of collective bargaining in automobiles has been not nearly so much the economic pressures of inter-firm competition as a clash of economic philosophies, a conflict over the issue of union responsibility, and a question of how far organized labor may "encroach" upon the functions of management. These three matters are closely inter-related, and we may therefore consider them in terms of the last-named issue — managerial prerogatives.

i. Areas penetrated by the union. Individual job rights. Among the chief union goals in automobiles has been, first, the establishment of individual worker rights on the job. What rules should govern job change — that is, layoff, re-hiring, transfer, and promotion? Management has wanted complete freedom to handle these matters on the basis of individual-worker merit, as judged by the foreman. The union has said that the application of this principle leads to discriminatory actions by foremen and uneven decisions among foremen. After negotiation the parties have agreed in general to the principle of seniority as a basic rule, with certain qualifications.[40] Again, what rules should govern the exercise of discipline in the plant? The union has argued that unlimited authority by supervisors is discriminatory. Management has again desired complete freedom. The parties have compromised by developing specific penalties which may be invoked by management, procedures for notifying workers of penalties, the right of workers through union stewards to challenge the penalties, and an elaborate grievance machinery. One authority believes that "in no area has management felt its authority more strongly challenged than in the imposition of disciplinary penalties."[41] Cooperative behavior among workers in automobile plants has declined, says management, because foremen now overlook many acts of insubordination. They fear their decisions may be overruled and their authority lessened in the eyes of the workers. The union replies that in pre-union days workers were afraid even to bring up grievances. The union's achievements have dissolved this fear. Nevertheless, underlying differences between the parties remain.[42]

Speed of operations. Another area of contention, almost equal in importance to job control, is the speed of operation. For example, when a production line is started after a model change, it begins slowly until the

[40] For example, in the bitter 1945–46 General Motors strike it appeared that the chief issue was economic, i.e., the union demand for a 30 per cent wage increase for which it would not settle unless the company agreed not to raise prices. Actually, in Chamberlain's opinion, a central issue was the union's demand for unqualified seniority in the transfer of workers to better or worse jobs. See Neil W. Chamberlain, *The Union Challenge to Management Control,* Harper and Brothers, 1948, p. 270.

[41] Chamberlain, *op. cit.,* pp. 270–271.

[42] For an excellent discussion of this problem, see Chamberlain, *op. cit.,* pp. 270–276.

"bugs" are gotten out and then steps up to "normal" speed. But what is "normal" speed? Both sides admit this is difficult to determine. As one union officer said: "A fair day's work is a hard thing to measure . . . I don't want any of our people standing around, I want them to work steady, but I don't want them to be like race horses either." [43] In practice, management has retained the right to set the speed, but the union has insisted on the right to challenge the speed through the grievance machinery. Quickie strikes and obvious slowdowns have followed management's failure to negotiate the issue. Since 1939, the U.A.W. has unquestionably slowed down the pace of operations.[44] Management argues this has meant lowering the pace *below* "normal." The union claims its actions have merely ended the "speed-up" and brought the pace *down to* "normal."

Wage rates. The basic wage issues between the parties have been four. First has been the *general level of wage rates.* The results of bargaining have been to keep automotive wage rates high, as they have always been, in the national wage-rate structure. Second has been the *determination of specific job rates and job-rate differentials.* In general, management has retained the right initially to set wage rates and production standards, but both have been made subject to the grievance machinery and negotiation.[45] Sometimes new rates have been jointly determined. If negotiation fails to resolve an issue, arbitration is sometimes resorted to. Current contracts generally provide for special rates for workers transferred to higher or lower classifications. Minimum hiring rates for new employees are generally specified in the contract. The third basic wage issue has been the matter of *inter-plant differentials* both within companies and between companies. The union has succeeded in narrowing differentials between the plants of the same company. But because its influence has been greater in the higher wage-rate centers than in the lower ones, some inter-area differentials have been widened.[46] The union's long-run objective is industry-wide uniformity. This issue is likely to move upward on the union's agenda in the future. The fourth issue has been the matter of *methods of wage payment.* In the 1920's

[43] R. J. Thomas, U.A.W. President in 1940, at Hearings, April 10, 1940, before the Temporary National Economic Committee, *Investigation of Concentration of Economic Power,* U.S. Congress, 76th, 3d Session, Senate, Part 30, Washington, D.C., 1940, p. 16377.

[44] As Walter Reuther said: "One of the purposes for which we organized our union was to slow down the assembly lines to a pace that was in keeping with the way a human being ought to work." Statement in *Investigation of the National Defense Program,* Part 28, p. 13179, as cited by Chamberlain, *op. cit.,* footnote, p. 285.

[45] The union proposal that production standards be jointly determined was one of the key issues in the bitter Chrysler strike of 1939. "Management's answer given in those days is the answer still given today: 'When (union) shop stewards handle the throttle of production, you have surrendered the plant.' " Chamberlain, *op. cit.,* p. 285.

[46] See W. H. McPherson, "Automobiles," Chapter 11, in *How Collective Bargaining Works,* pp. 614–615.

there was widespread use of group bonus incentive plans. They caused great worker dissatisfaction. Workers claimed they were a device whereby "the fast workers drove the slower." In the early 1930's, to offset interest in unionism, management shifted to a greater use of straight hourly rates. Since bargaining began in 1937, the trend away from incentive methods of payment has been accelerated. The union argues that setting incentive rates allows too much discretion to management's time study men and is subject to abuse; that it creates dissatisfaction among workers, which is difficult for the union itself to cope with; and that negotiation with management is simpler with hourly rates. Management believes that productivity per worker is lower on hourly rated jobs but agrees that bargaining is simplified.[47]

Union Security. In its competition with management for support of the rank and file, the union has constantly attempted to increase its power as an institution in the industry. The U.A.W. has wanted a closed shop or at least (under the Taft-Hartley Act) a union shop. It has argued that it cannot maintain internal union discipline and prevent quickie strikes as long as it is insecure. The "Big Three" have varied in their willingness to grant security to the union. Ford granted a union shop in 1941. Chrysler has never granted the union shop. However, it did grant the check-off in May, 1950. General Motors has been slow in granting any form of security. On May 23, 1950, however, it granted a modified union shop.[48]

"Off the job" security. In the postwar period the U.A.W. followed the Mine Workers in seeking private pensions. Management opposed this demand on the grounds that private plans are not as sound as the government's social security program and the union should use its efforts to expand the benefits of the national program. Several factors were involved in the union's making the pension issue an immediate objective after 1948. At that time federal payments lagged behind the cost of living and were inadequate. Lewis and the U.M.W. had secured a health and welfare program from an industry much less profitable than automobiles. The recession of 1949 intensified the workers' fear of insecurity (they expressed it in the phrase "too old to work, too young to die") and at the same time made "across the board" general wage-rate increases difficult to obtain. Ford granted pensions in September, 1949, soon after a fact-finding board recommended a similar settlement for the dispute in the basic steel industry. After a hundred-day strike, January 25–May 4, 1950,

[47] For a good discussion of this problem, see Chamberlain, *op. cit.*, pp. 276–279.

[48] Briefly: Present union members must remain in good standing in the union for the duration of the contract as a condition of employment; the same applies to present non-members who join within a limited time; present non-members do not need to join as a condition of employment; and new employees must join the union after a 90-day trial period, but at the end of one year may withdraw from the union and discontinue dues.

Chrysler granted the union demand. On May 23, 1950, General Motors fell in line. In general, the agreements provide pensions of $100 to $125 a month (including federal pension payments) after age 65 for qualified workers. The pension plans are company-financed and are funded, with joint administration.

Second to the fear of dependency when too old to work was the fear of ill health while still of working age. In the 1949 and 1950 negotiations the union obtained expansion of previous health and welfare gains. Workers now have protection covering, sickness, disability, hospitalization, life insurance, and paid vacations, jointly financed by companies and the union.[49]

Union responsibility. Throughout bargaining in this industry has run the issue of union responsibility for the acts of its members. Management has criticized the U.A.W. for unauthorized interruptions, sporadic quickie strikes, initiation of "phony grievances," and refusal to abide by contract decisions. Union leadership has been frank to admit that this issue has been a major headache for the union, too.

The causes of irresponsible unionism are numerous. One has been the desire of top union leadership to placate all union factions. If "a few of the boys blow off a little steam," the union is sometimes inclined not to take the matter too seriously. It has sometimes been unwilling or unable to overrule local groups. Second, the U.A.W. is confronted with the problems of "big unionism" in the same way that top management has often lacked adequate knowledge of what goes on down the line. Third, the numerous upheavals in individual plants in violation of the contract have been used by the U.A.W. to support its demand for greater security. Walter Reuther has argued that if the union had a closed shop, it would then discipline its own members, a proposal that has found little acceptance on management's side. Fourth, the newly acquired power by the rank and file has undoubtedly been abused on occasion. Fifth, and very important, management has sometimes failed in its responsibility to educate its foremen in the proper spirit and techniques of contract administration. The improper acts of these supervisors may well be no excuse for "wildcat" violation of the no-strike pledge by the union. But peaceful and amicable contract administration depends on a positive approach by both sides at all levels — and particularly at the bottom.

It is noteworthy that the number of wildcat strikes has diminished in the last few years.

ii. Areas retained by management. In general, management has retained control of the right to hire, the right to discipline and discharge for cause (subject to challenge), the right to assign tasks, the right to determine "the products to be manufactured, the location of plants, the

[49] For details of the pension plans, health and welfare benefits, and other selected contract provisions, see *Monthly Labor Review:* September, 1949, and April, 1951 (General Motors); April, 1951 (Ford); April, 1949, and April, 1951 (Chrysler).

schedules of production, the methods, processes and means of manufacturing,"[50] and does not share with the union decisions involving finance, the distribution of products, or the quality of products. Nor in practice has the union tried to interfere in the pricing of products, although Reuther made a public issue out of his demand in 1945–46 that G.M. could grant a 30 per cent wage increase "without raising prices." The union has attacked the "enormous profits" of the companies but has never actually tried to determine "reasonable profit." In fact, management has refused even to discuss this subject at most bargaining sessions.

It is in this connection that the previously mentioned conflict of economic philosophy is most important. This conflict is not between communist and private enterprise ideologies. True, there are still some communist splinters within the U.A.W. today. But the Reuther group is pretty securely in authority. It is a conflict between a tough-minded private enterprise philosophy of management's right and a union attitude that will accept no limits on its demands if the leaders believe a given policy is necessary for the welfare of the members or for the survival and progress of the union or themselves. If the union believes that joint determination of product pricing and plant investment decisions is needed to provide full employment for its members, it will demand such co-determination. Naturally this makes management worry about its own survival and leads to company policies of containment.

b. Crucial present human-relations matters. (1) Achievements. Despite the short bargaining history in automobiles, substantial progress has been achieved. The parties have gradually developed a new "common law" of shop rules governing working conditions. This law has established fundamental worker's rights on the job, which have lessened the worker's fear of arbitrary and discriminatory supervision. The development of health and welfare programs has lessened his fear of dependency by reason of illness. The expanding pension program has lessened his fear of old-age dependency.

The parties have found that it is possible to achieve "accommodation," i.e., the ability to live with each other. The major strikes which have occurred since 1937 appear now to have chastened both sides. The 1948 and 1950 G.M. settlements were undoubtedly the most successful between the two parties up to that time. They assured workers of participation in technological gains through an "annual improvement" factor, and protection against rising costs of living through an automatic adjustment to the government's official (B.L.S.) Consumers' Price Index.[51]

These agreements suggest emergent maturity, growing stability, and a greater degree of mutual confidence. After fourteen years of struggle the fact is today "that relations in many of the individual plants are whole-

[50] Chamberlain, *op. cit.*, p. 267.

[51] For details, see *Monthly Labor Review*, September, 1949, pp. 259–264, and April, 1951, pp. 405–406.

some and mutually satisfactory and . . . both parties do a successful job of contract administration."[52]

(2) Problems. Despite considerable progress, the problems facing the parties are still formidable. First, considerable suspicion and skepticism exist on both sides as to the long-run objectives of the other party. Management has been particularly concerned with the union's public discussion of a "new social and economic order." Many union leaders still criticize the motor companies for a "mechanistic" approach to industrial relations which overlooks the "human needs" of the industry. Some are convinced that management would still try to dispense with the union if it should get the opportunity. Second, the parties still have come to no real understanding on the basic issue of how far the union may penetrate into the functions formerly exercised solely by management. Management has made it clear that by now the unions have taken over or participate jointly in about all the areas of decision-making possible without crippling the ability of management to conduct its affairs efficiently. Third, the parties have not yet been able to agree on objective standards by which to evaluate worker performance, the setting of piece rates, the pace of assembly operations, and countless other operational matters. As long as subjective criteria are applied by both sides, differences of opinion will prevail. Fourth, the internal affairs of the U.A.W. still remain rather unstable.[53] Factionalism is considerably less today than formerly, but it is still disruptive. It weakens the ability of the union to carry out contractual agreements. Fifth, the relationship between union and management has differed greatly among the individual companies and has constantly changed over time. The attempt of the union to play one company off against the other or to take advantage of some temporary difficulty in one of the firms (management has of course done the same in reverse) has made for great unevenness in union-management relations and has aggravated tempers at bargaining sessions.

3. Appraisal. There can be no doubt that human relations in the automobile industry are better today than in past decades. It is too early in the bargaining history to make an adequate over-all appraisal. Can human relations continue to improve, can workers' needs continue to be met, without impairing the ability of management to manage? Can workers maintain loyalty to both companies and union? How far can the union go without altering the basic organization of productive processes? What will be the long-run effects on the nation's economic welfare if

[52] William H. McPherson's review of *Patterns of Union-Management Relations* by Frederick H. Harbison and Robert Dubin, *University of Chicago Law Review,* Vol. 15, No. 4, Summer, 1948, p. 1009.

[53] On June 23, 1951, the union's largest local, Ford Local 600 at River Rouge (60,000 members) staged an anti-Reuther "anniversary" celebration at which John L. Lewis labeled Mr. Reuther a "pseudo-intellectual nitwit." Neither the celebration nor Mr. Lewis's comment contributed to internal unity in the U.A.W.

organized labor should participate more and more in broad managerial decisions? These are questions for the future.

C. THE INLAND STEEL CONTAINER COMPANY

1. The setting for relations. The human-relations problems of labor and management at the industry level are only a part of the process of collective bargaining. Equally important are the problems at the individual firm and the individual plant levels. Until recently it was not easy to go behind the scenes to view the day-to-day relations of labor and management in individual plants and companies. Today it is possible through the increasing number of competent company analyses.[54] The individual company case study that we have chosen to present concerns the Chicago plant of the Inland Steel Container Company, a subsidiary of the Inland Steel Company.[55] Union-management relations at Inland Steel Container, 1937–50, constitute one of the most unusual cases on record of evolution from open conflict to cooperation.

a. Economic conditions. The Inland Steel Container Company's Chicago plant is a fabricating unit which through a highly mechanized process transforms sheet steel into various types of containers, such as steel barrels. The product market is competitive. This particular plant had experienced highly erratic earnings, due in part to the fact that demand had been subject to wide cyclical fluctuations and in part to the virtually constant internal labor strife that had characterized the plant.

b. The parties to bargaining. (1) General nature of the employer. At the time our story begins (1937), Inland Container was family-owned and had been for many years. Management policy was described as "dictatorial," harsh, and ruthless. The company sought out "hungry" workers without much industrial experience, from the South and other low-wage areas. It executed well the Machiavellian principle of "divide and rule." Wage rates were extremely low, for the steel fabricating industry. Favoritism by foremen was widespread. Differentials in wage rates existed between white and Negro workers performing the same tasks. Management fought union sentiment with unusual intensity.

In 1939, the family interests sold out to the Inland Steel Company, which still owns the plant.

(2) General nature of the union. As a result of its harsh policies, management had planted the seeds of bitter resentment among the workers. During the hard years of depression in the early thirties, the employees

[54] The National Planning Association, under the title "Causes of Industrial Peace Under Collective Bargaining," has thus far published about eight studies and has contributed much to our understanding.

[55] Based on William Foote Whyte, *Pattern for Industrial Peace,* Harper and Brothers, 1951, 245 pp. Our brief summary here does not do justice to Professor Whyte's exceedingly readable and competent account, which the student would do well to read in full.

could do nothing about their lot. But in 1937, encouraged by the sit-down strike in General Motors, workers in one department started a sit-down of their own one noon. Spontaneously, workers in all other departments joined. Stunned by this sudden turn of events, the family management recognized the new union after only four days. The new local promptly affiliated with the national organization that was to become the United Steelworkers of America (C.I.O.). Within a short time the local consolidated itself as a militant group, 100 per cent organized under Lucius Love, a Negro who had developed and proved unusual qualities of leadership.

2. The collective bargaining experience. *a. History and development.* The remarkable feature of the union-management story at Inland Steel Container is the above-mentioned reversal in relations. By 1945 there was complete deadlock and animosity, which resulted in a 191-day strike in 1946, numerous "quickie" stoppages, a host of phony, political-pressure grievances, and other evidences of basic conflict. In another year a notable change began to develop. Relations began to improve as the parties found ways of resolving their differences to the point of cooperation. In order to see how this evolution in human relations took place — and all within a few years — we shall use Professor Whyte's chronological outline, which divides the record of events into three parts.

(1) Disorganized Conflict, 1940–44. When Inland Steel took over in late 1939, it appointed new top management officials. They faced a chaotic organizational structure, unsystematic procedures, and low morale. The problems proved so overwhelming that there was little improvement as the months went by. The plight of middle management under the old family regime had been bad, and it was not much better now under the new order. As one official said, "Before you couldn't get a hearing; now you could get a hearing but no action." The foremen were in an untenable position. They couldn't get action from top management. They got pushed by the workers from below. When the union wanted something badly enough, it simply brushed past the foremen and middle executives, organized a demonstration, and marched into the general manager's office. If the union threatened enough, it got what it wanted. Encouraged by this show of authority, the union grew stronger and more demanding, but was not sure where it was going. Productivity declined and unit costs went up. The 1942 negotiations brought a crisis. The plant's general manager had orders from above not to grant a wage-rate increase, for the plant was losing money. The union demanded 10 per cent. The local plant manager believed he had to give something to avert a strike, and he hit upon a plan which he sold to the union. There would be a general 10-cent-an-hour increase. This looked good to the union. Most of the production workers were on incentive rates; that is, they had minimum base rates and were paid bonuses for exceeding

standard outputs. The 10-cent increase was applied to base rates but not to the incentive bonus rates. As a result, the incentive workers had higher guaranteed minima, but their earnings did not increase unless they turned out more production than before the increase. Thus the amount of bonus above the base rates was reduced. "This was a way of seeming to give away money without actually giving anything. The move proved terribly costly to management."[56] After the "increase" went into effect, the workers realized what had really happened. They felt they had been cheated. So they began to cheat on management. The company was paying for "down time" (time when the machines couldn't be run for one reason or another) beyond half an hour per day per worker at the regular guaranteed hourly minimum rate. Payments for "down time" now rose rapidly. Workers said the equipment was in bad shape. Slowdowns became frequent. Unit costs rose still higher. Grievances and complaints became endless. One official later said that the company at this time had no incentive on production, "just an incentive on down time." Foremen had no time for supervision. They spent their hours listening to complaints. Work stoppages broke out in various departments. Some were organized by the union; some were spontaneous. In the midst of this disorganization, management erred again. It tried to keep the union in check by going directly to the workers. The latter were quick to seize the opportunity to deal directly. Professor Whyte reports that ". . . it now became common practice for whole departments, if not the whole plant, to stop work and march on the top-management office."[57] Meanwhile, the union was not well disciplined. Sometimes the union officially endorsed the actions of the workers. At other times the union was helpless to stop actions it considered undesirable. The "union leaders had to run fast to stay ahead of the membership."[58] By 1943 the plant was losing so much money that the parent company decided to change Inland Container's top management again.

(2) Organized conflict, 1944–46. Two new top management men were appointed to straighten out Inland's tangled affairs. John Gossett was named as vice-president and general manager, and Robert Novy was named as general factories manager. Both were self-made men, who had come up from the ranks to managerial positions in sales or production. Before taking the job, Gossett visited the Chicago plant and was appalled at management's demoralization. He couldn't even get into the president's office for ten minutes because workers jammed the stairway while holding a "conference" with management. He decided then and there a firm hand would be required, backbone would have to be put into lower management, and some systematic procedures developed to make for consistency up and down the line.

It didn't take the union long to find out that the new management was going to be firm. Shortly after Gossett took office, three union officers, led

[56] Whyte, *op. cit.,* p. 22. [57] *Ibid.,* p. 26. [58] *Ibid.,* p. 27.

by Lucius Love, who had risen rapidly to leadership in the union, walked into the general manager's outer office to request a meeting. When Gossett came out, Love extended his hand.

> Gossett put his hands behind his back and leaned back against his secretary's desk.
> "What is your business here?" he asked curtly.
> "We want to discuss the general situation," Love explained.
> "There is nothing to discuss," Gossett said.

He went on to say that henceforth problems should be taken up in regular grievance meetings set up for that purpose. There would be no delegations to the general manager's office.

> Love tried again. The plant was in war production; its products were vitally needed. "Mr. Gossett," he said, "aren't you patriotic?"
> "Is that a subject for negotiation?" Gossett countered.
> . . . That was all. The men went out, stunned and boiling mad.[59]

This exchange made it clear to both sides that they were extremely far apart in their approach to common problems. The conflict within the plant would continue but would be more sharply organized on both sides. The union officers concluded that the new management had no respect for them. They would fight back with all the resources at their command. Gossett insisted that management, not the union, would have to run the plant.

Gossett ordered that henceforth all grievances must be written. This weakened the union's strength; some union stewards were not literate enough to handle written grievances. Further, it eliminated all the unwritten "gentlemen's understandings" that the union had obtained from the previous management. The union counterattacked. It harassed management by creating all manner of grievances. Management was confronted with an avalanche of paper work. The union also began a campaign of slowdowns. Management counterattacked in return. It threatened to discharge workers for loafing. Afraid of this move, the union shifted strategy from slowdowns to breakdowns. It was easy for workers to create "down time," but difficult for management to discover the causes.

Distraught foremen were figuratively run off their feet, trying to correct a loose nut here, a broken bolt there, or a missing part somewhere else. Management knew that the breakdowns were not accidental.

The inevitable explosion came on August 27, 1945. Workers refused to work overtime, even at time-and-one-half, claiming contract violation. The union was trying to break the new management, which responded by firing workers for insubordination. By September, 53 workers were gone. The plant shut down for nine weeks. The issue was arbitrated, but neither side won a clear-cut victory. The conflict continued and nervous tension mounted, while production lagged. Everyone knew that the conflict

[59] *Ibid.*, pp. 34–35.

could not go on this way indefinitely. In January, 1946, the plant shut down during the long general strike in the steel industry. When the rest of the industry resumed, Inland Container did not. Management pressed for twenty-one major changes in the contract. It held so little confidence in the possibility of working things out with the union that top Inland management considered selling the plant. If legal difficulties had not arisen, this move might have been taken. The strike was costly to management; it was costly to the union. Finally, after 191 days of shutdown, a new contract was signed which gave management a good deal of what it wanted. The union decided to sign what appeared to be a rather undesirable contract only because the workers were sure they could whip management in day-to-day operations regardless of the over-all agreement.

When production resumed, everyone expected relations to become still worse, but they did not. Both sides had learned to respect the "staying power" of the other. Slowly, almost imperceptibly, relations improved just a little. Gossett did not take undue advantage of his rather tough contract. He made a few concessions. He did not enforce the right to discharge workers outright but encouraged foremen to take up cases of discipline with union stewards. He agreed to discuss "other" problems with the union at grievance meetings. When management gave a little, so did the union. As union officer Love described it:

> "So Mr. Gossett finally began to give some to the union and that was the time I had been waiting for. I knew things couldn't go on like this forever. If we kept on fighting, we would kill each other off. I was hoping to see the day when we could live like people, so when Mr. Gossett began to give a little, I gave some too. That was easy to do then because half of the grievances we had in there didn't mean a thing and was just put in to make things hard for management." [60]

Soon after this development a remarkable change took place within the internal structure of management. Middle management had been driven hard by Gossett, who felt that pressure was necessary. But it had created hostility among his own colleagues. Resentments accumulated. One day Novy walked into Gossett's office and told him how his own subordinates felt. He listened carefully. He invited in all officials to "tell him off." They did. Instead of exploding, Gossett decided he had been too tough. He shifted his strategy to one of friendship and extreme tact. Not many bosses could do this. Gossett did, and in a very short time he created a surprising degree of harmony up and down the managerial hierarchy. Internal changes took place in the union, too. Convinced that management would remain firm regardless of losses, Love and others decided to ask management to correct some worker complaints on the production line. Formerly, this request would have gotten nowhere. This time it produced results. The parties remained considerably apart, but not so far as before the strike.

[60] *Ibid.*, p. 62.

(3) Organized cooperation, 1947 to date. Everyone recognized that the 1947 negotiations would be the key to either rapprochement or further conflict. Management, noting improvement in production, hoped to avoid a strike. The union approached negotiations expecting a strike. The rank and file felt that the union was losing ground to management. Workers' suspicions of management's long-run aims centered around the issue of wage-rate changes on incentive jobs. The "air hose" case will illustrate the problem. On a particular punch press, the worker stamped out covers from steel sheets. If the covers stuck together, he had to tap them loose, thus slowing up operations. One day some worker rigged up an air hose in such a way as to blow the covers loose out of the machine and onto a conveyor's device. The machine could then operate normally, and the employee could make higher earnings than before. After a while a time-study man noticed the change and had a metal air pipe installed to do the necessary blowing and loosening. Management claimed that this change altered the job content significantly and had the job retimed, with a resultant lowering of the incentive rate. This adjustment seemed logical to management, for this worker's earnings were not reduced under what they had been before the technological change was made. But to the workers and the union it looked as if management meant to cut incentive rates anywhere, any time. To protect the workers, the union felt that it had to secure the right to submit such a change to arbitration. If it couldn't get this right, the plant would be struck.

When negotiations began, a new figure entered the talks — an international union representative named Lawrence G. ("Jake") Shafer. He had to sell himself to management. He also had to sell himself to the local union committee. On one of the first issues, involving vacations, Shafer showed himself capable of holding his own in a highly technical discussion with management. This sold him to his own union people. Management made a minor concession without appearing to be weak. So far so good. Then the "air hose" case was argued strongly by both sides. But instead of losing their tempers and quitting, the parties, with Shafer in the lead, turned to other issues. Shafer interrupted often to talk of his hunting and fishing experiences. At first this puzzled management. Then Gossett and the others realized that Shafer was trying to ease the tension. The effect was remarkable. Not only did both sides join in the banter, but management decided it could trust Shafer. And in the exchange Shafer decided he could trust management. Despite this new confidence, tension began to rise on the next issue. The union wanted to have a voice in the appointment of worker representatives on the plant safety committee rather than have management exercise exclusive right to the naming of labor and management representatives. Management pointed out that, after all, the labor representatives were union members. Argument was long and tedious. There was no agreement. Love finally decided it was useless to talk further. He stood up. So did Shafer. Management saw that negotiations were about to break up over a minor issue; but it could not show weakness. So a management official stood up also, "took a deep breath and began talking to Shafer. He wasn't prepared to yield the point least of all under such obvious pressure, but he cast about for a possible adjustment."[61] During the next few minutes, it became clear that management would be glad to see worker representatives given copies of minutes of the safety committee's meetings so that they could make a full report at union meetings. Shafer then said, "What are we arguing about, then?" He sat down. So did the management official. "Love was left standing alone . . . he hesitated a moment longer. Then he too sat down. The immediate crisis had passed — although there was still no agreement in sight."[62] Leaders on both sides were *trying* to find areas of agreement. It was hard going, but some progress was made. After nine such meetings, the parties reviewed their situation and found they had finally reached agreement on every issue except the rate arbitration issue as illustrated by the "air hose" case. It could no longer be by-passed. Either the parties would resolve it or conflict would be resumed. Shafer began the discussion by expressing respect for management and indicating the union's interest in management's problems. The latter, he said, had dealt no cards under the table. Management returned this gesture and agreed that relations had improved greatly since the 191-day strike. This exchange of good will did not solve the arbitration issue, but it was important; it did pave the way for a long discussion of viewpoints during which tempers remained calm. Management discovered that the union's real concern was not so much about management's power to change incentive rates on existing jobs — something which after all didn't occur very often — but in setting rates on new jobs. This fact brought out a solution. In cases where job content was increased or decreased, management would continue to have the right to change rates on existing jobs. If the union questioned whether there had been a change in job content, that question (but not the rate as such) could be arbitrated. And management agreed that rates on *new* jobs must be in line with existing rates. It was now clear there would be no strike. A contract was signed.

The record shows that from this point on labor and management in Inland Container moved from agreement to integration and cooperation. How did they accomplish the transition? It is not possible to present the full story here, but an analysis of a few situations may serve to illustrate the process.

First was the union complaint of low morale in the Barrel Department. Some workers were missing out on the regular 15-minute relief periods when they had to help out elsewhere in the plant. The plant nurse took up time checking matters with workers when they were on incentive rates instead of waiting until lunchtime or the end of the shift. Instead of

[61] *Ibid.*, p. 102. [62] *Ibid.*, pp. 102–103.

ignoring these complaints, management recognized that the union was performing a service in bringing out complaints that otherwise might have been overlooked. Management instituted corrective measures immediately. Another morale-lowering factor had been management's failure to express appreciation to the workers in this department after output had risen due to the efforts of the union after the new contract was signed. When the union brought this matter to management's attention, the latter did not respond by saying something like "Aren't the men getting more money for their harder work? What more do they want?" Instead, management saw its error and gave public recognition to the department's achievements. Eventually management devised a system of publicly comparing all departments' output records over time; of comparing the whole plant's record with that of the company's other plants; and of expressing its appreciation with non-pecuniary rewards (such as plaques). In return for this attitude and these actions, management was rewarded by a union proposal for a system of worker suggestions for improvements in efficiency. Management offered to pay for these, but the union said it didn't want or need financial compensation.

A second issue came up when the union asked for a higher bonus rate on the production line in view of the greater over-all plant output. Management asked if the union could give assurance that there would be no letdown in production if the bonus went up. The union gave its assurance. Management (Gossett) replied, "That's good enough for me." In this we see the parties liquidating distrust and accepting each other's word at face value.

A third issue involved the old "air hose" problem, which came up as a grievance after the contract had been signed. The union said that it would drop the grievance if management would bring out the records so that it could be assured the man involved suffered no loss of earnings. The records were brought out. Earnings had not declined. The case was dropped. Formerly this case had been a "symbol of conflict," and no amount of logic could have settled the issue. Now it was settled easily.

A fourth problem was absenteeism. Before 1947, management might have discharged absentee workers outright. Now management called in the union. There was a joint examination of each case to see if absenteeism was excessive and, if so, why. In the next eighteen months, "only one worker was suspended (for a week) for absenteeism or lateness and no one was discharged. The record improved substantially and there was no need for penalties."[63] In nearly all cases, management and union agreed on the treatment of the case. The parties were now consolidating their gains and extending their confidence in each other.

A fifth issue will show how a "symbol of confidence" had replaced "symbols of conflict." It involved the receiving of sheet steel from Indiana Harbor, some miles away. The steel was brought over in trucks.

[63] *Ibid.*, p. 119.

If it arrived late, it could not be unloaded by the regular shift without overtime. If the workers refused to put in overtime, the steel had to be sent back. Since steel was in short supply, this meant that some departments might have to shut down for many hours with losses to both management and workers. Before 1947, the workers refused to work overtime, and the steel often had to be returned. Now Gossett called in Shafer. Shafer recognized the problem and asked the workers to work overtime, promising to see that the issue became a grievance if management took any advantage of this concession. From then on, the workers worked overtime when necessary. The steel got unloaded; management took no advantage; there was no grievance. The significance of this incident, as Professor Whyte points out, is that now management was actually utilizing the union to solve a production problem and the union in return accepted the responsibility.[64]

b. Crucial present human-relations matters. (1) Achievements. The most striking over-all accomplishment of the parties was their success in making the difficult transition from open conflict to cooperation. Each side was tough enough to command the other's respect. But they dealt straightforwardly and frankly with each other. They learned to forgo arguing about principles and abstract rights. They began to talk about one another's practical problems and how each could help the other solve them. There came to be proper, free, horizontal communication at all necessary levels between the two parties.

A second achievement was the correction of internal management weaknesses. Management became harmonious within itself. Middle management no longer felt bitter and frustrated. Foremen no longer felt caught in the crossfire between labor and management. At each management level adequate roles and statutes came to exist. Rewards and penalties commensurate with successful and unsuccessful performance came to be developed and accepted. Proper vertical communication was worked out within management from top to bottom and from bottom to top.

Third, the union obtained not only a sense of security within the plant but also a sense of ease and unity within itself. "I can now sleep at night knowing things won't pop out tomorrow," said one union officer in noting this change.

Fourth, top management was freed from the all-absorbing task of fighting the union and permitted to concentrate on production and market problems. At one period Gossett was spending 80 per cent of his time on union problems. After 1947, he was able to reduce this to 5 per cent.

Fifth, the area of joint action by the parties expanded so that more problems got analyzed and solved and the contributions of more people

[64] For an account of how these parties solved even more complicated problems, the student of industrial relations is particularly referred to Chapters 8 and 9, pp. 114–153, in Whyte, *Pattern for Industrial Peace.*

were brought to bear on the solutions. This took more time. But joint or bilateral decisions seemed to stick.

Sixth, the total effect of the change was followed by the rise of individual worker productively and total plant output. The Chicago plant of Inland Steel Container is no longer a marginal plant about to be abandoned but has become an efficient productive unit able to hold its own against the best of competitors.

Finally, there have been the achievements in personal satisfaction. Management officials can now take pride in their operations. They are recognized by the business community as successful in the managerial profession. Union officials take equal pride in having raised the incomes of union members and having protected their interests.

(2) Problems. The parties still face many problems. They face the task of consolidating the recent gains. They must continue to find areas where joint discussion may prove valuable to over-all plant efficiency and worker satisfaction. Some technical problems still remain formidable. An example is the determination of production standards in parts-making and assembly work. Time study still contains a large element of human judgment which makes for wide differences of opinion. The men who worked through the difficult years have the task of imparting the lessons learned to those who will replace or assist them.

3. Appraisal. Is the record at Inland Steel Container so unusual as to have little general application? In some respects it is. Both Gossett and Shafer were extraordinarily flexible men. The company is fairly small, with fewer than 1000 workers. Yet there are some lessons from Inland's experience which may well be applied to any collective bargaining situation in which human relations have deteriorated to the status of almost complete conflict and deadlock. First, we may note that the power struggle engaged in so vigorously by both sides prior to 1947 proved illusory. When one side made a proposal, the other immediately went on the defensive. As a consequence, neither side could gain. For example, even if management exercised its right to discharge workers for slowdown, the ill-will that was created prevented the desired rise in productivity. Professor Whyte observes that progress began to be made when both sides broke out of this power framework in the 1947 negotiations. Each side began to listen to the other's problems and tried to understand the reasons behind the other's viewpoint.

A second point to be noted is that bargaining requires careful planning, unity, skill, and patience on both sides. Shafer won management's confidence when he showed he had full control of his own union committee. Before this, management thought the union was uncontrollable. Shafer's use of safety valves — that is, his talk of generalities and his anecdotes of mishaps while fishing — were an important contribution to the lessening of tension. Gossett and others in management contributed likewise by adopting the technique of "disagreeing with respect." Professor Whyte points out the two different approaches to disagreement. In one, you not only disagree with someone but point out all the specific reasons as "proof of the other guy's stupidity." In the second approach, you listen carefully, express understanding of why the other person feels as he does, and then proceed to explain why your own experience has been different and hence gives you a different opinion on the matter. Management contributed further by adopting the "small minority" tactic in dealing with alleged failures on the part of the union. Using this tactic, management attacked neither the union as an institution nor its officers, but rather referred to the few in the union, as in any organization, who might have violated a regulation. Both sides made progress by "hearing the other guy out." This took patience; but it paid off, since lengthy discussions often brought out previously hidden reasons for a position.

Third, good human relations within a plant are an essential ingredient of high productivity. No matter how good the equipment or how hard management may press, productivity will remain low unless the workers believe they are fairly treated. During the period when workers hated management at Inland Steel Container, they held back production at great financial loss to themselves. As Professor Whyte says, "Money has only limited drawing power in a social system shot through with conflict and distrust." [65] Quite aside from this, the very emotional tension which surrounded turmoil and conflict produced fatigue which stifled output. When human relations improved, productivity improved too, without any basic changes in the wage structure or equipment.

Fourth, the familiar issue of "prerogatives" was shown to be relatively unimportant at Inland Steel Container. Much discussion in industrial relations today centers around the establishment of "management prerogatives," that is, those areas which management holds exclusively and which it defends against union penetration at all costs. The development of "prerogatives" usually involves discussion of broad principles. This kind of discussion was not very fruitful at Inland. The parties got nowhere dealing with abstractions. They did make progress when they tackled specific problems and worked out specific solutions. In 1947, management at Inland gave up some of its former authority; but it did not remain on the defensive. It originated action to be carried out by or through the union and thus utilized the union's resources as well as its own. What management gave up it got back through greater productivity and better understanding of problems out in the shop. It used the union as a means of communication both down to the production line and up from it. It learned about possible sources of trouble that could not have been learned of in any other way.

Fifth, we can observe from the experience of this plant how true is Professor Whyte's observation that "it takes time to build and maintain good

[65] *Op. cit.*, p. 194.

relations." Operating vice-presidents would not ordinarily be expected to spend 80 per cent of their time on human-relations problems. But Gossett did the first year. There is an important lesson in this for other executives. If management "looks on labor relations as an intrusion upon more important duties . . . it . . . will never do an effective job . . ."[66] An international union representative would not ordinarily spend almost all of his time in one plant; but Shafer did for a year. As he explained later, conditions at Inland were so bad that just a little time would have been a waste of time. In fact, he used the problems at Inland as an experiment to see what techniques could be developed for use elsewhere. The investment of time by both sides paid high dividends. It was an integral part in the remarkable transition from conflict to cooperation.

[66] *Ibid.*, p. 227.

PART THREE

The Labor Problems of American Government

Introduction: Some Aspects of Society's Problems

1. Who or what is "American society"? American society is all of us who live within the territorial boundaries of the United States. It is thus one of the world's national societies. If we were to think of all the people in all the nations and their dominions, we would of course be thinking of the international society.

All the members of the American society — whether workers or nonworkers, as we have defined those terms — have labor problems. These problems are experienced in varying degrees of directness by everyone, either as an individual or as a member of a particular private group (such as a union) or as a member of the society itself. A central theme of this book is that the problems of individual workers, unions, employers, and of unions and employers jointly, are also, in important part, the problems of society as a whole, and that society has the further significant problem of maintaining balance among the various individuals and groups that comprise it. It is therefore necessary for us to consider how our society is organized and what society has done and can do about its problems. It is the labor problems of people as members of the over-all group, society, with which we are concerned in this concluding part of the book.

2. What are the labor problems of the whole group? *a. General background.* American society is based and tries to operate on the principles of economic and political democracy. This means that most people have a high regard for the rights, integrity, and welfare of the individual. The problem may then be stated broadly in terms of seeing that every person gets a "break" and refrains from preventing other persons from getting their "breaks." More elegantly, the problem is to provide equality of economic and political opportunity for every individual and to protect him from undue coercion, i.e., from all coercions save those necessary to prevent him from unduly coercing others. And there is the further related problem of "making whole" those persons who have suffered from lack of equal opportunity or from undue coercion.

What is "undue coercion"? It may be defined as making some other, *unwilling* person or group do your will (1) through use of threats, physical force, fraud, or dishonesty, or (2) through use of other means, e.g., economic pressure, with the intent of injuring the other person rather than benefiting yourself.

Given the fact of scarce resources in relation to the wants of all the individuals in the society, competition is implicit in a society that practices economic and political democracy. And some degree of coercion is implicit in competition. The problem then is to keep competition within bounds, i.e., to eliminate "unfair" competition, so that there may be no undue amount of coercion.

Given the problem of providing equal opportunity to compete successfully and given the further problems of preventing undue coercion and of making whole those persons suffering undue coercion, the need for *cooperation* among individuals is evident. Individuals may act together in private groups, like unions or corporations. Or they may cooperate in and under a supreme organization known as government.

A group, private or public, possesses power by virtue of the fact that it is a group. It has the power to prevent strong individuals from coercing the weak. It also has the power to coerce weak or strong individuals. But the democratic ideal is not realized if the group exercises more coercion than that necessary to protect the weak or make them whole.

As we have said, government is the most powerful group that can be organized by the individual members of a society. Government is able not only to protect weak from strong individuals but also to prevent private groups from unduly coercing any individual. And by the same token government itself can be the supreme coercer.

But who is able to protect private individuals and groups from undue coercion by government? In a democracy at least, the individuals who are governed have this power. For government is not just an abstraction. It is also people. It is certain persons in one political party, out of two or more parties, who are elected by all the people. And if the voters think that the party in power has coerced any persons or groups too much or has failed to handle satisfactorily either of the other two general problems mentioned above, they can fire the government at the next election.

Government, then, is the ultimate agency of American society for trying to do something about the labor problems of any individual or private group. Government may in effect delegate some of its authority and responsibility for handling these problems to one or more private groups. For example, it may encourage workers to organize unions and protect unions from undue coercion, hoping that these organizations themselves will take care of individual workers' labor problems. But government retains the ultimate sovereignty. If the unions fail to cope with a given problem, such as old-age dependency, government can step in and deal directly with the problem itself. Or if the unions appear to be using their power in a socially undesirable manner, e.g., are unduly coercive of individual workers or employers, government is able to curb them.

Even though a particular party is at any one time the government, it is obligated to represent the whole of the society. One of the tenets of political democracy is due regard for the rights of minorities, i.e., an obligation to refrain from unduly coercing such groups.

It should be recognized that even in democracies the positive handling of the three general problems mentioned above — equality of opportunity, protection from undue coercion, and compensation for undue coercion — were not always considered as being part of the proper domain of government. The *laissez-faire* philosophy gave government mainly a negative role. True, government's courts and police officers were supposed to protect from and compensate for undue coercion. But it took a long time for the voters to understand that the most underprivileged and coerced individuals were precisely those who were too ignorant and poverty-stricken to be able to use the courts and the police power. And it was not until well into the nineteenth century that an approach to equality of opportunity was undertaken through universal free public schools. Gradually, however, government has taken more and more of a hand in trying to "solve" labor problems. Equalitarianism and the welfare of the common man have been its increasing concern.

b. Specific labor problems of government. What are the specific labor problems of society-through-government today? We may consider them, as we do in the chapters of Part Three, under two main heads: (1) the problems of workers as individuals; and (2) the problems arising out of the relations between unions and employers. In dealing with the problems of workers as individuals, government faces the task of protecting and helping workers who, through unions or otherwise, are unable to help themselves. Government tries to prevent undue economic coercion by passing and enforcing laws providing for minimum wage rates and maximum lengths of work periods and for special limitations on the employment of women and children. Government also attempts to prevent unemployment, accidents, sickness, and old-age dependency among workers, and, where it fails to achieve this objective, to provide compensation or relief for the workers who fall prey to these economic and physical mishaps. Finally, government tries to protect individual workers in their rights to form or join (or not to form or join) labor and managerial organizations (firms) of their own choosing.

In handling problems arising out of the relations between unions and employers, government becomes responsible for preventing coercion of unions by employers, or vice versa, and of preserving labor peace by providing principles, agencies, and procedures for the avoidance and settlement of labor disputes.

3. Problems faced by American government in dealing with labor problems. Government's attitude and policies on these labor problems are made known through all three of its branches — legislative, executive, and judicial. The legislators enact statutes in fairly general terms to deal with specific problems such as low wage rates. They also create administrative agencies which become part of the executive branch of government. The administrators' job is to give detailed interpretation and operational force to the intent of the legislators as expressed in the statutes. The justices on the courts decide whether the legislators' statutes and the administrators' rulings are within the limits prescribed by the federal or the state constitution or both. Apart from providing the ultimate interpretations of statutes, the courts also apply what is known as "common law" principles to cases between private individuals and groups where no particular statute is involved.

In trying to solve labor problems, government faces certain difficulties or obstacles, some of which are inherent in all government, and some of which are peculiar to our form of government. These difficulties include (*a*) the checks and balances among the three branches of government; (*b*) the existence of federal and state governmental jurisdictions; (*c*) specific constitutional limitations: (*d*) difficulties in drafting legislation; (*e*) administrative difficulties; (*f*) economic obstacles; and (*g*) general political obstacles.

a. Checks and balances and division of powers among governmental branches. The system of "checks and balances" established by the federal constitution among the legislative, executive, and judicial branches may well be a desirable implementation of democratic principles. But it may also operate toward preserving the status quo, blocking social progress, and increasing social lag; it tends to produce uncertainty about the validity of a given statute; and it may result in a great deal of wasted effort. The chief executive may veto the statute soon after its enactment. On the other hand, the highest court may declare a law unconstitutional some time after it has been passed by the legislators and approved by the executive. For example, the National Labor Relations Act was passed in 1935. But employers in general refused to obey the Act until 1937 (when the U.S. Supreme Court held it constitutional) because they had been advised by legal counsel that the Court would rule the statute unconstitutional. Thus, there was uncertainty for two years. And if the predictions of the employers' lawyers had been correct, there would have been social lag and there would have been a considerable waste of effort by the Congress and by the administrative agency, the National Labor Relations Board.

b. Division of authority among federal and state jurisdictions. The division of powers between the federal government and the several states makes for considerable duplication of effort as well as great lack of uniformity among the approaches taken in the different jurisdictions. Lack of uniformity tends to put at a competitive disadvantage the employers in the states having relatively "tough" laws. And until the U.S. Supreme Court in 1937 began to construe the interstate commerce clause of the constitution much more broadly than before, the federal government was limited in its ability to enact statutes providing uniform treatment for workers in various states.

c. Restrictions of federal and state constitutions. A federal law on labor or any other matter must pass muster before the federal constitution. A state law must run the gamut of the state's own constitution as well as of the federal one.

(1) Limitations on federal legislation. On federal statutes the federal constitution imposes three restrictions. First, federal laws must be within the power explicitly conferred, e.g., the power to tax and the power to regulate interstate commerce. Second, they must be reasonably related to the exercise of those specific powers. The latter must not be stretched to justify the enactment of unrelated statutes. Third, the laws must not violate specific constitutional provisions, among which in respect to labor legislation are Amendment I, which guarantees freedom of speech, assembly, and so on; Amendment V, which in effect says that no federal statute may deprive a person or group of freedom of contract or the right to acquire and use property unless "due process of law" is observed; and Amendment XIII, which prohibits slavery and servitude (except penal) and thereby says that workers cannot be forced to work against their wills.

Among these limitations the most important for labor legislation have been the commerce clause and the Fifth Amendment. The Supreme Court has greatly liberalized its interpretation of the interstate commerce clause. Today only labor in retail establishments or wholly local firms is in general beyond the reach of federal remedial legislation. As to the Fifth Amendment, the saving phrase is "due process of law." At first the Supreme Court gave it a narrow construction; statutes regulating the wage rates and work periods of economically weak workers were declared unconstitutional because they interfered with the freedom of employers and the workers to agree on whatever conditions of employment they saw fit. But gradually, as the need for protective legislation became more and more evident, "due process of law" was interpreted as meaning "social benefit." Freedom of labor contract *could* be abridged by a statute *if* sufficient public benefit could be proved and if the statute treated everyone the same, i.e., did not deny "equal protection of the law." On these grounds, many laws were held constitutional in the 1930's that would have been (or actually had been) invalidated in previous decades.

(2) Limitations on state statutes. State labor legislation is subject to Amendments I, XIII, and XIV of the federal constitution. The meaning of the First and Thirteenth Amendments is the same for state as for federal statutes. The meaning of the Fourteenth Amendment for state laws is the same in substance as that of the Fifth Amendment for federal legislation.

State constitutions contain much the same restrictions on state statutes as does the federal charter. We may also note, however, that some state constitutions do not confine themselves to broad political and governmental principles; they go into so much detail that they hamper statutory responses to the dynamic, changing conditions of the modern world.

d. Difficulties in drafting labor statutes. A well-drafted piece of labor legislation is difficult to obtain. It is necessary, first, that the objective of a given law be clearly understood and clearly stated (in a "declaration of policy"), and second, that the remainder of the law be framed in as clear and simple language as possible to carry out the declared purpose. With regard to this second point, it is desirable also that the law be confined mainly to a statement of rather general principles and rules to guide the administrative body. Legislators do not usually possess the expert knowledge which would permit them to embody in the law all the technical details necessary for successful operation. Furthermore, industrial conditions change very rapidly, and a detailed technical law might soon get out of date.

It is neither desirable nor necessary for an administrative body to be given a "blank check" in a law of a few words. The guiding principles and rules should be stated in clear detail. But too many labor laws in the past have suffered from "lawyer-itis." They have been overburdened with a mass of legalistic, sometimes meaningless, often conflicting language which has seriously hampered effective administration. Too late have the sponsors of such laws realized that there were numerous "jokers" hidden in profuse verbiage.

e. Difficulties of administration. No statute really means anything until it is given administrative interpretation and operation. The objective of any labor law will not be achieved unless the law is administered in accordance with the expressed intent and spirit of the legislators who enacted it and with a view to solving the problem at which the law was directed. Good administration can save and make effective even a poorly drafted statute. But poor administration can vitiate and discredit a well-drafted, well-intended statute.

If a good piece of labor legislation is to be well administered, the personnel of the administrative agency, from top to bottom, must be competent and public-spirited. They must not be political hacks; they should be chosen on the basis of adequate civil service standards. And they should try to serve the whole public rather than be biased toward any one group. Further, the administrative agency must be given enough funds by the legislators to do its job properly. Too often the legislators clear their social consciences by enacting a given statute; then they weaken or nullify its operation by appropriating too little money to provide an adequate staff and finance its activities. Some labor laws suffer in this respect less than others. Social security statutes, such as unemployment compensation, provide for contributions from employers; and a portion of the money thus received may be used to pay for some or all of the administrative costs. But the administration of other laws, e.g., on minimum wage rates, cannot be handled this way.

Given adequate funds for an adequately staffed agency, the administrator has the problem of obtaining sufficient and accurate information on which to base his directives and orders. To obtain such information he must not only have his own research staff or be able to call on an appropriate one in some other governmental agency. He must also usually hold hearings at which all the parties who may be affected by his orders have a full opportunity to present evidence and points of view. Such a procedure is especially important from the standpoint of human relations in a democracy. The orders will be much more acceptable if those subject to them feel that they have had a hand in working the orders out.

f. Political and economic considerations. This last point calls our attention to the fact that a labor law and its administration must be politically acceptable. That is, not only must a law be constitutional, administrable, and well administered; it must also be well received by at least a majority of the citizens. Otherwise it will be evaded or disobeyed. In making any political appraisal of government action, moreover, we must consider its effect on the balance between freedom and security (recall Chapter 3).

Still another requirement is that a labor statute must possess economic validity. It should not operate to worsen the disease it tries to cure; nor, if it helps the disease at which it is directed, should it set up another disturbance elsewhere. For example, a statute aimed at preventing unemployment should have enough economic validity to avoid creating additional unemployment. And a minimum-wage-rate law, in raising the rates and incomes of substandard workers, should not operate to produce significant unemployment among those or other workers.

When we come to make our own economic appraisals of government action, we shall employ the concepts developed in Chapter 3. That is, we shall consider such action in terms of its effects on resource allocation, income distribution, economic progress, and extent of resource utilization.

CHAPTER 22

Government and the Problems of Individual Workers

In Chapters 6–9 we dealt with the problems of individual workers: economic and technological unemployment; insufficient income; lack of physical well-being due to industrial and non-industrial causes; old-age dependency; and "political" unemployment, i.e., loss of job or inability to obtain a job because of the attitudes and policies of employers or unions.

In this chapter and the next we shall consider what measures the federal and state governments of the United States have taken in respect to these individual-worker problems. We shall find that some of the measures are preventive, in that they try to remove the causes of labor ills; while other measures are alleviative, that is, they are aimed at treating the maladies when they do occur, so as to ease the pain and suffering.

Government has tried to do something for individual workers, particularly certain classes of workers, because (1) in certain matters they have, for one reason or another, been unable or (in some cases) unwilling to handle their problems unaided; (2) the groups to which some of them belong, e.g., firms and unions, have been unable to cope with the problems adequately; and (3) the social conscience of the society represented by government has become sharpened.

This last reason for government action deserves special emphasis. If one reads the labor-problems textbooks of earlier decades (including the one written twenty years ago by the senior author of this volume), he finds that in most cases there are rather lengthy discussions of the pro's and con's of labor legislation. In other words, with the exception of certain laws (such as those on workmen's compensation for industrial accidents) most of the labor legislation now on the statute books was then highly controversial.

The situation is different today. Almost all the important labor laws confined to a brief highlighting of historical background, an outline of ago. The great majority of citizens and students have come to accept them. You who are reading these lines grew up with them. Although these measures were initiated largely by the Democrats, the Republicans have accepted the principle of labor legislation, and would not now repeal or seriously amend these statutes. Only one major legislative proposal (the one on a federal or federal-state health insurance and medical service plan) is controversial today. For the rest, our discussion can be confined to a brief highlighting of historical background, an outline of main features, an appraisal of the adequacy of the statutes and their administration, and an analysis of possible economic effects.

A. GOVERNMENT AND UNEMPLOYMENT

As already suggested, government's efforts to cope with workers' involuntary idleness caused by economic and technological changes have had two objectives: first, to prevent unemployment by dealing with some of the causes thereof; and second, to alleviate the effects of unpreventable unemployment. These objectives have given rise to four main kinds of measures: the collection of statistics on the extent of unemployment; attempts to improve the operation of the labor market; efforts to prevent or cure depressions and the general mass unemployment resulting therefrom; and unemployment compensation and relief programs.

The reasons, given above, for the enlarged scope of government action in respect to individual workers' labor problems apply with special force to the problem of unemployment. It came to be realized that no single firm, with or without a union, is big enough by its own policies and actions to prevent mass unemployment in the economy as a whole when total private spending declines substantially. Even if a few single firms, by virtue of making staple necessity products or by means of special managerial techniques, are able to regularize their employments seasonally or cyclically, other firms are not able to take similar preventive measures for their employees. Moreover, individual firms cannot be expected to stop making technological improvements of a labor-saving nature, nor in a private enterprise economy can firms be expected to *act together* in such a way as to prevent unemployment in the economy as a whole. Finally, it was realized that most workers' incomes are inadequate for proper saving against the risk of idleness; and that the resources of most individual firms and unions are insufficient to pay adequate benefits or relief to workers and members who become unemployed for any reason. In other words, a majority of the voters came to believe that unemployment was mainly a problem for government to handle.

1. Information on unemployment. In order successfully to apply preventive and relief measures the government must know the total amount of unemployment in the country; the amounts in various industrial areas and regions; the amounts among various age, sex, nationality, and other groups; the duration of idleness in the above classifications; and the proportions of all these groups that are unemployed.

In Chapter 5 and elsewhere, we have already discussed the work of two federal agencies — the Bureau of the Census in the Department of Commerce and the Bureau of Labor Statistics in the Department of Labor — in collecting information of this kind. Another federal agency which makes an important statistical contribution is the Bureau of Employment Security in the Department of Labor. This bureau administers the federal-state unemployment compensation system and the federal-state employment office program, both discussed below. In performing these functions it obtains a large volume of data on the extent and incidence of unemployment. This information unfortunately is incomplete because large numbers of workers are excluded from the coverage of the state unemployment compensation laws and because these laws vary a good deal in other respects.

2. Improving the operation of the labor market. Except in times of severe mass unemployment most firms have job vacancies because some employees quit, retire, or are discharged. At the same time some workers (e.g., those who have left their previous jobs or are entering the labor market for the first time) are looking for jobs. The sooner these workers are brought to the firms having vacancies, the better off both workers and firms are. But we have found in earlier chapters that the labor market is imperfectly organized. Individual workers are ignorant of most vacancies and are too inert or have too meager financial resources to learn about them. Firms have superior resources for finding job-seekers; but even here there is often difficulty. Consequently, there is a need for some agency that can bring job-seeking workers and worker-seeking firms together. The shorter the period of time between jobs and the better the job the worker gets, the better off he is; he is spared some of the costs of unemployment, and he is happier after he obtains work. Similarly, other things equal, the firm is better off in terms of output and profits. And society as a whole benefits from both parties' benefits.

a. Regulating private employment agencies. Where a need exists in a private enterprise economy, people can often make profits for themselves by setting up enterprises to produce a product or service which fills the need. This is exactly what happened in respect to the workers' need for jobs and the firms' need for workers. Private employment agencies were established with the aim of soliciting employers to tell the agencies of their job vacancies and of soliciting workers to come to the agencies for placement in the vacancies. In return for this dual service, the agencies required the workers who got the jobs to pay fees — a lump sum or a percentage of earnings on the jobs. Sometimes also the firms were charged fees. (Under the tight labor market conditions of recent years, many employers have been agreeing to pay workers' fees as well as their own.)

Now, such a procedure appears on its face to be perfectly reasonable and proper. But actually the system didn't work very well. The larger, "better" firms didn't patronize the private employment agencies; they preferred to recruit job applicants themselves, directly. Similarly, the "better" workers usually preferred to go job-hunting on their own. And in too many cases the persons who owned and operated the agencies were not of the highest caliber. It is easy to open an agency; not much capital is required. To many operators the profit rather than the service was the primary consideration; for the most part, they were too short-sighted to see that in the long run profit usually depends on quality of service. In short, most of these agencies failed to supply a service that was generally liked and used; hence they did not contribute greatly toward "clearing" the labor markets.

We may list here four specific abuses which developed in the operation of private agencies: exorbitant fees to workers; misrepresentation of facts (wage rates and other terms of employment, existence of strikes, and so forth) to workers about vacancies and to employers about workers; refusal to return fees to workers who failed to obtain satisfactory jobs; and the splitting of fees between the agencies and the foremen who, having purposely discharged certain employees in order to create vacancies, then hired the applicants sent by the agencies.

Given the inadequacy of the private agencies as a market-clearing device and given the above-listed abuses, three courses of action were open to government — and all three were tried: abolition of the private employment agencies; regulation of such agencies; and creation of government-operated (public) employment offices.

Attempts to abolish the private agencies were made, even before World War I, by the states of Washington and Idaho. But the United States Supreme Court said that complete prohibition violated the Fourteenth Amendment of the federal constitution. After the war New Jersey tried to regulate its private agencies by setting maximum fees for them. The conservative Court threw cold water on this measure also.

The possibilities of effective regulation, however, were by no means entirely wiped out by these decisions. It is still possible for states to do the following things. First, the *number* of new agencies may be *limited* by requiring the posting of a large forfeitable bond (as high as $5000 in certain states) to insure proper operation; requiring the payment of high license fees ($5000, for example, in Virginia); and issuing licenses only if three conditions are fulfilled — applicant of good character, premises of office suitable and wholesome (e.g., adequate equipment and not near lodging houses, restaurants, poolrooms, etc.), and actual need of community for the office's proposed services — a procedure used in Wisconsin, Minnesota, and New Jersey. Second, the *activities* of existing agencies may be *regulated* by formulating a code of proper operation, which will include such provisions as those of the California law, namely, no registration fees, adequate description of vacancies (including information about strikes), return of deposits within forty-eight hours, return of transportation costs if an out-of-town job fails to materialize, no splitting of fees with employers, and no assignment of wages to insure payment of fees. The agencies may be required to make regular reports on the number and kinds of jobs filled and the amount of fees collected, and to post their fee schedules and never exceed them. Appropriate state officials can be given the power to revoke licenses when the regulations have been disobeyed.

In spite of these regulatory possibilities, only a few states, such as California and Wisconsin, have secured relatively complete and effective control.

b. The federal-state system of public employment offices. Government control over private agencies may be highly desirable from the standpoint of protecting workers and employers from abuses. But regulation does not help much to clear the labor market. This function must be performed by government employment offices. Let us consider first some standards for such offices in the United States; second, the main steps in the development of the federal-state program; third, the chief features of that program; and fourth, its adequacy.

(1) Standards for public employment offices. (a) Particular offices. In any country a system of really effective public employment offices must meet a number of fundamental requirements. It must have the actual cooperation and confidence of employers and workers. This means getting employers to supply the offices with full information about all jobs they expect to fill from outside the plant. And it means getting not only the unemployed, but also those employed workers who are interested in better jobs, to register at the offices. To win this cooperation the system must see that all office quarters are externally inviting and internally clean, roomy, and completely equipped. Personnel must be interested in the work and thoroughly trained in the technique of placement. Appointments to the offices should be based on competence as discovered by civil service examinations. All odor of political patronage must be removed. Job vacancies reported by employers should be filled on the basis of the applicants' fitness rather than their need or political connections; that is to say, public employment offices should be on a business instead of a charitable or political basis. Each registered worker should be told of a number of different job vacancies. Different workers should be told of the same vacancy. Separate services and methods should be used for the various skills and grades of labor. No favoritism should be shown to either union or non-union workers. Standard and adequate forms, records, and procedure should be used. Each local office should assist in the administration of unemployment compensation by trying to get jobs for workers who have registered with the unemployment compensation offices as unemployed and by notifying the latter offices whether the workers have been willing to go after suitable jobs.

(b) Standards for a federal-state system of offices. The adequacy of any federal program for public employment offices may also be tested

by certain recognized criteria. Each individual office must, of course, fulfill the requirements set forth above. As to the division of the field among cities, states, and the national government, however, certain other considerations should also be borne in mind. Each office should serve its own community first and arise out of its needs. The state's functions should be to coordinate, set up standards for, inspect, clear information among, and help support the offices in the various communities. The federal service should function not by opening its own offices (except in unusual cases where the states cannot act) but by serving as a real coordinator of state services, on condition that the states conform to certain standards (such as the selection of personnel through the civil service, the use of the best methods of selection and placement, and the keeping of complete, accurate records); by exchanging information about conditions in each state and large city; by setting up district or sectional clearing houses; and by encouraging the opening of new offices where needed.

(2) Development of the federal-state employment service. With respect to conditions in the United States before the Great Depression, these desiderata seemed well-nigh utopian – and in a few respects still do. But successful experience in other industrial countries showed that they could be realized under proper allocation of authority, especially when combined with a comprehensive national system of unemployment insurance. The situation existing in the United States before the New Deal period was anything but satisfactory. As a matter of fact, only during the first World War had there been a national system of public employment offices which in any way approached adequacy. Among the states, Ohio was the pioneer, establishing five permanent municipal bureaus in 1890. The movement gradually spread during the next forty years, other states setting up offices in their cities and certain cities initiating their own exchanges without state action. By 1928 there were about 180 public employment offices being operated in 35 states and the District of Columbia. This does not mean, however, that 35 states had passed laws providing for state systems. A number of cities were still working independently, as may be gathered from the fact that at the beginning of 1931 only 31 states had statutes authorizing the establishment of public offices, and of these only 23 states had actually done as the laws directed. It remained for two important New Deal laws to stir the states into action — the so-called Wagner-Peyser Act of 1933, which established a federal employment service, and the Social Security Act of 1935, which gave federal stimulus to the passage of state unemployment compensation laws and which therefore made desirable the establishment of public employment offices for the clearing of jobs and the payment of benefits. By 1940 all the states had passed public employment office laws and were operating offices in cooperation with the United States Employment Service; and some progress had been made toward attaining the standards of effective operation.

By 1951 there were 1800 full-time and 2700 part-time offices, in various communities, being operated by the states and territories under grants from federal funds.

(3) The operation of the system. What do all these offices do? We must note, first, that the functions of all the offices within a given state are directed and coordinated by the central state employment agency. These local functions, as well as the direction and coordination by the state agency, must be in conformity with the standards laid down in the federal Wagner-Peyser Act as interpreted and enforced by the federal agency, the United States Employment Service. The U.S.E.S. is empowered to deny federal financial support to a state whose offices fail to measure up to the prescribed standards.

Under the latest Congressionally approved reorganization of federal agencies, the U.S.E.S. is now part of the Bureau of Employment Security in the federal Department of Labor. As to location, the Service has had a checkered career, having been shuttled back and forth between the Labor Department and the Social Security Administration as the political winds on Capitol Hill have veered about.

Placement of workers in job vacancies reported by firms is of course the major business of the public offices. To perform this function adequately, they must sell the service to both workers and employers. In order to sell the service, the offices must deliver, i.e., make the service desirable. This means several specific things. In respect to the employers, the offices study and analyze jobs. Beginning in 1938, the U.S.E.S. conducted and published the results of an Occupational Research Program. These publications contained specifications for key, standard jobs in many industries which might use the employment offices. Obviously, the placement personnel of the offices must know the content of any job for which they are asked to send applicants to a firm. One difficulty here, of course, is the fact that technological improvements often substantially change the contents of many jobs; the information assembled under the O.R.P. gets out of date. In respect to the workers, the employment offices provide counseling services in order to advise applicants on jobs. Here again it is clear that the placement officers must know what the jobs entail; and in addition they must know about the terms of employment in various plants, locally and elsewhere; the trends in employment opportunities in various industries and communities; the housing conditions; the transportation facilities; and many other matters relevant to proper job counseling. This counseling service is pointed particularly at certain groups, such as war veterans, handicapped workers, and young persons new to the labor market.

The second main function of the offices is to assist the federal-state agencies that have the task of administering the unemployment compensation system. Among the requirements that must be met by a jobless worker before he can receive his unemployment benefit is the "work test."

He must accept suitable work if it is offered to him. If a suitable job is not available (and if he meets certain other conditions), he is entitled to the compensation. Clearly the Employment Service is better fitted than any other single agency to know about suitable jobs for unemployed workers. Therefore it has been given the task of applying the work test to benefit claimants. Workers who become unemployed must register at their local public employment offices in order to establish their eligibility for benefits. If they do not get jobs, they must report periodically (e.g., at least every thirty days) in order to continue to be eligible for benefits.

It should be noted that the public employment offices do not themselves determine this eligibility. That is the job of the unemployment compensation offices. The function of the employment offices is to tell the compensation offices whether or not the workers seeking benefits have accepted *referrals* to job vacancies, i.e., have gone to the firms suggested by the employment offices and applied for the vacant jobs.

(4) Appraisal of the federal-state system. In the introduction to Part Three we stated several general requirements or standards for judging the adequacy of any given statute. And in the first part of our discussion of public employment offices we listed a number of specific standards for the operation and administration of a public employment service. Let us see if we can briefly appraise our federal-state system in the light of both these sets of criteria.

(a) Constitutionality. The federal and state laws that charter the federal-state employment service are constitutional. Their validity has never been challenged, for the only compulsion on firms and workers to use the service is in respect to the application of the work test for the unemployed. No one has seriously asserted that it is unreasonable to require unemployed workers to register with the public offices for jobs as part of the test of eligibility for benefits.

(b) Political acceptability. So far as we may judge, the statutes do not suffer from poor draftsmanship. They also meet the test of social equity or political acceptability. It is good human relations to help unemployed workers obtain suitable jobs, to help employed workers get better jobs, and to help employers fill job vacancies. There was a time during the thirties when employers feared that the heads and staff personnel of the offices would be appointed on the basis of political affiliation rather than ability; and that these people, displaying New Deal bias toward unions and other groups, would disregard employers' wishes as to the qualifications of job applicants. For the most part, these fears appear not to have been realized.

(c) Economic validity. The public employment office system is also "good economics." Its main economic goal is to remove or alleviate as much as possible the imperfections of the labor market that we noted in certain earlier chapters. That is, it tries to dispel ignorance, inertia, and

immobility among firms and especially among workers. Thereby its broad objective is to improve the allocation of the labor resource and raise total output and want-satisfaction.

(d) Administrability. Finally, are the laws administrable? The statutes can be administered if the offices have enough staff. Usually, however, because of inadequate appropriations by the legislators, the offices have been understaffed for the amount of work they have to do.

It is true that if all the country's firms and workers used the "exchanges" for all job vacancies and for all wanted jobs, the offices would be swamped and would require much larger staffs — in boom times to help both firms and workers, and in depressions to help unemployed workers. But it is unreasonable to expect all firms and workers to use the service. From either the economic or political standpoint, there is nothing wrong in the firms' use of their own resources to recruit their work forces. Thus, some firms rely on unions for most of their new employees; and others depend on suggestions from existing employees in order to have more congenial work forces. Similarly, there is nothing wrong in the attempts of energetic workers to shop around and find better jobs for themselves. However, this does handicap the service in developing a reputation of being a good place for employers to find good applicants and for workers to find good jobs. In practice many employers come to the service with only their poorer jobs, for which they themselves are unable to recruit applicants. And most of the workers registered at the offices are the unemployed and the poorer grades of the employed. Nevertheless, the employment service is performing a very important function if it operates as a supplement to the private job-seeking and worker-seeking efforts of workers and firms. It is highly desirable that some agency should take over the function of helping small or marginal firms; large firms with marginal jobs; and ignorant, non-aggressive, mediocre workers. It is precisely at the margin that the private labor market is least effective in bringing vacant jobs and idle workers together.

A public employment office system can perform its main function of placement entirely apart from any relation it may have with the administration of an unemployment compensation law. It may well be that it is the agency best fitted to apply the work test for unemployment benefits. But this function may also interfere with its major job of placement. The problem then is to find the "optimum combination" for both jobs, i.e., to find ways of applying the work test without interfering seriously with the placement function. The unemployment compensation people understandably wish to get the unemployed workers off the benefit rolls as quickly as possible in order to conserve the funds. This objective can be accomplished by referring the unemployed to jobs of any kind, with little regard for employers' requirements and wishes and for the workers' desires and qualifications. But if the employment service is to find favor with firms and workers, it must do a good job of placement. That is, it must recommend most workers, employed as well as unemployed, to satisfactory jobs, and it must find satisfactory job applicants for most employers. Workers and firms are concerned with getting round pegs in round holes even if the unemployment compensation offices are not. In the past there has been some tendency among many employment offices to yield to the compensation offices' point of view. Possibly the best solution is to leave the definition of "suitable work" (i.e., of an unemployed registrant's willingness to be referred to a job suited to his capacities) in the hands of the employment service.

c. *Improving the quality of the labor force; training workers.* Whatever the labor market procedure for bringing workers and jobs together, it is important that the workers' aptitudes be adequately trained for filling the jobs. Government action in this field is of course good economics and good politics (the latter in the broad sense of providing social equity by implementing the democratic principle of equal opportunity).

The improvement of labor quality and labor allocation through training has been and is being accomplished in a number of ways. First, federal and state laws have raised the minimum school-quitting ages, forbidden the employment of workers below certain ages, compelled those who have left regular school at early ages to attend part-time continuation schools, and provided educational facilities at no direct expense to those benefiting from them. In this way, there has been effected a great increase in the number and proportion of young people who complete grade school, high school, and college. Nevertheless, only about one child in three goes beyond grade school, and only about one in five finishes high school. Second, vocational training in specific occupations has been furthered under two federal laws. Under the Apprenticeship Act of 1937, the Bureau of Apprenticeship in the Department of Labor has organized the Federal Committee of Apprenticeship (composed of government, management, and labor representatives) under whose leadership basic standards of apprentice training have been established and put into effect by local groups in a good many communities. Under the Smith-Hughes Act of 1917 and the more recent George-Barden Act, the Vocational Division of the U.S. Office of Education administers a federal-state-local program of specific job training, designed to meet employers' needs. The apprenticeship program is intended mainly to aid young persons. The specific-job-training program is available not only to the young but also to older workers displaced by technological improvements. Third, a special plan of re-training disabled workers for useful employment has been in existence for many years under the Vocational Rehabilitation Act (amended in 1943). This program, also a federal-state one, is administered at the top by the Office of Vocational Rehabilitation of the Federal Security Agency. Fourth, in 1943 and subsequent years the Congress provided for the occupational training of both non-disabled and disabled veterans under the administration of the offices of the Veterans Administration.

3. The prevention of mass unemployment. As stated in Chapter 3, society is burdened with its largest economic loss during the prolonged mass unemployment of resources (labor and capital) that characterizes serious business depressions. At such times society also suffers from a grave threat to its political stability. Therefore, government is of necessity very much concerned with preventing cyclical unemployment. To serve society, as well as to maintain itself in power, government in modern times is bound to try to maintain reasonably full employment. And because its efforts to do so under our economic-political system may well be so imperfect as to overreach the mark, government must also be prepared to guard against inflation. Serious inflation of the general price level also makes for economic loss and political instability (because of the social inequities involved, for some groups suffer while other groups prosper during such periods). Society and its government thus have a twofold problem, which may be stated in the phrase, *full employment without inflation.*

a. Meaning of full employment. "Full employment" is a phrase that has gained great currency since about 1935. It is often used loosely, and we must avoid that error here. How shall we define it?

We do not adopt a definition proposed by the English social economist, Sir William Beveridge: a condition in which there are more jobs at "fair" wage rates than there are workers seeking jobs. We do not even go so far as to say full employment is a condition in which everyone seeking a job for which he is fitted at the current wage rate will find such a job. What we do mean is that, so far as the labor resource is concerned, there should be a minimum practicable amount of unemployment — an amount not in excess of that which necessarily occurs in a dynamic economy when technological improvements temporarily displace certain workers from certain jobs; when the demands for certain industries' or firms' products decline as other demands rise; or when either demand or supply conditions make for *seasonal* ups and downs in certain firms' outputs. This kind of unemployment is not cyclical or secular. It is "frictional"; it is due to lack of immediate, smooth adjustment within the labor resource when the above-mentioned kinds of change occur. Just how much labor unemployment is the "minimum" cannot be said with precision; but most economists put it at about 2 to 5 per cent of the available full-time work force, or about 1.5 to 3 million workers out of a resource of 65 million.

b. Attacking the causes of depressions. (1) Review of the causes. In Chapters 3 and 6 we talked about the conditions producing business downswings. Let us briefly summarize them here: *In the absence of government action* a downswing in total output, employment, money income, and prices occurs when there is a decrease in one or both of the two components of private spending: households' spending on consumption goods, and firms' spending on investment goods.

The total amount of consumption spending in any one period depends on how much disposable income (i.e., income after taxes) the households have just received and on their "propensity" to spend it on consumption goods rather than save it (buy securities with it, stock up on goods with it, or "hoard" it). Their propensity to buy consumption products depends chiefly on their notions about thrift and prudence, on their expectations about the level of future prices in relation to that of current prices, and on the degree of certainty with which they hold these expectations. It also depends on the degree of inequality in the distribution of incomes among the various households; the less unequal the distribution, the larger the fraction spent. Thus, anything that produces a decline in total disposable income or an unfavorable change in the conditions affecting the propensity to consume tends to reduce total consumption spending, and thereby to begin or worsen a depression.

The total amount of firms' investment spending on inventories and durable equipment depends on their expectations about future costs and sales revenues in relation to present ones. In other words, such spending depends on firms' profit expectations, and on the degree of certainty with which these are held. The main cost expectations are those affected by wage rates and interest rates. Revenue expectations are based on firms' estimates of future consumption spending, other firms' investment spending, and taxes on revenue. If expectations of profit become bleaker than previously, there will be a decrease in total spending on investment goods and a tendency for a depression to begin or worsen.

Given the propensities to consume and invest, a decrease in the quantity of money created by banks or any other source tends to cause both households and firms to lower the levels of their expenditures. The reduction of demand deposits (through banks' refusal to renew loans or make new ones) to the accounts of either of these two spending groups makes for lower money incomes, and thereby for decreased spending.

(2) Possible governmental measures. Let us consider what American government *might* do, as well as *has* done, to cope with these causes. The measures fall into two classes: *(a)* those affecting the private spending of households and firms; and *(b)* those having to do with government's own spending on goods and services.

(a) Measures dealing with private spending. i. Households' consumption spending. The level of disposable income. First, households' disposable incomes in any period are made higher if the households are able to borrow money to help purchase consumption goods (mainly durable) and common stocks. Therefore, anything the government can do to make this "installment" and "margin" buying easier tends to increase households' total spending. In this country the Federal Reserve Board, which administers the central banking (Federal Reserve) system, has been empowered by the Congress since before World War II to regulate the terms of consumer credit for the purchase of consumption goods and of stocks

on margin. If the Board were to ease its restrictions, there would be a tendency to raise the level of households' spending.

Second, a lowering of the *general level* of income, excise, sales, and other taxes by the federal, state, and local governments would raise the total income available for consumption spending (provided government expenditures were not reduced proportionately, i.e., provided the government were willing to run a deficit). This measure, however, could not be very effective unless the legislative branch of government were willing to delegate its constitutional powers over the tax level to some administrative agency, such as the Treasury Department, which could then act with the requisite speed. And such a delegation has yet to be made.

Third, the enactment of unemployment compensation and relief laws tends to put a floor under decreases in household spending. Large total benefit payments to the unemployed during depressions tend to prevent so great a decline as would otherwise occur.

The propensity to consume. The measures listed above have to do mainly with raising the level of disposable income. Now let us consider what might be done or has been done, in respect to increasing the percentage of disposable income spent on consumption goods, by raising the propensity to consume. Unemployment benefit payments have this effect to some extent, for they tend somewhat to make the distribution of income less unequal during depressions than it otherwise would be. Another way of achieving this result is to change the *structure* (as distinguished from the level) of tax rates in the direction of more "progressiveness," i.e., by "soaking the rich" harder than before. By this device, which has actually been used increasingly by the Congress and certain state legislatures since 1933 (but more as a social-equity plan than as a way of preventing or curing depressions), the distribution of incomes *after* taxes is made less unequal than it used to be. The propensity to spend for consumption is thereby raised. A third measure is to put a tax on hoarded savings in order to make it too expensive for households not to buy commodities or securities. This plan has not been tried by the Congress on a national scale, but during the worst of the depression years in the thirties a number of cities introduced stamp-scrip plans which in effect provided penalties for hoarding. The scrip was a special kind of paper money good at local stores. The holders of scrip, as long as they held it, were required periodically to buy and affix special local stamps to each piece.

The success of any of these measures depends a great deal on how households' expectations and feelings of confidence or certainty are affected when the measures are put into operation. Except through public statements by leading officials, the government is powerless to influence expectations directly. However, none of the programs mentioned above would be likely to produce unfavorable (downward) expectations, since the measures tend to favor the lower-income households, which do most of the consumption spending in the economy.

Both the level of total disposable income and the propensity to consume may be influenced by over-all changes in the general level of wage rates. However, because general wage-rate changes may also affect firms' investment spending, we shall defer discussion of wage policy until we have dealt with the spending of firms.

ii. Firms' investment spending. This spending is a crucial item in determining the level of economic activity in a private enterprise society. If it falls, business depression is very likely to ensue. And if, in the midst of a depression, firms considerably raise their spending, recovery is almost certain to follow. During a downswing, firms greatly diminish their borrowings from banks or their use of their own funds for the purchase of machines, materials, and labor. Households' incomes and consumption spending thereby also decline. During an upswing the opposite developments take place. Banks increase their demand deposits (quantity of checkbook money) in response to firms' requests for loans to buy more machines, materials, and labor. Households receive higher incomes (as wages, interest, profits) and raise their consumption spending. Therefore government should normally find it highly desirable to prevent decreases in investment spending when employment is reasonably full, and to encourage such spending when unemployment is above the critical point.

As previously noted, firms' expectations of profit (based on the expected relationships between future costs and future revenues) plus the degree of certainty or confidence with which the expectations are held are fundamental in affecting their decisions on investment spending. However, even less than with households can government exert any significant direct influence on these expectations. But indirectly the effects of government actions may be very substantial. Government measures may operate to raise or lower many future cost items, such as wage payments and interest charges. Government may also change anticipated revenues by its wage-rate and tax policies. And by enacting or threatening various regulations and controls, government may produce uncertainty and lack of confidence among businessmen.

Apart from wage-rate policy, which is discussed below, there are two chief kinds of measures which the federal government can use to stimulate the investment spending of firms; namely, measures having to do with the quantity of money available for lending by banks to firms and with the rate of interest payable on such loans, and measures having to do with business taxes.

Control over interest rates. Monetary policies. When the country's banks obtain more cash, additional loans may be credited to the accounts of borrowing firms. The banks have received an increase in *excess reserves.* Under the Federal Reserve Act a certain percentage of the total dollar volume of demand-deposit liabilities of any bank must be held as liquid reserves against the deposits. If the reserves exceed the required percentage, the amount above the requirement is called "excess reserves." Normally it is to the interest of the bank, i.e., it is profitable for the bank, to expand its loans or demand-deposit liabilities until the excess reserves have disappeared, i.e., until total reserves are just about the required percentage of demand deposits.

When the supply of loan funds increases, the interest rate on new loans or demand deposits tends to fall. Such a fall may well provide an inducement for non-banking firms to borrow more money from the banks. A lowering of the interest rate makes for lower interest payments on borrowed capital, and thereby smaller total costs for the firms.

Government has the power to raise the excess reserves of banks (thus paving the way for an increase in the quantity of demand-deposit money) and to lower the interest rate. Two agencies, the Federal Reserve Board and the Treasury Department, have received a delegation of this power from the Congress. Both agencies are authorized to buy (or sell) existing government securities (bonds and short-term notes) in the open market at their discretion. If these are purchased in sufficient quantities, two closely related things happen: The banks receive additional reserves; and the security prices are forced up. This rise in security prices produces a fall in the interest rates on the securities. (The securities bear fixed amounts of return or interest-yield; the interest *rate* on a given security is found by dividing the amount of interest by the price of the security; therefore, when the price of the security rises, the fixed yield divided by the higher price gives a lower interest rate.)

The Federal Reserve Banks are also authorized to make loans to member banks; the Reserve Banks "rediscount" member banks' loans. If the governing body of the banking system, the Reserve Board, orders the Reserve Banks to lower the rediscount (interest) rate, there is normally an inducement for the member banks to borrow more from the Reserve Banks, thus increasing the members' excess reserves and tending to make them increase their loans to non-banking firms.

Within statutory limits, moreover, the Federal Reserve Board can increase excess reserves in the banking system by lowering the required percentages of reserves to demand deposits.

The Treasury is also able to operate so as to increase the quantity of demand-deposit money. It can sell *new* government securities to the banking system (if the latter is willing to buy). The banks do not usually pay cash for the new securities. They create demand deposits (loan money) to the credit of the government against which the government can write checks in paying its bills to firms having government contracts and to household members employed by the government. The country's households get an increase in money income, which tends to raise total spending unless the increase is hoarded.

But it is far from certain that any of these measures will achieve its purpose. The quantity of money may not rise and the interest rate may not fall. Why? Because, as previously suggested, the general expectations of profit and the general confidence or certainty of banks and nonbanking firms are crucial in determining whether banks wish to lend and other firms wish to borrow. The enlarging of banks' excess reserves and the lowering of the interest rate by government may therefore not furnish a sufficient inducement for an adequate rise, if any, in investment spending. Banks and other firms may remain bearish in outlook. And the government is usually powerless to change such expectations directly (by pleas, exhortations, and so forth). So we must conclude that, although the above-mentioned measures *may* be helpful and should by all means be tried, they are far from certain to meet with success.

Taxation policies. Firms' net revenues or profits and expectations thereof are affected by corporation income and excess profit taxes. As we have previously noted at several points, one of the chief incentives for firms' managements to expand and net-invest is the anticipation of higher profits. Therefore government may wish to lower such tax rates in times of actual or threatened depression, so that the incentive to expand may be heightened.

iii. Conclusions. Let us apply our criteria to the above-mentioned measures for stimulating households' and firms' spending during depressions. The program is constitutional. It also possesses economic validity. And from the broad political standpoint (freedom versus security), it involves very little social cost. For it interferes very little with the freedom of individual firms and households to make their own private economic and political decisions. We have just seen that this is a main reason why the measures may be ineffective.

iv. National wage-rate policy. Now let us consider the desirability of raising the general level of wage rates in the economy. This could be done through the voluntary agreement of a big union and a big industry (e.g., basic steel) which often sets a pattern for other industries; or it might be accomplished as a result of government pressure — applied either behind the scenes or through the recommendations of a fact-finding board in a big, pattern-setting labor dispute; or, of course, the government might legislate or decree a general change in wage rates.

As we saw in Chapter 15, American unions cleave to the so-called "purchasing power" theory of depressions. They profess to believe that depressions are caused mainly by a deficiency in households' consumption spending. This in turn, they say, is caused chiefly by a deficiency in wage income, which is almost two-thirds of all household income; and this wage-income deficiency in its turn is produced by a too-low general level of wage rates. Thus, unions in part rationalize their demands for general, economy-wide wage-rate increases by the argument that such a measure is necessary in good times to prevent depressions and in bad times to cure them.

It is clear that unions emphasize the demand or spending aspect of wage rates. On the other hand, management emphasizes the cost aspect. Management argues, as a rule, that a general wage-rate increase would increase firms' costs and thereby dampen their expectations of profit. There would then be an increase in unemployment rather than in employment. The thing to do in time of threatened or actual depression is to reduce the level of wage rates. Firms' expectations will then brighten. They will raise their investment spending and their employment of labor.

It is pretty clear that labor's views on this issue are based on an assumption that wage-rate increases are automatically translated into fuller pay envelopes (wage income) and higher consumption spending. Union economists believe that their arguments stem from the economic philosophy of the eminent English theorist, the late Lord Keynes.

Management is used to thinking in terms of individual firms. Every corporation executive has had experience with wage-rate increases in his own business. He accordingly assumes that what happens in his own firm, when other firms are not involved, must happen to all firms when all make wage-rate increases. When his own firm has been forced to raise wage rates all by itself, labor costs have gone up; and employment has often been reduced on one or the other (or both) of two counts: The firm has introduced labor-saving machinery and managerial methods in order to bring labor costs down again. Or the firm has raised its product prices in order to preserve the profit margin per unit of output; when product prices have risen, the quantities of the product sold have diminished; and lower physical sales volume has meant reduced output and employment. So the executive proceeds in his reasoning from the particular to the general; he concludes that what is true of one firm must be true of all.

Further, management's economists appear to hold the "neo-classical" view of the economic process in the society as a whole. That is, they tacitly assume that total spending in the economy is a constant amount. (If total spending is constant, the quantity of money must be constant; price expectations must be constant, never cumulatively downward or upward; and complete certainty about the future must prevail.) Given this assumption, a general wage-rate increase at a time of full employment will reduce total output and employment; and a general wage-rate cut during a depression will increase output and employment. In the first case, the wage-rate increase will cause product prices to rise because of the increases in labor cost; and with no change in total spending fewer units of every product will have to be bought, thus reducing total output and employment in the economy. In the second case, a general wage-rate reduction will lower labor costs and product prices; then, with no change in total spending, more units of every product will be purchased, and total output and employment will rise. (This reasoning also assumes the flexible product prices of perfect or near-perfect competition.)

Let us look critically at the union and management views. In respect to the former, there appear to be at least two serious errors. First, the union economists' interpretation of Lord Keynes' reasoning seems to be incorrect. As a reading of his masterwork (*The General Theory of Employment, Interest, and Money*) shows, Lord Keynes doubted that, given a downswing in business activity, a general decrease in wage rates would bring recovery. He stated that such a move might worsen output and employment because firms might be led to expect further wage-rate cuts and therefore not only not rehire but lay off employees in the hope of obtaining lower labor costs in the future. There might be decreases in wage income and a decline in the demand for firms' products. Keynes also stressed the political impossibility of obtaining the unions' consent to wage-rate cuts. But Keynes did not claim, as his unorthodox followers do, that the proper move during depression is to *raise* money-wage rates. He recognized that a wage-rate increase means increased costs as well as a possible upward shift in wage income and total demand. Instead, he believed in a stable level of wage rates, and he relied on government's deficit spending and a lowering of the interest rate by government as ways to push the economy toward full output and employment. The unionists' error appears to lie in carrying too dogmatically and rigidly the view of Keynes that wage rates in general are not only an element of firms' costs but also an element in the demand for firms' products. Many American "Keynesians" stress the demand side of wage-rate changes much more than the cost side.

Apart from Keynesian economics, a second flaw in the union view lies in the implicit assumption that a general wage-rate increase is automatically translated into a general rise in consumption spending. There are two gaps in the chain of union reasoning: first, a wage-rate rise will produce more wage income only if the total number of hours worked per period is not reduced more than proportionately; second, a rise in wage income will produce more consumption spending only if households' expectations are favorable and certain enough to cause them to spend rather than hoard the increase.

As we know, wage income per period of time is made up of two main components: the wage rate, broadly defined, multiplied by the number of hours during the period. The critical component here is number of hours of employment. If this item increases, or is not reduced, or is reduced by a smaller percentage than the percentage of wage-rate increase, then wage income will be higher after than before the wage-rate increase. But if the hours worked are reduced more than proportionately to the wage-rate increase, then wage income is smaller than before.

What, then, determines the number of hours worked after wage rates are raised? It is the cost-price and profit expectations of firms and the degree of certainty with which they are held. If business confidence is jolted by the general wage-rate increase and profits are expected to fall, firms' investment spending may be so reduced that the decrease in work hours is more than proportionate to the wage-rate increase. Then wage income goes down, and so may consumption spending. Here we have a fall in the two items of private spending: investment and consumption expenditures. There is a decline in total output and employment.

However, firms' expectations and confidence may not suffer so severely. After World War II, for example, there were several rounds of general wage-rate increases, with no ensuing reductions in total hours worked; total wage income rose. Why? Because firms expected with considerable certainty that business would continue good. Their investment spending went on apace. However, if expectations and confidence are disaffected, although only moderately, there is some decline in investment spending but not enough to reduce work hours by so large a percentage rise in wage rates. Then wage income rises somewhat; and in the absence of hoarding by households, so does consumption spending. Here the loss from investment spending must be compared with the rise in consumption spending. The net effect may be a small loss or a small gain or no change in total output and employment.

But can't a general wage-rate increase raise consumption spending and employment by making the distribution of income less unequal and thereby raising the propensity to consume? Probably not. Under the institutions of a private enterprise economy, firms try to protect their profit margins by raising product prices when forced to increase wage rates. This means little or no change in income distribution. The real wage rates of workers go up but little, if at all, when their money rates are made to rise during short periods. As shown above, there may be no unfavorable effects on employment after money rates are increased; but this result is not likely to occur because of a rise in the propensity to consume.

Thus, we reach three important conclusions about the effect of a general wage-rate change on employment and on households' consumption spending. *(a)* Whatever happens, the wage-rate change affects employment only through changes in firms' investment spending (including banks' willingness to lend for such spending) and in houesholds' consumption spending. *(b)* The effect of the wage-rate change on these items of spending depends on what the change does to firms' and households' expectations and confidence. *(c)* No one can predict what will happen to expectations and confidence. No one has yet invented an expectation-detector.

Consider now the prevailing view of management. Here again we may spot flaws in logic. In the first place, it is incorrect to apply to all firms together conclusions which may be valid for a particular firm considered by itself. In economics the whole is almost always greater than the sum

pectations and confidence so as to cause them to postpone investment expenditure.

There is a final question: Will not the fear of having to build up reserves for guaranteed wages, or of having to pay guaranteed wages out of current earnings, move firms to regularize their operations so as to provide actual employment? If you have to pay out wages anyway, why not try to keep the orders coming in and get some profit out of your wage expenditures? The answer is that the causes of a business downswing are beyond the control of any one firm. Only a few firms making staple necessity products like soap and soup are so favorably situated in terms of stable demand over the cycle that they can afford to guarantee employment and wages. But, ironically, *their* workers do not need the guarantee.

Conclusion. On the basis of the foregoing analysis we may conclude that, from the purely economic standpoint, wage-rate policy has little reliability as a way of preventing or curing unemployment in time of business depression. There is the further consideration that, from the broad political standpoint (freedom versus security), government interference with employers' unilateral wage-rate decisions (where there are no unions) and with joint union-employer bargained decisions on wage-rate changes might well entail a considerable social cost. And this cost might well be substantially above the realized social utility, in view of the doubtful economic reliability of the measure. Furthermore, this social cost might be a distinctly increasing one. In some countries (such as Australia and New Zealand) where wage-rate changes have been under government control, the governments have found it necessary also to interfere in the setting of product prices in order better to insure profitable operations for firms. Not very much freedom of private decision-making may be left in the end.

(b) Government spending and budget control. If all the above-discussed measures have little reliability for preventing or curing depression unemployment, there is one possible solution left (short of complete government ownership, control, and operation of productive resources, i.e., socialism). This is government manipulation of its own spending on goods and services in such a way as to compensate for the reductions in private consumption and investment spending that cause depressions.

i. Nature. Such compensatory manipulation means using the government budget of revenues versus expenditures so as to run deficits when depression exists or threatens. It should be clearly understood that, in our present meaning, the amount of government expenditure must be considered not as an item by itself, to be added to private spending in the economy. It must be considered *in relation* to the amount of revenue obtained by government from the private part of the economy through taxation and through the *cash* sale of government securities to the private economy. In other words, the government budget of expenditure *and* receipts is the important thing. Obviously, if the government balances its budget, i.e., if its own spending is just equal to the amount of reduction in private spending that it has caused by taxation and cash bond sales, there is no net change in the total spending of the whole society. If government wishes to reduce over-all spending, it must run a budget surplus; the amount by which it reduces private spending through taxation and cash bond sales must be greater than the amount of government spending. Conversely, if over-all spending is to rise, there must be a budget deficit; government spending must exceed receipts.

If the government decides to have a budget surplus in order to prevent inflation, it is clear that, for the duration of the period over which it is pursuing this goal, the excess funds must be "sterilized," i.e., not spent. And if a deficit is chosen in order to prevent depression and resource-unemployment, it is clear that the funds represented by the amount of the excess of spending over receipts must be obtained from some source other than taxation or the sale of government securities for cash.

There are two ways to finance a deficit. First, as the agency possessing sovereign, exclusive control over the issuance of currency, the federal government can simply print enough more money at the Bureau of Engraving. That is, the government can pay its bills with new money, which is sometimes called non-interest-bearing debt. This method clearly requires careful administration by wise, honest officials because it is so easy and tempting to print and issue much more than enough such money, with resulting wild inflation.

The second method of obtaining the deficit funds — the more "respectable" but also more expensive way — is to borrow them from the banking system. This borrowing, it should be very clearly understood, is not the same thing as that involved in the cash sale of government securities to households and non-banking firms. In the latter there is merely a shift of spending-money from the private to the public sectors; the economic effect is essentially the same as that produced by taxation. (True, under taxation the households and firms lose their money forever and are left with nothing but non-negotiable tax receipts; whereas when they pay cash for government bonds, they get in return nicely engraved certificates that are negotiable and redeemable, i.e., the holders can re-sell the bonds for cash or can receive repayment of the principal with interest at the end of the loan period. But somebody else — maybe even the bondholders — may well have to pay enough in taxes to cover interest and amortize the principal for repayment. Thus, in terms of the whole society the chief economic effects of cash bond sales and of taxation are the same.) But when the government borrows from (sells its securities to) the banking system, the banks do not usually pay cash (currency) for the securities. They create *demand deposits,* i.e., set up loans, to the credit of the government, and the government can pay its bills by writing checks against these credits. And this process means that the banking system has created new money just as surely as the government itself would have done if it had decided to print additional quantities of new currency.

Government deficits can be created either by increasing government expenditure while leaving the level of taxation unchanged or by lowering taxes while leaving government spending unchanged or by any combination of these. For the creation of surpluses, taxes may be raised with unchanged spending or spending may be lowered with unchanged taxation, or some combination of these may be used.

When the government spends its funds, it buys the services of workers for its departments and bureaus, for its construction projects, for the making of defense materials, and so on; and it buys the machines and materials involved in these projects.

ii. Utilities and costs. The great advantage of using government budget control to compensate for unfavorable declines or increases in total private spending is that, other things equal, the total flow of spending (including that of government) can be held relatively constant in the economy as a whole. In other words, a wisely and competently administered system of budget control might be successful in preventing both deflation and inflation, i.e., in holding resource-utilization at the "full" level without inflation.

But would the system be wisely and competently administered? The answers to this question get us into a consideration of possible costs. If the system is to achieve its objective rather than fail or even worsen any tendency to deflation or inflation, two related requirements must be met: the budget deficit or surplus must be of the correct amount; and the government's spending or its mopping up of a part of private spending must be done at the right time. Both requirements are very difficult to fulfill. Are any men wise and prophetic enough to know what and how much to do when? And on the assumption that there are, are any men so public-spirited that they would spend for the benefit of the whole society rather than of any special private group or political party? There are no sure answers to these questions.

Let us turn to another possible disadvantage. Thus far we have implicitly assumed that private spending would not be unfavorably affected by the government deficits or surpluses. In respect to surpluses this may well be true; for surpluses are to be devised when households and firms are psychologically expansive, and people think of surpluses as good business for any spending unit. And even if increased taxation were used to obtain surpluses and were to dampen business initiative, i.e., change the prevailing mood from one of too much optimism, this result would probably not be unfavorable; for surpluses would be employed to avoid the inflation that comes in the end from too much private optimism.

On the other hand, there is the possibility that budget deficits would have unfavorable effects. They might lower private units' inclination to spend; this might well happen even if the method of creating the deficits involved mainly a substantial lowering of the tax scale. The reason is that most of the private units would carry over to the subject of government deficits their reasoning and conclusions about their own deficits. Every household and firm knows that it cannot for long run deficits and have big debts; sooner or later it will be declared insolvent. Most households and firms are likely, then, to believe that the same thing is true for the federal government. They are unlikely to understand that the internal debt of a sovereign authority is a different sort of thing because, in effect, the country's people owe the debt to themselves, paying interest on and amortizing the debt to themselves out of tax funds collected from themselves (in most cases the same class of people). They are apt to forget that no private firm, however large, has the power to levy taxes from its customers the way government can. Again, they may fail to recognize that over the period of a whole business cycle there would be surpluses as well as deficits and that the former might well cancel out the latter, thus leaving no net increase in the public debt at the end of the period. Because of this lack of understanding, and especially if the debt-servicing taxes must be high because the debt is huge, the private units are likely to suffer a loss in incentive to work and invest. Thus, repugnance to taxation and the very idea of deficits may be enough to reduce private spending still more below the full-employment amount, i.e., even below the level at which it was when government started trying to help by creating deficits. The private reasoning and conclusions are wrong; but if people *behave* as if they were right, the effect is the same. However, the remedy at such times is not fewer deficits but more education.

Every voter faced with the alternatives of government interference or non-interference in the field of maximizing want-satisfaction from the standpoint of full utilization of resources will have to make up his own mind whether the various government measures mentioned in this section involve net social gain or loss. Fortunately the alternatives seem to be divisible. But to make rational choices in the voting booths the voters must have knowledge of what the true costs and utilities of each alternative are. In this case they may well decide that, of all the government measures presented in this chapter for enlarging the citizens' satisfaction, the ones for maintaining full employment without inflation possess the highest net social advantage.

At least, they might so decide if they were very much concerned with preserving the American system of economic and political democracy. For it is to be doubted that failure to prevent the mass unemployment of a year like 1932 would long be tolerated by the citizens directly affected. The victims of unemployment come to look on "freedom" as a luxury that has little practical significance other than the freedom to starve or to live at low levels as wards of the state. They become easy prey to any demagogue that might arise to promise them the alleged joys of living under an authoritarian government which guarantees full employment.

iii. Some administrative matters. It is sometimes asked, Who or what agency would administer the program of trying to change government revenues and expenditures in such a way as to have a proper deficit under depressed conditions and a proper surplus under inflationary conditions? Under the Constitution the Congress has the sole power to levy federal taxes and approve federal expenditures. The President proposes a budget, but the Congress disposes. And the Congress takes a lot of time making appropriations and changing tax laws; committees of both Houses hold hearings covering months, and there is much debate on the legislative floors. This undoubtedly is good democracy. But time is of the essence in compensatory government spending.

There seems to be a way out — one suggested by experience under the Reciprocal Trade Agreement Act of 1934 and its subsequent re-enactments. Under this program the Congress, which under the Constitution has sole power to make tariffs and treaties, delegated some of its authority to the Department of State. And the latter, subject to the general directives of the delegating legislation, has negotiated a great many tariff-reduction treaties with other nations, without the need for specific Congressional ratification on each one. Periodically, usually every two years, the Congress has reviewed the actions of its delegatee; and, finding the actions satisfactory, has yet to revoke its delegation.

Here, then, is said to be a method of handling the administration of the budget deficit (or surplus, if the latter is called for). The Congress could delegate to the Treasury Department some of its own authority to spend and tax. It could keep a constant or period check-up on the way the delegation was being used; and if it did not like what it found, it could revoke the delegation. But wise and timely use of the compensatory-budget policy might be expected under adequate general directives. It is claimed that this administrative device would greatly improve the policy's chances for success.

A second administrative problem is that of coordinating the tax and expenditure policies of the various state and large city governments with federal policy. All the important lower levels of government would have to cooperate with the overall policy, for the aggregate of their spending is large, and failure to work together might well negate or endanger the federal measures.

Third, on what items should government deficit funds be spent? The governments could of course simply distribute such funds directly to the households. But it might seem better to have something to show for the outlays, e.g., new roads, harbor improvements, power dams, and so on. In this way the government could be surer that the money would be spent in the first instance. It could not be certain that the households would not hoard a significant portion of the funds if they received the money directly rather than via wage payments made by the private contractors, steel mills, and other plants which were helping produce "public works." Of course, once the money had reached the nation's households in the latter, indirect manner, there would be no certainty that the funds would not be hoarded and that the level of employment would not slip back to its previous low level. But the country would have the public improvements to show for its initial effort in any case. And the chances are that the hoarding leakages would not be very serious.

Finally, how long would the government have to continue running deficits? The answer to this question depends on how the expectations and confidence of firms and households are affected by the program. If expectations and confidence were significantly improved, one deficit might be enough; and even that one might not have to be very large. This was the idea behind the original talk of "pump-priming" which was heard a good deal during the early and middle thirties. On the other hand, if ignorance of the nature and suspicion of the purpose of deficit spending were prevalent, expectations might be made less favorable and confidence further impaired, so that successively larger and fruitless deficits would be required, with full employment still unrealized in the end.

iv. Summary appraisal. On the basis of the material presented above, informed proponents of the compensatory government spending program make the following appraisal. The measure would undoubtedly be held constitutional by the Supreme Court. It possesses a high degree of economic validity. It would be difficult to administer successfully, from the standpoint of proper timing and amount of deficit. The proposal has the support of most unionists but not of most employers (chiefly because management has not been educated to understand the difference between the finances of government and those of private economic units). Adequate economic education (not propaganda) is needed for the success of the program. Most important of all, from the freedom-versus-security standpoint, the measure stands high in that it operates only from the top, i.e., it does not interfere with firms' or households' freedom to make all kinds of economic decisions. It helps to make freedom worth having. That is, by helping to achieve and maintain reasonable full employment, it helps to preserve democracy.

v. Progress of the proposal in the United States. How close has the United States come to approving the proposal? Not very close. The fact that there *may* be future periods of stagnation (such as the one caused by the domestic political uncertainties of the thirties), together with the virtual certainty that there will be future cyclical fluctuations in economic activity, has led many American citizens to believe that the federal government should adopt a more positive and coordinated program to attain full employment of resources. A bill (sometimes known as the Murray Full Employment Bill) was introduced in the Congress in 1945 with the objective of providing government investment financed by budget deficits whenever labor employment was expected to fall below the "full" level. Fear of increased government action, plus the failure of the heralded postwar depression to materialize, led to the passage of nothing but a statement of public policy, with a very modest implementation. Nevertheless, the Employment Act of 1946 does mark an important milestone in the relation of government to full resource-utilization. It stated the responsibility of government to help private industry avoid depressions and inflations. And it created a Council of Economic Advisers whose duty it is to keep the President and through him the Congress informed on the state of the nation's economic health. On the basis of the Council's studies the President makes semi-annual and special economic reports and recommendations to the Congress, which are then to be studied and further reported on by a Joint House-Senate Committee.

c. Avoiding inflationary booms. Some pages back we said that the twofold aim of government should be (1) reasonably full employment and (2) avoidance of inflation — in other words, full employment without inflation. Inflation of the general price level is socially undesirable for two main reasons. First it is bad economics, for in the absence of government controls it leads straight into depressions and their mass unemployment of resources. Under a private enterprise economy during a business upswing or recovery period, there is such a mass mood of optimism that investment spending (and to some extent consumption spending) overreaches itself. Then, when events fail to bear out profit and other expectations, the mass mood turns unfavorably downward, and the economy is precipitated into a downswing and depression. Second, inflation of the general price level is bad human relations. A serious inflation works economic inequity on the white-collar, unorganized, fixed-income groups in the society. These groups fall far behind the organized groups (e.g., unionists and farmers) in their efforts to keep up with increases in the cost of maintaining their planes of living.

For both reasons it is desirable for government to take a hand. But in the light of human relations or of political as well as economic considerations, government's proper role in peacetime must be sharply distinguished from that which should be acted under the emergency conditions of war (hot or cold).

(1) In peacetime. Even though the nation is not threatened with or actually engaged in war, it is nevertheless desirable that government try to curb or prevent inflationary booms, for the reasons given above. But peacetime efforts must be made with due regard for the preservation of economic and political democracy; interference with private decision-making should be minimized. Otherwise the social cost of control is likely to be much too high.

The desirable kind of control may be attempted by the same sorts of measures, now working in reverse, as those discussed above for increasing the consumption spending of households, the investment spending of firms, and government spending on goods and services. When inflation threatens (or exists), the problem is to keep the aggregate expenditure of all three groups at (or reduce it to) just the level needed for reasonably full employment.

When private consumption and investment spending, plus the existing level of government spending, give a total in excess of that needed for reasonably full employment without inflation, the most important government measure is to run a budget surplus. By raising the level of tax rates or by lowering its own spending on goods and services or by some combination of these two devices, government can try to produce a surplus which is equal to the amount by which government estimates total previous spending has exceeded the desired level.

Our previous appraisal of the pro's and con's (utilities and costs) of government budget control are applicable here and need not be repeated. We may emphasize, however, that over the whole period of what would be a normal peacetime business cycle the proponents of budget deficits for depressions and surpluses for booms believe that the deficits and the surpluses would pretty much cancel each other out. In other words, over the period of a whole cycle there would not necessarily be any net increase in the government debt. Whether or not this would actually come to pass would depend on how budget control would affect private expectations and spending. In the absence of adequate economic knowledge among firms and households the reaction to deficits might be unfavorable; the private sector of the economy might decline to be "primed." In this event the deficits might well have to be so large and continuous that their total would be considerably larger than the total of the surpluses. However, as previously suggested, the remedy would seem to lie not in abandoning the proposal but in broadening the scope of economic education.

(2) In time of war and emergency defense. When the country is engaged in or threatened with total war, its survival, power, and prestige are in jeopardy. At such times economic considerations rise a great deal in importance relative to considerations of individual liberty and social equity or human-political relations. The extent of this shift in relative importance depends directly on the direness of the emergency faced by the society and on the sense of urgency felt by its citizen-members. But in any case government is compelled to establish some kinds of government action that have not been found suitable during full peace, and the voters become willing to accept some degree of authoritarianism.

Inflation is particularly bad for wartime. Not only does it involve the social costs that we mentioned above for peacetime. It hurts the morale and hinders the cooperation of all human beings involved in the war effort on the home front. Social inequities of peacetime become inequalities of sacrifice during wartime. Among workers there is an increase in labor turnover and idleness due to hunting for better-paying jobs in order to keep earnings in pace with rising costs of living. Strikes for wage-rate increases tend to rise greatly. All these and other developments lead to lowered output at a time when maximum production is needed.

We may think of the war or emergency defense situation in terms of an "inflationary gap." At the "top" of the gap, so to speak, is an amount (say $300 billion) which represents the total spending power of the economy — the greatly increased amount the government has to spend on war goods plus what households and firms will spend if the government does not take some of their buying power away from them. At the "bottom" of the gap is another total amount (say $220 billion) which represents the aggregate value of total produceable physical output at current prices. The question is, then, What shall government do with this gap (of say, $80 billion)?

There are a number of possible approaches. One is to do nothing. Then we have a bad inflation. No one except favorably situated organized groups, who can beat the game, wants to see this happen. A second approach is to tax the firms and households very heavily. Take the $80 billion and more from them and use the revenues for government spending. Then the government will not have to ask the banks to create new money, which is of course inflationary money. This is good economics. But it is bad politics. Unless the emergency is very acute, the private economic units will object vigorously to such rough treatment. As a matter of fact, no government engaged in total war has ever had the political fortitude to rely solely on this measure.

A third possibility is to use some other kind of money, in addition to the existing, usual kind. Require that the households use this new sort of money as well as the usual kind for the purchase of civilian goods. And limit the quantity of this additional kind of money severely, so that the total amount issued will just buy the total quantities of civilian goods available. Then, if the households have extra or "hot" amounts of the usual kind of money, they can either buy war bonds with it (transfer it to the government) or spend it on certain civilian goods (such as entertainment) for which the government says the new kind of currency is not needed and the prices of which do not interest the government. The name for the special kind of money is *ration coupons* or *tokens.*

It will be noted that the second and third measures just mentioned involve bringing the "top" or spending level of the inflationary gap down to the "bottom" or product-value level. The first or do-nothing approach leaves the gap open, like the bottom of an elevator in relation to the top. As fast as the bottom level rises (because the physical volume of output gets multiplied by higher and higher prices), the top level goes up too (because workers and other income-receivers receive higher and higher prices for their services and because the government has to spend more and more due to the higher prices it has to pay for the products it insists on having).

A fourth proposal sometimes made has to do with raising the bottom level up to or toward the top, i.e., closing or reducing the gap, with little or no upward movement of the top level. The proposal is that physical production be increased so much that higher output multiplied by the existing product prices will give a total goods value equal or nearly equal to total spending. The trouble with this notion is that increased output requires additional resources. Then, if more labor and capital were available and hired, wage and interest income would rise also. The top, spending level thus rises along with the bottom, goods-value level. Only if *productivity* were to rise (which is increased average output per worker, a very different thing from just increased total production) because of technological improvements or harder and more efficient work by labor, would this proposal have validity. But it is doubtful if productivity rises much at such times. Experienced workers are drafted and are replaced by green hands (women, handicapped, and superannuated workers). And when firms produce on government order, some of the incentive for technological progress is absent.

A fifth measure is to try to curtail unessential private spending by using in reverse all the valid Federal Reserve Board and Treasury Department measures mentioned above in respect to controlling depressions during peacetime.

Because of the limitations of the programs thus far discussed, there is finally a sixth approach to the inflationary gap. This is to hold the gap open but to prevent it from becoming wider and from moving upward like the elevator. The measures employed for this purpose are usually called "direct controls." They include authoritarian or semi-authoritarian (*i*) allocation of resources to uses desired by government; and (*ii*) control of changes in the prices of labor, materials, machines, and products. Under the first, critical materials and machines are given to manufacturers and other users on the basis of a special system of priorities. As a certain portion of the existing or potential work force is drafted for service in the armed forces, less authoritarian efforts are made to "freeze" essential labor in existing war work and draw other workers to it. Under the second type of control, stabilization agencies are created to minimize general upward movements in the levels of wage rates and materials and product prices, and to correct inequities within the structure of wage rates and prices.

In the next chapter, which includes a review of federal and state legislation on wage rates, we shall consider the nature of the wage-rate-control decisions of the National War Labor Board during World War II and of the Wage Stabilization Board during 1950–52.

4. Unemployment compensation. *a. Nature.* All governmental statutes providing for financial compensation to wage-earners who, because of exposure to the various risks of industry, are injured economically or physically (or both) come under the heading of *social insurance.* Unemployment compensation legislation belongs in this group of laws, which also includes government financial provisions for industrial accidents, occupational diseases, non-industrial accidents and sickness, and old-age work incompetence.

Government-fostered compensation for these industrial risks is called "insurance" because it is based on the principle (common to private insurance against, say, the risks of death and fire) of wide diffusion of risk; premiums or contributions are paid in to a common fund by many people so that those who happen to suffer from the risks can be given more money compensation from the accumulated fund than most could provide for themselves as individuals. The term "social" insurance is used in connection with such compensation because the purpose is broadly humanitarian; because all people are asked to contribute to the funds, directly or indirectly, so that the burden may be widely distributed; and because, under most socially conceived systems, the largest contributions come from the wealthier people, who are best able to contribute.

Unemployment compensation legislation stands in the twilight zone between measures for the prevention of unemployment and measures for the relief and alleviation of unemployment. In England, Germany, Italy, and many other European countries, the main purpose has appeared to be money relief for the jobless rather than regularization of employment, whereas certain American proposals and laws have stressed the latter aim, even in the face of the mass unemployment of the thirties. That is to say, although the object of most unemployment-benefit laws in America is mainly to pay benefits to help relieve the effects of unemployment among workers, the systems are organized in such a manner that employers are to be stimulated to provide more steady work. Prevention and relief are thus supposed to be combined in some degree.

It is doubtful whether public or private systems of making money payments to wage-earners for involuntary idleness deserve strictly to be called unemployment "insurance." Unemployment "compensation" or "benefits" appears to be a more apt appellation because, with the possible exception of seasonal idleness, unemployment is not a risk like that of death or accidental injury or sickness or property damage; it does not meet all the requirements of an insurable risk. It is true that unemployment insurance does try to diffuse the risk over a large number of individuals, but it differs from true insurance in certain other respects. First, the average incidence of unemployment (i.e., the average "mortality") is not predictable or calculable. Depressions vary in length and severity. A bad depression can make a holocaust of statistical probabilities of unemployment and can bankrupt an unemployment compensation fund, just as a big ring of arsonists in large cities or a tremendous epidemic of a fatal disease could work havoc with insurance against fire, illness, or death. Unemployment compensation can be called "insurance" only if it applies to non-depression unemployment. Second, unless depression unemployment is excluded, it is impossible to establish premiums the sum of which, when paid in, will with certainty be enough to cover all disbursements to those suffering the insured loss, provide for administrative and operating costs, and set up adequate reserves.

These facts of course provide no good argument for not having a compensation system for depression unemployment. Government can find the money somewhere, even through deficit financing.

b. Development of the American system. By 1930 more than 40 million European workers had been covered by government unemployment compensation programs. In the United States no workers were covered. There was no government system here at that time because only a small minority of the citizens wanted one. Almost all employers and unions were against it, perhaps because it represented a considerable departure from the "American way" of everybody for himself, with little paternalistic interference by government.

But the Great Depression was a very stern teacher. By 1932 the A.F.L. had reversed its position; its unions had learned how utterly inadequate their own out-of-work benefit plans were to tide members over prolonged periods of idleness. And many employers came also to bow before social and political necessity and economic helplessness. In 1932 Wisconsin took the lead by enacting the first state legislation. (Bills had been *introduced* in a number of states as early as 1916.) In 1933 there were 83 bills pending in 23 states. But it remained for the first New Deal administration and Congress to give the movement its big push. In June, 1934, President Roosevelt appointed a Committee on Economic Security to make a detailed study of various proposals and measures on different kinds of social insurance, including unemployment compensation, and to develop recommendations for Congressional action. A bill was introduced in January, 1935, and by August of that year the Social Security Act was enacted. Since that date its original provisions have been amended four times (in 1939, 1944, 1946, and 1950).

As we shall see, the American system of unemployment compensation is a federal-state one. Hence to complete our brief account of the development in this country we must tell what happened after Wisconsin's initial move. Nothing happened until after the enactment of the federal Act. But then, for two years, there was a great rush to jump on the bandwagon. Some of the more "progressive" legislatures swung into action almost immediately. Other states hung back to see what the 1936 presidential election would do to the New Deal administration (a Republican victory might, they thought, lead to the amendment or repeal of the federal Act) and what, in any case, the United States Supreme Court, of rather conservative bent, would do to the federal and state laws. They learned that both the voters (in November, 1936) and the Court (in May, 1937) approved the social security legislation. So before the fall of 1937 there were unemployment compensation laws on the statute books of all 48 states and of the District of Columbia, Alaska, and Hawaii — 51 laws in all.

Undoubtedly the main immediate stimulus to such fast, unanimous action was the provision in the federal Act taxing all the covered employers of each state, no matter whether the state had its own law or not. If the state had an unemployment compensation law, the workers of the firms in that state got benefits out of the payroll taxes paid by the firms. In the absence of a state law, these tax funds would leave the state for use elsewhere. Therefore it behooved the employers to pressure the state legislatures to enact their own statutes.

c. Early issues and problems. Once the voters and their government have chosen to inaugurate any plan of social insurance — old-age security, accident compensation, unemployment insurance, or whatever — certain important policy questions have next to be decided in respect to how the plan is to operate. These basic questions are always the same no matter how much the details differ; and in our discussion of each program we shall follow the same outline.

(1) Coverage. The first question is, What workers shall be subject to the plan? In the usual terminology, what is the coverage of the program? From this broad question, certain particular issues arise, such as the following: Shall the coverage be universal for all industries? Or shall certain industries like agriculture and domestic service be excluded because of the administrative difficulties involved in collecting contributions and paying benefits? In any covered industry, shall all firms be included, regardless of size, i.e., number of workers employed? Shall all employees, from corporation presidents to common laborers, be covered; or shall the program be confined to wage-earners below the rank of supervisor? Shall white-collar workers be included?

(2) Contributions. Second, where shall the money come from for the payment of benefits? What shall be the system of contributions? In respect to the United States, a number of specific questions flow from this general one. Shall government contribute at all; and if so, what percentage of the total? If government is to contribute, how shall its share be apportioned between the federal government and the state governments? Shall the workers contribute; and if so, how much? Or should the entire initial expense be borne in the first instance by the covered employers? Should employers' contributions, and workers' contributions (if any), be flat-rate, with perhaps only a few differentials based on age and sex; or should they be in proportion to the workers' earnings, so that higher contributions are paid in behalf of or by the more highly skilled and highly

paid workers? The flat-rate system is much simpler to administer. But the other plan is based more on ability to pay and might appear more equitable. Should employers' contributions vary on the basis of their ability to regularize employment, i.e., on the basis of how much unemployment their respective work forces actually have experienced; or should all employers in all industries contribute the same amounts?

It will be seen that almost all the issues in respect to contributions raise one broad, basic question: Who is to bear the cost of the unemployment produced under the private enterprise system? The answer to this fundamental question of course follows from one's economic-political-social philosophy. If you believe that private business is responsible for unemployment and is able by its own efforts to prevent it, then you hold that only employers should be asked to contribute to the payment of unemployment compensation to their employees. And you hold that the amount of each employer's contribution should be directly related to his recorded success in preventing joblessness among his own employees. But if you believe *(a)* that unemployment is mainly the result of the way the whole private enterprise system operates, *(b)* that it is impossible for most firms to regularize their employment even in prosperity years and certainly not in the years when serious declines in total spending produce the mass unemployment of depression, and *(c)* that unemployment is therefore a social cost paid for the privilege and advantages of having economic and political democracy, then you look for the least expensive and most socially equitable way of distributing this cost. And you probably conclude that this objective is best achieved by requiring most of the contributions for benefit payments to be made by those best able to bear the expense — the higher-income groups. This would mean progressive income taxes; but enough of the lower-income groups would have to be taxed (i.e., the tax base would have to be broad enough) to provide sufficient reserves. Furthermore, if you believe that people don't really appreciate benefit payments of any kind unless they themselves make some contribution, you will vote for such a broad base on this principle alone. And even if you do not approve of the progressive tax, you will wish workers to contribute along with employers.

(3) *Reserves.* Third, what happens to the funds amassed from the contributions or taxes, between the time of collection and the time when part of the monies are paid out as benefits? From this general problem such specific questions as the following must be answered. Shall the funds be segregated or pooled in one over-all reserve? If segregated, shall they be kept separate for each plant, or for each firm, or merely for each industry? Under a pooled-reserve plan, the benefits for workers can be higher than under segregation. The contributions of firms who are fortunate enough or managerially competent enough to have regular, stable employment can be used to pay benefits to the unemployed workers of less fortunate or less able firms. Under segregation, each unit — plant,

firm, or industry — has its own reserve for its own unemployed workers. And when this reserve is used up, no more funds are available for the unit. The narrower the segregation lines, the smaller the benefits and the shorter their duration. The main argument in favor of segregation is that it stimulates each employer to try to stabilize his own employment. What shall be done with the reserves that are accumulated in prosperous years? How shall they be invested so as not to affect the course of the business cycle unfavorably, i.e., so as not to cause changes in total spending which might produce or worsen a depression?

(4) Benefits system. Fourth, what sort of benefits system shall be established? What conditions shall determine eligibility for receiving benefit payments? What conditions shall disqualify applicants for benefits? What shall be the lengths of "waiting periods"; that is, how many days or weeks must workers who have become unemployed wait until they are eligible to receive unemployment compensation — three days, one or two weeks, or what? Long waiting periods of course conserve reserves; but they may work hardship on the jobless. Shall unemployed workers be permitted to refuse any kind of job and still get benefits? Or shall they be compelled to act as strikebreakers or take a job in a far-off community or work in their own city at jobs much inferior to their previous ones under penalty of becoming disqualified for benefits? What if they are on strike; are they eligible?

How high shall the general level of benefits be? Shall it be kept low in order to enable the system to care for the prolonged mass unemployment of a depression? Or shall it be made so high that, while adequate to handle all frictional unemployment, it is unable to carry much serious depressional unemployment, thus forcing long-idle workers to go on some other, "charitable" kind of relief? A closely related question is, What shall be the lengths of the benefit periods — ten weeks, twenty weeks, or what? And shall this period be the same for all unemployed workers, or shall it vary in relation to the amount of contributions built up for or by each?

What shall be the structure of the benefit system as to amount of compensation? Shall there be flat-rate benefits, the same for all the unemployed, with perhaps a few differentials based on age and sex; or shall the benefits be based on amounts of previous earnings and contibutions? A system of flat-rate benefits is much easier to administer, for it avoids much record-keeping, calculating, and red tape. But a system based on previous earnings and contributions might seem more equitable because it relates the size of the benefit for a given worker to his previous, customary plane of living. Again, shall the benefits paid to an unemployed worker vary in relation to the number of dependents he has?

(5) Administration. Finally, how shall the whole system be administered? What government agencies shall be set up and how shall they operate? In the United States an important question always is, Shall there be an exclusively federal system, with headquarters at Washington and

with regional offices and local sub-offices? Or shall each state have and administer its own plan, with no participation by the federal government? Or shall there be a combination federal-state system? The main arguments for an exclusively federal administrative set-up are that (*i*) there should be uniformity in coverage, contributions, benefits, and administration for all areas, and only a federal program can achieve this; (*ii*) a federal system would be financially stronger, not only because of greater resources but also because of a much wider diffusion of risk from region to region and industry to industry; (*iii*) a higher class of administrative personnel could be obtained; and (*iv*) only under a federal plan can workers who move from state to state be adequately cared for. The main arguments against this approach are that (*i*) it concentrates too much power and control in a federal bureaucracy; (*ii*) such control fails to give enough attention to special local conditions, needs, and problems; (*iii*) uniform treatment is not always desirable or possible; and (*iv*) action at the state level would permit more experimentation with various methods of handling problems. The arguments for a federal-state system are that it combines some of the best features and avoids some of the worst faults of an exclusively federal or state system.

Shall public employment offices be made an important part of the administrative set-up for unemployment compensation? If so, shall they have the entire responsibility for determining employees' eligibility for the receipt of benefits? Or shall they be given only partial responsibility, in the form of applying the "work test," i.e., determining whether or not workers have refused to look for "suitable" work and are therefore unqualified to receive compensation? If there is a state or federal-state system, how shall the interstate movement of workers be handled?

d. Main features of the United States program. Let us learn briefly how these questions have been answered by the Congress and the state legislatures. As we have seen, the Social Security Act of 1935 gave expression to the country's desire to have a government system of unemployment compensation. In passing the Act, the Congress considered the above-mentioned arguments in respect to an all-federal, an all-state, and a federal-state system and concluded that the last was the best for a country of the United States' size, heterogeneity, and governmental structure.

Actually the Social Security Act did not create an unemployment compensation system as such. It simply did two main things: (1) Title III of the Act provided for money grants to each state to pay for the cost of administering the state unemployment compensation law (if any). The amount of federal money going to each state for this purpose was to depend on its population, the number of workers covered by its law, the actual cost of administration, and other relevant factors. This Title of the Social Security Act also set up certain standards to which state statutes and their administrations had to conform in order that the federal grant might be received. (2) Title IX of the original Act, which in a few years came to be superseded by the Federal Unemployment Tax Act (which was made part of the Internal Revenue Code), provided for a tax of 3 per cent on the first $3000 of wage payments made during a calendar year by covered employers in covered industries to each covered employee. But it was also provided that, if the state in which a federally taxed employer operates has an unemployment compensation law and taxes the employer thereunder, the employer receives a credit or offset against the federal tax. The maximum amount of this credit (called the "normal" credit) is 90 per cent of the amount of the federal tax. Thus, if the 3 per cent federal tax amounted to $30,000 on an annual taxable payroll of $1,000,000 and if the state payroll tax on the employer were 2.7 per cent or $27,000, the employer would *not* pay a total tax of 5.7 per cent, or $57,000 to the federal and state governments together. He would pay only a total of 3 per cent or $30,000, of which 0.3 per cent or $3000 would go to the federal government, and 2.7 per cent or $27,000 to the state. Of course, if the state tax were 3.0 rather than 2.7 per cent, this employer would pay $3000 to the federal government and $30,000 to the state government — a total of $33,000. This is because the maximum credit against the 3.0 per cent federal payroll tax is 90 per cent thereof.

In addition to the so-called normal credit the Act provides for special credits for employers whose state taxes have been reduced because of their success in stabilizing their employments. See Table 40 for illustrations of the Federal Unemployment Tax Act's tax-offset provisions.

Thus, the objectives of the unemployment compensation provisions of the two Acts mentioned above were to stimulate states to pass their own laws and to provide the necessary amount of federal control and coordination. As we saw in our sketch of the development of the American system, the first goal was speedily achieved. We shall also learn that the second one has been rather well realized.

TABLE 40 *Illustrations of the Tax-Offset Provisions*

Federal-State Tax Relationships	Assumed Payroll of $1,000,000		
	If State Tax Is 3 Per Cent	If State Tax Is 2.7 Per Cent	If State Tax to Employer Is Actually 2 Per Cent under Experience-Rating or Individual Reserve Plan
1. Amount of state tax actually paid	$30,000	$27,000	$20,000
2. Amount of nominal federal tax — 3 per cent	30,000	30,000	30,000
3. Normal credit against federal tax (cannot be more than state tax paid or more than 90 per cent of federal 3 per cent tax)	27,000	27,000	20,000
4. Additional credit against federal tax	—	—	7,000
5. Net federal tax actually paid (lines 2 — 3 — 4)	3,000	3,000	3,000
6. Total federal-state taxes actually paid (lines 1 + 5)	33,000	30,000	23,000

(1) Administration. Let us consider the main features of the federal-state administrative arrangements as well as the chief ways in which the state and territorial laws are operated.

(a) Federal-state relationships. Under the Acts mentioned above, the collection of the 3 per cent federal payroll tax (actually 10 per cent of 3 per cent, because all the states have laws) is administered by the Bureau of Internal Revenue of the federal Treasury Department. This Department also disburses funds to the state governments to pay them for the expenses they will incur in administering their laws. Theoretically, it is from these tax monies that the administrative grants to the states are made. But in practice, it should be understood, the funds collected under the federal payroll tax are not segregated except in a bookkeeping sense. Like all other federal tax monies, they go into the general fund of the Treasury. And like all other disbursements made by the Treasury, the grants made to the states for administration must be out of funds specifically appropriated by the Congress. Every year the Bureau of Employment Security (B.E.S.) of the Department of Labor (see below) submits an estimate to the Congress as to how much money each state will need for administering its unemployment compensation act. If the Congress were to "forget" to appropriate funds directly earmarked for this purpose, the Treasury would be powerless to send administration checks to the states. The Congress has never had such a lapse of memory. But it has sometimes appropriated less than the amounts requested (also sometimes less than the total amounts collected by the federal payroll tax). In this case the B.E.S. must pro-rate the total appropriation among the states.

We see, then, that the Treasury is not free to make administration-cost disbursements on its own motion and that there is another federal agency (other than the Congress) which has an important say on the matter. The job of the Bureau of Employment Security is to see that the states conform to the minimum standards set forth in the Social Security Act. If the Bureau finds a lack of conformity in a given state, it can require the Treasury to suspend administrative grants from the state until the latter's waywardness has been corrected.

These standards for state performance are as follows: (*i*) administrative methods designed to insure full payment of unemployment compensation to eligible covered workers; (*ii*) payment of the benefits through public employment offices or other approved agencies; (*iii*) deposit by the state of all tax monies collected from its employers in the federal Treasury; (*iv*) use of funds withdrawn from the Treasury solely for the payment of unemployment benefits, i.e., not for administration or any other purpose; (*v*) observance of the rule that an unemployed worker shall not be denied benefits if he refuses to accept a job offered by the public employment office when such job would make him a strikebreaker, offers a lower wage rate and other terms of employment which are substantially less favorable than those prevailing for similar work in the locality, or requires as a condition of employment that he join a "company" union or resign from a "regular" union; (*vi*) fair hearings, before impartial tribunals of appeal, for workers whose claims for compensation have been denied; (*vii*) use of administrative funds solely for the purposes and in the amounts found necessary by the B.E.S.; (*viii*) selection of state administrative employees on a merit rather than political basis; and (*ix*) the making of whatever reports on operations the B.E.S. may require.

The Bureau of Employment Security has not had too much difficulty in getting the states to fulfill these standards. Once in a while, however, it has discovered disregard or evasion and has had to ask the Treasury to withhold administrative grants. This action, supplemented by conferences with the administrative officers of the state agencies, has always been enough to bring the offending states back into compliance with the standards.

As indicated above, the states cannot keep their unemployment tax collections at home. These funds must be deposited in the Unemployment Trust Fund of the Treasury Department. The states request the Secretary of the Treasury to release funds from their accounts for the payment of benefits to their unemployed workers. What happens to their deposits between time of deposit and time of withdrawal is considered below (under Reserves).

The federal-state system of public employment offices, discussed earlier in this chapter from the standpoint of improving the operation of the labor market, is a part of the federal-state system of unemployment compensation. The United States Employment Service, as previously noted, is within the federal Bureau of Employment Security. And the state employment services are integrated with the state unemployment compensation operations.

(b) State administration. i. Type of agency. In 32 of the 51 state-territorial jurisdictions, unemployment compensation is administered by special separate agencies created along with the acts. In the other 19 jurisdictions the laws vest administration within existing labor departments; even here, however, special bureaus have usually been established. In 30 of the 51 jurisdictions the top administrator is a board or commission, usually of three members. In the remaining 21, a single person is the head. Administration in about 40 jurisdictions is faciliated by the desirable adjunct of advisory councils, composed of representatives of the unions, the employers, and the general public.

ii. Appeals procedure. An important feature of state administration is the appeals procedure. Under it workers and employers can obtain reviews of decisions (on eligibility, coverage, amounts and durations of benefits, and so on) made by the state's administrative offices. All but four states have a lower and a higher level of appeal. Beyond these the courts, of course, have the ultimate decision.

In recent years the numbers and percentages of appealed cases have in general risen, thus throwing excessive burdens on administrative staffs and causing long delays.

iii. The place of public employment offices. The use of the public employment offices to apply the work test was mentioned earlier in the chapter. It should be emphasized again that the state employment office officials as such do not usually have the complete or final decision on workers' eligibility for benefits. They merely inform the unemployment compensation officials on whether the unemployed workers accepted referrals to job vacancies and took the jobs if offered. It is then up to the unemployment compensation officers to use this information, together with that pertaining to other criteria of eligibility, in deciding whether or not qualification for benefits has been established.

iv. Administering benefits for interstate workers. One of the difficulties of the federal-state system was dealing with the so-called "interstate" workers: (*a*) those whose occupations in such interstate companies as oil-well-drilling companies and bus corporations took them regularly across state lines; (*b*) those who lived in one community, such as Camden, New Jersey, and commuted regularly across a state line to work in another city, such as Philadelphia; and (*c*) the so-called "multi-state" workers, who terminated employment at frequent intervals and migrated from state to state, accumulating and leaving behind benefit rights in each place of work.

To handle the problems involved with these kinds of workers, the federal B.E.S. and the states have tried to work out cooperative methods and uniform procedures. In respect to workers who cross lines because of the nature of their occupations, about 35 states have signed an Interstate Coverage Arrangement involving a uniform definition of employment and the payment of contributions and benefits in the worker's state of residence. For interstate commuters, contributions and benefits are usually paid in the state of work. For migratory workers an Interstate Benefit Plan has been in operation among all the states since 1938. Under this plan a worker who has accumulated benefit rights in one state and moved to another may file a claim in an office of the latter. This second state then sends all necessary information to the first state, which determines eligibility and sends benefit payments to the claimant.

A special variant of the migrating-worker problem is involved when the claimant has worked in two or more states during his base year and, while earning enough in all of them together to qualify for benefits in any of the states, has not received enough wages in any one state to qualify exclusively for benefits there. To handle this problem, about 45 states have subscribed to an Interstate Wage Combining Arrangement, under which one state handles eligibility and pays benefits as if all the wages had been earned in that state.

(2) Coverage. (a) Under the federal tax provisions. The Federal Unemployment Tax Act makes the above-described federal levy on firms having eight or more workers in all employments except self-employment, family employment, agriculture, domestic service, government employment, casual work, employment in a non-profit organization (such as a college), and railroads. Because government workers have relatively regular employment and because railway employers are covered under their own special law (see below), the large exclusions are among workers in very small firms, in agriculture, and in homes and clubs.

(b) Under the state-territorial laws. Because of the important influence of the federal tax on state action, the coverage of the state laws is in general much like that of the federal levy. However, some of the states have narrowed the fields of their exclusions. In respect to size of firm, 22 states still retained the eight-or-more-employees provision in 1951. But a number had reduced this kind of exclusion to firms having fewer than three, four, and six workers; and 17 states included all sizes of firms in all covered industries. This broadening of coverage resulted from recognition of the fact that in many industries the small firms are the unstable ones, with high rates of insolvency, and therefore present special employment hazards for their workers.

In respect to industrial coverage, the states have again emulated the federal approach. However, we find again that some state laws have become broader. Thus, a number include "industrialized" agriculture, domestic service in homes or clubs where four or more are employed, and certain kinds of state and municipal workers.

In terms of the entire labor force, coverage is far from complete. In 1951 the labor force, as we saw in Chapter 5, numbered about 65 million. Among these persons roughly 14 million were self-employed or unpaid family workers in cities or rural areas, and about 49 million were employed by firms, including government. In the latter group about 15 million were not covered by unemployment compensation. This figure, added to the 14 million just mentioned, gives a total of 29 million excluded persons, or about 45 per cent of the total labor force.

(3) Contributions. Under the United States federal-state program the contributions to the unemployment reserve funds come overwhelmingly from payroll taxes on covered employers. The nominal employer contribution on federal account is the previously mentioned 3 per cent, the actual contribution usually 0.3 per cent. The federal government levies no tax on employees. The significant new things to be noted in respect to contributions or payroll taxes are in the state-territorial laws.

(a) Employer versus worker contributions. All state laws tax covered employers' wage payments or payrolls, but very few tax employees' earnings. At one time or another since 1935, employee contributions have

been specified in eleven state statutes. But only nine of these states actually collected the taxes, and five of the nine soon amended their laws to drop worker contributions. Of the remaining four which still impose taxes on employees, only one (Alabama) uses the receipts wholly for unemployment compensation reserves; the tax is one per cent of earnings (or less if the worker's firm has had a good record in stabilizing employment). Two others (Rhode Island and California) use the receipts from the one per cent employee tax to finance the cash benefit payments for sickness which are tied to their unemployment compensation system (see the next chapter). The fourth state, New Jersey, uses three-fourths of its one per cent tax for sickness benefits and one-fourth for unemployment compensation.

(b) Experience rating for employers. In the early years most of the state laws provided a normal tax of 2.7 per cent on covered employers' payrolls. Only two jurisdictions (Michigan and the District of Columbia, with 3 per cent) exceeded this percentage. However, from the beginning there was evidence of the belief that considerable unemployment is the result of individual firms' decisions; that firms can prevent much unemployment if they take the pains to introduce regularizing programs; that the laws should be framed so as to give firms an incentive to introduce such preventive measures; and that this can be done by varying each firm's tax or contribution rate on the basis of his previous year's record for unemployment among his employees. In short, almost from the beginning most states began experimenting with departures from flat-rate taxes, uniform for all covered employers.

This plan is commonly known as *experience rating* (though the term *merit rating* is also sometimes used). The idea probably came in part from the states' success in handling the first kind of social insurance used in the United States — "workmen's compensation" or insurance against industrial accidents (see the next chapter). The states found that employers tended to introduce and operate accident-prevention programs if they were given contribution rates related to the accident experience in their plants. Hence the states were inclined to apply the same principle to the hazard of unemployment. They professed to believe that, in terms of preventability, unemployment was much the same sort of risk as industrial accidents.

By 1948 all the 51 jurisdictions had introduced some kind of experience rating. In their laws four main methods are set forth for measuring experience: (*i*) the *reserve-ratio* method, which in substance expresses the relation of the benefits paid out of an employer's account to the reserves remaining in his account (this is by far the most common method); (*ii*) the *benefit-ratio* method, which relates the benefits paid out of an employer's account in a given period to his total *payroll* during the period; (*iii*) the *benefit-wage-ratio* method, which relates the total amount of *wages* paid by an employer to those of his workers receiving benefits during a year to his total payroll during the year; and (*iv*) the *payroll-variation* plan, under which employers' contributions are reduced when and after their total payrolls (and hence their "normal" contributions) have been so high as to build up "unnecessarily" large reserves, and under which, conversely, reductions in total payrolls give the signal for increasing their tax rates.

Are employers who have had particularly unfavorable employment records assessed contributions in excess of the usual 2.7 per cent? At first most of the states had such arrangements, but by 1950 only ten did. This meant that in most states the *average* tax rate for *all* employers was below 2.7 per cent. In 1950 the average contribution rate for all covered employers in all the 51 jurisdictions was 1.5 per cent, and the range among the jurisdictions was from 0.5 per cent for Delaware and Texas to 2.7 per cent for Alaska, New York, Rhode Island, and Washington.

The effect of the rise of experience rating may be seen from the facts that (*i*) whereas in 1941 the average contribution rate of employers in all 51 jurisdictions was 2.6 per cent, in 1950 it was the above-mentioned 1.5 per cent; and (*ii*) whereas in 1941 the total receipts from all the employer contributions in all the jurisdictions were 95 per cent of what they would have been if all the employers had been taxed at the 2.7 per cent standard rate, in 1950 they were only a little more than half of standard-rate revenue.

(4) Reserves. We have already noted that all states must send the funds collected from employer taxes to the federal Unemployment Trust Fund, there to be held for disbursement as benefit payments. There are, then, three things to consider here: (*a*) Are the funds collected by each state and deposited in the federal Unemployment Trust Fund pooled in a general reserve, or are each firm's or industry's contributions segregated in its own special reserve fund and used to pay benefits only to its own workers? (*b*) What does the Treasury do with the unused reserves in the Fund? (*c*) How adequate are the reserves?

(a) Kind of reserve fund. The overwhelming majority of state laws provide for over-all pooling of contributions in a single reserve within the federal Trust Fund. In the early years a small number of states followed Wisconsin in having individual-employer reserve accounts; each firm's contributions were used solely for benefit payments to its own workers. But today no state has this plan in pure form. The few laws originally providing for individual-firm accounts have since been modified to permit a compromise between the individual-firm reserve and the pooled reserve. That is, a portion of each firm's contributions is allotted to a pooled reserve available for benefits to any firm's workers, and the remainder is placed in each firm's separate account, to be used only for its own employees. This change came from a recognition both of the need for applying the broad insurance principle of risk-sharing, and of the fact that an individual-firm-reserve plan is little more than a com-

pulsory savings program for each firm, because it is impossible for any one firm to control all the variables which cause unemployment among its workers.

(b) Investment of reserves. Whatever the type of reserve fund, the taxes or contributions collected from employers under the state laws must, as we have seen, be deposited in the federal Unemployment Trust Fund. The Treasury is required to invest these reserves in federal interest-paying securities, and the accrued interest is credited to each state's account.

By 1944 it was found that the 0.3 per cent federal tax on payrolls was yielding considerably more than was necessary to carry the cost of administering the state acts. In that year, with the end of the war foreseen, it was also (wrongly) anticipated that there would be a high rate of unemployment of considerable duration while firms reconverted to peacetime production. Therefore, the Congress decided to permit states whose reserves might get low to obtain interest-free loans from the surplus in the administration fund. It also authorized additional appropriations if the surplus were used up. Successive re-enactments extended this provision through 1951.

(c) Adequacy of reserves. Thanks to the high employment that has existed during the war and postwar years, the reserves are in general more than adequate. (As a matter of fact, it was this condition, rather than any deep-seated belief in the validity of the experience-rating principle, which led a number of states to adopt experience rating and the reduced contribution rates which it usually involves.) In the thirteen years after 1937 the states' reserves in the Unemployment Trust Fund — deposits plus accrued interest credits minus benefit withdrawals — rose from about $300,000 to about $8,000,000. If no further contributions had been collected after the end of 1950, the total reserves available from the Trust Fund could have financed benefit payments for about six years in the country as a whole, provided that unemployment would be no more severe after 1951 than it was, on the average, from 1946 to 1950. On the other hand, if the country were to be struck with a mass-unemployment depression in which 25 per cent of the covered workers lost their jobs, then the reserves at the end of 1950 would have been large enough to pay standard benefits of maximum duration (as defined in the respective state laws) to the unemployed for less than two years.

But these data for the country as a whole are not very meaningful. The fact is, there is no general reserve fund; that is, each state's reserves are separate, and one state's deposits cannot be used to pay benefits to workers in any other state. Therefore, some states' reserves would be much more quickly exhausted than others'. The reserves of Massachusetts and Rhode Island, for example, would have financed benefit payments for less than a year and four months, if unemployment in those states had averaged the same after 1950 as from 1946 to 1950. At the other extreme, under the same assumptions, Iowa, Colorado, and New Mexico could have paid benefits for more than 20 years. (Thirty-six jurisdictions were above the United States average, 15 below.) By the same token the states whose reserves were relatively low could withstand a severe depression much less well than the high-reserve states.

(5) Benefit provisions. Now let us consider perhaps the most interesting and important set of provisions in the federal-state unemployment compensation system. The main purpose of paying benefits to unemployed workers is to compensate them for the losses suffered, through no fault of their own, from impersonal economic and technological changes. Those who enact and administer the statutes must, therefore, make sure that the workers who claim such benefits have been in the labor force, are able and willing to work, and have not left or lost their jobs through fault of their own.

It is also socially desirable that the unemployed workers take jobs when they become available. Hence the legislators and administrators must not make the benefits too high, in relation to previous wage income, and must limit the periods over which they are receivable. There are thus two main items of concern on benefits: *(a)* Given the fact of working in a covered firm, which employees are eligible and which are ineligible to receive benefits? *(b)* Given coverage and eligibility, what benefits are available and for how long?

On these matters the respective state laws are rather complicated. Furthermore, because the Social Security Act established no minimum standards and because of wide differences in state wealth and attitudes, the acts vary a good deal among themselves. Therefore, only a bare summary is possible below.

(a) Eligibility. Under all the state-territorial acts an unemployed worker's eligibility to receive a benefit payment after he loses his job depends on three things: *(i)* his experience in covered employment during a past period known as the "base period"; *(ii)* certain other qualifying and disqualifying provisions; and *(iii)* a "waiting period," if any.

i. Previous employment and/or earnings. In order to qualify for benefits the worker must either have been employed for some minimum period of time (20 weeks is the most usual) or have earned some minimum amount of money (such as a flat amount of, say, $300, or some multiple of his potential weekly benefit payment) or have fulfilled some combination employment-earnings requirement during the base year. "Base period" or "base year" is defined in most states as a four-quarter span ending about three months before the worker applies for benefits. This requirement means, of course, that unemployment benefits are payable only to established members of the work force. Fly-by-nights and new workers just out of school are excluded.

ii. Other qualifications and disqualifications. In addition to satisfying the standards just mentioned, an unemployed worker claiming benefits under his state law must show the administrative personnel that he is physically and mentally able to work and that he is willing to accept suitable work. "Suitable work" is defined legislatively and administratively as work which is not too far away geographically, or too strange, low-wage, difficult, or unsafe occupationally; nor may the work be immoral. All state laws must of course conform to the standards of governing "suitable work," as set forth in the Federal Unemployment Tax Act (refer to page 656). These provisions aim to keep the states neutral in labor disputes, prevent the undermining of employment standards, and avoid the use of government as an agency for "busting" unions.

A main test of ability and willingness is registration and periodic attendance at the appropriate public employment office. But a number of states insist that the employee be "actively" in search of a new job on his own account.

What if an unemployed unionist refuses to take a job which would involve his disobedience to union rules and standards? Is he refusing suitable work? The federal-state statutes are silent on this specific point, but administrative decisions tend to avoid disqualification for refusal to work under non-union conditions.

Refusal to accept suitable work, then, disqualifies a worker for benefits. So does discharge from his job for "misconduct," voluntary quitting of job without "good cause," and going on strike in a "labor dispute." The quoted words are defined legislatively in fairly specific terms and are applied administratively to particular cases. There is no space here for detailed discussion.

What happens to a worker who is disqualified by the unemployment compensation office? He is penalized in varying degrees of severity. Most states postpone the payment of benefits for a certain number of weeks, such as seven. A growing number, although still a minority, cancel benefits for the duration of the period over which the worker would otherwise be entitled to compensation. Certain states also reduce the amount of benefit when it does become payable. Some students believe that the laws and their administration have become unnecessarily harsh in this respect, partly because of the diminished reserves resulting from application of the experience-rating principle and partly because of overzealous worship of reserves. Other students believe that such provisions are necessary to prevent abuse of the system by would-be malingerers among the unemployed.

iii. Waiting period. Almost all the states decided in the early years to specify periods of two weeks or more (from the dates when unemployment began) during which no jobless worker could be paid benefits. These were called "waiting periods." There were several reasons for the establishment of waiting periods. It was believed that many newly unemployed workers either would soon find other jobs or would have sufficient resources of their own to tide them over short periods of idleness; and the states wished to conserve their funds for the payment of compensation to those unemployed for longer periods. Moreover, having little or no experience with administering unemployment benefit systems, the states wished to give the administrative offices time to process claims. In recent years, however, the claim-processing time has diminished and reserves have increased. Therefore, most states have reduced the length of the waiting period. In 1951 three states (Maryland, Nevada, and North Carolina) had no waiting periods, and in only two (Colorado and Montana) was the period as long as two weeks. The remainder of the state laws specified one week.

(b) Amounts of benefits. How high are the benefits (in absolute amounts and in relation to regular earnings) which the state laws allow eligible covered workers to receive? In answering this question we must distinguish between the totally unemployed and the partially unemployed.

i. Totally unemployed workers. In establishing benefit amounts for total unemployment the states follow a dual principle: *(a)* In general the benefit is related to the level of previous earnings; the higher a worker's weekly earnings were in some recent period of employment, the higher his weekly benefit when unemployed. *(b)* But the states also set forth minimum and maximum amounts of benefits for any unemployed worker. This is a bow in the direction of the flat-rate principle. It would be fair to say, nevertheless, that the proportion-of-earnings principle is the more important.

In respect to benefits related to previous wage income, most of the earlier laws provided that the benefit should be 50 per cent of normal full-time weekly wages; a few specified two-thirds. The objective, of course, was to provide a minimum plane of living but to keep the benefits too low to serve as an acceptable alternative to the earnings of employment, i.e., too low to remove the incentive to find another job. By 1940, however, the states changed their laws so as to achieve this objective indirectly. Instead of specifying the benefit as a percentage of *weekly* earnings, they said it should be a fraction (such as 1/20 or 1/26) of the wage income received during the high-wage *quarter* of a worker's base period. A few states even used a fraction of the previous *annual* earnings.

The reason for this change was to relieve employers of the burden of reporting weekly wage payments. Under the Old Age and Survivors' Insurance program, as we shall see in the next chapter, firms have to make only quarterly payroll reports. The states therefore moved over to paying benefits on the basis of employers' reports on quarterly wages.

It should be noted, however, that this change emphasizes a special factor in the calculation of benefit payments — the possibility that a worker did not work full-time throughout his high quarter. If the benefit is a fraction of a worker's *full-time weekly* earnings, no allowance is made for absenteeism. But if *actual quarterly* earnings are the base, the benefit is reduced to the extent of absenteeism or part-time work on the job during the thirteen weeks.

In respect to the flat-rate principle, the minimum weekly benefits among the states in 1951 ranged from $3 to $15; and the maxima ranged from $20 to $30, the most common being $25.

From 1940 to 1951 the cost of living rose about 72 per cent, and average weekly money earnings about 136 per cent. During this period the states also raised the amounts of their weekly benefit payments, as well as their weekly minimum and maximum benefit amounts. In 1940, unemployment benefits averaged about $10.60 per week, in 1951, about $21.70; this was a rise of 105 per cent. Thus, it appears that the increase in weekly benefits more than kept up with the rise in living costs but lagged behind the increase in money earnings. In other words, benefit payments were a smaller fraction of earnings in covered employments during 1951 than during 1940.

This *relative* decline in benefits took place despite an increasing tendency of states to provide extra benefits for dependents. In 1951 about a dozen jurisdictions permitted small but appreciable amounts of this sort, such as $2.00 per week for each dependent, up to a total of $6.00.

ii. Partially unemployed workers. Under most state laws a worker is defined as partially unemployed if his actual weekly earnings at less than full-time work are lower than the weekly benefit he would receive if he were totally jobless. Such a worker is commonly given a benefit equal to the difference between the actual weekly earnings and the appropriate weekly benefit. The most usual amounts are $3.00 to $5.00.

(c) Duration of benefits. All state laws limit the number of weeks during which an eligible covered unemployed worker may receive benefits during their benefit years. (The "benefit year" of a worker is commonly defined as the 52-week period which begins when he files a valid claim to unemployment compensation.) In the early years the periods were rather restricted; the great majority of states had maximum limits of 16 weeks or less. The reasons for these restrictions were the same as those listed above in respect to long waiting periods. However, since the war the same conditions that led to a reduction in the lengths of waiting periods produced an extension of benefit periods. In 1951, although 22 states still had maximum durations of 20 weeks or less, the most common maximum benefit period was 26 weeks. But this was not so liberal as it sounds, because only about 15 states actually allowed all recipients (no matter what their previous earnings and present benefit amounts) to run to the stated maximum limit. In the other states the workers' *total* benefits were restricted to some fraction (e.g., ¼, ⅓, or ½) of their respective total earnings during the four quarters of their base years. If, for a given worker, this sum divided by the weekly benefit allotted to him were used up in, say, 12 weeks, he would be finished as a benefit-receiver, even if the maximum duration permitted in his state were 26 weeks.

(d) Appeals. Workers who claim benefits under the federal-state system and are dissatisfied with the decisions of their local unemployment com-

pensation offices as to their eligibility for benefits or as to the amounts and durations of benefits allotted to them have the right to appeal from such decisions, as noted above (pages 657–58).

e. Railroad unemployment insurance. Our review of unemployment compensation in the United States would be incomplete without a very brief view of the special system provided by the federal Railroad Unemployment Insurance Act of 1938 for interstate railway workers. Originally these employees were covered by the federal-state program initiated by the Social Security Act of 1935. The railroad Act has been amended several times, the most important amendment occurring in 1947 when the Congress decided to extend the benefits and to treat idleness due to temporary sickness in the same way as unemployment. Our discussion considers the provisions as they stood in 1951.

The cost of the joint unemployment-sickness disability system is financed solely by a 0.5 per cent tax on railroad employers' payrolls. Originally the tax had been 3 per cent, and for some time before 1948 had varied from 3 to 0.5 per cent, depending on the reserves in each railroad's account. Of the total tax collections each year, 90 per cent goes into the Railroad Unemployment Insurance Account, from which the benefits are paid; and the other 10 per cent goes into the Administration Fund (except that any amount above $6 million in the Fund is transferred to the Account). The Fund covers all the costs of administering the benefits system and of operating the offices of the Railroad Employment Service.

To be eligible for benefits, railroad workers (who numbered more than 1.5 million in 1951) must meet the following requirements: (1) earnings of $150 or more in their base years; (2) no disqualifications because they *(a)* left their jobs voluntarily without good cause; *(b)* failed to accept or seek suitable work, as defined below; *(c)* made false benefit claims; *(d)* were directly engaged in a strike which violates the Railway Labor Act; *(e)* earned more than specified amounts in train and engine service during or immediately preceding the period for which benefits are being claimed; or *(f)* are receiving other social insurance compensation under any state or federal law.

The definition of "suitable work" is limited not only by the three items set forth as state law standards by the Social Security Act, but also by certain qualifications peculiar to the Railroad Unemployment Insurance Act. Work is unsuitable here if its acceptance would (1) require a worker to engage in activities in violation of law; (2) require him to do things so contrary to the reasonable provisions of his union's constitution, bylaws, or regulations that he would be subject to expulsion from the union; or (3) cause him substantially to lose his seniority rights under a collective bargaining agreement.

The duration of benefits is up to 130 days. But this number of days actually amounts to 26 weeks because during the benefit period not all the days of the week are compensated. In the first two weeks of unemployment, benefits are paid for all days of unemployment in excess of seven. Thereafter, during each two weeks of total unemployment only 10 of the 14 days are compensated; benefits are "on the five-day week."

The amount of benefit is defined in daily terms and varies in accordance with the amount of wages earned during the base year. The range is from $1.75 per day (for previous annual earnings of $150 to $199.99) to $5.00 per day for annual earnings of $2500 or more.

Administration of the Act rests mainly with the Railroad Retirement Board, which, as will be shown in the next chapter, also administers the Railroad Retirement (i.e., pension) Act. This three-man Board (composed of one labor representative, one employer representative, and one representative of the public) operates through nine regional and about 100 district and branch offices over the country, which handle the claims for benefits and also the employment service.

As in the federal-state system for non-railroad workers, the Treasury collects the payroll taxes, disburses the funds from which benefits are paid, and invests the unused portions of the tax collections in government securities.

f. Appraisal of the American system; current unemployment compensation issues. (1) Constitutionality. Unemployment compensation legislation in the United States has successfully hurdled the constitutional obstacles. The United States Supreme Court, by a 5–to–4 decision in May, 1937, decided that the taxation provisions of the Federal Unemployment Tax Act were constitutional (*Steward Machine Co. v. Davis,* 57 Sup. Ct. 883). It denied the contentions of the Alabama company that the taxes were arbitrary and not uniform; that they coerced the states and invaded states' rights; and that they burdened employment relations in violation of the "due process" clause of the Fifth Amendment. The taxes were for a public purpose and for the public good.

At the same time the Court validated the Alabama state unemployment compensation law. In the cases of *Carmichael v. Southern Coal & Coke Company* and *Carmichael v. Gulf States Paper Corporation* (57 Sup. Ct. 868), the majority held that the Alabama Act did not violate the "due process" and "equal protection" clauses of the Fourteenth Amendment. The reasoning was essentially the same as in the federal case.

(2) Economic-political validity. (a) General considerations. Anyone who tries to appraise the adequacy of a piece of legislation and its administration is bound to do so in the light of what he believes this sort of government action should try to achieve and in the light of what he believes are the best ways to achieve the objectives he considers desirable. In the case of unemployment compensation, he must decide whether the objective should be mainly the prevention of unemployment or mainly relief. If he believes that an unemployment compensation system can contribute in a major way to the prevention of unemployment and if he therefore chooses prevention as the chief objective, he will approve of contributions

or taxes solely on employers' payrolls and he will approve of varying the contribution rates on the basis of employers' success in achieving and maintaining high-level employment. On the other hand, possibly because he believes that individual firms can do very little to prevent unemployment, he may look on unemployment compensation mainly as a way of providing relief to the unemployed with the least damage to their morale and self-esteem. Then, if he favors payroll taxes at all, he will approve of uniform rates on all firms and he will press for such other measures as universal coverage, flat benefit rates, and pooled reserves. He may also favor a plan whereunder government contributes, through progressive income tax rates on a broad base, all or an important fraction of the funds out of which benefits are paid. In short, he conceives of the general objective as the provision of adequate relief benefits at the least social cost.

Given the goal of relief, there is a further decision to be made: Should the objective be to pay benefits indefinitely through periods of possibly prolonged depressional unemployment, or merely to handle the frictional idleness of more prosperous times? He who chooses the former alternative will doubtless favor such measures as high tax rates, modest benefits, substantial waiting periods, benefit periods of long or indefinite duration, and large reserves. He who holds the opposite view will hold to opposite measures and may well believe that government can prevent depressions through deficit spending (recall pages 639–43); or that, if this fails and depressions do occur, government deficits can be used to pay continued unemployment benefits through the compensation system after workers' regular benefit periods under the law have run out.

After fifteen years of unemployment compensation in this country, each of the broad pairs of alternatives mentioned above still provides controversial issues for students of unemployment compensation as well as for pressure groups, like unions and employers' associations, whose members' interests are directly affected. (The authors are inclined toward the second of each pair of alternatives.) There is no fundamental disagreement, however, on another basic matter: The system must not diminish the incentives for workers to work or for firms to produce and expand.

(b) Allocation of resources. Now let us briefly consider some specific economic matters in respect to the existing federal-state system. First, how is the allocation of labor and capital affected? Does the system make for greater or less mobility among covered workers and among the owners of capital? Or is there no appreciable social gain or loss from this standpoint?

In the absence of definitive objective research, one's answers to these questions must be hypothetical and tentative. It is necessary to distinguish between periods of high employment and periods of mass unemployment. During the latter, almost all firms' operations are reduced; they have few if any vacancies. Therefore, the problem of mobility is relatively insignificant at such times. But during years of high employment the existence of unemployment compensation may well to some extent diminish the incentive for unemployed workers to look for other jobs. It would take very strict and careful laws and administration to make workers' mobility as high as it would be in the absence of the laws. (We may assume that the public employment service would operate in the absence of unemployment compensation.) As things now stand, it is doubtful that "suitable work" is defined and administered in such a way as to make for "normal" mobility.

The existence of a federal-state system rather than a wholly federal one also probably tends to lessen labor mobility. This is because, although most states have signed a cooperative agreement to facilitate the payment of benefits to workers who migrate from state to state, some jurisdictions have not subscribed to the arrangement; and even in those that have, workers have experienced long delays in receiving their benefit checks.

We conclude that, from the standpoint of resource allocation, the American unemployment compensation system may well to some extent diminish the total want-satisfaction experienced from economic goods in the country because it may add somewhat to the mis-allocation of resources produced by other conditions. But the extent of the loss from this source is doubtless small and minor.

(c) Distribution of income and economic progress. In terms of the analysis made in Chapter 3 (pages 37–41), unemployment compensation *can* be a measure for effecting a redistribution of income in favor of the lower-income households. And thereby it can increase the total want-satisfaction of the society unless it so diminishes the incentives to produce and expand that total output is smaller than it otherwise would be.

The kind of system under which a significant income redistribution and gain in want-satisfaction could be made would be one providing for benefit payments out of funds accumulated by progressive income taxes. And this kind of system is also the one which might impede economic progress and produce a net loss in total satisfaction if the tax rates were too steeply progressive.

But this kind of system does not exist in the United States. The taxes are on covered firms' payrolls. This means that the covered firms experience an increase in labor costs (including the clerical costs of filling in forms and making reports). Unless this increase is counteracted by improved management or machines, it will tend to result in higher product prices. Then the households as consumers must pay more. Thus, non-covered workers and non-workers, as well as more covered workers, must pay for the unemployed workers' benefits. It would appear, then, there is very little if any progressiveness under such a tax system.

However, although the non-worker households and the households of non-covered workers help to pay for the unemployed covered workers' benefits, while receiving no direct return themselves, they do not pay much. The tax rates on payrolls are very low and the increase in product prices from this source are slight. There is thus no significant redistribution of income in favor of covered workers or against any other group. And by the same token there is no significant deterrent to normal economic progress. The American system seems mainly to provide a method for compulsory savings by the workers themselves against the risk of unemployment.

Although the system occasions no significant rise in total want-satisfaction from the redistribution of income and no significant decrease in satisfaction from impediments to economic progress, it undoubtedly does make for a net increase in welfare or satisfaction. This comes from the fact that the savings are available for relieving unemployment in·a dignified, self-respecting manner.

(d) Extent of resource utilization. We must next ask whether the unemployment compensation system affects total spending in the economy as a whole and thereby does what no single firm can do — change the level of total output and employment. Does the system make the price and profit expectations and the confidence of households and firms different from what they otherwise would be, thus changing total consumption and investment spending? Does the system affect government spending on goods and services?

Compared to other conditions influencing expectations and certainty, the taxation of payrolls, the amassing of reserves, and the payment of benefits would appear to have little effect. The introduction of the system may have had some initial dampening influence on business confidence, expectations, and investment spending. Not so now. It is an accepted part of our social organization. Even a rise in tax rates would probably be taken in stride by most firms. In respect to consumption spending, the enhanced feeling of security may well have led to a modest rise in the propensity of covered households to consume during high-employment years. During depression years both the level of disposable income and the propensity to consume are likely to be higher than in the absence of unemployment compensation. This is the "floor" under total spending produced by the system (provided, of course, that benefits are steadily paid).

But what about the large unused reserves accumulated during prosperous years? Doesn't this amount to government-induced and government-maintained hoarding? Doesn't this compulsory saving mean a decrease in total spending which reinforces any existing tendencies toward a business downswing? No. Consider what happens to the contributions collected by the states from the covered firms. Under the law they are invested in government bonds. That is, the Treasury in behalf of the federal Unemployment Trust Fund buys these securities. So now the Fund has the engraved pieces of paper and the general fund of the government has the money. But the money does not lie idle or hoarded. It is used in part to pay the salary of government employees, in part for snorkel submarines, in part for new roads in various states, and so on. But how do the states get funds for benefit payments if the money is spent like this by the federal government? The Trust Fund sells some of its bonds to the Treasury, which gets the money from the general fund, whose resources are built up from many sources as approved by the Congress. Thus, the funds that circulate into and out of the system are used, not hoarded. Total spending does not fall (or rise) because of the reserves.

The same holds true for the 0.3 per cent tax collected directly by the federal government. Part is sent at once to the states, which spend it for salaries and other items of administration. The remainder is held in Washington and invested and used as described above.

(e) Freedom versus security. Under the unemployment compensation system there is a gain in security for the covered workers and for society. The opportunity or real cost of the increase in security is of course some loss in individual liberty. Employers must pay taxes, fill out forms, and make reports; workers must report to employment offices; and so on. But the gain in security would appear significantly to exceed the loss in freedom. Society experiences a net gain in total welfare. This is especially true because during depressions the freedom of unemployed workers to take or leave a job means little to them, in any case.

From this over-all appraisal we are compelled to conclude that American society, through government, has induced a considerable gain in total want-satisfaction through the operation of its unemployment compensation system.

(3) The laws and their administration. One question remains: Is the net gain as large as it might be? Could the gross gain be enlarged, or could the social cost be lessened? Here we have to appraise the main features of the laws and their administation. There are five main issues.

First, is a federal-state system better than a wholly federal one? Each kind has its utilities and its costs, as previously outlined. The states think the existing system provides the largest net utility; the federal authorities believe the opposite. So do the authors. But each student and each voter will have to decide for himself.

Second, should coverage be extended to the workers of small-size firms and to such uncovered industries as agriculture, domestic service, and government? The social gains to be experienced from universal or near-universal coverage would seem to outweigh by a considerable margin the additional costs of covering the now-excluded workers. When unemployed, these workers need compensation just as much as, if not more than, the employees now covered.

Third, should the present specific tax on employers' payrolls be dropped in favor of a general progressive income tax, broad enough in its base to provide sufficient funds for unemployment compensation? On this question we express no opinion except to repeat that unemployment is a social cost arising out of an economic-political system that confers many benefits; its relief should be treated as a social problem; all persons and groups may therefore be asked to help solve the problem; those most able (the higher-income classes) may well be asked to help more than the less able; but a progressive tax system must not be such as to diminish the incentives to produce and expand.

Fourth, if the payroll tax is selected, should experience-rating tax differentials and individual-employer reserves be discontinued in favor of wholly pooled reserves, especially under an all-federal plan? Those (including the authors) who stress relief rather than prevention as the main objective of an unemployment compensation system, and who dispute the ability of firms individually to achieve general employment regularization, believe that a net social gain would follow an affirmative answer to the above question. A uniform tax need not be high. In fact, the more general the pool, the lower the tax or premium need be. Under a broad federal pooled fund the workers in distressed areas and industries could be paid given benefits of a given duration at considerably lower cost than under segregated state and industry reserves. Or to say the same thing differently, with a given cost higher benefits could be paid for more weeks to such workers. All this is simply an expression of good insurance principles.

Fifth, should simpler methods than those now in use be employed to determine eligibility for a benefit and to calculate the amount? In terms of social equity, there may well be good cause for relating amount of benefit to amount of previous earnings. But the system used for railroad employees seems simpler than those found under the state laws. And if need and relief are the main considerations in paying benefits, the wage qualifications for benefits might well be simplified or dropped.

5. Anti-discrimination laws: F.E.P.C. legislation. In previous chapters we saw that during past decades many individual workers have suffered loss of jobs, lack of promotion to better jobs, failure to obtain new jobs, and general repression of freedom to join or stay out of labor organizations or do other things, because of the discriminatory and autocratic policies of certain employers and unions. Has government tried to do anything about these problems?

There have been two main kinds of efforts. First, the federal government and certain state governments have enacted or tried to enact legislation forbidding discrimination against workers by employers, unions, and employment agencies in respect to job tenure on the basis of race, religion, national origin, or ancestry. Second, the federal government and certain state governments have passed laws forbidding employers and unions to discriminate against workers on the basis of membership or non-membership in labor organizations. We shall deal very briefly here with only the first kind of legislation. The second kind will be considered in Chapters 24 and 25.

From 1945 through 1949, eight states (New York, New Jersey, Massachusetts, Connecticut, New Mexico, Oregon, Rhode Island, and Washington) passed compulsory Fair Employment Practice acts, commonly known as "F.E.P.C." laws because of the impetus given to such legislation during the war by President Roosevelt's Fair Employment Practices Committee. In addition, two states (Indiana and Wisconsin) have statutes providing for voluntary compliance with F.E.P.C. principles. Under the latter laws the state labor commission or commissioner may investigate discriminatory hiring and other job practices, publicize the results, and make recommendations to the legislatures.

Each of the compulsory laws prohibits firms, employment agencies, and unions from discriminating against Negroes and other racial groups. The board or commission administering the law holds hearings, on its own motion or upon complaint of affected persons or groups, to investigate allegations of such discrimination. If it then decides that discrimination has been practiced, the board orders the guilty party or parties to "cease and desist" from such actions. If the party fails to comply with the order, the board is authorized to ask an appropriate court for a command for compliance. Then, if the court issues a compliance order, refusal to accept the order is contempt of court and punishable by fine or imprisonment or both.

Every year from 1946 to 1952 President Truman asked the Congress for an F.E.P.C. law. By the spring of 1952 his request had not been granted.

CHAPTER 23

Government and the Problems of Individual Workers (concluded)

B. OLD-AGE DEPENDENCY: PENSIONS

1. Development of approach. *a. In Europe.* We have already noted how the process of industrialization and urbanization created new problems of old-age dependency. It was logical, therefore, that the older industrial countries of Europe should be the first to interest themselves in methods of alleviating the distress of dependent older workers. Earliest efforts began around 1850; and by 1935, European governments had tried out a variety of alternative approaches. The first legislative efforts (in Belgium, France, and Italy) provided for *voluntary pensions.* Government was merely the bookkeeper. Workers were given the opportunity to purchase small annuities through regular voluntary contributions. This approach contributed little to a solution of the problem. Too few workers could take advantage of the plan. A second approach was made when a few governments provided *subsidized voluntary pension plans.* But again, experience showed, too few workers could make regular contributions; and even if they could, the benefits were still inadequate. A third development came in 1891, when Denmark led the way in providing *non-contributory old-age assistance grants.* The grants were not earned but were an outright gift to the superannuated needy. Fourth came a move for the establishment of *compulsory contributory old-age insurance,* led by Germany in 1889. Workers as well as employers were compelled to contribute to a system which in turn provided earned retirement benefits as a right rather than as charity.

Between 1880 and 1935 some 20 European countries had tried out at least one of these four approaches. The trend over the period was unmistakably toward earned pensions and away from gratuitous grants, for two major reasons. For one thing, there was widespread resistance among workers to a "means" or "need" test, which was required when government simply gave charity payments. At the same time, there was increasing resistance among taxpayers to the financial strain resulting from the rising percentage of the older population qualifying as needy and therefore entitled to benefits. European experience over three-quarters of a century, especially that of Great Britain, where the principle of contributory insurance was adopted in 1925, contributed much to our thinking in the United States when we attacked the old-age dependency problem in 1935.

b. In the United States. (1) Old-age assistance. Prior to 1935 there was no federal legislation in this country providing for dependent older workers. Responsibility for this group rested with the states. Until after 1900 the states themselves gave little attention to the problem; this was in keeping with a long-standing tradition that aid to the destitute aged was a private and not a public responsibility. The needy aged without friends or relatives, who had to turn to the community for help, were taken care of through state or county "almshouses" or "poorhouses," whose low standards of care stigmatized a nation proud of its high living standards. After 1900 the states, beginning with Massachusetts in 1903, began to study alternatives to the degrading "poorfarms." However, by 1929 only ten states had laws providing regular money grants, i.e., "outdoor relief," to aged indigents. Even in these states the benefits were pitifully meager, and the eligibility requirements were so severe that only a few could qualify.

The depression beginning in 1929, however, brought about a major change in public attitude and hence in state-government policy. By 1935, when the federal Social Security Act was passed, 28 states had legislation providing some form of monetary benefits to the needy aged.

(2) Old-age and survivors' insurance. The term *insurance* is generally used to denote a system of benefits to which the worker is entitled as a right because of his own contributions. This is in contrast to *assistance,* which generally refers to outright gifts or charity grants based on need. Prior to the 1930's there was no voluntary or compulsory federal or state *insurance* plan in operation in this country for non-government employees. Paradoxically, the federal government and many state and local units did have insurance plans in operation for public employees.

(3) Early issues, pro and con. (a) The approach before 1930. In contrast to European experience, this country was slow to adopt the policy of public responsibility for the dependent older worker. This was not due to mere indifference. It was due to a long-standing tradition that extensive government aid to the superannuated was both unnecessary and unwise. It was deemed unnecessary because it was believed that, in an expansive economy such as ours had been, the hard-working citizen could and would provide for his own old age; to reward the lazy and improvident would be to help those who contributed least to the community. It was considered unwise because the institution of the family would normally assume responsibility for those few of its members who, though hard-working, might through fortuitous circumstances end up penniless in their advanced years.

However, many students of the problem opposed the traditional view with increasing vigor after 1900. They cited strong counter-arguments based on long-run changes in our society, including the declining ability of the individual to adjust to the constant changes in a complex money economy; the greater element of dependency inherent in an urban society; and the shrinking role of the family as a security factor in view of declining average family size. There is evidence that these latter arguments, which favored greater public responsibility for the needy aged, were in the ascendancy even before the economic crisis which followed 1929.

(b) The impact of depression on public policy. The traditional American attitude toward old-age dependency was drastically altered in the 1930's. For one thing, the long-run forces noted above were having a cumulative effect. For another, the depression brought a number of overwhelming events in its train. Those who had been diligent and thrifty saw their lifetime savings swept away. The average worker became patently less and less able to provide a living for his immediate family, let alone for superannuated members. Private philanthropy proved hopelessly inadequate in the face of the widespread distress; and the financial straits of many local and state governments prevented adequate public assistance from this source to needy workers of all ages. By 1934, opposition to government's (especially federal government's) assumption of responsibility for the dependent aged needy had all but disappeared. Instead it was desperately sought. The principal question was the type of policy to be adopted.

(c) What form of government intervention? To help resolve the question of what form of old-age-benefits program should be developed, the President in June, 1934, referred the matter to his Committee on Economic Security. Its report was transmitted by the President to the Congress in January, 1935, and served as the basis for subsequent legislation. The first question faced by the Committee was whether the existing program of state-local institutional care, i.e., the "indoor" or "poorfarm" approach, should be expanded, or whether a non-institutional program, i.e., based on regular "outdoor" money payments to the dependent aged, should be developed. The latter would obviously tend to preserve normal home life. There was little argument on this question. The institutional approach was rejected as wasteful and inhumane. A second major question was whether the new program should be an insurance program based on contributions and paying earned benefits as a right, or whether it should be an assistance program based solely on need, with benefits constituting charity grants. An insurance program had much in its favor. It would be in keeping with the traditional view that every worker should contribute to his own retirement. Since benefits would be based on earnings, retirement income would tend to reflect the worker's earning power and customary standard of living. It would make possible

higher benefit payments. It would avoid the much disliked "means test." It would check the increasingly heavy drain of current "relief" expenditures on general tax funds. Adequate benefits would encourage superannuated workers to leave the labor market, which was already glutted, whereas low-level charity grants might simply subsidize older workers in the market. The regularity and certainty of insurance payments would help stabilize consumer expenditures.

The arguments in favor of an assistance program based on need were equally impressive. An assistance program could be put into operation quickly, whereas it would take years to set up an insurance program and get it into operation. The current plight of thousands of older workers was desperate. It would be administratively easy to reach all the superannuated, since eligibility would be based on need, whereas it would be administratively difficult to extend the insurance program based on payroll deductions to many groups of workers such as domestic servants and farm workers. In the future many workers would move from covered to uncovered occupations under the insurance program and fail to qualify for insurance benefits. Further, many persons whose incomes were derived from sources other than wages would end up dependent and in all equity should be provided for.

It soon became clear that both types of programs were needed; and both were included in the Social Security Act passed by Congress in 1935 — the Old-Age and Survivors Insurance (O.A.S.I.) program as the basic long-run program, and the Old-Age Assistance (O.A.A.) plan to meet current needs and to fill in where O.A.S.I. was lacking.

(d) Some issues in an insurance program. Once the decision had been made to develop an insurance program, numerous additional issues had to be settled. First, should the program be contributory or non-contributory? The decision was made in favor of a contributory program, in view of European experience and the traditional American approach. Second, should there be a single federal system or separate state systems encouraged by federal grants (as in unemployment compensation)? Those who supported separate state systems cited the advantage of experimentation and flexibility. But very strong arguments were advanced against the state program. The relatively high mobility of a large segment of the American labor force would pose some very difficult administrative problems, would make sound actuarial calculations almost impossible, and would give rise to excessive costs. Such a program would make for a variety of benefit standards, creating inequities between workers in the same interstate industry, and would make for varying competitive business costs between states. The accumulation of separate state reserve funds would create investment problems of serious proportion. Experimentation, while possibly desirable in the case of compensation for sickness or unemployment, would not apply to insurance benefits since 50 to 75 years would be required to test the program. The arguments against separate

state insurance programs proved overwhelming. The Congress therefore adopted the single, all-federal plan.

A third problem covered the relation of benefits to contributions. Should the program be modeled along the lines of private insurance, which would limit benefits to the insured worker and base benefits solely on contributions; or should the program be "social" insurance, which would somewhat favor the lower paid workers, as well as provide for dependents and survivors? The original program in the Act of 1935 was based chiefly on the "private" insurance principle. A shift to the "social" insurance approach was made in the amendments of 1939, as we shall note later.

(e) Some issues in the assistance program. What kind of assistance program would best serve the needs of those aged workers who were already 65 years old and dependent, or who, though under 65, would not qualify under the proposed insurance program in the future? One proposal called for annual federal "relief" grants to the states, with no state contributions. This approach was discarded on the grounds that it would completely destroy local responsibility; might lead to political abuses; would probably result in lax administration; and would prove a hardship for the high-income states because they would contribute to general tax funds out of proportion to benefits received. An alternative was an all-federal program of direct payments to the needy aged. But this plan, too, was discarded because of state opposition and because the task of administering such a plan without local participation would be formidable. Another alternative was for federal grants to the states on a matching basis. This would provide a sound financial underpinning, since the federal grants would be based on a nation-wide tax basis, but would still allow the states to vary benefits according to their own needs and resources. This alternative was adopted. The two programs, insurance and assistance, will be discussed in some detail below.

2. Old-age and survivors' insurance. The following discussion is concerned with the O.A.S.I. program, as amended in 1950. The 1950 amendments represent the second major change in the program since the original Act of 1935. The student may trace in Table 41 the evolution of selected aspects of the program to date.

a. Administration. (1) Agencies. The old-age insurance program is administered by the Bureau of Old-Age and Survivors Insurance. This Bureau is a major unit of the Social Security Administration, which is a part of the Federal Security Agency. The B.O.A.S.I. handles the tremendous bookkeeping task of recording all wage credits in separate accounts for each individual worker. It passes on all claims for benefits, calculates the amounts due, and checks on violations of the Act. The actual collection of tax contributions from employer and worker is performed by the U.S. Treasury's Internal Revenue Bureau, and the Treasury Department issues checks to beneficiaries in accordance with certification from the

TABLE 41 — *Selected Provisions of the O.A.S.I. Program, 1935, 1939, 1950*

SUBJECT	ORIGINAL ACT OF 1935	1939 AMENDMENTS	1950 AMENDMENTS
I. *COVERAGE* A. Industrial classification	Major exclusions include: self-employed (rural and urban); agricultural hired labor; domestic servants; casual workers; government workers; employees of non-profit (religious, charitable, educational) institutions; and certain maritime workers[1]	Major exclusions include: self-employed (rural and urban); agricultural hired labor[2]; domestic servants; casual, government, and nonprofit workers[3]	Major exclusions include: self-employed (rural only); professionals; and irregularly hired agricultural, domestic, and urban workers
B. Per cent of employed civilian labor force	49 per cent	51 per cent	74 per cent
C. Millions of workers		24,100,000 (1940)[4]	45,600,000 (June, 1951)
II. *BENEFITS* (monthly) A. Types of monthly benefits	*Primary* to insured worker	*Primary* to insured worker *Secondary* to: 1. Dependent wife 2. Dependent children 3. Dependent widow 4. Widow with dependent children 5. Dependent parents	*Primary* to insured worker *Secondary* to: 1. Dependent wife 2. Dependent children 3. Dependent widow 4. Widow or divorced wife with dependent children 5. Dependent parents 6. Dependent widower 7. Dependent husband
B. Amount of benefits	Minimum $10; maximum $85	*Single person:* Minimum $10; no maximum[5] *Couple:* Minimum $15; maximum $85 "*Family*": Mimimum $20; maximum $85 *Average:* About $26 as of August, 1950	*Single person:* Minimum $20; maximum $80[6] *Couple:* Minimum $30; maximum $120 "*Family*": Minimum $40; maximum $150 *Average:* About $45 in 1951; after 1960 about $50
C. Basis for computing benefits	1½ per cent of first $3000 taxable wages; one-twelfth of 1 per cent on next $3000–$45,000; one twenty-fourth on all above $45,000 (in any one year only first $3000 counted)	40 per cent of first $50 monthly earnings in covered employment; 10 per cent on next $200; plus 1 per cent increment for each year in which worker received $200 or more	50 per cent of first $100 of "average monthly earnings"; 15 per cent of all over $100 up to $300. (No increment for years in covered employment as before.)
D Outside earnings permitted while receiving benefit after 65	None permitted in covered employment	Up to $15 per month in covered employment. No restriction on non-covered employment.	Up to $50 monthly in covered employment, to age 75, after which no limit. No restriction on non-covered employment.

III. *ELIGIBILITY REQUIREMENTS*			
A. Types of insured status	"Fully" insured	"Fully" insured "Currently" insured	"Fully" insured "Currently" insured
B. Eligibility rules			
1. "Fully" insured	At least one day in covered employment in each of five different years after 1936	At least one quarter of coverage for each 2 calendar quarters elapsing after 1936 (or after age of 21, if later) and up to age 65 (or died), or 40 quarters since 1936. Minimum of 6 quarters required.[7]	At least one quarter of coverage for each 2 calendar quarters elapsing after 1950 (or after age of 21, if later) and up to age 65 (or died), or 40 quarters since 1936. (Minimum of 6 quarters required.) Any quarter earned since 1936 may be counted.
2. "Currently" insured	No "currently" insured status in original Act.	At least 6 quarters of coverage out of last 12 quarters immediately preceding age of 65 (or died)	At least 6 quarters of coverage out of last 13 quarters ending with quarter in which 65 (or died)
IV. *FINANCING*			
A. Tax rate	1 per cent on both employer and employee (originally scheduled to rise to 3 per cent each by 1949 but "frozen" by Congress at 1 per cent through 1949)	1 per cent on both employer and employee, 1939–49; raised to 1½ in 1950	1½ per cent on both employer and employee; scheduled to rise, beginning in 1954, to 3¼ per cent on each by 1970
B. Tax base	Tax rate applied to first $3000 in any one year	Tax rate applied to first $3000 in any one year	Tax rate applied to first $3600 in any one year

[1] Railroad employees not specifically excluded in the Social Security Act, but were specifically excluded by the Railroad Retirement Act of 1935 providing for a separate retirement system.

[2] Definition of agricultural labor more restrictive so as to exclude certain borderline activities formerly considered as covered. Also specifically excluded for first time were student nurses, interns, newsboys under 18, employees of foreign governments, domestic servants in fraternities and sororities.

[3] Maritime employment on foreign vessels and certain fishermen still excluded.

[4] Mainly as a result of growth in covered employments in the 1940's the percentage of the employed civilian labor force covered just prior to the 1950 amendments had risen to 59 percent, the number to 35 millions. Of the 35 million workers on jobs covered by O.A.S.I. on September 1, 1950, approximately 90 per cent were fully insured, and about 10 per cent "currently" insured. An additional 25 to 30 million were insured but not currently in jobs covered by the O.A.S.I. program; e.g., armed forces, unemployed in the home, in non-covered employment, etc. (Source: Wilbur J. Cohen, Technical Adviser to the Commissioner for Social Security, Washington, D. C.; and I. S. Falk, director of Division of Research and Statistics, Social Security Administration.)

[5] No statutory maximum. On assumption of 45 years of covered employment at $250 average monthly wage, single person could receive pension of $58 per month.

[6] For all persons receiving benefits prior to January 1, 1951, and for all new primary beneficiaries who acquire less than 6 quarters of coverage after December 31, 1950, the maximum primary benefit possible is $68.50. For all those who qualify for benefits after January 1, 1951, the maximum primary insurance is $80.

[7] In Act of 1935 first benefits scheduled for January 1, 1942. The 1939 amendments advanced this date to January 1, 1940.

B.O.A.S.I. The B.O.A.S.I. has steadily decentralized its operations. Today it has nearly 500 permanent field offices and over 1500 itinerant offices. An appeals procedure has been established with 12 regional hearing referees from whose decisions appeals may be taken to an Appeals Council of three members in Washington, D. C. The Council is independent of the Bureau and reports directly to the Commissioner of the Social Security Administration.

b. Coverage. The coverage of the present O.A.S.I. program in terms of industrial classifications is very broad, especially as a result of the 1950 amendments which added an additional 10 million workers to the system for a total of about 46 million workers in 1951 and raised the per cent of the nation's labor force covered from approximately 50 per cent to nearly 75 per cent. Since the exclusions today are a minority, they may be noted here. The program excludes about 8 million self-employed farm-owners and *irregularly* employed farm laborers; 2.5–3 million urban self-employed, e.g., professional persons; and about 1 million *irregularly* employed domestic service workers and unpaid family workers. Between 5 and 6 million government workers (federal, state, local) and railroad workers are excluded but have their own public retirement systems. It should be noted that the 1950 amendments extended *compulsory* coverage to 7.8 million additional workers including 4.7 million urban self-employed (non-professionals); 850,000 *regularly* employed farm workers; and 1 million *regularly* employed domestic workers. *Voluntary* coverage was also granted to about 2 million additional workers, principally employees of non-profit organizations and state and local governments not previously included in public retirement programs. All employers in covered employments are included regardless of size. The extended coverage in 1950 met the criticism that small urban business proprietors were being forced to provide for their few employees but could not provide for themselves. Although the number of occupations now excluded may be expected to decrease somewhat in the future, it may be noted that current exclusions are largely due to administrative barriers, the assumption that certain groups can provide for their own retirement, or the objections of the groups themselves to inclusion (e.g., professionals).

c. Contributions or taxes. Employer and employee must each currently pay 1½ per cent on taxable wages. This rate will continue through 1953, after which the rate will rise at five-year intervals until it reaches 3¼ per cent for each in 1970. The rate of tax is applied to the first $3600 of wages paid to each worker in each calendar year. Tax collections are quarterly. The total tax collection amounted to about $2.5 billion in 1950 and is expected to rise to somewhat over $6.0 billion by 1970.

The 1950 amendments extended coverage to some groups which presented special difficulties in tax collection. Three of these groups may be noted. The *self-employed workers* now covered must pay their own tax once a year as a part of their regular income tax. The rate of tax, effective 1951–53, is 2½ per cent and will rise after that by five-year intervals to 4⅜ per cent in 1970. The tax base for the self-employed is the same as for employees; namely, the first $3600 of net income. The tax on *regularly employed domestic workers* will be paid by the householder. For purposes of determining liability for tax payments, the householder must have paid a domestic $50 in cash during the calendar quarter and employed the domestic at least 24 days during that quarter or during the preceding quarter. In such case the householder must set aside 1½ per cent of wages paid the domestic, plus 1½ per cent withheld from wages on each pay day, and send the total amount at the end of each calendar quarter to the local Collector of Internal Revenue. Thus some domestics may be covered one quarter and not the next. The definition of *domestic* is broad and includes such categories as cooks, maids, cleaning women, butlers, companions, governesses, laundresses, gardners, chauffeurs, etc. The tax rate and tax base for *regularly employed agricultural workers* is the same as for workers generally. The significant determination of these workers is whether they come within the category of "regularly employed." Coverage begins after an employee has worked for the same employer continuously for one calendar quarter. Such a worker is covered from the beginning of the next quarter if he works at least 60 days in the second quarter and earns $50 or more of wages in that quarter. Coverage continues for every succeeding quarter in which he meets these qualifications. Coverage ends in the quarter when the worker fails to work 60 days or more or earns less than $50 in wages.

d. Reserves. (1) How handled. The contributions of employers and workers are placed in an O.A.S.I. Trust Fund. (Technically the Internal Revenue Bureau turns collections over to the Treasury's general revenue fund and the Congress appropriates an equivalent amount for the Trust Fund including penalties and interest on invested funds.) The Trust Fund is managed by a Board of Trustees consisting of the Commissioner of the Social Security Administration, the Secretary of Labor, and the Secretary of the Treasury. The Fund is invested in U.S. Government securities and the interest credited to the Fund. When O.A.S.I. was first established, the government assumed no obligation to make up any deficits which might occur. In 1943 this obligation was assumed, although up to the present this protection has not been needed.

(2) Recent volume. Since 1936, annual collections have exceeded benefit payments and expenses. In the fiscal year 1950–51 income totaled $3.4 billion and outgo totaled $1.6 billion. The accumulation in the reserve fund at the end of 1951 amounted to nearly $15 billion. It should be noted, however, that despite the rising tax rate over the next 20 years, the recent liberalization of benefits, together with the increasing numbers who will qualify for benefits and the increasing proportion of the labor force in the older age groups, will serve to check rising annual surpluses.

(3) Some questions of reserve policy. (a) The level of tax payments.

The income of the Trust Fund, 1936–49, was based on the low tax rate of 1 per cent which was not raised to 1½ per cent until 1950. This low rate was criticized in some quarters because it did not constitute the "true" long-run costs of the system, inasmuch as future outgo will rise as the system "matures." The rapid growth in the Trust Fund under the low rate was thus somewhat misleading. In actual practice the low rate of 1936–49 simply meant that the tax rate would have to be raised more steeply in later years, which is exactly what the Congress provided in the 1950 amendments.

(b) Use of current O.A.S.I. income for current government expenses. Some critics have objected to the present method of handling O.A.S.I. tax revenues. They point out that annual surpluses are invested in government securities. The Treasury uses the income derived from the sale of these securities for general government expenses. By providing the Treasury with an easy source of funds, this process encourages extravagance and deficit spending and permits the government to by-pass the unpleasant task of seeking new revenue sources. Further it is said to involve a form of "double taxation." Since current O.A.S.I. tax funds are used to defray current expenses, future O.A.S.I. obligations will require additional taxes.

In actual practice no fiscal legerdemain is involved. The sale of securities to the O.A.S.I. Trust Fund merely *replaces* the current need for additional taxation or borrowing; no double taxation is involved. If the Treasury borrowed from private sources, it would have to pay out interest. By selling securities to the O.A.S.I. Trust Fund the Treasury pays the interest to the Fund, thus actually lowering the cost of the retirement program.

e. Benefit payments. (1) Eligibility requirements under the 1950 amendments. Eligibility of a covered superannuated worker to receive benefits under the amended O.A.S.I. program depends on the number of quarter-years within a specified past period during which the worker has earned the specified amount of wage income. On this basis, workers may acquire two types of insured status: "fully" insured, and "currently" insured. The "fully" insured status may be of two categories: "fully" but not "permanently" insured, and "fully and permanently" insured. A fully but not permanently insured worker must have had at least one quarter of coverage for each two calendar quarters elapsing after January 1, 1951 (or after age 21, if later), and up to age 65 (or death). A minimum of six quarters and a maximum of 40 quarters are required. Any quarter earned since January 1, 1937, may be counted. A fully and permanently insured worker must have had any 40 quarters of covered employment since January 1, 1937, before age 65 (or death). Once 40 quarters have been earned, no additional quarters are required to receive benefits. A currently insured worker is one who has had at least six quarters of covered employment during the thirteen-quarter period ending with the quarter in which he reaches 65 (or dies).

The details of the eligibility requirements are rather complicated. It will be sufficient for us to note, in addition to the above, that the effect of the 1950 amendments was significantly to liberalize the standards. Many persons already retired and ineligible under the old law may now draw benefits. Many of those near retirement who would not have had enough quarters under the previous Act will now be eligible when they reach retirement age. And those covered for the first time under the 1950 amendments will be able to qualify much more quickly.

(2) Types of benefits. Two types of monthly benefits are paid, *primary* and *secondary.* Monthly primary benefits are paid to insured workers aged 65 and over, and are based on previous earnings in covered employment. Secondary benefits are paid to dependents of living insured workers and to surviving dependents of deceased insured workers. These benefits are paid every month and range from 50 to 75 per cent of the worker's primary benefit. In addition, a third type of payment, one *lump-sum benefit* equal to three times the deceased's monthly primary benefit, may be paid to a survivor of a deceased insured worker. This is in addition to any monthly benefit to which the survivor may be entitled.

(3) Amount of benefits. (a) The "social" nature of benefit determination. Primary and secondary benefits are determined by a conversion schedule which translates accredited, previously received average monthly wages into allowable insurance benefits. The schedule provides for a descending percentage allowance for average monthly wages as one moves up the income scale. For example, a worker who is credited with $100 of average monthly wages for purposes of computing benefits, may receive a benefit of $50, or 50 per cent of average earnings. But an individual credited with $200 of monthly earnings may receive only $65 a month in benefits or 33 per cent, and an individual who has earned the maximum amount allowable toward benefits, namely $300, will receive a benefit of $80, which is only 27 per cent of earnings. This is one of the "social" aspects of the benefit program, in that it favors the lower-income workers over the higher-paid.

(b) Basis for determining wages for benefit purposes. For the purpose of computing benefits, a worker is credited with 50 per cent of his first $100 of "average monthly wages" and with 15 per cent of all over $100 up to $300. "Average wages" are determined by dividing the total wages received in covered employment after the base year of 1937 or 1950 (whichever yields the higher benefit) by the number of calendar months which have elapsed in the interim. Since all months will be counted in the interim period, including those in which the worker may not have been in covered employment, the "average wages" for social security purposes may be considerably below the actual wages received over the period. The 1950 amendments raised potential benefits by permitting use of either 1937 or

1950 as the base year. For most workers, the 1950 base will prove more favorable, since it eliminates the years 1936–40 when wages were relatively low and unemployment widespread.

(c) Minimum and maximum benefits. The minimum primary benefit is $20 a month; the maximum is $80 (there is no specific statutory maximum but under the computation formula the primary maximum comes to this figure). The average primary benefit will average around $45 a month in the early years after 1950, and after 1960 will average around $50. The minimum "family" benefit, which may include both primary and secondary benefits, is $40 a month; and the maximum is $150.

(d) Contrast in 1950 amended rules and previous benefit provisions. Under the rules prior to the 1950 amendments, the amount of benefit was based on earnings *and* the number of months in employment. Under the new provisions the amount of benefit is based entirely on earnings. The old formula will be used for some time in certain cases but will nevertheless be raised to a higher level in accordance with a conversion table published in the 1950 amendments. The new formula will be effective after June, 1952, inasmuch as the new rules provide that a worker must have at least six quarters of coverage *after* 1950.

(4) Outside earnings permitted. Any eligible person, 65 and over, may earn up to $50 a month in covered employment while receiving benefits. Persons 75 and over may earn *any* amount in covered employment and still receive benefits.

(5) Workers entitled to simultaneous benefits. In some instances an individual may qualify for a benefit in his own right for work in covered employment and also for a derivative benefit as a dependent of an insured person. If the earned benefit is the larger, he may receive this but will lose the derivative benefit. If his own benefit is the smaller, he may take this plus the difference between the amount of his own benefit and the larger derivative benefit.

f. Appraisal. (1) Constitutionality. The constitutionality of the old-age insurance provisions of the Social Security Act of 1935 were attacked almost immediately on the grounds that in taxing for purposes of social welfare the federal government was infringing upon power reserved to the states. The issue was carried from lower courts to the U.S. Supreme Court. In its significant 1937 decision (*Helvering v. Davis,* 301 U.S. 619) the court held that the Tenth (taxation) Amendment was not violated; it was proper for the Congress to raise and spend money "in aid of the general welfare." Speaking for the Court's majority, Justice Cardozo said that the problem of social security was a national one. It was appropriate that the Congress should interest itself in providing greater security for all citizens.

(2) Economic-political considerations. Having considered union, employer, and union-employer private pension plans in preceding chapters, it is now necessary for us to make an appraisal of the country's retirement-

compensation set-up in terms of over-all economic-political welfare. Our analytical framework for this purpose was given in Chapters 2 and 3.

We may note that the pension movement represents a reaction to the insecurities bred by the technological resolution. It is a partial swing of the pendulum back to the attitudes and strivings toward security that characterized the medieval centuries, and away from the individual, private enterprise type of economic-political adventuring of the eighteenth and nineteenth centuries. In short, it is part of the shift of households' preferences from freedom toward security.

Given this shift in preferences plus a government responsive thereto, society's problem becomes one of satisfying the preferences at least social cost. In the present context this means that the voters must be aware of alternative ways of providing pensions and must know the costs as well as the utilities of each method. Only then can a rational choice be made (if the alternatives are divisible, which they are).

There are five alternative methods of providing retirement income for superannuated persons: saving by individual workers; private union pension plans; private employer or employer-union pension plans; old-age insurance; and old-age assistance. The method of individual savings has undeniable utility; let no one minimize the moral and general political value of this exercise of self-reliance and freedom. The trouble is — and here we come to the cost — that more than a third of all American households are unable or unwilling to save (recall pages 116, 133). Under this system, therefore, we have the evils noted earlier in this chapter. There is an additional difficulty: To provide a minimum retirement income these days, savings of about $20,000 per retired couple would be necessary. If every couple were able and willing to save that much, there would be a tremendous rise in national savings, with a corresponding decline in consumption spending. Would firms' investment spending be high enough to use all these savings? If not, we should be launched into a severe, prolonged depression unless government took a hand through deficit spending.

Some sort of group action therefore seems called for. Union pension plans have demonstrated their inadequacy. In practice, the costs of this system have outweighed its utilities. But what about company plans, with or without unions? The retirement incomes they provide undeniably have utility for those who receive them. But the costs are truly imposing.

For one thing, company plans place an additional obstacle to optimum resource allocation because they foster immobility in the labor force. Workers lose their pensions when they leave their employers — unless their pension rights are "vested." Under vesting a worker who quits his firm for a more attractive job takes along with him the accrued contributions made by the employer to his pension account. But vesting is not usual because it makes a private pension plan much more expensive and robs the plan of much of its attractiveness to the employer. Moreover, company pension systems tend to make for discrimination on the part of employers in the hiring of older workers, as shown in Chapter 9.

Another drawback to company pension plans is the fact that fewer than half of all American workers could be covered in this way. Some industries like canning, construction, and longshoring have such seasonal and casual employment that company plans are wholly impracticable. In many other industries many firms are too small and financially weak to bear the costs of the plans.

Private pension plans in the long run do not alter the distribution of income in favor of workers. They may in fact do just the opposite. The added labor costs which they involve do not come out of employers' profits, as unions profess to believe, but are reflected in higher product prices, at least under conditions of high employment. Such price increases bear most heavily on the lower-income groups.

Private company pension plans might affect economic progress unfavorably. Unless workers are to be the victims of a colossal hoax, i.e., if they are to be sure to receive their promised pensions, the companies must fund their pension obligations and build up adequate reserves, either in their own treasuries or through insurance companies. In any case, these reserves should not be invested in risky common stocks. And the reserves will have to be very large. Then we may witness a large diminution in the flow of the "venture" investment capital which is needed for economic progress.

Finally, private pension plans might, if widespread enough, become a force making for business depression. The basic reason is the same as that mentioned just above in respect to economic progress: the necessity for safe plans through adequate reserves. There is a question as to whether the reserves would not have to be so large that new private net investment could not be found for the large rise in savings. This large increase in saving could be worked under a pay-as-you-go plan, that is, under a provision for pension payments out of current revenues. But only a few firms have such stable product-demands, year in and year out, that they can pay as they go without enormously jeopardizing the safety of their plans. The only organization big enough and strong enough to do this safely is government itself.

We are driven to the conclusion, then, that private pension plans have little social merit except possibly as a modest adjunct to a governmental system. Fortunately, the recent plans resulting from the union pension drive of 1947–50 are tied in with the federal plan in the matter of benefits: the companies pay only the differences between the lower federal benefit and the higher total nominal company benefit.

The federal O.A.S.I. program supplemented by the federal-state old-age assistance system is the best least-social-cost approach for this country. Its coverage is by far the most extensive; it causes no discrimination against older workers; it offers little or no impediment to labor mobility (only perhaps between covered and uncovered occupations) and thus no threat to the proper allocation of labor resources; and it holds no menace for economic progress or high levels of employment. In respect to income distribution, it is neutral if not slightly regressive; for the pension funds of the O.A.S.I. are built up from taxes paid by workers and employers. In the end the workers also pay most of the employers' taxes through higher product prices. And this is regressive. But old-age assistance payments come in significant fraction from progressive income taxes; and this may cancel out the other program's regressiveness.

However, the fact that a federal system of retirement benefits represents the most socially desirable approach to the problem of old-age dependency does not necessarily mean that the program now in effect is the best that can be devised. The 1950 amendments to the old-age security laws went a considerable distance in broadening coverage, raising benefits that had become inadequate because of the postwar inflation, and eliminating inequities among various groups of workers in respect to contributions and benefits. But critics of the new program stress a number of continuing inadequacies. In respect to coverage, they say that the whole labor force — not just 75 per cent of it — should be made subject to the Act. And the O.A.S.I. program should be fully coordinated with the retirement systems covering railroad employees and government civilian employees (federal, state, and local). As for contributions, they say that the $3600 limit on the tax base is too low and should be about $5500. The present base favors the higher-paid workers, who receive more than $3600 per year. The lower-paid workers, receiving less than $3600, are taxed on their whole incomes, while the higher paid workers are taxed only on the first $3600 of their incomes. Some critics assert, moreover, that the general level of benefits is still too low and that the principle of *social* insurance is still inadequately observed for various age and income classes. These critics wish benefit payments to individual retired workers or survivors to be based more on need than on previous earnings and contributions.

(3) *Administration.* There has been general approval of the administration of the O.A.S.I. program to date. Administrative costs have been kept low, amounting in recent years to less than 4 per cent of income and less than 12 per cent of outgo. These costs should decline further in the future. The B.O.A.S.I. has done a creditable job in keeping separate accounts for millions of workers (over 83 million social security numbers issued to date), in applying the complex eligibility rules, in calculating benefits, and in explaining the details of a highly intricate program to claimants and beneficiaries.

3. Railroad retirement and survivors' insurance. In 1937 the Congress, as customary, did something special for interstate railroad workers. This time it was in the field of retirement benefits. Through the Railroad Retirement Act and its companion Carriers' Taxing Act, both of which have been amended several times, the administration of the program is in the hands of the Railroad Retirement Board and the Treasury. Funds for pension payments are accumulated by an excise tax on the railroads' payrolls and an income tax of equal amount on railroad workers' wage compensation. There is no government contribution. Beginning in 1952, the tax on each was 6¼ per cent. The original Act, like the O.A.S.I., provided for tax percentages on a rising graduated scale from 1937; but the amendments to the Act also raised the rates. Benefit requirements are "softer" and benefit amounts are generally higher than under the O.A.S.I., except for short-service workers. But usually railroad employees are long-service ones. (Retired railroaders of less than ten years' service, the minimum qualifying period of service, were put under the O.A.S.I. program in 1951.) Normally, benefits are payable when a railroader reaches the age of 65. But those having 30 or more years of service may retire at the age of 60. Permanent total disability at any age is compensable if the employee has had ten years of service. As under the amended O.A.S.I., the maximum wage that can be credited toward a retirement benefit is $300 per month. Other than this, there is no limit or maximum placed on the amount of the pension. Thus, under the computation formula of this program a worker of 40 years' service whose wage income had averaged $300 per month would receive a pension of about $220 per month. The Act also provides a schedule of minimum benefits, as well as benefits for spouses and survivors.

4. Old-age assistance. In contrast to the all-federal O.A.S.I. program, which provides benefits as an earned right, the Social Security Act establishes a federal-state public assistance program to provide various kinds of security for special groups of workers solely on the basis of their needs. The largest of these groups is composed of superannuated workers who cannot qualify for O.A.S.I. benefits. Other groups covered by the public assistance program will be considered later.

a. Administration. The principal role of the federal government in old-age assistance is to provide financial aid to the states through matching grants and to encourage them to develop adequate aid plans. The program is state-administered, but federal supervision is exercised by the Bureau of Public Assistance in the Social Security Administration of the Federal Security Agency. The Bureau's responsibilities are to allocate federal funds, review all state programs to insure conformance with federal requirements, develop standards for adequate care for the needy aged, and assist the states in administering their programs. Funds for public assistance are appropriated by the Congress from general revenues. Federal-state assistance in general is provided to individuals or families in their homes; but in recent years it has also been extended to persons in public or private institutions. Assistance usually takes the form of money payments to recipients but may also be made directly to "vendors" who provide goods or services (e.g., medical care) to recipients.

In order to secure federal approval of an old-age assistance program, each state must meet the following requirements: no age requirement higher than 65 years of age; no restriction which excludes any citizen of the United States; no residence requirement of more than five years out of the nine preceding years and one year immediately before an applicant applies for assistance; statewide coverage; state financial participation in the program; administration or at least supervision by a single state agency; and hearings and appeals procedures for persons denied assistance.

It will be noted that the above requirements can be met fairly easily by the states. Lacking is any uniform national yardstick as to the minimum amounts each state may provide its aged needy and as to the criteria to be applied in determining need. All the states have qualified for federal matching grants.

b. Benefit payments. (1) Eligibility. As we noted above, the principal uniform national requirement is that assistance grants may be given only to those persons 65 years of age and over and in need. Need is determined by the state agencies. As would be expected, the various states have adopted a wide range of standards. Only about half make citizenship a requirement. Some states have adopted the maximum residence requirement allowed by the Congress; others have no residence requirement at all. Most states define need in very general terms. A large majority of states have some property qualification; that is, persons having more than a specified maximum value of property are not regarded as needy or eligible. But this value varies all the way from denying assistance to persons with more than $300 of property to denial only if the value exceeds $5000. About one-third of the jurisdictions have no limitation on either income or property as a factor in eligibility. Some states practically ignore the existence of relatives who are financially able to support an applicant; others deny assistance if such relatives are available.

Certain general trends have been gradually emerging in the assistance programs. Centralized state controls have been growing at the expense of local unit administration, and the tax contributions of local units have declined proportionately. Eligibility requirements have been relaxed. Amounts of benefit payments have been liberalized. The responsibility required of relatives has been lessened. Benefits have been extended both to needy aged in their own homes and to those institutionalized. Adequate standards for determining needs have been slowly developed, and excessive investigation into the private lives and resources of the aged has declined a good deal.

(2) Amounts. (a) Average payments. In mid-1951, about 2.7 million persons were receiving monthly federal-state assistance payments averaging about $44 per person. Among the states, the monthly payments

averaged all the way from around $20 in the lowest (Mississippi) to about $73 in the highest (Colorado). Many states provided supplementary grants to large dependent families. In almost all states payments to urban recipients were higher than to those in rural areas. This accounts in part for the generally lower level of payments in the Southern states.

(b) Federal matching contributions. The maximum amount of federal participation in various types of benefits and the formulas applied for each one are presented in Table 42. Data for earlier years are included to enable the student to observe the major changes in the O.A.A. program since 1939. The table reveals that over the years the federal government has gradually increased the maximum amount of assistance which it would contribute and has increased its proportionate share up to certain limits. Federal-state expenditures on old-age assistance in 1950 totaled $1.6. billion, of which the federal government contributed 54 per cent.

c. Appraisal. Because of its decentralized nature the federal-state old-age assistance program has varied greatly over time and among the states in respect to quality of administration and in accomplishment. It has undoubtedly relieved much distress among the needy aged who are unable to qualify for O.A.S.I. benefits. The program has suffered from two serious deficiencies. First, the level of assistance has been inadequate in view of rising living costs in recent years. Second, there has been a serious lack of uniformity between the states (and in some instances within states) arising from differences in financial ability, attitudes toward social welfare, and the determination of what constitutes need. The increase since 1939 in the proportion of assistance advanced by the federal government, however, has helped to raise the level of benefits in the low-income states. Some progress had been made by 1951 toward uniformity, inasmuch as 30 state agencies had agreed on the basic consumption items needed to provide "minimum essentials."

C. PHYSICAL WELL-BEING

1. Other public assistance. The federal government through the Social Security Administration offers the states additional matching grants to meet the needs of four special groups of workers who would not otherwise be included in federal-state welfare services. Three of these will be discussed here, and the fourth group — the permanently and totally disabled — will be discussed later, in subsection 4.

As in the O.A.A. program, the role of the federal government in these additional forms of public assistance is limited to financial aid, encouragement, and guidance. The programs are state and locally administered. The maximum amount of federal participation, together with the basis for determining it, is presented in Table 42.

a. Aid to dependent children. All states but three have qualified for federal aid to dependent children. The three exceptions have separate

TABLE 42

Selected Aspects of Federal Participation in Public Assistance, 1939–1950

	1939	1946	1948	1950
I. Maximum amount of federal participation (per recipient)				
A. Dependent aged (65 and over)	$40	$45	$50	$50
B. Dependent blind	40	45	50	50
C. Dependent children				
(1) First child	18	24	27	27
(2) Each additional child	12	15	18	18
(3) Dependent parent or relative with whom child lives	None	None	None	27
D. Dependent disabled (permanently and totally 18 and over)	None	None	None	50
II. Formula for federal participation				
A. Dependent aged	½ of payments up to $40	⅔ of first $15, ½ of remainder	¾ of first $20, ½ of remainder to $50	¾ of first $20, ½ of remainder to $50
B. Dependent blind	"	"	"	"
C. Dependent children				
(1) First child	½ of payments up to $18	⅔ of first $9, ½ of remainder to $24	¾ of first $12, ½ of remainder to $27	¾ of first $12, ½ of remainder to $27
(2) Each additional child	½ of payments up to $12	⅔ of first $9, ½ of remainder to $15	¾ of first $12, ½ of remainder to $18	¾ of first $12, ½ of remainder to $18
(3) Dependent parent or relative with whom child lives	None	None	None	¾ of first $12, ½ of remainder to $27
D. Dependent d sabled (totally and permanently)	None	None	None	¾ of first $20, ½ of remainder to $50

all-state programs. About 1.6 million children under 18 years of age (2.1 million recipients, if allowances to some parents are considered) were receiving monthly benefits in 1951. The average payment was around $70 and ranged from a low of about $27 in Mississippi to a high of $110 in Massachusetts. In 1950 the federal-state program expended about $600 million, of which the federal share was 46 per cent.

b. Aid to the blind. All states but one have qualified for federal grants to aid the blind. About 100,000 persons received such aid in 1951, or slightly over one-third of the nation's estimated blind population. Monthly benefits averaged around $47 and ranged from a low of $22 (Kentucky) to a high of $83 (California). Total expenditures in 1950 were $47 million, with the federal government providing about 43 per cent.

c. Maternal and child health and welfare services. The scope of services provided by the states with the help of federal matching grants in this category is very broad. Included are maternity and child health services, particularly in backward areas, nursing services, immunization of school children, health clinics, medical care for crippled children, and so on. Federal appropriations have been relatively low, but in the 1950 amendments to the Act the Congress provided that funds would be raised from around $22 million annually to $42 million by 1952. The number of children reached by these services totals well over two million annually.

d. General assistance. For purposes of comparison it may be well to note here the additional expenditures of the states and local governments for welfare purposes in the absence of federal aid. This category of "general relief" or "home relief" covers aid to individuals or families when their needs are not otherwise provided for. Variation among the states is extreme since the unifying influence of federal participation is lacking.

Average payments per case in recent years have been around $45, but the range has been from a low of about $11 (Mississippi) to a high of $70 (New York).

In 1950, expenditures for the four types of federal-state assistance discussed above amounted to slightly over $2.0 billion. On their own, the states and local governments spent nearly $400 million additionally for general assistance. If all five categories are considered together, the federal government contributed 44 per cent of the total amount spent on public assistance programs.

2. Compensation for industrial accidents. *a. Development.* Government policy to compensate workers injured in industry developed in European countries as early as the 1880's. Social policy in the United States developed much more slowly. Not until 1902 did the first state, Maryland, enact legislation to provide cash and medical benefits for workers suffering from plant injuries. Opposition to this protection, plus the fact that some early state legislation was held unconstitutional, checked the drive for compensation laws until about 1910. After that year the movement spread rapidly.

Within five years, 26 states had enacted such legislation. Today all states have workmen's compensation laws.

(1) Basis for opposition to workmen's compensation. The slow development of workmen's compensation was due to strong opposition from the employers. This opposition was based on several propositions. First, it was believed that the payment of benefits to injured workers would encourage carelessness and increase the number of accidents. The remedy would aggravate the disease. Second, it would encourage malingering. Subsidized workers would be likely to stay away from their jobs as long as possible. It would be difficult to determine whether such idleness was due to inability or unwillingness to work. Third, since abuses would be likely to occur in making compensation claims, business costs would be raised unnecessarily, with obvious competitive disadvantages to the first states to enact compensation laws. Finally, employers said, workers had protection under the common law which prevailed in the absence of specific legislation.

Under the common law, injured workers could sue for damages in the courts. If the employer was found negligent, the employee might be granted damages by the court. Occasionally there were very large and spectacular awards. But for every case favoring the worker, there were many in which the employer was relieved of all liability.

The great difficulty that injured workers had in obtaining court redress lay in the theory of common law defenses against liability. This theory was made up of three major doctrines. One was *voluntary assumption of risk.* If the worker knew of the job risk involved when he voluntarily accepted the job, this fact relieved the employer of responsibility. Another was the doctrine of *contributory negligence.* If the worker contributed in any way to his own injury through thoughtlessness or carelessness, the employer was absolved. Third, was the *fellow servant* rule. If a worker sustained an injury through the negligence of a fellow worker, the employer was again relieved of blame. So strong were these common law defenses that it was an exceptional case when employer liability was proven. The average worker had neither the means nor the knowledge to institute long and costly legal proceedings against a large corporation. As a consequence, workers injured in American industry prior to 1910 had no practical means of obtaining compensation. Although the common law appears strangely inequitable to us today, it must be remembered that it was carried over from the days of handicraft economy and was not initially intended to be applied to modern factory conditions. When the common law was first developed by the English courts, the primary concern was the protection of property rights won by the English middle classes at great cost from the crown.

(2) The decline of opposition to state compensation laws. The opposition of employers to government intervention in behalf of disabled workers declined after 1910. A number of factors account for this. For one

thing, public opinion was aroused over the hardships imposed by the inequities of the common law. The pressure of trade unions drove a wedge into the anti-compensation forces; the federal government provided compensation for many of its own employees as early as 1908, and a few of the more progressive industrial states also took action. Perhaps of greater importance was the fact that the courts themselves began to liberalize the common law thus confronting employers with a rising number of awards and damage suits. "Employers increasingly insured their liabilities and mounting rates led many of them to prefer the definite and possibly lower costs of a compensation system to the indefinite and high costs of employers' liability insurance."[1] Finally, the experience of the first few states which pioneered the compensation movement demonstrated that workers did not become careless nor did accidents increase, thus allaying the worst fears of many employers.

(3) *Theory behind workmen's compensation.* The basic theory behind modern compensation laws is found in the doctrine of employer *liability without fault,* i.e., the employer is required to compensate injured workers even though he may not have been at fault. This approach rests on a number of propositions. First is the *impossibility of determining the causes of specific accidents.* Intensive research has revealed that the causes of industrial accidents are usually multiple and not susceptible of precise determination. Courts of law are not well equipped to make highly technical determinations nor can they handle the thousands of cases which arise annually. Second is the factor of *accident prevention.* The employer has sole authority over his property. He is the only one who can order changes in production methods, equipment, and tools; he is the only one who can enforce safety regulations. Financial liability for the cost of accidents is the best inducement for employers to reduce accidents. Third is the principle of *rehabilitation,* i.e., restoring the worker's earning power as quickly as possible regardless of who may have been at fault. Formerly the workers were often unable to return to work and became a burden on their families or on the community, simply for lack of proper medical attention. This meant loss of manpower to industry and loss of income to the workers' families. Rapid rehabilitation reduces the total cost of injuries. Fourth is the principle of *cost-sharing.* To avoid high premium payments the employer is induced to spend money to improve working conditions. He shares in the costs of injury. At the same time he will be likely to add at least some of his costs to his product prices. Thus the consumer also shares some of the costs, particularly in purchasing products from very hazardous industries. The injured worker not only suffers in terms of physical well-being, but, since his compensation is less than normal wages, he and his family bear part of the costs. Fifth is the principle of *reducing the unknown element in accident costs*

[1] Domenico Gagliardo, *American Social Insurance,* Harper and Brothers, 1949, pp. 395–396.

for both employer and employee. Under workmen's compensation the employer knows the extent of his liability and can provide for it as a part of business costs. The worker knows the extent of compensation to which he is entitled and can adjust his life during disablement accordingly.

b. Administration. Workmen's compensation for the great majority of employees is a state program. Its constitutionality has been upheld as within the police powers of the states to protect their citizens against hardship and promote the general welfare. The federal government has legislated solely for its own employees.

All states have enacted compensation laws. Almost all have established central commissions to administer them. The quality of administration has varied greatly from extremely competent to extremely lax. The task of administration includes determining and publishing the amount of compensation required for particular types of injuries; setting forth procedures for making claims and appeals; hearing appeals; analyzing causes of accidents; making recommendations to legislatures for improvements in the programs; and supervising the settlement of claims. In recent years compensation payments have totaled over $500 million annually.

c. Coverage. No state law covers all employments. Coverage is restricted in five major ways. First, there are limitations by *occupation or industry.* In almost all states, agricultural workers, domestic servants, casual employees, and professional persons are excluded. Interstate railroad workers are excluded at their own request because of their belief that they can obtain larger (even though less certain) damages under employer liability laws and because of the conflict in jurisdiction between state and federal authority. Exemption of domestic servants is based on administrative difficulties. Exemption of professional persons is based on the assumption that they do not need legislative protection. Second, coverage often depends on the *hazardousness of an industry.* Some states limit coverage solely to hazardous industries. In such states as New York this criterion exempts few industries. In some agricultural states, however, it is a very restrictive criterion. Third, there are exemptions based on *type of injury.* Almost all laws limit liability for injuries which result from intoxication, insubordination, or are self-inflicted. Fourth, there are exclusions based on *size of employer.* In 30 states, employers with less than a specified number of employees are exempted. The range is from two in Oklahoma to 15 in South Carolina. The remaining 18 states have no numerical exemption. Fifth, there is *compulsory versus elective coverage.* A compulsory compensation act "is one which requires every employer within the scope of the . . . law to accept the act and pay the compensation specified."[2] In the case of an elective law the employer has the option of either accepting or rejecting the act; but if he rejects it, he loses the customary common law defenses (i.e., assumption of risk, con-

[2] U.S. Department of Labor, Bureau of Labor Standards, *State Workmen's Compensation Laws as of September, 1950,* Bulletin 125, 1950, Washington, D.C., p. 2.

tributory negligence, and fellow-servant negligence). At present 28 of the states have compulsory and 20 have elective laws. In most elective states the majority of employers have elected to accept statutory liability. The exceptions, however, are sufficiently large to make the actual coverage less than potential. As a consequence, the exact number of workers covered by state compensation laws is unknown. The number in private industry was estimated at between 30 and 35 million in 1947.[3] If covered government employees are added, it has been estimated that roughly three out of four non-agricultural employees are now covered by state or federal workmen's compensation laws.[4]

d. Contributions or taxes. Under the principle of workmen's compensation, the employer, in order to limit his liability, must insure his risks. Insurance may be carried through a private company, a competitive state insurance fund, or a monopolistic state fund (required in eight states); or the employer may qualify for self-insurance, i.e., satisfy the state authority that sufficient reserves have been set aside to cover risks. Six states do not permit self-insurance. The cost of the insurance varies with the accident experience of the industry. The private insurance companies have developed a risk and rate schedule containing different rates for over 700 industrial or occupational classifications. Within each, a given employer pays a premium based on merit-rating, which means a higher or lower rate depending on the employer's individual accident record.

e. Benefit payments. (1) Alternative approaches. There are two alternative approaches to the payment of benefits. One is a policy of "full compensation," including costs of rehabilitation, current wage loss, and future wage loss from permanent or partial disability. The other approach is a policy of "rehabilitation" which pays the worker the full costs of medical care and provides partial compensation for current wage loss but would not attempt to pay for all current or future economic losses. The states have universally adopted the latter approach on the grounds that calculation of "full compensation" would be impossible; and even if such computation were possible, the costs would be too heavy and might well encourage malingering. Nevertheless, the increasing liberalization of medical-care benefits in recent years represents a definite trend in the direction of "full compensation" and away fom the meager partial compensation of many years ago.

(2) Types of benefits. Benefit payments are of two types: cash benefits to compensate for wage loss, and medical benefits for treatment to restore earning capacity.

(3) Amount and period of benefits. Almost all the state acts provide for weekly cash benefits based on a percentage of prior earnings with a specified minimum and maximum. The majority of states provide for a

[3] Arthur H. Reede, *Adequacy of Workmen's Compensation,* Harvard University Press, 1947, ch. ii and pp. 379–380. Quoted in Domenico Gagliardo, *op. cit.,* p. 403.

[4] *Monthly Labor Review,* October, 1950.

maximum of between $20 and $30 a week, with a few above $40. The higher the worker's average weekly wage, the lower is the *percentage* received in compensation benefits. In addition, most states provide for a maximum number of payments, usually between 400 and 575 weeks. In respect to the most serious type of non-fatal injury — permanent and total disability — about 40 per cent of the states provide benefits for life. In the remaining states, dollar maxima of between $5000 and $10,000 are provided. Lump-sum payments are paid to survivors in case of death to the insured. Nearly all states require a waiting period of one week before benefits can begin.

The exact amount of weekly cash compensation for a particular type of injury is determined and published in most states by the legislature or the state compensation authority, so that all persons know the extent of liability. The most notable change in benefit payments since the beginning of the compensation movement has been the expansion in the level and scope of provisions for medical care. This has resulted from greater emphasis on the "rehabilitation" aspects of compensation. Today about one-half of the states provide no limits on the amount of medical payments; the worker "gets as much as he needs," although some states do place a time limit on medical claims. Many students of compensation hold that, despite progress to date, this country has far to go before medical care for the injured may be considered adequate.

(4) Benefit payments by severity of injury. There are five levels of benefit payments based on the severity of an injury. The two least serious are *temporary partial* and *temporary total disability.* By definition, full recovery is made from these injuries within the time limits of the state law. A third category with higher benefits is *permanent partial disability,* which involves the loss of use of some body member. A fourth category is *permanent total disability,* which involves total destruction of a worker's future earning power. Eighteen states today pay life benefits for complete incapacity. In the others, payment is limited as to time or amount or both. The time periods range from 260 to 1000 weeks and the money limitation from $6000 in North and South Carolina to $14,000 in Rhode Island.

The fifth category is *accidental death.* The benefits paid vary widely. A few states provide benefits to a surviving widow for life or until remarriage. A majority of states limit payments by time or amount or both. In 33 states the time limit ranges from 200 to 600 weeks. In those limiting payments by amount, the maxima range from $6000 to $12,000.

(5) Supplementary benefits. Almost all states provide additional benefits to a surviving parent with dependent children. A growing number of states (13 in 1951) also provide supplemental benefits in permanent and total disability cases.

(6) Special payments for rehabilitation. An increasing number of states (18 in 1951) also provide special awards to assist workers in need of rehabilitation. Wisconsin, for example, pays up to 40 weeks of benefits

during training periods. Several states have free rehabilitation centers. After exhaustion of state assistance many workers today can obtain additional training aid under the federal-state Vocational Rehabilitation program mentioned in Chapter 22.

f. Appraisal. We now have nearly a half-century of experience out of which to evaluate workmen's compensation legislation and its administration. Injury frequency rates have declined despite greater mechanization of industry. Carelessness has not increased as the early opponents of compensation feared. The costs of accidents have been more equitably shared by the community. Opposition to the principle of compensation has all but disappeared. The chief remaining problem is one of adequacy. Because of limitations on coverage, many workers are still unprotected. In some states which permit employers to elect to stay out of the state program, workers must still undertake time-consuming and costly court suits to secure compensation. Occupational and size-of-employer exclusions are still too large. The level of benefits has lagged somewhat behind the rise in living costs. The most significant advance since the first enactments has been the growth of medical aid. Next to accident prevention, rehabilitation of injured workers through proper medical care is the major contribution of workmen's compensation to social welfare.

The student should remember that even if full compensation were made for all work-connected injuries, we would still have a long way to go to compensate for lost time in industry due to accidents, inasmuch as accidents away from work account for more wage loss today than accidents on the job, a fact which we shall discuss in more detail later in this chapter.

3. Compensation for occupational diseases. The states did not include occupational diseases among compensable injuries in the early development of workmen's compensation legislation. The addition of this category came slowly for several reasons. First, the difficulty of diagnosing the exact nature of some diseases is much greater than for most bodily injuries. Second, many diseases do not become apparent until months or even years after inception. Meanwhile, the worker may have worked for many firms in whose employ the disease may or may not have been aggravated. Under such circumstances it is difficult to allocate liability among employers. Third, since some diseases are not curable, it was feared in the early days that inclusion might prove an intolerable financial burden.

Over the years there has been gradual acceptance of the theory that occupational diseases should be compensated for in the same way as bodily injury, and that compensation should be made by the worker's current employer regardless of who was to blame. Employers protect themselves by means of periodic physical examinations for both new and old employees. Today 41 states include diseases in their compensation acts. In 24 states all diseases are covered; in 17, only selected diseases. The administration, coverage, and amount of benefits are in general similar to those discussed above for bodily injuries.

4. Compensation for disability from non-industrial accidents and sickness. *a. Permanent and total disability. (1) Extent of the problem.* For many years students of insecurity have pointed out that persons suffering permanent and total disability were among the least protected in the nation. It has been estimated that on any given day there are at least 2 million workers who are completely disabled and have been for six months or longer.[5] Yet since only about 5 per cent are disabled from work-connected accidents, they lack protection of workmen's compensation laws. A recent study of the National Safety Council found that, out of 46,500 deaths among workers from accidents in 1949, some 15,000 occurred at work and 31,500 or 78 per cent occurred away from work. Of 4.4 million injuries, 1.8 million occurred at work; 2.6 million occurred away from work.[6] Workers experiencing disablement are not eligible for unemployment compensation. If under 65, they cannot qualify for either O.A.S.I. or O.A.A. benefits. Unless protected by private insurance, which is not widely held because of its high cost and restricted benefits, these workers must depend on relatives or turn to public charity.

To meet the needs of the permanently disabled, there has been a growing demand for the inclusion of permanent disability compensation (with the age factor removed) in the all-federal O.A.S.I. program. The reasons for integrating disability with O.A.S.I. are that it would lower administrative costs, since much of the same wage information and procedure would be called for; the forced retirement of workers under 65 would need to be coordinated with their O.A.S.I. benefits after they reached 65; and inclusion would insure adequate financial support for the program.

Very strong opposition, however, has been voiced against the inclusion of disability insurance in any part of the government's security program. It is argued that the experience of private life insurance companies and foreign governments in this field casts serious doubt on the possibility of administering such a program without very high costs; adequate benefits would encourage malingering and discourage rehabilitation; this type of disability is very difficult to determine, and in some cases impossible; and in a year of widespread unemployment all sorts of excuses and devices would be used to get on the disability roll.

The arguments, pro and con, were analyzed by the U.S. Senate's Advisory Council on Social Security. In its report in 1948 the Council recommended inclusion of permanent and total disability benefits in the O.A.S.I. program. The majority of the Council members believed that

[5] Advisory Council on Social Security on its report to the Committee on Finance, U.S. Senate, 1948.

[6] National Safety Council, *Accident Facts,* 1950, p. 25.

sufficient administrative safeguards could be developed to prevent potential abuses from becoming realities; experience would overcome difficulties in applying eligibility rules; combining the two programs would reduce administrative costs; there was a similarity of risk; and integration would "facilitate the maintenance of benefit rights for disabled workers for purposes of future old age and survivors insurance payments."

After lengthy discussion, the Congress in the 1950 amendments to the Social Security Act compromised the views of those who opposed any form of permanent disability insurance and those who advocated an extensive program integrated with O.A.S.I. Aid to the totally and permanently disabled was made a new and fourth category in the federal-state public assistance program. The extent of federal participation is shown in Table 42. By the end of 1951 there were 110,000 permanently and totally disabled persons receiving monthly assistance payments averaging around $45 and ranging from a low of $17 in Mississippi to a high of $66 in Oregon. Total federal-state expenditures in 1950 were $10 million, of which the federal contribution was nearly 50 per cent.

b. Temporary disability: Health insurance. (1) State laws. As stated in Chapter 22, four states (California, New Jersey, New York, and Rhode Island) have passed legislation providing benefits for unemployment due to non-occupational disability, i.e., sickness or non-work-connected injury.[7] The legislation is known variously as "health insurance," "unemployment compensation disability benefits," and "cash sickness insurance."

(a) Administration. Because of the similarity in procedures and use of wage records, three of the states have coordinated the administration of temporary disability insurance with unemployment insurance. In the exception (New York) the program is administered by the Workmen's Compensation Board.

(b) Coverage. Disability is generally defined as the inability to do "regular or customary work," but there is considerable variation in the precise definitions used.[8] The industrial coverage is in general the same as for unemployment insurance, which means exclusion of farm workers, domestic servants, employees of non-profit organizations, interstate railroad workers, and government employees. Coverage is compulsory in Rhode Island. In the other three states, employers, with the consent of employees, may insure themselves if they provide equal or better protection. In three states, employers of four or more workers are covered; and in the fourth state (California) employers of one or more in covered employment are included.

(c) Contributions or taxes. In California and Rhode Island employers make no special contribution for the health benefits, and in New York

[7] A temporary disability law was passed by the legislature of the State of Washington and signed by the Governor March 21, 1949. It was disapproved by the voters in a general referendum March 7, 1950.

[8] The states generally deny or limit benefits in cases of pregnancy, self-inflicted injury, or injury sustained when engaged in illegal acts.

they are assessed only the costs (if any) of providing benefits in excess of employee contributions. Only in New Jersey are employers taxed a specific amount, 0.25 per cent of annual payroll. In California and Rhode Island, employees contribute 1.0 per cent of annual wages up to the first $3000. In New Jersey they pay 0.75 per cent, in New York 0.5 per cent, on the first $60 of weekly wages.

(d) Benefit payments. The amount of weekly benefits in all four states is roughly between a minimum of $10 and a maximum of $25 weekly,[9] specific amounts being computed as a per cent of high-quarter wages. Three states have a maximum benefit period of 26 weeks. One allows 31 weeks. In all four states there is a waiting period of seven days for each disability. Benefits may not be obtained concurrently with workmen's compensation in three states; Rhode Island, however, has permitted duplication up to 85 per cent of weekly wages. In Rhode Island and New York workers may receive state disability benefits and sick pay from private employers simultaneously; in the other two states, sick pay from the employer requires an equivalent reduction in state benefits.

(e) Appraisal. Because of the recency of state temporary disability laws, it is too early to appraise adequately this new development in social legislation. Rhode Island's law became effective in 1943, California's in 1946, New Jersey's in 1949, and New York's in 1950. Some very liberal provisions in the state acts have had to be tightened up to prevent serious drains on funds. On the other hand, the predictions of opponents that there would be wholesale abuses and malingering have not been confirmed. Although benefits are modest, there is general agreement that distress for low-income workers has been alleviated. This new development in social legislation promises to grow in the near future.

(2) Proposals for broad governmental program. (a) Nature. The recognition that sickness (both work-connected and non-work-connected) is a major cause of lost time in industry has brought forth many proposals and counterproposals for a national health program. These proposals differ from state temporary disability insurance in that they are concerned less with weekly cash benefits to compensate for wage loss, though these are sometimes included, than with the provision of adequate medical care, with emphasis on prevention as well as treatment. Five major proposals since 1939 will be reviewed briefly.

(i) The Wagner National Health Bill of 1939.[10] The original proposal of Senator Robert Wagner of New York was for the federal government to encourage the states to develop state programs for temporary disability compensation. This was to be accomplished by federal matching grants similar to those under the public assistance program. The amount and duration of cash benefits and other details were to be left to the states.

[9] California raised the maximum to $30 in 1951.

[10] For a detailed discussion of this and other national health proposals see Domenico Gagliardo, *op. cit.*, pp. 460–490.

The Wagner Bill would also have granted federal matching funds for the development of state health programs including medical care and disease control, construction of hospitals, the training of medical personnel, and expanded maternal and child health services.

(ii) The Capper Bill, 1940. Senator Arthur Capper of Kansas proposed federal grants-in-aid to the states to encourage the development of disability laws which should provide both cash sickness benefits and payments for medical care, with expenditures favoring the latter in the ratio of three to one. Both insured individuals and their dependents would be covered. Medical care would include the services of physicians in home or office, surgical care, hospital treatment, nursing care, and even dental care under certain conditions. Financing would involve contributions by employers, employees, and the states, as well as by the federal government.

(iii) The Wagner-Murray-Dingall Compulsory National Health Insurance Bill, 1945. This proposal would have established a compulsory, all-federal, nation-wide health insurance program designed to finance payment for a wide range of "personal health services." These included the services of general physicians, specialists, and dentists; home-nursing service; diagnostic and therapeutic laboratory benefits; certain types of appliances, including eyeglasses; and hospital benefits. The beneficiaries were to have free choice in the selection of doctors, in so far as the latter would join the system. A federal tax of 1.5 per cent each on employer and employee was to be levied to finance the plan. The program was to be integrated with O.A.S.I. The level of benefits would be related to the worker's status under O.A.S.I., i.e., whether "currently" or "permanently" insured or already receiving retirement or survivor's benefits.

(iv) The revised Wagner-Murray-Dingall Bill, 1947. Under different sponsorship the 1945 proposal was greatly modified and re-introduced in Congress in 1947. The revised proposal de-emphasized the federal role and expanded the role of the states. The latter were to be encouraged to develop and administer state health plans. Federal standards were to be developed and applied by a National Health Insurance Board. The latter would operate the plan in states which failed to present an acceptable plan. The states were to be given wide freedom to make contracts for medical care with medical societies, clinics, and hospital associations. The federal government was to finance the program through general revenue or by a special tax, and monies would be allocated to the states on the basis of population, with some allowance for need. In a special message to Congress on April 22, 1949, the President with additional modifications recommended passage of this revised proposal.

(v) The Taft National Health Bill, 1947.[11] This bill, offered by Senator

[11] An additional bill was offered by Senator Lister Hill of Alabama and others, in 1949. It proposed that the federal government finance membership in private voluntary non-profit medical insurance plans for all workers unable to pay for such

Robert A. Taft of Ohio as a counterproposal to the compulsory national health insurance plan, proposed a system of federal grants-in-aid to the states to encourage the development of programs for the provision of medical care to low-income families. The states were given very wide latitude. They could subsidize medical care, establish free health centers, make contracts with local medical groups, or even enact compulsory health insurance plans. In addition, the Taft bill would bring together all federal health activities into a single agency; subsidize medical research, the expansion of medical schools, and the construction of hospitals; and enlarge the activities of the U.S. Public Health Service.

None of these five proposals was enacted by the Congress. By 1951 the lines had been drawn sharply between those who urged the passage of a compulsory health insurance program and those who were just as strongly opposed. Apparently in an effort to reconcile the two sides, the President on December 29, 1951, appointed a fifteen-member President's Commission on the Health Needs of the Nation to review the issues involved, determine the "total health requirements" of the nation, and recommend ways of meeting them. The attempted inclusion on the Commission of a representative of the American Medical Association, the sharpest critic of compulsory health insurance, presumably recognized that the views of the medical profession would somehow have to be incorporated in any federal health program. However, the physician who was appointed to the Commission refused to serve. There was as yet no sign that the majority of A.M.A. members had decided to modify their bitter opposition to government action in the field.

In studying the relative merit of arguments on both sides of this issue, the student should keep in mind the distinction between *compulsory temporary disability insurance* designed to compensate workers for loss of earnings due to ill health and *compulsory health insurance* designed to provide health care (medical, dental, nursing, hospital) by means of payments to the vendors of such service. Confusion sometimes arises because some health care plans have also included temporary disability insurance.

(b) Arguments for compulsory health insurance. The arguments favoring a broad governmental program of compulsory health insurance include the following:

(i) Present medical care is too inadequate, too unevenly distributed, too expensive for middle- and lower-income groups. Rising costs have placed adequate medical care above the reach of the income groups which need it most. One study in 1942 revealed that, whereas the average family with an income of more than $5000 a year spent $241 on medical care, the families with less than $1000 average income spent only $42.[12]

insurance. It proposed a federal survey of areas lagging in health services to determine the extent of health needs and to develop plans for meeting them.

[12] Study by the Division of Research, Consumer Income and Demand Branch, Office of Price Administration, Washington, D.C., 1942. Quoted in Gagliardo, *op. cit.*, p. 450.

Yet the frequency of sickness is much higher among the low-income groups than among the high.[13] Some areas in the United States have numerous medical personnel; some have very few. For example, New York State has one physician for every 500 persons; Mississippi, one for every 1500 persons.[14] The unpredictability of illness makes financial planning by most families very difficult. While 50 million people are covered by some form of voluntary health insurance, this insurance provides only limited protection for hospitalization and little or no protection for other medical services. Only about 3.5 million have adequate all-round health insurance, and most of these are in the high-income classes.[15]

(ii) Compulsory health insurance is a method of payment and not a new approach to medical care. The objective of the compulsory health insurance proposal is to provide the financial means for adequate care. The compulsory aspects are designed to secure maximum sharing of risk — a policy that has worked successfully in state workmen's compensation for nearly 50 years. The program would "not interfere in the personal relationship between doctor and patient . . . would not disturb the freedom of doctors and hospitals to determine the nature and extent of treatment . . . would not require doctors to become employees of the government . . . patients would be free to choose their own doctors and doctors will remain free to accept or reject patients."[16]

(iii) The program is financially feasible and economically sound. Costs would not be prohibitive but could be financed by a 3 or 4 per cent tax on payrolls. The nation already spends about 4 per cent of its income for health care. The proposed program would obtain better care for the same money. Actually to obtain adequate national health we should be willing to spend even more than 4 per cent of the national income. The real cost of ill health in terms of suffering, lost man-days in industry, and unnecessary deaths cannot be calculated, but it is much more than is involved in a 4 per cent payroll tax. The net effect of national financing would be to spread the burden.

(iv) The program would improve the quality of medical care and reduce the volume of sickness. People who now get no care would be able to obtain it. Many areas not now served by adequate medical personnel, due to the inability of patients to pay or to lack of medical facilities, would be properly cared for. By getting patients early enough, doctors would be able to prevent the development of many serious illnesses.

(c) Arguments against compulsory health insurance. The arguments advanced against compulsory health insurance include the following:

(i) Under private practice America already has the best medical care

[13] U.S. Public Health Service, National Health Survey of 1935 as cited by Domenico Gagliardo, *op. cit.*, p. 444.

[14] *The Nation's Health,* Federal Security Agency, Washington, D.C., 1948, p. 10.

[15] Message of the President to the Congress, April 22, 1947.

[16] Message of the President to the Congress, April 22, 1947.

in the world. Numerous studies show that the sickness rate in the United States is extremely low compared with rates in other countries. This record has been achieved under existing private medical practice. The sickness frequency rate should continue to decline. Many of the deaths labeled "unnecessary" for "political" reasons are merely evidence of medical progress which enables citizens to live into advanced years.

(ii) Present costs of medical care are not beyond the financial reach of average families. All but a few indigent persons (who may obtain charity care) can afford medical attention in the United States. It is true that U.S. families spend about 4 per cent of the national income for medical care. But they also spend 6 per cent for alcoholic beverages and another 6 per cent for recreation. Families can obtain excellent medical care if they wish to give health a high enough priority in their scales of preference and in their budgets.

(iii) Costs would be excessive. The proposed 3 or 4 per cent payroll tax would be only the beginning. Experience abroad suggests that this rate would have to be raised very much higher and would impose a very inequitable burden on those families which already give good health a high place in their budgets. The costs of administration would detract considerably from the share of the national income available for diagnosis and treatment.

(iv) The quality of medical service would be lowered. Despite political announcements to the contrary, medical personnel would rapidly be forced into the status of government employees. Standard fees would deny doctors their basic freedom to give the best possible treatment to every patient regardless of ability to pay. The time of doctors would be diluted by patients with imaginary ills. It would be difficult to give sufficient time to those genuinely ill. Medical care is being extended to backward areas. The "evening up" process should continue in the future.

(v) Private, voluntary plans for medical and hospital care, e.g., Blue Cross and Blue Shield, have been growing very rapidly. They should be given an opportunity to show whether or not they can fill the alleged need.

(d) The problem of sufficient personnel and facilities. Both sides agree that the nation does not now have enough doctors and hospitals to put a compulsory plan into immediate operation. The proponents would provide federal financial aid to train more medical personnel and build more facilities. The opponents argue that, if this is accomplished, then there is no need for so drastic a change in present practices.

D. WAGE RATES, HOURS, AND WORKING CONDITIONS

1. Federal laws. *a. The Fair Labor Standards Act.* This Act, enacted by the Congress in 1938, was the first major effort of the federal government to regulate the wage rates and work periods of workers engaged in interstate commerce. Very significant amendments were enacted in October, 1949, effective January, 1950.

(1) Administration. Administrative authority is vested in the U.S. Secretary of Labor, and responsibility is delegated by him to the Wages, Hours, and Public Contracts Divisions of the U.S. Department of Labor headed by an Administrator. The divisions are decentralized, with regional offices in major cities and with numerous local offices.

(2) Coverage. (a) Inclusions. The original Act of 1938 applied to all employees (not otherwise exempted) who are engaged in interstate commerce or in the production of goods for interstate commerce. The term "production" was applied even to occupations "necessary" for the production of goods. The scope of the Act was thus very broad. It was so applied by the Administrator and upheld by the courts. To illustrate: Workers employed by a firm making a product sold only intrastate but used by a firm selling interstate were covered. Service workers such as window washers employed by a firm producing electric power for sale across state lines were covered. The 1949 amendments defined the term "production" to cover workers engaged *in* interstate commerce as in the 1938 Act. But coverage of workers engaged in production *for* interstate commerce was to be inclusive *only in so far as* they are engaged in "closely related processes or occupations directly essential to production of goods for interstate commerce." Apparently the Congress intended to narrow the coverage of the Act somewhat by exempting a few activities on the borderline between local and interstate business. The exact meaning of this 1949 redefinition, however, remains obscure. Clarification will have to await court interpretation. In any event, the net change is certain to be slight.

(b) Exclusions and exemptions. (i) Industry groups. The Act exempts numerous large industry groups including agriculture, intrastate transportation, and local retail and service trades. Employees of air carriers and sea food canneries were formerly exempt from both wage and hour provisions but are now exempt only from the hours limitation. *(ii) White-collar managerial employees.* The Act exempts administrative, executive, and professional employees. *(iii) Sub-minimum workers.* Apprentices, learners, and handicapped workers may be employed at wages below the Act's wage standard with the approval of the Administrator. *(iv) Employees in seasonal industries.* Employers engaged in activities designated as seasonal may work employees up to 12 hours a day, 56 hours per week, for a maximum of 14 weeks in a calendar year without incurring the Act's overtime penalties. *(v) Employees under labor-management guaranteed annual wage plans.* Partial exemption from overtime penalties is granted to employers operating under collectively bargained guaranteed annual wage plans. Such an employer may work employees up to 12 hours a day or 56 hours a week without paying overtime, providing he guarantees dur-

ing a 52-week calendar period anywhere from 1840 hours to 2080 hours of work or from 46 to 52 normal weeks of employment of not less than 30 hours per week. In the original Act such employer could not work employees over 2080 hours annually. Under the 1949 change, he may work employees 160 hours over 2080 if necessary, thus enjoying greater flexibility for emergencies and special circumstances. The extra hours over 2080 must be paid for at time-and-one-half. *(vi) Total exemptions.* It was estimated that there were about 30 million wage and salary workers engaged in interstate commerce in 1950. Of these, 21 million were subject to the Act, and 9 million were wholly exempted.

(3) Protective provisions. The Act is intended to give workers protection through three major provisions: minimum wage rates, maximum hours of work, and child labor restrictions. The first two provisions are discussed here. Child labor regulation will be considered later in the chapter.

(a) Minimum wage-rate standards. The Act of 1938, effective October 24, 1938, provided for an ascending schedule of minimum wage rates as follows: during the first year, 1938–39, 25 cents an hour; during the next six years, 1939–45, 30 cents an hour; after October 24, 1945, 40 cents an hour. Effective January 25, 1950, the amended Act raised the minimum to 75 cents an hour. Under the original Act, during the 1939–45 period, minimum wage rates for particular low-wage industries could be and were set somewhat higher than the statutory minimum, but in no case above 40 cents an hour. The Administrator was authorized to do this upon the recommendation of tripartite industry committees, which he was empowered to establish as he saw fit. The rising trend in wages and prices made the 40-cents-an-hour minimum in 1945 anomalous. Even in 1950 the increase to 75 cents an hour affected only about 1,500,000 workers directly out of an estimated total of 21 million wage and salary employees subject to the amended Act.

(b) Maximum hours. The F.L.S.A. originally provided for a standard work-week of 40 hours. This provision was retained in the amended Act. Hours worked over this standard by any covered worker must be paid for at the penalty rate of one and one-half the worker's regular rate. The student should keep in mind that the Act places no restriction on the maximum number of hours per week that can be worked; it merely requires premium pay for hours over the standard work-week. In the original 1938 Act, the 40-hour standard was reached in successive stages. The standard was 44 hours in 1938–39; 42 hours in 1939–40; and 40 hours after October, 1940. Two special exemptions from the hours standard have already been discussed for seasonal workers and employees under guaranteed annual wage plans.

(4) Some controversies in interpreting the Fair Labor Standards Act. (a) The "overtime-on-overtime" issue. The original F.L.S.A. did not define "regular rate" for determining overtime. Much of the time and

energy of the administrator and his staff had to be devoted to defining this term in particular cases. On some points, including those discussed here, considerable confusion and legal controversy arose.

The overtime-on-overtime issue (recall page 527) reached the Supreme Court in 1948[17] in two cases involving the International Longshoremen's Association. Here the dispute revolved around certain hours regularly worked within a standard work-week of 40 hours but paid for at premium rates because they were considered to be "undesirable" hours. Included were night and week-end work, holiday work, and meal periods worked. If the worker put in more than 40 hours a week, he was clearly entitled under the Act to time-and-one-half the "regular rate" for the regular hours. Then should the "regular rate" include just the rate on non-premium hours, or should it include the premium rates since they were regularly worked? The workers naturally argued for inclusion. The employers said this would be paying "overtime on overtime." The Court held in favor of the workers. But in so doing it opened the way for a flood of suits for back pay. Billions of dollars were involved. To relieve employers of this unexpected development the Congress in July, 1949, passed an "Overtime on Overtime Act" which amended the F.L.S.A., invalidated the suits and listed specific types of wage payments which are not to be considered part of "regular pay" in calculating overtime under the F.L.S.A. Among the exclusions were payment for time ordinarily not worked; work on Saturdays, Sundays, holidays; any payment for hours over eight per day; and extra payments in connection with certain profit-sharing and bonus plans. The new definition of "regular pay" was incorporated in the October, 1949, amendments to the F.L.S.A.

(b) The "portal-to-portal" pay issue. The question of what should be included in the "regular rate" was raised in a different way in connection with time spent on an employer's premises but for which the worker was not paid. In several decisions involving the mining industry in 1944,[18] the U.S. Supreme Court held that time spent in going to and from the mine face or workings should be considered as time worked"; should be compensated for at not less than the F.L.S.A. minimum; and if such travel time involved hours over 40, should be paid for at time-and-one-half the regular rate in accordance with the F.L.S.A. In other words, workers in such industries were to be paid for all time spent on the employer's property, from portal to portal.

Later the same doctrine was applied to manufacturing in a case which involved "walking" and "clean-up" time.[19] Before this, most employers had not paid workers for all time on the premises but only for time spent "at work." The Court's decision resulted in hundreds of claims for back

[17] *Bay Ridge Operating Co., Inc. v. Aaron* and *Huron Stevedoring Corp. v. Blue* (334 U.S. 446, 1948).

[18] *Tennessee Coal Co. v. Muscoda Local* (321 U.S. 590, 944) and *Jewell Ridge Coal Co. v. Local 6167* (325 U.S. 161, 1945).

[19] *Anderson, et al. v. Mt. Clemens Pottery Co., et al.* (66 Sup. Ct. 1187, 1946).

tain productivity increases, whereas the N.W.L.B. did not. Here again the issue had not risen during the war. This sort of wage-rate increase was not deemed inflationary, at least from the cost side, because it was not to be permitted to serve as the basis for raising employers' product prices.

2. State laws. *a. Minimum-wage-rate laws.* Prior to 1937, unfavorable U.S. Supreme Court decisions on constitutionality under the Fourteenth Amendment discouraged the states from further attempting to establish minimum-wage-rate regulations. In 1937, however, the U.S. Supreme Court upheld the minimum wage law of the State of Washington.[21] This decision proved to be a turning point. Today 26 states (plus the District of Columbia, Alaska, Hawaii, and Puerto Rico) have enacted minimum-wage-rate protection for their workers. Almost all the laws cover women workers. Five of the states (plus Hawaii and Puerto Rico) cover both women and men. Nearly all the laws apply to minors. Industrial coverage is generally broad, the principal exemptions being agriculture and domestic service.

In some states minimum wage rates are set by statute; in others they are established by wage boards after hearings on particular industries. Fifteen of the states attempted to keep up with the wage-price spiral of 1945–50 by raising their minima, about half setting wage rates of 60 cents or more and about half setting 70 cents or more. The progressive states thus raised their protection above the federal level until 1949. Since the rise in the F.L.S.A. minimum to 75 cents an hour, the state levels now generally lag below the federal by from 5 to 20 cents an hour. The lag is particularly wide in states where a change in minimum wage rates requires legislative action, in contrast to states which have delegated this authority to permanent or *ad hoc* wage boards. The principal protection of state minima in recent years has been in such local intrastate low-wage-rate industries as retail trade, hotels, restaurants, and laundries.

b. Hours. As in the case of minimum-wage-rate legislation, the unconstitutionality of the early laws made the states slow to continue enacting statutes regulating the lengths of work periods. The turning point in hours regulation came in 1908 when the U.S. Supreme Court upheld a law of the State of Oregon.[22] Since then the states have intervened extensively to protect workers, particularly women, from excessive hours which might endanger health.

(1) Hours regulation for women. Today, 43 states have laws which limit women's employment to 8 hours a day or 48 a week, or both. Nine states have set the maximum day at 9 hours with a weekly maximum of 50 to 54 hours; nine others have a daily limit of 10 hours with work-weeks of from 50 to 60 hours. One state has no daily limit but restricts hours to 54 per week. Twenty-three states now limit the employment of women

[21] *West Coast Hotel Co. v. Parrish* (300 U.S. 391, 1937).
[22] *Muller v. Oregon* (208 U.S. 412, 1908).

on night work. Of these, 13 prohibit night work outright in certain industries. Four states permit night work but require employers to meet certain standards. About half the states prohibit employment of women for more than six days a week.

(2) Hours regulation for men. In general the states have not intervened in the hours worked by men. The regulations which do exist are concerned principally with limiting hours either in industries, such as transportation, in which public safety is a factor (usually the limit is 10 hours) or in industries, such as mining, in which extreme hazards are a factor. In the latter the 8-hour day is generally required.

c. Working conditions. About half the states limit the employment of women and minors in occupations deemed injurious to health. For example, mining is banned for women in nearly all states where mining is important. Other regulations for women cover weight-lifting (9 states), rest periods (8 states), and seating requirements (46 states). Industrial homework for both men and women is regulated in nearly all states. The states have almost no legislation regulating working conditions for men.

d. Special regulations for women and children. Twelve states have passed "equal pay for equal work" laws to prevent discrimination based on sex in wage rates paid to women. Because of the difficulty of determining whether wage-rate differentials between men and women are based on sex or on job content, the effect of this legislation to date has been slight.

All states restrict the employment of underage children in industry and all require compulsory school attendance — generally to the age of 15 or 16. The laws restricting hours per day or per week for women generally apply to children up to the age of 16 or 17. Many states prohibit the employment of children in many occupations; and in the interests of their health and welfare, nearly all ban night work for children.

3. Economic appraisal of federal-state peacetime protective wage-hour legislation. *a. Minimum wage rates.* When we begin thinking about the economic effects of minimum-wage-rate laws, we must remember that here we are not dealing with the general, economy-wide wage-rate increases which we discussed in Chapter 22. Over-all, minimum wage rates such as those discussed above probably do not affect directly more than 5 to 10 per cent of the workers in covered industries. In terms of all industries, covered and non-covered, the percentage is considerably smaller. Furthermore, within a given covered industry the percentages of workers affected in different firms are very different. As we saw in Chapter 8 in spite of the union drive toward intra-industry and intra-locality uniformity, nominal wage rates vary a great deal among firms. The relatively high-rate employers will have few if any workers below the established minimum rate. The low-rate ones will have relatively large percentages. Again, except where there are strong unions (which is usually not the case in industries affected by minimum rates), the workers in a given firm who are already above the established minimum rate will not receive increases proportional to those gained by their low-skilled, sub-minimum brethren. For example, the skilled and semi-skilled Southern cotton textile workers received much less than the unskilled under the F.L.S.A. from 1939 to 1941; the inter-occupational wage-rate differentials in this industry were narrowed a great deal.

These things being so, we must resort to "particular" rather "aggregative" economic analysis. We have here no question of whether the initiation of minimum wage rates is inflationary or deflationary. The main question is this: In any firm in which the introduction of a minimum rate affects a substantial number of workers, will we find any resulting decline in employment? To answer this question, we must recall from Chapter 8 how employment *might* be adversely affected. (1) A firm might raise the prices of its products, with resulting reductions in quantities sold to consumers. Then employment would fall. (2) A firm might introduce improvements in managerial techniques or more efficient machines. Here, too, employment would tend to decline.

What is the likelihood of these things happening in the real world? It is true that the firm's product demand and employment may rise or fall for other reasons (e.g., an increase or decrease in consumption spending) than the rise in production cost occasioned by the minimum wage rate. But we must rule out such other circumstances in order to concentrate on the issue at hand.

Assume first that the firm is unable or unwilling to introduce technological improvements. Then the cost increase will *tend* to be followed in some degree (probably by an equal number of pennies per unit of product) by a product-price increase. This tendency exists because, given no change in the total demand for all products, management is institutionally and emotionally inclined to follow a cost increase by an equivalent price increase in order to preserve the profit margin per unit of output. (We must remember that the *percentage*-amount by which the product price rises, following an uncounteracted labor-cost increase of a given *percentage*-amount, depends on the technologically determined proportion which labor costs are of total costs. In any case, the percentage rise in product price is less than the percentage increase in labor cost.) But this result is by no means a certain one. The morale and health of the affected workers may be so improved that they become more efficient and productive. Then labor cost — and product prices — need not rise much, if at all. And sales and employment need not fall. (Remember too that, *if* product price rises, the extent of the drop in sales and employment depends on the degree of elasticity of demand for the products.) Furthermore, because a minimum wage rate affects different firms in varying degree, the firm may be forced to absorb out of profits most or all of the cost increase if, as is usually true in industries seriously affected by minimum wage rates, there is keen competition among firms. Here a single firm cannot afford to get out of line.

The other way in which a rise in cost and price can be avoided is for management to install improved methods and machines. But although employment does not fall here because of a rise in product price, it may well decline because of the labor saved — unless all the existing labor is essential and cannot be "shaved" or unless the cost reduction is so large that the product price can be lowered and sales increased substantially. (Here again the price elasticity of demand is a factor.) But, except in keenly competitive industries, firms are not inclined to reduce prices when costs fall.

The introduction of technological improvements is of course usually beneficial to society as a whole. But the short-run effect on employment in the firm may be unfavorable.

Some students favoring or opposing minimum-wage-rate legislation sometimes study affected industries to try to learn how valid an analysis like the above is under real-world conditions. They usually manage to find cases which superficially appear to support their points of view. But a moment's thought must impress one with the futility of such studies. Over a period of time in the real world, all the conditions affecting output and employment are variable. It is usually impossible to isolate the effects of any one of them.

b. Shortened work periods. By itself, a reduction in the length of the work-day or work-week for a particular firm does not raise costs per unit of product unless the firm's operations are sufficiently mechanized to make machine costs important and unless, therefore, the fixed machine costs are spread over fewer units of product, i.e., unit overhead cost rises. Here the increased leisure (decreased number of labor hours) means mainly a reduction in output with no drop in the number of men hired.

But there is also a reduction in weekly earnings. Workers don't like this, so they often ask that the hourly wage rate be raised proportionately to the hours reduction; take-home pay is thus preserved. For this case the economic analysis is essentially the same for a particular firm as that given above under minimum wage rates.

Suppose, however, that by statute or otherwise a reduction in the lengths of work periods is introduced simultaneously throughout the economy. Here again, with no change in hourly wage rates there may be a small increase in unit machine costs. The main result of this shift toward leisure is a reduction in output, with little if any reduction in the total employment of men as such. On the other hand, if at the same time a proportionate rise in wage rates were put into effect, the economic analysis presented in Chapter 22 on general wage-rate increases would be applicable.

CHAPTER 24

Government and Workers in Group Relations

A. NATURE OF GOVERNMENT APPROACH

In the two previous chapters we dealt with legislation enacted and administered by government for the benefit and protection of individual workers. This sort of government action has little to do with workers in their labor relations activities. It aims to help and protect all covered workers whether they are union members or not. It does not deal with them directly in their relations with unions or in their relations, through unions, with employers.

1. Government and private rights and duties. In this chapter and the next, however, we do consider government action in the field of labor relations. We are concerned here with what the attitudes and policies of the federal government and of state and local governments have been in respect to (*a*) the rights of individual workers to form and/or join unions for collective dealing with employers; (*b*) the rights of individual workers *not* to form and/or join such unions; (*c*) the rights of individual workers vis-à-vis the unions (as entities) that they have formed and/or joined; (*d*) the rights of employers in their relations with non-union and union workers and with the unions; and (*e*) the rights of the public as consumers and citizens in relation to collective bargaining between unions and employers.

This enumeration of the persons and groups on whom our interest focuses in these chapters suggests three things.

First, there are five categories of such persons and groups with which government must be concerned — unions as entities; firms as entities; individual union members; individual non-union workers; and that great, all-inclusive group, the consuming public, which is organized only through its governments, but which may be conceived as being in practice something apart from the governments as entities.

Second, in a democracy like ours all these persons and groups are related to each other and held together in a web of mutual, interacting, reciprocal rights and duties or responsibilities which it is government's right and duty to enforce. The rights of each person or group involve the duties of some other person or group; and vice versa. For example, government enforcement of the workers' right or freedom to organize in unions involves a reciprocal duty or obligation on the part of employers not to interfere with this right by most of the methods reviewed on pages 480–484 of Chapter 18. And government enforcement of unions' responsibility not to interfere maliciously with employers' operations establishes employers' rights in such relationships.

Third, government, as the supreme authority, is the only agency in a position to enforce these reciprocal rights and duties evenhandedly, with equal regard for the weak and unorganized, on the one hand, and for the strong and organized, on the other. It is true that a strong union or a strong employer is usually in a position to enforce its own rights directly vis-à-vis other groups. But in the absence of government action only a strong sense of social equity and trusteeship can make it exercise sufficient self-discipline to prevent it from overreaching itself and trampling on the rights and liberties of others. It is also true, as we saw in our review of union history, that government — being more than an abstraction, i.e., being composed of human beings having this prejudice or that bias — has often failed to enforce evenhandedly the rights and duties of all persons and groups. But almost always in a democracy this shortcoming eventually gets rectified by what is often referred to as an "aroused electorate." Sometimes, of course, the new government then swings the pendulum too far in the opposite direction.

In any case, as pointed out in earlier chapters, in the field of labor relations as in other fields the basic democratic ideal to which government must aspire is this: To have no more coercion of any person or group by any other person or group (including government itself) than that amount necessary to insure the full exercise of socially agreed-on rights and the complete fulfillment of socially sanctioned responsibilities. In other words, government should coerce or restrain private persons like workers and private groups like unions and corporations only to the extent necessary to keep these private persons and groups from unduly coercing and repressing each other.

2. Phases of government attitudes and policies. In the survey of union history presented in Chapters 10 and 11, we sketched the development of governmental attitudes and policies on workers' rights to organize and on union activities. Because of the reciprocal nature of the rights and duties of unions and employers (as well as non-unionists and consumers) our discussion in those chapters also inevitably dealt, even if only indirectly or by implication, with governmental attitudes and policies toward these other groups in the labor relations field.

In that survey we learned that five main periods were discernible in respect to the governmental approach. Although in any one period there were significant differences in attitudes and policies among the three branches of government and among the various governmental jurisdictions (federal, state, and local) within the country, the general attitude in each period was unmistakable.

Up to 1830, the chief attitude was one of denying the workers' right to collective action and of *suppressing* such action. Unions were regarded as conspiratorial, monopolistic restraints on free trade and competition. This attitude, of course, greatly favored employers and non-unionists, if not the general public.

During the hundred-year period from 1830 to 1930, the general attitude was one of *grudging tolerance* toward unionism. Workers were permitted to create and join labor organizations; but the activities of the unions were circumscribed in most governmental jurisdictions. In the main, government (especially the judicial branch) was a friendly ally of employers rather than of workers and their unions.

From 1930 to 1935 the effective governmental attitude was generally one of *friendly or benevolent neutrality.* Government, following the change in public sentiment brought on by the long, grim depression, became much more friendly to the principle of collective action among workers and shifted much of its support away from employers. But as yet there was not much really active and direct promotion and encouragement of unionism by government. The main idea was to keep government (particularly the judicial branch) from operating as an ally of anti-union employers. These employers were to be deprived of some of their important legal weapons, such as the injunction against unions. But their non-governmental anti-union measures were to be left untouched. Unions (through strikes and boycotts and measures connected therewith) and employers (through strikebreakers, company unions, and other measures) were to be left free to fight it out on the economic field of battle.

This attitude of friendly neutrality did not last long. Political conditions were such that government came to emphasize the friendliness more than the neutrality. From 1935 to 1947 its approach for the most part may fairly be said to have been one of *union encouragement.* In the minds of those who had this attitude there seems not to have been much differentiation between the concept of the union interest and the concept of the public interest. It now became official policy, as expressed chiefly in the National Labor Relations Act and its administration, not to let organized workers and employers work matters out through their own devices, with government sitting on the sidelines as a benevolent neutral or offering its friendly services to both sides for the mediation of unsettled disputes. Rather did government choose to remove most of the employers' weapons while leaving the unions largely untrammeled, perhaps in the hope that eventually the power of unionism would be built up to a point equaling or exceeding that of employers.

Given government aid and given also the enormous assistance of a tight labor market during and after World War II, that hope was by way of being realized. By 1947, however, to a majority of the country's voters a distinction between the interests of unions and the interests of the general public had come to be evident. They felt that many unions had failed voluntarily to impose discipline and restraint on themselves and had used their weapons and exercised their policies too often without regard for the interests of other persons and groups, including the public. So the representatives of these voters in the federal government and in some of the state governments decided to impose certain responsibilities on all unions, toward the end that a better balance in the public interest would be struck between organized workers, unorganized workers, organized employers, and consumers. Not only did government prohibit or restrict certain union policies and weapons; it also sought to protect the public by intervening more actively and strongly in major union-employer disputes. This period, we said, may also be known as one of *active government neutrality*. By "active" neutrality we mean that government was considerably less aloof than in 1930–35. Government was not by any means hostile to organized labor or, for that matter, to most employers. But there was little inclination to stand on the sidelines and, come what may, let the two parties fight things out. It was coming to be understood that in basic industries such a policy would too dangerously jeopardize the public welfare.

Thus, a major question at mid-century was not, *should* government intervene? but rather, *how far?* Most voters appeared not to regard complete non-intervention as a reasonable alternative. Nor were a majority inclined to view complete intervention (as in Nazi Germany or Soviet Russia, where free unions and free private employers were abolished and the state became all-powerful) as any more reasonable. In terms of our analytical framework of Chapter 3, the voters and their governments in this country were groping for an optimum combination of private freedom and collective security in the hope of maximizing the labor-relations satisfaction of the society.

3. The common law. As we know, there are three main branches of government concerned with union-employer relations: legislative, executive-administrative, and judicial. The first enacts statutes, the second interprets and administers them, and the third provides the ultimate interpretation, including that of constitutionality. But the judicial branch has another very important function, one that is distinct from statutory interpretation. In the absence of any statute on a particular subject a court deals with individual and group rights and duties in terms of the *common law*. In the early days, there were few if any statutes on union-employer relations. Therefore, it is not surprising that, in the history of governmental attitudes and policies toward workers' rights to organize and toward union and employer activities, the first branch of government to deal with these matters was the judicial one.

a. Definition of common law. The common law may be defined as a set of legal precedents and principles embodied in the court decisions of judges on various topics from generation to generation. The common law that has guided American court rulings, in the absence of legislative enactments or statutes on particular subjects, began in medieval England. That is, a common law ruling today is based on the decisions of both early English and more recent American judges. Suppose that some dispute comes before one or more judges in an American court today. They first consider whether there are one or more statutes applicable to the case. If there is no legislation on the subject, they next go to their "law books," i.e., the records of previous cases, to learn whether there have been previous decisions on similar disputes. If previous rulings can be found, the judges select those that seem most parallel with and applicable to the present case. They then apply the principle of these precedent cases to the case in current dispute and hand down their decision.

Of course, the dispute now before the judges may be more or less novel. Its facts may seem not to parallel those in any previously decided cases. Then the judges must create precedent. But even here they are not adrift on an open sea without compass or rudder. There are certain general principles of the common law on which they may rely, e.g., the rule that injury by one firm to a competitor is lawful unless it can be proved that the damage was willfully and maliciously inflicted as the main objective of the first firm's actions rather than merely incidental to the main objective of improving its profits position.

b. Human aspects of the common law. In any field (labor or non-labor) the application of common law precedents and principles to the facts of a particular case allows rather wide latitude and discretion to the judges sitting on the case. It is not hard to understand that in practice the meting out of justice does not usually conform to the ideal concept of the Blind Goddess. To change the figure, there is no mechanical, automatic way of sifting evidence and weighing facts; you don't put the facts into a hopper at one end of a machine, the precedents and principles into another, drop a coin in a slot, and receive from still another slot a card on which is printed the perfect answer. On the contrary, human judgments, beliefs, biases, and prejudices enter at almost every stage — in the questioning of witnesses, the selection of information considered important out of testimony, and the selection of precedent cases and principles. One judge may have a conservative bent because of the way he was brought up by his family, the kind of schools he attended, the wife he married, or for a variety of other reasons. Similarly, another judge may be of a "liberal" turn of thought (because of repression by his parents during childhood, lack of social acceptance by fellow students during his adolescence, or some other condition). Each is unconsciously guided in all his choices by all the factors that affect his way of looking at things. The same facts in a given case will be interpreted variously by different judges on a multi-judge court. That is why there are dissenting opinions in so many cases.

The significance of this for labor cases is obvious. Unionism has long been a controversial matter. It generates strong emotions. A judge who really questions the desirability of unionism, however sincerely and selflessly, has a difficult time controlling this prejudice and being objective in an important union-employer dispute. So does a pro-labor judge.

We do not mean to suggest that the great majority of judges do not try hard to do honest jobs on all kinds of cases, including those involving unions. We do mean to say that as human beings they are susceptible to previous mental conditioning, to the present beliefs and attitudes of friends and associates, and to trends in domestic and international events.

It is socially benefical for judges to be responsive to trends in events. Otherwise there is an overlong lag between the trends of events and the trend in court decisions. It is not good for judges to disregard the wishes expressed by voting citizens on various issues like unionism. If they do, the citizens lose respect for the law and the courts. Fortunately, however, most judges are quite able to listen and read perceptively. They watch the election returns just as elected government officials do. There may well be some lag in their adjustment to events like the Great Depression and the consequent defeat of the Republicans. But most of them do adjust. Only impatient people wish to "pack" the courts (add new judges) in order to obtain decisions consonant with the expressed wishes of the voters.

For all government officials, including judges, a more difficult thing than keeping up with the majority is safeguarding the rights of minorities. It may be that the conservative labor decisions of courts before the New Deal did reflect the attitude of the majority of voters toward unionism. Yet it is hard to see how some of the decisions could have been justified except on the assumptions that most voters did not wish the rights of minorities to be respected and that the judges concurred with this view. It is especially the responsibility of the courts to insure that this principle of democracy is honored.

c. Basic common law principles. Whether or not a given judge has and yields to a pro- or anti-labor bias or to a pro-small-business or a pro-big-business bias in any particular common law case, he is bound to pay attention to certain fundamental principles of common law, even if only to rationalize his bias. Therefore, in order to understand the reasoning of various judges in various court cases on unionism we must understand what these principles have been and are.

(1) The outlook of the common law. The principles of common law were established to define rights and duties in a particular kind of social organization.

In the first place, it is clear that the common law, particularly during the past 150 years in Britain and America, has been designed for a private enterprise society, particularly an atomistic one of a great many small businesses and households. The principles would sound strange indeed for the governing of a socialist, government-run economy.

Second, it is fair to say that the common law has focused mainly on one special aspect of human rights and duties — the right to acquire and hold income-producing property. There has been considerably more emphasis on this than on non-property human rights, such as freedom of speech and assembly. The latter rights seem to have been handled mainly by constitutions and statutes. Under the common law the terms "freedom of contract" and "freedom of trade" are very familiar; and in spite of the fact that they apply also to the buying and selling of labor services, they have mainly meant freedom to buy and sell income-producing goods and property.

Third, property has meant physical things, such as plant and equipment and materials, *and* the right to acquire and hold those things. The common law has given scant recognition to the concept held by some persons that workers have property rights or investments in their jobs. The workers don't own the jobs, say almost all the judges; the places and machines where they work belong to the owner-employers. How then can the workers be said to have property rights in particular jobs at particular plants and firms? To be sure, the skills and abilities that workers have acquired through their own and others' investments are their own properties, to be disposed of as they see fit (subject to the legal restrictions imposed on the use of all property). Freedom of contract and trade (buying and selling) applies to these things. Any individual worker has the right to sell (or not to sell) his labor skill and energy on terms that he considers proper (or improper). But the legal right of workers to sell their skills to any particular firm is no more established than that of a firm to sell its products to any particular customer. This is because firms and customers as buyers have freedom of contract also.

Fourth, no person has an *absolute* freedom or right to use his property as he sees fit. His freedom is subject to the common law principle to be summarized below. His rights are *relative* to the rights of other persons.

Finally, freedom to acquire, hold, and use property in a private enterprise society means, because of the scarcity of property as a whole, competition among individuals and groups. In respect to this competition for the possession of income-producing property, the common law imposes two related limitations. First, competition must be "fair." Certain methods are legal, others illegal. Second, competition ("trade") must not be "restrained" by methods aimed at monopoly. The relation between these two restrictions is plain: Unfair competition eventually creates monopoly or restraint of trade.

(2) Principles establishing limitations on the right to use one's property. What are unfair methods of competing and using one's property? The answer to this question will enable us to understand the general common

law approach to the relation of workers, unions, employers, and consumers.

(a) Individual action. Let us first consider two individuals who are competing with each other, i.e., whose respective rights are in conflict. Suppose that the first is a small firm, A, that in exercising his own competitive rights has put the second (another small firm, B) out of business. Has firm B any common law redress against firm A for having experienced this misfortune? He has if he can prove to the judge of the court one or the other or both of two things: *(i)* His rival had as his main objective malicious injury of this sort. That is, firm A's main purpose was not merely to increase his own profits (or lessen his own losses) or to win a competitive race in which the accepted rule is "the devil take the hindmost." If this had been the purpose, the injury to firm B would have been only *incidental to* and *justifiable under* lawful competition in the use of property; firm B would have no legal redress. But if firm A had definite malice toward firm B and deliberately went out of his normal competitive way to destroy him, we have a different case. Firm A is legally in the wrong. He has committed a "tort" and is liable to damages. (*ii*) Regardless of motive or purpose, firm A used illegal *methods* of competition. He failed to abide by the rules of the competitive game. What are illegal competitive methods? One is fraud, such as dishonest advertising about one's own or one's rivals' products. Another is violence, such as beating up rival salesmen or breaking competitors' plate glass show windows or damaging their delivery wagons. On the other hand, firm A's peaceful, honest, non-coercive persuasion of customers that his product was better than that of firm B would not make his conquest illegal. But suppose firm A, although careful not to use violence or fraud in competing with B, had made veiled threats against B or B's customers. Would this be unlawful coercion and intimidation? Probably, if the judge of the court liked firm B better than firm A or were extremely upright and ethical. Probably not, under opposite circumstances. Or suppose that firm B had been too small to supply all the products that its customers needed; the latter needed to buy also from firm A, which (let us now assume) was much larger. And suppose then that A had told B's customers they couldn't buy from A at all unless they said "no" to B's salesmen. Here again we have a borderline case. Some judges would find firm A guilty of unlawful economic coercion; others would say, in effect, "I'm sorry for you, Mr. B, but that's the way it goes when you tangle with a big fellow like Mr. A."

In short, competitive injury by one individual to another is unlawful and merits legal redress when (*i*) the first's *main* objective was such injury; *or* (*ii*) even in the absence of such a purpose, the first used unlawful methods resulting in such injury.

It should be noted that an aggrieved party does not have to prove *both* malicious objective *and* below-the-belt methods. One of the two is enough. Thus, suppose that a given economic-political contestant is able to prove, when sued, that his motives were pure. Nevertheless, if he can be shown to have used foul means toward his noble objective, under the common law he is legally reprehensible. The common law theory is not like the communist; the ends never justify the means. On the other hand, if bankrupt firm B can prove that A set out to ruin it as a *main* objective, then all A's methods, even the exercise of constitutionally guaranteed rights like freedom of speech, become tainted with the illegality of the unlawful purpose.

How does a judge determine the motive or purpose of a person or firm? How can a judge search into a man's mind and learn whether his objective was mainly to destroy or hurt the other person or to reap gain for himself? The answer reveals the close relationship between means and ends: Actually, a judge cannot delve into another person's mind to determine the motive. He can only infer the motive or purpose from the acts (means or methods) that the person has employed. If fraud or violence have been used, the judge is likely to conclude that the motive was malicious. If no foul play is found, the judge may well infer that the person's main purpose was self-improvement and that any injury to others was only incidental. Some judges have been forthright enough to say that in these cases they consider only the means employed.

(b) Collective action. The common law on the respective rights and duties of competing or opposing groups like unions and associations of firms is the same as on competing individuals, only "more so." It is "more so" because in the common law mind (especially in the minds of nineteenth-century judges in England and America) a group, being a *combination* of individual competitors or contestants, has much more *power* to commit evil, i.e., injury to other competitors or contestants in the economic arena. That is, the acts and motives of combinations were to be subject to special scrutiny and the above-stated common law principles were to be applied with particular rigor.

Fear or mistrust of organized groups led the judges to develop the so-called *doctrine of conspiracy.* A "conspiracy" was defined as a combination of two or more persons ("persons" could mean either legal entities like corporations, or individual human beings like workers) to accomplish an illegal purpose or to gain some objective, not in itself illegal, by unlawful means.

As already suggested, all the principles explained above in respect to the conflict of rights among individuals apply with special force to the conflict of rights between a group and an individual outside the group, or between organized groups.

d. Modes of applying the common law. There are three different ways or modes of action whereby the courts may make application of common law principles: (1) criminal actions; (2) civil actions; and (3) actions in equity.

(1) Criminal actions under common law. Under the first, the executive

branch of government is "the party of the first part." On its own motion or upon complaint by a private person or group, the government brings a criminal prosecution in an appropriate court against the person or organization accused of malicious, unlawful activities. There is testimony by government's and defendant's witnesses, with direct and cross examination by government's and defendant's attorneys. If no statute is involved in the case and if the accused is an organized group, the judges apply the common law doctrine of criminal conspiracy. The principles of this doctrine are those explained above. The use of the word "criminal" simply means that if the accused is found guilty, he is subject to the criminal penalties of imprisonment or fine or both.

(2) Civil actions. This sort of action is brought before a court by a private person or group that considers itself aggrieved or injured by the acts of another person or group and therefore seeks redress. The first is a "plaintiff," the second a "defendant." The court hears testimony by the witnesses of each side, under direct and cross examination by the respective attorneys. In deciding the case the judge applies the principles of the common law; and if the "accused" is an organized group, the doctrine of civil conspiracy is said to apply. The word "civil" simply means that, if judgment is made for the plaintiff, the "guilty" party is "punished" by an award of money damages, which are paid to the plaintiff. In other words, civil damages for the plaintiff here replace criminal fine or imprisonment.

(3) Actions in equity. The injunction. An injunction is an order or writ issued by a court in equity commanding an individual or a group of individuals to do or to refrain from doing certain acts. It originated centuries ago in the British Courts of Chancery, and the idea then, as now, was to provide a quicker and more equitable solution to legal problems of conflicting rights than would result from the operation of ordinary processes of law. In this country, where there are no separate or special courts of chancery or equity, injunctions are granted or refused by the same judges that try civil and criminal cases — judges "sitting in equity."

The nature of the injunction can best be understood by reference to certain *principles* or conditions *of equity* which are supposed to govern the courts in issuing and maintaining them. In the first place, the injunction is an extraordinary measure, to be used only when there is "inadequate remedy at law." The usual legal process open to a plaintiff is a civil action, in which a court judgment gives money damages and the defendant's property is attached to satisfy it. But if the defendant has no property, the plaintiff is left without redress, for he cannot attach the defendant's person. In the past another disadvantage of civil action, especially in suits against voluntary, unincorporated associations like labor unions, was the costly and time-consuming necessity for a "multiplicity of suits"; in some courts separate actions had to be taken against many individual defendants.

In the second place, an injunction is obtainable when irreparable damage is threatened. This simply means that certain property and property rights have such intangible and peculiar values to the owner that if they are destroyed or impaired, the loss cannot be calculated in money and the injury can never be repaired. Under such circumstances the equitable thing is not to wait until the damage is actually done and then go to court, but, upon reasonable assurance that it is seriously threatened, to restrain individuals from committing the injury.

A third principle, however, modifies this concept somewhat: Injunctions should not issue if the loss threatened to the complainant is less than the loss sustainable by the defendant in case it is granted. The best equity practice requires the posting of a bond by the complainant to reimburse the defendant in case it turns out that the latter has been wrongfully enjoined.

A fourth principle of equity is the doctrine that anyone who pays for an injunction must come into court "with clean hands" — must have put his own house in order and be himself guiltless of any unlawful conduct.

Fifth, an exceedingly important development in this country has been the gradual extension, by the courts, of the definition of *property* to include not only tangible wealth, but also *good will* and *the right to do business.* That is to say, courts came to the place where they granted injunctions, not merely to prevent irreparable damage to the physical property of a person or group, but also to keep some other persons or groups from ruining his business by blocking his access to various markets. To put business expectancies into the same category with physical wealth is greatly to broaden the scope of injunctions.

Sixth, the common law doctrine of conspiracy governs the issuance of injunctions against a group just as it governs judicial decisions in other cases arising out of acts of combination. The courts must be convinced that conspiracy exists; and they base their judgment, as usual, on the legality of purpose and the means employed up to that point in the dispute.

Still another principle has been that the injunction must be *served* to those against whom it is directed. It is not supposed to bind those who are not notified. In the earlier years this principle was narrowly construed, but in later years everybody in any way connected with the dispute was included by using the blanket words "all other persons in combination with them."

Finally, there must be some way of enforcing injunctions and securing obedience to their provisions. One of the chief principles of equity, long recognized, is that violation of an injunction constitutes contempt of court. The contempt may be committed in the presence of the court or so near thereto as "to obstruct the administration of justice," in which case it is called "direct" contempt, or it may be committed beyond the judicial precincts, in which case it is "indirect." In either event it has always been settled court law that the judge who grants the injunction has the power and discretion to punish any violation thereof by fine or imprisonment. Here, as in all other steps in equity procedure, the judge acts alone, without a jury (unless jury trial for such contempts is required by statute).

From the time when an injunction is first requested to the time when it is either vacated or made permanent, there are about six *procedural steps.* It is necessary to know something about these in order to understand certain complaints about labor injunctions in this country. A person or group who wants an injunction against another person or group goes to his lawyer and describes the situation. The lawyer takes out of his files a form, more or less standardized, on which the alleged acts already committed are filled in, together with reasons for requesting the injunction. The whole complaint or bill in equity, as it is called, is buttressed with sworn statements or affidavits of witnesses. The first step, then, is the presentation of the complaint to an appropriate judge. If on the basis of the evidence presented to him the judge believes that great and irreparable damage is imminent, he may, without hearing the other side, issue an *ex parte, temporary restraining order* to halt the threatening acts. This is the second step. It is then the duty of the judge to have the other side notified for a joint preliminary hearing, which is supposed to be held five or ten days after the temporary order is granted. Actually, avoidable or unavoidable delays may make the interval considerably longer. The preliminary hearing, which is the third step, seldom involves the testimony and cross-examining of witnesses; it is usually only a battle of affidavits, those of one side commonly being in flat contradiction to those of the other. Out of this bewildering maze of conflicting statements the judge must make a decision — whether to vacate the temporary restraining order or grant a *temporary (interlocutory) injunction.* His ruling constitutes step number four. If a temporary injunction is issued, it may continue or modify the original order. If the defendant is not whipped by this time, as the facts show he usually is, the fifth step is an actual trial, begun three weeks or more after the preliminary hearing. Here witnesses testify and are cross-examined; and on the basis of the evidence adduced in this manner the judge, still without a jury, rules the injunction void or permanent. This final step usually completes the procedure, although in cases believed to be crucial by either party there is still the possibility of appeal to higher courts, which may drag the dispute along for years.

4. The plan of discussion. In the three remaining sections of this chapter and the next, we shall discuss three aspects of government policy and action in the field of labor relations. Section B deals with the relation of government to the worker's right to form and join unions, and with the relation of government to the various policies and tactics that unions, once organized as entities, adopt and try to carry out vis-à-vis individual workers, employers, and the consuming public. Section C is concerned with the relation of government to the measures used by employers vis-à-vis individual workers (who do or do not wish to join unions), unions as entities, and the public. Section D is concerned with government attitudes and policies on the joint relations of unions and employers under conditions of labor relations peace and of labor relations war.

In each of these sections we shall deal, first, with the common or court law, and second, with the statutory law or legislation.

B. GOVERNMENT AND COLLECTIVE ACTION BY WORKERS

As previously suggested, any discussion of the rights and responsibilities of workers and unions implies some consideration of the rights and duties of employers. In Section C we shall focus on the employers; our focus here is on the workers and unions, and our interest centers in two related matters: First, how free, under government, have workers been to organize and join unions? Second, what have been the attitudes and policies of government on union activities, especially those (such as strikes and boycotts) which affect the public?

1. The common law. Unions are combinations of workers. The workers organize to exert collective pressure on employers. A union's immediate objectives are to improve the condition under which the members work and live and to increase and maintain the security and the pressure-exerting power of the union as an organizational entity. In other words, as we saw in Chapters 14–16, unions ask employers for such employee benefits as higher wage rates, shorter work periods, better physical working conditions, pensions, and seniority; and they also demand for the union things like the union shop and the check-off.

Normally, unions do not achieve these objectives merely by asking for them. As we have seen, they have to make employers aware that saying "no" to union demands is not desirable. That is, they have to make it clear that the alternatives to saying "yes" are costly rather than attractive. How can unions do this? They must be able and prepared to exert pressure.

What does the pressure consist of? For one thing it often involves making day-to-day shop life miserable for all levels of management. This is a tactic of infiltration. But the main pressure devices are the strike and the boycott and all the activities connected therewith, as described in Chapter 16. These are the direct frontal and enveloping assaults that can usually inflict the heaviest and most spectacular losses on employers. Keep the employer continuously off the labor and product markets, and you have him on the ropes before very long.

a. Labor combinations as such. "What one worker may lawfully do, a group of workers acting in concert may not lawfully do." This, in substance, was the common law rule on workers' collective action to raise wage rates, as enunciated by the judge in America's first noteworthy court case involving a labor union — the *Phildalephia Cordwainers* (shoemakers) case of 1806. The employing or master cordwainers in this case resisted a demand by their journeymen for higher piece rates and got the city officials to prosecute the local union. The judge, fearing the economic power of the union to raise wage rates and shoe prices, held the combination of workingmen to be a criminal conspiracy in restraint of trade, i.e., in restraint of a free market. He said, in effect, that it was all right for any one worker as an individual to refuse to work for any master who paid a wage rate lower than the one deemed acceptable by the workers. But a combination of all workers to refuse to labor for wage rates lower than those collectively believed acceptable had a much more serious effect on the whole community. It was a conspiracy against the common welfare and therefore unlawful.

For about thirty-five years this judicial attitude prevailed in Pennsylvania and other states. There was considerable doubt about the right of unions to exist as such. Workers presumably might combine to form mutual benefit societies, i.e., to pool their financial resources for the payment of sickness and death benefits. But any economic action, such as striking or boycotting or threatening to do so for higher wage rates or shorter work periods or for closed shops against non-union workers, was considered illegal. Inasmuch as workers form and join unions mainly to exert such economic pressure, the very existence of unionism was in jeopardy.

Union workmen did not take these decisions lying down. Crowds of them publicly hanged judges in effigy. And as shown in Chapter 10, they formed local political parties to try to get statutes enacted that should do away with such common law nonsense. They were not successful with the statutes. But they did succeed in impressing most judges that perhaps the courts had been a bit too harsh.

In 1842, in what had been and in fact continued to be a conservative jurisdiction, namely Massachusetts, Chief Justice Shaw of that state expressed the shift in judicial attitude in his decision in the landmark case of *Commonwealth v. Hunt.* In refusing to declare that a strike of Boston shoe-workers for a closed shop was unlawful, he rejected the notion that a combination of workmen who use economic pressure to gain their ends is a criminal conspiracy as such. He gave one of the clearest definitions of conspiracy to date when he said that the existence of a conspiracy depended on the objectives of the combination and on the means or methods used in pursuit of the objective. The economic power of a labor union was not *per se* inimical to the public welfare. If used mainly to help the organization and its members, the fact that other persons or groups (such as employers and non-union workers) incidentally got hurt in the process did not establish that the use of such power was illegal. And if the union refrained from unlawful methods such as fraud and violence, it could not be judged a conspiracy.

Shaw's decision meant a great deal to the labor movement. From now on, even though they were not regarded as socially "nice," unions were not to be considered as outlaws. They were to be tolerated. And if they behaved carefully, they might henceforth go about their business of putting the economic screws on employers and non-unionists.

b. Specific aims and tactics of unions. It would of course be a mistake to conclude that after 1842 the courts gave organized labor all the rope it needed, including enough to get itself eventually hanged. As just stated, unions had to be careful. And in some states — such as Massachusetts, New Jersey, and Pennsylvania — they had to be considerably more careful than in more liberal states, such as New York. They had to watch their steps in federal courts, too, for the next ninety years. In other words, the judges in most jurisdictions were still conservatively predisposed against unions. Such judges tended to condemn as unlawful certain union objectives and tactics that minority dissenting judges in those jurisdictions (such as Holmes of Massachusetts) and majority judges in the liberal jurisdictions tended to consider lawful.

(1) The strike. Under strike conditions the conflicts among the rights of unionists, non-unionists, employers, and consumers are brought into sharp focus. During practically all of the pre-New Deal period of grudging toleration, when courts were asked to settle these conflicts, the basis of decision was the traditional doctrine of conspiracy as enunciated by Shaw. As applied to strikes, this doctrine, in general, made all strikes illegal where the primary purpose was believed by judges to be to injure employers or non-unionists or consumers rather than to benefit the strikers, or where the means used by unionists to win the strike were believed to involve fraud, violence, or intimidation.

Viewed as mere collective quitting of work in a plant, every strike in private industry is legal, as no court has denied since the celebrated *Commonwealth v. Hunt* decision. This fact has led many persons to believe that workers may strike for "a good reason, a bad reason, or no reason at all" — in short, that workers have an *absolute* right to strike. But the truth is that strikes always involve much more than the mere collective stoppage of labor. For one thing, the workers expect the stoppage to be temporary; they expect to resume work after achieving their demands. For another thing, after the strikers make certain demands on the employer, and after he refuses to grant those demands and the workers walk out, they do a variety of things calculated to bring him to terms. It is these later acts which determine a strike's legality and make the "right to strike" a *relative* rather than an absolute thing. The strikers' rights are relative to the rights of the other parties, and although no court in peacetime will compel striking employees in private industry to go back to work as individuals (this would be "involuntary servitude" and a violation of the Thirteenth Amendment), it may make them cease conducting the strike if it decides that the strike constitutes an unjustifiable and unlawful interference with others' rights. In other words, if a judge says that the purpose of a strike is unlawful, then all collective activities in support of the strike become tainted with illegality. And if workers cannot prosecute a strike, they have lost it. They had better go back to work — just as surely as if the government had ordered them to do so. (Of course it may be difficult for the men to get their jobs back. Under the common law an employer usually has no legal obligation to take them back.)

Before the New Deal period, then, what strike *purposes* did the courts declare legal or illegal, i.e., what strikes were considered justifiable or unjustifiable interferences with employers' and non-union workers' rights? And what strike *methods* were held legal or illegal?

(a) Legality of purpose. As regards purpose, all strikes were lawful in the State of California, where the courts looked only to the means used. In other states and in federal courts a variety of liberal and conservative decisions were made. In general, when the proved motive was to increase wage rates, shorten hours, or improve working conditions, all courts, federal and state, held the strike motive legal. No such unanimity existed regarding other purposes. Although it is hardly possible to generalize on the matter, because the courts of a given state sometimes reverse their earlier decisions, it may be said that in federal jurisdictions, in the New England states, and in New Jersey, Pennsylvania, and Maryland, strikes to enforce a closed shop and secure the discharge of non-union laborers were illegal under the common law. Other strike purposes which received judicial disapproval in those jurisdictions were sympathetic strikes; strikes against working on non-union-made materials; strikes to compel the payment of fines levied on employers or union members; strikes to secure the discharge of foremen; strikes in violation of trade agreements; and strikes against attempts of employers to make their employees sign "yellow dog" contracts not to join the union. The courts of New York (and sometimes those of Wisconsin, Minnesota, Illinois, Ohio, and other midwestern states) were usually more liberal. Although sympathetic strikes were not often allowed, strikes for closed shops and against non-union materials frequently received judicial approbation so long as the union did not possess or use a complete, injurious monopoly of labor.

Thus far, the discussion has been confined to private industry. Workers in public employment, such as federal employees, postal clerks, firemen, and policemen, and in quasi-public industries, such as seamen and railroad employees, have commonly been put in separate categories regarding the right to strike. The public safety and welfare is here a paramount consideration. The usual attitude toward strikes of public employees (both before and during the New Deal period) is exemplified in the famous telegram sent by Governor Coolidge to Samuel Gompers at the time of the Boston police strike: "There is no right to strike against the public safety by anybody, at any time, anywhere." Seamen who quit work at sea can be held for mutiny, and railroad train crews who abandon their trains under conditions which endanger human life can be held for criminal negligence. The right of railway and public utility workers to strike may be subject to special limitation even when circumstances are not such as to menace human welfare directly, because of the very fact that they are employed in businesses "affected with a public interest." Thus far no court has ever actually prohibited such employees from quitting work in concert, but federal judges have enjoined them from "conspiring or combining to quit," which, of course, amounts to the same thing.

After 1935 the courts shifted appreciably toward more liberal interpretations of legality of purpose in strikes. Federal courts were somewhat less hasty in condemning strikes on grounds of the strikers' alleged interference with employers' rights. The same division existed, as in pre-New Deal years, between liberal and conservative state courts (e.g., the courts of New York as compared with the courts of New Jersey), yet even in New Jersey there was an occasional decision permitting a strike for the closed shop.

(b) Legality of means. With regard to the means used in conducting strikes, it should be borne in mind that the common law doctrine of conspiracy made all methods used by the strikers illegal if the purpose of the combination had been proved illegal. Thus, when the motive behind the strike was held to be restraint of trade or inducement of employees to break their "contracts" with their employers, federal courts forbade such things as the payment of strike benefits and peaceful persuasion, which were in themselves lawful. When the purpose of the strike passed judicial scrutiny, however, the legality of the strike was determined finally by court review of the strikers' acts. (It is of course true that the nature of these acts often helps courts to decide whether or not the purpose is legal.) There was rather general agreement among state and federal courts as to what tactics were lawful and unlawful. Peaceful persuasion of strikebreakers, prospective employees, and customers of the employer was *per se* legal. Fraud, violence, and usually intimidation and threats of violence were illegal. Definition of the two latter terms varied, however, because of their vagueness. Liberal courts held that intimidation was accomplished only by actual physical violence or threats of violence, while conservative courts declared that people were intimidated by gestures, looks, grimaces, epithets, jeers, and the mere force of numbers. Whenever employers or workers were made to fear injury to property or person, intimidation was said to exist.

During 1937 the legality of the *sit-down strike* came to the lower courts and to the U.S. Supreme Court for decision. Practically all the federal and state courts that were asked to grant injunctions against sit-down strikers did so, affirming the employers' claims that such strikers were unlawful trespassers on the employers' property and denying the unions' argument that the workers had property rights in their jobs and were peaceably exercising those rights. The courts said in effect (see the decisions in the *General Motors, Chrysler, Fansteel Metallurgical, Douglas Aircraft,* and *Apex Hosiery* cases), that if workers had property rights in their jobs, employers could be forced to buy back their jobs from the workers when the employers wished to lay the workers off or when the workers wanted to quit; or workers could sell their job property rights to other workers, thus making the right to work like any other commodity.

(2) Picketing under the common law. The chief method commonly employed by strikers to "persuade" other workers or the public is *picketing* the employer's plant or place of business. (Picketing is of course commonly used also by unions in prosecuting a secondary boycott. This discussion is therefore also applicable to that subject, dealt with later on.) It is usually done by a few individuals who take their turns on regular "beats" and bring their case to the attention of others by word of mouth or by display of banners, placards, and handbills. Sometimes, however, *mass picketing* is carried on, in which event large numbers of strikers and their sympathizers deploy at the entrances to the plant or store. In such cases, the factor of mob psychology makes the likelihood of violence much greater, especially when the crowd is provoked by the frequently unwarranted roughness or gruffness of employer-controlled workers, police, or special guards.

The legal status of picketing before 1921 was rendered very hazy by the courts. This was mainly because the word had been defined differently in different jurisdictions. All judges were agreed that picketing which was not peaceful was unlawful, but they failed to concur on the proposition that *peaceful picketing* was lawful, some holding that the two words were a contradiction in terms and others believing that peaceful picketing meant the same thing as *peaceful persuasion.* As a matter of fact, the use of the word *picketing* did nothing but becloud the issue, for in the end each court had to discover the specific acts committed and to decide whether they involved peaceful persuasion or violence, threats, intimidation, and so on. When the U.S. Supreme Court of those days finally spoke on the matter, it tried to banish the term from the vocabulary of labor law. In the famous *American Steel Foundries* decision of 1921 it pointed out that *picketing* was a "militant" and "sinister" term. *Peaceful persuasion* would be permitted, but must be defined. Each strikebreaker or new employee should have a right to "a clear passage on an unobstructed street" and "no one may be persistently dogged." Even persuasion from large groups of pickets was held to constitute intimidation, and to prevent this, and at the same time allow the strikers to engage in "missionary" work, only one man at each entrance to the plant was permitted, and each of these should have "the right to observe, communicate, and persuade" without allowing his arguments and appeals to become "abusive, libelous, or threatening." However, all this "is not laid down as a rigid rule." Each subsequent case would have to "turn on its own circumstances," and the decisions should be specific.

In the case of *Truax v. Corrigan,* decided a few weeks later, the Supreme Court held that an Arizona law which, as interpreted by the highest court in that state, legalized mass picketing and countenanced placarding of doubtful veracity, was unconstitutional. Taking the hint, the courts of almost every state outlawed mass picketing and limited the number of "missionaries," although not always to one.

These restrictions did not hold indefinitely. During the New Deal period the state courts had some disposition to permit more pickets to operate than were usually permitted in pre-New Deal days and to permit them to do more things. In other words, some of the courts limited their prohibitions to actual violent acts and were not seriously concerned by mass picketing if it was not openly violent. It remained for the "new" U.S. Supreme Court to establish and clarify a very liberal doctrine on picketing. By 1941, in the *Thornhill, Carlson,* and *Swing* cases,[1] the Court had upheld as a constitutional, free-speech right under the First Amendment all picketing "disentangled from violence"—whether conducted en masse, or in furtherance of secondary boycotts, or by non-employees ("stranger picketing"), or in violation of certain local ordinances.

Many students of the law believed that this new free-speech justification of peaceable, non-fraudulent picketing represented too extreme a swing of the pendulum away from the conservative restrictions of the 1920's. They asserted that although the injection of the First Amendment into labor disputes may well have been a desirable and salutary thing, it is wholly unreasonable and illogical for anyone to take the position that freedom of speech and assembly are *absolute* rights guaranteed by the Constitution against all limitation. The law, they pointed out, has always held that such rights are *relative* to the objectives of the organization exercising such rights. In other words, if a union's objective is judged to be unlawful by a court, then any act, even a constitutionally guaranteed one, must be held unlawful if used toward such an objective. Picketing is more than the exercise of free speech, even if the picketing is perfectly peaceable and honest. It is a method of applying economic pressure and coercion to employers, non-unionists, and consumers. It usually injures these other parties; and such injury is illegal unless justified by the union's direct economic interest in a given case, i.e., unless the main objective of the union can be shown to be its own economic betterment and therefore lawful.

The U.S. Supreme Court did not turn a wholly deaf ear to these arguments. Only a year after its decisions in the three cases cited above, it

[1] *Thornhill v. Alabama,* 310 U.S. 88; *Carlson v. California,* 310 U.S. 106; *A.F. of L. v. Swing,* 61 Sup. Ct. 568.

began to modify its attitude. In 1942 a case came up from Texas.[2] In that state a restaurant owner named Ritter was having a house built, about a mile and a half away from the restaurant, by non-union labor. The Carpenters' local union peacefully picketed Ritter's place of business, rather than the construction job. The union sought to deprive him of customer patronage, food supplies (which were normally delivered by union truckers who now refused to cross the picket lines), and employees (who were also unionized and declined to cross the lines) in order to make him use union labor on his house. The highest Texas court sustained an injunction against this picketing, holding that the union's direct economic interest would have justified peaceful picketing of the construction job but not of the restaurant. The union then appealed the case to the U.S. Supreme Court, claiming a deprivation of the right of free speech guaranteed by the First and Fourteenth Amendments to the federal Constitution. A majority of the nine justices on this highest tribunal upheld the Texas injunction, asserting that the union had no dispute with Ritter as a restaurant-owner and that the Texas court had correctly tried to confine the exercise of free-speech picketing to the sphere of the union's direct economic interest, namely construction. This decision can only mean that under court law, as well as under the Constitution, the right to picket peacefully is a relative rather than an absolute one.

Thus the Court soon seceded from the baldness of its position on picketing as stated in its *Thornhill* decision of 1940. With the *Ritter* decision of 1942, with a number of subsequent decisions [3] by the U.S. Supreme Court upholding state court rulings on the application of state statutes restricting picketing, and with certain subsequent federal and state statutes to be noted below, the legal status of picketing is not very much different from what it was before 1940. The rigors of the *American Steel Foundries* decision of 1921 have been removed; peaceable mass picketing as such, for example, is not taboo. Neither is stranger picketing as such. But the pendulum has undeniably swung back to a middle ground. If the objective of the picketing is unlawful, then all picketing in support thereof is unlawful, no matter how mild and peaceable in itself.

(3) The boycott. From our discussion in Chapter 16 it will be recalled that secondary boycotts by unions are a much more effective coercive weapon than primary boycotts; and that there are two kinds of boycotts — consumer boycotts (which aim to get extra-union consumers to cease patronizing the employer with which the union has a dispute) and factor

[2] *Carpenters' and Joiners' Union v. Ritter's Cafe*, 315 U.S. 722 (1942).

[3] See, for example, *Giboney v. Empire Storage & Ice Co.*, 336 U.S. 490, 1949; and *Building Service Union v. Gazzam*, 70 Sup. Ct. 784, 1950. In the *Giboney* case, a union picketed a wholesale union ice company in Missouri in order to make it stop selling to non-union retail peddlers. If the company had yielded, it would have violated a state anti-trust statute. The objective being bad, all picketing in connection therewith was bad. In the *Gazzam* case, picketing to compel self-employed persons to observe union hours standards was held unlawful.

boycotts (whereby union workers refuse to work with materials supplied by an employer with whom the union has a dispute).

The consumer boycott once rivaled the strike as a way of bringing employers to their knees. It was used mostly to help win strikes (i.e., as a means) and was often continued in case the strikes were lost; sometimes, however, it was the main weapon and arose in the absence of strikes. In either case, the aim of the workers was to keep the employer from having free access to the commodity market (thus reducing his sales and profits), just as the aim of strikes was to hurt the employer by barring him from the labor market. After 1912, however, this kind of boycott, except on a local scale, declined in frequency and effectiveness owing to the almost unanimous disfavor in which it had been held by the courts.

On the other hand, the factor boycott, although equally effective, fared better in most courts. Under the common law most judges found more direct economic-interest justification for its use by unions. Consequently, except for statutory restrictions, there has been little abatement in its use.

Both kinds of boycott fitted into the conspiracy doctrine with ease, both as to purpose and means. If it could be shown that the main purpose was to ruin the employer (or if the boycott unjustifiably interfered with the employer's rights), the boycott was a conspiracy and illegal. Or if coercion, fraud, violence, intimidation, and threats had been used to induce others to join in the boycott, the means were illegal and the combination a conspiracy. On this basis the courts agreed that, in the absence of unlawful acts, *primary* boycotts were legal because only the immediate employees were involved. Before 1911, however, there was no concurrence on the legal status of secondary boycotts. The situation at that time is best described by the words of the Supreme Court in the *Buck Stove* case, which arose out of a widespread and damaging secondary boycott conducted with all the resources of the American Federation of Labor:

> Courts differ as to what constitutes a boycott that may be enjoined. All hold that there must be a conspiracy causing irreparable damage to the business or the property of the complainant. Some hold that a boycott against the complainant by a combination of persons not immediately connected with him in business can be restrained. Others hold that the secondary boycott can be enjoined, where the conspiracy extends not only to injuring the complainant, but secondarily coerces or attempts to coerce his customers to refrain from dealing with him, by threats that unless they do they themselves will be boycotted. Others hold that no boycott can be enjoined unless there are acts of physical violence, or intimidation caused by threats of physical violence.[4]

The position taken by the Court in this case was essentially the same as that set forth three years before in the *Danbury Hatters* case,[5] namely, that the secondary boycott constituted a conspiracy in restraint of the

[4] *Gompers v. Buck Stove and Range Company,* 221 U.S. 418, 1911.
[5] *Loewe v. Lawlor,* 208 U.S. 274, 1908.

employer's and third parties' interstate trade, together with an unjustifiable interference with the rights of the consuming public. Not only was the purpose bad, but also the means employed, however innocent in themselves. Such things as circulars, notices, fair and unfair lists, and placards had been held intimidating and therefore illegal in themselves in the *Danbury* case, but the *Buck Stove* decision made it clear that *all* means (even informing union members about the progress of the boycott, as Gompers did in the American Federation of Labor magazine and convention) were illegal when employed to promote an unlawful boycott. "To hold that the restraint of trade could be enjoined and not the means would be to render the law impotent." Words used by a powerful labor organization "acquire a force far beyond the right of free speech of one man." They were "verbal acts" and therefore enjoinable.

These two decisions throttled labor's use of the boycott, which up to that time had been a very effective weapon. Most of the agitation for the Clayton Act resulted from the Court's use of the Sherman Act to outlaw all secondary boycotts. Similarly, much of labor's demand for the legislation that came to be enacted in the Norris-La Guardia Act of 1932 was based on the Supreme Court's unfriendly interpretation of the Clayton Act's provisions on boycotts.

In respect to the decisions of state judges in the absence of statutory law, the courts of Arizona, California, Montana, New York, Oklahoma, and Wisconsin have declared that peacefully conducted boycotts of all kinds are lawful; and in Missouri, although the legal status of secondary boycotts is doubtful, it has been held that the printing and distribution of circulars for boycott purposes may not be enjoined. The courts of most other states, however, have looked with disfavor on secondary consumer boycotts and, to some extent, on factor boycotts.

The legality of the union label as a negative boycott tool was never seriously questioned by the courts. Most of the cases involving its use came up over the attempts of some employer or rival union to "pirate" a label and employ it on their own products. In the absence of statutory regulation, the common law in most states refused to enjoin or grant damages for its unauthorized use, but many states passed protecting laws, and these were almost always upheld by the courts.

c. The labor injunction. In Section A of this chapter we learned that the conspiracy doctrine could be applied in three kinds of court action, one of which was the issuance of injunctions by courts sitting in equity. It was not until the last decade of the nineteenth century that this kind of government operation assumed first-rate importance in labor disputes. In 1894 the American Railway Union, led by Eugene Debs, who was later to run several times for the Presidency of the United States on the Socialist ticket, conducted a violent strike against the Pullman Company; the strike threatened to stop the operation of most railroads as well as the carrying of the mails. The federal government broke the strike by obtaining injunctions in federal courts against prosecution of the stoppage. Union leaders, including Debs, who disobeyed the injunctions were jailed for contempt of court. And without leadership the strike collapsed.

Anti-union and strike-bound union-recognizing employers were not slow to grasp the lesson of the *Debs* case. After 1895 an increasing number turned to the courts for writs against all kinds of union weapons — strikes, boycotts, and accompanying measures. And most of the courts of the pre-New Deal decades were not loath to grant employers' prayers.

Of all the legal weapons used by firms in those days, the injunction was the one that aroused the most bitterness and fear among unionists. This was in part the result of the preventive and effective nature of injunctions. An employer could halt a union army in its tracks, almost before it launched its offensive. He did not have to wait until the war was won or lost and then try to collect uncertain damages from the union. But the main reason for the unions' hatred of this governmental measure was certain violations, by the judges themselves, of the basic principles of equity that we explained earlier in this chapter.

Let us see what these alleged abuses were. First, a number of objections were raised to the customary injunction *procedure.* Bills of complaints were said to be largely standardized and to allege numerous wrongful acts that often never happened. Certain affidavits of one side or the other were bound to be false, it was claimed, because they so flatly swore to opposing statements. Courts insufficiently observed the "clean hands" and "equal loss" principles, especially when they failed to require employers to post bonds or forfeits. They also granted injunctions on trivial pretexts, thus violating the spirit of the "no adequate remedy" and "irreparable damage" principles. It was unfair, moreover, to grant a temporary restraining order on the insufficient and biased evidence presented by employers, especially because a preliminary hearing might not be held for several weeks and the strike might be absolutely crushed in the meantime, even though the order were vacated later on. Furthermore, appeals were decided at such late dates that, except when fundamental principles of law were at issue, the decisions which actually determined labor's success or failure in specific disputes were those of the lower rather than of the supreme courts. It was also too much to expect decisions in contempt cases to be just. Granted that courts should be empowered to enforce their rulings, why should the same judge who granted the injunction try cases arising out of disobedience thereto? It was practically impossible for him, as a human being, to be impartial under such circumstances. In all other criminal cases punishable by fine or imprisonment the accused person was assured trial by jury.

A second count against injunctions rose out of their so-called "blanket" nature. Instead of confining themselves to specific persons and to specific unlawful acts, as did certain judges in a few jurisdictions like Massachusetts, many judges issued orders which ended with such clauses as "all persons combining and conspiring with them [the unionists] and all other persons whomsoever" and "any interference whatsoever with the operation of the complainant's business." It is true that such injunctions did include all possible law-breaking persons and all possible law-breaking acts. But they also prohibited many law-abiding unionists and others from carrying on lawful activities, such as the payment of strike benefits and the exercise of civil liberties in peaceable fashion. Injunctions such as Judge Anderson's coal strike order of 1919 and Judge Wilkerson's railway shopmen's strike order of 1922 left exceedingly bitter memories in unionists' minds and in no wise increased their respect for the law.

d. The common law and intra-union democracy. It cannot be said that court law did much to uphold or maintain democracy within unions or to protect rank-and-file union members from arbitrary acts of despotic officials. With regard to internal organization and government, unions were held by the courts to be the same as any other voluntary, unincorporated association: The provisions of constitution and bylaws regarding membership requirements, discipline, conduct of business, and other affairs were matters to be determined by action of members. So long as these provisions broke no government law and were administered honestly and regularly, and so long as no member's property or civil rights were violated through the bad faith or fraud of officers or other members, the courts would decline to intervene. However, if a union member or a group of union members could establish the fact of expulsion, suspension, or other disciplinary measures contrary to the agreed-on rules of the union or resulting in the wrongful loss of property interests in the union, the courts usually granted, not money damages, but an order requiring reinstatement or removal of the disciplinary action. Even then, court relief was provided only when the judges had been satisfied that the union members had exhausted all remedies for redress afforded within the unions themselves.

Most students of the problem of intra-union democracy have come to the conclusion that the prevailing judicial attitude toward intra-union relations is archaic. Modern unions exercise great control over the lives of their members; they determine whether, when, where, and on what terms the members work. Any organization possessing such power is a real autocracy unless its members have a voice in determining these policies and unless minority groups have protection against overriding majorities. To treat unions as if they were old-fashioned private clubs or fraternities is to be blind to the realities of the modern economic world.

2. Statutory law and unionism. Having reviewed the attitudes and principles of the common law on workers' freedom to organize and on unions' freedom to use certain measures vis-à-vis employers, non-union workers, consumers, and union members, let us now consider the enactment and administration of federal, state, and local statutes and ordinances which deal with such matters.

a. Federal statutes. In surveying federal labor relations legislation it is desirable to distinguish laws covering non-railroad workers from those dealing with railroad employers. In respect to the first group, the statutes that interest us are the Sherman Act of 1890, the Clayton Act of 1914, the Norris-La Guardia Act of 1932, and the National Labor Relations Act of 1935, as amended by the Labor-Management Relations (Taft-Hartley) Act of 1947. In respect to railroad workers, we shall consider the Erdman Act of 1898 and the Railway Labor Act of 1926, as amended in 1934 and 1951.

(1) Laws covering non-railroad workers. Federal statutes bearing on labor relations cover all workers whose productive activity is a part of the stream of interstate commerce. The U.S. Supreme Court was at first inclined to define "interstate commerce" rather narrowly. But in its 1937 decision in the *Jones and Laughlin Steel Corporation* case (in which employers had challenged the constitutionality of the National Labor Relations Act) and in a number of subsequent cases under this and other statutes, the Court showed its awareness of the interdependence among our society's economic units and of the necessity for a considerable amount of uniform, centralized control over these units. Only purely local firms like independent groceries and dry-cleaning establishments might be said to be exempt from the operation of the federal statutes.

By 1890, when the first federal statute affecting non-railroad unionism was passed, the common law had already established the free rights of workers to form and join unions for collective action. That is, ever since Shaw's decision of 1842 in *Commonwealth v. Hunt,* it was established that *government itself* ought not to interfere and would not interfere with workers' efforts to organize. True, local government officials here and there, acting as agents of powerful employers and misusing local ordinances, sometimes acted to break up or restrict union organizing activities. And certain judges, in their decisions in particular common law cases, so hamstrung union measures that the right to organize had little substance. But these, in the main, could be considered perversions of general public policy. As a consequence, no federal statute affecting labor had or needed a provision saying that henceforth government would permit workers to act collectively.

This statement must not be construed to mean that no federal statute contained a declaration of government policy to the effect that workers should be free to organize. On the contrary, the Norris-La Guardia Act of 1932, the National Industrial Recovery Act of 1933, and the National Labor Relations Act of 1935 (as well as earlier statutes for railroad workers) had such declarations. But these statements meant that workers should be able to organize free of *employers'* interference. As such, we consider them under Section C of these chapters, which deals with employers' weapons and tactics.

(a) The Sherman Act before 1914. The Sherman Act was a federal legislative response to popular demand for regulation of monopolies and "trusts" created by business enterprisers. The first section states that "every contract, combination in the form of trust or otherwise, or conspiracy, in restraint of trade or commerce among the several states, or with foreign nations, is hereby declared to be illegal." Obviously, although this general statement makes no specific mention of labor combinations or labor controversies, the language is broad enough (in the words "or otherwise, or conspiracy") to cover them. Certain writers have studied the congressional hearings and debates which preceded the passage of the Act, in order to learn whether or not the legislators really meant the law to include labor organizations, but have found no conclusive evidence on either side. The point is mostly academic, however, because in interpreting statutes the courts are not bound to follow legislative intent and because even the most liberal members of Congress would not have meant to exempt every conceivable act of labor combination from court control under the Sherman Act.

It is the actual interpretation of the Sherman Act by the U.S. Supreme Court in important cases coming up after 1890 which is significant. The first noteworthy decision was that of the federal courts in the *Debs* case. Here it was held that the union activities constituted a conspiracy in restraint of trade within the meaning of the Sherman Act. The common law principle of menace to the public welfare, however, also played a large part in settling the issue. It remained for the celebrated *Danbury Hatters* case to convince labor that all its tactics were covered by the Act and that here was a most serious obstacle to the attainment of its objectives. In a suit brought against the United Hatters' Union by D. E. Loewe and Company, a Connecticut hat manufacturing firm, because of a successful secondary boycott instituted in twenty-one states, the U.S. Supreme Court declared that the union's acts definitely showed an unlawful conspiracy in restraint of interstate trade under the Sherman Act and awarded for the plaintiff triple damages of almost $300,000 against the union's members. Unjustifiable restraint of trade was said to be the proved purpose of the combination. It was illegal and therefore a conspiracy, and all acts employed to promote it, even the most harmless ones, were also illegal. Although the Court pointed out that because of the general language of the Sherman Act it had been necessary to fall back upon common law interpretation, the *Danbury* decision appeared to be so broad and unequivocal that organized labor was profoundly shaken. Union after union expressed the opinion that labor's rights had been trampled on and that every union effort to improve conditions would be condemnable if the Sherman Act were not amended. Agitation for legislative relief began at once. It was intensified a few years later when another important Supreme Court decision went against the workers:[6] A nation-wide boycott conducted through the American Federation of Labor against the Buck Stove and Range Company of St. Louis was held to violate the provisions of the Sherman Act, and the officers of the A.F.L. were forbidden even to speak or write anything in furtherance of the boycott.

(b) The Clayton Act. For a while labor believed that it had attained its long and persistently sought statutory relief in the Clayton Act of 1914. This Act was hailed by most union chiefs (whether sincerely, or merely for the benefit of judges or union members, it is impossible to tell) as a signal achievement and blessing; and Samuel Gompers, president of the American Federation of Labor, declared it to be labor's Magna Charta and Bill of Rights, the most significant piece of legislation since the abolition of slavery. According to Gompers, the *Danbury* and *Buck Stove Company* decisions had made it possible for the federal government actually to dissolve any labor organization in the country under the Sherman Act. But now, under the Clayton Act, unions, instead of existing only at the sufferance of the Department of Justice, were to be largely exempt from the operation of the anti-trust laws. If union men really believed that the Clayton Act removed the court-interpreted restrictions of the Sherman Act, they were headed for a jolting disappointment and rude awakening, for in decisions on new cases after 1914 the U.S. Supreme Court pursued the even tenor of its common-law way and interpreted the new statute in accordance with the old, well-established doctrine of conspiracy. But it is difficult to understand how labor leaders could have been so misled, unless they were deceived by their legal advisers or dishonest with themselves; for a dispassionate reading of the labor sections of the Act seems to justify no exuberant hope. Certain labor economists have expressed the opinion that the Act is dishonestly worded. Rather must it be said that the language is indefinite and vague. A liberal court might interpret it very favorably to labor; it was the workers' misfortune that most of the important, precedent-setting decisions were made by a preponderantly conservative Supreme Court.

The provisions of the Clayton Act which were thought to help labor appear to be quite modest. A review of Congressional hearings and debates indicates that most of the framers of the bill had no intention of exempting all labor acts from the anti-trust laws, but wished merely to set down in authoritative legislative enactment what was already good and accepted common law. It is desirable, however, to scrutinize the important passages of the Act itself in order to see whether or not labor's extravagant hopes or claims were justified. Section 6 is outstanding. It begins by declaring that "the labor of a human being is not a commodity or article of commerce." But no court had ever held that labor was a com-

[6] *Gompers v. Buck Stove and Range Company,* 221 U.S. 418, 1911.

modity and was for that reason subject to the Sherman Act. It goes on to state that "nothing contained in the anti-trust laws shall be construed to forbid the existence and operation of labor organizations . . . or to restrain individual members of such organizations from lawfully carrying out the legitimate objects thereof; nor shall such organizations be held to be illegal combinations or conspiracies in restraint of trade, under the anti-trust laws." This passage merely restates the common law, namely, that in themselves labor unions are legal; they become conspiracies only when they unlawfully (by illegal means) try to pursue illegitimate objects (injury to employers, non-unionists, or the public).

The other labor provisions of the Clayton Act (Sections 16–25) attempted to limit the issuance of labor injunctions by federal courts. The fact that organized labor tried to get free of liability under the Sherman Act mainly through restrictions on these courts' equity powers is indicative of labor's fear of the injunction.

Section 20 was hailed as the second most important part of the law. It dealt with the subject-matter of injunctions and with the parties to the action rather than with procedural matters, which were handled in Sections 16–19 and 21–25. Certain labor activities which were unlawful under the Sherman Act were apparently made non-enjoinable by the language of Section 20. According to the decision in the *Danbury Hatters* and the *Buck Stove Company* cases, even peaceful persuasion, the primary boycott, and peaceful assembly were illegal if they resulted in a restraint of trade. This was but the common-law view that, if the purpose of a combination is illegal, all means employed to attain the purpose are also illegal. But the second paragraph of Section 20 stated that federal courts should not prohibit these three comparatively harmless methods of prosecuting labor warfare. Indeed, even peaceably conducted secondary boycotts seemed to be legalized. The words are unmistakable in meaning and seem designed to forestall any more decisions as extreme as that in the *Danbury Hatters* case. This admittedly would have been a gain for wage-earners because it crystallized the liberal court view that trade is not unreasonably restrained by peaceful methods.

The first paragraph of Section 20 also seemed to aid labor to a certain extent. A wide area of allowable conflict in labor disputes was apparently given statutory sanction by the provision that injunctions could issue only under extraordinary circumstances in cases "between an employer and employees, or between employers and employees, or between employees, or between persons employed and persons seeking employment, involving or growing out of a dispute concerning terms or conditions of employment . . . ." This seems to mean that labor conflicts as such were to be permissible, not only between an employer and his own employees, but also on a district or nation-wide front between groups of employers and groups of workers. That is to say, workers in various trades or critics or industries might join in a dispute over terms of employment provided they did not disobey the other portions of the Act. Liberally construed, this might mean that even sympathetic strikes are not *per se* illegal.

Section 17 of the Clayton Act prohibited the issuance of temporary restraining orders without notice to the other party unless the employer could show by affidavit that immediate, irreparable injury was threatened. This was merely a statement of the best existing equity law and had no appreciable effect, for more *ex parte* orders were granted after 1914 than ever before. The same section also commanded that preliminary hearings be held within ten days, a provision which was fairly well obeyed. Section 18 required security or bond to be given by complainants so as to reimburse defendants for any costs or damage incurred from vacated, wrongful injunctions. Formerly such security was at the discretion of the judge, and it remained so. Section 19 demanded specificity as to persons and acts enjoined; but, as suggested on page 742, the blanket injunction did not disappear. Sections 21 to 25, inclusive, dealt with the contempt-of-court problem, providing in substance that indirect contempts which were also criminal offenses under United States statutes should be tried by juries instead of judges. This "gave with one hand and took away with another," for all offenses which were criminal by statute had to be tried by jury anyway.

In summary, the Clayton Act by no means gave labor a sweeping immunity from the operation of the anti-trust laws. It merely said that labor groups, as such, and lawful acts for lawful objects would not be considered conspiracies in restraint of trade. It then failed to define specifically what it meant by "lawful" acts and objects. This vagueness of language is found in many passages throughout the Act. It did seem, however, to set down in statute form the best common-law and equity practices and to prohibit courts in the future from calling peaceful assembly and peaceably conducted strikes and boycotts an unreasonable or illegal restraint of trade. Such modest gains should have caused union men to express only moderate jubilation.

At any rate, labor's exaltation of spirit was short-lived. The shouting had hardly died down when the conservative majority of judges sitting on the U.S. Supreme Court bench began to hand down decisions which turned unionists' joy into consternation and indignation. The rulings in four cases particularly — the *Duplex Printing* case, the *American Steel Foundries* case, the *Coronado Coal* case, and the *Bedford Cut Stone* case — plainly showed that labor combinations were still very much subject to the anti-trust laws.[7] The *Duplex* case arose from a strike and an interstate boycott conducted against the Duplex Printing Company (which

[7] See *Duplex Printing Company v. Deering*, 254 U.S. 349, 1921; *American Steel Foundries v. Tri-City Central Trades Council*, 257 U.S. 184, 1921; *United Mine Workers v. Coronado Coal and Coke Company*, 259 U.S. 344, 1922; 268 U.S. 295, 1925; *Bedford Cut Stone Company v. Journeymen Stone Cutters' Association*, 274 U.S. 37, 1927.

manufactured printing presses in a Michigan plant) by New York members of the Machinists' union in an effort to compel the firm to recognize the union. The boycott took the form, mostly, of getting New York printing establishments not to buy Duplex presses, thus destroying the main market. The Court held that the Clayton Act did not contain any prohibitions against calling such a boycott a conspiracy in restraint of trade under the meaning of the Sherman Act. Section 6 protected labor combinations only when they used lawful means for legitimate objects. In this case both means and purpose were illegal, for threats had been used and the aim was to injure the Duplex business. Furthermore, Section 20 did not mean to legalize industrial conflict carried on by employees in one city against an employer in another city and state. "Congress had in mind particular industrial controversies, not a general class war."

This decision left the law just where it had been before 1914, except that the Court did not state that peaceful persuasion and assembly and primary boycott were illegal merely if they caused a restraint of trade. In the *American Steel Foundries* case, however, which arose out of alleged violent picketing against strikebreakers by union strikers, judicial interpretation was given to "peaceful persuasion." Although the Court was careful to say that its ruling applied only to the case at hand, it declared that more than one picket at each factory gate constituted intimidation and was unlawful. Nothing was said about restraint of trade, but labor's cause may have been helped by the statement that the Clayton Act recognized a single employee's helplessness against large modern corporations and made it legal for many to combine to do what one man may lawfully do. However, Shaw of Massachusetts had said this 80 years earlier.

The two *Coronado Coal* decisions were based on a suit for triple damages under the Sherman Act brought by an Arkansas coal and coke company. This company had gone bankrupt as a result of the violent organizational strike activities carried on by District 21 of the United Mine Workers' union. The Supreme Court held in the end that the acts committed by the strikers were an illegal interference with interstate commerce and punishable under the anti-trust statutes. Although legal technicalities led to repeated orders for new trials and the case was finally compromised out of court, a dictum of the Court after the first suit (i.e., a verbal bonus, thrown in for good measure) established the fact that unincorporated labor organizations could henceforth be sued as entities and held liable for damages under the Sherman Act.

The *Bedford* case gave rise to one of the most severely conservative decisions ever handed down by the Supreme Court in a labor case. In accordance with a union rule that no member should work on stone cut by non-unionists, the Journeymen Stone Cutters' union refused to let its members in other states work with stone quarried and cut in the Bedford

Company's Indiana plant; in other words the union called strikes against "scab" stone in a secondary factor boycott case. But picketing was not used against contractors or non-unionists, and violence, threats, and fraud were avoided. The union's sole efforts during the strike were directed toward peacefully persuading its own members to abide by the union rule. Nevertheless, the Court held that the purpose of the action was to destroy the interstate markets of the Bedford Company in retaliation against the latter's refusal to employ members of the union, and therefore, even though the ultimate aim was a benefit to the union and no illegal tactics were used, the organization was guilty of conspiracy to restrain trade. It is obvious that this decision practically nullified any gain which labor had attained or hoped to attain from the Clayton Act. In effect it reduced unions once more to the status which they held after the *Danbury* decision: Any action could be interpreted as being an illegal restraint of interstate trade, and labor's hands could be completely tied by court action. As the liberal Mr. Justice Brandeis pointed out in his vigorous dissenting opinion, with Mr. Justice Holmes concurring, Congress surely did not mean that the Clayton and Sherman Acts should "impose restraint on labor which reminds of involuntary servitude," nor was it meant that these statutes should bear more severely on labor than on corporations; yet in the *Standard Oil, American Tobacco,* and *United Shoe Machinery* cases the same Court, by developing its celebrated "rule of reason," interpreted the Sherman Act to mean that only "unreasonable" restraints of trade are unlawful. It is difficult to comprehend how the Stone Cutters acted unreasonably in the *Bedford* case.

(c) The Norris-La Guardia Act. The outcry raised by organized labor at this decision was almost as loud as the protests following the *Danbury* ruling. No union man doubted now that the Clayton Act had been a hollow victory. But with faith in the efficacy of legislative relief still unshaken, labor leaders began a movement for a new law which should be specific and definite where the Clayton Act had been vague. Conservative courts should not have leeway to interpret the statute contrary to the wishes of the sponsors. Congress was more or less cold to labor's protests up to 1930, but the deepening gloom of depression helped to instill a more responsive attitude, and early in 1932 an overwhelming vote in both Houses gave labor the Norris-La Guardia Act, a law which on its face appeared to supply many of the things the workers had been demanding. Remembering what happened to the former "Magna Charta," however, union leaders were wary of heaping encomiums on the new statute and waited to see how it was treated in the courts. It is true that the new law was long known as the "anti-injunction bill" and that fear of labor injunctions was perhaps the ostensible reason why unions worked for its passage. But injunctions, as well as damage suits, are based on the anti-trust laws and the common law doctrines of restraint of trade and conspiracy,

and the fundamental reason for labor's support of the bill was its fear of repetitions of the *Bedford* case.

Slightly more than half of the Norris-La Guardia Act imposed restrictions on the manner in which federal courts might grant injunctions. The rest of the statute dealt with the subject-matter of injunctions — what might or might not be enjoined — and made no mention of the Sherman Act or the anti-trust laws as such, preferring doubtless to confine its prohibitions to the formerly neglected specific points. The matters of substance which seem to be important are embodied in Sections 4, 5, 6, and 13.

Section 4 contained nine specific actions by unions which might not be enjoined by federal courts; all of them had been declared unlawful and in restraint of trade at one time or another in the cases mentioned above or in other federal court proceedings. According to the provisions of Section 4, no United States court might prohibit workers, singly or in combination, from ceasing to work or refusing work; becoming or remaining a member of a union, regardless of any promise not to do so; paying or withholding strike or unemployment benefits; aiding by lawful means any person participating in a labor dispute who is involved in court action; giving publicity to the facts of any labor dispute by advertising, speaking, or patrolling, or any other method not involving fraud or violence; assembling peaceably or organizing to act in promotion of labor interests in a labor dispute; advising or notifying any person of intention to do any of the acts just mentioned; agreeing with other persons to do or not to do any of the above acts; advising, urging, or otherwise — without fraud or violence — inducing other persons to join in doing or not doing the above acts, regardless of any previous promise made by the other persons to refrain from such acts.

Section 5 of the Norris-La Guardia Act struck directly at the old common law principle which held that an act which was lawful when done by a single person became unlawful when done in concert by a group. Section 5 stated that no persons engaged in a labor dispute should be judged a conspiracy because of doing in combination any of the acts enumerated in Section 4.

In Section 6 an effort was made to forestall any repetition of what happened in the *Danbury* and *Coronado* decisions, as regards "blanket" responsibility for things done by individual union members; hereafter no federal court should hold liable any member or officer of a union for the unlawful acts committed in the course of a labor dispute by any other officer, member, or agent of the union "except upon clear proof of actual authorization, participation, or ratification of such act."

Finally, Section 13 of the Act, by going into great detail as to what might constitute a "labor dispute" and who might participate therein, attempted to guard against an injunction like the one in the *Duplex* case, which was partly based on the fact that the union boycotters were not employees of the Duplex Company.[8] Section 13 declared that all the restrictions set forth in the preceding sections should apply to all labor disputes involving "one or more employers or associations of employers" and "one or more employees or associations of employees" who were "in the same industry, trade, craft, or occupation" and who might have "direct or *indirect*[9] interests" in the dispute. Furthermore, "the term 'labor dispute' includes any controversy concerning terms or conditions of employment, or concerning the association or representation of persons in negotiating, fixing, maintaining, changing, or seeking to arrange terms or conditions of employment, regardless of whether or not the disputants stand in the proximate relation of employer and employee." The provisions of this section undoubtedly made the "area of allowable conflict" national. Apparently this area might even be permitted to go beyond the limits of a given industry; not only might machinists in New York City now further a machinists' controversy in Michigan, but carpenters or railway engineers might enter in, even though their interests were indirect. In other words, sympathetic action such as stranger picketing appeared to be legalized under this statute.

Now let us consider the provisions of the Act dealing with injunction procedure. There appeared to be a few provisions which would be of benefit to labor. Most of them, however, merely set forth in statute form what had always been good practice; nevertheless, if all federal courts could be made to observe good equity practice, a real gain would be registered. Among the new provisions of the Act, Section 7 required the testimony of witnesses for preliminary hearings and not only for final trials. It was also made necessary for an employer to prove that public officers are unable or unwilling to furnish adequate protection for his property. Temporary restraining orders without notice to the other party might be granted only upon testimony under oath which would be sufficient to justify the issuance of a preliminary injunction after a two-sided hearing, and such orders were to become void after only five (instead of ten) days. The bond and security provisions, as well as the specificity provisions, of the Clayton Act were reiterated in Sections 8 to 10. Sections 11 and 12 dealt with contempt of court and marked an actual advance, Section 11 requiring a jury trial for all indirect contempts and Section 12 allowing defendants in all such contempt proceedings to demand another judge if the contempt should arise from an attack on the character and conduct of the original judge.

The Sherman and Clayton Acts allowed the courts to decide what labor activities were lawful, with the result that almost everything was held unlawful if any degree of restraint of trade could be proved. The new

[8] It is true that the *American Steel Foundries* decision granted the right of unions to undertake organization work by lawful means in non-union plants where there are no union members.

[9] Italics are not in the original.

Act evidently intended to give labor the same right as corporations, namely, to restrain trade "reasonably," for it set up a list of specific acts which might not be enjoined and which accordingly might not be considered as evidence of intent to restrain trade unreasonably. As regards the means which might be employed with third parties, labor was to be permitted to use anything except "fraud" and "violence," and these are terms much less vague than "threats," "coercion," or "intimidation."

Right after 1932 a number of decisions by some of the lower federal courts (particularly those of the federal Court of Appeals for the Seventh Circuit) continued to be unfavorable to unions. Other federal courts, however, interpreted the Act in accordance with the spirit or intent of the legislators who passed it, and in time virtually all federal courts followed the latter example. In 1938 the U.S. Supreme Court spoke for the first time on the constitutionality of the Norris-La Guardia Act. Sections 4 and 13 of the Act were upheld in the case of *Lauf v. E. G. Shinner & Co.* In reversing the adverse decision of the Seventh Circuit Court of Appeals, the Supreme Court approved the legality of union picketing activities against an employer who had refused to sign a union agreement and in whose shop the union had little or no membership. In other words the stranger picketing as carried on by the union was not fraudulent or violent, and a "labor dispute" existed within the meaning of the Act.

This decision on the Norris-La Guardia Act itself had been foreshadowed in 1937 by the Supreme Court's upholding of a decision by Wisconsin's highest court on a provision of a Wisconsin statute modeled on the federal Act. In *Senn v. Tile Layers' Protective Union,* an organization which had no members in an employer's small shop had picketed the shop in order to obtain recognition and to compel the employer himself to stop working at the trade. The Court held that this was a labor dispute within the meaning of the Wisconsin law and refused to say that this law violated the Fourteenth Amendment.

After 1938 the court decisions under the Norris-La Guardia Act continued liberal. In part the reason may have been the greater specificity of the Act as compared with the Clayton Act. But mainly it was because new, more liberal judges had ascended the bench and because existing judges had been impressed by the election returns of 1932 and 1936.

(d) The Sherman Act after 1935. The Norris-La Guardia Act did not make the Sherman Act a dead letter in respect to union activities. The former focused on relieving unions from easy blanket injunctions. But there was still the possibility of damage suits and criminal prosecution under the Sherman Act. Here, too, unions' fears were allayed. At least as important, therefore, as the above-mentioned decisions under the Norris-La Guardia Act were two new Supreme Court rulings under the Sherman Act: first, that in the *Apex Hosiery Company* case, and second, that in the *Hutcheson* case.

The Supreme Court's decision in the *Apex* case [10] came during the 1939 term. It was this case that really quieted many of the fears raised among union men by the *Bedford* decision. Here the applicability of the Sherman and Clayton Acts was at issue; the Norris-La Guardia Act was not in question. The case arose out of a violent, property-destroying, sit-down strike conducted for seven weeks, in May and June, 1937, by the Hosiery Workers in the plant of the Apex Hosiery Company of Philadelphia. Production was completely stopped, and 130,000 pairs of finished hosiery (90 per cent for interstate orders) could not be shipped to customers. Only eight of the company's employees were avowed members of the union; the plant was seized and held mainly by union members from other Philadelphia employers' plants.

Clearly the facts of the case would have furnished even moderately conservative judges with ample grounds for following the *Duplex* and *Bedford* decisions: Not only were the means used by the union plainly unlawful, but the company's interstate trade was also stopped completely.

The final decision, by the U.S. Supreme Court with its recently liberal majority, went against the company, however. The importance of judges' attitudes was also demonstrated in the course of the case through the lower courts. At first the company asked a federal district court for an injunction against the strikers on the ground that the Sherman Act was applicable. The liberal judge refused the request, holding that mere stoppage of one company's interstate trade was not enough to justify resort to the anti-trust laws. The Third Circuit Court of Appeals, then preponderately conservative, reversed the district court's decision and granted an injunction on the grounds that illegal means had been used by the union (the old common law doctrine) and that the Sherman Act should be as applicable to interstate commerce as the recently validated National Labor Relations Act. The strike was then forcibly broken up. Nevertheless the company signed an agreement with the union. But it reserved the right to sue for damages, which it did, asking $712,000 under the Sherman Act. The federal district judge, guided by the Third Circuit Court's decision on the injunction, granted the judgment. But the Third Circuit Court meanwhile had experienced a change in personnel; it reversed the district court; on appeal, and finally the case went up to the Supreme Court, which by a 6 to 3 decision denied redress to the company.

The noteworthy items in the decision may be listed as follows: *(i)* The strikers' acts (means) were willfully and wantonly lawless, but redress would have to be sought in the Pennsylvania state courts. *(ii)* The purpose of the strike was to interfere with the company's interstate trade. *(iii)* But this purpose and these means were not enough to constitute a

10 *Apex Hosiery Company v. Leader and A.F. of Full Fashioned Hosiery Workers*, 60. Sup. Ct. 982.

violation of the Sherman Act, in general. *(iv)* Unions *are* subject to the Sherman Act in general. *(v)* But the same "rule of reason" applies to them as to corporations: It must be proved that unions' acts have an effect on the prices of a commodity in the market; that the acts create a monopolistic condition in the commodity market; and that the acts tend to discriminate against certain purchasers of the commodity in the market. In other words, as with corporations, only "unreasonable" restraints inimical to the public interest are unlawful under the Sherman Act. *(vi)* It was not shown that any such effects on the general market followed the strike. The company's output was only a very small percentage of total hosiery products, and the market prices of hosiery did not rise when Apex was prevented from reaching the market. Therefore, the union's acts in this case were not subject to the Sherman Act. *(vii)* To rule otherwise would be to call illegal any strike which interfered with the interstate shipment of products.

Plainly this decision in spirit reversed the *Duplex, Bedford,* and *Coronado* decisions of the Court, even though Associate Justice Stone, who wrote the decision, claimed that it did not.

In *obiter dicta* to the decision, the Court majority went on further to clarify the applicability of the federal anti-trust laws to union activities. The Court would *not* consider unlawful *(i)* the restraints on competition among workers inevitably arising out of their organization in unions; and *(ii)* restraints on competition among employers brought about by strikes or collective bargaining agreements on wages and other terms of employment. To hold otherwise would be to negate the public policy expressed in such statutes as the Norris-La Guardia Act and the National Labor Relations Act. But the Court *would* consider unlawful under the Sherman Act *(i)* union activities in collusion with employers to fix prices and monopolize markets; and *(ii)* union acts which by themselves try to attain such monopolistic objectives.

Early in 1941, organized labor was given additional satisfaction by the Supreme Court's decision in the so-called *Hutcheson* case.[11] Here the Carpenters' union had tried to win a jurisdictional dispute against the Machinists' union in the plants of the Anheuser–Busch corporation by conducting a peaceable strike and secondary boycott. The federal Department of Justice had brought a criminal prosecution under the anti-trust laws, but the Court denied that the Sherman and Clayton Acts forbade such acts as the unionists committed in this case, even though some of the unionists were not employees of the company. The Court thus recognized that the Norris-La Guardia Act, although it dealt with injunctions rather than with criminal prosecutions, was one of "three interlacing statutes" determining labor's rights in any anti-trust question, and in so

[11] *United States of America v. Hutcheson and others,* U.S. Sup. Ct. No. 43, Feb. 3, 1941.

doing, reversed the previous *Duplex* and *Bedford* decisions, which had gone against unions partly because unionists other than the company's employees had been involved in the strike-boycott activities. To state the matter differently, the Supreme Court henceforth not only would apply "the rule of reason" of the *Apex* case to labor activities but also would interpret the Sherman and Clayton Acts on labor matters in the light of the liberal Norris-La Guardia Act.

In summary, organized labor had cause for jubilation over the swing to liberalism in the *Apex* and *Hutcheson* decisions: Unions were henceforth to be treated the same as corporations under the Sherman and Clayton Acts (perhaps even more liberally). But labor's gratification was tempered by the Court's statements that under certain circumstances unions were subject to, rather than entirely immune from, the Acts' provisions.

(e) The amended National Labor Relations Act. Our discussion of federal statutes on the rights and duties of unions and union workers has thus far been presented pretty much in chronological form. However, in view of the way in which our whole survey in these two chapters is organized (the rights and duties of unionists, the rights and duties of employers, and the rights and responsibilities of unions and employers jointly), it is not consistent with our purpose to continue here a chronological story of New Deal and post-New Deal legislation.[12] This is because the first major New Deal labor statute — the original National Labor Relations Act, sometimes called the Wagner Act, after the name of its Senatorial sponsor — focused mainly on the rights and duties of employers; and this law will therefore be considered in the next chapter. The chief federal statute that is relevant to our present discussion is the Labor-Management Relations Act of 1947, i.e., the so-called Taft-Hartley amendments to the N.L.R.A.

The amended N.L.R.A. had two sets of provisions affecting what unions are permitted to do: those protecting employers from abuses of union power, and those protecting individual union members and non-union workers against abuses of union power. We shall consider the Act's relevant provisions in that order. First, however, we must deal with the underlying philosophy of the Act.

i. Philosophy of the amended N.L.R.A. The amended N.L.R.A. undoubtedly is the most comprehensive statute ever enacted by Congress for the regulation of labor relations. It is a complex measure that attempts to deal with a very broad range of problems. And because it is an omnibus measure, it cannot be described by oversimplifications such as "a slave labor law" or a "statute of managerial revenge against labor" or "a Magna Charta for management." The law calls for analysis. Many of its provi-

[12] However, the broad story of the chronological development is contained in Chapter 11. The student is invited to review pages 239–42 and 242–48 in order to have the historical sequence in mind before beginning the present survey.

sions are subject to controversial interpretations. Uncertainty will cloud their status until they have been given full administrative application and judicial review.

The Taft-Hartley Act of 1947 had a history. Immediate precedents for federal regulation of labor relations were available in the Railway Labor Act and in the original National Labor Relations Act. The latter measure was founded upon the assumptions that many labor disputes affect interstate commerce and that the conduct of employers in labor relations contributes substantially to such disputes. The new law built on these assumptions, finding that the conduct of unions and their members also contributes to disputes and should be subject to federal control.

Moreover, there had been a shift of public opinion away from unreserved support of relatively unregulated unionism having governmental support and encouragement, which was the underlying philosophy of the original National Labor Relations Act of 1935. This shift was also shown in the drift of state labor legislation after 1940. A main reason for this change had been the great strike wave of 1945–46, which involved the most important sections of American industry, including the railroads. These strikes dramatically revealed the new-found power of the unions, exerted with maximum effect in an inflationary sellers' market for labor. Without judging the merits of the controversies, it can be said that their impact brought about widespread public demands for regulation of unions. Thus, the Taft-Hartley amendments were primarily a union-control measure, whose omnibus character reflects an accumulation of grievances (rational and otherwise) against unions and a broad attempt to correct them with a single measure.

The philosophy of the 1947 law may be summarized as follows. First, it represented an attempt to establish in law a balance between and a mutuality of rights and obligations in the conduct of labor relations affecting commerce. Second, the public was recognized as a party at interest with rights and obligations of its own. Third, the members of unions as well as non-union employees also became parties at interest, with correlative rights and obligations. Fourth, the attainment of this balancing of rights and obligations was mainly to be achieved, according to the Act, by regulation of certain activities of unions, their officials, and their members; and only to a lesser extent by some redefinition of the rights and obligations of employers. Thus the law endeavored primarily to make labor unions more responsible at law for the greatly increased power they had acquired in recent years.

ii. Provisions restricting union activities in relations with employers. Procedural and administrative provisions. Under the basic philosophy of the original, union-encouraging N.L.R.A., five main anti-union measures of employers were prohibited (see page 786). They were called "unfair labor practices," and their prohibition was to be accomplished by the following procedure: Upon complaint by a union against an employer to an appropriate regional office of the National Labor Relations Board (the three-man agency of public representatives set up by the Act for its administration), the office made a preliminary investigation to learn whether there seemed to be any grounds for the union's charges. If grounds appeared to exist, the office issued a complaint against the employer, and hearings were held before a trial examiner from the National Board. Then facts were obtained through the direct and cross examination of witnesses by an attorney of the regional office and by the employer's attorney. On the basis of the record thus developed, the trial examiner either dismissed the case or wrote an intermediate report containing findings of fact and recommendations on how the case should be decided. Copies of his report were sent to the union and the employer, both of whom had 20 days within which to file exceptions. Unless the employer accepted the recommendations and promised to comply therewith, the next step was action by the Board in Washington. After expiration of the 20-day period the Board decided the case on the basis of the record, the examiner's analysis, any briefs or oral arguments that the parties cared to present, and (sometimes) further evidence if the Board decided to reopen the record. The Board then either dismissed the case or accepted or modified the trial examiner's recommendations. If the Board decided against the employer, it directed an order to him requiring him to "cease and desist" from continuing the unfair practices of which he had been found guilty and ordering him, in appropriate circumstances, to make restitution to injured employees (e.g., the re-hiring and payment of back wages to workers discharged for union activities). The Board was authorized by the Act to obtain enforcement of such orders in an appropriate federal circuit court of appeals. The employer too was empowered to obtain, on his own motion, circuit court review of the Board's order if he considered the decision unjust. No matter who initiated the court action, the court was required under the Act to accept the Board's findings of fact if they were supported by the evidence presented in the record of the hearings. The court could modify or set aside the order or remand the case back to the Board for further hearings or for modification of the order if it found the order wholly or partially unsubstantiated by the evidence or if it found that the Board had exceeded or misinterpreted the powers granted to it under the Act.

Under the 1947 amendments, this procedure for the prevention of unfair labor practices by employers, although changed in certain fairly important respects, was retained in essence. And it was made applicable to the unfair labor practices of unions (see below), which were included in the Act in that year. The main procedural and administrative changes were as follows: *(a)* The personnel of the Board itself was increased from three to five men representing the public. *(b)* The chief administrative officer for the operations of the Washington and regional offices was to be the General Counsel rather than an executive secretary, as previously. The

Counsel's office, moreover, was separated entirely from that of the Board; the former was not to be subject to the control of the latter. The Board was to become wholly a judicial body, with the Counsel exclusively initiating, directing, and controlling all investigations, prosecutions, and enforcement functions. The only operating staff under the Board itself was to be the trial examiners, which are the "lower" judges, and the legal assistants to the Board members. This separation of the judicial from the prosecuting function was largely the result of employers' criticism of the old Board set-up, which had combined judge, jury, and prosecutor in one agency. *(c)* The Board's Counsel no longer was to have exclusive power to prevent the unfair labor practices of employers or unions. An aggrieved party was authorized to take direct action in federal courts, through a request for an injunction or for damages. *(d)* Counsel was forbidden to act on complaints involving charges more than six months old. *(e)* Back pay for suspended or discharged employees was not to be ordered if employers had taken such disciplinary action "for cause." *(f)* In cases where back pay was properly payable to unjustly disciplined workers, unions rather than employers were to be assessed with the pay if the unions were shown to have been the cause of such unjust discipline. *(g)* Compaints by employers or others against the unfair labor practices of unions were to be given priority in the preliminary investigations of the Counsel. And if this kind of investigation established grounds for the charges, Counsel was empowered to ask a federal district, if necessary, for a five-day temporary injunction against such alleged unfair practices. *(h)* Individual workers or groups of workers, rather than just unions or employers, might file complaints against unions or employers. *(i)* Unions were not to be heard as complainants if they failed to comply with the amended Act's requirements in respect to filing financial reports and other information with the Secretary of Labor and filing non-Communist affidavits of officers with the N.L.R.B.

Unfair labor practices of unions vis-à-vis employers. Section 8 of the original N.L.R.A. was devoted to listing the unfair labor practices of employers. This became Section 8(a) of the amended Act; and a new subsection 8(b) was added to set forth the unfair labor practices of unions, which were to be handled under the modified procedure summarized above.

Section 8(b) enumerates twelve union measures that the N.L.R.B. was asked to consider as unlawful. Eight of these have to do with union activities against employers, and will be considered here. The other four deal with unions in relation to individual members or individual nonunionists and will be reviewed later on.

All eight of the prohibited employer-oriented activities were among those that most federal courts had permitted and all federal statutes had been silent on from 1935 to 1947. Henceforth, however, unions affecting interstate commerce would have to take them into account.

(a) It would be an unfair practice for a union to coerce an employer into selecting representatives agreeable to the union for the purpose of negotiating contracts or settling agreements with the union. The employer was to have just as much freedom in choosing his representatives as the union workers had been given under the first N.L.R.A. in choosing theirs. No strike or other pressure or threat thereof to influence the employer's choice was to be permitted.

(b) Under the old law, employers had the duty to bargain with a certified union representing the employees in the bargaining unit. No corresponding duty was laid upon the union, however. Certain unions, such as the United Mine Workers and the International Typographical Union, had at times followed the practice of laying down terms unilaterally and refusing to bargain over them. At other times unions had not bargained in good faith because they believed they could get a better break from some government agency to which their disputes would be referred. These tactics now were made an unfair labor practice.

(c) It became an unfair labor practice for a union to conduct a strike or a factor or consumer secondary boycott against an employer, where an objective of such economic action was one or more of the following: *(i)* to compel an employer or self-employed person to join a union or an employers' association; *(ii)* to force an employer or other person to participate in a boycott against some other firm or person; *(iii)* to make another employer deal with a union if the union had not been certified by the N.L.R.B. as the proper bargaining agency for the employer's workers; *(iv)* to make any employer deal with a union when the N.L.R.B. had already certified some other union as the appropriate bargaining agency for his workers; or *(v)* to force an employer to assign a particular kind of work to one union as against another union (in an inter-union jurisdictional dispute) unless the first union had been certified as the proper bargaining agency for the workers now performing the work.

From 1935 to 1947 under the Norris-La Guardia Act and the Wagner Act, unions had been doing all these things with legal impunity, as a rule. A main reason for union excesses leading to the above restrictions had been the rivalry between A.F.L. and C.I.O. unions, unforeseen at the time the original N.L.R.A. was enacted, plus the liberality of the Norris-La Guardia Act and of court decisions on picketing. Many innocent employers had been caught helplessly in the middle, and the general public also suffered. For example, the A.F.L. Brotherhood of Electrical Workers, powerful in the construction industry, was also a rival of the United Electrical (etc.) Workers for representation rights in the plants of manufacturers of electrical products. When beaten in Westinghouse, the A.F.L. union ignored the N.L.R.B. certification and tried to coerce the corporation into recognizing it rather than the U.E. Its coercion took the form of a secondary factor boycott against Westinghouse products in the construction industry. Such action ignored the democratic rights of the company's workers and left the company itself almost helpless. Coercion of this sort was made an unfair practice by the 1947 amendments. Now the pendulum swung back, particularly in respect to secondary boycotts. The legal status of this form of coercion harked back almost to that existing during the 1920's; that is, it promised to do so if this prohibition were strictly enforced. In short, the 1947 Act substantially amended the Norris-La Guardia Act as well as the original N.L.R.A.

(d) It now became an unfair labor practice for a union to attempt to exact money or other valuable gains from an employer for work not actually performed. This provision was directed against featherbedding practices, such as employment of stand-by crews who do no work, and other devices aimed at forcing employment of unnecessary men who do no work. It is doubtful that the provision would apply to rules that restrict output or compel spreading the job over a minimum-sized crew.

Other restrictions. In addition to prohibiting the above-listed unfair practices, the amended N.L.R.A. placed other limitations on unions' freedom of action vis-à-vis employers.

There were *certain prohibitions and restrictions on what a union and an employer could agree on in a contract,* even if both parties wished to. At least two of the items listed above as unfair union practices were to be held unfair only if a union tried to *coerce* an *unwilling* employer into agreeing to them. Thus, if an employer were to agree to let the union dictate his representatives for collective bargaining, nothing in the Act prohibited such an agreement. The employer would make no complaint, and the N.L.R.B. would normally have no case. But if the employer resisted and complained to the Board, the union could be told to "cease and desist." Similarly, an employer or self-employed person could agree to a union demand that he join a union or employers' association. Again there would be no one to complain to the Board (except perhaps individual, unorganized persons, who would be unlikely to have the necessary knowledge and financial resources). On the other hand, in respect to the other unfair practices (such as recognizing an uncertified union or preferring the "wrong" union in a jurisdictional dispute or helping a union in a secondary boycott), an employer could not with impunity come to an agreement with a union, because normally powerful, watchful third parties, other unions or other firms, would be on hand to complain to the Board. Moreover, the words of the Act on payments for work not performed ("high" featherbedding) make it clear that the Congress meant such a union demand to constitute an unfair practice even if an employer agreed to it. The Act said it would be an unfair practice for a union to "cause" (rather than "coerce") an employer to pay for unperformed work. However, there might be no one sufficiently interested or able to complain to the Board about such an agreement. It should also be noted that this provision was not directed against such minor items as call-in pay, pay for time lost during machine breakdown, paid vacations and holidays, paid rest and lunch periods, and employment-wage guarantees. Rather was it designed to eliminate major featherbedding items like the hiring of unneeded crews of musicians and electricians.

Under the amended Act there were other union measures which, while not listed as unfair labor practices in Section 8(b), were nevertheless prohibited or restricted by other sections. Chief among these were such basic union-security items as the closed shop, the union shop, maintenance of membership, and the check-off of union dues, fines, and assessments. These union policies of course affect individual union members and individual non-union workers and accordingly must be remembered for our discussion below which covers the relations between unions and these individuals. But they are also relevant here because they limit what unions can demand from employers and get them to agree to.

The original (Wagner) N.L.R.A. made it an unfair labor practice for an employer to discriminate against workers, in respect to hiring or job tenure or terms of employment, on the basis of their membership or non-membership in any labor organization. But attached to this prohibition was a proviso which permitted employers to agree with a union to discriminate against non-union workers. In other words, employers were permitted to agree to a closed union shop or any other form of union security if they wished to — and a good many did, particularly in certain industries like construction and printing. Many other employers however, objected to the union security demands and succeeded in obtaining from the Republican-dominated Congress, in 1947, amendments which in substance outlawed the closed shop agreement and placed certain restrictions on the union shop agreement and on the check-off. The union shop (and presumably the maintenance of membership) agreement was permitted only in the following circumstances: if a petition to the N.L.R.B. showed that 30 per cent of the workers in a bargaining unit certified by the Board wished to have such an agreement, and if thereafter, in an election conducted by the Board, a majority of all the workers eligible to vote in the unit chose to ask the employer for such a contract. (The amended Act did not permit such an agreement to require newly hired employees to join the union sooner than 30 days after they were hired.) With respect to the check-off, the amendments permitted an agreement for the check-off of union membership dues (including initiation and reinstatement fees and some kinds of assessments, but not including fines) only if the employees voluntarily gave the employer a written authorization therefor and if such authorizations were made for not more than one-year periods at a time, or to the period up to the termination of the agreement, whichever was shorter.

Two other Taft-Hartley provisions relating to the union shop should also be noted. First, once a union shop election had been conducted by the N.L.R.B., no new election could be held within a year after the first one. Second, after such lapse of time the petition and election procedure could be used by employees wishing to rescind the previous action, i.e., throw out the union shop.

A final item on which union-employer agreements were restricted was that which is sometimes broadly characterized as "union welfare funds," such as the one set up by the Musicians' union out of "royalties" paid on phonograph records by record-producing companies and the one set up by the Mine Workers out of "royalties" paid by coal-mining firms on produced coal. Such funds, said the Act, could be agreed to by employers only under the following conditions: if the union fund was of the trust type; if the basis of benefit payments was set forth in detailed written agreements; if the benefits were restricted to employees and their dependents; if the trust funds covered medical and hospital care, insurance against death, sickness, accidents, and disability, unemployment, and superannuation; if a separate fund was provided for pensions; if the plans received annual audits; and if the funds were jointly administered by union and employer, with provision for a neutral person to break any union-employer deadlock.

Union trust funds established prior to January, 1946, were exempted from most of these limitations. In this way, certain unions like the Musicians were relieved from full compliance.

These limitations, moreover, would apply only to *union* trust funds. They would not cover benefit payments (such as group life insurance) which were made directly by employers to union members, even though the plans had been established by union-employer agreement.

In addition to placing limitations on the subject-matter of union-employer bargaining, the 1947 amendments contained another group of restrictions which may be characterized as *those intended to make unions more responsible* in their relations with employers, members, and the public.

First, the obligation of both parties to bargain collectively was declared to embrace meeting to discuss in good faith wages, hours, and other conditions of employment,[13] with the aim of reaching agreement. Neither party was to be obliged to accept a given proposal or to make a concession. Further, the duty to bargain collectively provided that either side might modify or terminate the agreement, and perhaps strike or lockout the establishment, only if it had met the following requirements: had given the other party 60 days' advance notice of the proposed termination or modification, the 60-day period to precede the expiration date of the agreement, or if no expiration date existed, then 60 days prior to the date the termination or modification was to take effect; had offered to meet with the other party to negotiate a new agreement; had notified the

[13] This implies no express limitation upon the topics a union may introduce for bargaining, including matters often described by employers as "prerogatives exclusive with management."

federal Mediation and Conciliation Service and the similar state agency, within the first 30 days of the 60-day period, that a dispute existed, if agreement could not be reached within the first 30 days; and had maintained the existing contract fully in effect for the full 60 days or until the expiration date if it should occur after the 60 days had passed.

The intent of this proposal was to compel employers and unions affected by the Act to delay resort to economic warfare during a 60-day cooling-off period (or until the expiration date of the contract). The provision applied to disputes concerning changes in existing contracts. Employees who struck in violation of these conditions would lose their status as employees so far as Sections 8, 9, and 10 of the Act were concerned; that is, such employees would be deprived of the benefits of the Act. Finally, this part of the Act compelled resort to mediation (within 30 days) in all unresolved disputes involving changes of existing contracts.

Second, the law permitted an employer or a union to bring suit in the federal courts for violation of collective agreements between them. Such suits could now be filed regardless of diversity of state citizenship between the parties, and, where the union was defendant, regardless of whether it was an incorporated body or not. Furthermore, each party was made legally responsible for the acts of its agents, though the Act provided no definition of what an agent actually is. Finally, the Act specifically declared that previous authorization or subsequent ratification of the acts of supposed agents was not to be controlling in the determination of whether the activities in suit were committed by an agent.

This provision applied formally to both parties to collective agreements. Actually, it was of particular importance in making labor unions liable to damage suits in the federal courts for striking in violence of no-strike clauses and, further, for wildcat strikes. Wildcat strikes in violation of such clauses became actionable regardless of whether responsibility was fixed upon the union itself.

In addition, unions were also made liable to damage suits in the federal courts for losses brought about by commission of strikes and boycotts undertaken for purposes described above as unfair labor practice of unions.

Third, as a condition of investigating of a union's claim to representation as certified bargaining agent or a union's complaint against an employer for unfair labor practices, the N.L.R.B. was required first to make sure that the union had filed with Secretary of Labor copies of its constitution and its by-laws and a report that included the following information: names of its three principal officers and others receiving over $5000 a year, with actual amounts; manner of their selection; amounts of initiation fees and dues of members; details regarding admission and expulsion of members, elections, authorizations of bargaining demands, strike expenditures, and ratification of contracts; and a financial statement, for the last fiscal year, regarding assets, liabilities, receipts, disbursements, and purposes of such outlay. This information must be kept up to date for each year, with annual financial reports.

Fourth, as another pre-condition to investigation of any question concerning a union's claim to certification as bargaining agent or its anti-employer complaint, the Board was required to have on file an affidavit, no more than a year old, from (*a*) each officer of the union in question and (*b*) each officer of any national or international labor organization of which it is an affiliate or unit, that he was not a member of the Communist Party, was not affiliated with it, and was neither a member nor supporter of any organization believing in or teaching the overthrow of the United States government by force or other illegal or unconstitutional methods. False affidavits were to be liable to action under the criminal code.

Fifth, the Act made it unlawful for any labor organization, as well as for any business corporation, to make certain political contributions or expenditures. The restriction applied to presidential and congressional elections, to primary elections pertaining to selection of presidential and congressional candidates, and to associated political conventions and caucuses. By specifying "contributions *or* expenditures," the provision suggested that certain political activity as such by the organization (as distinguished from its members) was precluded, as well as direct financial outlays in behalf of parties or candidates. On this basis, endorsements, petitions, publicity, and vote-getting campaigns by unions might be affected.

Sixth, it was made unlawful for any individual employed by the federal government or by any of its agencies or corporations to participate in any strike. Violation was to mean immediate discharge, forfeiture of civil service status, and ineligibility for re-employment for three years. This provision did not preclude federal employees from joining a union or prohibit such unions from attempting to bargain collectively.

iii. Provisions restricting unions in relations with individual members and non-unionists. Whether because they were afraid of big unionism and wished to weaken it or because they were sincerely concerned over the attenuated, disappearing rights of the individual person, unionist or non-unionist, in a society of large organizations, the members of the 1947 Congress included in their amendments to the original N.L.R.A. several provisions aimed at protecting such individuals from union power and possible autocracy.

First, Section 7 of the original N.L.R.A. was a short paragraph stating in general terms the rights of workers to form, join, assist, and bargain collectively through labor organizations, free of interference by employers. This was the same kind of statement that had appeared as a declaration of public policy in the Norris-La Guardia and National Industrial Recovery Acts. But now something new was added — a statement that individual workers should have and did have the right to be free *not* to form and join unions. Clearly this addition gives notice to unions that they must modify their coercive practices in respect to non-unionists.

Second, the amended Act sets forth specific prohibitions against undue coercion by unions and puts teeth into enforcement of the restrictions. The list of unfair labor practices of unions, in Section 8(b) included these four items: (*a*) While maintaining unions' rights to establish their own rules for eligibility to membership, the Act forbade them to "restrain or coerce" individual workers in the exercise of both general rights stated in Section 7. Specific union acts to be outlawed were not mentioned here, however. (*b*) But the next paragraph, in conjunction with other portions of the amended Act, made it clear that the Congress wished to protect individual non-unionists' employment opportunities by prohibiting the closed shop and restricting the prevalence of the union shop (by means of the election procedure discussed above). In other words, no union could demand that an employer refuse to hire a non-unionist; and unless a union shop had been obtained in the prescribed manner, no union could demand that an employer discharge or otherwise discipline or discriminate against a non-unionist already hired. (*c*) Even if a union shop had been duly won, this same paragraph (8,b,2) also tried to protect union members against possible abuse of the union's expulsion or suspension power. It prohibited the union from asking employers to discharge or otherwise discriminate against or discipline ex-union members or would-be members on any ground other than that such workers had refused to pay initiation fees and periodic dues which were the same for them as for the members in good standing. In other words, so far as the Act was concerned, union officialdom could toss a member out of the organization for any reason — or no reason at all. But it could not lawfully demand his discharge or demotion by the employer if the ousted member was willing to continue paying regular dues; his job was to be kept safe for him. (*d*) In protection of both existing and would-be union members, the Act forbade unions to charge, under an approved union shop agreement, initiation fees which the N.L.R.B. might find excessive or discriminatory.

Section 14(b) of the amended N.L.R.A. also made it possible for even more onerous restrictions to be placed on the security arrangements of unions that claim jurisdiction over workers whose employers are in interstate commerce and are therefore subject to the N.L.R.A. Suppose that such unions operate in a state which has legislated complete prohibitions (rather than restrictions) on the closed shop, the union shop, maintenance of membership, and the check-off (see below for a summary of state legislation). Then Section 14(b) of the Taft-Hartley Act says that the state statute takes precedence. A union successfully following the federal procedure could have a union shop under the federal law — but not in a state prohibiting such a shop altogether.

Third, in respect to the settlement of grievances the Congress also tried to give individual union members and non-union workers employed in a unionized plant some protection against the arbitrary use of power by a union machine. Section 9(a), which in general dealt with questions of union representation and election, provided that, although a duly certified and recognized union should be the exclusive bargaining representative of all the workers in the bargaining unit in respect to wage rates and other terms of employment, any individual employee or group of employees in the unit was to have the right to present grievances to the employer and obtain settlement thereof, without the intervention of the union. However, the settlement of the grievances could not be inconsistent with the terms of the union-employer agreement. And union representatives were given the right to be present during the presentation and settlement. Through these last two qualifications it was hoped that labor-relations snarls would be avoided.

iv. Experience with the amended Act since 1947. Political acceptability. Organized labor was vehemently opposed to any change in the Wagner Act, under which it had fared so well. Perhaps most employers and non-unionists were in favor of the 1947 amendments. But many were indifferent or found their operations hampered rather than helped by the added legal tape. And many employers, faced with a tight labor market and fearing bad reactions from hard-to-replace or hard-to-get workers, declined to take advantage of their own legal prerogatives and of the unions' legal disabilities under the amended statute.

But the important A.F.L., C.I.O., and unaffiliated unions covered by the new law had long memories of previous employer anti-unionism. They feared that anti-unionism might be revived if and when the country experienced substantial unemployment again. And in any case, they resented the imposition of any curbs on their strength. Accordingly, they used all their individual and collective political power to obtain its repeal. And until the latter part of 1951 President Truman and his administration were committed to this end. The unions, however, failed to establish that they had suffered much from the amendments (except possibly in their efforts more fully to organize the South). And in the absence of such a showing, the public at large remained apathetic and the Congress refused to respond affirmatively to labor's request for wholesale repeal. By the end of 1951 most unionists, as well as the Democratic administration, were beginning to consider favorably the possibility that a better plan would be to undertake piecemeal revision of the Act — amendment or repeal of specific sections that could be shown to have failed of their purposes or to have become outmoded and useless or subject to widespread evasion.

N.L.R.B. and court decisions; legislative changes. Effects. Let us see what has happened to the important specific provisions of the Labor-

Management Relations Act of 1947. There is space here for only a short summary.

In accordance with the intent of the Act the N.L.R.B. in several cases has ordered unions to stop refusing to bargain in good faith with employers. In most of these cases the unions had insisted, as a condition of entering into an agreement, that the employer must agree to a closed shop (which was made illegal under the Act) or to a union shop, without going through the required election procedure. Such insistence was held to be evidence of refusal to bargain in good faith on the proper subjects of collective bargaining.

We said above that, if strictly enforced, the unfair labor practices paragraphs of the 1947 Act on secondary boycotts would place unions under virtually the same legal restrictions as before 1933. Has this happened? Not completely. The N.L.R.B. and court interpretations of these provisions have been rather moderate. True, in many cases the Board has found unions guilty of conducting unlawful secondary boycotts and has ordered them to cease carrying on all activities connected therewith (as the courts used to do under the conspiracy doctrine), including peaceful non-mass picketing and the publication of lists of employers who are "unfair" or whom "we don't patronize." And employers have for the most part been relieved of union picketing designed to force them to accept a union or join an employers' association or recognize a non-certified union.

But at least three loopholes have been found in the Act. The first lies in narrowing the definition of secondary boycotts. The Teamsters have fared well here. If this union has a dispute with a trucking employer, it is permitted to picket his trucks and the products carried therein, not only at his home base but also at the business places of any customers to which the trucks may have been driven by non-strikers. Pressure is thus exerted on the customers. But the Board has ruled that, so long as the picketing is confined to the trucks carrying the "hot" cargo, the boycott is only primary. Second, the N.L.R.B. has held that, if employers have previously agreed in their union contracts not to use "scab" materials and products, the ban on secondary boycotts is not violated when unions ask such employers to live up to such promises in respect to the products sold by employers with which the unions have disputes. This is an enormous loophole if unions can get employers to include such clauses in their agreements. Third, in furtherance of a boycott unions can picket any employer, such as a railroad, or any employees, such as supervisors, who are excluded from the coverage of the statute by the definitions of "employer" and "employee" written in the statute.

The ban on featherbedding has had little force. One reason is the disinclination or inability of affected employers or workers to lodge complaints against unions who might be committing such an unfair practice. Another is the administrative difficulty of defining in a practical way "payment for work not performed." The Board has held lawful the payment of wages to workers who merely were physically present but did no actual work, such as stand-by musicians. Apparently featherbedding would officially exist only if workers were paid while absent from the employer's place of business.

The Board has used sparingly its power to issue orders against jurisdictional strikes and thereby to determine inter-union jurisdictional disputes. It was pretty much relieved of the necessity of invoking this power by the action of the A.F.L. construction unions and the C.I.O. in voluntarily setting up their own systems of settlement, as explained in Chapter 12.

The prohibition on the closed shop has not been effective. Before 1947 more than 4.5 million unionists worked under closed shop arrangements, and it is doubtful that this number has diminished significantly, if at all. The great majority of employers who had agreed to this form of union security before the N.L.R.A. was amended had become accustomed to the closed shop — or even liked it. Furthermore, they disliked disturbing their relationships with their unions. Hence they filed very few complaints. Individual non-union workers, having slender resources, were also disinclined to file complaints. As a result, there were and are numerous bootleg closed shops. True, the closed shop issue did reach the N.L.R.B. in cases involving at least three important closed shop industries — maritime, construction, and printing. In each of these the Board won a technical victory. Employers were not to agree to hire exclusively through union hiring halls unless these did not discriminate against non-unionists. But in practice the employers ask no questions, and the union usually supplies only union men.

On the other hand, the amended Act's provisions on the union shop generally met with union-employer compliance. The N.L.R.B. had some trouble with conservative unions like the Mine Workers and with left-wing unions like the United Electrical Workers. The U.E., for example, demanded this form of security but legally could not obtain it because their officers had refused to file the non-Communist affidavits required by the Act. But by and large, the Act's procedures were observed. During the period from August, 1947, to October, 1951, about 46,000 union shop polls were conducted by the Board. In 97 per cent of these the petitioning union was rewarded with a union shop authorization. Of about 6.5 million workers eligible to vote in these elections, 85 per cent actually voted; and of these, 91 per cent favored the union shop. In the face of this overwhelming evidence of workers' interest and willingness, a rather surprised Congress made its first change in the amended Act. It struck out the election requirement for union-employer agreement on the union shop. However, the Act still said that such agreements are not legal unless the union's officers have complied with the non-Communist affidavit requirement. And any rescinding of such an agreement must still be obtained through an election.

It appears also that there has been substantial compliance with the Act's check-off requirements. But these provisions seem to have had little effect on union security.

The requirements of the Act on welfare funds may have led to some tightening of the provisions and administration of these funds. How much, it would be hard to say.

What success has the Act had in raising the level of union responsibility for keeping the peace? It is difficult to learn whether the 60-day cooling-off period has made for an increase in the number of non-strike labor settlements. However, it is quite clear that, given the high-employment conditions of 1947–51, employers have not taken much advantage of their opportunities to sue unions for damages from wildcat strikes and other breaches of contract. It may well be that the possibility of such suits has produced greater union self-discipline. Here again the answer is not clear. We may note, however, that the unions have been increasingly reluctant to include the customary no-strike promise in agreements negotiated since 1947.

The great majority of unions have complied with the requirement to file financial and other reports with the Secretary of Labor. However, a few of the large, important unions (mainly in the building trades) have chosen to ignore this provision. Thereby they lose the benefits of the Act. But these organizations feel securely intrenched and doubt that they need the Act for survival and progress.

In respect to the non-Communist affidavit, the situation has been mixed. Most unions have complied, but a number of large unions have refused. Some of these are conservatives in leadership; here the officers' stand is based on the principle that it is undemocratic to require *any* test of loyalty, whether the test be non-membership in or non-affiliation with the Communist Party, the Holy Rollers Church, or whatnot. Other unions are left-wing in leadership; here the motive for non-compliance may be based partly on principle and partly on dislike of choosing between truth and falsehood. The conservative unions are usually so strong that they do not need the support of the N.L.R.A., which they lose by non-compliance. The left-wing unions, however, are not in this position, and they have lost considerable strength through adherence to their policies.

The ban on union contributions and expenditures for political purposes does not seem to have been effective. For one thing, "expenditures" is too broad a term. In 1948 the U.S. Supreme Court held that this part of the prohibition was unconstitutional when applied to the publication of editorials in union periodicals advising members how to vote on candidates for election to the Congress. It would seem, then, that the prohibition is valid only in respect to the campaign funds of particular political parties and candidates. But if the C.I.O. and the A.F.L. have their own private organizations for getting out the labor vote in behalf of particular candidates, these organizations can receive union members' contributions and can make any expenditures they wish for this political purpose.

How effective has the Act been in protecting individual union members and non-union workers against abuses of union power? First, in a number of cases the N.L.R.B. has found unions guilty of the unfair labor practice of "restraint and coercion" against non-unionists and rival union members. It has ordered these unions to desist from using physical violence, threats of physical violence, and threats of economic reprisal where strikes were in progress, organization campaigns were being conducted, or elections between rival unions were in the offing. In such decisions the Board may be said to have taken a middle ground in comparison with the decisions made by the courts under the common law in the years before the Norris-La Guardia Act. Second, the Board has given force to the Act's provision that a union cannot cause an employer to discipline or discriminate against members for any reason other than non-payment of dues and fees. Third, in spite of these significant gains for the protection of individual workers, unions' discrimination against certain dissenters and minority groups (such as Negroes) within the ranks of their members or would-be members has been allowed to persist because of the Act's provision that nothing shall interfere with unions' rights to prescribe their own rules for membership, as long as the rules are applied uniformly to all applicants and members.

(f) The Anti-Racketeering Act of 1946. Congress in 1934 passed an anti-racketeering law that made it a felony to obtain money or property through use of threats or force, where such acts affected trade or commerce. Force or coercion connected with the payment of wages by a bona-fide employer to a bona-fide employee were excepted from coverage. Thus a threat to strike, or the coercion implied in an actual strike, did not become a crime under the original Act. However, a threat to strike could constitute a crime under the statute if the purpose was to "shake down" employers for the profit of racketeering union officials, providing the threat affected interstate commerce. This principle was sustained in *U.S. v. Compagna, et al.* (CCA–2; 1947), a case involving blackmail of motion picture producers and distributors.

However, the principle was not sustained in a Supreme Court case in which the Teamsters union had used threats and violence to compel truck operators to pay a full day's wage to union men for each non-union truck crossing the New Jersey state line en route into New York City.[14] In that case, the Court held that conspiracy under the Act involves the aim of obtaining money without rendering adequate service, and that violence is subject to state and local law and not to control under the Act. The union, in this instance, stood ready to furnish service in exchange for the

[14] *United States v. Local 807, International Brotherhood of Teamsters, et al.*, (315 U.S. 521) (1942).

wage payments; agreement had been made between bona-fide employers and employees; and in the opinion of the Court, the union employees were acting within their rights to insist upon the union scale even if the employer rejected their offer to work. Actually, coercion and threats had been employed, acts of violence had been committed, payments of money had been obtained, and no services had in fact been rendered in exchange. Thus the reasoning of the Court appears to rest, in exempting the case from the Act, on the grounds that a bona-fide agreement had been reached, an offer of services had been proffered in good faith, while the acts of violence involved were *intrastate* rather than *interstate* and hence not covered by the language of the statute.

The limitations implied by this decision helped bring about a strengthening of the law in 1946. As amended, acts of robbery and extortion that affect or obstruct interstate commerce become felonious. Robbery is defined as unlawful taking of property without consent, by use of threatened or actual violence; extortion is defined as obtaining property by consent exacted through wrongful use of threatened or actual force. More important, the amended law eliminates the original clause exempting wages paid to bona-fide employees by a bona-fide employer if obtained by actual or threatened force or violence. Removal of the exemption may lay unions and their members open to punitive actions where a strike or threat to strike, if it affects interstate commerce, is used to compel an employer to pay wages for work not actually performed, regardless of a bona-fide employer-employee relationship.

(2) *Statutes covering interstate railway workers.* On the subject of protecting employers and individual workers from abuses of union power, there is little to note in the legislation governing labor relations on the interstate railroads of the United States. This fact does not necessarily mean that there is no need for such protection. It does point to the political potency of the twenty-odd unions having members in this industry. In the past, but especially since 1933, railway labor laws have reflected the influence of these unions much more than that of the carriers.

We note here, then, only the following points: First, the Railway Labor Act of 1926 (sometimes known as the Watson-Parker Act), as amended in 1934, prohibited all forms of union security, including the closed shop, the union shop, and the check-off. The brotherhoods covering train operation were so well organized that they felt reasonably secure without these measures. But the unions in the non-operating fields were actively afraid of these union-security devices because at that time they were not strongly organized. Many railroads, such as the Pennsylvania, had company unions among the shop crafts, clerical workers, and freight handlers. The weaker non-operating organizations feared that railroad management would use the union security measures to entrench the company unions.

Fifteen years later all this had changed. The operating organizations were as strong as ever, and the non-operatives had used the Act to drive out virtually all company unions and enroll the great majority of non-operating workers in their organizations. There was now little to fear from railroad management. The sole remaining threat to the security of some of the railway unions was raiding by rival unions. Consequently, union security measures became attractive, and the unions asked the Congress to provide them. Accordingly, in 1951 the Railway Labor Act was amended to permit carriers and certified unions to agree on the union shop and on the check-off union dues, fees, and assessments (but not fines). In general the provisions of the amended Section 2 of the Act were similar to those of the Taft-Hartley amendments to the N.L.R.A. But there were three significant differences: (*a*) No elections had to be held to determine whether the employees in the bargaining unit wished to have the union shop. (*b*) The period within which any existing non-union employee or newly hired non-unionist had to join an appropriate union was set at 60 days. (*c*) Regardless of these provisions, operating employees were to be permitted to continue changing their memberships from one union to another (e.g., an engineer could change from the Locomotive Engineers to the Locomotive Firemen and back again) if and as they wished, so long as they belonged to some appropriate organization.

b. State statutes regulating union activities. (1) Scope. Because modern economic society is so big and complicated and its economic units so interrelated, and because the United States Supreme Court through its definitions of interstate commerce has given such broad scope to the application of federal labor statutes like the N.L.R.A., one might be led to conclude that intrastate industry is insignificant and that state labor relations legislation is unimportant. Both conclusions would be erroneous.

In respect to intrastate industry, we may note that about 25 per cent of the nation's labor force is employed in local retail stores and service establishments, local and intrastate transport and public utilities, and other intrastate firms. (Agricultural and domestic workers are excluded from the coverage of both federal and state labor relations laws).

In respect to the state legislation, the statutes must be important if so many intrastate workers are subject to them. Their importance is greatly increased by three things: (*a*) From the beginning the N.L.R.B. adopted the policy of granting jurisdiction, to state agencies administering state labor relations acts, over firms like big stores and brokers who, though technically subject to a broad interpretation of interstate commerce, were predominantly local in nature. One reason for this was that the Board did not have enough money and people to handle such firms. Another was that the Board really believed the state agencies could take better care of such cases. In its 1947 amendments to the N.L.R.A., the Congress approved this sort of delegation, but limited it to states whose laws were consistent with Taft-Hartley principles. This limitation restricted cooperation with states like New York, whose labor relations acts still adhered to the pattern set by the original Wagner Act. (*b*) As previously noted, the Taft-Hartley amendments contained a provision granting precedence to state-law provisions on union security, even in respect to interstate firms having plants within the states. (*c*) The Supreme Court has ruled that state laws can regulate various aspects of labor relations in interstate (as well as intrastate) plants if the Congress has enacted no federal statute which would cover the interstate plants in such matters. For example, certain state laws regulate the internal affairs of unions.

(2) History. Only about half the states have given serious attention to union-employer relations. Some of these, however, are the most populous and most highly industrialized.

Understandably, the temper of much state legislation has been influenced by federal labor relations enactments. From 1931 to 1938, about fifteen states passed statutes very similar to the federal Norris-La Guardia Act. Then from 1937 to 1945, seven states (Connecticut, Massachusetts, New York, Pennsylvania, Rhode Island, Utah, and Wisconsin) enacted laws modeled on the original N.L.R.A.; at the time of enactment, therefore, these seven "little Wagner Acts" were concerned with restricting employer rather than union activities.

But in 1939 Pennsylvania and Wisconsin amended their statutes so as to control union activities. And in the same year Michigan and Minnesota passed laws like these amended acts. That is to say, in that year the number of "little Wagner Acts" was reduced to five; and four acts that might be termed "little Taft-Hartleys" came into being. In 1943 Colorado and Kansas joined the latter group, followed soon by Hawaii and Puerto Rico. In 1947 Massachusetts partly and Utah wholly deserted the earlier camp for the later one. All these statutes could be called "labor relations acts" in the sense of the original or the amended N.L.R.A. Almost all created counterparts of the N.L.R.B. to administer their laws; but Kansas and Michigan left administration to regular law enforcement officers or to suits in courts, thereby making the laws largely inoperative because of the delays and expenses for grievants involved in court litigation.

Between 1939 and 1948, however, fifteen other states passed laws which certainly *affected* labor relations, although they are not to be designated formally as labor relations acts. All these statutes were aimed at curbing or controlling unionism. Because they were concerned mainly with prohibiting or limiting the various forms of union security, they were sometimes known as "right-to-work" laws. Most of them appeared near the end of the war or just after. The reasons for their enactment were the same as those previously listed to explain the enactment of the Taft-Hartley amendments to the N.L.R.A. However, it should be noted that most of the severest restrictions were enacted by the states south of the Mason-Dixon line and west of the Mississippi river — states where economic activity is less industrialized and attitudes more individualistic than elsewhere.

Beginning in 1948, the pendulum reversed its direction once more. It did not swing back to its 1937 position; nor is it likely to. But because of the greatly increased effectiveness of the C.I.O.'s and A.F.L.'s organizations for political action and education, and because of the significantly reduced frequency and severity of strikes, a number of state legislatures were induced to repeal or modify their union-regulating statutes. Outright repeal of legislative restrictions occured in Delaware, Louisiana, Maine, Missouri, and New Hampshire. In Michigan and Massachusetts there was some relaxing of regulatory measures.

(3) *Nature of major provisions.* There is no space here for a detailed analysis of state law provisions as they existed in 1951. Nor for the most part need we distinguish between the labor relations acts and the right-to-work acts as such. It will be sufficient to note the general nature of the restrictions and controls.

(a) *Restrictions on strikes, picketing, and boycotts.* As of 1951, several states severely restricted the right of unions in public utilities to strike for any reason. In a number of states strikes in other industries for particular objectives (such as the closed shop, "sympathy" for other unionists, and jurisdictional supremacy) were banned. Some states required that any strike, to be lawful, had first to be approved by a majority of the workers involved. All these measures are "conservative," even in terms of the common law as it was before 1930. Sit-down strikes, slowdowns, and sabotage were prohibited also, but these had always been illegal under the common law.

All picketing in furtherance of an unlawful purpose was banned in most of the states having labor-control laws. Among the specified unlawful purposes (in addition to those mentioned above) were secondary boycotts, union-security strikes (such as those to coerce workers into joining a union or to coerce employers into discriminating against nonunionists), strikes against employers' recognition of unions certified by state labor boards, strikes in violation of labor agreements with employers, and picketing the homes of workers.

Most of the states also prohibited mass picketing no matter whether the purpose of the strike was lawful or unlawful. Some laws even required that non-mass picketing must be authorized by a majority vote of the workers involved.

(b) *Restrictions on union security arrangements.* All states permitted the check-off of union dues and fees under restrictions similar to those imposed by the amended N.L.R.A. In other words, the automatic, involuntary, indefinite check-off was prohibited.

In respect to the closed shop and the union shop, one must distinguish between the labor relations acts and the right-to-work acts. Most of the former permitted both kinds of shops under certain restrictions. Only three states required elections among the workers of the bargaining unit (a three-fourths approval being needed in Colorado, a two-thirds approval in Wisconsin, and a majority in Kansas). Some states, like Massachusetts and Pennsylvania, require unions to be non-discriminatory as to membership requirements before they can have such union security. All the right-to-work state statutes prohibited all form of union-security shops.

(c) Regulation of unions' internal affairs. About a dozen states had provisions, similar to those in the amended N.L.R.A., requiring the unions to file financial reports with state agencies and also to distribute the reports to their members. Other regulations on unions' internal affairs varied greatly among the states. Colorado required the state industrial commission to pass upon the propriety of union fees and dues. It also specified the periodicity and procedures of elections for officers and demanded union incorporation; but these requirements were held unconstitutional by the state supreme court. Kansas, Minnesota, and Wisconsin also regulated union elections. Kansas and Texas required the registration and licensing of union business agents and organizers, but the U.S. Supreme Court held the Texas requirements unconstitutional under the First Amendment.

c. Local ordinances. All communities of any size have their own laws for the protection of citizens from various molestations, misdemeanors, and crimes. Under these, many things as vagrancy, door-to-door peddling, the distribution of advertising matter, the holding of public meetings, marching and parading, and trespassing on private and public property are regulated and controlled.

During organization campaigns, strikes, and boycotts, union organizers and officers have to sell the union cause to potential members and to the public. They need to distribute advertising, hold meetings, perhaps parade, and so on.

It is easy to see that law-enforcement officers can, if they wish, use against unions the city ordinances that relate to these activities. They can pick up and jail union organizers and officers on charges of loitering or vagrancy. They can refuse permits for the distribution of leaflets and for public meetings and parades. And they can be rough in so doing.

In the pre-New Deal years all these things did happen in many cities, especially those of modest size where one or more big employers dominated the local officialdom and demanded active anti-unionism. But elective and appointive officials can read election returns and other barometers of popular feeling and attitude even more sensitively than court judges. So, except in outlying areas of the South and West, the harassment of union men engaged in their lawful activities has tended to disappear within the last couple of decades.

A few decisions of the U.S. Supreme Court in 1939 hastened the change of heart among local authorities. In the *Lovell* case, the Court declared that freedom of the press and of speech was infringed by a local ordinance of Griffin, Georgia, which required permits for the distribution of leaflets. Henceforth, presumably, such ordinances could not be invoked against union-organizing activities. In the *Hague* decision, the Court outlawed

Jersey City's notorious methods of breaking up organization work through use of disorderly conduct, illegal assembly, and anti-placard ordinances.

It required four agencies of the federal government to establish union organization rights in "bloody Harlan" County of Kentucky during the 1930's. The La Follette Committee of the Senate conducted extensive hearings and brought to light many of the brutal, illegal methods used by the sheriffs and their deputies to help the coal companies resist unionization. The National Labor Relations Board ordered the Clover Fork Coal Company to re-hire discharged unionists and to cease its anti-union practices. The Circuit Court of Appeals upheld the Board's order. The Department of Justice instituted criminal prosecutions against certain coal companies and deputy sheriffs for conspiring to deprive citizens of rights guaranteed by federal law. In this action the local jury disagreed, but so much national publicity had been focused on Harlan County that finally the companies decided to recognize the United Mine Workers and concluded a collective agreement with the union. Discharged unionists were re-hired, company unions were disestablished, and the union persuaded the Labor Board to drop its cases against the companies.

CHAPTER 25

Government and Workers in Group Relations (concluded)

C. GOVERNMENT AND EMPLOYERS

Our task in this concluding chapter is, first, to consider (a) the common and statutory law on the union-oriented policies of employers, and (b) government attitudes and policies on union-employer relations with the public; second, to appraise the adequacy of all the government policies considered in this and the preceding chapters.

1. The common law. *a. General approach.* In the absence of statutory restrictions, employers had a distant advantage, under the common law, over unions and over workers who wished to form or join unions. This was true whether an employer wished to smash a union outright or was merely engaged in a temporary conflict with it over the terms of a new contract. In part, the reason for this superiority lay in the pro-employer attitudes of most judges before 1930 and in the greater financial strength of employers. But the main reason seems to have lain in the nature of the common law itself. The common law was devised to balance the rights and responsibilities of competing, conflicting *individuals.* If its principles (recall pages 724–27) were applied rigidly, as they usually were, it inevitably favored the stronger individuals. To the common law a big strong corporation was an individual person just the same as a weak worker. It took some time for judges to recognize that affording equal protection of the law to all individuals really meant treating the weak unequally.

Why was this? At common law an employer had the right to use his property (plant and equipment) as he saw fit, subject only to the restriction that he must not *intentionally,* i.e., as a main objective, injure other persons in so doing. *Incidental* injury was lawful. By the same token an individual worker had the right to try to use *his* property (labor skill and energy) as and wherever *he* saw fit, subject again only to the restriction that he must not intentionally harm anyone in so doing. This seems like equal treatment under the law. But it did not work out that way. This common law principle meant that an individual employer could employ or refuse to employ, for work on his property, any worker for any reason that suited him — color of eyes, membership in the Methodist Church, membership in a labor organization, or whatnot. It also meant that an individual worker could work or refuse to work for any firm for any reason he saw fit. But clearly, unless an individual worker had as good alternative opportunities for employment as the individual employer had for getting suitable workers, the application of this principle worked relative hardship on the worker. We have seen that an individual worker's alternatives are usually much more limited than those of an employer. Therefore the common law favored the employer.

Consider now collective action among workers who have organized a union. Here an individual employer may well lose his economic advantage in dealing with the workers. But under the common law he gains an additional legal advantage: Unless the employer acts in concert with other employers in some sort of employers' association, he is not subject to the doctrine of conspiracy. But the union with which he is faced is so subject.

b. Specific applications of the common law. Let us briefly note how the common law was applied to certain particular measures used by employers in their relations with unionists and unions.

Employers were perfectly free to form associations for the operation of uniform policies in respect to unions. Penalties for non-observance of uniform, voluntarily, and mutually agreed-on policies were enforceable in the courts against recalcitrant employers. As a voluntary organization, such an association was subject to the conspiracy doctrine; the motives and methods of the group vis-à-vis unions was subject to the tests explained in Chapter 24. An employers' association was free to try to operate "open shop" and avoid union recognition. But the main purpose of the combination could not lawfully be to destroy the union; and the methods could not legally include violence, fraud, and threats of violence. Here again we seem to have equality of treatment. But in practice it was usually more difficult to apprehend wrong-doing in employers' organizations than in unions because the membership of the former was in hundreds or less, while the membership of unions often ran into tens and even hundreds of thousands. In short, secrecy was much easier to preserve and conspiracy harder to prove.

Lockouts by individual employers or associations thereof were always legal. Particular tactics used to win a lockout might be held unlawful. But the right of employers to withhold their property from employment by unionists was never questioned.

Under the common law, employers had full right to try to win strikes through the use of non-union workers and professional strikebreakers. If a striking or locked-out union had the right to try by peaceful means to bar an employer from access to the labor and product markets, he had a corresponding right to try to obtain and maintain such access.

The common law also protected the employer in his efforts to avoid unionization before a strike or lockout occurred. (1) He was free to hire and use labor spies in order to learn workers' sentiments and unionists' plans. (2) He was legally free to use a blacklist of union workers or a whitelist of non-unionists for hiring and employment-tenure purposes, if such lists were developed and employed by him alone for his own purpose. This right was implicit in the right to use his property as he saw fit. But if such lists were circulated among a number of employers, the group might be liable under the conspiracy doctrine if the main purpose could be proved to have been deprivation of employment opportunities for union men. Nevertheless, in practice it was very difficult for union workers to obtain civil damages or criminal convictions in such cases. Because the lists could be circulated and used in almost complete secrecy, evidence of their use and of malicious intent was extremely hard to get. (3) Discriminatory discharge or other discipline of workers for union activity was wholly legal at common law under the property-use principle. (4) Employers were also entirely free to ask their existing workers as well as job applicants to sign, as a condition of obtaining and retaining jobs with the employers, "yellow-dog" contracts — promises not to join or aid unions. In other words, the contracts were lawful instruments. It was not the contractual aspect of the yellow-dog practice that made it so valuable to employers, however. Although an employer could sue his employees if they breached the agreement, it was practically impossible to prove damages in such instances. In short, perhaps the chief obligation of workers to carry out their written promises was moral rather than legal. And in truth, the psychological effect on the average employee of signing an anti-union contract was probably not inconsiderable. It remained for the Supreme Court, in its celebrated injunction decision in the case of *Hitchman Coal and Coke Company v. Mitchell,*[1] to show employers the real worth of the contracts as an anti-union weapon. It was here definitely established that union organizers would not be allowed to solicit members among employees who had signed agreements not to join unions while continuing in employment. In the *Hitchman* case the Court held that the agents of the United Mine Workers, by trying to seduce the company's miners into joining the union, not only used methods which were not above-board, but also interfered unjustifiably with the employer's rights. The union's right peaceably to ask other workers to join was not sufficient to support incitement to break contracts. "The right of action for persuading an employee to leave his employer is universally recognized." Although the federal courts continued to restrain union organizing activities which conflicted with anti-union contracts, certain

[1] 245 U.S. 229, 1917.

state courts were more liberal. Basing their decisions on the declaration by Chief Justice Taft, in the *American Steel Foundries* case, that the Supreme Court had not meant to prohibit all union efforts to persuade non-union men to go on strike and that the determining factor in the *Hitchman* case had been the deceptive means employed, judges in New York and Ohio held that unions might legally try to induce "contract" workers to join the union and participate in strikes.[2] Indeed, the New York court took the liberal and realistic position that anti-union contracts, being terminable at will and reserving unlimited discharge privileges for employers, were so one-sided that they could not expect the same protection as real commercial agreements. The courts of many other states, such as Massachusetts and Pennsylvania, however, followed the federal decisions and enjoined all union interference with anti-union contracts. So serious did the situation seem to organized labor, and so incensed did unions become over what they believed was a direct alliance between most courts and employers, that widespread efforts were made to secure state and federal statutory relief. Labor claimed that the judiciary had with few exceptions made it lawful for employers to operate a shop closed against union men, at the same time that it had held unlawful most union efforts to secure a shop closed to non-union men. In the eyes of the courts, the employers' methods of discrimination against unionists did not constitute coercion or intimidation, yet unions' methods of discrimination against non-unionists were commonly held to involve coercion and therefore constituted a conspiracy. The property right thus was believed to transcend the labor right. (5) Employers who wished to organize "company unions" or employee representation plans had a perfect legal right to do so under the common law.

From the summary given above, it is evident that in most jurisdictions the application of common law principles gave employers in most industries a formidable advantage in conflicts with unions. Small wonder that the latter worked long and vigorously for statutory relief from law made by judges.

2. Statutory restrictions on employers' activities and decisions. As we know from Chapter 11, organized labor succeeded finally in obtaining such relief. The statutory restrictions on employers were insignificant before the Great Depression had changed most men's thinking. But when the tide turned, it did so sweepingly.

As in Chapter 24, we shall consider first federal legislation, then state legislation. And because legislative efforts to redress labor's legal disabilities came first in respect to interstate railroads, we shall deal with

[2] Cf. *Interborough Rapid Transit Company v. Lavin,* 247 N.Y. 65, 1928; *Interborough Rapid Transit Company v. Green,* 227 N.Y.S. 258, 1928; *La France Electrical Construction and Supply Company v. Brotherhood of Electrical Workers,* 108 Ohio 61, 1923.

them before reviewing what was done to control non-railroad employers.

a. Federal statutes. (1) Laws applying to interstate railroads. (a) The Erdman Act. The first effort by the Congress to curb anti-union railroad employers came in the Erdman Act of 1890. This statute, although relying for enforcement only on existing federal law-enforcement officers and the courts (rather than on a special administrative body), contained a provision (Section 10) declaring it a misdemeanor for railroad employers to discharge employees on account of membership in unions or to make non-membership a condition for securing employment. But the United States Supreme Court decided, in the case of *Adair v. United States,*[3] that such a limitation of the employer's absolute right was unconstitutional, i.e., that it constituted deprivation of property without due process of law under the Fifth Amendment.

(b) The Railway Labor Act of 1926. The Congress made another try in 1926, when it passed a new Railway Labor Act (the Watson-Parker Act). One of the main provisions of this Act stated that union representatives for collective action should be self-chosen "without interference, influence, or coercion" by employers. In other words, the Congress wished to forbid the use of all discriminatory tactics by the railroads against members of the railway unions. The administration of the provision was still left to the courts. Nevertheless, in 1930 the U.S. Supreme Court ruled in a split decision that this prohibition was constitutional (in the case of the *Texas and New Orleans Railroad v. Brotherhood of Railway Clerks*[4]) and thus paved the way for similar provisions in the National Labor Relations Act of 1935. In this case, the railroad had tried to foster a company union and break the bona-fide Clerks' organization by discharging unionists, revoking their passes, otherwise discriminating against unionists, and paying non-unionists to support the company union. The Clerks then sued for an injunction, got it, and won the appeal.

(c) The 1934 amendments to the Railway Labor Act. The enactment of the 1926 statute and its favorable interpretation by the Supreme Court may perhaps be attributed chiefly to the political potency of the railroad unions. But the depression would have produced the same result. The Norris-La Guardia Act, discussed in Chapter 16, was passed in 1932; and then in 1933 came the Democratic New Deal administration, with its union-encouraging attitude. The way was paved for statutory restrictions on non-railroad employers and for a stronger Railway Labor Act. This Act was importantly amended in 1934.

i. Basic philosophy of the amended Act. Fundamentally, the framers and supporters of the Railway Labor Act wished to establish an enduring labor peace on the railroads by making collective bargaining between outside unions and railroad managements the normal, universal labor-relations practice. Not only did they wish to ensure continuance of this practice in the train-operation branch, where it had been well-nigh universal

[3] 208 U.S. 161, 1908.

[4] 50 Sup. Ct. 427.

because of the strategic position of the Big Four Brotherhoods, but also to introduce it in the shops, yards, and offices, where non-unionism still existed in a good many railway companies because of the economic weakness of these workers in the face of their employers' opposition to unions in these branches of the industry.

ii. Provisions. Only those parts of the Railway Labor Act which deal with interstate railroad workers' freedom to organize without interference from railroad managements are considered here.

The language of the Act was strengthened in its prohibitions against railroads' interference with, influence on, or coercion of their employees in making free choices as to what labor organizations to belong to. This meant that the fostering of company unions, the use of yellow-dog contracts, and all kinds of anti-union discrimination were banned. However, union representatives who lost work time traveling or conferring on union business might be given free transportation and compensatory pay by the carriers.

The majority-rule principle was included in a "permanent" federal statute for the first time in the clause. "The majority of any craft or class of employees shall have the right to determine who shall be the representative of the craft or class for the purposes of this Act." Although the word "class" might permit an administrative body to designate, on an industrial-union basis, an entire shop or division or railroad system as the "appropriate" unit for collective bargaining, the word "craft" was emphasized because of the dominant craft unionism of organized railroad labor.

"Teeth" were furnished for the first time in an employer-curbing law; railroad employers found guilty of any of the prohibited anti-union acts could be fined or imprisoned, or both, for each day of violation.

For the first time, also, administration was delegated in part to a special, full-time agency rather than merely of the courts. A National Mediation Board of three impartial, full-time expert members was established to handle the union-election (but not the carrier-curbing) parts of the Act (as well as the dispute-settlement provisions described in a subsequent section).

In 1936 the Act was amended to cover air carriers and their employees. And in 1940, coal companies and their employees whose work did not extend beyond the mine tipple were expressly excluded from the Act's coverage.

iii. Administration. The operation of the National Mediation Board (whose organization, located in Washington, includes a secretarial staff and statistical and technical divisions) in settling disputes over bargaining representatives was made relatively easy by the fact that railroads were used to government regulation in labor relations and other fields and by the fact that collective bargaining between employers and outside unions had long been an accepted feature of worker-employer relations in the train-operation branch of the industry. In other words, even in the non-operating railroad fields, employers were not inclined to consider the law an undue hardship; to be hostile to the Board; or to fight outside unionism with the vindictiveness, obstinacy, and bitterness characteristic of many non-railroad employers in those days. It was not that labor disputes did not arise on the railroads, but that management and unions normally believed in peaceable negotiation and settlement without resort to strikes.

As a result of this attitude, relatively few anti-union discrimination cases were brought to the courts for decision. Few unionists were discharged or demoted; few were asked to sign disguised yellow-dog contracts; and few railroads actively supported company unions in their shops. One railroad that opposed the Board's certification of an outside union for collective bargaining and tried to hold on to its company union lost its appeal to the U.S. Supreme Court. In denying this railroad's contentions that railroad shop operations did not involve interstate commerce, that the railroad was under no "legally enforceable obligation" to recognize the outside union as sole bargaining agency, and that such a requirement of the Railway Labor Act violated the "due process" clause of the Fifth Amendment, the Court upheld the constitutionality of the Railway Labor Act's provisions under discussion here (*Virginian Railway Co. v. System Federation No. 40,* 57 Sup. Ct. 592, March, 1937).

The main problems which the Mediation Board had to face in administering the employer-curbing parts of the Act may be enumerated as follows.

How should the majority representatives of a given group of workers be discovered — by holding an election or by checking the union membership roll against the employer's payroll? The Board used both methods, about two-thirds of its certifications being based on elections and the other third on written authorization of union members.

What should constitute a "majority" — more than half of the *eligible* voters, or simply more than half of those *actually voting*, or, in case more than two labor organizations might be involved, simply a plurality of the actual voters? The Board apparently did not have to make a decision on the third of these alternatives, but, with regard to the first two, it began by holding to a majority of all eligibles. However, after the federal district court's favorable decision in the *Virginian* case, it changed its ruling and gave certification to majorities of actual voters in subsequent elections.

What should constitute a "craft or class" of employees? In spite of the insignificance of the craft-industrial union struggle on the railroads, and in spite of the fact that crafts were rather well defined in the industry because of the prior existence of union-employer agreements, the Board found many small groups or sub-crafts that wanted separate representation and bargaining. Its policy was to deal with each case on its own merits, but in general it adhered to existing definitions and refused to split up workers into small sections lest collective bargaining become an interminable, stultifying experience for management and the public.

What should be done with an existing trade agreement between a union and a railroad if another union claimed to represent a majority of the workers and won an election from the first union? The Board ruled that the newly certified union should operate under the existing contract until its expiration.

One of the Board's annoying problems was the jurisdictional rivalry among certain A.F.L. and non-affiliated unions (e.g., the Street and Electric Railway Employees and the Trainmen or the Locomotive Engineers) over certain groups of workers. There was, of course, nothing the Board could do about it except hold elections, but the disputes consumed a disproportionate amount of its time and energies.

Under the operation of the Railway Labor Act, outside unions won about 85 per cent of the elections, and company unionism largely disappeared from the railroad labor relations set-up. The National Mediation Board did a good job of administering the pro-union and other parts of the Act. But the most important factor making for labor peace in the industry before World War II appeared to be the general acceptance of outside unionism by employers. In short, there was labor democracy; and consequently, for the most part, there were good labor relations. Disputes there were, of course, but not as a rule on the basic, embittering issues found in certain non-railroad industries.

(2) Laws applying to non-railroad employers. (a) The Norris-La Guardia Act. In Chapter 24 we discussed the relation of the Norris-La Guardia Act (Section 4 and subsequent sections) to the rights of unionists, i.e., to the things they were to be allowed to do without being subject to injunctions. One of these was joining or staying in a union in spite of having signed a yellow-dog contract not to do so. Section 3 of this Act removed the protection of federal courts from these contracts. That is, although this section did not prohibit employers from using them, it did tell employers that no federal court would (*i*) grant damages to any firm against a union or against workers if a union had caused the firm's employees to breach these contracts; or *(ii)* issue an injunction for a firm against such a union or such workers. In short, Section 3 of the Norris-La Guardia Act removed federal courts from the role of an ally of employers in respect to employers' use of anti-union contracts.

(b) The National Labor Relations (Wagner) Act of 1935. From the standpoint of number of employers and workers covered and of effects on labor democracy, labor relations, and labor peace, the most important federal labor law was (and is) the National Labor Relations Act. This statute was enacted about a year after the Railway Labor Act received its significant amendments in 1934. It embodied in relatively permanent form the concepts and the experiences of the federal government in respect to the temporary labor-relations agencies that had been set up during the two-year life of the National Industrial Recovery Act of 1933.

In respect to the rights and duties of employers, the original (Wagner)

Act of 1935 was not very much changed by the Taft-Hartley amendments of 1947. It might be said that all the items listed in Chapter 24 (pages 760–61), which limited employers' freedom to make agreements with unions on certain subjects, represented substantial alterations. They did, to be sure. But these changes are to be thought of mainly as restrictions on the rights and powers of unions. Such restriction was the major objective of the Congress at that time. It was from that point of view that we discussed them in Chapter 24. Our treatment here will be mainly in terms of the 1935 Act.

i. Basic philosophy of the Act. The labor-relations concepts which underlay the Wagner Act were essentially the same as those for the amended Railway Labor Act. But they were more significant in the non-railroad context because the anti-unionism of employers here was much more important.

The general beliefs of those who sponsored and supported the Act on its way through Congress were that labor peace based on a one-sided autocracy of employers had no solid foundation; that lasting labor peace in a political democracy can be obtained only when it is two-sided — i.e., based on a real labor democracy under which employers freely recognize unions of their workers' own selection and deal with them, in good faith and with a will to agree, on the basic terms of employment so vital to the workers' well-being; and that, since the workers in most non-railroad industries were too economically weak to organize and secure recognition from union-hating employers, they must be helped by government restrictions on the anti-union tactics used by such employers.

It should also be carefully noted that the original N.L.R.A., like the Railway Labor Act, represented a step considerably farther along the road of union-encouragement than the Norris-La Guardia Act of 1932 had been. The main idea of the latter was to make government, especially its courts, a *neutral* rather than an ally of employers in union-management relations. Under that Act, unions were supposed to be able to help themselves in fair fights with anti-union firms as well as with union-recognizing ones. But the theory of the Wagner Act was that most workers who wanted unions where none existed and most unions who wanted such workers as members (or who already had some workers as members) needed government help against powerful anti-union employers. Government was to be an ally of unions rather than a neutral between them and employers.

ii. Provisions. The original National Labor Relations Act established a National Labor Relations Board of three non-labor, non-employer members with two main functions: first, to prevent employers from engaging in certain "unfair labor practices"; and second, to conduct elections among employees in order to ascertain which representatives should have the right to bargain collectively with employers on the basic terms of employment.

In Section 7 the Act asserted briefly the general right of workers to organize their own unions free of employers' interference and discrimination. In Section 8 were enumerated five "unfair practices" of employers which the Board was empowered to prohibit: interference with, restraint of, or coercion of employees in their self-organization and collective-bargaining activities; domination of, interference with, or financial contribution to the formation or operation of any labor organization (except that under Board regulations employees might confer with employers during working hours without loss of pay); discrimination, with regard to conditions of employment, aimed at encouraging or discouraging membership in any labor organization (except that closed-shop and union-shop agreements between employers and outside labor organizations were to be permissible); discharge of or discrimination against employees because they might have filed charges or given testimony under the Act; and refusal to bargain collectively with the duly accredited majority representatives of employees.

The election-holding function of the Board was covered in Section 9 of the Act. It was provided that the representatives of the majority of a group of employees should be the exclusive collective-bargaining agency for all the employees with regard to the basic terms of employment. Individual workers or minority groups, however, were to be permitted to present grievances to employers. In ascertaining the majority choices of employees, the Board was empowered to designate the nature and extent of the appropriate bargaining unit — craft, plant, or employer unit — and to use secret ballots or other suitable methods.

In performing its two main functions the Board was "empowered" rather than "directed" to act. That is to say, the Board *might* move to prohibit unfair practices and to hold elections; the Act did not state that the Board *should* do so.

Sections 10–12 gave the Board certain powers of procedure and enforcement. The Board was to establish such personnel and such regulations as it might deem desirable to effectuate the provisions of the Act. It might subpoena witnesses and require submission of records, and it might utilize court orders to secure obedience to requests for information. Obstructive tactics were to be punishable by fine or imprisonment. If, after full hearings upon complaint, the Board should decide that an employer had been guilty of an unfair labor practice, the Board was authorized to utilize the procedure explained in Chapter 24 (pages 756–57).

Two other provisions of the Act are also noteworthy. The right to strike was expressly preserved (Section 13); and the protection of the Act was to hold for employees not immediately on their jobs because of strike, lockout, or discriminatory discharge, unless they had obtained "regular and substantially equivalent" jobs elsewhere.

iii. Administration. Essential procedure. In October, 1935, the N.L.R.B. began active administration. In addition to the main office in Washington, the Board created regional offices in 20 major industrial cities, each of which, under a regional director, was staffed with attorneys, examiners, and clerical help.

The procedure developed for handling complaints of employers' unfair labor practices was the same as that described in Chapter 24 for handling the unfair practices of unions. The procedure for determining whether an election for the choice of a collective bargaining representative by a group of workers was also essentially similar. Unless the employer was willing to have election (this was called a "consent" election), the regional office of the Board held hearings on an election petition filed by a union. At the hearings, evidence for and against holding the election was heard from the employer, the petitioning union, and any rival unions that chose to testify. After the hearings, the Board decided whether, when, where, and in what manner an election should be held. It ruled upon the scope of the bargaining unit (see below). Then it notified all the interested parties about the time and place of the election, which was in due course conducted by Board representatives. The majority union (see below) was finally certified to all concerned as the official collective bargaining representative for the workers in the unit. Thereafter the employer was obligated to deal with it.

It will be noted that the Labor Relations Act did not authorize the Board to mediate labor disputes. This work of trying to bring together the disputants was reserved to the Conciliation Service in the Department of Labor, because the framers of the Act felt that mediation should be a separate function not to be confused and mingled with the quasi-judicial function entrusted to the Board. In practice, however, the regional directors employed the mediatory process to a certain extent. They did not try to bring the disputants together on any basis contrary to the Act's provisions, but they did try to persuade employers to discontinue their use of the unfair practices. Thus the regional directors might satisfy the complaining employees and avoid further hearings and litigation.

Administrative problems and rulings under the Wagner Act. The list of problems which the National Labor Relations Board had to face almost from the moment it began to function is long and varied and can only be summarized very briefly here under four main heads: the problems involved in interpreting the Act's terms in accordance with its spirit; the problems arising out of the A.F.L.–C.I.O. rivalry; the problems arising out of anti-union employers' opposition; and the problems of enforcement in the courts.

Interpretation. The problems of interpretation were of four types. First, the Board had to give concrete, practical meaning to the words "interference, restraint, coercion, and discrimination." What specific acts of employers tended to discourage membership in labor organizations of the workers' own choosing — and were therefore unlawful? Second, the Board had to determine under what specific circumstances employers were dominating, interfering with, or contributing financial support to the formation or operation of a labor organization. Third, the Board had to decide on methods of discovering what collective bargaining representatives were desired by majorities of workers; and in so doing, the Board had to decide what workers were eligible to vote and what the bargaining units should be — plant, craft, shop, and so on. Fourth, the Board had to tackle the knotty problem of employers' refusal to recognize and bargain in good faith with duly certified majority representatives of their workers. When was an employer giving such representatives the "run-around"? What could be done about securing bona-fide collective bargaining for such representatives?

With regard to the first of these problems of interpretation, the Board, in the course of its hearings on complaints of unionists who believed they had been discriminated against, ran into an astonishingly large number of anti-union practices, some crude and common, some subtle and unusual. Most of them were mentioned in Chapter 18 and need no further enumeration. It is enough to say here that in its decisions in discrimination cases, the Board ordered employers to "cease and desist" from one or more of the following: using their own or hired spies in connection with union activities inside or outside plants; using professional strikebreakers, sluggers, and the like, to promote violence and fight unionism; using personal interviews and written media to propagandize against unionism in such ways as to cause workers to fear losing their jobs, houses, or store accounts, or in such ways as to cause workers to believe false things about unionism (e.g., "all union officers are racketeers and reds who live off the workers' dues"); causing or aiding public authorities or private citizens to work or act against unionism; discharging, demoting, laying off, or otherwise discriminating against unionists with regard to tenure of employment, where the evidence clearly showed no other substantial grounds for such action; getting workers to sign special individual labor contracts which, although making no mention of unions in the crude way of the old yellow-dog agreement, indisputably caused workers to avoid union affiliation; refusing to reinstate discharged, demoted, or striking unionists when ordered to do so by the Board; using blacklists or other means to prevent discharged unionists from securing employment elsewhere; and making reinstatement of strikers conditional upon renunciation of union affiliation.

An important measure which the N.L.R.A. empowered the Board to use in order to get employers to cease their discrimination tactics was reinstatement, with back pay, of employees proved to have been discharged or demoted because of unionism. Only if the discharged employees had found new, regular, similar jobs, were they not entitled to such damages, under Board rulings. The Board also was empowered to order the reinstatement of strikers who had gone out because of companies' anti-union practices. Back pay in strike cases, under Board orders as approved by the U.S. Supreme Court, was to begin from the first day of the strike caused by an unfair labor practice of the employer. In the Republic Steel Corporation case, the Board, in telling the company to reinstate thousands of workers who had gotten themselves blacklisted because of the "Little Steel" strike of 1937, even ordered the company to reimburse federal relief agencies which had helped care for some of the men during the strike. The Supreme Court refused to allow this particular kind of damages, however. In the *Fansteel Metallurgical Corporation* case the Board ordered the reinstatement of sit-down strikers who had engaged in violence; but this order was also vetoed by the Supreme Court, as was likewise the Board's order for reinstatement of workers who had struck in violation of a collective agreement (*Sands Manufacturing Company* case).

With regard to the problem of interpreting "domination of, interference with, or financial support of" a labor organization, the Board ordered employers to withdraw recognition from or to disestablish their company unions if the evidence showed that the employee-representation plans or other forms of company unions had been initiated under pressure and influence of employers; that the plans had never been submitted to the whole bodies of workers for approval or disapproval; that the employers were continuing to influence and control the operation of the plans; that the employers were paying for secretarial and other expenses, such as salaries for employee representatives beyond the average hourly earnings to which they were entitled under the Act for time spent on the plans; that the employers used outside agencies, such as lawyers, to promote and control the plans; and in short, that the company unions, if left to their own resources, were unable to stand on their own feet and act as adequate agencies for true collective bargaining. In these interpretations the Board was upheld by the United States Supreme Court — e.g., in the *Pacific Greyhound Lines* case and the *Pennsylvania Greyhound Lines* case.

A special aspect of this problem was the collusive-contract issue, particularly under the A.F.L.–C.I.O. conflict. Some of the company unions were dealing with their employers under contracts or agreements of specific duration, apparently similar in form to regular union trade agreements, and some of these were closed-shop arrangements, even with check-off of dues. Nevertheless, if after complaint by workers and investigation by the Board it appeared that such a union did not represent a majority of the workers, the Board disregarded the agreement and ordered an election for the democratic determination of representation. The issue became very important when two or more outside unions were involved, for the Board would have been hard-pressed to prove that the one favored by the employer was a company-controlled union. Yet that, in fact, is what the matter amounted to, if the employer, feeling that one of the two or more unions was more tractable or otherwise more desirable than the others, signed with it an agreement without having satisfied himself that it had enrolled a majority of his workers. Thus, in the race to "sign up" employers, certain A.F.L. unions, particularly the Electrical Workers, "sold" closed-shop contracts to certain companies, such as the National Electric Products Company near Pittsburgh and the Consolidated Edison Company of New York, without having bothered first to sell the union to a majority of the workers. Upon complaint by the rival union and upon discovery through investigation that the first organization was in the minority at the time of contract-signing, the Board felt that its plain duty was to declare such contracts void and to order the holding of democratic elections to discover which union actually did have the majority.

The Supreme Court usually agreed with the Board that members of unfavored unions who were discharged by employers because of collusive agreements with favored unions should be reinstated. The Court also agreed that elections should be held. But, as in the *Consolidated Edison Company* case, the Court was at first unwilling to approve the setting aside of the contracts themselves. Nevertheless, late in 1940 the Court unanimously came to uphold the Board's invalidation of a closed-shop contract; it was proved, in the *Tool and Die Makers* case, that the employer and his agents had engaged in unfair labor practices in assisting an A.F.L. union, the successor of a company union, to organize and obtain a closed-shop agreement at the same time that a contract was refused to the C.I.O. majority union.

With regard to the problem of determining collective bargaining representatives — the Board made significant decisions on certain basic issues.

In the first place, it did not always use the election method. In various cases, evidence of majority support for a particular union among the workers in a given bargaining unit was accepted from signed petitions, signed union membership cards, signed requests for strike benefits, signed authorizations to employers to check off union dues, union membership rolls, employer admission that the union had a majority, and uncontradicted testimony of union secretaries. But if employers or non-unionists strongly contradicted the paper claims of unions; if the unions themselves asked for ballot elections; if the unions, fearing employer retribution, refused to reveal members' names; or if the unions' evidence was not recent enough — then the Board decided to have elections by secret ballot. In 1940, elections came to be the only method employed by the Board.

Second, the question of eligibility to vote in elections was determined by such rulings as these: all workers on the payroll before the beginning of a strike; all workers on the payroll at date of election ruling by the Board; all workers on the payroll before the beginning of hearings on the case; all workers on the payroll during the last payroll period before the election date; and only plant or non-office workers below the rank of supervisor allowed to vote.

Third, the elections were to take place at dates from 10 to 30 days following the Board's election order, depending on circumstances, or after effects of the employers' unfair practices had worn off.

Fourth, the form of the ballot was important. When only one union (an outside union) was involved in a case, the Board gave workers the opportunity to vote for or against the given union. When two or more outside unions were involved, the Board at first directed the workers to choose between them; but during the second half of 1937 the Board also gave workers in such cases an opportunity to indicate dislike of both or all the rival unions. "Inside" unions were given places on ballots unless the employers had been found guilty of dominating them in violation of the Act. No blank spaces were provided for workers to write in the names of any organization not party to the case, the Board holding that ample opportunity for all interested groups to appear had been provided during the hearings.

Fifth, the Board had to decide what was meant by the term "majority." For non-election certification, it ruled that a majority of the workers in the given unit had to be included in the union lists. For election certifications, it ruled at first (before July, 1936) that any labor organization had to obtain a majority of the workers eligible to vote. (Thus, if there had been 100 eligible workers in a given voting unit, a labor organization would have had to obtain 51 votes in an election in order to be certified as the official collective-bargaining representative.) Thereafter, for a while, in accordance with the lower court decision in the *Virginian Railway* case, it ruled that, so long as a majority of the eligible voters actually voted, it would certify the organization that got a majority of these votes even though the organization were not chosen by a majority of all eligible voters. In other words, it would certify the representative selected by a majority of the majority of eligibles. (Thus, if only 51 out of 100 eligible voters had actually participated in an election, the Board nevertheless would have certified a union which received 26 votes.) Following the experience of the Electrical and Radio Workers' Union in an election at the Camden plant of the R.C.A.–Victor Company in 1936, when a company-inspired campaign to boycott the election resulted in participation of fewer than half of the eligible voters, the Board, not wishing to permit anti-union employers to intimidate voters into a denial of the democratic procedure envisaged by the Act, adopted a third ruling, under which the representative chosen by a simple majority of those actually voting would be certified. The number voting might or might not be a majority of the eligibles; that matter was up to the workers, once the election had been announced. But the purpose and spirit of the law were not to be defeated by subversive, coercive tactics of anti-union employers. (Thus, if an employer should succeed in keeping 90 out of 100 eligible voters away from the polls, the union which got 6 out of the 10 votes cast would be certified and the employer would have to deal with it.)

Sixth, run-off elections were provided in cases where three or more unions were on ballots and none was voted a majority. Through one or more run-offs, contests were reduced to two unions, one of which could then get a majority of valid votes cast.

Seventh, as already indicated, it was the workers, not the employers, who were to be free to choose the workers' representatives. Therefore, even though a contract or trade agreement might be in existence between an employer and a union, the Board would order an election if it were indicated that a majority of the workers wished to switch their affiliation to another union. With respect to its own certifications, the Board indicated that they should run for a year before the re-opening of representation issues.

Eighth, although the Board was apparently empowered by the Act to investigate any labor dispute affecting interstate commerce and to call for elections on its own motion in order to settle the dispute, it hesitated to set such a precedent, for a later, anti-union board might use the procedure to defeat unionism. At first the Board decided to hold elections only upon petition from unions, believing that unions should be given time and opportunity to conduct their organizing campaigns and that unions would petition for elections when they felt they had enrolled majorities of workers. In other words, the Board originally decided not to let employers ask for elections. Granting that employers were often seriously inconvenienced by conflicting claims and organizing activities of rival unions and that such conflicts should be settled as promptly as possible by democratic elections, the Board nevertheless held at first that to permit employers to petition for elections would be to allow anti-union companies to defeat the purpose of the Act. Thus, if an employer, knowing that thus far the union had not enrolled a majority of his workers, could obtain an election at his own pleasure, the union would lose, and owing to the psychological effects of such a defeat, its offensive would doubtless be halted in mid-air. But a growing realization that many employers who would have been dealing in good faith with some union were helpless in the face of A.F.L.–C.I.O. strife led the Board in 1939 to decide that thereafter it would entertain election petitions from employers in cases where two or more bona fide unions claimed majorities but neither had asked for an election.

Ninth, the Board was given the power to determine the "appropriate unit" — employer, craft, plant, or subdivision thereof — for collective bargaining. This meant, in the first place, that the issue of craft versus industrial unionism was placed squarely in its lap. For the first year of the Board's existence, the issue did not loom large. But the A.F.L.–C.I.O. conflict made it of paramount importance. Abstractly, more or less as a matter of rationalization in its written decisions, the Board stated that each case must turn on its own circumstances, and that the decision of the Board, in any case involving choice of union for bargaining representation, as to whether the workers should vote by crafts or by the plant as a whole would be based in consideration of the following: history of labor relations and employer-worker dealings in the industry; forms of existing self-organizations; rules of eligibility to membership in existing self-organizations; and relative extent to which alternative units might serve the interests of the workers, as shown by relationships among the processes of production, by the degree of common skill possessed, by the extent of wage uniformity, and by the extent of territorial closeness or separation among plants of a company. Concretely, as a matter of practical politics and economics, the Board had to make decisions calculated to offend as few as possible of the groups who might seek to have the Act amended and the Board's power curbed. Clearly the criteria just listed were vague and might sometimes point to different decisions. The Board therefore had great leeway in making its rulings on the "unit" question, and like most judges, arbitrators, and administrators, it appeared to reach them on the basis of expediency and rationalize them later on the basis of more or less abstract principles. Thus, up to October, 1937 (i.e., before the A.F.L. started its public denunciations of the Board), the three board members ruled that in mass production plants all non-supervisory workers constituted the voting unit, regardless of whether they were in the direct production process or in auxiliary and maintenance operations. Thereafter, however, two of the three Board members ruled that the latter groups of workers (such as electricians, molders, and machinists) should vote separately from the production workers; and that, especially if there had been a previous history of craft bargaining in the industry, they should be permitted to choose between the industrial union claiming all the workers and the craft unions claiming only the workers in their respective trades. Such a ruling (which came to be known as the "Globe doctrine," from the case in which it was first advanced, *Matter of Globe Machine and Stamping Company*) was defended by the argument that it preserved democracy for the small craft minorities in these plants. It was attacked by the argument that it gave the craft minorities the power, through strikes and other measures, to defeat the will of the production workers' majorities, and that when minorities could foil majorities, there would be denials of democracy.

Bargaining-unit problems were not confined to the issue of craft versus industrial unionism. A second problem was whether the unit should be the plant, the employer, or the industry. In the anthracite coal industry, for example, should the several mines of a large company be separate bargaining units, or should the company be treated as one unit, or should the industry as a whole be the unit? The Board decided in this case that the industry should be the unit because of the long history of industry-union collective bargaining. Similarly, the Pacific Coast longshore employers' association was selected as the unit to deal with the C.I.O. longshoremen; this decision stepped on the toes of the few A.F.L. locals that had had agreements with small local longshore employer groups. On the other hand, when an industry was very spottily organized — e.g., some employers dealt with a C.I.O. union, some with an A.F.L. union, and some with no union at all — the Board could not use the industry as a bargaining unit but had to choose the employer or the plant. Until 1941, the Board chose the employer unit if the union had majorities in *almost* all the plants of a company (*Pittsburgh Plate Glass* decision). After 1940, however, the Board favored the plant unit unless *all* plants of a company were well unionized (*Libbey-Owens-Ford* decision). Here the majority-minority issue of democracy was especially important because labor policy of a multi-plant employer is centrally determined. (The Supreme Court upheld the *Pittsburgh* ruling in April, 1941, a few days after the Board reversed itself.)

The election rulings as such were not usually subject to court review, because the holding of elections was considered by the Supreme Court to be only a step toward the objective of collective bargaining.

With regard to the problem of how to deal with employers who refused to bargain collectively with majority representatives of their workers and sign agreements with them, the Board refused to be sidetracked by the subterfuges of anti-union employers. It ruled repeatedly that, in accordance with the history of collective bargaining between unions and management who met with open minds to settle the terms of employment, employers must not only agree to listen to the demands of duly accredited workers' representatives, but also make counter-proposals and bargain with them, not merely to fulfill the letter of the law, but to reach an agreement in good faith. If possible, there must be a compromise meeting of minds, based on the will to agree. Tactics of delay and irritation, refusal to bargain at length on the union's proposals, or refusal to offer and support with adequate factual and other material his own proposals were condemned as evidence of an employer's bad faith and insincerity. The Board made it clear, of course, that the Act did not and could not require an employer to reach an agreement with an accredited union; to have done so would have violated the law on freedom-of-contract and would have made an employer submit to any original demands a union might make, no matter how absurd. But there must be an honest effort to find reasonable common ground.

During its first years the Board had made no official ruling that an agreement once reached between an employer and a union must be reduced to writing and signed by both parties. One of the subterfuges of certain anti-union employers had been a refusal to sign a trade agreement or union contract. Some employers would meet and bargain with union leaders and come to general understandings, but would refuse to incorporate them in bilateral written agreements; a few employers would go so far as to write out the terms and post them on bulletin boards as unilateral "statements of company policy," signed only by the management. Inasmuch as such tactics provided obvious evidence of incomplete recognition and bad faith, and inasmuch as employers, by denying to unions "the fruits of achievement," could undermine the loyalty of the union members and start the unions toward destruction, the Board finally ruled — in 1938 and thereafter, in such cases as *Inland Steel Company* and

H. J. Heinz Company — that the normal end of good-faith bargaining was a bilateral signed agreement and ordered the companies to put their agreements with the unions in writing. This decision was upheld by the Supreme Court in January, 1941.

A.F.L. versus C.I.O. The problems of the Board arising out of the conflict between the A.F.L. and the C.I.O. have already been touched upon in the discussion of the closed-shop and bargaining-unit issues. Before this conflict became open and bitter, the Board had refused to enter into union jurisdictional disputes at the job level, holding that these were matters for determination within the labor movement. But when the labor movement split wide open, the rival-union issue became unavoidable. Friends of organized labor felt that this development was most regrettable, for it took much of the Board's time and energy away from its main function — the curbing of anti-union tactics and the protection of the workers' right of self-organization.

Opposition of employers. The opposition of union-resisting employers was manifested in many ways. At the outset, several employers' associations advised their members to ignore and disobey the Act. In the fall of 1935, the National Lawyers' Committee of the American Liberty League made public its unofficial decision that the Act was unconstitutional on a number of counts. In other words, many employers proceeded on the belief that a law is unconstitutional until validated by the U.S. Supreme Court, and since they also believed that the Court would invalidate the Act, they behaved as if there were no such law. But many employers failed to reckon with the political-economic conditions which influence the attitudes of the courts. After the rise of unionism in 1936–37 and after the President's drastic proposal for reorganization of the judiciary, the Supreme Court, in April, 1937, found that manufacturing involved interstate commerce and thus denied the main argument of the Act's attackers. Soon after the Act was held constitutional (*Jones and Laughlin Steel, Fruehauf Trailer,* and *Friedman-Harry Marks Clothing* decisions; 57 Sup. Ct. 615), the Board's offices were flooded with cases, and the regional and national directors worked overtime deciding them. But the anti-unionists fought on. They delayed answering complaints; sought to block proceedings through legal technicalities and subterfuges; tried to secure, in the lower federal courts, injunctions restraining the Board from carrying out its activities (a tactic that the U.S. Supreme Court forbade after January, 1938); lobbied extensively in Congress to secure cuts in the Board's financial appropriations; and undertook a large-scale propaganda campaign in an attempt to discredit the Board and have the Act amended in various ways.

Enforcement in the courts. The problems of the Board in securing enforcement arose out of the attitudes of certain employers and judges. The Board issued two kinds of orders: negative orders requiring employers to "cease and desist" carrying on unfair labor practices; and positive orders requiring affirmative action by employers, such as reinstatement of discharged employees. Many employers complied with the Board's orders, but many others fought them in the courts, either in federal district courts through injunction proceedings or in federal circuit courts through requests for review. By the end of 1937, district courts had granted 22 out of 95 prayers for temporary injunctions restraining the Board, but only 3 of the 22 were upheld by circuit courts of appeal, and in January, 1938, the Supreme Court refused to uphold these three injunctions and decided that district courts were to have no further jurisdiction over Board cases. The Supreme Court decision upholding the Act in April, 1937, had also helped to reduce the number of court injunction actions attempted by employers.

The review of Board orders in federal circuit courts of appeal, either on the Board's motion to secure compliance or on an employer's motion to set aside, was the sort of action provided for in the Act. Here the N.L.R.B. fared well. By 1947, considerably more than half of its decisions had been upheld completely; less than a third had been modified; and less than a fifth had been denied. In short, the Board met with increasing success in securing court enforcement once the Supreme Court had spoken.

iv. Appraisal of the Wagner Act and its administration. It is difficult to appraise the original N.L.R.A. separately from its administration because, as we have repeatedly said, almost any statute has meaning and becomes effective only in terms of the interpretation and operation provided by the agency set up to administer it. And even if we look only at the Act as administered, evaluation is made hard because of the Act's controversial character and because of the changes that have occurred since 1935 in the attitudes and policies of employers, unions, and the public.

Economic validity. What are some probable or possible effects of employer-curbing and union-encouraging legislation on the allocation of resources, the distribution of income, economic progress, and the extent of resource utilization? That is, does such legislation make for improvement, or for the reverse, or for no significant change in these four elements of total want-satisfaction in the society? (Recall Chapter 3.)

We have seen that this legislation, particularly when administered under conditions of high employment, led to a notable increase in the strength of American unionism. Hence what our question really asks is this: Does the growth of union power affect these elements of want-satisfaction favorably? Is unionism an economic blessing or bane?

There is no space here for a rigorous and detailed analysis, but some suggestive generalizations may be offered. To begin with, our answers on each of the four elements must depend on what the unions that were created or expanded under favoring legislation *have been doing.* One set of policies would make for one kind of answer to our question; other policies might lead us to other answers. In short, our generalizations must be based on unions as we find them.

In respect to *resource allocation,* the following matters seem worthy of mention here. As we saw in Chapter 3, a misallocation of resources, with consequent loss in total economic want-satisfaction, occurs (in the absence of unionism) when firms hire labor-hours under conditions of monopsony, and when there are impediments to free mobility among the workers who own and offer the labor-hours.

Under monopsonistic hiring of labor, more than the socially desirable amount of workers and other resources tend to be employed in the firms faced with relatively elastic labor supplies; and fewer than the socially desirable amount of workers and other resources tend to be employed in firms having relatively inelastic labor supplies. Moreover, wage rates and other terms of employment tend to be poorer in the first than in the second group of firms. If, then, unions of similar bargaining skills are organized in both groups of firms, wage rates tend to fall *relatively* in the "over-employed" firms and to rise *relatively* in the "under-employed" firms. This is because of the differences in the elasticities of labor supply. With these changes in relative wage rates go changes in employment. Employment tends to fall further in the under-employed firms and rise further in the over-employed ones. In other words, unionism tends to worsen the allocation of resources from this standpoint.

Consider now the loss in want-satisfaction from the standpoint of immobility among workers. We have seen that even in the absence of unionism there is a considerable degree of inertia and ignorance of alternatives among workers (Chapter 8). Do union policies tend to increase this immobility? On balance, the answer again seems to be "yes." Looking only at horizontal (inter-firm and inter-locality) mobility, we find that union policies on such matters as seniority and private pension plans tend strongly to hold workers to their existing employers, even in tight labor markets; that unions' successes in handling workers' grievances and in removing various elements in job dissatisfaction tend to diminish the things that *push* workers into looking for other jobs; and that unions' successes in establishing standard, uniform terms of employment among various firms tend to diminish the things that *pull* workers away from their existing employers. True, in the absence of unionism many employer policies (Chapter 18) tend to diminish labor mobility; and so do inertia and ignorance among workers. But union policies almost certainly *add* significantly to this "natural" degree of immobility. Against this powerful tendency we must note some offsets, such as the increased knowledge of alternative employment opportunities afforded by union hiring halls and employment offices; and the legal restrictions on union-security devices such as the closed shop. But the net effect of unionism is almost certainly in the direction of immobility and therefore of an increase in resource misallocation.

In respect to *income distribution* as such (i.e., without regard to the other elements affecting total economic want-satisfaction, such as economic progress), it appears that the net influence of unionism (including the threat of unionism where none yet exists) is in the direction of a less unequal distribution of money claims on the goods that afford want-satisfaction — and therefore is in the direction of higher total satisfaction than would exist in the complete absence of unionism. From Chapter 3 we remember that the distribution of income or money claims on satisfaction is more unequal than the distribution of the capacity to enjoy satisfaction, and that a net rise in total satisfaction tends to occur if the first of these distributions is brought closer to the second. It appears that unions have been able to lessen the inequality of income distribution. They have produced this result, first by direct bargaining with employers on the economic front for higher money wage rates and other money benefits, and second, by exerting political pressure for benefit plans operated by government and for more steeply progressive personal income taxes.

In respect to *economic progress*, the record of unionism is anything but impressive. The short-run, opportunistic, pragmatic approach of most unions to their own particular problems has thus far precluded much consideration of the secular or long-run effects of their policies on the economy as a whole. In their narrow preoccupations they seem implicitly to have assumed that a progressive, expanding economy as a whole is an automatic, impersonal, certain thing, beyond the reach of any of their particular policies. They usually behave as if anyone can always have more of everything. That is, they act as if there were no such thing as the principle of real or opportunity cost (i.e., foregone alternatives), as explained in Chapter 3. Yet by and large, most American unions have stood in the forefront of the ranks of those whose policies are inimical to the two main elements of economic progress — net capital formation and technological innovation. Featherbedding rules and opposition to new machines and to incentive-wage plans are but three items in a long list. True, many such policies can be explained as security measures, ways of obtaining protection against the ruthlessness of a competitive system and against unfriendly employers. But these policies cannot be *explained away*. Two wrongs do not make a social good. One looks with satisfaction and hope, therefore, at the recent pronouncements of a few labor leaders who not only indicate an awareness of the problem but also a willingness to engage in non-collusive, bilateral union-management cooperation to solve the problem.

Finally, in respect to *extent of resource utilization*, union wage policy is the most important item for analysis. Such an analysis has already been made, in Chapter 23. The student should review that material at this point.

Political acceptability. The main criterion of the Wagner Act's social desirability must be in human-relations or broadly political terms. Did it contribute to good union-management relations? Or did it foster labor strife and widen the rifts between employers and workers and workers' unions? Did the public suffer under it?

Any answers to these questions must be based on one's personal concept of what socially beneficial labor relations are. Our own tentative standards on this matter were sketched in Chapter 2 and in the last part of Chapter 3 (in the section on freedom versus security).

It must also be borne in mind that, in applying one's criteria, the matters of timing and of the passage of time are important. By this we mean that in a world of change a law that may be desirable when enacted may turn out to be less desirable or even wholly undesirable some years later. In a democracy, moreover, when the voters and their representatives perceive abuses and problems in one or more sectors of the society, they pass laws to remedy the abuses and solve the problems. Sometimes the legislation which they hope will be remedial creates as many problems as there were before. But in any case, it is very rare in a democracy to find legislation for the handling of *anticipated* abuses and problems. Almost always bridges are crossed when the voters come to them.

The anti-union attitudes and activities of many employers and the attitudes and decisions of many courts seemed to involve abuses and problems that needed legislative action. First the Norris-LaGuardia Act was passed, to make the federal courts more neutral in labor relations. Our own preference would have been to allow considerably more time to establish the fact that employers' weapons were still too potent to permit unions to help themselves, without positive government assistance. In other words, we would have waited to see whether or not unionism could grow strong through its own efforts. (At this point the student will observe that we have started with a basic premise: unionism as a principle is good for society. We believe this because we think adherence to democratic principles demands that men be free to associate in unions and other organizations. If unions sometimes do things injurious to society, they can be punished or regulated like any other associations, such as corporations.) But we can be tolerant of those who wished to enact a more positive law like the Wagner Act; we do not consider them unreasonable. For one thing, the Democrats might well have felt uncertain about being returned to power in 1936; they wanted the law on the books before the next election. For another thing, honest men could reasonably have believed that without direct government prohibition of employers' harsher anti-union measures, unionism could not have grown and labor conflict would have spread unrest throughout the land.

Should the Act have been so "one-sided," whenever passed? Didn't the Congress know enough about the abuses of which unionism was capable to include in the Wagner Act a list of union unfair practices, along with employer unfair practices? This is a hard question. Some abuses by certain unions, e.g., featherbedding, were certainly recognized in 1935. The effects of secondary boycotts were well known. But when unionism as a whole is still weak and employers still much stronger than unions in general, many union activities do not loom as important as they do after the locus of power has shifted. A reasonable case can be made, it seems, for tackling employer abuses first. Perhaps this *was* the proper timing.

Administration. Now let us consider the administration of the Wagner Act. Before the Taft-Hartley amendments of 1947 were enacted, chronologically speaking there were really two sets of administrators, i.e., two Boards. The first set of three men operated from 1935 to 1939–40, the second from 1939–40 to 1947, after the members of the first group had resigned or had not been reappointed. We must distinguish these two groups — their attitudes, problems, and work of administration.

Employers became quite bitter about the rulings of the first Board. Moreover, several relatively objective students came to conclude that its members were unnecessarily pro-union. Employers not only critized the Board with the assertion that it could not be neutral when it was judge, jury, and prosecutor all in one; they said further that the Board was a "kangaroo court," with a decided radical, pro-C.I.O. bias, and that it disregarded the rules of evidence, relied a great deal on hearsay, and intimidated witnesses, workers, employers, and public officials to obtain the modicum of evidence needed to support its pre-conceived decisions in various cases.

Specifically, the employers' criticisms included the following charges: *(a)* The Board should have permitted petitions for elections by employers caught helplessly in the middle between rival organizing drives of A.F.L. and C.I.O. unions. *(b)* The Board should not have prohibited as an unfair practice employers' fair statements to their workers about unions' undesirable characteristics. Unions were permitted to make all sorts of anti-employer statements; why shouldn't this sort of thing cut both ways? *(c)* The Board was too eager to choose multi-plant and multi-employer bargaining units. *(d)* In cases of alleged discrimination by firms against union members, the Board ordered the reinstatement of the unionists with back pay when in many instances the evidence showed that the workers deserved the discipline they received, entirely apart from the happenstance of union membership, or that the union itself has stirred up the trouble leading to the disciplinary action. *(e)* The Board had a bias against any labor organization which was not affiliated with the A.F.L. or C.I.O. and was confined to a single plant or firm; almost invariably such an organization was called a "company union," whether or not the evidence supported such a conclusion. *(f)* The Board was very wrong in certifying unions of foremen as units with which employers had to bargain. How could upper management tolerate unions in and conflict with lower management?

The Board was not spared some criticism by the A.F.L. and the C.I.O. The C.I.O. did not like the "Globe doctrine" for craft union elections in mass production plants. But most of its criticisms were confined to specific cases and to certain delays under Board procedure. Unlike employers and the A.F.L., it did not try to get the Act amended in order to make the Board behave differently. The two chief criticisms of the A.F.L. were that the Globe doctrine was not rigorous enough, and that the Board had no business invalidating as "company union" agreements some of the contracts that A.F.L. unions had signed with employers at the employers' requests. The A.F.L. wanted the Wagner Act amended on these two matters.

In present-day perspective there seems to be some justification for concluding that the first N.L.R.B.'s heart did perhaps bleed too much for labor — and particularly for the C.I.O. But any fair-minded judgment must be relevant to the years in which that Board operated: and we can recognize how difficult it must have been for the Board members to remain truly neutral when experience had shown them how rough and how subtle employers could be in their anti-unionism, how disrespectful and resentful employers were about the job that the Board was given to do, and how myopic and ineffectual most of the A.F.L. unions had been in organizing the unorganized workers before the advent of the C.I.O.

Whether or not the charges leveled at the first Board had substantial foundation, its members and executive secretary were replaced by new men. Some personnel changes were also made in the regional offices. It was because of this second Board that policy was changed to allow employers to petition for elections when caught in a rival union conflict and to present non-coercive anti-union views to employees. These and other changes made the second Board less un-neutral. But they failed to mollify most employers. It was not that the Board was still considered to be extremely biased. Employers came to see more clearly that, from their point of view, the Act itself was the thing requiring considerable change. As we know, this change was effected in 1947.

Before outlining the 1947 amendments, let us try to give a short answer to the questions posed at the beginning of this discussion. It is of course impossible to be even reasonably certain about what would have happened in the field of labor relations if there never had been a National Labor Relations Act, or if the original Act had been like the 1947 amended one. Our conclusion is that the Norris-La Guardia Act, as interpreted by the courts, made for considerably more overt labor-management strife in the short run than the Wagner Act, although in the long run it undoubtedly fostered labor peace; that the short-run effect of the Wagner Act was to stir up union-management friction but (because of the election and other democratic, peaceable procedures) to reduce overt conflict; that the long-run effect of this Act was definitely in the direction of labor peace; and that from the present perspective it might have been better to start in 1935 with a statute somewhat like the 1947 amended one.

(c) The amended N.L.R.A. of 1947. Changes in employers' rights and duties. The changes affecting what employers may and may not do under the 1947 Act may be considered in three categories.

As previously stated, the later statute retained the Wagner Act's five unfair labor practices of employers. But one of these, number three, was amended. As already pointed out, an employer originally was forbidden to *discourage* membership in a labor organization but was permitted to make closed-shop and other union-security agreements. Under the new Act he may not *encourage* membership in a union through the closed shop; and he may agree to the union shop and the check-off only under the conditions described in Chapter 24. The fifth unfair labor practice of employers was amplified in this manner: Not only must an employer not refuse to bargain collectively with a duly certified union. If he reaches an agreement after bargaining (the law does not say he *must* reach an agreement), he may not refuse to put it in writing if the union so requests. And, like a union (Chapter 24), if an employer wishes to terminate or modify an existing agreement, he must give 60 days' notice before the termination date (and also notify federal and state conciliation agencies within the next 30 days if an agreement has not been reached by that time).

In addition to the restrictions on union-shop and check-off agreements, there were limitations on other items to which an employer may contract with a union (Chapter 24).

The amended Act also had new things to say about the employees and bargaining units with whom an employer must or must not bargain. First, supervisors and foremen were removed from the definition of "employee." They could form unions if they wished. But upper management was to be free, if it wished, to break such unions and refuse to deal with them. Second, the N.L.R.B. was restricted in its power to determine appropriate bargaining units. The Board was forbidden to certify as a bargaining agency any union which admitted to membership (or was directly or indirectly affiliated with a union admitting to membership) plant guards and watchmen. This was because guards enforce rules against the ordinary workers. But guards might be certified in their own exclusive, unaffiliated unions. Again, the Board was prohibited from including professional employees in the same bargaining unit with non-professional workers unless a majority of the former voted for such inclusion. And the Congress gave a helping hand to A.F.L. craft unionists by telling the Board that it must not deny to skilled craft employees a separate bargaining unit simply because such employees had been included in a broader unit by some *previous* Board decision. If the Board wished to continue this policy of inclusion, in any unit, it must hold an election and receive majority approval from the craft workers. In this way, earlier Board determinations of all-embracing units could be overturned by the craft unionists. The Act did not mention *new* decisions on scope of bargaining units, i.e., in plants where previous determinations had not been made; but surely the Board, in order not to be later overturned, would hold separate craft elections in these cases as well.

(d) The Byrnes Anti-Strikebreaking Act. Although the N.L.R.B. had

included employers' use of professional strikebreakers in the list of unfair practices which it tried to prohibit through its administrative orders, Congress deemed it desirable to aim a specific law at this objectionable anti-labor weapon. The so-called Byrnes Act, passed in 1936, provided

> That whoever shall knowingly transport or cause to be transported, or aid or abet in transporting, in interstate or foreign commerce, any person with intent to employ such person to obstruct or interfere, in any manner, with the right of peaceful picketing during any labor controversy affecting wages, hours, or conditions of labor, or the right of organization for the purpose of collective bargaining, shall be deemed guilty of a felony and shall be punishable by a fine not exceeding $5000, or by imprisonment not exceeding two years, or both, in the discretion of the court.

Careful reading of this short statute reveals three loopholes for judicial hamstringing in the word "knowingly" and in the phrases "with intent to employ" and "peaceful picketing." Late in 1937 the Act was in fact deprived of force by a federal judge and jury in Connecticut, who refused to convict the Remington Rand Company and Pearl Bergoff, the "King of Strikebreakers," for alleged use of thugs in breaking a strike in the company's Middletown (Connecticut) plant in 1936. The judge and jury believed that the strikebreakers were bona-fide millwrights.

After this alleged miscarriage of justice, unionists worked for a stronger federal law on the matter, and in 1938 the Congress amended the Act to read as follows:

> That *(a)* it shall be unlawful to transport or cause to be transported in interstate or foreign commerce any person who is employed or is to be employed for the purpose of obstructing or interfering by force or threats with (1) peaceful picketing by employees during any labor controversy affecting wages, hours, or conditions of labor; or (2) the exercise by employees of any of the rights of self organization and collective bargaining.
>
> *(b)* Any person who willfully violates or aids or abets any person in violating any provision of this Act, and any person who is knowingly transported in or travels in interstate or foreign commerce for any of the purposes enumerated in this Act, shall be deemed guilty of a felony, and shall, upon conviction thereof, be fined not more than $5000 or imprisoned not more than two years, or both.
>
> *(c)* The provisions of this Act shall not apply to common carriers.

b. State legislation on employers' activities. Toward the close of Chapter 24 we reviewed the history of state statutes on labor relations. We found that from 1935 to 1940 the state legislatures put certain restrictions on employers in their relations with unions. Let us summarize these restrictions by taking up, in order, the anti-union measures discussed in respect to the common law at the beginning of these chapters.

None of the states limited employers' rights to form associations, or the employers' right to lock out their employees. But in the 1920's some states began to try to curb the tactics used by many firms to win lockouts and strikes. By 1935 about a dozen states had required that employers, in advertising for labor during strikes and lockouts, must state the existence of labor trouble. Public and private employment offices were also sometimes required to make plain to job-hunters that strikes or lockouts were being conducted. These laws were held constitutional by the courts, but in practice the enforcement was lax, and employers usually had a loophole for evasion, in that they could claim the strike had been defeated and the dispute ended by the time enforcement action got under way. About twelve states passed laws during these years intended to prohibit the importation of strikebreakers from other states. These statutes were often nullified by the courts through declaration of unconstitutionality or through injunctions forbidding enforcement. Failing in prohibition, a few states tried regulation, such as laws forbidding the arming of guards. These laws, too, were nullified by lack of enforcement.

There were also certain efforts to restrict employers' anti-unionism in the absence of strikes or lockouts. Before 1935, there were about five states and a number of cities which tried to regulate industrial espionage by statute, the chief method being a licensing system under which private detective agencies were allowed to operate only upon evidence of competence and "character." Revocation of license for specific cause at the discretion of the administrative agency was provided for. These laws were held constitutional by state and federal courts. Of doubtful constitutionality, however, were the laws of three states which required employers to give workers hearings before disciplining or discharging them on the basis of information received from spies. In actual practice, the enforcement of regulatory measures against industrial espionage was made very difficult by the nature of the business. The best intentions in the world seemed to be of little avail in the face of the secrecy and evasiveness of employers and spy agencies. Complete prohibition might have been somewhat more effective, but it seemed certain that any such laws would be held unconstitutional in the courts.

By 1935 more than thirty states had forbidden or restricted the use of the blacklist and whitelist. These laws had on occasion been held constitutional. A number of states also required employers to give employees a statement of the reason for discharge, and these statutes were also constitutional. But in spite of all this, the laws were ineffective. One reason was the poor wording of the laws. Another was the court ruling that it was illegal to circulate the list, but not illegal to make use of it once received. The main difficulty, however, was inability to prove that discharge or refusal of job came from the use of a blacklist, and inability to discover who supplied the information.

In the early years of the century about twenty states enacted statutes forbidding anti-union discrimination along the lines of the Erdman Act for interstate railroads (page 781). But, as with the Erdman Act, enforcement was left to the courts. And neither the state courts nor the United States Supreme Court liked these laws. They declared them unconstitutional. But employers' effectiveness in using yellow-dog contracts was limited by a number of state "little Norris-La Guardia" acts, as previously explained. On the other hand, employers' use of company unions as an anti-union measure remained untouched by state legislation until 1937, when, over a period of some ten years, certain states passed "little Wagner" and "little Taft-Hartley" acts (pages 772–75).

There is no space here for an analysis of the details of these later statutes. In general, they contain lists of employer unfair labor practices which are essentially similar to those in the original and amended National Labor Relations Act. Under these laws the use of strikebreakers, blacklists, labor spies, yellow-dog contracts, and many other formerly legal kinds of anti-union discrimination can be and have been curbed or prohibited, either directly by the statute or by administrative decision. Some of these statutes are more restrictive on firms' anti-unionism than the federal law, others more lenient. All but two are administered by special labor relations agencies rather than by regular law-enforcement officers and the courts; where administrative boards exist, they have legislative authorization to hold elections and certify collective bargaining representatives in appropriate bargaining units. On the whole these states statutes on employers' tactics have proved to be desirable supplements to the federal law.

D. GOVERNMENT AND THE SETTLEMENT OF UNION–EMPLOYER DISPUTES

In this section, our focus of interest may perhaps best be understood if we make one important assumption: Let us suppose that all unions and employers are dealing with each other in good faith. Employers are not using any devices or dodges to avoid union recognition and collective bargaining; they engage in no unfair labor practices. Unions are not trying to hamstring employers or teach them lessons; there are no union unfair labor practices. Under these circumstances, then, there are two main matters of public concern, two things on which government must or should have policies: (1) It is possible for unions and their employers to love each other too well, in the sense that they do not love the public enough. That is, under conditions of labor-relations peace, union-management cooperation may develop into union-management collusion, so that the public suffers from too-high product prices and restricted output. (2) No matter how good the attitudes and intentions of both unions and managements, conditions do arise (such as a substantial decrease in product demand or a considerable price inflation) which bar the peaceful settlement of issues between the parties. Negotiations are broken off, and there is resort to the use of economic force, namely strikes or lockouts.

If the struck company or industry is large and if it produces essential products, the public welfare again becomes a matter of concern to the public's agency, government.

1. Collusion during labor peace. *a. Nature and extent.* There are no data available for making even a guess on the extent of union-management collusion in the United States. The *possibility* exists wherever *(i)* all or most of the firms in a product market have been organized by a union; *(ii)* a high degree of union-management cooperation (or at least a stable, peaceable relationship) — has existed for some time; *(iii)* there are a good many rather small firms; and *(iv)* the union is regarded as the most important if not the sole element which can bring stability into an otherwise chaotic competitive situation among the firms.

Whether collusion (defined as "high," double-barreled monopoly) *actually* develops in any industry or market seems to depend, in the absence of government controls, mainly on the social attitudes of the union leaders and of the employers. This same thing of course holds where there are other opportunities for anti-social policies; for example, many labor leaders have opportunities for racketeering, graft, and extortion, but not many take advantage of such opportunities.

b. Government attitudes and policies. One reason why the extent of union-employer collusion is not known is that it is not easy to detect. Another is that there is no federal or state statute dealing directly with it as such.

Under the common law, proved collusion would be regarded as a conspiracy to restrain trade. But a criminal court ruling under the common law would require prosecution by some law-enforcement officer, who is usually ill-equipped to harbor the necessary suspicion and to gather the requisite evidence. A civil action requires an injured complainant. Such persons do exist sometimes, not among ignorant consumers, but among those who would like to enter the collusive business but cannot because entry is barred, or who, managing to enter, decide for some strange reason to buck the monopoly.

The chief statute governing collusion is the Sherman Act whose administration in respect to union-employer matters lies mostly with the Department of Justice. Once in a while some crusader in that agency will decide to go after unions that he suspects of being parties to collusive arrangements. But in recent years his ardor has usually been cooled off by decisions of the "liberal" Supreme Court. However, not all the decisions have been unfruitful. In *United States v. Brims* (272 U.S. 549, 1926) the Court unanimously condemned, under the Sherman Act, a three-barreled collusive agreement in the Chicago area among the Carpenters' union, the building contractors, and the organized firms making woodwork (these also organized by the Carpenters), whereby wood products made by outside non-union firms were excluded from the market.

And in 1945, in *Allen Bradley Co. v. Local Union No. 3* (325 U.S. 797, 1945), the Court ruled against a similar set-up arranged by the A.F.L. Electrical Workers.[5]

2. Strikes and threats of strikes. *a. Extent of work stoppages in the United States.* The data presented in Table 43 show the number of work stoppages, the number of workers directly made idle, and the number of days lost from such stoppages for certain periods and years from 1881 through 1950. It will be seen that postwar inflationary years created more stoppages than any others, 1946 being the peak year in all respects.

TABLE 43 *Work Stoppages in the United States, 1881–1950*

Period	Average Number per Year of Stoppages	Average Number per Year of Workers Involved (in thousands)	Average Number per Year of Man-days Idle (in millions)
1881–85	530	175	
1886–90	1,410	370	
1891–95	1,440	390	
1896–1900	1,390	385	
1901–05	2,900	585	
1906–10	3,020	475	
1911–15	3,110	775	
1916–21	3,500	1,800	
1922–27	1,160	685	
1928–32	760	290	7.7
1933–37	2,500	1,280	18.8
1938–42	3,030	1,128	12.2
1943–48	4,236	2,712	40.8
1919	3,630	4,160	—
1946	4,985	4,600	116.0
1950	4,843	2,410	38.8

Source: G. I. Griffin, *Strikes*, Columbia University Press, 1939; U. S. Bureau of Labor Statistics.

Strikes unquestionably cause serious losses in national output and total want-satisfaction. The data in Table 43, moreover, by no means indicate the full effects in terms of men and days lost, for in many other firms in which there are no strikes work is slowed down or stopped because of inability to obtain customary materials and equipment. A strike in a single key industry like bituminous coal can eventually paralyze most industrial activity if it goes on long enough. After such a strike is over, the economy may well recover to full employment; but the loss in national income from the stoppage is not recoverable.

Nevertheless, it is possible to exaggerate losses from strikes. If the student will refer to Table 31 (page 175), he will have a better perspective on the relative importance of work stoppages in terms of economic waste.

b. Statutory and administrative intervention in strike situations by government. We have already considered the common and the statutory law

[5] These decisions, along with the later ones under the Sherman Act, mentioned in Chapter 24, suggest that unions' monopolistic practices are virtually exempt under the Sherman Act *unless* carried out in collusion with employers.

in respect to what unions and employers may do in prosecuting strikes and lockouts. We are concerned here with government attitudes and policies on settling stoppages that have gotten under way and on stepping into disputes that are near the stoppage stage in order to prevent overt conflict.

(1) Kinds of intervention. In the following pages, four methods or plans of government intervention are discussed and analyzed, each illustrating a certain degree of voluntarism or compulsion in respect to unions and employers: (1) mediation and conciliation; (2) voluntary arbitration; (3) fact-finding reports, with or without recommendations for settlement; and (4) compulsory arbitration.

(a) Mediation and conciliation. When an official (or agency) intervenes in a labor controversy, proffers his good offices to hear both sides, and gives tactful suggestions as to a common ground for settlement, without any hint of coercion, the procedure is described by the words *mediation* and *conciliation.* In the usage of some students of labor relations the two terms are synonymous. Others, however, confine the meaning of "concilation" to situations in which the government official or other neutral person makes no positive suggestions and exerts no personal pressure for settlement when he deals with the disputants. To these students, "mediation" implies a considerably more active role for the neutral. Although equipped and backed with no legal sanction whatsoever (the parties remaining wholly free to accept or reject his efforts and suggestions), the mediator does much more than merely listen to the parties and subtly pull them together as a peacemaker. He devises and proffers his own suggestions for a fair settlement and exerts his personal influence to get the disputants to accept them.

This may well be a proper distinction between the terms. The two extremes are easily identifiable. But the dividing line between them is very hard to recognize.

In any case, both mediation and conciliation have much in common. To be successful, both the mediator and the conciliator must be acquainted with the economic and technological nature and problems of the plant or industry, be well liked personally and respected for impartiality, inspire confidence, be sympathetic and tactful, and have fertile ideas for face-saving compromises.

There is no fixed procedure for mediators and conciliators to follow. One mediator may prefer to keep the parties in separate rooms and meet with them at different times, not calling them together in plenary session until at or near the end of his work, when he is sure he has developed a mutually satisfactory compromise. The advantage of this method is that it usually induces each side to reveal to the mediator the concessions it is willing to make, whereas it would not do so before the other party. Another mediator may prefer to meet with both sides in joint sessions, hammering out a settlement by making suggestions and inducing open negotiation thereon.

(b) Voluntary arbitration. Mediation or conciliation is often successful; it soothes ruffled feelings, injects new points of view, and enables the parties to withdraw from untenable positions into which their emotional zeal has driven them. But sometimes it fails; sometimes there is too much bitterness or stubbornness to allow compromise.

In that case, the mediator usually suggests to the parties that they voluntarily agree to submit their dispute to a third, neutral person for a final and binding decision. Such a person may be chosen by mutual agreement of the parties, or they may both agree to let the third person be selected by the mediator or the agency for which he works or some other outside person or agency with prestige and a reputation for fairness. This person is usually known as the "arbitrator," sometimes as the "referee" or "umpire." Sometimes an arbitration board of three or five men is preferred to a single person. Such a board may be composed of neutrals only; or it may include equal numbers of labor and management representatives, with one or more neutrals holding the balance of decision and with a neutral as chairman.

Getting the parties to agree to the mere idea of arbitrating their differences is usually a difficult task for the mediator. Each side will be weighing what it thinks it can get by this method against what it believes it can achieve by overt economic warfare. But even if they agree on the idea of arbitration, still other difficulties remain. It is hard to induce the parties to agree on the *stipulation* or *submission* to arbitrate, i.e., on the document which sets forth the issues in dispute and the decision-making powers of the arbitrator. And the selection of the arbitrator often raises difficulties; each side will try to get a person or a board that it believes will be sympathetic to its arguments and point of view.

This method of settling labor disputes is known as *voluntary arbitration.* It is "voluntary" because no one — government or any private person or agency — compels the parties to submit their dispute. But the word "arbitration" means compulsion, in this sense: Once the parties have agreed to submit the dispute, they bind themselves to accept the arbitrator's decision or award, whether they like it or not. In fact, "voluntary arbitration" is a short expression for "voluntary submission of the dispute, with compulsory acceptance of the award."

Arbitration is fundamentally different from mediation or conciliation. It is judicial in procedure, rather than diplomatic. Instead of listening to each group and gradually leading them to a common ground, the third or outside party learns each side's case in open hearing, with rebuttals, and then, like a judge, hands down a decision on the merits of the arguments presented — decision which presumably requires obedience from both parties. Needless to say, however, an arbitrator to be effective must inspire respect for his impartiality and economic and technical knowledge.

Looking at the whole field of labor disputes which are amenable to settlement by voluntary arbitration, we must make some important distinctions. There are two main classes of union-employer disputes: *(i)* those arising during the life of an existing collective bargaining agreement over its interpretation and application; and *(ii)* those arising at the expiration of an existing agreement, over the terms of a new one. The first kind of dispute is much more frequent, and in the aggregate these are very important in determining the kind of labor relations that exist between union and employer. But in respect to any one dispute, the second classification is much more important because a new agreement determines the basic conditions of employment and labor relations for the period of time that it will cover. The first class of dispute is handled under the grievance procedure discussed in Chapter 20. The automatic terminal point of this procedure is arbitration by a third person, either a "permanent" full-time umpire or a person chosen *ad hoc*, i.e., just for the particular case. In any event, the arbitrator is a private, non-governmental person. For the second class of dispute, arbitration is far from being automatic. A very few unions (such as the A.F.L.'s Street and Electric Railway Employees and the A.F.L.'s Typographical Union and their employers) have clauses in their contracts providing for the arbitration of unsettled terms of new contracts. Here the arbitrators are private persons, even though sometimes selected with the help of government agencies. But usually unions are loath to bind themselves in advance. When an unsettled dispute arises, resort to governmental mediation is required under the law (see below); and if mediation fails, arbitration is proffered, as stated above.

The kind of dispute settlement by arbitration in which we are interested here is that covered by federal and state legislation.

(c) Fact-finding. This method of handling unsettled labor disputes in basic industries involves governmental creation of boards (usually composed wholly of three or more neutral persons) to investigate the merits of the parties' contentions on the issues in dispute. The boards are *ad hoc*. They may be set up under statutory authority or under the general powers or prestige of the federal or state chief executive. The statute may provide for the compulsory submission of the dispute and for the compulsory submission of evidence. The boards may have the power to subpoena witnesses and evidence. During the period of investigation both sides are required not to engage in a work stoppage. This "cooling-off" period usually extends for some time after the close of the board's hearings, i.e., during the time needed by the board to submit and make public its report. Sometimes the statute provides that the board shall make recommendations as to desirable terms of settlement. Sometimes only findings of fact are permitted; but boards can often slip recommendations into such findings. In any case, at the end of the cooling-off period the

parties are free to accept *or* reject the findings and the recommendations, if any.

Fact-finding established by statute may be called "compulsory investigation" or "compulsory submission of the dispute, with voluntary acceptance of the award." It is thus in some sense the opposite of voluntary arbitration, which involves voluntary submission of the dispute and compulsory acceptance of the decision.

When, however, a state or the federal chief executive creates a *non-statutory* board (as in the case of the basic steel industry board mentioned at the beginning of Chapter 1), the parties are not compelled to submit their dispute. The appearance of the parties and their submission of evidence are voluntary acts, as well as their acceptance of any recommendations. In other words, such situations cannot be described by the term "compulsory investigation."

The major objectives of fact-finding include the diminution (cooling-off) of accumulated tensions between the parties, the informing of the public through the publicized report of the fact-finders, and the pressure of informed public opinion on both parties toward settlement of their differences.

(d) Compulsory arbitration. This kind of dispute settlement involves complete government intervention and compulsion at every step. The full term is "compulsory submission of the dispute and compulsory acceptance of the award." The decisions in all covered cases are made by a government arbitration agency, usually a full-time, permanent board or court. Under legislation requiring this sort of settlement, work stoppages by all covered parties are prohibited at all times — before, during, and after the arbitration proceedings. Full evidence must be presented to the board and all witnesses must appear before it. Awards can be enforced by all the resources of the government.

(2) Relative merits of the different measures. What are the utilities and the costs of each kind of government intervention in labor disputes? Here again is a question on which each student will have to make his own judgments, depending on his framework of values and preferences. As pointed out in Chapter 3, however, any rational choice among alternatives demands a knowledge of their utilities and their costs. We shall try to present the main advantages and disadvantages here.

In the broadest sense, the alternatives are no-government intervention on the one hand, and government intervention on the other. Or we may say that the alternatives are freedom versus security. Whatever we call the alternatives, we know from Chapter 3 that rational choice also requires alternatives to be divisible. Fortunately for society, they are. We can have some of each. Then the problem becomes one of finding the optimum quantities of both, in combination.

(a) Complete laissez faire. The main general utility of no-government

intervention is the freedom of economic and political decision that it provides. Under non-intervention, no one in Washington or in any state capital can tell unions or employers what to agree on, or when to agree, or indeed whether they shall come to any agreement at all. But this very important utility in terms of democracy is accompanied by a very serious cost in a society like ours — the loss in output and want-satisfaction that is experienced from strikes, particularly those in big basic industries. Is the utility worth this cost?

(b) *Compulsory arbitration.* At the other extreme is complete government intervention. Let us make the dubious assumption that all serious strikes can actually be prevented. If a union or an employer disobeys an arbitration award, the government can break the stoppage and teach an unforgettable lesson by using injunctions, armed forces, imprisonment, fines, and so forth. Let us make the further doubtful assumption that management and workers will be just as productive under these conditions as in a free society. Then the great utility of this alternative is uninterrupted production and a noteworthy rise in total want-satisfaction. But this utility is also accompanied by very large costs.

First is the serious restriction on the freedom to make economic decisions. This restriction is not likely to be confined to the freedom of unions and employers to negotiate such agreements as they please and to strike and lock out as they please in order to get what they want. (As we saw in Chapter 19, the freedom to strike and to lock out is an essential part of free collective bargaining and normally makes for agreement and labor peace.) It is likely, as it did in Australia and New Zealand (where a compulsory arbitration has long existed), to push government into controlling product prices, because government, still believing in the private enterprise profits system, wishes product prices to be high enough to provide adequate profit margins for firms. Here again is a deprivation of freedom in economic decision-making. (It should be noted that, as Australia and New Zealand have demonstrated, restrictions on economic freedom need not be accompanied by deprivations of political liberty. Those nations are still thoroughly democratic in the political sense.)

Second, real collective bargaining, a notable day-to-day, close-to-home expression of democracy, is almost certain to wither on the vine under compulsory arbitration. Why should unions and employers bother to negotiate agreements when a major force toward agreement, namely freedom to strike and to lock out, has been removed and when the government has the final word on all terms of employment? Better hasten to the arbitration court, let the lawyers proceed with their arguments, and get it over with.

Third, intra-union democracy is also likely to suffer. Why should union members bother going to union meetings when any union policies that they might help to establish must yield to those of government?

Is the utility of compulsory arbitration worth these costs?

(c) Mediation, voluntary arbitration, and fact-finding boards. Now let us consider the utilities and costs of three kinds of government intervention that stand somewhere between the two extremes of no intervention and complete intervention. Mediation, by its very nature, exerts little pressure against free decision-making. Neither does voluntary arbitration, for both parties are free to accept submission or to refuse it among the three alternatives available to them — agreement, work stoppage, and submission to arbitration. True, once the parties have agreed on submission, they give up their freedom to reject the award. But they have voluntarily agreed to relinquish this freedom. Statutory fact-finding involves some restriction on economic freedom; but this is only temporary, during the cooling-off period, including the hearings. The other kind of fact-finding involves even less limitation on liberty. Nevertheless, in so far as the recommendations of fact-finding boards are effectively enforced by public opinion, it is not improbable that some of the costs of compulsory arbitration, such as a noteworthy weakening of collective bargaining, will be experienced. However, this measure should be reserved only for the most essential industries, like railroads and bituminous coal. All in all, the cost of these measures in terms of lost democracy is relatively small. On the other hand, as experience has shown, these measures have succeeded in producing very many dispute settlements in all sorts of plants and industries, large and small, basic and fringe. In other words, they have demonstrated high utility.

Is not the net utility (gross advantage minus cost) of these three measures, which are often used together, notably higher than that of either of the extreme ones? Do they not come close to providing an optimum combination of freedom and security for a society that believes in democracy?

(3) Federal legislation. Now let us see what the federal government has done to help settle union-employer disagreements. As usual, we shall distinguish statutes covering interstate railways from those designed for other industries.

(a) Interstate railroads. The Act of 1888 marked the first effort of the federal government to handle labor disputes in the railroad industry. It provided for voluntary arbitration, which, if accepted by the disputants, was to be accompanied by compulsory investigation through the Commissioner of Labor and two temporary appointees of the President. Their decision was to be published if the President so decided, but could not be legally enforced. Although this Act remained on the books ten years, it was wholly inoperative. It was superseded by the Erdman Act of 1898, which specified, first, mediation by the chairman of the Interstate Commerce Commission and the U.S. Commissioner of Labor upon application of one or both of the disputants, and second — in case the mediatory efforts were unsuccessful — voluntary arbitration by a temporary board composed of one employer's representative, one labor man, and a neutral

chairman chosen by these two or appointed by the Commissioner of Labor. The arbitration board had compulsory fact-finding powers, and the award was binding and enforceable through court action. The courts, moreover, were empowered to modify the decision if necessary. Up to 1906 the Erdman Act appeared to be following in its predecessor's footsteps, having been applied in only one case. In that year, however, it finally swung into action, and by 1913 had been instrumental in settling sixty-one cases. The great majority of these were dealt with through mediation. A certain amount of dissatisfaction with the Act was felt, nevertheless, because, although employers and unions were almost unanimous in praising the mediation work, the mediators were not permitted to offer their services unless called upon, and because the possibility of court review of arbitration awards weakened the power of the arbitrators selected. Furthermore, the new policy of regional "concerted action" among the railway Brotherhoods seemed to make desirable the establishment of a more permanent and powerful agency for settling emergency conflicts.

In 1913, therefore, the Newlands Act set up a full-time President-appointed Board of Mediation and Conciliation. The arbitration provisions, however, were left almost unchanged. For three years the law operated satisfactorily, with mediation achieving over 70 per cent of the settlements, as before. In 1916, however, the Act broke down completely. The Brotherhoods had demanded a basic eight-hour day and refused to arbitrate the question with the railroad employers. A nation-wide strike was ordered, and so serious was this threat that President Wilson hastily prevailed upon Congress to pass the famous Adamson Act, which gave the unions their shorter basic work day. The Supreme Court held this law valid as an emergency railroad measure,[6] and then, before a new law could be passed to repair the Newlands Act, war was declared and the government soon took over the railroads. Labor relations were so liberally administered during the war that all serious trouble was avoided.

The Transportation Act of 1920 was the first postwar effort toward labor peace on the railroads. Disputes over the terms of new agreements were to go to the Railroad Labor Board, composed of nine Presidential appointees — three from the public, three representing the railroads, and three the workers. Although the law did not forbid strikes or require a compulsory waiting period, it did endow the Board with compulsory fact-finding powers. The Board's decisions were not binding, however; this was where public opinion was to step in and play its role.

Grievances and disputes over the interpretation of existing contracts were to go, for conciliation or voluntary settlement, to bi-partisan Regional Boards of Adjustment. Failure to reach agreement on these Boards meant that the case had then to be referred to the Railroad Labor Board.

Unfortunately, none of the characters performed as the playwrights expected them to. As a result, what was to have been a drama with a

[6] See *Wilson v. New,* 243 U.S. 332, 1917.

happy ending turned into a farce with an unhappy ending. To begin with, the Boards of Adjustment were never cast; the unions wanted them to be national, while the employers insisted they be local. This failure meant just so much more work for the Railroad Labor Board. Instead of acting as a court of appeals, it had to take original jurisdiction in the host of cases arising during the turbulent years between 1920 and 1923. Consequently, it was swamped, and there were many long delays. In the second place, the members of the Board, like many other federal officers during that administration, appear to have been miscast. They seem not to have been equipped for the roles of conciliators and investigators. The effect of all this was to shake the confidence of all the other employer and employee performers and more or less to disgust the public audience, especially those who had front seats. Unions and employers (particularly the Pennsylvania Railroad) began to flout the Board's rulings, and it became apparent by 1925 that a new law would have to be enacted.

The failure of the Railway Labor Board led to the passage, in 1926, of the (Watson-Parker) Railway Labor Act, which abolished the Board and set up a stronger system. With regard to settlement of grievances and of the relatively minor union-employer disputes arising out of inability to agree on the meaning or interpretation of parts of existing trade agreements, the Act tried to prevent a recurrence of the 1920–25 experience with the Labor Board, in the following ways: *(i)* To encourage the settlement of disputes by the parties themselves, temporary regional bipartisan Boards of Adjustment (composed of equal numbers of employer and worker representatives) were to be established, such as those which worked successfully during the war and which were supposed to be created under the previous Act. All cases of trade-agreement and working-rule interpretation not settled by direct bargaining were to be decided by majority votes of the Boards. Unlike the 1920 Act, the 1926 law made creation of these joint groups mandatory. Through their action it was hoped that the central agency, described below, would not be overwhelmed by a host of minor cases, as the 1920 Board had been. *(ii)* For any of these interpretative cases which could not be solved by the Boards of Adjustment, a Board of Mediation was established, made up of five high-salaried members appointed for five years by the President and removable by him in case of unsatisfactory work.

With regard to settlement of the major disputes — the deadlocked points arising from the negotiation of new union-employer agreements — the Act directed this Board of Mediation to try, on its own motion if necessary, to bring the disputants together by mediatory methods. But although the chief emphasis was on mediation, the Act provided for voluntary arbitration in stubborn cases which refused to yield to mediatory treatment. Upon mutual consent of railroads and unions, unsettled controversies were to be submitted to Boards of Arbitration set up temporarily for each case as it arose and composed of three or six men, whichever number might be agreed on. One or two were to be selected by each side, and the neutral one or two members were to be chosen by the other arbitrators or, in case of disagreement, by the Board of Mediation. The award was made binding by the provision that it be filed in a federal district court and, in the absence of protest by either side within ten days, be made a judgment of the court. If either side should protest, the award was to be argued in a circuit court, whose decision was to be final and binding unless both parties privately agreed to a change later on. The inclusion of federal courts in the arbitration system would appear to be a weakness, as it was in the Erdman Act, if it were not for the fact that the 1926 law restricted the scope of court review to questions of law; that is, the Board of Arbitration award could not be modified or set aside by a federal judge unless it had been made in a way not in accordance with the procedure laid down in the Act.

A last-ditch measure of dispute settlement remained under the Watson-Parker statute. Whenever the permanent Board of Mediation might find its mediatory efforts futile and might be unable to get both parties to agree to arbitration, it was required to notify the President that an emergency threatening to interrupt interstate commerce existed. If he should consider it necessary, the President might then appoint an Emergency Board of Investigation with compulsory fact-finding powers, which was to report to him within 30 days. From the time such a Board was created, no strike and no change of employment or other conditions by either side were permitted for 60 days. The President might publicize the findings if he desired, but they were not binding on the disputants after the time limit was up.

It will be seen that the Act of 1926 combined direct collective bargaining, mediation, voluntary arbitration, and compulsory investigation, with chief emphasis on the first two. There was nothing especially novel about it, but it seemed to take to heart the lesson common to the experience of all countries, namely that a settlement brought about in a voluntary, mediatory way is much more valuable and effective than one secured under governmental duress.

Up to 1934, the Railway Labor Act had worked rather well. Both unions and railroads seemed to like it, and the public undoubtedly benefited because after 1926 good will between these groups was apparently restored, whereas from 1920 to 1925 they had been becoming more and more irritated with each other. Nevertheless, between 1926 and 1934 certain flaws in the Act and its administration became visible as things actually worked out. These faults arose mainly in connection with the provisions for the settlement of grievances and the interpretation of existing agreements. In the first place, difficulty was experienced in getting the Boards of Adjustment set up in the non-train-operation branches of certain anti-union railroads; the railroads wanted their company unionists on the Boards, and the outside unions wanted their men to be the labor members. Second, even where the Boards were set up, they often failed to reach settlements, thus necessitating appeals to the Board of Mediation and overburdening this Board when its time should have been free for the more basic disputes. Third, if and when the Boards of Adjustments did reach settlements, there were no provisions for prompt enforcement or for putting the decisions into effect without delay.

Consequently, Congress amended the Railway Labor Act in 1934 in the following ways: *(i)* Through the employer-restraining provisions discussed in a preceding section, efforts were made to have collective bargaining between interstate railroads and outside unions universal in all branches of the industry. *(ii)* A *standing* National Railroad Adjustment Board was created, to be composed of 18 members chosen by national outside unions and 18 members selected by the railroads; the Board to operate in four main divisions of the industry (train and yard service, shops, etc.) Delay or refusal to designate Board members was handled by the provision that, in case unions or railroads failed to appoint them within 60 days after the Act's passage, they should be named by the National Mediation Board. *(iii)* Grievances and disputes over interpretation of agreements were to be settled by majority votes of the Adjustment Board, and in case of tie votes the cases were to go, not to the National Mediation Board (as under the 1926 Act), but to single referees — impartial umpires to be selected by the Adjustment Board or, if the latter was unable to reach an agreement, by the National Mediation Board. *(iv)* Awards or settlements made by the Adjustment Board, with or without referees, were to be binding within reasonable time limits. If railroads failed to comply in time, action for enforcement could be taken in federal district courts, where the Adjustment Board's findings of fact were to be *prima facie* evidence. The five-man Board of Mediation established by the 1926 Act was replaced by a three-man National Mediation Board whose main duties were the discovery and certification of collective bargaining representatives in cases where two or more rival unions were claiming bargaining rights; and the mediation of union-employer disputes arising out of the negotiation of *new* trade agreements. (The 1926 provisions for Emergency Boards remained unchanged.)

So far as the settlement of union-employer disputes is concerned, then, the amendments of 1934 improved the administrative arrangements; introduced promptness and compulsion into the settlement of grievances and agreement-interpretation disputes; and left the 1926 Act as it had been with regard to settlement of basic, new-agreement disputes.

From 1934 to 1941 the Act worked better than any previous law on railway labor relations, partly because of the amendments and partly because of the National Mediation Board's unusually able administrative personnel. The railroads criticized the operation of the National Railroad Adjustment Board somewhat, however, claiming that the procedure for settlements was becoming unduly legalistic; that the decisions of the referees were often pro-labor, or at least impractical; and that the probability of securing pro-union decisions from referees was leading unions to deadlock many cases that previously would have been settled by joint union-employer negotiations, without referees.

In 1936 the Act was amended to cover air transport lines and their employees.

From 1941 to 1952 the country's experiences under the Railway Labor Act became increasingly unfavorable and depressing. The number of work stoppages, of workers involved therein, and of man-days lost therefrom rose a great deal in the late war years and after. These increases were not so great as those registered in non-railroad industries; but they were ominous because of the essential nature of the industry, the earlier favorable experience in labor relations, and the existence of an Act that had been especially designed for the industry and had previously operated with success. This rise in strike activity occurred over unsettled grievances under existing agreements as well as over the terms of new agreements.

There were at least three other pieces of evidence of unsatisfactory relations. In the first place, on the First (train-operating) Division of the Railroad Adjustment Board there was a backlog of about two years' work; that is, there were that many unsettled grievances. And this was in spite of the appointment of two special panels a few years earlier to help the main Board. Delays in handling individual cases were almost interminable. Both railroad management and the unions seemed to prefer taking their chances with the Board to bargaining settlements between themselves. For another thing, the National Mediation Board was getting an increasing number of new-agreement cases. This betokened a breakdown in bargaining at all levels — local, regional, national. Although the Board was continuing its success in mediating many of the smaller, less important disputes or in getting the parties voluntarily to accept arbitration, it was failing to do so or being by-passed in the big national disputes involving wage rates, rules, and working conditions. These issues assumed the proportions of "movements," which the 16 non-operating organizations and the four or five operating brotherhoods, acting pretty much in concert after 1940, began initiating and "progressing" every year or so. The unions wished to get these big disputes to the emergency boards as soon as possible — or beyond, as we shall see. Finally, the emergency board procedure for settling disputes on the terms of new contracts seemed also to be breaking down. When the Act was passed, this procedure was designed to be used sparingly, for real emergencies; and real emergencies were not expected to occur every year, much less every month or so. It had also been anticipated that the prestige of the boards, plus the force of public opinion, would lead the carriers and unions to accept the boards' recommendations. At first, the Act worked as planned. There were few emergency boards before 1941, and their recommendations were in general accepted by both sides. But beginning in 1941, things changed. The number of boards was greatly increased. The last one appointed in 1951 was No 98. In 1950 there were eleven boards; in 1949, twelve. Nor were their recommendations being accepted; the unions in general rejected them while the railroads accepted them, whether considered favorable or not. Moreover, in 1950 six of the eleven emergency boards were created to handle actual or threatened strikes over grievances rather than over new contracts, as originally designed.

To what cause may this unfortunate trend in events be ascribed? It is desirable to distinguish primary from secondary causes. The main *primary* reason is the advance of technology, which has reduced employment in the industry from about 2 million workers in the 1920's to only 1.3 million in 1952. Technology has introduced competitive carriers — motor trucks, buses, airplanes, and passenger automobiles — which have taken much freight and passenger traffic away from the railroads. It has also provided many labor-saving devices on the railroads themselves, e.g., diesel locomotives that pull much longer trains much faster than before. With the decline in employment, the railroad unions have felt it necessary to fight vigorously for the preservation of members' jobs through all kinds of restrictive rules. These restrictions are extremely irksome to management and tend to worsen union-employer relations.

The chief *secondary* causes of the unsatisfactory labor situations on the railroads are these: *(i)* There is a multiplicity of bargaining units and too little effective centralization of bargaining. Covering the 120 Class I railroads are 21 "standard" railway unions, plus numerous miscellaneous organizations. The standard unions are craft in structure, and the claimed jurisdictions of some overlap considerably. In the past 15 years, it is true, a considerable amount of centralization has developed in bargaining over new contract demands. There is a Railway Labor Executives Association. The non-operating unions have been "progressing" wage rate and rules movements pretty much as a unit; and frequently two or more of the operating Brotherhoods have done the same. There are Eastern, Southeastern, Western, and national Carriers' Conference Committees. But most of the railroad union leaders have insufficient delegations of authority from their general chairmen and rank-and-file members to making binding settlements. *(ii)* The railroads' freight and passenger rate structure, i.e., the schedule of prices they charge for their products, is regulated by the Interstate Commerce Commission, a federal agency entirely separate from the boards which handle cases involving the railroads' most important cost item, labor. The carriers never know, in bargaining over or agreeing on wage rates and other demands, whether the increased labor costs will be permitted to serve as a basis for raising their product prices. This uncertainty makes it difficult for them to engage in free open bargaining. *(iii)* One of the railroads' chief competitors, motor transport, is not regulated or treated by government nearly so severely as the railroads. The competitive disadvantage of the railroads is undoubtedly worsened by this fact. *(iv)* Management's attitude on the railroads has stiffened during the past five years or so. Management has been demanding rules changes on its own account; offense now goes with defense. No longer do the unions gain their objectives without much fighting. This change should be of long-run benefit to the relationship; it is never good for one side to be stronger and more aggressive than the other. But in the short run the change has worsened the relationship. *(v)* As in other industries after 1940, wage-rate settlements on the railroads were made pretty much across the board in cents per hour. This way of making increases preserved the inter-craft wage-rate differentials in pennies but not in percentage terms. As a result, the more skilled classifications came increasingly to feel a sense of inequity and a loss of relative prestige. *(vi)* Because successive emergency boards rarely have the same personnel, there has been a considerable lack of uniformity, sometimes almost direct conflict, in their recommendations. This has not added to the prestige of the boards or to the esteem and respect with which their findings are regarded by the parties and the public. *(vii)* There has been a most unfortunate trend toward political settlements worked out at the very top of administrative government, "The White House." This began in 1941 when President Roosevelt, busy with world affairs, decided to take the quickest way of settling rail labor trouble. The rail unions had rejected an emergency board's recommendations, but instead of insisting that they go along with the board, the President tossed its recommendations aside and "mediated" a settlement more favorable to the unions. The same sort of thing happened again in 1943. President Truman tried, without signal success, to break the organizations of this habit. They had found it pleasant, heady, and profitable, so why should they voluntarily give it up? Clearly, if there is a more rewarding place to go, the unions are not going to be satisfied with a mediocre way-station like an emergency board. It is bad enough that there have to be such boards; the boards themselves are a threat to good-faith bargaining, because they represent an alternative from which one party or the other may get a better settlement than it could through bargaining or striking. But some such system seems to be needed because of the necessity for keeping the railroads running.

It is sometimes claimed that the hourly earnings of railroad workers have not kept pace with those of most non-railroad workers and that therefore the former are justifiably embittered. But the data of the federal Bureau of Labor Statistics indicate that, whereas in 1939 the hourly earnings of rail employees were only within the first third of all manufacturing industries ranked on the basis of amount of average gross hourly earnings, in July, 1951, they were within the top fifth of all industries.

What remedies are there for the unhappy circumstances outlined above? The carriers, who have consistently felt impelled to accept emergency board recommendations, have recently proposed compulsory arbitration. The Donnell Bill was introduced into the Congress toward this end. Before committing themselves to such a precedent-shattering policy, however for such a public-interest industry as the railroads, most students would prefer to see one more grand effort to make the present legislation operate in the spirit in which it was originally conceived and intended. Because the industry is so vital, only top-flight performers should be appointed to the agencies involved in the Act's administration; in no other agencies are more able, knowing, and respected men required. For the same reason, another governmental measure should be coupled with the above; there should be legislation providing for evenhanded treatment and regulation of all competing transportation media and for their proper coordination.

(b) Non-railroad industries. We may divide into two parts — peacetime and wartime (including emergency defense) — our brief discussion of government intervention in labor disputes in non-railroad industries. Some laws and agencies are primarily designed for peacetime conditions, although of course they are not discarded when the nation is at war or is engaged in a major defense effort. Other statutes are passed and other agencies established only for the latter conditions; usually they supplement rather than replace the normal peacetime set-up.

i. "Permanent" peacetime legislation. The most recent labor-dispute intervention measures for non-railroad industries are contained in the Taft-Hartley amendments of 1947 to the National Labor Relations Act. We may usefully distinguish two parts of this legislation: that dealing with the mediation of labor disputes for all non-railroad interstate industries, whether or not disputes in such industries "imperil the national health and safety"; and that conceived solely for disputes affecting the "national health and safety," e.g., in bituminous coal.

Mediation and conciliation. The most important permanent non-railroad mediation agency in the United States from 1914 to date has been what is now known as the Federal Mediation and Conciliation Service. Until 1947 this agency was known as the Conciliation Service and functioned as a semi-autonomous bureau within the U.S. Department of Labor. Over the years it employed from 50 to 200 mediators or "commissioners," and this staff won considerable respect from both unions and employers, successfully adjusting about 80 per cent of some 40,000 disputes into which they were called by one or both parties or into which they went on their own motion.

However, the Service did not escape criticism. Employers were much less enthusiastic about it than unions, partly just because the Service functioned within the labor-minded Department of Labor and partly because the Service had frequently hired ex-union officials as mediators. More neutral observers came to believe that the agency was rather badly understaffed both as to the number of mediators and as to their quality and competence. Much larger appropriations by the Congress were held to be essential if the coverage of the Service were to be adequately extended and if the salary scale for mediators were to be raised sufficiently to attract first-class personnel.

In 1947 the Congress acted to improve the settlement of union-management differences and, as one step in that direction, to enlarge the scope and heighten the prestige of the Mediation Service. In the Taft-Hartley amendments, as we have seen, it required good-faith bargaining by both unions and employers; a 60-day notice if either side wished to terminate or modify an existing contract; and a notification to the federal Service (and to any state mediation agency that might exist) if a new agreement was not succesfully being negotiated by 30 days after the original notice. These provisions were in part aimed at giving the Service more business.

The amended Act also had something to say on the Service itself. It gave the Service its present name. It took it out of the Department of Labor and established it as an independent agency. It set an annual salary of $12,000 for the director and required him to staff his agency under civil service regulations and procedures.

In the past few years there has been an improvement in the quantity and quality of services that the agency performs. Observers question, however, whether it has come within hailing distance of achieving the stature that such an agency should have in a society like ours.

Disputes affecting national health and safety. Under the Taft-Hartley amendments of 1947, a special class of labor disputes is established, termed "national emergencies," and reserved for special procedures. It embraces strikes or lockouts that, if permitted to occur or to continue, will "imperil the national health and safety." The President is to determine whether a dispute falls into this category.

If the President so finds in the case of a dispute, he may appoint a board of inquiry to make findings of fact without recommendations. Upon receipt of the report, the President may then direct the Attorney General to petition any district court of the United States to enjoin the strike or lockout. The court is empowered to issue an injunction if it finds that the dispute affects an entire industry, or a substantial portion of it, and imperils the national health and safety. If the injunction is issued, it is subject to appeal. The injunction order against strike or lockout action terminates the legality of a stoppage in progress or forbids the parties to begin a stoppage.

Upon issuance of the order, the President may reconvene the board of inquiry. Within sixty days from this date, the board is to report all the facts, including the employer's last (not necessarily best) offer of settlement. This report is to be made public. Within 15 additional days, the National Labor Relations Board is to take a secret ballot among the employees of each employer involved, to determine their wishes regarding the last offer of settlement. Within five days, the Board is to certify the results to the Attorney General.

If settlement is not yet reached, then with certification of the election results the Attorney General is required to request the court to discharge the injunction; and upon such action by the court the President is to submit a full report with recommendation to the Congress.

This provision does not outlaw strikes or lockouts that threaten public health and safety. They may occur before the injunction is granted, and they may occur at the end of the whole procedure, barring special legislation by the Congress. However, such strikes or lockouts are illegal under the Act if they occur prior to the expiration of the 60-day notice period (or expiration date of the agreement, if later than 60 days) applicable to changes in all existing contracts affected by the Act; or if they occur during the period when the injunction is in force.

Thus again in this section of the law the theory of delay is invoked in the case of disputes involving national emergencies. In such disputes the following appears to be the likely sequence over time: If the dispute concerns changes in existing contracts, at least 60 days must elapse before a stoppage can legally begin; within the first 30 of these 60 days, the dispute, failing of settlement, must go to mediation and conciliation, and within the whole 60 days or thereafter the President can appoint the board of inquiry, though the stoppage could legally occur after the end of this initial 60-day period; there then follows an indeterminate period during which the Board investigates and makes a preliminary report to the President; if the President then seeks an injunction and it is granted, a pending stoppage becomes illegal and a threatened stoppage must be deferred; at this point the board may be reconvened, and an additional sixty days' delay begins; 15 days more must then elapse for the balloting; within five more days, certification of the results must occur; the Attorney General is then (the date is not stipulated) to procure discharge of the injunction. Thus the injunction forbidding the strike covers at least 80 days $(60 + 15 + 5)$.

Disputes falling into the class of national emergencies are so determined by the President and the courts. Obviously, the class is indefinite and could cover several industries.

Presidential intervention under the above-described provisions took place in eight non-railroad disputes from March, 1948, to the end of 1951. That is not to say, however, that these were the only emergency disputes in non-railroad industries after the Act was amended. The dispute in the basic steel industry in 1949, for example, was handled outside the Taft-Hartley amendments.

Let us analyze briefly what happened in the eight disputes in which the Taft-Hartley provisions were invoked. Three of the eight were in bituminous coal, and two in the maritime industry. In five of them, both a fact-finding board and the 80-day injunction were used; in three, only a board was needed. In three, the N.L.R.B. tried to hold elections to learn whether the employees would accept the employer's last offer; in one of these three disputes, the election was boycotted, while in the other two the employer's last offer was overwhelmingly rejected. Finally and most important, the Act had only a 50–50 record in settling the eight disputes during the over-all intervention period: In four cases settlement occurred within this period; in four others, it did not. However, in two of these last four cases settlement came soon after the end of the period, without strikes.

ii. Wartime or emergency-defense intervention. Special boards. During wars or emergency-defense periods it is of urgent importance that strikes should not occur and that production should continue without interruption. Accordingly, in all such crises during this century the federal government has superimposed special dispute-settlement agencies on those available in peacetime. There was the War Labor Board of World War I, the National War Labor Board of World War II, and the Wage Stabilization Board of the Korean emergency-defense period. Apart from mediation work and apart from dispute settlement under the Railway Labor Act, such agencies inevitably become the chief medium for the peaceful settlement of labor disputes.

So great is the need for sustained output during such periods that a wartime board like the two mentioned above inevitably comes to exercise the powers of compulsory arbitration. It is true that, as at the beginning of World War II, employers and unions voluntarily agree to accept the board's jurisdiction and decisions. But the end result is compulsory adjudication. Unions and employers must submit their unsettled disputes to the board and, in one way or another are compelled to accept its directive order or decision. All the costs of compulsory arbitration mentioned previously, including the decay of real collective bargaining, come to be evident. But these costs, noxious to most people in terms of peacetime life, are rather willingly borne as part of the price exacted for speedy, total victory.

A defense-period board does not necessarily become a compulsory arbitration agency. The decisions of the Wage Stabilization Board in 1951–52 were in the form of "recommendations." Nevertheless, they tended to become much more than mere suggestions. Thus, in April, 1952, the Steelworkers insisted that the basic steel industry adopt in full the Board's recommendations in the steel dispute. When the companies refused, the President seized the industry, intending to apply the recommended wage increases. Only a successful court fight by the companies prevented this result.

Seizure of employers' plants. The main sanction that government has for enforcing the orders of a board during war-emergency periods is taking over the employer's operations. This is commonly known as "seizure." When the government "seizes" a plant, firm, or industry, it does not replace the various levels of management with army officers or the workers with army privates. Nor does the government usually take the profits; it only threatens to. (But the government does usually bear accounting losses, if any.) The whole procedure is a paper operation under which top management's freedom to make decisions offensive or unfavorable to the government and the nation is withdrawn. Top management is supposed to run the business as usual. But it now reports to some army assistant-secretary or general, who tells it what to do on labor matters.

The government seizes the employer's property no matter which side — the union or the employer — has refused to obey the board's order. This might seem unfair to the employer in cases in which the union is the offender. But it is the employer's plant which the government wishes to keep going. And technically it is unlawful for union members in a seized plant to strike; they are government employees as long as the seizure is in effect.

Once compliance with the Board's decisions has been obtained, the employer's property is formally returned to him.

Seizure in wartime is legal under Presidential emergency powers. Sometimes special legislation, such as the War Labor Disputes (Smith-Connally) Act of 1943, is passed to provide a definitive statutory basis. Under this Act, which expired early in 1946, about 35 cases of non-compliance with War Labor Board decisions (the union defied the Board in about 60 per cent of these) were referred to the President for seizure. The two that got the biggest headlines were the bituminous coal mines and Montgomery, Ward and Company.

Seizures are occasionally used in peacetime, but here there must be a statutory basis. The 1948 railroad seizure is an example, based on an old 1916 law. The 1952 steel case showed that, short of war, the President's *general* powers are not enough.

This governmental measure is a drastic one, justifiable only in wartime or for only the most essential industries in peacetime. It should have three main objectives: immediate labor peace in the firm or industry; avoidance of settlements provocative of labor warfare at some later date (this means fairness to both sides, no matter who defied the authorities); and return of the property to the employer as soon as possible. These standards are often more honored in the breach than in the observance. One reason why unions like seizure is that sometimes the government official in charge of the property negotiates a settlement with the union whereby the latter obtains more than it could have from the private management. (This was what happened in 1946, when Secretary of the Interior Krug negotiated with John L. Lewis while the government held the mines.) One reason why employers sometimes like seizure is that strikes are forbidden, and the government bears any losses but gives management the profits. But seizure should be conducted in such a way as to make both union and employer want to get the government out of firm or industry at the earliest possible moment. That is, seizure should be made to be a much less attractive alternative for both sides than the negotiation of an agreement between them. For example, government might take the profits (and perhaps refuse to bear any losses) and might appropriate all dues money collected from the union members during the period of seizure. Such a measure might of course require a constitutional amendment to establish its legality.

(4) State legislation. If we consider state dispute-settlement legislation as a whole, we find all kinds of government intervention. Some of the statutes are well-drafted, evenhanded in spirit, and ably administered; others are not. Space limitations make possible here only a short summary of this legislation.

Only about ten states, almost all highly industrialized (e.g., California, Michigan, New York, and Pennsylvania) have special agencies operating under statutory authority to mediate labor disputes. Some of these, notably New York, have done first-rate work in the field. All have satisfactory working arrangements with the Federal Mediation and Conciliation Service for a division of the field.

A few cities, particularly New York, Newark, and Toledo, have developed special mediation machinery.

A few states require unions to notify employers and state agencies of intention to strike. The notice must be filed a specified number of days before the strike can begin; that is, these laws provide for compulsory cooling-off periods. Experience has shown, however, that this requirement has strengthened rather than weakened unions' bargaining power. Whether serious about striking or not, unions file notice in order to coerce employers into yielding to their demands.

Colorado in 1915 provided for compulsory fact-finding during its required 30-day cooling-off period. This statute has not worked very well except in respect to mediation work by the investigatory board or agency. Strong unions have sometimes ignored the law's requirements, while weak unions have used the law to obtain more than they could otherwise have done.

Before the rise of modern big unionism, Kansas was the only state to experiment with compulsory arbitration and prohibition of strikes, establishing in 1920 a Court of Industrial Relations to settle disputes in all industries "affected with a public interest." However, after two or three years of fair success the Court ran into difficulties with the Mine Workers' leaders and members; and the U.S. Supreme Court held that the law was unconstitutional in respect to such industries as food and clothing. By 1925 a new governor and legislature, although permitting the act to remain on the books, decided to ignore it. It is still on the statute books, and it is still a dead letter. But about a dozen other states now have compulsory arbitration and no-strike laws, all of which are confined to essential services, such as hospitals and public utilities. Arbitration awards hold for one year. There are rather heavy penalties for disobedience. Accumulated experience is beginning to show that these statutes, instead of hampering unions to any great extent, are enabling them in many cases to obtain more from tribunals than they could get by bargaining or striking. The laws seem also to be inducing a partial atrophy of bargaining.

Along with some of these statutes (and in a few states, in the absence of compulsory arbitration laws) are provisions authorizing the governor to seize public utilities and other essential plants in case of strikes.

E. A PROPER ROLE FOR GOVERNMENT

1. Lack of coordinated policy. At various points in these last four chapters we have analyzed and appraised various governmental measures. Let us now look at and evaluate these policies as a whole. When we do this, we may well reach the conclusion that there has been no such thing as a well-thought-out, balanced, integrated national labor policy. We have a patchwork pattern of federal and state labor legislation and administration. There is not very much consistency among the state laws, between state and federal laws, or among the federal laws themselves.

However, this situation should not surprise us. Nor should it depress us too much; it has its utilities as well as its costs. In a democracy, problems are met as they arise. New problems cannot often be foreseen. The passage of time brings changes in legislators — and in legislators' views. A well-coordinated program for one period might come to be a disjointed one later on. Some variety in state legislation may well be desirable if it grows out of the differing needs of various groups of citizens. Only in a dictatorship can an over-all integrated program be devised and installed and changed quickly. And there is no guarantee that the highly integrated program of a dictatorship will be free of error.

But to understand the reasons for lack of integration in a democracy, and perhaps to condone it a bit, is not to consider it desirable or to excuse our lawmakers for not trying harder to achieve a closer approach to integration.

2. A frame of reference. One of the reasons for this lack of integration is the lack of an integrated, uniform frame of reference among those who enact and administer our labor laws. It is doubtless too much to expect agreement among all persons and groups on what this frame of reference should be. But is it too much to believe that a sizable majority can come to some agreement?

Let us see if we can develop the main elements or outlines of an acceptable frame of reference for a democracy like ours. The first thing we have to do is to define the role of government. How far should government go in dealing with labor problems and labor relations? How much should be left in private hands? It seems to the present authors that the answer lies in adherence to the general principle of preserving as much individual liberty and private decision-making as possible. This means, as we have repeatedly said, that government should interfere with and coerce its citizens and their organizations only so far as is necessary to prevent their unduly and unfairly coercing each other.

But the principle, as stated, is still far too abstract to be useful. What does it mean operationally? First, it means that government should handle problems which experience or common sense shows cannot or will not be solved by private decisions. This principle justifies old-age insurance, unemployment compensation, and other forms of social insurance. But what about health insurance and medical benefits, in which private initiative has made significant progress in recent years? Very well; give it a chance to demonstrate that it can cover as many workers' families as cheaply or almost as cheaply as it is estimated that government could. If it succeeds, then the principle of preserving private decision-making would dictate that health insurance and medical benefits should be left in non-governmental hands.

Second, where decisions are left in private hands, there is always danger that the common good will be neglected. Individual persons and groups often think only of their own immediate needs and forget to be socially responsible. Then government is justified in trying to correct abuses, including preventing the economically and politically strong from harming the weak.

Third, since freedom of private decision-making includes freedom to form and join organizations, government should protect this right of association.

Fourth, thc exercise of this right often produces large and powerful organizations, e.g., corporations and unions. These are among the strong elements from which government must sometimes protect the weak, e.g., individual workers. But there are at least three other proper relationships of government to such organizations, because one or more of these groups is often in serious conflict with one or more others. *(a)* Government should strive to treat these conflicting organizations evenhandedly and to attain balance between them. *(b)* Government should try to minimize the conflicts (as well as collusions) among these groups and to devise ways of protecting therefrom the weak, unorganized public, whose only strong representative or agent is government itself. *(c)* In doing these things government should try to make collective bargaining and union-employer compromise the most attractive alternative open to either side.

3. Applications to the labor problems of American society. These principles justify much and condemn some of the labor legislation considered in the last four chapters. As stated above, they justify most social insurance, modest minimum wage legislation, and statutes protecting women and child workers. They provide a rational basis for prohibiting most of the employer and union unfair labor practices in the amended National Labor Relations Act. But they raise serious questions about the propriety of the provisions in that Act which forbid employers and unions to agree to certain items like the closed shop. However, these principles might well justify a requirement that, where closed shops are in force, unions may not restrict their memberships in any way, e.g., bar Negroes or any other workers for any reason.

These principles justify efforts by government to settle union-employer disputes through mediation. They also furnish a solid basis for attempts to use stronger measures for really basic industries like railroads and bituminous coal. It is to be doubted that the Taft-Hartley procedure is the best that could be devised. (Injunction measures may induce employers not to bargain in good faith.) But that some effort short of compulsory arbitration should be made to protect the public from stoppages in basic industries seems hardly open to question. The best plan would be one also providing strong incentives for both parties to make timely voluntary agreements rather than cause delays, run to government (including the White House), and otherwise hamstring honest collective bargaining. Whether a suitably devised form of government seizure, such as that mentioned above, would be desirable may be open to question. But the principle of keeping the industry operating while encouraging true bargaining seems wholly sound.

Among all the problems considered in this book, three seem to stand out: *(a)* the maintenance of full employment without inflation; *(b)* an equitable (this does not at all mean equal) distribution of the national output; and *(c)* harmonious, cooperative, non-collusive union-management relations. Failure to solve these problems brings a serious threat to the democratic way of life. In respect to the first, government has an all-important role to perform. Yet, as we saw, the role is one that does not itself in turn threaten democracy. The second problem can be handled in part by union-employer decisions, in part by governmental ones. So also can the third; here again there need be no serious threat to democracy.

Throughout this volume we have stressed two criteria or standards of analysis: the human-relations or psychological one (Chapter 2), and the economic one (Chapter 3). As we have seen, the two need not be in conflict. When they do seem to conflict, it is usually because economics is too narrowly defined or because, whatever the definition, too short a view is taken of human desires and their satisfaction. Adequate satisfaction for all sorts of human desires does not necessarily have unfavorable effects on the allocation and utilization of resources, or on economic progress. It is part of government's job to show that this is true.

INDEX